Kitchen & Bath
Source Book

Welcome to the Kitchen & Bath Source Book...

McGraw-Hill is proud to present the 1993 edition to you. This reference is the showcase for the very latest building products and design ideas for today's kitchen and bathroom.

The Kitchen & Bath Source Book is the most useful guide of its kind. Inside these pages you'll find a variety of kitchen and bath products from major building product manufacturers. This comprehensive information will give you a broad selection of the product lines available and will also quickly direct you to select just the right building product for all your remodeling and new construction needs.

McGraw-Hill's Kitchen & Bath Source Book offers you:

- Thousands of products, design ideas and specifications shown in full color.

- National Kitchen & Bath Association (NKBA) guidelines to assist you in planning your kitchen and bath, including the latest trends in design and safety. It's like having your own team of kitchen and bath professionals to council you every step of the way!

- A listing of 1,300 Certified Kitchen and Bath Designers and 2,000 Dealers — for easy reference.

- To better serve you, we have included a research information card at the front of your Kitchen & Bath Source Book.

We hope you enjoy McGraw-Hill's Kitchen & Bath Source Book. We are confident that this valuable reference tool will help you choose just the right products when planning your new kitchen or bathroom.

Sincerely,

Robert D. Daleo
Publisher
Sweet's Group/McGraw-Hill, Inc.

Sweet's Group

The Consumer edition of the Kitchen & Bath Source Book is distributed by Macmillan Publishing Company.

Cover photo: Celeste Design & Associates

Senior Vice President-General Manager
Robert D. Daleo

Vice President/Publisher
Susan F. Leiterstein

Vice President-Product Management
Gloria H. Glowacki

Vice President-Operations
William H. Johnston

President-Sweet's Electronic Publishing
Stuart Griffin Burgh, AIA

Vice President-International
Ken D. Hutt

Director-Client Services
Jeffrey O. Britt

Director-Systems Development
William E. Keller

Director-Publishing Operations
Thomas H. Koster

Director-Market Analysis
Jane T. Morrison

Director-Technical Services
Stanley Shapiro

Director-Market Research
Alma L. Weinstein

Director-Manufacturing-Sweet's/Corp. Mfg.
James L. Celeste

Business Manager
Robert B. Doll

Manager-Design/Production
Thomas S. Herrschaft

National Consultant Manager
Martin W. Reinhart, AIA, CSI

Regional Publishers

New York, NY 10020
1221 Avenue of the Americas
212 512 3181
Irwin C. Gross

212 512 3137
Katherine E. Louis

Miami, FL 33174
8700 West Flagler Street, Suite 100
305 223 4470
John A. Fox

Cleveland, OH 44115
1255 Euclid Avenue, 3rd Floor
216 574 2135
Gary E. Darbey

Chicago, IL 60601
180 North Stetson Avenue, Suite 700
312 616 3213
Joseph J. Pepitone

San Francisco, CA 94105
221 Main Street, Suite 800
415 882 2885
Nancy E. Harmon

Consultant Staff

New York
Joseph V. Bower, AIA, CSI
Robert C. Chandler, AIA
Dorothy H. Cox, CSI
Raymond. M. Hennig, AIA, CSI
Alex E. Goldfine, AIA
E. Michael Hollander, AIA
Chicago
Robert C. Boettcher, AIA, CSI
Daniel C. Colella, AIA
Richard Jamiolkowski, P.E., IES, IEEE
Gary B. Keclik, AIA
Richard J. Mazzuca, AIA, CSI
Wayne W. Puchkors, AIA, CSI
Peter G. Schramm, AIA
G. Robert Steiner, S.E., ASCE,CSI
Anaheim
Albert J. Thomas, AIA, CSI
Monterey Park
William White, AIA, CSI

Sweet's Information Services

Sweet's Catalog Files
General Building & Renovation
  Selection Data
Industrial Construction & Renovation
Homebuilding & Remodeling
Contract Interiors
Accessible Building Products
Engineering & Retrofit
Mechanical Engineering & Retrofit
Electrical Engineering & Retrofit
Civil/Structural Engineering & Retrofit
Canadian Construction
Building Products for Export
Sweet's Light Source
Kitchen & Bath Source Book
Building Systems & Controls
SweetSource

For information on obtaining any of the above Catalog Files, call toll-free: 1 800 442 2258

Officers of McGraw-Hill, Inc.
Chairman, President & Chief Executive Officer:
Joseph L. Dionne;
Executive Vice President-Operations:
Harold W. McGraw III;
Executive Vice President, General Counsel and Secretary:
Robert N. Landes;
Senior Vice President, Treasury Operations:
Frank D. Penglase

ISBN 0-07-607064-6

Kitchen & Bath Source Book

Table of Contents

To Find Information Quickly

The Kitchen & Bath Source Book is organized in an easy-to-use format. Catalogs are grouped by similar product type to help you quickly locate information on manufacturers and products for your kitchen and bath projects.

Coding System

Catalogs are assigned a four-character code indicating their position in the Kitchen & Bath Source Book.

As an example: C123

Refer to the Indexes

The Kitchen & Bath Source Book contains complete Firms and Products indexes:

The Firms index is an alphabetical list of manufacturers and their catalog codes.

The Products index is an alphabetical list of all products within the Book. Manufacturers and their catalog codes appear for each product heading.

ADDITIONAL SERVICES PROVIDED BY THE NATIONAL KITCHEN & BATH ASSOCIATION

The National Kitchen & Bath Association (NKBA), a major industry resource, has provided a valuable reference for your use with Sweet's Kitchen & Bath Source Book.

Highlighted in your 1993 edition, you will find a directory of:

- 1,300 Certified Kitchen and Bath Designers.
- 2,000 Kitchen and Bath Dealers.

The NKBA has also furnished important tips, guidelines and rules addressing the latest trends in design and safety—all invaluable tools when planning your kitchen and bath—making the 1993 Kitchen & Bath Source Book the complete guide for designing and constructing your kitchen or bathroom.

Conversion Tables

The following tables are furnished to assist you in utilizing the information provided by building product manufacturers.

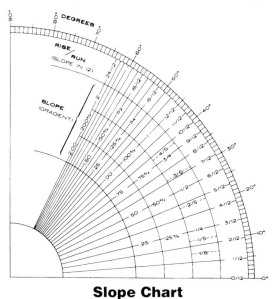

Slope Chart

Basic SI Units (Systéme International d'Unités)

physical quantity	name of unit	symbol for unit
length	metre	m
mass	kilogramme	kg
time	second	s
electric current	ampere	A
thermodynamic temperature	kelvin	K
luminous intensity	candela	cd
area	square metre	m^2
volume	cubic metre	m^3
density	kilogramme per cubic metre	kg/m^3
velocity	metre per second	m/s
angular velocity	radian per second	rad/s
acceleration	metre per second squared	m/s^2
pressure	newton per square metre	N/m^2
kinematic viscosity, diffusion coefficient	square metre per second	m^2/s
dynamic viscosity	newton second per square metre	$N\ s/m^2$
electric field strength	volt per metre	V/m
magnetic field strength	ampere per metre	A/m
luminance	candela per square metre	cd/m^2

Symbols for units do not take a plural form.

Distance

Imperial		Metric		Metric		Imperial	
1 inch	= 2.540	centimetres		1 centimetre	=	0.3937	inch
1 foot	= 0.3048	metre		1 decimetre	=	0.3281	foot
1 yard	= 0.9144	metre		1 metre	=	3.281	feet
1 rod	= 5.029	metres			=	1.094	yard
1 mile	= 1.609	kilometres		1 decametre	=	10.94	yards
				1 kilometre	=	0.6214	mile

Weight

1 ounce (troy)	= 31.103 grams		1 gram	=	0.032 ounce (troy)
1 ounce (avoir)	= 28.350 grams		1 gram	=	0.035 ounce (avoir)
1 pound (troy)	= 373.242 grams		1 kilogram	=	2.679 pounds (troy)
1 pound (avoir)	= 453.592 grams		1 kilogram	=	2.205 pounds (avoir)
1 ton (short)	= 0.907 tonne*		1 tonne	=	1.102 ton (short)

*1 tonne = 1000 kilograms

Capacity

Imperial

1 pint	=	0.568 litre
1 gallon	=	4.546 litres
1 bushel	=	36.369 litres
1 litre	=	0.880 pint
1 litre	=	0.220 gallon
1 hectolitre	=	2.838 bushels

U.S.

1 pint (U.S.)	=	0.473 litre
1 quart (U.S.)	=	0.946 litre
1 gallon (U.S.)	=	3.785 litres
1 barrel (U.S.)	=	158.98 litres

Area

1 square inch	= 6.452 square centimetres
1 square foot	= 0.093 square metre
1 square yard	= 0.836 square metre
1 acre	= 0.405 hectare*
1 square mile	= 259.0 hectares
1 square mile	= 2.590 square kilometres
1 square centimetre	= 0.155 square inch
1 square metre	= 10.76 square feet
1 square metre	= 1.196 square yard
1 hectare	= 2.471 acres
1 square kilometre	= 0.386 square mile

1 hectare = 1 square hectometre

Volume

1 cubic inch	= 16.387 cubic centimetres
1 cubic foot	= 0.0283 cubic decimetres
1 cubic yard	= 0.765 cubic metre
1 cubic centimetre	= 0.061 cubic inch
1 cubic decimetre	= 35.314 cubic foot
1 cubic metre	= 1.308 cubic yard

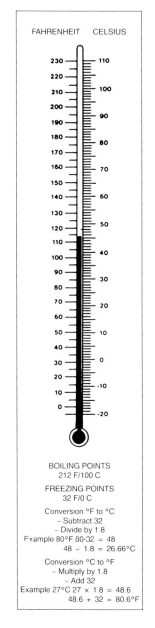

FAHRENHEIT   CELSIUS

BOILING POINTS
212 F/100 C

FREEZING POINTS
32 F/0 C

Conversion °F to °C
– Subtract 32
– Divide by 1.8
Example 80°F 80-32 = 48
48 ÷ 1.8 = 26.66°C

Conversion °C to °F
– Multiply by 1.8
– Add 32
Example 27°C 27 × 1.8 = 48.6
48.6 + 32 = 80.6°F

Conversion Tables

Inches/Feet to Millimetres

inches	millimetres	inches	millimetres	inches	millimetres	inches	millimetres	ft.	in.	millimetres
1/64	0.3969	1 27/32	46.8313	4 21/32	118.269	8 15/16	227.012	3	7	1092.20
1/32	0.7938	1 7/8	47.6250	4 11/16	119.062	9	228.600	3	8	1117.60
3/64	1.1906	1 29/32	48.4188	4 23/32	119.856	9 1/16	230.188	3	9	1143.00
1/16	1.5875	1 15/16	49.2125	4 3/4	120.650	9 1/8	231.775	3	10	1168.40
5/64	1.9844	1 31/32	50.0063	4 25/32	121.444	9 3/16	233.362	3	11	1193.80
3/32	2.3813	2	50.8000	4 13/16	122.238	9 1/4	234.950	4	0	1219.20
7/64	2.7781	2 1/32	51.5938	4 27/32	123.031	9 5/16	236.538	4	1	1244.60
1/8	3.1750	2 1/16	52.3875	4 7/8	123.825	9 3/8	238.125	4	2	1270.00
9/64	3.5719	2 3/32	53.1813	4 29/32	124.619	9 7/16	239.712	4	3	1295.40
5/32	3.9688	2 1/8	53.9750	4 15/16	125.412	9 1/2	241.300	4	4	1320.80
11/64	4.3656	2 5/32	54.7688	4 31/32	126.206	9 9/16	242.888	4	5	1346.20
3/16	4.7625	2 3/16	55.5625	5	127.000	9 5/8	244.475	4	6	1371.60
13/64	5.1594	2 7/32	56.3583	5 1/32	127.794	9 11/16	246.062	4	7	1397.00
7/32	5.5563	2 1/4	57.1500	5 1/16	128.588	9 3/4	247.650	4	8	1422.40
15/64	5.9531	2 9/32	57.9438	5 3/32	129.381	9 13/16	249.238	4	9	1447.80
1/4	6.3500	2 5/16	58.7375	5 1/8	130.175	9 7/8	250.825	4	10	1473.20
17/64	6.7469	2 11/32	59.5313	5 5/32	130.969	9 15/16	252.412	4	11	1498.60
9/32	7.1438	2 3/8	60.3250	5 3/16	131.762	10	254.000	5	0	1524.00
19/64	7.5406	2 13/32	61.1188	5 7/32	132.556	10 1/16	255.588	5	1	1549.40
5/16	7.9375	2 7/16	61.9125	5 1/4	133.350	10 1/8	257.175	5	2	1574.80
21/64	8.3344	2 15/32	62.7063	5 9/32	134.144	10 3/16	258.762	5	3	1600.20
11/32	8.7313	2 1/2	63.5000	5 5/16	134.938	10 1/4	260.350	5	4	1625.60
23/64	9.1281	2 17/32	64.2938	5 11/32	135.731	10 5/16	261.938	5	5	1651.00
3/8	9.5250	2 9/16	65.0875	5 3/8	136.525	10 3/8	263.525	5	6	1676.40
25/64	9.9219	2 19/32	65.8813	5 13/32	137.319	10 7/16	265.112	5	7	1701.80
13/32	10.3188	2 5/8	66.6750	5 7/16	138.112	10 1/2	266.700	5	8	1727.20
27/64	10.7156	2 21/32	67.4688	5 15/32	138.906	10 9/16	268.288	5	9	1752.60
7/16	11.1125	2 11/16	68.2625	5 1/2	139.700	10 5/8	269.875	5	10	1778.00
29/64	11.5094	2 23/32	69.0563	5 17/32	140.494	10 11/16	271.462	5	11	1803.40
15/32	11.9063	2 3/4	69.8500	5 9/16	141.288	10 3/4	273.050	6	0	1828.80
31/64	12.3031	2 25/32	70.6438	5 19/32	142.081	10 13/16	274.638	6	1	1854.20
1/2	12.7000	2 13/16	71.4375	5 5/8	142.875	10 7/8	276.225	6	2	1879.60
33/64	13.0969	2 27/32	72.2313	5 21/32	143.669	10 15/16	277.812	6	3	1905.00
17/32	13.4938	2 7/8	73.0250	5 11/16	144.462	11	279.400	6	4	1930.40
35/64	13.8906	2 29/32	73.8188	5 23/32	145.256	11 1/16	280.988	6	5	1955.80
9/16	14.2875	2 15/16	74.6125	5 3/4	146.050	11 1/8	282.575	6	6	1981.20
37/64	14.6844	2 31/32	75.4063	5 25/32	146.844	11 3/16	284.162	6	7	2006.60
19/32	15.0813	3	76.2000	5 13/16	147.638	11 1/4	285.750	6	8	2032.00
39/64	15.4781	3 1/32	76.9938	5 27/32	148.431	11 5/16	287.338	6	9	2057.40
5/8	15.8750	3 1/16	77.7875	5 7/8	149.225	11 3/8	288.925	6	10	2082.80
41/64	16.2719	3 3/32	78.5813	5 29/32	150.019	11 7/16	290.512	6	11	2108.20
21/32	16.6688	3 1/8	79.3750	5 15/16	150.812	11 1/2	292.100	7	0	2133.60
43/64	17.0656	3 5/32	80.1688	5 31/32	151.606	11 9/16	293.688	7	1	2159.00
11/16	17.4625	3 3/16	80.9625	6	152.400	11 5/8	295.275	7	2	2184.40
45/64	17.8594	3 7/32	81.7563	6 1/16	153.988	11 11/16	296.862	7	3	2209.80
23/32	18.2563	3 1/4	82.5500	6 1/8	155.575	11 3/4	298.450	7	4	2235.20
47/64	18.6531	3 9/32	83.3438	6 3/16	157.162	11 13/16	300.038	7	5	2260.60
3/4	19.0500	3 5/16	84.1375	6 1/4	158.750	11 7/8	301.625	7	6	2286.00
49/64	19.4469	3 11/32	84.9313	6 5/16	160.338	11 15/16	303.212	7	7	2311.40
25/32	19.8438	3 3/8	85.7250	6 3/8	161.925	12	304.800	7	8	2336.80
51/64	20.2406	3 13/32	86.5188	6 7/16	163.512	13	330.200	7	9	2362.20
13/16	20.6375	3 7/16	87.3125	6 1/2	165.100	14	355.600	7	10	2387.60
53/64	21.0344	3 15/32	88.1063	6 9/16	166.688	15	381.000	7	11	2413.00
27/32	21.4313	3 1/2	88.9000	6 5/8	168.275	16	406.400	8	0	2438.40
55/64	21.8281	3 17/32	89.6938	6 11/16	169.862	17	431.800	8	1	2463.80
7/8	22.2250	3 9/16	90.4875	6 3/4	171.450	18	457.200	8	2	2489.20
57/64	22.6219	3 19/32	91.2813	6 13/16	173.038	19	482.600	8	3	2514.60
29/32	23.0188	3 5/8	92.0750	6 7/8	174.625	20	508.000	8	4	2540.00
59/64	23.4156	3 21/32	92.8688	6 15/16	176.212	21	533.400	8	5	2565.40
15/16	23.8125	3 11/16	93.6625	7	177.800	22	558.800	8	6	2590.80
61/64	24.2094	3 23/32	94.4563	7 1/16	179.388	23	584.200	8	7	2616.20
31/32	24.6063	3 3/4	95.2500	7 1/8	180.975	24	609.600	8	8	2641.60
63/64	25.0031	3 25/32	96.0438	7 3/16	182.562	25	635.000	8	9	2667.00
1	25.4000	3 13/16	96.8375	7 1/4	184.150	26	660.400	8	10	2692.40
1 1/32	26.1938	3 27/32	97.6313	7 5/16	185.738	27	685.800	8	11	2717.80
1 1/16	26.9875	3 7/8	98.4250	7 3/8	187.325	28	711.200	9	0	2743.20
1 3/32	27.7813	3 29/32	99.2188	7 7/16	188.912	29	736.600	9	1	2768.60
1 1/8	28.5750	3 15/16	100.012	7 1/2	190.500	30	762.000	9	2	2794.00
1 5/32	29.3688	3 31/32	100.806	7 9/16	192.088	31	787.400	9	3	2819.40
1 3/16	30.1625	4	101.600	7 5/8	193.675	32	812.800	9	4	2844.80
1 7/32	30.9563	4 1/32	102.394	7 11/16	195.262	33	838.200	9	5	2870.20
1 1/4	31.7500	4 1/16	103.188	7 3/4	196.850	34	863.600	9	6	2895.60
1 9/32	32.5438	4 3/32	103.981	7 13/16	198.438	35	889.000	9	7	2921.00
1 5/16	33.3375	4 1/8	104.775	7 7/8	200.025	36	914.400	9	8	2946.40
1 11/32	34.1313	4 5/32	105.569	7 15/16	201.612	37	939.800	9	9	2971.80
1 3/8	34.9250	4 3/16	106.362	8	203.200	38	965.200	9	10	2997.20
1 13/32	35.7188	4 7/32	107.156	8 1/16	204.788	39	990.600	9	11	3022.60
1 7/16	36.5125	4 1/4	107.950	8 1/8	206.375	40	1016.00	10	0	3048.00
1 15/32	37.3063	4 9/32	108.744	8 3/16	207.962	41	1041.40	11	0	3352.80
1 1/2	38.1000	4 5/16	109.538	8 1/4	209.550	42	1066.80	12	0	3657.60
1 17/32	38.8938	4 11/32	110.331	8 5/16	211.138			13	0	3962.40
1 9/16	39.6875	4 3/8	111.125	8 3/8	212.725			14	0	4267.20
1 19/32	40.4813	4 13/32	111.919	8 7/16	214.312			15	0	4572.00
1 5/8	41.2750	4 7/16	112.712	8 1/2	215.900			16	0	4876.80
1 21/32	42.0688	4 15/32	113.506	8 9/16	217.488			17	0	5131.60
1 11/16	42.8625	4 1/2	114.300	8 5/8	219.075			18	0	5486.40
1 23/32	43.6563	4 17/32	115.094	8 11/16	220.662			19	0	5791.20
1 3/4	44.4500	4 9/16	115.888	8 3/4	222.250			20	0	6096.00
1 25/32	45.2438	4 19/32	116.681	8 13/16	223.838			21	0	6400.80
1 13/16	46.0375	4 5/8	117.475	8 7/8	225.425			22	0	6705.60

Millimetres to Inches/Feet

millimetres	inches	millimetres	inches	millimetres	inches	millimetres	inches	millimetres	inches
1	0.0394	91	3.5827	181	7.1260	271	10.6693	361	14.2126
2	0.0787	92	3.6221	182	7.1654	272	10.7087	362	14.2520
3	0.1181	93	3.6614	183	7.2047	273	10.7480	363	14.2913
4	0.1575	94	3.7008	184	7.2441	274	10.7874	364	14.3307
5	0.1969	95	3.7402	185	7.2835	275	10.8268	365	14.3701
6	0.2362	96	3.7795	186	7.3228	276	10.8661	366	14.4094
7	0.2756	97	3.8189	187	7.3622	277	10.9055	367	14.4488
8	0.3150	98	3.8583	188	7.4016	278	10.9449	368	14.4882
9	0.3543	99	3.8976	189	7.4409	279	10.9843	369	14.5276
10	0.3937	100	3.9370	190	7.4803	280	11.0236	370	14.5669
11	0.4331	101	3.9764	191	7.5197	281	11.0630	371	14.6063
12	0.4724	102	4.0158	192	7.5591	282	11.1024	372	14.6457
13	0.5118	103	4.0551	193	7.5984	283	11.1417	373	14.6850
14	0.5512	104	4.0945	194	7.6378	284	11.1811	374	14.7244
15	0.5906	105	4.1339	195	7.6772	285	11.2205	375	14.7638
16	0.6299	106	4.1732	196	7.7165	286	11.2598	376	14.8031
17	0.6693	107	4.2126	197	7.7559	287	11.2992	377	14.8425
18	0.7087	108	4.2520	198	7.7953	288	11.3386	378	14.8819
19	0.7480	109	4.2913	199	7.8347	289	11.3780	379	14.9213
20	0.7874	110	4.3307	200	7.8740	290	11.4173	380	14.9606
21	0.8268	111	4.3701	201	7.9134	291	11.4567	381	15.0000
22	0.8661	112	4.4095	202	7.9528	292	11.4961	382	15.0394
23	0.9055	113	4.4488	203	7.9921	293	11.5354	383	15.0787
24	0.9449	114	4.4882	204	8.0315	294	11.5748	384	15.1181
25	0.9843	115	4.5276	205	8.0709	295	11.6142	385	15.1575
26	1.0236	116	4.5669	206	8.1102	296	11.6535	386	15.1969
27	1.0630	117	4.6063	207	8.1496	297	11.6929	387	15.2362
28	1.1024	118	4.6457	208	8.1890	298	11.7323	388	15.2756
29	1.1417	119	4.6850	209	8.2284	299	11.7717	389	15.3150
30	1.1811	120	4.7244	210	8.2677	300	11.8110	390	15.3543
31	1.2205	121	4.7638	211	8.3071	301	11.8504	391	15.3937
32	1.2598	122	4.8032	212	8.3465	302	11.8898	392	15.4331
33	1.2992	123	4.8425	213	8.3858	303	11.9291	393	15.4724
34	1.3386	124	4.8819	214	8.4252	304	11.9686	394	15.5118
35	1.3780	125	4.9213	215	8.4646	305	12.0079	395	15.5512
36	1.4173	126	4.9606	216	8.5039	306	12.0472	396	15.5906
37	1.4567	127	5.0000	217	8.5433	307	12.0866	397	15.6299
38	1.4961	128	5.0394	218	8.5827	308	12.1260	398	15.6693
39	1.5354	129	5.0787	219	8.6221	309	12.1654	399	15.7087
40	1.5748	130	5.1181	220	8.6614	310	12.2047	400	15.7480
41	1.6142	131	5.1575	221	8.7008	311	12.2441	401	15.7874
42	1.6535	132	5.1969	222	8.7402	312	12.2835	402	15.8268
43	1.6929	133	5.2362	223	8.7795	313	12.3228	403	15.8661
44	1.7323	134	5.2756	224	8.8189	314	12.3622	404	15.9055
45	1.7717	135	5.3150	225	8.8583	315	12.4016	405	15.9449
46	1.8110	136	5.3543	226	6.8976	316	12.4409	406	15.9832
47	1.8504	137	5.3937	227	8.9370	317	12.4803	407	16.0236
48	1.8898	138	5.4331	228	8.9764	318	12.5197	408	16.0630
49	1.9291	139	5.4724	229	9.0158	319	12.5591	409	16.1024
50	1.9685	140	5.5118	230	9.0551	320	12.5984	410	16.1417
51	2.0079	141	5.5512	231	9.0945	321	12.6378	411	16.1811
52	2.0472	142	5.5906	232	9.1339	322	12.6772	412	16.2205
53	2.0866	143	5.6299	233	9.1732	323	12.7165	413	16.2598
54	2.1260	144	5.6693	234	9.2126	324	12.7559	414	16.2992
55	2.1654	145	5.7087	235	9.2520	325	12.7953	415	16.3386
56	2.2047	146	5.7480	236	9.2913	326	12.8346	416	16.3780
57	2.2441	147	5.7874	237	9.3307	327	12.8740	417	16.4173
58	2.2835	148	5.8268	238	9.3701	328	12.9134	418	16.4567
59	2.3228	149	5.8661	239	9.4095	329	12.9528	419	16.4961
60	2.3622	150	5.9055	240	9.4488	330	12.9921	420	16.5354
61	2.4016	151	5.9449	241	9.4882	331	13.0315	421	16.5748
62	2.4409	152	5.9843	242	9.5276	332	13.0709	422	16.6142
63	2.4803	153	6.0236	243	9.5669	333	13.1102	423	16.6535
64	2.5197	154	6.0630	244	9.6063	334	13.1496	424	16.6929
65	2.5591	155	6.1024	245	9.6457	335	13.1890	425	16.7323
66	2.5984	156	6.1417	246	9.6850	336	13.2283	426	16.7716
67	2.6378	157	6.1811	247	9.7244	337	13.2677	427	16.8110
68	2.6772	158	6.2205	248	9.7638	338	13.3071	428	16.8504
69	2.7165	159	6.2599	249	9.8031	339	13.3465	429	16.8898
70	2.7559	160	6.2992	250	9.8425	340	13.3858	430	16.9291
71	2.7953	161	6.3386	251	9.8819	341	13.4252	431	16.9685
72	2.8347	162	6.3780	252	9.9213	342	13.4646	432	17.0079
73	2.8740	163	6.4173	253	9.9606	343	13.5039	433	17.0472
74	2.9134	164	6.4567	254	10.0000	344	13.5433	434	17.0866
75	2.9528	165	6.4961	255	10.0393	345	13.5827	435	17.1260
76	2.9921	166	6.5354	256	10.0787	346	13.6220	436	17.1654
77	3.0315	167	6.5748	257	10.1181	347	13.6614	437	17.2047
78	3.0709	168	6.6142	258	10.1575	348	13.7008	438	17.2441
79	3.1102	169	6.6535	259	10.1969	349	13.7402	439	17.2835
80	3.1496	170	6.6929	260	10.2362	350	13.7795	440	17.3228
81	3.1890	171	6.7323	261	10.2756	351	13.8189	441	17.3622
82	3.2284	172	6.7717	262	10.3150	352	13.8583	442	17.4016
83	3.2677	173	6.8110	263	10.3543	353	13.8976	443	17.4409
84	3.3071	174	6.8504	264	10.3937	354	13.9370	444	17.4803
85	3.3465	175	6.8898	265	10.4331	355	13.9764	445	17.5197
86	3.3858	176	6.9291	266	10.4724	356	14.0157	446	17.5591
87	3.4252	177	6.9685	267	10.5118	357	14.0551	447	17.5984
88	3.4646	178	7.0079	268	10.5512	358	14.0945	448	17.6378
89	3.5039	179	7.0472	269	10.5906	359	14.1339	449	17.6772
90	3.5433	180	7.0866	270	10.6299	360	14.1732	450	17.7165

Firms

Catalogs are coded by position within the volume in numerical sequence, e.g., C345

Catalogs are coded by position within the volume in numerical sequence, e.g., C345

NOTE: Index headings listed below are based on the manufacturers' descriptions of their products as those descriptions appear in the catalogs distributed by Sweet's. SWEET'S MAKES NO REPRESENTATIONS OR WARRANTIES OF ANY KIND, EXPRESS OR IMPLIED, INCLUDING BUT NOT LIMITED TO IMPLIED WARRANTIES OF MERCHANTABILITY OR FITNESS FOR ANY PARTICULAR PURPOSE AS TO THESE INDEX HEADINGS OR AS TO THE PRODUCTS DESCRIBED BY THESE INDEX HEADINGS. Users of Sweet's Files should not rely on these index headings in connection with selecting products. Users of Sweet's Files should refer to the manufacturers' catalogs for further information regarding characteristics of products indexed below.

---

a

Accessible products for the disabled
see
> bathroom accessories: —disabled persons' use
> bathroom accessories: —grab bars—specific materials
> cabinets: —bathroom vanity—disabled persons' use
> cabinets: —kitchen—residential—disabled persons' use
> faucets—applications: —disabled persons' use
> hospital equipment: —grab bars, safety toilet seats, safety towel bars
> mirrors: —tilting
> plumbing fittings and trim: —disabled persons' use
> showers: —disabled persons' use
> showers: —seats—wall-mounted
> washroom accessories: —disabled persons' use
> washroom accessories: —grab bars

Acoustical products—properties
fire-resistant
see
> specific products

Acoustic isolation and control
partitions
see
> partitions—properties: —sound-insulating or retarding—specific type

Admixtures
plasticizers
see
> sealers

Air conditioners
central station units
> Amana Refrigeration, Inc. C481
packaged—unitary
see
> heaters—unit
packaged—window or through-wall
> Amana Refrigeration, Inc. C481

Air conditioning equipment
see
> air conditioners
> dehumidifiers
> heat pumps

Air distribution equipment
see
> fans
> ventilators

Air handlers
see
> air conditioners

Air/liquid treatment equipment
see
> air conditioners
> dehumidifiers
> waste handling equipment and systems
> water conditioning equipment

Air pollution control
see
> air conditioning equipment
> vacuum cleaning systems

Alarms and alarm systems
horns, sirens, bells and chimes
see
> bells, buzzers, chimes (entrance and alarm)

Aluminum products
see
> specific products

Appliances—residential—kitchen
see
> kitchen appliances—residential
> kitchen or kitchenette units

Architectural artwork
moldings and cornices
see
> moldings and cornices

Ash handling equipment
see
> vacuum cleaning systems

Asphalt
product information—manufacturers
see
> specific products

Association catalogs
see
> product information—associations

Audio and visual equipment
see
> intercommunicating systems

b

Barbecue grills
see
> grills—barbecue

Bar furniture and equipment
see also
> ice making machines
elbow rests, tops
> Du Pont Co. C468
sink
> Barclay Products Ltd. C567
> Elkay Mfg. Corp. C561

Barrier-free design products
see
> bathroom accessories: —disabled persons' use
> bathroom accessories: —grab bars—specific materials
> cabinets: —bathroom vanity—disabled persons' use
> cabinets: —kitchen—residential—disabled persons' use
> faucets—applications: —disabled persons' use
> hospital equipment: —grab bars, safety toilet seats, safety towel bars
> mirrors —tilting
> plumbing fittings and trim: —disabled persons' use
> showers: —disabied persons' use
> showers: —seats—wall-mounted
> washroom accessories: —disabled persons' use
> washroom accessories: —grab bars

Bars
grab
see
> bathroom accessories: —grab bars, safety toilet seats, safety towel bars—metal
> hospital equipment: —grab bars, safety toilet seats, safety towel bars
> washroom accessories: —grab bars

Bases
flooring
see
> flooring—specific materials

Bases *cont.*

shower
see
   showers: —stalls and receptors—specific material

Bathroom accessories
see also
   washroom accessories

cabinets and mirrors
see also
   mirrors
Basco, Inc. C585
Broan Mfg. Co., Inc. C587
Contractors Wardrobe, Inc. ...... B181; Inside Back Cover
Merillat Industries, Inc. C530
NuTone C590
Ultracraft Div., Alside C534
Wellborn Cabinet, Inc. C536

cabinets and mirrors—with lighting fixtures
see also
   lighting—application: —cabinets and mirrors
Basco, Inc. C585
Broan Mfg. Co., Inc. C587
Merillat Industries, Inc. C530
NuTone C590
Wellborn Cabinet, Inc. C536

clothes lines—retractable
Basco, Inc. C585

disabled persons' use
Basco, Inc. C585
Merillat Industries, Inc. C530

dispensers—facial tissue
Basco, Inc. C585
JADO Bathroom/Hardware
  Mfg. Corp. C581

dryers—hand or hair
see
   washroom accessories: —dryers—specific type—hand or hair

fans for
see
   fans: —kitchen or bathroom

fittings for
see
   plumbing fittings and trim

grab bars, safety toilet seats, safety towel bars—metal
see also
   hospital equipment: —grab bars, safety toilet seats, safety towel bars
   plumbing fittings and trim: —toilet seats
Basco, Inc. C585
Olsonite Corp. C590A

holders—toothbrush and/or tumbler—metal
Artistic Brass C579
Basco, Inc. C585
JADO Bathroom/Hardware
  Mfg. Corp. C581
NuTone C590

holders—toothbrush and/or tumbler—plastic
Basco, Inc. C585

hooks—coat or robe
Artistic Brass C579
Basco, Inc. C585
JADO Bathroom/Hardware
  Mfg. Corp. C581
NuTone C590

mirrors
see
   mirrors

shelves
see
   shelving: —bathroom or washroom—specific material

Bathroom accessories *cont.*

toilet paper holders, soap dishes—metal
Artistic Brass C579
Basco, Inc. C585
JADO Bathroom/Hardware
  Mfg. Corp. C581
NuTone C590

toilet paper holders, soap dishes—plastic
Basco, Inc. C585

towel holders
Artistic Brass C579
Basco, Inc. C585
JADO Bathroom/Hardware
  Mfg. Corp. C581
NuTone C590
Strom Plumbing, Sign of the Crab C584

towel holders—warmers for
Epanel C588

vanity cabinets
see
   cabinets: —bathroom vanity

water closets
see
   toilets

Bathroom planning and design
see
   consultants and services: —kitchen and bath planning and design

Baths—recirculating
see
   bathtubs: —hydro-massage combination

Baths—steam
see
   saunas and equipment
   steam bath rooms

Bathtubs

accessories
Jason International, Inc. C574

enclosures for
Aristech Chemical Corp. C591
Basco C592
Century Shower Door, Inc. C593
Du Pont Co. C468
Jason International, Inc. C574
Wilson: Ralph Wilson Plastics Co. C479
Work Right Products, Inc. C597

enclosures for—sliding door
Basco C592
Century Shower Door, Inc. C593
Jason International, Inc. C574
Work Right Products, Inc. C597

enclosures for—swinging door
Basco C592
Century Shower Door, Inc. C593
Work Right Products, Inc. C597

fiber glass, plastic
Aristech Chemical Corp. C591
Jacuzzi Whirlpool Bath C663
Jason International, Inc. C574
Swirl-way Plumbing Group C667

fittings for
see
   faucets—applications: —bathtub
   plumbing fittings and trim

hydro-massage combination
Aristech Chemical Corp. C591
Jacuzzi Whirlpool Bath C663
Jason International, Inc. C574
Swirl-way Plumbing Group C667

Bathtubs *cont.*

wall liners for, surrounds
see
   bathtubs: —enclosures for

Bathtub/shower—prefabricated unit
Aristech Chemical Corp. C591
Jason International, Inc. C574

Bells, buzzers, chimes (entrance and alarm)
Broan Mfg. Co., ... ii
NuTone C590

Bidets
see also
   faucets—applications: —bidet
Duravit/Santile International
  Corp. C568

Blenders
see
   kitchen appliances—residential: —blenders

Blocks—glass
Weck, Glashaus Div. B689

Blowers—centrifugal or axial
see
   fans
   ventilators

Bookcases
residential
Wellborn Cabinet, Inc. C536

Books and publications
see
   product information—associations

Bookstacks
see
   bookcases

Building paper
see
   vapor barriers/retarders

Bullet-resistant equipment and systems
see
   specific products

Burners
range
see
   ranges and ovens—residential: —cooktops—specific type

Buzzers
see
   bells, buzzers, chimes (entrance and alarm)

Entrances

doors
see
> *doors—application*
> *doors—operation*
> *doors—properties*
> *doors—swinging—by materials/construction*

Exercise equipment

see
> *health club equipment*

Exhaust systems

air
see
> *fans*
> *ventilators*

Extrusions

see
> *specific products*

f

Facings, refacings or veneers

see
> *panels—building*
> *surfacing and paneling—interior*

Fans

see also
> *ventilators*

fan-light combination
Broan Mfg. Co., Inc. ii
NuTone C590

kitchen or bathroom
Broan Mfg. Co., Inc. C484
NuTone C590

ventilating or exhaust
Broan Mfg. Co., Inc. C484
NuTone C590

wall, ceiling or pedestal
Broan Mfg. Co., Inc. ii
NuTone C590

Faucets

see
> *faucets—applications*
> *faucets—types*

Faucets—applications

bathtub
Alsons Corp., Masco, Inc. C578
Artistic Brass .C579
Grohe America C563
Jacuzzi Whirlpool Bath C663
JADO Bathroom/Hardware
   Mfg. Corp. C581
Luxcetz C583
Strom Plumbing, Sign of the
   Crab C584

bidet
Artistic Brass .C579
JADO Bathroom/Hardware
   Mfg. Corp. C581

disabled persons' use
Alsons Corp., Masco, Inc. C578

lavatory
Artistic Brass .C579
Grohe America C563
Jacuzzi Whirlpool Bath C663
JADO Bathroom/Hardware
   Mfg. Corp. C581
Luxcetz C583

Faucets—applications *cont.*

lavatory *cont.*
Strom Plumbing, Sign of the
   Crab C584

sink—kitchen
Blanco A012
Elkay Mfg. Corp. C561
Franke, Inc., Kitchen
   Systems Div. C562
Grohe America C563
JADO Bathroom/Hardware
   Mfg. Corp. C582
Luxcetz C583

sink—service, laundry
Grohe America C563

Faucets—types

metering, self-closing
Grohe America C563

**mixing—pressure-balancing,
thermostatic**
Grohe America C563
JADO Bathroom/Hardware
   Mfg. Corp. C581

pushbutton
Grohe America C563

single supply
Alsons Corp., Masco, Inc. C578
Artistic Brass .C579
Elkay Mfg. Corp. C561
Grohe America C563
Jacuzzi Whirlpool Bath C663
JADO Bathroom/Hardware
   Mfg. Corp. C581
Strom Plumbing, Sign of the
   Crab C584

swivel spout
Blanco A012
Elkay Mfg. Corp. C561
Grohe America C563
JADO Bathroom/Hardware
   Mfg. Corp. C582

wall-mounted
Grohe America C563

water-saving
JADO Bathroom/Hardware
   Mfg. Corp. C582

Fiber glass-reinforced materials—custom-shaped

see
> *specific products*

Files, filing cabinets

see
> *office equipment*

Finishes—metal-protective

see
> *coatings—metal-protective*
> *sealers: —metal*

Fireplaces

outdoor
see
> *grills—barbecue: —outdoor—built-in or portable*

Fire protection equipment and systems

partitions
see
> *partitions—properties: —fire-rated: —fire-resistant—specific type*

Fitness equipment

see
> *health club equipment*
> *saunas and equipment*
> *steam bath rooms*

Fittings

see
> *plumbing fittings and trim*

Floor cleaning and maintenance equipment

vacuum cleaning systems
see
> *vacuum cleaning systems*

Flooring

see
> *flooring—properties*
> *flooring—treatments, maintenance and resurfacing*
> *flooring—vinyl*

Flooring—properties

acid or alkali-resistant—residential use
Armstrong World Industries,
   Inc. C285

grease-resistant—residential use
Armstrong World Industries,
   Inc. C285

Flooring—treatments, maintenance and resurfacing

see also
> *sealers*
> *toppings—traffic-bearing*
Unelko Corp. A011

Flooring—vinyl

sheet or roll
Armstrong World Industries,
   Inc. C285

tile
Armstrong World Industries,
   Inc. C285

Floor toppings

see
> *toppings—traffic-bearing*

Food service equipment— commercial or institutional

compactors—waste
see
> *waste handling equipment and systems*

dispensers
see
> *dispensers*

ice making machines
see
> *ice making machines*

sinks
Du Pont Co. C468

ventilators
see
> *ventilators: —hoods—specific type*

waste handling equipment
see
> *waste handling equipment and systems*

Food waste disposers

see also
  waste handling equipment and systems

residential
Franke, Inc., Kitchen
  Systems Div. C562
In-Sink-Erator C501
Jenn-Air Co. C502
KitchenAid, Inc. C503
Maytag Co. C507

Forgings

see
  specific products

Fountains—soda

beverage dispensers
see
  dispensers

Freezers—residential

see also
  refrigerator-freezer combination: —residential—
    specific type

built-in
Amana Refrigeration, Inc. C481
Sub-Zero Freezer Co., Inc. C514

free-standing
Amana Refrigeration, Inc. C481
Sub-Zero Freezer Co., Inc. C514

undercounter
Amana Refrigeration, Inc. C481
Sub-Zero Freezer Co., Inc. C514

Fume hoods

see
  ventilators: —hoods—specific type

Furnaces

see
  heaters—unit

Furniture

see
  bar furniture and equipment
  bookcases
  cabinets
  desks
  hospital equipment
  laboratory equipment
  office equipment
  tables

g

Garbage disposal equipment

see
  food waste disposers
  waste handling equipment and systems

Generators

steam
see
  steam bath rooms: —equipment for

Generic information

see
  specific products/materials

Glass blocks

see
  blocks—glass
  glass—form: —block

Glass-ceramic

see
  specific products

Glass—film finish for

see
  glass—properties

Glass—form

bent, curved
Weck, Glashaus Div. B689

block
Weck, Glashaus Div. B689

**patterned, carved, decorative, etched or
textured**
Weck, Glashaus Div. B689

Glass products

see
  specific products

Glass—properties

anti-glare/shading
Weck, Glashaus Div. B689

burglar-resistant
Weck, Glashaus Div. B689

diffusing
see
  glass—form: —patterned, carved, decorative,
    etched or textured

fire-resistant
Weck, Glashaus Div. B689

heat-absorbing
Weck, Glashaus Div. B689

insulating panel
Weck, Glashaus Div. B689

security and detention
see
  glass—properties —burglar-resistant

sound-resistant
Weck, Glashaus Div. B689

Glazing

see
  glass—form
  glass—properties
  plastic—form
  plastic—properties

Glazing film

see
  glass—properties
  plastic—properties

Government agency catalogs

see
  product information—associations

Grab bars

see
  bathroom accessories: —grab bars—specific
    type
  hospital equipment: —grab bars, safety toilet
    seats, safety towel bars
  washroom accessories: —grab bars

Grills—barbecue

see also
  ranges and ovens—residential: —cooktops/
    grills—convertible

indoor—built-in or portable
Jenn-Air Co. C502

outdoor—built-in or portable
Jenn-Air Co. C502

Gypsum

see
  specific products

h

Handicapped persons' products

see
  bathroom accessories: —disabled persons' use
  bathroom accessories: —grab bars—specific
    materials
  cabinets: —bathroom vanity—disabled persons'
    use
  cabinets: —kitchen—residential—disabled
    persons' use
  faucets—applications: —disabled persons' use
  mirrors: —tilting
  plumbing fittings and trim: —disabled persons'
    use
  showers: —disabled persons' use
  showers: —seats—wall-mounted
  washroom accessories: —disabled persons' use

Hardware—bathroom, washroom

shower
see
  showers: —rods, hardware and tracks

Healthcare furniture

see
  hospital equipment

Health club equipment

see also
  saunas and equipment
  steam bath rooms: —equipment for
Finlandia Sauna Products,
  Inc. C642

Heaters—unit

electric
Amana Refrigeration, Inc. C481
NuTone C590

electric—with lighting
NuTone C590

gas-fired
Amana Refrigeration, Inc. C481

oil-fired
Amana Refrigeration, Inc. C481

Heaters—water

heat pumps—non-reversible
see
  heat pumps

Heat pumps

window or through-wall
Amana Refrigeration, Inc. C481

Holders

toilet paper
see
  bathroom accessories: —toilet paper holders,
    soap dishes—specific material
  washroom accessories: —holders—toilet paper

Hoods

see
  ventilators

Hose

connectors
see
  piping and tubing accessories

Hospital equipment

air conditioning units
see
air conditioners

desks—registration, reservation
see
intercommunicating systems—specific type

grab bars, safety toilet seats, safety towel bars
see also
bathroom accessories: —grab bars, safety toilet seats, safety towel bars—metal
plumbing fittings and trim: —toilet seats
Olsonite Corp. C590A

kitchen equipment
see
food service equipment—commercial or institutional

plumbing fittings
see
plumbing fittings and trim

Hotel, motel equipment

appliances—compact
see
kitchen or kitchenette units

bathroom
see
bathroom accessories

Hvc terminal units
see
heaters—unit

i

Ice making machines

residential
Elkay Mfg. Corp. . . . . Inside Front Cover
KitchenAid, Inc. C503
Sub-Zero Freezer Co., Inc. C514; C515

Intercommunicating systems
NuTone C590

Iron
see
specific products

Ironing boards
see also
laundry equipment—specific type: —iron-ironing board—built-in
NuTone C590

k

Kitchen appliances—residential

blenders
NuTone C590

can openers
NuTone C590

combination food preparation center
NuTone C590

mixers
NuTone C590

Kitchen equipment—residential
see
cabinets: —kitchen—residential
consultants and services: —kitchen and bath planning and design

Kitchen equipment—residential
cont.
see cont.
dishwashers—residential
fans: —kitchen or bathroom
food waste disposers: —residential
freezers—residential
kitchen appliances—residential
kitchen or kitchenette units
kitchen planning
ranges and ovens—residential
refrigerator-freezer combination: —residential—specific type
refrigerators
sinks—residential
ventilators: —hoods—residential kitchen—specific type

Kitchen or kitchenette units
Merillat Industries, Inc. C530

Kitchen planning
Merillat Industries, Inc. C530
NKBA, National Kitchen & Bath Association A105

L

Laboratory equipment

plumbing fittings
see
plumbing fittings and trim

sinks—strainers for
see
strainers

work surfaces for
Du Pont Co. C468

Laundry equipment—residential use

dryers
Amana Refrigeration, Inc. C481
KitchenAid, Inc. C503
Magic Chef, Inc. C506
Maytag Co. C507

iron-ironing board—built-in
see also
ironing boards
Broan Mfg. Co., Inc. ii
NuTone C590

washer/dryers—combination
Amana Refrigeration, Inc. C481
KitchenAid, Inc. C503
Magic Chef, Inc. C506
Maytag Co. C507

washers
Amana Refrigeration, Inc. C481
KitchenAid, Inc. C503
Magic Chef, Inc. C506
Maytag Co. C507

Lavatories and accessories

cabinets for
Wellborn Cabinet, Inc. C536

fittings and trim for
see
plumbing fittings and trim

lavatories
Barclay Products Ltd. C567
Du Pont Co. C468
Duravit/Santile International Corp. C568
Strom Plumbing, Sign of the Crab C584

tops for
Du Pont Co. C468
Wilson: Ralph Wilson Plastics Co. C479

Lavatories and accessories *cont.*

vanity top and bowl—molded—one piece
Du Pont Co. C468

Lead products

product information—manufacturers
see
specific products

Lighting
see
fans: —fan-light combination
heaters—unit: —electric—with lighting
lighting—application
luminaires—types
wiring devices—electrical

Lighting—application

cabinets and mirrors
see also
bathroom accessories: —cabinets and mirrors—with lighting fixtures
Basco, Inc. C585
Broan Mfg. Co., Inc. . . . . ii; C587
Merillat Industries, Inc. C530
NuTone C590
Wellborn Cabinet, Inc. C536

Lights

window
see
glass
plastic

Limestone products
see
specific products

Linings or liners

coatings and waterproofing
see
waterproofing membranes

Liquid waste disposal or treatment equipment
see
waste handling equipment and systems
water conditioning equipment

piping for
see
piping and tubing—application: —gas, water, electrical or sewer system

Louvers
see
ventilators

Lumber—treated
see
wood—treated

Luminaires—types

fan
see
fans: —fan-light combination

Piping and tubing—form
prefabricated
Geberit C580

Piping and tubing—materials
plastic
Geberit C580

Piping and tubing—properties
chemical-resistant
Geberit C580

Planning service—manufacturers
see
kitchen planning

Planning services—professional consultants
see
consultants and services

Plastic
see
plastic—form
plastic—properties

Plastic—form
colored
Du Pont Co. .C468
corrugated or flat sheet
Aristech Chemical Corp. C591
Du Pont Co. .C468
Wilson: Ralph Wilson Plastics
Co. C479
film
see
glass—properties
patterned or textured
Du Pont Co. .C468
sheet, coil
Du Pont Co. .C468

Plastic materials—custom-molded
see also
specific products
Du Pont Co. .C468

Plastic—properties
chemical-resistant
Du Pont Co. .C468
fire-resistant
Du Pont Co. .C468
heat-absorbing
Du Pont Co. .C468
moldable
Aristech Chemical Corp. C591
Du Pont Co. .C468
shock-resistant
Du Pont Co. .C468

Plumbing fittings and trim
see also
piping and tubing accessories
disabled persons' use
Alsons Corp., Masco, Inc. C578
Olsonite Corp. C590A
faucets/fixture trim
see
faucets
levers—toilet tank
Artistic Brass C579

Plumbing fittings and trim *cont.*
shower or spray
Alsons Corp., Masco, Inc. C578
Artistic Brass C579
Grohe America C563
Jacuzzi Whirlpool Bath C663
JADO Bathroom/Hardware
Mfg. Corp. C581
Strom Plumbing, Sign of the
Crab C584
shower or spray—group—column, wall-mounted
Grohe America C563
Jacuzzi Whirlpool Bath C663
thermostatic
see
plumbing fittings and trim: —valves—mixing—
pressure balancing, thermostatic
toilet seats
Beneke Div., Sanderson
Plumbing C586
Mayfair C589
Olsonite Corp. C590A
valves—diverter
Artistic Brass C579
valves—mixing—pressure balancing, thermostatic
Grohe America C563
JADO Bathroom/Hardware
Mfg. Corp. C581

Plumbing fixtures
see
bar furniture and equipment: —sink
bathtubs
bidets
lavatories and accessories
showers
sinks—commercial or institutional
sinks—residential
toilets

Plywood
product information—manufacturers
see
specific products

Pollution control equipment and systems
see
air conditioners
pumps: —sewage ejector or sump—specific
type
vacuum cleaning systems
waste handling equipment and systems
water conditioning equipment

Prefinished paneling
see
surfacing and paneling—interior

Preservatives
see
marble: —preservatives, treatments and
cleaners

Primers
metal
see
coatings—metal-protective

Product information—associations
see also
specific products

Product information—associations *cont.*
cabinets—kitchen
NKBA, National Kitchen &
Bath Association A105
kitchen and bath/planning and design
NKBA, National Kitchen &
Bath Association A105

Publications
see
product information—associations

Pumps
heat
see
heat pumps—unitary/split
sewage ejector or sump
Zoeller Co. .C576

Purifiers
water
see
water conditioning equipment: —purifiers

r

Ranges and ovens—commercial or institutional
see
kitchen or kitchenette units

Ranges and ovens—residential
accessories for
Jenn-Air Co. .C502
cooktops
Amana Refrigeration, Inc. C481
Elmira Stove Works A013
Jenn-Air Co. .C502
KitchenAid, Inc. C503
Magic Chef, Inc. C506
Maytag Co. .C507
Russell Range C510
Viking Range Corp. C517
cooktops/grills—convertible
see also
grills—barbecue
Amana Refrigeration, Inc. C481
Jenn-Air Co. .C502
KitchenAid, Inc. C503
Magic Chef, Inc. C506
Maytag Co. .C507
electric
Amana Refrigeration, Inc. C481
Jenn-Air Co. .C502
Magic Chef, Inc. C506
gas
Amana Refrigeration, Inc. C481
Elmira Stove Works A013
Jenn-Air Co. .C502
Magic Chef, Inc. C506
Viking Range Corp. C517
kitchenette combination
see
kitchen or kitchenette units
ovens—built-in
Amana Refrigeration, Inc. C481
Jenn-Air Co. .C502
KitchenAid, Inc. C503
Magic Chef, Inc. C506
Maytag Co. .C507
Viking Range Corp. C517
ovens—built-in—double
Amana Refrigeration, Inc. C481
Jenn-Air Co. .C502

Ranges and ovens—residential
cont.

ovens—built-in—double *cont.*
KitchenAid, Inc. C503
Magic Chef, Inc. C506
Maytag Co. C507
Viking Range Corp. C517

ovens—microwave
Amana Refrigeration, Inc. C481
Jenn-Air Co. C502
Magic Chef, Inc. C506
Maytag Co. C507
Sharp Electronics Corp. C512

ovens—microwave/conventional combination
Amana Refrigeration, Inc. C481
Jenn-Air Co. C502
Magic Chef, Inc. C506
Maytag Co. C507
Sharp Electronics Corp. C512

ovens—microwave—kitchenette units
Amana Refrigeration, Inc. C481

ovens—self-cleaning
Amana Refrigeration, Inc. C481
Elmira Stove Works A013
Jenn-Air Co. C502
KitchenAid, Inc. C503
Magic Chef, Inc. C506
Maytag Co. C507
Viking Range Corp. C517

ranges—built-in
Amana Refrigeration, Inc. C481
Jenn-Air Co. C502
Magic Chef, Inc. C506
Viking Range Corp. C517

ranges—griddle/broiler/oven combination
Jenn-Air Co. C502

ranges—microwave/conventional oven combination
Amana Refrigeration, Inc. C481
Jenn-Air Co. C502
Magic Chef, Inc. C506

ventilating hoods
see
> ventilators: —hoods—residential kitchen—
> specific type

Receptors—shower
see
> showers: —stalls and receptors—specific
> material

Refacings or facings
see
> panels—building
> surfacing and paneling—interior

Reference books and publications
see
> product information—associations

Refrigerator-freezer combination

residential
Amana Refrigeration, Inc. C481
Jenn-Air Co. C502
KitchenAid, Inc. C503
Magic Chef, Inc. C506
Maytag Co. C507
Sub-Zero Freezer Co., Inc. C514; C515

residential—built-in
Amana Refrigeration, Inc. C481
Jenn-Air Co. C502
KitchenAid, Inc. C503
Magic Chef, Inc. C506
Maytag Co. C507
Sub-Zero Freezer Co., Inc. C514; C515

Refrigerators
see also
> refrigerator-freezer combination

commercial or institutional
see
> kitchen or kitchenette units

residential
Amana Refrigeration, Inc. C481
Jenn-Air Co. C502
KitchenAid, Inc. C503
Magic Chef, Inc. C506
Maytag Co. C507
Sub-Zero Freezer Co., Inc. C514; C515

residential—built-in
Amana Refrigeration, Inc. C481
Jenn-Air Co. C502
KitchenAid, Inc. C503
Magic Chef, Inc. C506
Maytag Co. C507
Sub-Zero Freezer Co., Inc. C514; C515

residential—ice, chilled water dispensers
Amana Refrigeration, Inc. C481
Jenn-Air Co. C502
KitchenAid, Inc. C503
Magic Chef, Inc. C506
Maytag Co. C507
Sub-Zero Freezer Co., Inc. C514; C515

residential—kitchenette combination
see
> kitchen or kitchenette units

Rods and bars

shower
see
> showers: —rods, hardware and tracks

Room assemblies

partitions for
see
> partitions

Rooms—steam
see
> steam bath rooms

Rustication
see
> panels—building—materials
> stone—specific type

Rust inhibitors
see
> coatings—metal-protective

S

Sandwich panels or walls
see
> panels—building—materials

Saunas and equipment
see also
> doors—application: —sauna
Finlandia Sauna Products,
> Inc. C642

School equipment

laboratories
see
> laboratory equipment

Scuppers
see
> drains

Sealers

metal
see also
> coatings—metal-protective
Unelko Corp. A011

Seats—toilet
see
> bathroom accessories: —grab bars, safety toilet
> seats, safety towel bars—metal
> hospital equipment: —grab bars, safety toilet
> seats, safety towel bars
> plumbing fittings and trim: —toilet seats

Security and bullet-resistant equipment
see
> glass—properties —burglar-resistant
> panels—building—properties: —bullet or
> burglar-resistant
> partitions—properties: —bullet or burglar-
> resistant

Service basins
see
> sinks—commercial or institutional

Sewage treatment equipment and systems
see
> pumps: —sewage ejector or sump—specific
> type
> waste handling equipment and systems
> water conditioning equipment

Sheets, strips, plates, coils

glass
see
> glass—form

plastic
see
> plastic—form

Shelving
see also
> storage equipment

bathroom or washroom—glass
JADO Bathroom/Hardware
> Mfg. Corp. C581
NuTone C590

bathroom or washroom—metal
Basco, Inc. C585

wood or wood fiber, plywood
Merillat Industries, Inc. C530
Wellborn Cabinet, Inc. C536

Shower/bathtub modules
see
> bathtub/shower—prefabricated unit

Showers

cabinets and enclosures
Aristech Chemical Corp. C591
Basco C592
Century Shower Door, Inc. C593
Du Pont Co. C468
Jacuzzi Whirlpool Bath C663
Jason International, Inc. C574
Strom Plumbing, Sign of the
> Crab C584
Wilson: Ralph Wilson Plastics
> Co. C479
Work Right Products, Inc. C597

disabled persons' use
Alsons Corp., Masco, Inc. C578
Basco, Inc. C585

Showers *cont.*

doors
see
> *doors—application: —shower*

fittings
see
> *plumbing fittings and trim*

group
see
> *plumbing fittings and trim: —shower or spray—
> group—column, wall mounted*

rods, hardware and tracks
Basco, Inc. C585
Strom Plumbing, Sign of the
Crab C584

seats—wall-mounted
Alsons Corp., Masco, Inc. C578
Steamist Co., Inc. C673

stalls and receptors—fiber glass, plastic
Basco C592
Jacuzzi Whirlpool Bath C663
Jason International, Inc. C574
Swirl-way Plumbing Group C667

Shutters and louvers—ventilating
see
> *ventilators*

Sinks—commercial or institutional

fittings and trim for
see
> *plumbing fittings and trim*

food service
see
> *food service equipment—commercial or
> institutional: —sinks*

tops for
Du Pont Co. C468

Sinks—residential

bar
see
> *bar furniture and equipment: —sink*

ceramic, composite
Blanco A012
Du Pont Co. C468
Elkay Mfg. Corp. C561

fittings for
see
> *plumbing fittings and trim*

food waste disposers for
see
> *food waste disposers*

stainless steel
Blanco A012
Elkay Mfg. Corp. C561
Franke, Inc., Kitchen
Systems Div. C562

tops for
Du Pont Co. C468
Wilson: Ralph Wilson Plastics
Co. C479

Skylights—operation

ventilators—power-driven
see
> *ventilators: —adjustable—manual or power-
> operated*

Slate products
see
> *specific products*

Soap dispensers and holders
see
> *bathroom accessories: —toilet paper holders,
> soap dishes—specific materials*
> *washroom accessories: —dispensers—soap*

Solar energy conversion—components for—passive

glazing—insulating
see
> *glass—properties: —insulating—specific type*

panels—building
see
> *panels—building—properties: —insulating*

Solid waste handling equipment
see
> *waste handling equipment and systems*

Sound control
see
> *acoustic isolation and control*
> *specific products or materials*

Space dividers—interior
see
> *partitions*

Spas and equipment
Finlandia Sauna Products,
Inc. C642

Stainless steel
see
> *specific products*

Stalls—shower
see
> *showers*

Steam bath rooms

equipment for
see also
> *health club equipment*
Jacuzzi Whirlpool Bath C663
Steamist Co., Inc. C673

Steel products
see
> *specific products*

Stone
see
> *marble*

Stone products
see
> *specific products*

Stone—simulated/manufactured
see
> *moldings and cornices: —stone or simulated
> stone*
> *surfacing and paneling—interior: —stone—
> simulated*

Storage equipment
see also
> *office equipment*
> *shelving*

cabinets with doors
Merillat Industries, Inc. C530
Wellborn Cabinet, Inc. C536

Storage equipment *cont.*

cabinets with drawers
Merillat Industries, Inc. C530
Wellborn Cabinet, Inc. C536

Store fronts

fire-rated
Weck, Glashaus Div. B689

fire-resistant
Weck, Glashaus Div. B689

Strainers
see also
> *drains*
> *piping and tubing accessories: —strainers*

basket type
Elkay Mfg. Corp. C561

Sun controls
see
> *glass—form*
> *glass—properties*
> *plastic*

Surfacing and paneling—interior
see also
> *panels—building*

fire-resistant
Du Pont Co. C468

marble or simulated marble
Du Pont Co. C468

moldings and trim for—plastic, composite
see also
> *moldings and cornices: —plastic, composite*
Du Pont Co. C468

plastic—molded
Du Pont Co. C468

plastic—sheet or tile
Du Pont Co. C468

stone—simulated
Du Pont Co. C468

t

Tables

tops for
Du Pont Co. C468

Telephone equipment
see
> *intercommunicating systems*

Theft detection equipment and systems
see
> *security and bullet-resistant equipment*

Tile or tile form
see
> *flooring—specific material*
> *panels—building—materials —specific materials*
> *surfacing and paneling—interior*

Toilets

partitions
see
> *partitions—application: —toilet, urinal*

sewage removal pump compartments
Zoeller Co. C576

units
Barclay Products Ltd. C567

Toilets *cont.*

units *cont.*
Duravit/Santile International
Corp. C568

Toilet seats
see
plumbing fittings and trim: —toilet seats

Toppings—traffic-bearing
liquid applied or troweled
Unelko Corp. .A011

Tops
see
cabinets: —tops for
counters: —tops for
laboratory equipment: —work surfaces for
sinks—commercial or institutional: —tops for
tables: —tops for

Towel bars—safety
see
bathroom accessories: —grab bars, safety toilet
seats, safety towel bars—metal
hospital equipment: —grab bars, safety toilet
seats, safety towel bars
washroom accessories: —grab bars

Towels
holders
see
bathroom accessories: —towel holders

Tracks
shower cubicles
see
showers: —rods, hardware and tracks

Treatments
see
coatings—specific type
flooring—treatments, maintenance and
resurfacing
marble: —preservatives, treatments and
cleaners

Troughs—drainage, wash
see
drains

Tubing
see
piping and tubing—materials

Tubs
bath
see
bathtubs

U

Urinals
screens, partitions
see
partitions—application: —toilet, urinal

Utility line accessories
see
piping and tubing accessories
wiring devices—electrical

V

Vacuum cleaning systems
centralized, automatic operation
Broan Mfg. Co., Inc. ii
NuTone C590

Valves
see
plumbing fittings and trim
mixing
see
plumbing fittings and trim: —valves—mixing—
pressure balancing, thermostatic

Vanity cabinets
see
cabinets: —bathroom vanity: —washroom vanity

Vapor barriers/retarders
liquid or mastic
Unelko Corp. .A011

Vapor retarder systems
see
vapor barriers/retarders

Ventilators
see also
fans
adjustable—manual or power-operated
Broan Mfg. Co., Inc. C484
NuTone C590
ceiling, wall, window
Broan Mfg. Co., Inc. C484
NuTone C590
fans—kitchen
see
fans: —kitchen or bathroom
hoods—residential kitchen
Amana Refrigeration, Inc. C481
Broan Mfg. Co., Inc. . . . . ii; C484
Jenn-Air Co. C502
KitchenAid, Inc. C503
Maytag Co. .C507
Merillat Industries, Inc. C530
NuTone C590
Viking Range Corp. C517
hoods—residential kitchen—fan and light combination
Broan Mfg. Co., Inc. C484
Elmira Stove Works A013
Jenn-Air Co. C502
NuTone C590
hoods—residential kitchen—plate warmer
Broan Mfg. Co., Inc. C484
roof
Broan Mfg. Co., Inc. C484

Vinyl or vinyl fabrics
see
specific products

W

Wainscoting
see
surfacing and paneling—interior

Wall coverings—flexible
see
surfacing and paneling—interior

Wall coverings—rigid
see
surfacing and paneling—interior

Walls
blocks for
see
blocks—specific material
fans for
see
fans: —wall, ceiling or pedestal
fire-resistant
see
partitions—properties: —fire-resistant
interior
see
partitions
panels
see
panels—building
ventilators for
see
ventilators: —ceiling, wall, window

Wardrobes
doors for
see
doors—application: —closet—folding, sliding,
swinging: —closet—mirrored

Washroom accessories
see also
bathroom accessories
bottle openers
Basco, Inc. C585
disabled persons' use
Basco, Inc. C585
dispenser cabinets—toilet tissue
Basco, Inc. C585
dispensers—facial tissue
Basco, Inc. C585
dispensers—soap
Elkay Mfg. Corp. C561
dryers—electric—hand or hair
Broan Mfg. Co., Inc. ii
grab bars
Basco, Inc. C585
holders—toilet paper
Basco, Inc. C585
holders—toothbrush and/or tumbler—metal
Basco, Inc. C585
holders—toothbrush and/or tumbler—plastic
Basco, Inc. C585
hooks—coat or robe
Basco, Inc. C585

Waste handling equipment and systems
see also
food waste disposers
water conditioning equipment

Waste handling equipment and systems *cont.*

compactors—residential or institutional
Broan Mfg. Co., Inc. ii
Jenn-Air Co. C502
KitchenAid, Inc. C503

Water closets
see
toilets

Water conditioning equipment
see also
waste handling equipment and systems

piping for
see
piping and tubing—application: —gas, water,
electrical or sewer system

purifiers
Elkay Mfg. Corp. .... Inside Front Cover

Water conservation equipment
see
plumbing fittings and trim

Waterproofing membranes
see also
vapor barriers/retarders

fluid
Unelko Corp. A011

protection for
see
toppings—traffic-bearing

Wax—floor or wall
see
flooring—treatments, maintenance and
resurfacing

Whirlpools
see
bathtubs: —hydro-massage combination
spas and equipment

Windows—replacement
glass blocks for
Weck, Glashaus Div. B689

Wiring devices—electrical
wall plates
NuTone C590

Wood
see
specific products

Wood—treated
hardwoods
Bally, Michigan Maple Block C539

Wood treatments
see
wood—treated

Woodwork
moldings, cornices, door and window trim
Du Pont Co. C468

Woven wire mesh
see
specific products

Z

Zinc
see
specific products

If you don't use one of these...

you better use one of these.

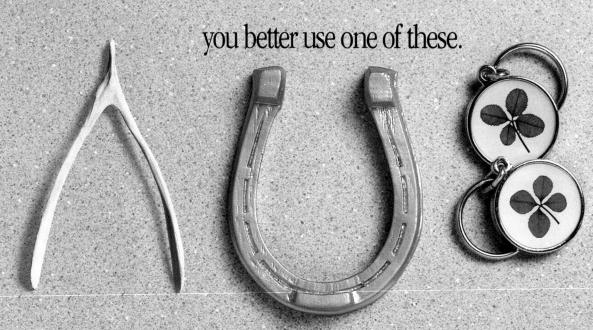

Maybe even all of them, if you're dreaming of a special new kitchen. Because you should ask a lot of the firm you hire to make that dream a reality:

- Will they spend the time to understand what you really want?
- Can they provide new and exciting ideas for making your kitchen look and *work* better?
- Will they do top-quality work at a fair price?
- Do they offer all the services you need?
- Do they have a showroom where you can see the latest trends and products?

Working with a member of the National Kitchen and Bath Association is the only way to be certain you'll get the right answer to each of these questions. So why test your luck?

Go with a sure thing — the total professionalism of every NKBA member. It's the best way to get exactly what you want.

Now that's our idea of a charmed life.

For information on NKBA members in your area, call toll-free: **1-800-FOR-NKBA**.

687 Willow Grove Street, Hackettstown, New Jersey 07840 FAX: (908) 852-1695

CREATING YOUR DREAM KITCHEN OR BATHROOM

More than four million kitchens will be built or remodeled in 1993. Some of the projects will be dreams come true. The rest can be nightmares.

When you stop and think about the effects that every alteration has on a room, you realize just how complicated remodeling or building can be. Besides the logistical questions, many decisions must be made in terms of color, hardware, appliances, lighting, plumbing fixtures, countertops, and the overall style of your new room.

"With so many decisions to make and so much to think about, the average consumer needs a professional to organize this project — someone who understands all of the complexities involved," said Donna M. Luzzo, Director of Communications for the National Kitchen & Bath Association (NKBA). "Kitchen and bathroom design is a specialized trade. It requires a good deal of experience and know-how to accomplish successful projects."

The first step in creating a successful new room is a simple one — find an NKBA member to design and coordinate the construction of your room.

"Someone remodeling a kitchen or bathroom wants the project to get off to a good start, and a kitchen and bath professional is definitely the way to go," said Luzzo. "An NKBA member will coordinate every aspect of the design and installation. They are experienced at working with contractors, electricians, plumbers, etc., and can efficiently schedule the jobs involved. And, most important, they are experts at working with the client. They listen to client needs and translate them into the kind of rooms they want."

To help consumers get ready for a remodeling and help them work with a kitchen or bathroom designer, the NKBA offers a 16-page brochure to consumers for $3. NKBA will also send a directory of kitchen/bathroom designers at no charge. Contact NKBA at 687 Willow Grove St., Hackettstown, N.J. 07840, or 1-800-FOR-NKBA.

NEW BATHROOM GUIDELINES REFLECT SAFETY/COMFORT

For much too long, the bathroom has been a miserable space accommodated in the smallest area of the home with the least amount of money. In the past, bathroom planning standards were based on minimum requirements established by the Department of Housing and Urban Development (HUD), which focused solely on the space required for the basic fixtures, and little or no consideration was given to the human anatomy of the user and his/her safe, comfortable movement in the space.

In the years ahead, successful bathroom designers will plan rooms that are designed around the people that will use them, rather than the fixtures that will be installed in them, according to the National Kitchen & Bath Association (NKBA).

"The bathroom is no longer a room reserved for simple personal hygiene," said Annette M. DePaepe, CKD, CBD, NKBA Director of Societies. "Today, people spend more time in the space. Some gather in a family group to enjoy the therapeutic pleasure of a hydromassage bath or sauna; others use the bathroom as a secluded spot away from hectic family and job responsibilities."

In keeping with the changing needs of the American family and issues such as safety and universal design, the NKBA has developed new planning guidelines for bathroom design which are based on the space required for the user(s) to function in the room comfortably and safely. The following is a complete list of these new planning guidelines.

NATIONAL KITCHEN & BATH ASSOCIATION'S
27 RULES OF BATHROOM DESIGN

1. A clear walkway of at least 32 inches must be provided at all entrances to the bathroom.

2. No doors may interfere with fixtures.

3. Mechanical ventilation system must be included in the plan.

4. Ground fault circuit interrupters specified on all receptacles. No switches within 60 inches of any water source. All light fixtures above tub/shower units are moisture-proof special purpose fixtures.

5. If floor space exists between two fixtures, at least six inches of space should be provided for cleaning.

6. At least 21 inches of clear walkway space exists in front of lavatory.

7. The minimum clearance from the lavatory centerline to any side wall is 12 inches.

8. The minimum clearance between two bowls in the lavatory center is 30 inches, centerline to centerline.

9. The minimum clearance from the center of the toilet to any obstruction, fixture or equipment on either side of toilet is 15 inches.

10. At least 21 inches of clear walkway space exists in front of toilet.

11. Toilet paper holder is installed within reach of person seated on the toilet. Ideal location is slightly in front of the edge of toilet bowl, the center of which is 26 inches above the finished floor.

12. The minimum clearance from the center of the bidet to any obstruction, fixture or equipment on either side of the bidet is 15 inches.

13. At least 21 inches of clear walkway space exists in front of bidet.

14. Storage for soap and towels is installed within reach of person seated on the bidet.

15. No more than one step leads to the tub. Step must be at least 10 inches deep, and must not exceed 7¼ inches in height.

16. Bathtub faucetry is accessible from outside the tub.

17. Whirlpool motor access, if necessary, is included in plan.

18. At least one grab bar is installed to facilitate bathtub or shower entry.

19. Minimum useable shower interior dimension is 32″ × 32″.

20. Bench or footrest is installed within shower enclosure.

21. Minimum clear walkway of 21 inches exists in front of tub/shower.

22. Shower door swings into bathroom.

23. All shower heads are protected by pressure balance/temperature regulator or temperature-limiting device.

24. All flooring is of slip-resistant material.

25. Adequate storage must be provided in plan, including: counter/shelf space around lavatory, adequate grooming equipment storage, convenient shampoo/soap storage in shower/tub area, and hanging space for bathroom linens.

26. Adequate heating system must be provided.

27. General and task lighting must be provided.

KITCHEN DESIGN CHANGES WITH THE TIMES

Home life, as we know it, is a far cry from what went on at the Cleaver residence, or in the Cunningham household, even at the Brady's "hip" pad.

In the past 40 years, lifestyles have undergone a lot of change. And no room in the house exemplifies that change better than the kitchen.

The walls have come down; more appliances have gone in; what we cook, when we cook and who cooks bears little resemblance to what went on two or three generations ago.

Yet, despite the great changes in lifestyle and kitchen use, little attention had been paid to the guidelines followed for kitchen design. Recognizing the need for updated planning standards, the National Kitchen & Bath Association (NKBA) conducted in-depth research into today's kitchens. As a result, today's kitchen planners have a new set of rules to follow in order to meet the needs of their 1990s clients.

"The kitchen did not used to be considered part of the social portion of the home," said NKBA Director of Communications Donna M. Luzzo. "Rather, kitchens were planned as walled-off spaces intended for use by a full-time homemaker who was the primary, from-scratch cook in the household."

Conversely, according to the NKBA, today most families consist of two working parents, creating a need for shared cooking and clean-up responsibilities. The walled-off space of the past has opened into other rooms. And families and guests are gathering in the kitchen to socialize and carry on activities other than cooking.

These changes make an impact on how a kitchen needs to be arranged; as do a host of others, according to Luzzo.

"Microwave ovens, side-by-side refrigerators and dishwashers are commonly found in kitchens," she said. "In addition, our recent research found that more than 700 utensils and food items are kept in the room. That's 400 more items than 40 years ago."

What does it all mean? More cabinet storage is necessary, for one. And the kitchen must become a comfortable setting for today's on-the-go families to gather, unwind, entertain and work in together easily.

The NKBA has established the following 31 rules for planning safe, functional kitchens. Whether remodeling on your own, or working with a professional kitchen planner as recommended by the NKBA, use these rules as guidelines to ensure a functional kitchen plan that will serve the needs of your family.

If you would like a directory of kitchen design firms, contact the NKBA at 1-800-FOR-NKBA and one will be sent to you at no charge.

NATIONAL KITCHEN & BATH ASSOCIATION'S
31 RULES OF KITCHEN DESIGN

1. A clear walkway at least 32″ wide must be provided at all entrances to the kitchen.

2. No entry or appliance door may interfere with work center appliances and/or counter space.

3. Work aisles must be at least 42″ wide, and passage ways must be at least 36″ wide for a one-cook kitchen.

4. In kitchens 150 square feet or less, at least 144″ of wall cabinet frontage, with cabinets at least 12″ deep and a minimum of 30″ high (or equivalent), must be installed over counter tops. In kitchens over 150 square feet, 186″ of wall cabinets must be included. Diagonal or pie-cut wall cabinets count as a total of 24″. Difficult to reach cabinets above the hood, oven or refrigerator do not count unless specialized storage devices are installed within the case to improve accessibility.

5. At least 60″ of wall cabinet frontage with cabinets which are at least 12″ deep and a minimum of 30″ high (or equivalent) must be included within 72″ of the primary sink centerline.

6. In kitchens 150 square feet or less, at least 156″ of base cabinet frontage, with cabinets at least 21″ deep (or equivalent) must be part of the plan. In kitchens over 150 square feet, 192″ of base cabinets must be included. Pie-cut/lazy Susan cabinets count as a total of 30″. The first 24″ of a blind corner box do not count.

7. In kitchens 150 square feet or less, at least 120″ of drawer frontage or roll-out shelf frontage must be planned. Kitchens over 150 square feet require at least 165″ of drawer/shelf frontage. (Measure cabinet width to determine frontage.)

8. At least five storage items must be included in the kitchen to improve the accessibility and functionality of the plan. These items include, but are not limited to: wall cabinets with adjustable shelves, interior vertical dividers, pull out drawers, swing-out pantries, or drawer/roll-out space greater than the minimum 135″.

9. At least one functional corner storage unit must be included. (Rule does not apply to a kitchen without corner cabinet arrangements.)

10. Between 15″ and 18″ of clearance must exist between the countertop and the bottom of wall cabinets.

11. In kitchens 150 square feet or less, at least 132″ of usable countertop frontage is required. For kitchens larger than 150 square feet, the countertop requirement increases to 198″. Counter must be 16″ deep to be counted; corner space does not count.

12. No two primary work centers (the primary sink, refrigerator, preparation center, cooktop/range center), can be separated by a full-height, full-depth tall tower, such as an oven cabinet, pantry cabinet or refrigerator.

13. There must be at least 24″ of counter space to one side of the sink, and 18″ on the other side. (Measure only countertop frontage, do not count corner space.) The 18″ and 24″ counter space sections may be a continuous surface, or the total of two angled countertop sections. If a second sink is part of the plan, at least 3″ of counterspace must be on one side and 18″ on the other side.

14. At least 3″ of counter space must be allowed from the edge of the sink to the inside corner of the countertop if more than 21″ of counter space is available on the return. Or, at least 18″ of counter space from the edge of the sink to the inside corner of the countertop if the return counter space is blocked by a full-height, full-depth cabinet or any appliance which is deeper than the countertop.

15. At least two waste receptacles must be included in the plan, one for garbage and one for recyclables; or other recycling facilities should be planned.

16. The dishwasher must be positioned within 36″ of one sink. Sufficient space (21″ of standing room) must be allowed between the dishwasher and adjacent counters, other appliances and cabinets.

17. At least 36″ of continuous countertop is required for the preparation center, and must be located close to a water source.

18. The plan should allow at least 15″ of counter space on the latch side of a refrigerator or on either side of a side-by-side refrigerator. Or, at least 15″ of landing space which is no more than 48″ across from the refrigerator. (Measure the 48″ walkway from the countertop adjacent to the refrigerator to the island countertop directly opposite.)

19. For an open-ended kitchen configuration, at least 9″ of counter space is required on one side of the cooktop/range top and 15″ on the other. For an enclosed configuration, at least 3″ of clearance space must be planned at an end wall protected by flame-retardant surfacing material, and 15″ must be allowed on the other side of the appliance.

20. The cooking surface can not be placed below an operable window unless the window is 3″ or more behind the appliance, and/or more than 24″ above it.

21. There must be at least 15″ of landing space next to or above the oven if the appliance door opens into a primary family traffic pattern. 15″ of landing space which is no more than 48″ across from the oven is acceptable if the appliance does not open into traffic area.

22. At least 15″ of landing space must be planned above, below, or adjacent to the microwave oven.

23. The shelf on which the microwave is placed is to be between counter and eye level (36″ to 54″ off the floor).

24. All cooking surface appliances are required to have a ventilation system, with a fan rated at 150 CFM minimum.

25. At least 24″ of clearance is needed between the cooking surface and a protected surface above. Or, at least 30″ of clearance is needed between the cooking surface and an unprotected surface above.

26. The work triangle should total less than 26′. The triangle is defined as the shortest walking distance between the refrigerator, primary cooking surface, and primary food preparation sink. It is measured from the center front of each appliance. The work triangle may not intersect an island or peninsula cabinet by more than 12″. No single leg of the triangle should be shorter than 4′ nor longer than 9′.

27. No major household traffic patterns should cross through the work triangle connecting the three primary centers (the primary sink, refrigerator, preparation center, cooktop/range center).

28. A minimum of 12″ × 24″ counter/table space should planned for each seated diner.

29. At least 36″ of walkway space from a counter/table to any wall or obstacle behind it is required if the area is to be used to pass behind a seated diner. Or, at least 24″ of space from the counter/table to any wall or obstacle behind it, is needed if the area will not be used as a walk space.

30. At least 10% of the total square footage of the separate kitchen, or of a total living space which includes a kitchen should be appropriated for windows/skylights.

31. Ground fault circuit interrupters must be specified on all receptacles that are within 6′ of a water source in the kitchen. A fire extinguisher should be located near the cooktop. Smoke alarms should be included near the kitchen.

BATHS UP, KITCHENS DOWN IN RETAIL SELLING PRICE

Results of the 1992 Kitchen/Bath Industry Trends Survey, released by the National Kitchen & Bath Association (NKBA), indicate that the average bathroom selling price is rising nationally. At the same time, the national average selling price of kitchen projects is down slightly.

The selling price reflects the total cost charged to retail customers or builders for complete kitchen and bathroom projects in newly-constructed or remodeled homes. Included in the selling price are all or most of the following items: labor, cabinets, fixtures/fittings, countertops, flooring, lighting, and appliances. The 1992 Survey tabulated information provided by 300 NKBA-member firms.

According to Paul L. Kelley, NKBA Vice President of Industry Relations and Marketing, the 1992 Trends Survey, which addresses business conducted in 1991, revealed that the average bathroom selling price at this time is $9,215, and the average kitchen selling price $16,491.

The Survey data also indicates that small kitchen jobs (less than 150 square feet) presently represent a larger portion of all kitchen projects installed compared to previous years, perhaps explaining the decrease in average price. Interestingly, small sized (under 35 square feet) bathroom projects now account for 17 percent of the total, up from just one percent of the total reported in the 1990 Survey.

KITCHEN HIGHLIGHTS

The gap between the popularity of wood cabinets (75 percent) and laminate cabinets (22 percent) is narrowing. The 1990 figures were 87 and 11.5 percent, respectively. Oak is the most popular wood species for cabinetry (54 percent), but maple (15 percent) is up dramatically since the 1990 Survey. Laminate leads all other countertop materials (54 percent), followed most closely by solid surfacing (30 percent).

BATHROOM HIGHLIGHTS

As in the kitchens surveyed, wood cabinets are installed most often (68 percent). Oak (59 percent) leads all other wood species, with cherry (24 percent) and maple (12 percent) in the second and third positions. Both cherry and maple have gained popularity — in the 1990 Survey, the figures tabulated were 11 percent and 3 percent, respectively. Paint (30 percent), wall paper (28 percent) and tile (16 percent) continue as the wall covering materials of choice, although the order of preference has changed since 1990, when wall paper topped the list at 66 percent.

COLOR

White is still the most important color in both kitchens (48 percent) and bathrooms (62 percent). These figures represent a rise of almost 13 percent in white kitchens installed, when expressed as a portion of total, since the 1990 Survey. White baths have risen a corresponding 19 percent. Wood-toned kitchens and pastel baths are the second most popular choices. Almond is the third most-often chosen color for both kitchens and bathrooms.

SURVEY CHANGES IN 1992

The NKBA Design Trends Survey, which has been conducted annually since 1986, becomes more comprehensive each year, reflecting changes in the kitchen and bathroom industry and incorporating emerging design issues. In the 1992 Survey, for example, new questions sought data on the use of new and replacement windows (32 percent) as well as recycling considerations (37 percent) in kitchen design.

HOW DOES YOUR KITCHEN RATE?

How functional and fashionable is your kitchen? Answer these questions from the National Kitchen & Bath Association to find out how the most important room in your home rates.

A. STORAGE SYSTEM

1. Do your cabinets feature time-saving accessories such as roll-out shelves, divided drawers and lazy Susans?   YES   NO

2. Is there enough cabinet shelf space?   YES   NO

3. Is the cabinet door style and color up-to-date?   YES   NO

4. Is there a place to sort recyclables?   YES   NO

B. COUNTERTOP

1. Is there enough counter space?   YES   NO

2. Is the countertop material undamaged and in good shape?   YES   NO

3. Is the counter color/pattern up-to-date?   YES   NO

C. MECHANICAL ELEMENTS

1. Do you have enough electrical outlets?   YES   NO

2. Is there a good ventilation system in the cooking area?   YES   NO

D. APPLIANCES/FIXTURES

1. Are all of your appliances a pleasant color that looks good?   YES   NO

E. ROOM ORIENTATION

1. Is there a casual dining/conversation area in the room?   YES   NO

2. Is the kitchen arranged so that "People Traffic" is directed away from the cook's activities?   YES   NO

If you answered "no" more than "yes," you may need a new room. Take the first step and contact a member of the National Kitchen & Bath Association to ensure a successful project. They are competent to design and install complete kitchens, and subscribe to a strict Code of Conduct. Bring this evaluation with you, and your NKBA Kitchen Dealer or Certified Kitchen Designer will help you use your NO answers to make planning decisions regarding room shape and size, appliance and material selection as well as mechanical specifications. For a complete list of NKBA members contact: NKBA, 687 Willow Grove St., Hackettstown, N.J. 07840   or   1-800-FOR-NKBA.

DOES YOUR BATHROOM PASS THE TEST?

How does your bathroom rate? Is it beautiful...functional...safe? Answer this brief survey from the National Kitchen & Bath Association to find out if your bathroom makes the grade.

A. FIXTURES

1. Is the shower safe (non-slip floor, grab bars, bench seat, temperature-controlled faucet)? YES NO

2. Is the bathtub safe (easy to get into, faucets within reach, non-slip bottom, grab bars)? Yes NO

3. Are all the fixtures an attractive color? YES NO

B. STORAGE SYSTEMS

1. Is the cabinet door style and color up-to-date? YES NO

2. Do cabinets include a well-organized storage system? YES NO

3. Is there space for towel storage in or near the bathroom? YES NO

C. MECHANICAL ELEMENTS

1. Is there an efficient ventilation system in the room? YES NO

2. Is there adequate lighting in the right place(s) for your bathroom activities (shaving, make-up application, reading)? YES NO

3. Are all the electrical outlets protected with ground fault circuit interrupters to prevent electrical shock? YES NO

D. MAJOR SURFACES

1. Are all the surfaces easy to keep clean? YES NO

E. ROOM ORIENTATION

1. Is the existing bathroom big enough? YES NO

2. Can two people use the bathroom comfortably and conveniently at the same time? YES NO

More "nos" than "yeses" on your score card may indicate that you need a new bathroom. Take the first step and contact a member of the National Kitchen & Bath Association to ensure a successful project. They are competent to design and install complete bathrooms, and subscribe to a strict Code of Conduct. Bring this evaluation with you, and your NKBA Bathroom Dealer or Certified Bathroom Designer will help you use your NO answers to make planning decisions regarding room shape and size, fixture and material selection as well as mechanical specifications. For a complete list of NKBA members contact: NKBA, 687 Willow Grove St., Hackettstown, N.J. 07840 or 1-800-FOR-NKBA.

IMPORTANT

The kitchen & bathroom remodeling job is going to bring you and your family a host of decisions. Where should the refrigerator go? How much light will we need? Should we include a bidet, a whirlpool? All these questions should have sound answers which any of the NKBA (National Kitchen & Bath Association) members can provide for you. A complete listing of these individuals can be found in this book.

Please fill out the brief questionnaire below and return it to us. This information is for demographic purposes only. By doing so, we can provide manufacturers with a profile of those involved in the planning, design and selection of products for their upcoming kitchen and bathroom projects.

1. Are you remodeling a kitchen or bathroom?
❑ Kitchen ❑ Bathroom ❑ Both ❑ Other: _____

2. What is the amount you estimate spending on your remodeling job?
❑ Less than $5,000 ❑ $10,000 - $19,999
❑ $5,000 - $9,999 ❑ $20,000 or More

3. How will the remodeling be completed?
❑ We will purchase the products and complete the remodeling ourselves
❑ We will purchase products, then hire a contractor for installation
❑ We will go to one place for all products and installation

4. Which product(s) do you plan to replace:

❑ Bath Accessories	❑ Flooring-Tile/Marble	❑ Refrigerator
❑ Cabinets	❑ Flooring-Wood	❑ Range
❑ Countertops	❑ Freezer	❑ Shower Doors
❑ Dishwasher	❑ Lighting	❑ Shower Stall
❑ Disposer	❑ Medicine Cabinet	❑ Sink
❑ Faucets	❑ Microwave Oven	❑ Toilets
❑ Flooring-Resilient	❑ Oven	❑ Bathtub
❑ Vanity	❑ Vanity Top	❑ Windows

5. Which product(s) do you plan to add:

❑ Bidet	❑ His/Her Sinks	❑ Shower Door
❑ Cooktop	❑ Hot Tub	❑ Skylights
❑ Disposer	❑ Ice Machine	❑ Sound/Intercom System
❑ Flooring-Resilient	❑ Microwave Oven	❑ Steam Bath
❑ Flooring-Tile/Marble	❑ Medicine Cabinet	❑ Sun Room
❑ Flooring-Wood	❑ Sauna	❑ Water Purifier
		❑ Whirlpool Tub

6. What is the approximate value of your home?
❑ Less than $100,000 ❑ $200,000 - $249,999 ❑ $400,00 - $499,999
❑ $100,000 - $149,999 ❑ $250,000 - $299,999 ❑ $500,000 or More
❑ $150,000 - $199,999 ❑ $300,000 - $399,999

7. What is your approximate household income?
❑ Less than $30,000 ❑ $50,000 - $74,999 ❑ $100,000 - $149,999
❑ $30,000 - $49,999 ❑ $75,000 - $99,999 ❑ $150,000 or More

8. Are you a double income household?
❑ Yes ❑ No

9. How long have you lived in your home?
❑ Less than 2 Years ❑ 6 - 10 Years ❑ More than 20 Years
❑ 2 - 5 Years ❑ 11 - 20 Years

10. How helpful was this book to you in selecting products?
❑ Very Helpful ❑ Somewhat Helpful ❑ Not Very Helpful ❑ Not At All Helpful

11. Where did you buy this book?
Name of store or book club:_____

Location of Store: City_____

(Please fold and tape this form closed with the return address showing on the outside)

Fold here and seal with tape. Do not staple.

BUSINESS REPLY MAIL

FIRST CLASS MAIL PERMIT NO. 226 NEW YORK NY

POSTAGE WILL BE PAID BY ADDRESSEE

**SWEET'S GROUP
MCGRAW-HILL INC
ATTENTION ALMA L WEINSTEIN
1221 AVENUE OF THE AMERICAS
NEW YORK NY 10124-0026**

Fold here and seal with tape. Do not staple.

ELMIRA COUNTRY RANGES BUILT ONLY BY

Elmira Ranges Feature:

- Deluxe 8M and 12M BTU Sealed gas top burners or EGO Euro Electric elements.

- Big, automatic, electric, self-cleaning ovens.

- Cabinets above range house automatic clock, timer, 350 cfm exhaust hood and light.

- Four burner model fits neatly into a standard 30" opening.

- Colors available: "Country Blue", "Cast Iron Grey", Almond, White or Black. All units come with nickel trim.

- Warranty: 1 year parts and labor, 3 years on burners and elements. Elmira ranges use all standard industry components.

- Options: Griddle, "Country Motif" as illustrated.

Dimensions - Models 1850, 1870

Dimensions - Models 1855, 1875

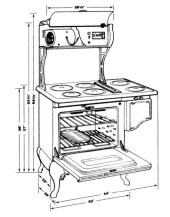

Call us at:
(519) 725-5500
for more information.

Or write:
**Elmira Stove Works
22 Church Street
Elmira, Ontario
N3B 1M3**

HEAVY GLASS

1038 1090 SHOWER DOORS

For the full story, contact Betty Byers, Alumax Bath Enclosures, P.O. Box 40, Magnolia, AR 71753; 800-643-1514.

Our finest frameless door: $\frac{3}{8}$-inch glass; uncluttered styling; gravity closing pivots; full water blockage; in-place adjustability; gold, silver, black finishes; immediate availabilities in both standard and custom bath enclosure models.

ALUMAX

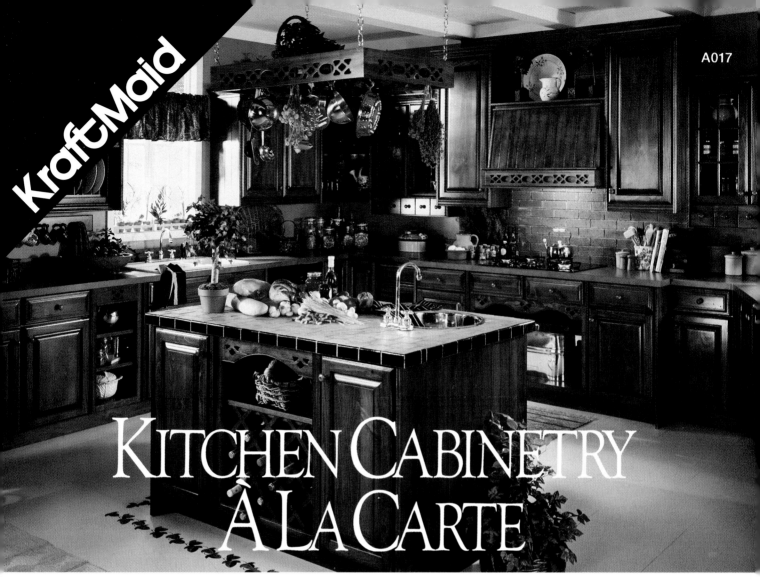

KraftMaid

A017

KITCHEN CABINETRY À LA CARTE

KraftMaid cabinetry looks fabulous in any kitchen.

But why stop there? KraftMaid's versatility looks great in baths, bedrooms, wall units or any room or office.

With KraftMaid's extensive line of traditional and contemporary cabinetry, optional features and finishes, you now have a new world of design possibilities at your fingertips!

Choose from over 55 beautiful door styles in a variety of classic hardwoods and high-tech laminates. Then add function by choosing the optional features you want.

For selection, style, finishes, and optional features, choose KraftMaid...America's cabinetry choice!

Call, 1-800-654-3008, 24 hours a day, 7 days a week.

KraftMaid Cabinetry, Inc., Middlefield, OH 44062

FROM INSPIRATION TO SENSATION

Creating Your
Dream Kitchen
Or Bathroom

OFF
TO A
GOOD
START

So, you've decided to create your dream kitchen or bathroom. Great idea. You'll finally be able to apply all of those wishes you've collected on your list over the years, like that kitchen island with a cooktop (and more of that invaluable countertop and cabinet space), or maybe you've always wanted a bathtub-for-two. Whether it's the kitchen or bathroom (or both), you can look forward to an exciting transformation into the room you've always wanted.

But when you stop and think about the effects that every alteration has on a room, you realize just how complicated remodeling or building can be. Take, for instance, the kitchen island with a cooktop. Where there's a cooktop, there's smoke and steam. And where there's smoke and steam, there has to be ventilation. So an overhead hood must be added, unless you have a downventing cooktop. Also, any time you have work space like the added countertop, you need electrical outlets. So wiring will be necessary for the outlets, as well as the cooktop and vent hood. And that's just the beginning.

Besides the logistical questions, many decisions must be made in terms of color, hardware, appliances, lighting, plumbing fixtures, countertops, and the overall style of your new room.

With so many decisions to make and so much to think about, you need a professional to organize this project — someone who understands all of the complexities involved. That's where the National Kitchen and Bath Association (NKBA) comes in.

FINDING THE NKBA MEMBER FOR THE JOB

The first step in creating your new room is a simple one — find an NKBA member to design and coordinate the construction of your room. You want your project to get off to a good start, and a kitchen and bath professional is definitely the way to go.

WHY?

The National Kitchen & Bath Association is an organization of professionals who focus specifically on kitchens and bathrooms. When you deal with an NKBA member, you'll benefit from specialized expertise, years of experience, a commitment to quality, and a high degree of professionalism. They maintain showrooms with products and complete designs on display so you can get a feel for the type and quality of work they can do.

A kitchen and bath professional can offer sound advice and suggest solutions to any problems that may arise, or, better yet, prevent problems from occurring. They also understand the ways families and individuals relate to their surroundings, and therefore may be able to troubleshoot and meet needs in ways that may not occur to those who don't specialize in kitchens and bathrooms.

An NKBA member will coordinate every aspect of the design and installation. They are experienced at working with contractors — electricians, plumbers, etc. — and can efficiently schedule the jobs involved. And, most important, they are expert at working with you, the client. They listen to your needs and translate them into the kind of room you want.

Don't take chances with your investment. When you make the decision for a new kitchen or bathroom, make the decision to find an NKBA member.

HOW?

NATIONAL KITCHEN NKBA & BATH ASSOCIATION

I t's easy to find an NKBA member, if you know what to look for. And easy identification begins with the NKBA logo, a symbol of quality, dedication and expertise in kitchens and bathrooms.

When visiting kitchen and bath showrooms, look for the logo in windows or on the counter.

If you know anyone who has recently remodeled, talk with them. Ask them who they used and if he or she is associated with the NKBA. Referrals are an excellent source for finding an industry professional, but be sure you're dealing with someone qualified in kitchens and bathrooms specifically — an NKBA member.

You can find all of the NKBA members in your area by contacting the National Kitchen and Bath Association at 687 Willow Grove Street, Hackettstown, New Jersey 07840, **1-800-FOR-NKBA**. They will provide you with a directory of NKBA firms who design, supply and install residential kitchens and bathrooms.

HAVE YOU FINISHED YOUR HOMEWORK?

Now that you have a name in mind (or possibly more than one — you may want to talk with several NKBA professionals to find the one with whom you feel most comfortable), you can go ahead and set up an appointment to discuss your project. But before you actually sit down with the designer, there are several things you should do in preparation. (This is the fun part.)

Chances are you've been thinking about this for a while, but if not, start reading magazines geared toward the home, remodeling, architecture, and especially those that focus on kitchens and bathrooms. Clip out pictures of kitchens or bathrooms that interest you — this will help the designer get a feel for the styles you like. You may even find features that would work in your new room.

Visit kitchen and bath showrooms to see the many options for new countertops and other surfaces, and to collect brochures on fixtures, cabinets, appliances and any other items or materials that interest you.

As you visit different showrooms in your search for ideas and NKBA designers, you should make notes on each one. The best way to find the NKBA member with whom you're most comfortable is to evaluate the designers and their showrooms. Use the following checklist to help you in your decision:

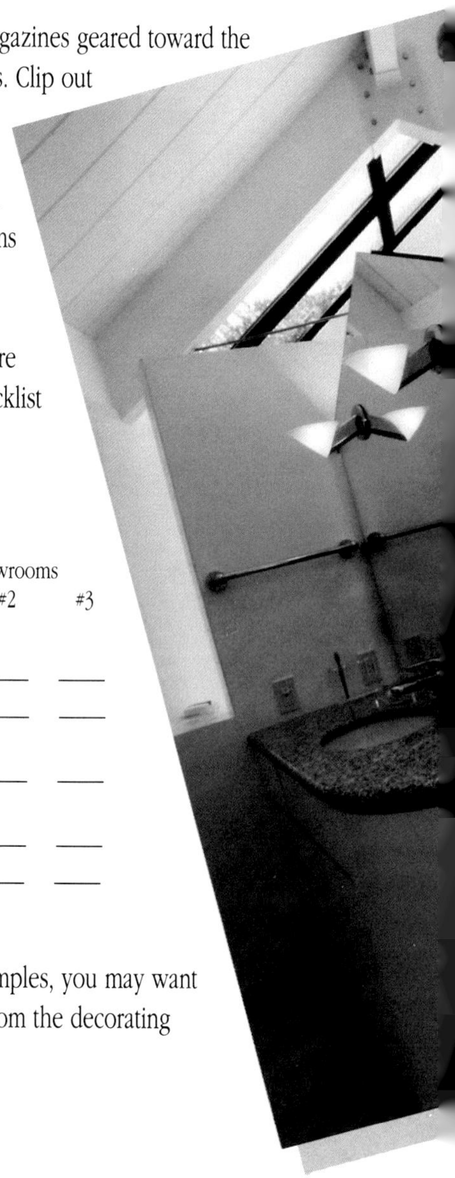

Evaluating the kitchen and bath dealership

	Showrooms #1	Showrooms #2	Showrooms #3
Showroom Clean and Neat	___	___	___
Displays Highlight Interesting Design	___	___	___
Displays Well-Constructed and Presented	___	___	___
Broad Range of Styles Offered	___	___	___
Staff Friendly and Helpful	___	___	___
Staff Knowledgeable About Products and Design	___	___	___

	Showrooms #1	Showrooms #2	Showrooms #3
Designers Ask Questions About Your Project	___	___	___
NKBA Membership Identified	___	___	___
Firm Has Been In Business for at Least Two Years	___	___	___
Firm Provides Complete Design and Installation Services	___	___	___
Referrals Provided	___	___	___

As you visit showrooms and gather notes, clippings, photographs, brochures and samples, you may want to organize them into an "idea file." As your file grows, you'll see a definite style emerge from the decorating trends you've chosen — *your* style.

KITCHEN PLANNING WITH YOUR NKBA SPECIALIST

You can save a lot of time and money, and greatly reduce guesswork by first evaluating your needs. Before even your initial consultation, write down some basic lifestyle facts.

Simple facts, like how many hours a week you work, will affect how often you cook and what appliances you use. If you work a lot of hours out of the home, you may cook less often, opting instead for microwave meals, in which case you'd need your microwave in a convenient location and a lot of freezer space.

Who uses your kitchen? Is it a setting for family gatherings, or the private domain of a gourmet chef? Will it function well with two or more cooks? Do you entertain often? All of these answers will affect the size, layout and type of equipment you need for your kitchen.

When preparing your evaluation, first consider your normal cooking habits. For instance, if your family shares in the meal preparation, you may need two sinks and built-in cutting and chopping boards strategically placed throughout the kitchen to maximize food preparation areas.

Will children be active in the kitchen? If so, easy-to-clean surfaces are a must. You may also want to consider a desk or counter setup for homework and after-school snacks.

If you like to entertain, often cooking for large groups of guests, you may need two ovens and a wide-shelved refrigerator.

Do you recycle? You'll need the separating and storage space, depending on your involvement and the requirements in your area.

All of the variables mentioned here (and others your designer will pose) will affect the layout of your kitchen. Each shape — U-shaped, L-shaped, Corridor, Island, One-Wall, or Peninsula — has its own functionality and advantages. Once the NKBA kitchen specialist has laid out your kitchen, he or she will guide you in selecting components. With all of the advances in materials, appliances and designs, this selection process would be overwhelming without the help of a professional.

Your decision-making becomes much easier once you have related your needs to your lifestyle. By providing your NKBA professional with a clear picture of what works best for your family, you'll be off to a head start.

BATHROOM PLANNING WITH YOUR NKBA SPECIALIST

Do you look forward to spending time in your bathroom? Sounds like a strange question to most people. Most bathrooms are cold and claustrophobic, places where comfort is either kept to a bare minimum, or simply not an option. But with the shift in society back toward the home also come changes in the bathroom.

Bathrooms have become more than a necessity. Their role has now expanded to that of "bodyroom," incorporating such amenities as whirlpool tubs, exercise equipment, dual-head showers, heat lamps and entertainment systems.

Before you talk to an NKBA professional about your new bathroom, evaluate your needs by first looking at who will use it, and how. The best way to do that is to examine present bathroom usage. Some NKBA members suggest taking notes as you use the room on a typical weekday and weekend. By mapping out your routine, you and your bath designer will be better-equipped to create a floorplan that is efficient and incorporates the features you need.

For example, you may think the first thing you do when you step out of the shower is to reach for your towel. Keeping a diary, however, might reveal that oftentimes the first move after exiting the shower is to drip, drip, drip across the hall to the linen closet. So, by simply focusing on details and making note of them, you've discovered the need for bathroom towel storage.

If several girls or women use the bathroom, adequate circuits and outlets are necessary for hair dryers and curling irons, as well as appropriate lighting for makeup application.

Special safety and convenience features should be considered for elderly, very young and handicapped family members. High water closet seats, grab bars and locking cabinets are practical options, and your designer will likely have other suggestions.

For family bathrooms which are shared by several people, privacy zones isolating the shower, tub, lavatory and water closet will allow simultaneous use.

Your NKBA bathroom specialist will take into consideration all of these factors and more. They have the experience to anticipate potential problems and point out options that may help you with your choices.

SETTING PRIORITIES

 hen your idea file is overflowing with clippings and photographs, you've thought about style and color, and evaluated your needs, there is one final step that will really help your NKBA professional: your "must-have" and "want" lists. You simply make two lists which include:

1) features you consider essential for your new room, and
2) features you'd like to have, if possible and if budget permits.

It sounds easy, right? Well, this one may force you to make some tough decisions and possibly even some sacrifices, but it is a very valuable step. Just listing and distinguishing the "must-haves" from the "wants" will help you focus on the features most important to you and your family. In fact, you may want to let each member of the family make their own lists. When you can actually see them on paper, it puts your needs into better perspective.

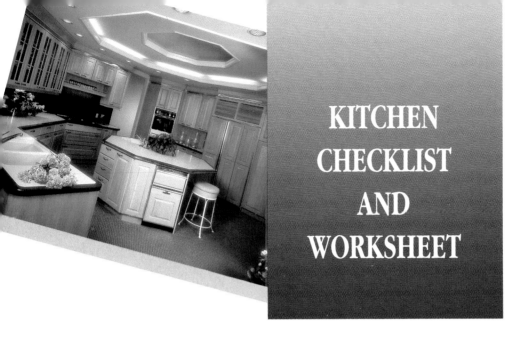

KITCHEN CHECKLIST AND WORKSHEET

Needs and Wants

Check the items you feel your kitchen must have in the "need" column, and the items you would like, if the budget and design allow, in the "want" column. (This should be used as a preliminary guideline; they may change along the way.)

	Need	Want		Need	Want
New cabinets	____	____	Recycling bins	____	____
New countertop	____	____	More workspace	____	____
New floor	____	____	More storage	____	____
New oven(s)	____	____	Pantry	____	____
New refrigerator/freezer	____	____	Wet bar	____	____
New cooktop	____	____	New window(s)	____	____
New microwave	____	____	Desk area	____	____
New dishwasher	____	____	Eating area	____	____
New sink(s)	____	____	Media/TV center	____	____
New light fixtures	____	____	Others _____	____	____
Cutting/chopping surfaces	____	____	_____	____	____
Waste disposal	____	____	_____	____	____
Trash compactor	____	____	_____	____	____

Lifestyle/Room Use

This worksheet will give you some things to think about in your initial planning, but it's only the beginning. Your NKBA kitchen specialist will conduct an in-depth interview with you in order to create a design that suits your lifestyle and satisfies your needs and wants.

Who is the primary cook? _____

How many other household members cook? _____

Do any of these members have physical limitations? _____

What type of cooking do you normally do?
 ____ Heat and serve meals
 ____ Full-course, "from scratch" meals
 ____ Bulk cooking for freezing/leftovers
 ____ Other _____

Do you entertain frequently? ____ Formally ____ Informally

Is the kitchen a socializing place? _____

Where do you plan to sort recyclables?
____ Kitchen ____ Laundry ____ Garage ____ Other

What type of feeling would you like your new kitchen space to have?
____ Sleek/Contemporary   ____ Warm & Cozy Country
____ Traditional   ____ Open & Airy
____ Strictly Functional   ____ Formal
____ Family Retreat   ____ Personal Design Statement

BATHROOM CHECKLIST AND WORKSHEET

Needs and Wants

Check the items you feel your bathroom must have in the "need" column, and the items you would like, if the budget and design allow, in the "want" column. (This should be used as a preliminary guideline; they may change along the way.)

	Need	Want		Need	Want
New vanity	____	____	Heat lamp	____	____
Separate shower	____	____	Bidet	____	____
New lavatory (sink)	____	____	New floor/wall surfaces	____	____
Tub for two	____	____	New countertops	____	____
Whirlpool tub	____	____	Customized storage	____	____
New water closet (toilet)	____	____	Others _____	____	____
Exercise area	____	____	_____	____	____
Entertainment center	____	____	_____	____	____
Linen storage	____	____	_____	____	____
Lighting fixtures	____	____	_____	____	____

Lifestyle/Room Use

This worksheet will give you some things to think about in your initial planning, but it's only the beginning. Your NKBA bathroom specialist will conduct an in-depth interview with you in order to create a design that suits your lifestyle and satisfies your needs and wants.

Who will use this bathroom (i.e., client, spouse, child, guests)?
_____

Type of bathroom?
__ Powder __ Children's __ Mastersuite __ Hall

How many will use it at one time? _____

What activities will take place in the bathroom?
__ Makeup application   __ Bathing
__ Hair care   __ Dressing
__ Exercising   __ Lounging
__ Laundering   __ Other _____

Would you like his and hers facilities? _____

Do you prefer the water closet and/or bidet to be isolated from the other fixtures? _____

Would you like a closet planned as part of your new bathroom?
    ___ Yes   ___ No

What type of feeling would you like your new bathroom to have?
___ Sleek/Contemporary   ___ Warm/Country
___ Traditional   ___ Open & Airy
___ Personal Design Statement

THE DESIGN CONFERENCE

O.K., you've done your homework — you stand ready with your ideas, lists, samples, photographs, maybe even rough plans. And now it's time to meet with your designer.

You may first meet with the NKBA member at the showroom to look over samples and displays, but then he or she will come out to your house and really get to work. Here's where you'll begin to see what sets NKBA specialists apart from other designers. The NKBA member will take careful and thorough measurements, right down to locating the pipes in the walls (something often overlooked by those who do not specialize in kitchen and bathroom planning).

He or she will look at your idea file and talk with you in depth about your needs. This is an opportunity for both of you to discuss thoughts and opinions, ask questions and determine a direction for your room design. Think of it as an exchange of ideas, a "design conference." This is another advantage of working with an NKBA member. He or she will work *with you* to achieve the best results, instead of simply dictating a design.

One very important determinant for your new room design is your budget. You should have a figure established as you go into this — one that's realistic for your situation. And the initial design conference is the time to talk budgets. Your NKBA specialist will let you know what can be achieved — in the way of materials, construction, appliances, etc. — for what you want to spend. And together, you can set priorities for your design that will allow your new dream room to stay within your budget.

When you both agree on a general direction and a budget, you can make arrangements for payment.

With many firms, payment begins with 50% at the signing of the contract, then 40% when installation begins, and the remaining 10% upon completion of the job. Financing can be arranged through a home improvement loan, or you may be able to negotiate the price into the mortgage when purchasing a home. Remember, your new room is an investment in your home's equity. It increases with the value of your home, and may be recovered when the home is sold.

LET THE TRANS-FORMATION BEGIN

From the first meeting, you'll begin to see how working with an NKBA member will make the project easier, and the results, better. When you've got the knowledge and experience of an NKBA professional on your side, you can rest assured that your new room will be everything you dreamed it would be, and more.

First, your NKBA specialist will design the complete layout, choose the final materials, and begin coordinating the contractors — all with your approval, of course. Then, the construction begins.

Living under construction is never easy, but your NKBA professional will do everything possible to minimize the inconvenience for you. Ask him or her for tips on living under construction. For example, setting up temporary facilities for cooking and cleanup. Your NKBA designer has experience in these matters and will undoubtedly have ideas to make you more comfortable during this phase.

And now it's only a matter of time before you see your dream room become a reality. Exactly how long depends on many variables (whether or not you are having cabinets custom-designed, for example), but in somewhere between two weeks and several months, you'll see the results.

You'll soon see your room taking shape. The ideas you've envisioned, the style you've developed, the colors you've decided upon, you'll see it all materialize at the hands of the craftsmen.

ANOTHER HAPPY ENDING

I t's evening, you're dining in your new kitchen, or soaking in your new whirlpool tub. You proudly gaze around the room. For the next few weeks you'll have to open an extra drawer or two looking for the silverware. Or you may catch yourself walking across the room to where the towels *used to* be. But you'll enjoy getting to know your new room and growing with it. After all, you created it (with a little help from NKBA).

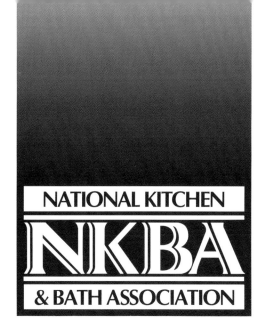

National Kitchen & Bath Association
687 Willow Grove St.
Hackettstown, New Jersey 07840
1-800-FOR-NKBA

A World of Style

Contractors
CW **W**ardrobe ®

A World of Style

Join us in a tour of exclusive mirror fashions selected by the design leaders of the Americas, Europe and Asia to add elegance and a spacious look to their homes, hotels, offices and condo projects. Join us in an examination of the mirror styles created and crafted by Contractors Wardrobe®.

Within these pages you'll see the reasons CW has earned its international reputation. First, for its total product quality...quality of mirror, of safety backing, of hardware. And, then, for its decorator sense—for continually originating the newest designs in mirror doors, with exclusive combinations of wood or aluminum or steel...in natural or colorful finishes...with high fashion, beveled edges available on expanses of unblemished, sparkling mirror.

3054 ENDORSEMENTS...

A Tribute to CW... The Mirage in Las Vegas is already a landmark in the Las Vegas skyline.

Lush tropical landscaping highlights a dramatic entrance which includes a lagoon with a five story waterfall and a volcano which erupts every few minutes, while a computerized misting system protects the delicately arranged tropical flowers.

The Tri-Towers configuration features 29 floors of 3,054 guest rooms and suites and CW is there.

The Model #500-A in Bright Gold was manufactured and supplied by Contractors Wardrobe for each of the suites and guest rooms (see pages 19 & 34 for specifications and details).

Mirage Hotel
Las Vegas, Nevada

1

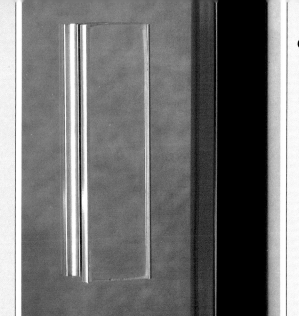

CW MIRROR HANDLE

Presenting...
DecoLite™

DECO LITE is the lat... custom design from ... its dramatically differe... has made it a trend-setter... decorating world. The... DECO LITE mirror doors boast of highly polished black anodize... frames... with a bright oriental,

Deco Lite™ with optional Beveled Edges

CW's mirror handle... designed to blend... with the mirror door pane... handle is standard w... mirror bi-pass wardrobe door... which require handles except the Royal Oak™.

red glazing vinyl between the spectacular black framing and the mirror. (Other colors of glazing vinyl are also available.) The result, as can be seen in these pictures, is high fashion that does justice to any area anywhere.

A DECO LITE Vanity Flair, minus the red vinyl, is available to complement the sliding doors. However, there is restrained use of the highly polished black framing in order to provide the vanity with the ...test edge to edge expense of mirror.

Deco Lite™

3

Style Lite®

Style Lite®

STYLE LITE is another outstanding example of the way CW designs lead the way in the decorating world. STYLE LITE gives a completely frameless look, a total-mirror look to your wardrobe doors. Just glance at the photos on the following pages. Note how the entire STYLE LITE series of glamor products gives a magical impression of pure mirror from top to bottom, from edge to edge! Truly different. Truly beautiful in its simplicity. The secret (and there is one, of course) is that behind the mirror panels are hollow tube extrusions of incredible strength which support the vast mirror expanse. About .300 of an inch of this special metal is folded over the top and bottom mirror edges. The metal is gently buffed and then Bright dipped (chrome type finish) to produce a mirrorlike shine. . .and all the eye sees is beautiful mirror, mirror everywhere.

The STYLE LITE door may also be had in polished gold. All STYLE LITES are available with a 1" bevel to surround it with jewel like reflections. And, if a decorating scheme calls for the greatest use of beveled mirror, then at modest cost a custom made beveled mirror fascia may be ordered to enhance the standard polished aluminum track and channel. As your assurance of quality, all beveling is done by CW's own craftsmen on its new state-of-the-art Bovone beveling machines.

Trim Line™ Bi-Pass with optional Beveled Edges
and optional Beveled Mirror Fascia

Trim Line™ Bi-Fold
with optional Beveled Edges

Style Lite® Walk-In

Style Lite® Vanity Flair
with optional Beveled Edges

California Oak™

Oak Fantasy®

Golden Oak™

Royal Oak®

8

Royal Oak® Bi-Pass

Oak

The look, the feel, the warmth of <u>solid</u> oak enhances an entire line of mirror wardrobe, doors and cabinets. As with all natural wood, each section of our oak is distinctive in graining.

CW's Oak doors are available in a variety of finishes; Medium Stain, Limed Oak, Dark Stain, Light Stain, Clear Lacquer and Unfinished. While unfinished oak is available, it is not recommended, due to the special finishing skills required. Certain doors are available in KD form, custom shapes, different woods and special finishes.

Royal Oak® Bi-Fold

9

10

Golden Oak™
Optional Bright Gold Mylar (inset)

Golden Oak™ Vanity Flair
with optional Beveled Edges

Oak Fantasy®

Oak Vanity Flair

900 Oak Walk-In

11

Oak Medicine Cabinet #1424

Custom Oak Vanity

California Oak™

Fantasy IV®

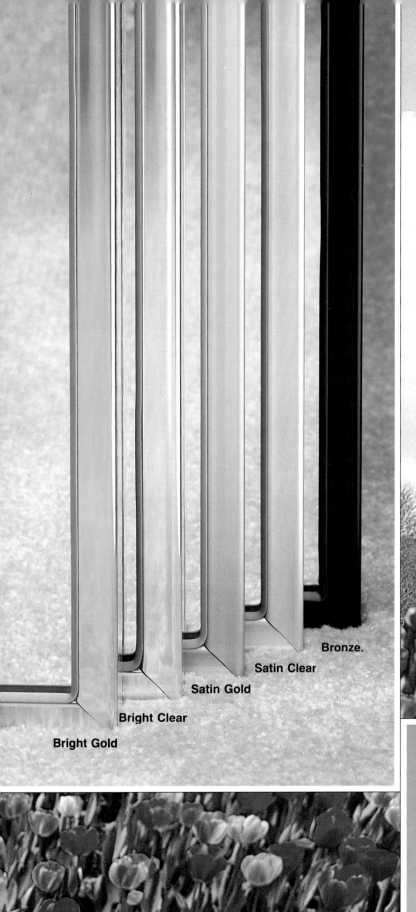

Bronze.

Satin Clear

Satin Gold

Bright Clear

Bright Gold

Fantasy IV®

Here are the first Cedar Backed Bi-Pass mirror wardrobe doors ever available. Fantasy IV™

This clever idea in wardrobe doors has frames of hollow tube extrusions and offers twin benefits. First the beauty and convenience of quality mirror wardrobe doors to enhance a room decor while adding a more spacious look. Second, the exclusive protection and aroma of genuine cedar which fully backs each panel!

As shown on these pages the Fantasy IV is available in many designer colors. . .and is manufactured with the heaviest float plate mirror available in a wardrobe door. . .¼″.

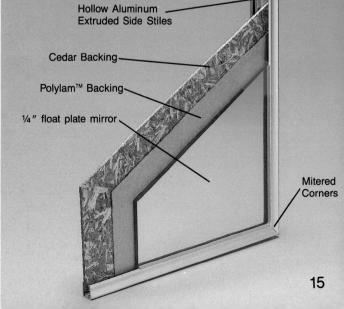

Hollow Aluminum Extruded Side Stiles

Cedar Backing

Polylam™ Backing

¼″ float plate mirror

Mitered Corners

15

3-way Vanity Door 1000

Aluminum

Aluminum has always been popular with those who prefer the traditional look. And CW has starred with a complete line of 3-way Vanities, Walk-in's and Bi-Pass wardrobe

700-A

doors, all hand crafted with heavy duty aluminum extrusions and durable state of the art finishes.

CW offers more aluminum wardrobe doors in a greater range of finishes than any other manufacturer.

400-A/450-A

Walk-In 900-A

17

550-A

400-A/450-A

500-A

Steel

A complete budget line!
There's no need to deny yourself the fashion, practicality and
decorative qualities of our mirror

products. Because our line of
Steel Framed doors is priced to fit
even the most modest budget.
In fact, you'll discover they're
about the least expensive way to
change any room from dull and
drab to totally new and glamorous!
Enjoy the spacious look of beauty
that only mirrors can bring...all
at a truly affordable price.

**400-S Champagne Gold
Also available as 700-S
Prefinished Wardrobe Doors**

20

Brittany Bi-fold with optional Beveled Edges

Tudor

400-S Bronze

400-S White

A World of Style
Around the World

To paraphrase a famous saying, "The sun never sets on the mirror doors of Contractors Wardrobe."

That means, of course, that you can go almost anywhere in the free world. . .from the Americas to Europe and across the time zones to far Asia. . .and you'll find the high fashion wardrobe doors of CW. CW is becoming the choice of the world because it has the step ahead styling. . .the solid quality and the ability to handle orders of any size quickly and reliably.

For example, the 5 star Nan Hoi hotel in Shekou, Guang

5 star Nan Hoi hotel in Shekou, Guang Dong province in the People's Republic of China

700 room Kowloon Hotel, Hong Kong

Dong province in the People's Republic of China selected CW mirror doors for its 500 rooms. The new Kowloon Hotel on the busiest island in the world, Hong Kong, chose CW mirror doors for its 700 rooms. And, in exciting Las Vegas, the magnificent Frontier installed 587 CW mirror doors. . .while the famous Riviera also selected them for its 933 additional rooms. . .over 1125 rooms in the breathtaking Resorts International Hotel in Atlantic City and 1520 rooms in the Orlando World Center Marriott in Orlando, Florida all have CW quality doors. Around the world, CW products are considered world-class.

Shouldn't you enjoy their benefits, too?

The famous Frontier.
Las Vegas.

25

A World of Quality
Custom Beveling

Here's the look that rivals the gleam of diamonds — the jewel like sparkle which only Beveling adds to your mirror edges. This close up shows a section of Golden Oak framing with a wide 1″ bevel. Notice how the beveling adds richness and an expensive look...how its faceted planes add star-like twinkling to the mirror. We believe you'll agree that beveling returns far more in beauty and enchantment than its modest additional cost.

Custom 1″ Bevel shown with Golden Oak™ section

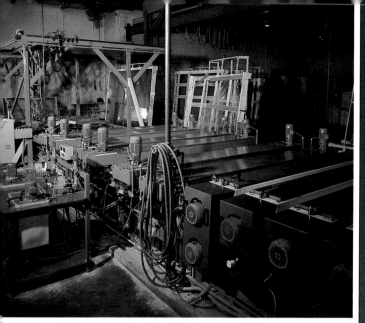

Silvering machine

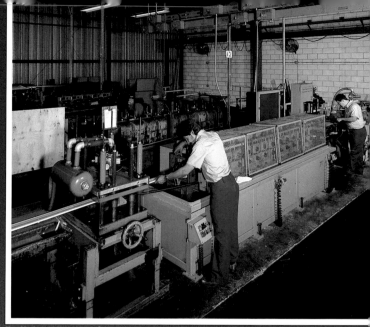

Roll forming machine

Bovone beveling machines

Wood milling machine

The beauty secret of beveling is the machine. . .and the craftsmen who use it. All of CW's beveling is handled in its factory by experienced and dedicated workers who consider themselves artists. They work with the world's newest, and probably finest, state-of-the-art Bovone mini-maxi beveling machines. This is your assurance of fine beveling. . .always.

Other important reasons CW mirror products are superior are: The world's most modern silvering line for changing quality "selected" plate glass into the finest mirrors.

The special tooled roll forming machines for turning the metal into correct shapes.

And, the wood milling machine for cutting and shaping fine woods into the custom shapes and designs needed for your CW doors or vanities.

Contractors Wardrobe®

Contractors Wardrobe was founded in 1973 and began designing and manufacturing its own product line in 1976. Today, the world wide operations of Contractors Wardrobe is guided from its corporate California headquarters which is located in CW's 121,000 square foot office and manufacturing structure.

CW also has warehouses in Miami, Florida, Phoenix, Arizona, The United Kingdom, and is represented in all 50 states. Additional fabrication facilities are in multiple locations in the United Kingdom and throughout Scandinavia.

Corporate Offices and Manufacturing

Specifications

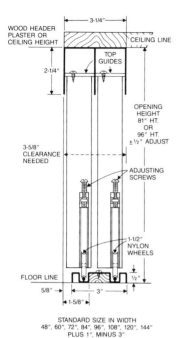

WOOD HEADER
PLASTER OR
CEILING HEIGHT

CEILING LINE

TOP
GUIDES

3-1/4"

2-1/4"

OPENING
HEIGHT
81" HT.
OR
96" HT.
±½" ADJUST

3-5/8"
CLEARANCE
NEEDED

ADJUSTING
SCREWS

1-1/2"
NYLON
WHEELS

FLOOR LINE

½"

5/8"   3"

1-5/8"

STANDARD SIZE IN WIDTH
48", 60", 72", 84", 96", 108", 120", 144"
PLUS 1", MINUS 3"

Deco Lite™

DECO LITE™ BI-PASS

As shown on front cover and pages 2 & 3
- Heavy gauge #6463 aluminum extrusions
- Deep polished black anodized standard with red glazing vinyl.
- Bottom and top tracks, aluminum extrusions, deep polished black to match
- Bottom rolled with jump proof tracks.
- 1-½" diameter wheels with hardened steel races and $\frac{5}{32}$" ball bearings in extra heavy 18 gauge steel housings.
- Injection molded top guides for smooth operation
- Full 1" adjustment to fit opening height, + or − ½"
- Available with beveled edges.
- Mitered corners
- Standard and custom sizes available.
- Standard opening width 48", 60", 72", 84", 96", 108", 120", 144", 168", 192"
- Standard opening height 81" and 96", + or − ½"

STYLE LITE® WALK-IN

As shown on page 7
- Heavy gauge #6463 aluminum extrusions
- Side styles as well as top and bottom rails Hollow Extrusions, (tubular) for added strength
- R-5 bright dip (chrome type finish) standard. Bright gold (polished brass look) and polished black anodized also available.
- Continuous piano hinge for strength and stability (eliminates sagging)
- Surface mounted for easy installation
- Magnetic catch to secure door in closed position
- Door is reversible, right or left opening
- Also available in standard aluminum frame or oak frame
- Available with beveled edges
- Mitered corners
- Matches entire STYLE LITE® series
- For installation specifications see Walk-In 900 diagram on page 34.
- Standard and custom sizes available
- Standard opening width 18", 24", 30", 36"
- Standard opening height 81"

STYLE LITE® BI-PASS

As shown on pages 4 & 5
- Heavy gauge #6463 aluminum extrusions
- Side styles as well as top and bottom rails Hollow Extrusions (tubular) for added strength
- R-5 bright dip (chrome type finish) standard. Bright gold (polished brass look) also available
- Bottom and top tracks, extruded aluminum finished to match
- Bottom rolled with jump proof tracks
- Mitered corners
- Injection molded top guides for smooth operation
- 1-½" diameter wheels with hardened steel races and $\frac{5}{32}$" ball bearings in extra heavy 18 gauge steel housings
- Full 1" adjustment to fit opening height, + or − ½"
- Available with beveled edges.
- For installation specifications see Deco Lite diagram above.
- Standard and custom sizes available
- Standard opening width 48", 60", 72", 84", 96", 108", 120", 144", 168", 192"
- Standard opening height 80½" and 96", + or − ½"

TRIM LINE™ BI-PASS

As shown on page 6
- Heavy gauge #6063 aluminum extrusions (#6463 for bright colors).
- R-5 Bright Dip (chrome-type finish), Bright Gold (polished brass look), Gloss White Paint, Gold Satin Anodized, standard. Tawny Brass also available
- Bottom and top tracks, extruded aluminum finished to match.
- Bottom rolled with jump proof tracks.
- Injection molded nylon top guides for smooth operation.
- 1-½" diameter wheels with hardened steel races and $\frac{5}{32}$" ball bearings in extra heavy 18 gauge steel housing.
- Full 1" adjustment to fit opening height, + or − ½".
- Available with 1" beveled long edges.
- Glazed with aircraft type two-way adhesive tape.
- Standard and custom sizes available
- Standard opening width 47", 59", 71", 83", 95", 107", 119", 143", 167", 191"
- Standard opening height 80½" and 96", + or − ½".

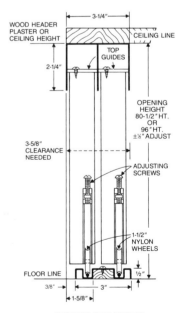

WOOD HEADER
PLASTER OR
CEILING HEIGHT

CEILING LINE

TOP
GUIDES

3-1/4"

2-1/4"

OPENING
HEIGHT
80-1/2" HT.
OR
96" HT.
±½" ADJUST

3-5/8"
CLEARANCE
NEEDED

ADJUSTING
SCREWS

1-1/2"
NYLON
WHEELS

FLOOR LINE

½"

3/8"   3"

1-5/8"

STANDARD SIZES IN WIDTH
47", 59", 71", 83", 95", 107", 119", 143"
PLUS 1", MINUS 3"

Trim Line™ Bi-Pass

ROYAL OAK® BI-PASS

As shown on pages 8 & 9

- Solid 2½" wide oak (milled from ⁶/₄ oak) surrounds each panel
- Panels stained and prefinished. 5 stage process
- Medium Oak stain standard. Limed Oak finish (white wash), Light Oak, Dark Oak, Unfinished and Lacquer Only also available.
- Solid brass European handles, flush mounted
- All corners glued and secured by 2½" Phillips wood screw
- All panels hand sanded for a custom look
- Matching Oak fascia preattached to top channel
- Full 1" adjustment to fit opening height, + or − ½"
- 1½" diameter wheels with hardened steel races and ⁵/₃₂" ball bearings in extra heavy 18 gauge steel housing
- Bottom rolled with jump proof tracks.
- Injection molded top guides for smooth operation
- Available with beveled edges.
- Mitered corners
- Heavy duty, extruded aluminum track and channel. Bright Gold anodized standard with all finishes except Limed Oak supplied with Gloss White.
- Standard and custom sizes available.
- Standard opening width 48", 60", 72", 84", 96", 108", 120", 144", 168", 192"
- Standard opening height 81" and 96", + or − ½"

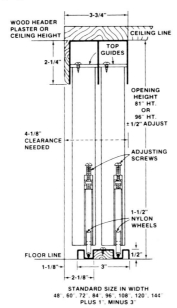

Royal Oak®

STYLE LITE®
VANITY FLAIR

As shown on page 7

- Heavy gauge #6463 aluminum extrusions
- Side Styles as well as top and bottom rails Hollow extrusions, (tubular) for added strength
- R-5 bright dip (chrome type finish) standard. Bright gold (polished brass look) and polished black anodized also available.
- Flush mount with all screws concealed
- Flush mount medicine Cans not included. Available at additional cost. 18" wide wings required to cover standard flush mount medicine cabinet. Units 72" or larger, 18" wings standard. Units smaller than 72", specify wing size at time of order.
- Vanity Flairs also available in standard aluminum frame or solid oak
- Available with beveled edges.
- Mitered corners
- Matches entire STYLE LITE® series
- Standard and custom sizes available
- Standard width 48", 60", 72", 84", 96"
- Standard height 36"

ROYAL OAK® BIFOLD

As shown on page 9

- Solid 2½" wide oak (milled from ⁶/₄ oak) surrounds each panel
- Panels stained and prefinished. 5 stage process
- Matching Oak fascia pre-attached to top track
- All panels hand sanded for custom look
- Solid brass European handles, flush mounted
- Mitered corners
- All corners glued and secured by 2½" Phillips wood screw
- Top and bottom tracks are extruded aluminum, bright gold anodized (polished brass look).
- Ball bearing pivot blocks
- Available with beveled edges
- Full length piano hinge allows smooth, rattle proof movement
- Spring loaded guide pins for easy installation
- Medium Oak stain standard. Also available in Limed Oak finish (white wash), Light Oak, Dark Oak, Unfinished and Lacquer only also available.
- Standard and custom sizes available
- Standard opening width:
  2 Panel: 24", 30", 36"
  4 Panel: 48", 60", 72"
- Standard opening height: 80¾"

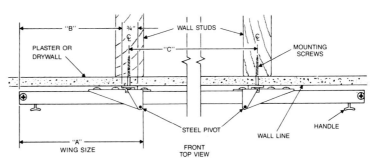

Style Lite® Vanity Flair

GOLDEN OAK™

As shown on page 10

- Solid 2$\frac{1}{8}$" wide oak (milled from $\frac{5}{4}$ oak) surrounds each panel
- Panels stained and prefinished. 5 stage process
- Matching oak fascia preattached to top channel
- All panels hand sanded for a custom look
- Mitered corners
- All corners glued and secured by two steel corner fasteners
- Medium Oak stain standard. Limed Oak finish (white wash), Light Oak, Dark Oak, Unfinished and Lacquer Only also available.
- Available with beveled edges.
- Full 1" adjustment to fit opening height, + or − $\frac{1}{2}$"
- 1$\frac{1}{2}$" diameter wheels with hardened steel races and $\frac{5}{32}$" ball bearings in extra heavy 18 gauge steel housing
- Injection molded top guides for smooth operation
- Heavy duty bronze steel track and channel standard with all finishes except Limed Oak supplied with Gloss White For installation specs see Royal Oak diagram page 31
- Gold or Chrome mylar trim available (see inset on page 10)
- Standard and custom sizes available.
- Standard opening width 48", 60", 72", 84", 96", 108", 120", 144", 168", 192"
- Standard opening height 81" and 96", + or − $\frac{1}{2}$"

GOLDEN OAK™ VANITY FLAIR

As shown on page 10

- Solid 2$\frac{1}{8}$" wide Oak frame matches Golden Oak Bi-Pass. #1424 Medicine Cabinet and Oak Frame mirrors available with Golden Oak Frame to match upon request.
- Surface mounted with all screws concealed.
- Flush mount medicine Cans not included. Available at additional cost. 18" wide wings required to cover standard flush mount medicine cabinet. Units 72" or wider, 18" wings standard. Units smaller than 72", specify wing size at time of order.
- Mitered corners
- Finger-pull routed in each side wing.
- Adjustable magnetic catch
- Available with beveled edges.
- Also available in Oak Fantasy and Style Lite series.
- All corners glued and secured by two steel corner fasteners.
- Medium Oak stain standard. Limed Oak finish (white wash), Light Oak, Dark Oak, Unfinished and Lacquer Only also available.
- Standard and custom sizes available.
- Standard width 48", 60", 72", 84", 96"
- Standard height 36"

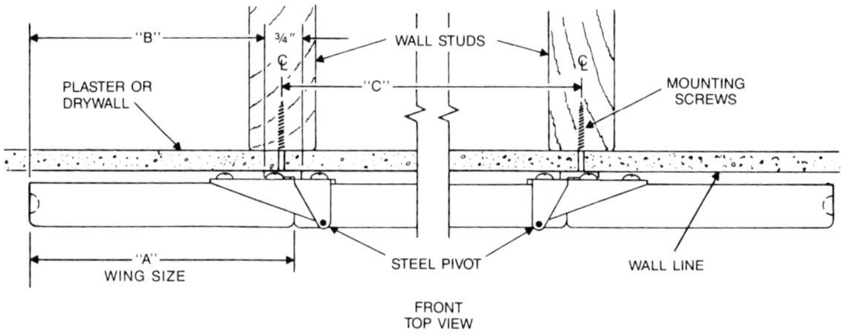

Golden Oak™ Vanity Flair

OAK WALK-IN

As shown on page 11

- Solid 2$\frac{1}{8}$" wide oak frame matches Oak Fantasy Bi-Pass, Oak Vanity Flair. #1424 Medicine Cabinet and Oak Frame Mirrors available with Oak Fantasy frame to match upon request.
- Continuous piano hinge for strength and stability (eliminates sagging).
- Surface mounted. All screws concealed
- Door is reversible; right or left opening
- Routed finger pull on frame edge.
- Adjustable magnetic catch.
- Back side finished in smooth, prefinished white hardboard
- Available with beveled edges.
- Mitered corners
- Panels stained and pre-finished. 5 stage process.
- Medium Oak stain standard. Limed Oak finish (white wash), Light Oak, Dark Oak, Unfinished and Lacquer Only also available.
- Standard and custom sizes available.
- Standard width 18", 24", 30", 36"
- Standard height 81" and 96"

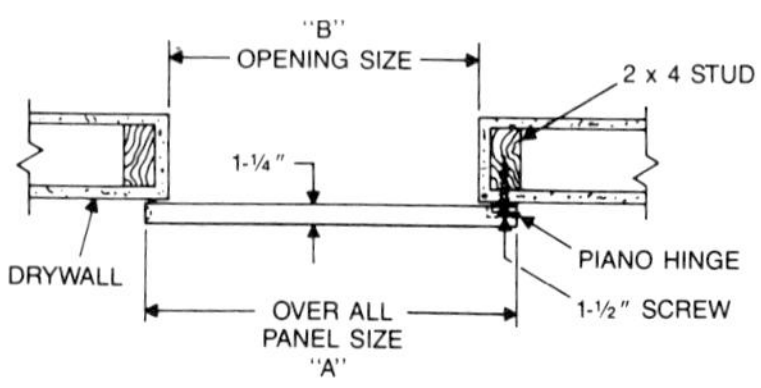

Oak Walk-In

OAK FANTASY®

As shown on page 11

- Solid 2$\frac{1}{8}$" wide oak (milled from $\frac{6}{4}$ oak) surrounds each panel
- Panels stained and prefinished. 5 stage process
- All corners glued and secured by two steel corner fasteners.
- Medium Oak stain standard. Limed Oak finish (white wash), Light Oak, Dark Oak, Unfinished and Lacquer Only also available.
- Available with beveled edges.
- All panels hand sanded for a custom look
- Matching Oak fascia preattached to top channel
- 1$\frac{1}{2}$" diameter wheels with hardened steel races and $\frac{5}{32}$" ball bearings in extra heavy 18 gauge steel housing
- Bottom rolled with jump proof tracks
- Full 1" adjustment to fit opening height, + or − $\frac{1}{2}$"
- Injection molded top guides for smooth operation
- Mitered corners
- Heavy duty, extruded aluminum track and channel. Deep Bronze anodized standard with all finishes except Limed Oak supplied with Gloss White For installation specs see Royal Oak Diagram page 31
- Standard and custom sizes available
- Standard opening width 48", 60", 72", 84", 96", 108", 120", 144", 168", 192"
- Standard opening height 81" and 96", + or − $\frac{1}{2}$"

OAK VANITY FLAIR

As shown on page 11

- Solid 2$\frac{1}{8}$" wide Oak frame matches Oak Fantasy Bi-Pass, #1424 Medicine Cabinet and Oak Walk-In door. Matching Oak Frame mirrors available.
- Surface mounted with all screws concealed.
- Flush mount medicine Cans not included. Available at additional cost. 18" wide wings required to cover standard flush mount medicine cabinet. Units 72" or wider, 18" wings standard. Units smaller than 72", specify wing size at time of order.
- Mitered corners
- Finger pull routed in each side wing.
- Adjustable magnetic catch
- Available with beveled edges.
- Also available in aluminum or STYLE LITE frame
- For installation specifications see Golden Oak Vanity Flair diagram above
- Medium Oak stain standard. Limed Oak finish (white wash), Light Oak, Dark Oak, Unfinished and Lacquer Only also available.
- Standard and custom sizes available
- Standard width 48", 60", 72", 84", 96"
- Standard height 36"

CUSTOM OAK VANITY

As shown on page 12
- Solid 2⅛″ wide oak frame matches Oak Fantasy Bi-Pass, Oak Vanity Flair, #1424 Oak Medicine Cabinet and Oak Walk-In. Matching Oak Frame mirrors available.
- Continuous piano hinge for strength and stability (eliminates sagging)
- Both wings swing open. Center panel stationary giving a three way effect to walk-in closets.
- Surface mounted for easy installation.
- Adjustable magnetic catch
- Flush mounted available (requires cased and squared opening)
- Slight upcharge for special push latch
- Wing panels 1½″ shorter than center to clear floor or carpeted areas.
- Also available in aluminum frame
- Medium Oak stain standard. Limed Oak finish (white wash), Light Oak, Dark Oak, Unfinished and Lacquer Only also available.
- Available with beveled edges
- Standard and custom sizes available
- Standard opening width 60″, 72″, 84″, 96″
- Standard opening height 81″

#1424 RECTANGLE MEDICINE CABINET

As shown on page 12
- Solid 2⅛″ wide oak frame matches Oak Fantasy Bi-Pass, Oak Vanity Flair and Oak Walk-In. Matching oak frame mirrors available.
- Continuous piano hinge for strength and stability (eliminates sagging).
- Routed finger pull
- 24-gauge steel can with shelves
- Available with beveled edges.
- Also available in Golden Oak to match Golden Oak Bi-Pass, and Golden Oak Vanity Flair.
- Magnetic catch to secure door in closed position
- Door is reversible; right or left opening
- Fits between standard 2 × 4 stud spacing, 16″ on center
- Door size 16 × 26
- Medium Oak stain standard. Limed Oak finish (white wash), Light Oak, Dark Oak, Unfinished and Lacquer Only also available.

CALIFORNIA OAK™

As shown on page 13
- Solid 1¼″ wide oak (milled from ⁵⁄₄ oak) surrounds each panel
- Panels stained and prefinished. 5 stage process
- Medium Oak stain standard. Limed Oak finish (white wash), Light Oak, Dark Oak, Unfinished and Lacquer Only also available.
- All corners glued and secured by 2½″ Phillips wood screw
- All panels hand sanded for a custom look
- Matching Oak fascia preattached to top channel
- 1½″ diameter wheels with hardened steel races and ⁵⁄₃₂″ ball bearings in extra heavy 18 gauge steel housing
- Bottom rolled with jump proof tracks.
- Full 1″ adjustment to fit opening height, + or − ½″
- Injection molded top guides for smooth operation
- Mitered corners
- Heavy duty, bronze steel track and channel standard with all finishes except Limed Oak supplied with Gloss White For installation specs see Royal Oak diagram page 31
- Standard and custom sizes available
- Standard opening width 48″, 60″, 72″, 84″, 96″, 108″, 120″, 144″, 168″, 192″
- Standard opening height 81″ and 96″, + or − ½″

TUDOR

As shown on page 21
- Heavy duty 24 gauge steel one piece head channel and 26 gauge frames available in Aztec Gold or White
- Steel back braces are hot melted (glued) to each panel to provide added strength and rigidity and to help prevent warpage.
- Full 1″ adjustment to fit opening height, + or − ½″
- Bottom rolled with jump proof track
- 1½″ diameter wheels with hardened steel races and ⁵⁄₃₂″ ball bearings in extra heavy 18 gauge steel housing
- Prefinished panels are interchangeable with mirror panels at any time with minimum labor.

FANTASY IV®

As shown on pages 14 & 15
- Heavy gauge #6063 aluminum extrusions (#6463 for Bright colors)
- Side styles are Hollow Extrusions, (tubular) for added strength
- Gold Satin anodized or Clear Satin anodized standard. R-5 Bright dip (chrome type finish), Bright Gold (polished brass look) and Bronze anodized also available
- Bottom and top tracks extruded aluminum finished to match
- Clear ¼″ plate mirror (6mm) standard.
- Each panel fully cedar backed
- One piece hand glazed vinyl color coordinated to match frame
- Bottom rolled with jump proof tracks.
- Mitered corners
- Injection molded top guides for smooth operation
- 1½″ diameter wheels with hardened steel races and ⁵⁄₃₂″ ball bearings in extra heavy 18 gauge steel housings
- Full 1″ adjustment to fit opening height, + or − ½″
- For installation specifications, see Deco Lite diagram on page 30.
- Available with beveled edges.
- Standard and custom sizes available
- Standard opening width 48″, 60″, 72″, 84″, 96″, 108″, 120″, 144″, 168″, 192″
- Standard opening height 81″ and 96″, + or − ½″

700-A

As shown on page 17
- Heavy gauge #6063 aluminum extrusions (#6463 for Bright colors)
- Bottom and top tracks extruded aluminum finished to match
- Gold satin anodized or Clear Satin anodized standard. R-5 Bright dip (chrome type finish), Bright Gold (polished brass look), Bronze anodized and Gloss White paint also available.
- Bottom rolled with jump proof tracks.
- Mitered corners
- Injection molded top guides for smooth operation
- Back sealed to help prevent warpage
- Textured prefinished surface
- 1½″ diameter wheels with hardened steel races and ⁵⁄₃₂″ ball bearings in extra heavy 18 gauge steel housings
- Full 1″ adjustment to fit opening height, + or − ½″
- Alpine White board standard. Numerous other colors and textures available.
- Panels are interchangeable with mirror panels at any time with minimum labor.
- Steel back braces are hot melted (glued) to each panel to provide added strength and rigidity and to help prevent warpage. For installation specifications see Deco Lite diagram, page 30.
- Standard and custom sizes available
- Standard opening width 48″, 60″, 72″, 84″, 96″, 108″, 120″, 144″, 168″, 192″
- Standard opening height 81″ and 96″, + or − ½″

3 WAY VANITY DOOR 1000

As shown on page 16

- Heavy gauge #6063 aluminum extrusions (#6463 for Bright colors)
- Full length mirror side panels adjust to any position and pivot out to give the 3-way effect. Center mirror panel slides in either direction, giving easy access to center of the wardrobe.
- Gold Satin anodized or Clear Satin anodized standard. R-5 Bright dip (chrome type finish), Bright Gold (polished brass look) and Bronze anodized also available
- For walk-in closets minimum recommended width, 72″. Specify equal panels at time of order.
- Square and/or cased openings recommended.
- Mitered corners
- One piece hand glazed vinyl color coordinated to match frame.
- Sliding center panel is bottom rolled on 1½″ diameter wheels with hardened steel races and 5⁄32″ ball bearings in extra heavy 18 gauge steel housing.
- Jump proof track.
- Standard and custom sizes available
- Standard opening width 48″, 60″, 72″, 84″, 96″, 108″, 120″, 144″
- Standard opening height 81″ and 96″

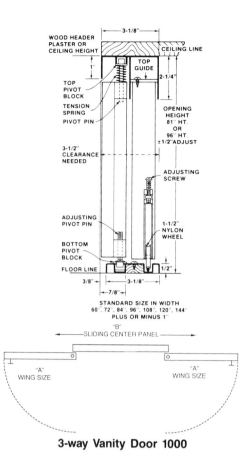

3-way Vanity Door 1000

WALK-IN 900-A

As shown on page 17

- Heavy gauge #6063 aluminum extrusions (#6463 for Bright colors)
- Gold Satin anodized or Clear Satin anodized standard. R-5 Bright dip (chrome type finish), Bright Gold (polished brass look) and Bronze anodized also available
- Frame aesthetically matches 400-A/450-A Slider, Fantasy IV, Deco Lite and 3-Way Vanity Door 1000.
- Mitered corners
- One piece hand glazed vinyl color coordinated to match frame
- Continuous piano hinge for strength and stability (eliminates sagging)
- Surface mounted for easy installation
- Magnetic catch to secure door in a closed position
- Back side finished in smooth prefinished white hardboard
- Also available with oak or STYLE LITE® frame
- Standard and custom sizes available
- Standard opening width 18″, 24″, 30″, 36″
- Standard opening height 81″ and 96″

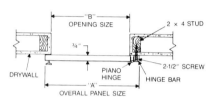

Walk-In 900-A

400-A/450-A

As shown on pages 17 & 18

- Heavy gauge #6063 aluminum extrusions (#6463 for Bright colors)
- Gold Satin anodized or Clear Satin anodized standard. R-5 Bright dip (chrome type finish), Bright Gold (polished brass look), Gloss White paint, Tawny Brass, Bronze anodized and Polished Black anodized (450-A only) also available.
- Bottom and top tracks extruded aluminum finished to match
- Bottom rolled with jump proof tracks
- Mitered corners
- One piece hand glazed vinyl color coordinated to match frame.
- Injection molded top guides for smooth operation
- 1½″ diameter wheels with hardened steel races and 5⁄32″ ball bearings in extra heavy 18 gauge steel housing.
- Full 1″ adjustment to fit opening height, + or − ½″.
- Panels are completely interchangeable with #700-A series
  For installation specifications see Deco Lite diagram, page 30.
- Standard and custom sizes available
- Standard opening width 48″, 60″, 72″, 84″, 96″, 108″, 120″, 144″, 168″, 192″
- Standard opening height 81″ and 96″, + or − ½″

550-A

As shown on page 18

- Heavy gauge #6063 aluminum extrusions (#6463 for Bright colors)
- Side styles are Hollow Extrusions (tubular) for added strength
- Gold Satin anodized or Clear Satin anodized standard. R-5 Bright dip (chrome type finish), Bright Gold (polished brass look) and Bronze anodized also available.
- Clear ¼″ plate mirror (6mm) standard
- One piece hand glazed vinyl color coordinated to match frame
- Bottom rolled with jump proof tracks
- Mitered corners
- Injection molded top guides for smooth operation
- 1-½″ diameter wheels with hardened steel races and 5⁄32″ ball bearings in extra heavy 18 gauge steel housings
- Full 1″ adjustment to fit opening height, + or − ½″
  For installation specifications see Deco Lite diagram on page 30.
- Available with beveled edges
- Standard and custom sizes available
- Standard opening width 48″, 60″, 72″, 84″, 96″, 108″, 120″, 144″, 168″, 192″
- Standard opening height 81″ and 96″, + or − ½″

500-A

As shown on page 18

- Heavy gauge #6063 aluminum extrusions (#6463 for bright colors)
- Side styles Hollow Extrusions, (tubular) for added strength
- Gold Satin anodized or Clear Satin anodized standard. R-5 Bright dip (chrome type finish), Bright gold (polished brass look), Gloss White paint and Bronze anodized also available.
- Wide style design incorporates handle in side style eliminating the need for a handle to obstruct the mirror
- Bottom and top tracks, extruded aluminum finished to match
- Bottom rolled with jump proof tracks
- Injection molded top guides for smooth operation
- 1½″ diameter wheels with hardened steel races and 5⁄32″ ball bearings in extra heavy 18 gauge steel housing.
- Full 1″ adjustment to fit opening height, + or − ½″
- For installation specifications see Deco Lite, page 30
- Standard and custom sizes available.
- Standard opening width: 48″, 60″, 72″, 84″, 96″, 108″, 120″, 144″, 168″, 192″
- Standard opening height 81″ and 96″, + or − ½″
- Available with beveled edges

STEEL FRAME MIRROR DOOR 400-S

As shown on pages 20, 22 & 23

- Heavy duty 24 gauge steel one piece head channel and 26 gauge frames available in Aztec Gold, Champagne Gold, Bronze or White
- Full 1″ adjustment to fit opening height, + or − ½″.
- Bottom rolled with jump proof track
- 1½″ diameter wheels with hardened steel races and ⁵⁄₃₂″ ball bearings in extra heavy 18 gauge steel housing
- Mirror rests upon ¼″ thick vinyl cushion inside top & bottom molding to help insure against breakage.
- Panels are completely interchangeable with #700-S series.
- Standard opening width: 47″, 59″, 71″, 83″, 95″, 107″, 119″, 143″, 167″, 191″
- Standard opening height: 80½″ or 96″, + or − ½″

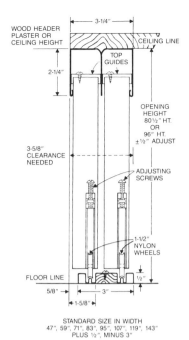

400-S / 700-S

700-S

(Not Shown)

- Heavy duty 24 gauge steel one piece head channel and 26 gauge frames available in Aztec Gold, Champagne Gold, Bronze or White
- Steel back braces are hot melted (glued) to each panel to provide added strength and rigidity and to help prevent warpage.
- Full 1″ adjustment to fit opening height, + or − ½″
- Bottom rolled with jump proof track
- 1½″ diameter wheels in extra heavy 18 gauge steel housing
- Prefinished panels are interchangeable with mirror panels at any time with minimum labor.
- Standard opening width: 47″, 59″, 71″, 83″, 95″, 107″, 119″, 143″, 167″, 191″
- Standard opening height: 80½″ or 96″, + or − ½″

BRITTANY™ BI-FOLD

As shown on page 21

- Heavy duty 26 gauge steel frames available in Aztec Gold and White
- Bottom and top tracks, extruded aluminum finished to match.
- Low friction steel pivot rods, adjustable screw type, held by steel clamps.
- Positive stop, steel hinge allows for smooth rattle-proof movement.
- Spring loaded nylon roller guide pins for easy installation and bind free action.
- 3mm float plate mirror with polished edges.
- Available with ½″ beveled long edges.
- Glazed with aircraft type two-way adhesive tape
- Standard and custom sizes available.
- Standard opening width:
  2 panel: 24″, 30″, 36″
  4 panel: 48″, 60″, 72″
- Standard opening height: 80¾″

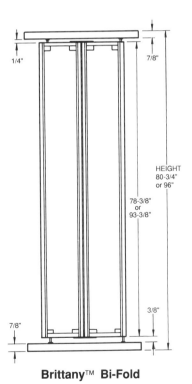

Brittany™ Bi-Fold

TRIMLINE™ BI-FOLD

As shown on page 6

- Heavy gauge #6063 aluminum extrusions (#6463 for bright colors)
- R-5 Bright dip (chrome type finish), Bright Gold (polished brass look), Gold Satin and Gloss White paint standard. Tawny Brass also available.
- Bottom and top tracks, extruded aluminum finished to match.
- Low friction steel pivot rods, adjustable screw type, held by steel clamps.
- Positive stop, steel hinge allows for smooth rattle-proof movement.
- Spring loaded nylon roller guide pins for easy installation and bind free action.
- 3mm float plate mirror with polished edges.
- Available with ½″ beveled long edges.
- Glazed with aircraft type two-way adhesive tape
- Standard and custom sizes available.
- Standard opening width:
  2 panel: 24″, 30″, 36″
  4 panel: 48″, 60″, 72″
- Standard opening height: 80¾″ or 96″

The Facts of Quality

12 Panel T-Display

The mirror. The mirror used in CW products is of unsurpassed clarity, quality and longevity. The reason: our mirror is made from the highest quality selected float plate glass on the most modern mirror line. It's the only one with the capability to clean glass so thoroughly—the only one to apply the base and finish paint coats by special "curtain coaters"—the only one to provide longer baking time for longer curing which reduces edge degradation.

The backing. Our mirrors are Safety Backed with "Polylam™," an exclusive CW quality process. This multi-layered backing consists of woven polypropolene and a white polyethelene sealer approximately 1 mil thick. This combination is designed to eliminate water, moisture and foreign substances from contacting the backside of the mirror.

The result. When our exceptional mirror is combined with exclusive "Polylam™" backing, black spots and de-silvering are virtually eliminated, resulting in truly long lasting beauty.

And for safety, all CW mirror products meet the most stringent impact tests because they have the heaviest backing...and fully comply with U.S. Government Safety Standards 16 CFR 1201 Category II 400 lb. Impact Test for both 3 mm and 4 mm, per reports M84-1917-4 and 5 respectively, dated Feb. 21, 1984. In addition, they complied with ANSI Z97-1-1984/Uniform Building Code, per report M86-2370-1, dated Feb. 19, 1986. They have also complied with the Category II Boil Test per report M79-1193-7, dated Oct. 3, 1979

Our guarantee. All CW products are covered by a 5 year Limited Warranty. Copies are available upon request.

Contractors Wardrobe reserves the right to change without notice, product specifications, prices and/or to discontinue products or designs.

The attractive T-Display shown above is available to the Trade.

Pallet Pack

The CW order department

Quality control and design meeting

600-S PIVOT
WOOD
STRIP
• HIDES HARDWARE
• BRIGHT DIP...
• EASY INST
• BALL BEARING PIVOT
• 24, 30, 36, 48, 60, 72
• BEVEL EDGES
6'8 & 8'0 HT

Contractors Wardrobe®

Manufacturers • Designers

26121 Avenue Hall • Valencia, CA 91355
(805) 257-1177 • Fax# 805-257-4907

Corporate Offices and Manufacturing: Valencia, California
Warehouse locations: Miami, Florida; Phoenix, Arizona; United Kingdom
Fabrication facilities: Throughout the United Kingdom and Scandinavia.

Stocked and sold by:

Toll free: 800-382-1156 • In California: 800-382-3354

B689

BuyLine 8644

WECK® GLASS BLOCKS

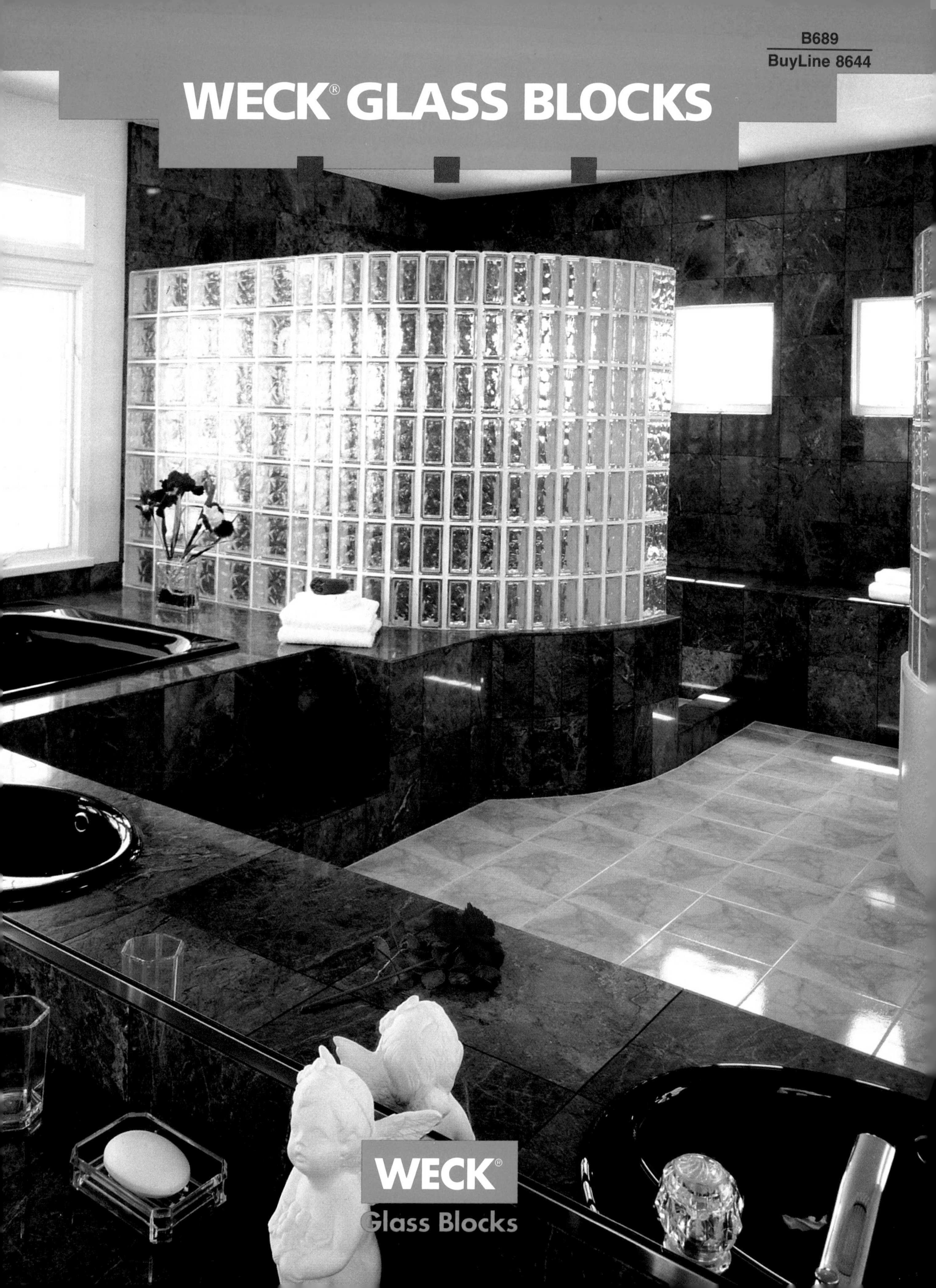

WECK®

Glass Blocks

INTRODUCING... THE UNFORGE

TABLE BATHROOM

Deliver unexpected drama and your bathroom will never be forgotten. With the widest range of shapes and finishes available, WECK® blocks will let you use:

• Soaring walls with no structural gaps, just beautiful glass all the way. • Smooth wall ends with no post construction. Nobody can resist touching the cool sweep and graceful arc of new WeckEnd blocks. • Dramatic step-downs with the new DoublEnd blocks for a feeling of privacy with open space that goes on and on. Tight-radius turns with AllBend blocks let you use dramatic lighting effects, sunlit columns, or space plan options never before possible. With the WECK® touch, you'll have bathrooms that make a statement of elegance!

Photography: Jim Jensen
Architect: Bryan Peters, AIA
Installation: Glass Block Designs

With WECK®'s new Designer Shapes you can have it your way! The curves, the angles, the circular columns. The beautifully finished wall-ends, smooth corners, whatever your creativity demands for striking drama with light and structure! The most beautiful edges and corners ever known can now accent your designs. New for you from WECK®'s engineered superiority.

AllBend

DoublEnd

Corner Block

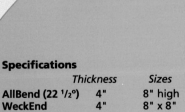

WeckEnd

Specifications

	Thickness	Sizes
AllBend (22 1/2°)	4"	8" high
WeckEnd	4"	8" x 8"
Double End	4"	8" x 8"
Corner (90°)	4"	6" high
Corner (90°)	4"	8" high
Corner (90°)	3"	8" high

Notes:
- All dimensions nominal
- Designer Shapes available in Nubio and Clarity
- 3" thick corner also available in Nubio Goldtone

AllBend

Smoothly curved 22 ¹/₂° angle blocks combine to make curves and corners, or columns with as small as a 12" radius. May be used with other WECK blocks to give you the look and the angles you choose. Available in Clarity or the distorted Nubio patterns. Compared to blocks with exposed seams, AllBend installs more easily and beautifully.

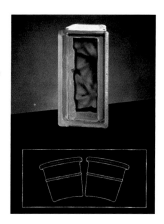

Functional and striking, these metric blocks are available in three distinctive patterns. Produced to metric dimensions, variable mortar joints will yield 7 ³/₄" or 8" rows. Available in distinctive Regent, Metallic, or Welle patterns, the blocks exterior measurements are 7 ¹/₂" x 7 ¹/₂" x 3 ¹/₈".

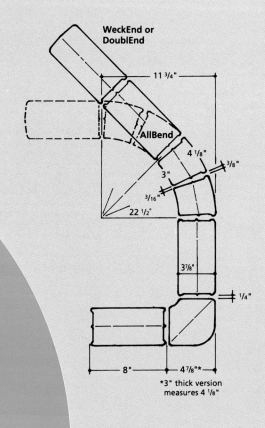

WeckEnd or
DoublEnd

11 ³/₄"

AllBend

4 ¹/₈"

³/₈"

3"

³/₁₆"

22 ¹/₂°

3⁷/₈"

¹/₄"

8"   4⁷/₈"*

*3" thick version
measures 4 ¹/₈"

Regent

Welle

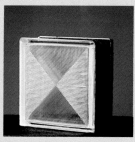

Metallic

Nubio

Nubio Corner Block

WeckEnd

DoublEnd

AllBend

Aktis

NUBIO

Intersecting random wave pattern, provides an attractive appearance and excellent privacy. Smooth exterior surface for easy cleaning.

Matching designer shapes provide beauty and flexibility to create angles, curves or finished jambs and/or heads. 45 and 60 minute fire ratings are available.

AKTIS

Elegant crystalline pattern provides privacy and good light transmission, at reasonable cost. Smooth exterior surface.

Series	Size Nominal	Fire Rating minutes/ max. size sq. ft.	U/R Values	Light Transmission %	Shading Coefficient	Sound Loss Decibels	Compressive Strength psi	Weight per block lbs	Installed Weight Per Sq. Ft.
NUBIO					**CLEAR**				
Standard and Firestop Series (3⅞″ thick)									
	4″ x 8″	45/120	.48/2.08	72-74	.65	41	700	3.6	23.8
	6″ x 6″	45/120	.48/2.08	72-74	.65	41	850	3.5	20.8
	8″ x 8″	45/120	.48/2.08	72-74	.65	42	850	6.4	19.5
	8″ x 8″	60/100	.45/2.22	57	.55	42	1000	7.7	22.7
	12″ x 12″	—	.48/2.08	72-74	.63	42	850	15.3	18.7
Thinline Series (3⅛″ thick)									
	4″ x 8″	45/120	.53/1.89	79	.66	41	700	2.9	18.6
	6″ x 6″	45/120	.53/1.89	79	.66	40	850	3.1	17.2
	6″ x 8″	45/120	.53/1.89	79	.66	41	850	4.5	17.9
	8″ x 8″	45/120	.53/1.89	79	.66	41	850	5.4	15.9
Corner (6″ – 3⅞″ thick) (8″ – 3⅞″ and 3⅛″ thick)									
	6″ High	—	.53/1.89	54	—	39	800	3.4	20.2
	8″ High	—	.53/1.89	50	—	39	750	4.1	18.1
WeckEnd and DoubleEnd (3⅞″ thick)									
	8″ x 8″	—	—	70	.65	42	850	6.2	19.1
AllBend (3⅞″ thick)									
	8″ High	—	.48/2.08	68	.65	41	700	3.6	23.8
					GOLDTONE				
Standard Series (3⅞″ thick)									
	8″ x 8″	45/120	.48/2.08	52	.12	42	850	6.4	19.5
Thinline Series (3⅛″ thick)									
	6″ x 6″	45/120	.53/1.89	52	.12	40	850	3.1	17.2
	6″ x 8″	45/120	.53/1.89	52	.12	41	850	4.5	17.9
	8″ x 8″	45/120	.53/1.89	52	.12	41	850	5.4	15.9
Corner (3⅛″ thick)									
	8″ High	—	.53/1.89	32	.12	36	650	3.9	17.7
AKTIS						**CLEAR**			
Standard Series (3⅞″ thick)									
	8″ x 8″	45/120	.48/2.08	72-74	.65	42	700	6.4	19.5
Thinline Series (3⅛″ thick)									
	4″ x 8″	45/120	.53/1.89	79	.66	41	700	2.9	18.6
	6″ x 6″	45/120	.53/1.89	79	.66	40	850	3.1	17.2
	6″ x 8″	45/120	.53/1.89	79	.66	41	850	4.5	17.9
	8″ x 8″	45/120	.53/1.89	79	.66	41	850	5.4	15.9

Size Nominal	Fire Rating minutes/ max. size sq. ft.	U/R Values	Light Trans-mission %	Shading Coeffi-cent	Sound Loss Decibels	Com-pressive Strength psi	Weight per block lbs	Installed Weight Per Sq. Ft.
CLEAR								
Standard and Firestop Series (3⅞″ thick)								
4″ x 8″	45/120	.48/2.08	72-74	.65	41	700	3.6	23.8
6″ x 6″	45/120	.48/2.08	72-74	.65	41	850	3.5	20.8
6″ x 6″	90/100	.31/3.23	51	.53	43	3000	11.2	51.6
8″ x 8″	45/120	.48/2.08	72-74	.65	42	850	6.4	19.5
8″ x 8″	60/100	.45/2.22	57	.55	42	1000	7.7	22.7
12″ x 12″	—	.48/2.08	72-74	.63	42	850	15.3	18.7
Thinline Series (3⅛″ thick)								
4″ x 8″	45/120	.53/1.89	79	.66	41	700	2.9	18.6
6″ x 6″	45/120	.53/1.89	79	.66	40	850	3.1	17.2
6″ x 8″	45/120	.53/1.89	79	.66	41	850	4.5	17.9
8″ x 8″	45/120	.53/1.89	79	.66	41	850	5.4	15.9
Corner (6″ – 3⅞″ thick) (8″ – 3⅛″ and 3⅞″ thick)								
6″ High	—	.53/1.89	54	—	39	800	3.4	20.2
8″ High	—	.53/1.89	50	—	39	750	4.1	18.1
WeckEnd and DoubleEnd (3⅞″ thick)								
8″ x 8″	—	—	70	.65	42	850	6.2	19.1
AllBend (3⅞″ thick)								
8″ High	—	.48/2.08	68	.65	41	700	3.6	23.8
GOLDTONE								
Standard Series (3⅞″ thick)								
8″ x 8″	45/120	.48/2.08	52	.12	42	850	6.4	19.5
CLEAR								
Fire Stop Series (3⅞″ thick)								
8″ x 8″	60/100	.31/3.23	48	.54	48	2850	11.2	30.6
CLEAR								
Standard Series (3⅞″ thick)								
6″ x 6″	45/120	.48/2.08	72-74	.65	41	850	3.5	20.8
8″ x 8″	45/120	.48/2.08	72-74	.65	42	850	6.4	19.5
12″ x 12″	—	.48/2.08	72-74	.63	42	850	15.3	18.7
Thinline Series (3⅛″ thick)								
8″ x 8″	45/120	.53/1.89	79	.66	41	850	5.4	15.9
CLEAR								
Standard Series (3⅞″ thick)								
8″ x 8″	45/120	.48/2.08	48-55	.41	42	850	6.4	19.5

Series

CLARITY

This see-through block provides a dramatic grid effect, undistorted vision, and maximum light transmission.

Matching designer shapes provide beauty and flexibility to create angles, curves or finished jambs and/or heads. 45, 60 and 90 minute fire ratings are available.

Clarity

Clarity Corner Block

Clarity WeckEnd

FORTRESS

Extra-heavy block; minimizes vandalism. Available with small line pattern or in Clarity.

Fortress

X-RIB

Vertical ribs on one face and horizontal on the other for privacy.

X-Rib

SPRAY

Grid pattern offers privacy, reduces glare.

Spray

PART 1   GENERAL

1.01 WORK INCLUDED
A. WECK GLASS BLOCKS
B. WECK GLASS BLOCKS with (45, 60 or 90) minute listed U.L. fire rating.
C. Integral joint reinforcing.
D. Miscellaneous metal anchors and/or fire rated hollow metal frames.
E. Mortars and sealants.

1.02 RELATED WORK
A. Section (_____-_____) Masonry.
B. Section (_____-_____) Lintels.
C. Section (_____-_____) Sealants.

1.03 REFERENCES
A. ASTM C153B2, Hot Dipped Zinc Coating.
B. ASTM C144, Aggregate for Masonry.
C. ASTM C150, Portland Cement.
D. ASTM C207, Hydrated Lime for Masonry.
E. ASTM C207, Mortar for Unit Masonry.
F. Underwriters Laboratories Building Materials Directory, 1992 Edition.

1.04 SUBMITTALS
A. Submit WECK Catalogue.
B. Submit _____ WECK GLASS BLOCK of each type for approval.

1.05 ENVIRONMENTAL REQUIREMENTS
A. Maintain materials and ambient air temperatures to a minimum of 40°F prior to, during and 48 hours after completion of work.
B. Protect WECK GLASS BLOCK from moisture prior to construction.

PART 2   PRODUCTS

2.01 ACCEPTABLE MANUFACTURERS
A. J. WECK GmbH u. Co.

2.02 GLASS UNITS
A. _____ x _____ x _____ Inch.
B. _____ x _____ x _____ Inch with (45, 60 or 90) minute listed U.L. fire rating.
C. Color (Cleartone or Goldtone) _____
D. Pattern _____
E. Edge Coating – White latex based paint.

2.03 ACCESSORIES
A. Joint Reinforcing: Ladder type, hot dipped galvanized, 2-9 gauge parallel longitudinal wire at 2″ o.c. for 3⅞″ wide block or 1⅝″ for 3⅛″ wide block and cross rods welded at 8″ o.c.
B. Panel Anchors: 20 gauge x 1¾″ x 24″ hot dipped galvanized steel with staggered perforations as supplied by Glass Masonry, Inc.
C. Perimeter Chase: Masonry recess, aluminum channel or steel channel.
D. Fire rated hollow metal frames as supplied by Glashaus, Inc.
E. Adjustable masonry anchors and wire ties.
F. Asphalt Emulsion: Karnac 100 or equal.
G. Expansion Strips: ⅜″ x 3½″ polyethylene plastic or glass fiber (for fire rating) as supplied by Glass Masonry, Inc.
H. Sealant: Silicone Type _____ Color.
I. Backer Rod: As recommended by sealant supplier.

2.04 MORTAR MATERIALS
A. Shall be prepared according to ASTM C270 for Type S Mortar. Mortar to have 1 part Portland Cement (Type 1), 1 part lime and 4½ to 6 parts of fine sand passing No. 20 sieve and free of iron compounds to avoid stains. Use white Portland Cement and silica sand for white joints. Mix mortar drier than normal and only an amount that will be used in ½ to 1 hour. Glass block will not absorb water the same as brick. Do not use retempered mortar. Do not use antifreeze compounds or accelerators.
B. Add _____ mortar color per manufacturer's instructions. Side walls of WECK GLASS BLOCK must be same color as mortar. If mortar is not white, strip paint and re-paint with colored latex paint.
C. Add Laticrete 8510 to increase waterproofing qualities of mortar.

PART 3   EXECUTION

3.01 PREPARATION
A. Vertify that pocket recesses or chases provided under other sections are accurately located and sized.
B. Establish and protect lines, levels and coursing.

3.02 INSTALLATION
A. Arrange coursing pattern to provide consistent joint work throughout.
B. Locate and secure perimeter metal chase.
C. Coat sill under units with asphalt emulsion as a bond breaker.
D. Mortar joints must be solid. Furrowing not permitted. Neatly tool surface to a concave joint.
E. Place panel reinforcing in horizontal joint above first course of block and not more than 18″ o.c. for Standard Series, every other course for Thinline Series and every course for Fire Stop Series. Panel anchors if used shall be installed in the same joints as reinforcing.
F. Isolate panel from adjacent construction on sides and top with expansion strips. Keep expansion joint voids clear of mortar.
G. Maintain uniform joint width of ¼″ ± ⅛″.
H. Maximum variation from plane of unit to next unit — 1/32″.
I. Maximum variation of panel from plane — 1/16″.
J. Do not use retempered mortar.
K. Do not tap glass block with steel tools.
L. When mortar has set, pack backer rod in jamb and head channels. Recess to allow for sealant. (Back-up for sealant at fire rated frames is mortar.)
M. Apply sealant.

3.03 CLEANING
A. Remove excess mortar from glass surfaces with a damp cloth before set occurs.
B. Number 4 steel wool can be used to remove remaining mortar.

For technical or installation information request our Design Guide.

Glass Blocks

Glashaus Inc.

415 West Golf Road
Suite 13
Arlington Heights, IL 60005

708/640-6910
FAX: 708/640-6955

Printing: Active Graphics — Chicago
9/92

C285
BuyLine 8604

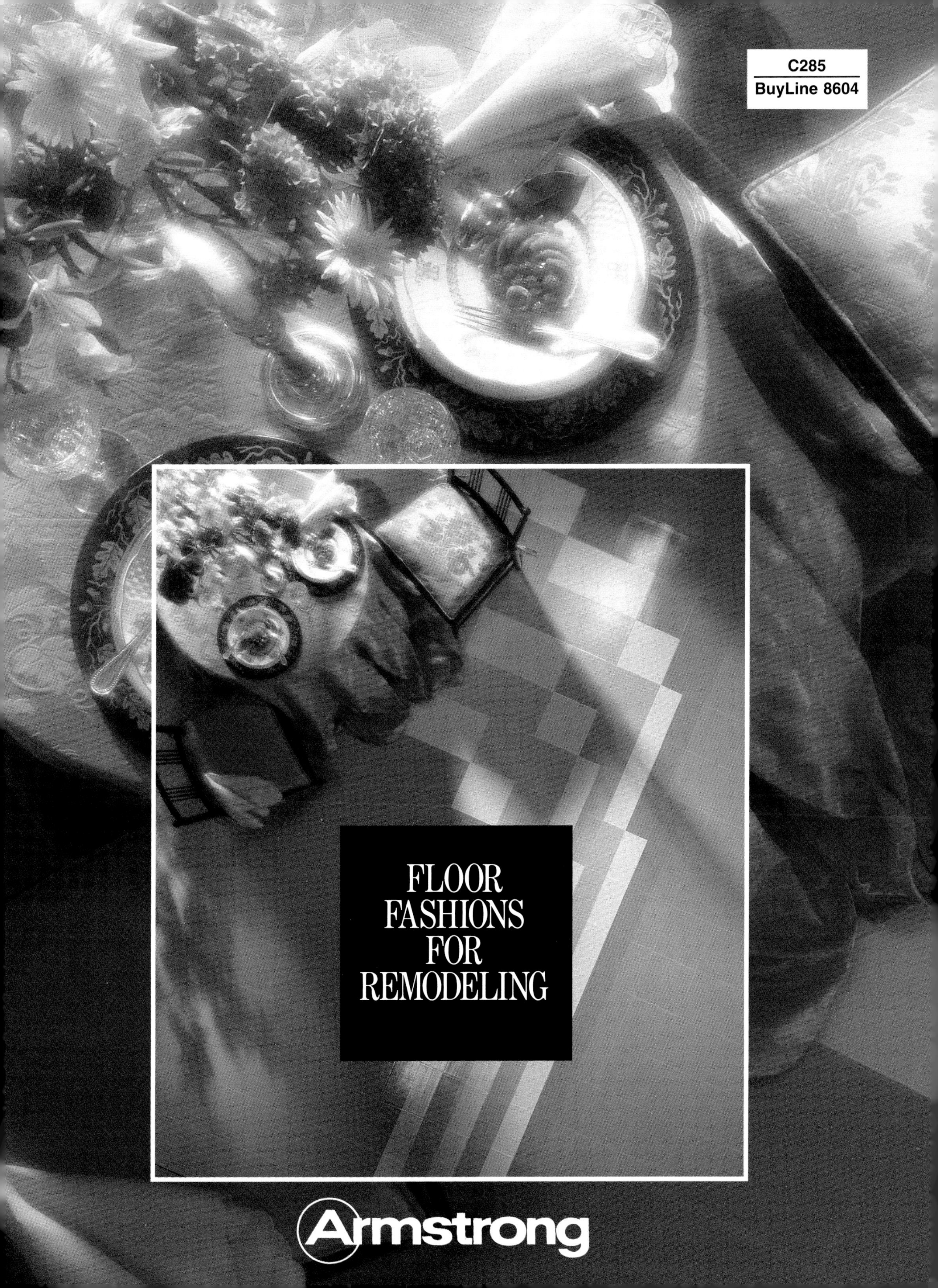

FLOOR FASHIONS FOR REMODELING

Armstrong

These are some of the elements with which you turn good ideas and smart remodeling solutions into reality . . . dream kitchens, luxurious baths, long-awaited hideaways. They're all home improvements intended to improve and expand on life itself. And it's up to you—the homeowner and the remodeler—to find the designs that will achieve your goals. ■ Armstrong can help with floors that are designed to complement and coordinate with today's interior finishes. Our designers work with leading designers around the world to give you the options of color and style that allow and encourage truly unique design statements. Let us show you how vinyl flooring can bring splash, sophistication and excitement to your remodeling project.

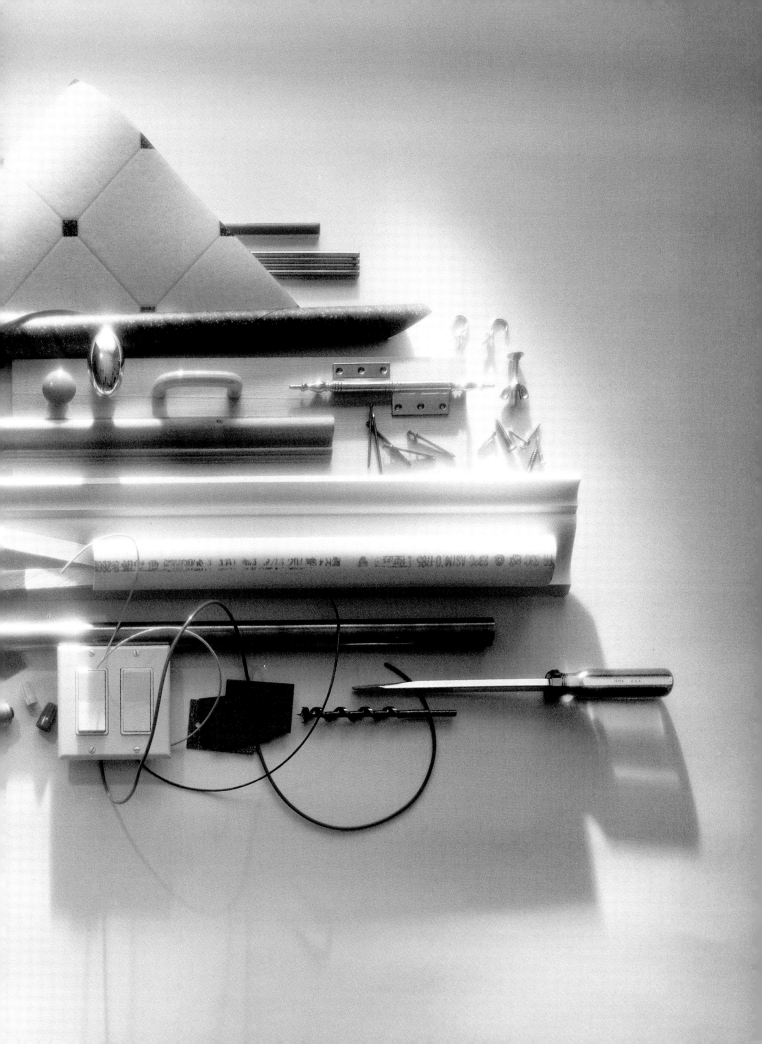

Bringing the outdoors in is an "in" trend. Once the province of the garden, luscious blooms and vine-laced walls now combine with the shimmering brightness of Designer Solarian II Rosita, floral prints and a medley of pinks.

N

eo-traditionalism is a borrowing from our heritage to create something fresh and new. This Designer Solarian floor is a striking counterpoint to luscious blue and white porcelains and damask draperies in a room decorated in a rich traditional style.

Floor design copyrighted by Armstrong

G lints of steel, glass and chrome, luxurious towels and a mock exotic zebra print fabric create a handsome bath. The palette of neutrals, grays and whites is set off by the sculptured pattern of Designer Solarian II Subtle Visions.

Floor design copyrighted by Armstrong

Today's sophisticated country kitchen is light, bright, open and colorful. The pastel blush and subtle pattern of this Designer Solarian floor offer just the right touch of country for a look that's homey, warm and whimsical.

Floor design copyrighted by Armstrong

A n intimate eating place by the fire takes on a rich elegance amid eclectic furnishings and antique accessories. The subtle patterns of hand-painted velvet and china blend beautifully with this Visions Solarian floor.

Floor design copyrighted by Armstrong

Good / Better / Best Terminology

In an effort to simplify the shopping process, Armstrong divides residential sheet floors into three distinct categories: GOOD, BETTER, and BEST. Each floor is manufactured with the same high standards but offers its own set of performance features and benefits.

Here is an explanation of how we determine whether each of the floors is Good, Better, or Best in terms of Maintenance and Durability.

MAINTENANCE

	EASY CARE	HOUSEHOLD STAIN RESISTANCE	TRAFFIC STAIN RESISTANCE
	BEST Requires vacuuming with an occasional wash using Armstrong Once 'n Done No-Rinse Floor Cleaner.	**BEST** Common household stains including hair dye, shoe polish, mustard, ketchup, permanent marker, etc., **will not** stain the floor.	**BEST** Foot traffic, including asphalt driveway sealer, **will not** permanently stain floors.
	BETTER Requires damp mopping with an occasional wash with Armstrong Once 'n Done No-Rinse Floor Cleaner.	**BETTER** May experience slight discoloration from some household stains such as hair dye, shoe polish, mustard, ketchup, and permanent marker when left on floor over time.*	**BETTER** May experience slight discoloration from foot traffic — including asphalt driveway sealer.
	GOOD Requires regular washing with Armstrong Once 'n Done No-Rinse Floor Cleaner.	**GOOD** May experience discoloration from some household stains such as hair dye, shoe polish, mustard, ketchup, and permanent marker when left on the floor over time.*	**GOOD** May experience discoloration from traffic stains — including asphalt driveway sealer.
SOLARIAN SUPREME	BEST	BEST	BEST
DESIGNER SOLARIAN II	BEST	BEST	BEST
DESIGNER SOLARIAN	BEST	BEST	BEST
VISIONS SOLARIAN	BEST	BEST	BEST
CROWNE CORLON	GOOD	BETTER	BETTER
STARSTEP SOLARIAN	BETTER	BETTER	BEST
SOLARIAN SELECT	BETTER	BETTER	BEST
SUNDIAL SOLARIAN	BETTER	BETTER	BEST
PREVAIL	GOOD	BETTER	BETTER
SUCCESSOR	GOOD	BETTER	BETTER
TIMESPAN	GOOD	GOOD	GOOD

*Test performed 72 hours after staining.

CleanSweep Guarantee

We guarantee that Solarian Supreme, Designer Solarian II, Designer Solarian and Visions Solarian are the easiest to clean of any sheet vinyl flooring. These floors only require vacuuming with an occasional wash using a no-rinse floor cleaner, and will not permanently discolor from household or traffic stains, including asphalt driveway sealers and carpet dyes. If you're not completely satisfied that these floors are the easiest to clean, Armstrong will replace the floor.

SCUFF RESISTANCE	DAMAGE RESISTANCE	INDENTATION RESISTANCE	
BEST Resists scuffing even in high traffic areas.	**BEST** Resists cuts, tears, and gouges from moving appliances and dropping utensils.	**BEST** **	
BETTER May experience slight scuffing in high traffic areas.	**BETTER** May experience some minor cuts, tears, and gouges from moving appliances and dropping utensils.	**BETTER** May experience slight indentation** from spiked and stiletto heels, furniture, and appliances.	
GOOD May experience scuffing in high traffic areas.	**GOOD** May experience cuts, tears, and gouges from moving appliances and dropping utensils.	**GOOD** May experience indentation** from spiked and stiletto heels, furniture, and appliances.	

BEST	BEST	BETTER	**BEST**
BEST	BEST	BETTER	**BEST**
BEST	BEST	BETTER	**BEST**
BEST	BEST	BETTER	**BEST**
GOOD	BEST	BETTER	**BETTER**
BEST	BETTER	BETTER	**BETTER**
BEST	GOOD	BETTER	**BETTER**
BEST	GOOD	GOOD	**BETTER**
GOOD	BETTER	GOOD	**GOOD**
BETTER	GOOD	BETTER	**GOOD**
GOOD	GOOD	BETTER	**GOOD**

**All floor coverings will indent or chip from spiked and stiletto heels and sharp furniture or appliance feet. In this category, no floor deserves a best rating.

F-4077-193L

Printed in United States of Ame

C468
06600/DUP
BuyLine 0665

CORIAN®

Corian®. The ultimate surfacing material.

For more than 25 years, Du Pont CORIAN has set a standard of beauty, performance and value that no other material can equal. CORIAN is easier to care for than marble or granite, and more durable than any laminate or coating. With all of the elegance of natural stone—and none of the limitations—it truly is the ultimate surfacing material.

Du Pont technological innovation combines a patented blend of natural materials and a high-performance acrylic—methyl methacrylate—to create CORIAN. The result is a solid material of lustrous beauty in an endless array of color combinations. Beneath the elegant appearance of CORIAN, however, lies a material whose strength, design flexibility and convenience have made it the leading choice of demanding architects and designers for a quarter century.

An unprecedented, 10-year installed warranty.

Du Pont now backs CORIAN with the best warranty program in the business—the industry's first installed limited warranty that guarantees the product quality of CORIAN plus its fabrication and installation. To ensure your CORIAN project is covered by Du Pont's installed limited warranty, the material must be fabricated and installed by a Du Pont Certified or Approved Fabricator/Installer. Please see an Authorized CORIAN Distributor for more details, or call Du Pont at 1-800-4CORIAN.

Properties.

CORIAN gives architects and designers the freedom to create beautiful interiors plus the confidence that it will stand up to the most demanding applications. The properties of CORIAN include:

- **Impact resistance:** CORIAN resists fracture, chipping and cracking better than marble, stone or polyester products.

- **Stain resistance:** The nonporous surface of CORIAN resists stains. It is unaffected by food stains and common disinfectants, and stubborn stains from cigarette burns, marking pens and hair dyes can be removed easily with routine care.

- **Heat resistance:** While CORIAN withstands heat better than many surface materials, use of a hot pad is recommended before placing hot cookware or electrical cooking appliances on a CORIAN surface.

- **Class I flammability rating:** CORIAN has a Class I flammability rating, making it suitable for virtually any horizontal or vertical application.

- **NSF compliance:** The National Sanitation Foundation has accepted CORIAN under NSF Standard # 51: "Plastic Materials and Components Used in Food Equipment." This sanction means CORIAN is ideal for use in food service, lodging, healthcare and educational institutions.

- **Resistance to germs and mildew:** Independent laboratory tests clearly show that nonporous CORIAN will not support the growth of fungi, mildew, and bacteria such as staph or other germs.

Additional information on radioactive compounds and HIV (AIDS) clean-up is available through a line of bulletins issued by Du Pont.

Applications.

No matter what the application—if it calls for durability and beauty—CORIAN is the ideal choice, with over 25 years of proven performance.

- sinks • countertops and work surfaces • vanities • lavatories • tub and shower surrounds • walls and partitions • wainscotting • windowsills • baseboards • molding • thresholds • desk and laboratory tops

In hotels, restaurants, hospitals, universities and homes, CORIAN is the elegant, durable choice.

Fabrication procedures.

CORIAN products can be fabricated in the shop or on-site. Because CORIAN has working characteristics similar to those of fine hardwood, skilled technicians can form CORIAN to fit your specifications exactly. Installers can cut, drill, sand, rout and form CORIAN, using normal woodworking power tools to create innovative shapes and surface effects. CORIAN can also be thermoformed more readily than other solid materials, creating endless possibilities for flowing forms and rounded edges.

CORIAN may be combined with wood, brass, tile, acrylics and other CORIAN colors for a wide variety of unique designs and edge treatments. Fabrication and installation information is available from your CORIAN distributor, or you can call Du Pont at **1-800-4CORIAN**.

Sheet and shape.

CORIAN is readily available from distributors in both sheet and precast shapes. Sheet sizes range up to 760 x 3680mm (30" x 145") in thicknesses of

6mm (¼"), 13mm (½"), and 19mm (¾"). Shaped products include one-piece vanity tops and bowls, kitchen sinks and lavatories.

Easy to care for.
Easy to maintain.

CORIAN is the perfect material for almost any surface because it is so easy to clean and maintain. CORIAN is nonporous, so most stains wipe right off with soap and water. More stubborn stains—even cigarette burns or scratches—can be sanded away with fine sandpaper, or even an abrasive household cleanser. This procedure is not possible with laminates or cultured marble products. Even in cases where damage is severe, CORIAN can be repaired to look like new.

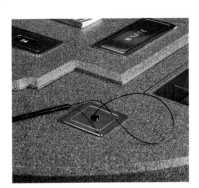

A wealth of beautiful, designer colors.

CORIAN is available in classic and versatile colors to complement any interior.

- Cameo White • Dawn Beige • Bone
- Dusty Rose • Taupe • Peach • Misty Green • Pearl Gray • Glacier White
- Sierra Midnight • Sierra Dusk
- Sierra Sandstone • Sierra Pink Coral
- Sierra Sapphire • Sierra Jade • Sierra Black Pearl • Sierra Garnet • Sierra Burnt Amber • Sierra Evergreen
- Sierra Oceanic • Sierra Sunset

Accessories.

CORIAN Joint Adhesive–for bonding CORIAN to CORIAN. Available in a variety of colors.

Silicone Sealant for CORIAN–for installing backsplashes and reveal edges; and for sealing tub and shower seams. Available in a variety of colors.

CORIAN inlay colors.

Inlay colors, made of acrylic resin-based material, can be used to add decorative elements by routing out the desired design, filling with inlay color, and sanding the finished area. Available in a variety of colors.

*Metric conversions are approximate.

Corian® Technical Data*

A wide variety of convenient sizes and kits.

Sheet products:
Sheets available in three thicknesses: 6mm (¼"), 13mm (½"), and 19mm (¾").

For vertical operations:
6mm (¼") sheet; 760mm (30") wide; and in lengths of 1524mm (60"), 1830mm (72"), and 2490mm (98"). Also, 25mm by 2490mm trim strips (1" x 98").

For horizontal applications:
13mm (½") and 19mm (¾") sheet; 760mm (30") wide; and in lengths of 2490mm (98"), 3070mm (121"), and 3680mm (145"). Also available in 13mm (½") sheet; 560mm (22") plus 205mm (8") wide; and 2490mm, 3070mm and 3680mm long.

Tub surrounds and shower wall kits:
Three separate products are available for wet wall applications.

- Commercial tub kit:
  Four panels, 6mm x 760mm x 1524mm, up to 2490mm (¼" x 30" x 60", up to 98"); plus a selection of trim strips for decorative trim.

- Standard (residential) tub kit:
  Four panels 6mm x 745mm x 1524mm (¼" x 29⁵⁄₁₆" x 60); plus one decorative batten strip, 6mm x 152mm x 1448mm (¼" x 6" x 57").

- **Shower wall panels:** (Custom applications) Standard 6mm sheets, 760mm up to 2490mm in length (¼" x 30" x 98"). Can be custom-cut for wall panels, ceiling panels and trim strips.

Integral vanity top and bowl:
The molded one-piece construction available in a variety of sizes and bowl locations combines the smooth, continuous surface of the vanity and bowl eliminating hard-to-clean crevices.

Lavatories:
CORIAN lavatories are available in five styles and are an excellent choice in combination with CORIAN sheet vanity tops or conventional vanity top material. Lavatories include topmounted, undermounted, or seamed undermounted models.

Sinks:
Single- or double-bowl units offer complete flexibility of color and placement. Beveled, undermount or seamed undermount installation may be used. Euro-style double-bowl drainboard sinks are also available.

How to specify CORIAN.
The following suggested write-up is included to assist you when specifying CORIAN.

- **One-piece CORIAN vanity top and bowl:** Vanity bowls and tops shall be of a one-piece, monolithic design, made of CORIAN (methyl methacrylate binder) manufactured by Du Pont. Color and pattern shall be selected by the architect and physical properties shall conform to the manufacturer's standard specifications. The material shall be homogenous, not coated or laminated.

Installation shall be in a work-manlike manner, in accordance with the manufacturer's instructions.

- **Surfaces:** Surfaces shall be CORIAN. Color and pattern shall be selected by the architect. CORIAN sheets shall be ½" (13mm) or ¾" (19mm) for countertops. Backsplashes, where specified, ¼" (6mm), ½" (13mm), or ¾" (19mm). Wall coverings shall be ¼" (6mm) unless otherwise specified. Physical properties shall conform to the manufacturer's standard specifications. The material shall be homogenous, not coated or laminated. Installation shall be in a workmanlike manner, in accordance with the manufacturer's instructions.

When specifying CORIAN for applications that are wider than 30" (760mm) or require a seam, specify Du Pont Joint Adhesive for CORIAN. It can be used to form a smooth, inconspicuous seam for joint applications. Silicone sealant should be used for caulking tub and shower wall seams and edges.

Literature and samples.
A variety of literature and samples, including the CORIAN Product Catalog, are available from your CORIAN distributor, or you can call Du Pont toll-free at 1-800-4CORIAN.

Available worldwide.
For more information, write or call:
Du Pont Polymers
Wilmington, DE, 19898
1-800-4CORIAN

Table I. Technical Data—CORIAN Solid Surface Products

PROPERTY	TYPICAL RESULT	TEST
Tensile Strength	6000 psi	ASTM-D-638
Tensile Modulus	1.5×10^6 psi	ASTM-D-638
Elongation	0.4% min.	ASTM-D-638
Hardness	94	Rockwell "M" Scale ASTM-D-785
	56	Barcol Impressor ASTM-D-2583
Thermal Expansion	3.02×10^{-5} in./in./°C (1.80×10^{-5} in./in./°F)	ASTM-D-696
Gloss (60° Gardner)	5-75 (matte–highly polished)	ANSI-Z124 HUD Bulletin UM73
Color Stability	No change—200 hrs.	NEMA-LD-3-3.10
Wear & Cleanability	Passes	ANSI-Z124 HUD Bulletin UM73
Boiling Water Surface Resistance	No visible change	NEMA-LD-3-3.05
High Temperature Resistance (500°F)	No change	NEMA-LD-3-3.06
Izod Impact (Notched Specimen)	0.28 ft.-lbs./in. of notch	ASTM-D-256 (Method A)
Stain Resistance: Sheets	Passes	ANSI-Z124 HUD Bulletin UM73
Impact Resistance: Sheets	No fracture	NEMA-LD-3-3.03
	¼" slab—36" drop ½ lb. ball ½" slab—36" drop 1 lb. ball ¾" slab—35" drop 2 lb. ball	
Point Impact: Bowls	No cracks or chips	ANSI-Z124 HUD Bulletin UM73
Weatherability	No change—1000 hrs.	ASTM-D-1499
Specific Gravity*	1.8 Standard Color 1.69 Sierra Colors	
Water Absorption	24 hrs. Long-term 0.04 0.4 (¾") 0.09 0.8 (¼")	ASTM-D-570
Flammability		ASTM-E-84

| | STANDARD COLORS | | | | | SIERRA COLORS | |
| | ¼"** | | ½" | ¼"*** | ¾" | ½" | ¾" |
Flammability	Masonry	Gypsum	Sheet	Gypsum	Sheet	Sheet	Sheet
Flame Spread	15	25	5	20	5	15	15
Smoke Developed	20	25	10	5	15	25	30
Class	1	1	1	1	1	1	1

*Approximate weight per square foot for standard colors: ¼" (6mm) 2.35 lbs. • ½" (13mm) 4.7 lbs. • ¾" (19mm) 7.0 lbs. For Sierra colors: ¼" (6mm) 2.2 lbs. • ½" (13mm) 4.4 lbs. • ¾" (19mm) 6.6 lbs.

** ¼" (6mm) results reflect material adhered to both masonry surfaces and standard grade ½" (13mm) thick Gypsum Board using Panel Adhesive for Du Pont CORIAN® and tested as a composite.

*** ¼" (6mm) results reflect material adhered to both masonry surfaces and standard grade ½" (13mm) thick Gypsum Board using Silicone Adhesive for Du Pont CORIAN® and tested as a composite.

CORIAN®
Living With The Best™

DU PONT

A sophisticated but colorful approach makes this kitchen a great place to spend time. Island countertop is GIBRALTAR® Solid Surfacing.

HOW TO TURN A KITCHEN INTO A VISUAL FEAST

All other countertops are clad with Pebble laminate. The edge treatment is painted Perma-Edge Molding®, with an insert strip of Metalwork laminate.

Just start with one of the over 230 WILSONART laminates. Each has been chosen to reflect the latest in global design trends, and is available in numerous aesthetic and performance options. So no matter what your design destination, we can provide the suitable point of departure.

For a brochure with complete product information plus great ideas for kitchen and bath design, and rapid Rocket Chip℠ delivery of samples, just call 1-800-433-3222, or 1-800-792-6000 in Texas.

WILSONART®
BRAND DECORATIVE LAMINATE
Bringing new solutions to the surface®

© 1992, RWP Co.

HOW TO BATHE A ROOM WITH LASTING COLOR

Begin with GIBRALTAR Solid Surfacing. Its solid, monolithic look is available in over 30 solid colors and stone-like patterns which uniquely match or coordinate with WILSONART® laminates. And the beauty of GIBRALTAR lasts — the fact is, it's the most durable solid surface on the market.

For a brochure with complete product information plus great ideas for kitchen and bath design, and rapid Rocket Chip℠ delivery of samples, just call 1-800-433-3222, or 1-800-792-6000 in Texas.

▲ A geometric motif is executed in several laminate colors on panels throughout the room, and in the shower stall with GIBRALTAR surfacing in Platinum, Platinum Stardust and Black Stardust.

◄ Countertop is shaped, rounded GIBRALTAR surfacing in Platinum, with an edge detail of Black Stardust.

Traditional Japanese design influences help make this bath a serene refuge from everyday cares.

GIBRALTAR®
SOLID SURFACING

From the Makers of WILSONART® Brand Decorative Laminate

© 1992, RWP Co.

Amana®
ALL THE RIGHT PIECES

Because you're always looking for an edge in kitchen design, Amana offers you four brand names featuring innovative products that can elevate your latest work from great to spectacular. Amana has all the right pieces for your next project. Let us help you solve the puzzle.

Amana®

Modern Maid®

Caloric®

Speed Queen™

1-800-843-0304
FAST FACTS

Call Amana's toll-free number today to promptly receive the most current information on the products you are specifying.

Amana

Modern Maid

Caloric

Speed Queen

The pieces all fit together when you specify Amana, Modern Maid, Caloric or Speed Queen.

We have the image, products, and sales and service network to support your design specifications.

Look to us for the solution to any of your puzzles, from the casual to the elegant, from the simple to the complex.

■ *Refrigerators:*
  Freezer on the top
  Freezer on the bottom
  Side-by-side
  Freestanding
  Built-in

■ *Microwave Ovens:*
  Over-the-Range
  Full-Size Countertop
  Built-in
  Microwave Convection
  Portable and Compact

■ *Ranges:*
  Freestanding
  Slide-in
  Double Deck
  Electric or Gas

■ *Dishwashers*

■ *Dehumidifiers*

Freezers:
  Chest
  Upright

1-800-843-0304
FAST FACTS

Call Amana's toll-free number today to promptly receive the most current information on the products you are specifying.

Synergy

- *Room Air Conditioners*

  Cooktops:
  Quartz Halogen
  All Radiant
  Solid Disk
  Electric Downdraft
  Gas Downdraft
  Gas on Glass

- *Central Heating & Cooling Products*

- *Built-in Toaster/Housing*
  Range Hoods

- *Wall Ovens:*
  Convection
  Single Electric
  Double Electric
  Combination
  Single Gas
  Double Gas

Washers & Dryers

KOHLER COLOR COORDINATES PARTNER

DESIGN BY REFINEMENT

From traditional to contemporary design, Amana has the appliances for your specific project.

Our products are built with integrity to ensure quality and your satisfaction.

Amana
A **Raytheon** Company

1-800-843-0304
FAST FACTS

Call Amana's toll-free number today to promptly receive the most current information on the products you are specifying.

Powerful Proof That Bosch Dishwashers Are The Best.

A company called Bosch.

As a leading manufacturer of appliances in Europe, Bosch is committed to developing products that perform efficiently and economically. Each year, we invest millions of dollars in research. Much of this money is used to develop appliances that not only make life easier, but also offer maximum protection to the environment.

This new line of thinking is fully realized in our new Bosch dishwashers, now available for the first time in the U.S. As you'll see, these machines measure up to every other product that Bosch has introduced in America during the last eight decades.

The closest thing to silence.

The ideal dishwasher would be completely silent. Once you listen to a Bosch dishwasher, we think you'll agree that our engineers have come closest to the ideal.

To eliminate internal vibration, which is the primary source of noise, a heavy duty insulation wrap is permanently bonded, under extreme pressure, to the outside of the stainless steel tub as well as to the inner door. The motors are completely insulated. In addition, a layer of sound absorbing material fits snugly between the inner and outer lining walls.

The result of this rather elaborate insulation process is dramatic. You could run eight Bosch dishwashers at the same time and they would still be quieter than one dishwasher made by other manufacturers.* When it comes to performance, we have sound proof that Bosch dishwashers are best

SMU 7052 US Deluxe (White); SMU 7056 US Deluxe (Black); (Almond door panel optional accessory SMZ 4034)

- *Six programs at the touch of a button: Rinse and Hold, Quick Wash, Economy, Regular Wash, Light/China, Pots and Pans*
- *Stainless steel inner liner and inner door*
- *Height adjustable upper rack with two double cup layers*
- *Multi-flexible bottom rack can accommodate large pots and pans*
- *Additional rack in lower basket for larger utensils.*
- *Capacity for twelve complete place settings*
- *Four spraying levels for efficient, thorough rinse and clean*
- *Convection drying system for even, gentler drying*
- *Two-pump system conserves water*
- *Deluxe control panel indicator lights*

- *Optional rack for long stemmed glasses (SMZ 2004)*
- *UL approved*
- *Made in Germany*

Deluxe SMU 7052 US (White)

Saves over 1,500 gallons of water per year.

To conserve water, Bosch engineered a unique washing system that draws the maximum cleaning power out of every drop of water.

Instead of the standard one-pump system that requires a large reservoir, Bosch uses a revolutionary two-pump system that circulates water through four spraying levels.

By making each drop of water work twice as much, a Bosch dishwasher, used just once a day, will save over 1,500 gallons of water per year compared to other dishwashers.* When it comes to conservation, that's

Deluxe SMU 7056 US (Black) For specifications see SMU 7052 US

Rinse and wash water is channeled through four spraying levels.

water proof that Bosch dishwashers are best.

A clear difference.

Perhaps the most impressive feature of the new Bosch dishwashers is how clean they get your dishes. To accomplish this, while at the same time using only half as much water as other dishwashers, requires unequaled performance features.

Cleaning.

Bosch dishwashers eliminate the need for hand rinsing with an exclusive triple filter system that includes a self-cleaning micro-filter.

Before washing,

the dishwasher boosts the temperature of the water up to 161° F, and automatically pre-activates the detergent.

Different wash programs can be selected at the touch of a button including special programs for economy wash, light/china, pots and pans and more.

Every program delivers the activated wash water at four separate spraying levels. These levels are pressure adjusted to deliver more spraying power to pots and pans and a more delicate spray to glassware.

Stainless steel inner liner and inner door will not rust through, chip or bleach.

Based on comparisions with leading U.S. manufactured dishwasher models available in June '92. Test comparisons conducted by an independent laboratory. Test data furnished upon request.

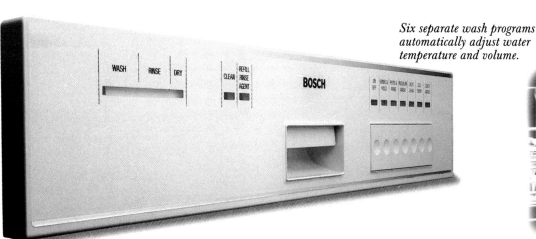

Six separate wash programs automatically adjust water temperature and volume.

Height adjustable upper rack can accommodate tall glassware.

Drying.

Bosch dishwashers feature convection drying that creates an internal air flow for even, gentle drying. Because it draws no outside air into the interior, this allows no dust into the system.

Hygienics.

Most dishwashers have plastic or porcelain coated inner liners, which are susceptible to rust, chipping and bleaching. Bosch dishwashers feature an inner liner and inner door made of stainless steel. They come with a 25-year warranty against rust through. (Please refer to instruction manual for warranty details.)

Perhaps even more unique is the combi-nation of stainless steel and our specially designed gasket system, which prevent dirt and bacteria from collecting inside the machine between washes.

Flexible arrangements.

Bosch dishwasher are designed to accommodate an incredible array of dishes. All models have flexible, heigh adjustable upper dish racks and mult flexible bottom dish racks that provide space for pots, pans —even a wok. They can hold up to twelve complete place settings.

The deluxe mode has an additional rack that provides more space for cups or larger utensils. A optional rack for long stemmed glasses, providing over 12 inches of additional space, is also available for both models (SMZ 2004).

SMU 4052 US (White) For specifications see SMU 4056 US

Even the dish racks did not escape the Bosch engineers' pursuit of superior quality and performance. Rather than the typical PVC coating found on many other dishwashers, Bosch dish racks are coated with nylon, which is more pliable and cut resistant.

new line of thinking.

Bosch dishwashers can be found in kitchens throughout Europe. Known for their innovative performance features, Bosch dishwashers are built to the highest quality standards. Every Bosch dishwasher is designed to fit all types of American and European cabinetry.

All Bosch dishwashers are designed to fit American and European kitchen cabinetry.

**SMU 4052 US (White)
SMU 4056 US (Black)
(Almond door panel optional accessory SMZ 4034)**

- *Four-program push button control panel: Rinse and Hold, Economy, Regular Wash, Pots and Pans*
- *Rotary knob start*
- *Stainless steel inner liner and inner door*
- *Height adjustable upper rack with two double cup layers*
- *Flexible bottom rack can accommodate large pots and pans*
- *Capacity for twelve complete place settings*
- *Four spraying levels for efficient, thorough rinse and clean*
- *Convection drying system for even, gentler drying*
- *Two-pump system conserves water*
- *Optional rack for long stemmed glasses (SMZ 2004)*
- *UL approved*
- *Made in Germany*

SMU 4056 US (Black)

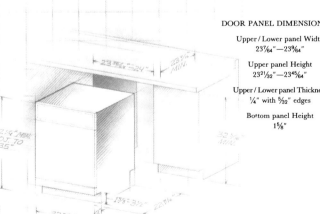

DOOR PANEL DIMENSIONS

Upper / Lower panel Width
23⅛" — 23¾"

Upper panel Height
23²¹/₃₂" — 23⁴⁵/₆₄"

Upper / Lower panel Thickness
¼" with ⁵/₃₂" edges

Bottom panel Height
1⅝"

Our engineers continually seek new ways to save on energy and water consumption. The built-in temperature booster, for example, allows you to turn your home's water heater down to 120° F (20° less than the standard setting, yet still hot enough for hot showers).

And, to demonstrate the extremes to which Bosch goes to protect our environment, we build our dishwashers from parts that are all recyclable.

At Bosch, we know what you expect from a quality dishwasher. We take great satisfaction in introducing a new line of dishwashers that go beyond your expectations.

SMI 7052 US

Bosch Dishwashers
The Integrated Series

The Bosch Integrated Series represents the optimum design approach for integrating dishwashers into the kitchen environment. It creates the prefect harmony between the convenience of innovative dishwashers and the beauty of breathtaking cabinetry. The prefect balance of form and function.

Bosch has engineered an unusual amount of flexibility into the installation of these dishwashers, allowing you to tailor the appearance of the dishwasher to

match the grid of the kitchen design. This is accomplished through these special features:

• A control panel that can be adjusted to match a drawer height of up to 6".

• A cabinet door mounting technique that can be used with virtually any kitchen cabinet, regardless of toe-kick dimensions.

• A dishwasher door that is recessed to accept a 3/4" thick door panel, providing

SMI 7056 US

a "flush" European look. Extra heavy-duty door springs handle the additional weight of the cabinet door panel for a smoothly balanced operation.

The final result is a designers dream, an uninterrupted flow of the horizontal lines, textures and colors of the cabinetry while providing the convenience, performance and reliability of a Bosch dishwasher. And Bosch dishwashers are easy to install in all types of

The Bosch Integrated Series dishwashers let you take kitchen design to a new level. They enhance the beauty of the kitchen, yet also add to the functionality with ultra quiet operation and a two-pump system that conserves up to 50% of the water used by other dishwashers. *

Bosch . . .leading the industry in innovation.

BOSCH

The Bosch Integrated Series features:

- SMI 7052 US Deluxe 6 Program Dishwasher (White)

- SMI 7056 US Deluxe 6 Program Dishwasher (Black)

- Ultra quiet operation, up to eight times quieter than other dishwashers*

- Two-pump system conserves up to 50% of the water used by other dishwashers*

- Six programs at the touch of a button: Rinse and Hold, Quick Wash, Economy, Regular Wash, Light/China, Pots and Pans

- Stainless steel inner liner and inner door (with a 25 year replacement guarantee, see owners manual for details)

- Height adjustable upper rack with two double cup layers

- Multi-flexible bottom rack can accommodate large pots and pans

- Additional rack in lower basket for larger utensils

- Capacity for twelve place settings

- Four spraying levels for efficient, thorough rinse and clean

- Convection drying system for even, gentler drying

- UL approved

- Made in Germany

Available Accessories:

SMZ 3022 US Cabinet Door Mounting Kit

SMZ 2004 US Optional Rack for long stemmed champagne glasses (up to 13" high)

BOSCH

Robert Bosch Corporation,
2800 South 25th Avenue,
Broadview, IL 60153

For dealer listing call: 1-800-866-2022

*Based on comparisons with leading U.S. manufactured dishwasher models available in June, 92. Test comparisons conducted by an independent U.S. laboratory. Test data furnished upon request.

Bosch is a registered trademark licensed by Robert Bosch GmbH.

@1992, Robert Bosch Corporation

321275 1092

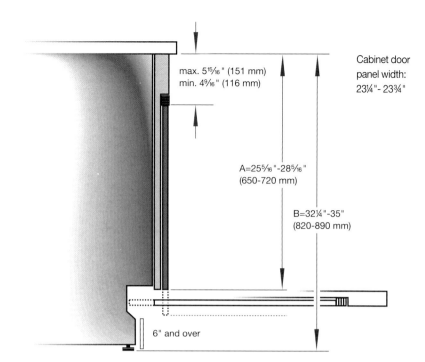

If the cabinets you're specifying fall within these dimensions, then all the hardware necessary to mount the cabinet door panel will be included with the dishwasher. (The continuous toe-kick of the cabinet will cover the bottom section of the dishwasher)

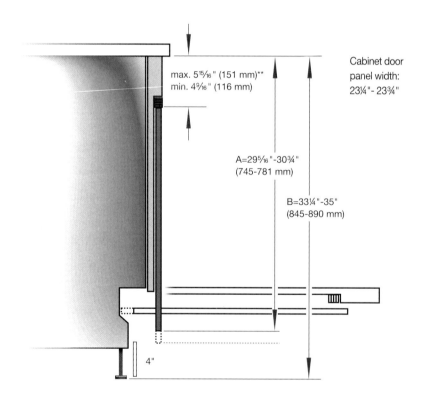

If the cabinets you're specifying fall within these dimensions, then you need to order the accessory door mounting kit **#SMZ3022 US** (You will also need an additional toe-kick plate from the cabinet supplier in order to cover the bottom section of the dishwasher).

For framed kitchens order a custom made door panel equal in width to 23¼".

After determining the type of installation you need from the above diagrams, order the same style kitchen door panel as the surrounding cabinets (except without handles or hardware).

**Note: For cabinets with a drawer height of over 6", order a door panel equal in length to Dimension A minus 4-11/16" (4-9/16" for the control panel + 1/8" panel spacing).

C484
BuyLine 8612

BROAN RANGE HOODS

RANGEMASTER™

Powerful, Quiet Ventilation For Professional Style Ranges.

The Broan Rangemaster™ range hood is the perfect answer to the higher ventilation requirements of professional quality home ranges. The Rangemaster's powerful blower systems can deliver up to 1200 CFM of quiet, efficient kitchen ventilation. Its heavy gauge construction and choice of either stainless steel or appliance-matching colors give the Rangemaster durability and a clean, functional appearance that complements all professional ranges.

Professional features — premium performance

- Infinite solid state speed control with exclusive blower memory.
- A choice of sizes to match any range — 18" high and 24" deep with widths from 30" to 72" in 6" increments.
- Exclusive Heat Sentry™ automatically turns blower to high speed when excess heat is detected.
- Dual warming lamps keep food hot until serving time.
- Optional stainless steel backsplash with shelves for food warming or condiment storage.
- Extra large filter area with easy-to-clean, removable aluminum filters that fit in dishwasher.
- Easy-to-clean stainless steel interior with no sharp edges.
- Economical dual level fluorescent lighting — select bright cooktop lighting or softer illumination.
- Optional soffit chimneys are available for installations without soffits.

All controls are mounted for easy operation. Filters are easy to remove and clean.

Optional backsplash with condiment shelves that fold down for food warming.

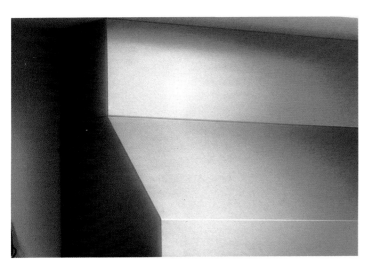

Optional soffit chimney available in a variety of widths and matching colors.

Powerful and quiet ventilation for even the largest range

■ Internal-mounted centrifugal blowers are HVI certified at 600 CFM, or 1200 CFM to match range size and cooking needs.

■ External roof or wall-mounted 900 CFM fan system also available. (Model 338, See page 15)

Ordering Instructions:

Range hood, blower, backsplash and soffit chimney are ordered separately. Blower includes installation rough-in kit.

Range Hood Selection Table

WIDTH	STAINLESS STEEL	WHITE	BLACK	ALMOND
30"	603004	603001	603023	603008
36"	603604	603601	603623	603608
42"	604204	604201	604223	604208
48"	604804	604801	604823	604808
54"	605404	+	+	+
60"	606004	+	+	+
66"	606604	+	+	+
72"	607204	+	+	+

Options Selection Table

	BACKSPLASH	SOFFIT CHIMNEY			
WIDTH	STAINLESS STEEL	STAINLESS STEEL	WHITE	BLACK	ALMOND
30"	RP3004	RN3004	RN3001	RN3023	RN3008
36"	RP3604	RN3604	RN3601	RN3623	RN3608
42"	RP4204	RN4204	RN4201	RN4223	RN4208
48"	RP4804	RN4804	RN4801	RN4823	RN4808
54"	RP5404	RN5404	+	+	+
60"	RP6004	RN6004	+	+	+
66"	RP6604	RN6604	+	+	+
72"	RP7204	RN7204	+	+	+

+Available as special order

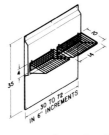 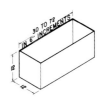 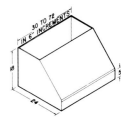

Blower Selection Table and Specifications

MODEL	MOUNTING	CFM	VOLTS	Hz	AMPS*	DUCT SIZE
325	Internal	600	120	60	7.6	7" Round
326	Internal	1200	120	60	8.1	4-1/2" x 18-1/2"**
338++	External	900	120	60	6.0	9" Round

++ Model 338K rough-in kit required for mounting.
* Includes 4.5 Amps representing all lights.
** Transitions to 10" round available. (see accessory section)

Replacement Bulbs:
Fluorescent: F14T12/SW (Soft White) Any F14T8 or F14T12 15" long preheat fluorescent lamp will fit.
Heat Lamps: 250 Watt, R40 Infrared (Bulbs and lamps not included).

3

ECLIPSE™

An Entirely New Concept In Superior Downdraft Cooktop Ventilation From Broan.

Universal design allows choice of cooktops*

- Rises to a height of 7" over cooktop surface.
- Vents smoke, vapors or airborne grease.
- Quiet, powerful 500 CFM or 900 CFM performance.

Flush with cooktop when not in use — easily raised or lowered

- Touch the cover top and the unit automatically raises.
- Touch a button and the unit automatically lowers flush with the cooktop.

Aesthetically appealing, functional design

- Ideal for island or peninsula cooktops.
- Beautifully complements contemporary kitchen design.
- Available with satin aluminum, white or black covers to coordinate with cooktop design.
- Side-mounted infinite speed control with solid state blower memory.
- Uses standard 6" round duct work to simplify installation around floor joists.
- Equipped with access panel for easy cleaning and service.

Choice of blower location

- Interior Blower System rated 500 CFM.
- 900 CFM rated exterior-mounted fan keeps interior sound to a minimum. (Model 338. See page 15.)

Touch the Eclipse's cover and it raises automatically. Touch a button and the unit lowers flush to the cooktop.

Infinite speed control with solid state memory is conveniently side-mounted.

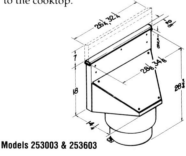

Models 253003 & 253603

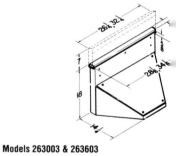

Models 263003 & 263603

*Cooktops, countertops and cabinets vary in dimension and support systems depending upon manufacturer. These factors may impact the Eclipse's ability to fit with every worktop/cabinet combination.

TO FIT NOMINAL COOKTOP SIZE	MODEL	DESCRIPTION	COVER COLOR
30"	253003	Interior Blower Unit	Satin Alum.
36"	253603	Interior Blower Unit	Satin Alum.
30"	263003	Exterior Blower Unit**	Satin Alum.
36"	263603	Exterior Blower Unit**	Satin Alum.
30"	253001C	Optional Cover	White
36"	253601C	Optional Cover	White
30"	253023C	Optional Cover	Black
36"	253623C	Optional Cover	Black

**Exterior unit utilizes Model 338 Exterior-Mounted Fan, Page 15. Ordered Separately.

SPECIFICATIONS

MODEL	VOLTS	AMPS	CFM	DUCT
25000	120	4.0	500	6" Round
26000	120	4.0	900	9" Round

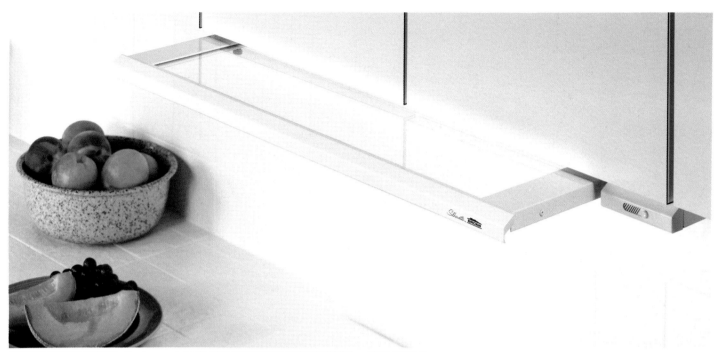

SILHOUETTE™

Dramatic Flair For Today's Euro-Style Kitchens.

Elegant style combines with extraordinary performance

Contemporary thin-line design unmatched by any other range hood.

Choice of black or white frame surrounding "see through" glass visor.

High capacity, dual centrifugal blower system.

Dual centrifugal blowers deliver superior air movement — HVI certified at 300 CFM.

Quietest high-performance system available at 4.5 Sones.

For vented installations only.

Quality and efficiency go hand in hand

Hood visor easily glides in and out.

Front-mounted infinite speed control with solid state memory.

Pull visor out to turn unit on automatically — push in to turn off.

Exclusive Heat Sentry™ automatically turns blower to high speed when excess cooking heat is detected.

■ Exclusive resilient motor mounts isolate blower motor to reduce noise and vibration.

Functional, compact design

Compact housing leaves ample shelf space behind cabinet doors.

Installs in standard width cabinets with flush or recessed bottoms.

24" fluorescent light (bulb not included) and prismatic glass lens delivers even cooktop lighting.

Washable foam filter is recessed for greater capture.

Duct connector with built-in damper included.

Premium features include fluorescent lighting with prismatic glass lens and the exclusive Broan Heat Sentry™.

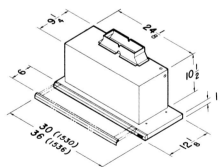

Allow 18 inches minimum from cooking surface to bottom of hood.

Silhouette

WIDTH	WHITE	BLACK
30"	153001	153023
36"	153601	153623

SPECIFICATIONS

VOLTS	AMPS	SONES	CFM	DUCT
120	3.7	4.5	300	3-1/4" X 10" (vertical)

Fluorescent Tube - 24", F20T12 (not included).

5

90000 SERIES

Precise Electronic Control On Our Highest Performance Range Hood.

State-of-the-art electronic controls combine with distinctive styling and superior performance to make the 90000 the industry's most advanced range hood.

The sleek electronic touchpad controls all hood functions. The advanced temperature monitoring system stays alert to changing ventilation requirements and adjusts blower speeds accordingly.

A high capacity, dual centifugal blower system with electronic solid state circuitry makes the 90000 the quietest high-performance system on the market. Available in ducted or duct-free configuration using our industry leading Microtek® System IV filter.

Advanced temperature monitoring systems

■ "AutoTemp" System adjusts blower speeds to match cooking conditions.
■ Heat Sentry™ System detects excess heat and automatically turns blower to highest speed.
■ High Heat Signal sounds when excessive temperatures are detected.
■ Heat Sentry System and High Heat Signal activate whether blower is on or off.
■ Test function pad enables user to check temperature monitoring systems.

Electronic control pad

■ Fingertip control of seven blower speeds.
■ Three light settings including "night light."
■ Flush-mounted for easy cleanability.
■ Indicator lights signal all hood functions.

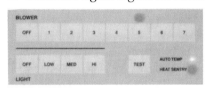 

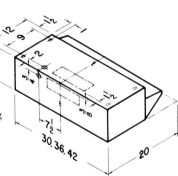

The Broan high capacity, dual centrifugal blower system delivers superior air movement — even in long duct runs. Yet, it's one of the quietest systems on the market.

90000 SERIES

WIDTH	WHITE	ALMOND	WHITE ON WHITE	BLACK	STAINLESS
30"	903001	903008	903011	903023	903004
36"	903601	903608	903611	903623	903604
42"	904201	904208	904211	904223	904204

Order Microtek® System IV filter 97007662 for Duct-free operation.

SPECIFICATIONS

VOLTS	AMPS	SONES VER.	SONES HOR.	CFM VER.	CFM HOR.	DUCT-FREE RHP INDEX	DUCT
120	4.5	5.5	6.0	360	350	59.09	3-1/4" x 10"

89000 SERIES

Infinite Speeds — Powerful, Quiet Performance.

Heavy-duty exhaust capacity ideal for convertible cooktops with barbecue grilles

- Dual centrifugal blowers.
- Vertical discharge HVI certified at 460 CFM, 6.0 Sones.
- Horizontal discharge HVI certified at 440 CFM, 7.0 Sones.
- Use with gas grilles under 14,000 BTU or electric grilles under 4,000 watts (Not for use with charcoal grilles).

Advanced fingertip control

- Infinite speed slide with exclusive solid state memory control.
- Automatic Heat Sentry™ turns blower to high when excess heat detected.
- Two-position light setting for bright cooktop lighting or soft "night light" illumination.

Sleek, contemporary styling with superior features

- Choice of genuine stainless steel or custom finishes.
- Unique motor mounting isolates blower to reduce vibration.
- Safety enhancing mitered sides and hemmed bottom edges.
- Duct connector with built-in damper.
- Twin 9-3/4" x 11-1/2" aluminum filters.

Special Order

Also available in 33" and 39" widths in stainless steel.

Choose 30", 33", 36", 39", 42" and 48" widths in hammered black, white, almond, harvest, avocado, coffee and Silver Lustre.

All finishes are baked enamel except Genuine Stainless Steel.

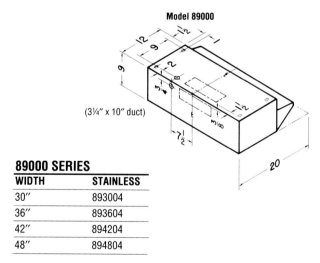

Model 89000

(3¼" x 10" duct)

89000 SERIES

WIDTH	STAINLESS
30"	893004
36"	893604
42"	894204
48"	894804

SPECIFICATIONS

VOLTS	AMPS	SONES		CFM		DUCT
		VER.	HOR.	VER.	HOR.	
120	6.0	6.0	7.0	460	440	3-1/4" x 10"

88000 SERIES

Premium Range Hood With Convertible Microtek® Convenience.

Advanced features and controls

- Infinite speed slide control.
- Exclusive solid state blower memory.
- Two-position light switch for bright working light or softer "night light."
- Broan Heat Sentry™ equipped for automatic high blower speed when excess heat detected.

Ducted or duct-free — engineered for impressive performance and installation flexibility

- Ducted exhaust capacity HVI certified at 360 CFM, 5.5 Sones vertical discharge.
- Horizontal discharge HVI certified at 350 CFM, 6.0 Sones.
- Dual centrifugal blowers for ultra-quiet performance.
- Unique motor mounting isolates blower to reduce vibration.
- Twin 9-3/4" x 11-1/2" aluminum filters.
- Duct connector with built-in damper included.
- Uses Microtek® System Filter No. 97007662 for duct-free installation (available separately).

Superbly crafted

- Mitered sides and hemmed bottom edges for safety and clean styling.

Special Order

88000 also available by special order in 30", 36" and 42" widths, in hammered black and Silver Lustre. 33", 39" and 48" widths available special order in all finishes.

All finishes are baked enamel except Genuine Stainless Steel.

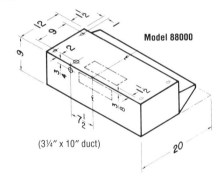

Model 88000

(3¼" x 10" duct)

88000 SERIES (65 *times better than ordinary duct-free range hoods*)

WIDTH	WHITE	ALMOND	WHITE ON WHITE	BLACK	STAINLESS
30"	883001	883008	883011	883023	883004
36"	883601	883608	883611	883623	883604
42"	884201	884208	884211	884223	884204

Also available in Harvest, Avocado and Coffee.

SPECIFICATIONS

VOLTS	AMPS	SONES VER.	SONES HOR.	CFM VER.	CFM HOR.	DUCT-FREE RHP INDEX	DUCT
120	4.5	5.5	6.0	360	350	59.09	3-1/4" x 10"

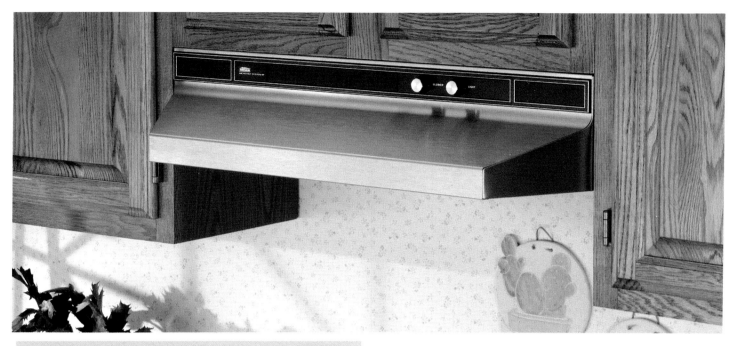

75000, 76000 & 77000 SERIES

Duct-Free Microtek® Convertibility.

Top-of-the-line features at a moderate price

- Dual centrifugal blowers for top efficiency.
- Infinite speed control for quiet performance.
- Contemporary styling with black matte control panel accenting stainless steel or popular appliance finishes.*
- Safety enhancing mitered sides and hemmed bottom edges contribute to sleeker styling.
- High strength polymeric lens houses 75 watt fixture for bright work area.

  *White control panel accents white on white models.

Convertible 76000 Series

- Duct connector with built-in damper included.
- Twin 11-5/8" x 6-5/8" aluminum filters.
- Duct-free convertibility using Microtek® System Filter No. 97007664 (available separately).
- Exhaust capacity HVI certified at 200 CFM, 5.5 Sones vertical discharge; horizontal discharge HVI certified at 200 CFM, 6.0 Sones.

Convertible 75000 Series

- Exhaust capacity HVI certified at 250 CFM, 6.5 Sones vertical discharge; horizontal discharge HVI certified at 250 CFM, 6.0 Sones.
- Other features same as 76000 Series.

Duct-Free 77000 Series

- Shipped ready for duct-free installation with Microtek® System Filter No. 97007664.

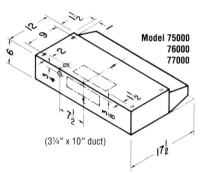

Model 75000
76000
77000

(3¼" x 10" duct)

75000 SERIES *(27 times better than ordinary duct-free range hoods)*

WIDTH	WHITE	ALMOND	WHITE ON WHITE	BLACK	STAINLESS
30"	753001	753008	—	—	753004
36"	753601	753608	—	—	753604
42"	754201	754208	—	—	754204

76000 SERIES *(25 times better than ordinary duct-free range hoods)*

WIDTH	WHITE	ALMOND	WHITE ON WHITE	BLACK	STAINLESS
24"	762401	762408	762411	762423	762404
30"	763001	763008	763011	763023	763004
36"	763601	763608	763611	763623	763604
42"	764201	764208	764211	764223	764204

Also available in Harvest, Avocado and Coffee.

77000 SERIES *(25 times better than ordinary duct-free range hoods)*

WIDTH	WHITE	ALMOND	WHITE ON WHITE	BLACK	STAINLESS
30"	773001	773008	—	—	773004
36"	773601	773608	—	—	773604

Also available in Harvest and Coffee.

SPECIFICATIONS

MODEL NO.	VOLTS	AMPS	SONES VER.	SONES HOR.	CFM	DUCT-FREE RHP INDEX	DUCT
75000	120	3.6	6.5	6.0	250	25.0	3-1/4" x 10"
76000	120	3.0	5.5	6.0	200	22.73	3-1/4" x 10"
77000	120	3.0	—	—	—	22.73	—

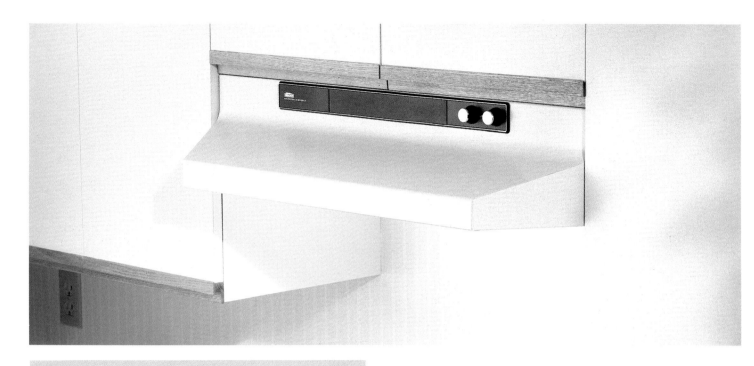

46000 SERIES

Microtek® System II Convertibility. The Most Efficient Duct-Free System In Its Price Range.

Step-up features and impressive performance from our popular economy hood

■ Contemporary styling with black matte control panel accenting popular appliance colors or stainless steel.
■ Infinite speed control for quiet performance.
■ Bright 75 watt light with high strength polymeric lens (bulb not included).
■ Safety enhancing mitered sides and hemmed bottom edges contribute to sleeker styling.
■ Mixed flow polymeric fan blade.

Ducted

■ Exhaust capacity HVI certified at 180 CFM, 7.0 Sones vertical discharge.
■ Horizontal discharge HVI certified at 180 CFM, 6.5 Sones.
■ Duct connector with built-in damper included.
■ 10-1/2" x 8-3/4" aluminum grease filter.

Duct-free

■ Easily converted by removing coverplate and installing Microtek® System Filter No. 97007696 (included).

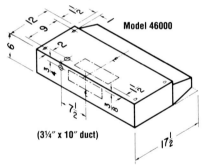

Model 46000

(3¼" x 10" duct)

46000 SERIES (*10 times better than ordinary economy duct-free range hoods*)

WIDTH	WHITE	ALMOND	STAINLESS
30"	463001	463008	463004
36"	463601	463608	463604
42"	464201	464208	464204

Also available in Harvest, Avocado and Coffee.

SPECIFICATIONS

VOLTS	AMPS	SONES VER.	SONES HOR.	CFM	DUCT-FREE RHP INDEX	DUCT
120	2.5	7.0	6.5	180	9.8	3-1/4" x 10"

40000/41000/42000 SERIES

Two-Speed Economy and Top-Of-The-Line Quality.

The industry's best economy range hood values

- Same shell and durable baked enamel finish as our intermediate models.
- Available in popular appliance colors and genuine stainless steel.
- Safety enhancing mitered sides and hemmed bottom edges contribute to sleek, contemporary styling.
- Two-speed rocker-type fan control.
- 75 watt light with high strength polymeric lens (bulb not included).
- Mixed flow polymeric fan blade.

Ducted 40000 Series

- Exhaust capacity HVI certified at 160 CFM, 5.5 Sones vertical discharge.
- Horizontal discharge HVI certified at 160 CFM, 6.5 Sones.
- Duct connector with built-in damper included.
- 10-1/2" x 8-3/4" aluminum grease filter.

Duct-Free 41000 Series/Microtek® System I

- Includes Microtek® System Filter No. 97007696 for the best duct-free filtration system in its class.
- All other features same as 40000 Series.

7" Round Ducted 42000 Series

- Washable 10-1/2" diameter aluminum filter.
- Use Broan #87 damper (available separately).
- Exhaust capacity HVI certified at 190 CFM, 5.5 Sones (vertical discharge only).
- All other features same as 40000 Series.

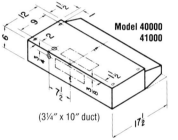

Model 40000 41000

(3¼" x 10" duct)

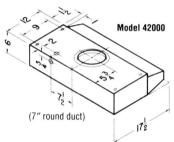

Model 42000

(7" round duct)

40000 SERIES Ducted

WIDTH	WHITE	ALMOND	STAINLESS
24"	402401	402408	402404
30"	403001	403008	403004
36"	403601	403608	403604

Also available in Harvest, Avocado and Coffee.

41000 SERIES Duct-Free *(9 times better than economy duct-free range hoods)*

RHP Index 8.7

WIDTH	WHITE	ALMOND	STAINLESS
24"	412401	412408	412404
30"	413001	413008	413004
36"	413601	413608	413604

Also available in Harvest, Avocado and Coffee.

42000 SERIES 7" Round Ducted

WIDTH	WHITE	ALMOND	STAINLESS
30"	423001	423008	423004
36"	423601	423608	423604

Also available in Harvest, Avocado and Coffee.

SPECIFICATIONS

MODEL NO.	VOLTS	AMPS	SONES VER.	SONES HOR.	CFM	DUCT-FREE RHP INDEX	DUCT
40000	120	2.0	5.5	6.5	160	—	3-1/4" x 10"
41000	120	2.0	—	—	—	8.70	—
42000	120	2.5	5.5	—	190	—	7" Round

Economy hoods are not convertible.

11

68000/67000 SERIES

48000/47000 SERIES

Sleek White Or Black Glass-Like Styling For Today's Contemporary Kitchens.

Complement Contemporary Kitchen Design With Straight-Side Styling.

7″ Round Ducted 68000 Series

- Handsome, easy-to-clean glass-like panel in black or white.
- Built-in, enclosed 75 watt light (bulb not included).
- Washable aluminum filter.
- Damper included.

7″ Round Ducted 48000 Series

- Straight-side styling in white, almond or genuine stainless steel.
- Built-in, enclosed 75 watt light (bulb not included).
- Washable aluminum filter.
- Damper included.

Duct-Free 67000 Series

- Includes combination duct-free filter.
- All other features same as 68000 Series.

Duct-Free 47000 Series

- Includes combination duct-free filter.
- All other features same as 48000 Series.

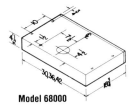

Model 68000

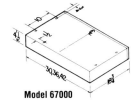

Model 67000

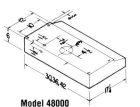

Model 48000

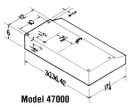

Model 47000

68000 SERIES 7″ Round Ducted

WIDTH	WHITE	BLACK
30″	683001	683023
36″	683601	683623
42″	684201	684223

67000 SERIES Duct-Free

WIDTH	WHITE	BLACK
30″	673001	673023
36″	673601	673623
42″	674201	674223

SPECIFICATIONS

MODEL NO.	VOLTS	AMPS	CFM	SONES
67000	120	2.0	—	—
68000	120	2.5	230	7.0

48000 SERIES 7″ Round Ducted

WIDTH	WHITE	ALMOND	STAINLESS
30″	483001	483008	483004
36″	483601	483608	483604
42″	484201	484208	484204

47000 SERIES Duct-Free

WIDTH	WHITE	ALMOND	STAINLESS
30″	473001	473008	473004
36″	473601	473608	473604
42″	474201	474208	474204

SPECIFICATIONS

MODEL NO.	VOLTS	AMPS	CFM	SONES
47000	120	2.0	—	—
48000	120	2.5	230	7.0

HIDEAWAY™

Pull-Out Style Disappears Flush To Cabinet Facing When Not In Use.

Expandable 24"-30" height accommodates 30" cabinet face frame with doors.

Light and blower turn on automatically when pulled out.

Exclusive design features built-in storage space.

Powerful but quiet dual centrifugal blower, HVI certified at 360 CFM horizontal or vertical discharge — 4.5 Sones.

Exclusive Heat Sentry™ turns blower to high speed automatically when excess cooking heat detected.

Bright cooktop lighting.

Install with rough-in kit Model No. 113123.

For vented installations only.

When not in use, the Hideaway disappears flush to cabinet facing.

The Hideaway provides ample storage space behind cabinet doors.

MODEL 113023 SPECIFICATIONS

VOLTS	AMPS	SONES	CFM	DUCT
120	3.7	4.5	360	3-1/4" x 10"

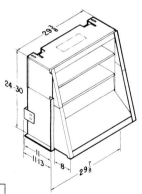

Model 113023

WOOD HOOD

Maintains The Natural Beauty Of All Wood Cabinetry.

■ Fits wood hoods with interior width from 28-1/4" to 28-7/8" (can be adapted to hoods up to 42" wide — order kit No. 97009790 available separately).

■ Powerful, dual centrifugal blower, HVI certified at 360 CFM, 4.5 Sones horizontal discharge; 360 CFM, 5.0 Sones vertical discharge.

■ Exclusive Heat Sentry™ turns blower to high speed when excess cooking heat detected.

■ Bright cooktop lighting with 24" fluorescent fixture (bulb not included).

■ Built-in duct connector with damper for 3-1/4" x 10" duct.

■ Install with rough-in kit Model No. 103123.

■ For vented installations only.

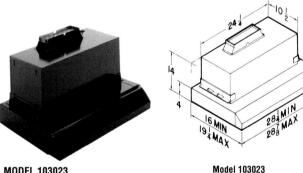

Model 103023

MODEL 103023 SPECIFICATIONS

VOLTS	AMPS	SONES VER.	SONES HOR.	CFM	DUCT
120	3.7	5.0	4.5	360	3-1/4" x 10"

MICROMATE™

Combination Range Hood/Microwave Shelf.

- Accommodates virtually every major brand microwave.
- Installs either ducted or duct-free using Microtek® System Filter No. 97007807 (available separately).
- Exclusive Heat Sentry™ protects microwave from excess heat build-up.
- Bright cooktop lighting.
- Quiet, high performance dual centrifugal blower.

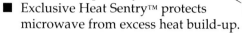

Model 123035

VOLTS	AMPS	SONES	CFM	DUCT-FREE RHP INDEX	DUCT
120	2.7	4.5	300	9.80	3-1/4" x 10"

Special Order
36" available in Hammered White, Hammered Almond, Hammered Harvest, Hammered Avocado and Hammered Coffee.

CANOPY HOOD/11000 SERIES

Infinite Speed, Convertible

- Ducted or Duct-free (Duct-free uses Microtek® Systems Filter No. 97007696).
- Textured hammered finish in popular appliance colors.
- Built-in light accomodates 100 watt bulb or 150 watt flood lamp (bulbs not included).

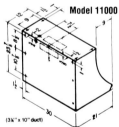

Model 11000

(3¼" x 10" duct)

11000 SERIES

WIDTH	HAMMERED WHITE	HAMMERED ALMOND	HAMMERED HARVEST	HAMMERED AVOCADO	HAMMERED COFFEE
30"	113036	113042	113047	113048	113049

VOLTS	AMPS	SONES VER.	SONES HOR.	CFM VER.	CFM HOR.	DUCT-FREE RHP INDEX	DUCT
120	3.0	6.0	6.5	190	200	9.80	3-1/4" x 10"

MODEL NO.	DESCRIPTION
634	Roof Cap (includes backdraft damper and birdscreen) 3-1/4" x 10" or up to 8" round
644	Aluminum Roof Cap (includes backdraft damper and birdscreen) 3-1/4" x 10" or up to 8" round
639	Wall Cap 3-1/4" x 10" duct (includes backdraft damper with birdscreen)
641	Aluminum Wall Cap fits 6" round duct (includes backdraft damper with birdscreen)
649	Aluminum Wall Cap fits 3-1/4" x 10" duct (includes damper with birdscreen)
643	Aluminum Wall Cap fits 8" round duct
87	Damper for 7" discharge hoods
97	7" Damper
99	9" Damper
35	Wall Hanging kit for mounting hoods to wall when cabinets are not used
411	3-1/4" x 10" to 6" Round Transition
412	3-1/4" x 10" to 7" Round Transition
413	3-1/4" x 10" to 8" Round Transition
401	3-1/4" x 10" Duct — 2" section
406	6" Round Duct — 2" section
407	7" Round Duct — 2" section
410	10" Round Duct — 2" section
415	7" Adjustable Elbow (4 per carton)
419	6" Adjustable Elbow
421	Damper Section, 10" round with damper
423	Vertical Transition, 4-1/2" x 18-1/2" to 10" round
424	Rear Transition, 4-1/2" x 18-1/2" to 10" round
425	Horz. Left Transition, 4-1/2" x 18-1/2" to 10" round
426	Horz. Right Transition, 4-1/2" x 18-1/2" to 10" round
428	3-1/4" x 10" Vertical Elbow
429	3-1/4" x 10" Horizontal Elbow
430	Short Eave Elbow for 3-1/4" x 10" duct (includes backdraft damper and grille)
431	Long Eave Elbow for 3-1/4" x 10" duct (includes backdraft damper and grille)
437	High Capacity Roof Cap — up to 1200 CFM
441	Wall Cap with gravity damper — 13-1/8" sq. takes 10" round

Model 338

- 900 CFM (at 0.1 static pressure)

  For indoor barbecues or extra duct runs. All aluminum, weatherproof construction. Thermally protected motor, 120 V. Requires 9" duct. Damper not included.

Model 334

- 470 CFM (at 0.1 static pressure)

  For conventional gas and electric range ventilation. All aluminum weatherproof construction. Thermal protected motor, 120V. Requires 7" round duct. Damper not included. For Roof Mounting use 434 Roof Conversion Kit, includes roof cap and flashing sheet.

SPLASH PLATES

Broan splash plates protect the kitchen wall from cooking splatter. Available in 24 gauge stainless steel or .019 (nominal) aluminum in enamel finishes.

Installs easily with four screws. For exact sizes, colors and model numbers refer to the Broan Price List.

Specifications represented in this catalog are subject to change without notice.

Broan -- The Single Source For All Of Your Kitchen Ventilation Needs.

Since 1932, Broan has been the leading innovator in the design and construction of premium kitchen ventilation products.

With more styles and features we're the number one manufacturer of home kitchen range hoods.

Broan's Microtek® System Filter

Thanks to its exclusive multi-filter design and the unique materials used in its construction, Broan's Microtek duct-free filter traps airborne particulates that ordinary duct-free range hoods merely recirculate into the kitchen. Combining properly matched air flow, superior capture performance and this unique filter, the Microtek System Range Hoods put an end to greasy cabinets, soiled curtains and grimy ceilings.

In short, the Microtek System represents your most effective ventilating alternative in situations where ducting is impractical.

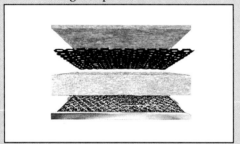

From our economy models to the top-of-the-line deluxe range hoods, only Broan offers you the proven effectiveness of the Microtek System for duct-free hoods. And only Broan can offer you the leading edge quality and styling you've come to expect from the acknowledged leader in range hood technology.

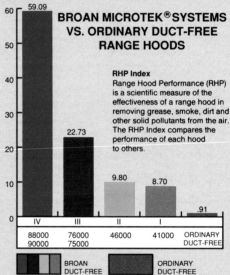

BROAN MICROTEK® SYSTEMS VS. ORDINARY DUCT-FREE RANGE HOODS

RHP Index
Range Hood Performance (RHP) is a scientific measure of the effectiveness of a range hood in removing grease, smoke, dirt and other solid pollutants from the air. The RHP Index compares the performance of each hood to others.

	IV	III	II	I	ORDINARY DUCT-FREE
	88000	76000	46000	41000	
	90000	75000			

BROAN DUCT-FREE — ORDINARY DUCT-FREE

* Test Method Report Available Upon Request

All Broan Range Hoods have been tested and certified by Underwriters Laboratory and the Home Ventilating Institute.

BROAN®

A NORTEK COMPANY
BROAN MFG. CO., INC. HARTFORD, WISCONSIN 53027

ALL THE COMFORTS OF HOME

99850148C
29L

Classic Supreme®
Designer Collection Dishwashers

C501
BuyLine 8621

The ultimate in understated elegance. Three contemporary motifs.

Classic Supreme 3000
(White)

Classic Supreme 3300
(Black)

Classic Supreme 3500
(Stainless Steel)

Sophisticated choices.

Classic Supreme® Designer Collection.

The embodiment of Eurostyle captured in impeccable all-white. The height of high-tech executed in a single sweep of lustrous stainless steel. Or the drama of deep, rich black. No chrome clutter. No color accents.

Whatever your kitchen vision, the Classic Supreme Designer Collection models bring it to life—beautifully. And make it easy to live with through the highest levels of engineered dependability and superior washing performance.

Designed for convenience.
Challenge this dishwasher to strip away tough, baked-on soil. Or to pamper fragile chinaware. No matter—four task-matched washing cycles deliver sparkling clean results.

And you can load just about anything from an over-sized platter to a champagne flute. Because a multi-position upper rack raises, lowers, or tilts—even when full.

While a unique easy-glide handle and latch mechanism opens and closes the door with ease.

Designer styling at its purest. Performance without compromise. Have it all with the new Classic Supreme Designer Collection.

Truly quiet. Total quality.
Each Designer Collection model has the exclusive QUIET SYSTEM™ sound package making them one of the quietest dishwashers on the market. Quality is measured many ways...the ultra-reliable 1/2 HP Emerson motor...the three-stage water filtration system with built-in food waste disposer and the Tri-Cote™ porcelain steel tank and door liner that guards against stains, scratches, and corrosion.

Cleans as great as it looks.
Dishes cleaner than the day you bought them. Because water is automatically heated to optimum washing temperatures. Then sent through upper and lower wash arms for maximum scrubbing power in every corner of the wash chamber. Finally, the exclusive CIRCA-DRY™ system circulates heated air for fast, even drying without hot spots.

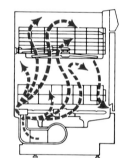

Specifications*

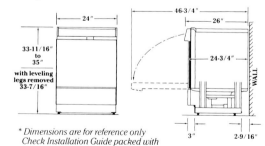

33-11/16" to 35" with leveling legs removed 33-7/16"

24"

46-3/4" 26" 24-3/4"

3" 2-9/16" WALL

Dimensions are for reference only Check Installation Guide packed with each model.

Manufacturer reserves the right to change specifications without notice.

Basic sizes for ¼" Custom Front Panels:
Door Panel Width 23⁹⁄₁₆"
Door Panel Height 18¹³⁄₁₆"
Lower Panel Width 23¹¹⁄₁₆"
Lower Panel Height 6⅝"

Basic Plumbing Data:
Water Supply–
• Inlet Water Temperature–120⁰F (49⁰C) minimum at the dishwasher.
• Inlet Water Pressure Operating Range– 20 to 120 psi.
• Inlet Water Tubing Size–1/2"OD minimum.

Basic Electrical Data:
• 115 volts AC, 60 Hertz.
• Maximum Amps–13.5; separate 15 amp 3-wire grounded circuit required.

Drain:
• ⁹⁄₁₆"ID minimum flexible hose from check valve; ⅝"OD minimum copper tubing may be run from ⁹⁄₁₆" hose if necessary.

ISE
IN-SINK-ERATOR

Built better. Backed better.™
4700-21st Street
Racine, WI 53406-5093

New Classic® Supreme 2000

State-of-the-art electronics...
convenient touch-pad cycle selection.

Presenting The New Classic® Supreme 2000 by In-Sink-Erator.

A solid-state electronic-control dishwasher that has all the quality features of the Classic Supreme. Plus a lot more. More convenience. More accuracy. And proven dependability. Here is a dishwasher whose efficiency speaks for itself, quietly.

At the heart of this high-tech wonder is an ingenious sensor system. A precision vacuum fluorescent digital display panel features large, illuminated words and numbers that are easily viewed, even in the brightest room. And this control panel has no buttons, grooves or recessed areas for dirt to collect.

Solid-state electronics make the Classic Supreme 2000 one of the easiest, most efficient and user-friendly dishwashers today.

User-Friendly Communications

Imagine…a dishwasher that tells you what cycle or option you've selected, how many minutes remain until the end of the cycle, then flashes the word CLEAN once a wash cycle is completed. If you interrupt a cycle to add dishes, simply close and lock the door and the machine restarts automatically. There's even a diagnostics feature with nine independent test sequences to assist a service technician.

Cycle Scheduling Flexibility

The Classic Supreme 2000 has four regular cycles: Pots & Pans, Normal Wash, Light Wash and Rinse & Hold. A special DELAY WASH feature allows you to load the dishwasher, program it, then delay the start of any wash cycle for up to nine hours to take advantage of economical, non-peak utility rates. The delay wash feature can also be programmed for delay periods of less than a full hour.

There is also a CYCLE MEMORY feature. The Supreme 2000 remembers the last cycle used and repeats it each time you press START. This eliminates the need to reprogram every time, especially convenient for daily routine dishwashing cycles.

Quiet Cleaning Power

The 2000, like all Classic Supreme dishwashers incorporates the exclusive QUIET SYSTEM™ sound package making it one of the quietest operating dishwashers available. Plus, a highly efficient wash system, unique three-stage filtration and automatic water heating for maximum cleaning power and consistently clean dishware.

Here is a dishwasher that's extremely quiet. A dishwasher that delivers beautiful results. A dishwasher that's the ultimate in electronic efficiency and ease. Here is the Classic Supreme 2000.

Specifications*

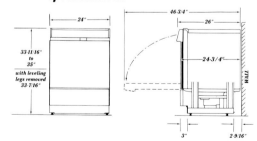

Dimensions are for reference only. Check Installation Guide packed with each model.

Basic sizes for ¼" Custom Front Panels:
Door Panel Width 23⁹/₁₆"
Door Panel Height 18¹³/₁₆"
Lower Panel Width 23¹¹/₁₆"
Lower Panel Height 6⅝"

Basic Plumbing Data:
Water Supply—
• Inlet Water Temperature— 120°F (49°C) minimum at the dishwasher.
• Inlet Water Pressure Operating Range— 20 to 120 psi.
• Inlet Water Tubing Size—½" OD minimum.

Basic Electrical Data:
• 115 volts AC, 60 Hertz.
• Maximum Amps—13.5; separate 15 amp 3-wire grounded circuit required.

Drain:
• ⁹/₁₆" ID minimum flexible hose from check valve; ⅝" OD minimum copper tubing may be run from ⁹/₁₆" hose if necessary.

Built to be Best.™
4700-21st Street, Racine, WI 53406-5093

GN-3 Dispenser System

New Steamin' Hot® Water Colors from In-Sink-Erator.

Model GN-3W in White

Presenting the GN Dispenser Series in Designer Colors

Model GN-3A

Model GN-3B

Model GN (Brass)
Also available in chrome

The extra touch of color that takes kitchens out of the ordinary!

Crisp alpine white. Creamy-rich almond. New midnight black. Polished brass and chrome. Five beautiful colors that make Steamin' Hot dispensers one of the most up-to-the-minute features in kitchens today.

Colors that blend effortlessly, elegantly into any decor. Completing the mood, never conflicting with it. And that's very important to those who always want what's new. What's best. And what's extra in kitchens.

How a dispenser works.
A super-heated water system and dispenser-in-one. Compact tank fits neatly under the sink. Connects to the kitchen's cold water line. Plugs into standard household outlet.

As the water in the tank is heated, some expands and enters the expansion chamber. When you press the handle, unheated water enters the tank at the bottom forcing 190° hot water out of the spout from the tank and expansion chamber.

Both the tank and expansion chamber are open to the atmosphere and are not under pressure.

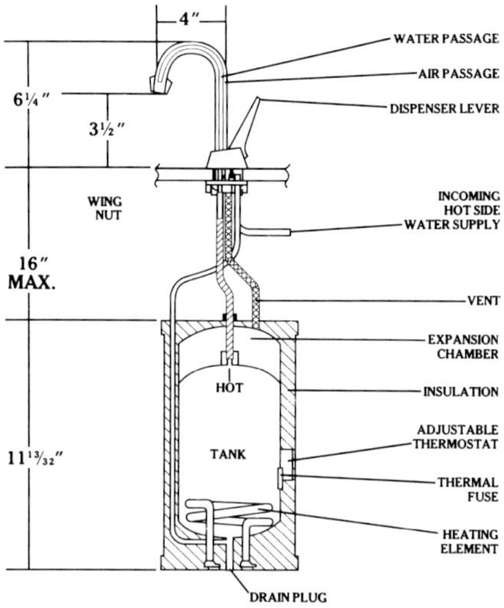

Specifications:
Capacity:
½ gallon, up to 60 cups of 190° F. water per hour.

Electrical:
750 watts, 6.5 amps, 115 volts A.C. U.L. listed—3-wire cord and 3-prong plug provided. (230)

Thermostat:
Snap-action, adjustable from 140°F. to 200°F. (factory pre-set at 190° F.)

Warranty:
1 year full parts and labor.

The extra touch of convenience.
The creative uses are unlimited. This super-heated water system and dispenser delivers 190° cooking-hot water instantly. For soups to sauces, to fresh-ground filter drip coffee. Or any recipe that calls for boiling water. Pure function. Pure style. It's why 94% of the people who own one wouldn't do without it.

In addition to the new GN-3 Designer Series, we offer a complete line of other quality hot water dispensers...from the economical HOT-1 to the popular H-770 and HC (hot/cold) dual purpose models.

Diagram labels:
- WATER PASSAGE
- AIR PASSAGE
- DISPENSER LEVER
- INCOMING HOT SIDE WATER SUPPLY
- VENT
- EXPANSION CHAMBER
- INSULATION
- ADJUSTABLE THERMOSTAT
- THERMAL FUSE
- HEATING ELEMENT
- DRAIN PLUG
- WING NUT
- HOT
- TANK
- 4″
- 6¼″
- 3½″
- 16″ MAX.
- 11¹³⁄₃₂″

Insulation:
Meets U.L. 94HF-1 flammability specification.

Valve:
Instant, self-closing.

Shipping wt.:
9 lbs.

Model HC Steamin' Hot® dispensers offer two conveniences in one.
The versatile, dual-purpose HC dispenser model features two levers. One for 190° cooking hot water instantly. The other for tap water for drinking or cooking. The cold water supply line can be connected to water filters, purifiers, chillers or other drinking water accessories (not available from In-Sink-Erator).

Available in white, almond, black, polished brass and chrome.

IN-SINK-ERATOR

Built to be Best.™

4700 21st Street, Racine, WI 53406-5093

America's preferred choice.

High performance, superb quality and outstanding warranties. All reasons why In-Sink-Erator is the first choice of builders, kitchen remodelers, plumbing contractors, architects, designers…and families nationwide. Disposers found in three out of four homes are made by In-Sink-Erator.

Making the best product possible.

In-Sink-Erator disposers have the best quality record of any kitchen appliance. Less than one out of 2,000 disposers ever require service during the warranty period. And if a problem should ever arise, the in-home service warranty is backed by over 2,500 factory-authorized service centers.

Compatible with septic tanks.

A big misconception about food waste disposers is that they can't be used in homes serviced by septic systems. Not so. You can enjoy the convenience of an In-Sink-Erator disposer in your home with the properly sized septic tank.

Good for the environment.

Disposers are the safe, easy and environmentally sound way to eliminate biodegradable food waste from the kitchen.

Classic® Series

Classic Features:

- Available in continuous-feed (Classic) or batch-feed (Classic LC) models.
- Powerful 1 H.P. motor offers maximum grinding efficiency.
- Full 7-year parts and in-home service warranty is one of the best available.
- Automatic reversing action offers anti-jam, trouble-free operation.

- Thick, upper shell contains sound-deadening insulation for extra quiet operation.
- Large cast nickel chrome shredder ring can handle the toughest grinding jobs.
- Large capacity, stainless steel grind chamber offers maximum resistance to corrosion.

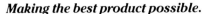

Performance Plus® Series

Model 77 and 17 Features:

- Available in continuous-feed (77) and batch-feed (17) operation.
- Heavy-duty ¾ H.P. motor offers the right level of power for efficient grinding.
- Full 5-year parts and in-home service warranty assures long-term protection.
- Exclusive automatic reversing action offers anti-jam, trouble-free operation.
- Sound-insulated upper shell provides quiet operation (Model 77).
- Large cast nickel chrome shredder ring can handle the toughest grinding jobs.
- Stainless steel grind chamber resists corrosion for longer life.

Better Model 333/SS Features:

- Rugged ½ H.P. motor offers excellent grinding power.
- Full 4-year parts and in-home service warranty provided.
- Large stainless steel grind chamber offers increased grinding capacity.

Good Model 333 Features:

- ½ H.P. motor is tough against any food waste.
- Full 3-year parts and in-home service warranty provides long-term protection.
- Long-life corrosion-resistant grind chamber.

Badger Models

Badger 5 Features:

- Full one-year parts and in-home service warranty.
- ½ H.P. motor for good grinding efficiency.
- Galvanized steel shredder ring for reliable grinding ability.
- Corrosion-resistant grind chamber.

Badger 1 Features:

- ⅓ H.P. motor.
- One-year full parts and in-home service warranty.

IN-SINK-ERATOR

Built to be Best.™

4700 21st Street,
Racine, WI 53406-5093

JENN-AIR

THE SIGN OF A GREAT COOK.

CONTENTS

APPLIANCE
MANUFACTURER'S
EXCELLENCE IN
DESIGN
MAJOR APPLIANCE
WINNER

The Jenn-Air Expressions™ Collection Cooktop was awarded First Place for major appliance design in the Appliance Manufacturers Fifth Annual Design Competition. One of the judges made this clear, saying, "This is the best-designed American cooktop available. It's easy to clean and easy to use."

First Place/Major Appliances

Jenn-Air's
Expressions' Collection
Cooktop

•EXCELLENCE IN DESIGN•

THE EXPRESSIONS™ COLLECTION COOKTOPS

Double cooktop Model C2200,[a] backlit controls, optional AC110 cartridge.

The most versatile, flexible cooktops ever created. A totally new Jenn-Air concept that's all about choices: yours. Styling that expresses your personality. An array of sizes, colors and options to harmonize with your kitchen and meet your diverse cooking needs. First, choose your size—single, double or triple. Next, choose controls (up to four different styles) and cooktop color at the same time (black, white or stainless steel). Now explore your options: cooktop cartridge choices (from halogen to conventional coils) and accessories. You've designed a beautifully unique cooktop, all yours and all Jenn-Air.

[a]Reference number only.

THE SINGLE COOKTOP:
Jenn-Air Performance In A Compact Space.

Your informal dining area, your rec room: our single cooktops make it easy to add the fun of Jenn-Air cooking in a compact space. Comes complete with PerimaVent™ downdraft ventilation system, Energy-Saver grill element and your choice of electronic or backlit controls. Adds optional cartridges and accessories for even more flexibility. Now you can get cooking in even a small space. Single-cooktop controls/color availabilities: electronic controls[a] (black or white); backlit controls (black, white or stainless steel).

Single cooktop Model C1200,[b] backlit controls.

Double cooktop Model C2000,[b] slimline controls, optional Model AC110 cartridge.

SLIMLINE CONTROLS

This slimline control module is a stylish space saver, whether you're remodeling or building a new home. For double cooktops only. Comes in black, includes black glass grill covers and standard grill element.

[a] Electronic controls available 4th quarter 1992.
[b] Reference number only.

4

See Pages 1A-2A for complete Expressions™ Collection specifications and features.

REMOTE CONTROLS

Remote controls install under your double cooktop at the front of the cabinet, giving your counter an uninterrupted flush surface. They're easy to use, easy to clean, and an excellent option for remodeling plans with limited cutout space. Black (shown) or white.

THE DOUBLE COOKTOP:
Just Right, Just About Everywhere.

There's no such thing as an average kitchen with a Jenn-Air double cooktop. You'll love its high-performance cooking flexibility and the choices it offers. Select slimline, remote, backlit or electronic controls. Then choose your cartridge and accessory options—and get into some serious gourmet food. Double-cooktop controls/color availabilities: electronic controls[b] (black or white); backlit controls (black, white or stainless steel); remote backlit controls (black or white); slimline controls (black).

Double cooktop Model CR2200,[a] remote controls, optional Model AR140 radiant cartridge.

Double cooktop Model C2200,[a] backlit controls, optional Model AH150 halogen cartridge.

[a] Reference number only.
[b] Electronic controls available 4th quarter 1992.

THE TRIPLE COOKTOP: *Possibilities Times Three.*

Triple cooktop Model CP3200,[a] backlit controls, optional Model AH150 halogen cartridges.

Your triple cooktop and its exciting selection of cartridge and accessory options will master any important occasion. Six-element cooking—on solid element, radiant, conventional coil or halogen cartridges. Four elements and a grill. Two grills, two elements. Even three grills. It's your choice. Dual downdraft ventilation systems mean you can place your grill in any of the cooking bays. Triple-cooktop controls/color availabilities: electronic controls[b] (black or white); backlit controls (black, white or stainless steel).

The PerimaVent™ downdraft ventilation system—a key to Jenn-Air performance—is featured in all Expressions™ Collection cooktops. Pulls smoke and cooking vapors down through the cooktop air grille, plus captures and vents wisps of smoke at the edges of your cooking area.

[a] Reference number only.
[b] Electronic controls available 4th quarter 1992.

Triple-cooktop electronic control module
Model CP340. Black or white (shown).

Double-cooktop electronic control module
Model CP240. Black (shown) or white.

Single-cooktop electronic control module
Model CP140. Black (shown) or white.

Jenn-Air electronic control modules provide advanced cooking capabilities in your choice of black or white. They're available for single, double or triple cooktops. And they offer some exciting advantages. A display to give you cooking information. Indicator lights to show you what's on. Touchpad control of eleven temperature levels and eight downdraft ventilation system fan speeds. A countdown timer. A probe that shows food temperature in 5° increments from 100° to 500° right in the information display. And a safety plus for curious little fingers: press the touch pad lock twice and your cooktop is locked.

BACKLIT CONTROL MODULE OPTIONS

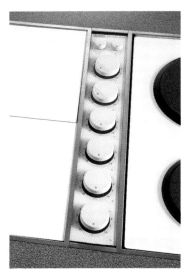

Triple-cooktop backlit control module
Model CP320. Black, white (shown) or stainless steel.

Double-cooktop backlit control module
Model CP220. Black (shown), white or stainless steel.

Single-cooktop backlit control module
Model CP120. Black, white or stainless steel (shown).

Backlit control modules are available in black, white or stainless steel for single, double or triple cooktops. Just press and turn a control knob, and the indicator ring around the knob glows as an element or grill/accessory is activated. Turn on your grill and the PerimaVent™ downdraft ventilation system automatically activates on Hi. Or use the manual ventilation control at the rear of the control panel to set the fan-speed level when you choose optional cartridges and accessories.

[a] Available 4th quarter 1992.

See Page 4 for information on slimline control module options and Page 5 for information on remote control module options (for double cooktops only).

Expressions™ Collection Cartridge Options[a]

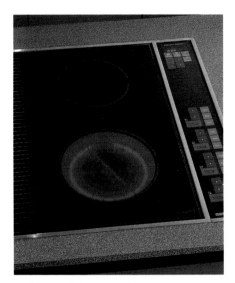

Model AH150 halogen cartridge.

Model AR140 Quick-Start™ radiant cartridge.

Model AS131 solid element cartridge.

Model AC110 conventional coil cartridge.

Jenn-Air cooktop cartridges replace like magic to let you explore new menus and cooking methods.

Model AH150 halogen cartridge with Haloring™[b] elements has circular infra-red lamps that match the round base of cookpots for optimum heat distribution. Instant visual response when turned on. Wipe-clean glass-ceramic cartridge surface. Black (shown) or Pearl White.[c]

Model AR140 Quick-Start™ radiant cartridge has two quick-on elements for high performance cooking. Wipe-clean glass-ceramic cartridge surface. Black or Pearl White[c] (shown).

Model AS131[d] solid element cartridge provides even heat. The large UltraPower™[e] element, with 25% more wattage, heats up fast. Wipe-clean glass cartridge surface. Black or white (shown).

Model AC110 conventional coils: the dependable choice of generations. Unplug the large element and use our wok or "big-pot" canning accessory options (see facing page). Black (shown), white or stainless steel.

[a] Use with Expressions™ Collection cooktops only. See Pages 20-21 for Designer Line cartridges.
[b] Haloring™ is a trademark of Ceramaspeed Limited.
[c] Pearl White cartridges available 2nd quarter 1992.
[d] Not shown is Model AS130 which contains two standard solid elements with stainless steel trim ring. The new cartridge AS131 with Ultra-Power™ element will be available 4th quarter 1992.
[e] UltraPower™ is a trademark of E.G.O. Products, Inc.

Jenn-Air cooktops change like magic when you change cooking methods. Our convertibility lets you switch from grilling to element cooking in seconds. Just remove the grill assembly and you're ready to insert a cartridge for four-element cooking. Or lift out one optional cooktop cartridge, plug in another, and presto: it's like having a completely different cooktop.

See Pages 1A-2A for complete Expressions™ Collection specifications and features.

Expressions™ Collection Accessory Options[a]

Model AO310 griddle.

Model A141A wok.

Our accessories add even more performance options to your cooking. They will add ease and enjoyment to just about any special cooking you do.

Model AO310 griddle has a nonstick DuPont SilverStone SUPRA® finish and an integral heating element for even heat distribution.

The **Model A141A** wok includes a heating element that replaces the large element in our optional conventional coil cartridge. Carbon steel bowl with nonstick finish. Lid, steaming rack and rice paddles included.

Model AO330 Energy-Saver grill assembly adds extra grilling capability to double and triple cooktops. Comes complete with heating element, Savorizer™ pan and grill grates with Excalibur® Finish.[b]

Model A145A "big-pot" canning element cooks lobsters, pasta, corn and more. The raised element plugs in to replace the large coil in Model AC110 conventional coil cartridge.

Model AO320 Rotiss-Kebab accessory turns four shish kebabs or other foods automatically on your electric grill. The motor-driven rotisserie includes Kebab wheels, Kebab skewers, spit, rotisserie meat skewers and motor.

A set of two extra grill covers is available in black or white tempered glass or stainless steel to protect your grill when not in use. Black glass (**Model AO345B**), white glass (**Model AO345W**), stainless steel (**Model AO340S**).

Model AO330 Energy-Saver grill assembly.

Model A145A "big-pot" canning element.

Model AO320 Rotiss-Kebab.

Model AO340S stainless steel grill covers.

[a] Use with Expressions™ Collection cooktops only. See Pages 20-21 for Designer Line accessories.
[b] Excalibur® is a registered trademark of Whitford Corp.

THE DESIGNER LINE
Quality Performance. Timeless Style. Unlimited Possibilities.

DESIGNER LINE *Downdraft* ELECTRIC COOKTOPS

Model C236 (30" wide) with optional Model A106 cartridge.

You'll command an almost unlimited array of cooking systems with our convertible cooktop **Model C236** (above). First, enjoy indoor grilling with Jenn-Air downdraft ventilation and Energy-Saver grill element. Then explore the optional cartridges and accessories accepted by both bays. Conventional coil to solid elements. Accessories for stir-frying, steaming and more. Hundreds of tasty possibilities—plus countertop or island/peninsula installation to suit your personal style. Black (shown) or white (shown) porcelain or stainless steel perimeter.

Model C236 in black with optional Model A121 cartridge.

See Pages 3A-5A for complete Designer Line cooktop specifications and features.

Consider the practical pleasures of convertible cooktop **Model C206** (right). Two permanently installed conventional coil elements are in the right side. Cook conventionally and enjoy indoor grilling at the same time with the standard grill element and downdraft ventilation system. And the left-side cooking bay accepts optional cartridges and accessories. Black or white (shown) porcelain or stainless steel.

Model C206 (30″ wide).

Model C316 (48″ wide) with two optional Model A125 cartridges.

Model C316 is the ultimate grill-range cooktop: it's tri-convertible! Downdraft ventilation and Energy-Saver grill element lets you grill indoors as you prepare other delights on almost any combination of optional cartridges and accessories. You'll serve a gourmet feast they'll never forget. Wooden cutting board covers utensil storage area. No ventilation for right hand cooking bay. Stainless steel perimeter with white or black (shown) accents.

11

Lanai™ Outdoor Grills With Downdraft Ventilation.

Model GO106 (18″ wide).

Model GO206 (30″ wide).

Bring electric grilling to outdoor cooking on your lanai, patio, deck or porch with a single or double Lanai™ outdoor grill. With the double grill **Model GO206** you can grill on both sides (2800-watt standard grill) or add grill accessories. Limited space? Enjoy our single

Lanai™ grill **Model G0106.** It has the same features as the double Lanai™ grill plus a 30-minute timer. Both grills accept cooker-steamer, griddle and grill cover optional accessories. Grills are non-convertible and not approved for indoor use. Black porcelain finish.

Designer Line Updraft Electric Cooktops For Use With Updraft Ventilation.

Model CU240 puts our finest updraft electric grilling cooktop at your service. Simply add a Jenn-Air high-performance ducted range hood or over-the-range microwave oven and you'll be ready to savor the pleasures of indoor grilling with the Energy-Saver grill element. Optional cartridges multiply the cooking possibilities with solid elements, conventional coils, halogen or radiant. Accessory options add even more delights. (Grills on left side only.) Black porcelain or stainless steel (shown) perimeter.

Model CU240 (30″ wide) with optional Model A100 cartridge.

See Pages 3A-5A for complete Designer Line cooktop specifications and features.

Model CCS447 (30" wide) with Model W130 wall oven and Model M437 microwave oven.

With backlit controls and an infinite number of settings, the low profile elements on **Model CCS447**[a] also provide flexibility in the size cookware used. Two UltraPower™ elements provide 25% more wattage for fast heat-up. The left-rear 9" element has 3200 watts, convenient for big pot cooking. The standard elements provide low settings for simmering or melting. Black or white (shown).

Model CCR466 (30" wide) with Model RH800 hood.

Bring uncluttered good looks to any kitchen with updraft cooktop **Model CCR466** and its expanse of translucent black glass ceramic. Four circular Quick-Start™ radiant elements are visible through the wipe-clean surface, with a surface indicator light to show when an element is on. The Hot Surface light indicates when the cooktop itself is hot, stays lit until cooktop has cooled. Black Ceran surface.

Dependable conventional coil elements, accessory options and a choice of three colors make updraft electric cooktop **Model CCE406** a favorite. It accepts the Model A141A wok and Model A145A "big-pot" canning element. Four surface-element indicator lights show which elements are on. Flush-mount edge. Black porcelain, almond porcelain or brushed chrome (shown).

[a] Available 2nd quarter 1992.
[b] UltraPower™ is a trademark of E.G.O. Products, Inc.

Model CCE406 (33" wide).

DESIGNER LINE *Updraft* GAS COOKTOPS For Use With Updraft Ventilation.

Model CCG456 (30" wide).

Model CCG456 sealed gas cooktop
in black with Model W130 wall
oven and M437 microwave oven.

Model CCG456 offers a winning combination: the responsiveness of gas cooking and the quick clean-up of sealed burners. You'll appreciate the durability of porcelainized cast-iron burner caps, porcelain-on-steel grates and porcelain-on-steel burner bowls. Four burners with BTU ratings from 9,000 to 12,000 (natural gas only) provide cooking flexibility. And this stylish cooktop installs nicely over Jenn-Air electric wall oven Model W130. Black or white (shown) glass.

Sealed gas burners on Models
CCG456 and CCG556[a] have automatic reignition feature should
burners momentarily go out.

Model CCG556 (36" wide).

Five burners hold it all, from small pans to large pasta pots or 12" skillets. **Model CCG556**[a] features five burners with BTU ratings from 6,000 to 12,000 (natural gas only). Low setting on small burner keeps food warm or melts food without scorching. All quick clean-up sealed burners with porcelainized cast-iron burner caps and porcelain-on-steel grates. Black (shown) or white glass.

[a] Availability 2nd quarter 1992.

See Pages 3A-5A for complete Designer
Line cooktop specifications and features.

Gas cooktop control pairs up with downdraft ventilation to offer you **Model CG206** convertible cooktop. Enjoy indoor grilling over the E-ven Heat™ grill burner, whether you use natural or LP gas. Convert your new cooktop to four burners by adding the optional two-burner module (Model AG200). Then choose from our gas grill/cooktop accessories, and explore all the delicious possibilities. Black (shown) porcelain or stainless steel perimeter.

Model CG206 (30" wide).

Model CG106 (18" wide).

Counter space at a premium? **Model CG106** convertible cooktop with downdraft ventilation packs many features into its 18" width. It grills with either natural or LP gas on an E-ven Heat™ burner, becomes a two-burner cooktop when you replace grill with our optional two-burner module (Model AG200). Accepts gas grill/cooktop accessories as well. Black porcelain (shown) or stainless steel perimeter.

Model CG205 (30" wide).

Master a new culinary repertoire with four-burner convertible cooktop **Model CG205.** Equipped with downdraft ventilation, it needs only optional grill assembly Model AG150 to add savory indoor grilling to your cooking adventures. The left bay accepts the grill, leaving two burners free for other foods. Add gas grill/cooktop accessories for more fun and variety. Uses natural or LP gas. White porcelain finish.

DESIGNER LINE *Downdraft* GRILL-RANGES

Model SEG196.

Quality and flexibility: downdraft Dual-Fuel™ grill-range **Model SEG196** (above) is the best of both worlds. Convertible gas surface cooking and indoor grilling with our E-ven Heat™ grill burner. Four-burner convenience when you add optional two-burner gas module Model AG200. Below, the self-cleaning electric **Selective-Use™ convection and bake/broil oven** lets you choose radiant cooking or convection at the turn of a dial. Flexible installation, too: slide your new grill-range into place for a built-in look, or choose freestanding installation with optional color side panels and backsplash. Black, white.

Model SEG196 in white.

See Page 6A for complete Designer Line grill-range specifications and features.

All-electric cooking, indoor grilling and convection baking in one beautiful package—that's **Model S176** downdraft grill-range with convertible cooktop. It grills indoors with the Energy-Saver grill element and accepts optional electric cartridges and accessories. The self-cleaning **Selective-Use™ convection and bake/broil oven** lets you bake like the finest chefs. And you'll appreciate the electronic oven controls, clock-controlled cooking and cleaning, and automatic self-clean door-lock mechanism. Installs as slide-in or freestanding. Black or white (shown).

Model S176 with optional Model A121 cartridge and optional Model A519 backsplash.

The user-friendly electronic touch control pad activates with a touch of your fingertip and a turn of a dial. Beeps when preheat is completed. Wipes clean in a snap.

Most of our grill-ranges accept optional lighted deluxe backsplash (**Model A519**, shown) or custom backsplash (**Model A507**). Pair backsplash with optional color side panels to create a free-standing grill-range.

Our **Model D156** downdraft grill-range with convertible cooktop offers all-electric cooking, indoor grilling, convection baking—and elegant ''drop-in look'' installation. The front supports are slightly recessed, so your cabinetry will extend below the oven door. Grills indoors with the Energy-Saver grill element, accept optional electric cartridges and accessories. Features a self-cleaning **Selective-Use™ convection and bake/broil oven** for the most versatile baking ever. All this, plus the ease of electronic oven controls, clock-controlled cooking and cleaning, and automatic self-clean door-lock mechanism. Black or white (shown).

Model D156 with optional Model A106 cartridge.

Model S156 with optional Model A125 cartridge.

Elegant simplicity is the theme of electric grill-range **Model S156.** It has a convertible cooktop with Energy-Saver grill element that accepts all optional cartridges and accessories. Grill indoors with downdraft ventilation. The **Selective-Use™ convection and bake/broil oven** will make your specialties even tastier. And you'll save steps and time with electronic-clock-controlled cooking and cleaning. Choose free-standing or slide-in installation. Black (shown) or white.

See Page 6A for complete Designer Line grill-range specifications and features.

FEATURES	COOKTOP MODEL NUMBERS							
COOKTOP[A]	**C1200**	**C1400**	**C2000**	**C2200**	**C2400**	**CR2200**	**C3200**	**C3400**
	COOKTOP COMPONENT MODEL NUMBERS							
CONTROL MODULE	CP120	CP140	CP200	CP220	CP240	CR220	CP320	CP340
BASE MODULE 1	CM100	CM100	CM200	CM200	CM200	CM200	CM200	CM200
BASE MODULE 2							CM100	CM100
Overall Width (in.)	19¼	19¼	29¹⁵⁄₁₆	30¹⁵⁄₁₆	30¹⁵⁄₁₆	27⅜	46¼	46¼
Overall Depth (in.)	21⅛	21⅛	21⅛	21⅛	21⅛	21⅛	21⅛	21⅛
Cutout Width (in.)	18¹¹⁄₁₆	18¹¹⁄₁₆	29⁷⁄₁₆	30⁷⁄₁₆	30⁷⁄₁₆	26⅞	45¾	45¾
Cutout Depth (in.)	20⅝	20⅝	20⅝	20⅝	20⅝	20⅝	20⅝	20⅝
Blower Assembly Clearance (below countertop)[B] (in.)	17½	17½	17½	17½	17½	17½	19	19
Total Connected Load[C] —KW —Amps (at 120/240 VAC)	4.35 18.1	4.35 18.1	8.45 35.2	8.45 35.2	8.45 35.2	8.45 35.2	12.80 53.3	12.80 53.3
Jenn-Air Golden Product Warranty	●	●	●	●	●	●	●	●
Downdraft Ventilation[D]	●	●	●	●	●	●	●	●
Indoor Grilling	●	●	●	●	●	●	●	●
Energy-Saver Grill[E]	●	●		●	●	●	●	●
Standard Grill[E]			●					
Accepts Grill/Cooktop Accessories[D]	●	●	●	●	●	●	●	●
Countertop/Island/Peninsula Installation	●	●	●	●	●	●	●	●
Single Cooktop	●	●	●					
Double Cooktop				●	●	●	●	
Triple Cooktop							●	●
PermaVent™ Downdraft Ventilation System	●	●	●	●	●	●	●	●
Variable-Speed Ventilation Fan	●	●	●	●	●	●	2	2
Slimline Controls			●					
Backlit Controls	●			●	●		●	
Remote Controls						●		
Electronic Touch Controls		●			●			●
Temperature Probe		●			●			●
Color Availabilities: (B=black, W=white, S=stainless steel)	B, W, S	B, W	B	B, W, S	B, W	B, W	B, W, S	B, W

NOTE: A control-module package (with color designation) and base module(s) must be selected to configure a cooktop. Use the control-module and base-module model numbers when ordering a cooktop configuration. One grill assembly is included in every control-module package. All cartridges and accessories are optional.

A. Cooktop reference number only.
B. Blower can be swiveled 90°.
C. All models are U.L. listed for 3-wire 120/240 VAC.
D. Can vent up to 60 equivalent feet with long duct run motor.
E. Energy-Saver grill has independent control of front and rear sections of grill (1400 watts each). Standard grill has unified control of entire grill element (2800 watts).

All Jenn-Air appliances are appropriately UL, AGA, CSA or CGA approved.

Model Availability Date:
Electronic Controls 4th quarter 1992

IMPORTANT

CUTOUT DIMENSIONS ARE CRITICAL

COOKTOP CONTROL-MODULE PACKAGES

SIZE	ELECTRONIC			ELECTROMECHANICAL		
	SINGLE	DOUBLE	TRIPLE	SINGLE	DOUBLE	TRIPLE
CONTROL-MODULE	CP140	CP240	CP340	CP120	CP200 CP220 CR220	CP320
Savorizer™ Liner Pan	1	1	1	1	1	1
Grill Element[A]	1	1	1	1	1	1
Wipe-Away Excalibur[B] Grill Grates	2	2	2	2	2	2
Color-Coordinated Grill Covers[C]	2	2	2	2	2	2
Color-Coordinated Air Grille	1	1	2	1	1	2
Temperature Probe	1	1	1			

NOTE: A control-module package (with color designation) and base module or modules must be selected to configure a cooktop. One grill assembly is included in every control-module package.

A. All control-module packages include an Energy-Saver grill element, except for Model CP200, which includes a standard element.
B. Excalibur® is a registered trademark of Whitford Corp.
C. All color-coordinated grill covers feature either stainless steel or tempered glass.

COOKTOP BASE MODULES

SIZE	SINGLE	DOUBLE	TRIPLE
BASE MODULE	CM100	CM200	CM100 + CM200
Removable Basin Pan Included	1	2	3
Air Filter Included	1	1	2
Remote Drain Jars Included	1	2	3
Ventilation Systems Included[A]	1	1	2

NOTE: Base module or modules and a control-module package must be selected to configure a cooktop.

A. Single- and double-bay modules include one downdraft ventilation system (blower). Since the triple-bay configuration is composed of a single-bay module plus a double-bay module, it includes two ventilation systems (which must be vented separately).

COOKTOP CARTRIDGE FEATURE CHART

Cartridge Type	AH150	AR140	AS131[C]	AC110
	Halogen	Quick-Start™ Radiant	Solid Element	Conventional Coil
Wattage[A] (Large element/ small element)	1800/1200	1700/1200[B]	2600/1500	2100/1250
Color Availabilities (B=black, W=white, S=stainless steel)	B, W	B, W	B, W	B, W, S

A. All cartridges rated 240V
B. Rated 240V. Also available with 208 rating (add –8 to end of model number.)
C. Model variation AS130 contains two standard solid elements with wattage of 2000 (large) and 1500 (small). Model AS131 contains UltraPower™ large element. UltraPower™ is a registered trademark of E.G.O. Products, Inc.

Model Availability Dates:
AH150 W and AR140 W available 2nd quarter 1992.
AS131 B/W available 4th quarter 1992.

COOKTOP ACCESSORY FEATURE CHART

Accessory Type	A141A	A145A	A0310	A0345B	A0345W	A0340S	A0330	A0320
	Wok	"Big-Pot" Canning Element	Griddle	Black[E] Grill Cover	White[E] Grill Cover	Stainless Steel Grill Cover[E]	Grill[F] Assbly	Rotiss Kebab
Wattage[A]	1800[B]	2100[C]	1300[D]				2800	

A. Plug-in accessories rated 240V.
B. Contoured element replaces large conventional coil element; not for use with other cooktop cartridges.
C. Raised element replaces large conventional coil element, not for use with other cooktop cartridges.
D. Integral heating element.
E. One set of 2 included to cover grill (order to cover grill assembly AO330) or griddle when not in use.
F. Includes Savorizer™ pan. Energy-Saver grill element and grill grates coated with Excalibur® finish.

IMPORTANT: Because of continuing product improvements, Jenn-Air reserves the right to change specifications without notice. Dimensional specifications are provided for planning purposes only. For complete details see installation instructions packed with product before selecting cabinetry, making cutouts or beginning installation.

EXPRESSIONS™ COLLECTION COOKTOP SPECIFICATIONS AND FEATURES

	A		B		C		D		E		F		G		H	
	CUTOUT WIDTH		CUTOUT DEPTH		DUCT OPENING		DUCT OPENING		DUCT OPENING TRIPLE ONLY		DUCT OPENING TRIPLE ONLY		DUCT OPENING TRIPLE ONLY		MIN. CABINET WIDTH	
	inches	cm	inches	cm	inches	cm	inches	cm	inches	cm	inches	cm	inches	cm	inches	cm
Single Bay w/3″ Control	18 11/16	47.48	20 5/8	52.37	6 5/16	16.03	14 7/16	36.68	—	—	—	—	—	—	21	53.34
Double Bay w/2″ Control	29 7/16	74.80	20 5/8	52.37	17 3/4	45.08	14 7/16	36.68	—	—	—	—	—	—	30*	76.20
Double Bay w/3″ Control	30 7/16	77.34	20 5/8	52.37	17 3/4	45.08	14 7/16	36.68	—	—	—	—	—	—	33	83.82
Triple Bay w/3″ Control	45 3/4	116.25	20 5/8	52.37	17 7/8	45.39	14 7/16	36.68	39 1/4	99.69	5 15/16	15.09	16 9/16	42.06	48	121.92

NOTE: 2″ or 3″ Control denotes nominal Control Glass Width.

Tolerances ± 1/16 inch OR ± .16 cm apply to dimensions A and B only.

*Some cabinets may require right side wall notched to provide required clearance to Control Panel.

Triple Bay Units require 2 separate duct systems. DO NOT CONNECT BOTH VENT BLOWERS TO THE SAME SYSTEM.

SINGLE

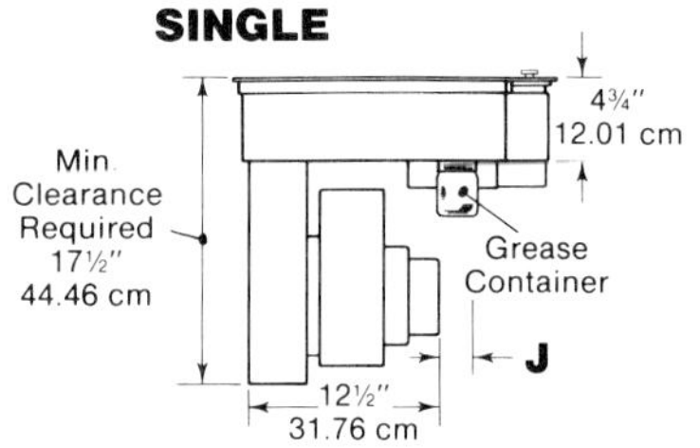

4¾″
12.01 cm
Min. Clearance Required
17½″
44.46 cm
Grease Container
J
12½″
31.76 cm

CONSULT DUCTING GUIDE FOR PROPER INSTRUCTION.

IMPORTANT: Dimensions Shown in Both Inches and Centimeters.

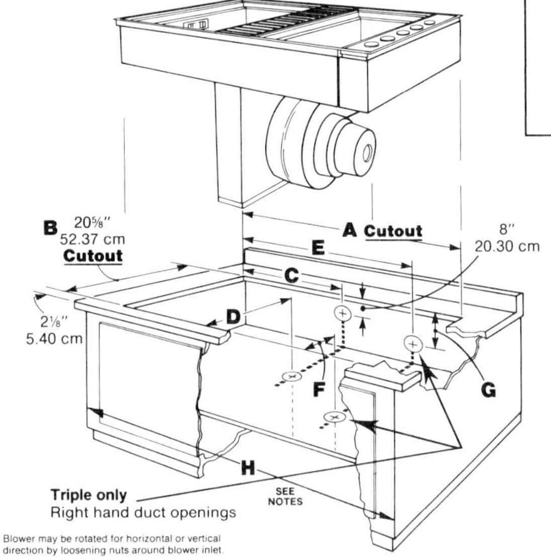

B 20⅝″
52.37 cm
Cutout
A Cutout
8″
20.30 cm
E
C
D
2⅛″
5.40 cm
F
G
H
Triple only
Right hand duct openings
SEE NOTES

NOTE: Blower may be rotated for horizontal or vertical direction by loosening nuts around blower inlet.

IMPORTANT

CUTOUT DIMENSIONS
(see above chart)
ARE CRITICAL

DOUBLE

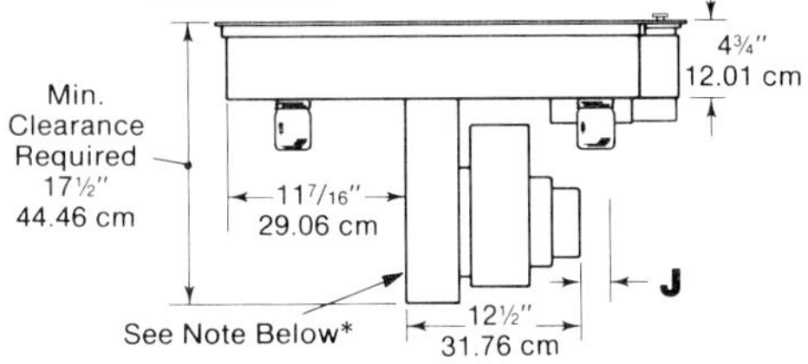

4¾″
12.01 cm
Min. Clearance Required
17½″
44.46 cm
11 7/16″
29.06 cm
J
See Note Below*
12½″
31.76 cm

TRIPLE

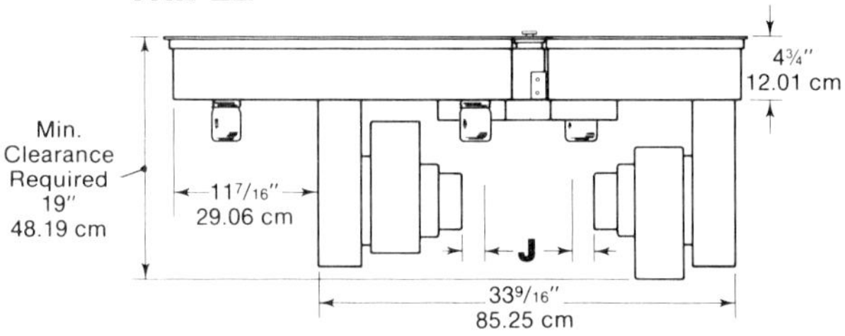

4¾″
12.01 cm
Min. Clearance Required
19″
48.19 cm
11 7/16″
29.06 cm
J
33 9/16″
85.25 cm

IMPORTANT

Dimension "J"—Provide 2″ min. (5.08 cm) cabinet clearance to motor for cooling purpose.

NOTE: Where possible 6″ (15.24 cm) is recommended for motor blower service.

Side Clearance—Grills installed near a side wall must allow a minimum clearance of 6″ (15.24 cm) between cooktop and sidewall for maximum ventilation performance. Minimum clearance of 1.0 inch (2.54 cm) is required to sidewalls and rear wall.

Electrical Hookup—The unit should be properly circuit protected and wired according to local electrical codes. See electrical wiring information. Unit power requirements are located on the data plate.

Access must be provided to remove and empty grease container(s).

CUTOUT DIMENSIONS FOR REMOTE

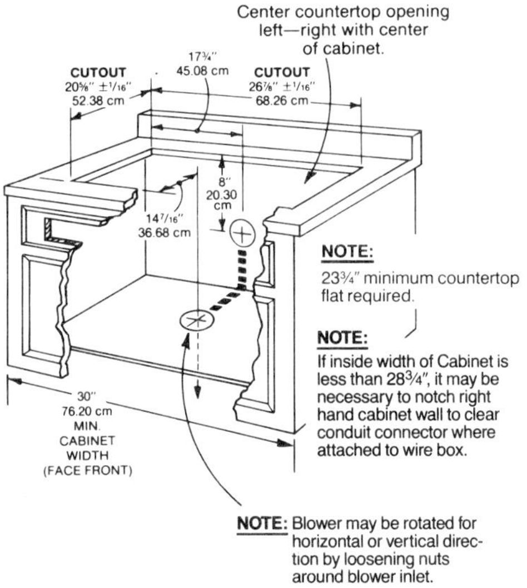

Center countertop opening left—right with center of cabinet.
17¾″
45.08 cm
CUTOUT
20⅝″ ±1/16″
52.38 cm
CUTOUT
26⅞″ ±1/16″
68.26 cm
8″
20.30 cm
14 7/16″
36.68 cm
NOTE:
23¾″ minimum countertop flat required.
NOTE:
If inside width of Cabinet is less than 28¾″, it may be necessary to notch right hand cabinet wall to clear conduit connector where attached to wire box.
30″
76.20 cm
MIN.
CABINET
WIDTH
(FACE FRONT)
NOTE: Blower may be rotated for horizontal or vertical direction by loosening nuts around blower inlet.

CABINET/FALSE FRONT CUTOUT

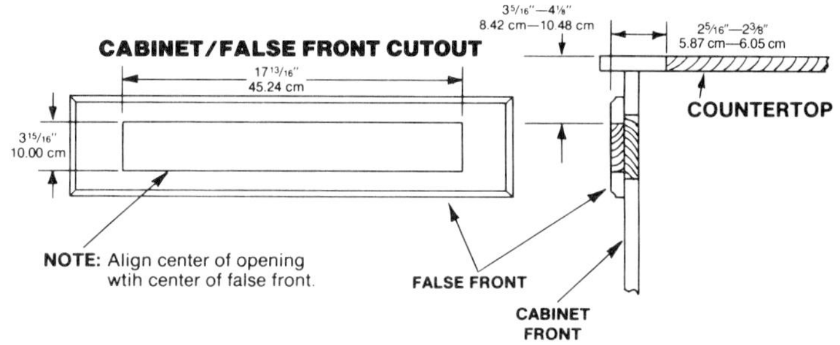

3 5/16″—4⅛″
8.42 cm—10.48 cm
2 5/16″—2⅜″
5.87 cm—6.05 cm
17 13/16″
45.24 cm
3 15/16″
10.00 cm
COUNTERTOP
NOTE: Align center of opening wtih center of false front.
FALSE FRONT
CABINET FRONT

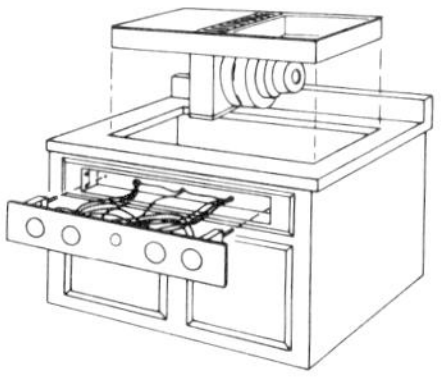

IMPORTANT:

Dimensions Shown in Both Inches and Centimeters.

IMPORTANT: Because of continuing product improvements, Jenn-Air reserves the right to change specifications without notice. Dimensional specifications are provided for planning purposes only. For complete details see installation instructions packed with product before selecting cabinetry, making cutouts or beginning installation.

DESIGNER LINE COOKTOP FEATURE CHART

COOKTOP FEATURES AND SPECIFICATIONS	DOWNDRAFT MODELS								UPDRAFT MODELS[A]					
	LANAI GRILLS		ELECTRIC			GAS			ELECTRIC				GAS	
	GO106	GO206	C206	C236	C316	CG106	CG205	CG206	CCE406	CCS447	CCR466	CU240	CCG456	CCG556
	18"	30"	30"	30"	48"	18"	30"	30"	33"	30"	30"	30"	30"	36"
Overall Width (in.)	18¹⁄₁₆	29⁷⁄₈	29⁷⁄₈	29¹⁵⁄₁₆	46¹³⁄₁₆	18¹⁄₁₆	29⁷⁄₈	29⁷⁄₈	33⁵⁄₈	30	30	29⁷⁄₈	30	36
Overall Depth (in.)	21½	21½	21½	21⁹⁄₁₆	21⁹⁄₁₆	21½	21½	21½	21⅝	21	21	21½	21	21
Cutout Width (in.)	17⅛	28⁷⁄₈	28⁷⁄₈	28⁷⁄₈	45¾	17⅛	28⁷⁄₈	28⁷⁄₈	33¹⁄₁₆	26⅝	29⁷⁄₁₆	28⁷⁄₈	26⁹⁄₁₆	32⁹⁄₁₆
Cutout Depth (in.)	20¹⁵⁄₁₆	20¹⁵⁄₁₆	20¹⁵⁄₁₆	20¹⁵⁄₁₆	20¹⁵⁄₁₆	20¹⁵⁄₁₆	20¹⁵⁄₁₆	20¹⁵⁄₁₆	21¹⁄₁₆	20	20⁷⁄₁₆	20¹⁵⁄₁₆	20¹⁄₁₆	20¹⁄₁₆
Blower Assembly Clearance (below countertop)[B] (in.)	15⅝	15⅝	15⅝	15⅝	15¹³⁄₁₆	15⅝	15⅝	15⅝						
Total Connected Load[C] —KW —Amps (at 120/240 VAC)	3.05 13.7	5.85 25.1	7.70 32.1	8.45 33.5	12.55 52.3				6.7 27.9	9.08 40.8	7.0 29.2	8.20 34.2		
BTUs (Natural/LP)[D] —Single unit, left side of double unit —Right side of double unit						8,000/ 8,000	8,000/ 8,000 10,000/ 9,000	8,000/ 8,000 10,000/ 9,000					9,500LF 10,000LR 12,000RF 9,000RR	9,500LF 10,000LR 6,000CR 12,000RF 9,000RR
Jenn-Air Golden Product Warranty	●	●	●	●	●	●	●	●	●	●	●	●	●	●
Downdraft Ventilation[E]	●	●	●	●	●	●	●	●						
Indoor Grilling			●	●	●	●	●	●				●		
Accepts Grill/Cooktop Accessories[F]	●	●	●	●	●	●	●	●	●			●		
Countertop Installation	●	●	●	●	●	●	●	●	●	●	●	●	●	●
Island/Peninsula Installation	●	●	●	●	●	●	●	●						
U.L. Approved for Outdoor Installation[G]	●	●												
Installs Over W130 Wall Oven										●	●		●	
Convertibility			●	●	●	●	●	●				●		
Number of Bays Accept Interchangeable Cartridges/Gas Surface Module			1	2	3	1[H]	2[I]	2[H]				2		
Number of Bays Accept Grill	Perma-nent[J]	Perma-nent[J]	1[K]	2[K]	2[K,M]	1[K]	1[L]	1[K,L]				1[K,L]		
Grill-Only Cooktop	●	●												
Energy-Saver Grill Element Included				●	●							●		
Standard Grill Element Included	●	2	●											
E-ven Heat™ Grill Burner Included						●[N]		●[N]						
Gas Surface Burners Included							4	2					4[O]	5[O]
Solid Elements Included										4[P]				
Conventional Coil Elements Included			2[P]						4[P]					
Quick-Start™ Radiant Elements Included											4[P]			
Electronic Pilotless Ignition						●	●	●					●	●
Flame Sensing Automatic Reignition													●	●
Convertible to LP Gas						●	●	●						
Backlit Controls										●				
Designer Line Styling	●	●	●	●	●	●	●	●	●	●	●	●	●	●
Color Availabilities (B=black porcelain, BC=brushed chrome, BG=black glass, L=almond porcelain, SB=stainless steel, black accents, SW=stainless steel, white accents, W=white, WG=white glass)	B	B	B, W, SB	B, W, SB	SB, SW	B, SB	W	B, SB	B, BC, L	WG, BG	BG[Q]	B, SB	WG, BG	WG, BG
Cooktop Perimeter Construction[R] (RF=roll formed, RFR=roll formed ring, ST=stamped)	ST	ST	ST	ST, RF	RF	ST	ST	ST	RFR		RFR	ST		

A. Proper operation requires use of range hood (Model CU240 requires a compatible high-performance ducted range hood such as Jenn-Air Models RH400, RH440, RH480). See Page 11A for Jenn-Air range hood specifications and features.

B. Blower can be swiveled 90°.

C. All electric models (except Models GO106, G0206 and CCR466) are U.L. listed and dual rated for 3-wire 120/240 VAC or 120/208 VAC, 60 Hz. For 120/208 VAC applications, appropriate grill element must be substituted prior to installation. Models GO106, GO206 and CCR466 are U.L. listed and rated for 3-wire 120/240 VAC only. Models GO106 and GO206 are available with 208V rating (add -8 to end of model number).

D. Regulator connection ½" N.P.T. (male pipe). Electric supply for pilotless ignition: 120 VAC, 60 Hz. Power cord supplied. Models CCG456, CCG556 use natural gas only. AGA and CGA approved.

E. Can vent up to 60 equivalent feet with long duct run motor.

F. Electric grill accessories are designed for use ONLY with electric cooktops. Gas grill accessories are designed for use ONLY with gas cooktops. These accessories are not interchangeable. Model CCE406 accepts Model A141A wok and Model A145A "big-pot" canning element only. Models GO106 and GO206 accept Model A302 griddle, Model A341 grill cover and Model A335 cooker-steamer only. Model CG205 accepts Model AG340 wok, Model AG150 grill assembly, and Model AG302 griddle (must be used in conjunction with Model AG150). Model CU240 accepts all cooktop cartridges plus A341 grill cover, A302 griddle, A312 Rotiss-Kebab, A141A wok and A145A "big-pot" canning element.

G. Not approved for indoor installation.

H. Optional two-burner module Model AG200 (black or white): 8,000 BTUs per burner (natural or LP).

I. Cooktop is shipped with four burners.

J. Grills are shipped with unit.

K. One grill is shipped with cooktop.

L. Grills on left side only. Model CG205 accepts optional grill assembly Model AG150 on left side only.

M. Model C316 does not accept grill in far righthand cooking bay.

N. Grill-grates coated with Excalibur® finish. Excalibur® is a registered trademark of Whitford Corp.

O. Sealed gas burners with automatic reignition.

P. Permanently installed (conventional coil elements remove for cleaning). Conventional element wattage: 8" elements, 2100; 6" elements, 1250. Solid element wattage: UltraPower™ elements: 9"-3,200, 6"-2,000; Standard elements: 7¼"-2,000; 6"-1,500; UltraPower™ is a registered trademark of E.G.O. Products, Inc. Radiant element wattage: 8" elements, 2100; 6" elements, 1200.

Q. Ceran translucent ceramic surface.

R. Stamped perimeter has rounded edge. Roll formed perimeter has square edge. Roll ring perimeter installs flush to countertop. Models CCS447, CCG456 and CCG556 have perimeterless glass ceramic surface. Model C236 stainless has roll formed perimeter. Models C236 black, C236 white have stamped perimeter.

Except as noted, all Jenn-Air cooktops are shipped complete with one grill assembly. All cartridges and accessories are optional.

Model Availability Dates:
Model CCG556 B/W availability 2nd quarter 1992.
Model CCS447 B/W available 2nd quarter 1992.

All Jenn-Air appliances are appropriately UL, AGA, CSA or CGA approved.

IMPORTANT: Because of continuing product improvements, Jenn-Air reserves the right to change specifications without notice. Dimensional specifications are provided for planning purposes only. For complete details see installation instructions packed with product before selecting cabinetry, making cutouts or beginning installation.

CONVERTIBLE COOKTOPS
Downdraft: Models CG206, CG205, C206, C236, GO206

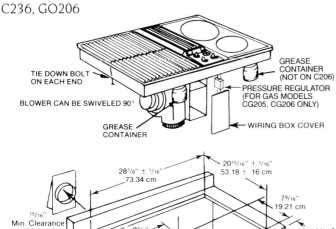

TIE DOWN BOLT ON EACH END

BLOWER CAN BE SWIVELED 90°

GREASE CONTAINER

GREASE CONTAINER (NOT ON C206)

PRESSURE REGULATOR (FOR GAS MODELS CG205, CG206 ONLY)

WIRING BOX COVER

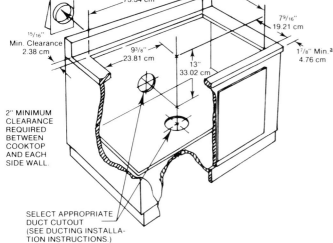

CONVERTIBLE COOKTOPS
Downdraft: Models CG106, GO106

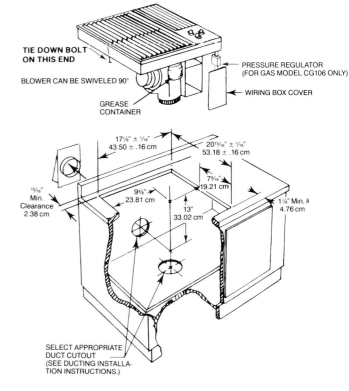

TIE DOWN BOLT ON THIS END

BLOWER CAN BE SWIVELED 90°

GREASE CONTAINER

PRESSURE REGULATOR (FOR GAS MODEL CG106 ONLY)

WIRING BOX COVER

SELECT APPROPRIATE DUCT CUTOUT (SEE DUCTING INSTALLATION INSTRUCTIONS.)

CONVERTIBLE COOKTOP
Electric, Updraft: Model CU240

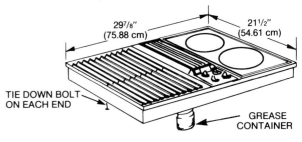

TIE DOWN BOLT ON EACH END

GREASE CONTAINER

CONVERTIBLE COOKTOP
Electric Downdraft: Model C316

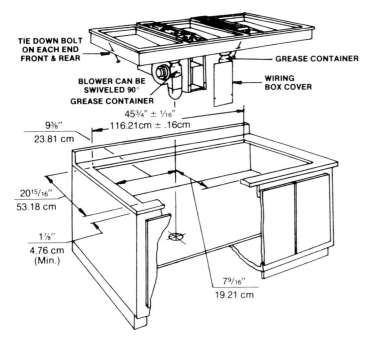

TIE DOWN BOLT ON EACH END FRONT & REAR

BLOWER CAN BE SWIVELED 90°

GREASE CONTAINER

GREASE CONTAINER

WIRING BOX COVER

RADIANT UPDRAFT COOKTOP
Electric, Updraft: Model CCR466

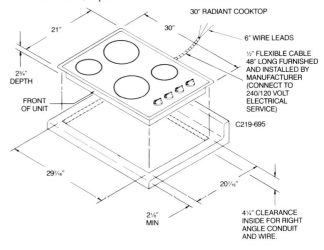

30" RADIANT COOKTOP

6" WIRE LEADS

½" FLEXIBLE CABLE 48" LONG FURNISHED AND INSTALLED BY MANUFACTURER (CONNECT TO 240/120 VOLT ELECTRICAL SERVICE)

C219-695

FRONT OF UNIT

4¼" CLEARANCE INSIDE FOR RIGHT ANGLE CONDUIT AND WIRE.

aMinimum distance from front edge of counter top and cut out.

NON-CONVERTIBLE SOLID ELEMENT COOKTOP
Electric, Updraft: Model CCS447

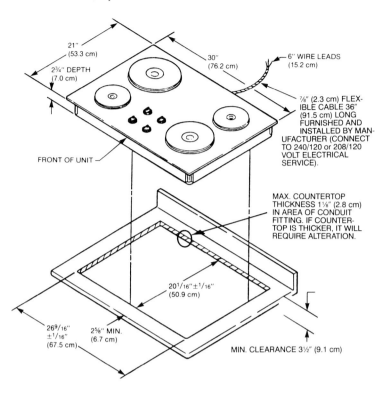

21"
(53.3 cm)

2¾" DEPTH
(7.0 cm)

30"
(76.2 cm)

6" WIRE LEADS
(15.2 cm)

⅞" (2.3 cm) FLEX-IBLE CABLE 36" (91.5 cm) LONG FURNISHED AND INSTALLED BY MANUFACTURER (CONNECT TO 240/120 or 208/120 VOLT ELECTRICAL SERVICE).

FRONT OF UNIT

MAX. COUNTERTOP THICKNESS 1⅛" (2.8 cm) IN AREA OF CONDUIT FITTING. IF COUNTER-TOP IS THICKER, IT WILL REQUIRE ALTERATION.

20 1/16" ± 1/16"
(50.9 cm)

26 9/16"
± 1/16"
(67.5 cm)

2⅝" MIN.
(6.7 cm)

MIN. CLEARANCE 3½" (9.1 cm)

NON-CONVERTIBLE CONVENTIONAL COIL COOKTOP
Electric, Updraft: Model CCE406

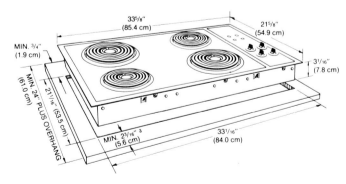

33⅝"
(85.4 cm)

21⅝"
(54.9 cm)

MIN. ¾"
(1.9 cm)

MIN. 24" PLUS OVERHANG
(61.0 cm)

21 1/16" (53.5 cm)

3 1/16"
(7.8 cm)

MIN. 2 3/16" a
(5.6 cm)

33 1/16"
(84.0 cm)

NON-CONVERTIBLE GAS COOKTOP
Gas, Updraft: Model CCG456

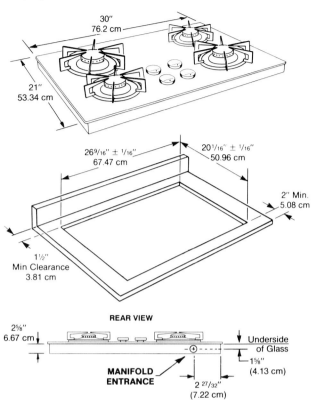

30"
76.2 cm

21"
53.34 cm

26 9/16" ± 1/16"
67.47 cm

20 1/16" ± 1/16"
50.96 cm

2" Min.
5.08 cm

1½"
Min Clearance
3.81 cm

REAR VIEW

2⅝"
6.67 cm

Underside of Glass

1⅝"
(4.13 cm)

MANIFOLD ENTRANCE

2 27/32"
(7.22 cm)

NON-CONVERTIBLE GAS COOKTOP
Gas, Updraft: Model CCG556

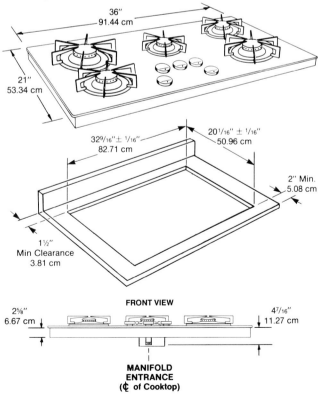

36"
91.44 cm

21"
53.34 cm

32 9/16" ± 1/16"
82.71 cm

20 1/16" ± 1/16"
50.96 cm

2" Min.
5.08 cm

1½"
Min Clearance
3.81 cm

FRONT VIEW

2⅝"
6.67 cm

4 7/16"
11.27 cm

**MANIFOLD ENTRANCE
(₵ of Cooktop)**

IMPORTANT: Because of continuing product improvements, Jenn-Air reserves the right to change specifications without notice. Dimensional specifications are provided for planning purposes only. For complete details see installation instructions packed with product before selecting cabinetry, making cutouts or beginning installation.

DESIGNER LINE GRILL-RANGE FEATURE CHART

GRILL-RANGE FEATURES AND SPECIFICATIONS	DOWNDRAFT					UPDRAFT[A]
	ELECTRIC				DUAL-FUEL™	ELECTRIC
	S136	S156	D156	S176	SEG196	SU146
Overall Height (in.)	35 1/2	35 1/2	35 1/2	35 1/2	35 1/2	35 1/2
Overall Width (in.)	29 15/16	29 15/16	29 15/16	29 15/16	29 15/16	29 15/16
Overall Depth[B] (in.)	26 3/8	26 3/8	26 3/8	26 3/8	26 3/8	26 3/8
Oven Interior Height (in.)	14 3/4	14 3/4	14 3/4	14 3/4	14 3/4	14 3/4
Oven Interior Width (in.)	21	21	21	21	21	21
Oven Interior Depth (in.)	18 9/16	18 9/16	18 9/16	18 9/16	18 9/16	18 9/16
Jenn-Air Golden Product Warranty	●	●	●	●	●	●
Downdraft Ventilation[C]	●	●	●	●	●	
Indoor Grilling	●	●	●	●	●[D]	●[D]
Accepts Grill Accessories[E]	●	●	●	●	●	●
Convertibility	●	●	●	●	●	●
Number of Bays Accept Interchangeable Cartridges/Gas Surface Module	2	2	2	2	2[F]	2
Number of Bays Accept Grill	2	2	2	2	1	1
Energy-Saver Grill Element Included		●[G]	●[G]	●[G]		●[H]
Standard Grill Element Included	●[G]					
E-ven Heat™ Grill Burner Included					●[I]	
Electronic Oven Touch Control			●	●		●
Electronic Clock with Timer	●	●	●	●	●	●
Self-Cleaning Oven	●	●	●	●	●	●
Clock-Controlled Cook and Clean	●	●	●	●	●	●
Automatic Self-Clean Latch			●	●		●
Bake-and-Broil Oven	●	●	●	●	●	●
Convection Oven		●	●	●	●	●
3-Rack Baking		●	●	●	●	●
Variable Temperature Broil	●	●	●	●	●	●
Glass Oven Door with Window	●	●	●	●	●	●
Accepts Optional Backsplash[J]	●	●		●	●	●
Accepts Optional Color Side Panels[K]	●	●		●	●	●
Island/Peninsula Installation[L]	●	●	●	●	●	●
Slide-In Installation	●	●		●	●	●
Drop-In-Look Installation[M]			●			
Gas Cooktop/Electric Oven					●	
BTUs (Natural/LP)						
Surface burners (right side)					10,000/ 9,000	
Grill burner (per half)					8,000/ 8,000	
Electronic Pilotless Ignition					●	
Convertible to LP Gas					●	
Designer Line Styling	●	●	●	●	●	●
Color Availabilities (B=black, W=white)	B, W	B, W	B, W	B, W	B, W	B

A. High-performance range hood required (such as Jenn-Air Models RH400, RH440, RH480). See Page 11A for range hood specifications and features.
B. Add 2" for door handle.
C. Can vent up to 60 equivalent feet with long duct run motor.
D. On left side only.
E. All grill-ranges are shipped with one grill. Electric grill accessories are designed for use ONLY with electric grill-ranges. Gas grill accessories are designed for use ONLY with gas grill-ranges. These accessories are not interchangeable.
F. Optional two-burner module (Model AG200): 8,000 BTUs per burner (natural or LP).
G. 2800-watt grill element.
H. 2500-watt grill element.
I. Grill grates coated with Excalibur® finish. Excalibur® is a registered trademark of Whitford Corp.
J. Deluxe lighted backsplash Models A519 (black), A519W (white): add 10 9/16" to range height. Custom backsplash Model A507: add 5 1/4" to range height.
K. Available in white (Model A501WT), black (Model A501BT) and almond (Model A501LT).
L. 24" "double toe space" base cabinets will not accept grill-ranges in slide-in installation. Use 24" flush back design or 27" or deeper base cabinets.
M. "Drop-in-look" refers to a range supported by four legs which extend to the floor. Lower front section is recessed to allow installation of custom cabinetry panel. Refer to installation instructions to determine size of panel.

Total connected load: All-electric models – 50 amp minimum circuit protection required; Model SEG196 – 30 amp minimum circuit protection required. All electric models are dual rated for 3-wire 120/240 VAC or 120/208 VAC, 60 Hz. For 120/208 VAC applications, appropriate electric grill element must be substituted prior to installation. **All Jenn-Air electric grill-ranges are shipped complete with one grill assembly. Model SEG196 includes gas grill burner and 2 surface burners. All cartridges, accessories, backsplashes, and side panels are optional.**

All Jenn-Air appliances are appropriately UL, AGA, CSA or CGA approved.

FREE-STANDING[a] GRILL-RANGE CUTOUT

Models S136, S156, S176, SEG196, SU146,

[a]Requires optional backsplash and side panels.

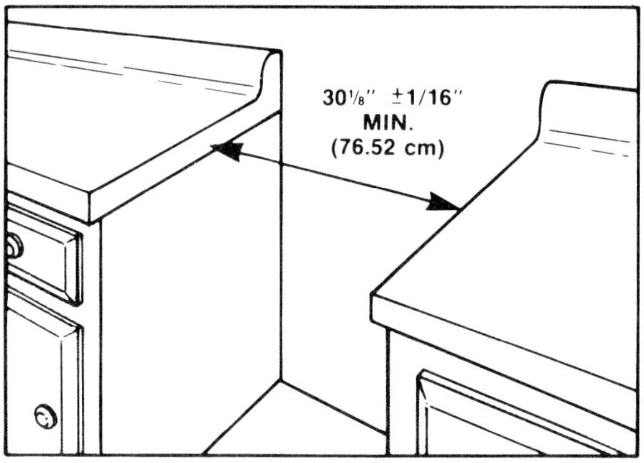

30 1/8" ±1/16"
MIN.
(76.52 cm)

SLIDE-IN OR "DROP-IN-LOOK" GRILL RANGE

Installation for All Grill-Range Models

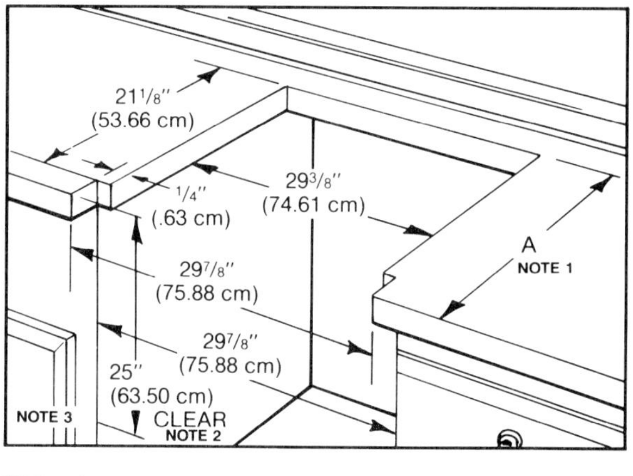

21 1/8"
(53.66 cm)
1/4"
(.63 cm)
29 3/8"
(74.61 cm)
A
NOTE 1
29 7/8"
(75.88 cm)
29 7/8"
(75.88 cm)
25"
(63.50 cm)
CLEAR
NOTE 2
NOTE 3

NOTE 1: If overhang is 1/2" to 1", dimension A=22 7/8". If overhang is 1" to 1 3/4", dimension A=23 3/16".
NOTE 2: 25" height dimension does not include additional height of base and legs.
NOTE 3: For European style cabinets (flush front) the required clearance for operation of the oven door is a minimum spacing between the cutout and the door, hinge or drawer of the cabinet.

IMPORTANT: Because of continuing product improvements, Jenn-Air reserves the right to change specifications without notice. Dimensional specifications are provided for planning purposes only. For complete details see installation instructions packed with product before selecting cabinetry, making cutouts or beginning installation.

DESIGNER LINE GRILL-RANGE/COOKTOP CARTRIDGES AND MODULE FEATURE CHART

Cartridge/ Module Type	ELECTRIC[A]				GAS[B]
	A100	A106	A121	A125	AG200
	Conventional Coil	Solid Element[C]	Quick-Start™ Radiant	Halogen	2-Burner Module[F]
Wattage[D] (Large element/ small element)	2100/1250	2600/1500	1700/1200[E]	1800/1200	
Color Availabilities (B=black, W=white, S=stainless steel)	B, W, S	B, W	B, W	B, W	B, W[G]

A. Cartridges designated "electric" are for use with electric-powered grill-ranges and cooktops only and retrofit all Jenn-Air grill-ranges and cooktops manufactured since 1977.
B. Module designated "gas" is for use with gas convertible cooktops and Model SEG196 Dual-Fuel™ grill-range only.
C. Model variation A105 contains two standard solid elements with wattage of 2000 (large) and 1500 (small). Model A106 contains UltraPower™ large element. UltraPower™ is a trademark of E.G.O. Products, Inc.
D. All electric cartridges rated 240V.
E. Rated 240V. Also available with 208 rating (add -8 to end of model number).
F. 8,000 BTUs per burner, natural or LP, if used on left side. 10,000 BTUs per burner, natural or LP, if used on right side.
G. White module has black grates.

Model Availability Dates:
A106B/W available 3rd quarter 1992.
A121W and A125W available 3rd quarter 1992.
AG200W available 2nd quarter 1992.

DESIGNER LINE GRILL-RANGE/COOKTOP ACCESSORY FEATURE CHART

Accessory Type	ELECTRIC[A]								GAS[B]				
	A141A	A145A	A302	A312	A335	A341	A350	A158	AG150	AG302	AG340	AG350	AG341
	Wok[C]	"Big-Pot" Canning Element[D]	Griddle	Rotiss-Kebab	Cooker-Steamer[E]	Grill Cover	Storage Tray[F]	Energy-Saver Grill[G]	Grill Assembly[H]	Griddle	Wok	Storage Tray[F]	Grill Cover
For Use with Grill			●	●	●	●			●	●			●
For Use on Gas Surface Burner											●		
For Use with Large Conventional Coil	●	●											
Wattage	1800	2100	2800	2800	2800			2800					
Color Availabilities (B=black, W=white)	B		B		B	B, W	B	B	B	B	B	B	B, W

A. Accessories designated "electric" are for use with electric-powered grill-ranges and cooktops only.
B. Accessories designated "gas" are for use with gas convertible cooktops and Model SEG196 Dual-Fuel™ grill-range only.
C. Contoured element replaces large element on a conventional coil cartridge; not for use with other cooktop cartridges.
D. Raised element replaces large conventional coil element; not for use with other cooktop cartridges.
E. For use with electric downdraft cooktops only. Not for use with electric updraft cooktops.
F. Holds one cartridge or accessory. Fits all cartridges, all accessories except Wok and Cooker-Steamer.
G. Has independent control of front and rear sections of grill (1400 watts each). Includes grill element, grates, grill-rocks and tray.
H. Includes gas E-ven Heat™ grill burner, 2 grill grates coated with Excalibur finish and tray. Excalibur is a registered trademark of Whitford Corp.

All Jenn-Air appliances are appropriately UL, AGA, CSA or CGA approved.

DESIGNER LINE EXTRAS

Model A905 Complete Cooking with Jenn-Air includes 192 pages of tested recipes and hints for electric cooking. Hardbound, full-color illustrations.

Model A913 Insulated Cookie Sheet measures 12" x 14". Two layers of aluminum insulated by an inner air layer help baked goods brown to perfection.

Part No. 2-0000001 Elco Cooktop Cleaning Cream cleans glass-ceramic cooktop surfaces.

Model A350 (Electric)/ **AG350** (Gas) Storage Tray holds one cartridge or accessory except wok and cooker-steamer. Not for use with Expressions™ Collection.

Model A911 Collo Electrol® maintains black matte surface of cast iron solid elements. **Model A912** Collo Luneta® removes stains and heat discoloration from stainless steel cooktop, cartridge and cookware surfaces.

DESIGNER LINE WALL OVEN FEATURE CHART

	SINGLE					DOUBLE			COMBINATION[A]			
	ELECTRIC					ELECTRIC			ELECTRIC			GAS
WALL OVEN FEATURES AND SPECIFICATIONS	**24″**	**27″**			**30″**	**24″**	**27″**		**27″**			**24″**
	W116	**W106**	**W136**	**W156**	**W130**	**W216**	**W206**	**W256**	**W227**	**W236[B]**	**W276[B]**	**WG206[C]**
Overall Height (in.)	29⅝	28⅞	28⅞	28⅞	28	46 5/16	51	51	48 7/16	48 7/16	48 7/16	46 5/16
Overall Width (in.)	23⅞	26¾	26¾	26¾	30½	23⅞	26¾	26¾	26¾	26¾	26¾	23¾
Overall Depth[D] (in.)	25 3/16	25	25	25	24	25 3/16	25	25	25	25	25	25⅛
Oven Interior Height (in.)	14	15	15	15	15	14U/12L	15[E]	15[E]	15[E]	15[E]	15[E]	14U/12L
Oven Interior Width (in.)	18	19	19	19	22	18[E]	19[E]	19[E]	19[E]	19[E]	19[E]	18U/18L
Oven Interior Depth (in.)	19	18	18	18	18	19[E]	18[E]	18[E]	18[E]	18[E]	18[E]	19U/19L
Cutout Height (in.)	28 11/16	28⅜	28⅜	28⅜	28⅛	45⅜	50½	50½	47⅞	47⅞	47⅞	45⅜
Cutout Width (in.)	22	25	25	25	30⅛[F]	22	25	25	25	25	25	22
Cutout Depth (in.)	24	24	24	24	24	24	24	24	24	24	24	24
Total Connected Load —KW —Amps (at 120/240 VAC)	3.6 15.0	5.7 23.8	5.7 23.8	5.7 23.8	3.5 14.6	6.5 27.1	11.4 48.4	11.4 48.4	6.9 35.3	7.1 35.3	7.1 35.3	
BTUs (Oven/Broiler; Natural/LP)[G]												16,000/ 16,000
Jenn-Air Golden Product Warranty	●	●	●	●	●	●	●	●	●	●	●	●
Catalytic Smoke Eliminator	●	●	●	●	●	U	U	B	L	L	L	
See-Through Oven Window	●	●	●	●	●	B	B	B	B	B	B	B
Formed Rack Guides	●	●	●	●	●	B	B	B	L	L	L	B
Large Capacity Oven		●	●	●	●		B	B	L	L	L	
Temperature Control Broiling		●	●	●			B	B	L	L	L	
Clock-Controlled Baking	●	●	●	●	●	U	U	B	L	L	L	
Self-Cleaning Oven	●	●	●	●	●	U	U	B	L	L	L	
Automatic Self-Clean Lock				●				B			L	
Broiler Pan Included	●	●	●	●	●	U	U	U	L	L	L	L
3-Rack Convection Baking			●	●			U	U		L	L	
Temperature Probe				●				U	U	U	U	
Electronic Clock with Timer	●	●	●	●	●	●	●	●	B	B	B	
Digital Clock with Timer												●
Electronic Touch Control				●				●	U	U	B	
Microwave Oven									U[H]	U[H]	U[H]	
Designer Line Styling	●	●	●	●	●	●	●	●	●	●	●	●
Color Availabilities (B= black, W=white)	B	B, W	B, W	B, W	B, W	B	B, W	B, W	B, W	B, W	B, W	B
Electronic Pilotless Ignition												●
Convertible to LP Gas												●
Undercounter Installation					●							

U=Upper, L=Lower, B=Both.

A. Model variations may be available for W227 (WM227), W236 (WM236) and W276 (WM277). Feature differences: unit includes M167 microwave which does not include probe. Probe added to lower oven of WM277. Microwave oven trim has chrome edge on white models of WM227 and WM236.
B. Order Trim Kit Model A517 to permit installation of wall oven Model W236 or W276 in cutout made for double wall oven Model W256. (Black models only.)
C. Single wall oven with separate broiler compartment.
D. Add 2″ for door handle (for Model WG206, add 1¾″).
E. Both oven cavities (lower oven only on combination ovens).
F. Minimum cutout width: 30⅛″; maximum: 30¼″.
G. Electric supply for pilotless ignition: 120 VAC, 60 Hz.
H. Microwave oven features for combination models W227, W236 and W276 are identical to M167 microwave oven *except* microwave includes a temperature probe. Microwave oven in WM227, WM236 and WM277 is identical to M167 microwave.

All Jenn-Air appliances are appropriately UL, AGA, CSA or CGA approved.

27″ DOUBLE WALL OVENS
Models W206, W256

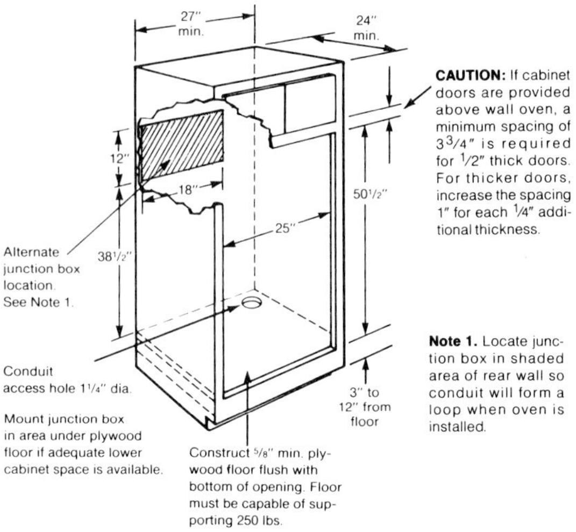

27″ min.
24″ min.
CAUTION: If cabinet doors are provided above wall oven, a minimum spacing of 3 3/4″ is required for 1/2″ thick doors. For thicker doors, increase the spacing 1″ for each 1/4″ additional thickness.
12″
18″
25″
50 1/2″
38 1/2″
Alternate junction box location. See Note 1.
Note 1. Locate junction box in shaded area of rear wall so conduit will form a loop when oven is installed.
Conduit access hole 1 1/4″ dia.
Mount junction box in area under plywood floor if adequate lower cabinet space is available.
3″ to 12″ from floor
Construct 5/8″ min. plywood floor flush with bottom of opening. Floor must be capable of supporting 250 lbs.

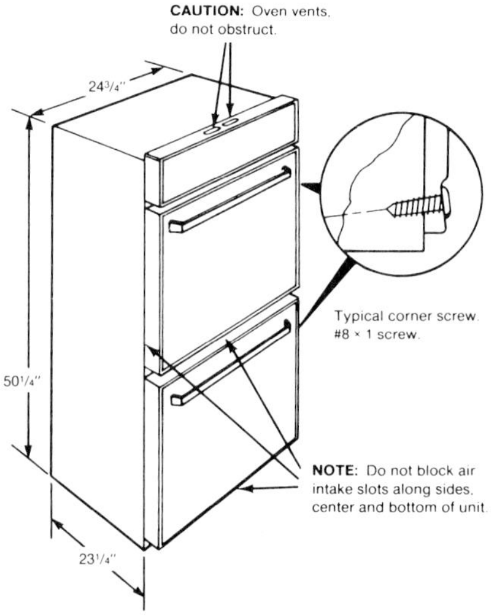

CAUTION: Oven vents, do not obstruct.
24 3/4″
Typical corner screw. #8 × 1 screw.
50 1/4″
NOTE: Do not block air intake slots along sides, center and bottom of unit.
23 1/4″

27″ COMBINATION WALL OVENS
Models W227, W236, W276

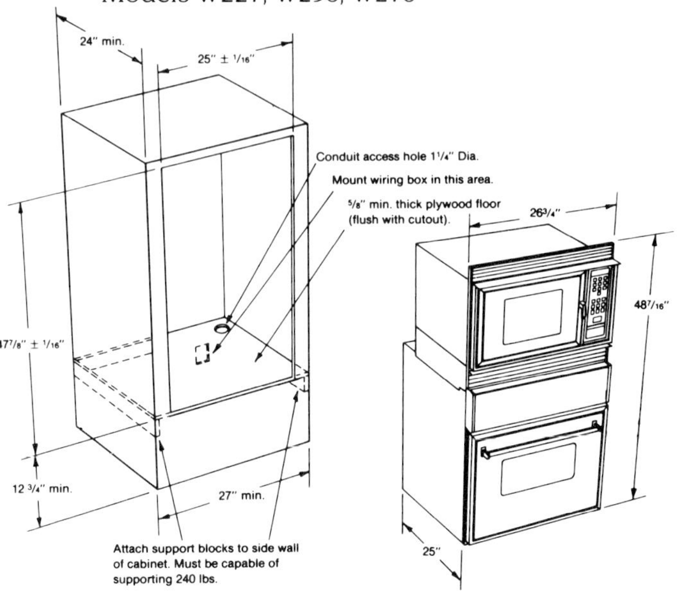

24″ min.
25″ ± 1/16″
Conduit access hole 1 1/4″ Dia.
Mount wiring box in this area.
5/8″ min. thick plywood floor (flush with cutout).
26 3/4″
48 7/16″
47 7/8″ ± 1/16″
12 3/4″ min.
27″ min.
Attach support blocks to side wall of cabinet. Must be capable of supporting 240 lbs.
25″

24″ DOUBLE WALL OVENS
Model W216

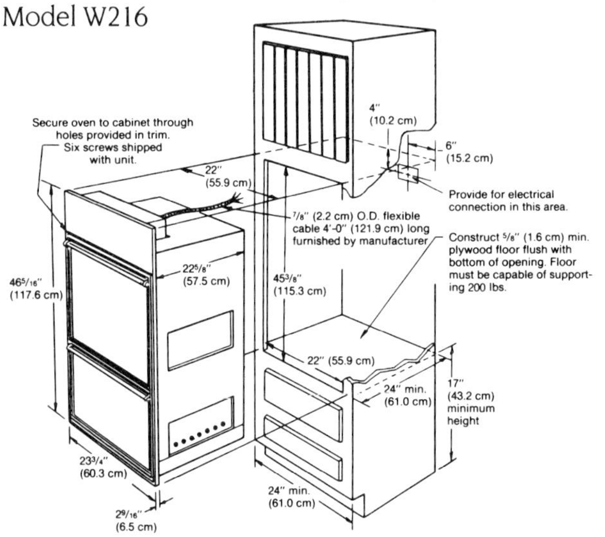

Secure oven to cabinet through holes provided in trim. Six screws shipped with unit.
4″ (10.2 cm)
6″ (15.2 cm)
22″ (55.9 cm)
Provide for electrical connection in this area.
7/8″ (2.2 cm) O.D. flexible cable 4′-0″ (121.9 cm) long furnished by manufacturer
Construct 5/8″ (1.6 cm) min. plywood floor flush with bottom of opening. Floor must be capable of supporting 200 lbs.
46 5/16″ (117.6 cm)
22 5/8″ (57.5 cm)
45 3/8″ (115.3 cm)
22″ (55.9 cm)
24″ min. (61.0 cm)
17″ (43.2 cm) minimum height
23 3/4″ (60.3 cm)
24″ min. (61.0 cm)
2 9/16″ (6.5 cm)

Revised 1-20-93

24" SINGLE WALL OVEN
Model W116

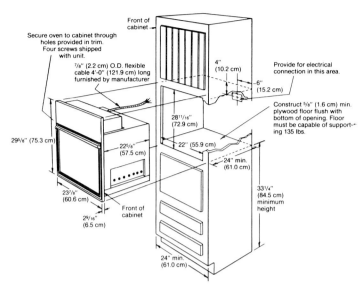

Secure oven to cabinet through holes provided in trim. Four screws shipped with unit.

Front of cabinet

⁷/₈" (2.2 cm) O.D. flexible cable 4'-0" (121.9 cm) long furnished by manufacturer

4" (10.2 cm)

6" (15.2 cm)

Provide for electrical connection in this area.

Construct ⁵/₈" (1.6 cm) min. plywood floor flush with bottom of opening. Floor must be capable of supporting 135 lbs.

28¹¹/₁₆" (72.9 cm)

29⁵/₈" (75.3 cm)

22⁵/₈" (57.5 cm)

22" (55.9 cm)

24" min. (61.0 cm)

33¼" (84.5 cm) minimum height

23⁷/₈" (60.6 cm)

Front of cabinet

2⁹/₁₆" (6.5 cm)

24" min. (61.0 cm)

30" SINGLE WALL OVEN
Model W130

WALL MOUNT INSTALLATION

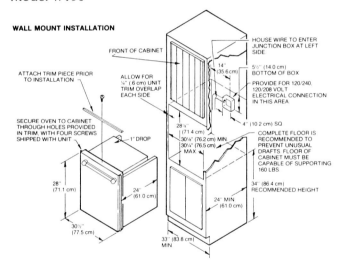

FRONT OF CABINET

ATTACH TRIM PIECE PRIOR TO INSTALLATION

ALLOW FOR ¼" (.6 cm) UNIT TRIM OVERLAP EACH SIDE

SECURE OVEN TO CABINET THROUGH HOLES PROVIDED IN TRIM, WITH FOUR SCREWS SHIPPED WITH UNIT

HOUSE WIRE TO ENTER JUNCTION BOX AT LEFT SIDE.

14" (35.6 cm)

5½" (14.0 cm) BOTTOM OF BOX

PROVIDE FOR 120/240, 120/208 VOLT ELECTRICAL CONNECTION IN THIS AREA

4" (10.2 cm) SQ

COMPLETE FLOOR IS RECOMMENDED TO PREVENT UNUSUAL DRAFTS. FLOOR OF CABINET MUST BE CAPABLE OF SUPPORTING 160 LBS

28" (71.1 cm)

1" DROP

24" (61.0 cm)

28¹/₈" (71.4 cm)
30¹/₈" (76.2 cm) MIN.
30¼" (76.5 cm) MAX

34" (86.4 cm) RECOMMENDED HEIGHT

24" MIN (61.0 cm)

30½" (77.5 cm)

33" (83.8 cm) MIN

UNDERCOUNTER INSTALLATION

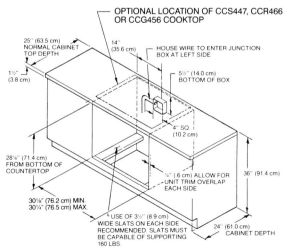

OPTIONAL LOCATION OF CCS447, CCR466 OR CCG456 COOKTOP

25" (63.5 cm) NORMAL CABINET TOP DEPTH

14" (35.6 cm)

HOUSE WIRE TO ENTER JUNCTION BOX AT LEFT SIDE

1½" (3.8 cm)

5½" (14.0 cm) BOTTOM OF BOX

4" SQ (10.2 cm)

28¹/₈" (71.4 cm) FROM BOTTOM OF COUNTERTOP

¼" (.6 cm) ALLOW FOR UNIT TRIM OVERLAP EACH SIDE

36" (91.4 cm)

30¹/₈" (76.2 cm) MIN.
30¼" (76.5 cm) MAX.

USE OF 3½" (8.9 cm) WIDE SLATS ON EACH SIDE RECOMMENDED. SLATS MUST BE CAPABLE OF SUPPORTING 160 LBS.

24" (61.0 cm) CABINET DEPTH

27" SINGLE WALL OVENS
Models W106, W136, W156

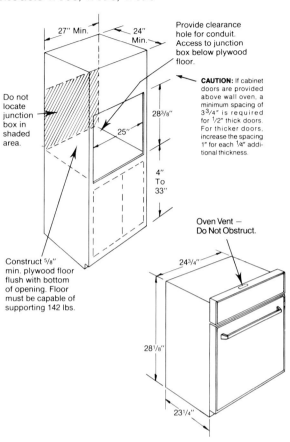

27" Min.

24" Min.

Provide clearance hole for conduit. Access to junction box below plywood floor.

Do not locate junction box in shaded area.

CAUTION: If cabinet doors are provided above wall oven, a minimum spacing of 3³/₄" is required for ½" thick doors. For thicker doors, increase the spacing 1" for each ¼" additional thickness.

28³/₈"

25"

4" To 33"

Construct ⁵/₈" min. plywood floor flush with bottom of opening. Floor must be capable of supporting 142 lbs.

Oven Vent — Do Not Obstruct.

24³/₄"

28¹/₈"

23¼"

24" GAS WALL OVEN WITH SEPARATE BROILER COMPARTMENT
Model WG206

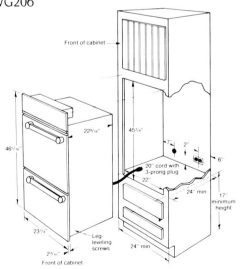

Front of cabinet

22⁹/₁₆"

45¹/₈"

46⁵/₈"

7"

2"

6"

20" cord with 3-prong plug

22"

24" min

17" minimum height

23¼"

Leg-leveling screws

24" min.

2¹/₈"

Front of cabinet

IMPORTANT: Because of continuing product improvements, Jenn-Air reserves the right to change specifications without notice. Dimensional specifications are provided for planning purposes only. For complete details see installation instructions packed with product before selecting cabinetry, making cutouts or beginning installation.

DESIGNER LINE MICROWAVE OVEN FEATURE CHART

MICROWAVE OVEN FEATURES AND SPECIFICATIONS[A]	BUILT-IN M167	OVER-THE-RANGE M417	M437	M446
Overall Height (front) (in.)	15¼	14⅝	14⅝	14⅝
Overall Height (back) (in.)	15¼	16½	16½	16½
Overall Width (in.)	21¾	30	30	30
Overall Depth (in.)	15¾	13	13	13
Jenn-Air Golden Product Warranty	●	●	●	●
Oven Capacity (cu. ft.)	1.1	1.0	1.0	1.0
Glass Door with Window	●	●	●	●
Power Output (watts)	750	750	750	750
Power Levels	10	10	10	10
2-Stage Memory Programming	●	●	●	●
Electronic Touch Controls	●	●	●	●
Temperature Probe/Hold		●	●	●
Digital Display with Clock/Timer	●	●	●	●
Preprogrammed Defrost Code				●
Quick Defrost	●			
Auto Defrost		●	●	
Programming Command Prompts		●	●	●
Oven Rack	●	●	●	●
Preprogrammed Codes[B]	●			
Preprogrammed Probe Code		●	●	●
Delay Start		●	●	●
Removable Glass Tray	●			
Designer Line Styling	●	●	●	●
Accepts Built-In Trim Kits[B]	●			
Below-Oven Work Surface Light		●	●	●
Built-In Exhaust System			●[C]	●
Provides Updraft Grilling Ventilation				●
Color Availabilities (B=black, W=white)	B, W	B	B, W	B

A. Model M446 is designed for use above all updraft gas and electric grill-ranges and grill-range cooktops. Model M437 is designed for use above all non-grilling gas and electric ranges and cooktops (not recommended over grill-ranges or cooktops with grilling capability unless the range or cooktop is equipped with downdraft ventilation.) Model M417 is designed for use above all gas and electric grill-ranges and grill-range cooktops with downdraft ventilation. 30" minimum clearance required between top of cooking surface and bottom of upper cabinet. 66" minimum clearance required between floor and top of microwave oven.

B. Preprogrammed codes include frozen convenience foods, reheat, defrost by weight, cook by weight and popcorn.

C. Trim kits to install M167 include: for 27" wide cabinet (cutout dimensions 18⅛" H x 24½" W, installed dimensions 19⅝" H x 26⅝" W) are A526B and A526W and A530W (has chrome trim around outer edge.). For 24" cabinet (cutout dimensions 15⅝" H x 22¼" W, installed dimensions 17" H x 23¾" W) is A424 (black only). For 30" cabinet (cutout dimensions 18⅛" H x 24½" W, installed dimensions 19⅝" H x 30" W is A626B and A626W.

Model Availability Dates:
A626 B/W available 2nd quarter 1992.
A530 W available 2nd quarter 1992.

MICROWAVE OVEN INSTALLATION ABOVE SINGLE WALL OVEN
Model M167

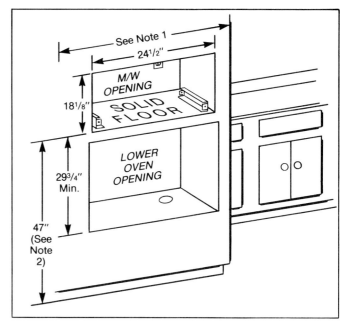

Note 1: When installing this Kit above a built-in oven in 27" cabinet, check built-in oven installation instructions to determine cutout dimensions for the (lower) wall oven.

Note 2: For a new installation, the 47" height dimension to the bottom of the cutout for the microwave oven is recommended. This places the microwave oven bottom at approximately 50" from the floor.

OVER-THE-RANGE MICROWAVE OVENS
Models M417, M437, M446

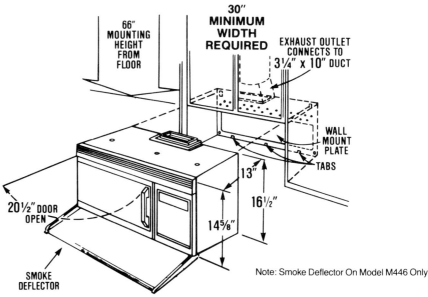

Note: Smoke Deflector On Model M446 Only

IMPORTANT: Because of continuing product improvements, Jenn-Air reserves the right to change specifications without notice. Dimensional specifications are provided for planning purposes only. For complete details see installation instructions packed with product before selecting cabinetry, making cutouts or beginning installation.

DESIGNER LINE RANGE HOOD FEATURE CHART

RANGE HOOD FEATURES AND SPECIFICATIONS	RH180	RH186	RH200	RH206W	RH400	RH440	RH480	RH800
Overall Height (in.)	5	5	7	7	7	7	7	11³/₁₆
Overall Width (in.)	30	36	30	30	22	30	30	30
Overall Depth (in.)	17⅝	17⅝	19¾	19¾	11¼	18¹¹/₁₆	19¾	11
Jenn-Air Golden Product Warranty	●	●	●	●	●	●	●	●
Touch Control Operation							●	
High-Performance Design^A					●	●	●	
Variable-Speed Fan			●	●	●	●	●	●
2-Speed Fan	●	●						
Auto On-Off Fan Control								●
Telescoping Hidavent™ Canopy								●
Lighting Levels	1	1	1	1	2	2	3	2
Vertical or Horizontal Air Discharge on 3¼" x 10" Duct	●	●	●	●	●	●	●	●
Vertical Discharge on 7" Round Duct	●	●	●	●				●
Adaptable to 7" Round Duct^B					●	●	●	
Ductless Installation	●^C	●^C	●^C	●^C				
Rating (vertical rectangular, CFM)^D	180	180	200	200	440	440	440	350
Rating (horizontal rectangular, CFM)^D	180	180	180	180	410	410	410	350
Rating (vertical round, CFM)^D	180	180	300	300				350
Cabinet Color Availabilities (B=black, L=almond, S=stainless steel, W=white)	B, L, S, W	B, W	B, L, S	W	B	B, L, S, W	B, L, S, W	B, W
Black-Glass-Look Front Panel			●	●		●	●	
Installs Under Custom Cabinetry					●			
For Use with Non-Grilling Cooktops	●	●	●	●				●

A. High-performance range hood (such as Models RH400, RH440, RH480) is required for use above updraft cooktops with indoor grilling.

B. Using transition; for vertical discharge only.

C. Model RH180 and RH186 shipped with aluminum filter and comes with charcoal pad for ductless installation. Order replacement charcoal filter RHF180. Models RH200 and RH206W convert to ductless installation. Order replacement charcoal filter RHF200. Running change Models RH200-02/RH206W-02. Order replacement charcoal filter RHF101. Running change Models RH200-03/RH206W-03. Order replacement charcoal filter RHF180.

D. Ducting configuration and length can affect air flow rates. Ratings shown are based on range hoods with correctly installed ducting.

Model Availability Date:
Model RH186 available 2nd quarter 1992.

All Jenn-Air appliances are appropriately UL, AGA, CSA or CGA approved.

Models RH180, RH186

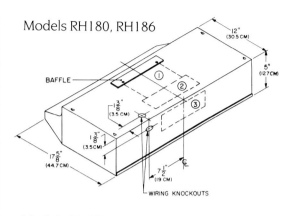

Models RH200, RH206W

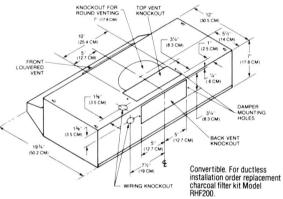

Convertible. For ductless installation order replacement charcoal filter kit Model RHF200.

Model RH400

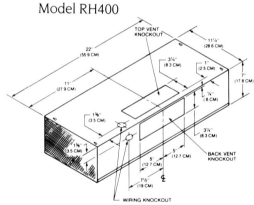

Model RH440

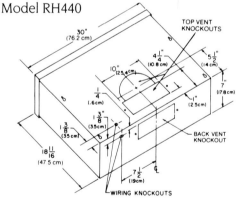

Model RH480

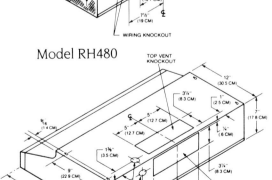

Model RH800

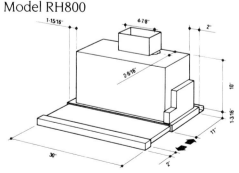

IMPORTANT: Because of continuing product improvements, Jenn-Air reserves the right to change specifications without notice. Dimensional specifications are provided for planning purposes only. For complete details see installation instructions packed with product before selecting cabinetry, making cutouts or beginning installation.

DESIGNER LINE SIDE-BY-SIDE REFRIGERATOR FEATURE CHART

Exterior Overall Dimensions

	JRS226	JRSD226	JRSD246
Height (add ½″ for door hinge and hinge cover) (in.)	66⅜	66⅜	66⅜
Width (closed) (in.)	33³⁄₁₆	33³⁄₁₆	36
Width (doors open 90°; incl. handle) (in.)	36	36	38¾
Depth (closed; excl. handle) (in.)	29¼	29¼	29¼
Depth (doors open 90°) (in.)	48²⁷⁄₃₂	48²⁷⁄₃₂	48²⁷⁄₃₂
Shipping Weight (approx. lbs.)	290	315	370

Interior Capacities (cu. ft. AHAM)

	JRS226	JRSD226	JRSD246
Total Volume	21.60	21.60	23.50
Refrigerator Compartment Volume	15.12	15.21	15.26
Freezer Compartment Volume	6.63	6.36	8.23
Total Shelf Area (sq. ft.)	29.10	29.00	27.50

General Features

	JRS226	JRSD226	JRSD246
Jenn-Air Golden Product Warranty	●	●	●
White or Almond Textured Steel Doors[A]	●	●	●
Accepts Custom Front Panels[B]	●	●	●
Optional Black Door Panel Kit	BDS22-02	BDS22D-02	BDS24D-02
Optional Decorator Trim Kit[B]	DTS22-02	DTS22D-02	DTS24-02
Optional White Trim Kit[B]		RDK226	RDK246
Adjustable Easy-Roll Wheels	●	●	●
Foam Insulation	●	●	●
Freezer/Refrigerator Lights	●	●	●
2 Door Stop Positions	●	●	●
Shelves with Three-Prong Supports	●	●	●
Roller Drawer System[C]			●
Crystal Gray Interior	●	●	
Crystal White Interior			●
Jenn-Air Designer Line Styling	●	●	
Jenn-Air Premier Designer Line Styling			●

Freezer Features

	JRS226	JRSD226	JRSD246
Total Door Shelves	6	5	5
Deep Storage Door Shelves with Easy-Off Fronts	6	4	4
Removable Wire Freezer Shelves	4	4	5
Adjustable Freezer Shelves			4
Bulk Storage Drawer	●	●	●[D]
2 Mini Cube Trays with Ice Service Bin	●		
Accepts Optional Ice Maker[E]	●		
Always Ice™ Automatic Ice Maker with Bin		●	●
Lighted Convenience Center (Chilled Water/Ice Dispenser)		●	●

Refrigerator Features

	JRS226	JRSD226	JRSD246
Total Shelves	5	5	4
Fixed Position Glass Shelf	1	1	1
Adjustable Cantilever Glass Shelves	4	4	3
Dairy Compartment with Butter Dish	●	●	●
2-Bottle Foldaway Wine Rack	●	●	
Shelf-Mount Wine Rack			●
Humidity-Controlled Sealed Crisper			●
Sealed Crisper	●	●	●
Temp Control Drawer	●	●	●
Deli Drawer	●	●	
Deep Storage Door Shelves with Easy-Off Fronts	2	2	2
Adjustable/Lift-Off Deep Storage Door Shelves	3	3	3
Shelf Tender	●	●	●
Lift-Out Egg Caddy	●	●	●
Door Shelf Cover		●	●

A. Add "W" to end of model number to indicate white cabinet; "L" to end of model number to indicate almond cabinet.
B. See right page for door Trim Kit information. Optional White Trim Kit includes white tape for door handle inserts, white escutcheon and white Jenn-Air nameplate.
C. For smooth movement of all freezer and refrigerator drawers.
D. Wire basket.
E. Order Model IMS105.

All Jenn-Air appliances are appropriately UL, AGA, CSA, or CGA approved.

Custom Panel Dimensions with Existing Trim[A]
(All dimensions shown in inches)

Freezer Door Dimensions

	JRS226	JRSD226	JRSD246
A1	11¹¹⁄₁₆	–	–
A2	–	11¹¹⁄₁₆	14⁷⁄₁₆
A3	–	11¹¹⁄₁₆	14⁷⁄₁₆
B	61³⁄₁₆	–	–
C	–	17³⁄₁₆	17³⁄₁₆
D	–	31¹¹⁄₁₆	31¹¹⁄₁₆

Refrigerator Door Dimensions

	JRS226	JRSD226	JRSD246
E	20¹⁵⁄₁₆	20¹⁵⁄₁₆	20¹⁵⁄₁₆
F	61³⁄₁₆	61³⁄₁₆	61³⁄₁₆

A. These dimensions apply to panels included in the optional Black Door Panel Kit and to any optional door panels of 0.125″ thickness.

Custom Panel Dimensions with Decorator Trim Kit
(All dimensions shown in inches)

Freezer Door Dimensions

	JRS226	JRSD226	JRSD246
A1	11⁷⁄₁₆	–	–
A2	–	11⁷⁄₁₆	14³⁄₁₆
A3	–	11⁷⁄₁₆	14³⁄₁₆
B	60⁹⁄₁₆		
C	–	16⅞	16⅞
D	–	31⁷⁄₁₆	31⁷⁄₁₆

Refrigerator Door Dimensions

	JRS226	JRSD226	JRSD246
E	20¹¹⁄₁₆	20¹¹⁄₁₆	20¹¹⁄₁₆
F	60⁹⁄₁₆	60⁹⁄₁₆	60⁹⁄₁₆

If a panel is more than 0.25″ thick, its edges must be routed to 0.25″ or less in thickness for installation.
When using a built-up or sculptured panel, an area adjacent to the door handles must be relieved to provide adequate clearance for fingers. The thicker the built-up panel, the more clearance is required.

DOOR PANEL CHART–SIDE-BY-SIDE REFRIGERATOR MODELS

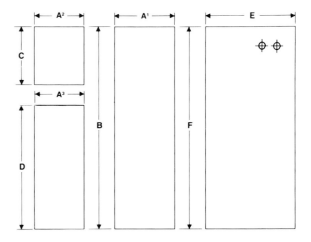

DESIGNER LINE TOP-MOUNT REFRIGERATOR FEATURE CHART

Exterior Overall Dimensions	JRT174	JRT192	JRT196	JRT216	JRT236	JRTD226
Height (add ½" for door hinge and hinge cover) (in.)	64½	65½	65½	65½	65½	65½
Width (closed) (in.)	29	31½	31 11/16	31 11/16	33 3/16	33 3/16
Width (doors open 90°; incl. handle) (in.)	30½	33	33	33	34½	34½
Depth (closed; excl. handle) (in.)	27⅝	27⅝	27⅞	30⅞	30⅞	30⅞
Depth (doors open 90°) (in.)	55 15/32	57 31/32	57 31/32	60 31/32	62 15/32	61 15/32
Shipping Weight (approx. lbs.)	230	245	250	270	285	310

Interior Capacities (cu. ft. AHAM)

Total Volume	16.50	18.60	18.50	20.90	22.50	22.00
Refrigerator Compartment Volume	11.71	12.90	12.83	14.54	15.61	15.15
Freezer Compartment Volume	4.82	5.67	5.67	6.39	6.80	6.36
Total Shelf Area (sq. ft.)	23.00	25.40	26.20	29.70	31.80	33.10

General Features

Jenn-Air Golden Product Warranty	•	•	•	•	•	•
White or Almond Textured Steel Doors[A]	•	•	•	•	•	•
Lefthand Door Available[B]						•
Reversible Doors	•	•	•	•	•	
Accepts Custom Front Panels[C]			•	•	•	•
Optional Black Door Panel Kit[C]			BDT21-02	BDT21-02	BDT23-02	BDT22D-02
Optional Decorator Trim Kit[C]			DTT21-02	DTT21-02	DTT23-02	DTT22-02
Optional White Trim Kit[C]						RDK226
Adjustable Easy-Roll Wheels	•	•	•	•	•	•
Foam Insulation	•	•	•	•	•	•
Refrigerator Light	•	•	•	•	•	•
160° Door Stop Position	•	•	•	•	•	•
Shelves with Three-Prong Supports		•	•	•	•	•
Roller Drawer System[D]						•
Crystal Gray Interior	•	•	•	•	•	
Crystal White Interior						•
Jenn-Air Designer Line Styling	•	•	•	•	•	
Jenn-Air Premier Designer Line Styling						•

Freezer Features

Deep Storage Door Shelves (F=full; S=split)	2	2	2	2	2	1F/2S
2-Position Shelf	•	•	•	•	•	•
Shelf Tender		•	•	•	•	•
2 Mini Cube Trays with Ice Service Bin	•	•	•	•	•	
Accepts Optional Ice Maker[E]	•	•	•	•	•	
Always Ice™ Automatic Ice Maker with Bin						•
Lighted Convenience Center (Chilled Water/Ice Dispenser)						•

Refrigerator Features

Total Shelves	4	5	5	5	5	5
Adjustable Cantilever Glass Shelves (S=split; F=full)	1F/2S	4S	4S	4S	4S	4S
Fixed Position Full Molded Shelf	1					
Fixed Position Glass Shelf		1	1	1	1	1
2-Bottle Foldaway Wine Rack					•	
Shelf-Mount Wine Rack						•
Sealed Crispers	2					1
Humidity-Controlled Sealed Crispers		2	2	2	2	1
Temp Control Drawer	•	•	•	•	•	•
Energy Saver Switch	•	•	•	•	•	•
Dairy Compartment with Butter Dish	1	1	1	1	2[F]	1
Fixed Deep Storage Door Shelves	3½	3½	1	1	1	1½
Adjustable/Lift-Off Deep Storage Door Shelves			5	5	4	3
Shelf Tender	•	•	•	•	•	•
Lift-Out Egg Storage (C=Caddy; R=Rack)	R	C	C	C	C	C
Door Shelf Cover					•	•

Custom Panel Dimensions with Existing Trim[A]
(All dimensions shown in inches)

Freezer Door Dimensions	JRT196	JRT216	JRT236	JRTD226
A	31 7/16	31 7/16	32 15/16	32 15/16
B	19⅞	19⅞	19⅞	19⅞

Refrigerator Door Dimensions

C	31 7/16	31 7/16	32 15/16	32 15/16
D	39⅞	39⅞	39⅞	39¼
E	–	–	–	16½
F	–	–	–	14⅝[B]

A. These dimensions apply to panels included in the optional Black Door Panel Kit and to any optional door panels of 0.125" thickness.
B. Dimension is 14 5/16 for lefthand refrigerator.

Custom Panel Dimensions with Decorator Trim Kit
(All dimensions shown in inches)

Freezer Door Dimensions	JRT196	JRT216	JRT236	JRTD226
A	31 3/16	31 3/16	32 11/16	32 11/16
B	19¼	19¼	19¼	19¼

Refrigerator Door Dimensions

C	31 3/16	31 3/16	32 11/16	32 11/16
D	39¼	39¼	39¼	39¼
E	–	–	–	16 3/16
F	–	–	–	14⅝[A]

A. Dimension is 14 5/16 for lefthand refrigerator.
If a panel is more than 0.25" thick, its edges must be routed to 0.25" or less in thickness for installation.
When using a built-up or sculptured panel, an area adjacent to the door handles must be relieved to provide adequate clearance for fingers. The thicker the built-up panel, the more clearance is required.

DOOR PANEL CHART–TOP-MOUNT REFRIGERATOR MODELS

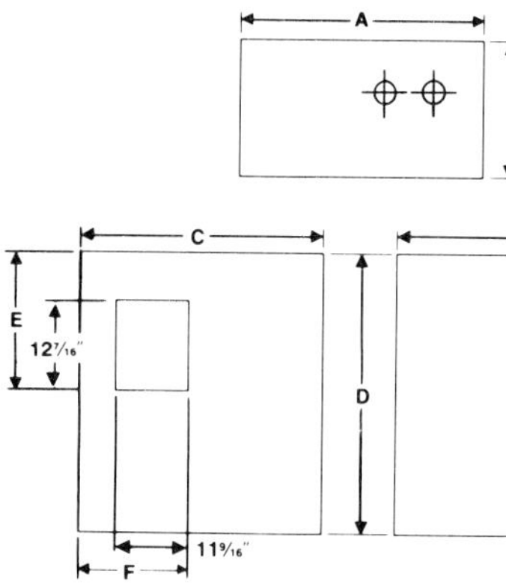

A. Add "W" to end of model number to indicate white cabinet; "L" to end of model number to indicate almond cabinet.
B. Add "L" to model number (before color indicator) to indicate lefthand door swing; "R" to indicate righthand door swing.
C. See above for door Trim Kit information. The optional White Trim Kit includes white tape for door handle inserts, white escutcheon and white Jenn-Air nameplate.
D. For smooth movement of all freezer and refrigerator drawers.
E. Order Model 1MT106.
F. Includes 2 dairy compartments, 1 butter dish.

Model Availability Dates:
JRT174 2nd quarter 1992

All Jenn-Air appliances are appropriately UL, AGA, CSA or CGA approved.

DESIGNER LINE DISHWASHER FEATURE CHART

BUILT-IN DISHWASHER FEATURES AND SPECIFICATIONS	DU430	DU466	DU486	DU506	DU599
Overall Height (min./max.) (in.)	34 35	34 35	34 35½	34 35½	34 35½
Overall Width (in.)	24	24	24	24	24
Overall Depth (excluding door depth) (in.)	23¼	23¼	24¹⁄₁₆	24¹⁄₁₆	24¹⁄₁₆
Custom Door Panel Insert Height (in.)	19⅛	19⅛	18⅜	18⅜	18⅜
Custom Door Panel Insert Width (in.)	23⁹⁄₁₆	23⁹⁄₁₆	23¹¹⁄₁₆	23¹¹⁄₁₆	23¹¹⁄₁₆
Custom Door Panel Insert Depth (in.)	¼	¼	¼	¼	¼
Accepts Custom Door Panels A	●	●	●	●	●
Access Panel Insert Height (in.)	3¹¹⁄₁₆	3¹¹⁄₁₆	4¹⁵⁄₁₆	4¹⁵⁄₁₆	4¹⁵⁄₁₆
Access Panel Insert Width (in.)	23⁹⁄₁₆	23⁹⁄₁₆	23¹¹⁄₁₆	23¹¹⁄₁₆	23¹¹⁄₁₆
Access Panel Insert Depth (in.)	¼	¼	¼	¼	¼
Fuse Requirements (amps) B	15	15	20	20	20
Water Supply C —p.s.i. —kg/sq. cm	15-120 1.06-8.44	15-120 1.06-8.44	15-120 1.06-8.44	15-120 1.06-8.44	15-120 1.06-8.44
Jenn-Air Golden Product Warranty	●	●	●	●	●
Heavy Wash Cycle	●	●	●	●	●
Normal Wash Cycle	●	●	●	●	●
Conserva Wash Cycle	●	●	●	●	●
Heated Dry	●	●	●	●	●
Rinse & Hold	●	●	●	●	●
Air Dry	●	●	●	●	●
Soft Food Disposer	●	●			
Food Disposer			●	●	●
Ultra-Mesh™ Filter D			●	●	●
Folding Upper Rack Dividers			●	●	●
Deep Upper Rack			●	●	●
Silverware Basket	●	●	●E	●E	●E
Metered Fill			●	●	●
Triple Sound Insulation			●	●	●
High Velocity Jetstream™ System			●	●	●
Porcelain Enamel Tub			●	●	●
Durable Plastic Tub	●	●			
4 Front Door Panel Colors Available F	●	●	●	●	●
Automatic Rinse Dispenser	●	●	●	●	●
Signal Light(s)			●	●	●
Built-In Water Heating Element	●	●	●	●	●
Cancel Cycle				●	●
Sani-Scrub Cycle				●	●
Delay Start				●	●
Electronic Touch Controls					●
Designer Line Styling		●	●	●	●
Color Availabilities (B=black, W=white)	B	B, W G	B	B	B, W

A. Installing ¼" custom door panels on Jenn-Air dishwasher Models DU430 and DU466 requires additional door panel trim kit. Product includes certificate for door panel trim kit (redeemable at no extra charge).
B. Electric supply (all models): 115 VAC, 60 Hz. All models U.L. listed.
C. ⅜" female pipe thread connection is attached to water valve. Water should be at 140°F when it enters dishwasher.
D. Only 100% filtered water is circulated over dishes.
E. Silverware basket contains small lidded items basket.
F. Models DU599 and DU466W include a reversible decorator front panel (black and white). Models DU430 and DU466 include a reversible panel (black and almond), plus a certificate which can be redeemed for a second reversible panel (white and harvest gold). All other models include four front door panel color options (black/white, almond/harvest gold).
G. For black dishwasher, order Model DU466. For white dishwasher, order Model DU466W.

Drain (all models): ½" I.D. flexible loop supplied (high drain loop on side).
Motor and Pump: Models DU486, DU506, DU599 — ⅓ h.p. reversible; direct-drive motor with high-efficiency pump. Models DU430 and DU466 — direct-drive motor with high-efficiency pump.

DESIGNER LINE TRASH COMPACTOR SPECIFICATIONS

TRASH COMPACTOR SPECIFICATIONS	TC406
Overall Height (in.) A	34¹⁄₁₆
Overall Width (in.)	15
Overall Depth (in.)	24
Cabinet Opening Height (min) (in.)	34⅜
Cabinet Opening Width (min) (in.)	15
Cabinet Opening Depth (min) (in.)	24
Custom Door Panel Insert Height (in.)	22¹⁵⁄₁₆
Custom Door Panel Insert Width (in.)	14⅝
Custom Door Panel Insert Depth (in.)	¼
Jenn-Air Golden Product Warranty	●
Colors Available (B=black, W=white)	B, W

A. Adjustable to 34¾". Toe plate also adjustable.

IMPORTANT: Because of continuing product improvements, Jenn-Air reserves the right to change specifications without notice. Dimensional specifications are provided for planning purposes only. For complete details see installation instructions packed with product before selecting cabinetry, making cutouts or beginning installation.

DESIGNER LINE 190° HOT WATER DISPENSER DIMENSIONS AND CONNECTIONS

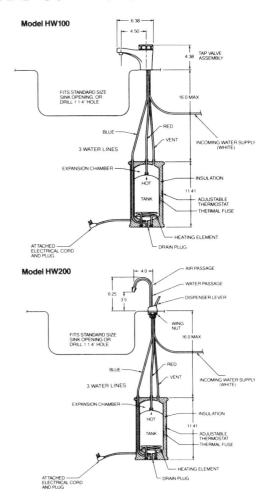

DESIGNER LINE DISPOSER FEATURE CHART

DISPOSER FEATURES AND SPECIFICATIONS	DELUXE MODELS			ECONOMY MODELS	
	GC440	GC460	GB460	GC410	GC431
Jenn-Air Golden Product Warranty	●	●	●	●	●
Quick-Mount Collar	●	●	●	●	●
½ H.P. Motor with Manual Reset	●	●	●	●	●
Continuous-Feed Operation	●	●		●	●
Batch-Feed Operation			●		
Dishwasher Drain Connection	●	●	●	●	●
Stainless Steel Sink Flange	●	●	●		
Sound Silencing Grinding Chamber	●	●	●		
Die-Cast Aluminum Grinding Chamber				●	●
Non-Corrosive Grinding Chamber	●	●	●		●
Nicron Shredder Ring	●	●	●		
Stainless Steel Shredder Ring					●
Galvanized Steel Shredder Ring				●	
Jam-Resistant Impeller Arms	●	●	●	●	●
2-360° Swivel Impellers				●	●
Positive Pressure Water Seal	●	●	●		
Space-Saver Design	●				

All Jenn-Air appliances are appropriately UL, AGA, CSA or CGA approved.

DUCTING DATA (GRILL-RANGES AND COOKTOPS)

DUCT LENGTH RECOMMENDATIONS (Maximum)[a]		
	5" Diameter[b]	6" Diameter or 3¼" x 10"[c]
All Electric[d]	10'[e]	60'
All Gas[f]	10'	60'

[a]**IMPORTANT:** See installation instructions shipped with product before selecting island cabinetry, making cutouts or beginning installation. Use 6" or 3¼" x 10" duct on island or peninsula installations. For best performance, it is suggested that no more than three 90° elbows be used with 6" or 3¼" x 10" duct. Each foot of flex duct counts as two feet of metal duct. Each flex elbow counts as two metal elbows. For longer duct runs of 31' to 60', the restricter ring on the blower inlet housing must be removed. 6" round or 3¼" x 10" duct must be used for ducting beyond 10' (up to 60').

[b]Count each 90° elbow as 4' of duct.

[c]Count each 90° elbow as 5' of duct.

[d]Ducting recommendations for updraft grill-ranges and updraft grill-range cooktops are dependent upon ducting requirements of range hood selected for updraft ventilation.

[e]When venting electric grill-ranges or cooktops, 5" diameter round duct may be used to vent straight out the back of the appliance and directly through the wall for 10' or less.

[f]When venting Model SEG196 and gas grill-range cooktops, 5" diameter duct must be used for runs of 10' or less.

THE LONG DUCT RUN

With Jenn-Air's more powerful blower, Jenn-Air downdraft grill ranges and grill-range cooktops can vent up to the equivalent of 60 feet.

Here's how it works.

For duct runs equivalent to 30' or less, install as received. For duct runs equivalent to 31' to 60', simply snap out the restricter ring on the blower inlet housing. Instantly, you have the power to vent up to the equivalent of 60' (using 6" round or 3¼" by 10" duct).

GRILL-RANGE COOKTOP DUCTING ACCESSORIES

Model A403 Surface Wall Cap—Single damper; down discharge. Fits 3¼" x 10" duct.

Model A405 Surface Wall Cap—Single spring-loaded damper; down discharge. Fits 5" diameter duct. Requires opening 5½" in diameter.

Model A406 Surface Wall Cap—Single spring-loaded damper; down discharge. Fits 6" diameter duct. Requires opening 6½" in diameter.

Model A453 Transition—5" round to 3¼" x 10" duct.

Model A456 Transition—5" to 6" round duct.

Model A463 Transition—6" round to 3¼" x 10" duct.

Model A495 Transition—90° angle for transition from 5" round to 3¼" x 10" duct.

Model A496 Transition—90° angle for transition from 6" round to 3¼" x 10" duct.

> **IMPORTANT**
> Downdraft grill-ranges and grill-range cooktops shown in this brochure are designed to be vented outdoors with 6" or 3¼" x 10" standard ducts. Short runs also may be ducted with 5" diameter duct. It is important that ducting instructions included with product be followed carefully. Failure to follow ducting recommendations or use recommended ducting accessories may result in substandard performance. Laundry-type wall caps never should be used.

TYPICAL COOKTOP DUCT ARRANGEMENTS
(Example shown, Expressions™ Collection)

TYPICAL GRILL-RANGE DUCT ARRANGEMENTS

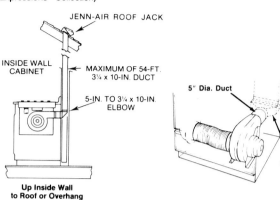

JENN-AIR ROOF JACK

INSIDE WALL CABINET

MAXIMUM OF 54-FT. 3¼ x 10-IN. DUCT

5-IN. TO 3¼ x 10-IN. ELBOW

5" Dia. Duct

A495

Up Inside Wall to Roof or Overhang

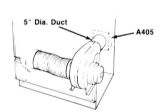

OUTSIDE WALL CABINET

5" Dia. Duct

A405

Directly to Outside

PENINSULA

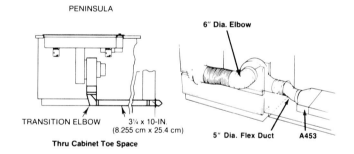

6" Dia. Elbow

TRANSITION ELBOW

3¼ x 10-IN. (8.255 cm x 25.4 cm)

5" Dia. Flex Duct

A453

Thru Cabinet Toe Space

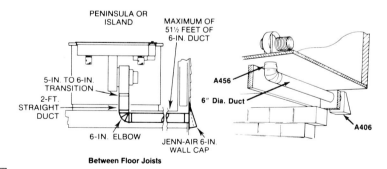

PENINSULA OR ISLAND

MAXIMUM OF 51½ FEET OF 6-IN. DUCT

5-IN. TO 6-IN. TRANSITION

2-FT. STRAIGHT DUCT

6-IN. ELBOW

JENN-AIR 6-IN. WALL CAP

A456

6" Dia. Duct

A406

Between Floor Joists

For venting up to the equivalent of 60', use standard steel ducting and elbows.

IMPORTANT: Because of continuing product improvements, Jenn-Air reserves the right to change specifications without notice. Dimensional specifications are provided for planning purposes only. For complete details see installation instructions packed with product before selecting cabinetry, making cutouts or beginning installation.

TYPICAL GRILL-RANGE DUCT ARRANGEMENTS

OPTIONAL GRILL-RANGE OR GRILL-RANGE COOKTOP DUCT ARRANGEMENT UNDER CONCRETE SLABª

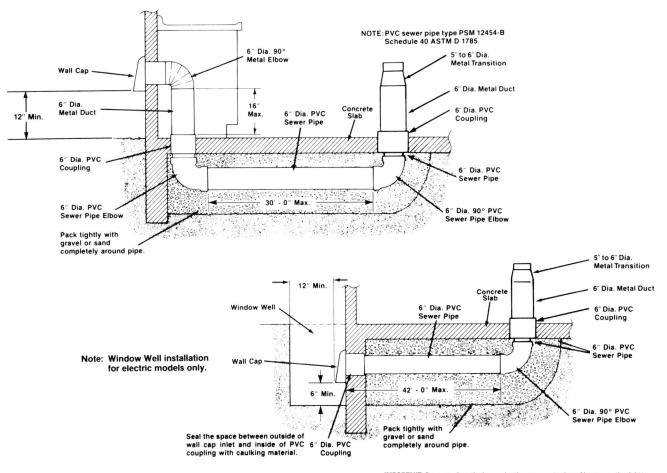

NOTE: PVC sewer pipe type PSM 12454-B
Schedule 40 ASTM D 1785.

Wall Cap

6" Dia. 90° Metal Elbow

5" to 6" Dia. Metal Transition

6" Dia. Metal Duct

6" Dia. Metal Duct

12" Min.

16" Max.

6" Dia. PVC Sewer Pipe

Concrete Slab

6" Dia. PVC Coupling

6" Dia. PVC Coupling

6" Dia. PVC Sewer Pipe

6" Dia. PVC Sewer Pipe Elbow

30' - 0" Max.

6" Dia. 90° PVC Sewer Pipe Elbow

Pack tightly with gravel or sand completely around pipe.

Note: Window Well installation for electric models only.

12" Min.

Window Well

Wall Cap

Concrete Slab

6" Dia. PVC Sewer Pipe

5" to 6" Dia. Metal Transition

6" Dia. Metal Duct

6" Dia. PVC Coupling

6" Dia. PVC Sewer Pipe

6" Min.

42' - 0" Max.

6" Dia. 90° PVC Sewer Pipe Elbow

Seal the space between outside of wall cap inlet and inside of PVC coupling with caulking material.

6" Dia. PVC Coupling

Pack tightly with gravel or sand completely around pipe.

ªConfiguration shown above is applicable only to grill-range or grill-range cooktop installation into slab construction. Using PVC ducting (vs. metal ducting) will reduce the maximum duct run recommendations to less than 60 equivalent feet.

IMPORTANT: Because of continuing product improvements, Jenn-Air reserves the right to change specifications without notice. Dimensional specifications are provided for planning purposes only. For complete details see installation instructions packed with product before selecting cabinetry, making cutouts or beginning installation.

DO	DON'T
Use 5" (12.7 cm), 6" (15.24 cm), or 3¼" x 10" (8.255 cm x 25.4 cm), pipe as recommended for your model	Use 4" (10.16 cm) dryer vent pipe or flex duct *
Use recommended wall caps	Use laundry type wall cap
Use no more than one 90° elbow with five inch (12.7 cm) duct or three 90° elbows with six inch (15.2 cm) or 3¼" x 10" (8.255 cm x 25.4 cm) duct.	Over run your system with too many bends and turns.
Duct system to the outside	Vent into an attic or crawl space
Mix 6" (15.24 cm) duct and 3¼" x 10" duct (8.255 cm x 25.4 cm) within the same system if necessary	Reduce back to 5" (12.7 cm) system after using 6" (15.24 cm) or 3¼" x 10" (8.255 cm x 25.4 cm).
Tape all joints securely with several wraps of tape	Butt joints, always use male-female connections in direction of flow.
Use one unit per duct system.	Exhaust more than one unit into a single system.

*Although not recommended, 5" or 6" metal flex duct may be used. Due to the irregular surface of flexible ducting, each foot of flex duct counts as two (2) feet of regular metal duct. Also, each elbow made in flex duct would count twice as much as standard metal elbow. The best idea with flexible ducting is to keep it as short and as straight as possible.

WALL CAPS/THERMAL BREAKS

Part 708786
Fits 5" (12.7 cm) Round Duct. Adds 2 ft. to duct length calculation.

PART 715557
Fits 6" (15.24 cm) Round Duct. Adds 2 ft. to duct length calculation.

MODEL A405
Fits 5" (12.7 cm) Round Duct. Requires 5¼" (13.34 cm) Dia. opening.

MODEL A406
Fits 6" (15.24 cm) Round Duct. Requires 6¼" (15.875 cm) Dia. opening.

MODEL A403
Single-damper, down discharge to fit 3¼" x 10" (8.255 cm x 25.4 cm) duct.

LEIGH PRODUCTS
P/N 5950
Roof Jack 10" x 10" (25.4 cm x 25.4 cm)

Model S136 with optional Model A100 cartridge.

Constantly recirculating air of the convection oven featured on most Jenn-Air grill-ranges and wall ovens, cooks foods more quickly. Meats are more flavorful and juicy, baked goods more golden-browned.

You and your family will enjoy delicious indoor grilling with the standard grill element and downdraft ventilation that grill-range **Model S136** features. Its convertible cooktop also accepts optional cartridges and accessories like the wok and "big-pot" canning element. You'll find that electronic-clock-controlled cooking and self-cleaning make the dependable bake/broil oven even more user friendly. And you can choose free-standing or slide-in installation—whichever suits your kitchen decor best. Black or white (shown).

U*pdraft* GRILL-RANGE

Even if your kitchen won't accommodate downdraft ventilation, the **Model SU146** updraft grill-range can add Jenn-Air quality and versatility to your cooking. Try out the optional cartridges and accessories: they'll multiply your options. Grill indoors with one of our high-performance ducted range hoods or over-the-range microwave ovens. Explore the possibilities of the **Selective-Use™ convection and bake/broil oven**. It has electronic oven controls, clock-controlled cooking and cleaning, and automatic self-clean door-lock mechanism. Free-standing or slide-in installation. Black.

Model SU146 with optional Model A100 cartridge.

DESIGNER LINE OPTIONAL CARTRIDGES, GAS MODULE AND ACCESSORIES[a]

Our popular optional grill-range and cooktop cartridges, modules and accessories
help build a complete cooking system with the flexibility to make every meal a masterpiece.

Solid Element Cartridge **Model A106**.[b] Cast iron elements heat evenly, retain heat. With 25% more wattage, the large UltraPower™[c] element heats up fast. Easy-clean glass cartridge surface. Black or white (shown).

Conventional Coil Cartridge **Model A100**. Accepts wok and "big-pot" canning accessories. Black porcelain, white porcelain (shown) or stainless steel.

Radiant Element Cartridge **Model A121**. This sleek beauty delivers high performance cooking on an easy-to-clean translucent glass-ceramic surface. Quick-Start™ heating elements are ready to use in seconds. Black, Pearl White[d] (shown).

Grill Cover Accessory **Model A341/ AG341**. Covers your grill when it is not in use. Black or white. Electric (shown) or gas.

Griddle Accessory **Model A302/ AG302**. Self-draining, family-sized, featuring superior nonstick DuPont SilverStone SUPRA®. Electric (shown) or gas.

Cooker-Steamer Accessory **Model A335**. Poach, blanch, steam or stew in this cooker-steamer on your downdraft electric grill-range or convertible cooktop. Includes see-through cover, two-position basket with handles.

[a] Use with Designer Line cooktops and grill-ranges only. See Pages 8-9 for Expressions™ Collection cartridges and accessories. Electric grill accessories are designed for use ONLY with electric cooktops. Gas grill accessories are designed for use ONLY with gas cooktops. Cartridges designated "electric" are for use with electric powered grill-ranges and cooktops and retrofit all Jenn-Air grill-ranges and cooktops manufactured since 1977.
[b] Not shown is Model A105 which contains two standard solid elements with stainless steel trim ring. The new cartridge Model A106 with UltraPower™ element will be available 3rd quarter 1992.
[c] UltraPower™ is a trademark of E.G.O. Products, Inc.
[d] Pearl White available 3rd quarter 1992.

See Page 7A for complete Designer Line cartridge, module and accessory specifications and features.

Model A125[a] halogen cartridge with Haloring™[b] elements has infra-red lamps for optimum heat distribution. Instant visual response when turned on. Wipe-clean glass-ceramic surface. Black (shown) or Pearl White.

Gas Two-Burner Module **Model AG200**. Four-burner versatility for your gas cooktop. Black (shown) or white.[c]

Grill Assembly **Model A158/AG150**. Electric includes Energy-Saver grill element with two grill rocks, two grill grates and storage tray. Gas includes E-ven Heat™ grill burner, two grill grates and storage tray. Electric (shown) or gas.

Rotiss-Kebab Accessory **Model A312**. This motor-driven rotisserie turns four shish kebabs or other foods automatically on your electric grill. Kebab wheels, Kebab skewers, spit, rotisserie meat skewers, and motor included.

Wok Accessory **Model A141A/AG340**. Healthful stir-frying and steaming in a fine carbon steel wok with nonstick finish. Lid, steaming rack and rice paddles included. Electric (shown) or gas.

"Big-Pot" Canning Element Accessory **Model A145A**. You'll want this one for canning or big cooking jobs with pots over 8" diameter. Replaces large conventional coil element.

[a] Pearl White available 3rd quarter 1992.
[b] Haloring™ is a trademark of Ceramaspeed Limited.
[c] White 2-burner module availabe 2nd quarter 1992. Grates are black.

DESIGNER LINE *Combination* WALL OVENS

Model W276[a] opens your way to kitchen mastery through user-friendly electronic controls. For the ease and speed of microwave cooking, the upper oven features electronic touch controls, ten power levels plus defrost, electronic clock with timer and a temperature probe. The electronic oven controls of the lower **Selective-Use™ convection and bake/broil oven** are an easy two steps to set and include convenient time functions such as clock-controlled radiant or convection cooking and self-cleaning. Black or white (both shown).

Model W276 in white.

Model W276 (27" wide).

[a]Refer to page 8A for information on model variations WM277, WM236 and WM227.

See Pages 8A-9A for complete Designer Line wall oven specifications and features.

Cook four ways with **Model W236**[a]. Its upper microwave oven has electronic touch controls, ten power levels plus defrost, electronic clock with timer and a temperature probe. While you're microwaving above, the large capacity **Selectiver-Use™ convection and bake/broil oven** lets you choose the cooking method you prefer at the turn of a dial. Lower oven includes electronic-clock-controlled cooking and self-cleaning. Black or white (shown).

Model W236 (27" wide).

Model W227 (27" wide).

If you prefer a combination wall oven with a radiant bake/broil oven below the microwave, we recommend **Model W227**[a]. The upper micorwave oven features electronic touch controls, ten power levels plus defrost, electronic clock with timer and a temperature probe. The large-capacity lower bake/broil oven has electronic-clock-controlled baking and self-cleaning. Black (shown) or white.

23

DESIGNER LINE *Double* WALL OVENS

Model W256 (27″ wide).

Model W206 (27″ wide).

Model W256 large-capacity double wall oven offers you bake/broil cooking in the lower oven and our versatile Selective-Use™ convection and bake/broil oven above. Both ovens have electronic oven controls, memory programming/programming recall, and clock-controlled cooking and self-cleaning. Doors lock automatically during self-cleaning function. The Selective-Use™ oven includes a temperature probe for accurate cooking. Black or white (shown).

Here's another way to double your cooking enjoyment: **Model W206.** A self-cleaning Selective-Use™ convection and bake/broil oven above, plus a standard-clean radiant bake/broil oven below. The upper oven features an electronic clock with timer for clock-controlled cooking and self-cleaning. The lower oven has a porcelain cavity. Black (shown) or white.

See Pages 8A-9A for complete Designer Line wall oven specifications and features.

DESIGNER LINE
Gas WALL OVEN

If you're looking for a wall oven that will bring Jenn-Air quality to your gas kitchen, space-saving **Model WG206** (below) is for you. It has a separate broiler compartment below and oven above. A digital clock times cooking, and an electronic pilotless ignition saves energy. Uses natural gas or converts to LP. Black.

Model W216 (24″ wide).

Even if your space is limited, you can enjoy the pleasures of Jenn-Air double wall oven cooking. Our 24″-wide **Model W216** allows you to prepare varied dishes at the same time in its upper bake/broil oven and lower bake oven. Includes an electronic clock with timer that controls cooking and self-cleaning of the upper oven (lower oven is standard-clean). Black.

Gas Model WG206 with separate broiler compartment (24″ wide).

Designer Line *Single* Wall Ovens

Here's the single wall oven that does it all. **Model W156** large capacity **Selective-Use™ convection and bake/broil oven** switches from convection to conventional radiant cooking with only a fingertip's pressure on the electronic oven controls. Other user-friendly features include memory programming/programming recall and a temperature probe for delicious results. Electronic-clock-controlled cooking and self-cleaning are standard. Black or white (shown).

Model W156 (27" wide).

Model W136 (27" wide).

Model W136 is our finest large capacity **Selective-Use™ convection and bake/broil oven** with conventional controls. It allows you to change from convection to bake/broil cooking at the turn of a dial, and offers both electronic-clock-controlled cooking and self-cleaning. Now you can convection bake whenever you want—just as the finest European chefs do. Black or white (shown).

If you prefer a 27" wide wall oven with radiant bake/broil cooking only, we suggest **Model W106** (not shown). It has all the features of Model W136 without convection capabilities. Black or white.

See Pages 8A-9A for complete Designer Line wall oven specifications and features.

Model W130 (30" wide) with Model CCR466 cooktop.

Our large-capacity **Model W130** (left) is the perfect oven to accompany your Jenn-Air cooktop. Performs beautifully on its own as well. The bake/broil oven is 30" wide, with an electronic clock and timer that control cooking and self-cleaning. Enjoy undercounter or in-wall installation with this versatile oven. Black (shown) or white.

If you are looking for a conventional radiant oven that can slip into the slimmest space, select **Model W116** (below). It includes performance features, such as electronic-clock-controlled cooking and self-cleaning, catalytic smoke eliminator and formed rack guides. A Jenn-Air oven just right for your kitchen—and just a slender 24" wide. Black.

Convection cooking, featured on many Jenn-Air grill-ranges and wall ovens, circulates fan-forced hot air to decrease cooking times and/or temperatures. Enjoy the convenience of three-rack cooking, juicier roasts, golden-brown baked goods.

Model W116 (24" wide).

Designer Line Microwave Ovens

Pair up your Jenn-Air wall oven with built-in **Model M167** microwave, or use it on your countertop. Its 1.1 cubic foot capacity will take on your biggest cooking tasks. In addition to the advanced programming features you want—like two-stage memory and four preprogrammed cook codes—the 750-watt oven includes a popcorn pad and removable glass tray and oven rack.

For a built-in look, use optional trim kits to install **Model M167** into the wall. Trim Kits are available for 24", 27" and 30" cabinets: **Model A424** (24") in black; **Model A526** (27") in black or white; **Model A530** (27") in white (has chrome trim around outer edge); and **Model A626** (30") in black or white.

Model M167 with Model A526 trim kit.

Model M167 in black.

Model M446.

Model M437.

Model M446 installs over all Jenn-Air updraft gas and electric grilling cooktops and grill-ranges. You'll enjoy its built-in high-performance exhaust system and smoke shield as well as the 1.0 cubic foot capacity and 750 watts. Programming is trouble-free with command prompts and electronic touch controls. Black.

Over-the-range microwave **Model M437** works beautifully above our non-grilling gas and electric updraft grill-ranges and cooktops, installs over our downdraft grill-ranges and cooktops as well. It has a built-in exterior exhaust system that can be converted for recirculating ventilation, if desired. Features 1.0 cubic foot capacity, 750 watts of power and a below-oven work surface light. Electronic touch controls let you program with ease. Black or white (shown).

Over-the-range microwave **Model M417** (not shown) has most of the same features as Model M437 in a nonventilated microwave oven. Your Jenn-Air downdraft grill-range or cooktop will look even better topped off with its 1.0 cubic foot capacity, 750 watts of power, electronic touch controls and below-oven work surface light. Black.

See Page 10A for complete Designer Line microwave oven specifications and features.

Model RH480.

Model RH480 is a high-performance hood designed for use with your updraft cooktop. Features touch controls, variable speed fan and an attractive black-glass-look front panel. Rated 440 CFM (vertical rectangular), 410 CFM (horizontal rectangular). Black, white, almond enamel (shown) or stainless steel.

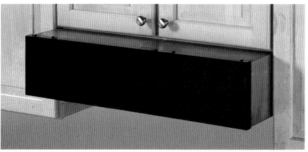

Model RH440.

High-performance design makes **Model RH440** another powerful choice for use with updraft cooktops. Black-glass-look front panel and variable speed fan. Rated 440 CFM (vertical rectangular), 410 CFM (horizontal rectangular). Black (shown), white, almond enamel or stainless steel.

Model RH400 (not shown) offers the power and advantages of Model RH440 and can be installed under custom cabinetry.

Model RH800.

Pull out the telescoping Hidavent™ canopy of our **Model RH800**[a] from its under-cabinet compartment and the fan starts automatically. Remembers selected fan setting, too. Rated 350 CFM (vertical rectangular or horizontal rectangular). Black (shown) or white.

[a] For use with non-grilling cooktops.

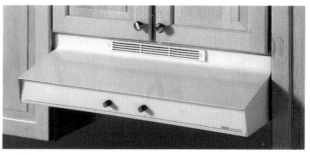

Model RH206.

Model RH206[a] has a variable speed fan, allows vertical or horizontal discharge or ductless installation with charcoal filter. Rated 300 CFM (vertical round), 200 CFM (vertical rectangular), 180 CFM (horizontal rectangular). White with gray controls.

Model RH200[a] (not shown) includes all the features of Model RH206 plus a black-glass-look front panel. Black, almond enamel or stainless steel.

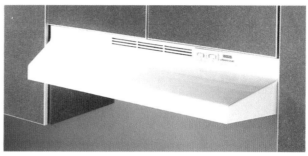

Model RH180.

Two fan speeds whisk odors away when you choose **Model RH180**[a]. This versatile model can ventilate indoors with charcoal filter or ventilate outside either vertically or horizontally. Rated 180 CFM (vertical round). Black, white (shown), almond enamel or stainless steel.

Model RH186[a] (not shown) has same features as RH180 but is 36" wide. Available in black or white.

See Page 11A for complete Designer Line range hood specifications and features.

DESIGNER LINE *Side-By-Side* REFRIGERATORS

Model JRSD246.

Because you appreciate the best, we present **Model JRSD246** (above), with Jenn-Air *Premier Designer Line* styling, 24 cubic feet of refrigerated volume and our unique roller drawer system. Well-organized special compartments like the humidity-controlled crisper, Temp Control Drawer and Bulk Storage freezer basket. Our convenient Always Ice™ Automatic Ice Maker, lighted Convenience Center and adjustable tempered glass shelves. And—as attractive as it is useful—this roomy side-by-side accepts our optional White Trim Kit, Black Door Panel Kit or your own custom front panels with our Decorator Trim Kit. White or almond textured steel doors.

All Jenn-Air Designer Line side-by-side refrigerators accept the Black Door Panel Kit. Shown here, Model JRSD246 with Black Door Panel Kit Model BDS24D-02.

Model JRSD226.

With a lighted Convenience Center, Deli Drawer, Temp Control Drawer and Bulk Storage freezer drawer, **Model JRSD226** adds 22 cubic feet of refrigerated volume to your kitchen—and does it beautifully. Features include Always Ice™ Automatic Ice Maker, adjustable tempered glass refrigerator shelves, crisper and wine rack. This refrigerator is at home in any decor—and you can personalize it with our optional White Trim Kit, Black Door Panel Kit or your own custom front panels with our Decorator Trim Kit. White or almond textured steel doors.

Every Jenn-Air side-by-side refrigerator features three adjustable/lift-off deep storage door shelves, two with easy-off fronts.

A convenient lift-out egg caddy is included with every side-by-side refrigerator you see here.

Model JRS226 is a fine addition to your kitchen, with Temp Control and Deli Drawers and a crisper making the most of its 22 cubic feet of refrigerator space. The freezer includes a handy Bulk Storage drawer and six Deep Storage door shelves with easy-off fronts. Adjustable tempered glass shelves make this refrigerator easy to use. It's customizable with optional automatic ice maker or Black Door Panel Kit. Or add custom-designed front panels with our Decorator Trim Kit for a one-of-a-kind look. White or almond textured steel doors.

Model JRS226.

DESIGNER LINE *Top-Mount* REFRIGERATORS

An integral addition to any kitchen decor, **Model JRTD226** accepts optional White Trim Kit, Black Door Panel Kit, custom front panels with our Decorator Trim Kit, or optional lefthand door. And its *Premier Designer Line* Styling is much more than skin-deep. Inside, 22 cubic feet of refrigerated volume keep foods at their best in our Temp Control Drawer, two crispers (one with humidity control) and four adjustable cantilevered tempered glass refrigerator shelves. Lighted Convenience Center and Always Ice™ Automatic Ice Maker are standard. White or almond textured steel doors.

Model JRTD226.

The specially designed roller drawer system featured on Model JRTD226 lets refrigerator drawers slide smoothly.

Model JRT236.

Maximum storage and versatile function distinguish **Model JRT236**. It boasts 23 cubic feet of refrigerated volume, including Temp Control Drawer and two humidity-controlled crispers, wine rack, four adjustable cantilevered tempered glass refrigerator shelves and two Deep Storage freezer door shelves. Accepts optional Automatic Ice Maker. Adapts to any kitchen style, too, because it accepts both optional White Trim Kit and Black Door Panel Kit, along with custom front panels using our Decorator Trim Kit. Locate it wherever you like: the reversible door opens on the right or left hand to allow flexible installation. White or almond textured steel doors.

See Page 13A for complete Designer Line top-mount refrigerator specifications and features.

Model JRTD226 with optional 0.25" custom wood panel (installed with optional Decorator Trim Kit Model DTT22-02; White Trim Kit Model RDK226W also shown).

Our Temp Control Drawer provides adjustable cooling levels for extra-cool refrigerator storage.

Model JRT196 packs features into 19 cubic feet of refrigerated volume. Four adjustable cantilevered tempered glass refrigerator shelves, two Deep Storage freezer door shelves, a Temp Control Drawer and two humidity-controlled crispers. Our optional Black Door Panel Kit or Decorator Trim Kit for custom front panels. And doors that open on the right or left hand. Ready to accept our optional Automatic Ice Maker. White or almond textured steel doors.

Model JRT216 (not shown) offers the features of Model JRT196 with 21 cubic foot capacity. White or almond textured steel doors.

Model JRT174[a] (not shown) includes 17 cubic foot capacity, two Deep Storage freezer door shelves, 3½ Deep Storage refrigerator door shelves and four refrigerator shelves (3 glass, 1 molded), plus lift-out egg rack. Temp Control Drawer, two crispers. Accepts optional Automatic Ice Maker. White or almond textured steel doors.

Model JRT192.

Model JRT192 has all the hallmarks of Jenn-Air quality. 19 cubic foot capacity, two humidity-controlled crispers, Temp Control Drawer and lift-out egg caddy. Four adjustable cantilevered refrigerator shelves. Two Deep Storage freezer door shelves. Accepts optional Automatic Ice Maker. White or almond textured steel doors.

Model JRT196.

[a] Available 2nd quarter 1992.

DESIGNER LINE DISHWASHERS

Model DU599 with white control panel.

Gentle enough for your fine china, tough enough to make utensils shine, Jenn-Air dishwashers **Model DU599** in white and black, does the job beautifully. Comes in your choice of four front door panel colors and accepts custom door panels to coordinate with most any kitchen style. Triple insulation makes it quiet. And design expertise makes it just about perfect for the most specialized washing, with high-velocity Jetstream™ cleaning system, food disposer, deep upper rack with fold-down dividers and silverware basket (with lidded small items basket), porcelain enamel tub, Ultra-Mesh™ water filter and Sani-Scrub cycle. All the features you want—plus 12-hour delay start, user-friendly electronic touch controls and signal lights to help you get the most from them.

Model DU506 is another multi-talented kitchen helper. It has 8-hour delay start, triple sound insulation, high-velocity Jetstream™ cleaning system and a food disposer. The porcelain enamel tub and deep upper rack with fold-down dividers and silverware basket (with lidded small items basket) are durable and functional. For top cleaning, you'll appreciate the Ultra-Mesh™ filter and Sani-Scrub cycle. Black control panel.

Model DU486 pampers dinnerware at heavy, normal and Conserva Wash cycles as well as heated and air dry. Its high-velocity Jetstream™ cleaning system and Ultra-Mesh™ filter make dishes sparkle. The deep upper rack with fold-down dividers and silverware basket (with lidded small items basket) keeps everything in place. Includes triple sound insulation, porcelain enamel tub and food disposer. Black control panel.

Three wash cycles (heavy, normal and Conserva Wash) plus heated dry and air dry are at your service with **Model DU466.** A durable plastic tub, soft food disposer, deep upper rack and silverware basket make it an excellent choice for your Jenn-Air kitchen. Black or white (shown) control panel.

Model DU430 Traditional Line dishwasher has everything you want in a basic dishwasher, plus Jenn-Air quality you can trust. Heavy, normal and Conserva Wash cycles, heated and air dry. Soft food disposer, deep upper rack, rinse dispenser and durable plastic tub. Black control panel.

Model DU599 with black control panel.

Model DU506.

Model DU486,

Model DU466 with white control panel.

Model DU430.

See Page 14A for complete Designer Line/Traditional dishwasher specifications and features.

COMPACTOR

Cut kitchen waste down to size: it's easy with Jenn-Air compactor **Model TC406.** Packs a week's trash from a family of four into one easy-carry package. Powerful, fast—it monitors itself with tilt-sensing anti-jam sensor and controls easily with toe release bar and fingertip handle. More than just functional, this compactor features a built-in solid air freshener compartment and comes with two reversible front panels (black/white, almond/harvest gold). Or install custom wood panels, if you prefer. Black or white (shown) control panel.

Model TC406.

DISPOSERS

Jenn-Air disposers whisk scraps and messes out of your way with 1/2 h.p. motor (manual reset) and jam-resistant impeller arms. Choose continuous feed and space-saver design with deluxe **Model GC440** or continuous feed with deluxe **Model GC460.** Deluxe **Model GB460** features batch feed. All three include a nicron shredder ring and are tough enough to grind nails in their sound-silencing non-corrosive grinding chambers. Our economy disposers do a great job as well, with continuous feed design and die-cast aluminum grinding chambers. Economy **Model GC410** features a galvanized steel shredder ring; **Model GC431**, a stainless steel shredder ring.

Deluxe disposers: Models GC440, GC460, GB460.
Economy disposers: Models GC410, GC431.

Model HW200 in black.

HOT WATER DISPENSERS

Save time, save steps with our 190° hot water dispenser. Delivers hot water at a touch in seconds, with a capacity of up to 60 cups an hour. Tops in installation and performance, too: a space-saving compact under-sink tank taps into your existing cold water supply, and the snap-action thermostat adjusts from 140°F to 200°F. Black, white or low-profile chrome (all shown).

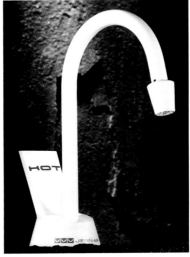

Model HW200 in white.

Model HW100 in low-profile chrome.

JENN-AIR GOLDEN PRODUCT WARRANTY HIGHLIGHTS
All Jenn-Air appliances carry a minimum warranty of:

1ST YEAR FULL WARRANTY PARTS & LABOR
2ND YEAR LIMITED WARRANTY PARTS ONLY

PLUS AN EXTENDED WARRANTY APPLIES TO THESE SPECIFIC PRODUCTS:

Electronic Control Cooktops, Grill-Ranges and Wall Ovens — 2nd year limited warranty (parts and labor) on any part of the electronic control panel.

Wall Oven with Microwave or Microwave Oven — 2nd year limited warranty (parts and labor), 3rd through 5th year limited warranty (parts and labor) on 8 major components of microwave oven.

Glass Ceramic Cooktop Cartridge — 3rd year limited warranty on glass-ceramic surface used in cooktop cartridges (parts only) if it fails due to thermal breakage.

Cast Iron Solid Elements (installed in cooktops, ranges or accessories) — 3rd through 5th years limited warranty (parts only) on solid elements.

Refrigerators — 2nd through 5th years limited warranty on any part of the refrigeration system (compressor, evaporator, condenser, or connecting tubing). Limited warranty covers repair of any break in interior liner excluding door liner. This extended warranty is limited to parts plus installation. Owner pays for service calls or trip charge to analyze system failure. Owner also is responsible for any shipping charges incurred (if applicable).

Dishwashers (all models) — 3rd through 5th years limited warranty (parts only).
- Electronic control panel components.
- Cabinet rust and wash system.

3rd through 10th years limited warranty (parts only).
- Dishwasher tub and door liner if leak develops due to rust or corrosion.

Food Waste Disposers — (Models GB460, GC460, GC440) — 3rd through 5th years limited warranty (parts only).

Warranties begin on the date of purchase.

THE ABOVE ARE WARRANTY HIGHLIGHTS. FOR COMPLETE WARRANTY INFORMATION, SEE YOUR JENN-AIR DEALER.

For the name of your nearest dealer call 1-800-JENN-AIR.

▨▨▨ JENN-AIR

3035 SHADELAND, INDIANAPOLIS, INDIANA 46226-0901
U.S. & Foreign Patents & Patents Pending
Specifications subject to change without notice.
Copyright 1992, Jenn-Air Company.

Shown on cover: Cabinets — QUALITY CUSTOM KITCHENS, INC. , New Holland, PA.
Flooring — Majestic Marble Imports, Distributors of Azuvi Tile, Indianapolis, IN.
Windows — Beveled Glass Designs, Indianapolis, IN.

Printed in U.S.A. REV. 4/92 Cat. 488L.

KitchenAid®

ARCHITECT SERIES

THE LOOK OF UNDERSTATED ELEGANCE. THE CAREFUL ATTENTION TO DETAIL THAT MAKES ANY CHOICE SEEM MADE-TO-ORDER FOR YOUR HOME. THE PERFORMANCE YOU EXPECT WHEN YOU SEE THE KITCHENAID NAME. THEY'RE ALL YOURS WHEN YOU CHOOSE APPLIANCES FROM TODAY'S ARCHITECT SERIES.

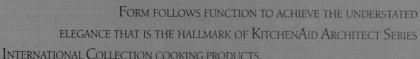

FORM FOLLOWS FUNCTION TO ACHIEVE THE UNDERSTATED ELEGANCE THAT IS THE HALLMARK OF KitchenAid Architect Series International Collection cooking products.

THE SELF-CLEANING 30-INCH OVEN, AVAILABLE IN CONVENTIONAL THERMAL OR VERSATILE Thermal-Convection™ VERSIONS, IS DESIGNED FOR FLUSH INSTALLATION IN American OR European-STYLE CABINETS OR UNDER A COUNTERTOP. Push-PUSH SELECTOR AND THERMOSTAT CONTROLS AND AN ELECTRONIC CLOCK GIVE YOU COMPLETE COOKING AND CLEANING FLEXIBILITY. THE CERAMIC GLASS COOKTOP WITH HALOGEN AND/OR RADIANT ELEMENTS, AVAILABLE IN 30-INCH AND 36-INCH SIZES, INSTALLS FLUSH TO COUNTERTOP FOR A SMOOTH, UNINTERRUPTED LINE THAT PLEASES THE EYE AND MAKES CLEANUP EASY. HALOGEN ELEMENTS PROVIDE INSTANT VISUAL RESPONSE, WHILE DUAL-CIRCUIT RADIANT ELEMENTS GIVE YOU A CHOICE OF COOKING SPEEDS.

INSPIRED CHOICES FOR YOUR MODERN KITCHEN, MODEL KEBN107Y THERMAL-CONVECTION OVEN IS SHOWN INSTALLED UNDER MODEL KECN507Y 30-INCH COOKTOP. THE BLACK CERAMIC GLASS SURFACE OF THE COOKTOP ECHOES THE MIRRORED BLACK DOOR OF THE STAINLESS STEEL OVEN. BACKLIGHTED CONTROLS COMPLETE THE MODERN LOOK.

INTERNATIONAL COLLECTION COOKING PRODUCTS

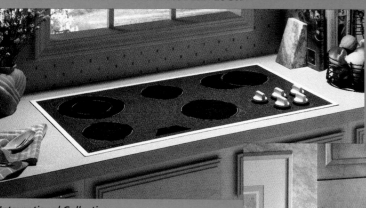

International Collection Model KECN567Y 36-inch cooktop increases cooking capacity with a fifth radiant element. Both 30-inch and 36-inch cooktops come in White or Black.

International Collection Thermal-Convection™ Oven is equally at home in this wall installation. Shown here in White, it is also available in Black or Stainless Steel styling.

THE DISHWASHER YOU'VE ALWAYS WANTED IS NOW YOURS
IN THE NEW KITCHENAID INTERNATIONAL COLLECTION. ELEGANTLY
EFFICIENT, THIS NEW DISHWASHER COMBINES A PREMIUM STAINLESS STEEL INTERIOR
WITH OUTSTANDING PERFORMANCE AND SLEEK STYLING THAT COMPLEMENTS BOTH
AMERICAN AND EUROPEAN-STYLE CABINETRY.

YOUR CONVERSATIONS WON'T HAVE TO COMPETE WITH THE DISHWASHER
WHEN YOU CHOOSE THE NEW KITCHENAID INTERNATIONAL
COLLECTION DISHWASHER; IT OPERATES AT A NOISE
LEVEL SLIGHTLY ABOVE A HUM. ITS SOPHISTICATED
STYLING IS VIVID EVIDENCE OF AN ATTENTION TO
DETAIL THAT DOESN'T STOP WITH APPEARANCE. THE
NEW VARIABLE WASH SYSTEM ACTUALLY MEASURES
AND ADJUSTS SPRAY PRESSURE TO DELIVER OUTSTAND-
ING PERFORMANCE EVEN WITH HEAVILY SOILED
UTENSILS. YET WATER USAGE IS MINIMAL... LESS THAN
SIX GALLONS IN THE NORMAL CYCLE. AND THAT
MEANS REAL SAVINGS FOR YOU.

IT ALL ADDS UP TO A MOST EXCITING DISHWASHER...
A KITCHENAID DISHWASHER, OF COURSE.

INTERNATIONAL COLLECTION DISHWASHERS

*International Collection Dishwasher Model KUDN230Y,
shown with optional European Toe-Kick Kit, is available
in your choice of immaculate all-white or dramatic
all-black styling.*

ARCHITECT SERIES DISHWASHERS CONTINUE THE TRADITION
FOR OUTSTANDING ATTENTION TO DETAIL THAT HAS DISTINGUISHED
KITCHENAID DISHWASHERS SINCE 1949. FOR EXAMPLE, A SIX-INCH HIGH CONTROL
PANEL MATCHES CABINET DRAWER HEIGHT, SO CABINETS AND DISHWASHER FLOW TOGETHER
IN AN UNINTERRUPTED LINE. YOU CAN TAKE YOUR CHOICE OF COLOR-COORDINATED
WHITE, ALMOND OR BLACK STYLING. A BUILT-IN TRIM FRAME ACCEPTS CUSTOM
PANELS FOR A TRULY INTEGRATED APPEARANCE. PERFORMANCE IS TOP
DRAWER, TOO. DISHES ARE WASHED CLEAN WITHOUT
PRERINSING AND USING 25% LESS WATER THAN
BEFORE, TO SAVE WATER AND ENERGY. WATER HEATING
IS AUTOMATIC. AND THE TRIDURA® PORCELAIN-
ON-STEEL TUB AND INNER DOOR ARE WARRANTED
FOR 25 YEARS!
MODEL KUDA23SY OFFERS STATE-OF-THE-ART
MICROCOMPUTER CONTROLS THAT LET YOU CREATE
THE CORRECT WASHING FOR EVERY LOAD AT A TOUCH.
SELECT WHITE, SHOWN, OR BLACK.

DISHWASHERS

*Model KUDA230Y,
available in Almond,
shown with custom
panels, or White gives
you easy push-button
operation plus Cycle
Monitor Lights which
show operating status
at a glance.*

BEHIND THE HANDSOME PANELED DOORS OF THIS
KITCHENAID ARCHITECT SERIES BUILT-IN IS HOME REFRIGERATION THAT
IS CONVENIENT, FUNCTIONAL AND EMINENTLY STYLISH AS WELL. ICE AND WATER ARE
DISPENSED NEATLY AND EFFICIENTLY THROUGH THE DOOR. THE ADJUSTABLE TEMPERATURE-
CONTROLLED WINTERCHILL™ MEAT LOCKER HELPS PROLONG FRESH MEAT STORAGE AND
THE LARGE CLEARVUE™ CRISPER AND UTILITY DRAWERS ARE HUMIDITY-
CONTROLLED TO HELP KEEP PRODUCE FRESH. DRAWERS AND BASKETS
MOVE IN AND OUT SMOOTHLY AND EASILY ON THE
EXCLUSIVE KITCHENAID ROLLERTRAC™ SYSTEM.
ARCHITECT SERIES REFRIGERATORS ARE
24 INCHES DEEP TO FIT FLUSH WITH CABINETS AND
ARE SHIPPED READY TO ACCEPT CUSTOM PANELS, SO
YOU CAN MATCH CABINETS, COLORS OR FABRICS, EVEN
SHOWCASE YOUR FAVORITE POSTERS OR THE KIDS'
ARTWORK, IF YOU LIKE. CHOOSE FROM 48, 42 AND
36 INCH WIDE MODELS, WITH OR WITHOUT ICE AND
WATER DISPENSERS WHICH ARE AVAILABLE IN BLACK
OR WHITE. ALMOND, WHITE OR BLACK GLASS-LOOK
AND STAINLESS STEEL PRECUT PANELS CAN BE
ORDERED FROM THE FACTORY.
48-INCH MODEL KSSS48DYW, SHOWN HERE,
OFFERS THE CONVENIENCE OF ICE AND WATER
THROUGH THE DOOR. 28.7 CUBIC-FOOT TOTAL CAPACITY
WITH A 10.6 CUBIC-FOOT FREEZER IS BIG ENOUGH FOR
A VERY HUNGRY FAMILY.

**BUILT-IN
REFRIGERATORS**

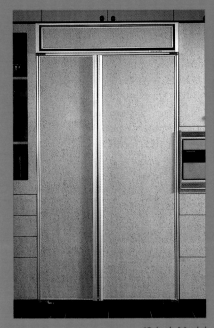

*42-inch Model
KSSS42MWX provides
24.3 cubic feet of total
food storage capacity
including a 9.0 cubic-foot
freezer. The automatic ice
maker puts a continuous
supply of ice crescents
at your fingertips.*

*36-inch Model
KSSS36DWX with
through-the-door ice
and water dispenser
offers a 20.1 cubic-foot
capacity with a 7.4 cubic-
foot freezer.*

ARCHITECT SERIES BUILT-IN OVENS ARE DESIGNED FOR BOTH SUPERLATIVE COOKING PERFORMANCE AND ENDURING AESTHETIC APPEAL. TWO-ELEMENT BALANCED BAKING AND ROASTING, VARIABLE TEMPERATURE BROILING AND VARIABLE SELF CLEANING ALL CONTRIBUTE TO THE QUALITY PERFORMANCE YOU EXPECT FROM A KITCHENAID OVEN.

CHOOSE A THERMAL-CONVECTION™ OVEN FOR BOTH CONVENTIONAL THERMAL AND EVEN-COOKING, EVEN-BROWNING CONVECTION OPERATION. IN THE CONVECTION SYSTEM, HEAT IS GENERATED BEHIND THE OVEN WALL AND CIRCULATED THROUGHOUT THE OVEN BY A FAN.

CONVECTION BAKING AND ROASTING TEMPERATURES ARE LOWER AND COOKING TIME SHORTER THAN IN THERMAL COOKING. CONVECTION BAKE USES THE REAR ELEMENT AND FAN, WHILE CONVECTION ROAST USES TWO ELEMENTS AND FAN. CONVECTION BROILING USES FAN-CIRCULATED AIR TO COOK EVENLY.

WHEN YOU WANT HIGH STYLE PLUS MAXIMUM COOKING FLEXIBILITY, CHOOSE ARCHITECT SERIES BUILT-IN OVENS.

MODEL KEBS277Y THERMAL-CONVECTION™ 27-INCH DOUBLE OVEN COMBINES MODERN TECHNOLOGY WITH TRADITIONAL KITCHENAID QUALITY. AVAILABLE IN WHITE, ALMOND OR BLACK. IF A SINGLE OVEN IS YOUR CHOICE, MODEL KEBS177Y OFFERS THE PERFORMANCE AND CONVENIENCE OF THERMAL-CONVECTION™ BAKING AND ROASTING.

BUILT-IN OVENS

The speed of microwave cooking and the flexibility of convection cooking unite in 27-inch Model KEMS377Y Superba™ Microwave/ Thermal-Convection™ combination oven, available in White or Black.

Choose Model KEMS378Y 27-inch Superba™ Microwave-Convection/ Thermal-Convection™ oven for microwave speed, convection versatility, and thermal baking and roasting all in one elegant oven. White, Almond, or Black.

WANT TO STAY ON TOP OF YOUR COOKING? ARCHITECT
SERIES GLASS SURFACE COOKTOPS ARE EXCEPTIONALLY PRACTICAL YET
DESIGNED TO BLEND SMOOTHLY INTO ALMOST ANY COUNTERTOP SETTING, IN EITHER
TRADITIONAL OR MODERN KITCHENS. COMPONENTS ARE SEALED INTO THE COOKTOP SO
CLEANUP IS SIMPLE: JUST WIPE THE SURFACE WITH A DAMP CLOTH OR SPONGE. COOKTOPS
ARE AVAILABLE IN GAS OR ELECTRIC, 36-INCH OR 30-INCH SIZE, AND IN WHITE,
ALMOND OR BLACK. OPTIONAL DOWNDRAFT SYSTEMS MAKE IT
POSSIBLE TO CONVERT COOKTOPS TO SELF-
VENTILATING OPERATION.

MODEL KGCT365X 36-INCH GAS
COOKTOP WITH COLOR-COORDINATED CAST-IRON
GRATES, SHOWN AT RIGHT, FITS VIRTUALLY ANY
33-INCH OR 36-INCH CUTOUT.

THE 36-INCH SLIDE-OUT VENT HOOD MODEL
KWVU265YBA WITH AUTOMATIC ON/OFF, THREE-
SPEED ELECTRONIC CONTROL AND FLUORESCENT
COOKING SURFACE WORK LIGHT IS THE ULTIMATE IN
EFFICIENT, CONVENIENT VENTING.

BUILT-IN COOKTOPS

Model KECC500W
30-inch electric cooktop
has Quick Star Radiant
elements and a glass-
ceramic surface for fast,
even cooking. Infinite-
Heat Push-to-Turn
controls let you "fine
tune" cooking heats.

Model KECC500W
30-inch electric ceramic
glass cooktop is also
available in Black.

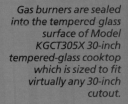

Gas burners are sealed
into the tempered glass
surface of Model
KGCT305X 30-inch
tempered-glass cooktop
which is sized to fit
virtually any 30-inch
cutout.

FREEDOM OF CHOICE TAKES ON A WHOLE NEW MEANING FOR YOUR KITCHEN. NOW YOU CAN DESIGN THE COOKTOP THAT'S RIGHT FOR YOUR KITCHEN AND THE WAY YOU COOK. JUST PUT TOGETHER ANY COMBINATION OF TWO-ELEMENT ELECTRIC OR TWO-BURNER GAS COOKTOP UNITS, ELECTRIC GRILL, AND SIDE-MOUNT DOWNDRAFT SYSTEM. CHOOSE FROM TEMPERED-GLASS CAST-IRON OR GLASS-CERAMIC RADIANT/HALOGEN ELECTRIC OR TEMPERED-GLASS SEALED-BURNER GAS UNITS. ALL ARE AVAILABLE IN WHITE, ALMOND OR BLACK. GRILL AND DOWNDRAFT VENT SYSTEMS COORDINATE WITH COOKTOPS.

SHOWN AT THE REAR: TWO MODEL KGCT025Y 12-INCH COOKTOPS, EACH WITH TWO SEALED GAS BURNERS, AND A MODEL KECT025Y 12-INCH ELECTRIC TEMPERED-GLASS COOKTOP WITH TWO HIGH-SPEED CAST-IRON ELEMENTS. ALL THREE COOKTOPS HAVE INFINITE-HEAT PUSH-TO-TURN CONTROLS SO YOU CAN "FINE TUNE" COOKING HEATS. MODEL KWVU265YBA 36-INCH SLIDE-OUT VENT HOOD WITH AUTOMATIC ON/OFF, THREE SPEED ELECTRONIC CONTROL AND FLUORESCENT COOKING SURFACE WORK LIGHT PROVIDES AN UPDRAFT VENTILATING SYSTEM.

IN THE ISLAND, MODEL KECG020Y DUAL-ELEMENT ELECTRIC GRILL WITH COLOR-COORDINATED INFINITE-HEAT PUSH-TO-TURN CONTROLS AND MODEL KSVD060Y SIDE-MOUNT DOWNDRAFT VENT SYSTEM WITH EASY-TO-USE FRONT CONTROL.

CREATE-A-COOKTOP SYSTEM

Model KECG020Y electric grill and Model KGCT025Y 12-inch sealed burner gas cooktop in White.

Model KECC027Y glass-ceramic cooktop with 6-inch radiant and 8-inch halogen element combines elegance and easy cleanup with fast boiling and uniform cooking.

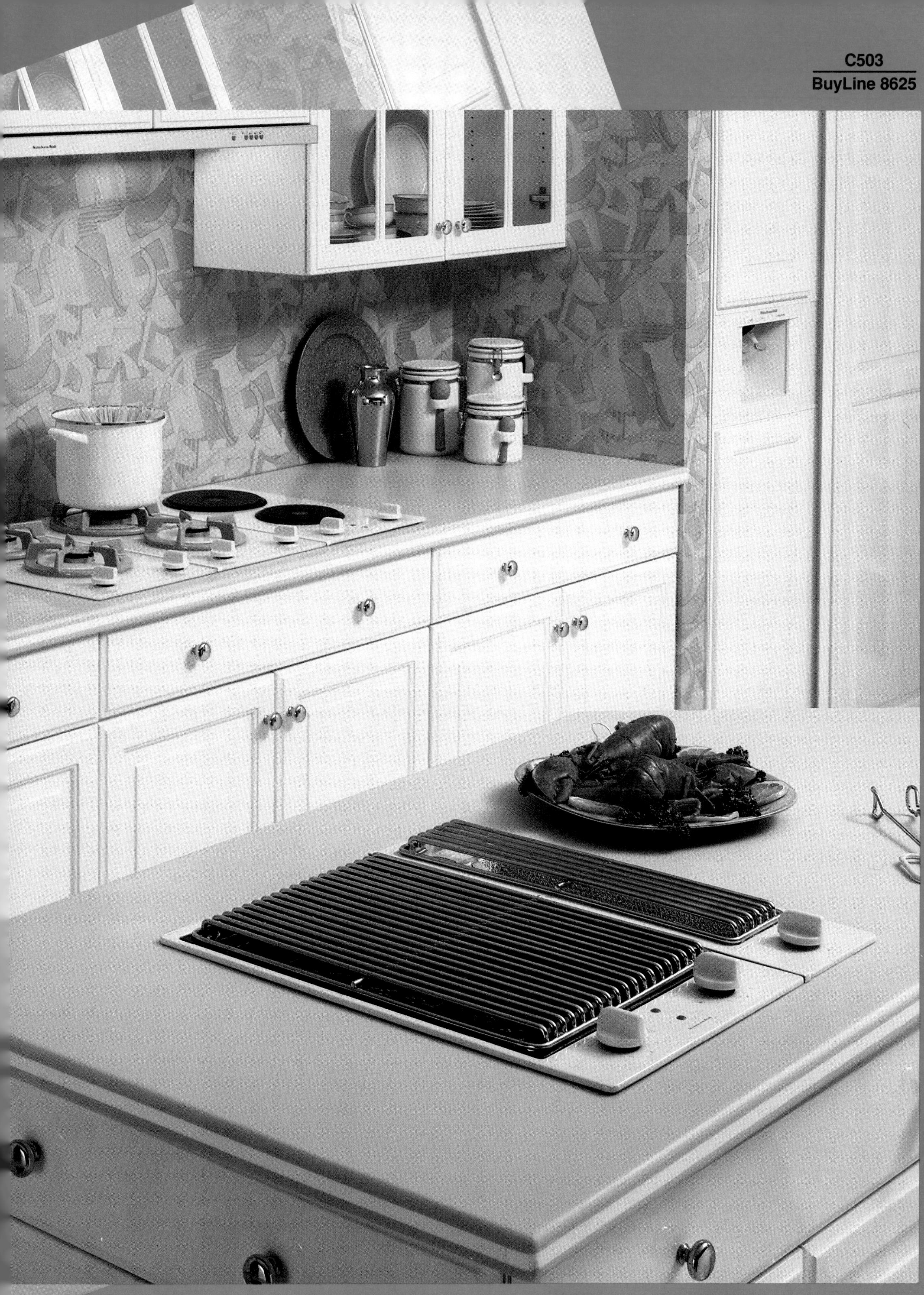

KitchenAid quality goes all the way – all the way to your laundry room, that is. With KitchenAid Superba® solid-state electronic laundry appliances, the proof is in the performance. Microcomputer controls deliver the correct washing and drying for any load at a touch. A broad selection of options provides the flexibility needed to custom-tailor washing and drying for special load requirements. Sleek, modern styling is at home in any setting.

Superba® Model KAWE960W solid-state clothes washer, shown, offers three pre-wash options, three rinse options, five wash/rinse water temperature combinations, and a selectable CYCLE SENTRY™ signal which alerts you to the end of the washing. The matching Superba® Model KGYE960W solid-state gas clothes dryer has four cycle selections, five CUSTOM DRY selections, and a QUICK PRESS option for Permanent Press garments.

LAUNDRY PRODUCTS

Choose the Superba® solid-state laundry pair with either electric or gas dryer. Both clothes washer and clothes dryer are available in White or Almond.

KitchenAid

KitchenAid Architect Series trash compactors take the unpleasantness out of the job no one wants to take on: taking out the trash. Compacting action reduces a week's worth of trash for an average family of four to a small, easy-to-handle package. The Activated Charcoal Filter and Odor Control Fan effectively deal with unpleasant trash odors. Architect Series trash compactors are available in 15-inch and 18-inch wide models to satisfy the needs of almost any kitchen. Optional color-coordinated control panels and the VARI-FRONT™ panel packs let you match your trash compactor to other appliances. The installed trim kit can also accept custom panels. Shown on the right is Model KUCS181T 18-inch trash compactor with exclusive LITTER BIN® Door.

TRASH COMPACTORS
ICE CUBE MAKER
INSTANT-HOT®
WATER DISPENSER
FOOD WASTE DISPOSERS

Hands full of trash? Just touch the toe-bar opener on the Model KUCC151T trash compactor and the trash drawer glides open automatically. Rear rollers make installation easy.

A must in the kitchen, a KitchenAid food waste disposer grinds away even bones and nut shells quickly and quietly. Choose from batch or continuous feed models, with motors up to one HP. Optional flange and stopper kits for continuous-feed models are available in White, Almond or Brass.

The heat's on – at the turn of a tap. The INSTANT-HOT® water dispenser, Model KHWS160V, available in White, Almond or Chrome, delivers up to 60 cups of 190°F water an hour. A great convenience in both kitchen and bathroom.

With the KitchenAid Model KUIS185T automatic ice cube maker, the iceman cometh – and keeps on coming, producing up to 51 pounds of clear ice daily. A lighted bin holds 35 pounds, refills automatically when the ice supply runs low.

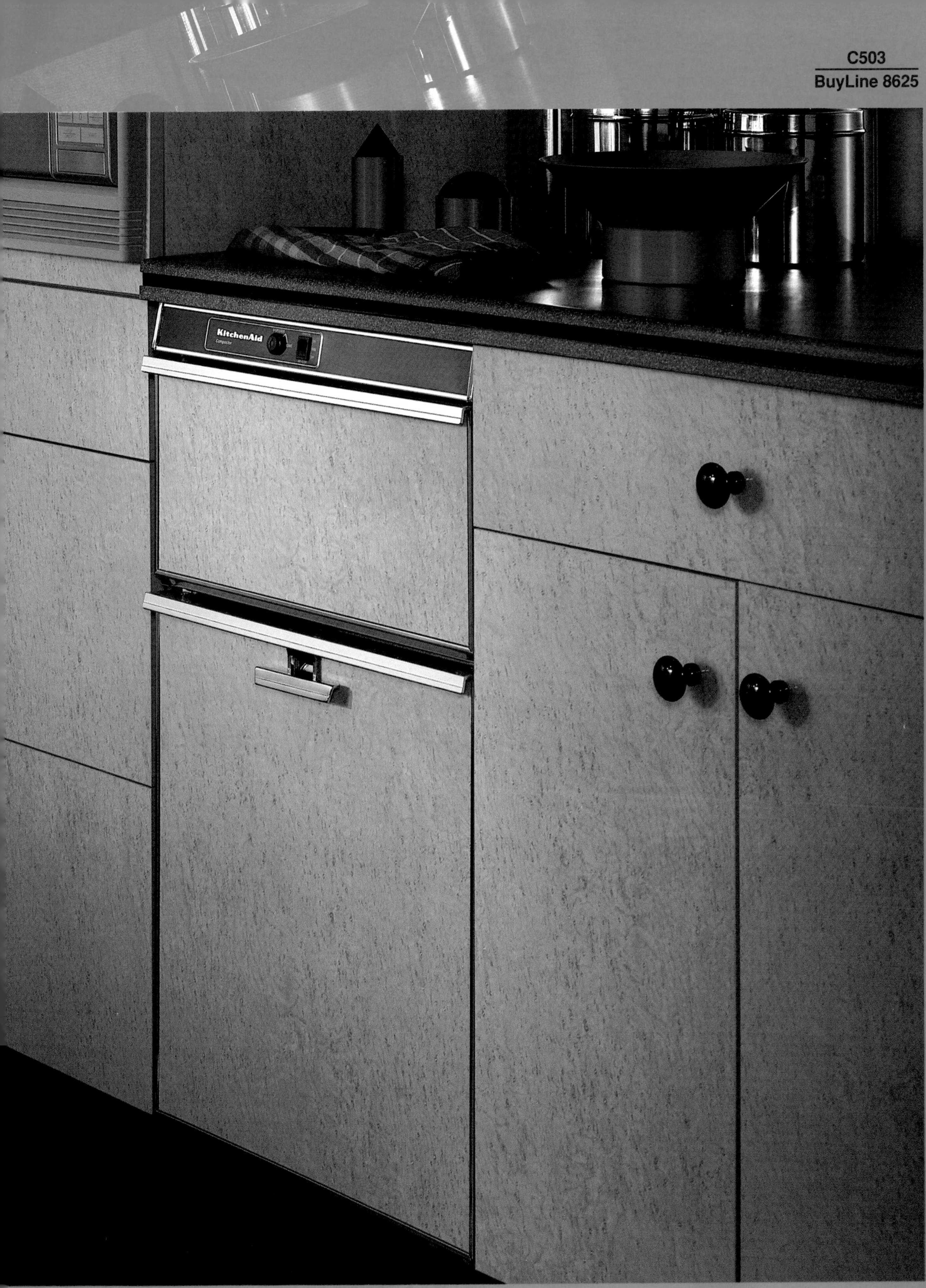
KitchenAid
Compactor

Cooktops
Models KECN567Y, KECN560Y, KECN507Y, KECC500W, KGCT365X and KGCT305X

COOKTOP DIMENSIONS All dimensions shown in inches.

Model	Overall			Cutout		
	Width (side to side)	Depth (back to front)	Height	Width (side to side)	Depth (back to front)	Height (min.)
International Collection – Electric KECN567Y – Ceramic Glass Surface, Halogen/Radiant Elements	35½	20	4	34⅞	19¼	—
KECN560Y – Ceramic Glass Surface, Radiant Elements	35½	20	4	34⅞	19¼	—
KECN507Y – Ceramic Glass Surface, Halogen/Radiant Elements	29½	20	4	28⅞	19¼	—
Electric KECC500W – Ceramic Glass Surface, Radiant Elements	30	21	3	29½	20½	3¼
Gas KGCT365X – Glass Surface	36	21¾	4½	33 to 34⅞	18¾ to 20⅝	3¼
KGCT305X – Glass Surface	30¾	21¾	4½	26½ to 29⅝	18¾ to 20⅝	3¼

NOTE: Power/Fuel supply connections extend below Glass Surface Cooktops and are not included in Overall Height dimension.

Electric
ELECTRICAL REQUIREMENTS
240 Volts AC, 60 Hz. Separate 2-wire with ground circuit. 4 ft. flexible steel conduit with product.

Gas
ELECTRICAL REQUIREMENTS
Separate 2-wire with ground circuit. 3½ ft. 120 Volt AC, 60 Hz., 3-wire cord, 3-prong plug with product (for ignition). **Natural Gas** as shipped; converts to LP gas with standard regulator.

Model	Electrical Ratings		Approx. Weights Lbs.	
	KW @ 240V	Circuit Amps (min.)	Net	Shipping
KECN567Y	8.5	40	46	59
KECN560Y	8.5	40	46	59
KECN507Y	7.3	40	37	45
KECC500W	7.6	30	37	45
KGCT365X	—	15*	56	70
KGCT305X	—	15*	50	62

*120 Volt electric service required for ignition.

Create-A-Cooktop System
Models KECC027Y, KECT025Y, KECG020Y, KSVD060Y and KGCT025Y

COMPONENT DIMENSIONS All dimensions shown in inches.

Model	Overall			Cutout		
	Width (side to side)	Depth (back to front)	Height (top to bottom)	Width (side to side)	Depth (back to front)	Height (top to bottom)
Electric KECC027Y – Glass-Ceramic Cooktop, Radiant/Halogen Elements	11¹⁵⁄₁₆	21¾	4¼	11	20½	4¼
KECT025Y – Tempered-Glass Cooktop, Cast Iron Elements	11¹⁵⁄₁₆	21¾	4¼	11	20½	4¼
KECG020Y – Electric Grill	13¹⁵⁄₁₆	21¾	4¼	13	20½	4½
KSVD060Y – Side-Mount Downdraft Vent System	5¹⁵⁄₁₆	21¾	4¼	4½	20½	4½*
Gas KGCT025Y – Tempered-Glass Cooktop, Sealed Gas Burners	11¹⁵⁄₁₆	21¾	4¼	11	20½	4½

*Plus Ductwork

Create-A-Cooktop System

Cutout Dimensions All dimensions shown in inches.

2 Cooktops
Width (side to side)	23
Depth (front to back)	20½
Height (top to bottom)	4¼

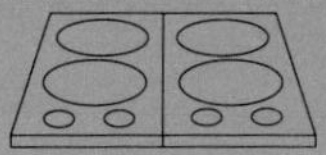

3 Cooktops
Width (side to side)	35
Depth (front to back)	20½
Height (top to bottom)	4¼

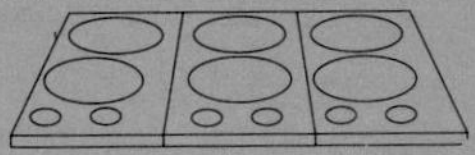

4 Cooktops
Width (side to side)	47
Depth (front to back)	20½
Height (top to bottom)	4¼

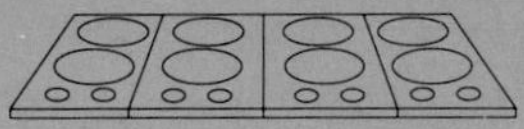

1 Cooktop with Vent
Width (side to side)	16⅞
Depth (front to back)	20½
Height (top to bottom)	4¼*

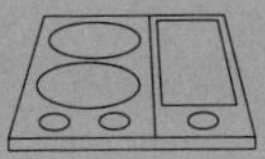

2 Cooktops with Vent
Width (side to side)	29
Depth (front to back)	20½
Height (top to bottom)	4¼*

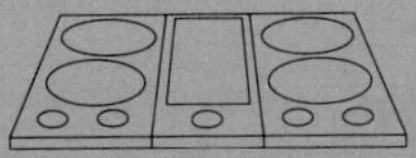

3 Cooktops with 2 Vents
Width (side to side)	47
Depth (front to back)	20½
Height (top to bottom)	4¼*

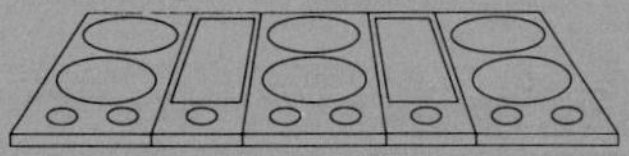

Cutout Dimensions All dimensions shown in inches.

1 Grill with Vent
Width (side to side)	18⅞
Depth (front to back)	20½
Height (top to bottom)	4¼*

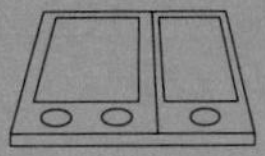

2 Grills with Vent
Width (side to side)	33
Depth (front to back)	20½
Height (top to bottom)	4¼*

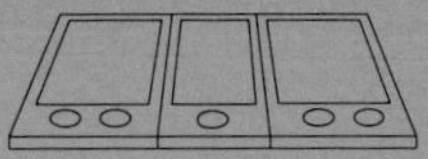

3 Grills with 2 Vents
Width (side to side)	53
Depth (front to back)	20½
Height (top to bottom)	4¼*

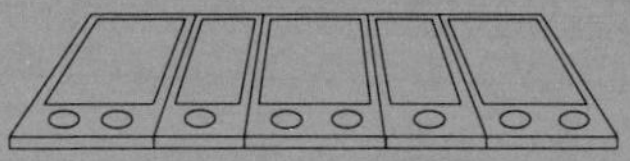

1 Cooktop, 1 Vent, 1 Grill
Width (side to side)	31
Depth (front to back)	20½
Height (top to bottom)	4¼*

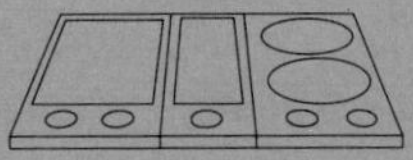

2 Cooktops, 2 Vents, 1 Grill
Width (side to side)	49
Depth (front to back)	20½
Height (top to bottom)	4¼*

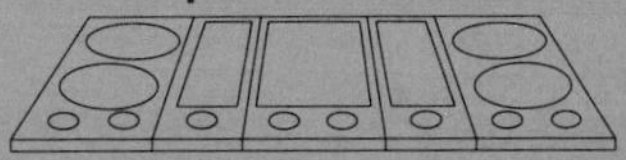

*Plus Ductwork. Use 6 in. or 3¼ in. x 10 in. duct with a maximum of 26 ft. To calculate length needed, add equivalent feet for each duct piece used in system.

CREATE-A-COOKTOP COMPONENTS

Model	Electrical Ratings		Approx. Weights Lbs.	
	KW @ 240V	Circuit Amps (min.)	Net	Shipping
Electric KECC027Y – Glass-Ceramic Cooktop, Radiant/Halogen Elements	3.2	20	17	20½
KECT025Y – Tempered-Glass Cooktop, Cast Iron Elements	7.0	40	18½	22
KECG020Y – Electric Grill	2.2	20	20	23½
KSVD060Y – Side-Mount Downdraft Vent System	—	15	16	20½
Gas KGCT025Y – Tempered-Glass Cooktop, Sealed Gas Burners	—	15	24½	28

SLIDE-OUT VENTILATION HOODS
Approx. weights shown in pounds.

Model	Net	Shipping
KWVU265Y	34	38
KWVU205Y	32	34

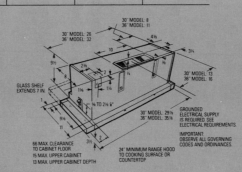

Dimensions shown in inches.

TWENTY ONE

Built-In Ovens

Models KEBN107Y, KEBS177Y, KEBS277Y, KEMS377X and KEMS378X

ELECTRICAL REQUIREMENTS

Dual rated, 240-208/120 Volts AC, 60 Hz. Separate 3-wire with ground circuit. 4 ft. flexible steel conduit with product. (4½ ft. with KEBN107Y.)

	Electrical Ratings			Approx. Weights Lbs.	
Model	KW @ 240V	KW @ 208V	Circuit Amps (min.)	Net	Shipping
KEBN107Y	3.4	2.6	30	134	154
KEBS177Y	3.1	2.3	30	153	172
KEBS277Y	6.1	4.6	40	260	290
KEMS377Y	4.5	3.8	40	236	266
KEMS378Y	4.8	4.1	40	241	271

OVEN DIMENSIONS All dimensions shown in inches.

	Overall					Cutout		
			Depth (back to front)					
Model	Width (side to side)	Height (bottom to top)	Door Closed (to edge of door)	Door Closed (to edge of handle)	Door Open	Width (side to side)	Height (bottom to top)	Depth (min.) (back to front)
International Collection KEBN107Y	29½	23¼	22¼	24	39	27⅞	22¾	24
Thermal-Convection™ KEBS177Y	26	29¾	26⅛	28⅛	43¾	24½	28½	23⅝
KEBS277Y	26	50	26⅛	28⅛	43¾	24½	49	23⅝
Combination KEMS377Y	26	50⅞	26½	28⅝	43¾	24½	49	23⅝
KEMS378Y	26	50⅞	26½	28⅝	43¾	24½	49	23⅝

Min. distance between cutout and cabinet doors 2½ in.

Dishwashers

Models KUDN230Y, KUDA235Y and KUDA230Y

ELECTRICAL REQUIREMENTS

115 Volts, 60 Hz. AC. Max. watts, 1420; max. amps, 12.5. Separate 15-amp, 3-wire grounded circuit required.

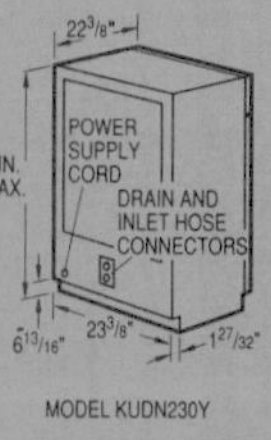

MODEL KUDN230Y

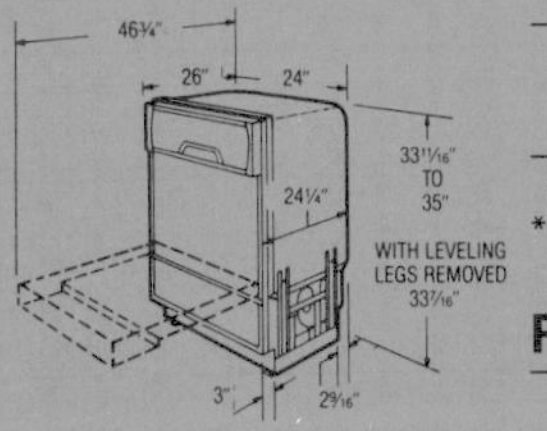

Superba® models require 23⅞" deep cutout; all others, 23½".

"23⅞" DEPTH CUTOUT REQUIRED. IF DRAIN LINE IS FLEXIBLE HOSE, THIS DIMENSION IS 22" ALTERNATE LOCATION.

IF DRAIN LINE IS COPPER, THE COPPER SHOULD BE 12" PLUS A 12" LENGTH OF FLEXIBLE HOSE ATTACHED TO THE END.

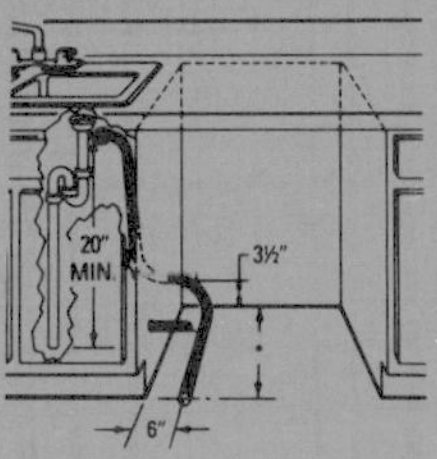

BASIC SIZES FOR CUSTOM FRONT PANELS Shown in inches, weights in pounds.

	Width		Height			
Model	Door	Lower	Door	Lower	Thickness	Max. Weight
KUDN230Y	23 7/32	NA	23 23/32	NA	5/32*	4
KUDA23SY, KUDA230Y	23 9/16	23 11/16	17 7/16	6⅝	¼**	7

*If panel is more than 5/32-in. thick, route outer edge; less, install spacer behind panel.
**If panels are more than ¼-in. thick, refer to Installation Instructions for routing information.

PANEL KITS

	Change-Out Control Panel Part Number		Change-Out Door Panel Part Number		
Model	Black	Stainless Steel	Almond/ White	Black/ Harvest Wheat	Stainless Steel
KUDN230Y	NA	NA	*	*	NA
KUDA23SY	NA	NA	4171200	4171201	4171198
KUDA230Y	4171325	4171389	4171200	4171201	4171198

*An optional Conversion Kit is available to convert this dishwasher to the flush, built-in look required for installations with European cabinets. White, part number 9741413; Black, 9741416.

DIMENSIONS ARE FOR PLANNING ONLY. FOR COMPLETE DETAILS, SEE INSTALLATION INSTRUCTIONS PACKED WITH PRODUCT. SPECIFICATIONS SUBJECT TO CHANGE WITHOUT NOTICE.

Trash Compactors
Models KUCS181T and KUCC151T

COMPACTOR DIMENSIONS All dimensions shown in inches.

Model	A	B	C	D	E	F	Net	Shipping
							Approx. Weights Lbs.	
KUCS181T	34⅛ to 35⅜*	17¾	24⅝ incl. door	34¼ min.	18	24 min.	195	210
KUCC151T	34¹⁄₁₆ to 34¾	14¹⁵⁄₁₆	24³⁄₁₆	34⅜ min.	15	24 min.	137	150

*Add 1½ in. when installed freestanding with maple wood optional top.

PANEL KITS

Model	Change-Out Control Panel Part Number			Change-Out Door Panel Part Number					
	Stainless Steel	White	Almond	Stainless Steel	Almond/ Harvest Wheat	Almond/ White	White/ Black	Black/ Harvest Wheat	Fresh Avocado/ Coffee
KUCS181T	—	7178062	4178063	4162888	—	4162889	—	4162890	4162887
KUCC151T	882681	4151847	4151848	882675	4151462	—	4151463	—	—

BASIC SIZES FOR ¼-in. CUSTOM FRONT PANELS All dimensions shown in inches.

Model	Width	Height
KUCS181T LITTER BIN® Door	17⁷⁄₁₆	7³¹⁄₃₂
Drawer	17⁷⁄₁₆	18¹⁵⁄₁₆
KUCC151T	14⅝	21⅞

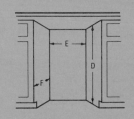

ELECTRICAL REQUIREMENTS

	KUCS181T	KUCC151T
Volts (AC)	115	115
Hertz	60	60
Rated Load (Max. Amps)	9	6.5

Special 15 Amp. 3-Wire grounded circuit required.

Food Waste Disposers
Models KBDS250X, KCDS250X, KCDI250X, KCDC250X, KCDC150X, KCDB250S and KCDB150S

DISPOSER DIMENSIONS All dimensions shown in inches.

Model	A	B*	C*	D	E
KBDS250X	16¹⁄₁₆	9⁷⁄₁₆	4	10¹⁄₁₆	7⅛
KCDS250X	13¹¹⁄₁₆	6¹³⁄₁₆	4	10¹⁄₁₆	7⅛
KCDI250X	13⁷⁄₁₆	6¹³⁄₁₆	4	9¹⁄₁₆	5¾
KCDC250X	12¾	6¹¹⁄₁₆	4	7²⁵⁄₃₂	5¾
KCDC150X	12¾	6¹¹⁄₁₆	4	8¹⁄₁₆	5¾
KCDB250S	12⅝	5¹⁵⁄₁₆	4	6⁵⁄₁₆	5
KCDB150S	11⅜	5¹⁵⁄₁₆	4	6⁵⁄₁₆	5

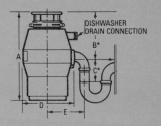

B* – Distance from bottom of sink to center line of disposer outlet. Add ½-in. when stainless steel sink is used.
C* – Length of waste line pipe from center line of disposer outlet to end of waste line pipe.
IMPORTANT: Plumb waste line to prevent standing water in the disposer motor housing.

Built-In Refrigerators
Models KSSS36DWX/DWW, KSSS36MWX, KSSS42DWX/DWW, KSSS42MWX, KSSS48DWX/DWW/DYW and KSSS48MWX

ELECTRICAL REQUIREMENTS
115 Volt AC, 60 Hz. Outlet should be positioned approx. 74 in. above floor.

PLUMBING REQUIREMENTS
¼-in. copper water supply line 1 in. above floor or through floor under refrigerator.

REFRIGERATOR DIMENSIONS All dimensions shown in inches.

	KSSS36DWX, DWW, KSSS36MWX	KSSS42DWX, DWW, KSSS42MWX	KSSS48DWX, DWW, DYW, KSSS48MWX
A	36	42	48
B	35⁵⁄₁₆	41⁵⁄₁₆	47⁵⁄₁₆
C	35	41	47

Model	Approx. Weights Lbs. Net	Shipping
KSSS36DWX, DWW	436	522
KSSS36MWX	431	517
KSSS42DWX, DWW	509	577
KSSS42MWX	504	572
KSSS48DWX, DWW, DYW	650	677
KSSS48MWX	645	672

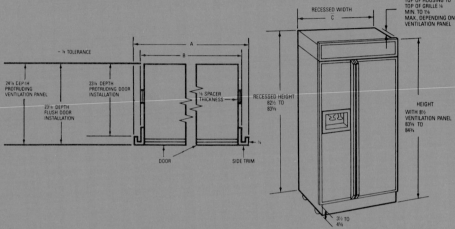

PANEL DIMENSIONS All dimensions shown in inches.

	Height	Width					
		KSSS36DWX, DWW	KSSS36MWX	KSSS42DWX, DWW	KSSS42MWX	KSSS48DWX, DWW, DYW	KSSS48MWX
8½-in. ventilation panel – std.	6	32⅜	32⅜	38⅜	38⅜	44⅜	44⅜
Freezer door panel	70⁷⁄₁₆	—	14¼	—	16¾	—	19¼
Freezer upper door panel	26¼	14¼	—	16¾	—	19¼	—
Freezer lower door panel	34⁷⁄₁₆	14¼	—	16¾	—	19¼	—
Refrigerator door panel	70⁷⁄₁₆	19¼	19¼	22¾	22¾	26¼	26¼
Door handle inserts – 2 required	68¹⁄₁₆	⅞	⅞	⅞	⅞	⅞	⅞

NOTE: Panels and handle inserts should be ¼ in. thick, with ⁵⁄₁₆ in. offset. Tolerance plus or minus ¹⁄₁₆ in.

If custom door panels greater than ¼ in. thick are used, it may be necessary to rout the handle side of panel a minimum of 3 in. in from the panel edge to provide a 2 in. minimum access to the door handle. Either the full length of the panel or a selected area(s) can be routed. Check with your builder.

FOR MORE DETAILS ON INSTALLATION AND PANEL DIMENSIONS SEE KITCHENAID PUBLICATION KSR604.

Convertible Ice Cube Maker
Model KUIS185T

APPROX. WEIGHTS
Net, 103 lbs.; shipping, 116 lbs.
WATER SUPPLY
¼-in. O.D. copper tube.
DRAIN
⅝-in. I.D. rubber tube.
ELECTRICAL REQUIREMENTS
115 Volts AC, 60 Hz.

CUSTOM PANEL DIMENSIONS
Dimensions shown in inches.

	Width	Height
Upper	17	11¼
Lower	17	11¹⁵⁄₁₆

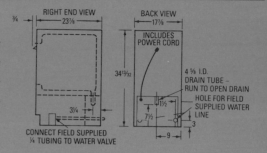

RIGHT END VIEW

BACK VIEW

INCLUDES POWER CORD

CONNECT FIELD SUPPLIED ¼ TUBING TO WATER VALVE

4 ⅝ I.D. DRAIN TUBE – RUN TO OPEN DRAIN HOLE FOR FIELD SUPPLIED WATER LINE

PANEL KITS

Model	Change-Out Control Panel Part Number		Change-Out Door Panel Part Number
	White	Almond	Stainless Steel
KUIS185T	4210583	4210584	819419

Laundry Products
Models KAWE960W and KGYE960W

LAUNDRY PRODUCT DIMENSIONS All dimensions shown in inches.

Model	Height (to top of control panel)	Height (to porcelain top/ work surface)	Width	Depth	Approx. Weights Lbs.	
					Net	Shipping
KAWE960W Clothes Washer	42	36	26⅞	25½	161	179
KGYE960W Clothes Dryer	42	36	29	27¾	124	140

KITCHENAID TRIPLE PROTECTION WARRANTY
KitchenAid
For the way it's made

KitchenAid warranty protection
your assurance of long-lasting performance

All KitchenAid Architect Series appliances are protected by liberal warranties. All are covered by at least a ONE-YEAR FULL WARRANTY on both parts and labor; most carry extended warranties. Your dealer can give you specific information on Architect Series product warranties.

KitchenAid®
For the way it's made.™

Magic Chef®

DESIGNER WHITE COLLECTION

Magic Chef
DESIGNER
WHITE
COLLECTION

MICROWAVE OVENS

- White control panel and white glass door
- Touch controls
- Defrost and cook by weight
- Automatic reheating
- Exclusive* recessed turntable/microwave stirrer system

VM11N-8P—1.0 cu. ft./600 watts over the range microwave/ vent hood combination.

REFRIGERATORS

Handles and Dispenser
- Color coordinated outside with white handles and ice and water dispenser
- Customized storage features

BDNS24L9—23.6 cu. ft. Side-by-side with trim kit installed for high-gloss white decorator panels (Order Kit No. **BPL24SD-N**).

RC24KN-3AW—23.6 cu. ft. Side-by-side with ice and water dispenser.
Also available with 21.7 cu. ft. capacity—**RC22KN-3AW**.

RB23KN-4AW—22.0 cu. ft. Top-Mount with Exclusive* Chef's Food Locker™ and ice and water dispenser.
Also available with 18.0 cu. ft. capacity—**RB18KN-4AW**.

M46N-14T—1.2 cu. ft./800 watts with double capacity removable rack.

M16N-10P—0.8 cu. ft./600 watts broils/browns/bakes.

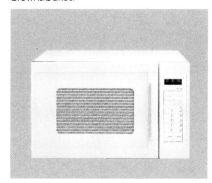

M15N-14T—0.8 cu. ft./600 watts, defrosts and cooks by weight.

DISHWASHER

DU96DN—
24" Built-In Dishwasher.

Touch Pad controls
- Exclusive* touch pad controls
- Special cycle for china and crystal
- Extra hot wash option
- Extra deep upper rack
- Third rack for kitchen and serving utensils

LAUNDRY

White control panel
- Exclusive* touch pad controls with visual readouts
- Exclusive* 20 lb. capacity washer/¾ hp, 2-speed motor
- 4-speed control washer
- Exclusive* Stain-Cleaner™ cycles—double wash action
- 7.0 cu. ft. dryer drum
- Wrinkle-out cycle
- Variable signal buzzer

Also available: Optional white handles for 17', 19', 21' and 23' Top-mounts (Order Kit No. GHK-N)

RB19KN-4A—18.5 cu. ft. Top-Mount with Exclusive* Chef's Food Locker.™ Automatic ice maker optional (Order Kit No. **IMKTM1**).
Also available with 20.9 cu. ft. capacity—**RB21KN-4A** or 22.5 cu. ft. capacity—**RB23KN-4A**.

W20N-5S/YE or YG20N-5—
20 lb. Capacity Laundry Pair.

* A Magic Chef Company Exclusive.

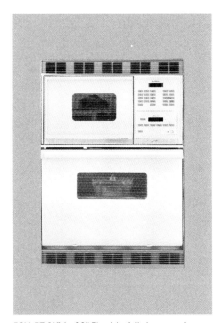

59N-5TVWM—30" Electric full-size oven/microwave combo with electronic controls and one-touch self-cleaning.
Also available: **54N-5TKVWM**—30" Gas wall oven microwave combo.

77N-5EVWW—27" Electric double wall oven with thin profile design for flush installation.
Also available: **77N-5EVWM**—27" Electric wall oven/microwave.

91N-4KLVW—24" Gas with continuous-clean oven.
Also available with standard oven—**91N-4KVW** and single oven—**90N-4KVW**.

BUILT-IN CONVENIENCE

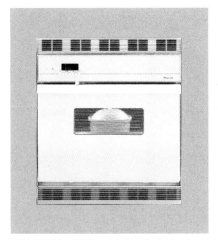

54N-5TKVW—30" Gas full-size single oven with electronic touch controls and one-touch self-cleaning.

59N-5TVW—30" Electric full-size single oven with electronic controls and one-touch self-cleaning.

79N-5EVW—27" Single Self-cleaning Electric with thin profile design for flush installation.

COOKTOPS

- Glass surface beauty
- Sealed burners and DuraGrates™ (Gas)
- Solid disc elements (Electric)
- Optional downdraft vent (HV30) available for electric cooktops
- Thin profile design for flush installation

82N-3K—30" Thin Profile Glass Gas Cooktop with Sealed burners/DuraGrates.™

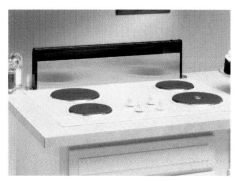

88N-2/HV30—30" Thin Profile Glass Electric Cooktop with Solid disc heating elements (88N-2) shown with optional downdraft vent (HV30).

Magic Chef®
Cleveland, TN 37311

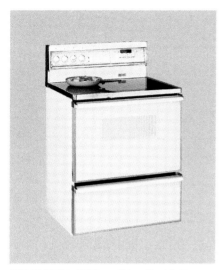

38N-6TVW-EV—30" Smoothtop Electric Range with electronic controls and one-touch self-cleaning oven.

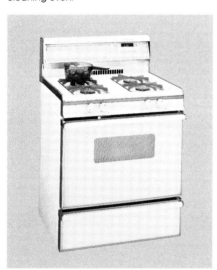

34N-5TKVW-EV—30" Sealed Burner Gas Range with electronic controls and one-touch self-cleaning oven.

24N-7CKVWV8-EV—Eye-Level Range with full-size self-cleaning oven, cooktop with sealed burners and deluxe touch control microwave oven.

Smoothtop
- Fast as a coil element
- Uses regular pots and pans
- High quality—5 year limited warranty on elements and smoothtop
- Easy to clean
- Electronic clock/ thermostat
- Electronic controls/ one-touch self-cleaning

Sealed Burners
- Sealed burners with 5 year warranty
- Burners are sealed to cooktop for easy cleaning
- Deluxe control knobs with infinite flame control
- High quality DuraGrates™

Infinite Flame Control

Electronic Controls
- Unique cooktop design overlaps counter on both sides (does not overlap at back)
- Self-cleaning oven
- Electronic clock and oven control
- Slanted easy-to-read control panel with recessed knobs

64N-4TKVW-EV—Gas Slide-in with electronic controls, one-touch self-cleaning oven and sealed burners.
Also available: **68N-4TVW**—Electric Slide-in with solid disc elements.

68N-6TVW—Electric Slide-in with electronic controls and smoothtop cooking surface.
Also available: **58N-6TVW**—Electric Drop-in with Electronic controls and smoothtop cooking surface.

58N-4TVW—Electric Drop-in with electronic controls, one-touch self-cleaning oven and solid disc elements.

SPECIFICATIONS

FREESTANDING RANGES

	34-Series		38-Series		Double Oven			64-Series		68/58-Series	
	Range	Oven	Range	Oven	Range	Microwave Oven	Lower Oven	Range	Oven	Range	Oven
Width	30"	22"	30"	22"	30"	18"	22"	30"	22"	30"	22"
Height	46"	15"	46"	15"	65¾"*	8"	15"	36½"	15"	36½", 27⅜" (58)	15"
Depth (not incl'd. Handle)	25⅝"	18"	25½"	18"	25½"	12½"	18"	26½"	18"	26½"	18"
Approx. Ship. Weight	215 lbs.		195 lbs.		300 lbs.			180 lbs.		205 lbs. (68) 175 lbs. (58)	
Total Connected Load/KW Rating	—		12.6 @ 240V 9.5 @ 208V		—			—		12.6 @ 240V 9.5 @ 208V	

*Pot Clearance 13¾" max.

WALL OVENS

	Upper Oven			Lower Oven			Cutout			Total Connected 120/240V	Load (KW) 120/208V	Approx. Ship. Wt. (lbs.)
Series	W	H	D	W	H	D	W	H	D			
77-M	14½"	10⁷⁄₁₆"	13⅛"	18"	14"	19"	24¾"	46⅛"	24" min.	6.4	5.1	220
90	18"	14"	19¼"	—	—	—	22½"	38"	24" min.	—	—	145
91	18"	14"	19"	18"	12"	19"	22"	45⅜"	24" min.	—	—	195
79	18"	14"	19"	—	—	—	24¾"	28⅛"	24" min.	3.6	2.7	140
77	18"	14"	19"	18"	12"	19"	24¾"	46⅛"	24" min.	6.5	4.9	215
59T	22"	15"	18"	—	—	—	30⅛"	28⅛"	24" min.	5.9	4.4	160
54T	22"	15"	19"	—	—	—	30⅛"	33¾"	24" min.	—	—	185
59-WM	14½"	10⁷⁄₁₆"	13⅛"	22"	15"	18"	30⅛"	42⅝"	24" min.	8.6	—	220
54-WM	14½"	10⁷⁄₁₆"	13⅛"	22"	15"	18"	30⅛"	43⅝"	24" min.	—	—	220

COOKTOPS

	Exterior		Cutout		Approx. Shipping Weight	Total Connected Load	
Series	W	D	W	D	Lbs.	120/240V	120/208V
88-2	30"	21"	26⅝"	20"	40	7	5.3
82-3	30"	21"	28⁵⁄₁₆"	19¹³⁄₁₆"	40	—	—

MICROWAVE OVENS

	M46 Series	M16	M15 Series	VM11
Height (Exterior)	15¼"	12¾"	12¾"	16¼"
Width (Exterior)	21⅞"	20⅜"	20⅜"	30"
Depth (Exterior)	15¹¹⁄₁₆"	14"	13¼"*	13"*
Volume Inside (cu. ft.)	1.2	0.8	0.8	1.0
Approximate Shipping Weight	70 lbs.	46 lbs.	42 lbs.	97 lbs.
Total Connected Load (for 120 volts)	11.5 Amps	10.5 Amps	10 Amps	12 Amps
Output Power (Watts)	800**	600**	600**	600**

* Excluding handle   ** IEC test method

REFRIGERATORS

	Outside Dimensions		Depth Dimensions		Total Volume (cu. ft.)		AHAM Shelf Area (sq. ft.)		Approx. Shipping Weight
Models	H	W	w/handle	w/door open	Total	Refrig.	Frz.	AHAM	Pounds
BDNS24L9	66⅜"	35¾"	29¼"	48¾"	23.6	15.14	8.41	28.1	324
RC24-3AW	66⅜"	35¾"	29¼"	48¾"	23.6	15.14	8.49	28.1	315
RC22-3AW	66⅜"	33"	29¼"	48¾"	21.7	15.17	6.46	26.2	300
RB23-4AW	65½"	33"	30⅝"	62⅜"	22.0	15.17	6.89	29.9	304
RB23-4A	65½"	33"	30⅝"	62⅜"	22.5	15.58	6.89	32.3	280
RB21-4A	65½"	31½"	30⅝"	60⅝"	20.9	14.50	6.39	30.2	274
RB18-4AW	65½"	31½"	27⅞"	57⅝"	18.0	12.36	5.67	24.2	265
RB19-4A	65½"	31½"	27⅞"	57⅝"	18.5	12.80	5.67	26.5	250

DISHWASHER

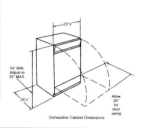

Dishwasher Cabinet Dimensions

	OUTSIDE DIMENSIONS			APPROX. SHIP. WT.
Model	H*	W	D	Pounds
DU96	34½"	23¾"	26¼"	100

*Adjustable from 34" to 35".
Drain hose included with each model.

DRYER

Approx. Shipping Weight 135 lbs.

Total Connected Load

Amps	Volt (3-wire)	Hz.
15	120	60

Gas dryers work with natural or LP gas (with available kit No. 63-6766).

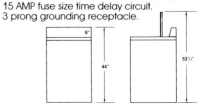

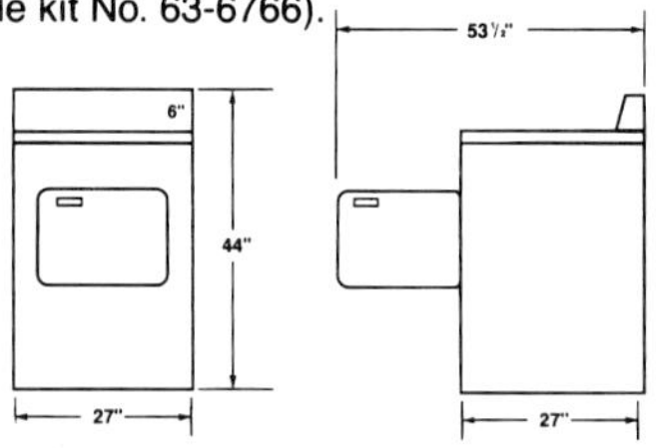

WASHER

APPROX. SHIPPING WEIGHT 185 LBS.

TOTAL CONNECTED LOAD

Amps	Volts	Hz.
11.5	120	60

15 AMP fuse size time delay circuit.
3 prong grounding receptacle.

M890-B484A

Magic Chef®
Cleveland, TN 37311

Design certified by the American Gas Association. Listed by Underwriters' Laboratories. Specifications subject to change at manufacturer's option.

Dimensional information for reference only. For actual installation, refer to instructions packed with product.

WALL OVENS & COOKTOPS

MAYTAG 30" ELECTRIC WALL OVENS

Built-in beauty! Nothing adds more contemporary appeal to a kitchen than a wall oven. And no wall oven offers quite the styling, convenience features and dependability of a Maytag.

   A wide range of models lets you choose the unit that most fits your cooking needs, kitchen decor and budget. And for the ultimate in contemporary styling, there's Maytag's Deco-White™ selection of wall ovens.

Model CWE9000 — Designed for under-the-counter installations, features include a self-cleaning oven, electronic digital clock, timer and a "delay-start" cook control. It also offers an automatic oven light, see-through oven window and a porcelain broiler pan and insert.

Deco-White™ CWE9000

MAYTAG 27" ELECTRIC WALL OVENS

Model CWE9900 — The top of the Maytag line! Features include a self-cleaning radiant oven that automatically converts to a convection oven at the touch of a pad. It also offers full computer touch control, an electronic digital clock, timer and a temperature probe to ensure precise cooking. In addition, there's a "delay-start" cook control, automatic oven light, see-through oven window and a porcelain broiler pan and insert.

Model CCE7010 — Combines the advantages of both radiant and microwave cooking. Features include a self-cleaning oven with an electronic digital clock, timer and a temperature probe. It also offers a "delay-start" cook control, automatic oven light and a see-through oven window. Plus! A deluxe, programmable Maytag microwave oven on top.

Model CWE6020 — Features include a self-cleaning oven, electronic digital clock, timer and a "delay-start" cook control. It also offers an automatic oven light, see-through oven window and a porcelain broiler pan and insert.

MAYTAG 24″ ELECTRIC WALL OVENS

Model CWE4700 —
Features include a self-cleaning oven, electronic clock, timer and a "delay-start" cook control. It also offers an oven light switch, see-through oven window and a porcelain broiler pan and insert. *Also available in the standard-clean model CWE4020.*

Deco-White™ CWE4700

Deco-White™ CWE5500

Model CWE5500 —
Double the dependability! Features include a self-cleaning upper oven, electronic clock, timer and a "delay-start" cook control. It also offers an oven light switch, see-through oven window and a porcelain broiler pan and insert. *Also available in the standard-clean model CWE5020.*

ELECTRIC WALL OVEN FEATURES	CWE9900	CWE9000*	CCE7010	CWE6020	CWE5500*	CWE5020	CWE4700*	CWE4020
Wall Oven Size	27″	30″	27″	27″	24″	24″	24″	24″
Microwave Oven			X					
Convection/Radiant Oven	X							
Radiant Oven		X	X	X	2	2	X	X
Self-Clean Oven	X	X	X	X	Upper		X	
Standard-Clean Oven					Lower	X		X
3 Heavy-Duty Racks, Multi-Levels	X				X	X		
2 Heavy-Duty Racks, Multi-Levels							X	X
Electronic Clock & 99 Minute Timer	X	X	X	X	X	X	X	X
"Delay-Start" Cook Control	X	X	X	X	X	X	X	X
Oven Window(s)	X	X	X	X	X	X	X	X
Oven Light	X	X	X	X	2	2	X	X
Pull-Off Control Knobs			X	X	X	X	X	X
Porcelain Broiler Pan & Insert	X	X	X	X	X	X	X	X
Black Glass Front	X	X	X	X	X	X	X	X
Temperature Probe	X		X					
Computer Touch Control	X							

*Models available in Deco-White™

All dimensions shown are for planning purposes only. Consult the Installation Instructions that accompany each product before cutting cabinets or countertops.

MAYTAG 24″ GAS WALL OVENS

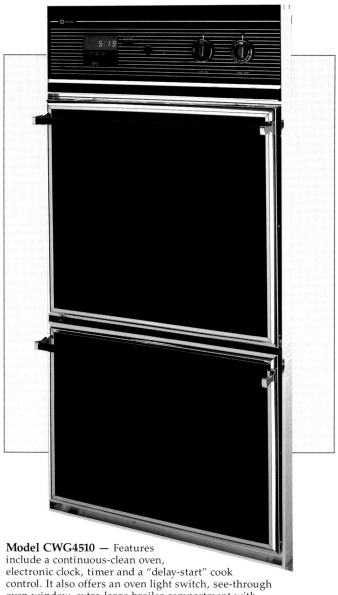

Model CWG4020 — Features include a continuous-clean oven, electronic clock, timer and a "delay-start" cook control. It also offers an oven light switch, see-through oven window and a porcelain broiler pan and insert. *Also available in the manual-clean model CWG3020.*

Model CWG4510 — Features include a continuous-clean oven, electronic clock, timer and a "delay-start" cook control. It also offers an oven light switch, see-through oven window, extra-large broiler compartment with window and a porcelain broiler pan and insert. *Also available in the manual-clean model CWG3510.*

GAS WALL OVEN FEATURES	CWG4510	CWG4020	CWG3510	CWG3020
Wall Oven Size	24″	24″	24″	24″
Continuous-Clean Oven	X	X		
Standard-Clean Oven			X	X
Electronic Clock & 99 Minute Timer	X	X	X	X
"Delay-Start" Cook Control	X	X	X	X
2 Heavy-Duty Racks, Multi-Level	X	X	X	X
Oven Window & Oven Light	X	X	X	X
Even-Heat Broiler	X	X	X	X
Broiler Compartment Window & Light	X		X	
Black Glass Front	X	X	X	X
Solid State Pilotless Ignition	X	X	X	X
Built-In LP Conversion	X	X	X	X

All dimensions shown are for planning purposes only. Consult the Installation Instructions that accompany each product before cutting cabinets or countertops.

MAYTAG EASY-CLEAN ELECTRIC COOKTOPS

The perfect complement to your
Maytag wall oven is a sleek, contemporary
Maytag cooktop. An array of models to
choose from, each is designed
with the quality construction,
attractive good looks and superior performance that typify all
Maytag appliances.

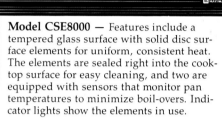

Deco-White™ CSE8000

Model CSE8000 — Features include a
tempered glass surface with solid disc surface elements for uniform, consistent heat.
The elements are sealed right into the cooktop surface for easy cleaning, and two are
equipped with sensors that monitor pan
temperatures to minimize boil-overs. Indicator lights show the elements in use.

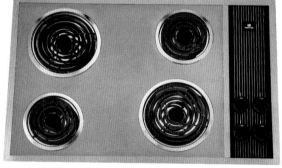

Model CSE6010 — Features include an easy-clean top
with four removable, heavy-duty coil elements. It also
offers a tempered glass control panel, surface indicator
lights, chrome reflector bowls, pull-off knobs and a
stainless steel trim.

Model CSE4000 — Features include a porcelain
enamel top with removable, heavy-duty coil elements.
It also offers a tempered glass control panel, infinite
set element controls, chrome reflector bowls and
pull-off knobs for easy cleaning.

Maytag's top-of-the-line electric cooktop offers the utmost in cooking
convenience and clean-up ease! Its smooth cooktop surface, elegant black styling
and flush-to-counter installation makes it perfect for today's modern kitchen.

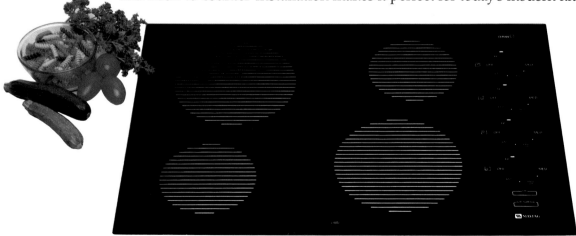

Model CSE9000 — Pots and pans slide easily from burner to burner!
Features include four high-speed radiant surface elements in a black
glass Ceran® top. It also features an element-in-use indicator light, infinite
set element controls and a "Hot Surface"light. Its smooth cooktop
surface and pull-off control knobs make cleaning simple!

MAYTAG EASY-CLEAN GAS COOKTOPS

Maytag's top-of-the-line gas cooktop gives you the ultimate in cooking performance. Its extra-large tempered glass surface and open design means greater flexibility. Clean-up is a breeze!

Model CSG9000 — The beauty of tempered glass! Features include a solid state pilotless ignition, sealed burners and porcelain enamel burner caps. It also offers porcelain enamel burner grates and removable, precision-set burner controls.

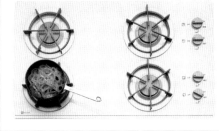

Deco-White™ CSG9000

Model CSG7000 — Features include a tempered glass surface, solid state pilotless ignition, sealed burners and porcelain enamel burner caps. It also offers porcelain enamel burner grates and removable, precision-set burner controls.

Deco-White™ CSG7000

Model CSG6000 — The convenience of a fifth burner or griddle! Features include a solid state pilotless ignition, porcelain enamel burner grates and removable, scratch-resistant burners. A lift-up surface and drip-retainer top make cleaning easy.

MAYTAG EASY-CLEAN GAS COOKTOPS

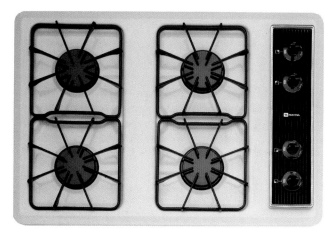

Model CSG5600 — Features include a solid state pilotless ignition, sealed burners and porcelain enamel burner grates. It also offers removable, precision-set burner controls, a lift-up surface and drip-retainer top.

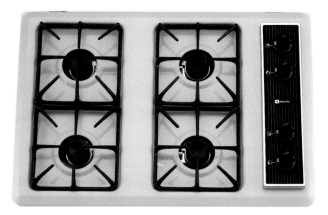

Model CSG5010 — Features include a solid state pilotless ignition, porcelain enamel burner grates and removable, scratch-resistant burners. It also offers removable, precision-set burner controls, a lift-up surface and drip-retainer top.

ELECTRIC COOKTOP FEATURES	CSE 9000	CSE* 8000	CSE 6010	CSE 4000
Cooktop Size	30"	30"	36"	30"
Tempered Glass Surface	X	X		
Radiant Surface Elements in Ceramic Glass	X			
Solid Disc Surface Elements		X		
Temp Sensor Control (2 Front Elements)		X		
Heavy-Duty Coil Surface Elements			X	X
Tempered Glass Control Panel	X	X	X	X
Pull-Off Control Knobs	X	X	X	X
White/Almond/Brushed Chrome			X	X
Drip-Retainer Top				X

*Model available in Deco-White™

GAS COOKTOP FEATURES	CSG* 9000	CSG* 7000	CSG 6000	CSG 5600	CSG 5010
Cooktop Size	36"	30"	36"	30"	30"
Tempered Glass Surface	X	X			
Tempered Glass Control Panel	X	X	X	X	X
Pull-Off Control Knobs	X	X	X	X	X
White/Almond/Brushed Chrome			X	X	X
Sealed Burners	X	X		X	
Removable Burners			X		X
Drip-Retainer Top			X	X	X
Lift-Up Cooktop			X		X
Precision-Set Burner Controls	X	X	X	X	X
LP Convertible	X	X	X	X	X
Solid State Pilotless Ignition	X	X	X	X	X

*Models available in Deco-White™

All dimensions shown are for planning purposes only. Consult the Installation Instructions that accompany each product before cutting cabinets or countertops.

MAYTAG DEPENDABILITY WARRANTY

Maytag wall ovens and cooktops come with a complete warranty that covers replacement and labor on all parts for one full year from date of purchase. A limited warranty provides free parts for two years. And for five years, there are free parts on solid disc elements, sealed gas burners, smooth top heating elements and glass cooking surfaces on cooktops and the touch pad and circuit boards on wall ovens. Unlike most warranties, your Maytag warranty moves with you and is valid anywhere in the United States. See your Maytag dealer for complete warranty details.

MAYTAG COOKTOP SPECIFICATIONS

ELECTRIC COOKTOPS ────────

Model CSE9000
  Radiant Surface Element: Two 8" — 2100 watts
  Two 6" — 1200 watts

Model CSE8000
  Solid Disc Surface Elements: Two 8" — 2000 watts
  Two 6" — 1500 watts

Model CSE6010 & CSE4000
  Coil Surface Elements: Two 8" — 2100 watts
  Two 6" — 1250 watts

CSE9000
RADIANT SURFACE ELEMENT
COOKTOP
CUTOUT DIMENSIONS
20⁷⁄₁₆"
29⁷⁄₁₆"

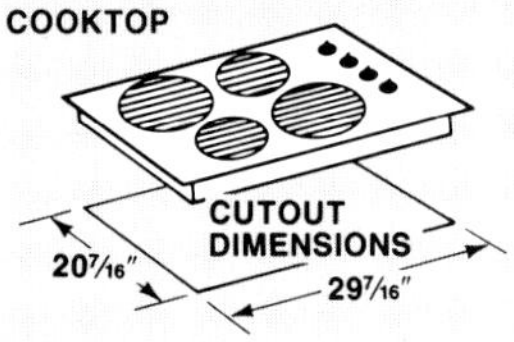

OVERALL: 30" W x 21" D x 2¾" H

CSE8000
SOLID ELEMENT
COOKTOP
CUTOUT DIMENSIONS
20"
26⅝"

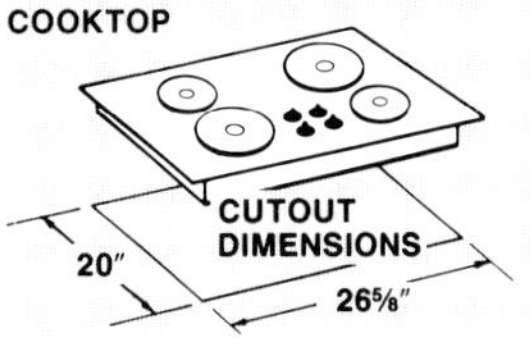

OVERALL: 30" W x 21" D x 2¾" H

CSE6010
ELECTRIC COOKTOP
CUTOUT DIMENSIONS
21¹⁄₁₆"
33¹⁄₁₆"

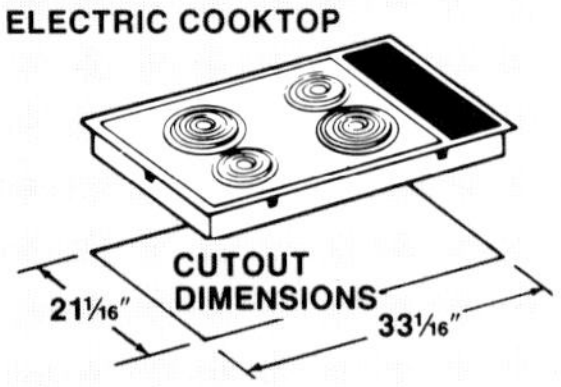

OVERALL: 33⅝" W x 21⅝" D x 3¹⁄₁₆" H

CSE4000
ELECTRIC COOKTOP
CUTOUT DIMENSIONS
19¹³⁄₁₆"
28⁵⁄₁₆"

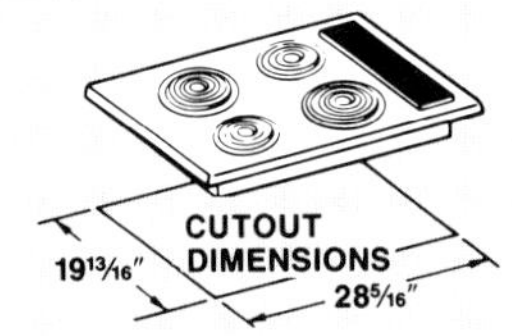

OVERALL: 30" W x 21" D x 3¼" H

GAS COOKTOPS ────────

Model CSG9000, CSG7000 & CSG5600
  BTU Rating — Sealed Burners: Nat. 9000/LP 8000

Model CSG6000
  BTU Rating — Standard Burners: Nat. 8000/LP 8000
  BTU Rating — Griddle: Nat. 6000/LP 5500

Model CSG5010
  BTU Rating — Standard Burners: Nat. 8000/LP 8000

CSG9000
GAS COOKTOP
CUTOUT DIMENSIONS
19¾"
34⅜"

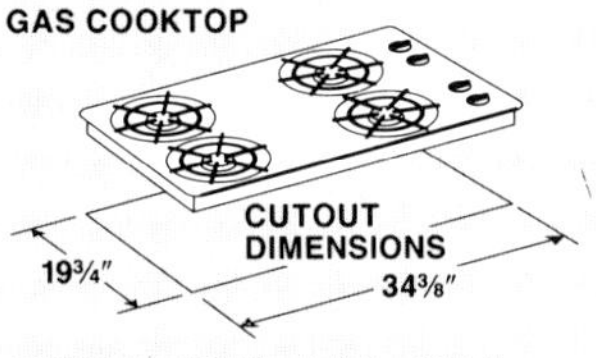

OVERALL: 36" W x 21" D x 3⅜" H

CSG7000
GAS COOKTOP
CUTOUT DIMENSIONS
19¾"
28⅜"

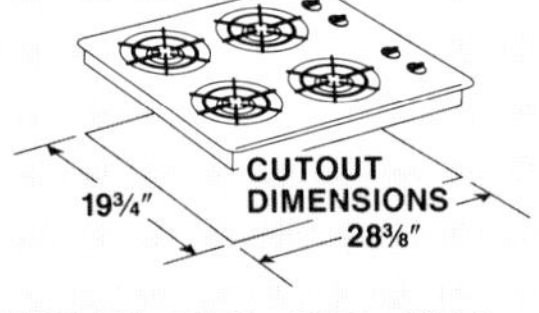

OVERALL: 30" W x 21" D x 3⅜" H

CSG6000
GAS COOKTOP
CUTOUT DIMENSIONS
19¾"
34⅞"

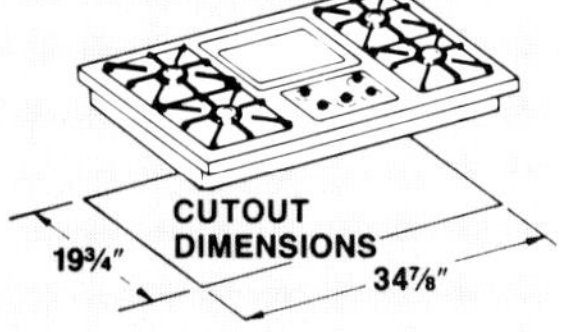

OVERALL: 36" W x 21" D x 3⁵⁄₁₆" H

CSG5600 & CSG5010
GAS COOKTOPS
CUTOUT DIMENSIONS
19¹³⁄₁₆"
28⁵⁄₁₆"

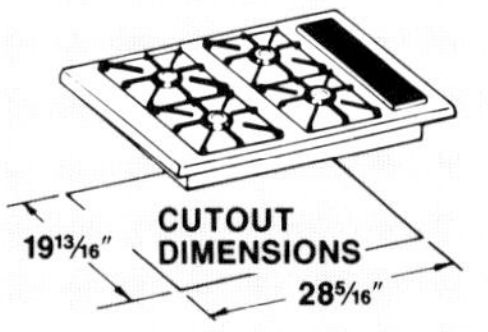

OVERALL: 30" W x 21" D x 3⅜" H

MAYTAG WALL OVEN SPECIFICATIONS

ELECTRIC WALL OVENS ────────

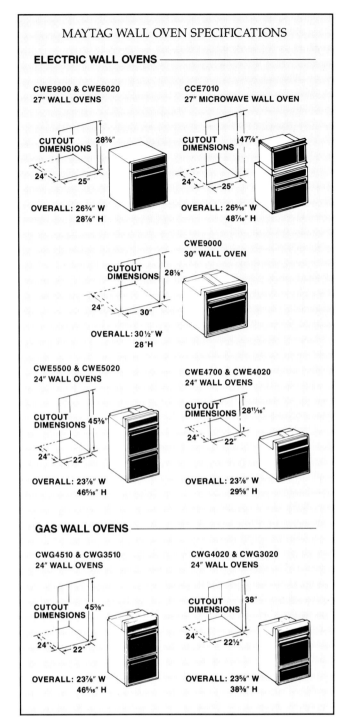

CWE9900 & CWE6020
27" WALL OVENS
CUTOUT DIMENSIONS
28⅜"
24"
25"

OVERALL: 26¾" W
28⅞" H

CCE7010
27" MICROWAVE WALL OVEN
CUTOUT DIMENSIONS
47⅞"
24"
25"

OVERALL: 26⁹⁄₁₆" W
48⁷⁄₁₆" H

CWE9000
30" WALL OVEN
CUTOUT DIMENSIONS
28⅛"
24"
30"

OVERALL: 30½" W
28" H

CWE5500 & CWE5020
24" WALL OVENS
CUTOUT DIMENSIONS
45⅜"
24"
22"

OVERALL: 23⅞" W
46⁵⁄₁₆" H

CWE4700 & CWE4020
24" WALL OVENS
CUTOUT DIMENSIONS
28¹¹⁄₁₆"
24"
22"

OVERALL: 23⅞" W
29⅝" H

GAS WALL OVENS ────────

CWG4510 & CWG3510
24" WALL OVENS
CUTOUT DIMENSIONS
45⅜"
24"
22"

OVERALL: 23⅞" W
46⁵⁄₁₆" H

CWG4020 & CWG3020
24" WALL OVENS
CUTOUT DIMENSIONS
38"
24"
22½"

OVERALL: 23⅝" W
38⅜" H

All dimensions shown are for planning purposes only. Consult the Installation Instructions that accompany each product before cutting cabinets or countertops.

Because of continuing product improvement, Maytag reserves the right to change specifications without notice.

MAYTAG COMPANY, One Dependability Square, Newton, Iowa 50208

MAYTAG *Jetclean™ Dishwashers*

Quiet Cleaning Load After Load, Year After Year!

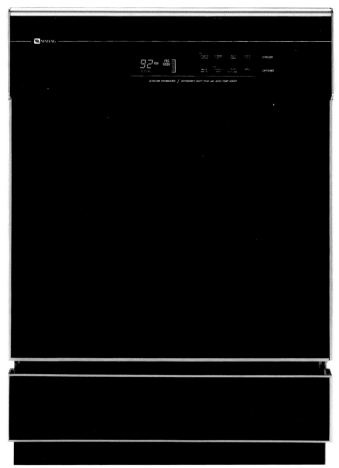

Elegant soft styling and non-glare, satin finish control panels make Maytag dishwashers at home in any decor.

We've designed Maytag dishwashers with wash cycle settings for a full range of cleaning jobs. There's a Normal Cycle for regular loads. For the toughest cleaning jobs, there's a Pots & Pans Cycle. Some models have a Light/China Cycle and a convenient Rinse & Hold Cycle. And to ensure the proper water temperature, a Temp Boost Sensor heating system.

Every Maytag dishwasher gives you two "forced air" fan dry settings. You can select either Heat Dry or energy-saver Air Dry. Both settings use an efficient dryer fan system to circulate air continuously throughout the dishwasher.

Maytag dishwashers are unsurpassed in capacity, loading flexibility and cleaning power. Whichever model you choose, you'll know it's been designed for dependably quiet operation.

You can also expect your new Maytag to add a touch of class to your kitchen. Dishwasher front panels include a full selection of today's most popular decorator colors. They can be customized with wood panels in the same finish as the rest of your kitchen cabinetry. You can select from two Deco-White™ models featuring all-white front panels and controls for the ultimate in contemporary styling.

Best of all, because they're quality Maytag dishwashers, you can count on that quiet cleaning operation load after load, day after day, year after year.

POWER SCRUB

NORMAL CYCLE

LIGHT CHINA

QUICK CYCLE

RINSE & HOLD

HEATED DRY

DELAY RESUME

DRAIN OFF

CYCLES

OPTIONS

Why Wash Your Dishes Before You Wash Your Dishes?

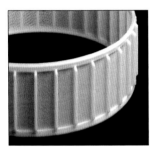

Micro-Mesh™ filter continuously traps and removes tiny food particles.

Patented "internal food disposer" handles both soft and hard food wastes.

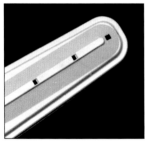

Smaller spray holes create a finer spray for greater scrubbing power.

Quiet "forced air" fan system dries dishes quickly and efficiently.

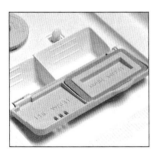

Dual-covered dispenser protects silverware from detergent damage.

Adjustable rinse aid dispenser adapts to various water conditions.

Maytag dishwashers have so much power that there's little need to rinse or pre-wash your dishes. Your utensils, dishes and cookware are cleaned from every direction with Maytag's full three-level wash system. Water comes powering out from the top, sides, and up from the bottom of your dishwasher. All in all, there's a total of 43 spray holes with high-velocity jets of water to clean vigorously.

Meanwhile, smaller spray holes in the wash arms provide a finer, more powerful spray for greater scrubbing power. Only burned-on foods may need extra attention. The patented, stainless steel "internal food disposer" handles both soft and hard food wastes with ease. And Maytag's Micro-Mesh™ filter continuously traps and removes tiny food particles. Every dish is washed and rinsed in 100% filter-cleaned water.

Our compact power module, which includes Maytag's long-life motor and pump, is so dependable that we guarantee it, as well as all other wash system components, for 5 full years.

All this and quiet as well. Maytag dishwashers are designed with sound-absorbing tubs and feature a unique sound-dampening insulation system. For even added sound control, we offer our *Dependably Quiet™Plus* models.

No Pre-Washing With Maytag!

Maytag's Flexible Racking Is Most Accommodating!

Nobody has more rack space! Maytag's MAX-Racks™ hold a party's worth of plates.

Bring on the odds and ends! Maytag's racking system is completely flexible.

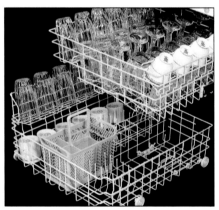

Goblets, tumblers, cups and more! Maytag's six tiers of racking hold all shapes and sizes.

Maytag's "largest ever" silverware basket loads by the handful. Removes for convenience!

Since there's no such thing as the "typical load" of dishes, Maytag dishwashers aren't designed in a typical way. Every aspect of the interior has been painstakingly engineered to make the most of available space while providing loading flexibility.

In the lower rack, you can place large dinner plates, bowls and other dishes in any location. There's room for taller items like bakeware and large platters on the left side, while smaller items like saucers fit conveniently behind the wash tower. And on some models, convertible bowl tines fold to provide either narrow or wide spacing for added convenience. Plus every model has a removable, heavy-duty silverware basket with a covered section for smaller, lightweight articles.

The upper rack has enough room for all your glasses, cups or bowls. Dishes are held in place by the rack's support wires and can be centered behind a single tine or angled to maximize space.

And our dish racks are built to last. They're made with heavy-gauge steel and coated with a durable nylon or vinyl coating to cushion and protect your dishes.

The DuraTip™ tines are rounded at the ends for lasting wear and protection. **And the specially-formulated co-polymer tub and door liner are so dependable, Maytag Company guarantees them against leaks for 20 full years.** That's a long time with nothing to worry about. Especially if you're a Maytag repairman!

92 MIN. PRE-WASH

POWER SCRUB	NORMAL CYCLE	LIGHT CHINA	QUICK CYCLE	CYCLES
RINSE &HOLD	HEATED DRY	DELAY RESUME	DRAIN	OPTIONS

JETCLEAN DISHWASHER / DEPENDABLY QUIET PLUS with AUTO TEMP BOOST

No other major brand is quieter than a Maytag Dependably Quiet™ Plus dishwasher!

- Additional 14 pounds of sound-absorbing material
- Additional insulation and sound-dampening pads
- Additional sound barriers to help keep noise where it belongs — in the dishwasher!

Model DWU9920 — Features include full touch controls, a display readout of the cycle time remaining and a delay-start function. It also offers Power Scrub and Quick Cycle options, a convenient Rinse & Hold Cycle, plus heat and no-heat drying. Other features include "Clean", "Heating" and "Rinsed Only" indicators, Auto Temp Boost water heating, nylon racks, deluxe racking, extra sound insulation and an adjustable rinse dispenser. This model also available in Deco-White.™

Model DWU9905 — Features include touch controls and cycle sequence indicator lights. It also offers a Quick Cycle option, convenient Rinse & Hold Cycle, plus heat and no-heat drying. Other features include Auto Temp Boost water heating, nylon racks, deluxe racking, extra sound insulation and an adjustable rinse dispenser.

Model DWU9200 — Simple push-button controls. Features include a delay-start function, Quick Cycle option, convenient Rinse & Hold Cycle, plus heat and no-heat drying. It also offers cycle sequence indicator lights, nylon racks and Maytag's deluxe racking system. Other features include a Temp Boost Sensor water heating option, extra sound insulation and an adjustable rinse dispenser.

At Maytag, we're doing our part to reduce noise pollution. Maytag's *Dependably Quiet™Plus* dishwasher models incorporate additional sound-absorbing pads and other sound barriers into their construction so you don't have to raise your voice in the kitchen to be heard.

As for durability, the DuraGuard™ racks are coated with wear-resistant nylon and guaranteed for 5 years. And our exclusive racking system is designed to give you even further loading options.

A convenient, delay-start function on some models lets you program the dishwasher to turn itself on automatically. Up to 12 hours in advance. It's just another convenient feature to make your dish washing easier.

From the traditional to the most contemporary, the understated elegance and distinctive styling of Maytag's *Dependably Quiet™Plus* dishwashers enhance any decor.

Deco-White™
Model DWU9920

Dependably Quiet™ Dishwashers

No other dishwasher on the market cleans more thoroughly while operating as quietly as a Maytag Jetclean™ dishwasher.

Every model, from the most economical to the top-of-the-line, is built with the same intense pride. The same dedication to quality. Whichever you choose, each is designed for years of trouble-free performance, lasting good looks and durability.

You can depend on it!

Model DWU7500 — Features include a Quick Cycle option, a convenient Rinse & Hold Cycle, plus heat and no-heat drying. It also offers in-use indicator lights, deluxe upper and lower racks, and convertible bowl tines. Other features include a Temp Boost Sensor water heating option, Sani-Rinse option and an adjustable rinse dispenser.

Deco-White™
Model DWU7400

Model DWU7400 — Features include a Pots & Pans Cycle, Normal Cycle and a Light/China Cycle. It also offers a convenient Rinse & Hold Cycle, deluxe upper and lower racks, and convertible bowl tines. Other features include a Temp Boost Sensor water heating option and a rinse dispenser. This model also available in Deco-White.™

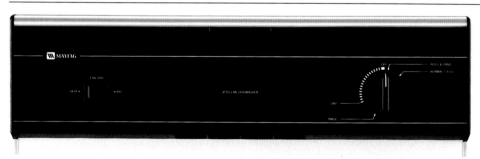

Model DWU7300 — Maytag dependability at a budget price! Features include a Pots & Pan Cycle, a Normal Cycle, automatic water heating, plus heat and no-heat drying. It also offers standard upper and lower racks, DuraTip™ tines and the same long-life motor, three-level wash system and co-polymer tub standard to all Maytags.

Maytag Dishwasher Specifications

ELECTRIC SUPPLY: 120 Volt; 60 Hz. All models require 15 amp fuse.

WATER SUPPLY: Water pressure should be 15-120 p.s.i. (1.06-8.44 kg / sq. cm). Water temperature should be 140°F. when it enters the dishwasher.

DRAIN: ½″ I.D. flexible drain hose furnished. High drain loop positioned on side of dishwasher.

MOTOR AND PUMP: ⅓ H.P. reversible; two-stage pump for circulation and draining.

WEIGHT (Crated/Uncrated):
Dependably Quiet™ Models — 100 lbs. (45 kg) / 85 lbs. (39 kg)
Dependably Quiet™ Plus Models — 115 lbs. (52 kg) / 100 lbs. (46 kg)
Added weight due to additional insulation.

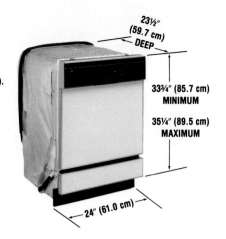

23½″ (59.7 cm) DEEP

33¾″ (85.7 cm) MINIMUM

35¼″ (89.5 cm) MAXIMUM

24″ (61.0 cm)

Trim Kit:
Door Panel Insert —
¼″ x 18⁹/₃₂″ x 23¹¹/₁₆″
(.64 cm x 46.4 cm x 60.2 cm)

Access Panel Insert —
¼″ x 4²¹/₃₂″ x 23¹¹/₁₆″
(.64 cm x 11.8 cm x 60.2 cm)

CYCLE	AVAILABLE ON MODEL(S)	CYCLE SEQUENCE							CYCLE TIME	WATER USAGE
Power Scrub	DWU9920	Pre-wash	Sani-Rinse	Sani-Rinse	Extended Main Wash	Sani-Rinse	Sani-Rinse	Dry	105 Minutes	11 (9 Imp.) Gallons 42 Liters
Pots & Pans	DWU9905, DWU9200, DWU7500, DWU7400, DWU7300	Pre-wash	Rinse	Rinse	Main Wash	Rinse	Rinse	Dry	99 Minutes	11 (9 Imp.) Gallons 42 Liters
Normal Cycle	All Models		Pre-wash	Rinse	Main Wash	Rinse	Rinse	Dry	84 Minutes	9 (7½ Imp.) Gallons 34 Liters
Light/China	DWU9920, DWU9905, DWU9200, DWU7500, DWU7400			Rinse	Main Wash	Rinse	Rinse	Dry	76 Minutes	7 (5½ Imp.) Gallons 26 Liters
Quick Cycle	DWU9920, DWU9905, DWU9200, DWU7500				Wash	Rinse	Rinse		17 Minutes	5 (4 Imp.) Gallons 19 Liters
Rinse & Hold	DWU9920, DWU9905, DWU9200, DWU7500, DWU7400				Rinse				7 Minutes	2 (1½ Imp.) Gallons 7 Liters

FEATURES	DEPENDABLY QUIET™ PLUS MODELS			DEPENDABLY QUIET™ MODELS		
	DWU9920	DWU9905	DWU9200	DWU7500	DWU7400	DWU7300
Touch Pads/Push Buttons	8	7	6	5	4	1
CYCLES:						
Power Scrub	X					
Pots & Pans		X	X	X	X	X
Normal Cycle	X	X	X	X	X	X
Light/China	X	X	X	X	X	
Quick Cycle	X	X	X	X		
Rinse & Hold	X	X	X	X	X	
WATER HEATING OPTIONS:						
Temp Boost Sensor	X	X	X	X	X	
Sani-Rinse	X	X	X	X		
Automatic Water Heating						X
FAN DRYING OPTIONS:						
Air Dry	X	X	X	X	X	X
Heat Dry	X	X	X	X	X	X
RACK OPTIONS:						
Upper Rack	Deluxe	Deluxe	Deluxe	Deluxe	Deluxe	Standard
Folding Shelf	X	X	X			
Lower Rack	Deluxe	Deluxe	Deluxe	Deluxe	Deluxe	Standard
High Side with Folding Shelf	X	X	X			
Convertible Bowl Tines	X	X	X	X	X	
OTHER OPTIONS:						
Nylon Rack Finish	X	X	X			
Rinse Dispenser	Adjustable	Adjustable	Adjustable	Adjustable	Standard	
Delay Start	X		X			
Indicator Lights	5	4	4	2	1	
Vacuum Fluorescent Display	X					
Touch Controls	X	X				
Available in Deco-White™	X				X	
Decorator Front Panels	All models come with Snow White/Black/Almond/Harvest Wheat decorator front panels (except Deco White™ models and model DWU7300 with Snow White/Black).					

All models listed here may not be available from every Maytag dealer. Because of continuing product improvement, Maytag reserves the right to change specifications without notice.

"QuickConnect" Disposers

The perfect complement to your new Maytag dishwasher is a quality Maytag food waste disposer.

Every model features "QuickConnect" mounting for easy installation. Heavy-duty, rust-resistant shredders grind everything from celery to chicken bones. And our jam-resistant impeller arms are made of high strength steel.

Our Batch Feed models feature Maytag's exclusive Auto-Start lid which turns on the unit when put in place. This prevents items from dropping into the disposer while it's operating. When the lid is removed, the disposer turns off.

Our Continuous Feed models are activated by a wall switch and feature an easy-load opening with a splash guard cover.

For more details, ask for a complete Maytag Food Waste Disposer specification sheet.

FEATURED CABINETRY BY THE GRABILL CABINET COMPANY

Fill your home with Maytag dependability! Maytag offers a complete line of quality kitchen and laundry products. There are models designed for every decor, lifestyle and budget.

MAYTAG
® THE DEPENDABILITY PEOPLE

782L-ADV JN 5/92 150 Printed in U.S.A.

MAYTAG COMPANY One Dependability Square, Newton, Iowa 50208

REFRIGERATORS

The ultimate in side-by-side refrigeration is expressed in the model RSW2400A with ice and water dispenser, pictured below, and the model RSD2400A (opposite page). Both models even have a convenient roll-out drawer which contains four sealed storage dishes that may be used in your microwave or oven.

And like all Maytag refrigerators, they feature a highlight you would never hear about on your own, our Whisper Cold™ compressor. We secure this high-capacity compressor on quieting rubber cushions with bolts, rather than simple metal tabs, so they won't break. This is an excellent example of Maytag's unending commitment to dependable construction. And just one of the many fine points of craftsmanship beneath the surface that distinguishes Maytag from all other brands.

RSW2400A

Upon closer inspection, you will discover that every side-by-side Maytag refrigerator boasts two slidable package "keepers", refrigerator door closers, a pull-out freezer basket and a freezer light. Note also the two sealed crispers, one of which is humidity selectable. Thus, you can tailor the different moisture needs of fruits and vegetables in their own preserving environments.

RSD2400A

Maytag refrigerators reflect the architectural tenet of maximizing the use of space, as demonstrated by the efficient placement of the wine rack. And the flexibility of adjustable shelves and bins.

Supporting this sophisticated design is adjustable cantilevered shelving, in every model, such as the RSD2400A, pictured at left. The sturdier construction of this design helps eliminate the rattles and shakes associated with ordinary refrigerators.

Along with the other sizes of refrigerators with the deluxe package of features, such as the model RSD2200A, pictured at right, you will find a double-walled meat keeper with temperature adjustment. Your fresh meats receive undivided attention as temperature and humidity are optimized, and the double wall helps prevent dry air from entering the chamber.

RSD2200A

Deco-White™ RSW2400

For the utmost in contemporary design, we point out one of our Deco-White™ models, pictured at left.

These models feature Maytag's convenient Thirst Aid™ Station ice and water dispenser, which offers many advantages over similar systems from other manufacturers.

The large fountain opening allows you to collect ice or water into pitchers or other large containers. Our molded foam insulation prevents freezing in the water line. And our unique design virtually eliminates ice jams.

Every Maytag top-mount refrigerator represents painstaking craftsmanship and attention to detail. Our egg cradle holds well more than a dozen and can be removed to the kitchen counter. The deep pockets of our bins, fixed into the refrigerator and freezer doors, always swing into use. And whatever model you select, you'll find an energy-saver switch to save you money as your seasonal climate turns cooler and less humid.

Many capacity choices are available with the deluxe feature package, such as model RTD1900A, pictured below. Every facet of the design enhances your use, such as the inclusion of a handy freezer light and versatile Sure-Lock™ shelves that adjust and conform to your needs.

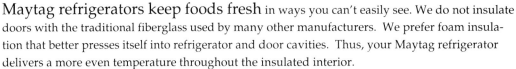

Maytag refrigerators keep foods fresh in ways you can't easily see. We do not insulate doors with the traditional fiberglass used by many other manufacturers. We prefer foam insulation that better presses itself into refrigerator and door cavities. Thus, your Maytag refrigerator delivers a more even temperature throughout the insulated interior.

RTD1900A

RTW2200A

Every possible convenience has been designed into the model RTW2200A, pictured at left. Of particular interest is the superior design of the ice maker.

The Maytag ice maker detects when ice cubes have frozen, then flash-heats them. Thus loosened, the ice is swept into the dispenser container. Even Maytag refrigerators that are not factory-equipped with this ice maker will accept it at a later date. The necessary internal elements are included in every model.

You will be comforted to know that every cubic foot of every refrigerator model is stocked with famous Maytag dependability. Sturdier steel and a triple-pronged locking design prevents shelves from twisting under heavy loads. Heavy-duty wire shelves are coated with a white epoxy finish to preserve shelf life. Hinges are stronger and heavier to keep doors from sagging. And door gaskets are reinforced with steel to prevent leaks.

RTD2300A

RTC1900A

The features are well illustrated in model RTC1900A, pictured at left, with its full-length handle trim and chrome door caps. It also features deep-door shelves with "keepers" that tighten up to condiments to stop them from tipping.

You will appreciate the two dairy compartments, as they maintain the proper temperature, so that butter remains spreadable. The split wire shelves enhance your flexibility in arrangement. Plus, this particular model adds an extra adjustable shelf in the freezer.

Tempered glass shelves and crisper tops shine in the model RTD1700A, pictured at right. You also receive the double-walled meat keeper with temperature adjustment. Note that this meat drawer is accepted in three different positions in the refrigerator. Again, adjustable shelves allow you to create the space to best suit your needs.

Regardless of which size or feature package catches your eye, your new refrigerator is solidly built on Maytag innovation. Our high-impact liner is an excellent example of using superior material to help prevent even hairline cracks to the refrigerator interior.

RTD1700A

As in the larger capacity models, you will still find slidable package "keepers" in both the refrigerator and freezer of the RTC1500A, pictured at left. The second crisper drawer is humidity controlled by you. And like all Maytag refrigerators, there's an adjustable meat drawer, covered dairy compartment, removable egg tray, no-frost freezer, adjustable freezer shelves and ice storage bin.

Every Maytag refrigerator measures up to certain standards of construction which exceed those of other manufacturers. We use galvanized steel, where others are content with plastic or cardboard. We use welds, where others use screws. We use screws, where others use nothing.

RTC1500A

Easy Ice™
Every Maytag refrigerator is designed to accept our ice maker, at your discretion.

Heavy-Duty Tempered Glass Shelves
Sturdier steel and cantilevered brackets eliminate twisting under heavy loads.

Thirst Aid™ Station With Pad-Lock
Our unique design allows you to easily fill pitchers or other large containers.

No-Break Bins
Practically indestructible and found throughout every Maytag refrigerator.

Strongbox™ Hinges
Stronger and heavier than regular hinges to prevent doors from sagging.

Adjustable Door Bin With Keeper™
Easily handles condiments from the refrigerator to the lunch table.

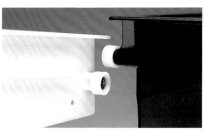

Roll-A-Drawers™
Maytag furnishes gliding rollers on every drawer in every refrigerator.

Egg Cradle
Nestles more than a dozen and removes to your cooking area.

Easy-Clean Access
Maytag's wide front wheels make light work of moving the refrigerator.

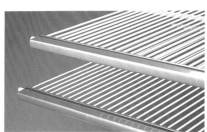

Heavy-Duty Wire Shelves
Coated with a white epoxy to preserve shelf life, the wires are closer together to prevent tipping of items.

High-Impact Liner
Maytag uses a liner material which helps prevent even hairline cracks.

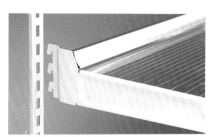

Sure-Lock™ Shelves
Maytag uses a triple-pronged locking design to insure stability.

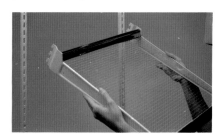

Create-A-Space™ System
Shelves relocate at your discretion, allowing you to be the interior designer.

Reinforced Airlock™ Seal
Strengthened with steel to prevent door gasket from leaking.

Textured Steel Reversible Doors
Hide hand and fingerprints for a cleaner look in your kitchen.

MAYTAG DEPENDABILITY WARRANTY

Maytag refrigerators come with a complete warranty that covers replacement and labor on all parts for one full year from date of purchase. There is a limited warranty that provides free parts for two years. And for five years, there are free parts and labor on some of the major components.

Unlike some warranties, your Maytag warranty moves with you and is valid anywhere in the United States (C.S.A. listed products warranted anywhere in Canada). See your Maytag dealer for complete warranty details.

FEATURES	TOP-MOUNT										SIDE-BY-SIDE					
REFRIGERATORS	RTD2300A	RTW2200A	RTD2100A	RTD1900A	RTC1900A	RTS1900A	RTD1700A	RTC1700A	RTS1700A	RTC1500A	RSW2400A*	RSD2400A	RSW2200A*	RSD2200A	RSD2000A	RSC2000A
Heavy Duty Adjustable Wire Shelf					3 split	2		3 split	2	2						2
Heavy Duty Adjustable Tempered Glass Shelf	4 split	4 split	4 split	4 split	1 split		4 split	1 split			3	3	3	3	3	1
Fixed Crisper Shelf (Glass/Opaque)	G	G	G	G	O	O	G	O	O	O	G	G	G	G	G	O
Temp. Adj. Meat Drawer (Double/Single) Wall	D	D	D	D	S	S	D	S	S	S	D	D	D	D	D	S
Crisper Drawers (Sealed/Moisture Control)	S/M	S/M	S/M	S/M	S/M	2S	S/M	S/M	2S	S/M	S/M	S/M	S/M	S/M	S/M	S/M
Wine Rack	•	•									•	•	•	•	•	
Microwave/Utility Drawer											•	•				
Covered Dairy Compartment	2	1	2	2	2	1	2	2	1	1	1	1	1	1	1	1
Deep Fixed Door Bins	1	1	1	1	3	3½	3	3	3½	2½	1	1	1	1	1	5
Deep Adjustable Door Bins	4	4	4	4							4	4	4	4	4	
Keepers	2	2	2	2	2		2	2		1	2	2	2	2	2	2
Energy Saver Switch	•	•	•	•	•	•	•	•	•	•	auto	auto	auto	auto	auto	auto
NO-FROST FREEZER																
Freezer Light	•	•	•	•							•	•	•	•	•	•
Heavy Duty Adjustable Wire Shelf	2	2	2	2	2	1	1	1	1	1	4	5	4	5	5	5
Deep Fixed Door Bins	2	2	2	2	2	2	2	2	2	2	5	6	5	6	6	6
Freezer Keeper	1	1	1	1	1		1	1		1						
Ice Cube Trays	4		4	4	4	4	2	2	2	2		4		4	4	4
Automatic Ice Maker	option	yes	option	option	option	option	option	option	option	option	yes	option	yes	option	option	option
EXTERIOR FEATURES																
Ice and Water Dispenser		•									•		•			
Reversible Doors	•	Special Order	•	•	•	•	•	•	•	•					•	•
Front Adjustable Wheels with Locks	•	•	•	•	•	•	•	•	•	•	•	•	•	•	•	•
Door Stops	2	2	2	2	2	2	2	2	2	2	2	2	2	2	2	2
Door Trim Kit "Option"	option	option	option	option	option						option	option	option	option		
Foam Door Insulation	•	•	•	•	•	•	•	•	•	•			•	•	•	•
Available in White and Almond	•	•	•	•	•	•	•	•	•	•			•	•	•	•
Shipping Weight (Lbs./Kg.)	314/142	328/149	306/139	282/128	270/122	268/121	260/118	254/115	249/113	240/109	373/169	358/162	345/156	330/150	321/146	310/141
Height (In./Cm.) NOTE: Does not include door hinge cover	65½/166	65½/166	65½/166	65½/166	65½/166	65½/166	64½/164	64½/164	64½/164	60/152	66⅜/169	66⅜/169	66⅜/169	66⅜/169	66⅜/169	66⅜/169
Width (In./Cm.)	33/84	33/84	31½/80	31½/80	31½/80	31½/80	29/74	29/74	29/74	29/74	35¾/91	35¾/91	33/84	33/84	31/79	31/79
Depth (In./Cm.) Including Handle	33/84	33/84	33/84	30/76	30/76	30/76	30/76	30/76	30/76	30/76	31⅓/79	31⅓/79	31⅓/79	31⅓/79	31⅓/79	31⅓/79
Depth (In./Cm.) with Door Open 90 Degrees	62⅜/158	62⅜/158	60⅞/155	57⅞/147	57⅞/147	57⅞/147	55⅜/141	55⅜/141	55⅜/141	55⅜/141	48¾/124	48¾/124	48¾/124	48¾/124	46¾/119	46¾/119
Total Shelf Area (Sq. Ft./Sq. M)	34.5/3.2	32.8/3.0	32.3/3.0	28.3/2.6	28.5/2.6	26.2/2.4	24.1/2.2	24.1/2.2	23.7/2.2	22.5/2.1	29.0/2.7	30.4/2.8	25.1/2.3	26.3/2.4	24.3/2.3	24.3/2.3
Total Volume (Cu. Ft./M)	22.5/.64	21.9/.62	21.0/.59	18.5/.52	18.6/.53	18.6/.53	16.5/.47	16.5/.47	16.5/.47	14.6/.41	23.5/.67	23.8/.67	21.6/.61	21.8/.62	20.2/.57	20.2/.57
Fresh Food Volume (Cu. Ft./M)	15.5/.44	15.0/.42	14.6/.41	12.8/.36	12.9/.37	12.9/.37	11.7/.33	11.7/.33	11.7/.33	10.5/.30	15.2/.43	15.2/.43	15.2/.43	15.2/.43	13.6/.38	13.6/.38
Freezer Volume (Cu. Ft./M)	7.0/.20	6.9/.20	6.4/.18	5.7/.16	5.7/.16	5.7/.16	4.8/.14	4.8/.14	4.8/.14	4.1/.12	8.3/.23	8.6/.24	6.4/.18	6.6/.19	6.6/.19	6.6/.19

For ease of installation, allow ½" clearance on sides and top.

*Models available in Deco-White™

All models listed in this brochure may not be available from every Maytag dealer. Because of continuing product improvements Maytag reserves the right to change specifications without notice.

MAYTAG *Full-Size Stacked Washers & Dryers*

Maytag Dependability In Half The Space!

Model LSE9900

Now you can bring the laundry room up from the basement and into the kitchen, the bath, the bedroom — even the hall closet!

At first glance, you may not even recognize a Maytag stacked washer & dryer as laundry equipment. With its sleek, contemporary styling and unobtrusive design, it's more like a work of art.

Imagine! Both a *full-size* Maytag washer and a *full-size* Maytag dryer are incorporated into one compact unit.

Specifically designed to fit small areas, a Maytag stacked washer & dryer lets you bring the laundry room up from the basement and into the kitchen, the bath, the bedroom — even the hall closet. Wherever there are a few square feet to spare. Wherever laundry piles up! That's where your laundry equipment makes the most sense.

And the features you'll find in a Maytag stacked washer & dryer are the same dependable features which have made Maytag washers and dryers America's *most preferred brand* in consumer preference surveys.

A full range of wash cycles assures you of the proper water temperature and agitation to clean all kinds of fabrics. Maytag's all-fabric drying, made possible by a high-velocity blower combined with a diagonal air flow, provides fast and even drying at temperatures that are gentle to your clothing and other laundry items.

And, like every product we make, a Maytag stacked washer & dryer is built to last longer and need fewer repairs. That's good news for you. Not so good for our repairman.

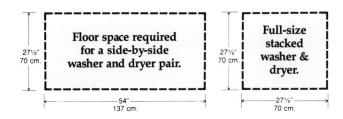

Floor space required for a side-by-side washer and dryer pair. 27½" 70 cm. 54" 137 cm.

Full-size stacked washer & dryer. 27½" 70 cm. 27½" 70 cm.

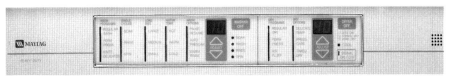

Deco-White™Model LSE/LSG9900

Model LSE/LSG9900 — Advanced computer touch controls! Simply activate the desired wash or dry cycle with the touch of a finger. The computer automatically selects the most commonly used wash and rinse temperature, wash time and water level. And the most commonly used drying temperature, drying time and drying level. The digital display indicates those selections. Yet, each selection can be tailored to meet your individual requirements.

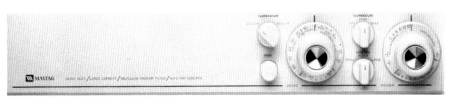

Deco-White™Model LSE/LSG7800

Model LSE/LSG7800 — Simple-to-operate rotary controls! The washer dial lets you select from Regular, Permanent Press and Delicate cycles. And the dryer dial lets you select from Regular, Permanent Press, Delicate and Air Fluff cycles. In addition, Timed-Dry and Press Care options offer even greater drying flexibility and control.

MAYTAG DEPENDABILITY WARRANTY

Maytag stacked washers & dryers come with a complete warranty that covers replacement and labor on all parts for one full year from date of purchase. A limited warranty provides free parts for two years. And for five years, there are free parts on replacements related to computer touch controls, cabinet rust and dryer drum.

In addition, there are free parts for ten years on the Dependable Drive® Transmission in our washers.

Unlike some warranties, your Maytag warranty moves with you and is valid anywhere in the United States (C.S.A. listed products warranted anywhere in Canada). See your Maytag dealer for complete warranty details.

Maytag Dryer Specifications

AIR FLOW: 180 CFM

EXHAUST: 4" duct permits a maximum of 50 feet rigid aluminum ductwork. Subtract 8 feet for each 90° elbow, 8 feet for an exhaust hood. Dryer vented out the back.

MOTOR: ¼ H.P.; 115 volt; 60 Hz; thermoprotected against overload; automatic reset.

HEAT SOURCE:
Electric — Nichrome helix coil, 240 volt 3-wire, 4600 watts, 30 amp fuse.
Gas — Single port burner 18,000 BTU/hr.; electric ignition; automatic shut-off.

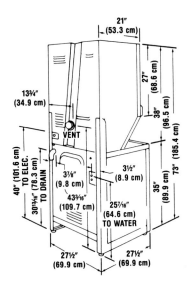

Maytag Washer Specifications

CAPACITY: Large 16 (13 Imp.) gal; 60.6 lit.

WATER USAGE: (regular full cycle) —
36 (30 Imp.) gal; 136 lit. — large
28 (23 Imp.) gal; 106 lit. — medium
24 (20 Imp.) gal; 91 lit. — small

MOTOR: ⅓ H.P.; 115 volt; 60 Hz; reversible; thermo-protected against overload; automatic reset.

POWER: 1-.17 kwh depending on cycle

HOSE LENGTHS: Inlet 5 feet (152 cm.); drain 4 feet (122 cm.)

INSTALLATION: Hot and cold connections with water pressure within 30-120 PSI range. At least 140°F. hot water; a drain; 115 volt electrical outlet properly grounded. Use standard 15 amp fuse.

UNCRATED WEIGHT: Approximately 340 lbs. (154 kg.)

DRYER FEATURES	LSE / LSG9900	LSE / LSG7800
Controls	Computer Touch	Rotary
Drying Control	Electronic	Auto
Temperature Selections	3	3
Adjustable Degree Of Dryness	X	X
Delicate Temperature Setting	X	X
Press Care	X	X
Air Fluff	X	X
Permanent Press Cycle	X	X
Cycle Signal	Adjustable	X
Eye-Level Loading	X	X
Cool-Down Indicator Light	X	
Self-Diagnostics	X	
Up-Front Lint Filter	X	X

All models available with either gas or electric dryers.

WASHER FEATURES	LSE / LSG9900	LSE / LSG7800
Controls	Computer Touch	Rotary
Warm Rinse Option	X	
Automatic Presoak/Soak Only Cycle	X	
Delicate/Knits Cycle	X	X
Permanent Press Cycle	X	X
Temperature Selections	5	3
Water Levels	3	3
Bleach Dispenser	X	X
Self-Cleaning Lint Filter	X	X
Fabric Softener Dispenser	X	X
Cycle Sequence Lights	X	
Tub Light	X	
Lid Lock	X	X
Self-Diagnostics	X	
White Porcelain Tub	X	X

All models available in white, almond or Deco-White™

Adequate clearance is necessary for proper installation. Please consult product installation instructions. Because of continuing product improvement, Maytag reserves the right to change specifications without notice.

MAYTAG
® THE DEPENDABILITY PEOPLE

783L-ADV JN 8/92 150M Printed in U.S.A.

MAYTAG COMPANY One Dependability Square, Newton, Iowa 50208

RUSSELL
RANGE

NNOVATION

RUSSELL RANGE leads the field in design innovation. We pioneered the domestic appliance industry as the **first** manufacturer to produce and market the unique ''Safe-Slide''™ top grate system. Each grate is designed to cover only one burner making the size and weight of each grate manageable. Our clean construction eliminates the exposure of unsightly hardware. RUSSELL RANGE manufactures the **only** commercial-style domestic cook-tops that **fit flush** into standard 24" cabinetry...

TANDARDS

RUSSELL RANGE has a commitment to quality that is unsurpassed in our industry. By employing master craftsmen on the cutting edge of modern technology, we achieve the most intricate detail and precise fit. The result is timeless beauty and complete satisfaction for the most demanding users. All RUSSELL RANGE products are setting the standards for quality and excellence now and for years to come...

ERSATILITY

RUSSELL RANGE blends innovation with bold styling to offer great flexibility in kitchen design. Along with A.G.A. certification for ''zero clearance'' installation, our cooktops are offered with either a square or bullnose front to create a clean, flush line with your choice of counter edges. Our dramatic stainless and black finish will enhance every kitchen design from Classic Country to Contemporary European to Hi-Tech Professional...

OFF

LITE

Hi

SIM

R

RUSSELL
RANGE

Mounts flush

Optional, easy to clean, stainless steel backsplash; required only for installation against combustible type wall.

Pilotless, high-power commercial stainless steel burners are rated up to 15,000 BTU's to satisfy a full range of cooking needs.

Versatile bullnose or square front designed to be compatible with your choice of counter edges.

Safe A.G.A. approved "push-to-turn" control knobs offer a true low simmer setting.

Modular, ed, cast ir Slide"™ to is an **indu**

ORMANCE...COMMITMENT TO QUALITY...

Optional custom-fitted, nickel plated wok ring locks into place over any burner.

Modular stainless steel or black porcelain support pans with removable drip bowls will fit any dishwasher.

A.G.A. certified for ''zero clearance'' and mounts **flush** into any standard 24'' deep cabinet.

:elain coat-
:Safe-
ate system
original.

Stainless steel leg-cover apron conceals leveling legs and creates a ''built-in'' appearance.

Ultra low simmer

Black porcelain finish

PERFORMANCE

RUSSELL RANGE's infinite flame control combines, high-power with ultra low simmer to take restaurant style cooking one step further. Our exclusive "Safe-Slide"™ top grate system blends the grace of sweeping curves with the durability of porcelain enameled cast iron. Our simple and comfortable "push-to-turn" knobs along with pilotless ignition, make operation safe and easy. The innovative modular design makes cleaning a snap...

Four burner model FSC 24-4

PRESTIGE

RUSSELL RANGE products are the gourmet's choice for outfitting a first class kitchen. Available solely through the most exclusive dealers nationwide, our cooktops are specified by top architects and kitchen designers. A RUSSELL RANGE cooktop will complete the most prestigious kitchen and please the most discerning homeowner. It is a source of pride and a symbol of quality and exclusivity...

RUSSELL RANGE COOKTOPS...

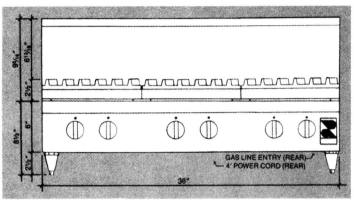

MODEL FSC 36-6

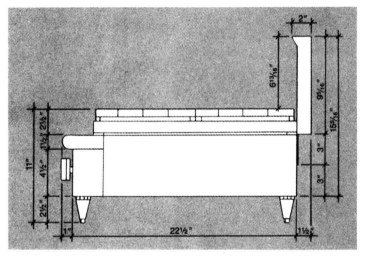

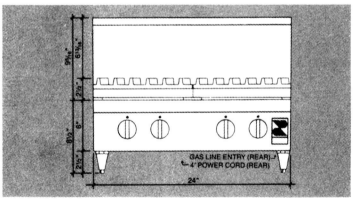

MODEL FSC 24-4

SPECIFICATIONS

- Electrical requirements: 1 amp, 120 volts, A.C. 60Hz
- 4-foot cord and 3-prong plug provided
- Shipping weight approx. 110 lbs. (FSC 36-6), 85 lbs. (FSC 24-4)
- Gas entry: bottom, right-rear corner
- All models are A.G.A. certified for ''zero clearance'' installation
- All models convert from natural gas to propane in the field with no additional parts
- Adjustable legs
- Pilotless electronic spark ignitors
- Stainless steel or black porcelain support pans and drip bowls available
- Black finish, heavy-duty, reversible cast iron griddle/grill optional
- All units must be vented properly
- Specifications subject to change without notice

SERVICE

All RUSSELL RANGE products come with a five year warranty on parts and one year warranty on labor and the support of a nationwide service team. We strive to insure that every customer has a reliable product with years of creative, worry-free cooking...

GAS LINE 1/2"
Gas Pressure
4" W.C. Nat.
10" W.C. L.P.

RUSSELL RANGE, INC.
325 SOUTH MAPLE AVE. #5
SOUTH SAN FRANCISCO, CA 94080

RUSSELL RANGE ® © 1990

SHARP®

CAROUSEL® II

M I C R O W A V E   O V E N S

R-1831, R-1830

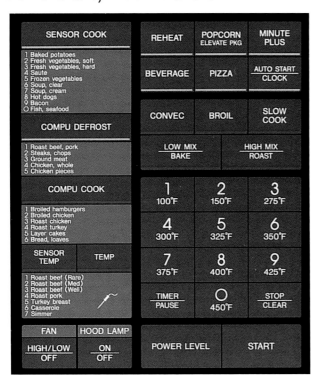

- ESP Sensor Cook automatically cooks favorite foods

- One-touch Pizza, Popcorn, Beverage and Reheat keys

- Auto-Touch® controls with 2-color display, clock, 99 minute 99 second timer, Auto Start, Timer/Pause, Minute Plus™; also programmable 4-stage cooking; 10 Variable Power levels

- Two combination settings with convection temperature control from 100°F to 450°F; Broil preheats oven, signals when ready

- Slow Cook expands timer up to 4 hours for slow cook recipes such as baked beans, marinated meats, chili and stews

- CompuDefrost™ is an easy defrost for meat, poultry; visual cues indicate when to turn over, cover or rearrange food

Carousel II Over The Range Convection Microwave Ovens are prime examples of space-efficient design, easy-to-understand features and one of the most versatile cooking systems on the market. Designed to install with ease, leaving the counter free and clear for maximum work space.

R-1831 is all white, an important element of style in today's modern or classic kitchens. R-1830 is available in sleek black. Generous 0.9 cu. ft. capacity has a 13" diameter turntable. Each unit features Sharp's advanced electronic controls for the hood lamp and powerful, built-in dual speed exhaust system; 310 cfm horizontal discharge, 300 cfm vertical discharge.

ESP™ Sensor Cook automatically cooks favorite foods — there's no manual setting of cooking times or power levels. Popcorn, Reheat, Beverage and Pizza keys offer Instant Start ease. Microwave, convection, combination and broil options create an unmatched system that turns out golden brown cakes and breads, plus moist, flavorful meat and poultry. Sensor Temp simplifies automatic temperature probe cooking so food is cooked to the desired degree of doneness. CompuCook™ computes convection and combination times/temperatures for perfect broiling, roasting and baking. Includes broiling trivet and rack for 2-level baking.

Installs ducted or non-ducted without needing recirculating kit and extra space. Optional RK-250 Filler Panel Kit with two 3" black panels for installation in spaces wider than 30". RK-210 Charcoal Filter for non-ducted installations. When mounted, oven top must be minimum of 66" from floor, 30" from cooking surface. Output power: 800 watts.

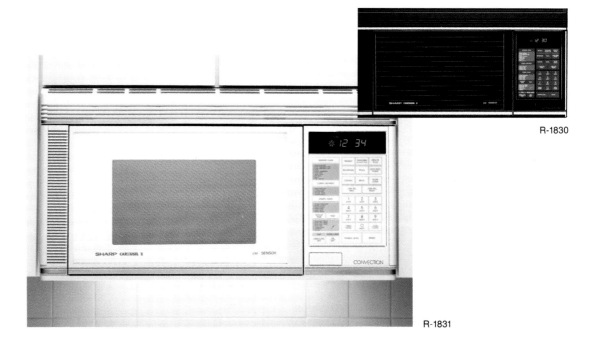

R-1830

R-1831

O V E R   T H E   R A N G E

Carousel II Over The Range Microwave Ovens have mastered the science of space-management and the art of microwaving ease. Each model avoids countertop congestion with its space-efficient Over The Range design. The 0.9 cu. ft. interior is equipped with a 12¾" diameter turntable for cooking food evenly without hot or cold spots. The black cabinet of the R-1420B is streamlined sophistication at its best. R-1421 is available in sleek white-on-white.

Timesaving features appeal to families with fast-paced schedules. Easy Reheat™ is a quick, no-work way to reheat a roll or muffin, dinner plate, vegetables, individual casserole or soup. CompuCook has 5 settings for automatic cooking of fresh or frozen vegetables, baked potatoes, hamburgers or chicken pieces. CompuDefrost makes freezer-to-table meals an everyday reality. Defrost meat or poultry without guesswork; instructions in the display advise when to cover, turn over, break apart or rearrange food.

Sensor Temp makes sure roasts, poultry and casseroles are cooked to the temperature of your choice; 7 preset food temperatures make temperature probe cooking easy. The 5 Variable Power levels ensure success with many foods.

Oven installs ducted or non-ducted without needing recirculating kit and extra space. Optional RK-250 Filler Panel Kit with two 3" black panels for installation in spaces wider than 30". RK-210 Charcoal Filter for non-ducted installations. When mounted, oven top must be minimum of 66" from floor, 30" from cooking surface. Output power: 800 watts.

R-1421, R-1420B

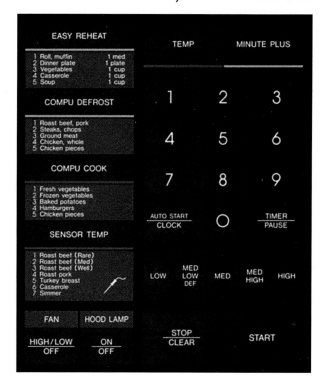

- Installation is simple, offering flexibility for home improvement projects or new home designs

- Advanced electronic controls for hood lamp and powerful 2-speed fan; built-in exhaust system features 310 cfm horizontal discharge, 300 cfm vertical discharge

- 10-key Auto-Touch controls are the ultimate in precision and ease; Auto Start, clock, 99 minute 99 second timer

- Minute Plus sets one minute of time per touch; Timer/Pause can be used as a kitchen timer or as a pause between stages to monitor food's progress, add ingredients or stir

- Easy Reheat is great for snacks or single servings

- Programmable for versatile 3-stage cooking

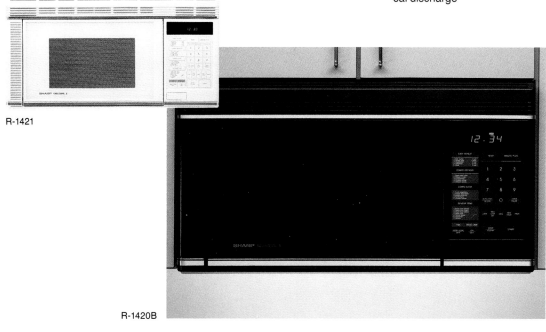

R-1421

R-1420B

O V E R T H E R A N G E

R-9H94
R-9H84

- 4-way cooking team browns, bakes, broils and crisps

- Auto-Touch controls with Auto Start, clock, Timer/Pause key and 99 minute 99 second timer

- Instant Start keys for Reheat, Popcorn, Dinner Plate, Beverage

- Minute Plus sets oven at HIGH with a single touch

- Deluxe ESP Sensor automatically cooks favorite foods

- New Cook & Simmer setting for homemade soups and sauces with the ease of the 90s

- Includes broiling trivet and rack for 2-level baking

- Optional Built-in Kit RK-90W (white) or RK-90 (black) for wall oven installation

Carousel II Convection Microwave Ovens bring together advanced capabilities with the best ideas in no-guesswork cooking, reheating and defrosting. Both the white and metallic charcoal finish cabinets set the standard for design. The 4-way cooking team browns, bakes, broils and crisps with convection, microwave and broiling options; two combination settings are perfect for roasting and baking.

Heading the impressive lineup of easy-to-use features is ESP Sensor Cook, which automatically determines cooking times and power levels for 8 varieties of microwave favorites. Instant Start keys continue the emphasis on ease, reheating foods, popping popcorn, heating a dinner plate or warming a beverage with one-touch convenience.

CompuDefrost is safe, efficient and always easy. Just touch the key to enter weight of meat or poultry and follow the commands in the display. New Cook & Simmer™ setting cooks soups and sauces automatically. Simply enter the number of cups of liquid in recipe and the simmer time — the oven takes it from there! Memory Plus™ stores the most often used cooking time.

Convection temperature control ranges from 100°F for proofing bread to 450°F for broiling. Broil key preheats oven, signals when ready. Slow Cook expands timer capacity up to 4 hours. Programmable 4-stage cooking. CompuCook computes times/temperature settings for automatic combination and convection cooking. Features Demonstration Mode and child lock. Large 1.5 cu. ft. capacity; 15⅜" diameter turntable. R-9H94 is white-on-white; R-9H84 is metallic charcoal. Output power: 900 watts.

R-9H94

R-9H84

C O N V E C T I O N

Carousel Convection Microwave Ovens offer a comprehensive lineup of capabilities plus the convenience of a space-efficient design. Sharp puts the emphasis on easy versatility with a 4-way cooking team. Brown, bake, broil and crisp with convection and broiling options. Two combination settings are perfect for roasting and baking, with convection temperature control from 100°F to 450°F. The 0.9 cu. ft. interior is equipped with a 13" turntable for 360° cooking.

CompuCook calculates microwave, convection and combination times and temperatures for no-guesswork, automatic cooking. CompuDefrost offers dependable, safe defrosting by weight of meat or poultry. It's easier than ever to monitor food as it cooks or defrosts with Sharp's new clear view see-through door.

Auto-Touch controls are designed for exacting control and total ease. Popcorn key pops a bag of microwave popcorn with a single touch. Broil setting preheats oven to 450°F and signals when ready. Slow Cook expands timer up to 4 hours. Programmable for easy sequencing of up to 4 cooking stages. The 10 Variable Power levels vary cooking speed for everything from fast reheating to delicate sauces.

Kitchen timer provides exact timing for cooking or other household tasks. Pause key stops the oven between stages to check on food, add ingredients or stir. Auto Start delays cooking up to 12 hours. Also features time of day clock and child lock. R-7A95 is white stone finish; R-7A85 is stone gray. Output power: 850 watts.

R-7A95
R-7A85

• Every option at your command — brown, bake, broil and crisp with the 4-way cooking team

• Two combination settings ideal for roasting and baking

• New clear view see-through door is great for watching food as it cooks or defrosts

• CompuCook and CompuDefrost make everyday cooking and defrosting easy — there's no guesswork

• Broil setting preheats oven to 450°F and signals when ready

• Optional RK-71 (for R-7A85) or RK-71W (R-7A95) Kit available for built-in installation†

R-7A85

R-7A95

CONVECTION

R-5X84
R-4X84

- Sharp's ESP Sensor Cook, Sensor Reheat and new Sensor Defrost sense when many foods are perfect

- One-touch Popcorn, Beverage and Dinner Plate keys are everyday work-savers

- Choice of 1.6 cu. ft. design with 16" turntable or 1.2 cu. ft. with 14⅛" turntable

- Auto-Touch controls with lighted display, 99 minute 99 second timer, Auto Start, Minute Plus and Timer/Pause

- Memory Plus stores the most often used cooking time

- Child lock is a welcome safety feature for parents, grandparents or caregivers

Carousel II Smart & Easy™ **Microwave Ovens** merge mistakeproof sensors and easiest-ever controls. Sharp's ESP Sensor and the innovative control panel take the guesswork out of cooking, defrosting and reheating for true ease and efficiency. Whether it's the extra-large 1.6 cu. ft. capacity R-5X84, or the generous 1.2 cu. ft. capacity R-4X84, each is an intelligent choice. Rotating turntable design ensures excellent results.

Smart & Easy Sensor Reheat offers automatic reheating by sensing vapor or humidity emitted by cooking food. Sensor Defrost is safe and ultra-easy. Just place steaks, chops, ground meat or poultry on the oven's special defrost/roast rack and touch the key! No need to enter weight or type of food to be defrosted. Deluxe Sensor Cook automatically cooks a wide variety of foods: baked potatoes, fresh vegetables, bacon, ground meat, fish/seafood, chicken, turkey breast and roast pork.

Popcorn, Dinner Plate and Beverage keys start with one-touch ease. New Cook & Simmer key is a work-saving idea that helps turn out perfect homemade soups and sauces. The user enters number of cups of liquid in recipe and the simmer time. The oven takes it from there, automatically calculating time to boil liquid, and then reducing power level for the simmer time. Stone gray cabinet is a sensible and stylish design choice. Programmable 4-stage cooking; 10 Variable Power levels. Optional Built-in Kits RK-81 (for R-5X84) and RK-41 (for R-4X84) for wall oven installation. Output power: 900 watts.

R-4X84

R-5X84

S M A R T & E A S Y

Carousel Auto-Touch Microwave Ovens. The clean-looking beauty of white is becoming a streamlined classic in today's kitchens. The R-5A95 and R-4A95 are style-setting designs offering a choice of sizes. R-5A95 is a 1.6 cu. ft. capacity oven with 16" turntable; R-4A95 is a 1.2 cu. ft. capacity oven with 14 1/8" turntable.

New Breakfast settings make the at-home "rush hour" run more smoothly. Select coffee/tea, fresh or frozen roll/muffin, hot cereal or scrambled eggs . . . breakfast is ready without any fuss. Snacks and Reheat settings automatically heat family favorites to just the right serving temperature.

CompuCook is the no-guesswork way to everyday cooking. It automatically calculates cooking times and power levels for 5 popular categories of microwaved foods. CompuDefrost quickly defrosts meats and poultry. Just touch the key to enter weight; visual cues in the display indicate when to turn over or check food. Versatile 4-stage cooking is easy and convenient. Pop microwave popcorn automatically with just one touch of the special Popcorn key.

Auto-Touch controls are designed for fingertip precision and ultimate ease. Auto Start delays cooking up to 12 hours. Minute Plus sets the oven at HIGH for one minute of cooking per touch. The 10 Variable Power levels vary cooking speed for everything from simple reheating to delicate sauces. Pause key stops the oven between stages; it's ideal for checking on food or adding ingredients. Kitchen timer provides exact timing. Also features clock, Demonstration Mode and child lock safety feature. Output power: 900 watts.

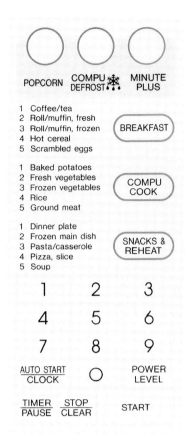

R-5A95
R-4A95

- White cabinets make a style statement of uncomplicated ease

- Optional RK-81W (for R-5A95) or RK-41W (R-4A95) Kit available for built-in installation†

- New Breakfast settings get the day off to a great start with quick, no-fuss morning meals

- Snacks and Reheat settings are ready for family favorites

- Programmable 4-stage cooking

- CompuCook and CompuDefrost provide automatic cooking and defrosting of frequently microwaved foods

- Popcorn key is one-touch easy

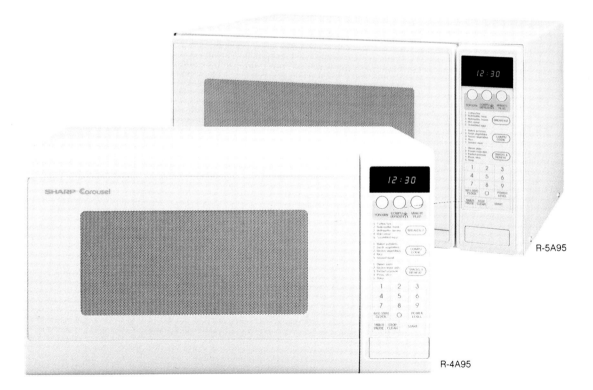

R-5A95

R-4A95

A U T O - T O U C H

Your Sharp Microwave Oven can be built into your kitchen wall or cabinet using the appropriate Sharp Built-in Kit. Complete hardware and easy-to-follow instructions are included. Prepare cabinet or wall opening according to the illustration below, providing access to a separate 3-pronged, 115-120v AC outlet, 15 amps or larger.

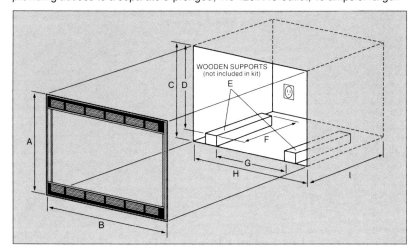

WOODEN SUPPORTS
(not included in kit)

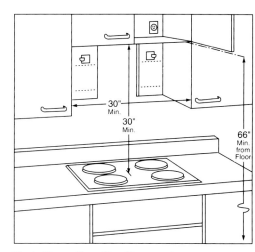

Each Sharp Over The Range microwave can be easily adapted for either outside ventilation (vertical or horizontal) or non-vented, ductless recirculation.

Make sure top of oven will be at least 66" from the floor and at least 30" from the cooking surface. A separate 15 amp or more electrical receptacle must be located in the cabinet directly above the microwave oven.

	A	B	C	D	E	F	G	H	I
RK-90, RK-90W	19	26	17 (+ height of wood)	17⅜"	nominal 2"×2" actual 1⅝"×2"×16"	16	18⅜"±⅛"	25¼"±⅛"	min. 20
RK-81, RK-81W	18	27	16⅞"±⅛"	—	not used	—	—	24¹³⁄₁₆"±⁷⁄₁₆"	min. 19
RK-41, RK-41W	17	23	15¹³⁄₁₆"±⅛"	—	not used	—	—	22³⁄₁₆"±⅛"	min. 18"
RK-71, RK-71W	20	22	14 (+ height of wood)	14³⁄₁₆"	nominal 2"×2" actual 1⅝"×2"×13"	13	16	21	min. 18

SPECIFICATIONS	R-1831, R-1830	R-1421, R-1420B	R-9H94, R-9H84	R-7A95, R-7A85	R-5X84, R-4X84	R-5A95, R-4A95
Oven Capacity:	0.9 cu. ft.	0.9 cu. ft.	1.5 cu. ft.	0.9 cu. ft.	R-5X84: 1.6 cu. ft. R-4X84: 1.2 cu. ft.	R-5A95: 1.6 cu. ft. R-4A95: 1.2 cu. ft.
Display:	2-color digital	Lighted digital	2-color digital	Lighted digital	Lighted digital	Lighted digital
Convection Oven Temperature Control:	100°, 150°, 275°- 450°F in 25° increments		100°, 150°, 275°- 450°F in 25° increments	100°, 150°, 275°- 450°F in 25° increments		
Cabinet:	R-1831: White painted R-1830: Black painted	R-1421: White painted R-1420B: Black painted	R-9H94: White R-9H84: Metallic charcoal	R-7A95: White stone R-7A85: Stone gray	Stone gray	White
Output Power:	800W	800W	900W	850W	900W	900W
Outside Dimensions: (WHD)	29⅞" × 16½" × 15"	29⅞" × 16½" × 15"	24⅝" × 14⅞" × 20¼"	20½" × 12" × 18¼"	R-5X84: 24" × 13¼" × 19" R-4X84: 21⅝" × 12¼" × 17"	R-5A95: 24" × 13¼" × 19" R-4A95: 21⅝" × 12¼" × 17"
Oven Dimensions: (WHD)	13⅝" × 8⅜" × 13½"	13⅝" × 8½" × 13½"	16⅛" × 9⅝" × 16⅛"	13¾" × 8⅛" × 13½"	R-5X84: 16⅞" × 9¼" × 17⅜" R-4X84: 15" × 8¼" × 16⅛"	R-5A95: 16⅞" × 9¼" × 17⅜" R-4A95: 15" × 8¼" × 16⅛"
Oven Interior:	Stainless steel with light	Acrylic with light	Stainless steel with light	Stainless steel with light	Acrylic with light	Acrylic with light
Approx. Weight:	Net: 74 lbs. Shipping: 87 lbs.	Net: 68 lbs. Shipping: 81 lbs.	Net: 60 lbs. Shipping: 66 lbs.	Net: 42 lbs. Shipping: 47 lbs.	R-5X84: Net: 47 lbs. Shipping: 55 lbs. R-4X84: Net: 38 lbs. Shipping: 43 lbs.	R-5A95: Net: 45 lbs. Shipping: 53 lbs. R-4A95: Net: 36 lbs. Shipping: 41 lbs.
AC Line Voltage:	120V, single phase, 60Hz, AC only	120V, single phase, 60Hz, AC only	120V, single phase, 60Hz, AC only	120V, single phase, 60Hz, AC only	120V, single phase, 60Hz, AC only	120V, single phase, 60Hz, AC only
AC Power Required:	1.6kW, 13.0A	1.6kW, 13.0A	1.55kW, 13.0A	1.4kW, 14.0A	1.52kW, 12.8A	1.52kW, 12.8A
Safety Compliance:	FCC, DHHS, UL listed	FCC, DHHS, UL listed	FCC, DHHS, UL listed	FCC, DHHS, UL listed	FCC, DHHS, UL listed	FCC, DHHS, UL listed
Supplied Accessories:	Broiling trivet, baking rack, temperature probe	Temperature probe	Broiling trivet, baking rack	Broiling trivet	Defrost/roast rack	
Optional Accessories: (Available at extra cost)	RK-250 Filler Panel Kit (2 3" black panels); RK-210 Charcoal Filter for non-ducted installations†	RK-250 Filler Panel Kit (2 3" black panels); RK-210 Charcoal Filter for non-ducted installations†	R-9H94: Built-in Kit RK-90W R-9H84: Built-in Kit RK-90 for in-the-wall installation†	R-7A95: Built-in Kit RK-71W R-7A85: Built-in Kit RK-71 for in-the-wall installation†	R-5X84: Built-in Kit RK-81 R-4X84: Built-in Kit RK-41 for in-the-wall installation†	R-5A95: Built-in Kit RK-81W R-4A95: Built-in Kit RK-41W for in-the-wall installation†

Specifications subject to change without notice. †Refer to Operation Manual for installation recommendations. Output wattage based on IEC-705 1988 Test Procedure.

Sharp Electronics Corporation
Corporate Headquarters and Executive Offices
Sharp Plaza, Mahwah, New Jersey 07430-2135
Phone: (201) 529-8703

Regional Sales Offices and Distribution Centers
Northeast: Sharp Plaza, Mahwah, New Jersey 07430-2135
Phone: (201) 529-8703

Midwest: 1300 Naperville Dr., Romeoville, Illinois 60441
Phone: (708) 759-8555
Western: 20600 One Sharp Plaza, South Alameda St., Carson, California 90810   Phone: (310) 637-9488

Southeastern: 725 Old Norcross Road, Lawrenceville, Georgia 30245   Phone: (404) 995-0717

R-1831, R-1830

LIMITED WARRANTY
7 years on magnetron tube
2 years on all other parts
2 years on related labor and in-home service
See Operation Manual or your dealer for complete details

R-9H94, R-9H84, R-7A95, R-7A85, R-5X84, R-4X84, R-5A95, R-4A95

LIMITED WARRANTY
5 years on magnetron tube
1 year on all other parts
1 year on related labor and carry-in service
See Operation Manual or your dealer for complete details

R-1421, R-1420B

LIMITED WARRANTY
7 years on magnetron tube
1 year on all other parts
1 year on related labor and in-home service
See Operation Manual or your dealer for complete details

Built~in Home Refrigeration
Designed for Beauty and Performance

The first choice in kitchens of distinction

In remodeling and new construction, the look of distinction in kitchens begins with the beauty of built-in appliances and built-in refrigeration by Sub-Zero. That's why leading custom kitchen designers choose Sub-Zero first. Classic in styling and unequaled for storage, convenience and quality, Sub-Zero true built-ins are the ultimate in elegant home refrigeration.

Enjoy the elegance of built-in refrigeration

Sub-Zero home refrigeration is designed to enhance the beauty of any decor by blending compatibly with other kitchen furnishings. This is possible because of its simple design . . . removable decorative panels and the fact it is the same 24″ depth as most base kitchen cabinets. A Sub-Zero is designed with a minimum of external hardware, making it hardly noticeable when built into a kitchen. It also has an exclusive toe-base feature, important in kitchen appliances, which lines up with kitchen cabinets.

All units are constructed with the 24″ depth which enables the face to fit flush with most standard base cabinets. A typical free-standing refrigerator protrudes into the room 4 to 6 inches beyond cabinets, creating an unsightly appearance and takes up valuable space in the room.

Sub-Zero built-ins are designed to accept removable exterior panels of any material on the front and sides. In doing so, the unit practically disappears into the overall kitchen, blending completely into the decor instead of dominating the kitchen appearance, as a free-standing unit does. And, because the panels are removable, they can be changed, should the room decor change.

These true built-in features mean your home refrigeration need not be an unattractive standout but can now complement the over-all style of the kitchen and function as an integral part of the total kitchen design. They allow individual styling and expression of your personal taste.

Built-in work savers

Truly an accent to the kitchen of distinction, Sub-Zero built-in refrigeration offers all of the time and work saving features that today's lifestyles require . . . like convenient usable storage, easy up-keep, simplified cleaning, automatic defrosting and automatic ice maker.

The shallow depth makes it easier to find what you are looking for, eliminating the need to search for items that have found their way to the back shelf area (as in other refrigerators). This, along with the fact that all shelves are fully adjustable, gives even greater flexibility for storage arrangements.

Easy up-keep is achieved because of the quality materials and craftsmanship used in the construction of a Sub-Zero, . . . interior, exterior and mechanical.

Cleaning is simplified because of two reasons: First the unit's built-in feature eliminates cracks and crevices that would normally collect dust and also eliminates the chore of pulling the refrigerator out to clean behind it.

Secondly, all shelves in Sub-Zero full-size units are removable to allow for ease of cleaning.

The automatic defrost feature is standard on all full-size models as well as the undercounter models (except

Model 550

249R). This eliminates the need to shut down the refrigerator to defrost and clean the unit.

Another standard feature of the full-size units is the automatic ice maker which produces an adequate supply of ice automatically without the need to handle awkward ice trays.

Many models to choose from

Whatever your space or usage requirements, Sub-Zero offers a selection of over 12 models to fit your needs and specifications. Choose from the popular side-by-side, the over-n-under (freezer on the bottom), the all-freezer and all-refrigerator units, compact undercounter refrigerators and an ice maker. Ranging in width from 18″ to 48″, Sub-Zero units offer capacities to 30.0 cubic feet. The combination all-refrigerator and all-freezer together provide as much as 40.0 cubic feet of food storage.

Sub-Zero 12-Year Protection Plan

Sub-Zero has always backed what it has manufactured, and offers a warranty package no one can match — the Sub-Zero 12-Year Protection Plan. From the day your Sub-Zero is installed, you have a full five-year (parts and labor) warranty and limited sixth through twelfth-year (parts) warranty on the sealed system, consisting of the compressor, condenser, evaporator, drier and all connecting tubing. You also have a full two-year (parts and labor) warranty on the entire product. (See warranty for non-residential use and other exceptions). Sub-Zero stands behind every refrigerator and freezer they manufacture, ensuring you of the finest in service and trouble-free maintenance.

Outstanding performance and craftsmanship

Sub-Zero is a leader in the industry in engineering functional refrigeration. Because Sub-Zero full-size units use a refrigerant in both the refrigerator and freezer compartments, proper and even temperatures are maintained more consistently throughout. This is the same type system used in some commercial refrigerators and is a standard feature in Sub-Zero home units, to insure top performance and operation. Complete factory testing of every Sub-Zero unit is your assurance of quality workmanship.

More than just refrigeration, Sub-Zero quality craftsmanship is a tradition, custom designed to enhance the value and elegance of your home for years to come.

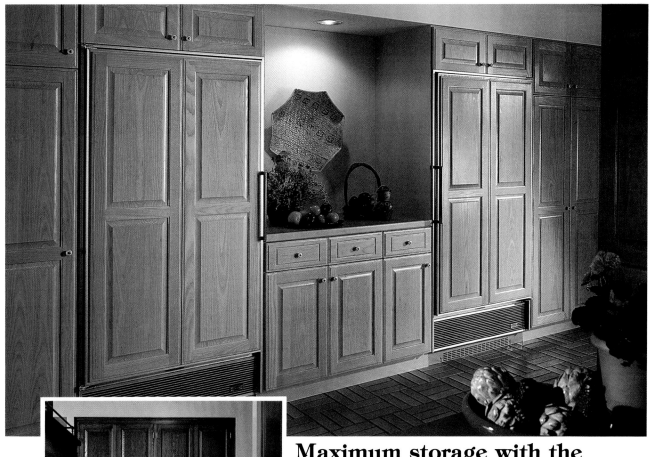

Maximum storage with the 500 SERIES Models 501R and 501F

For large families or those people who need maximum storage, Sub-Zero offers the convenience of its new Eurostyled all-refrigerator (Model 501R) and all-freezer (Model 501F) with a total storage capacity of 40 cubic feet. The "all-refrigerator's" 20 cubic foot capacity makes this exclusive unit the largest built-in all-refrigerator on the market. One of the advantages of these units is the flexibility of planning your kitchen. The units can be installed side-by-side or with a convenient counter between them or at opposite ends of the room, depending on your kitchen layout. Adjustable shelving in both the refrigerator and freezer gives even more storage versatility. The 501F has an automatic ice maker. The "all-refrigerator" Model 501R is also ideal for people who have existing freezer storage. **Separate detailed specification sheets on models 501R and 501F available upon request.**

501F

501R

ALL FREEZER
Model 501F—Automatic defrost. Freezer is equipped with automatic ice maker.
ALL REFRIGERATOR
Model 501R—Automatic defrost refrigerator.

Model	501F	501R
Capacity	20.0 cu. ft.	20.0 cu. ft.
Dimensions	Height 73" Width 36" Depth 24"	Height 73" Width 36" Depth 24"
Finished Roughing-In Dimensions	35½" x 72¾"	35½" x 72¾"
Weight (lbs.)	363 crated	376 crated

* Additional shelves available at extra cost.

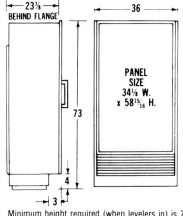

← 23⅞ →
BEHIND FLANGE

← 36 →

73

4

→ 3 ←

PANEL SIZE
34⅛ W.
x 58¹⁵⁄₁₆ H.

Minimum height required (when levelers in) is 72⁷⁄₁₆"

NOTE: Roughing-in width is 71½" when these models are installed side by side. If mullion is used to separate cabinets, add mullion width to 71½" dimension. Filler must be used when installed hinge to hinge.

One 115 volt, 60 cycle single phase, 15 amp. wall outlet must be provided.

Refer to 500 series "Installation Instruction" booklet for detailed installation and panel requirements.

3

Model 561

Model 561 Interior

SUB-ZERO ®

Side by Side Combination
Models 561 and 532

The new 500 series incorporates exciting engineering innovations, with built-in beauty and elegant Eurostyled interiors. This series also features the new satin-brushed aluminum exterior trim and simplicity of design. The elegant combination of white and clear interiors, together with the built-in appearance, offers breathtaking beauty.

Sub-Zero's model 561 features an 8.9 cu. ft. freezer and 12.5 cu. ft. refrigeration in convenient top-to-bottom, side-by-side storage. Its two compressors provide independent temperature control of the freezer and refrigerator compartments. The freezer compartment has four pull-out storage baskets, automatic ice maker with removable ice storage drawer and adjustable door storage.

Model 561

COMBINATION REFRIGERATOR-FREEZER
Model 561 — Automatic defrost model. Freezer compartment equipped with automatic ice maker.

Capacity:	12.5 cu. ft. Refrigerator 8.9 cu. ft. Freezer
Dimensions:	Height 84" Width 36" Depth 24"
Finished Rough-In Dimensions	35½" x 83¾"
Weight (lbs.):	480 lbs. crated

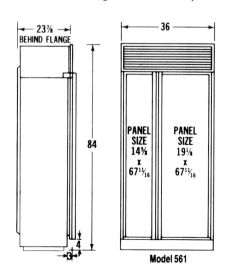

Model 561

One 115 volt, 60 cycle single phase, 15 amp. wall outlet must be provided.

Minimum height required (when levelers in) is 82⅞" (smaller grille recommended).

Refer to 500 series "Installation Instruction" booklet for detailed installation and panel requirements.

4

Model 532   Model 532 Interior

Sub-Zero's huge 30 cu. ft. combination refrigerator/freezer model 532 is one of the largest home built-in units made. It incorporates new engineering innovations and Eurostyled interior. It has an 11.2 cu. ft. freezer and 18.8 cu. ft. refrigerator with convenient top-to-bottom storage.

The freezer compartment has four pull-out storage baskets, an automatic ice maker with roll-out removable ice storage drawer and adjustable door storage. The refrigerator has four self-sealing crispers, each with independent humidity control. It also features an adjustable roll-out utility drawer, adjustable door storage shelves and adjustable glass shelves. This model also has two compressors to provide independent temperature control in both the freezer and refrigerator compartments.

This unit is available in the 48 inch format with water and ice dispensed through the refrigerator door. This is not an option but another addition to our full line called the Model 590.

Detailed specification sheets on model 532, 561 and 590 are available on request.

Optional solid panel grilles that accept matching panels are available for 532 and 561. The panel grille is standard on the 590. Detailed specification sheets on the three units and grilles available upon request.

Model 532

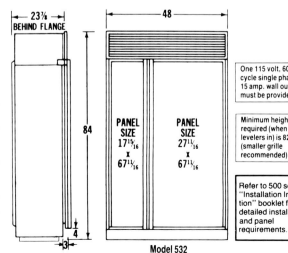

Model 532

COMBINATION REFRIGERATOR-FREEZER

Model 532—Automatic defrost model Equipped with automatic ice maker.

Capacity:	18.8 cu. ft. Refrigerator 11.2 cu. ft. Freezer
Dimensions:	Height 84″ Width 48″ Depth 24″
Finished Rough-In Dimensions:	47½″ x 83¾″
Weight (lbs.):	563 crated

23⅞″ BEHIND FLANGE

48

84

4

3

PANEL SIZE 17¹⁵⁄₁₆ x 67¹¹⁄₁₆

PANEL SIZE 27¹¹⁄₁₆ x 67¹¹⁄₁₆

One 115 volt, 60 cycle single phase, 15 amp. wall outlet must be provided.

Minimum height required (when levelers in) is 82⁷⁄₈″ (smaller grille recommended).

Refer to 500 series "Installation Instruction" booklet for detailed installation and panel requirements.

Model 532

Model 550

Model 550 Interior

![SUB-ZERO]

Over-N-Under (freezer on bottom)
Models 550 and 511

For those who prefer, Sub-Zero offers a convenient arrangement with freezer on the bottom. This design was prompted by the fact that the refrigerator section is used more often than the freezer, thereby providing the greatest convenience and best accessibility. The refrigerated top half offers full width storage on adjustable shelves while frozen foods below are easily accessible with a pull-out drawer.

The over-n-under units in the 500 series also incorporate exciting engineering innovations with built-in beauty and elegant Eurostyled interiors. These units also feature the new satin-brushed aluminum exterior trim and simplicity of design.

Sub-Zero's 22.1 cu. ft. model 550 over-n-under combination unit has a 6.4 cu. ft. slide-out, double-tier freezer drawer in the

Model 550

COMBINATION REFRIGERATOR-FREEZER
Model 550 — Automatic defrost model.
Freezer compartment equipped with automatic ice maker.

Capacity:	15.7 cu. ft. Refrigerator 6.4 cu. ft. Freezer
Dimensions:	Height 84″ Width 36″ Depth 24″
Finished Rough-In Dimensions	35¹/₂″x83³/₄″
Weight (lbs.):	468 crated

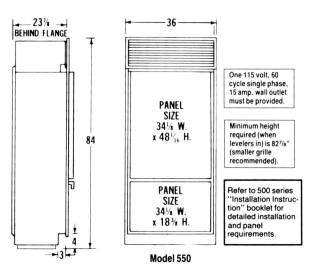

One 115 volt, 60 cycle single phase, 15 amp. wall outlet must be provided.

Minimum height required (when levelers in) is 82⁷/₈″ (smaller grille recommended).

Refer to 500 series "Installation Instruction" booklet for detailed installation and panel requirements.

PANEL SIZE 34¹/₈ W. x 48¹/₁₆ H.

PANEL SIZE 34¹/₈ W. x 18³/₈ H.

Model 550

(Optional panel grille shown)   Model 511

Model 511 Interior

bottom. The freezer has an automatic ice maker with removable ice storage container. The top pull freezer handle and double-tier design provide easy access. The refrigerator has two self-sealing crispers, each with independent humidity control. It has a roll-out utility drawer, adjustable glass shelves and fully adjustable door storage.

The model 511 features a 5.2 cu. ft. slide-out double-tier freezer drawer and a 12.7 cu. ft. refrigerator compartment. Again the freezer has an automatic ice maker with removable ice storage container. Like the model 550, easy freezer access is provided by top pull handle and roll-out double-tier design.

These over-n-under models are extremely versatile for kitchen designs used alone or in various combinations, such as the kitchen shown on the cover of this brochure.

Both units have two compressors which provides independent temperature control in both the refrigerator and freezer compartments. These units are backed by Sub-Zero's exclusive Twelve-Year Protection Plan.

Optional solid panel grilles that accept matching panels also available. Specification sheet available upon request. Detailed specification sheets on models 550 and 511 are available upon request.

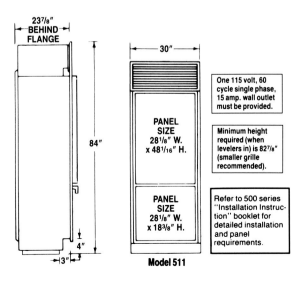

23⁷/₈″ BEHIND FLANGE

← 30″ →

One 115 volt, 60 cycle single phase, 15 amp. wall outlet must be provided.

PANEL SIZE 28¹/₈″ W. x 48¹/₁₆″ H.

Minimum height required (when levelers in) is 82⁷/₈″ (smaller grille recommended).

84″

PANEL SIZE 28¹/₈″ W. x 18³/₈″ H.

Refer to 500 series "Installation Instruction" booklet for detailed installation and panel requirements.

4″

→ 3″ ←

Model 511

COMBINATION REFRIGERATOR-FREEZER
Model 511 — Automatic defrost model. Freezer compartment equipped with automatic ice maker.

Capacity:	12.7 cu. ft. Refrigerator 5.2 cu. ft. Freezer
Dimensions:	Height 84″ Width 30″ Depth 24″
Finished Rough-In Dimensions	29¹/₂″x83³/₄″
Weight (lbs.):	375 crated

Model 511

Features of full-size, built-in units

1. Convenient Storage

All Sub-Zero units are 24″ in depth to conform to most kitchen base cabinet units. This not only improves appearance of finished installation but provides more accessible storage on interior shelves.

2. Sub-Zero 12-Year Protection Plan

Full five-year (parts and labor) warranty and limited sixth through twelfth-year (parts) warranty on the sealed system, consisting of the compressor, condenser, evaporator, drier and all connecting tubing; and a full two-year (parts and labor) warranty on the entire product from the date of installation. (Does not include installation.) (See warranty for non-residential use and other exceptions.)

3. Automatic Ice Maker

Makes and stores crescent-shaped ice pieces. Although several conditions affect the amount of ice that is produced in a given period of time, an adequate supply is provided. (Model 532 and 561 icemaker shown)

4. Automatic Defrosting

Automatically eliminates frost accumulation in both refrigerator and freezer sections.

5. Accepts Removable Decorative Door Panels

Front panels of virtually any material, not exceeding 1/4″ in thickness are easily installed. Raised panels may also be used when perimeter edge does not exceed 1/4″. **(We recommend routing, recessing or optional extended handles for finger clearance when using raised panels.) Refer to Installation Instruction Guide for detailed information. Only colored and stainless steel panels are available from the factory. (50# per door panel weight limit.)**

6. Side Panels

Unit is made to accept side panels if sides are exposed. Only colored and stainless steel panels are available from the factory.

7. Front-Vented

Allows for true built-in installation and eliminates over heating.

8. Removable and Adjustable Shelves

Cantilever type glass shelves in the refrigerator and wire shelves in the freezer for easy cleaning and flexible storage.

9. Deluxe Crispers

Spacious, self-sealing crispers have easy-glide roller design and adjustable, independent humidity control to assure food freshness.

10. Interiors

Award-winning Eurostyled white and clear interior.

11. Magnetic Door Gasket

Surrounds entire door with a pull that assures a positive seal.
NOTE — Because of a perfect seal, allow a slight delay before reopening door.

12. Right or Left Door Swing

Available, when specified, on all over-n-under and single door units (all side-by-side units are hinged on outside). Doors are not reversible.

13. Portable Egg Trays

Convenient and versatile, they may be carried to the table or preparation area.

14. Adjustable Dairy Compartment

Versatile, positive sealing compartment for dairy items.

15. Adjustable Utility Basket

Adjustable roll-out refrigeration basket offers handy storage for small items.

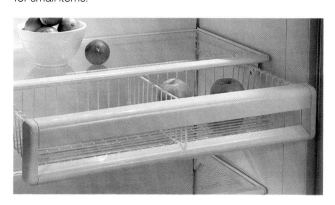

16. Clean Trim

No visible screws.

17. Colored Panels

Decorator front and side steel panels are available from Sub-Zero in the following colors: Harvest Gold, Almond, Avocado, Coffee, Stainless Steel and White.

18. Grilles

Standard grille height is 11″. Other available grille heights range from 10″ to 15″ in 1″ increments. Optional decorative, solid panel grilles that accept matching panels also available in these sizes.

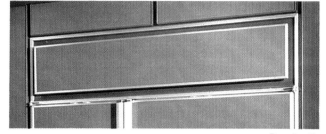

Panel grille

19. Toe Space Base

Integral part of cabinet. Inset is 4″ high by 3″ deep — meeting specifications of American Institute of Architects and conforming with most bases of kitchen cabinets.

20. Door Handles

Standard as shown in photographs throughout this literature.

21. Door Closers

All models equipped with door closers.

22. Door Stops

Although most installations do not require a door stop (door opens to 130°), an optional kit is available if needed. The Door Stop Kit allows the door to open to 90°.

23. Rollers

Unit has rollers and convenient leveling system for ease of installation.

24. Additional Shelves

Available at additional cost.

> **IMPORTANT:** For proper operation and use, the door must open at least a full 90°. A minimum 2″ filler should be used in corner installations to assure a 90° door opening. Remember to allow enough clearance in front of unit for full door swing.

Undercounter models

Sub-Zero undercounter refrigerators, freezers, combinations and ice makers are ideal for the bar, den, family room, yacht or office. They are designed to be installed under a counter. However, some may also be used as free-standing units.

All under-counter models are self-venting, have foamed-in-place insulation, have durable ABS easy to clean interiors and accept front door panels of practically any material to harmonize with cabinets or other equipment. They also have right to left door swings which are interchangeable in the field (kit required except model 245). All of these features and more are backed by Sub-Zero's 12-Year Protection Plan — providing a full five-year (parts and labor) warranty and limited sixth through twelfth year (parts) warranty on the sealed system, consisting of the compressor, condenser, evaporator, drier and all connecting tubing; and a full two year (parts and labor) warranty on the entire product from the date of installation. (Does not include installation.) (See warranty for non-residential use and other exceptions.)

The Sub-Zero combination models 245 and 801 provide automatic defrost, refrigerator storage, freezer storage and automatic ice making.

Sub-Zero also offers "all-refrigerator" and "all-freezer" undercounter units. The model 249RP "all-refrigerator" features automatic defrost, door storage and adjustable compartment shelving. Our model 249FF "all-freezer" features automatic defrost, adjustable compartment shelving and can be equipped with an automatic ice maker, but it must be installed at the factory.

A unit for those who desire primarily refrigerator storage with some freezer storage is the model 249R. This unit is a manual defrost, with a small full-width freezer, door storage and adjustable compartment shelving.

We also offer a built-in ice maker for those who entertain in style. Requirements for clear ice can be satisfied with the model 506, which provides an abundance of crystal-clear cubes in a unit that requires only an 18" width. Featuring a drop-down hopper-type door, this unit stores up to 35 pounds of 3/4" cubes. This unit requires a drain or pump.

Separate specification sheet on each undercounter model is available upon request.

Undercounter Model	249R	249RP	249FF	245	801	506
Capacity	4.4 cu. ft. Refrigerator .7 cu. ft. Freezer	4.9 cu. ft. Refrigerator	4.6 cut. ft Freezer	3.0 cu. ft. Refrigerator 1.9 cu. ft. Freezer	2.9 cu. ft. Refrigerator 2.6 cu. ft. Freezer	Stores 35 lbs. of ice
Unit Dimensions [Levelers in] (H × W × D in inches)	33^{13}/$_{16}$ × 23^7/$_8$ × 24	33^{13}/$_{16}$ × 23^7/$_8$ × 24	33^{13}/$_{16}$ × 23^7/$_8$ × 24	34 × 23^7/$_8$ × 24	33^5/$_8$ × 36 × 23^7/$_8$	34^{13}/$_{32}$ × 17^1/$_8$ × 23^7/$_8$
Weight (lbs.)	120 crated	117 crated	135 crated	139 crated	265 crated	110 crated

Note: Refer to "Installation Instruction" booklet for detailed water, electrical and other installation requirements.

Model 249R   **Model 249RP**   **Model 249FF** (ICEMAKER OPTIONAL)

Model 245   **Model 801**   **Model 506**

Installation specifications

Following are the installation specifications for all Sub-Zero full-size and undercounter models. The dimensions shown in the chart correlate with the schematic drawings. For further details refer to the **Installation Instruction Booklet.**

Schematic drawing

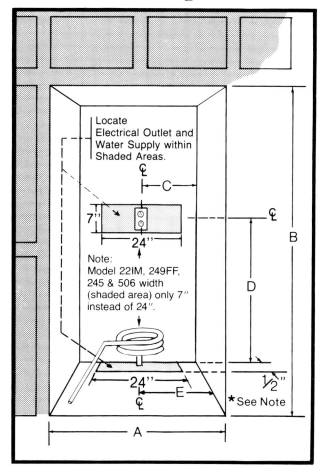

Locate Electrical Outlet and Water Supply within Shaded Areas.

Note:
Model 22IM, 249FF, 245 & 506 width (shaded area) only 7″ instead of 24″.

Door Clearance Schematic Drawing Top View

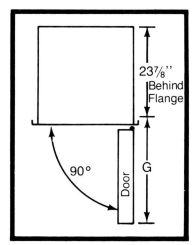

23⅞″ Behind Flange

90°

Door

G

Wood grille not available from Sub Zero.

Model No.	Finished Rough Opening Dimensions		Recommended Electrical Outlet Location		Water Supply Location	Door Panel Dimensions (width x height)	Minimum Door Clearance Requirement at 90°
	A	B	C	D	E		G
550	35½″	83¾″	18″	79″	18″	34⅛″ x 48¹/₁₆″ & 34⅛″ x 18⅜″	36¹/₁₆″
511	29½″	83¾″	15″	79″	15″	28⅛″ x 48¹/₁₆″ & 28⅛″ x 18⅜″	30⅛″
561	35½″	83¾″	18″	79″	18″	14⅝″ x 67¹¹/₁₆″ & 19⅛″ x 67¹¹/₁₆″	20¾″
532	47½″	83¾″	18″	79″	18″	17¹⁵/₁₆″ x 67¹¹/₁₆″ & 27¹¹/₁₆″ x 67¹¹/₁₆″	29¼″
501R	35½″	72¾″	18″	7″		34⅛″ x 58¹⁵/₁₆″	36¹/₁₆″
501F	35½″	72¾″	18″	7″	18″	34⅛″ x 58¹⁵/₁₆″	36¹/₁₆″
801	35½″	34½″	18″	3½″	18″	16⅞″ x 22⅞″ (both)	18½″
245	24″	34½″	5½″	4½″	12″	23½″ x 28⅛″	25¹³/₁₆″
249R	24″	34½″	12″	14″		23⅝″ x 30″	25⅜″
249RP	24″	34½″	12″	14″		23⅝″ x 30″	25⅜″
249FF	24″	34½″	5″	14″	18″	23⅝″ x 30″	25⅜″
506	18″	34½″	6″	6″	11″	17″ x 13³/₁₆″ & 17″ x 11¹⁵/₁₆″	11¾″

*NOTE: Water line may come directly thru wall, not higher than 3″ from floor.

(Optional panel grille shown)

How to buy

Sub-Zero home refrigeration can be seen and purchased at top custom kitchen dealers and appliance stores in all major cities across the United States and many Canadian cities. If not available in your area, feel free to contact Sub-Zero direct for the distributor nearest you. Call 800-222-7820.

Service

There are hundreds of authorized service centers throughout the country to provide warranty service and perform other service functions. These centers maintain a stock of Sub-Zero approved parts and a staff of qualified repair technicians. The service center nearest you may be found in the yellow pages or by contacting the dealer you purchased the unit from. If service cannot be found, contact Sub-Zero direct: 800-356-5826.

®

SUB-ZERO FREEZER CO., INC.

Post Office Box 44130
Madison, Wisconsin 53744-4130
608/271-2233

SUB-ZERO ®

Model 590
Ice & Water Refrigerator-Freezer

Innovative Excellence

SUB-ZERO ®

Sub-Zero has led the built-in home refrigeration industry for years with product enhancements which have set trends. Sub-Zero continues to redefine the art of built-in refrigeration for the 90's with the introduction of the distinctive Model 590 with its innovative version of ice and water through the refrigerator door.

The convenient placement and inconspicuous appearance of the ice and water dispenser and its controls were designed with you in mind.

And the ability to match your kitchen design has been assured with the Model 590. Like all Sub-Zero units, the Model 590 will fit flush with virtually all 24-inch cabinets and accept decorative side and front panels. Another exclusive feature of the Model 590 is the complementary color handle trim panels and glasswells which are offered at no charge.

Craftsmanship, a Sub-Zero trademark, is also built into each of these features:

•**Ice & Water Dispenser**– designed and practically placed for your convenience. A new industry feature, the water is <u>constantly</u> chilled within its huge 51 oz. reservoir.

•**Bulk Ice Dispenser**– conveniently located inside the refrigerator door when larger quantities are needed. This new industry feature is activated at the touch of a button.

•**Two Refrigeration Systems**– ensures independent, accurate freezer and refrigerator temperature control.

•**Decorative Door Panels**– front panels of virtually any material not exceeding 1/4" perimeter thickness are accommodated. Only color and stainless steel panels are available from the factory. (50# per door panel weight limit)

•**Automatic Defrosting**– freezer and refrigerator have own systems.

•**Adjustable Shelves**– cantilever type, easy to move and clean.

•**Spacious Crispers with Humidity Control**– four self-sealing crispers have clear view and individual controls.

•**Adjustable Door Shelves**– easy to adjust shelves provide complete flexibility on both doors.

•**Automatic Ice Maker**– an adequate supply of cresent-shaped ice is ensured.

•**Dairy Module**– a moveable, sealed environment for freshness.

•**Master Switch**– quick practical access is offered to shut unit off.

•**Rollers**– provides easy installation.

•**Positive Sealing Doors**– magnetic gaskets guarantee a tight seal.

•**Brushed Satin Trim**– offers clean design so there's no distraction from the beauty of your kitchen.

•**Portable Egg Containers**– easy access and convenient storage.

•**Panel Grille**– 11"panel grille is standard. Other sizes from 10" to 15" are available in one inch increments.

•**Solid Toe Plate**– allows custom finishing.

Refrigeration System Control and Bulk Ice Dispenser.

Ice & Water Dispenser with Night Light.

Model 590 shown with optional bright white handle trim panel and glasswell.

Sub-Zero 12 Year Protection Plan—full five-year (parts and labor) warranty and limited sixth through twelfth-year (parts) warranty on the sealed system, consisting of the compressor, condenser, evaporator, drier and all connecting tubing; a full two-year (parts and labor) warranty on the entire product from the date of installation. (Does not include installation. See warranty for other exceptions.)

Beauty — our award-winning interior is beautiful to the eye, but more importantly it is spacious with nearly 30 cubic feet of flexible storage for all your needs.
Refrigerator – 18.2 cubic feet.
Freezer – 11.2 cubic feet.

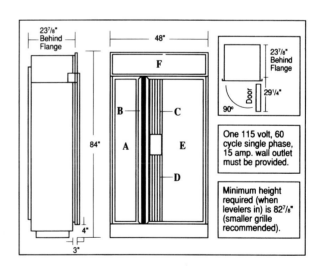

One 115 volt, 60 cycle single phase, 15 amp. wall outlet must be provided.

Minimum height required (when levelers in) is 82⁷/₈" (smaller grille recommended).

Capacity: Refrigerator 18.2 cu. ft. Freezer 11.2 cu. ft.	Dimensions: Height 84" Width 48" Depth 24"
Two Compressors	Finished Roughed-in Dimensions: 47¹/₂ x 83³/₄

Weight: 598 lbs. crated

| Door Panel Dimensions:
A 15 ¹/₈ w x 67 ¹¹/₁₆ h
B 2 ⁹/₁₆ w x 67 ¹¹/₃₂ h
C 6 ⁷/₈ w x 25 ⁷/₃₂ h | **D** 6 ⁷/₈ w x 31 ⁷/₃₂ h
E 20 ⁹/₁₆ w x 67 ¹¹/₁₆ h
Grille Panel Dimension:
F 46 ³/₁₆ w x 9 ³/₁₆ h |

B,C & D may not exceed .050" thickness

Due to our continuous improvement program, models and specifications are subject to change without notice.

Color
Selection Guide
for model 590 only

Complete Flexibility

Your Sub-Zero Model 590 will be shipped with handsome pin-striped pewter gray handle trim panels and glasswell. But an exclusive feature from Sub-Zero allows you to change this color scheme to accent your kitchen.

Ask your local dealer about specific color combinations. The eight glasswell and laminate handle trim panel alternatives we offer at no charge are:

Model 590 shown with standard pin-striped pewter gray handle trim panels and glasswell.

P1/G1	P2/G2
Bright White	Almond Buff
P3/G3	P4/G4
Camel	Adobe
P5/G5	P6/G6
Pewter Gray	Smoke Gray
P7/G7	P8/G8
Charcoal	Port Brown
	P9/G9
	Black Slate

*The colors illustrated here are only meant to give you an idea of the shades available and you should contact your dealer for more accurate color combinations and shading.

Note: Metal handle trim panels to match Sub-Zero supplied metal door and side panels are also available in white, almond, avocado, coffee, harvest gold and stainless steel at no charge.

Sales

In addition to the Model 590, Sub-Zero features a full line of built-in home refrigeration units with side-by-side, over-and-under and undercounter models which vary in size from 4.5 to 30 cubic feet of storage. For the dealer near you look in the yellow pages or call Sub-Zero at **800/222-7820** for your nearest distributor.

Service

Sub-Zero has an extensive service network throughout the United States and Canada to meet your needs. You can find them in the yellow pages or call us at **800/356-5826.**

SUB-ZERO FREEZER CO., INC.
P.O. Box 44130
Madison ,WI 53744 - 4130
(608) 271- 2233

Professional Performance For The Home

Freestanding Gas Ranges

Viking Professional Series ranges combine all of the advantages and performance of commercial cooking equipment with the convenience and safety features of a domestic range, providing the ultimate cooking experience for discriminating cooks.

Standard Features
- Heavy-gauge steel construction
- Heavy-duty porcelain/cast-iron removable surface grates
- Removable porcelain grate supports with integral burner bowls
- 15,000 BTU stainless steel removable surface burners
- Automatic ignition on all burners - no standing pilots
- Oven light(s)
- Thermostatically controlled griddle/simmer plate on selected models
- Removable pull-out drip trays with removable porcelain grease pan on griddle models
- Infinite surface burner controls with childproof push-to-turn knobs
- Gas infrared broiler for in-the-oven closed-door broiling
- Porcelain oven interiors
- Heavy-duty chrome-plated adjustable oven racks
- Heavy-duty porcelain broiler pan/grid
- Designed for zero clearance to cabinets
- A.G.A. design-certified for residential installation

Models
- VGR30-4B - 30" wide with four burners and one 24" wide oven
- VGR36-6B - 36" wide with six burners and one 28" wide oven
- VGR36-4G - 36" wide with four burners, 12" wide griddle, and one 28" wide oven
- VGR48-8B - 48" wide with eight burners and two 20" wide ovens
- VGR48-6G - 48" wide with six burners, 12" wide griddle, and two 20" wide ovens
- VGR48-4G - 48" wide with four burners, 24" wide griddle, and two 20" wide ovens

Options & Accessories
- Oven door windows (designate D after model number)
- 10" high stainless steel backguard (P30, 36, or 48-SS)
- Stainless steel high-shelf (HS30, 36, or 48-SS)
- Stainless steel island trim (R30, 36, or 48 IT-SS)
- Standard curb base front and side in six finishes (R30, 36, or 48CBF and R27CBS)
- Custom curb base for locally supplied trim (R30, 36, or 48CCB)
- Stainless steel countertop side trim (T27ST-SS)
- Hardwood cutting board (MCB)
- Stainless steel wok ring (WOK)

Finishes
- Black (BK), White (WH), Almond (AL), Stainless Steel (SS), Viking Blue (VB), and Forest Green (FG)

Built-In Gas Rangetops

Viking Professional Rangetops provide the discriminating cook with the performance of professional cooking equipment in a restaurant-style cooktop designed exclusively for home use. This commercial-quality product combines the safety and convenience of a domestic appliance in a built-in residential cooktop. The unique design of the Viking Rangetop blends commercial performance with distinctive styling, providing a variety of selections and options to complement any kitchen decor.

Standard Features
- Heavy-gauge steel construction
- Heavy-duty porcelain cast-iron removable surface grates
- Removable porcelain grate supports with integral burner bowls
- 15,000 BTU stainless steel removable surface burners
- Automatic ignition on all burners - no standing pilots
- Thermostatically controlled griddle/simmer plate on selected models
- Removable pull-out drip tray with removable porcelain grease pan on griddle models
- Infinite surface burner controls with childproof push-to-turn knobs
- Designed for built-in installation in standard depth cabinets
- A.G.A. design-certified for residential installation

Models
- VRT36-6BR - 36" wide with six burners
- VRT36-4GR - 36" wide with four burners and 12" wide griddle
- VRT48-6GR - 48" wide with six burners and 12" wide griddle

Options & Accessories
- 4" high stainless steel backguard (T36 or 48BG-SS)
- Stainless steel high-shelf (T36 or 48HS-SS)
- Stainless steel island trim (T36 or 48ITR-SS)
- Stainless steel countertop side trim (T24ST-SS)
- Hardwood cutting board (MCB)
- Stainless steel wok ring (WOK)

Finishes
- Black (BK), White (WH), Almond (AL), and Stainless Steel (SS)

Built-In Gas Thermal-Convection Ovens

Viking Professional built-in gas 36" wide ovens combine commercial-type styling and convection to create the designer's choice. The oven features a gas infrared broil burner and dual bake burners in a 3.3 cubic foot oven, the largest built-in wall oven cavity available. These features, along with two traditional cooking modes, two convection cooking modes and two special purpose functions provide the cook with capabilities unavailable in other gas ovens.

Standard Features

- Install as single, double stacked, or double side-by-side in standard depth residential cabinets
- Unique heavy-duty commercial-type size, design, and styling
- Distinctive, heavy-duty stainless steel trim at top and bottom
- Large commercial-type knobs/bezels
- Stainless steel or enamel/steel removable oven door with see-through window
- Heavy-duty commercial-type handle on oven door
- Door mounted die cast, chrome plated "Viking Professional" nameplate
- Porcelain oven interior with removable bottom and sides for easy cleaning
- Largest convection oven cavity available in residential built-in product
  - 24⅛" wide x 14⅛" high x 16½" deep
  - 3.3 cubic feet of overall space
- Conventional baking with dual burners and natural airflow
- Convection baking with dual burners and fan forced air
- 1500° F infrared broiling with new "low profile" burner - close door for smokeless broiling
- 1500° F infrared convection broiling with new "low profile" burner and fan forced air (especially effective with thicker cuts of meats) - close door for smokeless broiling
- Convection dehydration with low temperature bake setting and fan forced air
- Convection defrost with motorized fan forced air only (heat off)
- Pilotless electric ignition
- Oven "on" indicator light
- Convection fan switch
- Three heavy-duty, four-position oven racks for maximum convection baking capacity - can convection bake 6 dozen (72) cookies in one batch!
- Heavy-duty porcelain broiler pan/grid
- Oven light with switch
- High density insulation
- A.G.A. design-certified for residential installation

Model

- VGSO165 - 36" wide dual-burner thermal-convection oven

Finishes

- Black (BK), White (WH), and Stainless Steel (SS)

Built-In Gas and Electric Double Ovens

Viking Professional built-in 27" wide double ovens combine commercial-type styling with many home-wanted features. Gas models are self-cleaning and offer infrared broiling and natural airflow baking in both ovens. Viking electric models feature five conventional/convection cooking modes and two special purpose functions in addition to self-cleaning in both ovens. All models feature heavy-duty construction and easy-to-use commercial-type controls.

Standard Features

- Unique heavy-duty commercial-type styling
- Distinctive, heavy-duty perimeter trim
- Large commercial-type knobs
- Electronic clock/timer with commercial-type red digital L.E.D. display
- 99 minute timer
- Automatic time option for baking/roasting
- Automatic self-clean setting
- End of timing signal
- 12 hour alarm clock
- Removable oven doors with see-through windows
- Heavy-duty commercial-type handle on oven doors
- Porcelain oven interiors
- Self-cleaning ovens, upper and lower
- Self-clean indicator lights

Gas Model Features

- Conventional baking with natural air flow (both ovens)
- Infrared broil burner (both ovens) for closed door smokeless broiling
- Pilotless electric ignition
- A.G.A. design-certified for residential installation

Electric Model Features

- Conventional two-element baking
- Convection two-element baking with fan forced air
- Conventional broiling with large 6-pass element/reflector
- Convection broiling with large 6-pass element/reflector and fan forced air
- Convection cooking using only convection element in rear and fan forced air - especially effective for delicate dishes
- Convection dehydrating with low temperature convection cook setting and fan forced air
- Convection defrosting with motorized fan forced air only
- Three heavy-duty racks in both ovens for maximum capacity
- U.L. design-certified for residential installation

Models

- VGDO270 (gas) - 27" wide with two 19⅜" wide ovens
- VEDO275 (electric) - 27" wide with two 19⅜" wide ovens

Finishes

- Black (BK), White (WH), and Stainless Steel (SS)

Built-In Interior and Exterior Power Rangehoods

Undercounter Dishwasher

Viking Professional built-in rangehoods provide quiet, efficient ventilation while maintaining the elegance of the Viking kitchen. Crafted of the same high quality as other Viking appliances, they complete your kitchen design when used over the Viking Professional Series range or rangetop.

Viking Professional dishwashers are the choice for quiet operation, easy random loading, assured water temperature, and outstanding results. Manufactured of long life materials and heavy-duty components, the Viking dishwasher is one of the world's most quiet and energy efficient.

Standard Features

- Heavy-gauge steel construction and commercial-type styling
- Precision crafted and designed for super quiet operation
- Fluorescent lighting for even, shadowless illumination
- Models available in 600 to 1800 CFM
- U.L. design-certified for residential installation

Interior Power Rangehoods
- High-performance squirrel cage blowers with independent switches for custom ventilation control
- Removable blower housing for quick and easy cleaning
- Filterless centrifugal action grease removal system

Exterior Power Rangehoods
- Remote-mount exterior power ventilator(s) for quieter operation
- Infinite rotary switch for complete speed control
- Easy-to-clean commercial-type all metal baffle filter(s)

Models

Interior Power
- VRH30 (27"D) or VRHW300 (24"D) - 30"W wall hood
- VRH36 (27"D) or VRHW360 (24"D) - 36"W wall hood
- VRH48 (27"D) or VRHW480 (24"D) - 48"W wall hood
- VIH36 (30"D) or VRHI360 (27"D) - 36"W island hood
- VIH42 (30"D) or VRHI420 (27"D) - 42"W island hood
- VIH54 (30"D) or VRHI540 (27"D) - 54"W island hood

Exterior Power
- VRH30-EP (27"D) or VRHW300-EP (24"D) - 30"W wall hood
- VRH36-EP (27"D) or VRHW360-EP (24"D) - 36"W wall hood
- VRH48-EP (27"D) or VRHW480-EP (24"D) - 48"W wall hood
- VIH36-EP (30"D) or VRHI360-EP (27"D) - 36"W island hood
- VIH42-EP (30"D) or VRHI420-EP (27"D) - 42"W island hood
- VIH54-EP (30"D) or VRHI540-EP (27"D) - 54"W island hood
- VEPV900-RCK 900CFM exterior power ventilator

Options & Accessories

- Duct cover in six finishes (WDC30, 36, or 48 - wall hoods; IDC36, 42, or 54 - island hoods)
- Backsplash in six finishes - wall hoods (BSP30, 36, or 48-SS)
- Warming shelf panel - wall hoods (WSP30, 36, or 48)
- Heat lamp option - wall hoods (HLO-VRHW)
- Rear light option - island hoods (RLO-VRHI)
- Pot rack/decorative trim - wall and island hoods (PRDT-VRH)

Finishes

- Black (BK), White (WH), Almond (AL), Stainless Steel (SS), Viking Blue (VB), and Forest Green (FG)

Standard Features

- Formed stainless steel door and lower front panels
- Commercial-type heavy-duty stainless steel door handle
- Commercial-type knobs and bezels with easy-to-read graphics
- **Quiet Clean System** - one of the world's most quiet and efficient dishwashers
- Sound absorbing/heat retaining insulation
- Two Motor/Pump Assemblies
- Switch-Activated Dry Vent Door
- Fully useable graphite nylon racks - no lost space
- Two dual level cup racks in upper rack (left side cradles stemware)
- Large silverware/cutlery basket
- Automatic water heating system
- Main wash and final rinse heated to 140°F or Sani Cycle 165°F (optional choice)
- Multi-level wash system
- Stainless steel wash arms
- Triple filtration and waste removal system
- Natural airflow drying
- Choice of five cycles - Pots/Pans, Normal Wash, Light/China, Rinse/Hold, and Plate Warm
- Surgical stainless steel tank and inner door
- Zinc coated steel frame/base and base pan
- Counterbalanced compression door spring
- U.L. design-certified for residential installation

Model
- VUD140-undercounter dishwasher

Options & Accessories

- Formed black enamel/steel door and lower front panels (FK-VUD-BK)
- Formed white enamel/steel door and lower front panels with white knobs and white dry vent grill (FK-VUD-WH)
- 5" high lower panel in stainless steel, black, or white (LP5-VUD-SS, BK, or WH)
- 60 cm or 24" wide kickplates in black and white; dishwasher comes standard with 24" wide black kickplate (KP60-VUD-BK or WH; KP24-VUD-BK or WH)
- Tipguard bar for use when screws cannot anchor dishwasher (TG-VUD)

Finishes

- Stainless Steel (SS); see Options & Accessories for black and white fronts

Before purchasing this appliance, read important energy cost and efficiency information available from your retailer.

Specifications subject to change without notice.

F1184A   Viking Range Corporation, P.O. Drawer 956, 111 Front Street, Greenwood, Mississippi 38930 USA (601)455-1200   (M1192)

TECHNICAL PRODUCT MANUAL

Merillat®
AMERICA'S CABINETMAKER™

It's easy to understand why Merillat cabinets sell more than any other brand. ❧ We build them to meticulously high standards. And to meticulously strict tolerances. After all, when you specify a 30" cabinet, it doesn't do to get one that's 29 and 7/8". ❧ Plus, our corners are tight, square, and true, so your cabinets fit well and install easily. That not only will save you time and money. It will keep your customers and clients happy for years to come. ❧ For more information, or for assistance with your specifications, contact your Merillat distributor. Or just write to Merillat Industries, Inc., Customer Service, Dept. 4463, Adrian, MI 49221. It's as easy as that.

Just because your budget doesn't allow you to specify expensive custom cabinets, it doesn't mean you have to create a cheap excuse for a kitchen with little or no cabinet choices. ❧ Merillat cabinets come in almost every style imaginable — from traditional to contemporary, in both woods and laminates. And each is designed and priced to preserve your budget. As well as your reputation.

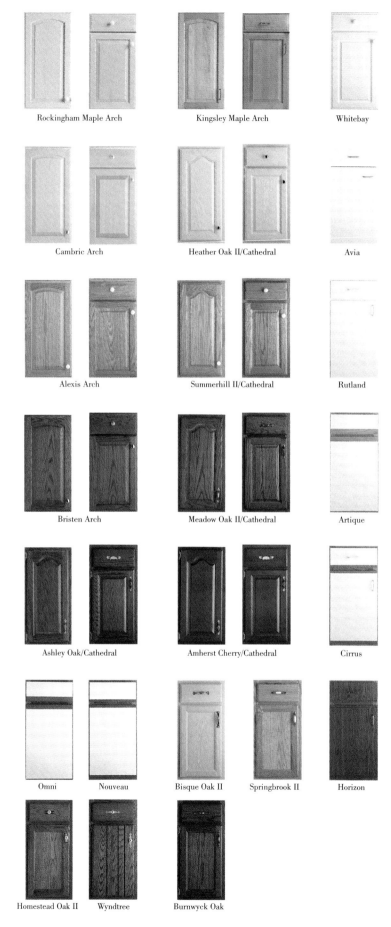

Rockingham Maple Arch

Kingsley Maple Arch

Whitebay

Cambric Arch

Heather Oak II/Cathedral

Avia

Alexis Arch

Summerhill II/Cathedral

Rutland

Bristen Arch

Meadow Oak II/Cathedral

Artique

Ashley Oak/Cathedral

Amherst Cherry/Cathedral

Cirrus

Omni

Nouveau

Bisque Oak II

Springbrook II

Horizon

Homestead Oak II

Wyndtree

Burnwyck Oak

Note: For Ashley Oak, Burnwyck Oak, and Amherst Cherry, check for availability.

ALEXIS. We craft our Alexis cabinets from durable oak and give them a light, subtle finish. Their simple squared, raised-panel doors and full-overlay design offer a clean look, although an elegant arched door design is also available for wall cabinets. Concealed hinges, roll-out trays, and adjustable shelves are standard.

BRISTEN. Like Alexis, Bristen is made with select oak. However, it's stained with a medium finish, which gives Bristen a classic, traditional feel. Squared, raised-panel, full-overlay doors are shown. An arched style is also available for wall cabinets. Concealed hinges, roll-out trays, and adjustable shelves are standard.

CAMBRIC. Cambric features a raised-panel, full-overlay door with a light, pickled oak finish. Arched wall cabinets are shown, although squared wall cabinet doors are also available. Like Alexis and Bristen, concealed hinges, roll-out trays, and adjustable shelves are standard with all Cambric cabinets.

◀ **A V I A .** Avia features a frameless design for a clean look. It's made from a durable laminate that resists moisture and scratches. Avia can be trimmed with pure white (shown), or with oak or gray trim. Concealed hinges, roll-out trays, and adjustable shelves are standard.

▶ **W H I T E B A Y .** Raised-panel doors and rounded inset corners give Whitebay a refined yet casual, traditional yet contemporary look. It's made from a durable laminate that resists stains, spills, and abrasions, as well as yellowing and warping. Concealed hinges, roll-out trays, and adjustable shelves are standard.

◀ **R U T L A N D .** Rutland offers both contemporary styling and an affordable price. Its durable laminate resists moisture and scratches. Adjustable shelves are standard.

▶ **K I N G S L E Y M A P L E .** Kingsley Maple features full-overlay maple doors on a frameless cabinet. It's available in a natural finish (shown) or a pickled finish called Rockingham Maple. Wall cabinets are available in the gentle arch shown, or in a squared design. Concealed hinges, roll-out trays, and adjustable shelves are standard.

◀ **H E A T H E R O A K I I .** Heather Oak II comes with a choice of cathedral (shown) or squared-style raised-panel doors in a pickled oak finish that gently enhances the grain of the wood. Concealed hinges, roll-out trays, and adjustable shelves are standard.

▶ **B I S Q U E O A K I I .** Bisque Oak II features the same pickled finish as Heather Oak II. Bisque Oak II, however, has recessed-panel doors for a simpler look. Concealed hinges, roll-out trays, and adjustable shelves are standard.

◀ **S U M M E R H I L L I I .** Summerhill II cabinets come with a choice of squared or cathedral-style raised-panel doors. Each features a light oak finish. Concealed hinges, roll-out trays, and adjustable shelves are standard.

▶ **S P R I N G B R O O K I I .** With its recessed-panel doors, Springbrook II works perfectly with traditional designs as well as contemporary. Concealed hinges, roll-out trays, and adjustable shelves are standard.

◀ **MEADOW OAK II.** These cabinets, in medium-stained oak, are available with your choice of squared or cathedral-style raised-panel doors. Concealed hinges, roll-out trays, and adjustable shelves are standard.

▶ **HOMESTEAD OAK II.** This medium-stained oak cabinet comes with recessed-panel doors for a traditional look and feel. Concealed hinges, roll-out trays, and adjustable shelves are standard.

◀ **ASHLEY OAK**⁎ Ashley Oak is available with your choice of squared or cathedral-style raised-panel doors. A recessed-panel design, called Burnwyck Oak* (with the same dark oak finish), is also available. Roll-out trays and adjustable shelves are standard on both styles.

▶ **WYNDTREE OAK.** Wyndtree features solid-planked oak doors in a medium finish for a true country feel. Roll-out trays and adjustable shelves are standard.

◀ **AMHERST CHERRY**⁎ Authentic cherry wood gives these cabinets their rich, warm glow. Cathedral-style doors are shown. Squared, raised-panel doors are also available. Solid cherry frames, roll-out trays, and adjustable shelves are standard.

▶ **HORIZON.** This is one of our most affordable cabinet styles. It features easy-to-care-for, oak-grained laminate doors on a solid oak frame.

◀ **OMNI.** Omni is made from a durable, almond-colored, moisture and stain resistant laminate. Medium-stained oak door and drawer trim, roll-out trays, and concealed hinges are standard. A similar style, called Artique, is also available. It features a white laminate with a light oak trim.

▶ **CIRRUS.** Both our Cirrus cabinet (shown) and our Nouveau style, a textured almond laminate with medium oak laminate trim, are economy-priced. They're ideal for times when you're working with a tight budget.

*For Ashley Oak, Burnwyck Oak and Amherst Cherry, check for availability.

◄ **HEATHER OAK.** For a traditional oak bath with a twist, consider Heather Oak with its pickled finish.

► **SUMMERHILL.** Like all Merillat finishes, Summerhill's light oak stands up to most household chemicals and the moisture from any bath.

◄ **OMNI.** With its smooth almond laminate and medium oak trim, Omni creates a clean looking bath.

► **WYNDTREE OAK.** Wyndtree Oak creates a bath with a casual feel and a country charm.

◄ **NOUVEAU.** With its economy price, Nouveau is ideal for designing a bath on a budget.

► **ASHLEY OAK.** Ashley Oak features a rich finish and raised-panel doors for an elegant looking bath.

◄ **WHITEBAY.** For a pure white bath, Whitebay cabinets offer a unique look and easy-to-clean laminate.

ADDITIONAL BATH STYLES (Turn to page 1 for door style photos) Alexis, Bristen, Cambric, Heather Oak II, Summerhill II, Springbrook, Springbrook II, Homestead Oak, Homestead Oak II, Meadow Oak, Meadow Oak II, Horizon, Burnwyck Oak, Rutland, Avia, Artique, Cirrus, Amherst Cherry, Kingsley Maple, Rockingham Maple, Bisque Oak and Bisque Oak II.

Note: "II" indicates traditional overlay styling with concealed hinges.

Customizers.

With our Customizers Program, you can easily add value and design intrigue to any of your projects. It's an affordable way to include the touches you usually get with expensive custom cabinets — including everything from functional units like swing-out pantry racks to accessories like decorative dishwasher panels and moldings. ❧ These are just a small sampling of our 100-plus Customizers. To see more, ask your distributor. Or write for our Customizers brochure.

▶ This handsome desk, assembled entirely with Merillat components, has several key features. Base and wall cabinets offer plenty of storage. Mullion glass doors are ideal for putting items on display. And appliance garages hide things away.

◀ With Merillat base swing-out shelves, the items in the back of blind corner base cabinets are easily accessible.
▶ Our cutting board knife tray kit hides knives safely away and adds extra work space. The cutting board is removable.

◀ This double wide roll-out tray with full extension guides allows easy access to big, bulky pots and pans.
▶ A spacious pantry not only eliminates clutter, it makes kitchen items easy to find.

◀ Our base wastebasket mounts easily on a roll-out tray, making it handy for recycling.

At Merillat, we offer a number of standard and speciality cabinets, in both framed and frameless designs, that add flair and function to any kitchen plan.

Most of our cabinets come with concealed hinges. Most base cabinets come with roll-out trays. And all of our wall cabinets have adjustable shelves. Both wall and base cabinets are available with single and double doors. We also offer double-faced cabinets that allow access from two sides, making them perfect for island and peninsula applications.

Our vanity, utility, pantry, and base lazy Susan cabinets add even more specialized storage space.

1. **PANTRY CABINET.** Provides up to 32 cubic feet of storage space.

2. **OVER-THE-PANTRY/REFRIGERATOR CABINET.** At 24 inches, it's twice as deep as regular wall cabinets.

3. **DOUBLE DOOR BASE CABINET.** Roll-out trays are standard. Additional trays, decorative end panels, and double-faced cabinets are also available.

4. **DIAGONAL WALL CORNER CABINET.** Also available as a double-faced cabinet.

5. **DOUBLE DOOR WALL CABINET.** Also available as a double-faced cabinet.

6. **FOUR DRAWER CABINET.** Includes three standard drawers and one extra deep drawer.

7. **SINGLE DOOR BASE CABINET.** Includes a single roll-out tray. Also available as a double-faced cabinet.

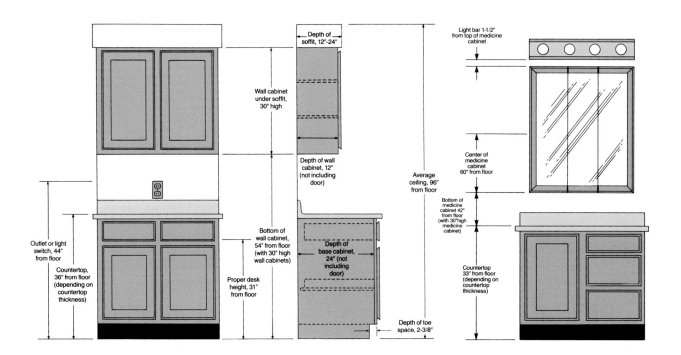

DIMENSIONS

FRAMED CABINETRY

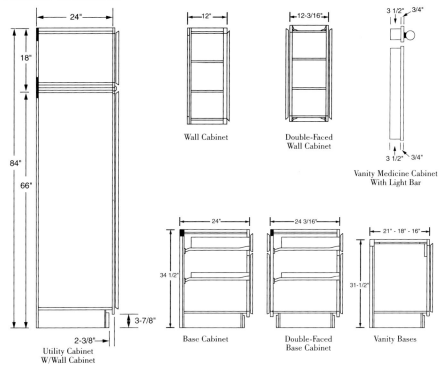

24"

18"

84"

66"

3-7/8"

2-3/8"

Utility Cabinet W/Wall Cabinet

12"

Wall Cabinet

12-3/16"

Double-Faced Wall Cabinet

3 1/2"   3/4"

3 1/2"   3/4"

Vanity Medicine Cabinet With Light Bar

24"

34 1/2"

Base Cabinet

24 3/16"

Double-Faced Base Cabinet

21" - 18" - 16"

31-1/2"

Vanity Bases

FRAMELESS CABINETRY

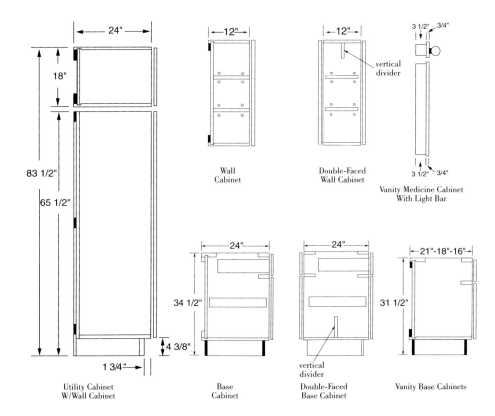

24"

18"

83 1/2"

65 1/2"

4 3/8"

1 3/4"

Utility Cabinet W/Wall Cabinet

12"

Wall Cabinet

12"

vertical divider

Double-Faced Wall Cabinet

3 1/2"   3/4"

3 1/2"   3/4"

Vanity Medicine Cabinet With Light Bar

24"

34 1/2"

Base Cabinet

24"

vertical divider

Double-Faced Base Cabinet

21"-18"-16"

31 1/2"

Vanity Base Cabinets

WHEELCHAIR-READY CABINETRY

Available in Horizon, Nouveau and Cirrus lines only, these Merillat cabinets have an extra high toe space (9″) which provides space for the wheelchair footrest to fit under the cabinet. Each base cabinet is equipped with easy-access roll-out trays which are laminated on the inside with an easy-clean surface.

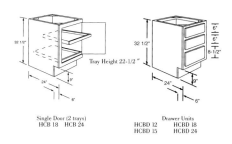

32 1/2"

Tray Height 22-1/2 ″

32 1/2"

6"
6"
8-1/2"

24"   9"

24"   9"

6"

6"

Single Door (2 trays)
HCB 18   HCB 24

Drawer Units
HCBD 12   HCBD 18
HCBD 15   HCBD 24

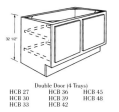

32 1/2"

Double Door (4 Trays)

HCB 27	HCB 36	HCB 45
HCB 30	HCB 39	HCB 48
HCB 33	HCB 42	

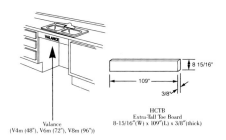

VALANCE

8 15/16"

109"

3/8"

Valance
(V4m (48"), V6m (72"), V8m (96"))

HCTB
Extra-Tall Toe Board
8-15/16″(W) x 109″(L) x 3/8″(thick)

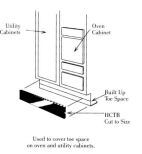

Utility Cabinets

Oven Cabinet

Built Up Toe Space

HCTB Cut to Size

Used to cover toe space on oven and utility cabinets.

Note: All depth measurements do not include door.

CABINET SIZES

FRAMED   FRAMELESS

WALL CABINETS

Wall cabinets are available in heights of 42″, 36″ (framed only), 30″, 24″, 18″, 15″ and 12″. Most cabinets are available in widths ranging from 9″ to 48″ in 3″ increments. Framed and frameless wall cabinets are 12″ deep, not including doors.

WALL BLIND CORNER CABINETS

Wall blind corner cabinets are available in heights of 42″, 36″ (framed only), 30″ and 24″. Most wall blind corner cabinets are available in widths of 24″, 27″, 30″, 33″, 36″, 42″ and 48″.

DOUBLE-FACE WALL CABINETS

Double-face wall cabinets are available in heights of 30″, 24″ and 18″. Most are available in widths of 18″, 24″, 30″, 36″, 42″ and 48″. Framed cabinets are 13¹⁵⁄₁₆″ deep, including doors. Frameless cabinets are 13½″ deep, including doors.

BASE CABINETS

All base cabinets are 34½″ tall. Most are available in widths ranging from 9″ to 48″, in 3″ increments. Framed and frameless base cabinets are 24″ deep, not including doors. Four drawer base cabinets are available in widths ranging from 12″ to 24″, in 3″ increments. Base Cabinets are also available in a three-drawer style in widths of 30″ and 36″

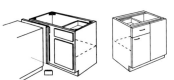 

BASE BLIND CORNER CABINETS

All base blind corner cabinets are 34½″ high. Most are available in widths of 24″, 30″, 36″, 42″ and 48″.

KITCHEN SPECIALITY CABINETS

Lazy susans: 36″ wide (requires this amount of wall space). **Range Hoods** (framed only): 30″ and 36″ wide. **Tilt-out Range Hoods** (frameless, Whitebay, Alexis, Bristen, Cambric and arch wall cabinets): 30″w x 24″h. **Glass Door Wall Cabinets** (frameless only): 30″ and 36″ wide. **Microwave Shelves:** 30″w x 22⅝″h (framed), 30″w x 18″h (frameless). **Wall Whatnot Shelves** (framed only): 30″ high. **Base Open Shelf Ends** (framed only): 34½″ high. **Pantries** (framed only): 36″w x 66″h x 24″d.

Utility Cabinets (framed): 24″w x 66″h, 18″w x 66″h. Available in 12″ and 24″ depths. **Utility Cabinets** (frameless): 24″w x 65½″h, 18″w x 65½″h. Available in 12″ and 24″ depths. **Oven Cabinets** (framed): 27″w x 66″h, 30″w x 66″h and 33″w x 66″h. All framed oven cabinets are 24″ deep. Up to four 6″ drawers can be added to framed oven cabinets. **Oven Cabinets** (frameless): 27″w x 65½″h, 30″w x 65½″h, 33″w x 65½″. All frameless oven cabinets are 24″ deep. Up to six 6″ drawers can be added to frameless oven cabinets.

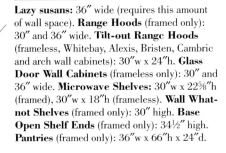

VANITY CABINETS

All vanity cabinets are 31½″ in height. Vanity bowl cabinets are available in depths of 21″, 18″ and 16″. Vanity bowl drawer cabinets are available in depths of 21″ and 18″.

BATH SPECIALITY CABINETS

Vanity Hamper (framed and frameless): 18″w x 31½″h x 21″d. **Vanity "Stack-On" Linen Storage** (framed and frameless): 18″w x 48″h x 21″d. **Vanity Wall Storage:** 25½″w x 48″h x 8″d and 24″w x 27⅝″h x 7″ (both of these are framed only), 24″w x 40″h x 8″d (frameless only).

Note: All depth measurements do not include doors, except where indicated.

FRAMED SPECIFICATIONS

GENERAL

1.01 Scope

1.01.01 The scope of this specification is to cover the design, construction and installation of all framed kitchen and bath cabinetry.

1.03 Submittals

1.03.01 Supplier will furnish shop drawings, which are taken from the architect's drawings, specifically calling out the cabinet nomenclature and sizes. Supplier shall also submit floor plans and elevations for the cabinets showing layout, dimensions and details of installation.

1.03.02 Submit cabinet door samples with manufacturer's range of colors for selection by the architect.

1.03.03 Submit manufacturer's literature on cabinets.

2. PRODUCT

2.01 Cabinets shall be "____" (specify door style) as manufactured by Merillat Industries, P.O. Box 1946, Adrian, MI 49221. Size and type as required to meet configurations indicated on drawings.

2.02 Certification

2.02.01 All cabinetry shall carry the Kitchen Cabinet Manufacturers Association (KCMA) certified cabinet seal and meet or exceed the "recommended minimum construction and performance standards for kitchen cabinets" outlined in the American National Standards Institute (ANSI) ANSI/KCMA A161.1-1990.

2.03 Materials-Case Construction

Depending on the door style selected, all Merillat cabinet frames shall be constructed of solid red oak or solid cherry. All door and drawer front veneered components shall be selected architectural grade sliced red oak or cherry, depending on style selected. "Solid hardwood" in these specifications refers to either solid oak or solid cherry, depending on cabinet line. No similar wood species such as ash or maple shall be substituted in any component or accessory. See specifications section 3.01 on cabinet frame for Rutland/Whitebay.

2.03.01 Cabinet frames shall have 3/4" thick x 1 5/8" wide solid hardwood rail and stile members. Center stiles shall be 3/4" thick x 3 1/4" or 6 1/4" wide solid hardwood. All frame joints shall be reinforced and precisely aligned with two 3/8" diameter birch dowels bonded with adhesive.

2.03.02 End panels shall be 3/8" thick-48 lb. industrial grade particleboard laminated inside and out with a water and household chemical resistant 2 mil rigid reverse printed vinyl. End panels shall be machined to accept tops, bottoms and backs.

2.03.03 Wall cabinets tops and bottoms shall be 1/2" thick-48 lb. industrial grade particleboard for extra strength and rigidity. These components shall be laminated on two sides with a water and household chemical resistant 2 mil rigid reverse printed vinyl. A dado joint and adhesive shall be used to join the tops and bottoms to the end panels.

2.03.04 Base cabinet bottoms shall be 3/8" thick-48 lb. industrial grade particleboard laminated with a water and household chemical resistant 2 mil rigid reverse printed vinyl on the interior side. The bottoms shall be joined to the end panels with dado joints and adhesive. Glue blocks shall be used to reinforce the bottoms of cabinets 27" or wider. The upper portion of base cabinets shall be strengthened with 1/2" gussets which maintain squareness.

2.03.05 All backs shall be 1/4" thick-50 lb. density particleboard with a water and household chemical resistant 2 mil rigid reverse printed vinyl laminated to the interior side. Wall cabinet backs shall be reinforced with 1/4" thick particleboard screw rails at the top and bottom. Wall cabinet backs shall be retained by a groove in the end panels; and glued and stapled to the tops and bottoms. Base cabinet backs shall be attached in the same manner, but the top of the cabinet shall have an 1 11/16" x 2 1/4" pine screw rail securing the back to the top of the cabinet.

2.03.06 All wall cabinets 24" and higher shall have adjustable shelves made of 1/2" thick-48 lb. density industrial grade particleboard. The shelves shall be laminated with a water and household chemical resistant 2 mil rigid reverse printed vinyl. The front edge of the shelf shall be laminated with oak grain melamine edgebanding. Cabinet sides shall be drilled for durable supports adjustable on 2 1/2" increments. Shelves are designed to support 15 lbs per square foot. Not to exceed 50 lbs per shelf.

2.03.08 All Nouveau, Cirrus and Horizon base cabinets, except sink bases, shall have half depth fixed shelves. The shelves shall be 1/2" thick-48 lb. density industrial grade particleboard with a water and household chemical resistant 2 mil rigid reverse printed vinyl laminated to the top surface. They shall be supported on the ends with shelf clips, but are not adjustable. The backs of the shelves shall be supported with staples driven through the cabinet backs. All shelves in base cabinets 27" or wider shall have a support apron for additional strength. Shelves are designed to support 15 lbs. per square foot. Not to exceed 50 lbs. per shelf.

2.03.09 The toe board shall be 3/8"-48 lb. density industrial grade particleboard and extend from the floor to the cabinet bottom. This not only supports the bottom but also effectively seals the toe space against vermin and insects. The toe board shall be covered with a 3/8" black vinyl covered particleboard strip which provides an easy cleaning, mop resistant finish.

3.03.10 Base lazy Susan cabinets shall have two 28" diameter revolving plastic shelves with reinforced bottoms, to provide 7.5 square feet of storage, with finger-tip accessibility. Shelves are designed to support 15 lbs. per square foot. Not to exceed 50 lbs. per shelf.

2.04 Drawer Construction (Horizon, Cirrus and Nouveau only)

2.04.01 All Horizon, Cirrus and Nouveau shall have 1/2" thick-48 lb. density particleboard drawer sides, which shall be rabbeted to accept 1/2" thick fronts and backs. All drawer components shall be laminated on the exterior side with a water and household chemical resistant 2 mil rigid reverse printed vinyl. The interior faces of the drawer sides shall be laminated with a water and household chemical resistant 4 mil semi-rigid reverse printed vinyl and the ends shall be wrapped around radiused edges of the drawer components.

2.04.02 Fronts and backs shall be 1/2" thick-48 lb. density particleboard with a water and household chemical resistant 2 mil rigid reverse printed vinyl on the outside and a water and household chemical resistant 4 mil semi-rigid reverse printed vinyl on the inside.

The drawer box shall be assembled with white glue and staples at each corner. The drawer core shall be secured to the drawer front with two or four screws.

2.04.03 All Horizon, Cirrus and Nouveau drawer bottoms shall be 1/4" thick-50 lb. density particleboard with a water and household chemical resistant 2 mil rigid reverse printed vinyl laminated on the interior side. Bottom shall be attached to the sides, front and back with adhesives and staples. The drawer slide "L" shaped lip shall be bent around the bottom to reinforce the drawer bottom.

2.04.04 Horizon, Nouveau and Cirrus base cabinet drawers are fitted with a dual-captive steel epoxy-coated side-mounted captive roller drawer system. The system consists of a pair of epoxy-coated 1.25mm steel slides that roll on close tolerance nylon rollers. The dual captive guide system and integrated adapter supports the drawer to a capacity rating of 75 lbs.

2.04.05 All other style drawer cores use the Merillat WhisperGlide® system and shall have 1/2" thick-48 lb. density particleboard sides that are attached to the 1/2" particleboard front and back. The drawer sides shall be laminated with a water and household chemical resistant 4 mil semi-rigid reverse printed vinyl on the interior and a water and chemical resistant 2 mil rigid reverse printed vinyl on the exterior surfaces. The top edges of the drawer sides, back and front shall be radiused and wrapped with a water and household chemical resistant 4 mil semi-rigid reverse printed vinyl. The corners of the drawer core shall be lap joined and bonded with adhesive and staples.

2.04.06 The drawer bottom shall be 1/4" thick-50 lb. density particleboard with 2 mil reverse printed wood-grained vinyl on the interior face. The bottom shall be attached to the sides, back and front with adhesive and staples. The drawer slide "L" shaped lip shall be bent around the bottom to reinforce the joints. The powder-coated steel WhisperGlide core member supports the drawer to a capacity rating of 75 lb.

2.04.07 All base cabinets except Cirrus, Horizon and Nouveau shall have roll-out trays consisting of 1/2" thick-48 lb. density particleboard sides which are laminated on the outside with a water and household chemical resistant 2 mil rigid reverse printed vinyl. The inside surface shall be laminated with a water and household chemical resistant 4 mil semi-rigid reverse printed vinyl and wrapped around the radiused top edge. The ends shall be rabbeted to receive the front and back. The tray front shall be 3/4" thick solid red oak finished with a tough coating of heat activated conversion varnish which is impervious to household chemicals. The tray front shall be rabbeted at the bottom edge to receive the bottom. The tray back shall be 1/2" thick-48 lb. density particleboard with a water and household chemical resistant 4 mil semi-rigid reverse printed vinyl on the interior and a water and household chemical resistant 2 mil rigid reverse printed vinyl on the exterior. The water and household chemical resistant 4 mil semi-rigid reverse printed vinyl shall be wrapped around the radiused top edge of the tray back. All four corners of the tray shall be attached with staples. The tray bottom shall be 1/4″ thick-50 lb. density particleboard with a water and household chemical resistant 2 mil rigid reverse printed vinyl on the interior face. The bottom shall be attached with adhesive and staples. The formed lip of the WhisperGlide guide reinforces this joint.

2.04.08 The exclusive Merillat WhisperGlide dual captive side-mounted roller drawer system shall be mounted on all drawer and tray cores with the exception of Horizon, Nouveau and Cirrus. The system shall consist of a pair of epoxy coated 1.25mm steel slices that roll on close-tolerance nylon wheels. The wheels shall be isolated from the metal slides with a pliable "O" ring tire which dampens the noise normally associated with most roller slide systems. The support channel half of the Merillat WhisperGlide shall be mounted to the oak front frame of the cabinet with a screw and snap into an adjustable plastic adapter on the inside back of the cabinet. The drawer and tray core half of the Merillat WhisperGlide shall be attached to the front and back of the core with screws. The "L" shaped bottom of this member wraps around the core to reinforce it and provide a finished edge. The epoxy-coated steel, dual captive WhisperGlide core member and integrated adapter supports the drawer to a capacity rating of 75 lbs.

2.05 *Door and Drawer Front Construction*

2.05.01 Horizon doors shall be 5/8″ thick-46 lb. density industrial grade particleboard laminated on two sides with wood-grained pattern low pressure melamine for balanced construction to prevent warpage. The melamine laminate is bonded to the particleboard and provides a water and household chemical proof surface. The vertical edges of the doors shall be edgebanded with a .4mm thick melamine wood-grained design edge-banding.
The horizontal door edges shall be machined with a coved/reverse bevel and banded with a soft-formed melamine wood-grained design edge-banding to form a finger pull.
Horizon doors shall be mounted on exclusive Merillat designed self-closing concealed hinges. Hinges shall have horizontal and vertical adjustments. Doors shall have pliable rubber bumpers to dampen noise.

2.05.02 Horizon drawer fronts have the same construction as Horizon doors.

2.05.03 Nouveau doors and drawer fronts shall be constructed the same as Horizon. However, Nouveau shall have an almond-colored textured melamine surface with an abstract tan-colored horizontal textured pattern. Nouveau shall have the same wood-grained melamine edgebanding and soft-formed handle as Horizon. Nouveau shall also utilize the same self-closing hinge as Horizon.

2.05.04 Cirrus doors and drawer fronts shall be constructed the same as Horizon. However, Cirrus shall have a white melamine surface. Cirrus shall have a natural finish wood-grained melamine edgebanding and soft-formed handle. Cirrus shall also utilize the same self-closing hinge as Horizon.
NOTE: Horizon, Cirrus and Nouveau cabinets have "full-overlay" contemporary styling where the doors and drawers conceal the cabinet front frame. Extra attention must be given to clearances in corners and near appliances when planning a kitchen with these cabinets.

2.05.05 Springbrook II, Homestead II, Bisque II and Burnwyck doors shall have 3/4″ thick and 2 5/16″ wide solid red oak stiles and

rails joined at the four corners with tongue and groove joints. The joints shall be bonded with adhesive. The frame shall be molded with a double-bead detail on the top and bottom and a coved/reverse bevel shall be machined on the top and bottom to serve as a finger grip. Sides shall carry a square edge profile. Burnwyck doors shall be machined with a coved/reverse bevel on all four sides. A 5/32″ thick plain-sliced veneered red oak plywood center panel shall be retained by a groove machined in the frame.

2.05.06 Omni doors shall be 5/8″ thick-46 lb. density particleboard with almond-colored melamine surfaces on both sides for balanced construction to prevent warpage. Three sides of the door shall be edged with a .4mm thick PVC banding. The fourth edge shall be capped with a 3/4″ x 1 1/2″ solid oak handle with integral finger grip. The oak shall be selected to insure a consistent horizontal grain pattern on all handles. The handle shall be attached to the door with 5/16″ x 1 3/4″ hardwood dowels and bonded permanently with adhesive. Omni doors shall be mounted on fully concealed self-closing hinges. These hinges feature strong two-point mounting and shall be adjustable in both the vertical and horizontal directions. Doors shall have pliable rubber bumpers to dampen noise.

2.05.07 Omni drawer fronts shall be constructed the same as the doors.

2.05.08 Artique doors and drawer fronts shall be constructed the same as Omni. However, Artique shall have a white melamine surface. Artique shall also utilize the same self-closing hinge as Omni.
NOTE: Omni and Artique cabinets have contemporary styling in which the doors and drawers conceal the cabinet front frames. Several of the cabinets, i.e., blind corner and BLS 36, have overlay panels on them to provide continuity. Extra attention must be given to clearances in corners and near appliances when planning a kitchen with these cabinets.

2.05.09 Summerhill II, Meadow II, Heather II, Ashley, and Amherst doors shall have 3/4″ thick x 2 5/16″ wide frame components hand-selected for uniform and pleasing grain patterns. These solid hardwood stiles and rails shall be joined at the four corners with tongue and groove joints. The joints shall be bonded with adhesive. The frame shall be molded with a double-bead detail on the top and bottom; and a coved/reverse bevel shall be machined on the top and bottom to serve as a finger grip. Sides shall carry a square edge profile. Ashley and Amherst doors shall be machined with a coved/reverse bevel on all for sides. The raised center panel shall consist of a 48 lb. density particleboard core with its edges machined in a coved shape. The front and back panel shall be covered with select hardwood veneers.
The veneer shall be bonded to the substrate using adhesive, heat and pressure. The resulting panel has the appearance of solid hardwood without the inherent problems of shrinkage and splitting. The panel is retained by a groove machined in the edge of the door frame.
This construction shall provide a strong door that resists the expansion, shrinkage and splitting associated with other types of raised panels. The veneered center panel shall provide the uniformity of grain and finish found in fine furniture. Doors shall have pliable rubber bumpers to dampen noise.

NOTE: Summerhill II, Meadow II, Heather II, Ashley and Amherst Cathedral-styled wall cabinets can be used with square raised panel base cabinets to design a more elegant, formal kitchen. The Cathedral doors are constructed the same as the square raised panel doors except for a wide 3/4″ thick x 4 1/8″ top rail which is shaped in a Cathedral arch. The raised center panel is machined to match.

2.05.10 Summerhill II, Homestead II, Meadow II, Bisque II, Springbrook II, Heather II, Burnwyck, Ashley, Wyndtree and Amherst drawer fronts shall be 3/4″ thick glued-up, solid hardwood lumber. The front of the panel shall be veneered with select furniture grade veneers. This technique combines the strength of solid hardwoods with the uniform grain patterns of fine veneers.

2.05.11 Wyndtree oak doors shall have 3/4″ thick red oak boards edge glued side-by-side to produce a solid oak panel. The panel shall be V-grooved on the front for decorative effect. At the bottom of the V-groove shall be a saw kerf that allows the panel to expand and contract without splitting. There shall be identical saw kerfs on the back door adjacent to the face kerfs. 5/8″ thick x 1 1/2″ wide oak battens shall be fastened to the back of the door with countersunk screws. These battens shall reinforce the door and prevent it from cupping. The outside edge of the door shall be machined with a reverse bevel finger grip and decorative cove shape.

2.05.12 Alexis, Bristen and Cambric doors shall have 3/4″ thick x 2 3/16″ wide frame components hand selected for uniform and pleasing grain patterns. These solid hardwood stiles and rails shall be joined at the four corners with tongue and groove joints. The joints shall be bonded with adhesive. The frame shall be molded with a single bead detail on the inside; and a shaped profile is machined on the outside perimeter. The raised center panel shall consist of a 48 lb. density particleboard core with its edges machined in a coved shape. The front and back of the panel shall be covered with select hardwood veneers.
The veneer shall be bonded to the substrate using adhesive, heat and pressure. The resulting panel has the appearance of solid hardwood without the inherent problems of shrinkage and splitting. The panel is retained by a groove machined in the edge of the door frame.
This construction shall provide a strong door that resists the expansion, shrinkage and splitting associated with other types of raised panels. The veneered center panel shall provide the uniformity of grain and finish found in fine furniture. Doors shall have pliable rubber bumpers to dampen noise.
NOTE: Alexis, Bristen, and Cambric arched-style wall cabinets can be used with square raised panel base cabinets to design a more elegant, formal kitchen. The arched doors are constructed the same as the square raised panel doors except for a wide 3/4″ thick x 4 1/8″ top rail which is shaped in a single arch. The raised center panel is machined to match.

2.05.13 Alexis, Bristen and Cambric drawer fronts shall be 3/4″ thick glued-up, solid hardwood lumber. Components are selected for uniform and pleasing grain patterns.

2.06 *Hinges*

2.06.01 All Springbrook II, Homestead II, Bisque II, Summerhill II, Meadow II and Heather II doors shall be mounted on concealed, nickle finish self-closing hinges which automatically close the cabinet door when it is within 10 degrees of the face frame. The safety feature helps prevent accidents caused by people bumping into cabinet doors that are left open inadvertently. Doors shall have pliable bumpers to dampen noise. Horizon, Nouveau and Cirrus shall have semi-concealed hinges. Omni and Artique shall have fully-concealed hinges.

2.06.02 All Merillat, Alexis, Bristen and Cambric doors shall be mounted on concealed, nickle finish self-closing hinges which automatically close the cabinet door when it is within 10 degrees of the face frame. The safety feature helps prevent accidents caused by people bumping into cabinet doors that are left open inadvertently. Doors shall have pliable rubber bumpers to dampen noise.

2.07 *Finishes*

2.07.01 Merillat oak cabinets are available in pickled, light, medium, and dark stain finishes. All contain pigments that accentuate the grain.

Merillat oak components shall be sanded to prepare the surface for staining. The penetrating stain shall be applied with a variety of specially designed electrostatic spray equipment (door and door fronts), mechanical spray devices (frames) or hand-spray equipment (accessories) tailored specifically to the type of part being finished. The stain shall be wiped to move it into the pores of the oak and to remove excess finish. A vinyl sealer shall be applied to prevent the oak from taking on or giving up moisture which could cause warping and cracking. The sealer also helps to bond the top coat to the product. The sealer shall be lightly sanded to prepare the surface for top coating. The high-solids, heat activated conversion varnish top coat shall create a durable envelope protecting the oak wood from chemicals, abrasion and detergents.

2.07.03 Merillat cherry cabinets are only available in a medium-toned dye stain finish.

Merillat cherry components shall be sanded to prepare the surface for staining. The dye stain shall be applied with mechanical spray (doors, drawer fronts, and front frames, and accessory components). The dye stain shall be brushed into the pores of the wood to provide grain definition and remove excess finish. A vinyl sealer coat shall be applied to prevent the cherry from giving up or taking on moisture, which could cause warping and cracking. The sealer also helps to bond the top coat to the product. The sealer shall be lightly sanded to prepare the surface for top coating. The high-solids, heat activated conversion top coat shall create a durable envelope protection for the cherry from chemicals, abrasion and detergents.

2.07.04 Some Merillat accessory items shall be top coated with lacquer.

3. **RUTLAND / WHITEBAY SPECIFICATIONS**

3.01 *Cabinet Frames*

3.01.01 Cabinet frames shall have 3/4″ thick x 1 1/8″ wide maple hardwood rail and stile members. Center stiles shall be 3/4″ thick x 2 1/4″, 5 1/4″ or 8 1/4″ wide solid maple hardwood. All frame joints shall be reinforced and precisely aligned with two 1/4″ diameter birch, dowels and bonded with precisely metered adhesive. Cabinet stiles and rails are grooved to accept end panels and both top and bottom panels. Cabinet frames extend 1/4″ beyond the end panels for trimability in the field. Merillat cabinets are within 1/32″ of tolerance to specified height and width.

3.02 *End Panels*

3.02.01 Merillat end panels shall be 3/8″ thick-48 lb. density industrial grade laminated inside and out with a water and household chemical resistant 2.5 mil rigid solid color vinyl. End panel shall be machined to accept tops, bottoms, and cabinet backs.

3.03 *Cabinet Tops and Bottoms*

3.03.01 Wall cabinets tops and bottoms shall be 1/2″ thick-48 lb. density industrial grade particleboard for extra strength and rigidity. These components shall be laminated on two sides with a water and household chemical resistant 2.5 mil rigid solid color vinyl. A dado joint and adhesive shall be used to join the tops and bottoms to the end panels and cabinet front frame creating a stronger more stable cabinet.

3.03.02 Base Cabinet bottoms shall be 1/2″ thick-48 lb. density industrial grade particleboard laminated with a water and household chemical resistant 2.5 mil rigid solid color vinyl on the interior side. The bottoms shall be joined to the end panels and cabinet front frame with dado joints and adhesive. Glue blocks shall be used to reinforce the bottoms of cabinets 27″ and wider. The upper portion of base cabinets shall be strengthened with 1/2″ thick gussets dadoed into front frame, back rail and end panels. Gussets maintain squareness.

3.03.03 All cabinet backs shall be 1/4″ thick-50 lb. particleboard laminated with a water and household chemical resistant 2.5 mil rigid solid color vinyl on the interior side. Wall cabinet backs shall be retained by a groove in the end panels. Base cabinet backs shall be attached in the same manner, but the top of the cabinet shall have an 11/16″ x 2 1/4″ pine screw rail securing the back of the cabinet. Base cabinet backs extend to the floor to provide added strength.

3.04 *Shelves*

3.04.01 All wall cabinets 24″ high and taller, under 42″ in width have adjustable shelves made of 1/2″ thick-48 lb density industrial grade particleboard. All wall cabinets 42″ and wider have fixed shelves dadoed into the end panels. The shelves shall be laminated with a water and household chemical resistant 2.5 mil rigid solid color vinyl. The front edge of the shelf shall be covered with a melamine edgebanding. Cabinet sides, for those cabinets with adjustable shelves, are precision drilled for durable locking shelf supports adjustable to 3 locations on 2 1/2″ increments. The shelf is supported in the center with adjustable supports in corresponding locations on the back of cabinet frame center stile.

3.04.02 All Rutland base shelves shall have half depth fixed shelves. The shelves shall be 1/2″ thick-48 lb. density industrial grade particleboard with a water and household chemical resistant 2.5 mil rigid solid color vinyl laminated to the top surface. Exposed shelf edge is laminated with melamine edgebanding. Shelves shall be supported on the ends with shelf clips, but are not adjustable. All shelves in base cabinets 27″ and wider shall have a support apron under shelf.

3.05 *Rutland Drawer and Drawer Cores*

3.05.01 All Rutland drawer sides, fronts, and backs shall be 1/2″ thick 48 lb. density industrial grade particleboard rabbeted to accept front and back. All drawer components shall be laminated on the exterior side with a water and household chemical resistant 2.5 mil rigid solid color vinyl. The interior faces of the drawer sides, fronts and backs shall be laminated with a water and household chemical resistant 4 mil semi-rigid

solid color vinyl and wrapped around the top radiused edges of the drawer components.

3.05.02 The corners of the drawer core shall be lap jointed and bonded with adhesive and staples. The drawer core bonded with adhesive and staples shall be secured to the drawer front with two or four screws depending on the drawer size.

3.05.03 Bottoms shall be 1/4″ thick-50 lb. density particleboard 2.5 mil vinyl laminated to the interior side. The bottom shall be attached to the sides, back and front with adhesive and staples. The drawer slide "L" shaped lip wraps the drawer bottom and reinforces drawer construction. The epoxy coated steel roller guide core member supports the drawer to a capacity rating of 75 lbs.

3.06 *Drawer Slides*

3.06.01 The Merillat Rutland drawer guide system is a side-mounted dual captive roller drawer system. The system consist of a pair of epoxy coated 1.25 mm steel slides that roll on close tolerance nylon rollers. The support channel half of the Merillat roller guide shall be mounted to the front frame of the cabinet with a screw. The rear of the channel snaps into an adjustable plastic adapter on the inside of the cabinet. The drawer core half of the Merillat roller guide shall be attached to the front and back of the core with screws. The "L" shaped bottom of this member wraps around the core to reinforce it and provide a finished edge.

3.07 *Whitebay Drawer Core and Tray Construction*

3.07.01 All Whitebay drawer cores use the exclusive Merillat WhisperGlide system and shall have 1/2″ thick-48 lb. density particleboard sides that are attached to the 1/2″ particleboard front and back. The drawer sides shall be laminated with a water and household chemical resistant 4 mil semi-rigid solid color vinyl on the interior and a water and chemical resistant 2.5 mil rigid solid color vinyl on the exterior surfaces. The top edges of the drawer sides, backs and fronts shall be radiused and wrapped with a water and household chemical resistant 4 mil semi-rigid solid color vinyl. The corners of the drawer core shall be laminated and bonded with adhesive and staples.

3.07.02 The drawer bottom shall be 1/4″ thick-50 lb. density particleboard with 2.5 mil solid color vinyl on the interior face. The bottom shall be attached to the sides, back and front with staples. The drawer slide "L" shaped lip wraps the drawer bottom and reinforces drawer construction. The epoxy-coated steel WhisperGlide core member supports the drawer to a capacity rating of 75 lb. load.

3.07.03 Drawers in base cabinets 30″ wide and over use a 3/8″ thick particleboard bottom for additional support.

3.07.04 All base cabinets shall have roll-out trays mounted with adapters attached to cabinet back. Trays are standard with all base cabinets except 9″ wide. Optional add-on trays are available for base cabinets.

3.07.05 Lap jointed assembly consisting of 1/2″ thick-48 lb. density industrial grade particleboard with 4 mil semi-rigid solid color vinyl wrapped around the radiused top edge to help prevent marring and chipping. The tray front shall be 3/4″ solid hardwood with a triple coating of heat activated conversion paint.

3.07.06 1/4″ thick-50 lb. density particleboard laminated with 4 mil vinyl on the interior side. The bottom is attached with adhesive and staples. The formed lip of the

	WhisperGlide tray member reinforces these joints.
3.08	*Toe Space*
3.08.01	The toeboard shall be 3/8″ thick-48 lb. density particleboard and extend from the floor to the cabinet bottom. This adds support to the bottom and effectively seals the toe space against vermin and insects. The toeboard shall be covered with a 3/8″ white vinyl covered particleboard strip.
3.09	*Rutland Door and Drawer Front Construction*
3.09.01	5/8″ thick 46 lb. density industrial grade particleboard laminated with water and household chemical/abrasion resistant white low pressure melamine. The white color has been developed specifically to provide maximum opacity and match the white used for most major appliances and countertop materials. The edges of doors and drawer fronts are edgebanded with a PVC edgebanding custom color matched to the front.
3.10	*Whitebay Door and Drawer Front Construction*
3.10.01	3/4″ thick-48 lb. density furniture grade medium density fiberboard. The one-piece medium density fiberboard is precision machined to exact tolerances. The component is laminated on the front side with a 16 mil vinyl foil that is thermo-formed to the door face. The back of the component is laminated with water and abrasion resistant white melamine. Both front surface and back are color matched and have been developed to provide the maximum opacity and resistant to abrasion, water and household chemicals and yellowing.
3.11	*Hinges*
3.11.01	Rutland doors are mounted on exclusive Merillat designed self-closing, nickle-plated, semi-concealed hinges and open to 110 degrees. Hinges shall have horizontal and vertical adjustments. Whitebay doors are mounted fully concealed, self-closing, nickle-plated hinges and open to 120 degrees. The hinges feature dowelled mounting and four-way adjustability.
4.	FIRE RESISTANCE
4.01	Overlaid particleboard and plywood used for cabinet construction has been tested in accordance with UL standard 723 "Test For Surface Burning Characteristics of Building Materials.
5.	FORMALDEHYDE EMISSIONS LEVELS
5.01	Formaldehyde emissions comply with requirements of 24 CFR, Part 3280 (August 9, 1984), the HUD rule on Manufactured Home Construction and Safety Standards and 29 CFR Part 1910 (May 27, 1992), the OSHA rule on Occupational Exposure to Formaldehyde.
5.02	Formaldehyde emissions for raw particleboard is restricted to 0.3 parts per million.
6.	INSTALLATION
6.01	Contractor shall verify all on-site dimensions and notify supplier of any variances or changes.
6.02	Install cabinets as indicated on the drawings. Install plumb and level with all joints tight, in accordance with instructions shipped with cabinets.
6.03	Shim cabinets as required and trim with molding to match cabinets.
6.04	Secure to walls with screws embedded one inch minimum in solid wood framing or blocking.
6.05	Install miscellaneous hardware and accessories as indicated on the drawings.
6.06	Clean cabinets and leave in perfect operating order with all doors, shelves and drawers aligned and plumb.

For further information, send to Merillat for a full product specification guide. (Merillat Industries, Inc., P. O. Box 1946, Adrian, MI 49221)

In keeping with our policy of continuous refinement, Merillat Industries reserves the right to alter specifications and styles without general notice or obligation to make similar changes in products previously produced.

FRAMELESS SPECIFICATIONS

GENERAL

1.01 Scope

1.01.01 The scope of this specification is to cover the design, construction and installation of all frameless kitchen and bath cabinetry.

1.03 Submittals

1.03.01 Supplier will furnish shop drawings, which are taken from the architect's drawings, specifically calling our the cabinet nomenclature and sizes. Supplier shall also submit floor plans and elevations for the cabinets showing layout, dimensions and details of installation.

1.03.02 Submit cabinet door samples with manufacturer's range of colors for selection by the architect.

1.03.03 Submit manufacturer's literature on cabinets.

2. PRODUCT

2.01 Cabinets shall be "____" (specify door style) as manufactured by Merillat Industries, P.O. Box 1946, Adrian, MI 49221. Size and type as required to meet configurations indicated on drawings.

2.02 Certification

2.02.01 All cabinetry shall carry the Kitchen Cabinet Manufacturers Association (KCMA) certified cabinet seal and meet or exceed the "recommended minimum construction and performance standards for kitchen cabinets" outlined in the American National Standards Institute (ANSI) ANSI/KCMA A161.1-1990.

2.03 Materials-Case Construction shall be 5/8″ thick-46 lb. density industrial grade particleboard laminated on both sides with a water and household chemical/abrasion resistant melamine.

2.03.01 End panels shall be 5/8″ thick-46 lb. density industrial grade particleboard laminated on both sides with water and household chemical/abrasion resistant melamine. The front exposed edge is covered with .4mm thick melamine edgebanding.

2.03.02 Cabinet tops and bottoms shall be 5/8″ thick-46 lb. density industrial grade particleboard. These components shall be laminated on both sides for stability and uniform appearance. 8mm dowels and adhesive shall be used in precision holes to join the tops and bottoms to the end panels. The front exposed edge shall be covered with .4mm color matched melamine edgebanding. 36″ wide bottoms for wall double-face cabinets shall be 3/4″ thick to provide maximum strength without the use of center dividers.

2.03.03 All backs shall be 1/4″ thick-50 lb. density particleboard with a water and household chemical resistant 4 mil thick vinyl laminated to the interior side. Maple product line shall have a maple grain melamine interior. Wall cabinet backs shall be reinforced with 1/2″ thick particleboard screw rails at the top and bottom. Wall cabinet backs shall be glued, stapled and retained by a groove in the end panels, top and bottom. Base cabinet backs shall be attached in the same manner. A 5/8″ thick back rail shall extend to floor for added strength.

2.03.04 All 24″ or higher wall cabinets shall have adjustable shelves made of 5/8″ thick-46 lb. density industrial grade particleboard. The shelf top and bottom shall be laminated with the same melamine as the cabinet interior. The front exposed edge shall be covered with a .4mm thick color matched melamine edgebanding. Wall cabinets shall be precision drilled to provide (three)

small (5/32″) diameter adjustable holes per shelf centered on 2 1/2″ increments. Each shelf shall be fitted with durable steel reinforced nylon shelf supports. This combination provides a clean, uninterrupted interior that accommodates easy storage of tall and short items. 3/4″ shelves shall be used on the following special cabinets W 332430, WBC 3630, WBC 3624, WDFB 3630, WDF 3624, WDF 3630. The extra shelf thickness on these deeper and wider cabinets omits the need for center dividers thus increasing storage flexibility while preventing sag.

2.03.05 Toe space shall be 5/8″ thick-46 lb. density industrial particleboard laminated with water and household chemical/abrasion resistant melamine to match cabinet finish. Toe boards shall be removable and held in place by metal clips mounted to cabinet sides. This can facilitate leveling of cabinet during installation and ensure complete clean up of kitchen spills. Toe board ends shall be edgebanded with .4mm thick melamine for a finished appearance.

2.03.06 Drawer core fronts, sides and backs shall be 1/2″ thick-48 lb. density industrial particleboard. Side shall be rabbeted to accept the front and back. All drawer components shall be laminated on the exterior side with a water and household chemical resistant 2.5 mil rigid vinyl. The interior faces of the drawer sides shall be laminated with a water and chemical resistant 4 mil semi-rigid vinyl and wrapped around the top radiused edges of the drawer components.

2.03.07 The drawer bottom shall be 1/4″ thick-50 lb. density particleboard with 2.5 mil vinyl on the interior side. The bottom shall be attached to the sides, back and front with adhesive and staples. The drawer slide "L" shaped lip wraps the drawer bottom and reinforces drawer construction. Drawer bottoms 30″ wide and over shall be 3/8″ thick-48 lb. density industrial particleboard with 2.5 mil thick vinyl on the interior side.

2.03.08 Roll-out trays shall be adjustable and mount on pre-bored holes in base and tall cabinets sides. One tray shall be 1/2″ thick-48 lb. density industrial grade particleboard. Sides shall be rabbeted to accept backs. All tray components shall be laminated on the exterior side with a water and chemical resistant 2.5 mil vinyl. The tray sides shall be butted to the tray front with four 6mm hardwood dowels and P.V.A. adhesive. The tray front shall be 1/2″ thick-48 lb. density industrial grade particleboard wrapped with 4 mil thick vinyl. The interior faces of the drawer sides and backs shall be laminated with a 4 mil vinyl and wrapped around the top radiused edges of the drawer components.

2.03.09 Door and Drawer fronts shall be 5/8″ thick-46 lb. density industrial particleboard laminated on both sides with water and household chemical/abrasion resistant white melamine. The vertical and horizontal edges shall be edgebanded with solid color PVC edgebanding.

2.03.09.01 Maple doors are constructed using solid 3/4″ maple rails and stiles, joined with tongue and groove joints at the corners, surrounding a 5/8″ thick center panel of solid maple. Maple center panel is cushioned in the rail and stile grooves with pads to allow for expansion and contraction. Wall cabinet doors are available in a

square raised panel or an elegant arched raised panel. Drawer fronts shall be 3/4″ thick solid maple.

2.03.10 Merillat's exclusive WhisperGlide side-mounted, wrap around roller drawer and tray system shall be mounted on all drawer and tray cores. The system shall consist of a pair of corrosion resistant white epoxy coated 1.25mm steel slides that roll on close-tolerance nylon wheels. The wheels shall be isolated from the metal slides with a pliable "O" ring tire which dampens the noise normally associated with most roller slide systems. Drawer and tray guides are rated to a capacity of 75 lbs.

2.03.11 Doors shall be mounted on fully concealed, self-closing, nickle-plated hinges. Hinges shall open to 120 degrees and provide six-way adjustability. The hinge shall close the cabinet door when it is within 10 degrees of the cabinet front.

3. FIRE RESISTANCE

3.01 Overlaid particleboard and plywood used for cabinet construction has been tested in accordance with UL standard 723 "Test For Surface Burning Characteristics of Building Materials".

4. FORMALDEHYDE EMISSIONS LEVELS

4.01 Formaldehyde emissions comply with requirements of 24 CFR, Part 3280 (August 9, 1984), the HUD rule on Manufactured Home Construction and Safety Standards and 29 CFR Part 1910 (May 27, 1992), the OSHA rule on Occupational Exposure to Formaldehyde.

4.02 Formaldehyde emissions for raw particleboard is restricted to 0.3 parts per million.

5. INSTALLATION

5.01 Contractor shall verify all on-site dimensions and notify supplier of any variances or changes.

5.02 Install cabinets as indicated on the drawings. Install plumb and level with all joints tight, in accordance with instructions shipped with cabinets.

5.03 Shim cabinets as required and trim with molding to match cabinets.

5.04 Secure to walls with screws embedded one inch minimum in solid wood framing or blocking.

5.05 Install miscellaneous hardware and accessories as indicated on the drawings.

5.06 Clean cabinets and leave in perfect operating order with all doors, shelves and drawers aligned and plumb.

For further information, send to Merillat for a full product specification guide. (Merillat Industries, Inc., P. O. Box 1946, Adrian, MI 49221)

In keeping with our policy of continuous refinement, Merillat Industries reserves the right to alter specifications and styles without general notice or obligation to make similar changes in products previously produced.

EXTRAS THAT DON'T COST EXTRA. *Merillat*

cabinets come with many standard features at no extra cost. Like

our exclusive self-closing hinges, which automatically shut the

door when it's within 30° of the cabinet front. Other standard

features include: ▶ *A durable fur-*
niture quality finish that protects the

wood on Merillat cabinets from dam-

aging moisture, spills and scratches.

 ◀ *With our WhisperGlide® Drawer*

and Tray Guide System, drawers

and trays glide smoothly and

quietly (shown in Alexis with pot

lid rack accessory). ▶ *All Merillat*

cabinets feature easy-clean interiors

that stand up to moisture and

most household chemicals. Stan-

dard adjustable shelves make it easier to customize

 *storage needs.* ◀ *Roll-out trays*

are a standard feature in most

Merillat cabinets. They allow access

to all those things in the back

without wading through all those things in the front.

Decorative hardware is available to complement your Merillat cabinetry. Actual colors
may vary slightly due to printing limitations. For full color accuracy please visit your
Merillat Dealer.

Merillat®

AMERICA'S CABINETMAKER™
A product of Merillat Industries

Rosemont

CREATE A WARM, INVITING
KITCHEN WITH ROSEMONT. THESE
ONE-PIECE PAINTED DOORS ARE
HIGHLIGHTED BY GROOVED
DETAILING FOR A SUBTLE
ELEGANCE THAT COMPLEMENTS
THE STYLE OF ANY HOME.

FINELY CRAFTED

FURNITURE

FOR THE KITCHEN

AND BATH

Trivera

WITH ITS BEVELED EDGES AND
POLISHED SHEEN, TRIVERA OFFERS
HOMEOWNERS A NEW DIMENSION IN
CABINETRY. OPTIONAL BEVELED
GLASS INLAYS ADD A STRIKING TOUCH
TO THE HANDSOMELY STYLED DOORS,
WHICH ARE AVAILABLE IN 16 SOLID
COLORS.

Royale

ROYALE'S FLOWING LINES AND RADIUS
EDGES ARE EMPHASIZED BY THE
REFRESHING CORAL COLOR OF
BAMBERG. THE GLOSSY LAMINATE
FINISH DRAWS OUT THE DETAIL OF
WARM PINE WOOD TO GIVE THESE
CONTEMPORARY DOORS A
CAPTIVATING APPEARANCE.

Bedford

WHAT A ROMANTIC COMBINATION...
SOLID MAPLE IN A LUSCIOUS IVORY
FINISH. HAND-SANDED AND -STAINED
FOR QUALITY ONLY A PERSONAL
TOUCH CAN GIVE, BEDFORD FEATURES
ATTRACTIVE, RAISED-PANEL DOORS
FOR AN ENDURING APPEAL.

Windsor

INSPIRED BY NATURE, WINDSOR'S
GOLDEN OAK FINISH ILLUMINATES A
KITCHEN WITH THE SPLENDOR OF A
SUNSET. THE WARM HONEY HUES
HIGHLIGHT THE GRAIN OF THE
BEAUTIFUL SOLID OAK, WHILE A
CONTOURED OUTLINE ADDS A
CHARMING TOUCH.

Samples of Selected Door Styles

SENECA

SENECA WOOD

SUSSEX

GENEVA

NOVA

ASPEN II

INNSBROOK

AMHERST

BERKSHIRE

FAIRLAWN

BRECKENRIDGE

LAKEWOOD

RICHMOND

OAKBROOK

HAMPSHIRE

A LIMITED WARRANTY TO CONSUMERS
Good Housekeeping
PROMISES
REPLACEMENT OR REFUND IF DEFECTIVE

THIS SEAL APPLIES TO
ULTRACRAFT®
KITCHEN CABINETS

KITCHEN CABINET
KCMA
MANUFACTURERS ASSOCIATION

CORTINA

ST. ANDREWS

MILAN

UltraCraft ®

6163 OLD 421 ROAD
LIBERTY, NORTH CAROLINA 27298
919-622-4281   800-262-4046

ALSIDE AND ULTRACRAFT ARE REGISTERED TRADEMARKS OF ALSIDE.
©ALSIDE, 1992   PRINTED IN U.S.A.   75-2000-01   3779

Premium Series

OXFORD

Light Oak

Western charm is displayed in this Oxford light oak kitchen enhanced with open shelving and offset heights. True quality craftsmanship reveals itself with knife door hinges and decorative edge profiles.

Wellborn's Oxford door style is available in a light, medium, natural, and pickle finish which is hand rubbed for wood grain enhancement. This traditional kitchen features our natural oak, a finish that reveals the true wood beauty. Valances and crown moulding combine to top these cabinets with tailored style, and matching end panels complete every turn. Useful as well as beautiful islands and peninsulas are easily created with our variety of cabinet styles and sizes. The inviting warmth and open space in this kitchen could make it the most lived in room in your home.

The three storage drawers in our **Oven Cabinets** are removable for double oven space.

This **Corner Sink Base** is equipped with two full-depth adjustable shelves for storage.

Brass accents enhance the cracked glass design in our **Leaded Glass Doors.**

Natural Oak

The finished plywood interior of this **Microwave Cabinet** reveals quality craftsmanship.

A **Base Lazy Susan** maximizes kitchen corner space storage.

A 30" or 36" wide **Drawer Range Base** is spacious for storing kitchen linens.

An elegant and functional serving center is designed with **Angle Wall and Base Cabinets.**

Medium Oak

Our creatively designed china cabinet features fret valances, bookcases and different height wall cabinets. The attention given to details such as counter top edge moulding and matching end panels allows us to offer the look of fine furniture. The richness of this medium oak finish combined with the sleek knife hinge makes the Oxford style appealing in any room of your home.

1/2" solid oak drawers slide smoothly on epoxy coated self closing guides.

Series Numbers:
2030 Natural
2031 Light
2032 Medium
2034 Pickle

5/8" thick shelves are fully adjustable and are secured with dual lock shelf clips.

KCMA
KITCHEN CABINET MANUFACTURERS ASSOCIATION

NKBA
NATIONAL KITCHEN & BATH ASSOCIATION

WELLBORN
W
People Who Care

Wellborn Cabinet, Inc.
P.O. Box 1210   Rt. 1, Hwy. 77S
Ashland, Alabama 36251
(205) 354-7151
Fax (205) 354-7022   Printed in U.S.A.

It is characteristic of stained wood finishes, especially the pickle white-washed, to age over time when exposed to sunlight and general household chemicals. Due to this aging process, minor differences may develop with color match when replacing doors on existing cabinetry or adding additional cabinetry at a later date. Due to the natural characteristics of wood and the lithographic printing process, slight color variations may occur in the photos reproduced in this brochure. Consult your local Wellborn dealership for actual wood sample color selection.

Red Oak

Maple

Bally
Wood Welded®

C539
BuyLine 8606

Because It's Wood

Red Oak

Bally
Wood Welded®

Whether you have selected our Hard Maple or Red Oak Butcher Block, Your choice is legendary for warmth and durability.

Now, with our new DURAKRYL™102 coating; our Butcher Block is more versatile than ever. This tough, non-toxic coating will repel most household agents including alcohol, bleach, even Paint Thinner!

Scientifically controlled Kiln Drying, Processing, and Finishing make "BALLY" Blocks an outstanding value.

Maple

Cut, sit or stand on genuine butcher block...

Because
It's Wood

Maple

Bally Red Oak and Hard Maple Butcher Block Tops

	AVAILABLE LENGTHS (INCHES)										
	18	24	30	36	42	48	60	72	84	96	120
25 INCH DEPTH											
30 INCH DEPTH	•	•	•	•	•						
36 INCH DEPTH	•	•	•	•	•						

25 INCH DEPTH   30 INCH DEPTH   36 INCH DEPTH

Bally Block Company   30 South Seventh Street, Bally, PA 19503   (215) 845-7511

Sinks That Make A Statement.

TRADITIONAL

To reflect the true elegance and beauty of your kitchen, choose our Traditional Gourmet Collection in shining stainless steel. As America's leading designer of stainless steel sinks, Elkay offers you the ultimate in quality. Each sink is carefully crafted from durable 18-gauge material and is machine ground and meticulously hand buffed to our exclusive Lasting Beauty™ finish that resists scratching, chipping, fading or cracking and is more forgiving to dropped glassware.

Our Traditional Gourmet Collection also features classic styling in single-, double- and triple-bowl configurations with large, 10"-deep bowls and optional ribbed drainboards. With so much to choose from, you're bound to find a brilliant complement to brighten your kitchen.

EGPI-4322-R

Elkay's new Gourmet Cuisine Centré makes food preparation a joy! Our exclusive design includes an innovative bi-level food prepration area, with a ribbed work surface, convenient disposer bowl and spacious 10"-deep bowl. Choose either a left- or a right-bowl model (EGPI-4322-R or L). Components separately: Regency Faucet (LK-4381-F-BK), Soap/Lotion Dispenser (LK-313-BK), Hot Water Machine (LKH-190).

EGPI-4322-R

DIMENSIONS IN INCHES

ILGR-6022-L-C

Featuring a ribbed drainboard and oversized compartments, this triple-bowl sink has a Hi-Arc faucet with contemporary spout styling, swivel aerator and retractable spray and hose. Shown here with left-side sink bowls, the package is also available with right-side sink bowls. Components available separately: Triple-bowl Sink (ILGR-6022-R or L), Faucet (LK-4124-F).

LGR-4322-C

A compact and efficient design makes this triple-bowl sink ideal for multiple cooking tasks. The Hi-Arc faucet allows quick and easy access to all compartments, while the retractable spray and hose make rinsing effortless. Components shown here are available separately: Sink (LGR-4322), Faucet (LK-4124-F).

ILFGR-5422-L

Make big chores into small work with our extra-wide, double-bowl sink, featuring our exclusive Lasting Beauty finish and a handy 19 3/4" ribbed drainboard. Shown here with left-side sink bowls, this model is also available with right-side sink bowls. Components separately: Sink (ILFGR-5422-L or R), Hi-Arc Faucet (LK-4324-F-BK), Soap/Lotion Dispenser (LK-313-BK).

ILGR-6022-L-C

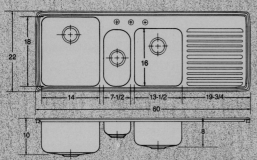

LGR-4322-C

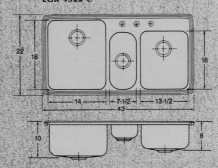

ILFGR-5422-L

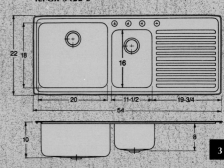

3

ILGR-5422-L

The two large sink bowls and expansive 19 7/8" ribbed drainboard offer ample room for so many tasks. Shown here with left-side sink bowls, this design is also available with right-side sink bowls. Components separately: Sink (ILGR-5422-L or R), Faucet (LK-4324-F-AL), Soap/Lotion Dispenser (LK-313-AL) and Strainer (LK-35-AL).

ILFGR-4822-L

For maximum versatility and unmatched durability, try this Elkay design featuring large and small bowls with a 17 1/2" ribbed drainboard. Shown with left-side bowls, it's also available with right-side bowls. Components separately: Sink (ILFGR-4822-L or R), Faucet (LK-4340-F-CR), Soap/Lotion Dispenser (LK-313-CR), Hot Water Machine (LKH-190).

ILGR-4822-L

If you have limited space, this sink offers unlimited options. Two large bowls make work comfortable and convenient, while the ribbed work space is ideal for rinsing, drying and food preparation. Shown here with left-side sink bowls, it's also available with right-side sink bowls. Components separately: Sink (ILGR-4822-L or R), Faucet (LK-4324-F-WH), Soap/Lotion Dispenser (LK-313-WH).

ILGR-5422-L

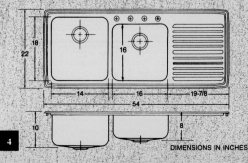

ILFGR-4822-L

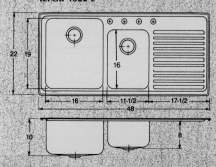

ILGR-4822-L

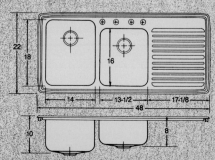

DIMENSIONS IN INCHES

4

LFGR-3722

Featuring a large and small bowl, this Elkay design offers virtually unlimited flexibility; clean and rinse in one bowl, prepare food in the other. Components separately: Sink (LFGR-3722), Faucet (LK-4350-F-BK), Soap/Lotion Dispenser (LK-313-BK), Hot Water Machine (LKH-190) and Strainer (LK-35-BK).

LGR-3722

An all-time favorite, this double sink with 10" bowl, Hi-Arc faucet and retractable spray and hose makes cleaning large pots and pitchers easier than ever. Components separately: Sink (LGR-3722), Faucet (LK-2453).

LFGR-3322

With a large and small bowl, this sparkling sink is great for smaller work spaces. And, for years of lasting brilliance, this model features our exclusive Lasting Beauty finish. Components separately: Sink (LFGR-3322), Faucet (LK-4361), Hot Water Machine (LKH-190).

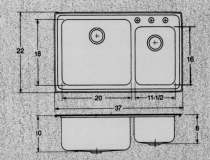

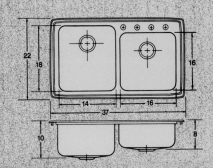

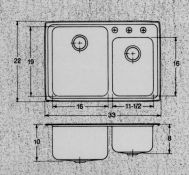

LGR-3322

One look at this shiny, compact sink and you'll know you've discovered the perfect addition to a small work area. Fits traditional kitchen counter areas. Components separately: Sink (LGR-3322), Faucet (LK-4324-F-BK), Soap/Lotion Dispenser (LK-313-BK).

ILGR-4322-L

Simple and convenient, this Elkay model is the first choice for those who need one spacious, durable sink compartment and a handy 20" ribbed drainboard. Shown with left-side bowl, it's also available with a right-side bowl. Components separately: Sink (ILGR-4322-L or R), Faucet (LK-4391-F-WH) and Escutcheon (LK-2725-WH).

LGR-3322

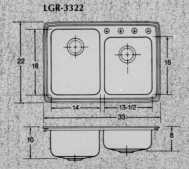

ILGR-4322-L

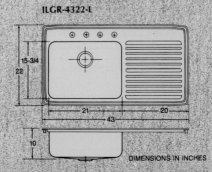

6

DIMENSIONS IN INCHES

CONTEMPORARY

Soft and elegant, yet durable and tough – that's Elkay's Contemporary Gourmet Collection. Like all our stainless steel sinks, the Contemporary Gourmet Collection won't chip, crack or fade. And our Lasting Beauty finish gives a soft, satin look that resists scratching.

Featuring a sleek, round-bowl design and European styling, these sinks will give your kitchen a fresh, modern look while performing radiantly well into the future. The optional left or right placement of the smaller bowl and the handy drainboards provide customized convenience and unmatched efficiency. Once you've owned an Elkay stainless steel sink, you'll see it's as beautiful as it is durable.

ILCGR-5322-L

Neatness and efficiency are the key advantages of this stainless steel sink. Featuring a large, double bowl, it also has a wide drainboard for drying dishes quickly and easily. Components separately: Sink (ILCGR-5322-L or R), Faucet (LK-4391-F-BK), Hot Water Machine (LKH-190), Strainer (LK-35-BK).

ILCGR-5322-L

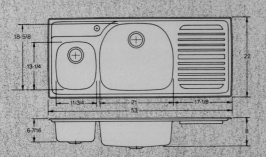

LCGR-3822-L

With a smaller yet functional bowl on the left, and a larger bowl on the right, this sink affords the busy cook ample work space. If you prefer the smaller bowl on the right, it's also available. Components separately: Sink (LCGR-3822-L or R), Faucet (LK-4381-F-CR), Soap/Lotion Dispenser (LK-313-CR).

ILCGR-4822-L

Need more space to create enticing entrees? Choose this Elkay design, with double-bowl configuration and spacious 16 15/16" right-side ribbed drainboard for cutting, rinsing and preparing food. Also available with left-side drainboard. Components separately: Sink (ILCGR-4822-L or R), Faucet (LK-4381-F-BK), Soap/Lotion Dispenser (LK-313-BK), Hot Water Machine (LKH-190).

LCGR-3322-L

Shown with our sophisticated Regency faucet, this stainless steel sink features a smaller bowl on the left or right side for added ease in food preparation. Components separately: Sink (LCGR-3322-L or R), Faucet (LK-4391-F-WH), Soap/Lotion Dispenser (LK-313-WH).

LCGR-3822-L

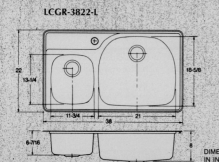

ILCGR-4822-L

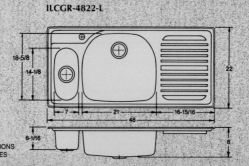

LCGR-3322-L

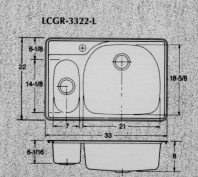

DIMENSIONS IN INCHES

ILCGR-4022-L

Rinse, clean, cut and slice! Our single-bowl sink provides you with the perfect bowl and ribbed 17" drainboard to do it all. Shown with left-side bowl, it's also available with right-side bowl. Components separately: Sink (ILCGR-4022-L or R), Faucet (LK-4350-F-AL), Soap/Lotion Dispenser (LK-313-AL) and Strainer (LK-35-AL).

LCGR-2522

Few sinks can offer the spacious and modern styling of our large, single-compartment sink. This single bowl provides the capacity for cleaning large pots and pans easily. Components separately: Sink (LCGR-2522), Faucet (LK-4350-F-WH) and Soap/Lotion Dispenser (LK-313-WH).

ILCGR-4022-L

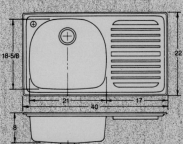

LCGR-2522

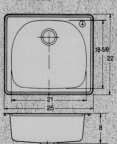

UNDERMOUNT

Elkay gives you the freedom to design your own kitchen, entertainment area or custom bath with our new Undermount Sink components. Make a statement of personal style by choosing from 10 unique designs crafted from the highest quality 18-gauge stainless steel and hand-ground to produce our exclusive scratch-resistant Lasting Beauty™ finish. Whether you're creating a food preparation area, bathroom sink or even a wet bar, the Elkay collection of shapes and sizes is the largest in the industry.

Elkay's undermount design affixes easily below any solid countertop. It leaves minimal space between the sink and the underside of the countertop, providing an integrated look with stainless steel durability.

So go ahead, take your pick – with Elkay Undermount Sinks the possibilities are endless.

ELU-2118

Add contemporary styling to extra-large capacity and you've got it all. This unique design offers ultrarounded corners to easily fit even the biggest of pots and pans. Pair it with any of the smaller components to create the ultimate kitchen work area.

ELU-2118

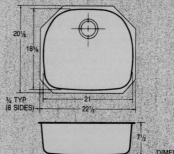

20⅛
18⅝
¾ TYP (8 SIDES)
21
22½
7½

DIMENSIONS IN INCHES

ELU-2115

When it comes to big kitchen work, this sink can take whatever you dish out – featuring a spacious rectangular bowl and an offset drain. The longer width design fits perfectly in narrower countertops.

ELU-1618

This full-capacity sink, with its 9-1/2"-deep bowl, features unique beveled back corners. And the heavy-duty 18-gauge steel construction helps make it as durable as it is functional. Choose a small companion sink for simple food preparation and cleanup.

ELU-1511

Elegant in form, this oval design is perfect as a stand-alone for the bath. As always, the vibrant stainless steel reflects and enhances the color of its environment.

ELU-2115

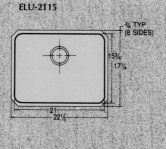

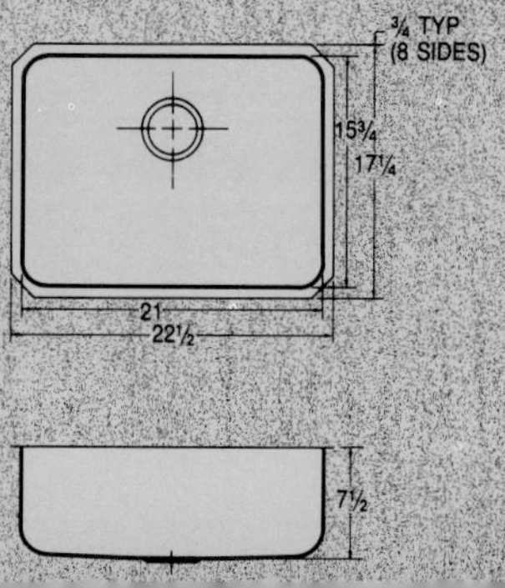

ELU-1618

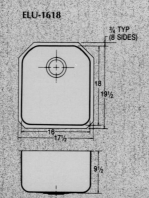

ELU-1511

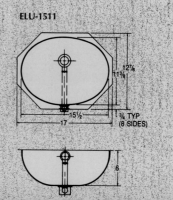

ELU-1316

A versatile design, small enough to fit in tight spaces yet large enough to handle the big chores. Couple it with a larger sink for ultimate capacity.

ELU-1418

The added size makes handling larger pots and pans easy. Pair it with a smaller sink to enhance the food preparation area.

ELU-1113

Contemporary, sophisticated styling. Use it as a second sink, or pair it with a larger bowl for the kitchen area.

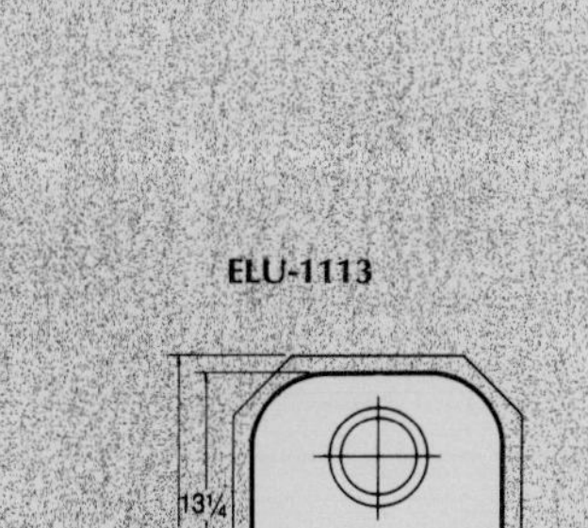

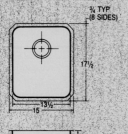

ELU-1316

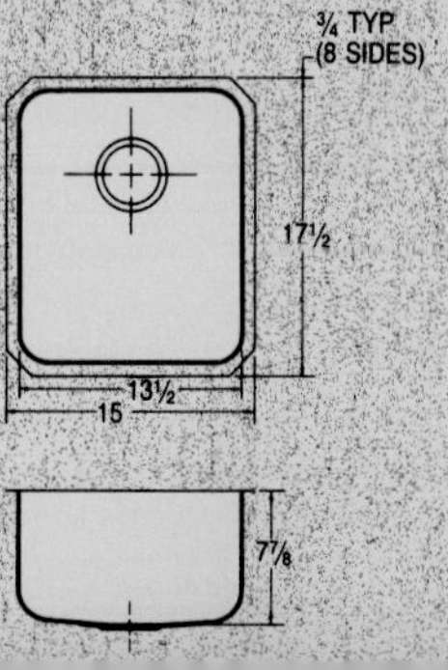

¾ TYP
(8 SIDES)

17½

13½
15

7⅞

ELU-1418

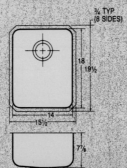

¾ TYP
(8 SIDES)

18
19½

14
15½

7⅞

ELU-1113

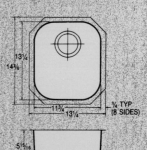

13¼
14¾

11¾
13¼

¼ TYP
(8 SIDES)

5¹⁵⁄₁₆

DIMENSIONS IN INCHES

ELU-1111

This uniquely stylish design is ideal as a corner sink for the kitchen or bar. The hand-ground satin finish makes it scratch-resistant, to keep it looking showroom-new for years.

ELU-715

This handy utility sink is a perfect companion to a spacious main sink. Ideal for cleaning fruits and vegetables.

ELU-714

Perfect as a side sink to accompany a larger bowl. And, like all of Elkay's durable stainless designs, it will never chip, fade or crack.

ELU-1111

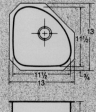

ELU-715

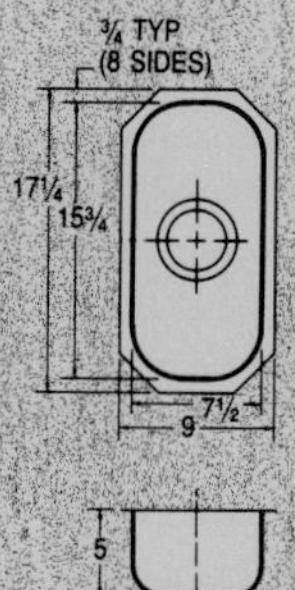

ELU-714

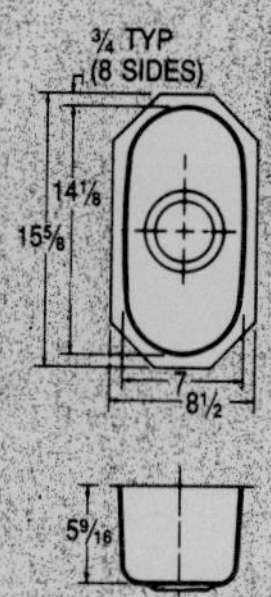

L USTERTONE

Deep, warm, classic tones. Elegant styling and a luxurious glow – that's Lustertone. Polished to a deep patina, our Lustertone sinks reflect your own good taste. And, like all our high-quality 18-gauge stainless steel sinks, the Lustertone Collection resists scratching and won't chip, crack or peel.

From versatile triple-bowl sinks to double-bowl sinks that make work equally easy from either side, to single-bowl sinks with spacious compartments with straight sides, our Lustertone sinks will stand up to any culinary wizardry you may cook up. These sinks blend beautifully with any decor, are easy to clean and are built to last. With Elkay Lustertone, you can make a classic statement and bask in the glow of Lustertone.

LCR-4322-C

For doing so many different tasks, you need a sink with many different options – like this triple-bowl design from Elkay. Package includes deluxe two-handle faucet with swivel aerator, retractable spray and hose, and pop-up drain outlets. Hardwood cutting board and rinsing basket.

LCR-4322-C

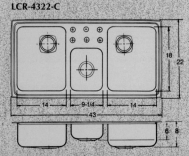

DIMENSIONS IN INCHES

14

PSMA-4322-C

Another triple-bowl sink to make your kitchen work a snap! This one, from our Pacemaker Starlight Series, is built with tough 20-gauge stainless steel. The components shown in this package are also available separately: Sink (PSMR-4322, 4 Hole), Faucet (LK-4301-F), Soap/Lotion Dispenser (LK-313-CR).

LMR-3322

Get double performance from this double-bowl sink. For cleaning and rinsing larger food items, use the right-side bowl. The bowl on the left is perfect for tasks that require less space, but easy access to water. Components alone: Sink (LMR-3322), Faucet (LK-4324-F-WH), Soap/Lotion Dispenser (LK-313-WH).

LR-250

These big bowls can accommodate any pot, pan, large roast or turkey with ease, making cleanup a snap. Components separately: Sink (LR-250), Faucet (LK-4391-F-AL), Soap/Lotion Dispenser (LK-313-AL).

PSMA-4322

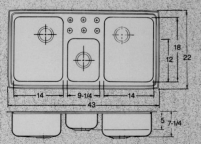

LMR-3322

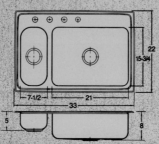

LR-250

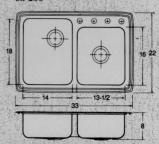

LR-3322

Overflow won't be a problem with this Elkay design, featuring a 7/16" drop-ledge and a raised faucet deck. Two large sink compartments offer all the room you need to clean and rinse dishes. Components alone: Sink (LR-3322), Faucet (LK-2433).

LCCRE-3232-C

Now you can take full advantage of your kitchen work space – with Elkay's unique corner sink package. Faucet with swivel aerator, soap dispenser and pop-up drain outlets complete the design and add to your cleaning ease. Components separately: Sink (LCCR-3232), Faucet (LK-4301-F), Soap/Lotion Dispenser (LK-313-CR), Pop-up Drain Outlet (LK-94).

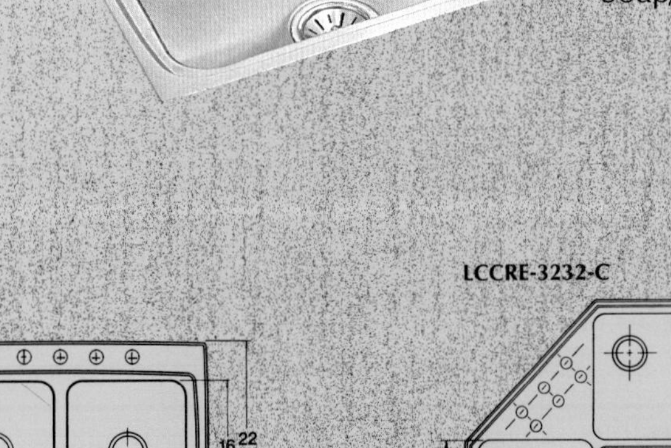

LR-2522

This single-bowl design is large enough to handle the biggest tasks. The straight sides and tight-radius corners maximize compartment space. Components alone: Sink (LR-2522), Faucet (LK-4391-F-BK), Soap/Lotion Dispenser (LK-313-BK).

LR-3322

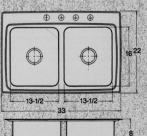

LCCRE-3232-C

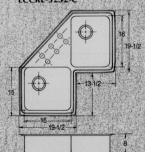

LR-2522

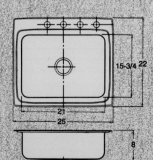

DIMENSIONS IN INCHES

DLH-2222-10-C

This single-bowl sink really cleans up! Specially designed for laundry rooms and work areas, this Elkay model has a 10" bowl but is also available with 12" bowl (DLH-2522-12-C). Components alone: Sink (DLR-2222-10, 10"-deep bowl or DLR-2522-12, 12"-deep bowl), Faucet (LK-2432).

LH-1722-C

Here's another single-bowl sink that stands up to the toughest hospitality and gardening jobs. Shown here as a package with a 22"-wide bowl (LH-1722-C) with Faucet (LK-2432). This sturdy sink is also available with a 20"-wide bowl (LH-1720-C). Components alone: Sink (LR-1722 or LR-1720), Faucet (LK-2432).

DLH-2222-10-C

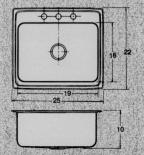

LH-1722-C

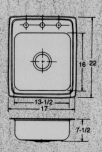

S C U L P T U R A

Make a colorful statement with Elkay's Sculptura® line. The fashionable tones, rounded bowls and sleek contours of Sculptura will add a smart, contemporary look to any work area. And all the Sculptura sinks are as durable as they are beautiful. The smooth, non-porous finish makes for easy cleaning, while the hi-tech Decostone material makes them long-lasting. Plus, Sculptura's exclusive textured finish on the sink bottom prevents pots and pans from skidding.

Add our coordinated accessories for a rich and colorful accent to your kitchen. The result is sure to be as original as you are.

DCGR-3322-R-W

Our cleanest classic, the White Sculptura double-bowl sink features a textured bottom to prevent pots and pans from skidding. Components separately: Regency Faucet (LK-4391-F-WH), Soap/Lotion Dispenser (LK-313-WH) and Strainer (LK-35-WH).

DCGR-3322-R

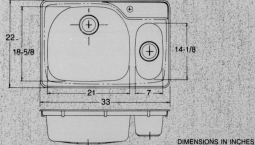

22
18-5/8
14-1/8
21
7
33

White

DIMENSIONS IN INCHES

DCGR-3322-R-A

Make an intelligent choice with our double-bowl Sculptura sink in Almond. Made of durable high-tech Decostone to be long-lasting. Components separately: Regency Pull-Out Faucet (LK-4350-F-AL), Soap/Lotion Dispenser (LK-313-AL), Strainer (LK-35-AL).

DCGR-3322-R-G

Make a strong statement with our Granite-look double-bowl Sculptura in Gray. Made with durable Decostone, it's highly resistant to heat and high temperatures. Components separately: Regency Pull-Out Faucet (LK-4350-F-CR), Soap/Lotion Dispenser (LK-313-CR), Strainer (LK-35) and Hot Water Machine (LKH-190).

DCGR-3322-R-T

Our Granite look now comes in a soft sandy Tan. A smooth, non-porous finish makes our Sculptura easy to care for. Just wipe with a soft cloth and gentle cleanser. Components separately: Regency Pull-Out Faucet (LK-4350-F-AL), Soap/Lotion Dispenser (LK-313-AL) and Strainer (LK-35-AL).

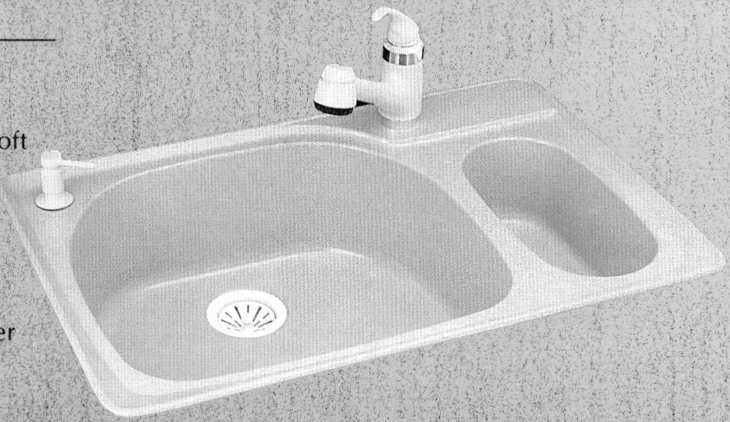

Almond

Desert Shadow (Gray)

Desert Sand (Tan)

DCGR-2522-W

Elkay's Sculptura in White makes a sunny addition to any kitchen. And its large single bowl offers ample room for cleaning, rinsing and preparing food items. Components separately: Regency Pull-Out Faucet (LK-4350-F-WH), Soap/Lotion Dispenser (LK-313-WH) and Strainer (LK-35-WH).

DCGR-2522-A

The single-bowl Sculptura, pictured here in Almond, offers all the durability and elegance of Elkay Decostone in the convenience of a single bowl. Components separately: Regency Pull-Out Faucet (LK-4340-F-AL), Soap/Lotion Dispenser (LK-313-AL) and Strainer (LK-35-AL).

DCGR-2522

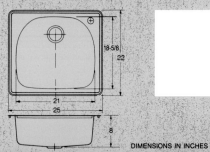

18-5/8
22
21
25
8

White

Almond

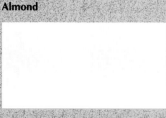

DIMENSIONS IN INCHES

DCGR-2522-G

Our simply stunning Granite look comes in Gray to suit a variety of kitchen decors. Like all our Sculptura sinks, this model is made of high-tech Decostone. Components separately: Regency Pull-Out Faucet (LK-4350-F-CR), Hot Water Machine (LKH-190) and Strainer (LK-35).

DCGR-2522-T

The durability of Decostone, the sophistication of our Tan Granite-look finish and the efficiency of our single bowl. . .all in this Sculptura. Components separately: Regency Pull-Out Faucet (LK-4350-F-AL), Soap/Lotion Dispenser (LK-313-AL) and strainer (LK-35-AL).

DCGR-2522

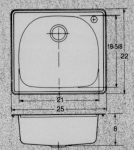

18-5/8
22
21
25
8

Desert Shadow (Gray)

Desert Sand (Tan)

HOSPITALITY

When it's your turn to relax, or to throw the party of the year, who better to turn to than Elkay to assist you with all your entertaining needs. And, because Elkay stainless steel coordinates so beautifully with any décor, it never looks out of place. Even if you change your décor, you never have to change your sink. And Elkay's Hospitality Collection sinks are specially crafted to make you feel comfortable while you entertain...with extra-deep bowls, far-reaching Hi-Arc faucets, handy swing spouts and compact design. Make sure one of our Hospitality sinks gets invited to your next party.

BILGR-2115-L

Add polish to your bar area with our Contemporary Gourmet bar sink and Brass-finish faucet. Available with sink bowl on the right or left, it features a 7 3/4" ribbed drainboard for food preparation. Components separately: Sink (BILGR-2115-L or R), Polished Brass Faucet (LK-2088-13-D), Strainer (LK-36).

BILGR-2115-L

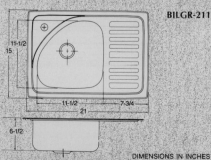

11-1/2
15
11-1/2   7-3/4
21
6-1/2

DIMENSIONS IN INCHES

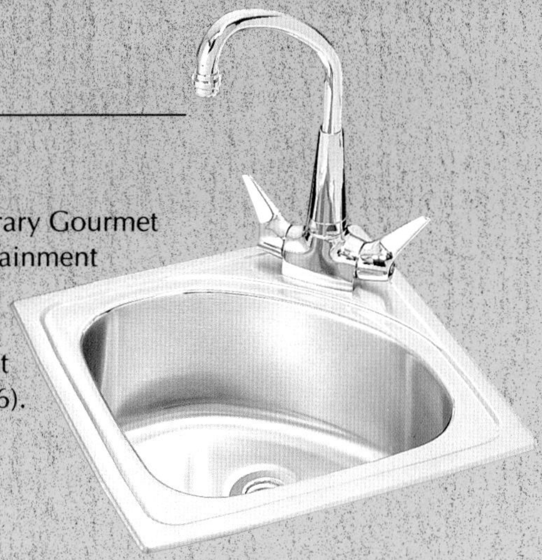

BLGR-1515

This compact Contemporary Gourmet sink can make any entertainment area much more inviting. Components separately: Sink (BLGR-1515), Faucet (LK-2223), Strainer (LK-36).

BLR-150-C

This Hospitality sink features a Hi-Arc bar faucet with two solid brass wing handles and strainer. Faucet height: 12 3/8". Components separately: Sink (BLR-15), Faucet (LK-2223), Strainer (LK-36).

BLH-15-C

Choose this elegant Hospitality sink with Hi-Arc faucet for contemporary styling. Shown here with Crystalac handles and strainer. Components separately: Sink (BLR-15), Faucet (LKA-2438), Strainer (LK-36).

BLGR-1515

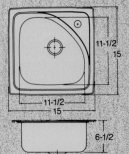

BLR-150-C

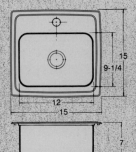

BLH-15-C

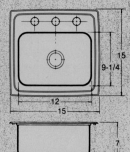

BPSH-15-C

This gleaming chrome sink is complemented by our Hi-Arc faucet with traditional spout styling, sparkling Crystalac handles and strainer. Components separately: Sink (BPSR-15), Faucet (LKA-2437), Strainer (LK-36).

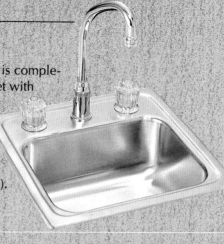

BPSRA-150-C

Another brilliant sink from Elkay! Shown with our 8″ Hi-Arc faucet bar, two forged brass wing handles and strainer. Components separately: Sink (BPSR-15), Faucet (LK-2088-8), Strainer (LK-36).

BCH-15-C

One of our most efficient sinks...shown with Elkay's Hi-Arc faucet and decorative Crystalac handles. Components separately: Sink (BCR-15), Faucet (LKA-2447), Strainer (LK-58).

BPSH-15-C

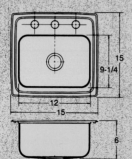

15
9-1/4
12
15
6

BPSRA-150-C

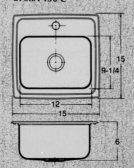

15
9-1/4
12
15
6

BCH-15-C

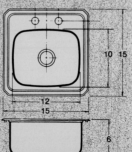

10   15
12
15
6

DIMENSIONS IN INCHES

24

F A U C E T S

Elkay offers you three superb choices: the elegant Regency Collection, the exceptionally versatile Calais Collection and the colorful Hi-Arc Collection.

The Regency Collection, in polished chrome or colored epoxy, combines exclusive detailing with advanced technology. And the newest edition, the Regency Pull-Out, features an innovative pull-out spray and single-lever design.

The Calais Collection adds sleek Eurostyling to any kitchen and offers an easy pull-out spray, modern spout and high-tech, state-of-the-art cartridge, ensuring long-lasting performance.

The Hi-Arc Collection blends color and functionality. With its 10-inch reach and 9-inch height, the Hi-Arc faucet makes it easy to fill large pots or vases. And you can select from four distinctive designer colors.

REGENCY PULL-OUT

Elegant lines and graceful design combine to make the Regency Pull-Out faucet. The single-lever design gives you a full temperature range with the touch of a finger. Choose from White, Almond and Black with Brass accents, or Chrome with Black accents.

LK-4350-F-AL

LK-4350-F-BK

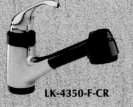

LK-4350-F-CR

LK-4350-F-WH

REGENCY PULL-OUT

Regency Pull-Out faucets are available in a full range of decorative colors including solid White, Almond and Black, or Chrome with Black Sprayer. The pull-out sprayer provides extended reach and our patented Hi'n'Dry™ cartridge ensures years of trouble-free operation.

LK-4340-F-CR

LK-4340-F-AL

LK-4340-F-WH   **LK-4340-F-BK**

REGENCY SINGLE-LEVER

Sophisticated and distinctive, our Regency Collection of faucets features a selection of colors and accents. Faucet shown here, Glossy Black with Brass accents, may also be ordered in White, Almond or Chrome with Brass accents.

LK-4381-F-BK

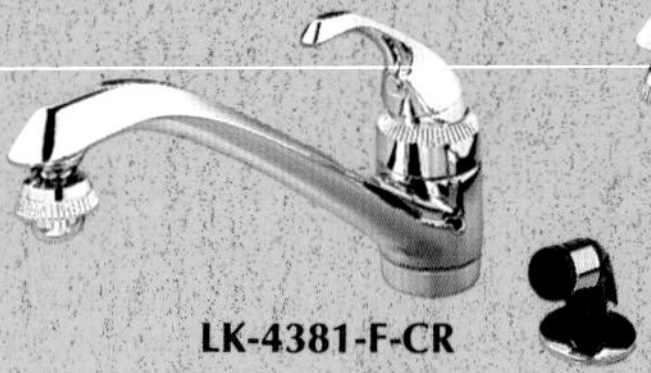

REGENCY SINGLE-LEVER

Another fine faucet from our Regency Collection, this time in White epoxy. As with all our Regency faucets, this comes in a variety of solid color options, with a 10" cast-brass swing spout and may be ordered with or without a handy spray hose.

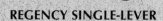

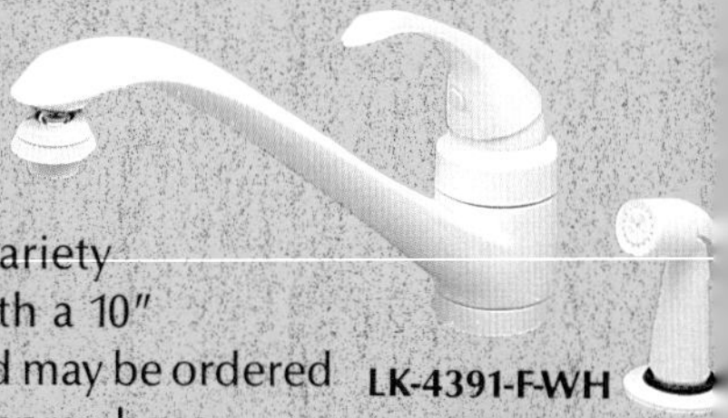

LK-4381-F-WH

LK-4381-F-CR

LK-4391-F-WH

LK-4381-F-AL

LK-4371-F-CR

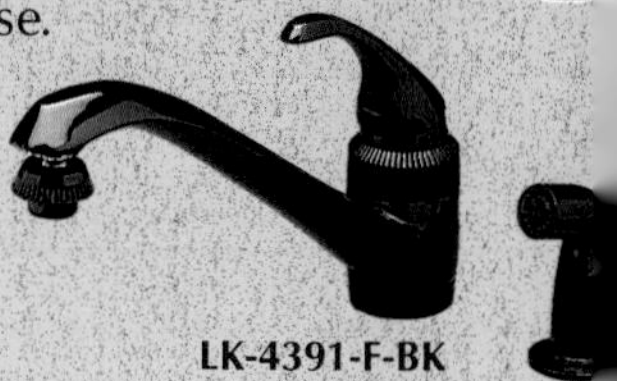

LK-4391-F-BK

LK-4391-F-AL

HI-ARC SINGLE-LEVER

Cleaning big kitchen items is easy with this faucet's 10" reach and 9" height. Hi-Arc single-lever faucet shown in Black. Also available in White, Almond and Brass.

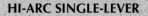

LK-4324-F-BK

LK-4324-F-WH

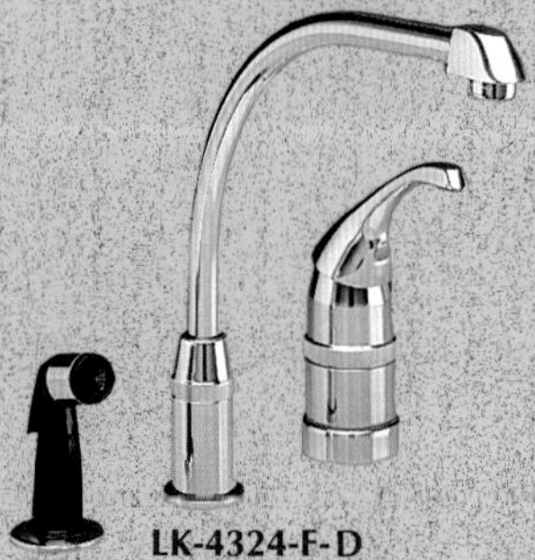

LK-4324-F-D

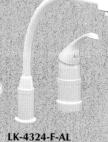

LK-4324-F-AL

CALAIS COLLECTION– SINGLE-LEVER

Our single-lever Calais faucet has a sleek, Eurostyled look. A convenient pull-out sprayer gives all the extended reach necessary for washing and rinsing, while its exclusive high-tech ceramic disk cartridge provides years of trouble-free use. Select from a variety of decorator shades including Almond, White, Chrome or Black.

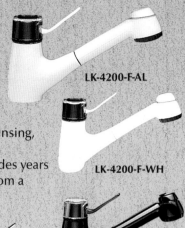

LK-4200-F-AL

LK-4200-F-WH

LK-4200-F-BK

LK-4200-F-CR

CALAIS COLLECTION – TWO-HANDLE

Our two-handled pull-out spray Calais model, shown here in Almond, is also available in White and Chrome. Featuring elegant Eurostyling, this faucet allows you to control water temperature quickly and efficiently.

LK-4230-F-AL

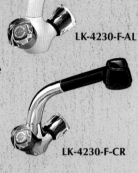

LK-4230-F-CR

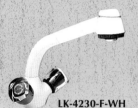

LK-4230-F-WH

HI-ARC SINGLE-LEVER

This Hi-Arc single-lever faucet has added convenience with a swivel aerator and retractable spray and hose.

LK-4124-F

HI-ARC TWO-HANDLE

Easy to clean and use, this attractive faucet features chrome metal wing handles and a handy swing spout with an extended 10" reach. Available with our hose/spray option (LK-2453) or without hose/spray (LK-2452).

LK-2453

DELUXE SINGLE-LEVER POST MOUNT

Our deluxe Post Mount features a 9" reach, swing spout, swivel aerator and hose/spray to make your kitchen chores easier. The single-lever faucet provides volume and water temperature control at your fingertips.

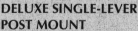

LK-4361-F

HI-ARC TWO-HANDLE

With its contemporary spout styling and 10" height, Elkay's Hi-Arc kitchen faucet adds efficiency to your space. Filling larger pots, vases and pitchers is a snap! Wing handles complement its sleek design.

LK-2433

A CCESSORIES

Details, details...it's all in the details. And with these fine Elkay accessories you'll give your kitchen that final touch of class right down to the details, while making food preparation and cleanup virtually effortless! With our handy Hot Water Machine and Aqua Chill®, and our useful cutting boards, drain trays, colanders, rinse baskets, soap/lotion dispensers and strainers, you'll look forward to working in the kitchen, and your kitchen will have that final polished look.

HOT WATER MACHINE AND AQUA CHILL

The convenience of instant hot or refreshing chilled water is now available in decorator colors and features our No-Lead design. With waterway systems designed to be completely free of lead-containing materials, the LKH-190 and LK-2156 dispensers ensure you that no lead is being added to your drinking water. Our Hot Water Machine heats water to 180°F for hot drinks, soups or gelatins, while our Aqua Chill refrigerates water to 40°F for fast refreshment. Our Standard Hot Water Machine (LKH-180) is available in Chrome only. Order both the dispenser (LK-2156) and chiller (ER-1) for the Aqua Chill.

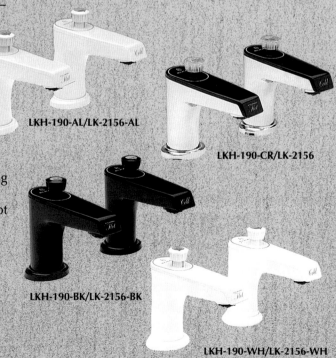

LKH-190-AL/LK-2156-AL

LKH-190-CR/LK-2156

LKH-190-BK/LK-2156-BK

LKH-190-WH/LK-2156-WH

COLANDER

If you own an Elkay Contemporary Gourmet sink, this colander is a must! It's great for straining, draining or storing vegetables and fruits. Available in White (SC-1407-WH) and Almond (SC-1407-AL. Fits models LCGR-3322, ILCGR-4822 and Sculptura DCGR-3322.

COLANDER

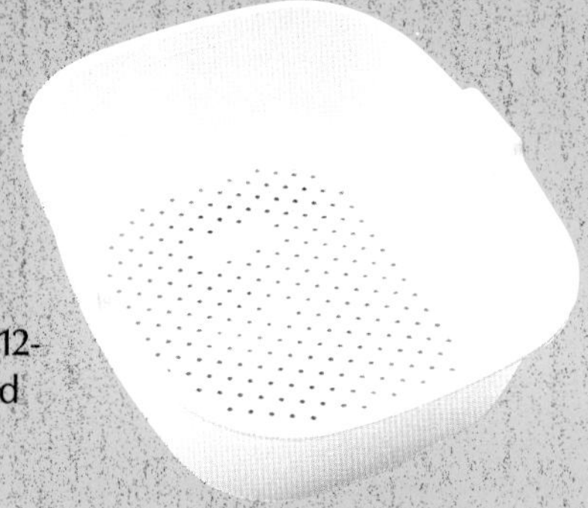

This colander fits our larger Contemporary Gourmet sinks for those with larger kitchen tasks. Available in White (LC-1412-WH) or Almond (LC-1412-AL). Fits LCGR-3822 and ILCGR-5322 models.

DRAIN TRAY

For our Elkay Contemporary Gourmet sink, make sure you own an Elkay drain tray, too. Perfect for rinsing and draining, it actually expands your counter work surface. Comes in two ever-popular colors: White (DT-2215-WH) and Almond (DT-2215-AL).

RINSING BASKET/TEAK CUTTING BOARD

With these special Elkay accessories, kitchen work becomes much more pleasurable. Our bright White, top-fitting rinsing basket measures 17 3/4" ×15 3/4" ×3 1/2". Simply order VB-1816. Our specially designed teak cutting board fits over the larger bowls of our Gourmet sinks and brings unique style and efficiency to your kitchen work area. Choose from two popular sizes: our large 17" ×13 1/2" model (CBT-1713) or our smaller 16 3/4" ×13 1/2" model (CBT-1613). Order rinsing basket and teak cutting board with all Traditional Gourmet sinks except ILFGR and LFGR models.

RINSING BASKET

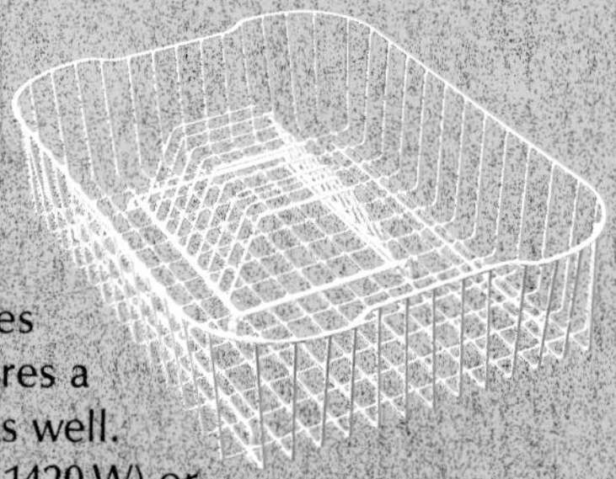

Durable and roomy, this vinyl-covered rinsing basket fits our Contemporary Gourmet sinks and is ideal for draining dishes or other items. It features a removable plate rack as well. Available in White (DB-1420-W) or Almond (DB-1420-A), it measures 14" × 20" ×4 5/8".

TEAK CUTTING BOARD

This carefully crafted teak cutting board adds natural beauty to your work area and is designed to fit over the large bowl of our Contemporary Gourmet sinks. It measures 22"×13" (CBT-2213).

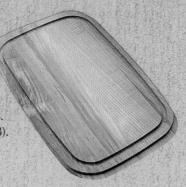

CUTTING SURFACE

Standard with every Gourmet Cuisine Centré, our custom-designed cutting surface fits neatly into the Centré's ribbed work area. The cutting surface is 11" × 16 1/2" and fits right- or left-side sinks (CBP-1116). Or choose our optional counter-top cutting surface, shown here. It measures 13"×19" and fits flush with our Gourmet Cuisine Centré and your countertop. (Model CBP-1319-L fits EGPI-4322-L; CBP-1319-R fits EGPI-4322-R.) Both cutting surfaces are made from the same tough high-density polymer.

STRAINERS

Specially designed as a fashionable finish to your Elkay sink: our newest strainers. We offer spicy colors to suit your personal tastes—White (LK-35-WH), Almond (LK-35-AL), Black (LK-35-BK), Gray (LK-35-GR), or Chrome (LK-35).

SOAP/LOTION DISPENSER

Creatively designed as an attractive complement to your sink area, our soap and lotion dispensers are always there when you need them. Choose from Chrome (LK-313-CR), White (LK-313-WH), Almond (LK-313-AL) and Black (LK-313-BK).

POP-UP DRAIN OUTLET

Elkay's remote-control drain outlets (LK-94) allow you to empty the sink bowls without putting your hands in the water. Fits 3 1/2" opening; 4 1/2" top diameter. Be sure to order extra drilling hole on sink ledge.

SINK SPECIFICATIONS

MODEL NUMBER	MINIMUM CABINET SIZE	HOLE DRILLINGS
TRADITIONAL		
EGPI-4322 – L or R	42"*	1, 3 or 4
ILGR-6022 L-C or R-C	42"	3 (package)
ILGR-6022 – L or R	42"	4
LGR-4322-C	42"	3 (package)
LGR-4322	42"	4
ILFGR-5422 – L or R	36"	3 or 4
ILGR-5422 – L or R	36"	3 or 4
ILFGR-4822 – L or R	30"	3 or 4
ILGR-4822 – L or R	30"	3 or 4
LFGR-3722-3	36"	3
LGR-3722	36"	3 or 4
LFGR-3322	30"	3
LGR-3322	30"	3 or 4
ILGR-4322 – L or R	24"	3 or 4
CONTEMPORARY		
ILCGR-5322 – L or R	36"	1, 2, 3 or 4
LCGR-3822 – L or R	36"	1, 2, 3 or 4
ILCGR-4822 – L or R	30"	1, 2, 3 or 4
LCGR-3322 – L or R	30"	1, 2, 3 or 4
ILCGR-4022 – L or R	24"	1 or 2
LCGR-2522	24"	1 or 2
UNDERMOUNT		
See Undermount section for sink size specifications, p. 10-13.		
LUSTERTONE		
LCR-4322-C	42"	6 (package)
PSMA-4322-C	42"	6 (package)
LMR-3322	30"	3 or 4
LR-250	30"	3 or 4
LR-3322	30"	3 or 4
LR-2522	24"	3 or 4
LCCRE-3232-C	–	6 (package) or 4
DLH-2222-10-C/DLH-2522-12-C	24"	3 (package)
LH-1720/1722-C	24"	3 (package)
SCULPTURA		
DCGR-3322-R-A	36"	1, 2, 3 or 4
DCGR-3322-R-W	36"	1, 2, 3 or 4
DCGR-3322-R-G	36"	1, 2, 3 or 4
DCGR-3322-R-T	36"	1, 2, 3 or 4
DCGR-2522-A	24"	1 or 2
DCGR-2522-W	24"	1 or 2
DCGR-2522-G	24"	1 or 2
DCGR-2522-T	24"	1 or 2
HOSPITALITY		
BILGR-2115 – L or R	24"	1
BLGR-1515	24"	1
BLR-150-C	24"	1 (package)
BLH-15-C	24"	3 (package)
BPSH-15-C	24"	3 (package)
BPSRA-150-C	24"	1 (package)
BCH-15-C	24"	2 (package)

* Can be installed in 30" cabinet with modifications to adjoining cabinet.

Elkay Manufacturing Company
2222 Camden Court
Oak Brook, Illinois 60521
708.574.8484 Telex RCA289234

...now in color.

∎∎∎ From the originator of undermount stainless steel sink systems comes the luxe of neutral color in durable quartz composite configurations.

Through your design professional.

Franke, Inc.
Kitchen Systems Division
212 Church Road, Dept. B
North Wales, PA 19454
800-626-5771

Kitchen Sinks
Faucets
Water Dispensing Systems
Disposers
Custom Accessories

∎ Technology   ∎ Quality   ∎ Design

■ ■ Franke Color Elements® the essence of flexible design, the confidence of color, plus the durability of bonded quartz.

■■■ Once again Franke introduces the perfect design solution for hardworking contemporary kitchens. Franke Color Elements are specifically designed for mounting beneath granite, marble, and man-made solid surfacing materials.

■■■ Components are made from an extremely tough quartz composite material that will withstand the rigors of hard daily use remaining chip and stain resistant through the long life of the sink. The durability of Franke's material is especially important when installed in costly countertop materials.

■■■ Each Element is designed to mount tightly with silicone to the under surface, eliminating gaps where food particles, dirt and grease could be trapped. The Franke mounting system ensures fast and solid installation.

■■■ Configurations include rectangular and elliptical models which can be mounted alone or in any desired combination. Select models include a handy grid drainer. A variety of accessory options are available. And, there is a complete line of Franke faucets, hot/cold water dispensers and waste disposers plus color-coordinated strainer baskets to complement the sink area.

■■■ Available in white or almond.

■■■ Design perfection and quality products. Isn't that what you expect from the name Franke?

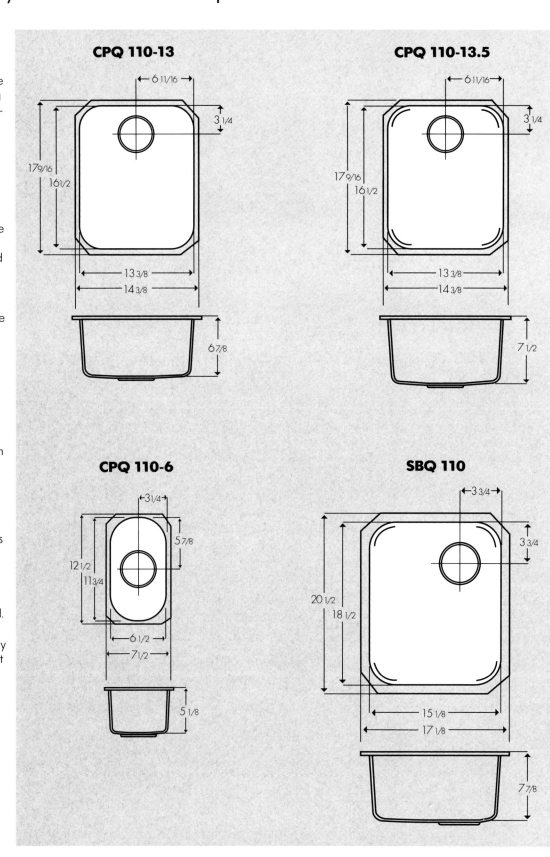

GROHE

for your family safety

Protect your family from accidental scalding in the shower or bath with a Grohmix Thermostat/Pressure Balance Valve...the ultimate in safety, comfort, luxury and quality.

Dial your water temperature just as you would the heat or air conditioning in your home... that simple...that worry-free.

Grohe manufactures an impressive collection of fine products for your kitchen and bath...affordable quality.

GROHE

for your bathroom

Elegant options.

Grohe lavatory faucets ... refined and distinctive, designed to fit your needs and tastes.

Select from Grohe's wide range of styles, color combinations, and handle options to create a complete and coordinated bath environment.

Grohe manufactures an impressive collection of fine products for your bath and kitchen...affordable quality.

G R O H E

for your kitchen

C563
BuyLine 7688

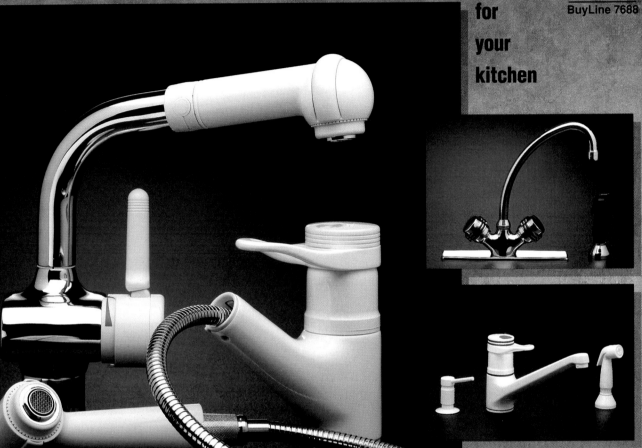

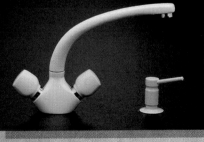

Grohe kitchen faucets... designed to fit your tastes, functional to fit your needs... available in a wide variety of combinations.

Color coordinated soap/lotion dispensers and side sprays are also offered.

Grohe manufactures an impressive collection of fine products for your kitchen and bath...affordable quality.

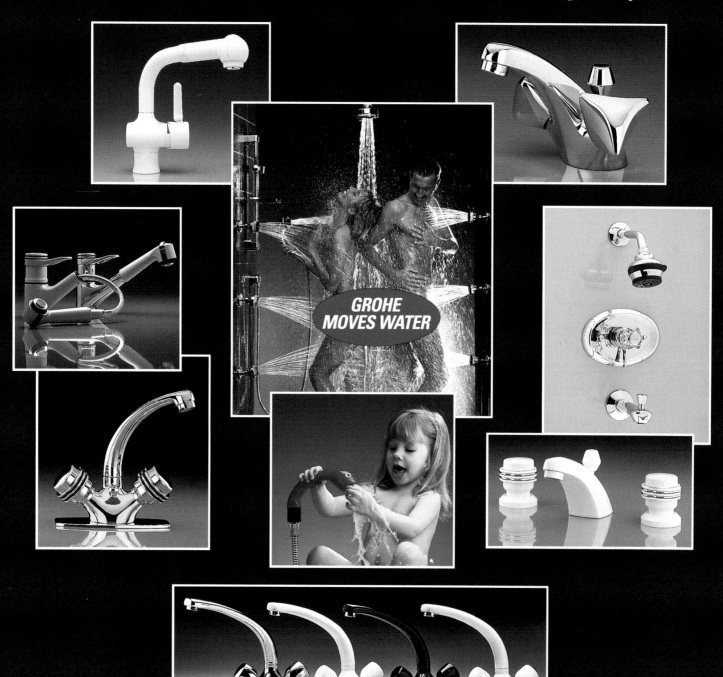

Decorated Victoria®

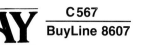

3-458WO **Victoria** with Olivia design   25"W x 20$^1/_2$"D x 32"H
Shown with: Argenti faucet **4202L**

3-458WK **Victoria** with Kimberly design   25"W x 20$^1/_2$"D x 32"H
Shown with: Argenti faucet **4202L**

3-458W   **Victoria** white pedestal   25"W x 20$^1/_2$"D x 32"H
Shown with: Argenti faucet **4202L**

3-458WV **Victoria** with Violet design   25"W x 20$^1/_2$"D x 32"H
Shown with: Argenti faucet **4202L**

3-458 Decorated **Victoria** is available in 8" drillings only.

Also available in undecorated:

3-458W	**Victoria** white pedestal 8" faucet drillings	25"W x 20$^1/_2$"D x 32"H
3-458B	**Victoria** bone pedestal 8" faucet drillings	(not shown)
3-454W	**Victoria** white pedestal 4" faucet drillings	(not shown)
3-454B	**Victoria** bone pedestal 4" faucet drillings	(not shown)

Barclay Products Limited
4000 Porett Drive • Gurnee IL 60031
(708) 244-1234   FAX (708) 244-1259

Victoria® Water Closets

Pub. No. VC 080
Barclay © 1990

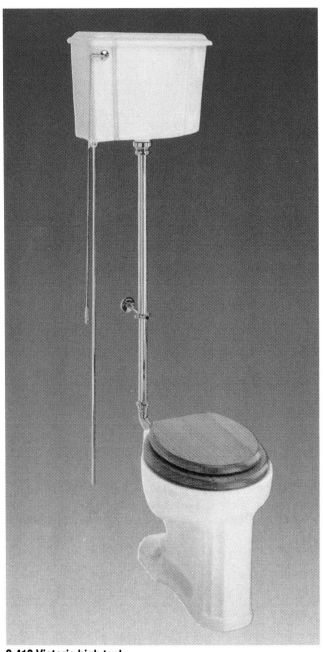

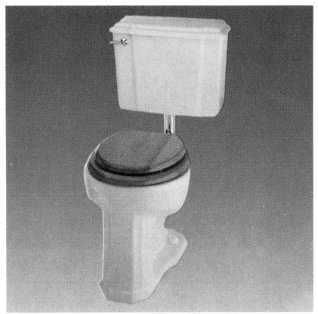

2-422 Victoria wall hung

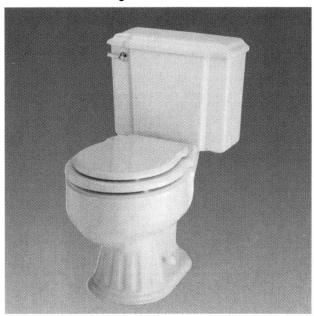

2-412 Victoria high tank

2-412WB	**Victoria** high tank with brass trim	
3300B	Oak closet seat with brass trim	
2-412WC	**Victoria** high tank with chrome trim	(not shown)
3300C	Oak closet seat with chrome trim	(not shown)

Shown above right:

2-422WB	**Victoria** wall hung with brass trim	
3300B	Oak closet seat with brass trim	
2-422WC	**Victoria** wall hung with chrome trim	(not shown)
3300C	Oak closet seat with chrome trim	(not shown)

2-402 Victoria water closet

2-402WB	**Victoria** white water closet	
9-402WB	**Victoria** white closet seat	
2-402BB	**Victoria** bone water closet	(not shown)
9-402BB	**Victoria** bone closet seat	(not shown)
	All the above have brass trim	
2-402WC	**Victoria** white water closet	(not shown)
9-402WC	**Victoria** white closet seat	(not shown)
2-402BC	**Victoria** bone water closet	(not shown)
9-402BC	**Victoria** bone closet seat	(not shown)
	All the above have chrome trim	

Barclay Products Limited
4000 Porett Drive • Gurnee IL 60031
(708) 244-1234   FAX (708) 244-1259

Hand Decorated

B̲ARCLAY
PRODUCTS LIMITED

C567
BuyLine 8607

3-718WPC Drop-in with Derrick design–Multi
20¾" O.D. x 17¾" O.D.

3-718WPB Drop-in with Derrick design–Black
20¾" O.D. x 17¾" O.D.

3-718WBF Drop-in with Barclay Flyer design
20¾" O.D. x 17¾" O.D.

3-718WRD Drop-in with Rubber Ducky design
20¾" O.D. x 17¾" O.D.

3-718WGF Drop-in with Golfer design
20¾" O.D. x 17¾" O.D.

Pub. No. VC 130
Barclay ©1991

Barclay Products Limited
4000 Porett Drive • Gurnee IL 60031
(708) 244-1234   FAX (708) 244-1259

Hand Decorated
Lavatory Basins

4-710WO **Lisbon** with Olivia design 18"W x 14 1/4"D x 7 1/4" H
4-711WO **Madrid** with Olivia design (not shown)

4-710WD **Lisbon** with Danielle design 18"W x 14 1/4"D x 7 1/4" H
4-711WD **Madrid** with Danielle design (not shown)

4-710WC **Lisbon** with Collette design 18"W x 14 1/4"D x 7 1/4" H
4-711WC **Madrid** with Collette design (not shown)

4-710WB **Lisbon** with Brigitte design 18"W x 14 1/4"D x 7 1/4" H
4-711WB **Madrid** with Brigitte design (not shown)

4-710WK **Lisbon** with Kimberly design 18"W x 14 1/4"D x 7 1/4" H
4-711WK **Madrid** with Kimberly design (not shown)

4-710WE **Lisbon** with Evelyn design 18"W x 14 1/4"D x 7 1/4" H
4-711WE **Madrid** with Evelyn design (not shown)

Pub. No. VC 061
Barclay © 1992

4000 Porett Drive   Gurnee, Illinois 60031   (708) 244-1234   Fax (708) 244-1259

Pedestal Lavatories

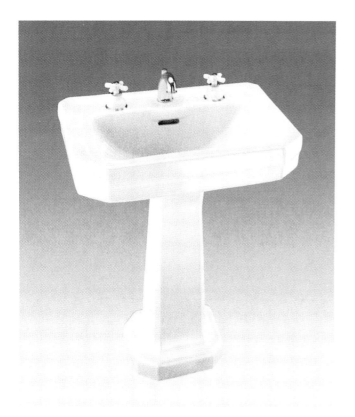

3-838 Constitution
Shown with: Argenti faucet **4202A**

3-818 Windsor
Shown with: Argenti faucet **4202L**

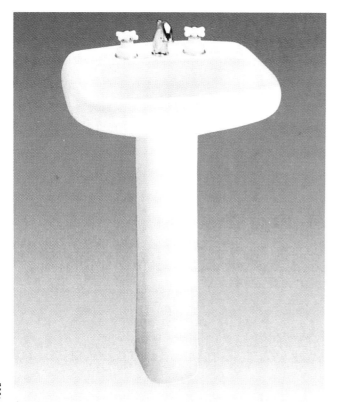

3-518 Chianti
Shown with: Argenti faucet **4208A**

3-838WH Constitution pedestal lavatory
26"W x 20½"D x 32"H

3-818WH Windsor pedestal lavatory
24½"W x 20"D x 32½"H

3-518W Chianti pedestal
23"W x 17½"D x 33" H

Barclay Products Limited
4000 Porett Drive • Gurnee IL 60031
(708) 244-1234   FAX (708) 244-1259

Italian Consoles

89196-WH
Deco single basin console – chrome legs
35⅞"W x 22¼"D x 32¼"H

81166-WH
Belle Epoque I
single basin console
42½"W x 22⅞"D x 32¼"H

81167-WH
Belle Epoque II
double basin console
47¼"W x 22⅞"D x 32¼"H

72166-WH
Aretusa single basin console 42⅛"W x 24"D x 32¼"H

Pub. No. VC 016
Barclay ©1992

Note: All consoles include basin and legs.
Faucets and plumbing accessories not included.

Barclay Products Limited
4000 Porett Drive • Gurnee IL 60031
(708) 244-1234   FAX (708) 244-1259

Bath Tubs

5960   White 5 foot tub – Chrome feet
Note: Tubs come with polished brass feet. Chrome feet available for an additional charge.
Shown with: **4010C**   Chrome old-style shower
                C145-54   D-Rod converto
                3321WH   Oak and white bath seat

5970   White 5½ foot tub – brass feet (not shown)

5962   Bone 5 foot tub – brass feet
Shown with: **4005B**   Brass telephone shower
                5599B   Brass tub waste & overflow

5972   Bone 5½ foot tub – brass feet (not shown)

Note: All tubs are made of acrylic reinforced with fiberglass.

5969   Red 5 foot tub – brass feet
Shown with: **4010B**   Brass old-style shower

5979   Red 5½ foot tub – brass feet (not shown)

Barclay Products Limited
4000 Porett Drive • Gurnee IL 60031
(708) 244-1234   FAX (708) 244-1259

Bar Sinks

Pub. No. MS 010
Barclay ©1991

5763BB   Brass Bar Sink Package includes:
    5762BP   Polished brass bar sink
    4800B   Brass bar sink faucet with blade handles
    5586B   Brass bar sink basket strainer

5763BL   Package same as above but with lever handle faucet
              (not shown)
All brass bar sinks are not coated and will tarnish. Customer care is required.

5763SL   Stainless Bar Sink Package includes:
    5762SP   Polished stainless bar sink
    4806L   Chrome bar sink faucet with lever handles
    5586S   Chrome bar sink basket strainer

5763SB   Package same as above but with blade handle faucet (not shown)

Barclay Products Limited
4000 Porett Drive • Gurnee IL 60031
(708) 244-1234   FAX (708) 244-1259

splish! splash!

C568
BuyLine 8636

DURAVIT

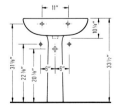

Pedestal: # 857.50
Basin: # 420.70
Stock Colors: White, Black
Accommodates: Single Hole,
                    Widespread

Non-stocked colors: Manhattan – 11, Amber – 41, Fogo – 47, Rose-Perle – 54, Jasmin – 72, Edelweiss – 78, Flannel – 79,
Opaline-Blue – 15, Opaline-Grey – 43, Opaline-Beige – 45, Opaline-Rose – 55.

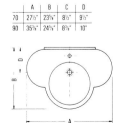

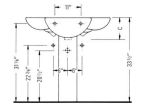

	A	B	C	D
70	27½"	23¾"	8½"	9½"
90	35⅜"	24⅜"	8⅜"	10"

Pedestal: # 857.40
Basin: 70, # 430.70
90, # 430.90
Stock Color: White
Accommodates: Single Hole, Widespread

Non-stocked colors: Manhattan – 11, Royal-Turquoise – 17, Royal-Rose – 53, Jasmin – 72, Edelweiss – 78, Flannel – 79.

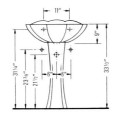

Pedestal: # 858.00
Basin: # 436.65
Stock Colors: White, Black
Accommodates: Single Hole,
                     Widespread

Non-stocked colors: Manhattan – 11, Amber – 41, Jasmin – 72, Edelweiss – 78, Flannel – 79, Opaline-Grey – 43,
Opaline-Beige – 45.

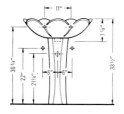

Pedestal:	# 2622.00
Basin:	# 2613.70
Stock Colors:	White, Black
Accommodates:	Single Hole

Non-stocked colors: Rose-Perle – 54, Jasmin – 72, Edelweiss – 78, Flannel – 79, Opaline-Blue – 15, Opaline-Grey – 43, Opaline-Beige – 45, Opaline-Rose – 55.

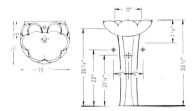

Accessoires Orchidee

Pedestal:	# 2622.00
Hand-Rinse-Basin:	# 2614.50
Stock Colors:	White, Black
Accommodates:	Single Hole

Non-stocked colors: Rose-Perle – 54, Jasmin – 72, Edelweiss – 78, Flannel – 79, Opaline-Blue – 15, Opaline-Grey – 43, Opaline-Beige – 45, Opaline-Rose – 55.

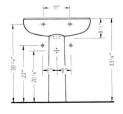

Pedestal:	# 2122.00
Basin:	# 2113.70
Stock Colors:	White, Black
Accommodates:	Single Hole, Widespread

Non-stocked colors: Manhattan – 11, Rose-Perle – 54, Jasmin – 72, Edelweiss – 78, Flannel – 79.

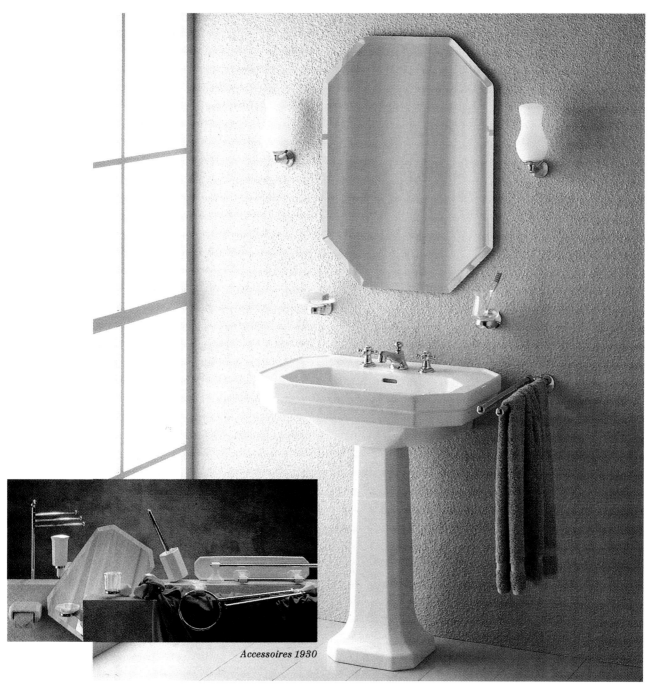

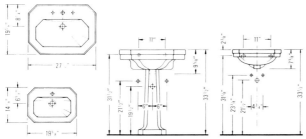

Accessoires 1930

Pedestal: # 857.90
Basin: # 438.70
Hand-Rinse-Basin: # 785.50
Stock Color: White
Accommodates: Single Hole, Widespread

Non-stocked colors: Manhattan – 11, Edelweiss – 78, Flannel – 79.

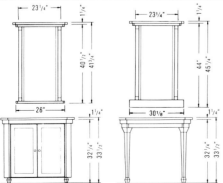

Commode for
Vanity basin: # 9551
Mirror with
Wooden Frame: # 9710
Console for
Vanity basin: # 9550
Mirror with Splash
Guard and Stone Top: # 9711

Stone top colors: Granite-Nero-Impala – 44,
Marble-Arabescato – 46, Wood-Finish – 16.

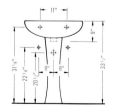

Pedestal:	# 2222.00
Basin:	# 2213.70
Stock Colors:	White, Black
Accommodates:	Single Hole, Widespread

Non-stocked colors: Manhattan – 11, Amber – 41, Rose-Perle – 54, Jasmin – 72, Edelweiss – 78, Flannel – 79,
Opaline-Blue – 15, Opaline-Grey – 43, Opaline-Beige – 45, Opaline-Rose – 55.

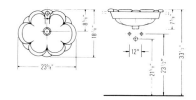

Vanity basin:　　　　# 477.60
Stock Colors:　　　　White, Black
Accommodates:　　　Single Hole

Non-stocked colors: Rose-Perle – 54, Jasmin – 72, Edelweiss – 78, Flannel – 79, Opaline-Blue – 15, Opaline-Grey – 43, Opaline-Beige – 45, Opaline-Rose – 55.

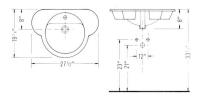

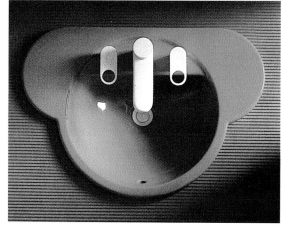

Vanity basin:　　　　# 469.70
Stock Color:　　　　White
Accommodates:　　　Single Hole,
　　　　　　　　　　Widespread

Non-stocked colors: Manhattan – 11, Royal-Turquoise – 17, Royal-Rose – 53, Jasmin – 72, Edelweiss – 78, Flannel – 79.

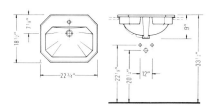

Vanity basin:　　　　# 476.58
Stock Color:　　　　White
Accommodates:　　　Single Hole,
　　　　　　　　　　Widespread

Non-stocked colors: Manhattan – 11, Edelweiss – 78, Flannel – 79.

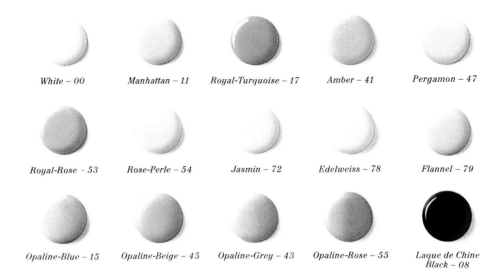

White – 00   Manhattan – 11   Royal-Turquoise – 17   Amber – 41   Pergamon – 47

Royal-Rose – 53   Rose-Perle – 54   Jasmin – 72   Edelweiss – 78   Flannel – 79

Opaline-Blue – 15   Opaline-Beige – 45   Opaline-Grey – 43   Opaline-Rose – 55   Laque de Chine Black – 08

White and black only stocked colors. Please contact Santile International Corporation for other color availability.

$\mathcal{S}$antile
International Corporation
6687 Jimmy Carter Blvd. • Norcross, Georgia 30071
Phone (404) 416-6224 • Fax (404) 416-6239

DURAVIT · B.P. 10 · F-67642 Bischwiller Cedex · Téléphone 88.90.61.00 · Télex 890.502 · Télécopie 88.90.61.01
DURAVIT AG · Postfach 240 · D-7746 Hornberg · Telefon 0 78 33/70-0 · Teletex 7 83 321 · Telex (17) 7 83 321 · Telefax 0 78 33/70-289

EDITION DORNBRACHT

CONTENT

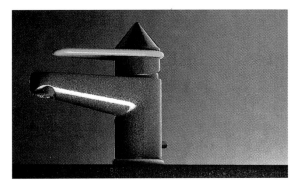

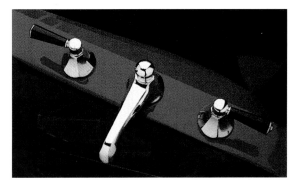

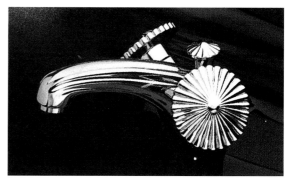

Design: Sieger Design.

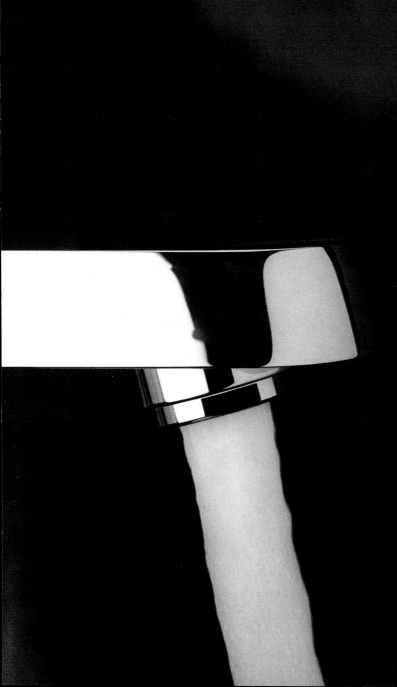

polarity. Harmonious quintes-
sence through perfect design:
Edition Fino.

El círculo en oposición a la
línea recta: tensión proporcio-
nada por su geometría – polari-
dad creativa. La quintaesencia
armónica de un diseño acabado:
Edition Fino.

Il cerchio contro la linea retta:
geometrie ricche di tensione, po-
larità creativa, la quintessenza
armoniosa del perfetto design:
Edition Fino.

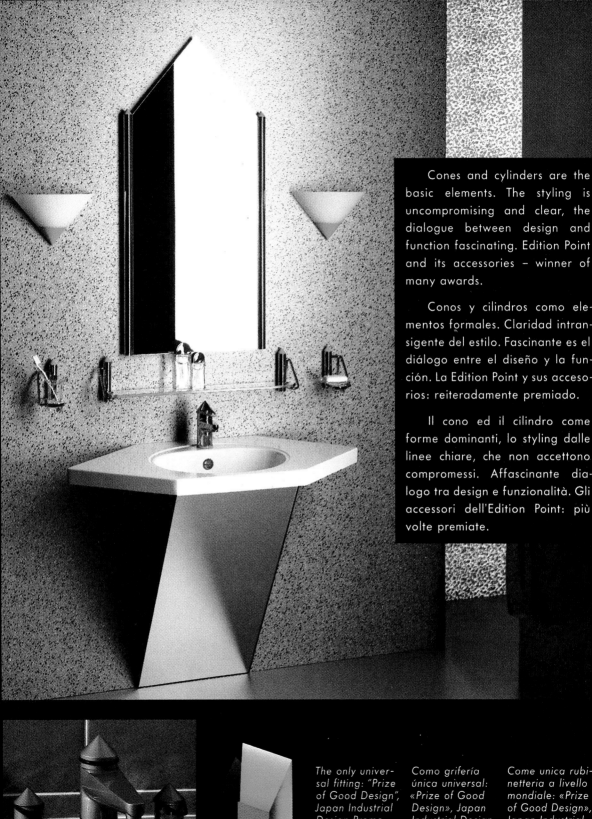

Cones and cylinders are the basic elements. The styling is uncompromising and clear, the dialogue between design and function fascinating. Edition Point and its accessories – winner of many awards.

Conos y cilindros como elementos formales. Claridad intransigente del estilo. Fascinante es el diálogo entre el diseño y la función. La Edition Point y sus accesorios: reiteradamente premiado.

Il cono ed il cilindro come forme dominanti, lo styling dalle linee chiare, che non accettono compromessi. Affascinante dialogo tra design e funzionalità. Gli accessori dell'Edition Point: più volte premiate.

The only universal fitting: "Prize of Good Design", Japan Industrial Design Promotion Association. In the Collection of the Design Museum, London.

Como grifería única universal: «Prize of Good Design», Japan Industrial Design Promotion Association. Incluido en el museo de diseño de Londres.

Come unica rubinetteria a livello mondiale: «Prize of Good Design», Japan Industrial Design Promotion Association. Esposta al museo del design di Londra.

Lever, ring and cone. Combine them in a variety of surface finishes and the finest materials. Top design brought to a most individual point: Edition Point.

Elevador, anillo y cono en superficies diversamente combinables de materiales nobles. Diseño cumbre, llevado de una forma individual al punto más alto de la perfección: Edition Point.

Le leve, gli anelli ed i coni in superfici variamente abbinabili, di materiali pregiati: un design personalizzato e portato al massimo della perfezione – Edition Point.

Design: Sieger Design.

The Modern Classic. Fittings and accessories in perfect harmony. Excitingly clear styling, made precious by selected high-quality finishes. No other fitting has achieved such wide acclaim, neither nationally nor internationally.

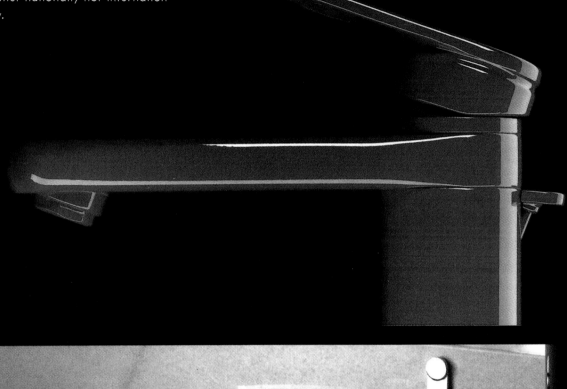

El clásico moderno. Griferías y accesorios en perfecta armonización. Estilo emocionantemente diáfano. Ennoblecido por medio de superficies de una primera calidad exquisita. Ninguna otra grifería fue tan galardonada tanto a nivel nacional como internacional.

Il classico moderno. Le rubinetterie e gli accessori in perfetta sintonia. Lo styling chiaro ed eccitante, impreziosito dalle superfici di alta qualità. Nessun'altra rubinetteria è stata così spesso premiata a livello nazionale ed internazionale.

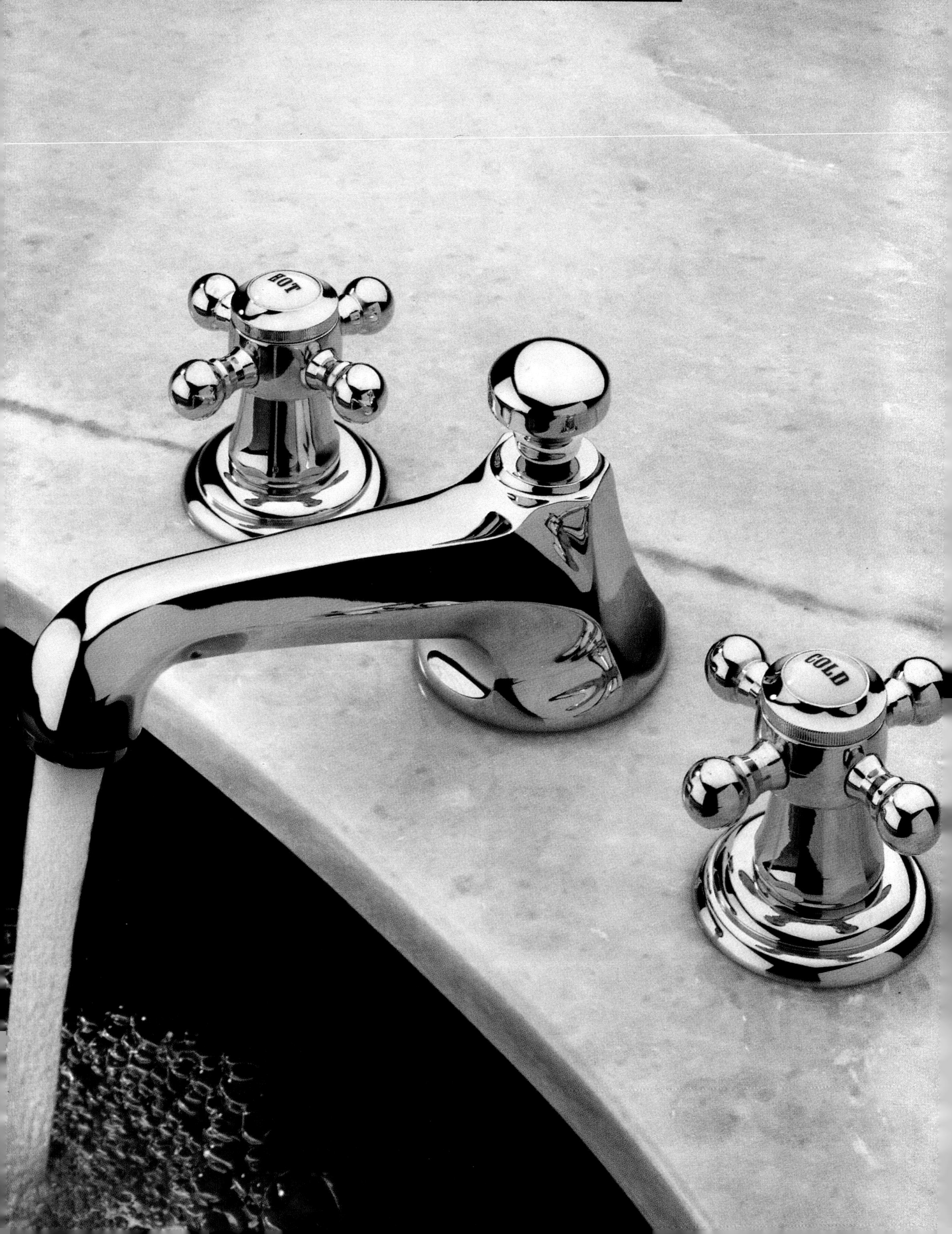
HOT
COLD

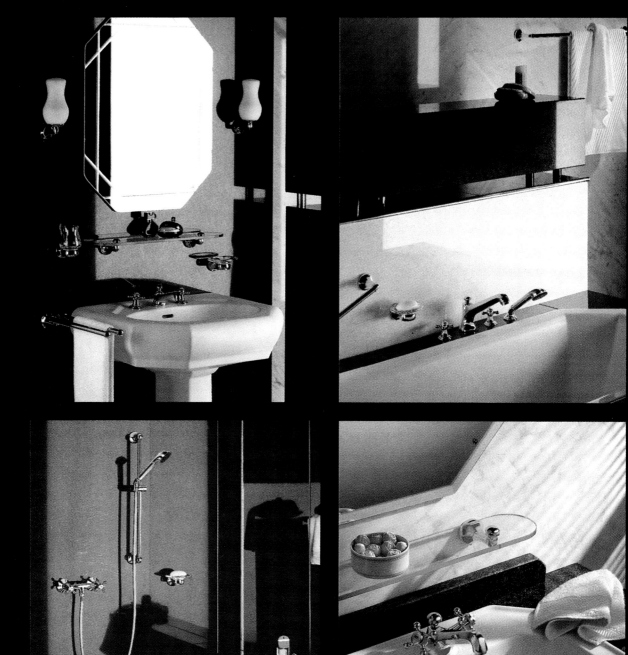

The original set of fittings and its accessories, nostalgic design at the peak of technical perfection. Cross-head handles with porcelain inlays, angular-section outlets, the finest surface finishes. For classical, luxurious bathroom design.

La grifería original y sus accesorios: diseño tradicional en armonía con la más alta perfección técnica. Tiradores en forma de cruz con placas insertadas de porcelana, salidas angulares, las superficies más nobles. Para un diseño del baño clásicamente lujoso.

La rubinetteria originale e i suoi accessori: design nostalgico abbinato a perfezione tecnica di altissimo livello. Le manopole a crociera con le piastrine di porcellana, i rubinetti a sezione angolare e le più pregiate superfici. Per un bagno classico e lussuoso.

EDITION MADISON / FLAIR

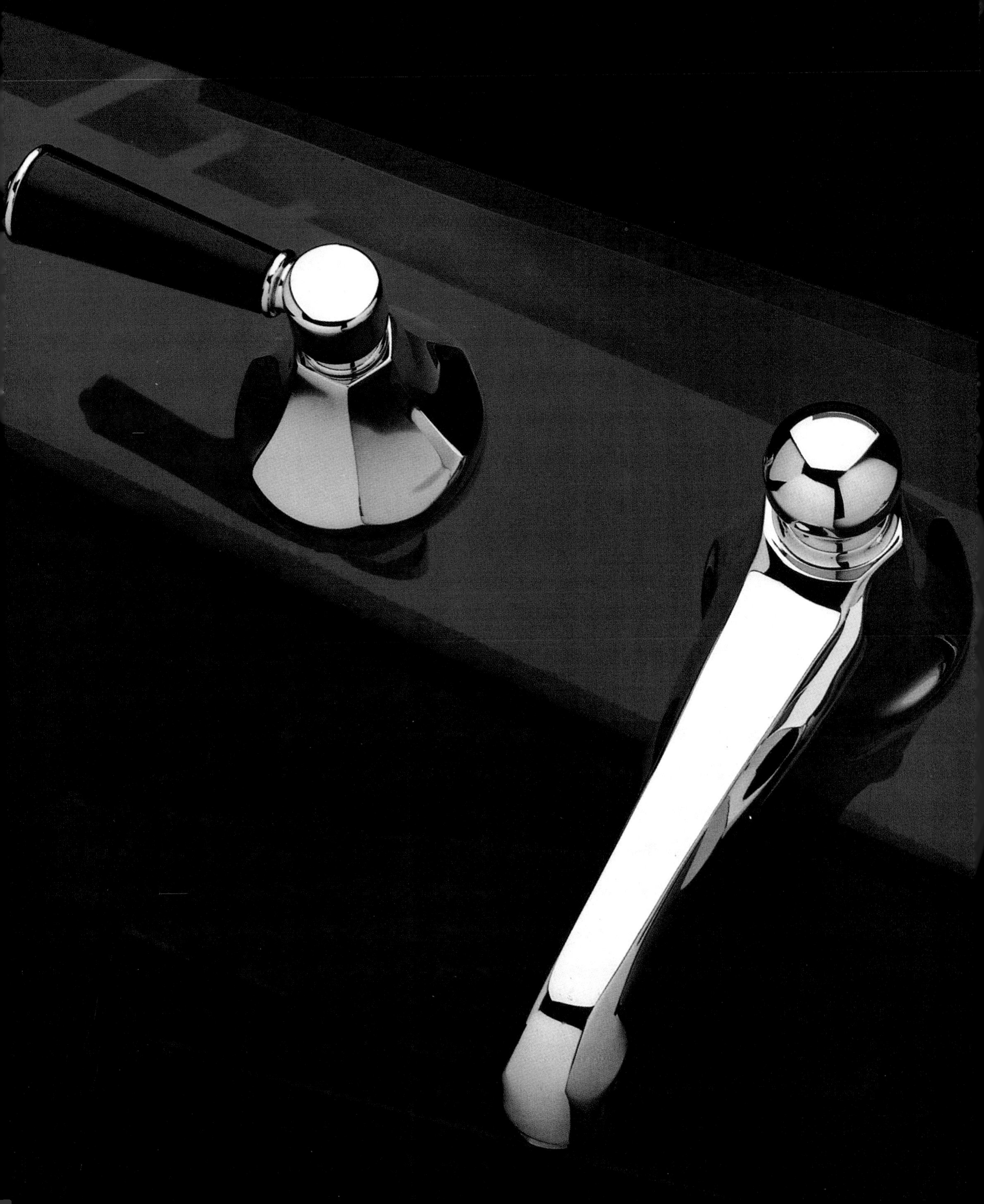

The distinctive variant of our great classic. With its stylish lever handles and striking lever inlays, it can be combined in a whole range of beautiful, choice finishes. For the inimitable flair of elegance in your bathroom.

La distintiva variante de nuestro gran clásico. Con tiradores elevables llenos de estilo y relevantes piezas elevables que se combinan diversamente con superficies de una belleza selecta. Para un inimitable instinto de la elegancia en el baño.

La versione elegante del nostro grande classico. Manopole a leva di grande stile, attacchi delle leve dalla forma marcata, abbinabili a combinazioni ricche di contrasti con superfici bellissime. Per un inimitabile tocco d'eleganza nel bagno.

nishes of the highest quality, nine
types of ring in nine fine finishes.
For maximum scope in your individual bathroom design.

Chic, encantadora y variada
como ninguna otra: seis superficies de grifería de alta calidad,
nueve tipos de anillos en nueve
superficies nobles. Para una
máxima en cuanto al diseño de un
baño individual.

Chic, affascinante e versatile
come nessun altro: sei superfici
per rubinetterie e nove tipi individuali di anelli con nove super-

Perfectly beautiful bathroom design: graceful the elegance of its lines, exclusive the surface finishes, individual the rings. The fittings and accessories a perfect match.

Diseño de baño de alta perfección y belleza: la elegancia que se desprende sus líneas, exclusivas las superficies, individuales los anillos. Perfecta la armonización de grifería y accessorios.

Creazione di alta perfezione e bellezza: eleganza fluida delle linee, esclusive le superfici con gli individuali tipi di anelli. In splendida armonia le rubinetterie con gli accessori.

EDITION COSMOS

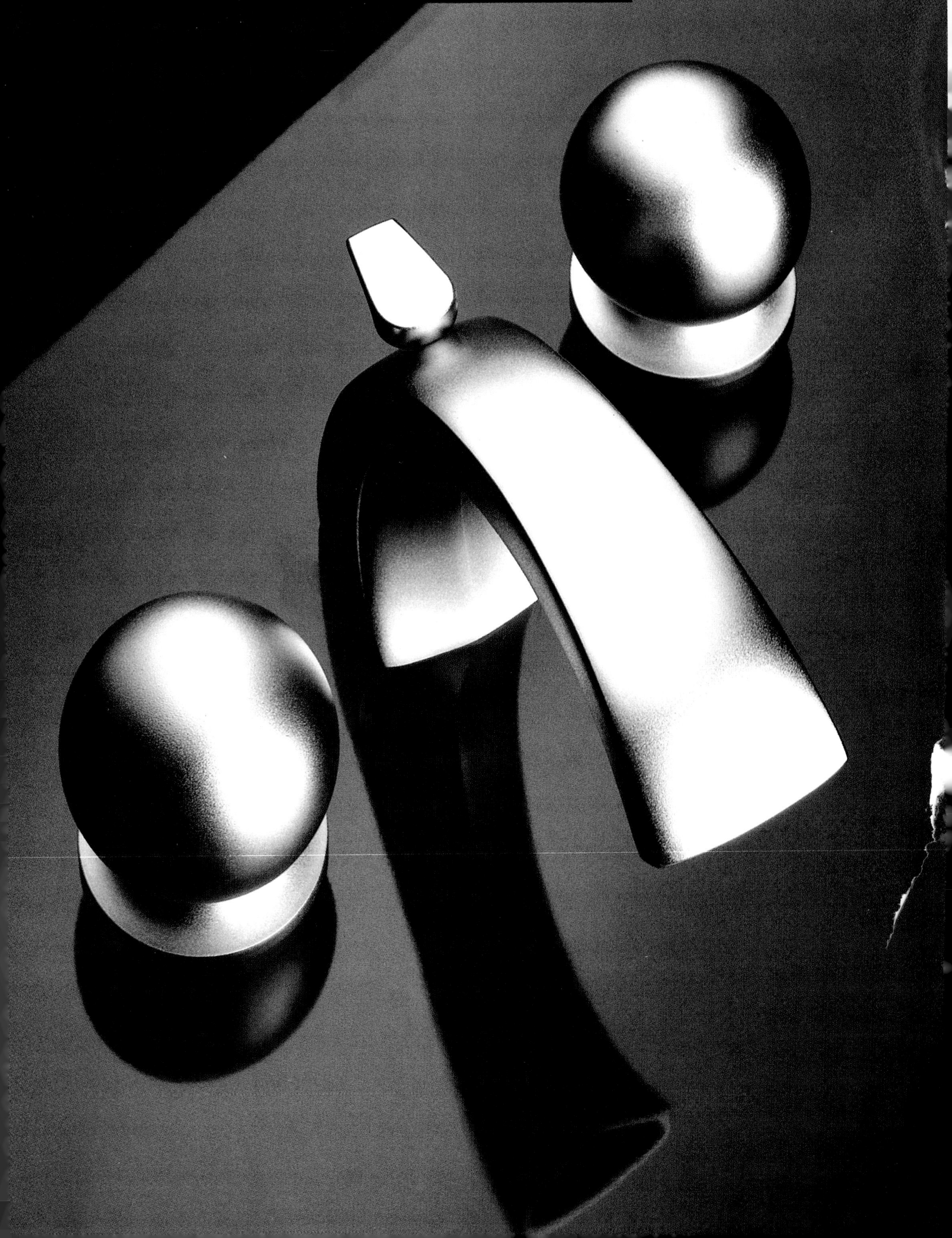

A futuristic, sensuous atmosphere for your bathroom: spherical handles, clear colors, gleaming finishes on the finest materials. Fittings and accessories – for visionary bathroom design.

Atmósfera del baño sensualmente futurista: tiradores de forma esférica, colores claros, superficies resplandecientes llevadas a cabo con materiales de alta calidad. Grifería y accesorios – para un diseño visionario del baño.

Per una atmosfera futuristica e sensuale nel bagno: le manopole sferiche, i colori chiari, le superfici splendenti di materiali pregiati. La rubinetteria e gli accessori per una creazione visionaria del bagno.

Our classic: dynamic expressiveness of design, appealing contrasts, flowing forms and square handles. Whether gold-plated or chrome, the aristocratic finishes make both fittings and accessories gems of exclusive bathroom furnishing.

Nuestro clásico: expresión de formas dinámicas, contrastes atractivos, formas fluidas y tiradores cuadrangulares. Dorado o cromado – superficies nobles hacen de la grifería y de los accesorios las piezas maestras de un diseño del baño exclusivo.

Il classico: linguaggio dinamico delle forme, contrasti affascinanti, forme fluenti e impugnature rettangolari. Le nobili superfici dorate che chromate fanno delle rubinetterie e degli accessori pezzi pregiati di un bagno dallo stile esclusivo e raffinato.

Classical elegance of timeless beauty. Harmonious lines, stylistic contrasts, exquisit surfaces. Perfekt the matching of fittings and accessories.

Elegancia clásica de una belleza intemporal. Armoniosa la configuración de sus líneas, de un estilo refinado los contrastes, noblemen-

te bellas las superficies. Perfecta la armonización entre la grifería y los accesorios.

Classica eleganza, bellezza senza tempo, armoniose linee, contrasti pieni di stile, finiture scelte. Perfetto abbinamento di rubinetterie e accessori.

Thrilling elegance, daring dynamics: shining dolphin backs that create a lively atmosphere in the bathroom, consistent how the fittings and accessories match, how noble the surfaces are.

Elegancia cargada de tensión, dinámica audaz: los resplandecientes dorsos de los defines aportan al baño un ambiente lleno de vida. Consecuente la armonización entre la grifería y los accesorios, nobles las superficies.

Eleganza ricca di tensione, ardite dinamiche: dorsi scintillanti di delfini donano al bagno un'atmosfera di allegra vivacità. Coerente abbinamento di rubinetterie e accessori. Finiture nobili.

The Mediterranean slant to the bathroom environment. Fittings and accessories in elegant forms, floral design and precious finishes. A sheer delight to the eye.

El ambiente del baño del estilo mediterráneo: grifería y accesorios en formas elegantes, diseño floral y superficies suntuosas. Una delicia óptica.

Un ambiente da bagno meditteraneo: la rubinetteria e gli accessori in eleganti forme dal design floreale e le superfici preziose. Un vero piacere per gli occhi.

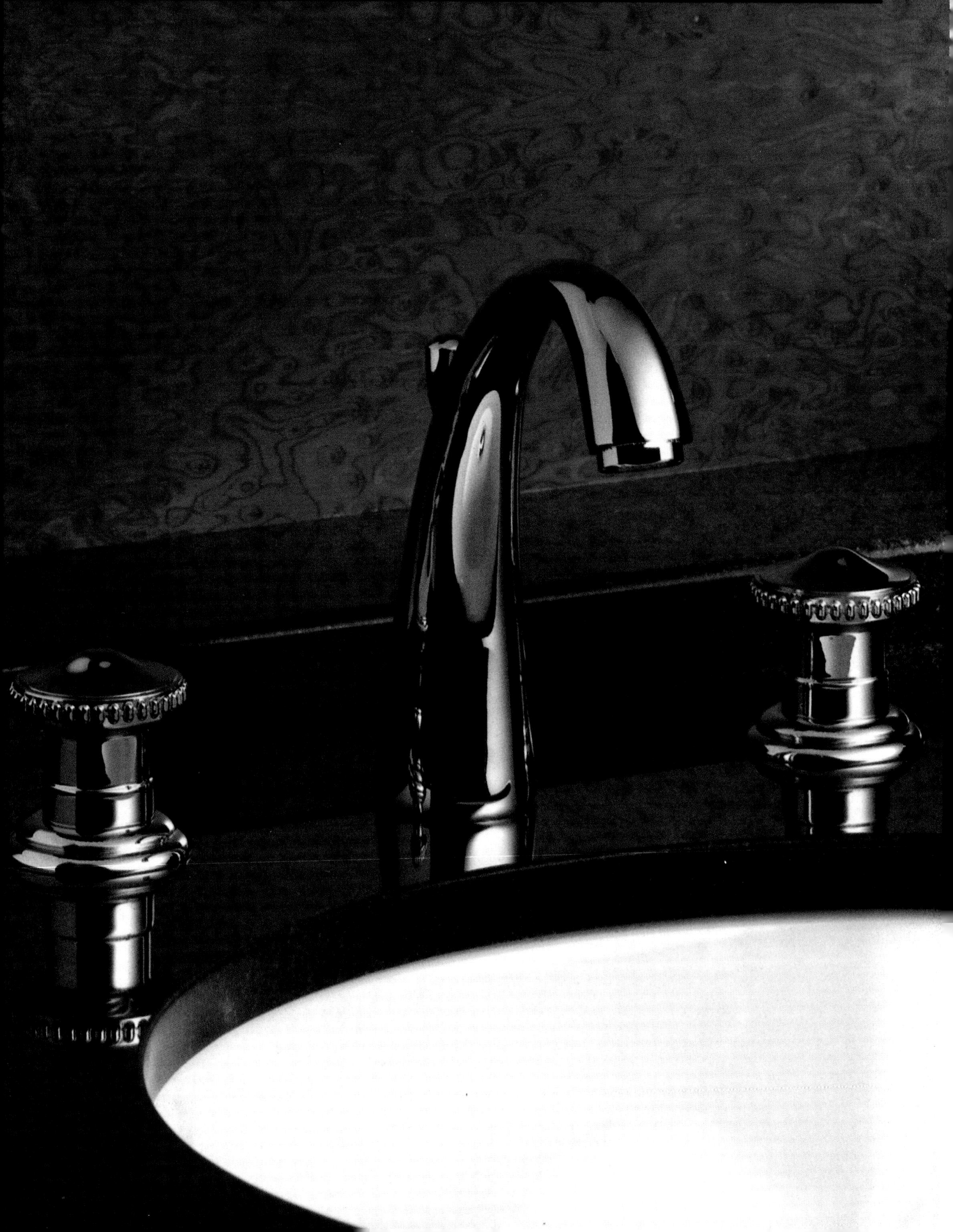

Princely bathroom design down to the finest detail. Whether is be the graceful curves of the outlets, the ring of beading on the handles or the very finest surface finishes, these fittings and accessories make a gem of your bath.

Un diseño de baño principesco hasta en el más refinado de los detalles: Tanto las salidas graciosamente arqueadas, los tiradores embellecidos a modo de corona de guirnaldas como las superficies más nobles – grifería y accesorios transforman el baño en una alhaja.

Un design per il bagno principesco fino nei minimi dettagli: i rubinetti dalle forme morbide ed arcuate, le manopole ornate di una corona di perle oppure le superfici pregiatissime. La rubinetteria e gli accessori fanno del bagno un vero gioiello.

MEMBER
PLUMBING MANUFACTURERS INSTITUTE

Underwriters Laboratories Inc.®
LISTED

NATIONAL KITCHEN
NKBA
& BATH ASSOCIATION

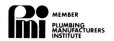

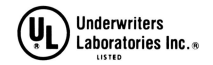

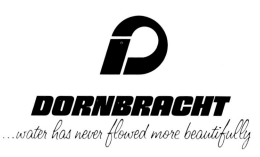

DORNBRACHT

...water has never flowed more beautifully

Dornbracht,
Postfach 14 54, D-5860 Iserlohn, Tel. 0 23 71/4 33-0,
Telex 827 761 adia d und 827 780 adia Export,
Telefax 0 23 71/43 32 32 und 0 23 71/43 31 32 (Export)

Represented exclusively by:

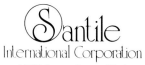

Santile
International Corporation
6687 Jimmy Carter Blvd.
Norcross, Georgia 30071
Phone (404) 416-62 24 · Fax (404) 416-62 39

Products specifically designed for the US Market comply to these approvals.

01.00.00.970.18

"*Our pride in this collection is passionate. The quality and value have never been higher.*"

Remo Jacuzzi

THE FIRST FAMILY OF LUXURY BATHING.

Behind Every JASON® Product Stands A Jacuzzi

Foreground: Remo Jacuzzi, President. Standing from left to right: Remo V. Jacuzzi, Vice President of Engineering; Paulo Jacuzzi, Technical Service; Jennifer Jacuzzi Peregrin, Vice President of Finance.

Our family name, Jacuzzi, has come to mean more than kinship. It began in 1915 when my father and his six brothers formed a business called Jacuzzi Brothers, Inc. But in the 1950s my family name became a household word when my uncle, Candido, invented the whirlpool bath.

For many years, I worked for the family business. Then in 1982, after all family members sold their respective interests in the business, I formed Jason International, Inc. Many experienced family members and employees have since joined us.

The first whirlpool baths were effective but primitive devices built solely for therapy.

Today, JASON whirlpool baths combine therapy with luxury and convenience to bring you the absolute state-of-the-art in whirlpool bathing. We've put complete, and incredibly quiet, operation at your fingertips. Our rich acrylic finishes are long lasting and so very easy to clean. Your back, indeed every part of your body, is considered in our designs. Integrated lumbar supports and armrests, recessed therapy jets...everything we do is designed to make your bathing experience more soothing and pleasurable. The new JASON collection within these pages is a testament of how far we've come.

We appreciate this opportunity to tell you about our heritage and our products - and for making us the first family of luxury bathing.

Remo Jacuzzi
President
JASON International, Inc.

THE CASARSA™

The Perfect Circle

Our newest bath of the Signature Series - and one of our most exciting. The CASARSA is named after Casarsa, Italy, site of the ancestral home built by Remo Jacuzzi's grandfather, Giovanni Jacuzzi. The circular shape makes this bath ideal for installation in a corner, platform, or island setting. There's ample room for two and a choice of four bathing positions, each with lumbar support. For the greatest relaxation, there are six therapy jets including two recessed Ultrassage™ back jets and two recessed opposing end jets. So a simultaneous back and foot massage can be enjoyed by both you and your bathing partner. As in all Signature Series baths, two silent air controls allow whisper-quiet operation. And the JASON digital control puts complete state-of-the-art whirlpool operation at your fingertips while you bathe in luxury.

CASARSA™

Full selection of colors with complementing fittings. Lumbar supports and armrests. One hp pump (120V, 20A). JASON digital control with programmable timer. Low water level and temperature sensors. Six therapy jets including two recessed Ultrassage™ back jets and two recessed opposing end jets. Two silent air controls. Textured floor. Shown in large photo with optional metal trim kit and two Double Cascade Spout® & faucet sets in bright brass. See page 23 for other options. Individually factory tested, IAPMO and UL listed.

├─── 72" (183 cm) diameter ───┤

height: 23" (58 cm)

THE FLORA™

Roman Goddess of Flowers

We named this bath the FLORA because it is internally shaped like the cup of a flower. And because it exudes a warm and gracious feeling like Remo Jacuzzi's sister, Flora. Designed for corner placement, the dimensions of the FLORA provide generous space for two. To ensure the greatest relaxation, there are six therapy jets including a recessed Ultrassage™ back jet and a recessed opposing end jet. Thus, you can enjoy a soothing lower back and foot massage at the same time. Two silent air controls bring life to a whisper. And, as in all Signature Series baths, the JASON digital control puts complete whirlpool operation at your fingertips. Could life be better?

FLORA™

Full selection of colors with complementing fittings. Lumbar supports. One hp pump (120V, 20A). JASON digital control with programmable timer. Low water level and temperature sensors. Six therapy jets including a recessed Ultrassage™ back jet and a recessed opposing end jet. Two silent air controls. Textured floor. Shown in large photo with optional metal trim kit and Double Cascade Spout® & faucet set in gold. See page 23 for other options. Individually factory tested, IAPMO and UL listed.

60" (152 cm)

60" (152 cm)

height: 20-1/2" (52 cm)

4

Ultimate Luxury Resort

Just off the coast of Venice and not far from the Jacuzzi ancestral home, lies la isola Lido, one of Europe's most fashionable and relaxing island resorts. And as one of our most fashionable and relaxing baths, we have named this the LIDO. This bath features five therapy jets including a recessed Ultrassage™ jet to provide you with a most soothing lower back massage. Also for your comfort are raised shoulder supports, armrests, and lumbar support. The JASON digital control puts complete whirlpool operation at your fingertips. Finally, two silent air controls let you calm the roar of the world.

LIDO™

Full selection of colors with complementing fittings. Lumbar support and armrests. One hp pump (120V, 20A). JASON digital control with programmable timer. Low water level and temperature sensors. Five therapy jets including a recessed Ultrassage™ back jet. Two silent air controls. Textured floor. Shown in large photo with optional metal trim kit with grip handles, Double Cascade Spout® & faucet set, and hand held shower in bright brass. See page 23 for other options. Individually factory tested, IAPMO and UL listed.

72" (183 cm)

36" (91 cm)
height: 20-1/2" (52 cm)

5

THE BON JOUR™

For A Good Day, Every Day

Here is yet another reason why JASON whirlpool baths are so esteemed. Elegant European styling with raised shoulders and sweeping armrests. The BON JOUR gives you room enough for two. The BON JOUR PETITE™ is a roomy, though more narrow bath, well-suited for remodeling installations. For the greatest relaxation, both baths feature six therapy jets including a recessed Ultrassage™ back jet and a recessed opposing end jet. You can enjoy a soothing lower back and foot massage at the same time. Two silent air controls. JASON digital control puts whirlpool operation at your fingertips. Should you start the day or end the day in the luxury of your JASON BON JOUR? Why not both?

BON JOUR™ & BON JOUR PETITE™

BON JOUR and BON JOUR PETITE are 42" and 36" wide, respectively. Full selection of colors with complementing fittings. Lumbar supports and armrests. One hp pump (120V, 20A). JASON digital control with programmable timer. Low water level and temperature sensors. Six therapy jets including a recessed Ultrassage™ back jet and a recessed opposing end jet. Two silent air controls. Textured floor. Shown in large photo with optional metal trim kit with grip handle, headrests, and Double Cascade Spout® & faucet set in gold. See page 23 for other options. Individually factory tested, IAPMO and UL listed.

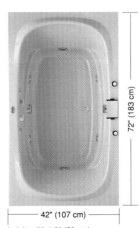

42" (107 cm)
72" (183 cm)
height: 20-1/2" (52 cm)

36" (91 cm)
72" (183 cm)
height: 20-1/2" (52 cm)

6

Two Can Say "It's Mine"

In Italian, mia means "mine." And that might suggest to you that this is a personal-sized bath. But such is not the case, and we can explain. As in other Signature Series baths, the MIA provides you with a recessed Ultrassage™ back jet and a recessed opposing end jet for simultaneous back and foot massage. Yet, in the MIA, these jets are offset from the center so that two of you can relax with a back massage while stretching out in comfort to enjoy the MIA's full length and shoulder room. Not to mention all the Signature Series features. Such as JASON digital control and two silent air controls. So yes, mia means "mine." And in this case, it means "mine" for two.

MIA™

Full selection of colors with complementing fittings. Lumbar supports and armrests. One hp pump (120V, 20A). JASON digital control with programmable timer. Low water level and temperature sensors. Six therapy jets including a recessed Ultrassage™ back jet and a recessed opposing end jet, both offset from center. Two silent air controls. Textured floor. Shown in large photo with optional metal trim kit with grip handle, and Double Cascade Spout® & faucet set in bright brass. See page 23 for other options. Individually factory tested, IAPMO and UL listed.

72" (183 cm)

48" (122 cm)

height: 23" (58 cm)

THE ANGELICA™

As Spacious As The Heavens

One of our most spacious baths, the ANGELICA is as wide as many baths are long. And here is a bath to set your mind free. With two optional Double Cascade Spouts® flowing, it's easy to imagine yourself (and your partner) in a hot spring with twin waterfalls at your feet. Of the six therapy jets, there are two recessed Ultrassage™ back jets so that each of you can enjoy a most therapeutic lower back massage. Each of you can also enjoy a foot massage from the therapy jets at your feet. Shoulder supports, armrests, lumbar supports, silent air controls, and JASON digital control…the ANGELICA gives you all the features that set the standards for luxury bathing.

ANGELICA™

Full selection of colors with complementing fittings. Lumbar supports and armrests. One hp pump (120V, 20A). JASON digital control with programmable timer. Low water level and temperature sensors. Six therapy jets including two recessed Ultrassage™ back jets and two recessed opposing end jets. Two silent air controls. Textured floor. Shown in large photo with optional metal trim kit with grip handles, and two Double Cascade Spout® & faucet sets in gold. See page 23 for other options. Individually factory tested, IAPMO and UL listed.

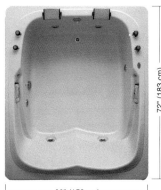

72" (183 cm)

60" (152 cm)

height: 20-1/2" (52 cm)

THE MADELINE™

An Oval In An Oval

Designed as an oval within an oval, it is a matter of style that makes the MADELINE so unique. The sculpted design brings comfort to your shoulders while the lumbar support brings relaxation to your back. Six therapy jets surround you with whirlpool action. Opposing, recessed end jets simultaneously provide you with soothing foot and back massage. There's even room for two. Also offered as a soaking bath without whirlpool features (see page 18).

MADELINE™

Full selection of colors with complementing fittings. Lumbar supports and armrests. 3/4 (.75) hp pump (120V, 20A). Variety of control options. Six therapy jets including two opposing recessed end jets. Two silent air controls. Textured floor. Shown in large photo with optional metal trim kit with grip handle, and Double Cascade Spout® & faucet set in bright brass. See page 23 for other options. Individually factory tested, IAPMO and UL listed.

72" (183 cm)

42" (107 cm)

height: 20-1/2" (52 cm)

THE BRITTANY™

High Sophistication Without A High Price

Brittany is a region of France and one of the most sophisticated areas of the world. We chose to name this bath the BRITTANY because of its sophisticated (and French influenced) design. We offer the BRITTANY in your choice of two sizes, the BRITTANY V and the BRITTANY VI. Both are spacious enough for two. Both feature a host of standard equipment such as built-in lumbar support and sweeping armrests. And both have recessed therapy jets at your back to comfortably massage you. In addition, the BRITTANY VI provides opposing recessed end jets for a most relaxing massage of your back and feet at the same time. Both baths are also offered as soaking baths without whirlpool features (see page 18).

BRITTANY™ V, VI

Full selection of colors with complementing fittings. Lumbar supports and armrests. 3/4 (.75) hp pump (120V, 20A). BRITTANY V has 60" length, five therapy jets (one recessed back jet). BRITTANY VI has 72" length, six therapy jets (two opposing recessed end jets). Both have two silent air controls, textured floor. Variety of control options. Shown in large photo with optional metal trim kit with grip handle, and Double Cascade Spout® & faucet set in polished chrome. See page 23 for other options. Individually factory tested, IAPMO and UL listed.

60" (152 cm)

42" (107 cm)
height: 20-1/2" (52 cm)

72" (183 cm)

42" (107 cm)
height: 20-1/2" (52 cm)

Song Of Joy

In Italy, a canto is a song. And singing is what you'll do when you experience the exceptional value in this fine bath. Because there are so many places to sit in the CANTO, each of the four therapy jets is recessed and located so that they can comfortably massage your back and feet at the same time. There's room for two, of course, and each of you can enjoy your own built-in lumbar support. Also offered as a soaking bath without whirlpool features (see page 18).

CANTO™

Full selection of colors with complementing fittings. Lumbar supports. 3/4 (.75) hp pump (120V, 20A). Four therapy jets, all recessed. Two silent air controls. Textured floor. Variety of control options. Shown in large photo with optional metal trim kit and Double Cascade Spout® & faucet set in bright brass. See page 23 for other options. Individually factory tested, IAPMO and UL listed.

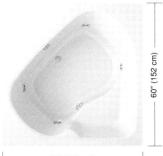

60" (152 cm)

60" (152 cm)

height: 20-1/2" (52 cm)

THE ASHLEY™

Extra Shoulder Room

A recent JASON design, the ASHLEY has become one of our most popular baths. It incorporates a bit more width for extra shoulder room. And it offers you recessed therapy jets on each end so you can enjoy simultaneous back and foot massage. Plus, these jets are offset from center so that two can stretch out in comfort and relaxation. Other superb JASON features remain – built-in lumbar supports and sweeping armrests.

ASHLEY™

Full selection of colors with complementing fittings. Lumbar supports and armrests. 3/4 (.75) hp pump (120V, 20A). Six therapy jets including two opposing recessed back jets. Two silent air controls. Textured floor. Variety of control options. Shown in large photo with optional metal trim kit with grip handle, and Double Cascade Spout® & faucet set in bright brass. See page 23 for other options. Individually factory tested, IAPMO and UL listed.

60" (152 cm)

48" (122 cm)

height: 20-1/2" (52 cm)

THE LORELLE™

Understated Spaciousness

The LORELLE is a spacious bath. Yet this quality seems understated in appearance if not in use. Here you'll find room that is sufficient for two. And, of course, JASON features to match. Lumbar support sweeps the entire width. And of the six therapy jets, two are recessed for a very comfortable back massage. Also offered as a soaking bath without whirlpool features (see page 18).

LORELLE™

Full selection of colors with complementing fittings. Lumbar support. 3/4 (.75) hp pump (120V, 20A). Six therapy jets including two recessed back jets. Two silent air controls. Variety of control options. Shown in large photo with optional metal trim kit with grip handles in polished chrome. See page 23 for other options. Individually factory tested, IAPMO and UL listed.

72" (183 cm)

48" (122 cm)

height: 20-1/2" (52 cm)

THE NINA™

A Big Idea For Small Space

In Italy, nina means "little girl." Like a little girl, this little bath can bring you great joy. Its small dimensions (and price) make it ideal for replacing a conventional 5' bathtub with the lasting luxury of a JASON whirlpool bath. Yes, this bath is small, but it's hardly short on "big bath" features. Built-in lumbar support and gracefully flowing armrests. Five therapy jets, one of which is recessed for complete massage of your back. Two silent air controls for whisper quiet operation. Also offered as a soaking bath without whirlpool features (see page 18).

NINA™

Full selection of colors with complementing fittings. Lumbar support and armrests. 3/4 (.75) hp pump (120V, 20A). Five therapy jets including one recessed back jet. Two silent air controls. Textured floor. Variety of control options. Shown in large photo with optional metal trim kit with grip handles in polished chrome. See page 23 for other options. Individually factory tested, IAPMO and UL listed.

60" (152 cm)

├── 32" (81 cm) ──┤

height: 20-1/2" (52

As Big Or As Small As You Want

With the ENCORE, you can choose from three sizes to fit your needs and space. All are classically designed. All are of the quality you expect from JASON. And all offer you many features you don't expect at this price. Built-in armrests and lower back lumbar support. Five therapy jets for full whirlpool relaxation, one of which is positioned and recessed for soothing massage of your back. Two silent air controls for whisper quiet operation. The ENCORE V and VI are also offered as soaking baths without whirlpool features (see page 18).

ENCORE™ V, V-1/2, VI

ENCORE V, V-1/2, VI have 60", 66", and 72" lengths, respectively. Full selection of colors with complementing fittings. Lumbar support and armrests. 3/4 (.75) hp pump (120V, 20A). Five therapy jets including one recessed back jet. Two silent air controls. Textured floor. Variety of control options. Shown in large photo with optional metal trim kit with grip handles in bright brass. See page 23 for other options. Individually factory tested, IAPMO and UL listed.

36" (91 cm) · 60" (152 cm)
height: 20-1/2" (52 cm)

36" (91 cm) · 66" (168 cm)
height: 20-1/2" (52 cm)

36" (91 cm) · 72" (183 cm)
height: 20-1/2" (52 cm)

THE EMILY™

Our Most Adaptable Design

The special design of the EMILY, with its end-drain configuration and reduced length, allows a beautiful installation in a corner, wall, platform, or island setting. Though compact in overall dimensions, this bath will surprise you with its very large bathing well. Of the five therapy jets, one is recessed for a comfortable massage of your back. Two others are positioned for a soothing massage of your feet. One of our most distinctive baths, certainly our most adaptable of the Decorator Series. Also offered as a soaking bath without whirlpool features (see page 18).

EMILY™

Full selection of colors with complementing fittings. Lumbar support and armrests. 3/4 (.75) hp pump (120V, 20A). Variety of control options. Five therapy jets including one recessed back jet. Two silent air controls. Textured floor. Shown in large photo with optional trim kit with grip handle and Double Cascade® Spout in bright brass. See page 23 for other options. Individually factory tested, IAPMO and UL listed.

60" (152 cm)

42" (107 cm)

height: 20-1/2" (52 cm)

16

A Classic

Designed with a distinctive relief at its border, the LARA is a classic complement to any decor. A bounty of standard equipment includes a built-in lumbar support and two silent air controls. Once you decide this style bath is perfect for you, then your choice is one of two sizes. The LARA V is a personal-sized bath. The LARA VI provides extra length if you need it. Both baths are also offered as soaking baths without whirlpool features (see page 18).

LARA™ V, VI

LARA V and LARA VI are 60" and 72" long respectively. Full selection of colors with complementing fittings. Lumbar support. 3/4 (.75) hp pump (120V, 20A). Four therapy jets. Two silent air controls. Textured floor. Variety of control options. Shown in large photo with optional metal trim kit in polished chrome. See page 23 for other options. Individually factory tested, IAPMO and UL listed.

60" (152 cm)

42" (107 cm)

height: 20-1/2" (52

SOAKING BATHS

The same construction quality and fine acrylic surfaces found in JASON whirlpool baths are also available in JASON traditional soaking baths without whirlpool features.

	MADELINE™	BRITTANY™ V, VI	CANTO™	LORELLE™	NINA™	ENCORE™ V,VI	EMILY™	LARA™ V,VI
CONSTRUCTION								
High gloss low maintenance fully pigmented acrylic surface.	S	S	S	S	S	S	S	S
Fiberglass reinforced structure.	S	S	S	S	S	S	S	S
Available in full color selection.	S	S	S	S	S	S	S	S
Leveling blocks.	S	S	S	S	S	S	S	S
Built-in lumbar support(s).	S	S	S	-	S	S	S	S
Built-in armrests.	S	S	-	-	S	S	S	-
Textured floor.	S	S	S	-	S	S	S	S
Integral tile-in lip.	-	O	O	-	-	-	-	-
ACCESSORIES								
Plated brass grip handle(s); polished chrome/bright brass/gold.	O	O	-	O	O	O	O	O
Powder coated brass grip handle(s); white/bone/quicksilver.	O	O	-	O	O	O	O	O
Metal overflow drain assembly; polished chrome/bright brass/gold.	O+	O+	O+	O+	O+	O+	O+	O+
Overflow drain kit; polished chrome/bright brass.	O+	O+	O+	O+	O+	O+	O+	O+
Hand held shower kit; polished chrome/bright brass/gold.	O+	O+	O+	O+	O+	O+	O+	O+
Removable headrest; white	O+	O+	O+	O+	O+	O+	O+	O+
Tile flange kit.	-	O	O	O	O	O	-	O
Lateral skirt.	-	O	-	O	O	O	-	O
For additional information, refer to page...	9	10	11	13	14	15	16	17

S = standard   O = optional   O+ = field installable option

NOTE: Soaking bath surfaces may subtly reveal the location where hydrotherapy fittings would be installed if the bath was constructed for whirlpool application. Field plumbing of a soaking bath to convert it to a whirlpool bath will void its warranty.

THE ALEXIA™
Combination Brazilian Shower/Bath

While living in Brazil, Remo Jacuzzi discovered the concept of combining a shower base and small bath into a single unit. Today, JASON offers you the ALEXIA as the embodiment of this concept. In a small space, the stylish ALEXIA provides a shower base, a small bath, and even a seat.

48" (122 cm)

36" (91 cm)

height: 12" (30 cm)

Molded seat. Left or right hand drain. Textured bottom. Tile-in lip on three sides. Shown in large photo with optional tempered glass enclosure. Overlfow drain kit, optional.

SHOWER BASES

Even with all the pleasure that a JASON bath will give you, there are times when there's no time for anything but a quick shower. With a JASON acrylic shower base to complement your JASON acrylic bath, you can enhance the beauty of your bathroom and two can bathe at the same time.

All JASON shower base surfaces are made with thick, quality acrylic. Shower bases of lower quality and price rely on a gel coat surface, which is merely a form of paint. Acrylic looks better and lasts far longer. The finish is more lustrous and easier to clean. And with the wide selection of JASON sizes and configurations — plus, of course, all the rich colors — you're assured of a perfect match to your bath and bathroom alike.

MODEL	DEPTH	WIDTH	HEIGHT
SHOWER BATH…			
ALEXIA	36" (91 cm)	48" (122 cm)	12" (30 cm)
SINGLE THRESHOLD…			
S3232S	32" (81 cm)	32" (81 cm)	6-1/2" (17 cm)
S3448S	34 (86 cm)	48 (122 cm)	5-1/2 (14 cm)
S3636S	36 (91 cm)	36 (91 cm)	6-1/2 (17 cm)
S3648S	36 (91 cm)	48 (122 cm)	6-1/2 (17 cm)
DOUBLE THRESHOLD LEFT OPENING…			
S3232L	32" (81 cm)	33-1/2" (85 cm)	6-1/2" (17 cm)
S3636L	36 (91 cm)	37-1/2 (95 cm)	6-1/2 (17 cm)
S3648L	36 (91 cm)	49-1/2 (126 cm)	6-1/2 (17 cm)
DOUBLE THRESHOLD RIGHT OPENING…			
S3232R	32" (81 cm)	33-1/2" (85 cm)	6-1/2" (17 cm)
S3636R	36 (91 cm)	37-1/2 (95 cm)	6-1/2 (17 cm)
S3648R	36 (91 cm)	49-1/2 (126 cm)	6-1/2 (17 cm)
TRIPLE THRESHOLD CENTER OPENING…			
S3232T	32" (81 cm)	35" (89 cm)	6-1/2" (17 cm)
S3636T	36 (91 cm)	39 (99 cm)	6-1/2 (17 cm)
S3648T	36 (91 cm)	51 (130 cm)	6-1/2 (17 cm)
NEO-ANGLE…			
S3838N	38" (97 cm)	38" (97 cm)	6-1/2" (17 cm)
S4242N	42 (107 cm)	42 (107 cm)	5-1/2 (14 cm)

NEO-ANGLE

With a door opening to the center of the shower, our NEO-ANGLE shower base helps you make any bathroom corner more beautiful, or can even be installed along a straight wall. Tempered glass enclosure is optional.

QUALITY DETAILS

High gloss low maintenance fully pigmented acrylic surface	Standard
Fiberglass reinforced structure	Standard
Available in a full color selection	Standard
Textured bottom (except S3232)	Standard
Integral tile-in lip	Standard
Metal drain assembly; polished chrome.	Standard
Metal drain assembly; bright brass/gold.	Optional
Tempered glass enclosure kits, clear glass doors and panels; with anodized silver or gold finish closely resembling polished chrome or bright brass respectively.	Optional

NOTE: Above options must be field installed

SQUARE CORNERED SHOWER BASES
Single, Double, Or Triple Threshold

The single threshold shower base is designed for wall enclosure on three sides, with a door located on the remaining side.

Triple threshold model with optional shower base drain.

The double threshold shower base is designed for wall enclosure on two adjoining sides. The door opening is normally on the longer of the two remaining sides.

The triple threshold shower base is designed for wall enclosure on one side, with a door located opposite the wall.

Glass enclosure kits are optional. Door openings may be either right or left hand.

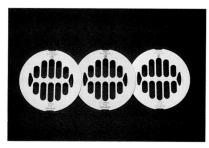

A metal drain assembly with polished chrome trim is standard. Bright brass or gold trim is optional.

THERAPY

While some baths are designed to simply look good, JASON baths are designed to feel good as well. JASON combines enduring aesthetics with baths of high therapeutic value. This is a noteworthy distinction between JASON whirlpool baths and competitive products.

Our overall goal is to provide you with a luxurious bath of soothing, therapeutic comfort. Many unique design details* aid us in this goal.

- Built-in lumbar supports and recessed back jets for comfortable support and massage of your lower back.
- Opposing end jets for simultaneous massage of your back and feet.
- Ultrassage™ therapy jets for the deepest, most therapeutic whirlpool massage. This feature is standard in Signature Series baths, optional in most Decorator Series baths.
- Built-in armrests for greater relaxation.
- Bathing wells that are spacious relative to the outside bath perimeter. This allows greater comfort, even in our smaller baths.

Trust The Quality

Besides the details mentioned above, each JASON bath is appointed with other standard features that you'll long appreciate. Rich, deep acrylic colors for lasting beauty. Three layers of fiberglass reinforcement for high strength and rigidity. Self-draining pumps and plumbing for better sanitation. Directionally adjustable jets, specially designed to never freeze in place. Quality fittings and components for years and years of reliable service.

The pump has a run-dry seal for protection if accidentally run without water. Every whirlpool bath is factory tested to assure that everything works exactly as it should. Every whirlpool bath arrives pre-leveled on an exclusive, fully supporting thermoformed base for a simple and solid installation.

Some design details are not available on some models.

The Signature Series

Signature Series designs represent the state-of-the-art in whirlpool bathing. Each Signature Series bath has a more powerful one hp whirlpool pump. Whirlpool operation is programmable and at your fingertips with the JASON digital control. A low water level sensor helps protect your bath and your bathroom. A temperature sensor aids your comfort by monitoring the water temperature of your bath. All are standard Signature Series features.

Many luxury options are available only in our Signature Series baths. A bather-operated heater, for example, can be incorporated into the JASON digital control — allowing you to set and maintain your desired water temperature. The digital control itself is available in six-speed version so you can select your favorite whirlpool action.

Options For All JASON Whirlpool Baths

For both Signature and Decorator Series models, there are many options which help you transform your bath into a very personal luxury.

To determine the standard and optional equipment for each bath, refer to the chart on page 23. Some options are pictured here.

With the help of your JASON dealer, and your imagination, your JASON bath can be equipped just about any way you want.

Programmable JASON Digital Control.
On Signature Series baths, a one-speed digital control is standard and a six-speed digital control is optional. With either, a button at your fingertips lets you set the desired whirlpool time. Then, while you bathe, a digital display informs you of the remaining whirlpool time and the water temperature. With the optional in-line heater, a separate button lets you set and maintain the desired water temperature.

JASON Touch Control.
Optional on all JASON whirlpool baths. The whirlpool "touch" control button is incorporated into the JASON emblem affixed to the bath. Includes a built-in 20-minute timer and protective sensor that shuts off pump if water level is too low. Choose either one-speed or three-speed version.

Metal trim package colors
To complement other bathroom fixtures, choose from a variety of metal trim options in either polished chrome, bright brass, or gold finish. Components vary slightly from model to model. Photo shows available escutcheon and jet nozzle combinations. Luxury kits include plated brass jet nozzles to replace standard color-coordinated jet nozzles. Attractive, two-color trim packages are also available. Choose either "polished chrome dominant" or "bright brass dominant" colors. Jet escutcheons and grip handles are provided in the dominant color, with air control knobs and jet nozzles in the highlight color. It is suggested that other bath options be selected in the dominant color.

& LUXURY

JASON Double Cascade Spout® & faucet set.
Elegantly restyled for 1992, this patented spout is an example of the JASON knack for combining technology and luxury. A beautiful option for most JASON whirlpool baths. Used to fill bath and/or provide aesthetic recirculation of water. Metal finished in polished chrome, bright brass, or gold. Also available in white, bone, and quicksilver powder-coated finishes.

JASON Ultrassage™ Jet.
Standard on Signature Series baths, optional on most others. Jet orifice rotates for deeper, soothing, therapeutic massage over your entire back. Color coordinated assembly. Escutcheon optionally available in polished chrome, bright brass, or gold.

Metal grip handles.
An attractive and useful option. Available for most models. Choose polished chrome, bright brass, or gold plated finish; white, natural bone, or quicksilver powder-coated finishes.

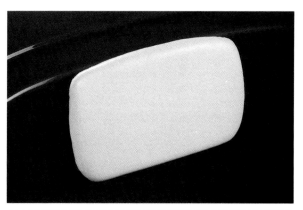

Removable headrests.
Two beautiful models to add comfort on your JASON bath. HR100 raised shoulder contoured model (black only) fits all Signature Series baths except FLORA. HR200 Ultrasoft universal model (white only) fits all JASON baths.

Hand held shower.
A luxury option for all models. Mounts at deck. Provided with extension hose. Facilitates bath cleaning. Choose polished chrome, bright brass, or gold.

Underwater light with mood lenses.
Sets the perfect mood for luxury bathing. Available as an option on all whirlpool models. 12V.

COLORS THAT GLOW WITH QUALITY

With JASON, you're assured of acrylic colors that are rich, deep, and lasting. Care is easy, too. Just wipe with a soft cloth and the finish will return to a high-gloss shine. And just look at the color selection JASON offers you.

Basic Colors

Classic White 001(WT) **Quicksilver 007(QS)** **Natural Bone 017(NB)**

Standard Colors

Morning Blue 011(GB) **Rose 012(RS)** **Smoke Grey 014(SG)** **Blush 016(SH)** **Coral Shell 018(CS)**

Ice Blue 019(IB) **Rouge 021(RG)** **Sea Green 022(SN)** **Peach 027(PH)** **Rose Bloom 029(RB)**

Classic Beige 031(CB) **Almond Bone 036(AB)** **Glacier Grey 038(GG)**

High Fashion Colors

Raspberry 013(RP) **Black 015(BK)** **Ruby Red 020(RY)** **Teal Green 026(TL)** **Style Grey 028(EG)**

Tawny Brown 033(TB) **Verde Green 035(VE)** **Royal Blue 039(RO)**

Unless optional metal fittings are specified, baths are shipped with fittings of complementary color. This color chart should be used as a preliminary reference only. Due to printing process, exact colors may vary from those presented here. To determine exact color, refer to your JASON dealer for an acrylic sample.

BATH FEATURES, OPTIONS & ACCESSORIES

	SIGNATURE SERIES							DECORATOR SERIES								
	CASARSA™	FLORA™	LIDO™	BON JOUR™	BON JOUR PETITE™	MIA™	ANGELICA™	MADELINE™	BRITTANY™ V, VI	CANTO™	ASHLEY™	LORELLE™	NINA™	ENCORE™ V, V-1/2, VI	EMILY™	LARA™ V, VI
CONSTRUCTION:																
High gloss low maintenance fully pigmented acrylic surface.	S	S	S	S	S	S	S	S	S	S	S	S	S	S	S	S
Fiberglass reinforced structure.	S	S	S	S	S	S	S	S	S	S	S	S	S	S	S	S
Pre-leveled thermoformed full-support base.	S	S	S	S	S	S	S	S	S	S	S	S	S	S	S	S
Available in a full color selection.	S	S	S	S	S	S	S	S	S	S	S	S	S	S	S	S
Color coordinated high fashion suction, jet & air fittings.	S	S	S	S	S	S	S	S	S	S	S	S	S	S	S	S
Individually factory assembled & tested to exacting standards.	S	S	S	S	S	S	S	S	S	S	S	S	S	S	S	S
Built-in lower back lumbar support(s).	S	S	S	S	S	S	S	S	S	S	S	S	S	S	S	S
Built-in armrests.	S	—	S	S	S	S	S	S	S	—	S	—	S	S	S	—
Textured floor.	S	S	S	S	S	S	S	S	S	—	S	S	S	S	S	S
Integral tile-in lip.	—	O	—	—	—	—	—	—	O	O	—	—	—	O	—	—
Factory plumbed for Double Cascade Spout® & faucet set.	S	S	S	S	S	S	S	S	S	S	S	—	—	—	S	—
PUMP and BATH CONTROLS:																
3/4 hp single-speed pump and 30-minute wall timer.	—	—	—	—	—	—	—	S	S	S	S	S	S	S	S	S
3/4 hp single-speed pump and air switch with 10-minute timer.	—	—	—	—	—	—	—	O	O	O	O	O	O	O	O	O
3/4 hp single-speed pump and electronic touch control with 20-minute timer & low water level sensor.	—	—	—	—	—	—	—	O	O	O	O	O	O	O	O	O
3/4 hp three-speed pump and electronic touch control with 20-minute timer & low water level sensor.	—	—	—	—	—	—	—	O	O	O	O	O	O	O	O	O
1 hp single-speed pump, digital control with programmable timer, low water level and temperature sensors.	S	S	S	S	S	S	S	—	—	—	—	—	—	—	—	—
1 hp six-speed pump, digital control with programmable timer, low water level and temperature sensors	O	O	O	O	O	O	O	—	—	—	—	—	—	—	—	—
1 hp three-speed pump and electronic touch control with 20-minute timer & low water level sensor.	O	O	O	O	O	O	O	—	—	—	—	—	—	—	—	—
1 hp one-speed pump and electronic touch control with 20-minute timer & low water level sensor.	O	O	O	O	O	O	O	—	—	—	—	—	—	—	—	—
In-line bath heater, 1.5 kw/120V, (temp settings programmable with digital controls above).	O	O	O	O	O	O	O	O	O	O	O	O	O	O	O	O
HYDROTHERAPY SYSTEM:																
Full size JASON directionally adjustable jets for more gentle massage.	S	S	S	S	S	S	S	S	S	S	S	S	S	S	S	S
Super quiet JASON air volume controls for optimal relaxation.	S	S	S	S	S	S	S	S	S	S	S	S	S	S	S	S
IAPMO & UL listed JASON hi-flow suction fitting protects bather.	S	S	S	S	S	S	S	S	S	S	S	S	S	S	S	S
Rigid PVC plumbing to ensure self-draining and hygienic operation.	S	S	S	S	S	S	S	S	S	S	S	S	S	S	S	S
Recessed back jet(s) for more comfortable hydrotherapy.	S	S	S	S	S	S	S	S	S	S	S	S	S	S	S	—
Opposing back and foot jets (except BRITTANY V).	S	S	—	S	S	S	S	S	S	S	S	—	—	—	S	—
ACCESSORIES:																
Metal trim kit; polished chrome/bright brass/gold/two-color. (see page 20).	O	O	O	O	O	O	O	O	O	O	O	O	O	O	O	O
Plated brass grip handle(s); polished chrome/bright brass/gold.	O	—	O	O	O	O	O	O	O	—	O	O	O	O	O	O
Powder-coated brass grip handle(s); white/bone/quicksilver.	O	—	O	O	O	O	O	O	O	—	O	O	O	O	O	O
Overflow drain assembly; metal in polished chrome/bright brass/gold; ABS in white/bone/quicksilver.	O+	O+	O+	O+	O+	O+	O+	O+	O+	O+	O+	O+	O+	O+	O+	O+
Overflow drain kit; polished chrome/bright brass.	O+	O+	O+	O+	O+	O+	O+	O+	O+	O+	O+	O+	O+	O+	O+	O+
Double Cascade Spout® & faucet set; polished chrome/bright brass/gold/white/bone/quicksilver.	O+	O+	O+	O+	O+	O+	O+	O+	O+	O+	O+	—	—	—	O+	—
JASON Ultrassage™ rotating jet for deep, therapeutic back massage, (Ø indicates location on end opposite pump only).	S	S	S	S	S	S	S	Ø	Ø	O	Ø	O	O	O	O	—
Hand held shower kit; polished chrome/bright brass/gold.	O+	O+	O+	O+	O+	O+	O+	O+	O+	O+	O+	O+	O+	O+	O+	O+
Bath light with mood lenses, 12V.	O+	O+	O+	O+	O+	O+	O+	O+	O+	O+	O+	O+	O+	O+	O+	O+
Removable headrests; two styles; white/black (see page 21).	O+	O+	O+	O+	O+	O+	O+	O+	O+	O+	O+	O+	O+	O+	O+	O+
JASON Heat Saver — maintains water temp. non-electrically, (except BRITTANY V and all multi-speed units.)	O	O	O	O	O	O	O	O	O	O	—	O	—	O	—	—
Tile flange kit.	—	O+	—	—	—	—	—	—	O+	O+	O+	—	O+	O+	—	O+
Lateral skirt.	—	—	O+	O+	—	—	—	—	O+	—	O+	O+	O+	O+	—	O+

NOTE: Above options must be factory installed unless otherwise noted and therefore must be specified with bath order.
LEGEND: S = Standard, O = Optional, — = Not available, O+ = Option available for field installation only, Ø = Location on end opposite pump only
Most baths and components are also offered for the electrical requirements of countries other than U.S.A., consult factory.

THE FIRST FAMILY OF LUXURY BATHING.

JASON INTERNATIONAL INC. • 8328 MACARTHUR DRIVE • NORTH LITTLE ROCK, ARKANSAS 72118

1-800-255-5766 (ORDER DESK) / 501-771-4477 / 501-771-2333 (FAX)

A vital contributor to JASON quality is your JASON dealer.
We stake our reputation on these fine people.

"QUALITY PUMPS SINCE 1939"

 ZOELLER CO.

Product information presented here reflects conditions at time of publication. Consult factory regarding discrepancies or inconsistencies.

MAIL TO: *P.O. BOX 16347* ● *Louisville, KY 40256-0347*
SHIP TO: *3280 Old Millers Lane* ● *Louisville, KY 40216*
(502) 778-2731 ● *FAX (502) 774-3624*

C576
BuyLine 8646

QWIK JON SEWAGE REMOVAL SYSTEMS

SERIES 100/102* - Economical sewage systems designed for built in or free standing installations.

MODELS:
Model 100 (Patented)
Model 102 Unlisted Pump, (Patented)

TYPICAL INSTALLATIONS

Versatile installation enables the pump compartment and piping to be concealed by the installation of a wall. **NOTE:** Access must be maintained to the pump compartment. **NOTE:** The Qwik Jon is designed to fit flush with any elevated floor made of standard 2″ x 6″ material (actual dimensions 1½″ x 5½″). And you can add a Lavatory-Bathtub-Shower with the installation of the 2″ adapt-a-flex seal (provided). Tub or shower requires built in installation. See Installation Instructions.

INSTALL A QWIK JON JUST ABOUT ANYWHERE

- Designed to accommodate a toilet, lavatory and a bathtub
- Use with a variety of toilet styles (1.6 Gallon residential flush, other installations use over 3 gallon flush)
- Perfect for basements, family rooms, warehouse, factories, room additions
- No need to destroy concrete floors
- Reduces construction costs
- Pumps any direction
- Fits just about anywhere

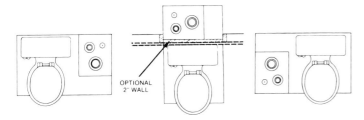

Code approved (Consult factory)

Basic Installation
Toilet, Fixtures and Piping Not Included

Built In Installation
Toilet, Fixtures and Piping Not Included

TECHNICAL INFORMATION

QWIK JON SYSTEMS INCLUDE:

Sewage Pumps

MODEL 100
Pump: Model WM 262
1/2 HP 115V 12 amps
Shaded pole
Weight: 25 lbs.

MODEL 102
Model WM 267
1/2 HP 115V 10.4 amps
Split phase
51 lbs.
UL Listed
CSA Certified

NOTE:
*Sewage Pumps WM262 & WM 267 are designed
for use in Qwik Jon units only. They are not
designed for use in any other application.

- Automatic preset mercury float switch
- Thermal overload protected motor
- Stainless steel screws, bolts & handle
- Non-clogging vortex impeller
- Passes 2" solids (sphere)
- UL listed 3-wire neoprene 10 ft. cord & plug
- Maximum temperature rating -130° F
  (54° C)

Tank

MODEL 100/102 (Pat. Pend.)
- Polyethylene
- Lt. gray finish
- Lightweight
- Wt. 26 lbs.

2" Back Flow Device and Union

- 2" back flow device (check local codes) required
  to prevent backflow of water and sewer gas
- No threading of pipe required
- Fits ABS, PVC and steel pipe
- Rated at 25 PSI
- Weight: 2 lbs.

ALL IN ONE CARTON

- Tank, lid & gasket
- ½ HP sewage pump
- Back flow device (check local codes)
- 2" Discharge & 3" Vent with adapt-a-flex seals
- 2" adapt-a-flex seal for additional fixtures
- Hardware pack and floor anchor kit
- Installation instructions
- Shipping weight:
  - 100 System - 63 lbs.
  - 102 System - 89 lbs.

ITEMS NEEDED BY INSTALLER

- Supply fittings, toilet gasket & waste pipe
- Toilet fixture
- Electrical source with ground fault interrupter
  protected receptacle
- Water source
- Tools
- Floor Flange seal extender kit MUST BE USED for
  built in installations —
  Part Number 100-0050 for ¾" floors
  Part Number 100-0051 for ½" floors

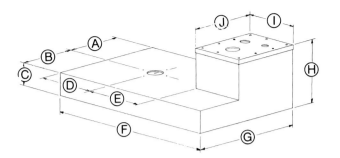

TANK DIMENSIONS

MODEL NO.	A	B	C	D	E
100/102	12¼	12¼	5½	12¼	14⅛
	F	**G**	**H**	**I**	**J**
100/102	41	25	16¼	14	17

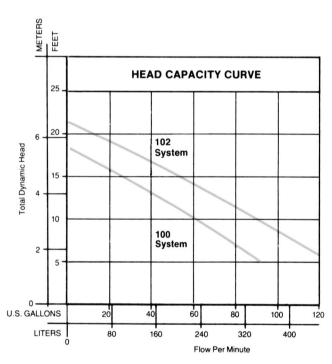

HEAD CAPACITY CURVE

Model	262(100)		267(102)	
Ft.	Meters	Gal.	Ltrs.	Gal.	Ltrs.
5	1.52	90	341	128	484
10	3.05	60	227	89	337
15	4.57	22.5	85	50	189
Lock Valve:		18 Ft.		21.5 ft.	

NOTE: Recommended for installations up to 16'
total dynamic head. Consult factory if installation is
above 15' vertical height in 2" pipe.

CAUTION
All installation of controls, protection devices and wiring should be done by a qualified
licensed electrician. All electrical and safety codes should be followed including the
most recent National Electric Code (NEC) and the Occupational Safety and Health Act
(OSHA).

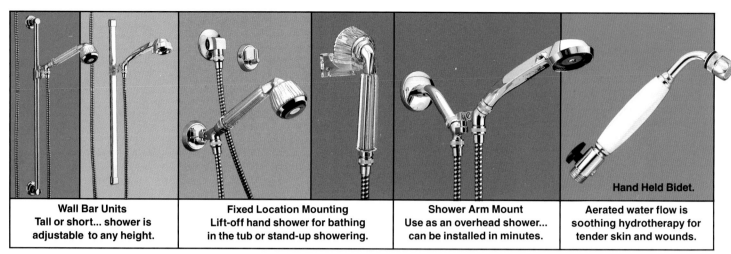

Wall Bar Units
Tall or short... shower is adjustable to any height.

Fixed Location Mounting
Lift-off hand shower for bathing in the tub or stand-up showering.

Shower Arm Mount
Use as an overhead shower... can be installed in minutes.

Aerated water flow is soothing hydrotherapy for tender skin and wounds.

Hand Held Bidet.

Create Personal Bathing Environments With Optional Mountings, Hand Showers and Finishes.

The Monterey Collection is a fashionable European styled ensemble, offered in four exotic finishes: Silver Plate, Polished Gold, Polished Brass, and Pure White. (Shown in lustrous Silver Plate.)

SHOWER HEADS

Choose from a broad selection:
- Invigorating massage action
- Adjustable
- Combination
- Full shower spray
- Designs from Contemporary to European Styling.

ROMAN TUB COLLECTION

DECK MOUNT SYSTEMS

These ensembles are designed for adding the luxury of a hand-held shower for tub-side showering. Featured at left is a classic hand shower which rests in a gracefully styled hand shower cradle.

TIP-UP BATH SEAT

Convenient for sit-down bathing or shaving legs... when not in use tip-up out of the way. Teakwood slats are mounted on brass frame.

SPECIAL FINISHES

In addition to polished chrome, Alsons bathing products are available in polished brass, antique brass, and polished gold.

Alsons™

525 E. Edna Place, P.O. Box 311, Covina, California 91723   (818) 966-1668   FAX: (818) 915-1033
42 Union Street, P.O. Box 282, Hillsdale, Michigan 49242   (517) 439-1411   FAX: (517) 439-9644

ARTISTIC BRASS™

rtistic Brass first introduced decorative, solid brass fittings for the bath over 30 years ago. Today, we are recognized for our reputation for producing unparalleled quality and distinctive design.

We provide the assurance of solid brass construction and our handcrafted quality. Each brass component is polished, assembled, and tested by hand. Our exclusive Marine™ Protective Finish and ceramic disc valves ensure years of trouble-free service, backed by our 5-year limited warranty.

Artistic Brass offers a wide selection of contemporary and traditional styles. Classics · Colonial · Architectural Accents · España · Eclectic

Each series has a complete range of matching accessories, tub and shower fittings, and Roman tub sets, as shown on the two illustrated pages in this brochure.

Our many innovative decorative finishes will enable you to create a coordinated ensemble of faucets and accessories for your home.

Shown are the three decorative metal finish options for the Classics and Colonial collections and selected Eclectic series. España styles are available in Polished Brass. In addition, the 12 contemporary dual metal finishes and color combinations are pictured with the Architectural Accents collection.

Welcome to the world of Artistic Brass, a company created on a bedrock of design, uncompromising quality and a dedication to the design needs of the most discriminating homeowners.

Polished Brass

Polished Chrome

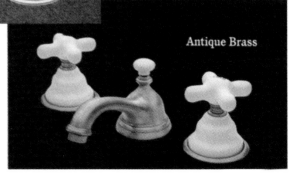

Antique Brass

605-L
4" Centerset

65-L
Widespread Lavatory Fitting

Clarion/65 Series

6005-L
Mini-Widespread

6046
Towel Ring

5046
Towel Ring

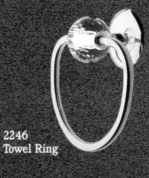

2246
Towel Ring

22-L
Widespread Lavatory Fitting

Regency/22 Series

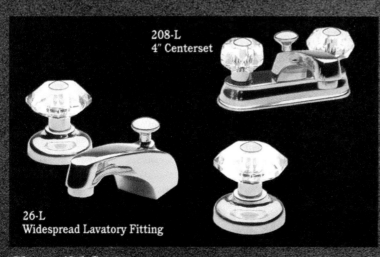

208-L
4" Centerset

26-L
Widespread Lavatory Fitting

Classic/26 Series

2646
Towel Ring

22-3D51
3-Handle Tub/ Shower
Combination

512-RTS
Roman Tub Spout

3004-L
Mini-Widespread

305-L
4" Centerset

34-L
Widespread Lavatory Fitting

Colonial Jamestown/34 Series

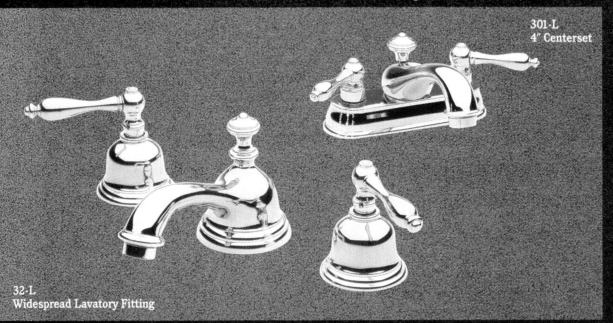

301-L
4" Centerset

32-L
Widespread Lavatory Fitting

Colonial Williamsburg/32 Series

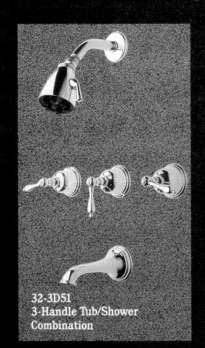

3002-L
Mini-Widespread

32-3D51
3-Handle Tub/Shower
Combination

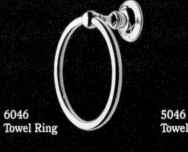

6046
Towel Ring

5046
Towel Ring

3211-RTS
Quick Connect
Roman Tub Spout

603-L
4" Centerset

68 Series
Almond

63 Series
Almond

68-L
Widespread Lavatory Fitting

Concord/68 Series

603-L
4" Centerset

63-L
Widespread Lavatory Fitting

Victorian/63 Series

6003-L
Mini-Widespread

330 Series
Almond

334-L
4" Centerset

6146
Towel Ring
White

6146
Towel Ring
Almond

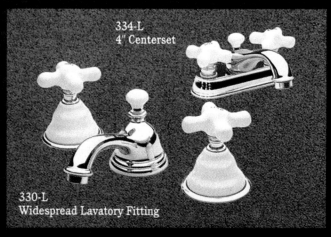

330-L
Widespread Lavatory Fitting

3200-RTS
Roman Tub Spout

Nostalgia/330 Series

Colonial

342-L
4" Centerset

3006-L
Mini-Widespread

3446
Towel Ring

340-L
Widespread Lavatory Fitting

Winchester/340 Series

5046
Towel Ring

6046
Towel Ring

407-L
4" Centerset

47-L
Widespread Lavatory Fitting

Fredericksburg/47 Series

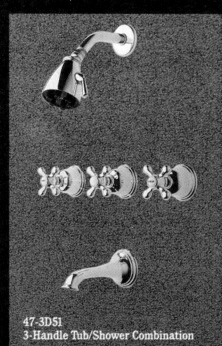

47-3D51
3-Handle Tub/Shower Combination

604-L
4" Centerset

64-L
Widespread Lavatory Fitting

Lexington/64 Series

6004-L
Mini-Widespread

ARTISTIC BRASS FAUCETS AND ACCESSORIES
CLASSICS, COLONIAL, ESPAÑA, AND ECLECTIC SERIES

Artistic Brass offers a wide range of fittings and accessories, featuring our exclusive Marine™ Protective Finish (MPF) and ceramic disc valves.

Please see your showroom representative for more details.

LAVATORY FAUCETS

Widespread Lavatory Fitting

4″ Centerset

Mini-Widespread
Styles available: 3002-L, 3004-L, 3006-L, 6003-L , 6004-L, 6005-L

TUB AND SHOWER FITTINGS

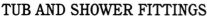

Tub Fitting   **Shower Fitting**

3-Handle Tub/Shower Combination

2-Handle Tub/Shower Combination

Single Control Shower Fitting with Pressure Balance Valve

Single Control Tub/Shower Combination Fitting with Pressure Balance Valve

DECK MOUNT ROMAN TUB FITTINGS

Roman Tub Spout   **Quick Connect Roman Tub Spout 3211-RTS Only**

Roman Tub Set Deck Mount

3-Handle Tub/Shower Combination with Roman Tub Spout

Roman Tub Set and Personal Shower with Retractable Hose

Roman Tub Set and Personal Shower with Cradle Bracket

*Bidet
Specify wall or deck mount.

**Trip Waste and Overflow

Tank Lever Handle

Wet Bar Faucet

Minispread Wet Bar Faucet
Styles available: 3002-WBF, 3004-WBF, 3006-WBF, 6003-WBF, 6004-WBF, 6005-WBF

ACCESSORIES

18″ Towel Bar   **24″ Towel Bar**   **30″ Towel Bar**

Robe Hook

Towel Ring

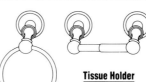
Tissue Holder

Wall Soap Dish

Toothbrush and Tumbler Holder

MARINE™ PROTECTIVE FINISH
An Artistic Brass Exclusive

The lustrous finish of each Artistic Brass fitting and accessory is protected by our exclusive Marine™ Protective Finish (MPF).

MPF is a crystal clear protective coating, 4 times thicker than conventional coatings, that protects the brass even in harsh salt air or hard water environments.

MPF's durability and resistance to corrosion not only meet and exceed industry standards but are backed by our 5 year limited warranty.

CERAMIC VALVES
- Quarter-turn, positive stop
- Non-rising stem
- Ceramic Disc
  Washerless
  Solid Brass Construction
  Guaranteed Long Life

MINI-WIDESPREADS
- Elegant alternative to 4″ centerset
- Styling of a widespread faucet
- Proportioned and engineered to fit 4″ drilled vanities
- Quick connect spout and one-piece valve body for easy installations

*Bidet: If required by local code, order vacuum breaker 5504.
**Trip Waste and Overflow: Shipped standard with grid-type drain.
If local code requires pop-up stopper-type drain, specify when ordering.
Certified by manufacturer: Complies with California Energy Standards and other states' standards of 3.0 gpm maximum.

Architectural Accents features 7 dual-metal finish combinations plus white, almond, and black color finishes with a choice of polished brass or polished chrome trim.

The decorative metal finishes are hand polished in an 8-step process and are protected by Artistic Brass' exclusive Marine™ Protective Finish.

The color finishes are high impact polymer resins which are bonded to solid brass, under high temperatures, in Artistic Brass' state-of-the-art infrared ovens. This thermoset process produces durable color finishes that are highly resistant to chipping and scratching.

PC/PB
Polished Chrome/
Polished Brass

PB/PC
Polished Brass/
Polished Chrome

PB/PC
Polished Brass/
Polished Chrome

SC/PB
Satin Chrome/
Polished Brass

SC/PB
Satin Chrome/
Polished Brass

SC/PC
Satin Chrome/
Polished Chrome

SB/PB
Satin Brass/
Polished Brass

AL/PB
Almond/
Polished Brass

BK/PB
Black/
Polished Brass

BK/PC
Black/
Polished Chrome

WH/PB
White/
Polished Brass

WH/PC
White/
Polished Chrome

PB
Polished Brass

PC
Polished Chrome

Architectural Accents I/Finishes

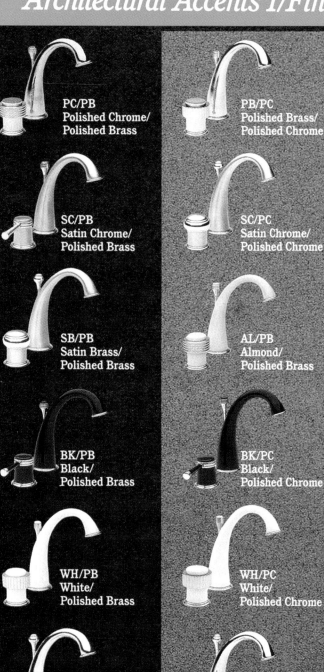

PC/PB
Polished Chrome/
Polished Brass

PB/PC
Polished Brass/
Polished Chrome

SC/PB
Satin Chrome/
Polished Brass

SC/PC
Satin Chrome/
Polished Chrome

SB/PB
Satin Brass/
Polished Brass

AL/PB
Almond/
Polished Brass

BK/PB
Black/
Polished Brass

BK/PC
Black/
Polished Chrome

WH/PB
White/
Polished Brass

WH/PC
White/
Polished Chrome

PB
Polished Brass

PC
Polished Chrome

80-L
Widespread Lavatory Fitting

Wave/80 Series/Architectural Accents II

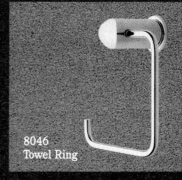

8046
Towel Ring

9935-P
Robe Hook

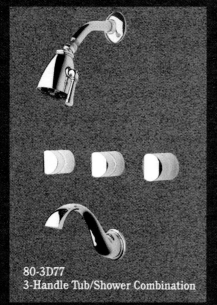

80-3D77
3-Handle Tub/Shower Combination

87-L
Widespread Lavatory Fitting

Ionic/87 Series/Architectural Accents II

3800-RTS
Quick Connect
Roman Tub Spout

75-L
Widespread Lavatory Fitting

Doric/75 Series/Architectural Accents I

78-L
Widespread Lavatory Fitting

Hellenistic/78 Series/Architectural Accents I

7835
Robe Hook

7500-RTS
Quick Connect
Roman Tub Spout

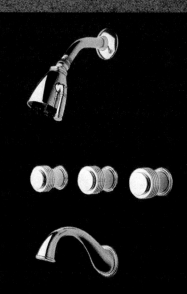

75-3D76
3-Handle Tub/Shower Combination

76-L
Widespread Lavatory Fitting

Corinthian/76 Series/Architectural Accents I

7006-L
Mini-Widespread

72-L
Widespread Lavatory Fitting

Diamond Cut/72 Series/Architectural Accents I

3955-P
Wall Soap Dish

9935-P
Robe Hook

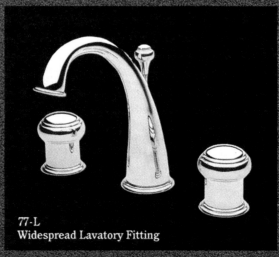

77-L
Widespread Lavatory Fitting

Ionic/77 Series/Architectural Accents I

Architectural Accents

9346
Towel Ring

9346
Towel Ring
Black Marble

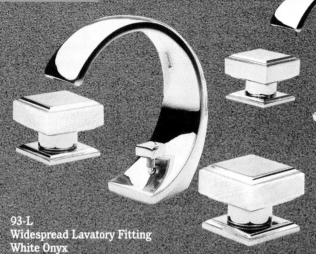

93-L
Widespread Lavatory Fitting
White Onyx

93-L
Widespread Lavatory Fitting
Polished Chrome/Polished Brass Finish

Cubist/93 Series/Architectural Accents III

Polished Brass/Polished Chrome Finish

Travertine

Black Marble

2246
Towel Ring

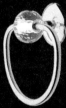

91-L
Widespread Lavatory Fitting

Crystal/91 Series/Architectural Accents II

9446
Towel Ring

94-L
Widespread Lavatory Fitting

Robie/94 Series/Architectural Accents III

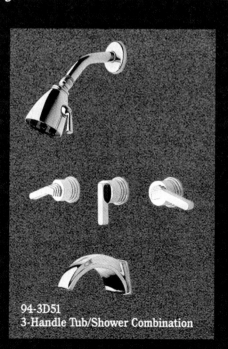

94-3D51
3-Handle Tub/Shower Combination

Onyx, marble, and travertine are products of nature.
The veining and color may vary from those shown.

95-L
Widespread Lavatory Fitting

Doric/95 Series/Architectural Accents II

3955-P
Wall Soap Dish

9935-P
Robe Hook

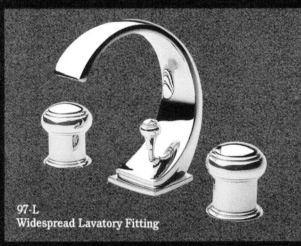

97-L
Widespread Lavatory Fitting

Ionic/97 Series/Architectural Accents II

92-L
Widespread Lavatory Fitting

Diamond Cut/92 Series/Architectural Accents II

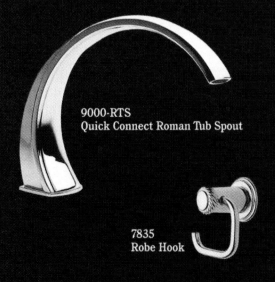

9000-RTS
Quick Connect Roman Tub Spout

7835
Robe Hook

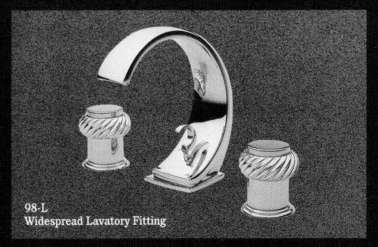

98-L
Widespread Lavatory Fitting

Hellenistic/98 Series/Architectural Accents II

Espana

48-L
Widespread Lavatory Fitting

Swan/48 Series

480-RTS
Roman Tub Spout

5046
Towel Ring

400-RTS
Roman Tub Spout

4046
Towel Ring

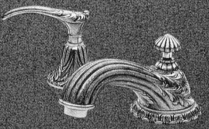

400-L
Widespread Lavatory Fitting

Barcelona/400 Series

450-L
Widespread Lavatory Fitting

La Reina/450 Series

4500-RTS
Roman Tub Spout

4546
Towel Ring

4646
Towel Ring
Brown Onyx

Green Onyx

Black Onyx

460-L
Widespread Lavatory Fitting
Brown Onyx

Onyx/460 Series

3246
Towel Ring

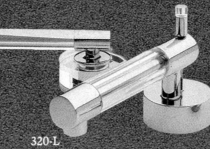

322-L
4" Centerset

320-L
Widespread Lavatory Fitting

Reflections/320 Series

312-L
4" Centerset

310-L
Widespread Lavatory Fitting

Delicious/310 Series

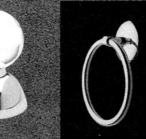

5046
Towel Ring

740-L
Widespread Lavatory Fitting

Wedgwood/740 Series

7446
Towel Ring

590-L
Widespread Lavatory Fitting

580-L
Widespread Lavatory Fitting

Grand Tour/Flanders & Picardy/580 & 590 Series

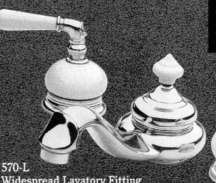

570-L
Widespread Lavatory Fitting

Grand Tour/Verona/570 Series

5846
Towel Ring

5946
Towel Ring

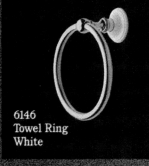

6146
Towel Ring
White

ARTISTIC BRASS FAUCETS AND ACCESSORIES
ARCHITECTURAL ACCENTS

Artistic Brass offers a wide range of Architectural Accents fittings and accessories, featuring our exclusive Marine™ Protective Finish (MPF) and ceramic disc valves.

Please see your showroom representative for more details.

LAVATORY FAUCETS

Widespread Lavatory Fitting

Mini-Widespread
Style available: 7006-L

TUB AND SHOWER FITTINGS

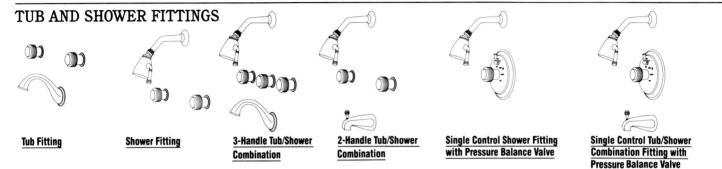

Tub Fitting

Shower Fitting

3-Handle Tub/Shower Combination

2-Handle Tub/Shower Combination

Single Control Shower Fitting with Pressure Balance Valve

Single Control Tub/Shower Combination Fitting with Pressure Balance Valve

---

DECK MOUNT ROMAN TUB FITTINGS

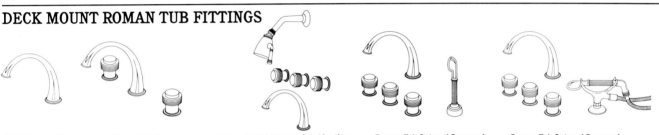

Quick Connect Roman Tub Spout

Roman Tub Set Deck Mount

3-Handle Tub/Shower Combination with Roman Tub Spout

Roman Tub Set and Personal Shower with Retractable Hose

Roman Tub Set and Personal Shower with Cradle Bracket

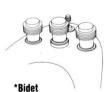

*Bidet
Specify wall or deck mount

**Trip Waste and Overflow

Tank Lever Handle

Minispread Wet Bar Faucet
Style available: 7006-WBF

ACCESSORIES

18" Towel Bar   **24" Towel Bar**   **30" Towel Bar**   **Robe Hook**   **Towel Ring**   **Tissue Holder**   **Wall Soap Dish**   **Toothbrush and Tumbler Holder**   **18" Shelf**

LONG BROACH STEMS

Architectural Accents tub and shower fittings are shipped standard with long broach stems for easy installation without critical tolerances.

ROMAN TUB VALVES AND QUICK CONNECT SPOUTS

- Easy rough-ahead installation of clamp-type valves and spout connector allows installation of handle trim and snap-on decorative spout after deck is finished.
- High flow capacity 3/4" valves

ANTI-SCALD PRESSURE BALANCE VALVES

- Maintains constant water temperature.
- Eliminates sudden bursts of scalding hot or freezing cold water.
- Automatically compensates for changes in water pressure.
- Meets code requirements.

---

*Bidet: If required by local code, order vacuum breaker 5504.

**Trip Waste and Overflow: Shipped standard with grid-type drain. If local code requires pop-up stopper-type drain, specify when ordering.
Certified by manufacturer: Complies with California Energy Standards and other states' standards of 3.0 gpm maximum.
Patents pending on all Architectural Accents products.

ARTISTIC BRASS™ A Masco Company
4100 Ardmore Avenue South Gate, California 90280
©1989 Masco Building Products Corporation Printed in U.S.A.

Innovative Drains for Today's Upscale Kitchen and Bathroom

C580
BuyLine 8619

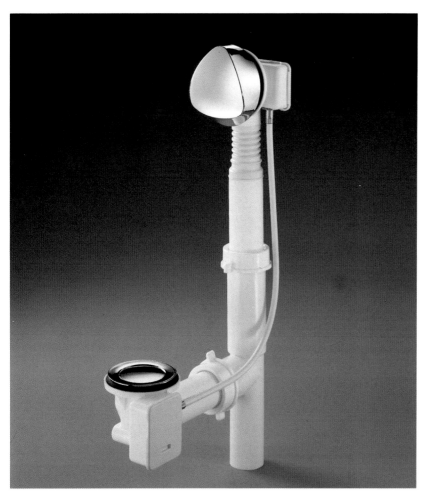

Geberit Remote Control Bath Waste and Overflow

European styling for today's up-graded bath designs. The remote control design puts the critical working parts outside the pipe, away from the water flow. This allows the water to flow freely, prevents clogging, and provides for years of reliable, maintenance-free performance.

A quarter turn of the European style con-toured handle provides a smooth, positive drain function that never needs adjustment. Fits bathtubs and whirlpools from 12" to 29" deep, whether acrylic, fiberglass, cast iron, stainless steel, or marble composition.

Available in the following popular finishes:
Chrome, Gold, Bright Brass, Antique Brass, Old Silver, Satin Brass, White, Bone, Grey, and Black.

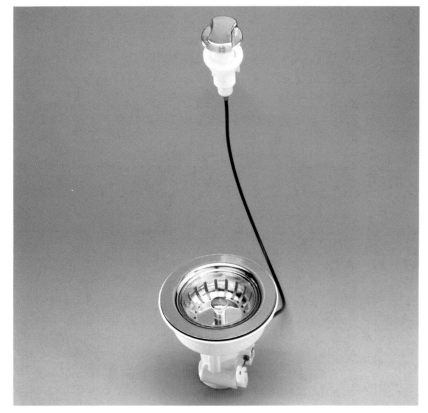

Geberit Remote Control Kitchen Sink Strainer

Now you can open the basket strainer and empty the sink by remote. No need to move dishes, pans, or, put hands in water.

Geberit's easy-to-operate drain is actuated by a rigidly mounted encased bowden cable made of nickel chromium steel. The non-corrosive drain fits in the standard 3-1/2" opening in all stainless steel, cast iron, enam-eled steel, and composite sinks. The normal deck hole accommodates the control knob, plus, it never needs adjustment. Manufac-tured to give long, trouble-free performance.

Available in six popular finishes:
Chrome, Bright Brass, White, Almond, Black, and Grey.

GEBERIT

Innovative Wastes & Traps to complement today's elegant kitchen and bathroom

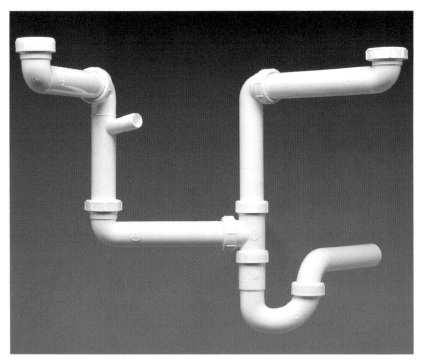

Geberit Space-Saving Kitchen Sink Waste & Trap.

End clutter and gain up to 40% more useable storage space under your kitchen sink. The GEBERIT space-saving trap is one of the best improvements you can make in new construction or renovation, adding tidy and efficient under-sink storage space.

Fabricated from heavy-gauge, non-corrosive polypropylene, these unique systems are hot water resistant, and will stand up to caustic household cleaning agents for long, trouble-free service.

Available in complete kits for both single- and double-bowl sinks.

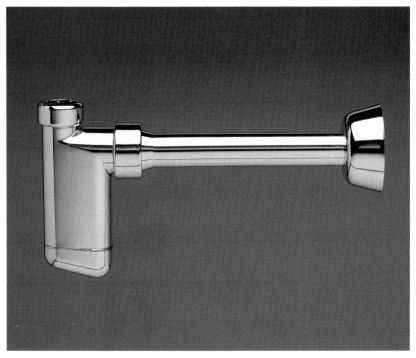

Geberit Decorative Lavatory Trap.

European styling to match the new look of today's bathroom decor. The GEBERIT Decorative Lavatory Trap fits all wall-hung and pedestal sinks. The unique design allows for straight line connections for easier installation and comes with a 13" outlet pipe and escutcheon. Fabricated from heavy-gauge polypropylene. The Lavatory Trap is hot water resistant, stands up to caustic household cleaning agents, and, is completely non-corrosive for long, trouble-free service.

Available in the following popular finishes: Chrome, White, Gold, and Bright Brass.

Geberit Manufacturing, Inc.
P.O. Box 2008, 1100 Boone Drive, Michigan City, Indiana 46360
Phone (219) 879-4466, (800) 225-7217, Fax (219) 872-8003

GEBERIT

USA Form #1396-11-92

GROUPE JADO

PLUMBING FITTINGS & ACCESSORIES

PRECISION ENGINEERING/INCOMPARABLE DESIGN

GROUPE JADO

SERIES ORIENTAL

Finishes Available

- ■ **Polished Brass**
- ■ **Silver Nickel/Gold**
- ■ **Polished Gold**

Widespread Lavatory Set...893/933

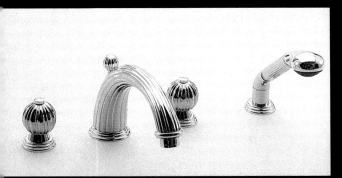
Roman Tub Set with Hand Shower...894/933

3 Valve Tub & Shower Set...855/931

Single Hole Lavatory Set...891/903

Hooded Tissue Holder...033/145   6" Ring...033/150   Robe Hook...033/010

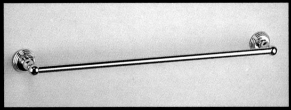
30" Towel Bar...033/800

For further information call:
(805) 482-2666
(800) 227-2734
FAX (800) 552-5236

GROUP JADO

GROUPE JADO

SERIES WALZ

Finishes Available

- ■ **Polished Chrome/ Ultra Gold**
- ■ **Ultra Gold**

Widespread Lavatory Set...838/004

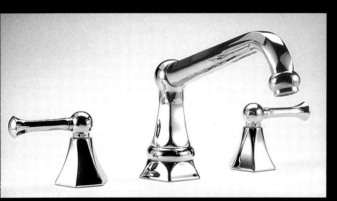

Roman Tub Set...838/005

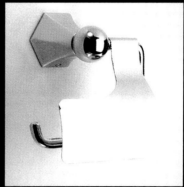

Hooded Tissue Holder...038/145

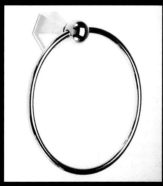

6" Towel Ring...038/150

30" Towel Bar...038/800

Shelf...038/612

For further information call:
(805) 482-2666
(800) 227-2734
FAX (800) 552-5236

GROUPE
JADO®

PO BOX 1329 ● Camarillo, California 93011

GROUPE JADO

SERIES SWAN/PERLRAND

Widespread Lavatory Set...893/902

Finishes Available

■ **Polished Brass**
■ **Polished Gold**

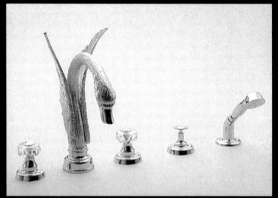

Roman Tub Set with Hand Shower...896/502

Roman Tub Set with Hand Shower...893/912

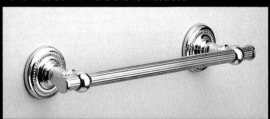

18" Towel Bar...501/460

Hooded Tissue Holder...501/145

Wet Bar Faucet...862/102

6" Towel Ring...501/150

Widespread Lavatory Set...896/303

For further information call:
(805) 482-2666
(800) 227-2734
FAX (800) 552-5236

GROUPE JADO

PO BOX 1329 ● Camarillo, California 93011

GROUPE JADO

SERIES RAINBOW

Single Hole Lavatory Set...830/905

Finishes Available
- **Silver Nickel/Gold**
- **White/Gold**
- **Interchangeable Rings**

Roman Tub Set with Hand Shower...834/335

24" Towel Bar...030/601

Shelf...030/612

Tumbler...030/141

Hooded Tissue Holder...030/145

Rope   Ribbed   Square
Ring Selection: If other than rope, please specify.

For further information call:
(805) 482-2666
(800) 227-2734
FAX (800) 552-5236

GROUPE JADO®

PO BOX 1329 ● Camarillo, California 93011

GROUPE JADO

SERIES GOLDEN GATE

Finishes Available

- ■ **Silver Nickel/Gold**
- ■ **Brushed Nickel/Gold**
- ■ **Black Chrome/Gold**

Widespread Lavatory Set – Flat Spout...843/912

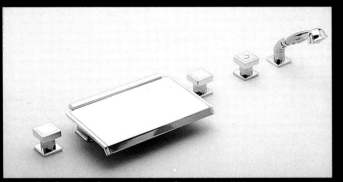

Roman Tub Set – Flat Spout – with Hand Shower...844/932

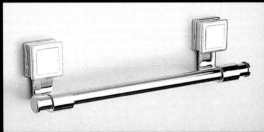

18" Towel Bar...031/460

3 Valve Tub & Shower Set...843/992

Robe Hooks...031/010

Hooded Tissue Holder...031/145

Widespread Lavatory Set – "C" Spout...843/902

For further information call:
(805) 482-2666
(800) 227-2734
FAX (800) 552-5236

GROUPE JADO®

PO BOX 1329 ● Camarillo, California 93011

G R O U P E
JADO
SERIES EVERGREEN

Finishes Available

■ **Silver Nickel/Gold**
■ **Brushed Nickel/Gold**

Widespread Lavatory Set...853/907

Roman Tub Set with Hand Shower...855/927

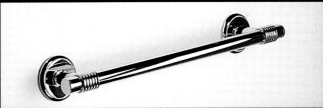

24" Towel Bar...411/601

Single Control Thermostatic Shower Set...875/907

3 Valve Tub and Shower Set...855/917

Widespread Lavatory Set with Straight Levers...853/997

6" Towel Ring...411/150

GROUPE JADO

SERIES VOGUE

Finishes Available

- **Polished Chrome/Gold**
- **Polished Chrome/ Dull Chrome**
- **White/Polished Chrome**

Single Control Lavatory Set…837/001

Single Control Roman Tub Set with Hand Shower…837/007

Robe Hook…037/010

6" Towel Ring…037/150

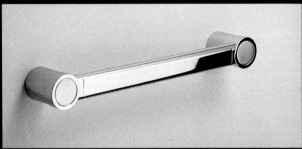

24" Towel Bar…037/601

Widespread Lavatory Set…837/011

Hooded Tissue Holder…037/145

24" x 32" Mirror…037/390

For further information call:
(805) 482-2666
(800) 227-2734
FAX (800) 552-5236

GROUPE JADO ®

PO BOX 1329 ● Camarillo, California 93011

G R O U P E
JADO

SERIES CLASSIC

Finishes Available

- ■ **Polished Brass**
- ■ **Polished Chrome**
- ■ **Brushed Nickel**

Widespread Lavatory Set – Cross Handle...853/938

Roman Tub Set with Hand Shower – Cross Handle...855/990

3 Valve Tub & Shower Set...855/948

6" Towel Ring...033/15(

24" Towel Bar...033/601

Hooded Tissue
Holder...033/145

Widespread Lavatory Set – Straight Lever Handle...853/948

For further information call:

(805) 482-2666

(800) 227-2734

FAX (800) 552-5236

G R O U P E
JADO

PO BOX 1329 ● Camarillo, California 93011

G R O U P E
JADO

SERIES COLONIAL

Finishes Available

■ **Polished Brass**
■ **Polished Chrome**
■ **Brushed Nickel**
■ **Polished Brass/White Porcelain**
■ **Polished Chrome/White Porcelain**

Widespread Lavatory Set with Straight Levers…853/908

Roman Tub Set with Hand Shower…855/848

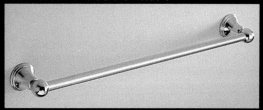

Kitchen Faucet Set…883/018

24" Towel Bar…508/601

3 Valve Tub & Shower Set…855/948

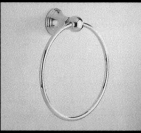

8" Towel Ring…508/200

Hooded Tissue Holder…508/145

31" x 20" Mirror…020/850

For further information call:
(805) 482-2666
(800) 227-2734
FAX (800) 552-5236

G R O U P E
JADO ®

PO BOX 1329 ● Camarillo, California 93011

GROUPE JADO

SERIES JETLINE

Widespread Lavatory Set – Lever Handle…848/901

Finishes Available
- **Polished Chrome**
- **Silver Nickel/Gold**

Roman Tub Set with Hand Shower – Knob Handle…849/912

Hooded Tissue Holder…512/145   6" Ring…512/150   Robe Hook…512/010

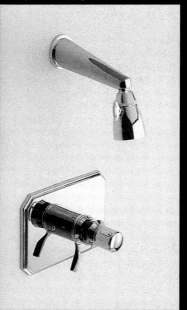

Single Control Thermostatic Shower Set…875/942

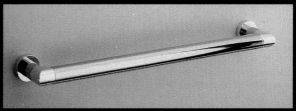

30" Towel Bar…512/800

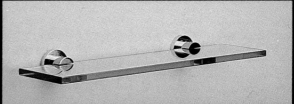

Shelf…512/612

For further information call:
(805) 482-2666
(800) 227-2734
FAX (800) 552-5236

GROUPE JADO ®

PO BOX 1329 ● Camarillo, California 93011

GROUPE JADO

LUXURY FORGED BRASS FROM GERMANY

PRODUCTS AVAILABLE

Single Hole LAV Sets

Widespread LAV Sets

Wet Bar Faucets

Single Hole Bidet Sets

3-Hole Bidet Sets

Roman Tub Sets

Roman Tub with Hand Shower

3 Valve Tub and Shower Sets

2 Valve Shower Sets

Single Control Thermostatic Shower Sets

3/4" Thermostatic Mixing Valve Sets

5-Port Diverters

4-Port Diverters

1/2" and 3/4" Wall Valves

Body Sprays

Wall Angle Stops

Hand Shower Systems

Robe Hooks

6" Towel Rings

18" Towel Bars

24" Towel Bars

30" Towel Bars

Tissue Holders

Tumbler Holders

Soap Dish Holders

24" Shelves

Mirrors

Facial Tissue Box

Waste Paper Baskets

Wire Soap Trays

1/4 Turn Ceramic Disc Cartridge – **LIFETIME WARRANTY**

For further information call:

(805) 482-2666

(800) 227-2734

FAX (800) 552-5236

GROUPE JADO®

PO BOX 1329 ● Camarillo, California 93011

WATERMASTER SERIES

GROUPE
JADO

WaterMaster by GROUPE JADO...A collection of faucets for todays contemporary kitchens.

Groupe JADO introduces a series of kitchen faucets combining not only outstanding contemporary design but proven reliable performance with state of the art technology.

The new WaterMaster Collection features 3 sophisticated designs with a variety of color choices and finishes that await your personal selection.

This fresh new faucet, elegant and contemporary, permits flexibility to move water flow to all areas of the sink with its convenient pull out hand held sprayer. Your choice of water flow, spray or stream, is available at the touch of a button. Together with its unique design and enduring reliability you also receive a LIFETIME MECHANICAL WARRANTY on your Drip Free Ceramic Disc Cartridge.

GROUPE JADO...*Uncompromising quality!*

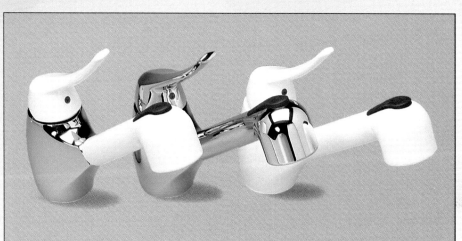

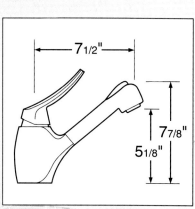

7 1/2"

7 7/8"

5 1/8"

GROUPE JADO's commitment to function and design has produced a contemporary, elegant European faucet with the ease of a single control and the versatility of a pull out sprayer.

Combined with the modern technology of a quarter turn ceramic disc cartridges for smooth and precise control water flow; JADO WaterMaster faucets also feature a two valve check system, preventing backflow siphonage.

All GROUPE JADO single control faucets are provided with coordinated 10" coverplates to cover unsightly plumbing holes that may exist in your kitchen sink or countertop. Additionally, all JADO faucets are designed with more than just esthetics in mind – making installation very simple and less time consuming is always a goal at GROUPE JADO.

GROUPE JADO...*Functional Elegance!*

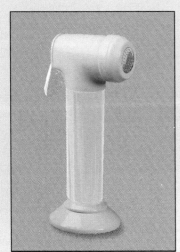

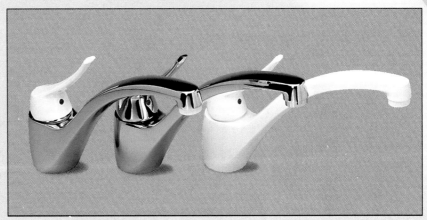

The same GROUPE JADO uncompromising quality and attention to detail is given to this elegant faucet.

It has been designed to compliment the international style and contemporary elegance of today's kitchen with a classically sculpted cast spout. This extra long spout will easily accommodate your larger cookware. For added mobility, it is also available with a companion side sprayer.

As with all WaterMaster faucets by GROUPE JADO, a LIFETIME MECHANICAL WARRANTY of the Ceramic Disc Cartridge accompanies this reflection of beauty.

GROUPE JADO...*Timeless Design!*

9 1/4"

8 1/16"

6 7/8"

4 1/8"

GROUPE JADO WaterMaster

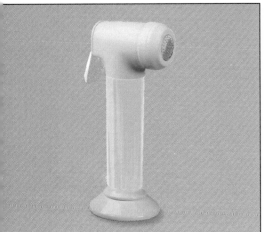
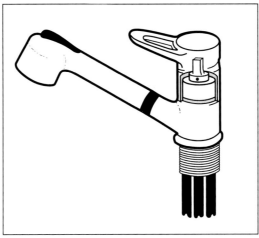

Special Features:

- All models operate by single control

- 2 pull-out spray models

- 1 solid swivel spout model with pull-out side spray

- Lifetime mechanical warranty on 1/4 turn ceramic disc cartridge

- All models equipped with built in backflow preventer

- All models comply with 2.2 gpm water conserving flow rate codes

- 10" cover plate included at no extra charge

- Available in polished chrome, white and polished chrome/white

GROUPE JADO proudly introduces the "WATERMASTER" series of kitchen faucets. The "WATERMASTER" series combines contemporary design, superior performance, state of the art technology and proven reliability.

As is true with GROUPE JADO bathroom and hardware products, the "WATERMASTER" Series is made with legendary European manufacturing precision and uncompromised quality.

Groupe JADO...Precision Engineering/Incomparable Design.

Distributor:

GROUPE JADO®
P.O. Box 1329, Camarillo, CA 93011

LUXCETZ

C583
BuyLine 8628

Luxcetz

Series GE

Series GH

The

New

Touch

of

Luxury

Series AO

With style and quality in mind, in creating the finest collection

Series GG

Series HO

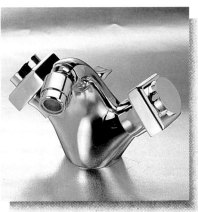

Built on a foundation of the latest in technology and decades of experience, our products consistently surpass standards set in the industry.

Featured with solid bass construction, each Luxcetz series is protected by polish-free epoxy coating, and our quarter-turn washerless ceramic disk valves are backed by a lifetime limited warranty.

For quality at its best, use .. Luxcetz.

Luxcetz has succeeded of decorative faucets.

Series DC

Series BG

Series AB

Series GC

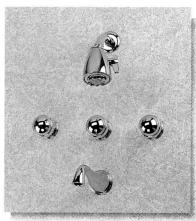

Series FF

Series HC

▶ The
New
Touch
of
Luxury

Luxcetz, Inc.
13001 Ramona Blvd., Suite K
Irwindale, CA 91706-3797
Tel: (818) 813-1087-9
Fax: (818) 813-1080

Strom Plumbing

BY
Sign of 🦀 the Crab

C584
BuyLine 8653

No. 91

SIGN OF THE CRAB specializes in solid brass plumbing and decorative accessories. Through years of careful development, our products include authentic reproduction items and new, designer-oriented products. Also available is the service that is necessary to see your project through to completion. We have custom-made many items to include stainless steel and brass products for the Sheraton Palace Hotel in San Francisco and the Beverly Wilshire Hotel in Beverly Hills.

Enclosed is a sampling of some of our items. Please write to us or call us for our complete catalog available at no charge to the trade. We welcome you to the world of STROM PLUMBING.

SIGN OF THE CRAB, LTD.
3756 OMEC CIRCLE, DEPT. 214
RANCHO CORDOVA
CALIFORNIA 95742

TELEPHONE: (916) 638-2722
FAX: (916) 638-2725

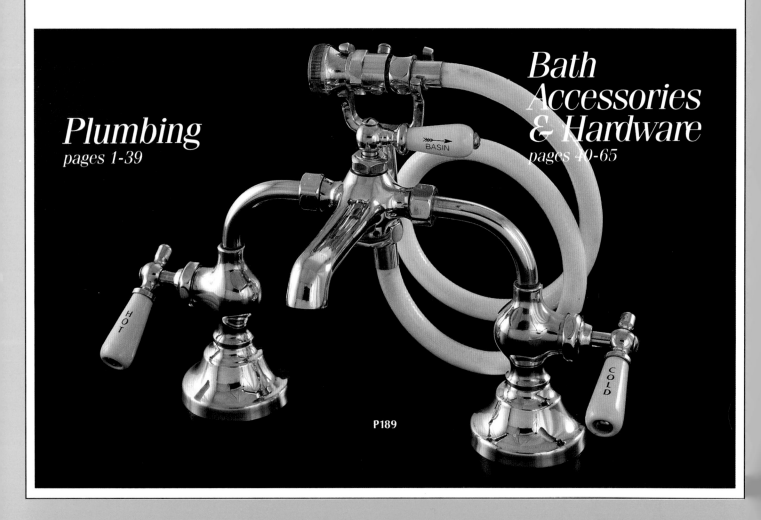

Plumbing
pages 1-39

Bath Accessories & Hardware
pages 40-65

P189

This redesigned P06, the Triumph, is our newest manufacturing breakthrough. It features solid brass components for lasting durability, replaceable seats and the highest quality valve in our industry.

Each of our faucets is solid brass, skillfully manufactured and 100% tested before it leaves our factory. With the optional "supercoat" protected finish, these faucets can be as care-free as any lifestyle, yet have the solid brass durability of the classics.

This deck mounted P341 faucet, a version of our P146, is especially designed for Roman Tubs with the convenience of a hand-held shower.

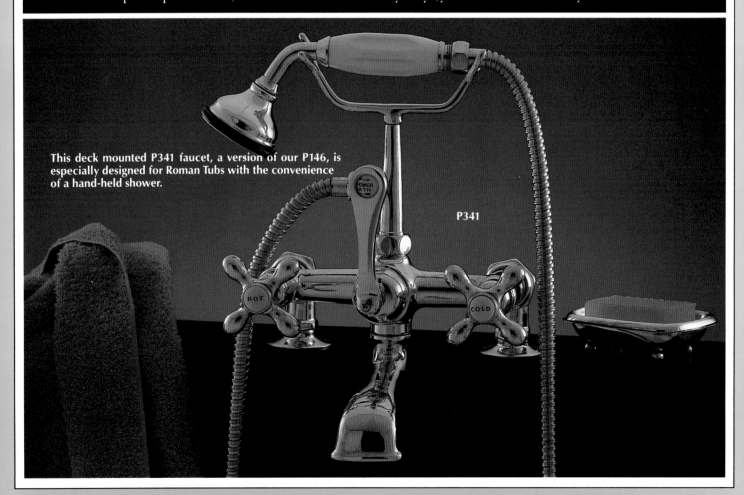

P341

P87

**P08-1
C CLAMP
ONLY**

**EXTRA BRACES
INCLUDE
C CLAMP,
BRACE &
ESCUTCHEON
P0008-12
P0008-24
P0008-36
P0008-48**

P51

GB215

P147

**P34
Shower Enclosure**

**P34P
Shower Enclosure
With P51 Porcelain
Shower Head**

P34 LEG TUB SHOWER ENCLOSURE SET, includes P06 LEG TUB FAUCET WITH DIVERTER, porcelain handles marked "Hot," "Cold" and "Shower," 3⅜" centers, P08 SHOWER ENCLOSURE WITH ADJUSTABLE CEILING 36" AND WALL 12" BRACES, ⅝" (1/4" IPS) heavy gauge polished brass tubing, 45" lgt. 25" wd., P09 SHOWER RISER (2 piece), ⅜" brass pipe size, 5' total hgt., 9"

extension with adapter includes fitting ½" pipe size shower head, P10 SHOWER HEAD, polished brass, 4⅞" dia., items may be purchased separately. Porcelain shower head available at additional cost, see price list for details.

P34P LEG TUB ENCLOSURE SET, same as P34, but with P51 porcelain shower head instead of P10.

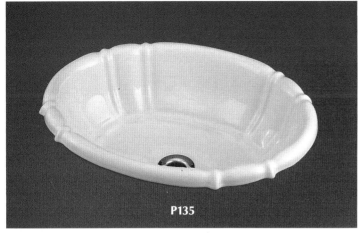

P135

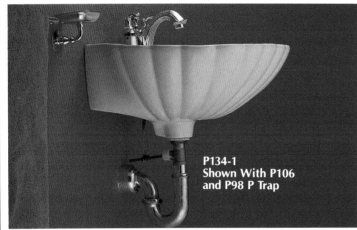

P134-1
Shown With P106
and P98 P Trap

P150
SHOWN WITH P103

P134
Shown With P103

P104
P54
P53
P64
Installed On
Pedestal Sink
P81

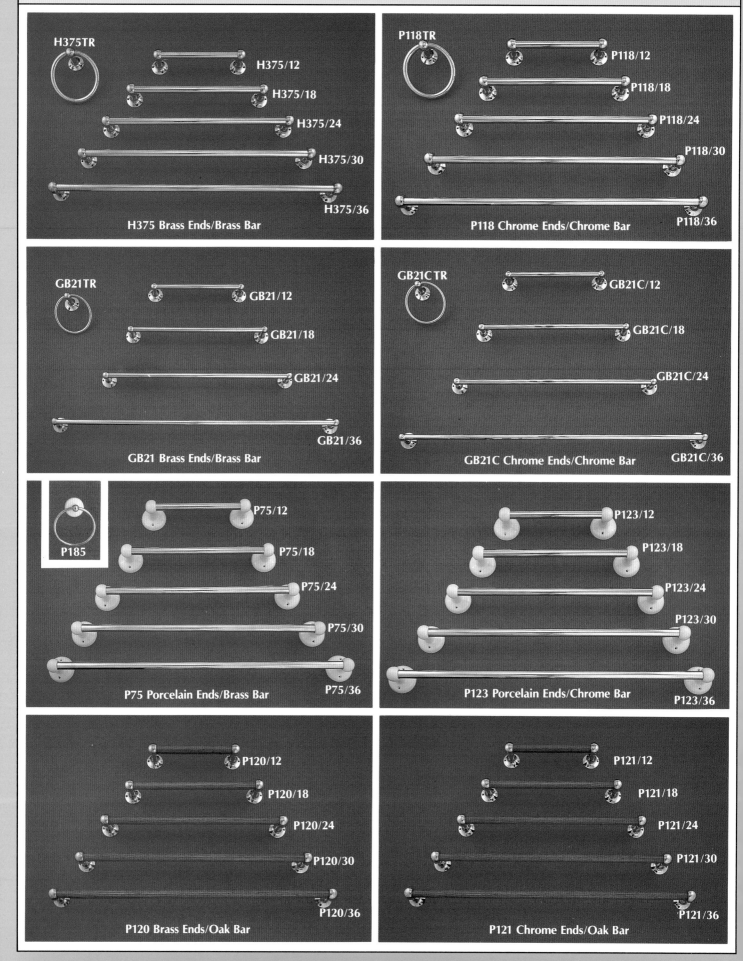

H375TR

H375/12
H375/18
H375/24
H375/30
H375/36

H375 Brass Ends/Brass Bar

P118TR

P118/12
P118/18
P118/24
P118/30
P118/36

P118 Chrome Ends/Chrome Bar

GB21TR

GB21/12
GB21/18
GB21/24
GB21/36

GB21 Brass Ends/Brass Bar

GB21C TR

GB21C/12
GB21C/18
GB21C/24
GB21C/36

GB21C Chrome Ends/Chrome Bar

P185

P75/12
P75/18
P75/24
P75/30
P75/36

P75 Porcelain Ends/Brass Bar

P123/12
P123/18
P123/24
P123/30
P123/36

P123 Porcelain Ends/Chrome Bar

P120/12
P120/18
P120/24
P120/30
P120/36

P120 Brass Ends/Oak Bar

P121/12
P121/18
P121/24
P121/30
P121/36

P121 Chrome Ends/Oak Bar

P368

P369

P370

P371

P333

P372

P333

P373

P374

P375

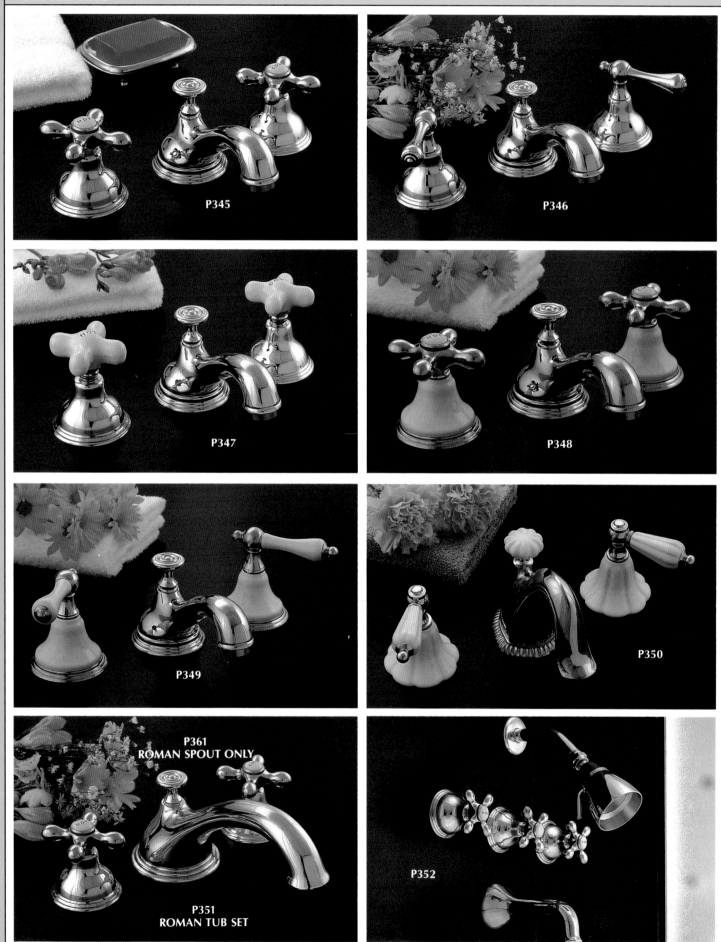

P345

P346

P347

P348

P349

P350

P361
ROMAN SPOUT ONLY

P351
ROMAN TUB SET

P352

Tri-View Medicine Cabinets with Light

MODEL LC-F3630SM-W SHOWN

These superbly crafted medicine cabinets are fabricated of heavy 20 gauge prime cold rolled steel. They are fabricated for <u>SURFACE</u> mounting. The tri-view doors are mounted with completely invisible European-style cabinet hinges. The cabinet body and doors are bonderized after forming to resist rust, spray painted with our special white color enamel paint, then baked at high temperature for durability.

Mirrors are ³/₁₆" first quality plate glass and are available in FRAMELESS POLISHED edge or FRAMELESS BEVELED edge. Doors can be completely frameless or have bright stainless steel trim at the top & bottom.

Integral light fixture is bright chrome plated and accepts standard G25 base bulbs. The fixture is four (4") high and one (1") deep and the face of the fixture is flush with the face of the mirrored doors. The chrome light socket base projects and additional one (1") in front of the mirrors. Optional brass light fixture is also available substitute "LB" instead of "LC" at the beginning of the part number.

Overall Size w x h	Mirrored Area Size w x h	Polished Stainless Steel Trim	Frameless Polished Edges	Frameless Beveled Edges	Fixed Metal Shelves	Number Of Bulbs
24" x 28"	24" x 24"	LC-S2424SM-W	LC-F2424SM-W	LC-BV2424SM-W	2	4
24" X 34"	24" X 30"	LC-S2430SM-W	LC-F2430SM-W	LC-BV2430SM-W	3	4
30" X 28"	30" X 24"	LC-S3024SM-W	LC-F3024SM-W	LC-BV3024SM-W	2	5
30" X 34"	30" X 30"	LC-S3030SM-W	LC-F3030SM-W	LC-BV3030SM-W	3	5
36" X 34"	36" X 30"	LC-S3630SM-W	LC-F3630SM-W	LC-BV3630SM-W	3	5
36" X 40"	36" X 36"	LC-S3636SM-W	LC-F3636SM-W	LC-BV3636SM-W	4	5
48" X 34"	48" X 30"	LC-S4830SM-W	LC-F4830SM-W	LC-BV4830SM-W	3	6
48" X 40"	48" X 36"	LC-S4836SM-W	LC-F4836SM-W	LC-BV4836SM-W	4	6
54" X 40"	54" X 36"	LC-S5436SM-W	LC-F5436SM-W	LC-BV5436SM-W	4	6
60" X 40"	60" X 36"	LC-S6036SM-W	LC-F6036SM-W	LC-BV6036SM-W	4	8
72" X 40"*	72" X 36"	LC-S7236SM-W	LC-F7236SM-W	LC-BV7236SM-W	4	9

* STANDARD WITH 4 DOORS, 3 DOOR CABINET OPTIONAL

Bi-View Medicine Cabinets

These superbly crafted medicine cabinets are fabricated of heavy 20 gauge prime cold rolled steel. They are fabricated for surface mounting.

The bi-view doors are mounted with completely invisible European-style hinges. The cabinet body and doors are bonderized after forming to resist rust, spray painted with our special white enamel paint, then baked at high temperature for durability. Mirrors are ³/₁₆" first quality plate glass and are available in FRAMELESS POLISHED edge or FRAMELESS BEVELED edge. Doors can be completely frameless or have bright stainless steel trim at the top & bottom.

MODEL BV2030DD SHOWN

Width	Size Height	Depth	Polished Stainless Steel Trim	Frameless Polished Edges	Frameless Beveled Edges	Fixed Metal Shelves
24"	24"	5¼"	S2424DD-W	F2424DD-W	BV2424DD-W	2
20"	30"	5¼"	S2030DD-W	F2030DD-W	BV2030DD-W	3
24"	30"	5¼"	S2430DD-W	F2430DD-W	BV2430DD-W	3
24"	36"	5¼"	S2436DD-W	F2436DD-W	BV2436DD-W	4
24"	42"	5¼"	S2442DD-W	F2442DD-W	BV2442DD-W	4

Custom Sizes Available in Quantity

Corner Medicine Cabinet

BODY: 20 gauge prime sheets of cold rolled steel.
FINISH: Bonderized after forming to resist rust and sprayed with a special white color enamel, baked on at a high temperature for durability.
MIRRORS: ³/₁₆" first quality plate glass
SHELVES: Adjustable glass shelves
DOOR STOP: Stop hinge-reversible swing door.
DOOR STYLES:
1. Polished brass frame
2. Polished stainless steel frame
3. Frameless polished edge mirror
4. Beveled frameless polished edge mirror

MODEL CR1436PE SHOWN

Polished Stainless Steel Frame	Polished Brass Frame	Frameless Polished Edge Mirror	Beveled Frameless Polished Edge Mirror	Overall Size W x H	Shelves
CR1430-W	CR1430PB-W	CR1430PE-W	CR1430BV-W	14" X 30"	2
CR1436-W	CR1436PB-W	CR1436PE-W	CR1436BV-W	14" X 36"	3
CR1442-W	CR1442PB-W	CR1442PE-W	CR1442BV-W	14" X 42"	4

SUGGESTED ARRANGEMENT FOR CORNER MEDICINE CABINET

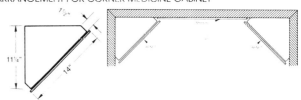

2

Tri-View Medicine Cabinets

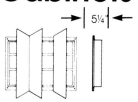

These superbly crafted medicine cabinets are fabricated of heavy 20 gauge prime cold rolled steel. They can be fabricated for both <u>SURFACE</u> and <u>PARTIALLY RECESSED</u> mounting. The tri-view doors are mounted with completely invisible European-style cabinet hinges. The cabinet body and doors are bonderized after forming to resist rust, spray painted with our special white color enamel paint, then baked at high temperature for durability.

Mirrors are ³⁄₁₆" first quality plate glass and are available in FRAMELESS POLISHED edge or FRAMELESS BEVELED edge. Doors can be completely frameless or have bright stainless steel trim at the top & bottom.

Size w x h	Wall Opening w x h	Polished Stainless Steel Trim	Frameless Polished Edges	Frameless Beveled Edges	Fixed Metal Shelves
24" x 24"	23 ¾" x 23 ½"	S2424XX-W	F2424XX-W	BV2424XX-W	2
24" x 30"	23 ¾" x 29 ½"	S2430XX-W	F2430XX-W	BV2430XX-W	3
30" x 24"	29 ¾" x 23 ½"	S3024XX-W	F3024XX-W	BV3024XX-W	2
32" x 24"	30" x 20"	S3224PR-W	F3224PR-W	BV3224PR-W	2
30" x 30"	29 ¾" x 29 ½"	S3030XX-W	F3030XX-W	BV3030XX-W	3
36" x 30"	35 ¾" x 29 ½"	S3630XX-W	F3630XX-W	BV3630XX-W	3
36" x 36"	35 ¾" x 35 ½"	S3636XX-W	F3636XX-W	BV3636XX-W	4
48" x 30"	47 ¾" x 29 ½"	S4830XX-W	F4830XX-W	BV4830XX-W	3
48" x 36"	47 ¾" x 35 ½"	S4836XX-W	F4836XX-W	BV4836XX-W	4
54" x 36"	53 ¾" x 35 ½"	S5436XX-W	F5436XX-W	BV5436XX-W	4
60" x 36"	59 ¾" x 35 ½"	S6036XX-W	F6036XX-W	BV6036XX-W	4
72" x 36"***	71 ¾" x 35 ½"	S7236XX-W	F7236XX-W	BV7236XX-W	4

MODEL BV3630SM-W WITH LS-36 LIGHT FIXTURE SHOWN

"XX" SUBSTITUTE "SM" FOR SURFACE MOUNTED OPTION OR "PR" FOR PARTIALLY RECESSED OPTION. ALL PARTIALLY RECESSED CABINETS REQUIRE A WALL DEPTH OF 3".
**STANDARD WITH 4 DOORS, 3 DOOR CABINET OPTIONAL.

Optional side mirror kits are available for surface mounted tri-views. Mirrors are ⅛" plate mirror, polished on all sides.

<u>TRI-VIEW HEIGHT</u>	<u>MIRROR KIT MODEL NO.</u>
24"	MKTV-24
30"	MKTV-30
36"	MKTV-36

Fully Recessed Tri-View Medicine Cabinets

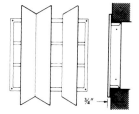

This tri-view cabinet is a <u>FULLY RECESSED</u> medicine cabinet which when mounted only protrudes from the wall a total of ¾". The doors are mounted with completely invisible European-style hinges which allows the door to sit flush against the wall. The body is heavy 20 gauge prime cold rolled steel bonderized to resist rust, sprayed with a special white color enamel then baked at high temperature for durability. Mirrors are ³⁄₁₆" first quality plate glass and are available in FRAMELESS POLISHED edge or FRAMELESS BEVELED edge. Doors can be completely frameless or have bright stainless steel trim at the top & bottom.

Size w x h	Wall Opening w x h	Polished Stainless Steel Trim	Frameless Polished Edges	Frameless Beveled Edges	Fixed Metal Shelves	Optional Adjustable Glass Shelves
24" x 24"	21 ¾" x 22"	S2424FR-W	F2424FR-W	BV2424FR-W	2	2
24" x 30"	21 ¾" x 28"	S2430FR-W	F2430FR-W	BV2430FR-W	3	3
24" x 36"	21 ¾" x 34"	S2436FR-W	F2436FR-W	BV2436FR-W	4	4
30" x 24"	27 ¾" x 22"	S3024FR-W	F3024FR-W	BV3024FR-W	2	2
30" x 30"	27 ¾" x 28"	S3030FR-W	F3030FR-W	BV3030FR-W	3	3
36" x 30"	33 ¾" x 28"	S3630FR-W	F3630FR-W	BV3630FR-W	3	3
36" x 36"	33 ¾" x 34"	S3636FR-W	F3636FR-W	BV3636FR-W	4	4
48" x 30"	45 ¾" x 28"	S4830FR-W	F4830FR-W	BV4830FR-W	3	N/A
48" x 36"	45 ¾" x 34"	S4836FR-W	F4836FR-W	BV4836FR-W	4	N/A
54" x 36"	51 ¾" x 34"	S5436FR-W	F5436FR-W	BV5436FR-W	4	N/A
60" x 36"	57 ¾" x 34"	S6036FR-W	F6036FR-W	BV6036FR-W	4	N/A
72" x 36"***	69 ¾" x 34"	S7236FR-W	F7236FR-W	BV7236FR-W	4	N/A

MODEL S3630FR-W WITH G25B436 LIGHT SHOWN

Custom Sizes Available

ALL CABINETS REQUIRE A WALL DEPTH OF 3 ¼"

**Standard with 4 Doors, 3 Doors Cabinet Optional

Slim Line Surface Mounted With Light

This elegant medicine cabinet is fabricated with a very slim profile and projects only 3-1/2" from the wall. The cabinet is equipped with an integral beveled mirror light fixture with four candelabra base (G16) bulb sockets.

The body is heavy 20 gauge prime cold rolled steel bonderized to resist rust, sprayed with our special white enamel paint then baked at high temperature. Mirrors are first quality 3/16" plate glass with a 1/2" bevel around the perimeter of the mirror. Mirrors on sides of cabinet are 1/8" plate with polished edges on all sides.

The cabinet door is equipped with a spring-loaded touch latch and is hung on completely invisible European-Style hinges.

Model No.	Size
LM423BV-W	16"w x 26⅛"h
LM425BV-W	16"w x 30⅛"h
LM426BV-W	16"w x 34⅛"h
LM427BV-W	18"w x 28⅛"h
LM428BV-W	18"w x 34⅛"h
LM429BV-W	16"w x 40⅛"h
LM431BV-W	18"w x 40⅛"h

Slim Line Surface Mounted Medicine Cabinets

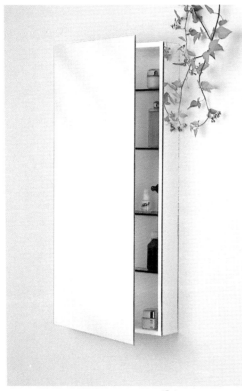

The new Slim Line surface mounted medicine cabinets are a very slim profile wall mounted cabinet that projects <u>only 3 1/2"</u>. The cabinets are available with mirrored sides or with our traditional luxurious painted enamel sides. The cabinet door is equipped with a spring-loaded touch latch and is hung on completely invisible European-Style hinges.
The body is heavy 20 gauge prime cold rolled steel bonderized to resist rust, sprayed with our special white enamel then baked at high temperature for durability. Mirrors are first quality 3/16" plate glass and are available in four different door styles. Mirrors on sides of cabinet are first quality 1/8" plate with polished edges on all sides. See additional door styles on page 7.

Polished Stainless Steel Frame	Polished Brass Frame	Frameless Polished Edge Mirror	Beveled Frameless Polished Edge Mirror	Overall Size w x h	Glass Shelves
WM321-W	WM321PB-W	WM321PE-W	WM321BV-W	13½" X 36"	3
WM323-W	WM323PB-W	WM323PE-W	WM323BV-W	16" X 22"	2
WM325-W	WM325PB-W	WM325PE-W	WM325BV-W	16" X 26"	3
WM326-W	WM326PB-W	WM326PE-W	WM326BV-W	16" X 30"	3
WM327-W	WM327PB-W	WM327PE-W	WM327BV-W	18" X 24"	3
WM329-W	WM329PB-W	WM329PE-W	WM329BV-W	16" X 36"	4
WM331-W	WM331PB-W	WM331PE-W	WM331BV-W	18" X 36"	4
WM333-W	WM333PB-W	WM333PE-W	WM333BV-W	18" X 42"	5

MODEL NUMBERS ABOVE ARE FOR CABINET WITH PAINTED ENAMEL SIDES. ADD "MS" TO THE ABOVE MODEL NUMBERS FOR CABINETS WITH MIRRORED SIDES.

MODEL WM331PE-W-MS SHOWN

AVAILABLE WITHOUT MIRRORED SIDES -
SEE TABLE AT RIGHT

Slim Line Recessed Medicine Cabinets

SLIM LINE medicine cabinets are the ideal cabinets for use in conjunction with wall mirrors or for side wall mounting where the side is exposed on entry to the bathroom. The SLIM LINE cabinet only protrudes from the wall 5/16", eliminating unsightly gaps between cabinet and wall mirror.

The cabinet door is equipped with a spring-loaded magnetic catch. Press gently and the catch releases opening the door. Close the door and the magnet holds it securely. The door is mounted with completely invisible European-style hinges which allow the door to sit flush against the wall.

The body is heavy 20 gauge prime cold rolled steel bonderized to resist rust, sprayed with our special white enamel then baked at high temperature for durability.

Mirrors are 3/16" first quality plate glass. See additional door styles on page 7.

Polished Stainless Steel Frame	Polished Edge Mirror	Beveled Edge Mirror	Wall Opening w x h x d	Overall Size w x h	Glass Shelves
FM321-W	FM321PE-W	FM321BV-W	12⅜ x 34¼ x 3¼	13½ x 36	3
FM323-W	FM323PE-W	FM323BV-W	14⅞ x 20¼ x 3¼	16 x 22	2
FM325-W	FM325PE-W	FM325BV-W	14⅞ x 24¼ x 3¼	16 x 26	3
FM326-W	FM326PE-W	FM326BV-W	14⅞ x 28¼ x 3¼	16 x 30	3
FM327-W	FM327PE-W	FM327BV-W	16⅞ x 22¼ x 3¼	18 x 24	3
FM329-W	FM329PE-W	FM329BV-W	14⅞ x 34¼ x 3¼	16 x 36	4
FM331-W	FM331PE-W	FM331BV-W	16⅞ x 34¼ x 3¼	18 x 36	4
FM333-W	FM333PE-W	FM333BV-W	16⅞ x 40¼ x 3¼	18 x 42	5

Suggested Arrangements for Slim Line Medicine Cabinets

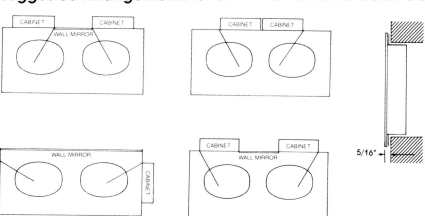

Slim Line Semi-Recessed Series Medicine Cabinets

The SR Series by BASCO is designed for recessing in very shallow walls. The cabinet only recesses into the wall 2" yet provides a fully 3" of storage depth.

The cabinet door is equipped with a magnetic touch latch and invisible European-style hinges. The body is heavy 20 gauge prime cold rolled steel bonderized to resist rust, spray painted with our special white enamel than baked at high temperature.

Mirrors are 3/16" first quality plate glass. See additional door styles on page 7.

Polished Stainless Steel Frame	Polished Brass Frame	Frameless Polished Edge Mirror	Beveled Frameless Polished Edge Mirror	Wall Opening W x H x D	Overall Size W x H	Glass Shelves
SR321-W	SR321PB-W	SR321PE-W	SR321BV-W	12⅜" x 34¼" x 2	13½" x 36"	3
SR323-W	SR323PB-W	SR323PE-W	SR323BV-W	14⅞" x 20¼" x 2	16" x 22"	2
SR325-W	SR325PB-W	SR325PE-W	SR325BV-W	14⅞" x 24¼" x 2	16" x 26"	3
SR326-W	SR326PB-W	SR326PE-W	SR326BV-W	14⅞" x 28¼" x 2	16" x 30"	3
SR327-W	SR327PB-W	SR327PE-W	SR327BV-W	16⅞" x 22¼" x 2	18" x 24"	3
SR329-W	SR329PB-W	SR329PE-W	SR329BV-W	14⅞" x 34¼" x 2	16" x 36"	4
SR331-W	SR331PB-W	SR331PE-W	SR331BV-W	16⅞" x 34¼" x 2	18" x 36"	4
SR333-W	SR333PB-W	SR333PE-W	SR333BV-W	16⅞" x 40¼" x 2	18" x 42"	5

MODEL SR321PE-W SHOWN · REQUIRES ONLY 2" WALL DEPTH

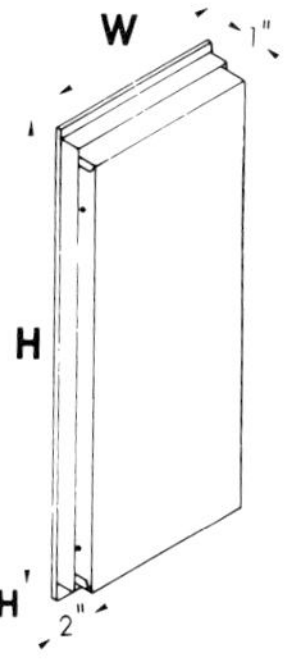

Stainless Steel Framed Medicine Cabinets

MODEL 378P-W SHOWN

BODY: Heavy 20 gauge prime sheets of cold rolled steel.
FINISH: Bonderized after forming to resist rust and sprayed with a special white color enamel, baked on at a high temperature for durability.
MIRRORS: First quality plate glass, with two coats of silver, then electrolytically copper clad as defined in U.S. Commercial Standard CS-27-36. Warranteed for 5 years against silvering defects.
SHELVES: Glass, adjustable ¼" thick with polished front edge.
DOOR STOP: Stop hinge-reversible swing door.

Recessed Model No.	Surface Model No.	Mirror Type	Wall Opening w x h x d	Overall w x h	Glass Shelves
360-W	SM360-W	⅛" Plate	12" x 18" x 3"	14⅛" x 20¼"	2
370-W	SM370-W	⅛" Plate	10" x 34" x 3"	12⅛" x 36¼"	4
371-W	SM371-W	⅛" Plate	14" x 18" x 3"	16⅛" x 22¼"	2
372P-W	SM372P-W	³⁄₁₆" Plate	14" x 20" x 3"	16⅛" x 22¼"	2
374P-W	SM374P-W	³⁄₁₆" Plate	16" x 22" x 3"	18⅛" x 24¼"	3
375P-W	SM375P-W	³⁄₁₆" Plate	14" x 24" x 3"	16⅛" x 26¼"	3
376P-W	SM376P-W	³⁄₁₆" Plate	18" x 24" x 3"	20⅛" x 26¼"	3
377P-W	SM377P-W	³⁄₁₆" Plate	14" x 34" x 3"	16⅛" x 36¼"	4
378P-W	SM378P-W	³⁄₁₆" Plate	16" x 34" x 3"	18⅛" x 36¼"	4
379P-W	SM379P-W	³⁄₁₆" Plate	16" x 40" x 3"	18⅛" x 42¼"	4
380P-W	SM380P-W	³⁄₁₆" Plate	16" x 58" x 3"	18⅛" x 60¼"	5
390P-W	SM390P-W	³⁄₁₆" Plate	22" x 28" x 3"	24⅛" x 30¼"	4
392P-W	SM392P-W	³⁄₁₆" Plate	22" x 34" x 3"	24⅛" x 36¼"	4

SURFACE CABINETS PROJECT 5" FROM WALL.
Custom Sizes Available in Quantity

**POLISHED BRASS FRAMES ARE AVAILABLE
ADD PREFIX "PB" TO ABOVE MODEL NUMBERS.**

Polished Edge And Beveled Edge Mirror Cabinet

MODEL BV378P-W SHOWN

BODY: Heavy 20 gauge prime sheets of cold rolled steel.
FINISH: Bonderized after forming to resist rust and sprayed with a special white color enamel, baked on at a high temperature for durability.
MIRRORS: First quality ³⁄₁₆" plate glass, with two coats of silver, then electrolytically copper clad as defined in U.S. Commercial Standard CS-27-36. Warranteed for 5 years against silvering defects. Edges polished or polished with ½" bevel.
SHELVES: Glass, adjustable ¼" thick with polished front edge.
DOOR STOP: Stop hinge-reversible swing door.

Beveled Edge Model No.	Polished Edge Model No.	Wall Opening w x h x d	Overall Size w x h	Glass Shelves
BV370P-W	PE370P-W	10" x 34" x 3"	12" x 36"	4
BV371P-W	PE371P-W	14" X 18" X 3"	16" X 22"	2
BV372P-W	PE372P-W	14" X 20" X 3"	16" X 22"	2
BV374P-W	PE374P-W	16" X 22" X 3"	18" X 24"	3
BV375P-W	PE375P-W	14" X 24" X 3"	16" X 26"	3
BV376P-W	PE376P-W	18" X 24" X 3"	20" X 26"	3
BV377P-W	PE377P-W	14" X 34" X 3"	16" X 36"	4
BV378P-W	PE378P-W	16" X 34" X 3"	18" X 36"	4
BV379P-W	PE379P-W	16" X 40" X 3"	18" X 42"	4
BV380P-W	PE380P-W	16" X 58" X 3"	18" X 60"	5
BV390P-W	PE390P-W	22" X 28" X 3"	24" X 30"	4
BV392P-W	PE392P-W	22" X 34" X 3"	24" X 36"	4

ALSO AVAILABLE SURFACE MOUNTED, SPECIFY PREFIX "SM". SURFACE CABINETS PROJECT 5" FROM WALL.
Custom Sizes Available in Quantity

Medi-Lock Box

Securely stores medicines and personal items under lock and key. Installs into any BASCO medicine cabinet 14" or wider.

Fabricated of 20 gauge steel and finished in our special baked white enamel. Equipped with a tumbler lock and furnished with two keys.

MODEL MLB-4	**SIZE:**	13"w x 5"h x 4"d
MODEL MLB-3	**SIZE:**	13"w x 5"h x 3"d

Light Fixture With Bright Chrome or Polished Brass Finish

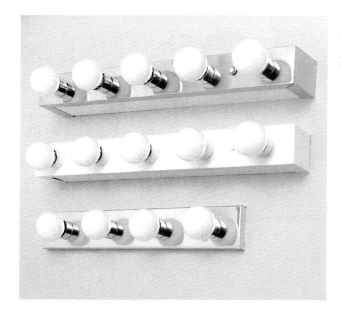

Basco's lighting fixtures are fabricated entirely of 20 gauge steel, chrome plated steel or brass plated steel. Heavy duty construction ensures durability and safety. All fixtures are U.L. approved. All fixtures use G25 lamps (Not Included). Optional convenience outlets available add suffix - CO to part numbers listed below.

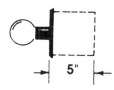

Length	Bright Chrome Model	Polished Brass Model	Size	Number of Bulbs
18"	LS-18	LS-18PB	3½" x 18" x 5" deep	3
24"	LS-24	LS-24PB	3½" x 24" x 5" deep	4
30"	LS-30	LS-30PB	3½" x 30" x 5" deep	5
36"	LS-36	LS-36PB	3½" x 36" x 5" deep	5
48"	LS-48	LS-48PB	3½" x 48" x 5" deep	6
60"	LS-60	LS-60PB	3½" x 60" x 5" deep	8
72"	LS-72	LS-72PB	3½" x 72" x 5" deep	9

Custom Sizes Available

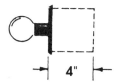

Length	Bright Chrome Model	Polished Brass Model	Size	Number of Bulbs
13"	G25B413	G25B413PB	4" x 13" x 1" deep	2
16"	G25B416	G25B416PB	4" x 16" x 1" deep	3
18"	G25B418	G25B418PB	4" x 18" x 1" deep	3
20"	G25B420	G25B420PB	4" x 20" x 1" deep	4
24"	G25B424	G25B424PB	4" x 24" x 1" deep	4
30"	G25B430	G25B430PB	4" x 30" x 1" deep	5
36"	G25B436	G25B436PB	4" x 36" x 1" deep	5
48"	G25B448	G25B448PB	4" x 48" x 1" deep	6
60"	G25B460	G25B460PB	4" x 60" x 1" deep	8
72"	G25B472	G25B472PB	4" x 72" x 1" deep	9

Custom Sizes Available

Length	White Enamel Model	Size	Number of Bulbs
16"	L4W-16	3½" x 16" x 4" deep	3
18"	L4W-18	3½" x 18" x 4" deep	3
24"	L4W-24	3½" x 24" x 4" deep	4
30"	L4W-30	3½" x 30" x 4" deep	5
36"	L4W-36	3½" x 36" x 4" deep	5
48"	L4W-48	3½" x 48" x 4" deep	6
60"	L4W-60	3½" x 60" x 4" deep	8
72"	L4W-72	3½" x 72" x 4" deep	9

Basco Door Styles

The six basic door styles listed are available on all BASCO swing door medicine cabinets.

Many combinations are pictured in our catalog matching various door styles with different size cabinets and body styles.
Since we are a custom medicine cabinet manufacturer we can fabricate any combination of door style with any body style or size.

Your inquiries regarding custom combinations or custom sizes are welcomed.

DOOR STYLES:

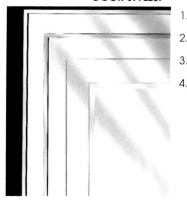

1.
2.
3.
4.

1. Polished brass frame
2. Polished stainless steel frame
3. Frameless polished edge mirror
4. Beveled frameless polished edge mirror
5. Plastic laminated door add "PL" to any Basco part number. PL door is fabricated of ½" thick medium density partical board finished with white melamine on the interior side. The front and edges are finished in Wilsonart Mica.
   Standard color is Wilsonart Frosty White Matte #1573. Other Wilsonart colors are available as selected by architect. (not shown)
6. Solid wood door with high quality unfinished birch veneer on the front and edges. Interior side of door is finished in white mica. Add "WD" to any Basco part number.

DOOR STYLE #6

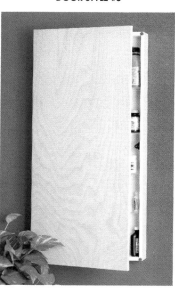

WM331WD-W SHOWN

7

Fixed Tilting Mirror

FIXED TILTING MIRROR

Basco's new design of fixed tilting mirror attempts to take the institutional look out of accessories for the handicapped. Mirrors are fabricated out of heavy 20 gauge prime cold rolled steel and painted a very appealing white enamel. Mirrors are 3/16" first quality plate mirror and are reinforced with a shock absorbing filler and a 20 gauge steel back. Mirrors project 4" from the wall at the top and 1" at the bottom. Mirrors are mounted on a concealed wall hanger fabricated of 20 gauge galvanized steel. Basco's L4W series light fixtures are especially made 4" deep to compliment the tilting mirrors and are also painted white to match the mirror.

Mirror	Size	Matching Light	Size	Bulbs
HTM-16x30-W	16" x 30"	L4W-16	16"w x 3½"h x 4"d	3
HTM-18x24-W	18" x 24"	L4W-18	18"w x 3½"h x 4"d	3
HTM-18x30-W	18" x 30"	L4W-18	18"w x 3½"h x 4"d	3
HTM-24x30-W	24" x 30"	L4W-24	24"w x 3½"h x 4"d	4
HTM-30x24-W	30" x 24"	L4W-30	30"w x 3½"h x 4"d	5
HTM-36x30-W	36" x 30"	L4W-36	36"w x 3½"h x 4"d	5
HTM-48x24-W	48" x 24"	L4W-48	48"w x 3½"h x 4"d	6
HTM-48x30-W	48" x 30"	L4W-48	48"w x 3½"h x 4"d	6

Other sizes available in quantity.

Medicine Cabinet With Tilting Mirror

This quality medicine cabinet is designed for the use by handicapped persons. The medicine cabinet mirror may be used in the upright position or tilted down to accommodate a seated person. The cabinet door is equipped with a latch to keep the door closed when mirror is tilted down. The tilted mirror is secured by an elbow hinge and a stainless steel piano hinge at the bottom.

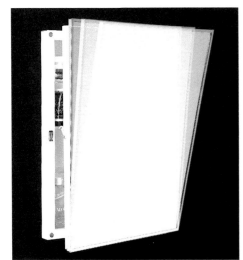

BODY: 20 gauge prime sheets of cold rolled steel.
FINISH: Bonderized after forming to resist rust and sprayed with a special white enamel, baked on a high temperature for durability.
MIRRORS: First quality plate glass, with two coats of silver, then electrolytically copper clad as defined in U.S. Commercial Standard CS-27-36. Warranteed for 5 years against silvering defects.
FRAME: Stainless steel.
SHELVES: Glass, adjustable.
DOOR STOP: Stop hinge.

Model No.	Wall Opening	Overall Size	Glass Shelves
372P-ATM - W	14" x 20" x 3"	16⅛" x 22¼"	2
SM372P-ATM - W	SURFACED MTD.	16⅛" X 22¼" X 5¾"	2
374P-ATM - W	16" x 22" x 3"	18⅛" x 24¼"	3
SM374P-ATM - W	SURFACED MTD.	18⅛" X 24¼" X 5¾"	3
375P-ATM - W	14" x 24" x 3"	16⅛" x 26¼"	3
SM375P-ATM - W	SURFACED MTD.	16⅛" X 26¼" X 5¾"	3

Other sizes available in quantity.

Surface Mount/Top Light

BODY: 20 gauge prime sheets of cold rolled steel.
FINISH: Bonderized after forming to resist rust and sprayed with a special white enamel, baked on a high temperature for durability.
MIRRORS: First quality plate glass, with two coats of silver, then electrolytically copper clad as defined in U.S. Commercial Standard CS-27-36. Warranteed for 5 years against silvering defects.
FRAME: Stainless steel.
SHELVES: Glass, adjustable.
DOOR STOP: Stop hinge.

Model No.	Overall Size	Mirror Size	Light
TL-SM-371 - W	16⅛" x 23½" x 7⅜"	16⅛" x 20¼"	(2) 60 watt incandescent bulbs (not included). U.L. approved.

STAINLESS STEEL GRAB BARS

Specifications: All grab bars are fabricated of heavy duty 18 gauge type 304 satin finish stainless steel tubing. Bars are heliarc welded to stainless steel flanges. Bars will withstand a force of 900 lbs. Flanges and cover plates are type 304 stainless steel with a satin finish. All bars have a 1½" wall clearance.

Construction: CONCEALED WITH SNAP-ON FLANGE
14 Gauge mounting flange 3" in diameter with 3 mounting holes.
20 Gauge type 304 stainless steel cover
CONCEALED WITH SET SCREWS
10 Gauge 4" deep 3" diameter flange with a minimum of 3 set screws 13 Gauge concealed mounting plate with 3 slotted mounting holes.
EXPOSED SCREW MOUNTING 10 Gauge mounting flange 3" in diameter with 3 mounting holes.

Optional Finishes: PEENED GRIPPING SURFACE:
ADD SUFFIX "P"
KNURLED GRIPPING SURFACE:
ADD SUFFIX "K"
BRIGHT POLISHED FINISH:
ADD SUFFIX "B"
BRASS WITH POLISHED FINISH:
ADD SUFFIX "BB"
BRASS WITH SATIN FINISH:
ADD SUFFIX "SB"

Specifying Instructions: When specifying grab bars insert the model numbers (SHAPES) into the double zeros at the end of the grab bar series number.

EXAMPLE: An exposed fastened 1½" grab bar 24" long is part number 8414H.

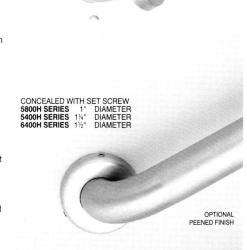

SNAP-ON CONCEALED MOUNTING
5100H SERIES 1" DIAMETER
5200H SERIES 1¼" DIAMETER
6200H SERIES 1½" DIAMETER

CONCEALED WITH SET SCREW
5800H SERIES 1" DIAMETER
5400H SERIES 1¼" DIAMETER
6400H SERIES 1½" DIAMETER

OPTIONAL PEENED FINISH

EXPOSED SCREW MOUNTING
5600H SERIES 1" DIAMETER
5000H SERIES 1¼" DIAMETER
8400H SERIES 1½" DIAMETER

OPTIONAL KNURLED FINISH

STRAIGHT BARS   MODEL   Straight
                11 thru 19   Horizontal
11 Straight horizontal 12"
12 Straight horizontal 16"
13 Straight horizontal 18"
14 Straight horizontal 24"
15 Straight horizontal 30"
16 Straight horizontal 32"
17 Straight horizontal 36"
18 Straight horizontal 42"
19 Straight horizontal 48"

MODEL   Straight with
21 thru 25   Centerpost

21 Horizontal 36" with center support
22 Horizontal 42" with center support
23 Horizontal 48" with center support
24 Horizontal 54" with center support
25 Horizontal 60" with center support

MODEL 26   Toilet Compartment 52"
MODEL 28   Toilet Compartment

MODEL 80
Toilet Straddle

MODEL 84
OR 26 ADJUSTABLE

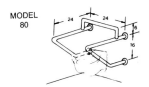

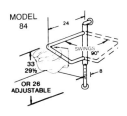

MODEL 51   Wall to Floor

MODEL 52   Wall to Floor (with socket)

LOOSE FLANGE SPECIFY EXTERNAL SLEEVE, IF REQUIRED

MODEL 33
90° Angle 16 x 32
LEFT HAND SHOWN

MODEL 32
90° ANGLE 16 X 32
RIGHT HAND SHOWN

MODEL 42
Shower Bar
RIGHT HAND SHOWN
TWO PIECES, UNLESS OTHERWISE SPECIFIED

LEFT HAND SHOWN
MODEL 57
Wall to Floor with Outrigger

MODEL 75
Wall to Floor Straddle

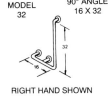

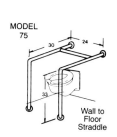

MODEL 92
RIGHT HAND SHOWN
Tub and Shower Bar

MODEL 69
Shower Compartment Bar

MODEL 46
Inside Corner Angle Bar

MODEL 41
Inside Corner Angle Bar

MODEL 44
RIGHT HAND SHOWN
TWO PIECES, UNLESS OTHERWISE SPECIFIED
Tub and Shower Bar

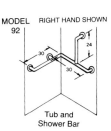
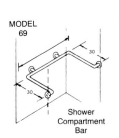
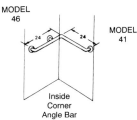
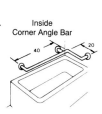

9

Europa Hotel Bath Accessories

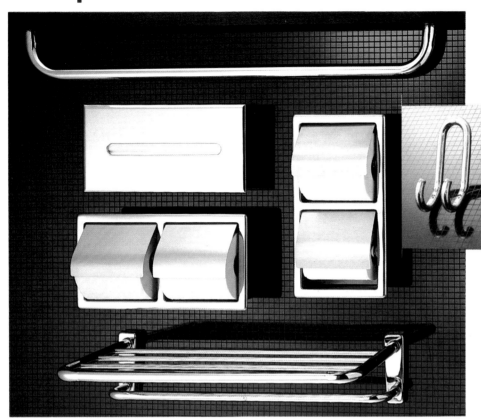

915P Towel Bar
Crafted of 1" diameter seamless 20 gauge type 304 stainless steel tubing polished to a bright finish. Concealed mounting hardware is solid brass. Available in 18", 24", 30", 36", length. (Custom sizes available)

925P Towel Bar
Same as 915P except ¾" diameter.

7925C Recessed Facial Tissue Cabinet
Polished chrome panel with galvanized steel storage box. Overall size: 11¾" x 6". Wall opening required: 10¾" x 5" x 2⅝".

7987P Horizontal Dual Hooded Toilet Paper Holder
Fabricated in one piece of type 304 stainless steel polished to bright finish. Furnished with chrome plated roller. Overall size: 12⅜" x 6½". Wall opening required: 11⅝" x 5¾" x 3".

7988P Vertical Dual Hooded Toilet Paper Holder
Same specifications as Model 7987P. Overall size: 6½" x 12⅜". Wall Opening required: 5¾" x 11⅝" x 3".

1680P Towel Shelf with Towel Bar
Superbly crafted entirely of type 304 stainless steel tubing and then polished to a bright finish. Heavy duty concealed wall brackets are fabricated of 11 gauge (.119) cadmium plated steel. Unique mounting system insures secure attachment to wall.
Sizes:
           18" x 9¼" x 4⅞"
           20¾" x 9¼" x 4⅞"
           24" x 9¼" x 4⅞"

1648P Chrome Robe Hook
Size: 2⅛" x 5½" x 2" Projection

All items available in polished brass finish. Add "PB" in front of part number.

Europa II Stainless Steel Bath Accessories

The Europa II series bath accessories are fabricated of type 304 stainless steel and are available in the following finishes:
Bright Polished - add suffix "P" to part number
Satin finish - add suffix "S" to part number
Bronze finish - add suffix "BZ" to part number
Polished Brass - add suffix "PB" to part number

1614*	Soap Dish and Bar with drain holes
1615*	Soap Dish without drain holes
1616*	Soap Dish with drain holes
1618*	Toothbrush Tumbler Holder
1626*	Shelf 6⅜" deep - available in 18" and 24" lengths
1630*	Toilet Paper Holder - plastic roller
1631*	Toilet Paper Holder - chrome roller
1630D*	Dual Toilet Paper Holder - plastic roller
1631D*	Dual Toilet Paper Holder - chrome roller
1641*	Square Towel Bar ¾" diameter - available in 18", 24", 30" and 36" lengths
1642*	Round Towel Bar ¾" diameter - available in 18", 24", 30", and 36" lengths
1643*	Double Robe Hook 2" projection
1644*	Single Robe Hook 2" projection
1645*	Towel Pin 4¼" long
1646*	Single Robe Hook 4¼" high
1650*	Towel Ring 5" wide x 4½" high
1651*	Towel shelf 8" deep - available in 18" and 24" lengths
1652*	Towel Shelf w/drying rod 8" deep - available in 18" and 24" lengths

*Add finish code "P", "S", "BZ" or "PB"

THE CONCEALED-MOUNTING SYSTEM
Post is welded to mounting bracket and flange to form an integral unit. Post assembly mounts on stainless steel wall plate and is secured with set screw on bottom.

POST ASSEMBLY
WALL PLATE mounts directly to wall
SET SCREW
Flange dimension is 2" x 2"

Contempo Chrome Bath Accessories

• FUNCTIONAL STYLING   • DELUXE EXPOSED SCREW DESIGN

The Contempo Series offers easy installation and modern design. BASCO makes these quality fixtures available to you at a price you're sure to enjoy. These triple chrome plated accessories are made of durable Zamac.

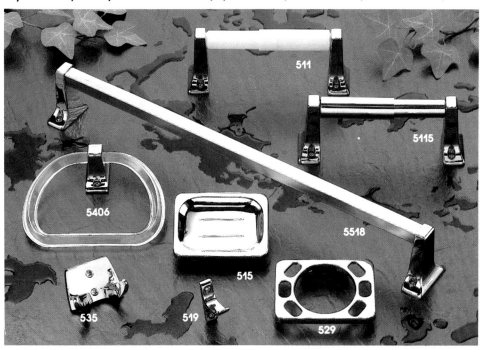

519	Robe Hook
5115	Paper Holder, Chrome Roller
511	Paper Holder, White Roller
535	Double Robe Hook
529	Chrome Toothbrush & Tumbler Holder
515	Chrome Soap Holder
5586	Soap Holder with 8" Grab Bar (not illustrated)
5406	Lucite Towel Ring
5406C	Chrome Towel Ring

⅝" Square Polished Stainless Steel Towel Bar Set

5518	18" Long
5524	24" Long
5530	30" Long
5536	36" Long

⅝" Square Aluminum Bar Towel Bar Set

5518A	18" Long
5524A	24" Long
5530A	30" Long
5536A	36" Long

Basco Shower Rods & Flanges

Shower Rods - Available in 3, 5 & 6 Foot Lengths

MODEL NO.	MATERIAL & FINISH	DIAMETER	WALL THICKNESS
1210	Anodized Aluminum	1"	.022
1210AB	Anodized Alum., Antique Brass	1"	.022
1210PB	Anodized Alum., Polished Brass	1"	.022
1212	Polished Stainless Steel	1"	.015
1213B	Polished Type 304 St. Steel	1"	.035
1213PB	Polished Brass	1"	.042
1214B	Polished Type 304 St. Steel	1"	.049
1215B	Polished Type 304 St. Steel	1¼"	.049
1216B	Polished Type 304 St. Steel	1¼"	.035
1217B	Polished Type 304 St. Steel	1½"	.035
1218B	Polished Type 304 St. Steel	1½"	.049

SHOWER ROD END FLANGES

MODEL NO.	DESCRIPTION	DIAMETER	ILLUSTRATION NO.
1200B	Concealed Screw Stainless Steel	1"	E
1201	Adjustable Chrome Plated Cast Zinc	1"	G
1201AB	Adjustable Antique Brass Cast Zinc	1"	A
1201PB	Adjustable Polished Brass Cast Zinc	1"	(Not Shown)
1202	Extended Exposed Screw Stainless Steel	1"	H
1203	Exposed Screw Chrome Plated Cast Zinc	1"	C
1203PB	Exposed Screw Solid Polished Brass	1"	B
1204B	Exposed Screw Polished Stainless Steel	1"	F
1205B	Exposed Screw Polished Stainless Steel	1¼"	F
1208B	Concealled Screw Chrome Pltd. Brass	1"	I
1209B	Concealled Screw Chrome Pltd. Brass	1¼"	I
1230B	Concealled Screw Stainless Steel	1¼"	E
1235B	Jumbo Exposed Screw Chrome Pltd. Steel	1"	D

Classic Chrome Bath Accessories

Most items available in a polished brass finish. Add prefix "PB" to model number below.

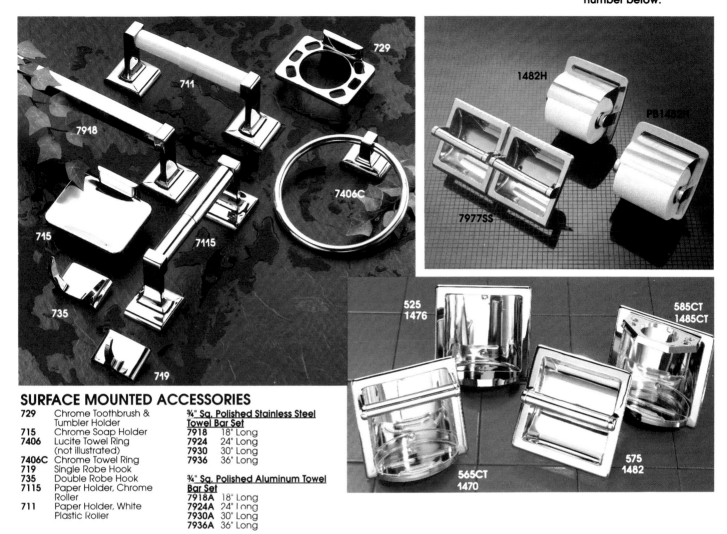

SURFACE MOUNTED ACCESSORIES

729	Chrome Toothbrush & Tumbler Holder	
715	Chrome Soap Holder	
7406	Lucite Towel Ring (not illustrated)	
7406C	Chrome Towel Ring	
719	Single Robe Hook	
735	Double Robe Hook	
7115	Paper Holder, Chrome Roller	
711	Paper Holder, White Plastic Roller	

¾" Sq. Polished Stainless Steel Towel Bar Set

7918	18" Long
7924	24" Long
7930	30" Long
7936	36" Long

¾" Sq. Polished Aluminum Towel Bar Set

7918A	18" Long
7924A	24" Long
7930A	30" Long
7936A	36" Long

BASCO'S very finest concealed screw accessories! The classic design of these chrome fixtures will supply you with a complete range of your bathroom needs. Made of durable Zamac, the quality craftsmanship of the Classic Series is unsurpassed. Available with ¾" square towel bars in stainless steel or aluminum. Our easy-to-install concealed screw fixtures are a must for any modern bathroom.

BASCO'S recessed accessories are crafted of solid brass and are luxuriously triple chrome plated, or made of highly polished stainless steel.

RECESSED MOUNTED ACCESSORIES

Standard Size
Chrome Plated Brass

Overall dimensions 6¼" x 6¼"
Wall Opening 5¼" x 5¼"

525	Soap Holder
565	Soap Holder & Grab Bar
575	Paper Holder with Chrome Roller
576	Paper Holder with Plastic Roller
525CT	Soap Holder with Protective Tray
565CT	Soap Holder & Grab Bar with Protective Tray
585CT	Toothbrush, Tumbler & Soap Holder with Protective Tray
PB1482	Recessed polished brass toilet paper holder. Overall Size: 6¼" x 6¼" Wall Opening: 5¼" x 5¼" x2"
PB1482H	Recessed polished brass toilet paper holder with hood. Overall Size: 6¼" x 6¼" Wall Opening: 5¼" x 5¼" x2"

Standard Size
Polished Stainless Steel

Overall Dimensions 6¼" x 6¼"
Wall Opening 5¼" x 5¼"

1470	Soap Holder and Grab Bar
1476	Soap Holder
1482	Paper Holder with Chrome Roller
1488	Paper Holder with White Plastic Roller
1485CT	Toothbrush, Tumbler & Soap Holder with Protective Tray
1482H	Recessed Polished stainless steel toilet paper holder with hood. Overall Size: 6¼" x 6¼" Wall Opening: 5¼" x 5¼" x 2"
7977SS	Recessed polished stainless steel dual toilet paper holder. Overall Size: 12⅝" x 6¼" Wall Opening: 11½" x 5¼" x 2"

Installation Clamp

For use with screw type recessed fixtures, this handy device simplifies installation by eliminating framework or setting in cement.

630	Installation Clamp with Retainer Spring
630LS	Installation Clamp, less Retainer Spring

Cement and Tile Installation

Add the suffix "L" to any model number. A special lug will be secured to the back of any recessed fixture ordered in this manner, permitting it to be set in cement.

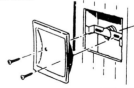

Part No. 630
Optional

40 AERO ROAD, P.O. BOX 237, BOHEMIA, N.Y. 11716
(516) 567-4404 • FAX (516) 567-4815

(Printed in USA)

1993

12

Expressions
By Beneke®

Model 250

Home of Dr. and Mrs. Albert Laws
Columbus, Mississippi

The Bathroom Seat As

Model 6150

Home of Mr. and Mrs. Tom Sneed
Columbus, Mississippi

The bathroom. A key element in contemporary home design. Accentuated with marbleized fixtures or warm country woods, the bath has become a showplace for fixtures, cabinetry, tile and, now, bathroom seats. Expressions by Beneke is a line of exquisitely styled seats crafted to complement the materials

An Element Of Design.

Model 1000/1000E

Home of Mr. and Mrs. James Teel
Columbus, Mississippi

Home of Mr. and Mrs. Bernie Imes, III
Columbus, Mississippi

Model 520

and colors that are part of today's bathroom designs.

Beneath the contemporary style lies traditional Beneke quality. With smooth color, fine woodworking detail, and unique designs, Expressions by Beneke represents the finest in bathroom appointments.

Home of Dr. and Mrs. Albert Laws
Columbus, Mississippi

Model 550

Home of Mr. and Mrs. Tom Whitaker
Columbus, Mississippi

Model 520

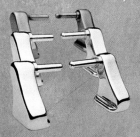

Metal Hinges
These heavy duty hinges offer both elegance and sophistication. Choose from chrome-plated, polished brass, or an antique brass finish. Available with models 6150, 550, 420, and 520. Specify chrome-plated, polished brass, or antique brass.

Model 250
This molded "raised frame cabinet" look provides a traditional approach in decorating today's bath. A perfect accessory for coordinating vanities, cabinetry, and molding. The heavy duty plastic hinge is color matched.

Model 6150
The marbleized seashell is a unique design available in a wide range of colors as a round front model. This seat coordinates with the fashionable china prevalent in luxury bath designs.

Model 1000/1000E
Hand-rubbed Southern oak extends the look of oak cabinetry and vanities. Our special moisture-resistant sealer, metal hinges, and attention to fine woodworking detail create a seat that is durable, long-lasting, and comfortable. We offer seats with golden oak, bleached oak, and weathered oak finishes. All our oak seats are available for round (Model 1000) or elongated bowls (Model 1000E).

Model 420/520 Stone Look
A bold statement in texture, this seat provides new flexibility in working with today's stone look countertops. With a rich, sophisticated look, it fits contemporary designs. Available for regular (Model 420) or elongated bowls (Model 520).

Model 550
Sleek, European styling in the bath. Designed to coordinate with today's marbleized countertops, the 550 creates a bath of drama, distinction, and comfort.

Model 420/520
Today's bathroom is a symphony of color. Now the bathroom seat is in perfect harmony. Available in an array of high fashion and fixture matched colors, this seat is a statement of luxury and sophistication. Available for regular (Model 420) and elongated bowls (Model 520).

*F*or a color reference chart, pricing information and the name of the representative in your area, contact our Customer Service department at 1-800-647-1042.

A division of Sanderson Plumbing Products Inc
P.O. Box 1367
Columbus, Mississippi 39703
(601) 328-4000 FAX: (601) 329-4362
Customer Service FAX: (601) 329-4399

Expressions
By Beneke®

An Element Of Bath Design

Photography by Bernie Imes, III
Columbus, Mississippi

Accessories compliments of
The Bath Station
Columbus, Mississippi

BATH CABINETS & LIGHTING

INCLUDING NEW MODELS

BROAN®

LE BACCARAT
Expressions

Vive Le Baccarat! The "arch de triumph" – a classic masterpiece of refined grace in the French tradition. An arch-top beveled mirror surrounded in clear, smoked or bronze finish frames the clear-mirror swing-door cabinet offered in both recessed and surface mount versions. Matching wall mirrors echo the arched motif and the mosaic beveled glass design.

LBC 10 Cabinet

Model		Overall Size W H D	Wall Opening W H D
RECESSED CABINET			
Clear	**LBC 10**	24x35⅜	16½x25¼x3⅞
Smoked	**LBC 20**	24x35⅜	16½x25¼x3⅞
Bronze	**LBC 30**	24x35⅜	16½x25¼x3⅞
SURFACE MOUNT CABINET			
Clear	**LBC 10SM**	24x35⅜	None
Smoked	**LBC 20SM**	24x35⅜	None
WALL MIRROR ONLY			
Clear	**LBM 15**	24x35⅜	None
Smoked	**LBM 25**	24x35⅜	None
Bronze	**LBM 35**	24x35⅜	None

Expressions OF LUXURY

Like sparkling jewels, our "Expressions" line of luxury cabinets are painstakingly handcrafted of the finest quality materials available, into exquisite designs that set a bold new hallmark of elegance for the bath.

Large, 8" diameter magnifying make-up mirrors may be conveniently mounted at desired height on the inside of any door.

Fully mirrored back walls lend a luxurious touch of elegance to the all stainless steel interiors. 1/4"-thick, smoked glass shelves can be easily adjusted to any desired position.

Fully concealed, 6-way adjustable hinges permit perfect alignment of mirrors and swing open a full 150° on cabinets equipped with magnifying make-up mirrors for convenient viewing. Hinges on models without make up mirrors open 110° for easy cabinet access.

All edges of the distortion-free plate mirrors are either polished or elegantly beveled to a jewel-like finish. Individual, custom construction of heavy-gauge stainless steel ensures a lifetime of use. Cabinets are hand-crafted one at a time, with custom fitting and assembly that produces unique styling for the most elegant homes.

2

These outstanding features are included in all the "Expressions" cabinets, pages 2, 3, 4, & 5.

PRC 2160 Cabinet with PRL 2060 Soffit Light

Our leader in luxury options – a polished-edge, clear mirror tri-view cabinet. Available in recessed or surface mount styles, in two widths, framed on the sides and bottom with a classic-patterned beveled mirror trim in clear or smoked finish. Above, an illuminating choice: a matching soffit light or matching strip light with clear or smoked mirror trim, or perhaps simply a beveled mirror strip to complete the framing. Color-correcting, instant-on fluorescent soffit light fixtures provide accurate daytime make-up lighting, while specular, parabolic light diffusers soften the light for a decidedly elegant atmosphere.

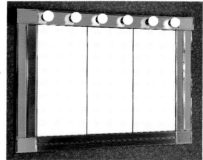

PRC2160 with PRT2060

PRIMEVÉRE
Expressions

	Clear Mirror Model	Smoked Mirror Model No.	Overall Size W H D	Wall Opening W H D	Lights
CABINET					
Recessed Unlighted	**PRC 1048**	**PRC 2048**	48x41	36⅞x32⅞x3⅞	None
	PRC 1060	**PRC 2060**	60x41	48⅞x32⅞x3⅞	None
Recessed Lighted	**PRC 1148**	**PRC 2148**	48x37⅜	36⅞x32⅞x3⅞	Use optional PRL or PRT Series Light
	PRC 1160	**PRC 2160**	60x37⅜	48⅞x32⅞x3⅞	Use optional PRL or PRT Series Light
Surface Unlighted	**PRC 1148SM**	**PRC 2048SM**	48x41	None	None
	PRC 1160SM	**PRC 2060SM**	60x41	None	None
Surface Lighted	**PRC 1148SM**	**PRC 2148SM**	48x37⅜	None	Use optional PRL or PRT Series Light
	PRC 1160SM	**PRC 2160SM**	60x37⅜	None	Use optional PRL or PRT Series Light
Matching Soffit Light	**PRL 1148**	**PRL 2048**	48x4¼x5⅜	None	Fluorescent F40C50 or Equivalent (Included)
	PRL 1160	**PRL 2060**	60x4¼x5⅜	None	Fluorescent F40C50 or Equivalent (Included)
Matching Strip Light	**PRT 1148**	**PRT 2048**	48x4¼x2	None	5 Bulbs up to 40W G25 or G40 (Not Included)
	PRT 1160	**PRT 2060**	60x4¼x2	None	6 Bulbs up to 40W G25 or G40 (Not Included)

CTC 1060 Cabinet with CTL 1060 Soffit LIght

CONTEMPRA
Expressions

A sophisticated sweep of art deco – the clean-lined Contempra, handsomely paired with an elegantly curved, matching soffit light of stainless steel and soft white with acrylic. Available in three widths, the Contempra's ample tri-view cabinet features beveled, clear-mirror doors and side trim. Specular, parabolic light diffusers soften the color-correcting, instant-on fluorescent light, directing it to both mirror and subject.

	Model	Overall Size W H D	Wall Opening W H D	Lights
CABINET	CTC 1036	36x32½	28⅞x30¾x4	Use Optional CTL Series Light
	CTC 1048	48x32½	40⅞x30¾x4	Use Optional CTL Series Light
	CTC 1060	60x32½	52⅞x30¾x4	Use Optional CTL Series Light
MATCHING SOFFIT LIGHT Stainless Steel & Acrylic	CTL 1036	36x8x5	None	Fluorescent F20T12/C50 or Equivalent (Included)
	CTL 1048	48x8x5	None	Fluorescent F40C50 or Equivalent (Included)
	CTL 1060	60x8x5	None	Fluorescent F40C50 or Equivalent (Included)

4

OBSIDIAN
Expressions

Simple elegance in basic black begins with the Obsidian's frameless, polished-edge mirror on a swing-door cabinet. Above, a matching top light pairs sleek stainless steel with crisp black laminate trim. Below, a thoughtful touch – the convenience of a matching black laminate cosmetic shelf. Match the cabinet, top light and/or cosmetic shelf in *single* or *multiple* installations to create modular walls of storage.

	Model	Overall Size W H D	Wall Opening W H D
CABINET	**MRC 110**	16x32⅝	14¼x31⅜x3¾
MODULAR *TOP LIGHT	**MRL 170**	16x7⅛x6	None
MODULAR COSMETIC SHELF	**MRS 170**	16x3¼x4⅝	None

MRC 110 Cabinets (2) with MRL 170 Top Lights (2) and MRS 170 Shelves (2)

LUMINAIRE
Expressions

Timeless texture of classic luxury – the rich, smooth, look and feel of marble-like White Corian®, perfectly accented with a simple mirrored trim. The Luminaire's modular swing-door cabinet,with its frameless, polished-edge mirror, can be matched with the modular quartz halogen top light and cosmetic shelf in single or multiple installations to extend the elegance to any dimension desired.

	Model	Overall Size W H D	Wall Opening W H D
CABINET	**MRC 110**	16x32⅝	14¼x31⅜x3¾
MODULAR *TOP LIGHT	**MRL 160**	16x7⅛x6	None
MODULAR COSMETIC SHELF	**MRS 160**	16x3¼x4⅝	None

*Lights use 2-50 PAR20/CAP/NFL50W

5

MRC 110 Cabinets (3) with MRL 160 Top Lights (3) and MRS 160 Shelves (3)

BROAN JOINS KOHLER COMPANY IN THE EXCITING KOHLER® COLOR COORDINATES™ PROGRAM

Cabinet 350NB(3); Light 745NB(3)

White (WH) — Teal (TL) — Navy Blue (NB) — Country Grey (CG) — Innocent Blush (CB) — Wild Rose (WR) — Mexican Sand (MS) — Raspberry Puree (RP) — Almond (AL) — Heron Blue (LB) — Black/Black (BL) — Tender Grey (TG)

All color names listed are trademarks of Kohler Co.

SPLASH IN THE BATH

Broan and Kohler combine to help you create an exciting color coordinated bathroom. As part of the Kohler Color Coordinates Program, you can match Broan bath cabinets with fixtures from Kohler and products from other Program participants to create a dramatically colorful bathroom environment. Broan color coordinated bathroom cabinets feature baked enamel soft-tone interiors and plate glass mirrors. "Enduro" frame is designed for long life in high moisture atmosphere. Top lights use up to 60W G-25 or G-40 bulbs (bulbs not included).

KOHLER COLOR COORDINATES

SPECTRUM SWING-DOOR CABINETS

Available with 2 adjustable shelves (14x18 wall opening), or 3 adjustable shelves (14x24 wall opening). Full piano hinge. Reversible. 2009 Series is convertible – may be recessed in wall or surface mounted. Includes built-in top light and two fixed shelves. Top light uses up to 60W G-25 or G-40 bulbs (bulbs not included).

SPECTRUM III TRI-VIEW CABINETS

Feature 3 plate glass mirrors for 3-way viewing, 3 storage areas and 2 fixed shelves. Models 3330 and 3336 series with built-in top lights can be recessed or surface mounted. Models 3230 and 3236 cabinets can be recessed or surface mounted. However, models SP132 and SP133 top lights for the 3230 and 3236 cabinets can be surface mounted only.

Cabinet 350TL(3); Light 745TL(3)

Cabinet/Light 2009RP

Cabinet 3336TG

Cabinet 3236CB; Light SP133CB

ORDERING INFORMATION

When ordering bath cabinets and top lights, indicate color by including color code after model number. For example, to order a surface mounted 352 series cabinet in Wild Rose (WR), ask for 352WR.

	Swing-Door Model	Overall Size	Wall Opening
CABINETS			
Recessed	**350 series**	18x27½	14x18x3½
	358 series	18x27½	14x24x3½
Surface	**352 series**	18x27½x5	None
Surface w/Built-in Top Lights:**	**2009 series**	19⅛x32¼x5	16¾x28¾x3½
MIRROR ONLY	**355 series**	18x27½	None
TOP LIGHTS **			
For Recessed	**745 series**	18x6½x3	None
For Surface	**746 series**	18x6½x5½	None

	Tri-View Model	Overall Size	Wall Opening
CABINETS			
Surface w/Built-in Top Light:**	**3330 series**	31x30⅜x5	28¾x27½x3½
	3336 series	37x30⅜x5	34¾x27½x3½
Surface	**3230 series**	30x30x4¼	27½x27x3½
	3236 series	36x30x4¼	33½x27x3½
	3248 series	48x30x4¼	45⅜x26⅞x3½
TOP LIGHTS **	**SP132 series**	30x6½x5¼	
	SP133 series	36x6½x5¼	
	SP134 series	48x6½x5¼	

**Raspberry Puree and Navy top lights on models 745, 746, SP132, SP133, SP134, 2009, 3330, 3336 equipped with gold tone panel. All other lights equipped with bright chrome panel.

7

Cabinet 473248; Light EA54828

EARLY AMERICAN ◤NEW◢

Charming, provincial floral pattern creates new decorating possibilities. Warm tone colors can be used to complement or accent your bathroom decor. Bright brass accent trim. White sides. Tri-view cabinet features 3-way viewing, 2 fixed metal shelves, plate glass mirrors, one touch magnetic catch and baked enamel interiors. Can be recessed or surface mounted. Matching top light features bright brass fittings and face plate insert and uses up to 60W G-25 or G-40 bulbs (bulbs not included).

	Tri-View Model	Overall Size W H D	Wall Opening W H D	Bulb Capacity
CABINET	473230	30x29¾x4	27½x27x3½	
	473236	36x29¾x4	33½x27x3½	
	473248	48x29¾x4	45⅜x27x3½	
TOP LIGHT	EA53028	30x8x9¾	None	3
	EA53628	36x8x9¾	None	4
	EA54828	48x8x9¾	None	5

Reversible swing door cabinet. Adjustable shelves on recessed units, fixed shelves on surface mount. Piano hinge. Magnetic catch. Recessed and surface mounted units available. Can be mounted to open left or right. Other features same as tri-view.

	Swing-Door Model	Overall Size W H D	Wall Opening W H D	Bulb Capacity
CABINET				
Recessed	**4730**	18x27½	14x18x3½	
	4738	18x27½	14x24x3½	
Surface	**4732**	18x27½x5	None	
TOP LIGHT				
For Recessed	**705EA**	18x8x7½	None	2
For Surface	**706EA**	18x8x11	None	2

8

Cabinet 4738 Light 705EA

Cabinet 471236; Light CT53618

Cabinet 4710; Light 705CT

NEW # COUNTRY FLORAL

Tri-view cabinet features innovative new design with light, airy floral pattern. Complements the Kohler Color Coordinates Program. Bright brass accent trim. 3-way viewing. Plate glass mirror doors. 2 fixed metal shelves. Recessed or surface mounted. Soft-tone baked enamel interior. Spring loaded magnetic door catches. Top light features bright brass fitting and clear halothane glass shades. Use 60W medium-based bulbs (bulbs not included).

	Tri-View Model	Overall Size W H D	Wall Opening W H D	Bulb Capacity
CABINET	471230	30x29¾x4	27½x27x3½	
	471236	36x29¾x4	33½x27x3½	
TOP LIGHT	CT53018	30x8x9¾	None	3
	CT53618	36x8x9¾	None	4

Swing door cabinet. Adjustable shelves. Piano hinge. Magnetic catch. Recessed and surface mounted units available. Reversible: can be mounted to open left or right. Other features same as tri-view.

	Swing-Door Model	Overall Size W H D	Wall Opening W H D	Bulb Capacity
CABINET				
Recessed	**4710**	18x27½	14x18x3½	
	4718	18x27½	14x24x3½	
Surface	**4712**	18x27½x5	None	
TOP LIGHT				
For Recessed	**705CT**	18x8x7½	None	2
For Surface	**706CT**	18x8x11	None	2

MAXIM

NEW

Classic formal design featuring an inlay of polished black marble-stone with bright brass trim. Tri-view cabinet features 3-way viewing, 2 fixed metal shelves, plate glass mirrors, one-touch magnetic door catches, and soft-tone baked enamel interiors. Can be recessed or surface mounted. Brass tone side panels. Matching top lights feature bright brass fittings and clear prismatic glass shades. Uses maximum 60W medium-based bulbs (bulbs not included).

	Tri-View Model	Overall Size W H D	Wall Opening W H D	Bulb Capacity
CABINET	666230	30x29¾x5½	27½x27x3½	
	666236	36x29¾x5½	33½x27x3½	
TOP LIGHT	BM63018	30x7¼x11½	None	4
	BM63618	36x7¼x11½	None	5

Swing-door cabinet. Piano hinge. Magnetic catch. Recessed and surface mounted units available. Reversible: can be mounted to open left or right. Other features same as tri-view.

	Swing-Door Model	Overall Size W H D	Wall Opening W H D	Bulb Capacity
CABINET				
Recessed	660BC	18x27½	14 x 18 x 3½	
	668BC	18x27½	14 x 24 x 3½	
Surface	662BC	18x27½x5	None	
TOP LIGHT				
For Recessed	76668	18x7¼x9¼	None	2
For Surface	76768	18x7¼x12½	None	2

TREASURES

Distinctive, Euro-styled cabinet with built-in light. Upscale design features back-to-back mirror doors, with mirrored interior, 3-way viewing from a 2-door cabinet. Can be recessed or surface mounted. Soft-tone baked enamel interior has 3 adjustable glass shelves. One-touch magnetic door catch. High gloss frame available in White, Black, Almond and Raspberry Puree with color coordinated side panels, plus striking gold accent stripe and gold faceplate. Built-in light uses up to 60W G-25 or G-40 bulbs (bulbs not included).

	Model	Overall Size W H D	Bulb Capacity
White	**3130WH**	31x30⅜x5	4
	3136WH	37x30⅜x5	5
Almond	**3130AL**	31x30⅜x5	4
	3136AL	37x30⅜x5	5
Black	**3130BL**	31x30⅜x5	4
	3136BL	37x30⅜x5	5
Raspberry	**3130RP**	31x30⅜x5	4
	3136RP	37x30⅜x5	5

Cabinet 3130BL

CASPAR

Sculptured contemporary extruded aluminum frame features choice of 3 decorator finishes: silver/brass, brass/brass, and silver/silver. 3-way viewing, plate glass mirror doors. 3 storage areas. 2 fixed metal shelves. Heavy gauge steel storage cabinet can be surface or recessed mounted. Built-in light section features brass faceplate with brass frame; silver faceplate with silver frame. Soft-tone baked-on enamel interiors. Spring-loaded magnetic door catches. Built-in top light. Uses up to 60W G-25 or G-40 bulbs (bulbs not included).

	Model	Overall Size W H D	Wall Opening W H D
Brass	**111930**	30x29⅜x5½	28¾x27½x3½
	111936	36x29⅜x5½	34¾x27½x3½
Silver	**112930**	30x29⅜x5½	28¾x27½x3½
	112936	36x29⅜x5½	34¾x27½x3½
Silver w/ brass strip	**113930**	30x29⅜x5½	28¾x27½x3½
	113936	36x29⅜x5½	34¾x27½x3½

Cabinet 111930

11

VICEROY

Bright brass or chrome metallic framing to complement today's bathroom accessories. Plate glass mirror doors feature "one touch" door release. Heavy gauge steel cabinet can be surface or recessed mounted. 2 fixed metal shelves. Soft-tone baked enamel finish. Built-in top light with matching faceplate. Uses up to 60W G-25 or G-40 bulbs (bulbs not included).

Brass Model	Chrome Model	Overall Size W H D	Wall Opening W H D	Bulb Capacity
171924	172924	23¾x29⅛x4⅝	22¾x27¾x3½	3
171930	172930	30x29⅛x4⅝	28¾x27¾x3½	4
171936	172936	36x29⅛x4⅝	34¾x27¾x3½	5
171948	172948	48x29⅛x4⅝	46¾x27¾x3½	6

Cabinet 171930

CORONA

Bright brass or chrome metallic framing to complement today's bathroom accessories. Plate glass mirror doors feature "one touch" door release. Heavy gauge steel cabinet can be surface or recessed mounted. Hinged right. Soft-tone baked enamel finish. 3 fixed metal shelves. Built-in top light with matching faceplate. Uses up to 60W G-25 or G-40 bulbs (bulbs not included).

	Brass Model	Chrome Model	Overall Size W H D	Wall Opening W H D	Bulb Capacity
CABINET	2012BR	2022CII	18x31x5	16¾x29x3½	3

Cabinet 2012BR

VERONA

Reflective, glossy metallic-framed cabinet in 2 contemporary finishes. Swing-door cabinet is reversible for right or left hand opening. Door features magnetic catch. Soft-tone baked enamel interior. Available with steel or molded storage cabinet. Reversible: can be mounted to open left or right. Available in brass or chrome. Matching top light uses up to 60W G-25 or G-40 bulbs (bulbs not included).

	Brass Model	Chrome Model	Overall Size W H D	Wall Opening W H D	Bulb Capacity
STEEL CABINET	310BR	310CH	17¼x27¼	14x18x3½	
	318BR	318CH	17¼x27¼	14x24x3½	
MOLDED CABINET	313BR	313CH	16x20	14x18x2½	
TOP LIGHT	747BR	747CH	17¼x5½x3		3

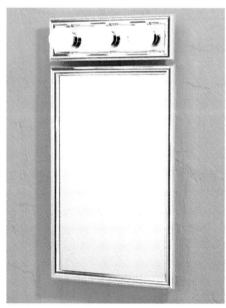

Cabinet 318CH; Light 747CH

OAKVIEW

Modern "country manor" design with genuine hardwood oak trim and sides in light honey oak or popular pickled oak finish. Surface mounted. 3-way plate glass mirror doors. 3 storage areas with 2 fixed metal shelves. Note: Models 107224 and 104224 are 2-door styles. Soft-tone baked enamel interior. Choice of matching top light: smoked glass shades or new clear ribbed prismatic glass shade with bright brass trim ring and fittings. Maximum 60 watt bulbs recommended (bulbs not included).

Light Honey Oak	Pickled Oak	Overall Size W H D	Bulb Capacity
CABINET			
107224	104224	25x32¼x5	
107230	104230	30x32¼x5	
107236	104236	36x32¼x5	
TOP LIGHT Smoked Shade			
SO42476	SO42446	25x6x11	3
SO43076	SO43046	30x6x11	3
SO43676	SO43646	36x6x11	3
TOP LIGHT Prismatic Shade			
SO82475	SO82445	25x6x11	3
SO83075	SO83045	30x6x11	3
SO83675	SO83645	36x6x11	3

Cabinet 107236; Light SO83675

Cabinet 104224; Light SO82445

OAKSHIRE 2

Genuine oak hardwood frame with traditional detailing. Surface mounted cabinet features traditional light honey oak frame with matching wood-tone sides. 3 plate glass mirror doors, 3-way viewing, and 3 storage areas with 2 fixed metal shelves. Soft-tone baked enamel finish. Matching top lights use up to 60W G-25 or G-40 bulbs (bulbs not included).

	Model	Overall Size W H D	Bulb Capacity
CABINET	117230	30x28½x5½	
	117236	36x28½x5½	
TOP LIGHT	SS40279	30x6x6½	4
	SS40379	36x6x6½	5

Cabinet 117236; Light SS40379

13

Cabinet 567248; Light GS54873

GOLDEN SAND

Natural honey oak frames complementary brown-toned inlay of "touchstone" simulating warm granite texture. Tri-view cabinets features 3-way viewing, 2 fixed metal steel shelves, plate glass mirrors, one-touch magnetic door catches, and soft-tone baked enamel interiors. Surface mounted. Matching wood-tone sides. Matching top lights feature bright brass fittings and clear-ribbed prismatic glass shades. Uses maximum 60W medium-based bulbs (bulbs not included).

	Tri-View Model	Overall Size W H D	Bulb Capacity
CABINET	567230	30x28½x5¼	
	567236	36x28½x5¼	
	567248	48x28½x5¼	
TOP LIGHT	GS53073	30x7¼x12¼	3
	GS53673	36x7¼x12¼	4
	GS54873	48x7¼x12¼	5

Reversible swing-door cabinet. Adjustable shelves. Piano hinge. Magnetic catch. Recessed and surface mounted units available. Can be mounted to open left or right. Other features same as tri-view.

	Swing-Door Model	Overall Size W H D	Wall Opening W H D	Bulb Capacity
CABINET				
Recessed	5670	17⅛x27⅛x2	14x18x3½	
	5678	17⅛x27⅛x2	14x24x3½	
Surface	5672	17⅛x27⅛x5½	none	
TOP LIGHT				
For Surface	707GS	17⅛x7¼x6¾	none	2
For Recessed	708GS	17⅛x7¼x10⅛	none	2

14

Cabinet 5670; Light 707GS

Cabinet 562248; Light WH54873

Cabinet 5620; Light 707WH

WHITE MARBLE

Natural honey oak frames complements white marble inlay of "touchstone" simulating high gloss marble finish. Tri-view cabinets features 3-way viewing, 2 fixed metal shelves, plate glass mirrors, one-touch magnetic door catches, and soft-tone baked enamel interiors. Surface mounted. Matching wood-tone sides. Matching top lights feature bright brass fittings and clear-ribbed prismatic glass shades. Uses maximum 60W medium-based bulbs (bulbs not included).

	Tri-View Model	Overall Size W H D	Bulb Capacity
CABINET	562230	30x28½x5¼	
	562236	36x28½x5¼	
	562248	48x28½x5¼	
TOP LIGHT	WH53073	30x7¼x12¼	3
	WH53673	36x7¼x12¼	4
	WH54873	48x7¼x12¼	5

Swing-door cabinet. Adjustable shelves. Piano hinge. Magnetic catch. Recessed and surface mounted units available. Reversible: can be mounted to open left or right. Other features same as tri-view.

	Swing-Door Model	Overall Size W H D	Wall Opening W H D	Bulb Capacity
CABINET				
Recessed	5620	17⅛x27⅛x2	14x18x3½	
	5628	17⅛x27⅛x2	14x24x3½	
Surface	5622	17⅛x27⅛x5½	none	
TOP LIGHT				
For Recessed	707WH	17⅛x7¼x6¾	none	2
For Surface	708WH	17⅛x7¼x10⅛	none	2

15

Cabinet 182248; Light SE24828

CANTERBURY

Surface mounted tri-view cabinet in traditional cathedral arch design features, 3-way viewing and 3 separate storage areas. 2 fixed metal shelves. Choose natural light honey oak or traditional colonial white frame with matching sides. Plate glass mirrors. Magnetic door catches. Soft-tone baked enamel interior. Matching top lights with clear ribbed prismatic glass shades and bright brass fittings. Maximum 60 watt bulbs recommended (bulbs not included).

	Honey Oak Model	White Model	Overall Size W H D	Bulb Capacity
CABINET	187230	182230	30x28½x5½	
	187236	182236	36x28½x5½	
	187248	182248	48x28½x5½	
TOP LIGHT	SE23078	SE23028	30x8x11	3
	SE23678	SE23628	36x8x11	4
	SE24878	SE24828	48x8x11	4

HENLEY

Swing-door cabinet features adjustable shelves on recessed models, fixed shelves on surface models, piano hinge, magnetic door catch. Hinged right.

	Honey Oak Model	White Model	Overall Size W H D	Wall Opening W H D	Bulb Capacity
CABINET					
Recessed	8570	8520	18¼x27¼	14x18x3½	
	8578	8528	18¼x27¼	14x24x3½	
Surface	8572	8522	18¼x27¼x5½	none	
TOP LIGHT					
For Recessed	76378	76328	18x8x8	none	2
For Surface	76478	76428	18x8x11½	none	2

16

Cabinet 8578; Light 76378

Cabinet 177930

Cabinet 2072

OAKHILL

Popular honey oak framed tri-view cabinet with built-in top light. One-touch spring-loaded magnetic door releases. Can be surface mounted or recessed. 3-way viewing plate glass mirrors. 3 storage areas. 2 fixed shelves. Soft-tone baked-on enamel finish, steel storage cabinet. Built-in top light features chrome faceplate and uses G-25 or G-40 bulbs (bulbs not included).

Model	Overall Size W H D	Wall Opening W H D	Bulb Capacity
177924	23¼x30x5½	22¾x27½x3½	4
177930	30x30x5½	28¾x27½x3½	4
177936	36x30x5½	34¾x27½x3½	5
177948	48x30x5½	46¾x27½x3½	5

OAKDALE

Swing-door cabinet with built-in top light features 3 fixed shelves and can also be resessed of surface mounted. Hinged right. Soft-tone baked-on enamel finish, steel storage cabinet. Built-in top light features chrome faceplate and uses G-25 or G-40 bulbs (bulbs not included).

Model	Overall Size W H D	Wall Opening W H D	Bulb Capacity
2072	18x31x5½	16¾x28¾x31½	3

AUTUMN

The warmth of honey oak enhanced by a new canopy design shields bulbs and delivers plenty of subdued lighting. Can be recessed or surface mounted. 2 fixed metal shelves. Plate glass mirrors. Matching oak frame and wood-tone sides completes this practical tri-view cabinet. Uses maximum 60W standard medium-based bulbs (not included).

Model	Overall Size W H D	Wall Opening W H D	Bulb Capacity
197230	30X29X5½	28¾X27½X3½	4
197236	36X29X5½	34¾X27½X3½	5
197248	48X29X5½	46¾X27½X3½	5

Cabinet 197236

SHENENDOAH

An elegant and spacious honey oak surface mounted cabinet that complements traditional oak vanity bases. Sturdily constructed with a solid oak frame and plywood interior. 2 fixed metal shelves. Plate glass mirrors. Etched glass shades and bright brass trim provide the finishing touch. Uses maximum 60W standard medium-based bulbs (not included).

	Model	Overall Size W H D	Bulb Capacity
CABINET	807230	30x32x5	
	807236	36x32x5	
	807248	48x32x5	
LIGHT	PL3077	30x7½x11½	4
	PL3677	36x7½x11½	4
	PL4877	48x7½x11½	5

18   Cabinet 807236; Light PL3677

GRAND OAK II

Can be recessed or surface mounted. 3 storage areas. Light honey oak framed plate glass mirrors, 2 fixed shelves, magnetic door catches. Surface mounted top lights use up to 60W G-25 or G-40 bulbs (bulbs not included).

Tri-View Model	Overall Size W H D	Wall Opening W H D	Bulb Capacity
CABINET			
277924	24x25	22¼x23x3½	
277930	29x28⅞	27½x27x3½	
277936	35x28⅞	33½x27x3½	
277948	47x28⅞	45½x27x3½	
TOP LIGHT			
SG32479	24x5⅝x5¼	None	3
SG33079	29x5⅝x5¼	None	4
SG33679	35x5⅝x5¼	None	4
SG34879	47x5⅝x5¼	None	4

Cabinet 277930; Light SG33079

GRANT

Light honey oak frame available with steel or molded poly-styrene storage cabinets in recessed and surface mounted styles. Reversible for left or right hand opening. Matching top light uses two G-25 or G-40 bulbs (bulbs not included).

	Swing-Door Model	Overall Size W H D	Wall Opening W H D
CABINET			
Recessed Steel	**8770**	16¼x24¼	14x18x3½
	8778	16¼x26¼	14x24x3½
Recessed Molded	**8773**	16¼x22	14x18x2½
Surface Steel	**8772**	16¼x24¼x5½	None
TOP LIGHT			
For Recessed Cabinet	**74279**	16¼x5½x3	None
For Surface Cabinet	**74379**	16¼x5½x6½	None

Cabinet 8778; Lights 74279

Contemporarily styled cabinets featuring genuine honey oak frames and beveled-edge plate glass mirrors. Interior features fixed shelves (tri-views) or adjustable shelves (swing-door) magnetic door catches and soft-tone baked enamel finish. Tri-view is surface mounted. Reversible swing-door can be mounted to open left or right. Matching top light has chrome centerplate and uses up to 60W G-25 or G-40 bulbs (bulbs not included).

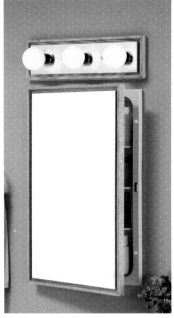

Cabinet 8378; Light 71829

Cabinet 158536; Light SA23629

KINGSTON

	Model	Overall Size W H D	Wall Opening W H D	Bulb Capacity
CABINET				
Recessed	**8370**	16½x26½	14x18x3½	
	8378	16½x26½	14x24x3½	
TOP LIGHT	**71829**	16½x5½x2¼	None	3

FOXWOOD

	Model	Overall Size W H D	Bulb Capacity
CABINET			
Surface	**158530**	30x26x5¾	
	158536	36x26x5¾	
	158548	48x26x5¾	
TOP LIGHT	**SA23029**	29½x5½x5¾	4
	SA23629	35½x5½x5¾	5
	SA24829	47½x5½x5¾	7

The warmth of natural light honey oak frames. The surface mounted Huntington features matching wood grain sides. The Chapel Hill offers reversible recessed or surface mounted units which can be mounted to open left or right. Matching top light features gold-tone accent panel and uses up to 60W G-25 or G-40 bulbs (bulbs not included).

Cabinet 8272; Light 75819

Cabinet 157036; Light SC53619

CHAPEL HILL

	Model	Overall Size W H D	Wall Opening W H D
CABINET			
Recessed	**8270**	17¼x27¼	14x18x3½
	8278	17¼x27¼	14x24x3½
Surface	**8272**	17¼x27¼x5½	None
TOP LIGHT (3 bulbs)			
For Recessed	**75719**	17¼x5½x3	None
For Surface	**75819**	17¼x5½x5⅜	None

HUNTINGTON

	Model	Overall Size W H D	Bulb Capacity
CABINET			
Surface	**157030**	30x34x5	
	157036	36x34x5	
	157048	48x34x5	
TOP LIGHT	**SC53019**	30x5½x7	4
	SC53619	36x5½x7	5
	SC54819	48x5½x7	7

Cabinet 828; Light 70123

Cabinet 878; Light 70373

BAKER STREET

Charming Victorian detail lends a distinctive period touch. Choose the classic colonial white or honey oak wood frame in the recessed or surface mount styles. Reversible for left or right hand opening. Plate glass mirrors. Adjustable shelves (recessed models) or fixed shelves (surface model). Matching top light and side light fixtures feature frosted glass shades, bright brass fittings and use medium-based bulbs (not included). Side lights also include brass towel ring.

	Honey Oak Model	Colonial White Model	Overall Size W H D	Wall Opening W H D	Bulb Capacity
CABINET					
Recessed	870	820	18x27	14x18x3½	
	878	828	18x27	14x24x3½	
Surface	872	822	18x27x5	None	
SIDE LIGHT	70173	70123	6½x13½x9½	None	1
TOP LIGHT					
For Recessed	70273	70223	18x8x9	None	2
For Surface	70373	70323	18x18x13½	None	2

COUNTRYSIDE

The traditional look with natural light honey oak trim. Includes 2 styles of cabinets.

The surface mounted model features sculptured oak sides and an open glass vanity shelf. The recessed model features a matching light fixture with antique brass fittings and frosted glass globes and 2 adjustable shelves. Recessed cabinets with a 14" x 24" wall opening feature 3 shelves. Recessed model is reversible for left or right hand opening.

Matching top lights with antique brass fittings and frosted glass globes feature elegant, traditional design. Maximum 60 watt clear bulbs recommended (bulbs not included).

Cabinet 1276; Light 74078 | Cabinet 1273

	Model	Overall Size W H D	Wall Opening W H D	Bulb Capacity
CABINET				
Surface	1273	18x38x5½	None	
	1274	18x27x5½	None	
Recessed	1276	18x27	14x18x3½	
	1278	18x27	14x24x3½	
TOP LIGHTS				
For Recessed	74078	18x8x6¼	None	2
For Surface	74178	18x8x10	None	2

OAK MALIBU

Natural oak frame available in honey oak and "pickled oak" finish. Ceramic door pull; plate glass mirror. Interior is soft-tone baked-on enamel. Adjustable shelves. Reversible: can be mounted to open left or right.

Choice of matching top lights with smoked glass globes or clear ribbed prismatic glass shades, and bright brass fittings. Medium-based 60 watt clear bulbs recommended (bulbs not included).

Cabinet 8878; Light 76378 | Cabinet 8840; Light 72446

	Honey Oak Model	Pickled Oak Model	Overall Size W H D	Wall Opening W H D
CABINET				
Recessed	8870	8840	18¼x27½	14x18x3½
	8878	8848	18¼x27½	14x24x3½
Surface	8872	8842	18¼x27½x5½	None
WALL MIRROR ONLY	8875	None	18¼x27½	None
TOP LIGHT				
Smoked Glass Globes				
For Recessed Cabinet	72476	72446	18¼x6½x9⅜	None
For Surface Cabinet	72576	72546	18¼x6½x11	None
Clear Glass				
For Recessed Cabinet	76378	76348	18¼x6½x9⅜	None
For Surface Cabinet	76478	76448	18¼x6½x11	None
SIDE LIGHT GLOBES				
For Recessed Cabinet	72676		6½x6x8	None

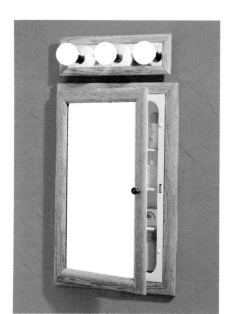

Cabinet 2371; Light 75719

SHERIDAN

Swing-door cabinet features double honey oak frame which covers cabinet return for that "built-in" look. Magnetic door catch. 3 shelves for ample storage. Plate glass mirrors. Reversible for left or right hand opening. Door pull. Interior is soft-toned baked enamel.

Matching top light has brass center plate and uses up to 60W G-25 or G-40 bulbs (bulbs not included).

	Model	Overall Size W H D	Wall Opening W H D	Bulb Capacity
CABINET	2371	18½x28½	14x24	
TOP LIGHT	75719	17¼x5½x1⅞	None	3

DUNHILL

Classic cameo oval provides grace and elegance. Available with the warmth of natural honey oak. Recessed storage with adjustable shelves. Plate glass mirrors. Magnetic door catch. Reversible for left or right hand opening.

Matching oak side light fixtures. Smoked glass shade. Clear 60 watt bulb maximum recommended (bulb not included).

	Model	Overall Size W H D	Wall Opening W H D
CABINET	1370	21x31	14x18
	1378	24x35¾	14x24
WALL MIRROR ONLY	1375	21x31	None
SIDE LIGHT	72676	6½x6x8	None

Cabinet 1370; Light 72676

ADANTE

The graceful arched oak framed cabinet features beveled plate glass mirror. Recessed cabinet with adjustable shelves, magnetic door catches and soft-tone baked enamel interior. Hinged right.

Matching side lights feature oak sconce and frosted glass shades. Uses standard medium-based bulbs. Max. 60W recommended (bulbs not included).

INTERIOR	Model	Overall Size W H D	Wall Opening W H D
CABINET	5470	18¾x33⅛	14x18x3½
	5478	18¾x33⅛	14x24x3½
SIDE LIGHT	73679	5⅜x13¼x7¼	None

Cabinet 5470; Light 73679

Cabinet 205236

SONATA

These 3-way frameless, beveled-edge plate glass mirror doors are cut in graceful, classic shapes to complement the traditional home. Other features include three family-size storage areas. Heavy gauge steel construction, concealed hinges, two fixed steel shelves, and bright stainless steel side panels. Surface mounted.

	Model	Overall Size W H D	Wall Opening W H D
CABINET	205230	30x32x5¼	None
	205236	36x32x5¼	None

LYRIC

Unique side light fixtures complement the gentle lines to complete a striking ensemble. Other features: a heavy gauge steel recessed storage cabinet, adjustable shelves, soft-tone baked enamel finish and magnetic door catches. Hinged right. Matching side lights feature beveled-edge mirror backplate and distinctive frosted glass shades with grey accent striping. Uses standard medium-based bulbs (bulbs not included). Maximum 75W recommended.

	Model	Overall Size W H D	Wall Opening W H D
CABINET	250	16x28	14x18x3½
	258	16x32	14x24x3½
SIDE LIGHT	72052	5x17½x6⅛	None

Cabinet 258; Light 72052

24

Cabinet 165248, Light HO34890

Cabinet 268, Light 73290

OPUS

Dramatically styled art deco surface mounted cabinet. Beveled-edge plate glass mirrors and mirror appliques for a unique, and very distinctive design. 3-way viewing and a steel cabinet, with soft-tone baked enamel finish. 2 fixed steel shelves. Matching top light fixtures use G-45 or G-40 medium-based bulbs (not included).

	Model	Overall Size W H D	Wall Opening W H D	Bulb Capacity
CABINET	165230	30x28¼x5¼	None	
	165236	36x28¼x5¼	None	
	165248	48x28¼x5¼	None	
LIGHT	HO33090	30x4½x5⅞	None	4
	HO33690	36x4½x5⅞	None	4
	HO34890	48x4½x5⅞	None	5

ETERNA

Swing door cabinets feature the same art deco styling of the Opus, and are recess mounted in standard wall openings. Reversible for left or right hand opening. Adjustable shelves. Full piano hinge. Magnetic door catch. Matching top light fixtures use G-45 or G-40 medium-based bulbs (not included).

	Model	Overall Size W H D	Wall Opening W H D	Bulb Capacity
CABINET	260	16x26	14x18x3½	
	268	16x26	14x24x3½	
LIGHT	73290	16x4½x2	None	2

25

Cabinet 151B; Light CL74829

BEL AIRE

Clean contemporary lines make the Bel Aire a big favorite with builders and designers across the nation. Perfect for today's popular, larger bathrooms. Three-way panoramic plate glass mirrors, stainless steel trim top and bottom; polished vertical edges. Two "his-n-hers" storage cabinets. Six adjustable plastic shelves in recessed models. Six fixed plastic shelves in surface mounted models. Magnetic door catches.

Choice of two matching strip lights: CL Series uses up to 60W G-16 ½ candelabra-base bulbs; BA or SB Series uses up to 60W G-25 or G-40 medium-based bulbs (bulbs not included).

	Model	Overall Size (A)	Dist. (B)	Wall Opening (C)x(D)x(E)	Bulb Capacity
CABINET					
Recessed	**131D**	36x36	18¼	8x33	
	151B	48x36	23¾	11¼x33¼x3½	
	171B	58x36	33¾	11¼x33¼x3½	
Surface	**136H**	36x36x5⅜	None	None	
	148G	48x36x5⅜	None	None	
TOP LIGHT					
For Recessed	**CL73629**	36x3¼x1¾	None	None	6
	CL74829	48x3¼x1¾	None	None	8
	BA93629	36x3¼x3	None	None	5
	BA94829	48x3¼x3	None	None	6
For Surface	**CL73729**	36x3¼x5	None	None	6
	CL74929	48x3¼x5	None	None	8
	SB63629	36x3¼x6½	None	None	5
	SB64829	48x3¼x6½	None	None	6

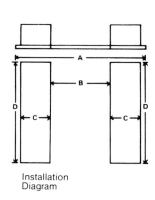

Installation Diagram

QUANTUM

Smart, frameless, beveled-edge plate glass mirrors softened with radius corners for more elegant appeal. Heavy gauge steel storage cabinet with soft-tone baked enamel. Magnetic door catches. Surface mounted. 3 storage areas. Concealed hinges. 2 fixed steel shelves. Built-in top light with matching faceplate. Uses up to 60W G-25 or G-40 bulbs (bulbs not included).

Model	Overall Size W H D	Bulb Capacity
455224	24¼x32¼x5¼	3
455230	30x36½x5¼	4
455236	36x36½x5¼	5
455248	48x36½x5¼	6

Cabinet 455248

LAFAYETTE

Modern styling with elegant beveled mirror featuring radius corners. Surface mounted with built-in top light for easy, low cost installation. Hinged right. Plate glass mirror door. 3 fixed steel shelves. Soft-tone baked enamel interior. Full piano hinge. Magnetic door catch. Top light uses up to 60W G-25 or G-40 bulbs (bulbs not included).

Model	Overall Size W H D	Bulb Capacity
1402	18⅛x32⅜x6	3

Cabinet 1402

27

Cabinet 355236; Light H033690

AURORA

Beveled-edge plate mirror doors with 2 beveled-edge cut glass design on left and right doors. 3-way panoramic viewing. Steel storage cabinet with 2 fixed steel shelves. Recessed or surface mounted. Magnetic door catches. Concealed hinge design. Soft-tone baked enamel interiors. Matching top light uses G-25 or G-40 bulbs (bulbs not included).

	Model	Overall Size W H D	Wall Opening W H D	Bulb Capacity
CABINET				
Recessed	355030	30x28¼	27⅝x24½x3½	
	355036	36x28¼	27⅝x24½x3½	
	355048	48x28¼	45⅝x24½x3½	
Surface	355230	30x28¼x5¼	None	
	355236	36x28¼x5¼	None	
	355248	48x28¼x5¼	None	
TOP LIGHT				
For Recessed	H043090	30x4½x2¼	None	4
	H043690	36x4½x2¼	None	4
	H044890	48x4½x2¼	None	5
For Surface	H033090	30x4½x5⅞	None	4
	H033690	36x4½x5⅞	None	4
	H034890	48x4½x5⅞	None	5

MIRAGE

Swing-door cabinet. Recessed. Reversible for left or right hand opening. Heavy gauge steel storage cabinet available in two sizes. Adjustable shelves. Piano hinge. Magnetic catch.

	Model	Overall Size W H D	Wall Opening W H D
CABINET	1410	16x26	24x18x3½
	1418	16x26	24x24x3½
TOP LIGHT	73290	16x4½x2	None

Cabinet 1410; Light 73290

28

HORIZON

Beveled-edge plate mirror doors. Recessed or surface mounted. Concealed hinge design. Steel storage cabinet with 2 fixed steel shelves. Soft-tone baked enamel interior. Matching top lights use 60W G-25 or G-40 bulbs (bulbs not included).

Model	Overall Size W H D	Wall Opening W H D	Bulb Capacity
RECESSED CABINET			
255024	24x24	21⅝x30⅜x3½	
255030	30x28¾	27⅝x24½x3½	
255036	36x28¼	33⅝x24½x3½	
255048	48x28¼	45⅝x24½x3½	
SURFACE CABINET			
255224	24x24x5¼	None	
255230	30x28¼x5¼	None	
255236	36x28¼x5¼	None	
255248	48x28¼x5¼	None	
TOP LIGHT For Recessed Cabinet			
HO42490	24x4½x2¼	None	3
HO43090	30x4½x2¼	None	4
HO43690	36x4½x2¼	None	4
HO44890	48x4½x2¼	None	5
TOP LIGHT For Surface Cabinet			
HO32490	24x4½x5⅞	None	3
HO33090	30x4½x5⅞	None	4
HO33690	36x4½x5⅞	None	4
HO34890	48x4½x5⅞	None	5

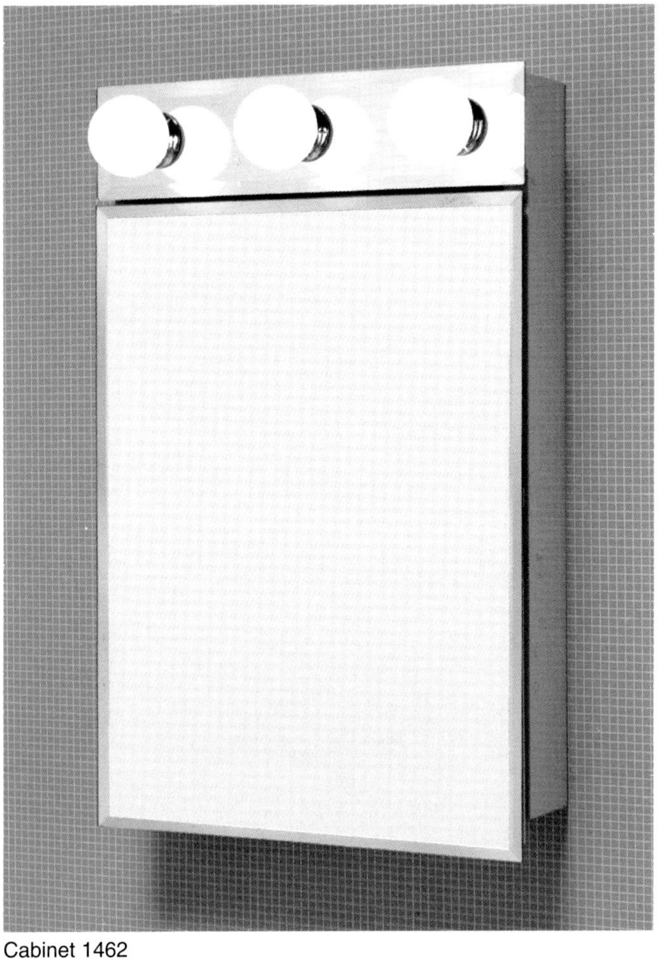

Cabinet 255236; Light HO33690

LAFAYETTE

Swing-door cabinet. Plate glass mirrors. 3 fixed steel shelves. Surface mounted with built-in top light for easy installation. Piano hinged on right. Magnetic catch. Soft-tone baked enamel interior. Top light uses up to 60W G-25 or 6-40 bulbs (bulbs not included).

Model	Overall Size W H D	Bulb Capacity
1462	18⅛x28⅜x6	3

Cabinet 1462

Cabinet 151224; Light SB22429   Cabinet 151230; Light SB23029

BEL AIRE 2

Modern Bel Aire styling for the cost-conscious buyer. Offers easy surface mounting with deluxe features: Silver aluminum frame surrounds 3 plate glass mirror doors; 3-way panoramic viewing; 3 storage areas, 2 fixed steel shelves, magnetic door catches; soft-tone interior. Model 151224 has two doors as shown. Matching top light uses up to 60W G-25 or G-40 bulbs (bulbs not included).

	Model	Overall Size W H D	Bulb Capacity
CABINET	151224	23⅜x30x5	
	151230	29x30x5	
	151236	35x30x5	
TOP LIGHT	SB22429	23⅜x3x5¾	4
	SB23029	29x3x5¾	4
	SB23629	35x3x5¾	5

STYLELINE 2

Surface mounted with built-in top light for easy, low cost installation. Plate glass mirror door with stainless steel trim top and bottom; polished vertical edges. 3 fixed steel shelves. Hinged right. Soft-tone baked enamel interior. Full piano hinge. Magnetic door catch. Top light features stainless steel face and uses up to 60W G-25 or G-40 bulbs (bulbs not included).

Swing-Door Model	Overall Size W H D	Bulb Capacity
565	18x28x6	3

Cabinet 565

30

Cabinet 155136; Light SB23729

VIENNA

Contemporary elegance trimmed in polished chrome. Surface mounted tri-view cabinet features 3 storage compartments each with 2 fixed steel shelves. Magnetic door catches. Soft-tone baked enamel interior. Matching chrome top lights accommodate up to 60W G-25 or G-40 bulbs (bulbs not included).

	Model	Overall Size W H D	Bulb Capacity
CABINET	155124	24x26x5½	
	155130	30x26x5½	
	155136	36x26x5½	
TOP LIGHT	SB22529	24x4x5½	3
	SB23129	30x4x5½	4
	SB23729	36x4x5½	5

 NEW # FOCUS

Simple elegant design. Surface mounted tri-view cabinet with built-in top light. Polished edge plate glass mirrors. 3 doors. 3 storage areas. 2 fixed steel shelves. Concealed hinges. Soft-tone baked enamel finish. Top light uses up to 60W G-25 or G-40 bulbs (bulbs not included).

Model	Overall Size W H D	Bulb Capacity
295224	24x28⅝x5¼	3
295230	30x32¾x5¼	4
295236	36x32¾x5¼	5

Cabinet 295236

TORINO

The timeless beauty of a classic shape. Available in three decorator styles: elegant frosted cut-glass *teardrop* motif; polished cut glass *art deco* design; and *plain beveled-edge*. Recessed steel storage cabinet features adjustable shelves, magnetic catches, soft-tone baked enamel interiors. Hinged right. Matching side light fixtures feature beveled-edge mirror back plate and frosted glass shade. Uses standard medium-based bulbs. Max. 75W recommended (bulbs not included).

	Model	Overall Size W H D	Wall Opening W H D
CABINET Teardrop	**5520**	16½x34½	14x18x3½
	5528	16½x34½	14x24x3½
SIDE LIGHT	**73591**	5⅜x13¾x6½	None

Cabinet 5520; Lights 73591

Detail of Cabinet 5520

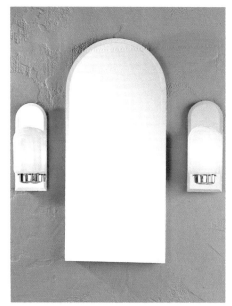

Cabinet 5518; Lights 73591

	Model	Overall Size W H D	Wall Opening W H D
CABINET Beveled Edge	**5510**	16½x34½	14x18x3½
	5518	16½x34½	14x24x3½
SIDE LIGHT	**73591**	5⅜x13¾x6½	None

Cabinet 5530; Lights 73591

	Model	Overall Size W H D	Wall Opening W H D
CABINET Art Deco	**5530**	16½x34½	14x18x3½
	5538	16½x34½	14x24x3½
SIDE LIGHT	**73591**	5⅜x13¾x6½	None

MIRAGE

Frameless beveled-edged mirrors in elegant styles. Recessed, with adjustable shelves, magnetic catches and soft-tone baked enamel interior. Reversible for left or right hand opening. Matching top lights, or side lights with beveled mirror sconce and tinted glass shade. Uses up to 60W G-25 or G-40 bulbs (bulbs not included).

	Model	Overall Size W H D	Wall Opening W H D
CABINET	1454	18x27	14x18x3½
	1456	17⅜x32	14x24x3½
MIRROR ONLY	1454WM	18x27	None
SIDE LIGHT	73190	5x12x6½	None

Cabinet 1454; Lights 73190

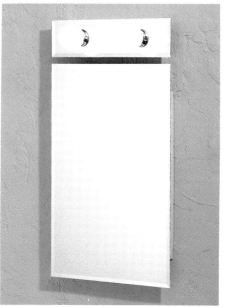

Cabinet 1450BC; Lights 73190

Cabinet 1451; Lights 73290

Cabinet 1452; Lights 73290

	Model	Overall Size W H D	Wall Opening W H D
CABINET	1450BC	16x26	14x18x3½
	1458	16x26	14x24x3½
MIRROR ONLY	1450WM	16x26	None
SIDE LIGHT	73190	5x12x6½	None
TOP LIGHT	73290	16x6½x2½	None

	Model	Overall Size W H D	Wall Opening W H D
CABINET Steel	1451	16x26	14x18x3½
	1459	16x26	14x24x3½
Molded	1453	16x20	14x18x2½
MIRROR ONLY	1451WM	16x26	None
SIDE LIGHT	73190	5x12x6½	None
TOP LIGHT	73290	16x4½x2	None

	Model	Overall Size W H D	Wall Opening W H D
CABINET	1452	16x26	14x18x3½
	1457	16x26	14x24x3½
MIRROR ONLY	1452WM	16x26	None
TOP LIGHT	73290	16x4½x2	None

33

DECORAH

Contemporary styling with a patterned mirror design. Elegant floral with soft gold- tone and soft white design. Recessed. Adjustable shelves. Frameless plate glass mirror. Reversible for left or right hand opening. Magnetic catches. Soft-tone baked enamel interior. Matching top light uses up to 60W G-25 or G-40 bulbs (bulbs not included).

	Model	Overall Size W H D	Wall Opening W H D
CABINET	**1420FL**	16x26	14x18x3½
	1428FL	16x26	14x24x3½
TOP LIGHT	**735FL**	16x4⅜x2	None

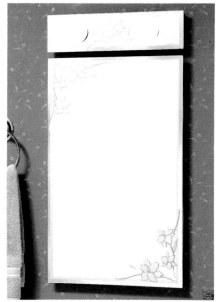

Cabinet 1420FL; Light 735FL

ADANTE – Beveled

Brilliant plate glass beveled-edge mirror is a perfect complement to popular pedestal sinks. Recessed cabinet features soft-tone baked enamel interior and adjustable shelves. Unit is reversible for use with optional arch top light for a dazzling 2-piece oval ensemble. Matching top light uses up to 60W G-25 or G-40 bulbs (bulbs not included).

	Model	Overall Size W H D	Wall Opening W H D
CABINET	**5410**	16½x26	14x18x3½
	5418	16½x31	14x24x3½
TOP LIGHT	**73960**	16½x6¼x2	None

Cabinet 5418

ADANTE – Horizon

Polished edge plate glass mirror cabinet: features a contemporary "Horizon" stencil design. Reversible for use with matching top light unit. Other features are the same as the Adante – Beveled. Matching top light uses up to 60W G-25 or G-40 bulbs (bulbs not included).

	Model	Overall Size W H D	Wall Opening W H D
CABINET	**5420**	16½x26	14x18x3½
	5428	16½x31	14x24x3½
TOP LIGHT	**73790**	16½x6¼x2	None

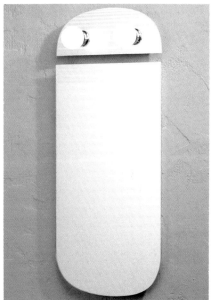

Cabinet 5420

Cabinet WF4070; Light 72876

Cabinet 2471IL

Choose from a wide selection of practical bath cabinets that feature great storage capacity for a moderate price. All feature plate glass sliding mirror doors, soft-tone baked enamel interiors and decorative door pulls.

OAK CHELSEA

Stylish replacement cabinet for standard wall openings. Features solid oak frame, ceramic door pulls and adjustable shelves. Recessed. Available with 3 bulb top light (bulbs not included).

	Model	Overall Size	Wall Opening
CABINET	WF4070	29½x21x3	26¼x17½
TOP LIGHT	72876	24¾x6x9	None

OAK HOLLYWOOD

Surface mounted cabinet features honey oak frame and matching wood-tone sides. Other features include built-in top light (bulbs not included), grounded outlet, on-off switch and gold-tone door pulls.

	Model	Overall Size
CABINET	2471IL	24¾x24½x9
	2871IL	28¾x24½x9

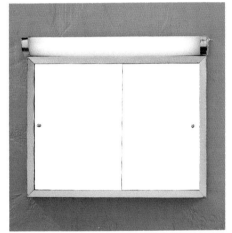

Cabinet SDL25

Cabinet 128LP

Cabinet 323LP

BEAUTY GLIDE

Stainless steel shadow box frame with adjustable shelves and chrome door pulls. Attached fluorescent light includes tubes. Grounded outlet and on-off switch.

Model	Overall Size	Wall Opening	Lamps (Watts)
CABINET			
Unlighted			
SD15	24x18¾	21½x17x3½	None
SD41	27½x19¼	26¼x17¼x3½	None
Fluorescent Top Lighted			
SDL25	24x21¼	21½x16½x3½	1 (20)
SDL82	27½x22	26¼x18¼x3½	1 (20)

ENSIGN

Stainless steel trim with built-in light (bulbs not included). Surface mounted with fixed shelves. Includes convenient grounded outlet and on-off switch.

Model	Overall Size	Mirror Size
CABINET		
124LP	24x23½x8¼	(2) 12x18
128LP	28x23½x8¼	(2) 14x18

FLAIR

Our economy leader includes fixed shelves, stainless steel trim, built-in light (bulbs not included) and on-off switch.

Model	Overall Size	Mirror Size
CABINET		
323LP	24x19½x8	(2) 12x14
327LP	28x19½x8	(2) 14x14

35

STYLELINE

Cabinet 410BC

Classic stainless steel frames and easy installation make the economical Styleline Series a builder's favorite. Unlighted cabinets are reversible: can be mounted to open from left or right.

Model	Mirror	Overall Size	Wall Opening
410BC	WINDOW	16x22	14x18x3½
420BC	WINDOW	16x22	14x20x3½
421BC	PLATE	16x22	14x20x3½
451	PLATE	16x22	14x18x3½
458	PLATE	16x26	14x24x3½
468	WINDOW	16x26	14x20x3½
490	PLATE	18x24	16x21½x3½
471FS*	PLATE	16x22	14x18x3½
478FS*	PLATE	16x26	14x24x3½
495	PLATE	20x30	16¼x26¼x3½

*Meets or exceeds all government specifications as published in Federal Spec #WW-P-541/8B.

Cabinet 407BC

Reversible recessed cabinet with fixed shelves. Polystyrene storage.

Model	Mirror	Overall Size	Wall Opening
407BC	WINDOW	16x22	16x18x2½
449BC	PLATE	16x22	16x18x2½

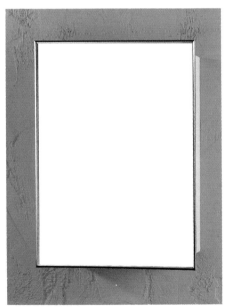

Cabinet 452SM

Surface mounted reversible cabinet with steel storage and fixed shelves.

Model	Mirror	Overall Size	Wall Opening
412SM	WINDOW	16x22x4¾	None
422SM	WINDOW	14x20x5	None
452SM	PLATE	16x22x4¾	None

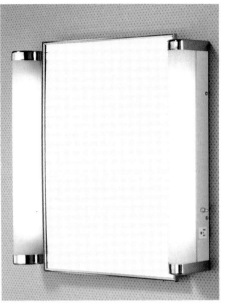

Cabinet 455FL

Recessed plate glass mirror cabinet with one-piece steel storage and adjustable shelves. Attached fluorescent side lights (tubes included) with grounded outlet and on-off switch.

Model	Overall Size	Wall Opening	Bulbs
455FL	21½x22¼x3½	16x18x2½	2

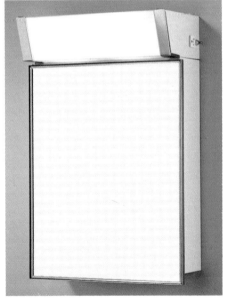

Cabinet 555IL

Surface mounted with steel storage and fixed shelves. Attached 2-bulb top light features grounded outlet and on-off switch (bulb not included).

Model	Mirror	Overall Size	Bulbs
555IL	PLATE	16x24X8	2

Cabinet 629

Cabinet 622

MIRROR CABINETS

Auxiliary storage with reversible frameless plate glass mirror doors. Model 629 has special low-profile (1/4" projection from wall) to fit flush with adjacent wall mirrors. Models 1430 to 1438 feature standard return flange. 3 adjustable shelves. Spring-loaded magnetic door release. Eurostyle concealed hinges. All fit standard wall openings.

Model	Overall Size	Wall Opening
1430	16x22	14x18x3½
1438	16x26	14x24x3½
629	15x36	14x34x4

HIDEAWAY

Steel swing-door can be wallpapered or painted to blend with wall for hidden storage. Reversible door for left or right hand opening. Rugged piano hinge with magnetic door catch. Adjustable shelves with soft-tone baked enamel interior.

Model	Overall Size	Wall Opening
622	17⅛x21½	14x18x3½

Cabinet 602, 605, 608 Pine Louver
UNFINISHED PINE - ARCH TOP

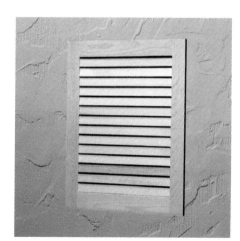

Cabinet 606, 607, 609 Pine Louver
UNFINISHED PINE - FLAT TOP

Cabinet 603 Pine Louver
WHITE POLYSTYRENE

LOUVER DOOR

This versatile auxiliary cabinet series offers added storage to mirrored walls. Rugged piano hinged doors are reversible for left or right hand opening. Steel cabinets feature adjustable shelves. Molded cabinets feature fixed shelves. Also feature soft-tone baked enamel interior and magnetic door catch.

Model	Cabinet	Overall Size	Wall Opening
602	Steel	16x24	14x18x3½
605	Molded	16x24	14x18x2½
608	Steel	16x28	14x24x3½

Model	Cabinet	Overall Size	Wall Opening
606	Steel	16x22	14x18x3½
607	Molded	16x22	14x18x2½
609	Steel	16x28	14x24x3½

Model	Cabinet	Overall Size	Wall Opening
603	Molded	16¼x22¼	14x18x2½

Cabinet (2) 631; PEM3636 Mirror; CL73629 Light Strip

Cabinet 672

AVANTI

Triangular-shaped corner cabinet adds storage and 3-way viewing when used in pairs with a simple wall mirror. Ideal for vanity nooks. Or use a single cabinet with wall mirror to make smaller areas look larger while adding storage space. Surface mounted. Reversible. 3 shelves. Special mirror channel built into cabinet receives mirror behind door to assure perfect fit. Stainless steel trim top and bottom, polished edge mirrors on sides.

Triangular Shaped

Stainless Steel Model	Gold Aluminum Model	Overall Size W H D
631	632	13x36x7¼

CORNER CABINET **NEW**

A handsome, compact, corner-mounted unit with genuine oak frame. Makes the most of limited space when installed with corner vanity cabinets.

Model	Overall Size W H D
672	19 ½ X33 ½ X10 ½

COMMODORE

Combination VM230M

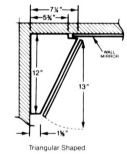

Light IL36; Mirror PEM3624; Cabinet V36

Match and install individual components to create a custom ensemble that precisely matches your lighting and storage needs. Components are channeled for easy installation. Light fixture includes grounded switch and outlet. Quality electrolytic mirrors feature polished edges and copper backing. Stainless steel trim.

INCANDESCENT LIGHT FIXTURES

Model	Overall Size	Lamp (Watts)
IL24	24x4x7½	(4) 60
IL30	30x4x7½	(4) 60
IL36	36x4x7½	(4) 60

WALL MIRRORS

Model	Overall Size
PEM2424	24x24
PEM3024	30x24
PEM 3624	36x24
PEM 4824	48x24
PEM3036	30x36
PEM3636	36x36
PEM4836	48x36
PEM6036	60x36

COMBINATION MIRROR & CABINET

Mirror Door	Styrene Door	Overall Size
	VM218P	18¼x32x4⅛
VM224M	VM224P	24¼x32x4⅛
VM230M	VM230P	30¼x32x4⅛
VM236M	VM236P	36¼x32x4⅛

STORAGE CABINETS

Model	Overall Size
V24	24¼x8¾x4¼
V30	30¼x8¾x4¼
V36	36¼x8¾x4¼
V48	48¼x8¾x4¼

MIRROR DOOR

Designed to meet the variety of needs presented by today's bathroom interiors. Available in either recessed or surface mounted models. Ideal in combination with wall mirror and light strips to provide extra storage and 3-way viewing.

Plate glass mirror, stainless steel trim top and bottom with polished vertical mirror edges. Steel storage cabinet with soft-tone; baked-on enamel finish. 3 fixed shelves.

Cabinet 625

Cabinet (two) 626; PEM3630 Mirror;
MB830-19 Light Strip

	Model	Overall Size	Wall Opening
RECESSED	**625**	13x36	11¼ x33¼
SURFACE	**626**	13x36x4¾	None

INDEX

Broan Quality Assurances

Steel construction for lifelong service and value. Most cabinets have heavy gauge steel cabinet storage, either deep-draw (recessed) or formed and welded (surface mounted). They are treated with a phosphate bath to inhibit rust and final finished with acid-resistant Hi-temp baked enamel. Cabinets with built-in or attached lighting are pre-wired at the factory and are listed by Underwriters' Laboratories, Inc. All mirrors are made from the finest silvering glass obtainable. Silvering is protected by electroplated copper backing. All products are shipped in specially engineered Hi-impact packaging able to withstand extra heavy duty handling to assure safe delivery.

Specifications represented in this catalog are subject to change without notice.

ALSO SEE OUR VANITY BROCHURE

Broan is proud to offer a complete line of matching vanities, vanity tops and other bathroom cabinetry all designed to complement Broan bath cabinets and lighting.

ITEM INDEX ON PAGE 39

A NORTEK COMPANY ®

BROAN MFG. CO., INC. HARTFORD, WISCONSIN 53027

ALL THE COMFORTS OF HOME

Discover Wrapture™
in the Bathroom

Model #250

epanel

Model #110

Model #320

he newest sensation in fine homes, hotels, health facilities and bath showrooms all over America is Ep'anel's new Wrapture towel warmer. Imagine the luxurious comfort to be experienced, after your bath or shower, with towels deep-warmed by Wrapture's unique paneled hearth design. Safe to the touch. With a 24-hour programmable timer offering pre-set convenience, Wrapture beats all other towel warmers cold.

The Wrapture line includes six free-standing models in contemporary and traditional designs, in oak, brass or chrome. Eight wall models are available – four hardwire and four plug-in. All 14 attractively priced styles are thermostatically controlled. Each has an analog clock timer affording the luxury of pre-selected on/off times, making towels from Wrapture warm, dry and ready when needed.

Discover Wrapture, available exclusively from Ep'anel, and enjoy an experience you can get wrapped up in.

Model #210

Model #240

Wrapture comes at an affordable price that beats other towel warmers cold.

Model #260

specifications

Model #260 - Oak with Brass Trim

Height - 37" • Width - 25" • Depth - 10"

Model #230 - Oak and Chrome
Model #240 - Oak and Brass

Height - 37½"• Width - 24½"• Depth - 10"

Model #110 - Chrome
Model #120 - Brass
Model #130 - Chrome and Oak
Model #140 - Brass and Oak

Height - 26½" • Width - 23¼" • Depth - 3½"

Model #250 - Solid Brass Frame

Height - 38" • Width - 25" • Depth - 9¼"

Model #310 - Chrome
Model #320 - Brass
Model #330 - Chrome and Oak
Model #340 - Brass and Oak

Height - 26½" • Width - 24" • Depth - 3¾"

Model #210 - Chrome
Model #220 - Brass

Height - 37½" • Width - 23¾" • Depth - 10"

Maximum operating temperature 155°. Built in back-up safety fuse. Thermostat automatically turns off at 155° and back on at 115°. Electromechanical timer module can be set to automatically turn on or off in 15 minute increments. The timer is equipped with a manual on/off switch, regardless of the time cycle programmed. A "real time" analog clock can be programmed to turn on 15-30 minutes before warm towels are needed, and automatically turned off at any pre-selected time. A red light glows when the unit is plugged in. A green light indicates the heaters are energized. Warm-up time approximately 15 minutes.

Heater rating 320 watts (1100 BTUs/hr)120 volts AC. Unit weight 12 to 14 pounds. Accommodates two 28" x 54" bath towels or one 28" x 54" bath towel, one 16" x 30" hand towel and one 18" x 18" wash cloth. More than 5½ sq. ft. of heating surface. **Made in USA.**

UL Listed

Wrapture™

a new sensation in fine homes, hotels, health facilities and bath showrooms.

epanel

products to make your life more livable

P.O. Box 115 ♦ 145 Route 31
Pennington, NJ 08534

1-800-5-EPANEL
609-466-1172
Fax 609-466-0773

SEATS TO MATCH OR ACCENT FIXTURES.

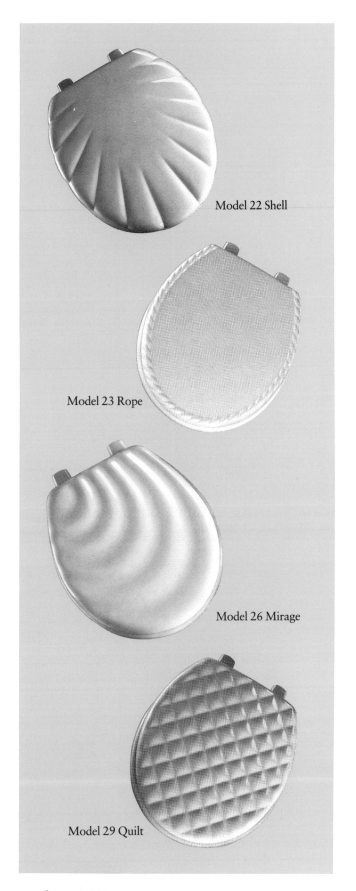

Model 22 Shell

Model 23 Rope

Model 26 Mirage

Model 29 Quilt

Model 22 Shell

The Model 22 features a sculpted shell design constructed of molded-wood for greater weight and durability. Dial-On® hinges ensure easy installation and a secure no-wobble fit. With a smooth, easy-to-clean, multi-coat enamel finish, the Model 22 resists chipping and scratching.

Model 122 Same seat for elongated bowl.

Model 23 Rope

The Model 23 features a sculpted rope design constructed of molded-wood for greater weight and durability. Dial-On® hinges ensure easy installation and a secure, no-wobble fit. The smooth, easy-to-clean, multi-coat enamel finish resists chipping and scratching.

Model 26 Mirage

The Model 26 features a sculpted mirage design constructed of molded-wood for greater weight and durability. Dial-On® hinges ensure easy installation and a secure, no-wobble fit. The smooth, easy-to-clean, multi-coat enamel finish resists chipping and scratching.

Model 29 Quilt

The Model 29 features a sculpted quilt design constructed of molded-wood for greater weight and durability. Dial-On® hinges ensure easy installation and a secure, no-wobble fit. With a smooth, easy-to-clean, multi-coat enamel finish, the Model 29 resists chipping and scratching.

For Your Sense Of Style   Mayfair® Division of Bemis Manufacturing Company, Sheboygan Falls, WI 53085   414-467-4621 or 800-558-7651 FAX: 414-467-8573

NuTone

KITCHEN & BATH GUIDE

The NuTone Food Center: One powerful built-in motor operates 10 appliances...makes cooking and storage easier!

The powerful, yet compact Food Center Power Unit installs easily *beneath* your countertop ... operates 10 of your most-used kitchen appliances!

You see only the flush Surface-Plate in Decorator White or Classic Stainless Steel. It's always conveniently there when you need it, but you have complete use of your counter when not using it.

Solid-State Infinite Speed Control assures the correct speed

Food Processor – 256N, shown on Power Unit 251WH with handsome Decorator White finish surface-plate.

Blender – 272, shown on Power Unit 251SS with classic stainless steel surface-plate.

For complete information on the NuTone Food Center, see Catalog FC-200.

for each lightweight, full size appliance – every one beautifully designed to handle food prep jobs with ease.

With no heavy, bulky motors, they're easy to put away in a cabinet when you are not using them. And instead of 10 cords to plug in and get tangled up, you have none!

Mixer – 271

Fruit Juicer – 173N

Knife Sharpener – 274

Ice Crusher – 281

Juice Extractor – 231

Coffee Grinder – 276

Can Opener – 279

Shredder-Slicer – 278N

NuTone Decorator Range Hoods help keep kitchens fresh, clean and beautiful!

With NuTone, there's no reason to put up with lingering cooking odors, smoke, heat, humidity or excessive grease in your kitchen.

You can keep it fresh and clean every day with a NuTone Range Hood. Mounted directly above your cooking surface, it collects and filters out airborne cooking by-products.

NuTone offers styling to match or complement any kitchen decor. Both ducted and non-ducted models are available, providing powerful air movement. And all NuTone Hoods are UL listed.

NuTone Range Hoods. Designer styling plus proven power and performance – *guaranteed!* mpp

SO-9100V Select-A-Matic Range Hood – five power unit choices plus night light.
Infinite speed switch for just the air delivery needed ...use Exterior or Interior Power Units shown on next page. Three sizes: 30", 36", 42". Baked enamel finishes in All White, Almond, White with black trim – plus Stainless Steel. Vents horizontally or vertically.

SO-9100V Series Range Hood Shell uses Exterior or Interior-Mounted Fans for the most choices in powerful kitchen ventilation.

NN8300 Convertible Twin Blower Hood with night light.
Right up to the time of installation you can decide to use it with 3 1/4" x 10" ducting ...or as a Non-Duct. *And no special kit is needed!*

Powerful, but quiet. Solid-state controls. Activated charcoal filters combined with grease filters included. 30" and 36" sizes in four enamel finishes plus stainless steel.

SH-1000WH Series Slide-Away Range Hood

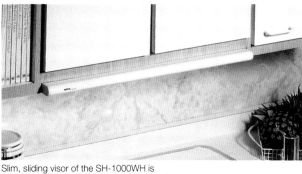

Slim, sliding visor of the SH-1000WH is virtually invisible ... until things get cooking!

SH-1000WH Slide-Away Range Hoods Easily install in a standard cabinet above range or cooktop. Ideal for remodeling an existing kitchen, as well as for new homes. Only the slim, squared-off Hood 'visor' is visible – a thin line underscoring your beautiful cabinetry.

To remove smoke, steam or cooking odors, just pull out the tempered glass visor. This turns on an exceptionally efficient dual-centrifugal blower to keep your kitchen fresh.

Easily accessible sliding controls operate variable speed fan, bright cooking light or night light. 30", 36". 320 CFM, 5.0 sones.
SH-1030WH 30", White.
SH-1036WH 36", White.

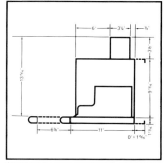

SH-1000 is easily installed in a standard cabinet above the range or cooktop

MM Series Decorator Range Hood

MM6500 Convertible Decorator Hood with night light One beautiful hood – three ducting options! Infinite speed control for quiet, efficient operation. Right up to the time of installation, you can decide to use it with 3¼" x 10" duct horizontally or vertically...7" round duct...or as a non-duct. 30", 36", 42" sizes. Four enamel finishes plus stainless steel.

Choose exterior or interior Power Unit for your SO-9100V Hood!
RF-35 Roof Fan
Strong centrifugal blower, 270 CFM. Uses 7" round duct. Aluminum damper opens and closes automatically.
WF-35 Wall Fan Housing is baked enamel on zinc-coated steel. Similar to RF-35.
WF-1N Wall Fan All aluminum housing with stainless steel fittings, rainshield included. 650 CFM.
RF-1N Roof Fan
1/8 HP motor, 620 CFM. Aluminum housing with 24" sq. self-flashing flange.

VP-400 Interior Power Unit Twin blowers for improved ventilation through long duct runs. 410 CFM, 6.5 sones vented horizontally; 420 CFM, 7.0 sones vertically

VP-400 Interior Power Unit

RF-35 Roof Fan

WF-35 Wall Fan

WF-1N Wall Fan

RF-1N Roof Fan

For complete information on the full line of NuTone Range Hoods, see Catalog HF-300.

3

NuTone Ironing Center 'hides' in the wall until you need it!

Board folds up into cabinet for storage

Board swivels 180° to face any direction

NUTONE BUILT-IN IRONING CENTERS mpp
Great idea — an ironing board that hides in the wall 'til you need it. Simply reach into the cabinet, pull down the board and you're ready to iron.

AVC-40NDR Deluxe Ironing Center Cabinet Board swivels a full 180° and adjusts up or down to just the right height. Features include: automatic safety timer, a safety shut-off switch, a convenient electric outlet for your iron, adjustable work light, garment hook, and a sturdy steel cabinet.

Recesses between 16" O.C. studs for a built-in look. Optional Surface Mount Frame available.

AVC-41NDR Economy Ironing Center Cabinet The built-in convenience you want in a non-electric model. Steel cabinet features board that adjusts up and down, storage shelf, and garment hook.

Customize your NuTone Ironing Center with your choice of three door styles. Order cabinet and door separately. All doors can be hinged for right or left opening.

AVC-M Attractive mirror door with pencil edge.

AVC-RP Traditional genuine oak raised panel door can be painted or stained.

AVC-W Smooth unfinished wood door – paint, paper or stain to match decor.

For complete information on the full line of NuTone Ironing Centers, see Catalog IC-800.

Specialty Heaters add comfort in those special areas

'Kickspace' Heater 9515 (120 Volts) – 9515X (240 Volts)
Fits under bathroom vanity ... kitchen cabinet ... many other areas where vertical space is limited. Quiet tangential blower wheel distributes heat evenly. Black louvered grille.

Two models give you a choice of volts – you select 750W or 1500W at installation with simple 'plug-in' of either one or two heating elements. Grille is 18 1/4" wide x 3 5/8" high.

'Register' Heater with Thermostat
9315T (120 Volts)
9315XT (240 Volts)
Compact fan-forced heater styled like conventional forced-air 'register'. Built-in rotary thermostat On/Off switch.

Select 750W or 1500W at installation with simple 'plug-in' of either one or two heating elements. Easily installed. Grille is 12" wide x 9 3/8" high.

9840 Hi-Wattage Wall Heater (240 Volts)
Fan-forced. Handy built-in switch lets you choose 2000W or 4000W as needed. Built-in rotary thermostat lets you dial the comfort level you want – or turn Heater Off. One-piece grille is 15 1/2" wide x 20" high.

For complete information on the full line of NuTone Heaters, see Catalog VH-360.

With a Built-In NuTone Pants Presser you can have professionally pressed pants any time!

NUTONE BUILT-IN PANTS PRESSER EPP-30

Effectively eliminates wrinkles and restores a sharp crease to pants in just 30 minutes.* Works great on neckties, scarves and handkerchiefs too. An excellent way to save on dry cleaning bills. Ideal for master bedroom, dressing room or guest room.

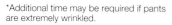

Reversible front panel is set in a chrome frame...rich oak-finished woodgrain look on one side, unfinished genuine oak veneer on the other. Unfinished side can be painted, stained or wallpapered. Panel may also be replaced with a mirror or color-coordinated laminate panel (purchase separately).

*Additional time may be required if pants are extremely wrinkled.

Easy to install. Recesses between 16" o.c. studs for a built-in look.

Thinline design blends with any decor. Black top panel with silver trim opens to reveal 30 minute timer, on/off indicator light plus a compartment for your watch, wallet, coins and keys.

Place pants in the NuTone Presser while you take a shower or before you go to bed. Set the timer for 30 minutes and forget it. Timer automatically shuts off unit when time has elapsed. Pants may be safely left in unit overnight.

For complete information on the NuTone Pants Presser, see Catalog EPP-30.

NuTone Radio-Intercom works for you in every room!

Located in the kitchen, the Master Station becomes the communication and entertainment center of your home

NuTone Radio-Intercoms
You can be in two places at once! NuTone Radio-Intercom gives you room-to-room intercom ... the security of answering your front door without opening it ... lets you listen in on the baby or to a sick room ... enjoy FM/AM radio in any room, poolside or on the patio!
Plus two new options: Video Door-Answering and Surveillance, and Home Control of electric outlets and lights – indoors and outside – can be added to *any* NuTone Radio-Intercom.

Imagine seeing, hearing and talking to callers at the front door from your bathroom, bedroom or anywhere you have a remote speaker in your home

NuTone offers a complete line of Radio-Intercom systems to meet every home or budget requirement.

IMA-4006

Door Speakers IS-58V, IS-69PB, ISB-64

VALUABLE HOMEOWNER'S WARRANTY

NUTONE PRODUCTS GUARANTEED FOR AS LONG AS YOU OWN YOUR HOME

For complete information on the NuTone Radio-Intercoms, see Catalog IR-700.

5

NuTone Bath Cabinets add sparkle, elegance and convenient storage to today's larger, more luxurious baths and powder rooms

NuTone lets you put an end to the "lookalike" bathroom! Classic designs are combined with useful features in a vast selection of quality Bath Cabinets.

Select from the stunning all-glass mirrored styles shown here ... or wood or metal framed cabinets, some with built-in lights or matching sidelights ... or a magnificent TriVista with all-around viewing.

Today there's no need to choose between a spacious all-glass look or convenient storage. Because all NuTone Bath Cabinets include the wonderful *bonus* of right-there storage ... the most appreciated luxury of all!

The Radiance Collection's modular design lets you create an infinite variety of custom combinations.

Turn your bath from ordinary to *extraordinary!* The NuTone Radiance series includes dazzling clear glass cabinets, mirrors, toplights and coordinating shelves. The mirrored glass is richly detailed with striking polished v-grooves and beveled edges. The cabinets can be recessed or surface mounted. Pair several modular pieces for a breathtaking ensemble for the master bath. Or, use a single cabinet and matching toplight for a smaller bath or powder room.

For example, in the elegant grouping shown on the facing page, two Radiance cabinets are surface mounted, separated by a matching mirror. The Radiance toplights and shelf unite the three units into a single, coordinated ensemble – to make any bath more luxurious, more spacious looking.

D-2000 Radiance Cabinet D-2000-LK-4 Radiance Toplight Beveled mirrors with striking v-grooves surround a double-sided mirror door. Inside ... a spacious cabinet with full mirror behind 3 adjustable glass shelves. A magnifying cosmetic mirror is also included. Add a coordinated toplight and the look is complete. Cabinet recesses. Overall dimensions: 24" x 33". Can be surface mounted with kit D-2000-SM.

D-2000-LK4 Radiance Toplight Handsome coordinating glass light for use with D-2000 recessed cabinet or D-2000-M mirror. Overall dimensions: 24" x 4" x 4".

Radiance models available:
D-2000 Cabinet
D-2000-SM Surface-Mounting Kit
D-2000-M Mirror
D-2000-LK4 Toplight
D-2000-LK8 Toplight
D-2000-S48 Shelf
D-2000-S72 Shelf

D-179 Reflections Graceful arched mirror-on-mirror cabinet creates a striking look for traditional or contemporary baths. Full 3/4" bevel around mirror. Recessed cabinet with ample storage, two adjustable glass shelves. Overall size: 19" x 30".

D-71 Viewpoint Brilliant, uncommonly elegant round mirrored cabinet is high-lighted with polished v-grooves and a 1/2" beveled edge. Recessed cabinet with two adjustable glass shelves. Overall size: 28" diameter.

D-2000 Radiance Cabinet
D-2000-LK-4 Radiance Toplight

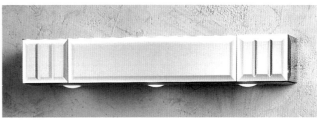

D-2000-LK4 Radiance Toplight

NuTone Radiance cabinets feature all the "extras" you want. Double-sided beveled mirror door, full mirror on back of cabinet, glass shelves, magnifying cosmetic mirror (6¾" round), specially designed European hinges that allow cabinet door to open a full 135° and push-to-release magnetic catches.

For complete information on the full line of NuTone Bath Cabinets, see Catalog BC-900.

Radiance D-2000 (two)/D-2000-SM (two)/D-2000-M, D-2000-LK8 (two)/D-2000-LK4 Valance Lights and D-2000-S72 Mirrored Shelf.
Put together a custom look for your bath with unique Radiance cabinets, mirrors, top lights and shelves. Components can be combined
in an almost infinite number of ways.

D-71 Viewpoint

D-179 Reflections

NuTone offers functional Bath Cabinet design options with enduring beauty, for every decor

NEW! 3130L Imperial TriVista

D-146 Reflections Distinctive octagonal beveled mirror-on-beveled-mirror creates three-tiered illusion. Overall size: 18" x 28".

D-169N Deauville Polished brass finish seamless aluminum tubing outlines graceful arched beveled mirror. Size: 17¾" x 29¾".

D-171 Continental Cabinet DL-171 Continental Top Light Polished Brass half-round frame adds rich detail to rectangular mirror door. Matching Toplight features mirror-chrome backplate. Cabinet 16" x 26", Toplight 16" x 5".

New! D-370L Bright Lights TriVista All-in-one cabinet with center beveled mirror door and mirrored toplight, two beveled-edge wing mirrors. Surface-mount steel cabinet has two adjustable shelves, convenience outlet and switch. Overall size: 35" x 26".

New! D-530LPC Beacon Handsome polished chrome finish frame outlines this surface-mount slider. Built-in light strip. Sturdy enameled steel cabinet with two adjustable shelves. Two sizes: 23¾" x 25" and 29¾" x 25".

New! 2130BE Aurora All-glass bi-view cabinet. Sturdy, enameled steel surface-mount cabinet. Two shelves and magnifying mirror. Overall size: 30" x 30¾".

New! 3130L Imperial TriVista Goldtone frame with dramatic black marble-look insert. Trio of 1/2" beveled mirror doors. Inside, there's storage plus two adjustable glass shelves, convenience outlet and switch. Two sizes: 30¼" x 30⅞" and 36¼" x 30⅞".

New! 3333-36HO Richwood TriVista Solid oak framed TriVista. Trio of mirrored doors for all-round viewing. Easy-to-open, push-to-release catches. Inside, there's generous storage with two adjustable shelves. Four sizes: 25¼" x 32", 31¼" x 32", 37¼" x 32", 49¼" x 32".

New! 3530BE Minuet TriVista Beveled-edge mirror doors open for ample storage and all-round viewing. Sturdy steel cabinet with two shelves. Surface-mounted. Overall size: 30" x 34½".

New! 3736LBE Hollywood TriVista Radius corner bevel-edge mirror doors, toplights for extra dramatic impact. European hinges. Steel cabinet surface mounts. Two shelves and convenience outlet. Two sizes: 30" x 33⅛" and 36" x 33½".

New! 3930LPB Park Avenue TriVista Polished Brass half-round frame surrounds three hinged mirror doors for all-round viewing. Built-in lights have reflective backplate for added brilliance. No visible hardware. Steel surface-mount cabinet. Two sizes: 29¾" x 30½", 35¾" x 30½".

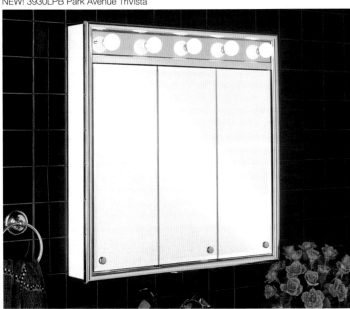

NEW! 3930LPB Park Avenue TriVista

NEW! 3530BE Minuet TriVista

For complete information on the full line of NuTone Bath Cabinets, see Catalog BC-900.

NEW! 2130BE Aurora

D-169N Deauville

D-146 Reflections

NEW! D-530LPC Beacon

D-171 Continental Cabinet
DL-171 Continental Top Light

NEW! D-370L Bright Lights TriVista

3333-36HO Richwood TriVista

NEW! 3736LBE Hollywood TriVista

NuTone HallMack Bath Accessories are styled to perfectly complement luxury bathroom decors

Everything you need to help create a stunning traditional or contemporary bath environment can be yours with HallMack by NuTone Bath Accessories.

The Sovereign Collection: superb quality, hot forged solid brass accessories, crafted in two distinctive finishes ... plus exquisite sidelights.

AristoChrome: fine-forged solid brass in Polished Brass or Polished Chrome finish.

Select from an array of beautiful, functional HallMack by NuTone accessories for luxurious convenience.

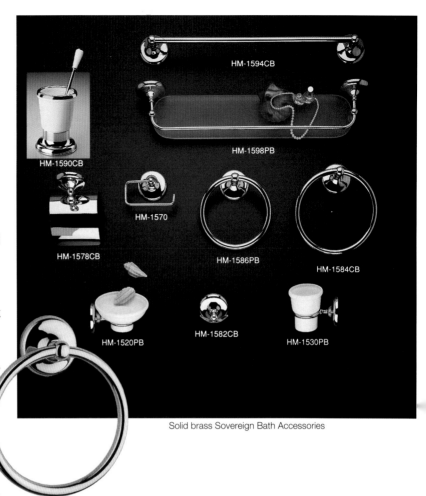

Solid brass Sovereign Bath Accessories

Sovereign Bath Accessories and Sidelights.

Choose your Sovereign accessories in classic Polished Brass or the contemporary look of Polished Chrome touched with Brass. Both styles are protected with clear lacquer that will stand up to years of use. Creamy white ceramic pieces and frosted glass add a distinctive touch. Concealed-screw surface mountings enhance Sovereign's flowing lines.

Stunning sidelights of frosted or white glass with either solid brass wall mounts or arched mirror back plates add the perfect illumination.

No matter which NuTone Sovereign pieces you choose, the results will be simply elegant!

Sovereign

DL-615	Sovereign Sidelight 5" wide x 12" high; extends 7 5/8" (Polished Brass only) Lamp wattage: 60W*
DL-1505	Sovereign Sidelight 6 1/2" W x 8 3/4" H extends 8 1/2" (Polished brass only) Lamp wattage: 60W*
HM-1502	Mirror Support Brackets. Set of 4. (Polished Brass only).
HM-1520	Soap Holder with ceramic soap dish
HM-1530	Tumbler Holder with ceramic tumbler
HM-1570	Paper Holder
HM-1578	Paper Holder with Hood
HM-1582	Double Robe Hook
HM-1584	Towel Ring 9" dia.
HM-1586	Towel Ring 7 3/4" dia.
HM-1590	Urn and Brush Ceramic urn 7 1/2" tall Brush 12 7/8" long with ceramic handle
HM-1594	Towel Bar - 5/8" round Lengths: 24" or 30"
HM-1598	Glass Shelf, frosted 24 3/4" long

*Lamps not included

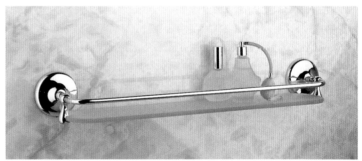

HM-1598 Glass Shelf

DL-1505 Sidelight

DL-615 Sovereign Sidelight shown with NuTone 790N Elegance Mirror (available separately) and HM-1502 Sovereign Mirror Support Brackets.

For complete information on the full line of NuTone HallMack Bath Accessories, see Catalog HM-1000.

10

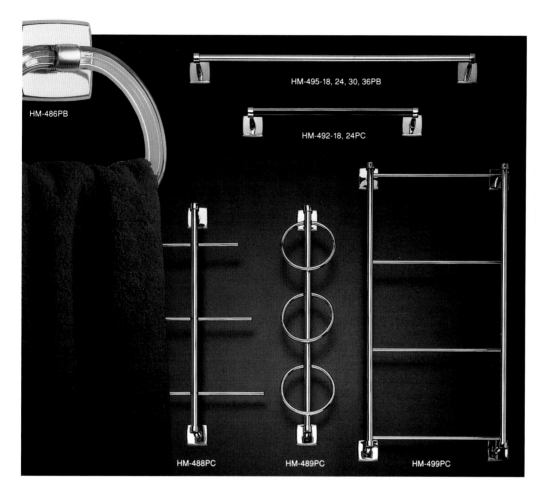

HM-486PB

HM-495-18, 24, 30, 36PB

HM-492-18, 24PC

HM-488PC   HM-489PC   HM-499PC

AristoChrome Bath Accessories in two beautiful finishes – Polished Brass and Polished Chrome.

HallMack by NuTone meets the demands of the most discriminating with the splendid craftsmanship of AristoChrome in fine-forged solid brass!

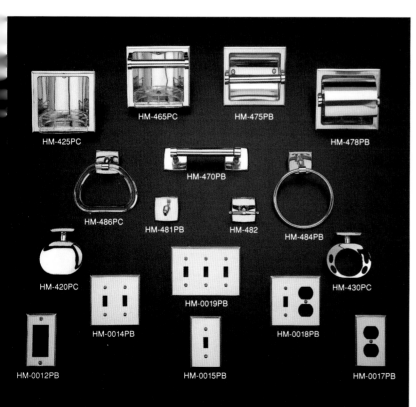

HM-425PC
HM-465PC
HM-475PB
HM-478PB
HM-470PB
HM-486PC
HM-481PB
HM-482
HM-484PB
HM-420PC
HM-430PC
HM-0019PB
HM-0014PB
HM-0018PB
HM-0012PB
HM-0015PB
HM-0017PB

AristoChrome

HM-420	Soap Holder
HM-425	Recessed Soap/ Tumbler Holder with removable polystyrene tray
HM-430	Toothbrush & Tumbler Holder
HM-465	Recessed Soap and Bar with removable polystyrene tray
HM-470	Surface-Mounted Paper Holder
HM-475	Recessed Paper Holder
HM-478	Recessed Paper Holder with Hood
HM-481	Single Hook
HM-482	Double Hook
HM-484	Towel Ring
HM-486	Towel Ring (clear lucite ring)
HM-488	Towel Tree* 15 1/2" W x 24"H
HM-489	Triple Towel Ring* 24" high
HM-492	Towel Bar* 3/4" hexagonal stainless steel bar Lengths: 18" & 24"

HM-495	Towel Bar 3/4" round bar Lengths: 18", 24", 30" & 36"
HM-499	Towel Ladder* 16 3/4" x 32"

Solid Brass Switchplates

Polished Brass finish

HM-0012PB	GFI Switch Plate
HM-0014PB	Double Switch Plate
HM-0015PB	Single Switch Plate
HM-0017PB	Duplex Receptacle Plate
HM-0018PB	Duplex Receptacle and Switch Plate
HM-0019PB	Triple Switch Plate

*Available in Polished Chrome only

For complete information on the full line of NuTone HallMack Bath Accessories, see Catalog HM-1000.

NuTone Exhaust Fans and Fan-Lights provide quiet, efficient ventilation to help make today's homes more comfortable

Powerful yet quiet! NuTone ventilation can rid your home of airborne contaminants, heat, smoke, humidity and stale odors from cooking, cleaning and showering.

NuTone's great selection of designs and decorator finishes please the most discriminating homeowner. And all are guaranteed for as long as you own your home. m̶p̶p̶

New! QT90. 90 CFM at 1.5 sones. Meets Washington State code requirements for houses from 1300-1800 sq. ft. (85 CFM at .25 static pressure.) For baths up to 85 sq.ft., other rooms to 115 sq. ft.

QT130 Twin blowers. 130 CFM vertical or 120 CFM horizontal – at a mere 1.0 sones! For baths up to 120 sq.ft., other rooms to 160 sq.ft.*

QT140L QuieTTest Fan-Light with Night Light 150 CFM at only 2.0 sones. 100W ceiling light, 7W night light. Can be used in tub or shower enclosures.** For baths to 140 sq. ft., other rooms to 185 sq. ft. White polymeric grille with shadow free glass lens, aluminum reflector.

QT150 QuieTTest Fan For baths up to 150 sq. ft., other rooms to 200 sq. ft. Powerful – 160 CFM at 2.5 sones! White polymeric grille.

QT200 QuieTTest Fan Ventilates rooms up to 250 sq. ft. 200 CFM at 2.0 sones. Horizontal or vertical ducting. White polymeric grille.

QT300 For rooms up to 375 sq. ft., 300 CFM at 4.5 sones.

QT80 For baths up to 75 sq. ft., other rooms to 100 sq. ft. 80 CFM at 1.5 sones. White polymeric grille.

QT110 For bathrooms up to 105 sq. ft., other rooms to 135 sq. ft. 110 CFM at 2.0 sones. White polymeric grille, 4" duct.

8663/8673 Series Fan-Lights
100 CFM at 3.5 sones. For baths to 95 sq.ft., other rooms to 125 sq.ft.
Genuine Wood Fan-Lights –
8663LG Round 8673LG Square
Oak-stained frames, brass finish grilles. Glass lens.
Decorator Metal Fan-Lights
8663MAB – Antique Brass
8663MBR – Polished Brass
8663MSA – Satin Aluminum
Can be used in shower or tub enclosure.** Uses 100W lamp.
Polymeric Fan-Lights –
8663P Round 8673P Square
White polymeric grille. 100W lamp. 7W night light. Can be used in shower or tub enclosure.**
8663F Fluorescent Fan-Light
Combines energy-saving fluorescent lamps with high performance. White polymeric grille.

8814 Exhaust Fan for large baths. Polymeric grille in white pebble finish. Can be used in shower or tub enclosure.** 110 CFM for baths up to 105 sq. ft.

8833 Concealed-Intake Bath Fan Brushed aluminum center panel can be painted or papered. For baths up to 75 sq. ft., other rooms to 100 sq. ft. 80 CFM, 3.5 sones.

8832WH/8832SA Bath Fan Mounts in ceiling or wall. Choice of white or silver aluminum grille. For baths up to 75 sq. ft., other rooms to 100 sq. ft. 80 CFM, 3.5 sones.

8145 Room-to-Room Fan Moves 220 cu. ft. of air every minute at peak setting. Solid-state speed control. Adobe white textured grille.

8070WH/8070SA 8" Automatic Fan 160 CFM. No duct Thru-the-Wall-Fan. Choose white or silver anodized aluminum grille.
8170WH/8170SA 10" 270 CFM.

8010WH/8010SA 8" Pull-Chain Fan 250 CFM. No duct Thru-the-Wall-Fan. Choose white or silver anodized aluminum grille.
8110WH/8110SA 10" 550 CFM.

8220 8" Round Vertical Discharge Fan 170 CFM, 4.0 sones.

8210 7" Round Vertical Discharge Fan 210 CFM, 6.5 sones.

8490 10" Round Vertical Discharge Fan 260 CFM, 5.5 sones.

8510 10" Round Fan For Walls or Ceilings 300 CFM, 7.5 sones.

8310 8" Round Fan 180 CFM, 5.5 sones.

Exterior-Mounted Fans

RF/WF-35 Roof/Wall Fans Strong centrifugal blower, 270 CFM. Uses 7" round duct. Aluminum damper opens and closes automatically.

WF-1N Wall Fan All aluminum housing with stainless steel fittings, rainshield included. 650 CFM.

RF-1N Roof Fan 1/8 HP motor, 620 CFM. Aluminum housing with 24" sq. self-flashing flange.

*Meets Northwest Energy Ventilation Code.

**UL Listed for use in a tub or shower enclosure when used with GFI branch circuit.

RF-40 Heavy Duty Roof Fan 1000 CFM. 1/8 HP motor. All-aluminum housing.

Deluxe Attic Cooling Fans

RF-69N Aluminum Attic Fan 1250 CFM. 22" dia. Automatic thermostat. Ball-bearing motor. Bird guard.

RF-59N Enameled Attic Fan Same as RF-69N, but with zinc-coated steel housing finished in baked enamel.

RF-68H Attic Fan 1530 CFM. Ball-bearing motor. Heavy-gauge aluminum housing. Bird guard. Automatic thermostat.

8673LG Wood Fan-Light

QT140L QuieTTest Fan-Light

8673P Polymeric Fan-Light

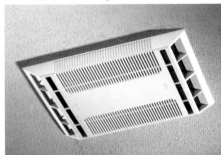

QT130, QT150, QT200, QT300 QuieTTest Twin Blower Fans

8814 Bath Fan

QT80, QT90, QT110 QuieTTest Fans

12

8663LG Wood Fan Light

8663MBR Polished Brass Fan-Light

8663P Polymeric Fan-Light

8663F Fluorescent Fan-Light

8833 Concealed-Intake Bath Fan

8663MAB Antique Brass Fan-Light

8663MSA Satin Aluminum Fan-Light

8832SA Bath Fan

8145 Room-to-Room Fan

8070SA, 8170SA Thru-the-Wall Automatic Fans

8010WH, 8110WH Thru-the-Wall Pull-Chain Fans

8210, 8220, 8490 Exhaust Fans

8310, 8510 Ceiling Exhaust Fans

RF35 Roof Fan

WF35 Wall Fan

RF-1N Roof Fan

WF-1N Wall Fan

RF40 Heavy Duty Roof Fan

RF68H Roof Fan

RF69N Roof Fan

RF59N Roof Fan

VALUABLE HOMEOWNER'S WARRANTY

NUTONE PRODUCTS GUARANTEED FOR AS LONG AS YOU OWN YOUR HOME

mpp

For complete information on the full line of NuTone Exhaust Fans, see Catalog VH-360.

NuTone Built-in Electric Heaters...turn the cold spots in your home into cozy warm...save heating the whole house

A NuTone auxiliary heater can make any room – the bath, nursery, den, family room – more pleasant in any season.

NuTone heaters save energy too! They make the room you're in warm and cozy, without turning up your whole-house thermostat.

Just look at the selection of models and finishes! Deluxe fan-forced multi-function units provide heat, light, ventilation – even a night light – singly, or in combination. There are silent radiant ceiling heaters, plus handsome wall heaters!

Build-in beauty, comfort and *quality* with NuTone Electric Heaters. *Guaranteed!* mpp

QT-9093AB and
9093AB Heat-A-Ventlites®

QT-9093 QuieTTest Heat-A-Ventlite®
Enjoy NuTone QuieTTest performance in this classic Heater, Fan, Light and Night Light combination fixture! 1500W heating element with blower evenly distributes heat. 110CFM at a quiet 2.5 sones. Bright 100W ceiling light, 7W night light. Four function Switch included.
QT-9093AB Antique Brass
QT-9093BR Polished Brass
QT-9093CH Chrome
QT-9093WH White

9093 Deluxe Heat-A-Ventlite® This combination Heater, Ventilator and Ceiling Light has been an industry standard for years. Now a handy Night Light makes it even better! 1500W heating element, aluminum blower, glass lens. Uses 100W lamp. Four function Switch included.
9093AB Antique Brass
9093BR Polished Brass
9093CH Chrome
9093WH White

9013NL Heat-A-Lite® Heat, bright light – and now a convenient Night Light, plus Switch to control all functions separately! Ideal for rooms with a separate ventilating fan. Chrome grill.

9965 Heat-A-Ventlite® Performance plus great contemporary styling! Heat, 100W Light, Ventilation and Night Light operate singly or in combination. White polymeric grille. Switch included.

9960 Heat-A-Lite® with Night Light. Same as 9965, but without vent fan.

9905 Heat-A-Vent® Same as 9965, but without lights. Switch included.

9427 Two-Bulb Heat-A-Vent®
Silent, instant warmth and ventilation ... together or separately. White Noryl® ceiling plate. Automatic reset thermal protection.

9417D One-Bulb Heat-A-Vent®
has same features as 9427, above.

9422 Two-Bulb Heat-A-Lamp®
Instant radiant heat with two 250W infrared lamps. Compact design for medium size bathrooms. White Noryl® ceiling plate. Automatic reset thermal protection.

9412D One-Bulb Heat-A-Lamp®
for smaller bathrooms. Uses 250W infrared lamp. White Noryl® ceiling plate.

9840 Deluxe Hi-Wattage Wall Heater Powerful 240 Volt Heater is perfect for larger rooms – offices, family rooms, vestibules! Handy built-in switch lets you choose 2000W or 4000W of cozy warmth. Built-in rotary thermostat. Light almond steel grille accented with black chrome louvers, bright chrome anodized aluminum frame.

Fan-Forced Wall Heaters
9810BWN Brown Wood-grain
9810WH White Strong, even heat from a 1000W instant heating element to warm an entire room. Handsome, heat-resistant Noryl® grille in choice of brown wood-grain or Bright White finish.

9815BWN, 9815WH 1500W Fan-Forced Wall Heater. Same features as 9810. **9819BWN, 9819WH** 1920W Fan-Forced Wall Heater. Same features as 9810.

9965 Heat-A-Ventlite®

9960 Heat-A-Lite®

9905 Heat-A-Vent®

9840 Hi-Wattage Wall Heater

9810WH, 9815WH, 9819WH
Wall Heaters

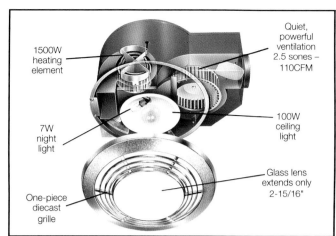

1500W heating element

Quiet, powerful ventilation 2.5 sones – 110CFM

7W night light

100W ceiling light

One-piece diecast grille

Glass lens extends only 2-15/16"

Cutaway view QT-9093CH

9417D One-Bulb Heat-A-Vent®

9427 Two-Bulb Heat-A-Ventlite®

9422 Two-Bulb Heat-A-Lamp®

9412D One-Bulb Heat-A-Lamp®

QT-9093BR, 9093BR

QT-9093CH, 9093CH, 9013NL

QT-9093WH, 9093WH Heat-A-Ventlite®

VALUABLE HOMEOWNER'S WARRANTY

NUTONE PRODUCTS GUARANTEED FOR AS LONG AS YOU OWN YOUR HOME

mpp

15

NuTone products add comfort, convenience, security and entertainment to your home

Central Vacs

Imagine vacuum cleaning so thorough you have to dust less often! So quiet you can vacuum while baby naps or the family watches TV. So convenient you don't have to lug around a heavy motor. All you carry is a lightweight hose and cleaning tool. Cleaning room-to-room, up and down stairs, basement, garage is easier. No wonder NuTone Central Vac is one of today's most-wanted features.

The power unit is built-in. NuTone offers *five* different systems. Sanitary, fully disposable soil bag models, and a bagless unit with the revolutionary NuTone Draw-down™ Cyclonic patented technology. Easy to install, they add value to any home.

On/Off inlets come in colors to blend with your home decor. Simply plug in the cleaning hose and the powerful motor is on – ready to wisk away dirt and dust.

Door Chimes

Express your personal decorating touch with a traditional or contemporary NuTone Chime. Chime tones range from two-note to chordtone to the beloved Westminster chime sequence ... or even one you can program to play any tune you can whistle, sing or hum!
There are even wireless extension chimes and a visual door signal for the hearing impaired!

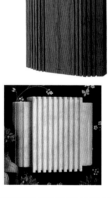

Paddle Fans
Add comfort and energy efficiency with an elegant NuTone contemporary or traditional fan. Light Kits are also available.

mpp This symbol identifies NuTone Maximum Performance Products – *guaranteed for as long as you own your home.*

For the name of your nearby NuTone sales outlet, **DIAL FREE** **1-800-543-8687** in the contiguous U.S., except in Ohio call 1-800-582-2030.

VALUABLE HOMEOWNER'S WARRANTY

NUTONE PRODUCTS GUARANTEED FOR AS LONG AS YOU OWN YOUR HOME

mpp

Send for FREE Full Line catalog

NuTone Inc., Dept. KBS-93
P.O. Box 1580, Cincinnati, Ohio 45201

Name	Title
Company	
Address	
City	State	Zip
Phone	9537

Product specifications subject to change without notice.   Form 9537, Printed in U.S.A.

NuTone

Olsonite ®

SOFT TOUCH

Comfortable, easy-care soft touch Olsonite seat combines thick urethane foam covered with heavy gauge, electronically heat sealed matte-finish vinyl. Full coverage lid with squared ring design provides extra style and superior durability.

SOFT SEAT

KS Available in a wide range of colors, Olsonite's KS Soft Seat adds the perfect modern touch. Easy-care, comfortable and engineered to last, comes complete with mathing top mount hinges.

SOFT TOUCH EMBROIDERED

Attractive soft-cushioned comfort on pastel colors, in two distinctive embroidered designs. Color-fast securely stiched embroidery on Olsonite's easy-clean, durable soft touch seat.

MONARCH

EMBT 60 Popular Monarch pattern with cheerful butterflies and flowers, securely stiched, accent Olsonite's superior design soft touch seat.

FLEURETTE

750 SP Spectacular fleurette pattern in a wide range of available colors firmly stiched on a padded vinyl insert. Pattern constructed with high thread count for enduring value.

OLSONITE CORPORATION   8801 CONANT   DETROIT, MICHIGAN 48211   (313) 875-5831   1-800-521-8266   FAX (313) 874-2846

1290

SPRING ROSE

EMBT 47 Lovely large rose with ribbon skillfully stiched. Olsonite's appealing Spring Rose pattern with high thread count for added value.

WOOD WITH EMBROIDERED INSERT

Wonderful embroidered vinyl panel inserted in the cover of our classic enamelled seat. Colored seat matches with thread color on vinyl insert background. Olsonite's wood with embroidered insert seats offer quite a decorative choice.

MONARCH

760 SP Enhanced beauty with timeless monarch pattern featuring butterflies and flowers mounted on a colored enamelled seat.

PEARLESCENT

70 Stunning elegance with Olsonite's lively white pearlescent seat, offered in a classic design built to fit regular bowls. Molded-in pearl-like finish will not chip, crack or peal. Deep lustre and flowing contours compliment most bowl designs.

SOLID OAK

HO66 Uncompromising quality for the discriminating consumer in this handcrafted solid oak seat. Classic, built-to-last finish complimented with brass hinges.

OLSONITE CORPORATION   8801 CONANT   DETROIT, MICHIGAN 48211   (313) 875-5831   1-800-521-8266   FAX (313) 874-2846

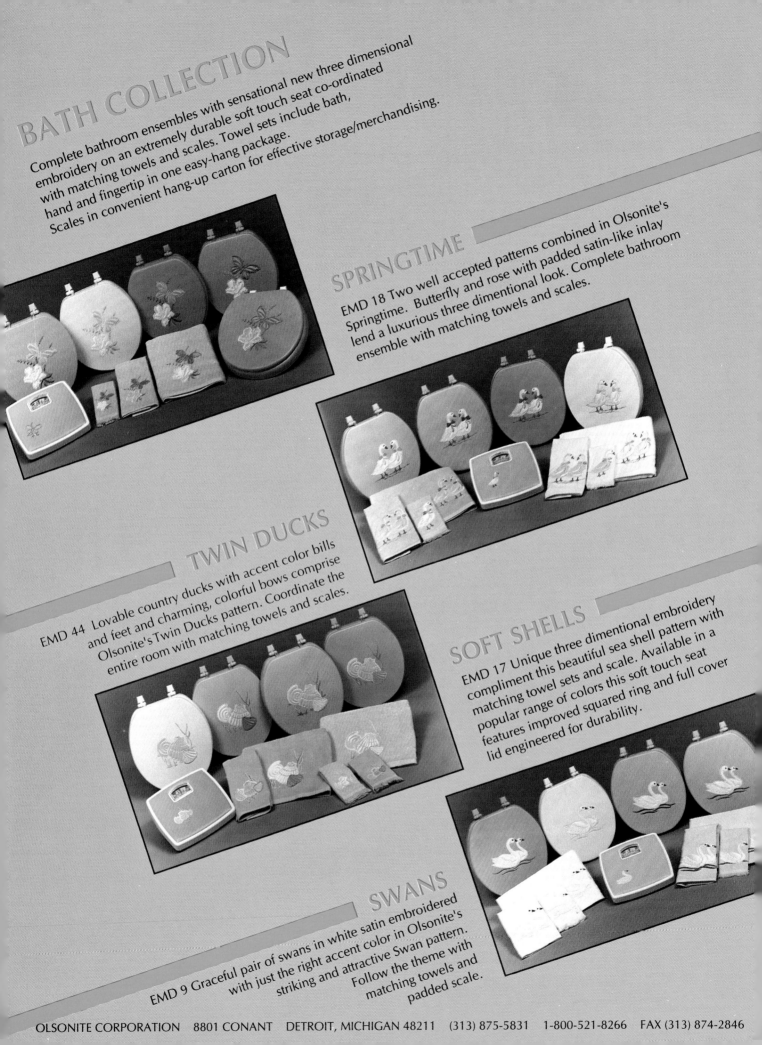

BATH COLLECTION

Complete bathroom ensembles with sensational new three dimensional embroidery on an extremely durable soft touch seat co-ordinated with matching towels and scales. Towel sets include bath, hand and fingertip in one easy-hang package. Scales in convenient hang-up carton for effective storage/merchandising.

SPRINGTIME

EMD 18 Two well accepted patterns combined in Olsonite's Springtime. Butterfly and rose with padded satin-like inlay lend a luxurious three dimensional look. Complete bathroom ensemble with matching towels and scales.

TWIN DUCKS

EMD 44 Lovable country ducks with accent color bills and feet and charming, colorful bows comprise Olsonite's Twin Ducks pattern. Coordinate the entire room with matching towels and scales.

SOFT SHELLS

EMD 17 Unique three dimensional embroidery compliment this beautiful sea shell pattern with matching towel sets and scale. Available in a popular range of colors this soft touch seat features improved squared ring and full cover lid engineered for durability.

SWANS

EMD 9 Graceful pair of swans in white satin embroidered with just the right accent color in Olsonite's striking and attractive Swan pattern. Follow the theme with matching towels and padded scale.

OLSONITE CORPORATION   8801 CONANT   DETROIT, MICHIGAN 48211   (313) 875-5831   1-800-521-8266   FAX (313) 874-2846

Quality, durability and color versatility in tub, shower and whirlpool surfacing.

ARISTECH ACRYLIC SHEET

■ *Altair I-300 is the most attractive plumbingware surface material available anywhere.*

That's a pretty bold statement, but it's a fact. Altair I-300 comes in a vast array of glossy colors. Other surface materials don't. Consumers can now choose from over thirty solid colors and soft marbles for any specific decor.

■ *Altair I-300 is easily maintained.*

Consumers will especially appreciate that the vibrant, high-gloss features of Altair I-300 are retained for years with minimal care using mild household cleaning materials. No back-breaking scrubbing is required to clean Altair I-300 because it's not a porous material. Dirt and grime can't penetrate the surface and cause discoloring. With just a few wipes, Altair I-300 looks brand new again... and stays that way year after year.

The plumbingware surface material of the future is available today...Altair® I-300 Acrylic Sheet, manufactured by Aristech Chemical Corporation.

Today all of the major plumbingware manufacturers have chosen Altair I-300 acrylic surfaces for their premier whirlpool, tub and shower units.

Designers, builders and remodelers are also discovering that when given a choice, more and more home buyers and remodeling customers are choosing Altair I-300 acrylic surfaces for their plumbingware products.

WHAT ARE THE ADVANTAGES OF ACRYLIC PLUMBINGWARE SURFACES?

Fact: Tubs, showers and whirlpools with Altair I-300 acrylic surfaces look better and last longer than units made from competitive materials. And when you get right down to the bottom line (and what customer doesn't), the long-term durability of acrylic translates into economic savings. Economics also play a leading role for builders since installation times are minimized.

■ *Altair I-300...a very durable plumbingware surface material.*
Altair I-300 has earned a reputation as a tough and durable acrylic surface. It has proven impact resis-

tance. Tests and field experience have shown that under normal use and conditions, it will not chip, crack or craze...and the colors won't fade over the years.

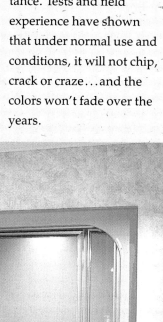

■ *Altair I-300 is economical, too.*
When you consider that Altair I-300 acrylic retains its appearance and physical properties years longer than other materials, it truly is the economical choice.

And Altair I-300 acrylic plumbingware surfaces have a "warm" feel. Unlike the cold sensation you get from contact with steel or cast iron, Altair I-300 retains heat naturally...making it an energy-efficient material.

So when you're specifying tubs, showers, modular tub/showers and whirl-pools, choose the surface material of the future... today. Aristech's Altair I-300.

For more information about where plumbingware products with Altair® I-300 surfaces are available near you, contact a manufacturer listed below.

SPAS

**Benson Pump/
Seven Sea Spa**
800 Central Ave.
University Park, IL 60466
708-534-6242

Blue Pacific
7630 South Union Ave.
Bakersfield, CA 93307
805-836-2779

**California
Acrylic Industries**
1462 E. 9th St.
Pomona, CA 91766
714-623-8781

Catalina Spas Inc.
275 W. Rider St.
Perris, CA 92571
714-940-4556

Clearwater Spas
P.O. Box 2140
Woodinville, WA 98072
206-483-1877

Colorado Made Spas
389 Wadsworth
Lakewood, CO 80226
303-233-7103

DFA
205 S. 28th St.
Phoenix, AZ 85034
602-225-0101

Delair Group
1 Delair Plaza
Delair, NJ 08110
609-663-2901

Dolphin Spas
717 N. McKeever Ave.
Azusa, CA 91702
818-334-0099

Gold Country Spas
3899 Security Park Dr.
Rancho Cordova, CA 95742
916-351-0721

Grecian Spas
7200 Hazard Ave.
Westminster, CA 92683
714-891-6641

Leisure Spas
P.O. Box 607366
Orlando, FL 32860-7366
407-297-0141

Marquis Corporation
596 Hoffman Rd.
Independence, OR 97351
503-838-0888

Pacific Pool
#8 12th St.
Blaine, WA 98230
604-533-4771

Quality Acrylic Spas
8993 Tara Blvd.
Jonesboro, GA 30236
404-603-0058

SSI/Alternate Eng.
2593 South Raritan St.
Englewood, CO 80110
303-936-1828

Saratoga Spa and Bath
33 Wade Rd.
Latham, NY 12110
206-383-1727

Spa-N-Save
1474 Grass Valley
Auburn, CA 95603
916-888-6077

Sundance Spas Inc.
13951 Monte Vista St.
Chino, CA 91710
714-627-7670

Tadd Manufacturing
P.O. Box 1186
Poplar Bluff, MO 63901
314-686-7266

IN CANADA

City Fiberglass Co. Ltd.
c/o Triac Industries
40 Minuk Acres
West Hill, Ontario,
Canada M1E 4Y6
416-281-9475

Donner Plastic Products
5721 Production Way
Langley, B.C.,
Canada V3A 4N5
604-530-2684

Leisure Mfg./Sunrise
417 Read Rd.
St. Catherines,
Ontario, Canada L1R 7K6
416-646-7727

Pacific Pool Water Products
6315 202nd St.
Langley, B.C.,
Canada V3A 4P7
604-533-4771

Technican Industries
383 Elgin St., Box 1870
Brantford, Ontario,
Canada N3T 5W4
519-756-3442

Waterworks
2351 Simpson Rd.
Richmond, B.C.,
Canada V6X 2R2
604-270-0485

PLUMBING-WARE

Aker Plastics Co. Inc.
1001 N. Oak Rd.
P.O. Box 484
Plymouth, IN 46563
219-936-3838

American Molds Dist.
900 Kirby
Wylie, TX 75098
214-442-6116

American Standard
605 S. Ellsworth Ave.
Salem, OH 44460
216-332-9954

**American
Whirlpool Products**
3050 N. 29th Ct.
Hollywood, FL 33020
305-921-4400

Aqua Glass
P.O. Box 412
Industrial Rd.
Adamsville, TN 31310
901-632-0911

Bath-Tec Corporation
P.O. Box 1118
Ennis, TX 75120
214-299-5625

Bremen Glass Company
1010 W. Dewey St.
Bremen, IN 46506
219-546-3298

Crane Plumbing
8290 South Central Exp.
Dallas, TX 75239
214-371-8700

Four Flags Bath Factory
5 Greenwood Ave.
Romeoville, IL 60441-1398
815-886-5900

Hamilton Plastics
P.O. Box 31, Hwy. 78 South
Hamilton, AL 35570
205-921-7858

Hessco
160 E. Foundation
La Habra, CA 90631
213-691-6478

Hydro Swirl
2150 Division St.
Bellingham, WA 98225
206-734-0616

Jacuzzi
100 North Wiget Lane
P.O. Drawer J
Walnut Creek, CA 94596
510-938-7070

Jetta Products Inc.
500-A Centennial Blvd.
Edmond, OK 73013
405-340-6661

Kohler Company
444 Highland Dr.
Kohler, WI 53044
414-459-1671

Kohler Company
P.O. Box 1987
Spartanburg, SC 29301
803-582-3401

Lasco Bathware
P.O. Box 1177
Lot 7 Halifax Cty. Ind.
South Boston, VA 24592
804-572-1200

Lasco Industries
3255 E. Miraloma Ave.
Anaheim, CA 92806
714-993-1220

Lifestyles
6100 237th Place S.E.
Woodinville, WA 98072
206-481-9000

National Fiberglass
5 Greenwood Ave.
Romeoville, IL 60441
708-257-3300

Novi American Inc.
P.O. Box 44649
Atlanta, GA 30336
404-344-5600

Pearl Bath Inc.
9224 73rd Ave. North
Minneapolis, MN 55428
612-424-3335

Premier Plastics
P.O. Box 359
Pontotoc, MS 38863
601-489-2007

Royal Bath
P.O. Box 671666
Houston, TX 77267
713-442-3400

Swirl-Way
P.O. Box 210
1505 Industrial Dr.
Henderson, TX 75252
903-657-1436

Trajet Whirlpool Baths
7025 Sarpy Avenue
Omaha, NB 68147
402-734-2268

Universal Rundle Corp.
P.O. Box 960
New Castle, PA 16103
800-955-0316

IN CANADA

Acryli Plastique J.R. Inc.
118 St. Pierre
Quebec, Canada G05 1V0
819-389-5818

Fiberez Canada
235 Saunders Dr.
P.O. Box 1057
Cornwall, Ontario,
Canada K6H 5V2
613-933-3525

Kohler Company
RR #3 Spallumcheen Dr.
Armstrong, B.C.,
Canada V0E 1B0
604-546-3196

Longevity Acrylics, Inc.
Richmond Road
RR #1 Summertown
Ontario, Canada K0C 2E0
613-931-1615

Maax Inc./Acrylica
600 Rue Cameron
St. Marie Beauce,
Quebec, Canada G6E 3C2
418-387-4155

Mirolin Industries
60 Shorncliffe Rd.
Toronto, Ontario,
Canada M82 5K1
416-231-9030

Sherlic
2755 Boudreau St.
Fleurimont, Quebec,
Canada J1J 3N1
819-562-3500

TCRV, Inc.
64 Grandes Fourches Nord
Sherbrook, Quebec,
Canada J1H 5G2
819-563-4030

**V & R Sensational Marble
Fiberglass Products**
29 Torbarrie Rd.
Downsview, Ontario,
Canada K3L 1G5
416-241-4441

ARISTECH
ACRYLIC SHEET
Quality that comes to the surface.

Altair I-300 is a registered
trademark of Aristech
Chemical Corporation,
Acrylic Sheet Unit,
7350 Empire Drive,
Florence, KY 41042.
Phone (800) 354-9858.
In Canada, call (416) 731-0500.

Altair I-300 is a registered trademark of Aristech Chemical Corporation.

Elegance by Design

Framed Glass Enclosures by Basco.

Shown: Custom Enclosure ▲

A Dramatic Departure from the Basic Bath.

Mirrored Sliding Enclosure

Polished silver delineates the classic style of obscure glass. A beautiful full body mirror and streamlined towel bar compliment its refined appearance.

◀Shown: unit #6150M

Neo-Angle Enclosure

The contemporary Neo-Angle enclosure fits perfectly into any corner for a more spacious bath. It's beauty comes compliments of a black onyx frame which elegantly surrounds tinted grey glass.

Shown: unit #160

Custom Enclosure

◀(Cover) Beyond the ordinary. The brilliance of clear glass adds a daring touch of style to this Basco original. A masterpiece, in it's own right, which exposes Basco's limitless versatility in custom enclosure designs.

Basco's fine collection of enclosure designs take bathrooms from basic to brilliant. The elements of function and form have never been so blended, as in these classic exhibits of elegance.

Door and Panel Enclosure

The simple elegance of Basco's spacious door and panel design stands as a contemporary alternative to the bypass shower enclosure.

◀Shown: unit #135

Etched Glass Enclosure

The rich anodized bronze finish surrounding this etched glass enclosure is a perfect complement to antique bronze fixtures. Our etched enclosures are also available in custom sizes to further enhance any bath design.

Shown: Unit #2150EE ▶

Pivot Shower Door

This clear glass enclosure is highlighted with a sand etched image that adds an exquisite touch to today's bath decors. The absence of hinges defines the clean, crisp design that's uniquely Basco.

◀ Shown: Unit#100 EE/200 EE

Bi-Fold Shower Door

Rich gold accentuates the beauty of obscure glass in this functional bi-fold enclosure. The door is designed to take-up less space, yet allow full access to the shower.

Shown unit #1000 ▶

7201 Snider Road | Mason, OH 45040 | 1-800-543-1938 | FAX 513-573-1919

FR-6/87

Contours

The Curved Glass Collection From Basco.

Unit #880 L, white painted finish with clear glass.

There's been an unexpected turn in bath enclosures. And it's called Contours. The European styled bath enclosure with a profile that actually curves.

The tempered glass panels, arced to a full 90 degrees, surround you in sheer elegance. Making your shower area larger and more spacious than you'd ever think possible.

What's more, Basco, the originator of curved bath enclosures, offers two Contours options: a symmetrical 37″ wide unit #660 and the more spacious 48″ x 36″ unit #880. Both are available with a durable fiberglass* base which meets **ANSI** code #Z124.1. The exact finished opening of the curved base assures easy installation of your Contours enclosure.

*#660 also available with acrylic base

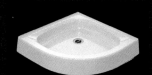
Base #601

Drain Kit #710

Base #800 L (Left)

Unit #660 CL, gold finish with clear glass.

Contours Glass Options: Clear, Bronze Tint and Grey Tint.
Contours also available in custom sizes.

UNIT NUMBER	COLORS							
	Silver	Gold	Black	White	Almond	Tender Grey	Sterling Silver	Red
Contours Bath Enclosure #660	Anodized Metal Finishes			Painted Finishes				
	●	●	●	●	●	●	●	●
Contours Base 37″ x 37″ x 6″ Fiberglass #600 Acrylic #601				●	●	●	●	
Contours Bath Enclosure #880 L (Left) #880 R (Right)	Anodized Metal Finishes			Painted Finishes				
	●	●	●	●	●	●	●	●
Contours Base 48″ x 36″ x 6″ Fiberglass #800 L (Left) Fiberglass #800 R (Right)				●	●	●	●	
Drain Kit #710	Polished Finishes							
	●	●						

Frameless Heavy Glass Enclosures

A Whole New Dimension In Luxury.

Unit #3872 CL, gold finish with clear glass.

Never before has luxury been so clearly defined than with Basco's new frameless heavy glass enclosures. Expertly crafted with 3/8" clear, tempered glass and exquisite styling, these enclosures turn a bathroom into a room of beauty.

What's more, Basco's leak resistant, heavy glass enclosures are readily available in standard heights in a variety of unit styles. We can even accommodate custom applications, which means your dream bath can become a reality. Additionally, each door is designed with a self-closing feature, combining elegance with ease.

Choose from gold, silver and black anodized finishes. Or to coordinate with today's most popular bath fixtures, select one of five painted finishes including white, almond, tender grey, sterling silver and red. A spectrum of options that give your bath luxury beyond measure. Only from Basco.

Unit #3816 CL, gold finish with clear glass.

The finishing touch: a clear acrylic handle to complement our frameless heavy glass door.

Unit #3813 CL Inline

Unit #3814 CL Double Threshold

Unit #3815 CL Double Threshold

A Stroke of Brilliance

Colours. The Painted Frame Collection by Basco.

The revolution taking place in the contemporary bath has prompted some rather colorful moves on our part.

The Colours collection of bath enclosures by Basco.

This elegant line of painted bath enclosures offers a brilliant example of what a little color can do for the common bath.

Of course, all this beauty is more than skin deep. High gloss enamel is electrostatically applied and heat bonded for a durable, lustrous finish that is scratch, crack and chip resistant.

And Colours is available in 5 elegant finishes to complement most popular bath fixtures. It's a stroke of brilliance for your bath.

Contours unit #660CL

White

Almond

Tender Grey

Sterling Silver

Red

Basco Colour Complements*

Basco Colour	Code**	Cross Reference		
		American Standard	Eljer	Kohler
White	WP	White	White	White
Almond	AP	Bone White	Natural	Almond
Tender Grey	GP	—	—	Tender Grey
Sterling Silver	SP	Sterling Silver	Platinum	Ice Grey
Red	RP	—	—	Antique Red

Painted frame color code should be added to end of unit number. For example, 3150CL-48**RP**.

*Shows close match to other manufacturers' colors.

Color matches are as accurate as modern printing techniques will allow. Please contact your Basco dealer to see actual color samples.

bema
BATH ENCLOSURE
MANUFACTURERS
ASSOCIATION

7201 Snider Road　Mason, OH 45040　1-800-543-1938　FAX 513-573-1919

Frameless Infinity Series

Basco's Innovative Design Rounds Another Corner.

Unit #4400, silver finish with clear glass.
Shower height, #4500 is also available.

Infinity is crafted with 1/4" glass for a luxurious look and effortless gliding action. Innovative, curved towel bars accentuate a cleaner, more elegant appearance. Plus, a new rounded header design adds yet another element of style to your exquisite bath. Infinity from Basco. A turning point in bath enclosures.

7201 Snider Road | Mason, Ohio 45040 | 1-800-543-1938

BASCO

Specifications

Materials and Construction:

A. Extruded aluminum shall be 6463-T5 alloy.

B. All exposed screws or fasteners shall be stainless steel to prevent rust and corrosion.

Glazing Materials:

A. Bath Enclosures

All glazing materials to be safety tempered glass with a minimum thickness or .156" on obscure framed panels, .188" on all clear panels, and .200" on obscure frameless panels or other safety glazing materials to conform to CPSC standard 16 CFC 1201 Category I and II.

B. Mirror Doors

Glazing to be .156" mirrors with Class I safety back.

Individual Unit Features:

A. Models 2150/3150 and 6150/7150

1. Fully adjustable sealed ball bearing rollers.
2. Safety tee-lock jamb to header connection.
3. Easy clean, self draining tub track.
4. Molded nylon panel bumpers and guide.
5. Nylon panel guide to be of sufficient height to prevent accidental dislodging of interior panel.
6. (Optional) Vinyl anti-jump insert to be installed in header.
7. Finish shall conform to Aluminum Association Specifications:
   a. AA-M22-C31-A21 for buffed clear bright anodized aluminum (models 6150/7150 and 2150/3150 Silver).
   b. AA-M22-C31-A23 for buffed color bright anodized aluminum (models 6150/7150 and 2150/3150 Gold, Bronze, and Black).

B. Models 8500/9500

1. Fully adjustable sealed ball bearing rollers.
2. Easy clean, self draining tub track.
3. Molded nylon panel bumpers and guide.
4. Nylon panel guide to be of sufficient height to prevent accidental dislodging of interior panel.
5. Finish shall conform to Aluminum Association Specifications:
   a. AA-M1-C31-A21.

C. Models 3400/3500

1. Fully adjustable sealed ball bearing rollers.
2. Safety tee-lock jamb to header connection.
3. Easy clean, self draining tub track.
4. Molded nylon panel bumpers and guide.
5. Nylon panel guide to be of sufficient height to prevent accidental dislodging of interior panel.
6. Finish shall conform to Aluminum Association Specifications:
   a. AA-M22-C31-A21 for buffed clear bright dip anodized aluminum (Silver).
   b. AA-M22-C31-A23 for buffed color bright anodized aluminum (Gold, Bronze, and Black).

D. Models 3600 and 100 Pivot Doors

1. All pivot plates shall be extruded aluminum, finished to match unit.
2. Pivot jambs shall have vertical vinyl seal.
3. All doors shall have continuous drip rail and vinyl wiper blade at bottom of panel. Drip rail to be attached with two sided silicone tape with no exposed screws.
4. Pivot doors to have 2" lateral adjustment, 1" plus and 1" minus.
5. Pull handle on Model 3600 shall be extruded aluminum with integral latch.
6. Pull handles on Model 100 to be extruded and finished to match unit. Latch to be full length magnetic strips in strike rail and strike jamb.
7. Finish shall conform to Aluminum Association Specifications:
   a. AA-M22-C31-A21 for buffed clear bright anodized aluminum (Silver).
   b. AA-M22-C31-A23 for buffed color bright anodized aluminum (Gold, Bronze, and Black).

E. Model 15

1. All doors shall have a continuous piano hinge permanently riveted to the hinge jamb and hinge rail in a finish to match the unit.
2. All doors shall have continuous water deflector and vinyl wiper blade at bottom of panel.
3. All doors shall have handles and adjustable catch in a finish to match the unit.
4. 15 Series door has optional adjustable jamb to provide ± 5/16" adjustment.
5. Finish shall conform to Aluminum Association Specifications:
   a. AA-M12-C31-A21 for clear bright anodized aluminum (Silver).
   b. AA-M12-C31-A23 for color bright anodized aluminum (Gold).

F. Thin-Line

Models 136, 146, 151, 161

1. Pivot jamb and strike jamb to have continuous vinyl seal.
2. Pull handles to be extruded aluminum with integral latch; finish to match unit.

Models 135, 145, 150, 160

1. Pivot jamb to have continuous vinyl seal. Strike jamb and strike rail to have continuous magnetic strip.
2. Pull handles to be extruded aluminum; finish to match unit.

All Models

1. All doors to have continuous drip rail and vinyl seal at bottom of panel. Drip to be attached with two sided silicone tape with no exposed screws.
2. Top pivot pin to have safety washer to prevent accidental dislodging of the door.
3. Finish shall conform to Aluminum Association Specifications:
   a. AA-M22-C31-A21 for buffed clear bright anodized aluminum (Silver).
   b. AA-M22-C31-A23 for buffed color bright anodized aluminum (Gold, Bronze, and Black).

Century

Century Shower Door

C593
10820/CEN
BuyLine 7554

CENTURY

Century Brasstec & Glasstec lines are available in the following finishes:

Century glass options include: clear safety glass, obscure, mirror, striped grey, striped bronze, grey tint, bronze tint, v-groove, beveled or custom.

Polished Brass

Satin Brass

Antique Brass

Polished Chrome

Satin Chrome

Polished Nickel

Satin Nickel

Polished Copper

24K Gold

Century has these distinct advantages that make it the clear leader in the industry:

Variety in design and formats including: sliding, hinged, framed & frameless.

Design dedicated assistance is available to answer questions and solve problems.

Quality and satisfaction is guaranteed with the unmatched Century Guarantee.

Delivery is the best in the business due to our multi-million dollar inventory.

Century aluminum finishes include: polished aluminum, gold anodized, fifteen standard paint colors or custom matching to your specifications.

Charcoal Granite

Grey Stone

Desert Stone

Dusty Rose

Teal Green

BronzeTone

Cobalt Blue

Royal Red

AlmondTone

Cameo Cream

Caramel

Linen White

Platinum Grey

Powder Grey

Black Onyx

Custom applications are a specialty at Century. We are the only manufacturer with full-time product designers to answer questions and solve problems, guaranteeing the best possible service and fit. We stock the widest possible selection of aluminum extrusions and glass options for immediate delivery to meet virtually any need. In addition, our brass line includes over 30 designer channels to fit any configuration.

Century Guarantee We at Century Shower Door guarantee your complete satisfaction with our products. We stand by our enclosures and our customers.

Brasstec enclosures are heavy gauge solid brass, in 1" or 1¼" frame
- Four different designs are available: sliding, hinged, framed & frameless
- Nine different finish options are available including polished, satin, or antique brass, polished or satin chrome, polished or satin nickel, copper & 24K gold.

Glasstec frameless enclosures are constructed of ⅜" or ½" tempered glass with a beveled glass design that seals tight to eliminate the need for channels.
- Patented hinge, header and hardware is available in solid brass and the full Century range of finishes, each individually crafted to customer specifications.
- Glasstec handles are available in standard and "Highline" styles as shown.

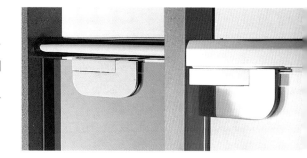

Centec frameless sliding enclosures feature a unique rounded header design constructed of heavy gauge anodized aluminum with ¼" tempered glass doors.
- Finishes include: polished aluminum, gold anodized, twelve standard painted finishes, custom-matched colors, and Stonetec painted granite finish.
- Centec features pass-through towel bars and low-maintenance bottom track.

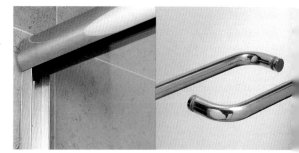

Lucette framed aluminum enclosures have been designed as a system to fit all standard formats and virtually any custom configuration you can dream up.
- Finishes include: polished aluminum, gold anodized, twelve standard painted finishes or custom colors, and the widest range of glass and sizes available.
- A system of over 72 extrusions provides angles & sizes to meet any need.

Crest framed aluminum enclosures are a low cost option for standard formats.
- Available in chrome anodized aluminum finish with a range of glass options.
- Crest is available in hinged & sliding door styles in standard configurations.

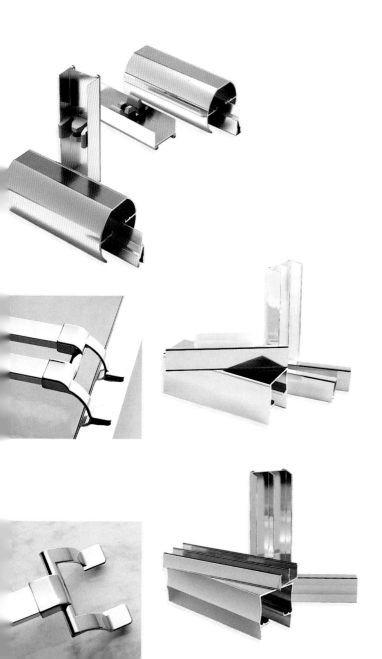

Century design options are endless. With Brasstec you can choose from four styles, four handle designs and nine finishes, all in solid brass. Create beautifully clear barriers with Glasstec enclosures in solid brass or aluminum and two handle styles. Century also offers three lines of aluminum framed and frameless enclosures to match any color scheme or budget.

CENTURY

Brasstec enclosures are heavy gauge solid brass, in 1" or 1¼" frame

■ Four different designs are available including: sliding, hinged, framed & frameless

■ Nine different finish options are available including polished, satin, and antique brass, polished and satin chrome, polished and satin nickel, copper & 24K gold.

■ Century offers the most extensive brass line available and the Century Guarantee.

Bras

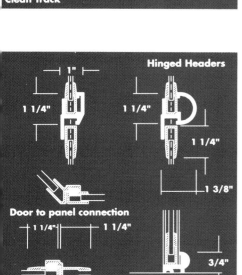

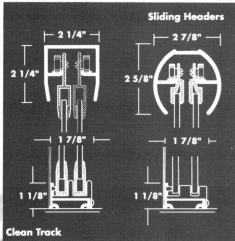

Specifications

PART 1 – GENERAL

1.1 SUMMARY
   A. This Section consists of standard and custom fabricated framed solid brass shower and tub enclosures.

1.2 SUBMITTALS
   A. Literature: Manufacturer's catalog cuts, detail sectional drawings and installation instructions.
   B. Shop drawings: Plan and elevations, bearing dimensions of actual measurements taken at the project.
   C. Selection samples: Sample card indicating Manufacturer's full range of finishes available for selection by Architect
   D. Verification samples:
      1. Samples of special order glass type.
      2. Sectional samples, illustrating brass finish.

1.3 DELIVERY, STORAGE AND HANDLING
   A. Deliver, store, and handle enclosure components following manufacturer's recommended procedures.

1.4 FIELD MEASUREMENTS
   A. Take field measurements before preparation of shop drawings and fabrication, to ensure proper fit.

PART 2 – PRODUCTS

2.1 MANUFACTURER
   A. Manufacture: To establish a standard of quality, design and function desired, Drawings and specifications have been based on Century Shower Door Inc., 250 Lackawanna Avenue, West Paterson, NJ 07424, (201)-785-4290, Product: "Brasstec", no substitution will be accepted.

2.2 COMPONENTS
   A. Frame and hardware: Extruded Architectural Bronze, copper alloy number 385.
   B. Glass: [select one of the following]
      1. Clear safety glass, conforming to ANSI Z97.1 and certified by Safety Glazing Certification Council.
      2. Custom glazing: [Optional glass types, include obscure glass, mirror glass, striped grey, striped bronze, grey tint, bronze tint, "v-groove" and other custom glass types are available, contact Century Shower Door for more information.]
   C. Hinge: Adjustable continuous piano hinge or pivot, as required.

2.3 FACTORY FINISH
   A. Frame and hardware: [select one of the following]
      1. Polished Brass, US 3 finish (Bright brass, clear coated).
      2. Satin Brass, US 4 finish (Satin brass, clear coating).
      3. Antique Brass, US 5 finish (Satin brass blackened).
      4. Polished Chrome plate, US 26 finish (Bright chromium plated).
      5. Satin Chrome plate, US 26D finish (Satin chromium plated).
      6. Polished Nickel plate, US 14 finish (Bright nickel plated).
      7. Satin Nickel plate, US 15 finish (Satin nickel plated).
      8. Bright Copper finish.
      9. Custom 24 K gold plate.

PART 3 – EXECUTION

3.1 INSTALLATION
   A. Install shower and tub enclosures in accordance with manufacturer's instructions. Install plumb and level, securely and rigidly anchored, with doors operating freely and smoothly.

Glasstec frameless enclosures are constructed of ³⁄₈" or ¹⁄₂" tempered glass with a beveled glass design that seals tight to eliminate the need for channels. ■ Patented hinge, header and hardware is available in solid brass and the full Century range of finishes, each individually crafted to customer specifications. ■ Glasstec handles are available in standard and "Highline" styles as shown.

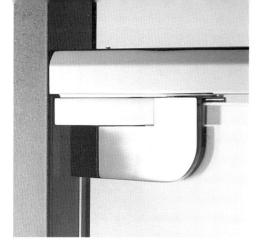

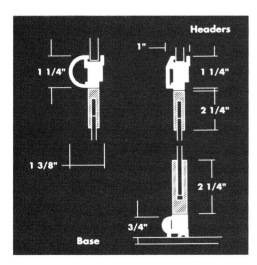

Headers

1"

1 1/4"

1 1/4"

2 1/4"

1 3/8"

2 1/4"

3/4"

Base

Corner Hinges   Offset Hinges

2 1/4"

4 3/4"   X   4 3/4"

2 1/4"

Specifications

PART 1 – GENERAL

1.1   SUMMARY
     A.   This Section consists of standard and custom fabricated 'heavy glass' shower and tub enclosures.

1.2   SUBMITTALS
     A.   Literature: Manufacturer's catalog cuts, detail sectional drawings and installation instructions.
     B.   Shop drawings: Plan and elevations, bearing dimensions of actual measurements taken at the project.
     C.   Selection samples: Sample card indicating Manufacturer's full range of finishes available for selection by Architect
     D.   Verification samples:
         1.   Samples of special order glass type.
         2.   Sectional samples, illustrating metal finish.

1.3   DELIVERY, STORAGE AND HANDLING
     A.   Deliver, store, and handle enclosure components following manufacturer's recommended procedures.

1.4   FIELD MEASUREMENTS
     A.   Take field measurements before preparation of shop drawings and fabrication, to ensure proper fit.

PART 2 – PRODUCTS

2.1   MANUFACTURER
     A.   Manufacture: To establish a standard of quality, design and function desired, Drawings and specifications have been based on Century Shower Door Inc., 250 Lackawanna Avenue, West Paterson, NJ 07424, (201)-785-4290, Product: "Glasstec", no substitution will be accepted.

2.2   COMPONENTS
     A.   Header, trim and hardware: Extruded Architectural Bronze, copper alloy number 385.
     B.   Glass: [*select one of the following*]
         1.   Clear tempered glass: 3/8 or 1/2 inch thick safety glass, ASTM C 1048 FT, complying with Class 1 clear, quality q3 glazing select, conforming to ANSI Z97.1.
         2.   Custom glazing: [*Optional grey tinted, bronze tinted, sandblasted, or etched glass is available, contact Century Shower Door for more information.*]
     C.   Hinge: Adjustable pivot hinge, solid brass matching selected frame finish. Hinge shall allow glass to come within 1/32 inch from sidewall, and be capable of 1/4 inch side to side adjustment and 3/16 inch front to back adjustment.

2.3   FACTORY FINISH
     A.   Header, trim and hardware:
         1.   Polished Brass, US 3 finish (Bright brass, clear coated).
         2.   Satin Brass, US 4 finish (Satin brass, clear coating).
         3.   Antique Brass, US 5 finish (Satin brass blackened).
         4.   Polished Chrome plate, US 26 finish (Bright chromium plated).
         5.   Satin Chrome plate, US 26D finish (Satin chromium plated).
         6.   Polished Nickel plate, US 14 finish (Bright nickel plated).
         7.   Satin Nickel plate, US 15 finish (Satin nickel plated).
         8.   Bright Copper finish.
         9.   Custom 24 K gold plate.

PART 3 – EXECUTION

3.1   INSTALLATION
     A.   Install shower and tub enclosures in accordance with shop drawings and manufacturer's instructions. Install plumb and level, securely and rigidly anchored, with doors operating freely and smoothly.

Centec frameless sliding enclosures feature a unique rounded header design constructed of heavy gauge anodized aluminum with ¼" tempered glass doors.

■ Finishes include: polished aluminum, gold anodized, twelve standard painted finishes, custom-matched colors, and Stonetec painted granite finish.

■ Centec features pass-through towel bars and low-maintenance bottom track.

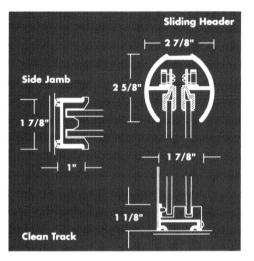

Side Jamb

Sliding Header

2 7/8"

2 5/8"

1 7/8"

1"

1 7/8"

1 1/8"

Clean Track

Specifications

PART 1 – GENERAL

1.1 SUMMARY
    A. This Section consists of standard and custom fabricated shower and tub enclosures, with frameless sliding glass doors.

1.2 SUBMITTALS
    A. Literature: Manufacturer's catalog cuts, detail sectional drawings and installation instructions.
    B. Shop drawings: Plan and elevations, bearing dimensions of actual measurements taken at the project.
    C. Selection samples: Sample card indicating Manufacturer's full range of colors available for selection by Architect
    D. Verification samples:
        1. Samples of special order glass type.
        2. Sectional samples of perimeter frame, illustrating custom finish.

1.3 DELIVERY, STORAGE AND HANDLING
    A. Deliver, store, and handle enclosure components following manufacturer's recommended procedures.

1.4 FIELD MEASUREMENTS
    A. Take field measurements before preparation of shop drawings and fabrication, to ensure proper fit.

PART 2 – PRODUCTS

2.1 MANUFACTURER
    A. Manufacture: To establish a standard of quality, design and function desired, Drawings and specifications have been based on Century Shower Door Inc., 250 Lackawanna Avenue, West Paterson, NJ 07424, (201)-785-4290, Product: "Centec", no substitution will be accepted.

2.2 COMPONENTS
    A. Perimeter frame: Extruded aluminum, alloy 6463-T5. [*Optional Brass-Centec is available with solid brass perimeter framing, contact Century Shower Door for more information.*]
    B. Glass: [*select one of the following*]
        1. Clear tempered glass: 1/4 inch thick safety glass, ASTM C 1048 FT, fully tempered, complying with Class 1 clear, quality q3 glazing select, conforming to ANSI Z97.1. [*Brass Centec is available with 1/4, 3/8 or 1/2 inch thick tempered glass*]
        2. Special order glazing: [*Optional "v-groove", grey tinted or bronze tinted glass is available, additionally, sandblasted glass or etched glass is available with Brass Centec.*]

2.3 Factory Finishes
    A. Frame and hardware: [*select one of the following*]
        1. Bright aluminum finish: Highly specular bright finish, clear anodized; Aluminum Association AAC31A21.
        2. Bright gold finish: Highly specular bright finish, colored anodized; Aluminum Association AAC31A21.
        3. Colored finish: Sprayed-applied thermo-set colored finish in manufacturers standard or custom color as directed by the Architect.
        4. Stonetec finish: Sprayed-applied thermo-set multi-colored 'granite pattern' finish in color selected by Architect from manufacturer's available range.
        5. Brass Finishes [Same finishes are available as *Brasstec* enclosures, *with optional solid brass framing.*]

PART 3 – EXECUTION

3.1 INSTALLATION
    A. Install shower and tub enclosures in accordance with manufacturer's instructions. Install plumb and level, securely and rigidly anchored, with doors operating freely and smoothly.

CENTURY

Lucette framed aluminum enclosures have been designed as a system to fit all standard formats and virtually any custom configuration you can dream up.

■ Finishes include: polished aluminum, gold anodized, twelve standard painted finishes or custom colors, and the widest range of glass and sizes available.

■ A system of over 72 extrusions provides special angles & sizes to meet any need.

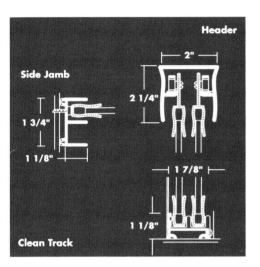

Side Jamb

Header

2"

2 1/4"

1 3/4"

1 1/8"

1 7/8"

1 1/8"

Clean Track

Over 72 different profiles guarantee that we can create the right enclosure for any need.

Specifications

PART 1 – GENERAL

1.1 SUMMARY
A. This Section consists of standard and custom fabricated shower and tub enclosures, with aluminum framed glass doors, both hinged and sliding types.

1.2 SUBMITTALS
A. Literature: Manufacturer's catalog cuts, detail sectional drawings and installation instructions.
B. Shop drawings: Plan and elevations, bearing dimensions of actual measurements taken at the project.
C. Selection samples: Sample card indicating Manufacturer's full range of colors available for selection by Architect.
D. Verification samples:
1. Samples of special order glass type.
2. Sectional samples of shower door frame, illustrating custom colored finish.

1.3 DELIVERY, STORAGE AND HANDLING
A. Deliver, store, and handle enclosure components following manufacturer's recommended procedures.

1.4 FIELD MEASUREMENTS
A. Take field measurements before preparation of shop drawings and fabrication, to ensure proper fit.

PART 2 – PRODUCTS

2.1 MANUFACTURER
A. Manufacture: To establish a standard of quality, design and function desired, Drawings and specifications have been based on Century Shower Door Inc., 250 Lackawanna Avenue, West Paterson, NJ 07424, (201)-785-4290, Product: "Lucette", no substitution will be accepted.

2.2 COMPONENTS
A. Frame: Extruded aluminum, alloy 6463-T5.
B. Glass: [*select one of the following*]
1. Obscure glass: Patterned safety glass, nominal 5/32 inch thick, conforming to ANSI Z97.1.
2. Clear safety glass, conforming to ANSI Z97.1 and certified by Safety Glazing Certification Council.
3. Custom glazing: [*Optional glass types, include mirror glass, striped grey, striped bronze, grey tint, bronze tint, "v-groove" and other custom glass types are available, contact Century Shower Door for more information.*]
C. Hinge [*with hinged doors*]: Continuous aluminum piano hinge, matching selected frame finish.
D. Track [*with sliding doors*]: Extruded aluminum, matching frame finish. Provide doors with adjustable rollers with ball bearings and nylon tires.

2.3 FACTORY FINISH
A. Frame: [*select one of the following*]
1. Bright aluminum finish: Highly specular bright finish, clear anodized; Aluminum Association AAC31A21.
2. Bright gold finish: Highly specular bright finish, colored anodized; Aluminum Association AAC31A23.
3. Colored finish: Sprayed-applied thermo-set colored finish in manufacturers standard or custom color as directed by the Architect.

PART 3 – EXECUTION

3.1 INSTALLATION
A. Install shower and tub enclosures in accordance with manufacturer's instructions. Install plumb and level, securely and rigidly anchored, with doors operating freely and smoothly.

CENTURY

Crest framed aluminum enclosures are a low cost alternative for all standard formats.

■ Available in chrome anodized aluminum finish with a full range of glass options.

■ Crest is available in hinged and sliding door styles in all standard configurations.

CENTURY

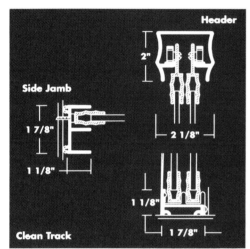

Header

Side Jamb

2"

1 7/8"

1 1/8"

2 1/8"

1 1/8"

1 7/8"

Clean Track

Specifications

PART 1 - GENERAL

1.1 SUMMARY
A. This Section consists of shower and tub enclosures in manufacturer's standard sizes, with aluminum framed glass doors, both hinged and sliding types.

1.2 SUBMITTALS
A. Literature: Manufacturer's catalog cuts, detail sectional drawings and installation instructions.

1.3 DELIVERY, STORAGE AND HANDLING
A. Deliver, store, and handle enclosure units following manufacturer's recommended procedures.

1.4 FIELD MEASUREMENTS
A. Take field measurements, to ensure openings fit manufacturer's unit sizes.

PART 2 - PRODUCTS

2.1 MANUFACTURER
A. Manufacture: To establish a standard of quality, design and function desired, Drawings and specifications have been based on Century Shower Door Inc., 250 Lackawanna Avenue, West Paterson, NJ 07424, (201)-785-4290, Product: "Crest", no substitution will be accepted.

2.2 COMPONENTS
A. Frame: Extruded aluminum, alloy 6463-T5, having diffuse bright finish, clear anodized; Aluminum Association AAC32A21.
B. Glass: [*select one of the following*]
   1. Obscure glass: Patterned safety glass, nominal 5/32 inch thick, conforming to ANSI Z97.1.
   2. Clear safety glass, conforming to ANSI Z97.1 and certified by Safety Glazing Certification Council.
C. Hinge [*with hinged doors*]: Continuous aluminum piano hinge, matching frame finish.
D. Track [*with sliding doors*]: Extruded aluminum, matching frame finish. Provide doors are adjustable rollers with ball bearings and nylon tires.

PART 3 - EXECUTION

3.1 INSTALLATION
A. Install shower and tub enclosures in accordance with manufacturer's instructions. Install plumb and level, securely and rigidly anchored, with doors operating freely and smoothly.

Options	Brasstec	Glasstec	Centec	Lucette	Crest
Sliding	■	■	■	■	■
Hinged	■	■		■	■
Standard Sizes	■	■	■	■	■
Custom Sizes	■	■	■	■	
Finishes					
Bright Aluminum		■	■	■	■
Anodized Gold		■	■	■	
Century Colors	■	■	■	■	
Stonetec			■		
Brass Finishes (8)	■	■	■		
24K Gold	■	■	■		
Glass					
$3/16''$ $5/32''$ Tempered	■		■	■	■
$3/8''$ $1/2''$ Tempered		■			
$1/4''$ Laminated	■			■	■
Obscure	■			■	■
Mirror	■			■	■
Bronze Tint	■	■	■	■	■
Grey Tint	■	■	■	■	■
Bronze Striped	■			■	■
Grey Striped	■			■	■
V-groove	■		■		
Custom Glass	■	■	■	■	
Transoms					
Steam Vent	■	■		■	
Grille	■			■	■

Century Shower Door, Inc. ■ 250 Lackawanna Avenue ■ West Paterson, NJ 07424 ■ 201 785 4290 ■ 800 524 2578

SS1190

Master Designed Shower Environments

WORK RIGHT

SS1190

If you can imagine it, Work Right creates it. In just about any size or shape you dream up. Enclose a tub for a peaceful hide-away. Transform a shower into an invigorating steam room. And place your shower center stage as the star of the master bath.

SS11135 with in-line panels

From traditional to contemporary, large or small—Work Right shower environments are featured in over one million of the finest hotels and homes throughout the world.

Open the door to beauty, luxury & ease

*L*eave it to the master designers at Work Right to offer the finest in modern shower environments. Like frameless doors that open the space visually like never before. Butted-glass corners for seamless transparency. And a modular framing system that can be used for either standard applications or custom enclosures.

Full Height Shower Door Model D-1000

FOR OPENINGS	HEIGHT	USE MODEL
20" to 21"	66 5/8"	D-1000-20
21" to 22"	66 5/8"	D-1000-21
..............Through..............		
34" to 35"	66 5/8"	D-1000-34

1" adjustable jambs,
header and curb available as option

Pivot Door Model D-2000

FOR OPENINGS	HEIGHT	USE MODEL
24 1/2" to 26 1/2"	67 1/4"	D-2000-24 to 26
26 1/2" to 28 1/2"	67 1/4"	D-2000-26 to 28
28 1/2" to 30 1/2"	67 1/4"	D-2000-28 to 30
30 1/2" to 32 1/2"	67 1/4"	D-2000-30 to 32
32 1/2" to 34 1/2"	67 1/4"	D-2000-32 to 34
34 1/2" to 36 1/2"	67 1/4"	D-2000-34 to 36

2" adjustable jambs, no header, with full curb

Stall Shower Model SS-11180

FOR OPENINGS	HEIGHT	USE MODEL
34" to 42"	69"	SS-11180-42
42" to 48"	69"	SS-11180-48
48" to 60"	69"	SS-11180-60
60" to 72"	69"	SS-11180-72*

panel and full height door in line or
*door centered between two side panels

Stall Shower Model SS-1190-34

FOR OPENINGS	HEIGHT	USE MODEL
Up to 34" x 34"	69"	SS-1190-34

panel and full height door at 90°

Stall Shower Model SS-1190-38/48

FOR OPENINGS	HEIGHT	USE MODEL
Up to 38" x 38"	69"	SS-1190-38
Up to 48" x 48"	69"	SS-1190-48

two panels and full height door at 90°

Stall Shower Model SS-11135-38

FOR OPENINGS	HEIGHT	USE MODEL
Up to 24" x 27" x 24"	69"	SS-11135-38

two panels at 135° neo-angle to full height door

Tempered glass is strong for added family safety.

Quality craftsmanship

Work Right shower environments are as beautiful inside as they are outside. We use only the best and most durable materials. Heavy extruded aluminum frames. Tempered safety glass. Vinyl seals. And nylon latches and rollers.

Then we add precision-engineered details developed over 20 years. Finally, we make Work Right showers a breeze to keep clean. Our frameless doors—swinging, sliding and pivot—eliminate grooves and corners that can gather dirt. And Work Right's unique open-track design lets you clean the base of sliding doors in just one wipe.

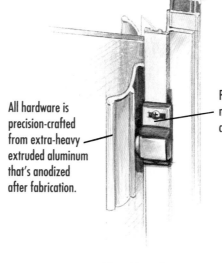

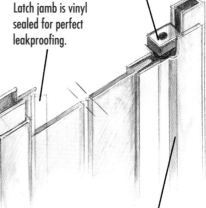

All hardware is precision-crafted from extra-heavy extruded aluminum that's anodized after fabrication.

Patented adjustable nylon catch system can't rust or jam.

New ball and joint hinge provides strong, silent, and watertight installations even for overheight doors.

Latch jamb is vinyl sealed for perfect leakproofing.

Adjustable jambs simplify installation with out-of-square walls, ceilings and floors.

Nylon and aluminum hinge assemblies provide strong, smooth, and quiet operation.

Not shown: Sloping drain bar sends excess water back into the shower, keeping floors dry.

SE1400

Since the glass door won't be hanging open in a bathroom walkway, sliding doors are ideal for young families, the senior set and hotels where guests come and go.

Best of all, sliders blend safety *and* style. You can design an enclosure wall up to 84". And you won't have those bulky frames at the hinge. So you can enjoy an uninterrupted feeling of airiness and spaciousness that only a continuous expanse of glass can provide.

All sliding models can be ordered as tub or shower enclosures.

Step into a world of indulgence

Now bathrooms short on space can be long on style with a Work Right sliding shower enclosure. If you're working with cramped quarters and don't have the room for a swinging door, consider a slider.

TE1600

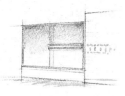

Sliding Tub/Shower Enclosure 1400 Series

FOR OPENINGS	USE MODEL	
Sliders	Tub 57 3/8" HT	Shower 70 3/8" HT
Up to 48"		SE-1400-48
48" to 60"	TE-1400-60	SE-1400-60
60" to 66"	TE-1400-66	

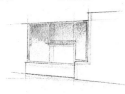

Sliding Tub/Shower Enclosure 1400 Series

FOR OPENINGS	USE MODEL	
Sliders up to 60" with 12" in-line panel	Tub 57 3/8" HT TE-1400-1-72	Shower 70 3/8" HT SE-1400-1-72
Sliders Up to 60" with 24" in-line panel	Tub 57 3/8" HT TE-1400-1-84	Shower 70 3/8" HT SE-1400-1-84

Sliding Tub/Shower Enclosure 1400 Series

FOR OPENINGS	USE MODEL	
Sliders up to 60" with two 12" in-line panels	Tub 57 3/8" HT TE-1400-2-84	Shower 70 3/8" HT SE-1400-2-84

Sliding Tub/Shower Enclosure 1400 Series

FOR OPENINGS	USE MODEL	
Sliders up to 60" with 36" end panel at 90°	Tub 57 3/8" HT TE-1400-3	Shower 70 3/8" HT SE-1400-3

Sliding Tub/Shower Enclosure 1400 Series

FOR OPENINGS	USE MODEL	
Sliders up to 60" with 12" & 24" end panels at 135° neo-angle	Tub 57 3/8" HT TE-1400-4	Shower 70 3/8" HT SE-1400-4

Tracks: 1400 Series ships with open track. To order a "W" shaped track use a 1200 Series designation. All resulting heights will be 3/8" less than the 1400 Series listings.

Glass: 1400 Series and 1200 Series use minimum 3/16" glass.

Custom color and glass etching are available from many local Work Right dealers.

Design and color options

High Light™ finished frames color-coordinate with today's bright and beautiful fixtures. Opt for buffed and bright dipped metals or powder-coated paints. In glass, choose from obscure to sparkling clear or warm bronzes to cool frosts. Plus, any model can be fitted with bars that accommodate the thirstiest towels. Ask your local dealer to help you customize your bathroom right down to the last detail.

Standard finishes include silver, gold, black, and white.

All the luxury at half the cost

*O*nly Work Right gives you a master-designed shower environment with sophisticated elegance—at an affordable price!

Shop and compare. Then come back to Work Right. Because you can get the upscale look and feel of heavy glass and chrome on brass at a fraction of the cost charged by other shower companies.

At Work Right, we believe your shower can add value and pleasure to your day—and to your home. That's why we use sturdy materials and employ talented craftsmen. The result is a shower environment that's master designed for the ultimate in beauty and functionality.

SE1600

Prestige® sliding door headers offer twice the framing options in just one piece. Use the rounded side to enhance curvacious porcelain. Or flip it to flat for a mirror-bright complement to the crispness of contemporary fixtures.

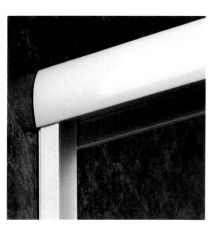

The Euro design Prestige frames are engineered to accommodate heavier glass and operate with an unmistakable feel of quality.

Prestige showers have no interior towel racks that can be mistakenly used for grab bars. Plus, tubular towel bars complement the soft curve of the frame.

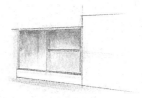

Prestige Tub/Shower Enclosure 1600 Series

FOR OPENINGS Sliders	USE MODEL Tub 57 3/8" HT	Shower 70 3/8" HT
Up to 48"		SE-1600-48
48" to 60"	TE-1600-60	SE-1600-60
60" to 66"	TE-1600-66	

Prestige Tub/Shower Enclosure 1600 Series

FOR OPENINGS Sliders	USE MODEL Tub 57 3/8" HT	Shower 70 3/8" HT
up to 60" with 12" in-line panel	TE-1600-1-72	SE-1600-1-72
Sliders Up to 60" with 24" in-line panel	Tub 57 3/8" HT TE-1600-1-84	Shower 70 3/8" HT SE-1600-1-84

Prestige Tub/Shower Enclosure 1600 Series

FOR OPENINGS Sliders	USE MODEL Tub 57 3/8" HT	Shower 70 3/8" HT
up to 60" with two 12" in-line panels	TE-1600-2-84	SE-1600-2-84

Prestige Tub/Shower Enclosure 1600 Series

FOR OPENINGS Sliders	USE MODEL Tub 57 3/8" HT	Shower 70 3/8" HT
up to 60" with 36" end panel at 90°	TE-1600-3	SE-1600-3

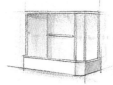

Prestige Tub/Shower Enclosure 1600 Series

FOR OPENINGS Sliders	USE MODEL Tub 57 3/8" HT	Shower 70 3/8" HT
up to 60" with 12" & 24" end panels at 135° neo-angle	TE-1600-4	SE-1600-4

Tracks: 1600 Series ships with open track.

Glass: 1600 Series use minimum 1/4" glass.

Work Right provides your builder—and you—with color chips, specification sheets, line drawings, installation and maintenance instructions, and design suggestions.

For smooth installation, each model is precut, predrilled and prepackaged with all parts. What's more, our qualified dealer/installers—over 200 nationwide—are trained and backed by comprehensive technical support. The result for you is product performance that's equal to your bath's unique and stunning style.

For complete design information, or the location of your nearest Work Right dealer/installer, call 800/358-9064 (800/862-4995 from California).

Guide Specifications

Part 1 General

1.1 Work included: Provide shower doors as needed for a complete and proper installation

1.2 Related work by others

  a. Shower receptor base (specify one — tile shower pan, pre-fab shower pan, bathtub)

  b. Wall surface (specify one — tile, marble, cultured marble, fiberglass/plastic, non-porous watertight material

  c. Sealants and caulking (specify a compatible sealant for aluminum and glass)

1.3 Quality assurance

  a. Mock up/sample installation Factory approved mock up sample will represent minimum quality for the work

  b. Source quality control Factory tests for metal hardness, finish and dimensional tolerance

  c. Code compliance
    ANSI Z.97.1
    CPSC 16CFR1201 II
    ASTM C1048-85
    USFS DD-G-1403B

1.4 Delivery, storage and handling by others

  a. Deliver to job site door(s) assembled and ready for installation

  b. Store off ground, under cover, protected from weather and construction activities

  c. Do not lay glass flat either in transport or storage

1.5 Sequencing/Scheduling

Shower door(s) are to be installed only after related work 1.2a and 1.2b is completed

Part 2 Systems

2.1 Specified system or equal
Work Right Products, Inc.
Lakeport, CA
(specify one: D-1000, D-2000, TE-1200, TE-1400, TE-1600, SE-1200, SE-1400, SE-1600, SS-11180, SS-1190, SS-11135)

2.2 Materials

  a. Shower door(s) shall be constructed of (specify clear, obscure, bronzed or custom etched) 3/16" or 1/4" tempered safety glass with all exposed edges polished and rounded

  b. Aluminum sections shall be 6463 T5 aluminum alloy with a minimum thickness of .062"

  c. Aluminum sections shall be buffed and bright dipped anodized or powder coat painted (specify finish or color)

  d. Swinging shower door(s) shall have vinyl seal at both the latch jamb and hinge jamb side of door

  e. Sliding shower enclosures shall have patented roller brackets at the top of each sliding panel

2.3 Fabrication

  a. Shop assembly of doors and sliding panels shall be completed prior to delivery to job site

  b. Fabrication of metal for out-of-plumb or out-of-level

conditions exceeding normal adjustments shall be done prior to installation

  c. Roller brackets for clear glass sliding panels shall be bonded to glass with silicone sealant 24 hours prior to installation, with screws torqued to 28 inchpounds

  d. Handles shall be secured by means of pressure fitting

  e. Sliding shower enclosures shall have one piece, pressure fitted handles and roller brackets

Part 3 Execution

3.1 Surface preparation
Prior to installation of unit, installer shall be sure that surface is free from foreign matter that could compromise the watertight bond of unit to surface (e.g., rust, dirt, grease, paint, mastic, taping compound, etc.)

3.2 Installation
Unit(s) shall be installed consistent with current manufacturer's guidelines and instructions

3.3 Field quality control
Installer shall be responsible to test that door operates smoothly and that at no time does the glass come into contact with metal during normal operation

3.4 Adjusting and cleaning
Installer shall be responsible for adjusting door operation and for securing the owner care and maintenance card to unit

MASTER DESIGNED SHOWER ENVIRONMENTS

Lakeport, CA
Call (800) 358-9064
California (800) 862-4995
Intl. (707) 263-0290
FAX (707) 263-4048

U.S. Pat. No. 3,827,737; 3,796,405; 3,787,936; 4,484,411

POP DG 002   1/92/150K

FINLANDIA SAUNA
The Pacesetter

We have built our reputation as "old country" Sauna builders since 1964, by believing that it takes individual attention to provide each customer with a quality piece of workmanship. Our FINLANDIA Sauna packages are custom cut with special care and experienced craftsmanship. It's the little extras that count — so we take the extra effort — such as nailing our benches from the bottom to make sure that our customers will have no worries (or burns) from protruding nails. We bevel our wall and ceiling boards for the tightest fit, to eliminate unsightly corner moldings. We countersink any surface nails, and we fill any visible nail holes.

FPC Packages Include

PRECUT WALL & CEILING BOARDS
1" x 6" (redwood) or 1" x 4" (cedar), full ¾" thickness, certified, kiln-dried T&G, cut to size with 2% bevel for tight fit.

BOARDS ARE CUT FOR HORIZONTAL INSTALLATION.

ASSEMBLED BENCHES of clear V.G. S4S kiln-dried 2" x 2" tops with ½" spacing, and 2" x 4" facing (much superior to standard 1" x 3" lightweight benches, in design and strength).

PREHUNG GLASS DOOR (FGD) 2'0" x 6'8" as per specs page 12.

ASSEMBLED HEATER FENCE

ASSEMBLED HEADREST/BACK-REST for upper bench(es).

TRIM AND BASE

SUPER DEK as per specs page 12 (enough for walking area of floor).

FINLANDIA SAUNA HEATER

PERIDOTITE STONES

CONTROL/CONTACTOR PANEL (if required by heater).

LIGHT wall mounted, vapor-proof.

VENTS (two sets) for installation in upper and lower wall areas.

ACCESSORIES thermometer #3444, wooden bucket #100, wooden dipper #106/40, bathing sign.

INSTRUCTIONS for building.

NAILS hot dipped, galvanized.

FPC 35
Seats 1 person.

FPC 44 or FPF 44
Seats 2 people.

FPC 46 or FPF 46
Seats 3 people.

FPC 56 or FPF 56
Seats 3 people.

FPC 66 or FPF 66
Seats 4 people.

◀ **FPC 68 or FPF 68**
Seats 6 people.

FPC 88 or FPF 88
Seats 7 to 8 people.

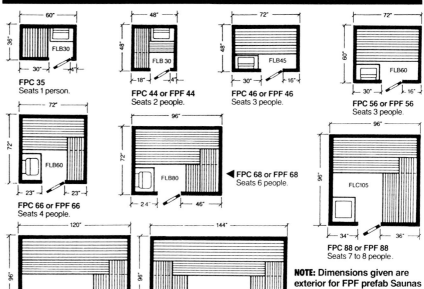

FPC 810 or FPF 810
Seats 8 to 9 people.

FPC 812 or FPF 812
Seats 12 people.

NOTE: Dimensions given are exterior for FPF prefab Saunas and interior for FPC precut packages. Specify right or left door hinge when ordering. We precut to size, you install on your framed, insulated wall and ceiling surfaces.

FPC 66 EXAMPLE Dimensions are interior measurements.

FPF
½" EXTERIOR SIDING (PLYWOOD) RUFF SAWN OREGON DOUGLAS FIR
CONCEALED LOCKING SYSTEM
3½" FIBERGLAS INSULATION
TYPE "C" FOIL (VAPOR BARRIER)
2" X 2" DRY OREGON DOUGLAS FIR
1" X 4" KD. T&G V.G. REDWOOD, CLEAR ALASKA YELLOW CEDAR, WESTERN RED CEDAR, OR WESTERN HEMLOCK
2" X 4" REDWOOD OR CEDAR BASE

FPC
1" X 4" KD. T&G CLEAR ALASKA YELLOW CEDAR, WESTERN RED CEDAR OR WESTERN HEMLOCK
1" X 6" V G REDWOOD
2" X 4" DRY FIR
½" DRYWALL
2" X 4" TREATED PLATE
1" X 2" BASE

FINLANDIA SPECIFICATIONS FOR ARCHITECTS/CONTRACTORS

GENERAL CONTRACTOR SPECIFICATIONS:

Framing of walls and ceiling shall be of dry Douglas Fir, construction grade no. 1 or 2, 16″ center. Use pressure treated plates (against concrete)

Ceiling shall be 7′0″ from finished floor to ceiling joists (16″ center)

Door shall be roughed in at 26″x82″ and must open out

Insulation of walls and ceiling shall be of R11 foil faced fiberglas batts (R19 if Sauna has exterior location)

Drywall shall be ⅝″ firewall (only if required by local building codes)

Added Vapor Barrier shall be of Type C (Reynolds) Construction foil over insulation or drywall—walls and ceiling (recommended as second vapor barrier)

Flooring shall be of hard surfaced, waterproof type—concrete, ceramic tile, heavy-duty seamless vinyl

Floor Drain is recommended for new construction and is essential for commercial and public Saunas

Exterior Walls shall be of drywall, paneling, tile, etc. and exterior painting, door finishing, etc. shall be included

ELECTRICAL CONTRACTOR SPECIFICATIONS:

(Must be licensed and bonded)

Roughin for Sauna controls, heater, room light shall be as per Finlandia wiring diagram (provided with control box or in heater box)

Hookup of controls, heater, light shall be as per Finlandia wiring diagram (see pgs. 8–9 for wire size, amperage, etc.) USE COPPER WIRE ONLY

FINLANDIA SAUNA CONTRACTOR SPECIFICATIONS:

Walls and Ceiling shall be 1″x4″ or 1″x6″ select, certified, kiln-dried (moisture content not exceeding 11%) T&G, v joint, clear, vertical grain Redwood, clear Western Red Cedar, clear Alaska Yellow Cedar, or clear Western Hemlock. All boards shall be blind nailed with 7p galvanized, hot dipped nails, or power stapled with galvanized staples.

The following specs shall include and match one of the four woods chosen above:

Benches shall be clear S4S kiln-dried 2″x2′ tops with ½″ spacing and 2″x4″ facing; glued and fastened with exposed nails countersunk. Bench tops shall be fastened from bottom to eliminate exposed metal)

Door shall be FGD 2′0″x6′8″ of vertical grain Douglas Fir rails and clear hermetically sealed, double glass, tempered (15¾x60″) with casing, jamb, and threshold of Redwood.

Door Hardware shall be (3) 4″x4″ butt hinges, Ives ball catch MP347B3. (2) wooden door pulls 3431

Vents shall be (2) 4″x10″ louvered V10 for upper wall placement and lower wall placement

Removable Flooring shall be Super Dek interlocking 12″ squares—sanitary, non-skid surface in terra cotta color—over walking area of base floor

Light shall be wall-mounted, vapor-proof Progress P5511, satin finish cast aluminum, rated for 75 watts

Sauna Heater shall be FINLANDIA model … as per room cubic footage and voltage requirements (see chart pgs. 8–9)

Heater Fence shall be of 2″x2″ & 1″x2″ and shall be placed 2½″ away from Sauna heater

Temperature Control/Contactor panel shall be model … from pg. 9

Accessories shall be … from pg. 10

Stones shall be a peridotite, heat tested, igneous type from Finland

Precut and Prefab Saunas shall be as per specifications pgs. 4–5

Warranty shall be 1 yr. on room materials and workmanship and 5 yr. limited warranty on Sauna heaters when installed according to Finlandia specifications and wiring information

Maintenance

Finlandia Sauna heaters and rooms require minimum care and maintenance. Basic household methods, including cleaning of Sauna room floor with a product such as Pine Sol, and occasional scrubbing of benches with a mild soap, is necessary for sanitary and odor-free atmosphere. When wood becomes dark or stained from perspiration, a light sanding will help to restore its beautiful appearance. Do not use sealers, paint, or varnish on interior wood, as toxic vapors could be dangerous in the high temperatures of a Sauna.

Note: When figuring room capacities for number of bathers, allow 2′ of bench space per person.

FINLANDIA SAUNA IS THE ONLY U.S. COMPANY WHICH OFFERS A CHOICE OF THE WORLD'S BEST SAUNA WOODS:

100% vertical grain California Redwood, clear Western Red Cedar, clear Alaska Yellow Cedar, and clear Western Hemlock. All are a full 3/4″ thickness (others use 1/2″ to 5/8″ thickness).

Our CALIFORNIA REDWOOD is 100% vertical grain (tight grain to prevent raising and slivering in the high heat), is the most fire resistant, most dry-rot resistant, most termite resistant, and does not warp. Redwood, however, does darken with age.

The best-known and most widely used of the West Coast cedars is WESTERN RED CEDAR. It has the most beautiful color variation, has a refreshing aroma, and is dry-rot resistant. Because it's the softest wood, it is least hot to sit on or lean against.

ALASKA YELLOW CEDAR is a beautiful white variety of cedar which does not dry-rot or warp. It has a silky smooth finish and a wonderful, refreshing aroma.

Our clear WESTERN HEMLOCK is an excellent wood for people who have wood allergies—it has no aroma and no resins.

Finlandia Sauna does not use inexpensive woods such as thin knotty spruce which has a tendency to cup, shrink, warp, and crack; (and some knots come loose when the pitch and resin around them dries in the high heat of the Sauna). Many European Saunas, however, are built from knotty spruce as it has been the available wood for centuries. Knotty spruce cannot be used for benches as it gets too hot, and the knots and pitch can burn the bather; so African Abachi is imported for benches. Abachi is a clear wood and it's comfortable for sitting; but, it has a peculiar, unpleasant odor. Finlandia uses only clear Western softwoods which have the proper matching wood for benches.

NOTE! Page numbers referenced on this page are from the complete 12 pg. brochure available from Finlandia Sauna.

Finlandia Sauna Products, Inc.

FINLANDIA sauna ® *The Pacesetter*

14010-B S.W. 72ND AVENUE, PORTLAND, OREGON 97224-0088
TELEPHONE TOLL FREE 1-800-354-3342, IN OR 503-684-8289, FAX 503-684-1120

■ *The International Designer Collection*

JACUZZI® WHIRLPOOL BATHS. YOU

You can see the dramatic difference.

Inch for inch, no other whirlpool can match the power—or the pleasure—of PowerPro® jets by Jacuzzi Whirlpool Bath.

You can feel the luxurious difference.

The result is powerful—but gentle—hydrotherapy for the whole body.

Our patented PowerPro jets make the difference.

Only Jacuzzi whirlpool baths have more of what you really buy a whirlpool for.

Jacuzzi jets turn a whirlpool bath into the luxurious, relaxing experience it is meant to be. But as you can see, not every jet is built the same. Some are too weak to do an effective job.

Only Jacuzzi PowerPro jets have the power to be gentle. They combine air and water from all directions, creating a broad, massaging circular pattern of bubbles. PowerPro jets are fully adjustable to focus on body areas that need special attention. You feel the soothing, penetrating, therapeutic difference every time you bathe. It's the complete relaxation experience you expect—and deserve—from your Jacuzzi whirlpool bath.

Jacuzzi Whirlpool Bath

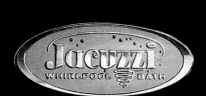

The Originator. The Innovator.

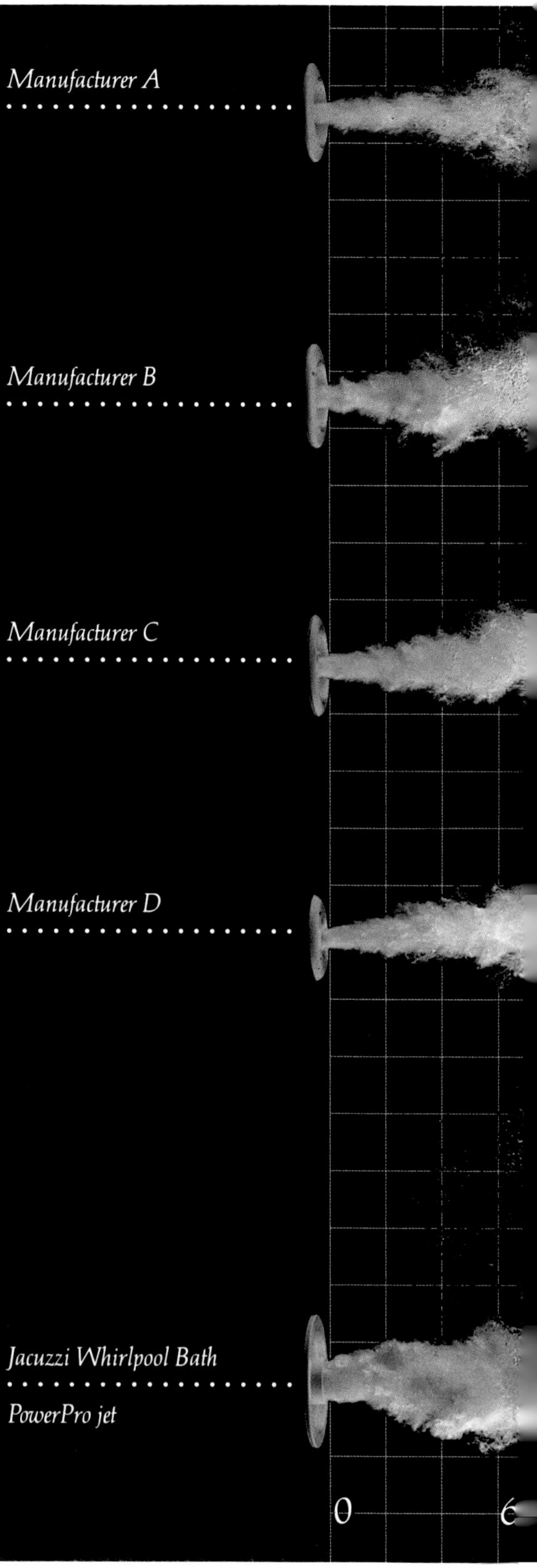

Manufacturer A
Manufacturer B
Manufacturer C
Manufacturer D
Jacuzzi Whirlpool Bath
PowerPro jet
0

Major jet systems in the whirlpool bath and spa industry were tested under identical conditions to evaluate the performance of each system's jet action. The test protocol was the same for each jet, and the photography, as shown, represents air/water travel and volume as actually occurred in the test.

12　18　24　30　36　42　48

The ultimate in hydrotherapy.

Any whirlpool bath can make bubbles. But only a Jacuzzi® whirlpool bath has the patented Power Pro® jet system that

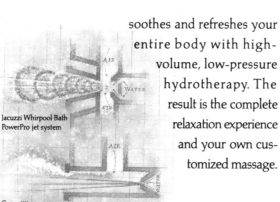

Jacuzzi Whirlpool Bath
PowerPro jet system

*Competitive
whirlpool jet systems*

soothes and refreshes your entire body with high-volume, low-pressure hydrotherapy. The result is the complete relaxation experience and your own cus-tomized massage.

The components of pleasure.

The total expe-rience of enjoyment in a Jacuzzi whirlpool bath is the

sum of many intelligently designed parts: ergonomic seating, the soothing sounds of the Water Rainbow® fill spout,

why we back up each one of our baths with an extensive warranty program and nationwide service network.

Whether the criterion is innovative design and technology or quality manufacturing, Jacuzzi® whirlpool baths provide the standard by which all other whirlpool baths are judged.

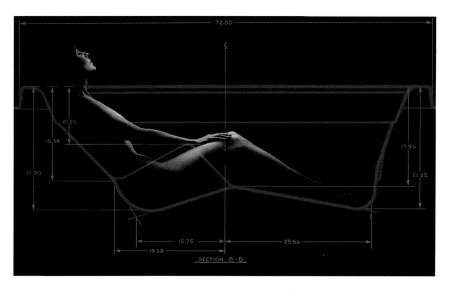

the Magic Touch® on/off switch, and the patented Silent Air induction system. Jacuzzi Whirlpool Bath has thought of everything, so you don't have to think of anything except unwinding.

So reliable, it's relaxing.

Your whirlpool bath should be a soothing experience. That's why our first priority is building a dependable, quality product every time. It is also

A tradition of trust.

At Jacuzzi Whirlpool Bath we're very proud that we invented the whirlpool bath

The original Jacuzzi Brothers

back in 1968. But we are even more proud of the reputation we've built since that time.

An international bestseller. Jacuzzi Inc. is the world leader in whirlpool baths, with 250 international patents and 10 factories worldwide. Now in Europe, Asia, North and South America, Jacuzzi Inc. provides a universal way to relax and retreat.

It's a good feeling to know that our hard work is leading to a very relaxing end—a luxurious bathing experience for each and every one of our customers.

Roy Jacuzzi
President and
Chief Executive Officer,
Jacuzzi Inc.

The Originator. The Innovator.

■ The ultimate luxury is the one you share, which is why Jacuzzi Whirlpool Bath created the dramatic Fontana™ whirlpool bath for two. The Fontana is as roomy as it is beautiful, with every detail designed with your pleasure in mind: the cascading waterfall, the European-style hand-held shower and the conveniently placed Magic Touch® fingertip jet control. Put them together and you have a special environment all your own, the ultimate refuge from a stressful world.

SPECIFICATIONS:

- *DIMENSIONS:* 72" long x 54" wide x 28" high.
- *MATERIAL:* High-gloss acrylic, fiberglass reinforced.
- *CONSTRUCTION:* Self-contained, completely preplumbed.
- *INSTALLATION:* Recessed in floor or platform.
- *WHIRLPOOL MOTOR/PUMP:* 1½ HP, 115V 20 AMP service required.
- *WATER CAPACITY:* 110 U.S. gallons.
- *FLOOR LOADING:* 58 lbs./sq. ft.
- *SHIPPING WEIGHT:* 298 lbs.
- *CERTIFICATIONS:* UL and IAPMO listed, factory pretested.

Product specifications subject to change without notice.

FEATURES:

- Four patented, fully-adjustable PowerPro® jets.
- Scalloped bath rim crests in a spectacular stairstep waterfall with built-in WaterRainbow.®
- An acrylic panel reveals a second Water Rainbow fill spout, for a dual cascade effect. The panel also houses a hand-held European-style shower.
- Roomy interior provides dual bathing comfort and ease.

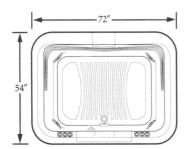

EURA · MIRA

■ Even at first glance, you can see that this is a vision in whirlpool bath design. Select the two-person Eura™ or the Mira™ for one. The fluid lines and uplifted contours set them apart from the ordinary. Both baths offer ample width and raised backrests for the ultimate in contoured comfort. And to enhance your bathing experience even further, you'll find luxurious features such as our Magic Touch® control and PowerPro® jet system. With the Eura and Mira, you can truly escape from it all.

SPECIFICATIONS:

- *DIMENSIONS:* EURA: 72" long x 42" wide x 19½" high. MIRA: 72" long x 36" wide x 19" high.
- *MATERIAL:* High-gloss acrylic, fiberglass reinforced.
- *CONSTRUCTION:* Self-contained, completely preplumbed.
- *INSTALLATIONS:* Recessed in floor or platform, or with optional matching skirt.
- *WHIRLPOOL MOTOR/PUMP:* ¾ HP, 115V 20 AMP service required.
- *WATER CAPACITY:* EURA: 75 U.S. gallons. MIRA: 65 U.S. gallons.
- *FLOOR LOADING:* EURA: 44 lbs./sq. ft. MIRA: 45 lbs./sq. ft.
- *SHIPPING WEIGHT:* EURA: 171 lbs. MIRA: 153 lbs.
- *CERTIFICATIONS:* UL and IAPMO listed, factory pretested.
Product specifications subject to change without notice.

FEATURES:

- Fully-adjustable PowerPro jets
- Raised backrest at each end
- Optional Water Rainbow® spout

EURA

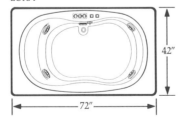

72" 42"

MIRA

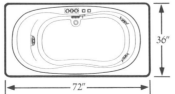

72" 36"

■ If you have ever wondered what to do with that problem corner, maybe you should consider a waterfall! The Fiore™ whirlpool bath features a double Water Rainbow® spout system which creates the sensual sight and sound of water gently cascading down the staircase waterfall sculpted into the bath design. With the contoured comforts of a corner bath for two, and a seat which opens to reveal an accessory area with mirrored interior and hand-held shower, the Fiore is a true breakthrough in whirlpool design and whirlpool pleasure.

SPECIFICATIONS:

- *DIMENSIONS:* 66" long x 66" wide x 21¾" high (27¾" high at corner).
- *MATERIAL:* High-gloss acrylic, fiberglass reinforced.
- *CONSTRUCTION:* Self-contained, completely preplumbed.
- *INSTALLATION:* Comes complete with matching skirt.
- *WHIRLPOOL MOTOR/PUMP:* 1½ HP, 115V 20 AMP service required.
- *WATER CAPACITY:* 90 U.S. gallons.
- *FLOOR LOADING:* 47.6 lbs./sq. ft.
- *SHIPPING WEIGHT:* 343 lbs.
- *CERTIFICATIONS:*
UL and IAPMO listed, factory pretested.

Product specifications subject to change without notice.

FEATURES:

- Four fully-adjustable PowerPro® jets
- Bath rim rises gracefully in the corner, creating a dramatic waterfall effect as a hidden Water Rainbow spout recirculates the water down a unique stairstep design sculpted into the bath
- Rounded seat opens to reveal an accessory area with vanity mirror. Concealed within are a second Water Rainbow spout to fill the bath, hot and cold valves, and a hand-held shower.
- Contoured bathing areas for two with sloping backrests for added comfort
- Curved matching skirt is removable to provide front service access
- Underwater interior lighting

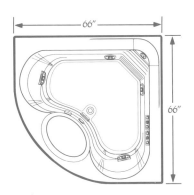

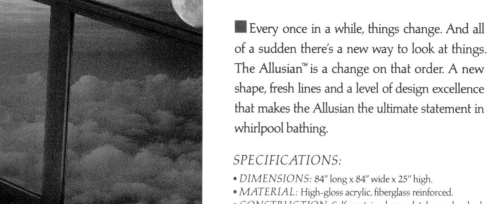

■ Every once in a while, things change. And all of a sudden there's a new way to look at things. The Allusian™ is a change on that order. A new shape, fresh lines and a level of design excellence that makes the Allusian the ultimate statement in whirlpool bathing.

SPECIFICATIONS:

- *DIMENSIONS:* 84" long x 84" wide x 25" high.
- *MATERIAL:* High-gloss acrylic, fiberglass reinforced.
- *CONSTRUCTION:* Self-contained, completely preplumbed
- *INSTALLATIONS:* Recessed in floor or platform. (Must provide service access to both pumps)
- *WHIRLPOOL MOTOR/PUMP:* Two 1 HP, 2-speed motors/pumps. Two dedicated 115V 20 AMP circuits required.
- *WATER CAPACITY:* 150 U.S. gallons.
- *RECOMMENDED WATER HEATER:* 100 gallons
- *FLOOR LOADING:* 46 lbs./sq. ft.
- *SHIPPING WEIGHT:* 649 lbs.
- *CERTIFICATIONS:* UL and IAPMO listed, factory pretested.

Product specifications subject to change without notice.

FEATURES:

- Six fully-adjustable PowerPro® jets
- Two Water Rainbow spouts: one to fill, the other to recirculate
- Two 12-volt interior lights with a choice of colored lenses
- Two acrylic covers with mirrored interiors and accessory area

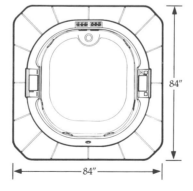

■ Classic, spacious whirlpool baths with beautiful swirling lines, the Viante™ and Viante Grande™ are fashioned for comfort as well as for style. Patented PowerPro® jets make for a bathing experience that's more than just relaxing—it's therapeutic.

SPECIFICATIONS:

- *DIMENSIONS:* VIANTE GRANDE: 60" long x 42" wide x 20" high. VIANTE: 60" long x 36" wide x 20" high, available May 1991.
- *MATERIAL:* High-gloss acrylic, fiberglass reinforced.
- *CONSTRUCTION:* Self-contained, completely preplumbed.
- *INSTALLATION:* Recessed in floor or platform, or with optional matching skirt.
- *WHIRLPOOL MOTOR/PUMP:* ¾ HP, 115V, 20 AMP service required.
- *WATER CAPACITY:* VIANTE GRANDE: 70 U.S. gallons.
- *FLOOR LOADING:* VIANTE GRANDE: 49 lbs./sq. ft.
- *SHIPPING WEIGHT:* VIANTE GRANDE: 155 lbs.
- *CERTIFICATIONS:*
  UL and IAPMO listed, factory pretested.
  Product specifications subject to change without notice.

FEATURES:

- VIANTE GRANDE: Four patented, fully-adjustable PowerPro jets
  VIANTE: Three patented, fully-ajustable PowerPro jets
- Unique scalloped European design
- Provides the luxury and style of a larger tub in a five-foot space
- Optional faucet and handles

VIANTE

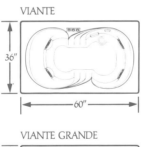

36"

60"

VIANTE GRANDE

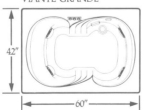

42"

60"

■ Seldom do luxurious comfort and state-of-the-art European design come together as dramatically as they have in the Ciprea™ whirlpool bath. Its unique bowed shape provides an unusually comfortable bath, and the extra room actually makes the Ciprea a pleasure that can also be shared. The Ciprea also features a recirculating Water Rainbow® spout that creates a cascade of water to delight both eye and ear.

SPECIFICATIONS:

- *DIMENSIONS:* CIPREA: 72" long x 48" wide x 20" high.
  MYA: 60" long x 38" wide x 20" high.
- *MATERIAL:* High-gloss acrylic, fiberglass reinforced.
- *CONSTRUCTION:* Self-contained, completely preplumbed.
- *INSTALLATION:* Factory installed matching skirt.
- *WHIRLPOOL MOTOR/PUMP:* ¾ HP, 115V 20 AMP service required.
- *WATER CAPACITY:* CIPREA: 75 U.S. gallons.
  MYA: 65 U.S. gallons.
- *FLOOR LOADING:* CIPREA: 46.5 lbs./sq. ft.
  MYA: 53.5 lbs./sq. ft.
- *SHIPPING WEIGHT:* CIPREA: 207 lbs. MYA: 141 lbs.
- *CERTIFICATIONS:*
  UL and IAPMO listed, factory pretested.
  Product specifications subject to change without notice.

FEATURES:

- Fully-adjustable PowerPro® jets
- Unique bowed interior and matching skirt for extra bathing space
- Water Rainbow spout mounted on side wall of bath to create a cascade of water (Ciprea only)
- Built-in armrests
- Side drain/overflow

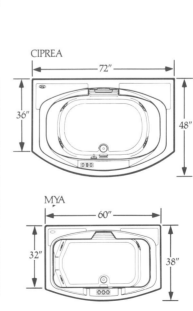

CIPREA
72"
36"
48"

MYA
60"
32"
38"

Leave it to the innovators at Jacuzzi Whirlpool Bath to create an entirely new concept in whirlpool bathing. Thanks to its revolutionary shape, the elegantly—and intelligently—designed Maurea™ whirlpool bath is as sleek and sophisticated as it is comfortable and functional. Not only does the Maurea easily accommodate two bathers side by side, it also features a contoured backrest and built-in armrests for complete relaxation. In addition, there is a special side seat for bathside grooming as well as a tastefully concealed vanity with mirror and accessory area. Top it off with the peaceful sounds of the cascading Water Rainbow® fill spout, and you have an environment that's nothing short of pure pleasure.

SPECIFICATIONS:

- *DIMENSIONS:* 72" long x 63" wide x 22" high.
- *MATERIAL:* High-gloss acrylic, fiberglass reinforced.
- *CONSTRUCTION:* Self-contained, completely preplumbed.
- *INSTALLATION:* Recessed in floor or platform.
- *WHIRLPOOL MOTOR/PUMP:* ¾ HP, 115V 20 AMP service required.
- *WATER CAPACITY:* 80 U.S. gallons.
- *FLOOR LOADING:* 51.5 lbs./sq. ft.
- *SHIPPING WEIGHT:* 320 lbs.
- *CERTIFICATIONS:* UL and IAPMO listed, factory pretested.

Product specifications subject to change without notice.

FEATURES:

- Four fully-adjustable PowerPro® jets
- Contoured backrest and built-in armrests for added comfort
- Integral seat for bathside grooming
- Water Rainbow fill spout with matching acrylic cover
- Built-in hot and cold water faucets

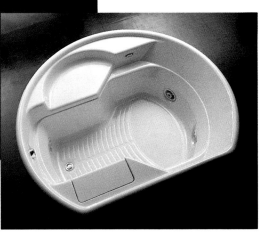

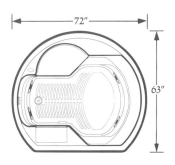

■ When can a totally new design be considered a classic? When it is the Opalia,™ a whirlpool bath so elegantly simple and gracefully shaped it transcends the merely fashionable. You won't find a single straight line in the Opalia, from its superb oval shaping and asymmetrically curved rim to its etched detailing and shell bottom design. The Opalia is the essence of comfort as well as beauty, with a spacious six-foot size and built-in armrests perfectly suited to luxuriant bathing for two.

SPECIFICATIONS:

- *DIMENSIONS:* 72" long x 44" wide x 22" high.
- *MATERIAL:* High-gloss acrylic, fiberglass reinforced.
- *CONSTRUCTION:* Self-contained, completely preplumbed.
- *INSTALLATION:* Recessed in floor or platform.
- *WHIRLPOOL MOTOR/PUMP:* ¾ HP, 115V 20 AMP service required.
- *WATER CAPACITY:* 98 U.S. gallons.
- *FLOOR LOADING:* 53 lbs./sq. ft.
- *SHIPPING WEIGHT:* 175 lbs.
- *CERTIFICATIONS:* UL and IAPMO listed, factory pretested.

Product specifications subject to change without notice.

FEATURES:

- Four fully-adjustable PowerPro® jets
- Interior contours with built-in armrests
- Attractive ribbed pattern on slip-resistant shell bottom
- Optional faucet and handles

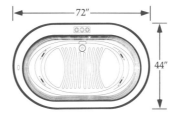

AURA

■ As the originator of whirlpool bathing you would expect Jacuzzi Whirlpool Bath to lead in innovative design. With the Aura,™ this tradition continues. A new level of comfort, extraordinary features and stunning design make the Aura the ultimate two-person lounger bath.

SPECIFICATIONS:

- *DIMENSIONS:* 72" long x 60" wide x 20" high.
- *MATERIAL:* High-glbss acrylic, fiberglass reinforced.
- *CONSTRUCTION:* Self-contained, completely preplumbed.
- *INSTALLATIONS:* Recessed in floor or platform.
- *WHIRLPOOL MOTOR/PUMP:* 1.5 HP, 115V 20 AMP service required.
- *WATER CAPACITY:* 125 U.S. gallons.
- *FLOOR LOADING:* 52 lbs./sq. ft.
- *SHIPPING WEIGHT:* 348 lbs.
- *CERTIFICATIONS:*
  UL and IAPMO listed, factory pretested.

Product specifications subject to change without notice.

FEATURES:

- Four fully-adjustable PowerPro® jets
- Two Water Rainbow spouts: one to fill, the other to recirculate
- Built-in hot & cold water faucets
- Two acrylic covers with mirrored interiors, concealing the controls and providing an accessory area for bathing items
- Two interior lights with a selection of colored lenses
- Two individual loungers

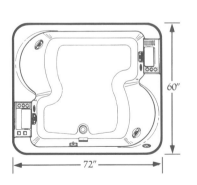

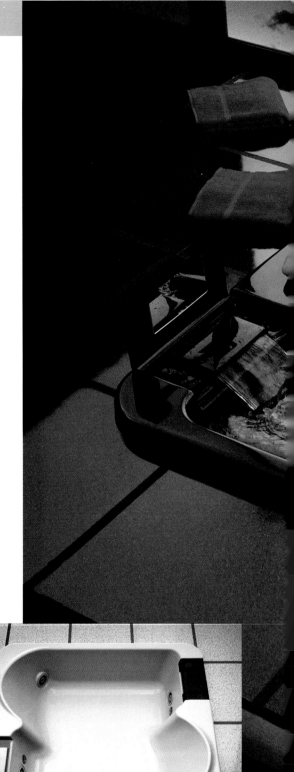

■ One of the most exciting designs we have ever introduced, the Amea™ whirlpool bath combines the distinctive lines of European style with the kind of practical innovations that have made Jacuzzi Whirlpool Bath the leader in whirlpool bathing. Its integral headrest and sloping backrest provide an extraordinary degree of comfort. The unique seat allows for bath-side grooming, or a convenient place to store bathing items.

SPECIFICATIONS:

- *DIMENSIONS:* AMEA 5.5: 66" long x 36" wide x 20" high. AMEA 6: 72" long x 36" wide x 28" high.
- *MATERIAL:* High-gloss acrylic, fiberglass reinforced.
- *CONSTRUCTION:* Self-contained, completely preplumbed.
- *INSTALLATION:* Recessed in floor or platform, or with optional matching skirt.
- *WHIRLPOOL MOTOR/PUMP:* ¾ HP, 115V, 20 AMP service required.
- *WATER CAPACITY:* AMEA 5.5: 55 U.S. gallons. AMEA 6: 65 U.S. gallons.
- *FLOOR LOADING:* AMEA 5.5: 44 lbs./sq. ft. AMEA 6: 45 lbs./sq. ft.
- *SHIPPING WEIGHT:* AMEA 5.5: 147 lbs. AMEA 6: 145 lbs.
- *CERTIFICATIONS:* UL and IAPMO listed, factory pretested.

Product specifications subject to change without notice.

FEATURES:

- Fully-adjustable PowerPro® jets
- Integral headrest for added comfort
- Integral seat for bath-side grooming or a convenient shelf to store bathing items
- Side drain/overflow
- Optional Water Rainbow® spout

AMEA 6

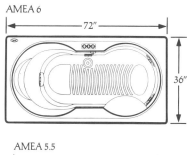

AMEA 5.5

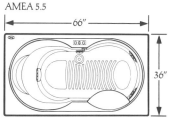

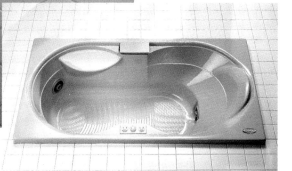

BIANCA

■ The Bianca™ provides a perfect place for just the two of you. A place to be alone—together. And to be away from it all. Of course, you'll find the Bianca just as enjoyable when you bathe by yourself. Our whirlpool system is famous for creating a very special experience. And with the Bianca, it's an experience that can bring two people together.

SPECIFICATIONS:
- *DIMENSIONS:* 72" long x 48" wide x 20" high.
- *MATERIAL:* High-gloss acrylic, fiberglass reinforced.
- *CONSTRUCTION:* Self-contained, completely preplumbed.
- *INSTALLATIONS:* Recessed in floor or platform, or by constructing a skirt.
- *WHIRLPOOL MOTOR/PUMP:* 1½ HP, 115V 20 AMP service required.
- *WATER CAPACITY:* 85 U.S. gallons.
- *FLOOR LOADING:* 48 lbs./sq. ft.
- *SHIPPING WEIGHT:* 179 lbs.
- *CERTIFICATIONS:* UL and IAPMO listed, factory pretested.

Product specifications subject to change without notice.

FEATURES:
- Four fully-adjustable PowerPro® jets
- Contoured backrest
- Side-by-side bathing space
- Optional faucet and handles.

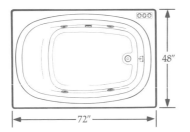

PRIMA II

■ The dramatic Prima II™ will dazzle your senses. It's a work of art, with contours as captivating as fine sculpture. And the luxury standard features of Prima II make it an equally captivating experience. Once you are inside, the Magic Touch® on/off switch enables you to activate the whirlpool with just a touch of your finger. The entire system is adjustable, to suit your every mood. The Prima II by Jacuzzi Whirlpool Bath—it'll take you to another world.

SPECIFICATIONS:

- *DIMENSIONS:* 72" long x 36" wide x 18" high.
- *MATERIAL:* High-gloss acrylic, fiberglass reinforced.
- *CONSTRUCTION:* Self-contained, completely preplumbed.
- *INSTALLATIONS:* Recessed in floor or platform, or with optional matching skirt.
- *WHIRLPOOL MOTOR/PUMP:* ¾ HP, 115V 20 AMP service required.
- *WATER CAPACITY:* 65 U.S. gallons.
- *FLOOR LOADING:* 46 lbs./sq. ft.
- *SHIPPING WEIGHT:* 161 lbs.
- *CERTIFICATIONS:* UL and IAPMO listed, factory pretested.

Product specifications subject to change without notice.

FEATURES:

- Three fully-adjustable PowerPro® jets
- Sloped backrest for reclining
- Optional Water Rainbow fill spout & faucet knobs

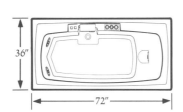

Soothing Cascade Shower

Restorative Steam Bath

Stimulating Hydromassage

Fully-adjustable Shower

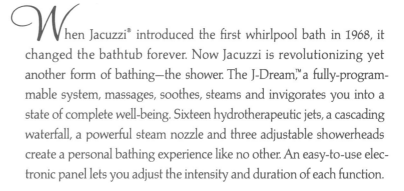

When Jacuzzi® introduced the first whirlpool bath in 1968, it changed the bathtub forever. Now Jacuzzi is revolutionizing yet another form of bathing—the shower. The J-Dream,™ a fully-programmable system, massages, soothes, steams and invigorates you into a state of complete well-being. Sixteen hydrotherapeutic jets, a cascading waterfall, a powerful steam nozzle and three adjustable showerheads create a personal bathing experience like no other. An easy-to-use electronic panel lets you adjust the intensity and duration of each function.

Step into the J-Dream and see how Jacuzzi has created the ultimate shower experience. Because the J-Dream is made by Jacuzzi, everything about it—from innovative design and technology to quality manufacturing—is simply the best.

■ *Soothing: The Cascade Shower*

Rest on the specially molded seat and relax as a soothing, cascading waterfall caresses your neck and shoulders. The cascade shower is specifically designed to release tension from the entire upper spine area, and create a feeling of well-being throughout your body.

■ *Restorative: The Steam Bath*

The touch of a finger activates a nozzle located under the molded seat to fill the J-Dream with full-bodied steam. In just minutes, you can enjoy all the cleansing benefits of steam heat—without stepping outside the shower. The steam may also be used simultaneously with any other function: the cascade, jets or shower spray.

■ *Stimulating: The Hydromassage*

Sixteen programmable hydrotherapy jets provide high-power hydromassage to invigorate and relax the body. Program the jets to pulsate in any one of six pre-determined configurations, adjusting both the spray pattern for each jet and the rate at which you want the jets to pulsate.

■ *Cleansing: The Shower Sprays*

Both the dual state-of-the-art high-output showerheads and the hand held shower offer a range of sprays from fine mist to full-flood. Even the shower temperature is programmable, so you won't have to set it each time. The hand held shower can also be adjusted vertically so even the tallest adult or the smallest child can shower in total comfort.

DIMENSIONS: 60" long x 36" wide x 84" high.

WATER RAINBOW ULTRA
Larger, bolder and more luxurious, the oval Water Rainbow® ultra fill spout offers the same soothing murmur of cascading water as our classic Water Rainbow fill spout. It also fills faster than conventional fill spouts, with a ¾" opening instead of the standard ½" variety. Choose from chrome or brass metallic finishes with Rope, Ring or Band handles.

ROPE

RING

BAND

■ *WATER RAINBOW*
Like the Jacuzzi® whirlpool bath itself, our Water Rainbow® fill spout has become synonymous with pure pleasure and relaxation. This private waterfall is equipped with flow control and shower diverter, and can be color-coordinated to complement your Jacuzzi whirlpool bath. Choose from lustrous chrome, gold or bright brass metallic finishes, or any one of fourteen color-matched Designer shades. Also available with Rope, Ring or Band handles.

■ *SUPER METRO*
Designed specifically for larger tubs, this impressive faucet is the essence of sleek and modern bathroom elegance. The Super Metro is fashioned of solid brass and finished in chrome or brass. Available with Rope, Ring or Band handles.

■ *SEA CREST*
The Sea Crest faucet is at
once graceful and dramatic.
It is also quite practical, as it
delivers hot water quickly to
the tub or lavatory. Fashioned
of solid brass and finished in
lustrous brass or chrome with
your choice of Rope, Ring or
Band handles.

ROPE

RING

BAND

CROSS

LEVER

■ *RENAISSANCE*

With its handsome shape and sculpted lines, the Renaissance faucet will remain a classic for generations. Choose from lever or cross grip handles. Available in chip-resistant white, silver or almond, as well as chrome or brass finishes. Constructed from solid brass.

■ *METRO*

Like a fine work of modern art, the Metro faucet is both bold and innovative. Fashioned of solid brass and finished in chrome, brass, white or almond, Metro faucets are available for both bath and basin.

■ *JACUZZI® SHOWER HEADS*

Choose a gentle rain or an invigorating spray—quality is evident in every detail of the Jacuzzi® shower heads. These solid brass fixtures, with your choice of brass or chrome finishes, match Jacuzzi® faucets for coordinated appeal. Choose between two different sizes.

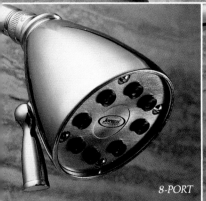

8-PORT

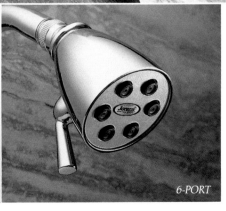

6-PORT

The Originator. The Innovator.

JACUZZI WHIRLPOOL BATH
Corporate Headquarters
100 North Wiget Lane
P.O. Drawer J
Walnut Creek, CA 94596
(800) 678-6889

U.S. Regional Offices
GREAT LAKES REGION: (708) 882-8788, 2500 W. Higgins Rd., Suite 1000, Hoffman Estates, IL 60195
CENTRAL REGION: (214) 931-7474, 17950 Preston Road, Suite 708, Dallas, Texas 75252
SOUTHEAST REGION: (404) 981-8222, 2500 Park Central Blvd., Suite B6, Decatur, GA 30035
NORTHEAST REGION: (201) 575-7710, 310 Passaic Ave., Suite 304A, Fairfield, NJ 07004

Outside the U.S. Contact
JACUZZI DO BRASIL: Telex 1179709/Telephone 011-55-409-1711/FAX 011-55-11-482-4836
JACUZZI CHILE: Telex 332-346-388/Telephone 011-56-2-577-5708
JACUZZI CANADA: Telephone: 416-675-3333/FAX 416-674-6351
JACUZZI EUROPE (ITALY): Telex 843-450-839/Telephone 011-39-434-85-141/FAX 011-39-434-85-278
JACUZZI U.K.: Telephone 011-44-1-997-4871/FAX 011-44-1-997-1507

SUMMARY OF LIMITED WARRANTY FOR BATH PRODUCTS: Jacuzzi Whirlpool Bath (Jacuzzi) provides a limited warranty to the consumer. The warranty applies to the bath, pump, motor and most attached fittings and plumbing. In general, Jacuzzi, without charge, will repair or replace (at our option) any new unit or component which proves defective in material or workmanship or does not operate in accordance with written performance specifications stated on the unit. Our warranty has specific limitations. Excluded from our warranty are certain damages including but not limited to: shipping damage; damage occuring during or after installation; damage resulting from installation or use not in accordance with our published instructions and specifications for the product; damage from use of chemicals, bath oil additives, or improper cleaning agents; incidental or consequential damages or losses, and damages from product modifications, careless handling or product use for other than personal, family or household purposes. Nor is Jacuzzi reponsible for minor blemishes, pitting, or crazing, or for costs incurred in the removal and/or installation of a unit. Our warranty does not cover damage or loss resulting from modification. A copy of our entire warranty is available from any of our authorized Dealers and Distributors. We urge each prospective consumer to read our warranty carefully to assure that he enjoys the full benefits of the protection our warranty provides and understands its limitations, the purchaser's obligations, and the obligation of others. Product Specifications subject to change without notice. Be sure to check for local code compliance.

IMPORTANT NOTICE REGARDING ALL WHIRLPOOL BATH INSTALLATIONS: Access must be provided to service equipment located under unit. Installation with control panel against wall is not recommended as this would impair service access. Install and operate each bath only according to instructions provided with product. Final electric and/or plumbing connections should be made by a professional for your safety and for conformance to local building codes.

The following are registered trademarks of Jacuzzi Inc.: Jacuzzi Whirlpool Bath and Jacuzzi, Allusian, Amea 5.5 and Amea 6, Aura, Bianca, Ciprea, Eura, Fiore, Fontana, J-Dream, Magic Touch, Maurea, Mira, Mya, Opalia, PowerPro, Prima II, Viante and Viante Grande, and Water Rainbow.

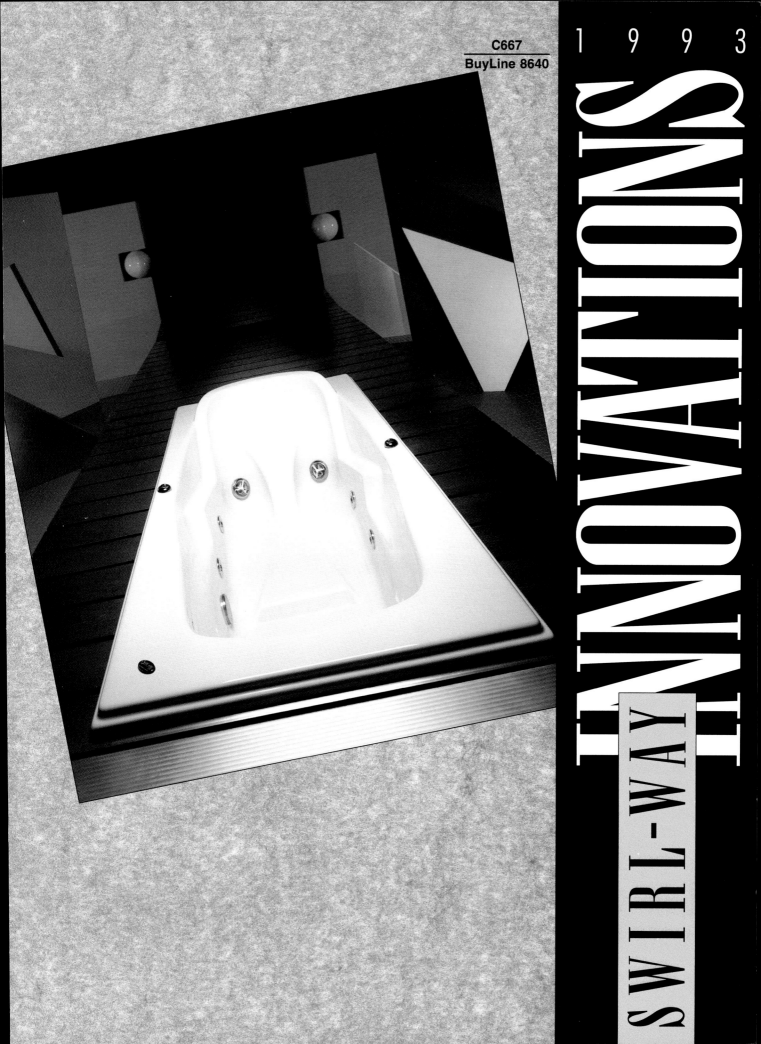

1 9 9 3

INNOVATIONS

SWIRL-WAY

A New Level of Comfort

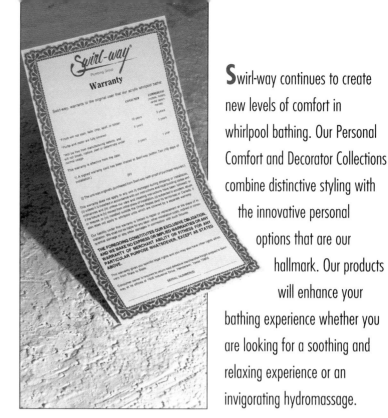

Swirl-way continues to create new levels of comfort in whirlpool bathing. Our Personal Comfort and Decorator Collections combine distinctive styling with the innovative personal options that are our hallmark. Our products will enhance your bathing experience whether you are looking for a soothing and relaxing experience or an invigorating hydromassage.

Your head and shoulders are cradled in comfort.

Micro'ssage™ jets complement our exclusive backrest.

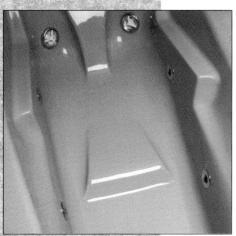

The leg support provides a gentle incline for full body relaxation.

The concepts of innovation, quality, durability, and value have been the guiding principles at Swirl-way for many years. Swirl-way products meet or exceed the most stringent safety and building codes to ensure years of trouble-free performance. Because we use only the best materials, we can offer the strongest guarantee in the industry — a 10-year limited warranty. We even warrant the pump and motor on our whirlpools for five years.

Take a look at our whirlpools and see why Swirl-way innovations provide the best in personal comfort, hydrotherapy, and aesthetic design.

Plumbing Group

For Dealer Locations, Call 1-800-999-1459

The Personal Comfort Collection whirlpool baths feature sculpted backrests and contoured leg supports for maximum relaxation. A combination of Micro'ssage™ and slim-line jets is standard and provides a soothing yet powerful hydromassage. Take a look at these whirlpools and see why Swirl-way innovations provide the best in personal comfort, hydrotherapy, and design.

Aspen

ASPEN

The streamlined Aspen whirlpool bath is designed for personalized comfort with contoured backrest and leg support. In addition, a total of eight jets, including two Freedom Series interchangeable jets, allow you to easily select the type of massage or whirlpool action you desire. Touch Sensor Plus is standard on the Aspen for personal 3-speed whirlpool selection.

71³/₄" x 36" x 22³/₄"

All dimensions are nominal. See spec sheet for exact dimensions.

ANDIAMO

Andiamo

The beautifully sculpted two-person Andiamo is Swirl-way's largest whirlpool. Armrests and leg supports are positioned to give total body relaxation for one or two bathers. Our exclusive backrest allows you to enjoy the hydrotherapy to full advantage. This luxurious model features four Micro'ssage™ and four slim-line jets. And with the new Touch Sensor Plus, a standard feature of the Andiamo, three-speed whirlpool action is at your fingertips.

71³/₄" x 48" x 24¹/₄"

AVALON

Avalon

In the quest to blend style and engineering into one design, the Avalon is an inspired solution. Its eight jets include two Micro'ssage™ jets that provide a gentle massage. Or you can convert the Micro'ssage™ to high volume directional or adjustable jets with our Freedom Series jets. Our new Touch Sensor Plus, standard on these designs, enhances the Freedom Series jets by providing convenient 3-speed whirlpool pump selection.

71¹/₂" x 40¹/₂" x 25¹/₂"

TOUCH SENSOR PLUS

The whirlpool bath designs from our Personal Comfort Collection feature the new Touch Sensor Plus. The Touch Sensor Plus combines the convenience of finger-tip on/off control, a 20-minute timer, and a low-water cut-off with a 3-speed pump. Now you can select the whirlpool intensity you want with the touch of a finger.

THE DECORATOR COLLECTION

DaVanti

DAVANTI
The dramatic and inviting DaVanti will be an impressive addition to your bathroom suite. With the option of our contemporary skirt to match the bath, you'll have the style you desire as well as easy access to the pump and drain.

60" x 60" x 21¼"

ARIANNA
The raised contours and gentle slope of our elegant Arianna whirlpool create an especially comfortable bathing experience. For added convenience, the air controls are located on the armrests.

71½" x 40½" x 25½"

Arianna

MILANO II
Lean back and let relaxation take over in the Milano, an extra wide whirlpool with armrests and sculptured drain. Two new 12" suede-soft pillows, standard on the Milanos, provide soothing comfort.

71½" x 47⅝" x 22½"

Milano II

MILANO I
59½" x 47" x 22¾"

AMBRIA
For maximum bathing capacity with a contemporary look, choose the distinctive Ambria. This sleek design is a blend of beauty and practicality with dual armrests and an optional front skirt.

59½" x 59½" x 22¼"

Ambria

LOMBARDI
The distinctive oval lines of our six-foot Lombardi whirlpool enhance any decor. How it fits into your life is up to your imagination. Ample size, air switch for control of whirlpool action, and center drain placement make this whirlpool an inviting possibility for two bathers.

72" x 44" x 20¾"

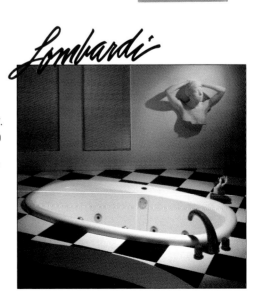

Lombardi

Cambio

CAMBIO

You can have the perfect blend of traditional beauty and soothing comfort with our five-foot oval whirlpool. Air controls are located on the armrests, and the wide circular design increases the bathing area.

60" x 42" x 20¾"

FLORENCE II

The redesign of the Florence, our popular and beautiful oval whirlpool within a rectangular deck, now includes contoured armrests and sculptured drain. An optional skirt and nailing flange are also available.

71⅝" x 42" x 19½"

Florence II

FLORENCE I
59⅝" x 42" x 20¾"

Trevi

TREVI

We've given this corner design added appeal with a personalized contoured seat. An optional removable skirt combines a sleek, contemporary look with convenient access to pump and motor.

59¼" x 59¼" x 23¼"

Verdi

VERDI

The Verdi gives you the look and feel of a large whirlpool in a smaller space. Our popular hourglass design provides maximum bathing area in a five-foot space.

59½" x 41½" x 22"

Sorrento

VERONA

Give yourself some time to relax in this classic hourglass whirlpool. In fact, we designed the Verona for convenience and comfort with armrests, shampoo shelf, and grab bar.

71¼" x 41⅝" x 22¾"

SORRENTO

This unique design, set diagonally within a 5½-foot area, is a beautiful way to make the most of your space. Why not take full advantage of the extra room and soothing incline to create the perfect retreat.

65¾" x 32" x 21¾"

Verona

THE DECORATOR COLLECTION

Asti

ASTI

The Asti adds a lot of style to even the smallest bathroom. This practical whirlpool incorporates all the features of our larger models and is available in all standard and special colors.

59¾" x 32" x 21"

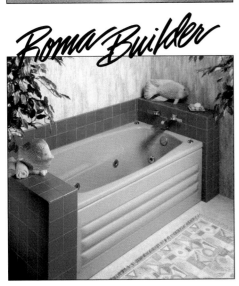

Roma Builder

ROMA BUILDER

The versatile Roma Builder is a six-jet whirlpool that fits the most demanding remodel design. Integrated tile flange, above-the-floor drain, and a new contemporary skirt make this model one of the easiest whirlpools to retrofit.

59¾" x 32" x 21¾"

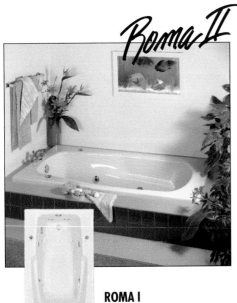

Roma II

ROMA II

Immerse yourself in the luxurious feel of warm swirling waters and realize the true beauty of a whirlpool bath. Traditional design combined with a comfortable back support make our Romas a popular choice.

71½" x 35½" x 20"

ROMA I
59¾" x 35¾" x 21"

36" x 36"
Single Threshold
Length O.D. ....35"
Width O.D. ....35"
#3636-ST

32" x 32"
Single Threshold
Length O.D. ....31"
Width O.D. ....31½"
#3232-ST

36" x 42"
Single Threshold Short Side
Length O.D. ....35"
Width O.D.........................41½"
#3642-STSS

42" x 36"
Single Threshold Long Side
Length O.D. ....41"
Width O.D.........................35½"
#4236-STLS

48" x 34"
Single Threshold Long Side
Length O.D. ....47"
Width O.D.........................33½"
#4834-STLS

SHOWER BASES

38" x 38" – Neo-Angle
Length O.D. ....37¼"
Width O.D. ....37¼"
#3838-TTNA

36" x 36" – Neo-Angle
Length O.D. ....35½"
Width O.D. ....35½"
#3636-TTNA

36" x 36" – Double Threshold
Length O.D. ....35"
Width O.D. ....35"
#3636-DT

38" x 38" – Neo-Angle
Length O.D. ....37½"
Width O.D. ....37½"
#3838-RTNA

36" x 36" – Neo-Angle
Length O.D. ....35½"
Width O.D. ....35½"
#3636-RTNA

48" x 32"
Single Threshold Long Side
Length O.D. ....47"
Width O.D. ....31½"
#4832-STLS

60" x 34"
Single Threshold Long Side
Length O.D. ....58¾"
Width O.D. ....33½"
#6034-STLS

Swirl-way shower bases are the practical choice for new construction or remodeling. We combine beauty and design with a quality material, acrylic, to produce a shower base that provides years of trouble-free performance and easy maintenance.

Our shower bases come in the same color selections as our whirlpools, giving you the flexibility to complete the most demanding design scheme. For convenient installation, our shower bases are compatible with today's most popular shower doors.

Now it's easy to achieve a designer look when you include our shower bases in your bathroom plans.

All dimensions are nominal. See spec sheet for exact dimensions.

FEATURES

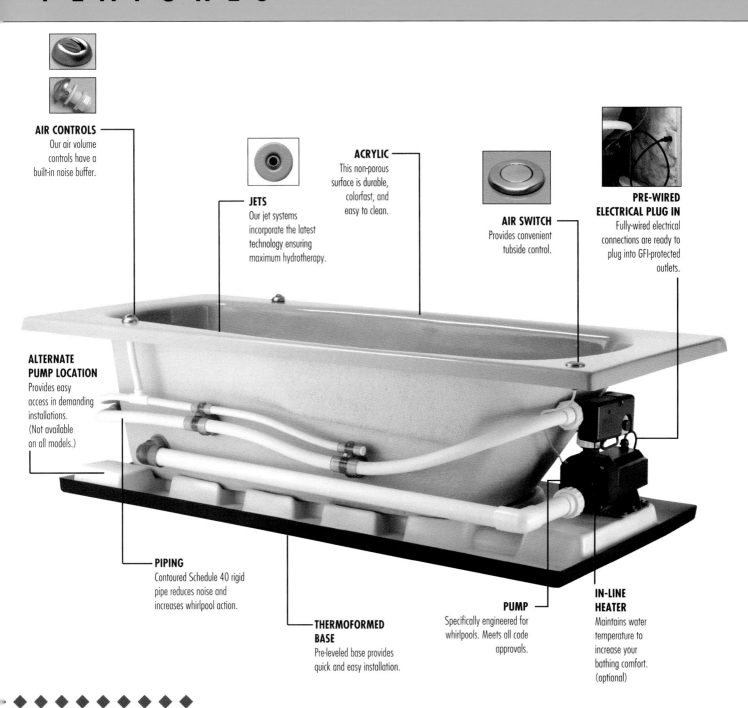

AIR CONTROLS
Our air volume controls have a built-in noise buffer.

JETS
Our jet systems incorporate the latest technology ensuring maximum hydrotherapy.

ACRYLIC
This non-porous surface is durable, colorfast, and easy to clean.

AIR SWITCH
Provides convenient tubside control.

PRE-WIRED ELECTRICAL PLUG IN
Fully-wired electrical connections are ready to plug into GFI-protected outlets.

ALTERNATE PUMP LOCATION
Provides easy access in demanding installations. (Not available on all models.)

PIPING
Contoured Schedule 40 rigid pipe reduces noise and increases whirlpool action.

THERMOFORMED BASE
Pre-leveled base provides quick and easy installation.

PUMP
Specifically engineered for whirlpools. Meets all code approvals.

IN-LINE HEATER
Maintains water temperature to increase your bathing comfort. (optional)

◆ ◆ ◆ ◆ ◆ ◆ ◆ ◆

Swirl-way whirlpools are engineered and designed for beauty, durability, and value. We listen to you, the customer, and respond to your demands with innovative features that make Swirl-way the preeminent name in quality whirlpool baths.

PACKAGING/PROTECTIVE LINER

To ensure the strongest packaging possible, Swirl-way uses specially engineered crates. For on-the-job protection, we include a corrugated cover that is pre-cut to be used as a mat on the tub floor and deck during construction. This covering includes a plastic liner to protect the sides. All cardboard pads are made from recycled materials.

TIMER
Swirl-way's convenient 30-minute timer is wall mounted and thermal insulated.

OPTIONS

TOUCH SENSOR PLUS

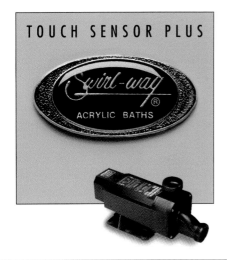

TOUCH SENSOR PLUS

Touch Sensor Plus features control of on/off functions and three whirlpool pump speeds. The package also includes a 20-minute timer and low-water cut-off to ensure proper operation.

THE FREEDOM SERIES

DIRECTIONAL JET

This jet has a movable eyeball so you can direct the jetstream to a specific area. The directional jet creates a more powerful vortex or whirlpool action.

ADJUSTABLE JET

This jet gives you fingertip control of direction and intensity. A twist of the jet nozzle changes a soft relaxing whirlpool into an invigorating powerful water massage.

COMFORT CONTROL PLUS

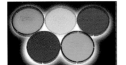

COMFORT CONTROL PLUS

Swirl-way's new Comfort Control Plus package features a digital control panel mounted at tub-side for easy use. Comfort Control Plus lets you select from six whirlpool pump speeds and the pulsation mode from our variable speed pump, set the timer and mood lights, and regulate the in-line heater for perfect water temperature. A low-water cut-off is also included. (Digital control panel not mounted on tub.)

COMFORT CONTROL

Digital control panel and variable speed pump can be purchased separately.

MICRO'SSAGE™ JET

This unique rotating jet produces a continuous circular massage. You can apply soothing relief to specific muscles or have a therapeutic total massage.

Now, Swirl-way's special massage and whirlpool jets can be purchased individually. Select from Micro'ssage,™ directional, or adjustable jets. You control the type of massage or whirlpool action you want by simply changing out the jet assembly.

The Freedom Series jets are available in four finishes to complement your whirlpool bath. Choose from chrome, polished brass, white, or bone.

COLOR KEYED JETS

Swirl-way offers color-coordinated jets for standard color whirlpool baths. Our jet system provides the ideal jet-to-pump ratio and maximizes the greatest potential of both the pump and jets.

METAL FINISH JETS

As an option, Swirl-way offers the following finishes:

| BRASS | SATIN BRASS | CHROME | ANTIQUE BRASS | GOLD |

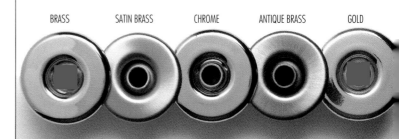

OPTIONS

◆ ◆ ◆ ◆ ◆ ◆ ◆ ◆

Your choice of options is almost endless. Swirl-way offers the widest selection of options in the industry so that you can customize your acrylic whirlpool bath to meet your own special needs. With finishing touches like these, you can reach a whole new level of comfort.

IN-LINE HEATER
Our heater is thermostatically controlled to maintain water temperature and increase your bathing comfort.

TIMER
Swirl-way's convenient 30-minute timer is wall mounted and thermal insulated.

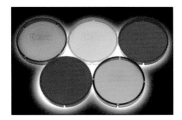

MOOD LIGHTS
Swirl-way offers five color filters to create that special ambience. With front access, it's simple to change the bulb and filter.

DRAIN KITS
Our cable-operated drain kits allow you to open and close the drain with ease. Colors available are polished brass, chrome, white, and bone.

NAILING FLANGE
Swirl-way can provide a code approved nailing flange for special installation needs. (The nailing flange will slightly alter the dimensions of the unit.)

PILLOWS
Nothing adds more comfort to your bathing experience than Swirl-way's new suede-soft 12" pillow.

REMOVABLE SKIRTS
The contemporary styling of our front panel skirts provides easy access to the underside of the tub and a perfect match to the designs and colors of our whirlpool baths.

COLORS

ACROSS THE SPECTRUM
Whether your bathroom is contemporary or traditional, Swirl-way has rich acrylic colors to complement your decor. You can select your Swirl-way acrylic whirlpool bath or shower base from an exciting array of standard and special colors or from our grouping of designer colors for unique decorating needs.

CODE COMPLIANCE

 Listed No. 2719

 State of Ohio and various other state and local approvals

 Listed No. SP-1179

 Listed 47E6 hydromassage bathtub

 Listed S.259 hydromassage bathtub

 When tested for compliance to the requirement of ANSI A112.19.7M and A112.19.8M for "Whirlpool Bath Appliances" and ANSI Z124.1 for "Plastic Bathtub Units" the tested units are found to comply and are acceptable for listing under the Terralab Engineers, Inc. follow-up service. Listed No. 15197

Swirl-way ®
Plumbing Group

For Dealer Locations, Call Toll Free: 1-800-999-1459

1505 Industrial Drive ▪ P.O. Box 210 ▪ Henderson, Texas, USA 75653-0210 ▪ FAX: 903-657-3450

Printed in the USA.

Uncover A New Dimension In Steam Bathing

STEAMIST®

transform yourself with a luxurious spa.

The pleasures of steambathing appreciated for centuries, have never been easier to enjoy in your own home.

Having your own personal steambath can help you sleep better and work better. Because above all, you'll feel better.

Entering this warm, moisturizing enclave will relax you before retiring. Linger and let stiffness and fatigue melt away under the soft fingers of soothing steam. After your steambath a shower will give you new life.

Steambathing contributes to a brighter, healthier outlook, increases blood circulation and metabolism, provides a haven from mental and physical stress.

Steamist will enhance the quality of life for both you and your family each and every day.

Steamist transforms your bath area as well

By adding a new level of convenience, beauty and practicality, your Steamist steambath will let you enjoy its pleasures without distractions.

Steamist controls are simple and unobtrusive. In a choice of polished chrome, brass or white finish, they complement the appearance of any bath decor.

And the easy-to-reach controls are just as simple to operate — At the press of a button, your steambath is ready. The controls regulate the time cycle and temperature automatically, holding the temperature precisely at your pre-set comfort level — allowing you to lose yourself completely and confidently, in your period of relaxation.

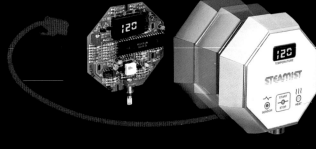

TC-130

Plug-in connections make it easy to install...

Our telephone type connectors make it a snap to install the Steamist generator. The plumbing hookup and electric lines are similar to that of your existing hot water heater, and the unit can be installed as far as 25 feet away from the bath area.

The compact steam generator hides quietly in the vanity, closet, or even an insulated attic or basement. In addition, low voltage controls are safe and easy to operate and the system is maintenance free.

A Relaxing Steambath with the Push of a Button

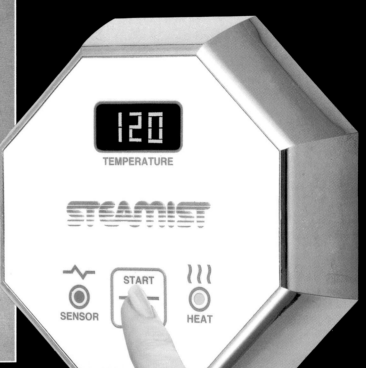

TC-130

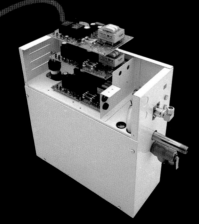

Steamist has been the leading manufacturer of personal steambaths for over 25 years, using our expertise to design convenience and reliability into a choice of contemporary systems. Steamist adds value to both your home and your well-being.

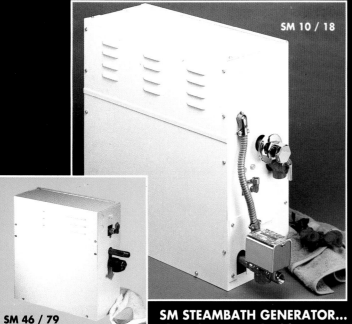

SM 10 / 18

SM 46 / 79

TC-130 DIGITAL TIMER AND TEMPERATURE CONTROL

This control operates on a pre-set time cycle and the start/stop feature allows complete control of your steambath from within. Located inside the steamroom, it is perfect for bathers who require an exact temperature.

TC-120 TIMER AND TEMPERATURE CONTROL

This control is pre-set for your steambath duration and maintains exact temperature. A simple control adjustment by you will change the temperature and keep it within 1 1/2°F. A start/stop keypad is located inside the steamroom.

SM STEAMBATH GENERATOR...
The Industry Standard for over 30 Years

The model # SM - 46 and SM - 79 offer exceptional flexibility of design by providing an adjustable kilowatt level to better size the unit to your bath area. The larger STEAMIST generators can be equipped with an optional auto drain to enhance the performance. All SM units feature Stainless Steel construction and Solid State circuitry and are designed to last for years of maintainance free operation. Conservative on water and electricity, STEAMIST generators are UL Listed and include a Five Year Limited Warranty.

STEAMIST • SM SERIES • RESIDENTIAL

Model No.	Maximum Cu. Ft. Range	KW Rating	Volt	Phase	Maximum AMPS	Wire Size 90 C Copper AWG	Line Fuse Req'd	Cabinet Dimensions H x W x L
SM-46	60 -130	4.5/6	208	1	29	8	40	15.5" x 6" x 15"
			240	1	25			
SM-79	135-300	7.5/9	208	1	44	8	50	15.5" x 6" x 15"
			240	1	38			
*SM-10	375	10.5	208	1	50	6	60	20.5" x 8" x 20"
			208	3	29	8	40	
			240	1	44	6	60	
			240	3	25	8	40	
*SM-12	410	12	208	1	58	6	70	20.5" x 8" x 20"
			208	3	33	8	40	
			240	1	50	6	60	
			240	3	29	8	40	
*SM-15	475	15	208	1	72	4	90	20.5" x 8" x 20"
			208	3	42	8	50	
			240	1	63	6	70	
			240	3	36	8	50	
*SM-18†	575	18	208	1	87	3	100	20.5" x 8" x 20"
			208	3	50	6	60	
			240	1	75	4	90	
			240	3	44	6	60	
*SM-24†	800	24	208	1	115			CONTACT MANUFACTURER
			208	3	67			
			240	1	100			
			240	3	58			
*SM-30†	1000	30	208	1	144			CONTACT MANUFACTURER
			208	3	84			
			240	1	126			
			240	3	72			

* Optional auto drain available for SM-10 thru SM 30
† UL Pending

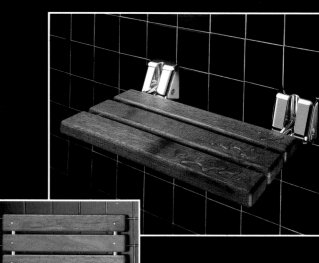

TILT-UP BATH AND SHOWER SEAT

The STEAMIST tilt-up bath and shower seat is designed to make your bathing as practical and comfortable as possible. This attractive seat combines natural hand rubbed exotic European wood on your choice of chrome, white or brass frame. It matches perfectly to any designer bathroom decor.
Dimensions: 19 1/4" x 13" D

Distributed by:

3/93

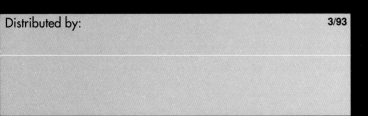

STEAMIST ®
a new dimension in bathing

East Coast Office:
One Altman Drive • Rutherford, NJ 07070
Telephone: (201) 933-0700 • Fax: (201) 933-0746

West Coast Office:
Telephone: (714) 533-6033 • Fax: (714) 533-8357

For further information about Steamist Heavy Commercial Steambath Generators, Steambath Enclosures, and other accessories, write for a full product line brochure.

DL
"SERIES"

STEAMIST ®

a new dimension in steam bathing

Temperature Control (VFD-400)

STEAMIST is the finishing touch for any bath environment!

People spend many hours enjoying the luxurious innovations that accentuate today's bath.

Finding time from the fast pace of life requires a setting for relaxation . . . Let STEAMIST "DL" Deluxe Series Steam Generators provide this oasis for you.

A simple touch of the keypad on a STEAMIST 60-Minute Timer will begin your experience.

Stepping into your steambath you have entered a new world, as steam billows up, feel sensations never encountered. Surrender to the tranquil environment of a STEAMIST steambath as muscles unwind and pores are cleansed, a serenity envelopes you; R-E-L-A-X, succumb to the experience as today's most sophisticated steambath stimulates circulation and metabolism providing a more energetic day at work or night on the town.

STEAMIST's Temperature Display and Control digitally reads out ambient temperature and a temperature adjustment knob allows you to raise or lower steamroom temperature. When you desire to interrupt or end the steambath prematurely just touch the keypad, the generator will now stop producing steam.

After your steambath, enjoy a cool shower and be ready to go out and conquer the world or take a warm shower and sleep like a baby. Either way, you'll discover the age old secret of steambathing.

The "DL" Deluxe system, for those who enjoy the finer things in life.

Timer Control (VFD-100)

Now the bathing enthusiast can experience a truly unique steambath environment with the DELUXE Generator and DELUXE Controls.

Select the duration of your steambath with the Deluxe Timer (VFD-100) that can be set up to 60 minutes in one minute increments. The control is easy to operate, touch one of the "Time" keypads on the Timer (VFD-100) to set the length of the steambath and then touch the Start/Stop keypad to begin your bath. It's as easy as that. Now once in the steamroom the Temperature Control will digitally read out the ambient temperature, a simple turn of the adjustment knob and you can raise or lower the steambath temperature. Never again be plagued with the problem of temperature accuracy, the Deluxe Temperature Control, (VFD-400) is accurate to within 1½°F.

The DELUXE steambath controls provide for easy-to-read and easy-to-use selection of Time and Temperature.

Simply touch the soft keypad of the Digital Timer located outside the bathing area to set the duration of your steambath. The Digital Temperature Display and Control with Start/Stop Switch is located within arm's reach inside the steamroom and will enable you to regulate temperature and digitally view ambient temperature.

Steamist has considered every detail including Designer Finishes of which chrome is standard, with brass and 24K gold available. Now anyone can custom coordinate their bath environment with matching Steamist DELUXE controls, medicated steamhead and escutcheon.

It has never been easier to enjoy one's self, totally immersed in steam. The steambath will become as important to your everyday health as a shower or bath. Enjoy this new adventure of steam in the comfort of your home spa. Beautifully designed controls will complement the most luxurious bath, no matter how lavish the design or materials used. A large bright display in each control provides essential information at a glance.

Steamist is designed to bring you comfort and pleasure for many years to come.

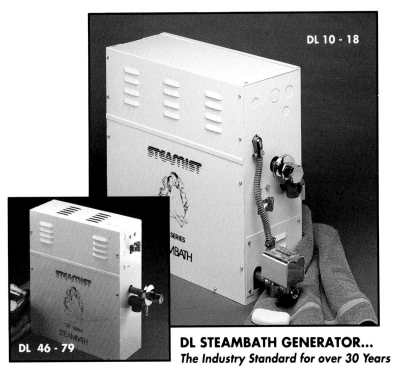

DL 10 - 18

DL 46 - 79

DL STEAMBATH GENERATOR...
The Industry Standard for over 30 Years

The model # DL - 46 and DL - 79 offer exceptional flexibility of design by providing an adjustable kilowatt level to better size the unit to your bath area. The larger STEAMIST generators can be equipped with an optional auto drain to enhance the performance. All DL units feature Stainless Steel construction and Solid State circuitry and are designed to last for years of maintenance free operation Conservative on water and electricity, STEAMIST generators are UL Listed and include a Five Year Limited Warranty.

STEAMIST • DL SERIES • RESIDENTIAL

Model No.	Maximum Cu. Ft. Range	KW Rating	Volt	Phase	Maximum AMPS	Wire Size 90 C Copper AWG	Line Fuse Req'd	Cabinet Dimensions H x W x L
DL-46	60 -130	4.5/6	208	1	29	8	40	15.5" x 6" x 15"
			240	1	25			
DL-79	135-300	7.5/9	208	1	44	8	50	15.5" x 6" x 15"
			240	1	38			
*DL-10	375	10.5	208	1	50	6	60	20.5" x 8" x 20"
			208	3	29	8	40	
			240	1	44	6	60	
			240	3	25	8	40	
*DL-12	410	12	208	1	58	6	70	20.5" x 8" x 20"
			208	3	33	8	40	
			240	1	50	6	60	
			240	3	29	8	40	
*DL-15	475	15	208	1	72	4	90	20.5" x 8" x 20"
			208	3	42	8	50	
			240	1	63	6	70	
			240	3	36	8	50	
*DL-18†	575	18	208	1	87	3	100	20.5" x 8" x 20"
			208	3	50	6	60	
			240	1	75	4	90	
			240	3	44	6	60	
*DL-24†	800	24	208	1	115	CONTACT MANUFACTURER		
			208	3	67			
			240	1	100			
			240	3	58			
*DL-30†	1000	30	208	1	144	CONTACT MANUFACTURER		
			208	3	84			
			240	1	126			
			240	3	72			

* Optional auto drain available for DL-10 thru DL-30
† UL Pending

Distributed by: FEB/93

APPROVED NKBA DEALER KITCHEN/BATH SPECIALIST MEMBERS

ALABAMA

Ashland

WELLBORN CABINET INC
PO Box 1210
Ashland, AL 36251

Auburn

AUBURN UNIVERSITY
Dept. Of Consumer Affairs
308 Spidle Hall
Auburn, AL 36849

JENNIFER C HEAD KITCHEN
& BATH DESIGN
703 Cary Drive
Auburn, AL 36830

Birmingham

CABINET SYSTEMS SOUTH
INC
410 Lorna Square
Birmingham, AL 35216

KITCHEN & BATH
SHOWPLACE
1811 Avenue F
Box 8243
Birmingham, AL 35218

Decatur

CLASSIC CABINETS INC
1415 Kathy Lane SW
Decatur, AL 35601

Hueytown

FIRST ALABAMA SUPPLY
COMPANY INC
PO Box 3322
Hueytown, AL 35023

Huntsville

A A DERRICK REMODELING
162 Export Circle
Huntsville, AL 35806

HOME DEPOT #0870
University Drive
Huntsville, AL 35806

Mobile

HOME DEPOT #0865
Mont Limar Drive
Mobile, AL 36609

Montgomery

REDLAND DESIGN
1067 B-1 Woodley Road
Montgomery, AL 36106

Oxford

THE KERR COMPANY
2009 Barry Street
Oxford, AL 36203

Tuscaloosa

CENTRAL SUPPLY COMPANY
711 21st Avenue
Tuscaloosa, AL 35403

CHARLES L HAMBY
BUILDING & REMODEL Inc
1207 18th Street
Tuscaloosa, AL 35401

COOPER CABINETS
PO Box 2757
813 31st Avenue
Tuscaloosa, AL 35403

MONTGOMERY WOODWORKS
INC
1033 19th Avenue E
PO Box 40390
Tuscaloosa, AL 35404

ALASKA

Anchorage

CENTRAL PLUMBING &
HEATING
212 East International Airport
Road
Anchorage, AK 99518

GALCO BUILDING
PRODUCTS
10010 Old Seward Highway
Anchorage, AK 99515

J & D INTERIORS
8300 Briarwood
Anchorage, AK 99578

ARIZONA

Chandler

HOME DEPOT #5495
West Germann Road Box 5001
Chandler, AZ 85226

Lake Havasu

VAN ROOY PLUMBING INC
3636 S Jamaica Boulevard
Lake Havasu, AZ 86403

Mesa

HOME DEPOT #0461
S Country Club Drive
Mesa, AZ 85202

HOME DEPOT 0456
E Superstition Springs
Mesa, AZ 85206

KITCHENS UNLIMITED INC
105 W Hoover Avenue #2
Mesa, AZ 85210

Peoria

HOME DEPOT #0459
W Bell Road
Peoria, AZ 85345

Phoenix

AMERICAN WOODMARK
CORPORATION
3831 E La Salle
Phoenix, AZ 85040

CLYDE HARDWARE
COMPANY INC
4808 N 15th Street
Phoenix, AZ 85014

COPPERSTATE CABINET
COMPANY
1932 W N Lane
Phoenix, AZ 85021

DESIGNER CABINETRY
4350 E Camelback Road
Suite 110-C
Phoenix, AZ 85018

DLM BUILDING & DESIGN
INC
4545 E Shea
Suite 200
Phoenix, AZ 85028

FINCH ASSOCIATES
2524 E Washington Street
Phoenix, AZ 85034

HOME DEPOT #0455
McDowell
Phoenix, AZ 85035

HOME DEPOT #0460
N Cave Creek Road
Phoenix, AZ 85022

HOME DEPOT #0462
W Camelback Road
Phoenix, AZ 85019

HOME DEPOT #0463
Thomas Road E
Phoenix, AZ 85016

QUALITY KITCHENS
817 W Indian School Road
Phoenix, AZ 85013-3103

STANLINE INC
2345 South 16th Avenue
Phoenix, AZ 85007

Scottsdale

GLORIA TROST INTERIORS
7304 E Rancho Vista Drive
Scottsdale, AZ 85251

HOME DEPOT #0457
E Indian Bend Road
Scottsdale, AZ 85253

SCOTTSDALE PLUMBING
COMPANY INC
7501 E Osborn Road
Scottsdale, AZ 85251

SUNVEK
8361 E Gelding Drive
Scottsdale, AZ 85257

UNELKO CORPORATION
7428 East Karen Drive
Scottsdale, AZ 85260

Tempe

D & J WOOD RESOURCES INC
2424 W University
PO Box 3135
Tempe, AZ 85280

HOME DEPOT #0458
W Warner Road
Tempe, AZ 85284

Tucson

ALBRITE BATH & KITCHEN
3640 E Fort Lowell Road
Tucson, AZ 85716

ARIZONA DESIGNS
KITCHENS & BATHS
2700 N Campbell Avenue
Tucson, AZ 85719

DAVIS KITCHENS INC
3391 E Hemisphere Loop
Tucson, AZ 85706

HOME DEPOT 0465
E Broadway
Tucson, AZ 85710

HOME DEPOT 0466
N Oracle Road
Tucson, AZ 85705

TUCSON OUTSTANDING
PRODUCTS
3820 S Palo Verde
Suite 105
Tucson, AZ 85714

ARKANSAS

Bentonville

CARR PLUMBING COMPANY
Route 4 Box 365
Bentonville, AR 72712

Jacksonville

WRIGHT'S CABINET SHOP
INC
2600 Cory Drive
Jacksonville, AR 72076

Jonesboro

BARTON'S OF JONESBOROS
PO Box 4040
Jonesboro, AR 72401

Little Rock

BATH AND KITCHEN
GALLERY
921 Rushing Circle
Little Rock, AR 72205

INTERIOR INSIGHT
10720 Rodney Parham
Little Rock, AR 72212

LAING SALES & SERVICE
INCORPORATION
200 West Roosevelt Road
Little Rock, AR 72206

PC HARDWARE &
MACHINERY INC
PO Box 949
1021 King Drive
Little Rock, AR 72203

North Little Rock

JASON INTERNATIONAL
8328 Macarthur Drive
North Little Rock, AR 72118

CALIFORNIA

Agoura

SG DESIGN
229 N Smoketree Avenue
Agoura, CA 91301

Alameda

INTERNATIONAL KITCHENS
ALAMEDA INC
2319 Lincoln Avenue
Alameda, CA 94501

R L ENTERPRISES
2425 Clement Avenue
Alameda, CA 94501

STUDIO BECKER KITCHENS
S.B.K. PACIFIC INC
1030 Marina Village Parkway
Alameda, CA 94501

THERESA EARLY AGLER
909 Marina Village Parkway
Suite 501
Alameda, CA 94501

Albany

A & R SALES GROUP
1325 Solano Avenue
Albany, CA 94706

HOUSE OF KITCHENS INC
1325 Solano Avenue
Albany, CA 94706

SHIRLEY A MASON
700 Calhorn Suite #202
Albany, CA 94706

Anaheim

ALLANTE' MANUFACTURING
1365 N Dynamics Street #C
Anaheim, CA 92806

BLOCK TOPS INC
4770 E Wesley Drive
Anaheim, CA 92807

CALIFORNIA FAMILY LIVING
1231 N Tustin Avenue
Anaheim, CA 92807-1603

HOME DEPOT 0607
W Lincoln Avenue
Anaheim, CA 92801

PORCELANOSA USA
1301 S State Street
College Boulevard Suite E
Anaheim, CA 92806

REBORN CABINETS INC
2821 E White Star Avenue
Suite K
Anaheim, CA 92806

Apple Valley

HITT PLUMBING COMPANY
INC
13608 Hitt Road
PO Box 638
Apple Valley, CA 92037

Atherton

KAREN SIRI DOUGLASS
11 Sargent Lane
Atherton, CA 94027

Azusa

D-DESIGNS & ASSOCIATES
623 N Azusa Avenue
Azusa, CA 91702

WBP ASSOCIATES
1001 W Kirkwall Road
Azusa, CA 91702

Bakersfield

SHAKIR ENTERPRISES
6261 White Lane 101
Bakersfield, CA 93309

Belmont

THE COUNTERTOP STORE
1475 Old County Road
Belmont, CA 94065

Berkeley

TRUITT & WHITE LUMBER
COMPANY
642 Hearst Avenue
Berkeley, CA 94710

Big Bear Lake

PINNACLE DOOR & FINISH
42106 Big Bear Boulevard
PO Box 536
Big Bear Lake, CA 92315

Brea

FORMICA CORP
2601 Saturn Avenue
Suite 103
Brea, CA 92621

KITCHENS & BATH SUPPLY
INC
2750 Satlen Street
Brea, CA 92621

Brisbane

GOLDEN WEST SALES
25 Park Lane
Brisbane, CA 94005

Buena Park

VENT-A-HOOD OF
CALIFORNIA INC
7050 Valley View Street
Buena Park, CA 90620

Burbank

CALIFORNIA KITCHENS INC
2305 W Alameda Avenue
Burbank, CA 91506

KITCHENS WITH TASTE
719 South Marioposa Street
Burbank, CA 91506-3103

Burlingame

PACIFIC HOME PRODUCTS
1805 Rollins Road
Burlingame, CA 94010

RICHARD JAMES
330 Primrose Road
Suite 303
Burlingame, CA 94010

SIGNATURE KITCHENS
344 Lorton Avenue
Burlingame, CA 94010

Calabasas

ELAINE TOMIKO TOMINAGA
4031 Meadow Lark Drive
Calabasas, CA 91302

I.C.C. KITCHEN DESIGN
CENTER
26668 Agoura Road
Calabasas, CA 91302

Camarillo

JADO BATHROOM &
HARDWARE MANUFACTURE
CORP
4690 Calle Quetzel
Camarillo, CA 93012

SHOWCASE KITCHENS &
BATHS
2650 Ventura Blvd
Suite 101
Camarillo, CA 93010

Campbell

GRIDLEY CONSTRUCTION
INC
19 S Third Street
Campbell, CA 95008

Canoga Park

HOME DEPOT #0612
Roscoe Boulevard
Canoga Park, CA 91304

Carmel

SEGER'S KITCHENS & BATHS
OF CARMEL
26386 Carmel Rancho Lane
Carmel, CA 93923

Carmichael

HOME DEPOT #0650
Madison Avenue
Carmichael, CA 95608

Carson

SUGATSUNE AMERICA, INC.
221 East Selandia Lane
Carson, CA 90746

Catheys Valley

MARIPOSA CUSTOM
FABRICATORS
PO Box 277
Catheys Valley, CA 95306

Cerritos

BATHROOM JEWELRY
16030 Arthur Street
Cerritos, CA 90701

EVANS ENTERPRISES INC
11304 South Street
Cerritos, CA 90701

HOME DEPOT 0608
Alondra Boulevard
Cerritos, CA 90701

Chico

GINNO'S KITCHEN &
APPLIANCES SYSTEMS
INCORPORATED
2505 A Zanella Way
Chico, CA 95928

Chino

HOME DEPOT 0619
Walnut Avenue
Chino, CA 91710

Chula Vista

BAY KITCHEN & BATH
REMODELERS
669 Palomar Street
Suite A
Chula Vista, CA 91911

HOME DEPOT #0677
East H Street
Chula Vista, CA 92010

City of Industry

BACCARO KITCHEN & BATH
CENTRE
18605 East Gale Avenue
Suite 110
City of Industry, CA 91748

Colma

HOME DEPOT #0625
Colma Boulevard
Colma, CA 94014

Commerce

AMANA REFRIGERATION
WEST COAST LA
6201 E Randolph Street
Commerce, CA 90040

Compton

WOLF RANGE COMPANY
19600 S Alameda Street
Compton, CA 90224

Concord

CREATIVE KITCHEN CENTER
1325 Galindo Street
Concord, CA 94520

DESIGN INNOVATIONS
1647 Williow Pass Road
Suite 332
Concord, CA 94520

EL MONTE KITCHEN
DESIGNS
1476 Wharton Way
Concord, CA 94521

HOME DEPOT 0634
Meridian Park Boulevard
Concord, CA 94520

STRICTLY CUSTOM
1001 Shary Circle
Unit 12
Concord, CA 94518

THE CABINET SHOP
288 Buchanan Field Road
Concord, CA 94520

Corona

HOME DEPOT #0601
McKinley Street
Corona, CA 91719

WESTECH CABINETS
143 Business Center Drive
Corona, CA 91720-1757

Corona Del Mar

KITCHENS DEL MAR
3536 E Coast Highway
Corona Del Mar, CA 92625

Costa Mesa

CONCEPTS II LTD KITCHEN
& BATH STUDIO
2915 Red Hill Avenue
Suite B-101
Costa Mesa, CA 92626-5929

EUROBATH & TILE
2915 Redhill Avenue
F 102
Costa Mesa, CA 92626

KITCHEN SPACES
2915 Redhill Avenue
Ste B105
Costa Mesa, CA 92626

ROHL CORPORATION
1559 Sunland Lane
Costa Mesa, CA 92626

Cotati

HEAVENLY BATHS &
KITCHENS TOO
7530 Commerce Boulevard # F
Cotati, CA 94931

Covina

ARTISTIC KITCHENS &
BATHS
310 E Rowland Street
Covina, CA 91723

HOME DEPOT #0605
W Azusa
Covina, CA 91722

Danville

SHOWPLACE KITCHENS &
BATHS
651 San Ramon Valley Boulevard
Danville, CA 94526

Discovery Bay

CIMARON PACIFIC
4911 Cabrillo Point
Discovery Bay, CA 94514

Downey

ALL AMERICAN HOME
CENTER
7201 E Firestone Boulevard
Downey, CA 90241

DOWNEY PLUMBING &
HEATING COMPANY
11829 S Downey Avenue
Downey, CA 90241

Dublin

RENOVATIONS DESIGN/BUILD
CENTER
7127 Amador Plaza Road
Dublin, CA 94568

THE PLUMBERY
11825 Dublin Boulevard
9778 Business Park Drive
Dublin, CA 94568

THE PLUMBERY
11825 Dublin Boulevard
Dublin, CA 94568

El Ajon

HOME DEPOT 0676
Arnele Avenue
El Ajon, CA 92020

El Cajon

CALDERA SPAS & BATHS
1080 W Bradley Avenue
El Cajon, CA 92020

El Segundo

WATER INC
321 Coral Circle
El Segundo, CA 90245

Encinitas

CABINET VISION INC
4405 Manchester Avenue
Suite 102
Encinitas, CA 92024

Escondido

HOME DEPOT #0675
W Valley Parkway
Escondido, CA 92029

Eureka

MIKE'S PLUMBING &
HEATING
1606 Koster Street
Eureka, CA 95501

Fairfield

HOME DEPOT #0637
Cadenasso Drive
Fairfield, CA 94533

Fallbrook

CLEAR WATER PLUMBING &
SUPPLY INC
616 E Alvarado
Suite D
Fallbrook, CA 92028

Fortuna

OESTER CABINETS
315 Fortuna Boulevard
PO Box 673
Fortuna, CA 95540-0673

Foster City

KB ASSOCIATES
1169 Chess Drive
Suite 1
Foster City, CA 94404

Fountain Valley

KITCHENS BY JONI
18384 Brookhurst
Fountain Valley, CA 92708

ORANGE COAST PIPE &
SUPPLY
17273 Mount Herrmann Street
Fountain Valley, CA 92708

Fremont

CUSTOM KITCHEN BATH
CENTER
40900 Fremont Boulevard
Fremont, CA 94538

HOME DEPOT #0623
Albrae Street
Fremont, CA 94538

WATER CONCEPTS SUB
DALE HARDWARE INC
3636 Thornton Avenue
Fremont, CA 94536

Fresno

KITCHENS ETC
1441 N Thesta
Fresno, CA 93703

NELSON DYE REMODELING
SPECIALISTS
4937 E Dakota Avenue
Fresno, CA 93727

Fullerton

HOME DEPOT #0682
S Placentia
Fullerton, CA 92631

HOME DEPOT #5699
DEPARTMENT 26 MERCHANT
W Coast
601 Placentia Avenue
Fullerton, CA 92631

Gardena

ALEXANDER CABINET
CENTER
17209-A S Figueroa Street
Gardena, CA 90248

HOME DEPOT #0611
182nd St
Gardena, CA 90248

Glendale

BERBERIAN KITCHENS &
BATHS
511 1/2 East Broadway
Glendale, CA 91205

GRUSHKIN DESIGN
ASSOCIATE
2132 Ashington Drive
Glendale, CA 91206

H & S CABINETS &
CONSTRUCTION
3609 N Verdugo Road
Glendale, CA 91208

HOME DEPOT #0649
5040 San Fernando Road
Glendale, CA 91204

Glendora

JB KITCHENS BATHS &
DESIGN
631 E Arrow Highway
Suite Q
Glendora, CA 91740

ROSE DESIGN AND
CONSTRUCTION BATH
KITCHEN DESIGN AND
REMODELING
536 W Heber Street
Glendora, CA 91740

Goleta

INTERIOR CABINET
CORPORATION
7330 Hollister Avenue
Goleta, CA 93117

Grand Terrace

SOUTHERN CALIFORNIA
KITCHENS
12036 La Cross Avenue
Grand Terrace, CA 92324

Grass Valley

THE WALDEN COMPANY
12012 Sutton Way
Suite G
Grass Valley, CA 95945

Greenbrae

BYGG INC
2100 Redwood Highway
Greenbrae, CA 94904

Hacienda Heights

FALCON CONSTRUCTION
14810 Orange Grove Avenue
Hacienda Heights, CA 91745-
3243

Half Moon Bay

BRUCE TURNER
PO Box 843
Half Moon Bay, CA 94019

Hawthorne

HOME DEPOT #0620
Oceangate
Hawthorne, CA 90250

Hayward

FRANK MULLIN BUFFINGTON
& ASSOCIATES
30525 Huntwood Avenue
Hayward, CA 94544

MID CONTINENT CABINETRY
OF CALIFORNIA INC
2388 Lincoln Avenue
Hayward, CA 94545

PREMIER KITCHENS
1881 Whipple Road
Hayward, CA 94544

RALPH WILSON PLASTICS
CO.(WILSONART)
30830 San Clemente Street
Hayward, CA 94544

SCHULER CORPORATION
26250 Corporate Avenue
Hayward, CA 94545

VENT-A-HOOD OF
CALIFORNIA INC
2506 Technology Drive
Hayward, CA 94545

Hillsborough

SHARON G FRIEDMAN
15 Horseshoe Court
Hillsborough, CA 94010

Huntington Beach

GARCIA CABINETMAKERS
5770 Research Drive
Huntington Beach, CA 92649

HOME DEPOT #0681
Edinger Ave
Huntington Beach, CA 92647

MICHAEL ANTHONY &
ASSOCIATES INC
4081 Diablo Circle
Huntington Beach, CA 92649

Imperial Beach

HOME DEPOT #0671
Saturn Boulevard
Imperial Beach, CA 92154

Industry

HOME DEPOT #0607
Gale Avenue
Industry, CA 91748

Irvine

A PLUS KITCHENS
15791 Rockfield Boulevard
Suite E
Irvine, CA 92718

PANASONIC HOME &
BUILDING
152 Technology Drive
Suite 220
Irvine, CA 92718

THE J M COMPANY KITCHEN
& BATH SHOWROOM INC
15333 Culver Drive
Suite 220
Irvine, CA 92714

La Habra

COURTNEY CABINETS
621-E E Lambert Road
La Habra, CA 90631

La Jolla

DESIGN STUDIO WEST
7422-24 Girard Avenue
La Jolla, CA 92037

KITCHEN EXPO
7458 La Jolla Boulevard
La Jolla, CA 92037

La Mesa

KITCHENS BY DE LUCA
7872 La Mesa Boulevard
La Mesa, CA 91941

KITCHENS PLUS
7943 University Avenue
La Mesa, CA 91941

La Mirada

HOME DEPOT #0684
La Mirada Boulevard
La Mirada, CA 90638

La Mirida

MAJOR LINES DISTRIBUTOR
15510 Heron Avenue
La Mirida, CA 90638

Lafayette

ARMSTRONG DESIGN
ASSOCIATES
942 Foye Drive
Lafayette, CA 94549

AUTOMATIC APPLIANCE &
KITCHEN CABINETRY
3458 Mount Diablo Boulevard
Lafayette, CA 94549

Laguna Hills

B & C CUSTOM HARDWARE
& BATH
23461
Laguna Hills, CA 92653

CABINETCRAFTERS (BELLA
GATO INC)
23331 Peralta Drive
Suite 1
Laguna Hills, CA 92653

KITCHEN CONCEPTS PLUS
26071 Merit Circle
S 109
Laguna Hills, CA 92653

Lake Forest

VALLEY KITCHENS
22541 Aspan
Suite A
Lake Forest, CA 92630

Lakeport

WORK RIGHT PRODUCTS INC
4615 Work Right Circle
Lakeport, CA 95453

Lakewood

B & B SALES BATES & BATES
3699 Industry Avenue
Lakewood, CA 90712

KASMAR PUBLICATIONS
11401 Carson Street #K
Lakewood, CA 90715

Livermore

O'KEEFE CONSTRUCTION
PO Box 2107
Livermore, CA 94551

Lodi

WOOD SPECIALTIES
2395 Maggio Circle
Lodi, CA 95240

Long Beach

C O D PLUMBING & HEATING
SUPPLY INC
2200 South Street
Long Beach, CA 90805

HOME DEPOT #0686
Atlantic
Long Beach, CA 90807

KITCHENS BY THE SEA
4403 Los Coyotes Diagonal
Long Beach, CA 90815

MR Z'S SPECIALTY KITCHENS
BATHS & Bars
1819 Redondo Avenue
Long Beach, CA 90804

PLUMBING WORLD
6152 Cherry Avenue
Long Beach, CA 90805

Los Altos

BARBARA CRICHTON
22170 Cloverlt Court
Los Altos, CA 94024

Los Angeles

BULTHAUP
153 S Robertson Boulevard
Los Angeles, CA 90048

C & H KITCHEN CABINETS
1016 S Wilton Place
Los Angeles, CA 90019

CLEVELAND WRECKING
COMPANY
3170 E Washington Boulevard
PO Box 23427
Los Angeles, CA 90023

COOPER-PACIFIC KITCHENS
INC
8687 Melrose Avenue
Suite G #776
Los Angeles, CA 90069-5701

CUSTOM KITCHENS AND
BATHS
743 N La Brea Avenue
Los Angeles, CA 90038

DESIGNTEK BATH KITCHEN
PLUS
147 N Robertson Boulevard
Los Angeles, CA 90048

GMA KITCHEN/BATH
CENTER
10549 W Pico Boulevard
Los Angeles, CA 90064

HARDEN INDUSTRIES
13915 S Main Street
Los Angeles, CA 90061

HIRSCH PIPE & SUPPLY
3317 W Jefferson Boulevard
Los Angeles, CA 90018

JOHN W AVRAM AND
ASSOCIATES
1328 S Santa Fe Avenue
Los Angeles, CA 90021

KITCHEN GALLERY
8687 Melrose Avenue
Suite G686
Los Angeles, CA 90069

L K DISCOUNT CABINETS
312 W 2nd Street
Los Angeles, CA 90012

MAR VISTA LUMBER
COMPANY THE KITCHEN
CENTER
3860 Grandview Boulevard
PO Box 661007
Los Angeles, CA 90066

MODERN CONCEPT KIT &
BATH SHOWROOM
3403 W 43rd Street
Los Angeles, CA 90008

PANEL-IT THE KITCHEN
STORE
6322 W. Slauson Avenue
Los Angeles, CA 90230

PHYLRICH INTERNATIONAL
1000 N Orange Drive
Los Angeles, CA 90038

SHOWCASE KITCHENS
2317 Westwood Boulevard
Los Angeles, CA 90064

SNYDER DIAMOND
DISCOUNT PLUMBING &
APPLIANCES
100 S Robertson
Los Angeles, CA 90048

THE DESIGN HOUSE
120 1/2 N Orlando Avenue
Los Angeles, CA 90048

THE FRENCH REFLECTION
INC
820 S Robertson Boulevard
Los Angeles, CA 90035

THE KITCHEN WAREHOUSE
2149 W Washington Boulevard
Los Angeles, CA 90018

THERMADOR/WASTE KING-A
MASCO COMPANY
5119 District Boulevard
Los Angeles, CA 90040

VIVID DESIGN
11950 San Vicente Boulevard
Suite 202
Los Angeles, CA 90049

Madera

WISHON BUILDERS
17212 Road 38
Madera, CA 93638

Menlo Park

GREAT KITCHENS
842 Santa Cruz Avenue
Menlo Park, CA 94025

HARRELL REMODELING INC
108 Gilbert Avenue
Menlo Park, CA 94025

KATHERINE MOLINA DESIGN
CONSULTANTS
648 Menlo Avenue
Suite #2
Menlo Park, CA 94025

Mill Valley

JANINE PECK
72 Meadow Road
Mill Valley, CA 94941

Millbrae

KITCHENS BATHS &
CABINETS
1795 El Camino Real
Millbrae, CA 94030

Milpitas

HOME DEPOT #0626
Landess Avenue
Milpitas, CA 95035

Mission Viejo

LIFETIME KITCHENS
23332-F Modero Road
Mission Viejo, CA 92691

Modesto

THE KITCHEN SOURCE
3507 Tully Road Suite B9
Modesto, CA 95356

Monrovia

HOME DEPOT 0602
W Huntington Drive
Monrovia, CA 91016

Montclair

PACIFIC FAUCETS
8966 D Benson Avenue
Montclair, CA 91763

RAY MAY BATH & KITCHEN
CENTER
4877 Arrow Highway
Montclair, CA 91763

Montebello

MERI T ONISHI
728 Sanchez Street
Montebello, CA 90640

SCHULER CORPORATION
1065 Vail Avenue
Montebello, CA 90640

Monterey

G O REMODEL STORE
1105 Del Monte Avenue
Monterey, CA 93940

M & S BUILDING SUPPLY
2456 Del Monte Avenue
Monterey, CA 93940

Moreno Valley

HOME DEPOT #0616
Pigeon Pass Road
Moreno Valley, CA 92387

Mountain View

KITCHENS BY MEYER, INC
278 Castro Street
Mountain View, CA 94041

LINDER DESIGN BUILD
939-A San Rafael Avenue
Mountain View, CA 94043

Napa

DESIGN SHOWCASE
686 Soscol Avenue
Napa, CA 94559

HILL ET AL
Walnut Street
Napa, CA 94559

LIMPIC'S CUSTOM
WOODWORKS
952 Third Street
Napa, CA 94559

Nevada City

KITCHEN & BATH
INNOVATION BY TONY
PO Box 1417
Nevada City, CA 95959

Newhall

KITCHENS ETC
23119 W Lyons Avenue
Newhall, CA 91321

Newport Beach

KITCHEN & BATH DESIGN
CENTER
3601 Jamboree Road
Suite 21
Newport Beach, CA 92660

KITCHEN DESIGN
1000 Bristol Street N 21
Newport Beach, CA 92660

REHABITAT
1800 Westcliff Drive #18
Newport Beach, CA 92660

North Highlands

SIERRA ELECTRONIC
DISTRIBUTING
4320 Roseville Road
North Highlands, CA 95660

North Hollywood

FAMILIAN PIPE & SUPPLY
MAJOR APPLIANCE DIVISION
12556 Saticoy Street S
North Hollywood, CA 91605

HARTER'S DISTRIBUTING
COMPANY
11211 Vanowen Street
North Hollywood, CA 91605

SNYDER DIAMOND
DISCOUNT PLUMBING &
APPLIANCES
12725 Vanowen Street
North Hollywood, CA 91605

WILLIAM A PEET & SON
PLUMBING
4849 Laurel Canyon Boulevard
North Hollywood, CA 91607

Norwalk

STANLINE INC
12851 Alondra Blvd
Norwalk, CA 90650

Novato

ARIANA WEST DESIGNS
212 San Felepe Way
Novato, CA 94945

J & J DESIGN
PO Box 5151
Novato, CA 94948

KEYS' CABINETRY
20-B Pimentel Court
Novato, CA 94947

MARIN KITCHEN WORKS INC
401 D Bel Marin Keys Boulevard
Novato, CA 94949

SPACIAL DESIGN
21 Pamaron Way
Suite A
Novato, CA 94949

Oakland

CUSTOM KITCHENS BY JOHN
WILKINS INC
6624 Telegraph
Oakland, CA 94609

FEDERAL BUILDING
COMPANY DESIGN-BUILD
GENERAL CONTRACTOR
3630 Park Boulevard
Oakland, CA 94610

ROCKRIDGE COMPANY
1865 Pleasant Valley Avenue
Oakland, CA 94611

SUPERIOR HOME REMODELING
4700 Telegraph Avenue
Oakland, CA 94609

Oceanside

HOME DEPOT #0679
Vista Way
Oceanside, CA 92056

Ontario

DIAMOND CAB DIV OF
WHITE CONSOL IND
1675 S Champange Avenue
Ontario, CA 91761

Orange

ANDERSON INTERNATIONAL
TRADING
1011 W Barkley Avenue
Orange, CA 92668

CAREFREE KITCHENS INC
453 North Anaheim Boulevard
Orange, CA 92668

HOME DEPOT #0615
W Katella Avenue
Orange, CA 92667

KITCHENEERING INC
514 W Katella Avenue
Orange, CA 92667

Orinda

DIANA L MECKFESSEL
25 Rheem Boulevard
Orinda, CA 94563

KITCHEN AND BATH DESIGN
2 Theater Square Suite 307
Orinda, CA 94563

Oxnard

HOME DEPOT #0604
Vineyard
Oxnard, CA 93030

KITCHEN QUEEN
CORPORATION
138 South
Oxnard, CA 93030

Pacific Grove

KITCHEN & BATH DESIGN
SHOWROOM
158 Fountain Avenue
Pacific Grove, CA 93950

Palm Desert

KITCHENS BY LYNN
43 754 Fairhaven
Palm Desert, CA 92260

KITCHENS OF THE DESERT
73405 El Paseo Drive
Palm Desert, CA 92260

Palm Springs

LUMBERMEN'S BUILDING
CENTER
3455 N Indian Avenue
PO Box 2008
Palm Springs, CA 92263

Palmdale

HOME DEPOT #0638
West Avenue P
Palmdale, CA 93551

Paramount

PACIFIC COAST INSTALLATIONS
INC
7110 Motz Street
Paramount, CA 90723

Pasadena

DACOR
950 South Raymond Avenue
Pasadena, CA 91109

KOKKEN-SCANDINAVIAN
KITCHEN DESIGN
54 W Green Street
Pasadena, CA 91105

SNYDER DIAMOND
DISCOUNT PLUMBING &
APPLIANCES
3660 E Colorado Boulevard
Pasadena, CA 91107

Petaluma

EXCEL DISTRIBUTING
1010 Lakeville Street
Petaluma, CA 94952

SILVERWOOD STUDIOS
PO Box 839
Petaluma, CA 94953

Pico Rivera

HOME DEPOT #0689
Whittier Boulevard
Pico Rivera, CA 90660

Pinedale

ERIC TIENKEN
7094 N Harrison 161
Pinedale, CA 93650

TRAFTON BUILDERS
7094 N Harrison 161
Pinedale, CA 93650

Pittsburg

VENEGAS COMPANY
2201 Harbor Street Unit L
Pittsburg, CA 94565

Placerville

KENSCO SUPPLY
7533 Green Valley Road
Placerville, CA 95667

Pleasant Hill

BUTLER JOHNSON
CORPORATION
94 Santa Barbara Road
Pleasant Hill, CA 94523

Pleasanton

BARBARA J. BRUNKEN
1753 Paseo Del Cajon
Pleasanton, CA 94566

HOME DEPOT 0629
Johnson Drive
Pleasanton, CA 94588

Pomona

THE AGITATOR SHOP INC
4238 E Mission Boulevard
Pomona, CA 91766

Poway

HOME DEPOT #5692
Kerran Street
Suite 1
Poway, CA 92064

Rancho Palos Verd

KARBACH KITCHENS
5935 Flambeau Road
Rancho Palos Verd, CA 90274

Redding

KITCHENS & BATHS BY
SHIRLEY
1301 Court Street
Suite B
Redding, CA 96001

Redondo Beach

HANK THE PLUMBER INC
1400 Aviation Boulevard
Redondo Beach, CA 90278

THE KITCHEN COLLECTION
241 Avenida Del Norte
Redondo Beach, CA 90277

Redwood City

CALIFORNIA DESIGN
ASSOCIATES
259 Sequoia Avenue
Redwood City, CA 94061

CANADA COLLEGE
4200 Farm Hill Boulevard
Redwood City, CA 94061

COULTER DISTRIBUTING
1605 Tacoma Way
PO Box 5128
Redwood City, CA 94063

DOROTHY H RODGIERS
937 Iris Street
Redwood City, CA 94061

PRACTICAL HOMEOWNER
PUBLICATION COMPANY
656 Bair Island Road
Redwood City, CA 94063

Richmond

AMY ROTHBERG
5726 Santa Cruz
Richmond, CA 94804

Riverside

EDWIN J ECCLESTON
235 E Shady Grove
Riverside, CA 92507

THE KITCHEN & BATH CO
2239 Business Way
Riverside, CA 92501

Rocklin

CABINETICS
4465 Granite Drive #540
Rocklin, CA 95677

HARRISON'S FINE PLUMBING
WARE
4467 Granite Drive #300
Rocklin, CA 95677

Rohnert Park

HOME DEPOT #0641
Redwood Drive
Rohnert Park, CA 94928

Rolling Hills Estates

AVINERI REMODELING
&CONSTRUCTION INC
700 Silver Spur Road #102
Rolling Hills Estates, CA 90274

Roseville

INNOVATIVE KITCHENS INC
1125 Orlando Avenue #C
Roseville, CA 95661

S San Bernardino

HOME DEPOT 0610
Hospitality Lane
S San Bernardino, CA 92408

S San Francisco

QUALITY KITCHEN
CABINETS
161 El Camino Real
S San Francisco, CA 94080

THE GENE SCHICK
COMPANY
1355 Lowrie Avenue
S San Francisco, CA 94080

Sacramento

C & C PLUMBING &
BUILDING SUPPLY INC
7232 Stockton Boulevard
Sacramento, CA 95823

CURTIS AND COMPANY
1152 Fernwood Street
Sacramento, CA 95691

HOME DEPOT #0651
Florin Road
Sacramento, CA 95823

KITCHEN CABINET
WAREHOUSE
1001 Richards Boulevard
Sacramento, CA 95814

KUSTOM KITCHENS DESIGN
CONSULTANT
1220
Sacramento, CA 95818

MK DESIGNS
PO Box 216295
Sacramento, CA 95821

NORTHSTAR KITCHENS &
BATH
610 22nd Street
Sacramento, CA 95816

PAMELA YOUNG
7712 La Mancha Way
Sacramento, CA 95823

PANATTONI INTERIORS
5615 H Street
Sacramento, CA 95819

THE PLUMBERY
9778 Business Park Drive
Sacramento, CA 95827

Salinas

TYNAN'S CUSTOM HOUSE
325 Front Street
Salinas, CA 93901

San Anselmo

KITCHENS & MORE BY
KRIKOR HALAJIAN
50 Stuyvesant Drive
San Anselmo, CA 94960

San Bernardino

HOME DEPOT 0683
W 21 Street
San Bernardino, CA 92405

San Bruno

DESIGNER'S BRASS
280 El Camino Real
San Bruno, CA 94066

SAN BRUNO LUMBER
COMPANY
101 San Bruno Avenue
San Bruno, CA 94066

San Carlos

CABINET WORLD INC
1501 Laurel Street
San Carlos, CA 94070

CLOSET DIMENSIONS
1480 Industrial Road
San Carlos, CA 94070

GENIE NOWICKI
480 Erlin Drive
San Carlos, CA 94070

HOME DEPOT #0628
Old County Road
San Carlos, CA 94070

San Clemente

KITCHEN & BATH DESIGN
CENTER ORANGE COAST
PLUMBING
1108 N El Camino Real
San Clemente, CA 92672

San Diego

BATH CAROUSEL
11305 Rancho Bernardo
RD 115
San Diego, CA 92127

CANAC KITHENS DESIGN
CENTER
1241 Morena Boulevard
San Diego, CA 92110

DIXIELINE'S CLASSIC
COLLECTIONS
7292 Miramar Road
San Diego, CA 92121

EUROPEAN KITCHEN &
BATH DESIGN
6440 Lusk Boulevard
Suite D106
San Diego, CA 92121

HOME DEPOT #0669
Carmel Mountain Rd.
San Diego, CA 92128

HOME DEPOT #0670
Othello Avenue
San Diego, CA 92111

HOME DEPOT #0674
Sports Arena Boulevard
San Diego, CA 92110

HOME DEPOT #0680
Genesee
San Diego, CA 92117

HOME DEPOT 0678
University Avenue
San Diego, CA 92115

KITCHEN IDEA CENTER
7341 Clairemont Mesa Boulevard
Suite #105
San Diego, CA 92111

KITCHENS PLUS
7160 Miramar Road
San Diego, CA 92121

KOVACH KITCHEN &
REMODELING
10382 Carioca Court
San Diego, CA 92124

NATIONAL BATH & KITCHEN,
A DIVISION OF PW HAMM
ENT., INC.
5328 Metro Street
San Diego, CA 92110

SAINT THOMAS CREATIONS
9240 Trade Place
Suite 300
San Diego, CA 92126

STANDARDS OF EXCELLENCE
2620 Financial Court
San Diego, CA 92117

San Fernando

HOME DEPOT 0609
Foothill Boulevard
San Fernando, CA 91342

San Francisco

ABBAKA
435 23rd Street
San Francisco, CA 94107

BK DESIGN CENTER
135 Rhode Island Street
San Francisco, CA 94103

CONTINENTAL KITCHENS &
BATHS
151 Vermont Street
Suite 8
San Francisco, CA 94103

CS BATH
566 Minnesota Street
San Francisco, CA 94107

DEALERNET
60 Elmira Street
San Francisco, CA 94124

DELUXE KITCHEN AND
BATH
2234 Taraval Street
San Francisco, CA 94116

FIXTURE PERFECT
2741 16th Street
San Francisco, CA 94103

FLOORCRAFT
470 Bay Shore
San Francisco, CA 94124

GILMAN SCREENS &
KITCHENS
228 Bay Shore Boulevard
San Francisco, CA 94124

JOANN CANNELL
2400 Pacific #507
San Francisco, CA 94115

KEN TOPPING HOME
IMPROVEMENTS
3101 Vicente Street
San Francisco, CA 94116

LAURE DILLON DECORATIVE
HARDWARE
PO Box 590126
San Francisco, CA 94159

MAJOR LINES OF CALIFORNIA
235 Bayshore Boulevard
San Francisco, CA 94124

NOVA DESIGNS
300 DeHaro Street at 16th Street
San Francisco, CA 94103

R B CABINETS & DESIGNS
4635 17th Street
San Francisco, CA 94117

STUDIO BECKER KITCHENS
1355 Market
Suite 239
San Francisco, CA 94103

THE BATH & BEYOND
135 Mississippi Street
San Francisco, CA 94107

THE MAJESTIC SHOWER
COMPANY
1795 Yosemite Avenue
San Francisco, CA 94124

TONY CADIAC HUI
1227 32nd Avenue
San Francisco, CA 94123

San Jose

CONCEPTS KITCHENS &
BATHS
466 Meridan Avenue
San Jose, CA 95126

HOME DEPOT #0622
Blossom Hill Road
San Jose, CA 95123

MAM DESIGN CENTER
1676 Monterey Highway
San Jose, CA 95112

ROTH WOOD PRODUCTS LTD
2260 Canoas Garden Road
San Jose, CA 95125

WILLOW GLEN KITCHEN &
BATH
351 Willow Street
San Jose, CA 95110-3223

San Leandro

GRAY & GRAY
16608 Kildare Road
San Leandro, CA 94578

HOME DEPOT #0625
Davis Street
San Leandro, CA 94577

KALLISTA INC
2701 Merced Street
San Leandro, CA 94577

San Marcos

DISTINCTIVE KITCHEN &
BATH DESIGN INC
730 Nordahl Road Suite 109
San Marcos, CA 92069

KATHERINE SHUMATE
PO Box 144
San Marcos, CA 92079

PALOMAR COLLEGE
1140 West Mission Road
San Marcos, CA 92069-1487

San Matco

R F LINDSTROM & SON
293 N Amphlelt Boulevard
San Matco, CA 94401

San Mateo

CENTURY DESIGNS
CONSTRUCTION
PO Box 101
San Mateo, CA 94401

INTRAPLAN DESIGN
161 West 25th Avenue
San Mateo, CA 94403

San Pedro

COOK'S KITCHEN CENTER
402 West 7th Street
San Pedro, CA 90731

San Rafael

ACCURATE BUILDING
& CONSULTING K & B
SHOWROOM
900 Anderson Drive
San Rafael, CA 94901

CTW DESIGNS
610 C Dubois Street
San Rafael, CA 94901

CULINARY DESIGNS
15 Dodie Court #M
San Rafael, CA 94901

EXCEL MARKETING GROUP
221 Point San Pedro Road
San Rafael, CA 94901

LAMPERTI ASSOCIATES
1241 Andersen Drive
San Rafael, CA 94901

NINA LILIENTHAL-MURPHY
21 La Vista Way
San Rafael, CA 94901

PISHRO INC KITCHEN AND
BATH
3070 Kerner Boulevard #J
San Rafael, CA 94901

SUNWORKS
425 Irwin Street
San Rafael, CA 94901

San Ramon

ROHL CORPORATION
NORTHERN CALIFORNIA
6090 Lakeview Circle
San Ramon, CA 94583

Santa Ana

BRASSTECH INC
320 E Alton Avenue
Santa Ana, CA 92707

HOME DEPOT #0606
MacArthur Boulevard
Santa Ana, CA 92704

HYDRABATHS
2100 S Fairview
Santa Ana, CA 92704

Santa Barbara

JACK'S KITCHEN'S
2919 Dela Vina
Santa Barbara, CA 93105

SANTA BARBARA KITCHENS
710 N Milpas
PO Box 21656
Santa Barbara, CA 93121

SANTA BARBARA PLUMBING
SUPPLIES
621 North Milpast Street
Santa Barbara, CA 93103

THE KITCHEN COMPANY
1717 State Street
Santa Barbara, CA 93101-2521

THIELMANN'S KITCHENS
AND BATHS
208 Cottage Grove Avenue
Santa Barbara, CA 93101

Santa Clara

HOME DEPOT #0630
Lafayette
Santa Clara, CA 95050

Santa Cruz

COUNTERCRAFT
834 17th Avenue
Santa Cruz, CA 95062

EASY CARE KITCHENS AND
BATHS
2557 Soquel Drive
Santa Cruz, CA 95065

JOANNA HOSTETLER
Paradise Park Slot 255
Santa Cruz, CA 95060

TRA WOODWORKING
1847-B Harper Street
Santa Cruz, CA 95062

Santa Fe Spring

ASSOCIATED CABINETS
12303 Florence Avenue
Santa Fe Spring, CA 90670

CAL-WESTERN DISTRIBUTING
11969 Telegraph Road
Santa Fe Spring, CA 90670

RALPH WILSON PLASTICS
COMPANY WILSONART
13911 E Gannet Street
PO Box 2336
Santa Fe Spring, CA 90670

UNIVERSAL GRANITE &
MARBLE INC
13875 Mica Street
Santa Fe Spring, CA 90670

Santa Monica

BAY CITIES KITCHENS,
BATHS, APPLIANCES
1412 14th Street
Santa Monica, CA 90404

GERMAN C SONNTAG
1303 Oak Street C
Santa Monica, CA 90405

JOSE SOLORIO
1028 7th Street
201
Santa Monica, CA 90403

SNYDER DIAMOND
DISCOUNT PLUMB &
APPLIANCES
1399 Olympic Boulevard
Santa Monica, CA 90404

Santa Rosa

DESIGN HOUSE KITCHEN &
BATH
3504 Industrial Drive
Santa Rosa, CA 95403

DESIGNERS' CHOICE
SHOWROOM DIVISION SANTA
ROSA HARDWARE COMPANY
INC
3646 Standish
Santa Rosa, CA 95407

LOSCO ENTERPRISES
PO Box 11608 S
Santa Rosa, CA 95406

WESTERN CABINETS
1845 Piner Road
Santa Rosa, CA 95406

YAEGER & KIRK
PO Box 1919
Santa Rosa, CA 95402

Santee

HOME DEPOT #0673
Town Center Parkway
Santee, CA 92071

Sausalito

SHARON BRENNAN
262 Santa Rosa Avenue
Sausalito, CA 94965

Scotts Valley

KITCHENS & BATHS BY
DESIGN
5276 A Scotts Valley Drive
Scotts Valley, CA 95066

SCARBOROUGH LUMBER &
BUILDING SUPPLY INC
20 El Pueblo Road
Scotts Valley, CA 95066

Seaside

KITCHEN STUDIO OF
MONTEREY PENINSULA
INCORPORATED
1096 Canyon Del Rey Boulevard
Seaside, CA 93955

Sierra Madre

BONNIE SCHUMAN
LANDSBERG
503 Key Vista Drive
Sierra Madre, CA 91024

Simi Valley

KITCHEN ETC. OF VENTURA
COMPANY
3885-H Cochran Street
Simi Valley, CA 93063

Soquel

HANSGROHE INC
2840 Research Park Drive
Suite 100
Soquel, CA 95073

South Pasadena

CYNTHIA BENNETT &
ASSOCIATES-KITCHEN
BATHS & REMODELING
501 Fair Oaks Avenue
South Pasadena, CA 91030

Spreckels

WESTERN CABINET &
COUNTER
PO Box 7188
Spreckels, CA 93962

Stockton

HOME DEPOT 5695
Tilly Lewis Drive
Building 1 Unit D
Stockton, CA 95206

KELLY'S PLUMBING SUPPLY
925 N Wilson Way
Stockton, CA 95205

MAZZERA'S INC
501 N Baker Street
Stockton, CA 95203

Suisun City

FISHER CONSTRUCTION
2526 Mankas Corner Road
Suisun City, CA 94585-3134

Sunnyvale

CUSTOM REMODEL SUPPLY
548 S Murphy Avenue
Sunnyvale, CA 94086

DREAM BATHS
149 San Lazaro Avenue
Sunnyvale, CA 94086

HOME DEPOT #0621
E El Camino Real
Sunnyvale, CA 94087

INTERNATIONAL KITCHEN
EXCHANGE
1175 E Homestead Road
Sunnyvale, CA 94087

KITCHENLAND INC OF
SUNNYVALE
984 W El Camino Real
Sunnyvale, CA 94087

THE BATH ROOM INC
1291 W El Camino Real
Sunnyvale, CA 94087

Sylmar

CHERYL HERRAN
13639 Sproule Avenue
Sylmar, CA 91342

Thousand Oaks

HOME DEPOT #0613
N Ventu Park Road
Thousand Oaks, CA 91320

Truckee

TRUCKEE-TAHOE LUMBER
COMPANY
PO Box 369
Truckee, CA 96160

Tulare

HOUCK INDUSTRIES INC
PO Box 179
Tulare, CA 93275

Tustin

DESIGNER KITCHENS INC
17300 E 17th Street
Suite A
Tustin, CA 92680

HOME DEPOT #0603
El Camino Real
Tustin, CA 92680

Ukiah

DESIGN WORKS
1023 W Perkins Street
Ukiah, CA 95482

Union City

HOME DEPOT #0635
Industrial Parkway W
Union City, CA 94587

Upland

CLASSIC KITCHENS & BATHS
669 E Foothill Boulevard
Upland, CA 91786

HOME DEPOT #0687
S Mountain
Upland, CA 91786

Valencia

GRUBER SYSTEMS
25636 Avenue Stanford
Valencia, CA 91355

ST ENCINO STARR GLASS
COMPANY
24854 Avenue Tibbetts
Valencia, CA 91355

Vallejo

HOME DEPOT #0633
Admiral Callaghan Lane
Vallejo, CA 94591

Van Nuys

HOME DEPOT #0685
Roscoe Boulevard
Van Nuys, CA 91406

KITCHEN & BATH
SPECIALIST INC
7820 Balboa Boulevard
Van Nuys, CA 91406

Ventura

BETTER KITCHENS & BATHS
1884 Eastman Avenue
Suite 106
Ventura, CA 93003

KITCHEN PLACES & OTHER
SPACES
1076 B Front Street
Ventura, CA 93001

Vernon

ANDRE COLLECTION
4955 Everett Court
Vernon, CA 90058

Walnut Creek

JACUZZI WHIRLPOOL BATH
100 N Wiget Lane
Walnut Creek, CA 94596

KITCHENS ETC
1501 N California Boulevard
Walnut Creek, CA 94596

SIMON STORES
1500 Botelho Drive
Walnut Creek, CA 94596

West Hollywood

KITCHEN DESIGN STUDIO
400 N Robertson Boulevard
West Hollywood, CA 90048

Westlake Village

BERNARD BUILDERS INC
31121 Via Colinas #1005
Westlake Village, CA 91362

BETTER HOMES AND
KITCHENS
31121 Via Colinas #1004
Westlake Village, CA 91362

PATRICIA FLUERY
4655 Lakeview Canyon Road
Westlake Village, CA 91361

Westminster

HOME DEPOT #0647
Westminster Boulevard
Westminster, CA 92683

Woodland

FISHER DESIGN & BUILDING
427 Main Street
Woodland, CA 95695

Woodland Hills

JON C BOURGAULT & SON
22714 Calvert Street
Woodland Hills, CA 91367

COLORADO

Aurora

RALPH WILSON PLASTICS
COMPANY Wilsonart
14675 E Wagontrail Drive
Aurora, CO 80015

Boulder

KITCHEN CONNECTION
2878 30th Street
Boulder, CO 80301

KITCHEN PLANNERS
1627 28th Street
Boulder, CO 80301

Brighton

DESIGN ADVENTURES
589 Poppy Drive
Brighton, CO 80601

Colorado Spring

KITCHEN'S AT THE DEPOT
76 S Sierra Madre St #B
PO Box 489
Colorado Spring, CO 80903-0489

Denver

ACOUSTA LITE
11100 E 55th Avenue D
Denver, CO 80239

BELL PLUMBING & HEATING
4201 East Evans Avenue
Denver, CO 80222

BIG 3 SUPPLY COMPANY
1001 W Bayaud Avenue
Denver, CO 80223

BRADLEY DISTRIBUTORS INC
3850
Denver, CO 80239

CABINET WAREHOUSE LTD
5175 Stapleton N Drive
Denver, CO 80216

CADKIT
12136 W Bayand Avenue
Suite 120
Denver, CO 80228

CASEY'S DESIGN CENTER
2055 S Raritan Street
Denver, CO 80223

DAHL'S, INC OF DENVER
280 S Santa Fe Drive
PO Box 9568
Denver, CO 80209

DARANT DISTRIBUTING
CORPORATION
1832 East 68th Avenue
Denver, CO 80229

EDWARD HANLEY &
COMPANY
1448 Oneida Street
Denver, CO 80220

EETCHEN MASTERS INC
5280 W 38th Avenue
Denver, CO 80212

FALKENBERG CONSTRUCTION
COMPANY
PO Box 38514
Denver, CO 80238

KITCHEN CONNECTION
639 Kalamath
Denver, CO 80204

KITCHEN GALLERY LTD
66 S Logan Street
Denver, CO 80209

LARSON DISTRIBUTING
COMPANY
5925 N Broadway
Denver, CO 80216

QUALITY DISTRIBUTORS
INC ARIZONA WHOLESALE
SUPPLY
11585 E 53rd Avenue
Unit 6
Denver, CO 80239

ROTH DISTRIBUTING
COMPANY INC
11440 E 56th Avenue
Suite 100 PO Box 390065
Denver, CO 80239

TANIA FENDEL
3850 E 17th Street
Denver, CO 80206

THE COMPLEAT KITCHEN
INC
1039 S Gaylord Street
Denver, CO 80209

THURSTON INC
2920 E 6th Avenue
Denver, CO 80206

TIMBERLINE KITCHEN AND
BATH INC
1842 South Broadway
Denver, CO 80210

WILLIAM OHS INC
5095 Peoria Street
Denver, CO 80239

WILLIAM OHS SHOWROOMS
INC
2900 E 6th Avenue
Denver, CO 80206

Dillon

KITCHENS BY DESIGN
121 Dillion Mall #103
Dillon, CO 80435

Englewood

BROADWAY KITCHEN
STUDIO
2885 S Broadway
Englewood, CO 80110

CHRISTOPHER'S BATH &
KITCHEN
2857 W Hampden Avenue
Englewood, CO 80110

DONNE ORIGINALS
8376 E Jamison Circle North
Englewood, CO 80112

MODERN PLASTICS INC
2750 S Raritan Street
Englewood, CO 80110

THE KITCHEN SHOWCASE
INC
6555 South Henton Street
Suite 309
Englewood, CO 80111

Evergreen

KITCHEN CENTERS OF
COLORADO INC
3755 Evergreen Parkway
PO Box 4299
Evergreen, CO 80439

PATRICIA H MAYOSS
KITCHEN DESIGNER
1571 Prouty Drive
Evergreen, CO 80439

Fort Collins

AAAH! THE KITCHEN PLACE
INC
226 South College Avenue
Fort Collins, CO 80524

ALLEN PLUMBING &
HEATING INCORPORATION
101 South Link Lane
PO Box 567
Fort Collins, CO 80522

INNOVATIVE KITCHENS A
DIVISION OF INNOVATIVE
COMPANIES
4401 Innovation Drive
Fort Collins, CO 80525

Glenwood Spring

MODERN KITCHEN CENTER
INC
5050 154 Road
Glenwood Spring, CO 81601

Greeley

KITCHEN & BATH
REVELATIONS INC
2126 W 9th Street
Greeley, CO 80631

Lafayette

TECHNI-KITCHEN & BATH
DESIGN
613 E Emma Street
Lafayette, CO 80026

Lakewood

BATH BEAUTIFUL ENT INC
65 Sheridan Boulevard
Lakewood, CO 80226

Littleton

KITCHEN DISTRIBUTORS INC
1309 W Littleton Boulevard
Littleton, CO 80120

Pueblo

KITCHEN'S DESIGN
1416 East 4th Street
Pueblo, CO 81001

QUALITY CUSTOM
WOODWORK INC
415 West 4th Street
Pueblo, CO 81003

Steamboat Spring

SKI COUNTRY KITCHENS
PO Box 770060
1475 S Lincoln
Steamboat Spring, CO 80477

Westminister

CHARLES MARTIN &
ASSOCIATES
7931 Bradburn
Westminister, CO 80030

CONNECTICUT

Avon

AVON PLUMBING & HEATING
COMPANY INC
124 Simsbury Road
P.O. Box 705
Avon, CT 06001

DESIGNER KITCHENS
HOLLAND CARPENTERS
195 W Main Street
Avon, CT 06001

Berlin

HOME DEPOT 6203
Wilbur Cross Highway
Berlin, CT 06037

Bethel

RING'S END INC
Taylor Avenue
Bethel, CT 06801

SECURED KITCHEN
INVESTMENTS
219 Greenwood Avenue
Bethel, CT 06801-2113

Bloomfield

CANAC KITCHENS OF
CONNECTICUT INC
1296 Blue Hills Avenue
Bloomfield, CT 06002

Branford

MURRAY COMPANY INC
29 Flax Mill Road
Branford, CT 06405

Bridgeport

F H HANNAN SUPPLY
COMPANY KITCHEN CENTER
PO Box 5124
Bridgeport, CT 06610

Bristol

A & L ASSOCIATES
10 Capenter Avenue
Bristol, CT 06010

DOUGLAS KITCHENS INC
270 Riverside Avenue
Bristol, CT 06010

ROBIN J. LENSI
77 Vermont Drive
Bristol, CT 06101

Centerbrook

DISTINCTIVE KITCHEN
DESIGNS
24 Main Street
PO Box 297
Centerbrook, CT 06409

Clinton

J & J SCHUM INC
11 E Main Street
Clinton, CT 06413

Collinsville

MINER LUMBER COMPANY
INC
41 Bridge Street
PO Box 227
Collinsville, CT 06022

Cornwall Bridge

NORTHWEST LUMBER &
HARDWARE INC
26 Kent Road
Cornwall Bridge, CT 06754

Cos Cob

AFFORDABLE KITCHENS
39 Orchard Street
Cos Cob, CT 06807

PUTNAM KITCHENS INC
406 E Putnam Avenue
Cos Cob, CT 06807

Danbury

KITCHEN BROKERS INC
132 Main Street
Danbury, CT 06810

LLOYD INC
23 S Street
Danbury, CT 06810

PDS ASSOCIATES
29 Park Avenue
Danbury, CT 06810

THE NUTMEG PLUMBING
SUPPLY COMPANY
11 17 Newton Road
Danbury, CT 06810

Darien

BLACK FOREST KITCHENS
1472 Post Road
Darien, CT 06820

RING'S END INC
181 West Avenue
PO Box 1066
Darien, CT 06820

Derby

HOUSATONIC LUMBER
COMPANY
23 Factory Street
Derby, CT 06418

E Woodstock

BRUNARHANS DESIGN
Woodstock Road
PO Box 208
E Woodstock, CT 06244

East Hartford

APPLIANCE DISTRIBUTORS
OF CONNECTICUT INC
570 Tolland Street
PO Box 280868
East Hartford, CT 06128

Fairfield

DOMESTIC KITCHENS INC
553 Commerce Drive
Fairfield, CT 06430

FAIRFIELD LUMBER &
SUPPLY
185 Thorpe Street
PO Box 400
Fairfield, CT 06430

HOME DEPOT #6206
Kings Highway Cut Off
Fairfield, CT 06430

Farmington

KITCHENS BY DESIGN
4 Eastview Drive
Farmington, CT 06032

Glastonbury

CUSTOM CABINET DESIGNS
INC H H MILLER KITCHENS
22 Kreiger Lane Unit #14
Glastonbury, CT 06033

NICK NAPLES REMODELING
SHOWCASE
141 Hebron Avenue
Glastonbury, CT 06033

Glostonbury

EHL EURO CONCEPTS
110 Commerce Street
Glostonbury, CT 06033

Granby

SUSAN K WALDMAN
MCQUILLAN
157 N Granby Road
Granby, CT 06035

Greenwich

CERAMIC DESIGN LTD
26 Bruce Park Avenue
Greenwich, CT 06830

FORM LTD
32 West Putnam Avenue
Greenwich, CT 06830

GEIMER CONSTRUCTION INC
24 Lake Circle
Greenwich, CT 06830

KENT STEYER ASSOCIATES
LTD
40 W Elm Street
Greenwich, CT 06830

Guilford

EMERSON SUPPLY INC
PO Box 1468
640 Boston Road
Guilford, CT 06437

Hamden

THE KITCHEN BARRON INC
1700 Dixwell Avenue
Hamden, CT 06514

Ivoryton

INNOVATIVE DESIGNS
90 Pond Meadow Road
Ivoryton, CT 06442

Madison

KITCHENS BY GEDNEY INC
84 Bradley Road
Madison, CT 06443

Manchester

CUSTOM KITCHEN CENTER
25A Olcott Street
Manchester, CT 06040

HERITAGE KITCHEN AND
BATH CENTER
254 Broad Street
Manchester, CT 06040

HOME DEPOT #6207
Buckland Hills Drive
Manchester, CT 06040

Meriden

CLASSIC KITCHEN & BATH
INC
464 Pratt Street Ext
Meriden, CT 06450

S J PAPPAS INC
718 Old Colony Road
Meriden, CT 06450

Middlebury

KITCHEN ELEGANCE INC
Route 64 Middlebury Hamlet
PO Box 809
Middlebury, CT 06762

Middlefield

NORTON KITCHEN & BATH
480 Meriden Road
PO Box 32
Middlefield, CT 06455

Milford

GREAT BEAR DISTRIBUTORS
354 11 Woodmont Road
Milford, CT 06460

Monroe

NEW ENGLAND KITCHEN
DESIGN CENTER INC
Village Square Shopping Center
Route 111
Monroe, CT 06468

Moodus

MOODUS LUMBER & SUPPLY
COMPANY
25 Falls Road
PO Box 413
Moodus, CT 06469

New Britian

VIKING ALUMINUM
PRODUCTS
33-39 John Street
New Britian, CT 06051

New Canaan

KITCHEN DESIGN STUDIO OF
NEW CANAAN
21 South Avenue 289 Oenoke
New Canaan, CT 06840

MARK A RUTTER &
COMPANY LTD
PO Box 1530
244 Elm Street
New Canaan, CT 06840

New London

GENERAL WOODCRAFT
531 Broad Street
New London, CT 06320

New Milford

MOODS OF WOOD LTD
147 Danbury Road
New Milford, CT 06776

RING'S END INC
140 Danbury Road
New Milford, CT 06776

Newington

ROGERS SASH & DOOR
COMPANY
385 Stamm Road
PO Box 310816
Newington, CT 06111

North Franklin

UNIQUE KITCHENS & BATHS
574 Route Thirty Two
North Franklin, CT 06254

North Haven

D'ELIA ASSOCIATES OF
CONNECTICUT INC
18 Corporate Drive
PO Box 264
North Haven, CT 06473

HOME DEPOT #6201
Universal Drive N
North Haven, CT 06473

THE KITCHEN COMPANY INC
370 Sackett Point Road
North Haven, CT 06473

Norwalk

FRONT ROW KITCHENS
INCORPORATION
73 Main Street
Norwalk, CT 06851

Norwich

DAVID HECHT CUSTOM
KITCHEN CENTRE
675 W Thames Street
Norwich, CT 06360

Old Lyme

PAUL DOLAN COMPANY INC
Halls Road
Old Lyme Shopping Center
Old Lyme, CT 06371

Orange

HOME DEPOT #6202
Boston Post Road
Box 228
Orange, CT 06477

Oxford

DAHLE EUROPEAN
CABINETRY
208 Christian Street
Oxford, CT 06478

Plainfield

NORTHEAST COUNTERTOPINC
101 Plainfield Pike
PO Box 131
Plainfield, CT 06374-0131

Quaker Hill

SCRIBNER'S KITCHEN &
BATH DESIGNS
44 Route 32
Quaker Hill, CT 06375

Ridgefield

ALTIMA INC KITCHENS
BATHS & MORE
722 Danbury Road
Ridgefield, CT 06877

CLARIS BERGMAN KITCHEN
& BATH
199 Ethan Allan Highway
Ridgefield, CT 06877

COLD SPRING DESIGNS
9 Brookside Road
Ridgefield, CT 06877

STRITTMATTER KITCHEN &
BATH
54 Danbury Road 283
Ridgefield, CT 06877

Rocky Hill

RAYBURN COMPANY INC
88 New Britian Avenue
PO Box 687
Rocky Hill, CT 06067

Seymour

L & M CUSTOM KITCHENS &
BATHS
151 Main Street
Seymour, CT 06483

South Windsor

ATLANTIC PLYWOOD
1590 John Fitch Boulevard
South Windsor, CT 06074

GENERAL BUILDING SUPPLY
K & B CENTER
75 Johnfitch Boulevard
Route 5
South Windsor, CT 06074

Southington

HOME DEPOT 6208
Queen Street
Southington, CT 06489

Stamford

FIRST GENERAL REMODELING
CENTER
980 Hope Street
Stamford, CT 06907

KITCHENS BY DEANE INC
1267 E Main Street
Stamford, CT 06902

MOHAWK KITCHENS
INCORPORATION
48 Union Street
Stamford, CT 06906

SURFACE TECHNIQUES INC
COUNTERTOP INC
432 436 Fairfield Avenue
Stamford, CT 06902

TODAY'S KITCHENS LTD
111 High Ridge Road
Stamford, CT 06905

Stratford

ENER-G TECH
400 Surf Avenue
Stratford, CT 06497

Torrington

DUCCI KITCHENS INC
379 Goshen Road
Route 4
Torrington, CT 06790

THE COLONIAL BRONZE
COMPANY
PO Box 207
511 Winsted Road
Torrington, CT 06790

Uncasville

KITCHEN BEAUTIFUL
150 Norwich PO Box 503
New London Turnpike
Uncasville, CT 06382

Wallinford

DAVENPORT ASSOCIATES
INC
367 Washington Street
Wallinford, CT 06492

Washington Depot

WASHINGTON KITCHENS
Routes 47 & 109
Box 384
Washington Depot, CT 06794

Waterbury

GIORDANO CABINETS INC
560 Chase Avenue
Waterbury, CT 06704

LES-CARE KITCHENS INC
One Les-Care Drive
P O Box 3008
Waterbury, CT 06705

LEWIS KITCHEN & BATH
CENTER, INC.
130 Scott Road
Waterbury, CT 06705

TORRINGTON SUPPLY
COMPANY
100 N Elm Street
Waterbury, CT 06723

Watertown

CABINET GALLERY
WATERTOWN BUILDING
SUPPLY
PO Box 299
Watertown, CT 06795

West Hartford

CONNECTICUT PLYWOOD
CORPORATION
9 Andover Drive
PO Box 330236
West Hartford, CT 06133

SIGNATURE CONSULTANTS
64 High Farms Road
West Hartford, CT 06107

WHAMSCO KITCHENS &
BATHS
1048 New Britain Avenue
West Hartford, CT 06110

West Haven

SPEAR NEWMAN INC
55 Railroad Avenue
West Haven, CT 06516

THE KITCHEN STUDIO
DIVISION WEST HAVEN
LUMBER
741 Washington Avenue
West Haven, CT 06516

Westbrook

COVENANT KITCHENS &
BATHS
1871 Boston Post Road
Westbrook, CT 06498

Weston

ALL SHOWER DOOR
COMPANY
226 Goodhill Road
Weston, CT 06883

Westport

KITCHEN SYSTEMS INC
993 Post Road East
Westport, CT 06880

Wilton

CREATIVE DESIGN
STRATEGIES INC
141 Scribner Hill Road
Wilton, CT 06897

KITCHENS BY BENSON INC
297 Danbury Road
Wilton, CT 06897

DELAWARE

Marydel

U L HARMAN INC
PO Box 56
Marydel, DE 19964

Millsboro

THE HOWLETT COMPANY
280 Old Landing Road
Millsboro, DE 19966

Newark

INNOVATIVE KITCHENS
DESIGN CENTER Inc
33 Possum Park Mall
Newark, DE 19711

Rehoboth Beach

DESIGNER KITCHENS INC
Route One Ames Plaza
PO Box 610
Rehoboth Beach, DE 19971

Seaford

CUSTOM HOME FASHIONS
INC
8 N Arch Street
Seaford, DE 19973

Stanton

W E SHONE COMPANY
Old Chdristiana Stanton Road
Stanton, DE 19804

Wilmington

A H ANGERSTEIN INC
315 New Road
Wilmington, DE 19805

BATH AND KITCHEN SUPPLY
PO Box 2680
Wilmington, DE 19805

CRAFT-WAY KITCHENS INC.
3913 Evelyn Drive
Wilmington, DE 19808

DU PONT CORIAN
1007 Market Street
Room N7545 2
Wilmington, DE 19898

ESPRIT DESIGN LTD
213 W 4th Street
Wilmington, DE 19801

GIORGI KITCHENS INC
218 Philadelphia Pike
Penny Hill
Wilmington, DE 19809

KITCHENS INC
2411 Lancaster Avenue
Wilmington, DE 19805

LEWIS ENTERPRIZES
522 Windley Road
Wilmington, DE 19803

MC KENZIE SUPPLY
COMPANY
212 S Kerr Avenue
PO Box 1849
Wilmington, DE 28402

THE KITCHEN & BATH
STORE INC
703 Philadelphia Pike
Wilmington, DE 19809

WILCO PLUMBING &
HEATING SUPPLY COMPANY
INC
15 S Poplar Street
Wilmington, DE 19899

Yorklyn

CATHY HODGINS INTERIOR
DESIGN
2892 Creek Roadchens &
Interiors,Inc
PO Box 404
Yorklyn, DE 19736

DISTRICT OF COLUMBIA

Washington

CHESAPEAKE KITCHENS INC
4620 Wisconsin Avenue N W
Washington, DC 20016

EJ'S BATHS BY DESIGN
4434 Connecticut Avenue NW
Washington, DC 20008

THE KITCHEN GUILD
5027 Connecticut Avenue NW
Washington, DC 20008

THE MCMAHON PLUMBING
COMPANY
1433 P Street N W
Washington, DC 20005-1940

THOMAS SOMERVILLE
COMPANY TSCO RETAIL THE
KITCHEN & BATH CENTER
4900 6th Street N E
Washington, DC 20011

W T WEAVER & SONS INC
1208 Wisconsin Avenue NW
Washington, DC 20007

FLORIDA

Alachua

DESIGN CABINETS &
FURNITURE INC
PO Box 1108
Alachua, FL 32615

Altamonte Springs

HOME DEPOT #0263
W State Road 436
Altamonte Springs, FL 32714

Alva

MONTGOMERY CABINETRY
COMPANY INC
2191 Dixie Lane
Alva, FL 33916

Boca Raton

BATH & KITCHEN
CREATIONS INC
3850 N.W. Boca Raton Boulevard
Suites 19 & 20
Boca Raton, FL 33431

BATHS OF DISTINCTION
#2081
5030 Champion Boulevard
Suite F4
Boca Raton, FL 33496

HOME DEPOT #0204
Glades Road
Boca Raton, FL 33434

INNOVATIVE CABINETRY
COMPANY
6590 W Rogers Circle
Studio #7
Boca Raton, FL 33487

THE PLUMBING EXPERTS
INC
303 NW First Avenue
Boca Raton, FL 33432

ULTIMATE KITCHEN AND
BATH INC.
1000 Clint Moore Road Suite 105
Boca Raton, FL 33487

Bonita Springs

GULFSHORE KITCHENS
8951 Bonita Beach Road
Bonita Springs, FL 33959

Boynton Beach

HOME DEPOT 0224
SW 8th Street
Boynton Beach, FL 33426

Bradenton

MANATEE CABINETS INC
8700 Cortez Road W
Bradenton, FL 34210

THE WOODCRAFTERS OF
MANATEE INC
6103 28th Street East
Bradenton, FL 34203

Bunnell

COASTAL CABINETS INC
519 N State Road
PO Box 535
Bunnell, FL 32110

Cape Coral

PARKWAY DESIGNS
CORPORATION
4409 S E 16th Place
Suite 10
Cape Coral, FL 33904

PLUMB PERFECT COMPANY
1953 S E 36th Street
Cape Coral, FL 33904-4457

Casselberry

HOME DEPOT #0262
SUS Highway 17 92
Casselberry, FL 32707

Clearwater

DEEM CABINETS INC
2114 Drew Street
Clearwater, FL 34625

HOME DEPOT #0241
US 19 North
Clearwater, FL 34623

HOME DEPOT #0246
U S Highway 19 N
Clearwater, FL 34625

HOME DEPOT #0247
US Highway 19 N
Clearwater, FL 34621

Coral Gables

LA ASSOCIATES
4200 Aurora Street
Suite B
Coral Gables, FL 33146

Dania

ALLMILMO CORPORATION
Dcota 1855 Griffin Road
A 460
Dania, FL 33004

DESIGNERS PLUMBING AND
HARDWARE INC
1855 Griffin Road A367
Dania, FL 33004

SAM JOLLEY'S PLUMBING
INC
55 N W 1 Avenue
Dania, FL 33004

Davie

HOME DEPOT #0222
S University Drive
Davie, FL 33324

Daytona Beach

HOME DEPOT #0233
Volusia Avenue
Daytona Beach, FL 32114

Deerfield Beach

DEERFIELD BUILDERS
SUPPLY
77 SE 2nd Avenue
Deerfield Beach, FL 33441

HOME DEPOT 0218
SW 12th Avenue
Deerfield Beach, FL 33441

Fort Lauderdale

ALLIED KITCHENS & BATHS
616 W Oakland Park Boulevard
Fort Lauderdale, FL 33311

BATHS & KITCHENS BY
LUCCI
4363 N Andrews Avenue
Fort Lauderdale, FL 33309

DESIGNER KITCHENS &
BATHS INC
2500 Wilson Drive
Fort Lauderdale, FL 33305

LIFESTYLE CABINETRY INC
2303 N E 26th Street
Fort Lauderdale, FL 33305

MILLERS FINE DECORATING
HARDWARE & PLUMBING
4244 Peters Road
Fort Lauderdale, FL 33317

THE KITCHENWORKS
117 NW 2nd Avenue
Fort Lauderdale, FL 33311

Fort Meyers

QUALITY MILLWORK
2570 Franklin Street
Fort Meyers, FL 33901

Fort Myers

BENN'S CABINETS INC
11350 Metro Parkway Unit 101
PO Box 061313
Fort Myers, FL 33906

HAMMER SALES LTD
13251 McGregor Boulevard
Fort Myers, FL 33919

HOME DEPOT 0267
S Cleveland Avenue
Fort Myers, FL 33907

KITCHEN CABARET INC
16295 S Tamiami Trail
Fort Myers, FL 33908

SAHARA CABINETS INC
2171 Flint Drive
Fort Myers, FL 33916

Fort Walton Beach

GULF SOUTH DISTRIBUTORS
INC
707 Anchors Street NW
Fort Walton Beach, FL 32548

LINN'S PRESTIGE KITCHEN'S
INC
218 Greenacres Road
Suite 100
Fort Walton Beach, FL 32547

MARBLE WORKS - KITCHEN
AND BATH CENTER
20 Ready Avenue
Fort Walton Beach, FL 32548

Gainesville

BEYOND THE BASIC BATH
INC
1244 NW 39th Avenue
Gainesville, FL 32609

PIONEER MILLWORK AND
MOLDINGS INC
4822 N W 33rd Place
Gainesville, FL 32606-5979

Gainsville

HOME DEPOT #0270
N W 4th Boulevard
Gainsville, FL 32607

Hialeah

DISCOUNT HOUSE
CORPORATION
7880 20 Avenue #46
Hialeah, FL 33016

HOME DEPOT #0209
N W 167th Street
Hialeah, FL 33014

HOME DEPOT #0212
W 49th Street
Hialeah, FL 33012

Hollywood

FLORIDA BUILDER
APPLIANCES
2847 Hollywood Boulevard
Hollywood, FL 33020

HOME DEPOT #0214
S State Road #7
Hollywood, FL 33023

Holy Hill

MODERNAGE INC
100 Modernage Boulevard
Holy Hill, FL 32117

Indian Harbor Beach

S&S FINE CABINETRY INC
131 Tomahawk Drive
Indian Harbor Beach, FL 32937

Indiantown

W & W LUMBER COMPANIES
PO Box 1
Indiantown, FL 34956

Islamorada

MR D'S ISLAND DESIGNS INC
83292 Highway #1
Islamorada, FL 33036

Jacksonville

FERGUSON ENTERPRISES INC
PO Box 47230
Jacksonville, FL 32247

HERITAGE WOOD PRODUCTS
INC
125 Stockcton Street
Jacksonville, FL 32204

HOME DEPOT #0226
Southside Boulevard
Jacksonville, FL 33256

HOME DEPOT #0227
Romana Boulevard
Jacksonville, FL 32205

HOME DEPOT #0228
Atlantic Boulevard
Jacksonville, FL 32225

HOME DEPOT #0229
Blanding Boulevard
Jacksonville, FL 32244

KITCHENS ETC BY REGENCY
8321 Atlantic Boulevard
Jacksonville, FL 32211

SEARS HIPS DISTRICT SALES
OFF #4476
3333 N Canal Street
Jacksonville, FL 32209

Jensen Beach

HOME DEPOT #0221
N W Federal Highway
Jensen Beach, FL 34957

Jupiter

EXECUTIVE DESIGNS INC
6389 Winding Lake Drive
Jupiter, FL 33458

Lake Park

HOME DEPOT #0220
Northlake Boulevard
Lake Park, FL 33403

Lake Worth

HOME DEPOT #0205
Lake Worth Road
Lake Worth, FL 33461

ROGER JORN ASSOCIATES
1010 Tenth Avenue N
PO Box 1429
Lake Worth, FL 33460

Lakeland

ERVOLINA ASSOCIATES INC
4809 Fox Run
Lakeland, FL 33813

FLORIDA KITCHEN DESIGNS
608 N Ingraham Avenue
Lakeland, FL 33801

Largo

A KITCHEN & BATH
SHOWROOM BY CURLY
1890 West Bay Drive #W4
Largo, FL 34640

A&B KITCHEN DESIGN INC
12517 Ulmerton Road
Largo, FL 34644

HOME DEPOT 0236
E Ulmerton Road
Largo, FL 34641

KITCHEN & BATH CONCEPTS
1642 N Missouri Avenue
Largo, FL 34640

THE CABINET CORNER INC
426 W Bay Drive
Largo, FL 34640

Lauderdale Lake

HOME DEPOT 0215
N State Road 7
Lauderdale Lake, FL 33313

Maitland

CLASSIC KITCHENS AND
BATHS INC
1455 S Orlando Avenue
Maitland, FL 32751

J.W. MARKHAM'S INC
668 N Orlando Avenue
Suite 1005
Maitland, FL 32751

Margate

HOME DEPOT #0223
N W 31st Street
Margate, FL 33063

SIRO DESIGNS
2010 NW 55th Avenue
Margate, FL 33063

Miami

ARD DISTRIBUTORS INC
1600 N W 159th Street
Miami, FL 33169

BACI BY REMCRAFT
12870 NW 45 Avenue
Miami, FL 33054

ERNIE DIEGUEZ
2253 N W 18th Street
Miami, FL 33125

ESQUEMA COLLECTION
IMEXPAIN USA
8275 N W 36 Street
Miami, FL 33166

HOME DEPOT #0207
S W 106th Avenue
Miami, FL 33157

HOME DEPOT #0210
W Kendall Drive
Miami, FL 33186

HOME DEPOT #0211
S Dixie Highway
Miami, FL 33157

HOME DEPOT #0219
W Flagler Street
Miami, FL 33144

HY TEK PRECISION
WOODWORKS INC
7375 N W 35th Street
Miami, FL 33122

RALPH WILSON PLASTICS
COMPANY WILSONART
1331 NW 82nd Avenue
Miami, FL 33126

TRIM LINE KITCHENS &
BATHS
10001 S Dixie Highway
Miami, FL 33156

Miami Springs

KITCHEN CENTER INC
3968 Curtiss Parkway
Miami Springs, FL 33166

Naples

DESIGN KITCHENS & BATHS
1673 Pine Ridge Road
Naples, FL 33942

HOME DEPOT #0280
Pine Ridge Road
Naples, FL 33942

KITCHEN KABINETS &
KOUNTERS INC
1460 Golden Gate Parkway
108
Naples, FL 33942

KITCHEN KONCEPTS INC
3906 Exchange Avenue
Naples, FL 33942

KITCHENS A'LA CARTE
3603 Ninth Street North
Naples, FL 33940

North Miami Beach

HOME DEPOT #0216
NE Miami Gardens Drive
North Miami Beach, FL 33179

Ocala

CLASSIC KITCHENS INC
3100 NE 70th Street
Ocala, FL 32670

JEMARKETING
COMMUNICATIONS INC
2405 SE 17th Street
Ocala, FL 32678

Orlando

FORMICA CORPORATION
7482 President Drive
Orlando, FL 32809

HOME DEPOT #0231
East Colonial Drive
Orlando, FL 32807

HOME DEPOT #0232
Southland Boulevard
Orlando, FL 32809

HOME DEPOT #0261
W. Colonial Dr.
Orlando, FL 32818

HOMETECH SUPPLY INC
10551 Satellite Boulevard
Orlando, FL 32837

RJF CABINETRY
11310 S Orange Blossom Trail
#C-305
Orlando, FL 32837-9409

Pensacola

CUSTOM CRAFT CABINETRY
INC
5125 W Jackson Street
Pensacola, FL 32506

KAY'S KITCHEN & BATH
DESIGNS
2901 N
Pensacola, FL 32501

SEARS ROEBUCK AND
COMPANY 4296
7171 N Davis Highway
Pensacola, FL 32504

SEVILLE CABINETRY &
REMODELING CENTER
801 B N Ninth Avenue
Pensacola, FL 32501

Pinellas Park

KITCHENS PLUS
9751 66th Street N
Pinellas Park, FL 34666

Plantationdale

JOHN M KENNEDY JR CKD
1550 N W 110th Avenue #351
Plantationdale, FL 33322

Pompano Beach

ATLANTIC CABINET CENTER
1216 E Atlantic Boulevard
Pompano Beach, FL 33060

HOME DEPOT #0208
N W Copans Road
Pompano Beach, FL 33064

Port Charlotte

HOME DEPOT #0250
Tamiami Trail
Port Charlotte, FL 33948

KITCHEN CLASSICS
4265 Tamiami Trail K
Port Charlotte, FL 33980

STOHLEMYER & SHOEMAKER
LUMBER COMPANY
1615 Market Circle
Port Charlotte, FL 33953

Port Orange

A CREATIVE TOUCH
CABINETRY
3925 S Ridgewood Avenue
Port Orange, FL 32119

Port Richey

HOME DEPOT 0238
US Highway 19
Port Richey, FL 34668

WOODY TUCKER PLUMBING
INC
6802 Jasmine Boulevard
Port Richey, FL 34668

Safety Harbor

R CARR INC
250 9th Avenue North
Safety Harbor, FL 34695

Saint Cloud

KARL'S KABINET SHOP INC
1324 Carolina Avenue
Saint Cloud, FL 34769

Saint Petersburg

HOME DEPOT #0242
34th Street NW
Saint Petersburg, FL 33713

KITCHEN CENTER PLUS INC
2900 4th Street North
Saint Petersburg, FL 33704

SHOWCASE CABINETRY INC
1984 Massachusetts Avenue NE
Saint Petersburg, FL 33703

SURFACE TECHNOLOGY
CORPORATION
1509 1/2 49th Street S
Saint Petersburg, FL 33707

Sarasota

AQUI INC
613 N Washington Boulevard
Route 301
Sarasota, FL 34236

ASGARD KITCHENS & BATHS
437 Burns Court
Sarasota, FL 34236

COOK'S CUSTOM CABINETRY
INC
1191 Palmer Wood Court
Sarasota, FL 34236

EUROTECH CABINETRY INC
1609 DeSoto Road
Sarasota, FL 34234

FOREST PRODUCTS SUPPLY
5330 Pinkney Avenue
PO Box 21359
Sarasota, FL 34276

HOME DEPOT 0235
Cattleman
Sarasota, FL 34233

JOANNA KAYE
2815 Marshall Drive
Sarasota, FL 34239

KITCHENS BY DESIGN OF
SARASOTA INC
4233 Clark Road #4
Sarasota, FL 34233

LAWRENCE CABINETS
215 Interstate Boulevard
Sarasota, FL 34240

RAY ROUTH INC
1502 N Lime Avenue
Sarasota, FL 34237

STANDARD PLUMBING'S
PLUMBING SHOWCASE
901 N Washington Boulevard
Sarasota, FL 34236

STOTTLEMYER &
SHOEMAKER LUMBER
COMPA
2211 Fruitville Road
Sarasota, FL 34237

THE CABINET MILL INC
2311 Whitfield Industrial Way
Sarasota, FL 34243

TOTAL BATH & KITCHEN
DESIGN INC
1760 East Avenue N
Suite B
Sarasota, FL 34234

VILLAGE WOODWORKING
6110 Clark Center Avenue
Sarasota, FL 34238

Sunrise

HOME DEPOT #5299
N W 2nd Street
Sunrise, FL 33323

KITCHENS UNIQUE INC
10795 N W 53 Street
Sunrise, FL 33351

Tallahassee

ANDY'S CABINETS &
MILLWORK INC
5120 Woodlane Circle
Tallahassee, FL 32303

MAYCO KITCHEN & BATH
2184 West Tennessee Street
Tallahassee, FL 32304

TALLAHASSEE KITCHEN
CENTER INC
PO Box 13004
Tallahassee, FL 32317

Tampa

BUILDER BRANDS DIRECT
6015 Benjamin Road
Suite 319
Tampa, FL 33634-5179

EUROPEAN KITCHEN
CENTRE
4218 4220 W Kennedy Boulevard
Tampa, FL 33609

GULF CENTRAL CORPORATION
7819 Professional Place
Tampa, FL 33637

HOME DEPOT #0237
W Hillsborough Avenue
Tampa, FL 33614

HOME DEPOT #0240
N Florida Avenue
Tampa, FL 33604

HOME DEPOT #0243
Adamo Drive
Tampa, FL 33619

HOME DEPOT #0245
N Dale Mabry Highway
Tampa, FL 33618

HOME DEPOT #5293
Sunstate Boulevard
Tampa, FL 33614

HOUSE OF CABINETS INC
3401 W Kennedy Boulevard
Tampa, FL 33609

TODAY'S KITCHENS OF
AMERICA
5011K W Hillsborough Avenue
Tampa, FL 33634

Vero Beach

DESIGN FIRST KITCHENS &
BATHS INC
951 Old Dixie Highway Suite
Vero Beach, FL 32960

FANTASY KITCHENS &
BATHS INC
943 20th Place
Vero Beach, FL 32960

THE KITCHEN SCENE
89 Royal Palm Boulevard
Vero Beach, FL 32960

West Melbourne

HOME DEPOT 0260
W Newhaven
West Melbourne, FL 32904

West Palm Beach

BMW DESIGNER KITCHENS
INC
1860 Old Okeechobee Road
Suite 510
West Palm Beach, FL 33409

HOME DEPOT #0225
S State Road 7 North
West Palm Beach, FL 33411

SBA CABINETWORK
4047 Okeechobee Boulevard
West Palm Beach, FL 33409

Winter Park

CENTRAL KITCHEN & BATH
1096 W Fairbanks
Winter Park, FL 32789

GEORGIA

Atlanta

BROOKWOOD KITCHENS INC
2140 Peachtree Road N W
Suite 310
Atlanta, GA 30309

BUCKNELL DESIGN STUDIO
6290 Rivershore Parkway
Atlanta, GA 30328

CANAC KITCHENS OF
GEORGIA
666 Miami Circle NE
Atlanta, GA 30324

CUSTOM SURFACES INC
1401 Tugaleo Drive
Atlanta, GA 30319

DESIGN GALLERIA LTD/FINE
CABINETRY
351 Peachtree Hills Avenue NE
Suite 234
Atlanta, GA 30305

FORMICA CORPORATION
1770 Century Boulevard
Suite A
Atlanta, GA 30345

HOME DEPOT #0109
Piedmont Road
Atlanta, GA 30305

HOME DEPOT 0103
Jonesboro Road SE
Atlanta, GA 30354

HOWARD PAYNE COMPANY
3577 Chamblee-Tucker Road NE
Atlanta, GA 30341

JACKIE NAYLOR INTERIORS
4287 Glengary Drive
Atlanta, GA 30342

KITCHEN STYLISTS
351 Peachtree Hills Avenue NE
313
Atlanta, GA 30305-4503

KITCHENSMITH INC
1198 N Highland Avenue NE
Atlanta, GA 30306

MASTER BATH & KITCHEN
3872 Roswell Road
Suite A-2
Atlanta, GA 30342-4400

NOLAND COMPANY
4084 Presidential Parkway
Atlanta, GA 30340

SAINT CHARLES OF
ATLANTA INC
3487 Northside Parkway NW
Atlanta, GA 30327

THE APEX SHOWROOM
DIVISION APEX SUPPLY
COMPANY INC
2500 Button Gwinnett Drive
Atlanta, GA 30340

THE HOME DEPOT INC USA
2727 Paces Ferry Road
Atlanta, GA 30339

THELEN KITCHEN & BATH
STUDIOS
5566 Chamblee Dunwoody Road
Atlanta, GA 30338

VENT-A-HOOD OF GEORGIA
1473 Spring Street N W
Atlanta, GA 30309

Austell

HOME DEPOT #0112
Austell Road
Suite 101
Austell, GA 30001

Columbus

CARGILL DESIGN REMODEL
1126 Virginia Street
Columbus, GA 31901

Decatur

HOME DEPOT #0101
Memorial Drive
Decatur, GA 30032

RALPH WILSON PLASTICS
CO.(WILSONART)
2323 Park Central Boulevard
Decatur, GA 30035

Doraville

HOME DEPOT #0115
Tilly Mill Road
Doraville, GA 30360

HUGHES SUPPLY INC BATH
STYLE DIVISION
6885 NE Expressway Access
Road
Doraville, GA 30362

Douglasville

HOME DEPOT #0107
Douglas Boulevard
Douglasville, GA 30133

Duluth

HOME DEPOT #0105
Shackel Ford Parkway
Duluth, GA 30136

Dunwoody

HARBOUR TOWNE
CONSTRUCTION INC
4629 Ellisbury Drive
Dunwoody, GA 30338

Fayetteville

SOUTH EAST PLUMBING
155 North 85 Parkway
PO Box 1043
Fayetteville, GA 30214

Kennesaw

HOME DEPOT #0106
Roberts Court Road
Kennesaw, GA 30144

RENEWED BY DESIGN
4305 Edgewater Drive
Kennesaw, GA 30144

Lawrenceville

GLW ENTERPRISES INC
1285 Rivershyre Parkway
Lawrenceville, GA 30243-4471

HOME DEPOT #5199
Old Norcross Road
Suite E
Lawrenceville, GA 30245

PLUMBING DISTRIBUTORS
INC
PO Box 1167
20 Collins Industrial Way
Lawrenceville, GA 30246

Lilburn

HOME DEPOT #0110
Highway 78
Lilburn, GA 30247

Marietta

FLETCHER SALES AND
MARKETING
PO Box 395
Marietta, GA 30061

HOME DEPOT 0111
Roswell Road
Marietta, GA 30062

HOPSON INTERIORS INC
1004 Cobb Parkway N
Suite A
Marietta, GA 30062

KITCHEN DESIGNERS INC
1468 Roswell Road
Marietta, GA 30062

Maritetta

HOME DEPOT 0104
Terrell Mill Road
Maritetta, GA 30067

Martinez

CRAWFORD KITCHENS INC
138D Davis Road
Martinez, GA 30907

KITCHENS BY JUDITH INC
3830 Washington Road
Martinez, GA 30907

MARTINEZ CABINET &
MILLWORKS INC
3825 Martinez Boulevard
Martinez, GA 30907

Morrow

HOME DEPOT #0114
Mount Zion Road
Morrow, GA 30260

Newnan

E G O PRODUCTS INC
PO Box 780
Newnan, GA 30264

Norcross

BERKELEY WOODWORKING
4600 Berkeley Lake Road
Norcross, GA 30071

CARAPACE CORPORATION
3250 A Peachtree Corner Circle
Norcross, GA 30092

DIVERSIFIED CABINET
DISTRIBUTOR
6292 Dawson Boulevard
Norcross, GA 30093

R C S INC
6490 Jimmy Carter Boulevard
Norcross, GA 30071

SANTILE INTERNATIONAL
CORPORATION
6687 Jimmy Carter Boulevard
Norcross, GA 30071

Roswell

FERGUSON ENTERPRISES INC
PO Box 1004
Roswell, GA 30077

HOME DEPOT #0108
Market Boulevard
Roswell, GA 30076

KITCHEN AND BATH
CONCEPTS
11444 Alpharetta Highway
Roswell, GA 30076

OLIVER WILLIAMS DAVIS
Box 1639
Roswell, GA 30077

Savannah

CUSTOM CABINETS BY
RIVERSTREET MILL
7601 Waters Avenue
Suite H
Savannah, GA 31406

HOME DEPOT #0120
Abercorn Expressway
Savannah, GA 31406

Smyrna

WHITE HOME PRODUCTS
INC
2401 Lake Park Drive Suite 220
Smyrna, GA 30080

St. Simons Island

KITCHEN & BATH CONCEPTS
OF ST. SIMONS, INC.
1627 Frederica Rd., Unit 16
St. Simons Island, GA 31522

Stone Mountain

SOUTHERN KITCHENS &
BATHS INC
602 Riverbirch Trace
Stone Mountain, GA 30087

Tucker

PLUMBING CENTER
3771 Lawrenceville Highway
Tucker, GA 30084

STANDARD KITCHENS OF
GEORGIA
2725 Mountain Industrial
Boulevard
Tucker, GA 30084

Tyrone

H A SANAK INC CABINET &
DESIGN
119 Palmetto Road
Tyrone, GA 30290

HAWAII

Aiea

AMERICAN CABINETRY INC
98-820 Moanalua Road
Aiea, HI 96701

GRAY DISTRIBUTING
COMPANY LTD
99-1267 Waiua Place
Aiea, HI 96701

KAIMANA CONSTRUCTION
DIVISION LAND DATA &
RESEARCH
99-1405 Koaha Place
Aiea, HI 96701

Hilo

ABC INTERIORS INC
154 Holomua Street
Hilo, HI 96720

HPM BUILDING SUPPLY
380 Kanoelehua Avenue
Hilo, HI 96720

QBP INC
411 East Kawili Street
Hilo, HI 96720

Honolulu

ALOHA STATE SALES
COMPANY INC
2829 Awaawaloa Street
Honolulu, HI 96819

AMERICAN CABINETRY INC
820 Hind Drive Shop 114
Honolulu, HI 96821

DESIGN CONCEPTS/CHERYL
L WROBEL
4614 Kilauea Avenue
Suite 333
Honolulu, HI 96816

DESIGN GUILD INCORPORATED
909 Kapahulu Avenue
Honolulu, HI 96816

DETAILS INTERNATIONAL
560 N Nimitz Highway
Suite 119B Mailbox 111
Honolulu, HI 96817

ELECTRICAL DISTRIBUTORS
LIMITED
PO BOX 2120
Honolulu, HI 96805

EUROKITCHENS
Four Waterfront Plaza 420
500 Ala Moana Boulevard
Honolulu, HI 96813

FIDDLERS
1020 Auahi Street
Honolulu, HI 96814

HAWAII CABINET REFACING
685 Auahi Street
Roon 205
Honolulu, HI 96813

HAWAII REMODELING
420 N Nimitz Highway #220
Honolulu, HI 96817

HIGHLINE KITCHEN SYSTEMS
4331 Lawehana Street
Honolulu, HI 96818

HOMEOWNERS DESIGN
CENTER
1030 Kohou Street #201
Honolulu, HI 96817

ISLAND PACIFIC DISTRIBUTORS
INC
1668 S King Street
Honolulu, HI 96826

JOHN COOK ASSOCIATES INC
1020 Auahi Street Building #4
Honolulu, HI 96814

KITCHEN & BATH
DESIGNWORKS
350 Ward Avenue 106
Honolulu, HI 96814

KITCHEN CONCEPTS PLUS
INC
770 Kapiolani Boulevard
Honolulu, HI 96813

KITCHEN DISTRIBUTION
CENTER
300 Coral Street
Honolulu, HI 96813

KITCHEN SOURCE
758 Kapahulu Avenue
Suite 270
Honolulu, HI 96816

KITCHENS BY ARTHUR
THOMSON
1210 Queen Street
Suite 12
Honolulu, HI 96814

KRAFT KITCHENS &
COUNTERTOPS INC
1130 N Nimitz Highway
Suite A144 Space D
Honolulu, HI 96817

LN SALES INC
1645 Dole #502
PO Box 22535
Honolulu, HI 96823

MARILYN MOSS &
ASSOCIATES INC
PO Box 10613
Honolulu, HI 96816-0613

MIDPAC LUMBER COMPANY
LTD
1001 Ahua Street
Honolulu, HI 96819

NATIONAL LAMINATES INC
2858 Kaihikapu Street
Honolulu, HI 96819

PACIFIC DYNAMICS
CONSTRUCTION
944 Ahua Street
Honolulu, HI 96819

REMODELING SPECIALISTS
HAWAII
3160 Waialae Avenue
Honolulu, HI 96816

RESIDENTIAL BUILDERS INC
151-B Puuhale Road
Honolulu, HI 96819

SERVCO PACIFIC INC
1610 Hart Street
Honolulu, HI 96817

SKYLIGHTS OF HAWAII INC
1824 Dillingham Boulevard
Honolulu, HI 96819

STUDIO BECKER KITCHENS
560 N Nimitz Highway
Suite 121-A
Honolulu, HI 96817

THE CABINETREE
1130 N Nimtz Highway
#A 153 A
Honolulu, HI 96817

Kahului

HONSADOR INC
250 Lalo Place
Kahului, HI 96732

Kailua

AFFORDABLE KITCHEN &
BATH
#9 Maluniu Avenue
Kailua, HI 96734

CYNDI W WONG
340 Lala Place
Kailua, HI 96734

HANCO SALES LTD
182 Aikahi Suite B
Kailua, HI 96734

Kailua Kona

KITCHEN CABINETS INC
74 5598 Luhia Street
Kailua Kona, HI 96740

Kailua-Kona

DURALITH PRODUCTS
PO Box 241 73-7776 Kandlani St
Kailua-Kona, HI 96745

Kamuela

ELIN TEICHNER &
ASSOCIATE
PO Box 1380
Kamuela, HI 96743

Mililani Town

TRAVIS A OWEN
95 195 Mohai Place
Mililani Town, HI 96789

Pearl City

BAYVIEW BUILDING
MATERIALS
96-1333 B Waihona Street
Pearl City, HI 96782

Waipahu

DIAMOND CABINETS
94-144 Leoole Street
PO Box 845
Waipahu, HI 96797

TOTAL BUILDING PRODUCTS
PO Box 33
Waipahu, HI 96797

IDAHO

Boise

ERNST HOME CENTER #261
6650 Glenwood
Boise, ID 83703

ERNST HOME CENTER #262
10175 Fairview Avenue
Boise, ID 83704

JAYMARK CABINETS INC
605 E 44th 6
Boise, ID 83714

Idaho Falls

ERNST HOME CENTER #242
1445 Northgate Mile
Idaho Falls, ID 83401

SAMONS OF IDAHO INC
1592 E 17th Street
Idaho Falls, ID 83404

Moscow

ERNST HOME CENTER #253
2242 W Pullman Road
Moscow, ID 83843

Nampa

ERNST HOME CENTER #235
1611 Caldwell Boulevard
Nampa, ID 83651

TREASURE VALLEY
WOODWORKING INC
12783 Orchard Avenue
Nampa, ID 83651

Pocatello

ERNST HOME CENTER #202
800 B Yellowstone Avenue
Pocatello, ID 83201

Twin Falls

ERNST HOME CENTER 236
870 Blue Lakes Boulevard N
Twin Falls, ID 83301

ILLINOIS

Addison

KITCHEN DISTRIBUTORS OF
AMERICA
133 S Route 53
Addison, IL 60101

Antioch

THE BATH WORKS
902 Main Street
Antioch, IL 60002

Apple River

GEE AND ASSOCIATES INC
3-162 Gen Jackson Court
Apple River, IL 61001

Arlington Heights

DETAIL KITCHEN & BATH
COMPANY
11 W College Drive
Suite C
Arlington Heights, IL 60004

LAMICO DESIGNERS
1732 Algonquin Road
Arlington Heights, IL 60005

LARSON & ASSOCIATES
8 N Forrest
Arlington Heights, IL 60004

MARKETING ALTERNATIVES
INC
3721 Ventura
Suite 180
Arlington Heights, IL 60004

PAGEL & SON DESIGNED
KITCHENS
914 S Arthur Avenue
Arlington Heights, IL 60005

REMODELING BY
REDDINGTON
1818 N Fernandez Avenue
Arlington Heights, IL 60004

Arthur

HORIZON HOME CENTER INC
E Route 133
PO Box 290
Arthur, IL 61911

Aurora

SUPERIOR CABINET
WAREHOUSE
971 W Industrial Drive
Aurora, IL 60506

Aviston

MARKUS CABINET
MANUFACTURING COMPANY
601 South Clinton
Aviston, IL 62216

Barrington

BARRINGTON HOMEWORKS
KITCHEN CENTER
301 E Main Street
Barrington, IL 60010

Belleville

SCHIFFERDECKER KITCHENS
& BATHS
747 E Main
Belleville, IL 62220

Bensenville

JENN AIR CENTRAL
DISTRIBUTING
401 Eastern Avenue
Bensenville, IL 60106

SPRING RAM AMERICA
534 N York Road
Bensenville, IL 60106

Berwyn

MARCELLES KITCHEN BATH
& TILE LTD
6519 W 26th Street
Berwyn, IL 60402

Bonfield

KITCHENS & BATHS BY
TAMARA
PO Box 183
Bonfield, IL 60913

Brookfield

LAMANTIA BUILDING &
SUPPLY CO INC
9100 Ogden
Brookfield, IL 60513

Buffalo Grove

ALAN L FOSS & ASSOCIATES
INC
160 Weidner Road
Buffalo Grove, IL 60089

Calumet City

THE HOUSEHOLD
ORGANIZERS
760 Burnham Street
Calumet City, IL 60409

Cary

KITCHEN WHOLESALERS INC
188 S Northwest Highway
Cary, IL 60013

Champaign

KITCHEN BATH & CABINET
COMPANY OF CHAMPAIGN
115 West Kirby
Champaign, IL 61820

Chicago

CHICAGO BRASS INC
2757 N Lincoln Avenue
Chicago, IL 60614

CHICAGO KITCHEN & BATH
INC
1521 N Sedgwick Street
Chicago, IL 60610

CITY KITCHENS
2231 N Clybourn
Chicago, IL 60614

CITY-SUBURBAN KITCHENS
& BATHS
3400 West 111th Street
Chicago, IL 60655

COMMUNITY HOME SUPPLY
COMPANY
3924 North Lincoln Avenue
Chicago, IL 60613

CONSUMERS SUPPLY
COMPANY
1110 West Lake Street
Chicago, IL 60607

CREATIVE DESIGNS
5868 N Broadway
Chicago, IL 60660

CREDA INC
5700 W Touhy
Chicago, IL 60648

DESIGN CONCEPTS
INTERNATIONAL MERCHANISE
The Merchandise Mart
Suite 1378
Chicago, IL 60654

DURA-OAK CABINET
REFACING SYSTEMS
5023 W Strong
Chicago, IL 60630

G & S SUPPLY COMPANY
5801 S Halsted Street
Chicago, IL 60621

GERBER PLUMBING
FIXTURES CORPORATION
4656 W Touhy Avenue
Chicago, IL 60646

KELLER AND ASSOCIATES
INC
4232 N Albany Avenue
Chicago, IL 60618

KITCHENS & BATHS BY DON
JOHNSON
Suite 1375
Merchandise Mart
Chicago, IL 60654

KRENGEL & ASSOCIATES INC
13101 The Merchandise Mart
Chicago, IL 60654

LUCKY STRIKE CABINET
COMPANY
3350 N Milwaukee Avenue
Chicago, IL 60641

MAX GERBER INC
2293 N Milwaukee
Chicago, IL 60647

MERCHANDISE MART
PROPERTIES INC
470 The Merchandise Mart
Chicago, IL 60654

PORCHER INC
13 160 Merchandise Mart
Chicago, IL 60654

QR INC PUBLISHING
KITCHEN & BATH CONCEPTS
20 E Jackson Boulevard
Chicago, IL 60604

THE BENCHMARK
SHOWCASE
13 185 Merchandise Mart
Chicago, IL 60654

TRIANGLE HOME PRODUCTS,
INC
945 E 93rd Street
Chicago, IL 60619

VANCE INDUSTRIES INC
7401 W Wilson Avenue
Chicago, IL 60656

Chicago Ridge

MIKOFF CUSTOM KITCHENS
& BATHS
10527 S Ridgeland Avenue
Chicago Ridge, IL 60415

Crystal Lake

SVENDSON & ASSOCIATES
10 W Terra Cotta Avenue
Crystal Lake, IL 60014

Danville

DANVILLE CASH & CARRY
LUMBER COMPANY
508 W Williams Street
Danville, IL 61832

Deerfield

DESIGNER KITCHENS &
BATHS INC
768 Osterman Avenue
Deerfield, IL 60015

Des Plaines

A B C KITCHENS & BATHS
454 NW Highway
Des Plaines, IL 60016

FORMICA CORPORATION
1400 E Touhy Avenue
Suite 430
Des Plaines, IL 60018

GEISER-BERNER PLMB HTG
& AIR COND
1484 East Rand Road
Des Plaines, IL 60016

REED KITCHEN DESIGNS
2434 Dempster Street
Des Plaines, IL 60016

THE CHICAGO FAUCET
COMPANY
2100 S Clearwater Drive
Des Plaines, IL 60018

Downers Grove

LARSON CABINETS INC
1310D 75th Street
Downers Grove, IL 60516

NORMANDY BUILDERS
734 Ogden Avenue
Downers Grove, IL 60515

STEPHENS PLUMBING &
HEATING INC
747 Ogden Avenue
Downers Grove, IL 60515

Dundee

KITCHENS AND BATHS BY
DESIGN
12 E Main Street
Dundee, IL 60118

Dunlap

WOODSIDE CABINET AND
MILLWORK
1715 W Woodside Drive
Dunlap, IL 61525

Dwight

HOGAN DESIGNS
RR 1 Box 10
Dwight, IL 60420

Edwardsville

KITCHENLAND EDWARDSVILLE
LUMBER COMPANY
201 W High Street
Edwardsville, IL 62025

Eldorado

STIDMAN LUMBER &
HARDWARE
813 S State
Box 40
Eldorado, IL 62930

Elgin

KITCHEN & BATH MART BY
BLOEDE'S
877 Villa Street
Elgin, IL 60120

RALPH WILSON PLASTICS
COMPANY WILSONART
1765 Holmes Road
Elgin, IL 60123

SEIGLES HOME & BUILDING
CENTER
1331 Davis Road
Elgin, IL 60123

Elk Grove Village

BRODERICK & ASSOCIATES
INC
1713 Elmhurst Road
Elk Grove Village, IL 60007

IMPO GLAZTILE
2200 E Devon
Elk Grove Village, IL 60007

MONARCH METAL
PRODUCTS
1901 Estes Avenue
Elk Grove Village, IL 60007

OAKTON DISTRIBUTORS INC
780 Lively Boulevard
Elk Grove Village, IL 60007

Elmhurst

KITCHENS & BATHS BY
PORTER DESIGN
575 7 W Street
Charles Road
Elmhurst, IL 60126

Elmwood Park

ABRUZZO KITCHEN & BATH
STUDIO
7612 W North Avenue
Elmwood Park, IL 60635

SPROVIERI'S KITCHENS
7506 W Grand Avenue
Elmwood Park, IL 60635

Evanston

CRANE PLUMBING/FIAT
PRODUCTS
1235 Hartney Avenue
Evanston, IL 60202

JOHN J CAHILL INC
1515 Church Street
PO Box 871
Evanston, IL 60201

KARLSON KITCHENS
1815 Central Street
Evanston, IL 60201

Evergreen Park

DEL-MONT BUILDERS INC
3360 W 95th Street
Evergreen Park, IL 60642

Fairbury

DESIGN EXPRESSIONS IN
CABINETRY
RR2 Box 127
Fairbury, IL 61739-9462

Fairfield

B-WAY HOME CENTER
900 Leininger Road
PO Box 340
Fairfield, IL 62837

Fairmount

HOMEWORKS
RR 1 Box 370B
Fairmount, IL 61841-9801

Forrest

KNAPP KITCHENS...AND
MORE
Corner Oak And Krack Streets
Forrest, IL 61741

Geneva

FAYEBOBS CUSTOM
CABINETRY
302 E State Street
Geneva, IL 60134

PAST BASKET CABINETRY
200 S Third Street
Geneva, IL 60134

THERMADOR
1601 Eagle Brook Drive
Geneva, IL 60134

Glen Ellyn

DRURY DESIGNS
244 Exmoor Avenue
Glen Ellyn, IL 60617

Glenview

DDK KITCHEN DESIGN
GROUP INC
600 Waukegan Road
Glenview, IL 60025

ELEGANT HARDWARE LTD
2731 Pfingsten
Glenview, IL 60025

GLENVIEW CUSTOM
CABINETS
2000 N Lehigh Avenue
Glenview, IL 60025

HOWELL BABBITT SALES INC
1870 Elmdale Avenue
Glenview, IL 60025

KITCHENS UNLIMITED INC
1232 Waukegan Road
Glenview, IL 60025

Grayslake

DESIGNING KITCHENS ETC
358 Mitchell Drive
Grayslake, IL 60030

Gurneeo

BARCLAY PRODUCTS
LIMITED
4000 Porett Drive
Gurneeo, IL 60031

Highland Park

NUHAUS KITCHEN BATHS &
LIFESTYLE ENVIORONMENT
1665 Old Skokie Road
Highland Park, IL 60035

Huntley

J H PATTERSON COMPANY
36 W Main Street
Huntley, IL 60142

Itasca

DANIELLE'S KITCHEN AND
BATH/CRYSTAL A FINE
NAME IN CABINETS
206 W Irving Park Road
Itasca, IL 60143

La Grange Park

TEACHERS' REMODELING
INC
1101 N Beach
La Grange Park, IL 60525

Lacon

ALLEN LUMBER COMPANY
220 Fifth Street
Lacon, IL 61540

Lake Bluff

DESIGN FIRST
708 Foster
Lake Bluff, IL 60044

Lake Forest

COURTYARD CABINETRY
516 N Western Avenue
Lake Forest, IL 60045

Lansing

MINK BROTHERS KITCHENS
18610 Burnham Avenue
Lansing, IL 60438

Libertyville

DESIGNS IN CONTEXT INC
1585 N Milwaukee Avenue
Suite 5
Libertyville, IL 60048

ROYAL FABRICATORS INC
1920 Industrial Drive
Libertyville, IL 60048

Lincolnshire

HOME IMPROVEMENT
CENTER
400 Knightsbridge Parkway
Lincolnshire, IL 60069

Lincolnwood

AIROOM INC
6825 N Lincoln Avenue
Lincolnwood, IL 60646

Lockport

JOLIET CABINET AND
FORMICA TOP COMPANY
INC
405 W Caton Fram Road
Lockport, IL 60441

Marion

P.D.W. INC
603 S Court
Route 37 So
Marion, IL 62959

Millstadt

CUSTOM MARBLE INC
850 S Mulberry
Millstadt, IL 62260

Morris

DESIGN CLASSICS IN
CABINETRY SIMMS SUPPLY
1427 Division Street
Morris, IL 60450

Morton

CREATIVE KITCHENS INC OF
MORTON
2001 W Jackson Street
Morton, IL 61550

IRON A WAY INC
220 W Jackson
Morton, IL 61550

Morton Grove

W W DESIGNS INC
9112 Parkside
Morton Grove, IL 60053

Mount Prospect

M J CONTRACTORS &
REMODELERS INC
15 North Elmhurst Avenue
Mount Prospect, IL 60056

Mundelein

CLASSIC CABINETRY
21196 Commercial Drive
Mundelein, IL 60060

Murphysboro

J WRIGHT BUILDING CENTER
INC
Williams Street
Po Box 412
Murphysboro, IL 62966

Naperville

KITCHEN & BATH DESIGN
GROUP
15 E Gartner Road
Naperville, IL 60540

PHIL WALZ PLUMBING INC
28 W 545 Ogden Avenue
Naperville, IL 60563

THE KITCHEN MASTER
CONST MASTERS INC
600 Industrial Drive
Naperville, IL 60563

WEGNER PLUMBING
COMPANY
701 Frontenac Road
Naperville, IL 60563

Niles

BETTER KITCHENS INC
7640 N Milwaukee Avenue
Niles, IL 60714

Northbrook

BATHLINES
571 Waukegan Road
Northbrook, IL 60062

COMPLETE BATH &
KITCHEN
310 Melvin Drive #20
Northbrook, IL 60062

WILLIAM B PARK INC
812 Skokie Highway
Northbrook, IL 60062

Northfield

K & B GALLERIES LTD
197 Northfield Road
Northfield, IL 60093

Oak Brook

ARTISTIC KITCHEN DESIGNS
610 Enterprise Drive
Oak Brook, IL 60521

ELKAY MANUFACTURING
COMPANY
222 Camden Street
Oak Brook, IL 60521

SLUSARZ CORPORATION
19W222 Governors Trail
Oak Brook, IL 60521

Oak Lawn

BUCHE CABINET CO-BDS INC
5516 W 110th Street
Oak Lawn, IL 60453

THE BATH HOUSE
4811 W 103rd Street
Oak Lawn, IL 60453

Oak Park

THE KITCHEN STUDIO INC
1107 9 Westgate
Oak Park, IL 60301

Olney

KKC INC
600 S Whittle Avenue
Olney, IL 62450

Palatine

CABINETS PLUS
706 E Northwest Highway
Palatine, IL 60067

GREAT ROOMS INC
20070 N Rand Road
Palatine, IL 60074

VAN HORN ASSOCIATES
330 W Colfax Street
Palatine, IL 60067

Palos Hills

KITCH'N BATH SHOWCASE
7630 W 111th Street
Palos Hills, IL 60465

Park Forest

ED'S HOME REMODELING
111 Berry Street
Park Forest, IL 60466

Park Ridge

KITCHENS & ADDITIONS INC
817 West Devon Avenue
Park Ridge, IL 60068

Peoria

WAHLFELD'S
1100 SW Washington Street
Peoria, IL 61602

River Grove

REYNOLDS ENTERPRISES INC
2936 River Road
River Grove, IL 60171

Rockford

ANDCO DISTRIBUTORS INC
2241 15th Street
PO Box 5625
Rockford, IL 61125

CITATION DISTRIBUTORS
INC
5245 27th Avenue
Rockford, IL 61109

DAHLGREN & JOHNSON INC
1000 Ninth Street
Rockford, IL 61104

HOME IMPROVEMENT
SYSTEMS INC
1125 5th Avenue
Rockford, IL 61104

KITCHEN DISTRIBUTORS OF
AMERICA INC
3224 S Alpine Road
Rockford, IL 61109

PIERCE LAMINATED
PRODUCTS
2430 N Court Street
Rockford, IL 61103

TELAMON REMODELING INC
616 N Madison Street
Rockford, IL 61107

VALLEY COUNTERTOPS
COMPANY
6067 11th Street
Rockford, IL 61109

Saint Charles

DOORS & DRAWERS OF
ILLINOIS INC
103 North 11th Avenue
Saint Charles, IL 60174

KITCHEN & BATH DESIGN
CONCEPTS
1519 E Main Street
Saint Charles, IL 60174

Schaumburg

C B S KITCHEN & BATH
REMODELING INC
P O Box 681218
Schaumburg, IL 60193

HANDY ANDY HOME
IMPROVEMENT CENTERS
INC
905 E Golf Road
Schaumburg, IL 60173

STERLING PLUMBING GROUP
1375 Remington Road
Schaumburg, IL 60173

Skokie

HOWARD MILLER
REMODELING
4503 West Oakton Street
Skokie, IL 60076

TARLOS KITCHENS & BATH
INC
8808 Gross Point Road
Skokie, IL 60077-1809

South Elgin

SCHRECK KITCHENS
CORPORATION
194 N La Fox Street
South Elgin, IL 60177

Spring Grove

TOTEM LUMBER &
MILLWORK
7701 Buvin
Spring Grove, IL 60081

Springfield

DISTINCTIVE DESIGNS FOR
KITCHENS & BATHS
226 Highland
Springfield, IL 62704

GARY BRYAN KITCHENS &
BATHS INC
3208 South Douglas
Springfield, IL 62704

REARDEN KITCHENS INC
2743 S Veterans Parkway
317
Springfield, IL 62704-6402

Streamwood

WICKS LUMBER STORE 025
1111 E Lake Street
Streamwood, IL 60107

Taylorville

BROWN & SONS INC
BROWN'S BARN
421 Springfield Road
Taylorville, IL 62568

Tinley Park

HOME BUILDING SUPPLY
CORPORATION
17532 Duvan Drive
Tinley Park, IL 60477

Vernon Hills

LEUCO TOOL CORPORATION
910 Woodlands Parkway
Vernon Hills, IL 60061

SCOTSMAN INDUSTRIES
775 Corporate Woods Pkwy
Vernon Hills, IL 60061

WICKES LUMBER COMPANY
706 Deerpath Drive
Vernon Hills, IL 60061

Villa Park

AMERICAN OAK CORP
150 E Saint Charles Road
Villa Park, IL 60181

DESIGNER'S SHOWCASE
135 W Saint Charles Road
Villa Park, IL 60181

West Dundee

E DAHLIN AND ASSOCIATES
LTD
547 S 8th
West Dundee, IL 60118

Westmont

CUSTOMWOOD KITCHENS
17 E Chicago Avenue
Westmont, IL 60559

Wheeling

CHICAGO CUSTOM CABINET
FRONTS INC
325 North Milwaukee Avenue
Wheeling, IL 60090

HERROLD KITCHEN & BATH
COMPANY INC
102 E Dundee Road
Wheeling, IL 60090

Wilmette

DE GIULIO KITCHEN & BATH
DESIGN
1121 Central Avenue
Wilmette, IL 60093

KARL G KNOBEL INC
1218 Washington Avenue
Wilmette, IL 60091

KITCHEN CLASSICS INC
519 Fourth Street
Wilmette, IL 60091

Winnetka

V J KILLIAN COMPANY
933 Green Bay Road
Winnetka, IL 60093

Wood Dale

GROHE AMERICA INC
900 Lively Boulevard
Wood Dale, IL 60191

Woodridge

CEREN DESIGNS LTD
6810 Route 53
Woodridge, IL 60517

Woodstock

JENSEN'S HOME IMPROVEMENT
CENTER
670 E Calhoun Street
Woodstock, IL 60098

INDIANA

Anderson

GENTRY'S CABINET INC
415 Main Street
PO Box 168
Anderson, IN 46015

Batesville

WALSMAN SUPPLY
COMPANY INC
1818 State Road 46E
PO Box 225
Batesville, IN 47006

Bloomington

ROGERS BUILDING SUPPLIES
PO Box 849
Bloomington, IN 47402

ROUTEN DESIGN ASSOCIATES
3915 Sugar Lane E
Bloomington, IN 47404

Bluffton

CLINE KITCHEN CENTER DIV
CLINE LUMBR
717 W Washington Street
Bluffton, IN 46714

Bremen

BREMTOWN KITCHENS
PO Box 409
Bremen, IN 46506

Brownsburg

KITCHEN AND BATH HOUSE
847 North Green Street
Brownsburg, IN 46112

Carmel

CARMEL KITCHEN
SPECIALISTS INC
606 Station Drive
Carmel, IN 46032

R K HUBER & ASSOCIATES
5020 Westwood Drive
Carmel, IN 46033

Chandler

HEIDORN CONSTRUCTION
INC
1455 Stevenson Station Road
Chandler, IN 47610

Columbus

ALEXANDERS' CABINETS &
APPLIANCES
1817 24th Street
Columbus, IN 47201

COLUMBUS CUSTOM
CABINETS INCORPORATION
8750 North US # 31
Columbus, IN 47201

Crawsfordsville

TOWN & COUNTRY
HOMECENTER INC
401 E South Boulevard
Crawsfordsville, IN 47933

Demotte

KAPERS BUILDING
MATERIALS
Highway 231 & Begonia Street
PO Box 517
Demotte, IN 46310

Elkhart

KITCHENS ETC INC
PO Box 2479
1150 North Nappanee Street
Elkhart, IN 46515

Evansville

CABINETS BY DESIGN
4619 Lincoln Avenue
Evansville, IN 47714

COUNTER DESIGN COMPANY
INC
2381 Cullen Avenue
Evansville, IN 47715

ELKO BUILDING SUPPLY
DIVISION
940 N Boeke Road
Evansville, IN 47711-4998

FEHRENBACHER CABINETS
INC
8944 Highway 65
Evansville, IN 47720

INDIANA WHOLESALERS INC
1000 N Contress
PO Box 5245
Evansville, IN 47716

KENTUCKY INDIANA
LUMBER
PO Box 4099
Evansville, IN 47711

KITCHEN INTERIORS
5545 Boonville Highway
Evansville, IN 47715

ODDJOB/CREATIVE
INTERIORS INC
1124 E Columbia Street
Evansville, IN 47711

Fort Wayne

EERDWARE WHOLESALERS
Nelson Road
PO Box 868
Fort Wayne, IN 46801

GIANT CUSTOM CABINETS
INC
7923 Lima Road
Fort Wayne, IN 46818

THE PANEL MART INC
4602 Lima Road
Fort Wayne, IN 46808

Goshen

DOORS & DRAWERS INC
64722 C R 27
Goshen, IN 46526

DUTCH MILLS INC
Po Box 805
Goshen, IN 46526

Grabill

DUTCH MADE INC
Roth Road
PO Box 310
Grabill, IN 46741

GRABILL CABINET
COMPANY INC
Corner State & Main Street
Box 40
Grabill, IN 46741

Greencastle

MUNCIE & ASSOCIATES
611 S Jackson
Greencastle, IN 46135

YE OLD CABINET &
APPLIANCE SPECIALTY
DIVISION MUNCIE &
ASSOCIATES
611 S Jackson Street
Greencastle, IN 46135

Greenwood

KITCHENS BY TEIPEN
586 S Street Road 135
Greenwood, IN 46142

WD BILL RUPEL CKD
4011 Tarry Lane
Greenwood, IN 46142

Hammond

SUPERIOR LUMBER
COMPANY
1014 165th Street
Hammond, IN 46324

Harlan

HARLAN CABINETS INC
12707 Spencerville Road
PO Box 307
Harlan, IN 46743

Highland

THOMPSON NELSON KIT
DSGN CENTER INC
9434 Indianapolis Boulevard
Highland, IN 46322

Indianapolis

ALDERMAN SUTDIOS INC
7316 Lantern Road
Indianapolis, IN 46256

BARBER CABINET COMPANY
INC
2957 South Collier Street
Indianapolis, IN 46241

BUILDING MATERIALS
SERVICE
PO Box 1981
Indianapolis, IN 46206-1981

CASEWORKS INC
9423 North Meridan Street
Indianapolis, IN 46260

CENTURY MARBLE
COMPANY INC
4347 W 96th Street
Indianapolis, IN 46268

CORSI CABINET COMPANY
INC
6111 Churchman Bypass
Indianapolis, IN 46203

DEFLECTO CORPORATION
7035 E 86th Street
Indianapolis, IN 46250

DELTA FAUCET COMPANY
55 E 111th Street
Indianapolis, IN 46280

DIAL ONE TREMAIN INC
9337 Castle Gate Drive
Indianapolis, IN 46256

HAWKINS CABINET
COMPANY INC
2125 S Keystone Avenue
Indianapolis, IN 46203

JACK MC DONOUGH &
ASSOCIATES INC
8535 E 30th Street
Indianapolis, IN 46219

JENN AIR COMPANY
3035 N Shadeland
Indianapolis, IN 46226

JIM JORDAN SHOWPLACE
KITCHENS
2206 Lafayette Road
Indianapolis, IN 46222

KITCHENS OF DISTINCTION
4842-4850 North College Avenue
Indianapolis, IN 46205

MARCUS & COMPANY
2727 East 86th Street
Suite 234
Indianapolis, IN 46240

MILLER MAID CABINETS INC
4805 Hardegan
PO Box 27086
Indianapolis, IN 46227

NAPPANEE WOOD
PRODUCTS
8270 Center Run Road
Indianapolis, IN 46250

RABB & HOWE CABINET TOP
COMPANY
2571 N Winthrop Avenue
Indianapolis, IN 46205

REESE KITCHEN DISTRIBUTING
INC
1057 E 54th Street
Indianapolis, IN 46220

SEARS ROEBUCK &
COMPANY 4012
4050 Lafayette Square
Indianapolis, IN 46254

STEWARD BOARMAN
KITCHENS INC
1627 Oliver Avenue
Indianapolis, IN 46221

Jasper

ACTUA
PO Box 420
One Aristokraft Square
Jasper, IN 47546

ARISTOKRAFT INC
#1 Aristokraft Square
Jasper, IN 47547

DECORA'
One Aristokraft Square
PO Box 420
Jasper, IN 47547

KITCHEN JEWELS INC
844 East 13th Street
Jasper, IN 47546

Kokomo

BUCKNER DISTRIBUTING INC
505 E Center Road
PO Box 2205
Kokomo, IN 46902

Lafayette

BIGGS PUMP & SUPPLY INC
181 Sagamore Parkway S
PO Box 7208
Lafayette, IN 47903

MR BUILD PLUS
2632 N Ninth Street Road#D
Lafayette, IN 47904

Lebanon

KITCHENS BY MICHAEL
118 N Lebanon Street
PO Box 108
Lebanon, IN 46052

Liberty

MILES RICHMOND INC
PO Box 360
Liberty, IN 47353

Martinsville

EARL GRAY & SONS INC
398 State Road 37 N
Martinsville, IN 46151

Maxwell

KLINE WOODWORKING INC
Highway 9 PO Box 12
Greenfield
Maxwell, IN 46154

Michigan City

DESIGN CENTER INC
8474 W US 20
Michigan City, IN 46360

Mishawaka

METROPOLITAN HOME
PLUMBING SERVICE
4014 Fir Road
Mishawaka, IN 46545

Mount Vernon

KUEBER'S CABINET SHOP
2300 Highway 62W
Mount Vernon, IN 47620

Muncie

KNAPP SUPPLY COMPANY
INC
420 S Ohio Avenue
PO Box 2488
Muncie, IN 47307-0488

PIPPENS KITCHEN BATH &
WINDOW CENTER
3400 W Purdue Road
Muncie, IN 47304

RICHARD'S KITCHEN & BATH
CENTER
4209 N Weeling Avenue
Muncie, IN 47304

UNITED HOME SUPPLY INC
1420 S Hoyt Avenue
Muncie, IN 47302

Nappanee

NAPPANEE WOOD
PRODUCTS
1205 E Lincoln Street
Nappanee, IN 46550

Newburgh

BAYER'S PLUMBING INC
7944 Bell Oaks Drive
Newburgh, IN 47630-2547

COMPLETE DESIGN
KITCHENS BY MITCHELL
4395 Highway 261
PO Box 396
Newburgh, IN 47629

LANCE CABINET SHOP
4222 Sharon Road
Newburgh, IN 47630

Noblesville

B & E CUSTOM CABINETS
INC
14000 State Road 32 E
Noblesville, IN 46060

Richmond

KEMPER QUALITY CABINETS
701 S N Street
PO Box 1567
Richmond, IN 47374

Rockport

PEERLESS POTTERY
N Lincoln Avenue
Rockport, IN 47635

Saint John

SAINT JOHN PLUMBING INC
9769 Wicker Avenue
PO Box 242
Saint John, IN 46373

Shelbyville

RISLEY'S KITCHEN
SPECIALISTS
212 E Broadway
Shelbyville, IN 46176

South Bend

LOUIE SEAGO & SONS
REMODELING SERVICE INC
2506 S Michigan Street
South Bend, IN 46614

Speedway

B & W PLUMBING &
HEATING COMPANY INC
2101 Cunningham Road
Speedway, IN 46224

Spencer

BRADFORD MANUFACTURING
640 E Franklin
PO Box 865
Spencer, IN 47460

Syracuse

BEEMER ENTERPRISES INC
PO Box 5
Syracuse, IN 46567

Terre Haute

KITCHENS AND INTERIORS
INC
13 A The Meadows
Terre Haute, IN 47803

Valparaiso

GARY R. SCHMITT &
COMPANY LTD
1603 E Lincolnway
Suite A
Valparaiso, IN 46383

SPESCO INC
52 Marks Road
Valparaiso, IN 46383

Vincennes

GALLERY OF KITCHENS,
DIVISION OF WARREN
HOMES INC
1721 Washington Avenue
Vincennes, IN 47591

Warsaw

CABINET HOUSE INC
417 East Winona Avenue
Warsaw, IN 46580

West Lafayette

PURDUE UNIVERSITY
SCHOOL OF CONSUMER &
FAMILY SCIENCE
Matthews Hall 221
West Lafayette, IN 47907

Westfield

WICKES LUMBER COMPANY
#372
16708 U S 31 N
Westfield, IN 46074

Whiteland

VINYLCRAFT INC
RR #1 Box 66 B 1
PO Box 218
Whiteland, IN 46184

IOWA

Ames

KITCHEN BATH & HOME
201 Main Street
Ames, IA 50010

KITCHEN BY DESIGN
212 Duff Avenue
Ames, IA 50010

Ankeny

PAMELA J BOWMAN
301 NE 12th Street Apt 37
Ankeny, IA 50021

Burlington

FOX APPLIANCE AND
KITCHEN CENTER INC
705 11 Jefferson Street
Burlington, IA 52601

Cedar Rapids

AR-JAY BUILDING
PRODUCTS
1515 Blairs Ferry Road N E
PO Box 10017
Cedar Rapids, IA 52410-0017

VALENTA PLUMBING &
HEATING
1100 H Avenue NE
Cedar Rapids, IA 52402

Davenport

BRAMMER MANUFACTURING
COMPANY
1701 Rockingham Road
PO Box 3547
Davenport, IA 52808

Denison

COLOR CENTER LTD
1711 E Highway 30
Denison, IA 51442

Des Moines

BUILDERS KITCHEN &
SUPPLY
130 E. 3rd Street
Des Moines, IA 50309

MOEHL MILLWORK INC
9943 Hickman Road
Des Moines, IA 50322

Fort Dodge

ATLAS KITCHEN & BATH
1903 1st Avenue S
Fort Dodge, IA 50501

Indianola

BORTS CUSTOM CABINETS
INC
1200 North 14th Street
Indianola, IA 50125

Iowa City

HAMM'S HEARTH & HOME
1134 S Gilbert Street
Iowa City, IA 52240

Marion

GREAT PLAINS SUPPLY INC
3115 7th Avenue
PO Box 347
Marion, IA 52302

Marshalltown

STEWART BUILDING CENTER
110 W Madison Street
Marshalltown, IA 50158

SWANCO ENTERPRISES INC
815 N 3rd Avenue
Box 1030
Marshalltown, IA 50158

Menlo

SARGENT'S CUSTOM
CABINETS
506 Shermen
Menlo, IA 50164

Newton

CURRY KITCHENS
1313 S 10th Avenue E
Newton, IA 50208

MAYTAG COMPANY
One Dependability Square
Newton, IA 50208

Northwood

FIELDSTONE CABINETRY INC
Highway 105 East
PO Box 109
Northwood, IA 50459

Ottumwa

BROWNS KITCHEN CENTER
303 East 2nd
Ottumwa, IA 52501

Sergeant Bluff

PIONEER CABINETRY
PO Box 774
105 Sargeant Square Drive
Sergeant Bluff, IA 51054

Sious City

CENTRAL KITCHEN SUPPLY
210 Pearl Street
Sious City, IA 51101

Sioux City

HANDY MAN REMODELING
CENTER
3460 Gordon Drive
Sioux City, IA 51106

HOUSE OF KITCHENS LTD
308 S Floyd Boulevard
Sioux City, IA 51101

Washington

WIDMER INTERIOR DESIGN
1602 E Washington Street
Washington, IA 52352

Waterloo

OMEGA CABINETS LTD
1205 Peters Drive
Waterloo, IA 50703

West Des Moines

CITY DESIGN
208 4th Street
West Des Moines, IA 50265

KANSAS

Eskridge

COUNTERTOPS UNLIMITED
INC
212 Main
PO Box 206
Eskridge, KS 66423

Independence

PRESTIGE INC
201 N Penn Suite 412
PO Box 731
Independence, KS 67301

WOODS LUMBER OF
INDEPENDENCE KS INC
915 N 8th
PO Box 528
Independence, KS 67301

Lenexa

CONTRACTORS APPLIANCE
INC
14308 W 96th Terrace
Lenexa, KS 66215

PAYLESS CASHWAYS INC
14303 W 95th Street
Lenexa, KS 66215-5210

Olathe

THE BROADWAY COLLECTION
1010 W Santa Fe
Olathe, KS 66061

Salina

CRESTWOOD INC
353 East Avenue A
Salina, KS 67401

Shawnee Mission

SHAWNEE MISSION
PLUMBING HEATING COO
11306 W 89th Street
Shawnee Mission, KS 66214

Topeka

DILLON'S CUSTOM
KITCHENS INC
1507 S W 21st Street
Topeka, KS 66604

Wichita

FIRST NATIONAL FIXTURES
CORPORATION
926 North Mosley
Wichita, KS 67214

STAR LUMBER & SUPPLY
COMPANY INC
PO Box 7712
Wichita, KS 67277

SUPERIOR PLUMBING OF
WICHITA INC
6837 East Harry St
Wichita, KS 67207

THE CRAMER COMPANY
811 E Waterman
Wichita, KS 67202

THE KITCHEN PLACE INC
7732 E Central
Wichita, KS 67206

KENTUCKY

Bowling Green

SIGNATURE KITCHEN AND
BATH
979 Lovers Lane
Bowling Green, KY 42103

Cresent Springs

BUILDERS CABINET SUPPLY
2464 Anderson Road
Cresent Springs, KY 41017

Elizabethtown

MOUSER KITCHENS INC
2102 North Highway 31 W
PO Box 2527
Elizabethtown, KY 42702

WALTERS CUSTOM
CABINETS
1340 Middle Creek Road
Elizabethtown, KY 42701

Erlanger

O'BRYAN KITCHENS INC
3420 Dixie Highway
Erlanger, KY 41018

Florence

ARISTECH CHEM CORP-
ACRYLIC SHEET UNIT
7350 Empire Drive
Florence, KY 41042

IN-XTERIOR DESIGN INC
6219 Apple Valley
Florence, KY 41042

WESTERN KITCHEN & BATH
CENTER
4971 Houston Road
Florence, KY 41042

Fort Mitchell

SIGNATURE KITCHENS
18 Pleasant Ridge Avenue
Fort Mitchell, KY 41017

Jamestown

WILKERSON'S DO-IT CENTER
263 N Main Street
PO Box 30
Jamestown, KY 42629

Jeffersontown

REV A SHELF INC
2409 Plantside Drive
PO Box 99585
Jeffersontown, KY 40299

Lexington

AUTO GRAPH COMPUTERIZED
DESIGN SYSTEM
651 Perimeter Drive
Suite 100
Lexington, KY 40517

CREATIVE KITCHEN & BATH
1141 Industry Road
Lexington, KY 40505

DESIGNER KITCHENS INC
1269 Eastland Drive
Lexington, KY 40505

R G COPPINGER &
ASSOCIATES
1429 New Circle Road N E
Lexington, KY 40504

Louisville

GENERAL ELECTRIC
APPLIANCES
Appliance Park
AP4-128
Louisville, KY 40225

KENTUCKY-INDIANA
LUMBER COMPANY INC
227 E Lee Street
Louisville, KY 40208

KITCHEN CRAFTERS
111 Street Matthews Avenue
Louisville, KY 40207

MILLER'S FANCY BATH
109 Horstbouane Lane
Louisville, KY 40222

MOUSER KITCHENS INC
12204 Shelbyville Road
Louisville, KY 40243

Murray

DEPARTMENT OF HOME
ECONOMICS
Oakley Applied Science Building
Murray State University
Murray, KY 42071

Owensboro

CABINETS BY DESIGN
3149 Commonwealth Court
Owensboro, KY 42301

Paintsville

KITCHEN SHOWCASE INC
450 Broadway
Paintsville, KY 41240

Springfield

BARBER CABINET COMPANY
INC
215 Progress Avenue
PO Box 271
Springfield, KY 40069

LOUISIANA

Baton Rouge

ACADIAN HOUSE KITCHENS
& BATHS
12888 Jefferson Highway
Baton Rouge, LA 70816

FERGUSON ENTERPRISES INC
8622 S Choctaw Drive
Baton Rouge, LA 70815

HIGHLAND CABINETS &
MILLWORKS INC
15717 Perkins Road
Baton Rouge, LA 70810

HOME DEPOT #0355
Airline Highway
Baton Rouge, LA 70815

Covington

POOLE LUMBER COMPANY
PO Box 1240
Covington, LA 70434

THE KITCHEN PLACE
1401 N Highway 190
Covington, LA 70433

Denham Springs

GOZA MILLWORKS INC
8726 Stephenson Drive
Denham Springs, LA 70726

Gretna

CABINETS BY DESIGN
429 Wall Boulevard
Suite 1A
Gretna, LA 70056

HOME DEPOT #0350
W Bank Expressway
Gretna, LA 70053

Harahan

CAMPBELL CABINET
COMPANY INC
220 Hord St
PO Box 23884
Harahan, LA 70183

SPECIALTY APPLIANCES
INCORPORATED
5400 Jefferson Highway
Harahan, LA 70123

Harvey

LOUISIANA GAS SERVICE
COMPANY
1233 Westbank Expressway
Harvey, LA 70058

Herahan

HOME DEPOT 0351
S Clearview Parkway
Herahan, LA 70123

Kenner

HOME DEPOT #0349
Veterans Boulevard
Kenner, LA 70062

Lafayette

TOP'S WOODWORK &
SUPPLY
5826 Johnston Street
PO Drawer 31810
Lafayette, LA 70503

Metairie

MARCHAND INTERIOR
SPECIALTIES INC
3517 Division Street
Metairie, LA 70002

PRECISION INTERIORS
3305 Metairie Road
Metairie, LA 70001

SEARS HOME IMPROVEMENT
#4926
4400 Veterans Highway
Metairie, LA 70002

New Orleans

CAMERON KITCHEN AND
BATH DESIGNS
8019 Palm Street
New Orleans, LA 70125

CLASSIC CUPBOARDS INC
4747 Earhart Boulevard
New Orleans, LA 70125

HOME DEPOT #0352
1-10 Service Road
New Orleans, LA 70128

LAGARDE INDUSTRIES, LTD.
4513 Eve Street
New Orleans, LA 70125

LAURENT'S SOLID SURFACE
2626 Music Street
New Orleans, LA 70117

LOUIS W HOWAT & SON INC
2001 Gentilly Boulevard
New Orleans, LA 70119

LOUISIANA POWER & LIGHT
COMPANY
317 Baronne Street (N-356)
New Orleans, LA 70112

MATTIX CABINET WORKS
INC
415 North Solomon Street
New Orleans, LA 70119

TOP'S WOODWORK &
SUPPLY INC
4344 Earhart Boulevard
New Orleans, LA 70125

Shreveport

DESIGNER KITCHENS &
FLOORS INC
6210-B Fairfield Avenue
Shreveport, LA 71106

EXTRA TOUCH KITCHENS
9050 Pradd Road
Shreveport, LA 71106

HOME DEPOT #0353
West 70th Street
Shreveport, LA 71108

Slidell

SUSAN M BRADFORD
106 Highway 190 West
Suite A-15
Slidell, LA 70460

MAINE

Alfred

ROUX'S KITCHEN & BATH
CENTER
PO Box 337
Route 202
Alfred, ME 04002

Auburn

PIONEER PLASTICS
CORPORATION
One Pionite Road
PO Box 1014
Auburn, ME 04211

Belfast

COASTAL PLUMBING &
HEATING INC
119 Northport Avenue
Route 1
Belfast, ME 04915

MATHEWS BROTHERS
COMPANY
Spring Street
Belfast, ME 04915

Boothbay

PROUTY PLUMBING INC
Back River Road
PO Box 257
Boothbay, ME 04537

Brunswick

BRUNSWICK COAL &
LUMBER
18 Spring Street
PO Box 250
Brunswick, ME 04011

East Holden

GRANVILLE LUMBER
CORPORATION
PO Box 1240
East Holden, ME 04429

East Waterboro

SYLCO KITCHEN & BATH
Junction Route 202 & 5
PO Box 34
East Waterboro, ME 04030

Ellsworth

ELLSWORTH BUILDERS
SUPPLY INC
RR 4 Box 4 State Street
Ellsworth, ME 04605-0004

SUNRISE BUILDING CENTER
Bar Harbor Road
Ellsworth, ME 04605

Kittery

BOLD CABINETRY
162 State Road
Kittery, ME 03904

Lewiston

BELLEGARDE CUSTOM
KITCHENS
516 Sabattus Street
Lewiston, ME 04240

DICK'S PLUMBING &
HEATING
693 Sabattus Street
Lewiston, ME 04240

DION DISTRIBUTORS
75 Westminster Street
PO Box 1668
Lewiston, ME 04241

Moody

LAVALLEY LUMBER
PO Box 476
Route 1
Moody, ME 04054

Norway

KITCHEN & BATH DESIGNS
INC
106 Main Street
PO Box 717
Norway, ME 04268

Rangeley

RANGELEY LAKES BUILDERS
SUPPLY COMPANY
PO Box 549
Rangeley, ME 04970

Rockland

E C HART & SON INC
101 Maverick Street
Rockland, ME 04841

MATHEWS BROTHERS
COMPANY
25 Rankin Street
Rockland, ME 04841

Sanford

LAVALLEY LUMBER
COMPANY
New Dam Road
PO Box P
Sanford, ME 04073

Van Buren

GAGNON'S HARDWARE &
FURNITURE INC
184 Main Street
Van Buren, ME 04785

Warren

LONNIE'S PLUMBING
COMPANY
846 Carroll Road
Warren, ME 04864

Waterville

CREATIVE KITCHENS &
DESIGNS
16 Main Street
Waterville, ME 04901

York

GERRITY BUILDING CENTER
Route 1
PO Box 867
York, ME 03909

MARYLAND

Annapolis

KITCHEN ENCOUNTERS/DESIGN
SOLUTIONS
302 Legion Avenue
Annapolis, MD 21401

Ashton

COUNTER INTELLIGENCE
INC
1204 Tucker Lane
Ashton, MD 20861

Baltimore

BALTIMORE GAS &
ELECTRIC COMPANY
1200-67th Street
Baltimore, MD 21237

BRIGGS & COMPANY
3921 M Vero Road
Baltimore, MD 21227

COX KITCHEN & BATH INC
5011 York Road
Baltimore, MD 21212

GREENBAUM AND
ASSOCIATES INC
1201 S Howard Street
Baltimore, MD 21230

HOME DEPOT 2502
Pulaski Highway
White Marsh
Baltimore, MD 21220

IKEA U.S. INC
White Marsh Mall
8352 Honeygo Blvd
Baltimore, MD 21236

JME CONSULTING INC
2106 Burdock Road
Baltimore, MD 21209

JOHN H MORGAN &
ASSOCIATES
3800 Timber View Way
Baltimore, MD 21136

KENWOOD KITCHENS INC
6231 Kenwood Avenue
Baltimore, MD 21237

LEE L DOPKIN STANDARD
PLUMBING
2100 West Coldspring Lane
Baltimore, MD 21209

LINTON ASSOCIATES
16 Beaver Oak Court
Baltimore, MD 21236

MILL VALLEY KITCHENS
3500 Clipper Road
Baltimore, MD 21211

NORTHEASTERN PLUMBING
& HEATING
808 North Chester Street
Baltimore, MD 21205

NORTHFIELD SALES
COMPANY INC
6413 15 Harford Road
Baltimore, MD 21214

RIDGE LUMBER COMPANY
8121 Belair Road
Baltimore, MD 21236

S D KITCHENS
1201 Greenwood Road
Baltimore, MD 21208

SARATOGA SUPPLY
COMPANY
1645 Warner Street
Baltimore, MD 21230

STACKS INC BUILD RITE
KITCHENS
7516 Belair Road
Baltimore, MD 21236

STUART KITCHENS INC
1858 Reisterstown Road
Baltimore, MD 21208

THE PARADIES DISTRIBUTING
COMPANY
3000 Waterview Avenue
Baltimore, MD 21230

THOMSON REMODELING
COMPANY INC
505 W Coldspring Lane
Baltimore, MD 21210

WELSH CONSTRUCTION
REMODELING COMPANY
3901 E Monument Street
Baltimore, MD 21205

Bel Air

DON ROOS CONSTUCTION
COMPANY
227 Gateway Drive
Suite D
Bel Air, MD 21014

THE VERY BEST IN KITCHEN
AND BATH
320 Bright Oaks Drive
Bel Air, MD 21015-6211

Beltsville

AMERICAN SYNTHETIC
SURFACES INC-ASSI
11270 Old Baltimore Pike
Beltsville, MD 20705

BRAY & SCARFF
11950 Baltimore Avenue
Beltsville, MD 20705

BUILDERS WHOLESALE FOR
KITCHENS & BATHS
10401 Tucker Street
Beltsville, MD 20705

COLONIAL DISTRIBUTORS
INC
5200 Sunnyside Avenue
Beltsville, MD 20705

CONTRACT KITCHEN
DISTRIBUTORS INC
12002 Old Baltimore Pike
Beltsville, MD 20705

MID SOUTH BUILDING
SUPPLY OF MD INC
5640 P Sunnsyside Avenue
Beltsville, MD 20705

TOWN & COUNTRY
BATHS/BATH & KITCHEN
REMODELING A DIVISION OF
EJ WHELAN &
6655 Mid Cities Avenue
Beltsville, MD 20705-1415

Bethesda

ANNE NISKANEN NISKANEN
DESIGN
5910 Onondaga Road
Bethesda, MD 20816

CASE DESIGN REMODELING
INC
4701 Sangamore Road
N Plaza Suite 40
Bethesda, MD 20816

NANCY THORNETT
ASSOCIATES
6701 Democracy Boulevard
Suite 809
Bethesda, MD 20817

SMITH THOMAS & SMITH INC
4713 Maple Avenue
Bethesda, MD 20814

Bladnesburg

CARAPACE CORPORATION
5335 Kilmer Place
Bladnesburg, MD 20710

Brandywine

DANS COMPANY INC
15402 Crain Highway
Brandywine, MD 20613

California

BEAUTIFUL KITCHENS
2006 Wildewood Center
California, MD 20619

Capitol Heights

MAJA INTERIORS INC
9100 H Edgeworth Drive
Capitol Heights, MD 20743

Chevy Chase

AAI - T/A KITCHENS INC
6809 Wisconsin Avenue
Chevy Chase, MD 20815

RICHARD M TUNIS INC
7032 Wisconsin Avenue
Chevy Chase, MD 20815

THOMAS W PERRY INC
8513 Connecticut Avenue
Chevy Chase, MD 20815

Clinton

CLINTON CUSTOM
KITCHENS INC
8904 Simpson Lane
Clinton, MD 20735

College Park

MARYLAND THERMAL
MASTER INC
5107 A Berwyn Road
College Park, MD 20740

METROPOLITAN BATH &
TILE INC
9035 Baltimore Avenue
College Park, MD 20740

Columbia

WASHINGTON APPLIANCE
WHOLESALERS INC
9545 Gerwig Lane
Columbia, MD 21046

Easton

CHARTER DISTRIBUTING INC
509 S Street
Easton, MD 21601

Ellicott City

DON ROOS CONSTRUCTION
COMPANY INC
10176 Baltimore National Pike
Ellicott City, MD 21042

GARVEY KITCHEN AND
BATH
3290 Pine Orchard Lane
Ellicott City, MD 21042

KITCHEN CONCEPTS BY
TRISH HOUCK
4474 Columbia Road
Ellicott City, MD 21042

KITCHEN GALLERY
10314-A Baltimore National Pike
Ellicott City, MD 21042

Forestville

GOODE KITCHEN & BATH
DISTRIBUTORS
5501 Marlboro Pike
PO Box 47391
Forestville, MD 20747

Frederick

DESIGNER KITCHENS &
BATHS INC
10 S Market Street
Frederick, MD 21701

NOLAND COMPANY
PO Box 664
Frederick, MD 21701

Gaithersburg

ALLSEASON PLUMBING
HEATING& A C INC
223 Muddy Branch Road #215
Gaithersburg, MD 20878

BARRONS GAITHERSBURG
LUMBER
23 W Diamond Avenue
Gaithersburg, MD 20877

KITCHEN WORKS & BATH
WORKS COMPAMY INC
10130 Little Pond Place
Gaithersburg, MD 20879-2802

KWC INC
8154 Beechcraft Avenue
Gaithersburg, MD 20879

SANFORD'S BATH GALLERY
7600 D Lindbergh Drive
Gaithersburg, MD 20879

Germantown

CORTIN COMPANY
13509 Jamieson Place
Germantown, MD 20874

FRANK GREEN & ASSOCIATES
19110 Gunnerfield Lane
Germantown, MD 20874

SOMERVILLE CONSTRUCTION
20130 Timber Oak Lane
Germantown, MD 20874

Glen Burnie

HOME DEPOT #2501
New Ordnance Road
Glen Burnie, MD 21060

Grantsville

CASSELMAN LUMBER
St Rt Box 32B
Grantsville, MD 21536

Hagerstown

GALLERY OF BATHS
101 East Baltimore Street
Hagerstown, MD 21740

HAGERSTOWN LUMBER
COMPANY INC
700 Frederick Street
Hagerstown, MD 21740

INNER SPACE
45 W Franklin Street
Hagerstown, MD 21740

Hanover

CLASSIC BUILDING
SPECIALTIES INC
7476 New Ridge Road - Suite D
PO Box 590
Hanover, MD 21076

Hebron

RICKARDS CABINETS INC
PO Box 520
Hebron, MD 21830

Hollywood

DEAN HOME CENTER
North On Route 235
Hollywood, MD 20636

Hughesville

COLONIAL WORKSHOP INC
PO Box 370
Hughesville, MD 20637

Jarrettsville

KITCHENS BY REQUEST
3802 Norrisville Road
PO Box 452
Jarrettsville, MD 21084

Kensington

CUSTOM CRAFTERS INC
4000 Howard Avenue
Kensington, MD 20895

Landover

INTERIOR WOODWORKING
3321 75th Avenue Road
Landover, MD 20785

Lanham Seabrook

CHESAPEAKE MARKETING
INC
9420 Annapolis Road
206
Lanham Seabrook, MD 20706

Laurel

CHEVY CHASE PRODUCT
CENTER INC
126 Lafayette Avenue
Laurel, MD 20707

Lutherville

KITCHEN & BATH CENTER
INC
1518 York Road
Lutherville, MD 21093

Millersville

KITCHEN DESIGN STUDIO
8213 Jumpers Hole Road
Millersville, MD 21108

North Beach

MAGIC HAMMER, INC.
3947 2nd Street
P.O. Box 1132
North Beach, MD 20714

North Bethesda

JACK ROSEN CUSTOM
KITCHEN INC
White Flint Mall Level 3
11301 Rockville Pike
North Bethesda, MD 20895

Odenton

CLASSIC KITCHENS INC
PO Box 354
Odenton, MD 21113

NEVAMAR CORPORATION
8339 Telegraph Road
Odenton, MD 21113

Owings Mills

KITCHEN & BATH WORLD
INC
10435 Reisterstown Road
Owings Mills, MD 21117

SUTTON CORPORATION
11438 C Cronridge Drive
Owings Mills, MD 21117

Pasadena

STUART KITCHENS INC
8031 Ritchie Highway
Pasadena, MD 21122

Phoenix

HAYES CONSTRUCTION
COMPANY
14307 Jarrettsville Pike
Phoenix, MD 21131

RACKL GILBERT ASSOCIATES
INC
4004 Sweet Air Road
Phoenix, MD 21131

Potomac

HOPKINS & PORTER
CONSTRUCTION INC
12944 C Travilah Road
Potomac, MD 20854

Rising Sun

CECIL COMMERCIAL
INTERIORS INC
38 Buckley Avenue
PO Box 648
Rising Sun, MD 21911

Rockville

BEAUTIFUL BATHS
11500 Schuylkill Road
Rockville, MD 20852

CABINET DESIGNS INC
712 E Gude Drive
Rockville, MD 20850

CREATIVE KITCHENS INC
1776 E Jefferson Street
Rockville, MD 20852

IDEAL INDUSTRIES
651 Southlawn Lane
Rockville, MD 20850

KITCHEN PLANNERS INC
12140-B Parklawn Drive
Rockville, MD 20852

KITCHEN TECHNIQ INC
12011 Nebel Street
Rockville, MD 20852

POTOMAC DESIGNS
6227 Executive Boulevard
Rockville, MD 20852

RUSSELL GLICKMAN
CONSTRUCTION COMPANY
LTD
15746 Crabbs Branch Way
Rockville, MD 20855

TRAVILAH SQUARE KITCHEN
& BATH INC
10070 Darnestown Road
Rockville, MD 20850

Saint Michaels

TIDAL BUILDING SUPPLY
1206 Talbot Street
Saint Michaels, MD 21663

Salisbury

BUYERS MARKETING
SERVICE INC
PO Box 2593
Salisbury, MD 21802

Savage

D & H DISTRIBUTING
COMPANY
8220 Wellmoor Court
Savage, MD 20763

Severna Park

BAY KITCHENS LTD
688 Ritchie Highway
Severna Park, MD 21146

Shady Side

FADELEY ASSOCIATES INC
P O Box 807
Shady Side, MD 20764

Silver Spring

GILDAY COMPANY INC
9162 Brookville Road
Silver Spring, MD 20910

MGD DESIGN BUILD
COMPANY
9232R Warren Street
Silver Spring, MD 20910

SHOWCASE KITCHENS INC
13824 Old Columbia Pike
Silver Spring, MD 20904

SURFACE TECHNOLOGY
CORPORATION
2730 Pittman Drive
Silver Spring, MD 20910

Temple Hills

ED'S KITCHEN AND CABINET
SHOP INC
7039 Allentown Road
Temple Hills, MD 20748

Timonium

BALLY SERVICES INC
200 W Padonia Road
Timonium, MD 21093

KITCHEN DISTRIBUTORS OF
MARYLAND
221-41 Greenspring Drive
Timonium, MD 21093

Towson

GARON'S FURNITURE
COMPANY INC Ethan Allen
Gallery
8725 Loch Caven Boulevard
Towson, MD 21204

Valley Lee

L & S CABINETS INC
Saint Route Box 159 1A
Valley Lee, MD 20692

Westminster

SCHAEFFER LUMBER
COMPANY
27 Liberty Street
PO Box 865
Westminster, MD 21158

White Plains

B & K CONCEPTS BY
WALDORF MARBLE INC
6309 Theodore Green Boulevard
White Plains, MD 20695

MASSACHUSETTS

Agawam

KITCHENS BY HERZENBERG
INC
South End Bridge Circle
Agawam, MA 01001

Amesbury

EASTERN LUMBER KITCHEN
& BATH CENTER
65 Haverhill Road
Route 110
Amesbury, MA 01913

Andover

ANDOVER KITCHEN & BATH
CENTER INC
2 Stevens Street
Andover, MA 01810

Arlington

FEINMANN REMODELING
INC
150 Gray Street
Arlington, MA 02174

Bellingham

SCANDIA KITCHENS INC
38 Maple Street
PO Box 85
Bellingham, MA 02019

Beverly

MOYNIHAN LUMBER OF
BEVERLY INC
82 River Street
PO Box 509
Beverly, MA 01915

SALEM PLUMBING SUPPLY
COMPANY INC
97 River Street
PO Box 510
Beverly, MA 01915

Boston

CANAC (KITCHENS) OF
BOSTON INC
877 Beacon Street
Boston, MA 02215

HARRISON SUPPLY
COMPANY
1011 Harrison Avenue
Boston, MA 02119

LEE KIMBALL KITCHENS INC
276 Friend Street
Boston, MA 02114-1801

Boxboro

WHITCOMB BROTHERS
265 Hill Road
Boxboro, MA 01719

Boylston

KITCHENS BY DESIGN
PO Box 670
200 Shewsbury Street
Boylston, MA 01505

Cambridge

JON SPECTOR & ASSOCIATES
INC
PO Box 801
Cambridge, MA 02238

Cohasset

RENEE C. LESIEUR
3 Grace Drive
Cohasset, MA 02025

Concord

ACORN STRUCTURES
PO Box 1445
Concord, MA 01742

Dalton

L P ADAMS COMPANY INC
484 Housantonic Street
Dalton, MA 01226

Danvers

BROWN'S KITCHEN & BATH
CENTER
56 North Putnam Street
Danvers, MA 01923

HOME DEPOT #2663
Newbury Street
Danvers, MA 01923

Dennisport

KITCHEN STUDIO DCM INC
66 Upper County Road
PO Box 1188
Dennisport, MA 02639

Duxbury

GOODRICH LUMBER INC
85 Rairoad Avenue
PO Box R
Duxbury, MA 02331

SOUTH SHORE CABINET
CENTER INC
PO Box 1608
122 Tremont Street
Duxbury, MA 02331

East Falmouth

COASTAL KITCHENS
130 Goeletta Drive
PO Box 174E
East Falmouth, MA 02536

East Longmeadow

KITCHENS BY CHAPDELAINE
87 Shaker Road
East Longmeadow, MA 01028

Everett

FABRIZIO BROTHERS INC
14 Garvey Street
Everett, MA 02149

Falmouth

JESSICA WASSETH FLYNN
PO Box 323
Falmouth, MA 02541-0323

Framingham

KITCHEN CENTER OF
FRAMINGHAM INC
697 Waverly Street
Framingham, MA 01701

Gloucester

BUILDING CENTER INC
1 Harbor Loop
PO Box 180
Gloucester, MA 01930

Granby

TOWN AND COUNTRY
INTERIOR
56 W State Street
Route 202
Granby, MA 01033

Greenfield

CLASSIC KITCHENS
6 French King Highway
Greenfield, MA 01301

RUGG LUMBER COMPANY
66 Newton Street
PO Box 507
Greenfield, MA 01302

Harwich

HACKBERRY & CHATHAM
506 Depot Street
Harwich, MA 02645

Harwich Port

FRANCIS E WOELFEL INC
432 Main Street
Harwich Port, MA 02646

Haverhill

WINDSOR KITCHENS LTD
1181 Boston Road Route 125
PO Box 8011
Haverhill, MA 01835

Hopkinton

CLARKE DISTRIBUTION
CORPORATION
100 South Street
Hopkinton, MA 01748

Hudson

RS LAMSON & SONS INC
29 Lake Street
Hudson, MA 01749

Hyannis

CLASSIC KITCHEN DESIGN
INC
200 Thornton Drive
Hyannis, MA 02601

JOHN HINCKLEY & SON
COMPANY
49 Yarmouth Road
PO Box 2110
Hyannis, MA 02601

R B CORCORAN COMPANY
349 Iyannough Road
Route 28 PO Box 340
Hyannis, MA 02601

Lawrence

JACKSON LUMBER &
MILLWORK
215 Market Street
PO Box 449
Lawrence, MA 01842

Leominster

SOLID SURFACES UNLIMITED
853 N Main St Suite 203
Leominster, MA 01453

Lexington

DRAKE CABINET &
REMODELING INC
(Rear) 401 Lowell Street
Lexington, MA 02173

Lynn

STANDARD OF LYNN INC
400 Lynnway
PO Box 830
Lynn, MA 01903

Marblehead

NORTHSHORE KITCHENS
PLUS
183 Tedesco Street
Marblehead, MA 01945

Marlboro

HOLLAND WOODWORKING
INC
40 Florence Street
Marlboro, MA 01752

Mashpee

KITCHEN DESIGN CENTER
Summerfield Park
Route 28
Mashpee, MA 02649

Mattapoisett

DESIGNER KITCHENS BY
ANGELA
92 North Street PO Box 85
Mattapoisett, MA 02739

MAHONEY'S BUILDING
SUPPLY CENTER
One Industrial Drive
Mattapoisett, MA 02739

Maynard

THE FAUCETORIUM
161 Main Street
Maynard, MA 01754

Melrose

HEARTWOOD KITCHEN &
BATH CABINETRY
99 Washington Street
Melrose, MA 02176

Millis

ELIZABETH A WENZEL
21 Bridge Street
Millis, MA 02054

Nantucket

MARINE HOME CENTER/MARINE
LUMBER CO
Lower Orange Street
Nantucket, MA 02554

Natick

FORMICA CORPORATION
190 N Main Street
Natick, MA 01760

KITCHEN INTERIORS
255 Worcester Road
Natick, MA 01760

Needham

ASQUITH COMPANY
166 Cresent Road
Needham, MA 02194

New Bedford

KITCHENS & BATHS
54 Nauset Street
New Bedford, MA 02746

REVERE SINK CORPORATION
12 Coffin Avenue
New Bedford, MA 02746

TAILORED KITCHENS
SUPPLY
100 Tarkiln Hill Road
PO Box 50004
New Bedford, MA 02745

Newton

EURO PLUS DESIGN
29 Crafts Street
Suite 510
Newton, MA 02160

MASTERPIECE KITCHEN &
BATH INC
381 Elliot Street
Newton, MA 02164

NATIONAL LUMBER
COMPANY
15 Needham Street
Newton, MA 02161

SPLASH
244 Needham Street
Newton, MA 02164

North Brattleboro

INEL KITCHENS & BATHS INC
560 Kelley Boulevard
Route 152
North Brattleboro, MA 02760

North Chatham

ACCENT ON KITCHENS
277 Orleans Road
Route 28
North Chatham, MA 02650

North Dartmouth

DARTMOUTH BUILDING
SUPPLY COMPANY INC
958 Reed Road
North Dartmouth, MA 02747

North Reading

FREDERICK SHOHET INC
51 Concord Street
PO Box 439
North Reading, MA 01864

RALPH WILSON PLASTICS
COMPANY WILSONART
29 Concord Street
PO Box 217
North Reading, MA 01864

Northampton

RUGG LUMBER COMPANY -
HAMPSHIRE DIVI
33 Hawley Street
Northampton, MA 01060

Norwell

KITCHEN CONCEPTS INC
159 Washington Street
Norwell, MA 02061

Norwood

GAGGENAU U S A
425 University Avenue
Norwood, MA 02062

REPUBLIC PLUMBING
SUPPLY CO. INC
890 Providence Highway
Norwood, MA 02062

Orleans

MID-CAPE HOME
CENT/NICKERSON LUMBER
15 Main Street
PO Box 99
Orleans, MA 02653

Osterville

KITCHEN & BATH DESIGNS
UNLIMITED INC
5 Parker Road
Osterville, MA 02655

Pittsfield

SHEDD INC
730 Tyler Street
Pittsfield, MA 01201

Plainville

RAPETTI FAUCETS GEORGE
BLOTCHER LTD
0 High Street
Plainville, MA 02762

Plymouth

DESIGNED INTERIORS
116 Long Pond Road
Plymouth, MA 02360

PILGRIM CUSTOM
COUNTERTOP
204 South Meadow Road
Plymouth, MA 02360

THE CABINET CONNECTION
INC
27 Samoset Street
Plymouth, MA 02360

Quincy

HOME DEPOT #2670
Willard Street
Quincy, MA 02169

Salem

BERGERON BATH &
KITCHEN
47 Canal Street
Salem, MA 01970

Sandwich

KITCHEN TECH INC
374 Route 130
PO Box 1030
Sandwich, MA 02563

Seekonk

HOME DEPOT #2661
Highland Avenue
Seekonk, MA 02771

Shrewsbury

CUCCARO ASSOCIATES INC
2 Wesleyan Terrace
Shrewsbury, MA 01545

MODULAR KITCHENS INC
33 Boston Turnpike
Route 9
Shrewsbury, MA 01545

Somerset

HORNER MILLWORK CORP
1255 G A R Highway
Route 6
Somerset, MA 02726

Somerville

THE WOODWORKING
STUDIO INC
57 Central Street
Somerville, MA 02143

South Attleboro

HOME DEPOT #2659
Newport Avenue
South Attleboro, MA 02703

South Dartmouth

COSTA'S QUALITY KITCHENS
6 McCabe Street
South Dartmouth, MA 02748

South Deerfield

ELDER LUMBER CORPORATION
1 N Street
South Deerfield, MA 01373

South Walpole

THE KITCHEN AND
BATHROOM
175 Summer Street
South Walpole, MA 02071

South Weymouth

KITCHENS UNLIMITED
1604 Main Street Rte 18
South Weymouth, MA 02190

Springfield

BAYSTATE STONE COMPANY
INC
1380 Main Street
Springfield, MA 01103

CUSTOM CABINET &
MILLWORK INC
784 Page Boulevard
Springfield, MA 01104

Sterling

KITCHEN ASSOCIATES INC
76 Leominster Road
Route 12
Sterling, MA 01564

Stoughton

RICHARD KUBLIN KITCHENS
489 Page Street
Stoughton, MA 02072

Stow

CREATIVE DESIGNS IN
KITCHENS INC
132 Great 3Road
Route 117
Stow, MA 01775

Taunton

KITCHEN CONCEPTS INC
451 Winthrop Street
Taunton, MA 02780

Waltham

BRICKMAN'S
419 Moody Street
PO Box 9160
Waltham, MA 02154

MR BUILD E STONE ENT INC
20 Riverview Avenue
Waltham, MA 02154

Ward Hill

RUNTAL NORTH AMERICA
INC
187 Neck Road
Ward Hill, MA 01835

Ware

AMERICAN CABINET WORKS
INC
148 Hardwick Pond Road
Ware, MA 01082

Watertown

ARCHITECTURAL CABINET
COMPANY
635 Main Street
Watertown, MA 02172

Wayland

SUPERIOR COLUMN &
DISTRIBUTION COMPA
25 Wayland Hills Road
Wayland, MA 01778

Wellesley

JARVIS APPLIANCE INC
958 Worcester Street
Wellesley, MA 02181

WESTON KITCHENS
868 Worcester Road
Wellesley, MA 02181

West Bridgewater

KITCHEN SALES INC
60 Manley Street
West Bridgewater, MA 02379

West Chatham

ARCHIBALD WOODWORKING
39 George Ryder Road
PO Box 282
West Chatham, MA 02669

West Hatfield

DANCO KITCHENS
INCORPORATED
10 West Street
West Hatfield, MA 01088

West Newbury

A & L ASSOCIATES
29 Pleasant Street
West Newbury, MA 01985

NORTHEAST ASSOCIATES
25 Pleasant Street
West Newbury, MA 01985

West Springfield

HOME DEPOT 2661
Daggett Drive
West Springfield, MA 07089

Westborough

KBQ INC
PO Box 1620
173 Flanders Road
Westborough, MA 01581

WESTBOROUGH DESIGN
CENTER INC
3 Ruggles Street
Westborough, MA 01581

Westwood

METROPOLITAN CABINET
DISTRIBUTORS
345 University Avenue
Westwood, MA 02090

PRATT & SON INC
91 Alder Road
Westwood, MA 02090

Weymouth

J B KITCHENS AND BATHS
1471 Main Street
Rte 18
Weymouth, MA 02190

Woburn

DESIGN BUILD SOLUTIONS
INC
3 Baldwin Green
Suite 204
Woburn, MA 01801

KITCHENS DIRECT/MOBEN
KITCHENS
600 W Cummings Park
Woburn, MA 01801

MICHIGAN

Adrian

MERILLAT INDUSTRIES INC
5353 U S 223
PO Box 1946
Adrian, MI 49221

Alpena

HISER KITCHEN & BATH
CENTER
3303 W Washington Avenue
Alpena, MI 49707

Ann Arbor

KITCHEN AND BATH
GALLERY Division of D & C
Supply
5161 Jackson Road
Ann Arbor, MI 48103

MARY CHRISTENSEN'S
KITCHEN & BATH DESIGN
CENTER
2335 W Stadium Boulevard
Ann Arbor, MI 48103

WASHTENAW WOODWRIGHTS
INC
5 Keppler Court
Ann Arbor, MI 48103

Auburn Hills

TREVARROW INC
1295 N Opdyke Road
Auburn Hills, MI 48326

Baroda

BARODA LUMBER COMPANY
PO Box 98
Baroda, MI 49101

Battle Creek

MILLER WHOLESALE INC
Box 1070
2450 W Columbia Avenue
Battle Creek, MI 49016

THE KITCHEN SHOP
492 Capital Avenue SW
Battle Creek, MI 49015

Bay City

HEPPNER KITCHEN CENTER
3909 N Euclid
Bay City, MI 48706

Belleville

CRAFTMASTERS KITCHENS &
BATHS
21620 Sumpter Road
Belleville, MI 48111

Belmont

DOTY FORSTER ENTERPRISES
6588 Rogue View Court
Belmont, MI 49306

Benton Harbor

WHIRLPOOL CORPORATION
Administrative Center
2000 M-63
Benton Harbor, MI 49022

Big Rapids

BIG RAPIDS CASH AND
CARRY
130 S Third
Big Rapids, MI 49307

Birmingham

KITCHENS BY JENSEN
563 S Eton
Birmingham, MI 48009

KITCHENS BY LENORE &
RICHARDS INC
912 S Woodward Avenue
Birmingham, MI 48009

Bloomfield Hills

BLOOMFIELD CUSTOM
KITCHENS INC
4068 W Maple Road
Bloomfield Hills, MI 48301

EUROSTYLE LTD
1030 N Hunter Boulevard
Bloomfield Hills, MI 48304

Brighton

CARE CRAFTED LTD
12619 E Grand River
Brighton, MI 48116

KSI KITCHEN SUPPLIERS INC
9325 Maltby Road
Brighton, MI 48116

Burton

RON'S KITCHENS & BATHS
G-4437 S Saginaw Street
Burton, MI 48529

Cadillac

COUNTRYSIDE KITCHEN &
BATH CENTER
7401 E 35 Mile Road
Cadillac, MI 49601

Canton

MANS KITCHEN & BATH
41816 Ford Road
Canton, MI 48187

Caro

GRAFF & SONS CABINET
GALLERY
1539 E Caro Road
Caro, MI 48723

Centerville

MILL RACE DISTRIBUTING
INC
240 W Main Street
PO Box 577
Centerville, MI 49032

Charlotte

CHARLOTTE KITCHEN
CENTER
630 W Lawrence Avenue
Charlotte, MI 48813

Chassell

ANDERSON & JARVI LUMBER
COMAPNY
U S 41
P O Box 439
Chassell, MI 49916

Chesaning

COX GREGORY AGENCY
16160 Briggs Road
Chesaning, MI 48616

SWARTZMILLER &
ASSOCIATES
137 S Saginaw Street
Chesaning, MI 48616

Climax

SHOWCASE KITCHENS &
INTERIORS
12717 P Avenue East
Climax, MI 49034

Coldwater

H & S SUPPLY INC
317 N Fiske Road
Coldwater, MI 49036

Coopersville

LEIGH A HARROW COMPANY
411 64Th Avenue
Coopersville, MI 49404

Davisburg

DAVISBURG LUMBER
COMPANY INC
13180 Andersonville Road
PO Box 16
Davisburg, MI 48350

Davison

KENNETH R LAWRENCE &
SON CONSTRUCTION INC
205 E Flint Street
Davison, MI 48423

PIONEER CABINETRY INC
PO Box 280
301 W Rising Street
Davison, MI 48423

East Detroit

DON HILL INC
15351 Camden
East Detroit, MI 48021

Elansing

MERIDIAN PLUMBING INC
2654 E Grand River
Elansing, MI 48823

Escanaba

DELTA DO IT CENTERS
6669 Highway 2-41-M35
Escanaba, MI 49829

Farmington Hill

ARTISTIC KITCHENS INC
29586 Orchard Lake Road
Farmington Hill, MI 48334

Flint

CASTLES BROTHERS
KITCHENS
1471 W Bristol Road
Flint, MI 48507-5591

FLINT KITCHEN & BATH
CENTER
G 3463 W Pierson Road
Flint, MI 48504

KEN'S KUSTOM KITCHENS &
BATHS
2501 Clio Road
Flint, MI 48504

OK PLUMBING & HEATING
COMPANY INC
5317 N Saginaw Street
Flint, MI 48505-2967

VIC BOND SALES
1240 East Coldwater Road
Flint, MI 48505

Flushing

STARLINE DISTRIBUTORS
G 5500 W Pierson
PO Box 158
Flushing, MI 48433

Fowlerville

FOWLERVILLE LUMBER
118 N Ann Street
PO Box 352
Fowlerville, MI 48836

Fraser

FABRI TOP COMPANY INC
33410 Groesbeck Highway
Fraser, MI 48026

SHOWCASE KITCHEN &
BATH INC
31435 Utica Road
Fraser, MI 48026

Freeland

RADKA'S KITCHEN & BATH
CENTER
4540 N. River Road
Freeland, MI 48623

Grand Blanc

BLESSING COMPANY
122 East Grand Blanc Road
Grand Blanc, MI 48439

Grand Rapids

GALLERY OF KITCHENS INC
5243 Plainfield Avenue N E
Grand Rapids, MI 49505

JACQUELINE NEAL
55 Ionia N W #1202
Grand Rapids, MI 49503

KITCHENS BY A & B
DISTRIBUTORS INC
5234 Plainfield N E
Grand Rapids, MI 49505

KITCHENS BY STEPHANIE
2880 Thornhills SE
Grand Rapids, MI 49546

KOZAK'S PLUMBING &
HEATING
2790 3 Mile Road N W
Grand Rapids, MI 49504

LIFESTYLE KITCHEN & BATH
2216 Wealthy Street SE
Grand Rapids, MI 49506

LUMBERMEN'S PLASTIC
DIVISION
4418 Stafford Avenue
Grand Rapids, MI 49508

STANDARD KITCHENS
1450 Kalamazoo SE
Grand Rapids, MI 49507

VICTOR S BARNES COMPANY
1927 Will N W
Grand Rapids, MI 49504

WILLIAMS DISTRIBUTING
COMPANY
PO Box 2585
Grand Rapids, MI 49501

WOODLAND HOUSE OF
KITCHENS INC
6619 S Division SW
Grand Rapids, MI 49548

Grandville

BELWITH KEELER
INDUSTRIAL SALES
4300 Gerald Road
Ford Freeway
Grandville, MI 49418

BELWITH-KEELER
INDUSTRIAL SALES
4300 Gerald R Ford Freeway
Grandville, MI 49468

CREATIVE SOLID SURFACES
2975 Chicago Drive
Grandville, MI 49418

INTERIORS BY CHERI
3901 Chicago Drive
Suite 120
Grandville, MI 49418

Grosse Point Woods

MUTSCHLER KITCHENS INC
20227 Mack Avenue
Grosse Point Woods, MI 48236

Gulfport

BAILEY LUMBER & HOME
CENTER
813 Pass Road
Gulfport, MI 39507

Hale

BERNARD BUILDING CENTER
INC
395 South Washington
Hale, MI 48739

Highland

FIVE STAR SUPPLY
1135 S Milford Road
Highland, MI 48357

Hillsdale

MC CALL HOME CENTER
123 E Carleton Road
PO Box 247
Hillsdale, MI 49242

Holland

CLASSIC KITCHENS AND
BATHS INC
650 Riley Street
Suite G
Holland, MI 49424

Howell

B & J ASSOCIATES
3987 S Woods Road
Howell, MI 48843

OPIE'S CABINET & DESIGN
CENTER INC
3220 E Grand River
Howell, MI 48843

Jackson

ROYAL CABINET INC
3900 Francis Street
Jackson, MI 49203

THE KITCHEN SHOP INC
407 First Street
Jackson, MI 49201

Kalamazoo

THE KITCHEN SHOP
2415 South 11th Street
Kalamazoo, MI 49009

Kentwood

ENTREE KITCHENS
3224 28th Street S E
Kentwood, MI 49508

Laingsburg

KIRKBY ASSOCIATES INC
120 W Grand River
PO Box 459
Laingsburg, MI 48848

Lansing

ACCENT KITCHEN BATH
CENTER INC
615 S Waverly
Lansing, MI 48917

CAPITOL CITY LUMBER
COMPANY
700 E Kalamazooa Street
PO Box 20277
Lansing, MI 48901

HEDLUND PLUMBING
COMPANY
6323 W Saginaw
Lansing, MI 48917

MCDANIELS SALES
COMPANY
3900 North East Street
Lansing, MI 48906

THE KITCHEN SHOP
5320 S Pennsylvania
Lansing, MI 48911

Lincoln Park

UNIQUE KITCHENS & BATHS
3504 Fort Street
Lincoln Park, MI 48146

Livonia

APPLIANCE DISTRIBUTORS
INC
13455 Stamford Court
Livonia, MI 48150

KITCHENS PLUS
31815 W Eight Mile Road
Livonia, MI 48152

KURTIS KITCHEN & BATH
CENTERS
12500 Merriman Road
Livonia, MI 48150-1923

Livonia Road

MATHISON KITCHEN &
BATH SUPPLY DIVISION OF
MATHISON HOME
28243 Plymouth Road
Livonia Road, MI 48150

Marquette

SCHWALBACH KITCHEN
SPECIALISTS
500 N Third Street
Marquette, MI 49855

Marshall

TRIMBILT KITCHENS
519 S Kalamazoo Avenue
Marshall, MI 49068

Midland

OWENS CABINET
1928 Stark Road
Route 3
Midland, MI 48640

Monroe

MATTHES KITCHENS & BATH
2351 W Albain Road
Monroe, MI 48161

WEINLANDER KITCHEN &
BATH
310 N Telegraph Road
Monroe, MI 48161

Mount Pleasant

CENTRAL PLUMBING &
HEATING INC
600 North Mission Street
Mount Pleasant, MI 48858

JOE MCDONALD'S HOUSE OF
CABINETS INC
5800 E Pickard
Mount Pleasant, MI 48858

Muskegon

DCN ASSOCIATES INC
4764 Maranatha Drive
Muskegon, MI 49441

STYLE TREND KITCHENS &
BATHS
792 W Laketon Avenue
Muskegon, MI 49441

Northville

LONG PLUMBING COMPANY
190 E Main Street
Northville, MI 48167-1692

Novi

MANSFIELD CABINETS
45033 Grand River
Novi, MI 48375

Okemos

WILLIAM S LUBAHN
4595 Arrowhead Road
Okemos, MI 48864

Petoskey

BOND A COVE
408 Petoskey Street
Petoskey, MI 49770

PRESTON FEATHER BD
CT/LIFESTYLES K&B
896 Spring Street
Petoskey, MI 49770

PUFF'S OF PETOSKEY
1200 Bay View Road
PO Box 807
Petoskey, MI 49770

SWEET'S KITCHEN CENTER
2429 US 31 North
Petoskey, MI 49770

Pinconning

LLOYD'S CABINET SHOP INC
1947 North M 13
Pinconning, MI 48650

Plymouth

KITCHENS BY STELLA
747 S Main Street
Plymouth, MI 48170

Pontiac

ACORN KITCHEN & BATH
DISTRIBUTORS
111 South Telegraph Road
Pontiac, MI 48341

Romulus

ISLAND CABINET TREE
27588 Dupre
Romulus, MI 48138

Royal Oak

CONSTRUCTION BY
CHAMPAGNE INC
304 South Kenwood
Royal Oak, MI 48067

FUTURISTIC FURNISHINGS
4329 Normandy Court
Royal Oak, MI 48073

MODERN COUNTER TOP
COMPANY
819 East 4th Street
Royal Oak, MI 48067

QUE VIE INC
4240 Woodward
Royal Oak, MI 48073

ROYAL OAK KITCHENS INC
4518 N Woodward Avenue
Royal Oak, MI 48073

Saginaw

REMER PLUMBING &
HEATING INC
5565 State Street
Saginaw, MI 48603

SAGINAW KITCHEN & BATH
CENTER
315 W Holland
Saginaw, MI 48602

Saint Clair Shores

RIVERSIDE KITCHEN & BATH
31499 Harper Avenue
Saint Clair Shores, MI 48082

WOODMASTER KITCHENS
26510 Harper
Saint Clair Shores, MI 48081

Saint Joseph

KITCHENAID INC
701 Main Street
Saint Joseph, MI 49085

Saline

BRIDGEWATER LUMBER
COMPANY
7895 E Michigan Avneue
Saline, MI 48176

Sault Ste Marie

ERICKSON APPLIANCE &
FURNITURE CENTER
2405 Ashmun Street
Sault Ste Marie, MI 49783

Southfield

FAIRWAY CONSTRUCTION
COMPANY
21348 Telegraph Road
Southfield, MI 48034

KITCHEN & BATH INC
16000 W Nine Mile Road
Suite 306
Southfield, MI 48075

Southgate

MICOLE CONSTRUCTION INC
13633 Longtin
Southgate, MI 48195

Spring Arbor

SPRING ARBOR APPL & TV
KIT & BATH
7650 Spring Arbor Road
Spring Arbor, MI 49283

Sturgis

DERAND KITCHENS INC
315 S Clay Street
PO Box 397
Sturgis, MI 49091

Swartz Creek

DICK HARRIS CKD/CBD &
ASSOCIATES
5404 Don Shenk Drive
Swartz Creek, MI 48473

THE KITCHEN SHOP OF
HAGER FOX
5376 Miller Road
Swartz Creek, MI 48473

Sylvan Lake

LIVING SPACES INC KITCHEN
& BATH DESIGN
2678 Orchard Lake Road
Sylvan Lake, MI 48320

WORLD WIDE CABINETS INC
2655 Orchard Lake Road
Sylvan Lake, MI 48320

Taylor

MASCO CORPORATION
21001 Van Born Road
Taylor, MI 48180

RADIO DISTRIBUTING
COMPANY
27015 Trolley Drive
Taylor, MI 48180

Three Oaks

HARBOR COUNTRY
KITCHENS & BATHS
8E Maple Street
Three Oaks, MI 49128

Traverse City

BROWN LUMBER & SUPPLY
COMPANY VISIONS KITCHEN
& BATH
1701 S Airport Road
Traverse City, MI 49684

CABINETS BY ROBERT
2774 Garfield
Traverse City, MI 49684

CHERRYLAND CUT STONE &
MARBLE COMPANY
699 N Three Mile Road
Traverse City, MI 49684

CREATIVE KITCHEN
747 Woodmerelace
Traverse City, MI 49684

KELLOGG WHOLESALE
BUILDING SUPPLY INC
2662 Cass Road
Traverse City, MI 49684

NORTHWOOD KITCHENS INC
10240 Cherry Bend Road
Traverse City, MI 49684

Troy

ALTIMA KITCHENS
2821 Rochester Road
Troy, MI 48083

Vassar

WEBER LUMBER &
MILLWORK INC
8586 W Sanilac Road
Vassar, MI 48768

Walled Lake

NEWMYER INC
3081 Haggerty Road
Suite 1
Walled Lake, MI 48390

Warren

H J OLDENKAMP COMPANY
4669 East 8 Mile Road
Warren, MI 48091

Waterford

ACCURATE WOODWORKING,
INC
7675 Highland Road
Waterford, MI 48327

Westland

RALPH WILSON PLASTICS
COMPANY
1500 Superior Parkway
Westland, MI 48185

Whitehall

JERJAN ENTERPRISES
1198 S Lake Street 305
Whitehall, MI 49461

Wixom

EW KITCHEN DISTRIBUTORS
INC
29750 Anthony Drive
Wixom, MI 48393

JENN-AIR DISTRIBUTING
PO Box 436
51740 Grand River Avenue
Wixom, MI 48393-9910

Woodhaven

GRAHL'S KITCHEN & BATH
21111 Allen Road
Woodhaven, MI 48183

MINNESOTA

Albert Lea

JIM & DUDES PLUMBING &
HEATING INC
724 West Clark Street
Albert Lea, MN 56007

Alexandria

ALEXANDRIA TECHNICAL
COLLEGE BETTY L RAVNIK
1601 Jefferson
Alexandria, MN 56308

Anoka

HIRSCH INC CABINETS BY
DESIGN
357 McKinley Street N W
Anoka, MN 55303

HUTTON AND ROWE INC
THE PLUMBERY
2126 2nd Avenue N
Anoka, MN 55303

Bemidji

BENCHMARK ENTERPRISES
7507 Filbert Lane N E
Bemidji, MN 56601

Bloomington

SUN RAY WOOD PRODUCTS
INC
9854 James Circle
Bloomington, MN 55431

Brooklyn Park

CABINET BROKERS INC
5116 Hamilton Lane
Brooklyn Park, MN 55443

Chanhassen

CHANHASSEN KITCHEN &
BATH
530 West 79th Street
PO Box 6
Chanhassen, MN 55317

Crookston

RED RIVER CABINETS
R R 1
Box 86
Crookston, MN 56716

Crystal

JP MILLWORK & DESIGN INC
5525 34th Avenue N
Crystal, MN 55422

Duluth

CONTARDO LINDQUIST &
COMPANY
926 East 4th Street
Duluth, MN 55805

HANNA INTERIORS INC
106 East Superior Street
Duluth, MN 55802

SUPREME KITCHEN & BATHS
4877 Miller Trunk Highway #1
Duluth, MN 55811

Eagan

WOODMASTERS INC
990 Lone Oak Road
Suite 150
Eagan, MN 55121

Eden Prairie

HALLMARK BUILDING
SUPPLIES INC
7582 Washington Avenue South
Eden Prairie, MN 55344

ROTH DISTRIBUTING
COMPANY
7640 Commerce Way
Eden Prairie, MN 55344

Edina

NORTH STAR SERVICES
4402 France Avenue S
Edina, MN 55410

Elk River

BRAD CAIRNS
19171 Zebulon Street
Elk River, MN 55330

Ely

W N PLUMBING & HEATING
203 E Conan Street
Ely, MN 55731

Fridley

PREFERRED KITCHENS INC
7221 University Avenue N E
Fridley, MN 55432

Golden Valley

CRYSTAL KITCHEN CENTER
668 N Highway 169
Golden Valley, MN 55427

Ham Lake

KNAPP WOODWORKING
16430 Highway 65 N E
Ham Lake, MN 55304

Hastings

IMPERIAL COUNTERS INC
725 Spiral Boulevard
Box 636
Hastings, MN 55033

Hopkins

GALAXY SALES INC
41 Tenth Avenue N
Hopkins, MN 55343-7569

VENT A HOOD OF THE TWIN
CITIES INC
1426 Main Street
Hopkins, MN 55343

Howard Lake

DURA SUPREME INC
300 Dura Drive
Howard Lake, MN 55349

Litchfield

RICK PLUMBING & HEATING
22 E 3rd Street
Litchfield, MN 55355

Maple Grove

JUNE VOLK
13301 Maple Knoll Way
Apt. 601
Maple Grove, MN 55369

Marshall

MINNESOTA CABINETS INC
1101 E College Drive
Marshall, MN 56258

Mendota Heights

ACCENT DESIGN STUDIO
1408 Northland Drive
Suite 305
Mendota Heights, MN 55120

Minneapolis

CARA UNDERHILL
7620 Logan Avenue S
Minneapolis, MN 55423

FANTASIA DIVISION OF SPS
COMPANY INC
IMS 275 Market Street
Suite 102
Minneapolis, MN 55405

INTERNATIONAL MARKET
SQUARE
275 Market Street
Minneapolis, MN 55405

KITCHENS BY PHOENIX INC
5435 Lyndale Avenue S
Minneapolis, MN 55419

MINNESOTA TILE
SKETCHBOOK
4825 France Avenue N
Minneapolis, MN 55429

NSS AT IMS
275 Market Street
Suite 156
Minneapolis, MN 55405

PARTNERS 4 DESIGN INC
275 Market Street
Suite 109
Minneapolis, MN 55405

PEARL BATHS INC
9224 73rd Avenue N
Minneapolis, MN 55428

PLYWOOD INDUSTRIES INC
2129 Broadway Street N E
Minneapolis, MN 55413

SAWHILL CUSTOM KITCHENS
& DESIGN INC
275 Market Street
Suite 157
Minneapolis, MN 55405

STEVEN CABINETS INC
2303 Kennedy Street NE
Minneapolis, MN 55413

VALLEY INTERIOR
PRODUCTS INC
4626 Lyndale Avenue N
Minneapolis, MN 55412

Minnetonka

BUDGET POWER
12201 Minnetonka Boulevard
Minnetonka, MN 55343

HIGHLINE DISTRIBUTING INC
11300 West 47th Street
Suite 100
Minnetonka, MN 55343

TRADE SHOWS INC
15235 Minnetonka Boulevard
Minnetonka, MN 55345

Mora

NORDENSTROM CONSTRUCTION
126 South Union
Mora, MN 55051

New Ulm

COVINGTON CABINETRY
1217 S Washington
New Ulm, MN 56073

North Saint Paul

ANDERSEN CABINET INC
2500 N Charles
North Saint Paul, MN 55109

Osseo

GREAT IDEAS (KITCHENS &
BEYOND)
8686 Jefferson Highway
Osseo, MN 55369

Owatonna

ADVANTAGE CABINETS, INC
Route 3 Box 326
Owatonna, MN 55060

Plato

PLATO HOME CENTER
119 E Main Street
PO Box 68
Plato, MN 55370

PLATO WOODWORK INC
200 3rd Street S W
PO Box 98
Plato, MN 55370

Plymouth

F C HAYER COMPANY
845 Berkshire Lane
Plymouth, MN 55441

GRAYBOW DANIELS
WESTBURNE
2400 Xenium
Plymouth, MN 55441

SANDRA M BARON
4745 Yorktown Lane North
Plymouth, MN 55442

Princeton

CRYSTAL CABINET WORKS
INC
1100 Crystal Drive
Princeton, MN 55371

Prior Lake

MINNESOTA WOODS AND
INTERIORS INC
6867 Boudin Street N E
Prior Lake, MN 55372-1433

Robbinsdale

SAWHORSE DESIGNERS AND
BUILDERS
4740 42nd Avenue North
Robbinsdale, MN 55422

Rochester

HANSON BUILDERS &
REMODELERS
2122 8th Ave. NE
P.O. Box 7287
Rochester, MN 55906

KITCHENS OF DISTINCTION
1115 7th Street N W
Rochester, MN 55901

UNITED BUILDING CENTERS
2751 7Th Street
Nw Box 6066
Rochester, MN 55903

Saint Cloud

ANNEGRET HAMILTON
803 20th Avenue N
Saint Cloud, MN 56303

Saint Louis Park

ANDERSEN CABINETS
5814 Excelsior Boulevard
Saint Louis Park, MN 55416

MINN STANDARD
SHOWRMS/DIV SPS CO INC
4301 Country Road-Highway 7
Saint Louis Park, MN 55416

Saint Paul

BONGARD CORPORATION
PO Box 130160
Saint Paul, MN 55113

BRUCE NELSON PLUMBING &
HEAT SER INC
1272 South Point
Douglas Road
Saint Paul, MN 55119

CLASSIC KITCHENS BY
LANCE FORMERLY SAINT
CHARLES OF MN
1146 Grand Avenue
Saint Paul, MN 55105

H B FULLER COMPANY
3530 N Lexington Avenue
Saint Paul, MN 55126

IRMITER CONTRACTORS &
BUILDERS LTD
1472 Grand Avenue
Saint Paul, MN 55105-2220

KITCHENS BY KRENGEL INC
1688 Grand Avenue
Saint Paul, MN 55105

NORCRAFT COMPANIES INC
30 E Plato Boulevard
Saint Paul, MN 55107

NORTH STAR SERVICES
688 Hague Avenue
Saint Paul, MN 55104

UNIV OF MINN-DESIGN,
HOUSING, APPAREL
240 McNeal/1985 Buford Avenue
Saint Paul, MN 55108

Sauk Rapids

DESIGN LINE CABINETS
2460 Quarry Road
PO Box 9
Sauk Rapids, MN 56379

Stillwater

MONSON INTERIOR DESIGN
PO Box 313
320 W. Myrtle Street
Stillwater, MN 55082

Victoria

OLSON CABINETS &
WOODWORKING
PO Box 177
Victoria, MN 55386

Waile Park

SIMONSON LUMBER WEST
900 W Division
Waile Park, MN 56387

Wells

JEAN VOKIEL
R1 Box 48
Wells, MN 56097

White Bear Lake

CABINET CRAFTERS INC
1350 Highway 96
White Bear Lake, MN 55110

Willmar

BRIARWOOD CABINETRY
2508 W Trott Avenue
Willmar, MN 56201

KITCHEN FAIR
313 West 5th Street
Willmar, MN 56201

MISSISSIPPI

Columbus

EXPRESSIONS BY BENEKE
PO Box 1367
Columbus, MS 39703

Greenwood

CUSTOM KITCHENS AND
DESIGN SPECIALTY Inc
PO Box 488
Greenwood, MS 38930

VIKING RANGE CORPORATION
111 Front Street
Greenwood, MS 38930

Gulfport

BUILDERS SPECIALTY
SUPPLY CO
1312 31st Avenue
PO Box 403-39502
Gulfport, MS 39501

Jackson

CREATIVE DESIGNS
5001 Highway 80 W
Jackson, MS 39209

FRIERSON BUILDING SUPPLY
4525 Lynch Street Extension
PO Box 10817
Jackson, MS 39289

KITCHEN KREATORS
LIMITED
K 13 B Lakeland Drive
Jackson, MS 39216

McComb

CITY PAINT & GLASS INC
334 - 25th Street
McComb, MS 39648

Yazoo City

ARCHITECTURAL
MILLWORKS INDUSTRIES
Route 6 Box 268
Yazoo City, MS 39194

MISSOURI

Bozeman

ERNST HOME CENTER #270
200 S 23rd Avenue
Bozeman, MO 59715

Bridgeton

BROCK'S APPLIANCE
11707 Natural Bridge Road
Bridgeton, MO 63044

DECORATIVE KITCHEN
SALES INC
11820 Saint Charles Rock Road
Bridgeton, MO 63044

Buffalo

C & C CABINET COMPANY
Route 3 Box 330
Buffalo, MO 65622

Camdenton

DESIGNED KITCHENS &
INTERIOR
Highway 5 N Ryland Center
Route 76 Box 830
Camdenton, MO 65020

Chesterfield

PERMA CERAM OF SAINT
LOUIS
109 Shady Valley
Chesterfield, MO 63017

SANFORD SPECIALTY SALES
COMPANY
16033 Aston Court
Chesterfield, MO 63005-4577

TRENCO INC
1928 Farm Valley Road
Chesterfield, MO 63017

Columbia

DESIGNER KITCHENS AND
BATHS
1729 West Broadway
Columbia, MO 65203

KERRY BRAMON REMOLDING
& DESIGN
1204 Rogers Street
Columbia, MO 65201

Des Peres

BUELER CUSTOM KIT &
CONSTRUCTION INC
13314 Manchester Road
Des Peres, MO 63131

CUTTER'S CUSTOM
KITCHENS & BATHS INC
12878 Manchester Road
Des Peres, MO 63131

Earth City

THOMAS CONSTRUCTION
COMPANY
4283 Shoreline Drive
Earth City, MO 63045

Fenton

ANCHOR SALES
1693 Fenpark Drive
Fenton, MO 63026

CONSTRUCTION APPLIANCE
SUPPLY
1606 Headland Drive
Fenton, MO 63026

Ferguson

MOEN GROUP
423 Tiffin
Ferguson, MO 63135

Florissant

EHRLICH'S KITCHEN AND
BATH
3236 Parker Road
Florissant, MO 63033

LASTING IMPRESSIONS HOME
REMODEL CTR
2168 North Waterford
Florissant, MO 63033

PHIL L MILLER PLUMBING
COMPANY
661 Sreet Ferdinand Street
Florissant, MO 63031

Four Seasons

H & S SALES INC
3 Acacia Court
Four Seasons, MO 65049

Jefferson City

CAPITAL SUPPLY COMPANY
418 W Elm Street
PO Box 455
Jefferson City, MO 65102

Kansas City

G W RYAN DISTRIBUTING
COMPANY INC
2201 E Truman Road
Kansas City, MO 64127

Kirkwood

BAYGENTS COMPANY
117 West Argonne
Kirkwood, MO 63122

JE REDINGTON COMPANY
639 Leffingwell
Kirkwood, MO 63122

SCHUMACHER KITCHEN &
BATH STUDIO
10030 Big Bend Boulevard
Kirkwood, MO 63122

Manchester

ROY E DUENKE CABINET
COMPANY
14436 Manchester Road
Manchester, MO 63011

O'Fallon

K & R WOOD PRODUCTS INC
61 N Central Drive
O'Fallon, MO 63366

O'Follen

NATIONAL SALES COMPANY
401 S Cool Springs Road
O'Follen, MO 63366

Pacific

ARCHWAY KITCHEN AND
BATH
PO Box 386
Pacific, MO 63069

Poplar Bluff

ARNDT CABINET COMPANY
INC
Route 1 Box 476
Poplar Bluff, MO 63901

Rockhill

WILLIAM A ROSE KITCHEN &
REMODELING CENTER INC
9807 Manchester Road
Rockhill, MO 63119

Rolla

POWELL'S LUMBER & HOME
CENTER
6th and Rolla Streets
PO Box 1039
Rolla, MO 65401

Saint Charles

CALLIER'S CUSTOM
KITCHENS & BATHS
INCORPORATED
4524 Parktowne Drive
Saint Charles, MO 63304

KITCHENS BY WEAVER INC
2281 First Capitol Drive
Saint Charles, MO 63301

Saint Clair

JERRY'S QUALITY
WOODWORKS
10 Bolte Lane
Saint Clair, MO 63077

Saint Louis

AHRENS & MC CARRON INC
4621 Beck Avenue
Saint Louis, MO 63116

ARNOLD-MISSOURI
CORPORATION
3905 Forest Park Boulevard
Saint Louis, MO 63108

BASSE CABINET COMPANY
7243 Sutherland
Saint Louis, MO 63119

BRIGHTMAN DIST COMPANY
10411 Baur Boulevard
Saint Louis, MO 63132

CALLIER'S CUSTOM
KITCHENS
2570 South Brentwood Boulevard
Saint Louis, MO 63144

CARDINAL BUILDING
MATERIALS
4565 McRee Avenue
Saint Louis, MO 63110

CRESCENT PLUMBING
SUPPLY COMPANY
640 Rosedale Avenue
PO Box 24140
Saint Louis, MO 63130

GLEN ALSPAUGH COMPANY
9808 Clayton Road
Saint Louis, MO 63124

ICI ACRYLICS INC
10091 Manchester Road
Saint Louis, MO 63122

INNOVATIONS FOR KITCHEN
& BATH
2025 S Big Bend
Saint Louis, MO 63117

J & J SALES REP INC SWAN
8393 Page Boulevard
Saint Louis, MO 63130

KARR-BICK KITCHENS &
BATH
2715 Mercantile Drive
Saint Louis, MO 63144

KITCHEN & BATH RESOURCE
STUDIO
2901 Olive Street
Saint Louis, MO 63103

MARGO INC
2039 Concourse Drive
Saint Louis, MO 63146

MODERN KITCHENS & BATHS
INC
3122 S Kings Highway
Saint Louis, MO 63139

MORGAN WIGHTMAN
SUPPLY COMPANY
5668 Anglum
Main PO Box 1
Saint Louis, MO 63166

RSI DISTRIBUTING INC
8110 Eager Road
Saint Louis, MO 63144

SHOWCASE KITCHENS AND
BATHS
1230 Macklind Avenue
Saint Louis, MO 63110

SOULARD PLUMBING SUPPLY
INC
78 N Gore Avenue
Saint Louis, MO 63119

THE SWAN CORPORATION
1 City Centre
Suite 2300
Saint Louis, MO 63101

THOMPSON'S HOUSE OF KIT
& BATHS IN.
5452 Southfield Center
Saint Louis, MO 63123

THOMPSON'S HOUSE OF
KITCHENS & BATHS INC
11718 Manchester Road
Saint Louis, MO 63131

W E BRANDT INC
3636 Geyer Road
Suite 200
Saint Louis, MO 63127

WEST END SALES INC
9252 Manchester Road
Saint Louis, MO 63144

Troy

ACTIVE PLUMBING SUPPLY
HOUSE BATHS SHOWROOM
684 S Lincoln Drive
PO Box 255
Troy, MO 63379

Webster Groves

NATIONAL KITCHEN & BATH
INC
280 E Kirkham
Webster Groves, MO 63119

MONTANA

Billings

AMERICAN APPLIANCE
COMPANY
2121 1st Avenue South
PO Box 1937
Billings, MT 59103

ERNST HOME CENTER #244
1313 Grand Avenue
Billings, MT 59102

Bozeman

BOZEMAN TV & APPLIANCE
INC
34 North Bozeman
Bozeman, MT 59715

MCPHIE CABINETRY
435 E Main
Bozeman, MT 59715

Chester

NORM'S CUSTOM
WOODCRAFT
Box 682
Chester, MT 59522

Great Falls

ERNST HOME CENTER #269
207 NW Bypass
Great Falls, MT 59404

THE CABINET COMPANY
801 9th Street S
Great Falls, MT 59405

Hamilton

SPECIALTY WOODWORKS
COMPANY
212 Pennsylvania Avenue
Hamilton, MT 59840

Kalispell

CAROL NELSON DESIGN
115 W Nevada
Kalispell, MT 59901

Missoula

DESIGN AND CONSULTATION
309 N Higgins
Missoula, MT 59802

ERNST HOME CENTER #274
3025 Paxson Street
Missoula, MT 59801

THURMANS KITCHEN &
BATH
3020 Reserve
Missoula, MT 59801

Polson

WEST SHORE CABINET
474 Rocky Point Road
PO Box 77
Polson, MT 59860

Whitefish

SHIRNO CABINETS
5729 Highway 93 S
Whitefish, MT 59937

NEBRASKA

Fremont

EVERLY PLUMBING &
HEATING
2505 E 23rd Avenue S
Fremont, NE 68025

Grand Island

THE KITCHEN GALLERY INC
2808 Old Fair Road
Suite G
Grand Island, NE 68803

Hastings

SHOWCASE
347 W 2nd
Hastings, NE 68901

Kearney

BABL COMPANY
1209 Avenue A
PO Box 280
Kearney, NE 68848

TASK LIGHTING CORPORATION
910 E 25th
PO Box 1094
Kearney, NE 68848

UNIVERSITY OF NEBRASKA
Kearney Department of Family &
Csmr Science OttoOlson206
Kearney, NE 68849

Lincoln

CROWL'S KITCHENS &
BATHS
137 S 9th Street
Lincoln, NE 68508

GREEN FURNACE &
PLUMBING COMPANY INC
2747 N 48th
PO Box 4556
Lincoln, NE 68504

HANDY MAN HOME
REMODELING CENTER
501 W Gate Boulevard
Lincoln, NE 68528

HYLAND BROTHERS INC
1060 N 33Rd Street
Lincoln, NE 68503

LINCOLN CABINET
624 K Street
Lincoln, NE 68508

MCEWEN ODBERT
CONSTRUCT & CABINET
COMPAMY
5034 Old Cherry Road
Lincoln, NE 68516

REYNOLDS KITCHEN DESIGN
INC
2406 J
Lincoln, NE 68510

WAYNE GIEBELHAUS
PLUMBING & HEATING
2231 Winthrop Road
Lincoln, NE 68502

McCook

CORKY'S MODERN
INTERIORS
214 Norris Avenue
McCook, NE 69001

Omaha

ARLON MILLER COMPANY
CUSTOM KITCHENS &
INTERIORS
3909 Farnam Street
Omaha, NE 68131

ASHTON WHOLESALE
SERVICE INC
1218 Nicholas Street
Omaha, NE 68601

EUROWOOD CUSTOM
CABINETS INC
4327 S 90th
Omaha, NE 68127

HEARN PLUMBING SERVICE
INC
10430 J Street
Omaha, NE 68127-1020

KITCHENS BY DESIGN
1263 South 120
Omaha, NE 68144

LARSON CUSTOM KITCHENS
10801
Omaha, NE 68137

MILLARD LUMBER INC
5005 South 135th Street
Omaha, NE 68137

NEBRASKA CUSTOM
KITCHENS
4601 Dodge Street
Omaha, NE 68132

WARD'S KITCHENS & BATHS
10908 Elm Street
Omaha, NE 68144

WOOD SPECIALTIES
12510 North 108th Street
Omaha, NE 68142

NEVADA

Fallon

KARENA NYGREN
PO Box 1223
Fallon, NV 89407

Las Vegas

EUROPEAN BATH &
KITCHEN
4850 W Flamingo Road 36
Las Vegas, NV 89103

KITCHEN STUDIO INC
610 1/2 E Sahara Avenue
Las Vegas, NV 89104

Reno

CABINET & LIGHTING
SUPPLY
6970 S Virginia Street
Reno, NV 89511

CLASSIC KITCHENS &
DESIGNS
PO Box 6874
Reno, NV 89513

ERNST HOME CENTER #243
3310 Kietzke Lane
Reno, NV 89502

KITCHENS & BATHS BY
LOUISE GILMARTIN
245 Vine Street
Suite B
Reno, NV 89503

Sparks

ERNST HOME CENTER #268
2400 Oddie Boulevard
Sparks, NV 89431

NEW HAMPSHIRE

Amherst

CURRIER KITCHENS
101 Route 101A
Amherst, NH 03031

D J B CORPORATION
71 Route 101A Windmere Place
Amherst, NH 03031

Claremont

LAVALLEY'S CLAREMONT
BUILDING SUPPLY
Pleasant & Mulberry Streets
Claremont, NH 03743

Concord

KITCHEN FASHIONS
Lamplighter Plaza # 8
133 Loudon Rd.
Concord, NH 03301

Farmington

ANGELO SASSI & SON
PLUMBING & HEATING
COMPANY
PO Box 591
Farmington, NH 03835

Hampton Falls

CABINETRY BY LANE
WOODWORKS
97 Lafayette Road
Hampton Falls, NH 03844

Hillsboro

EAGLE ASSOCIATES INC
Route 9W
PO Box 1429
Hillsboro, NH 03244

Jaffrey

MASTER DECORATING
Park Place
Jaffrey, NH 03452

Keene

GRASHOW'S
147 Winchester Street
Keene, NH 03431

HAMSHAW LUMBER INC
3 Bradco Street
Keene, NH 03431

Londonderry

FREDERICK SHOHET OF NEW
HAMPSHIRE INC
10 Burton Drive
Londonderry, NH 03053

Manchester

SUNDEEN'S BUILDING
CENTER
271 Mamoth Road
Manchester, NH 03103

Nashua

DREAM KITCHENS
139 Daniel Webster Highway
Nashua, NH 03060

HOME DEPOT #3481
Daniel Webster Highway
Nashua, NH 03060

RIVERSIDE MILLWORK
COMPANY INC
332 Amherst Street
Nashua, NH 03060

Newington

ADAPTATIONS UNLIMITED
2001 Woodbury Avenue
Newington, NH 03801

Newport

LA VALLEY BUILDING
SUPPLY INC
Box 267 Guild Road
Newport, NH 03773

North Conway

CHICK HOME BUILDING
CENTER
PO BOX 3060
Mtn. Valley Mall Blvd.
North Conway, NH 03860

R L MEAD INC
PO Box 560
East Conway Road
North Conway, NH 03860

Peterborough

UPCOUNTRY KITCHENS &
BATHS
PO Box 367
23 Elm Street
Peterborough, NH 03458

Portsmouth

AREA KITCHEN CENTRE
105 Bartlet Street
Portsmouth, NH 03801

STANDARD PLUMBING
& HEATING SUPPLY
CORPORATION
430 W Road
PO Box 1267
Portsmouth, NH 03801

Rye

MABIE ENTERPRISES INC
116 Central Rd
Rye, NH 03870-2522

Salem

HOME DEPOT #3480
South Broadway
Salem, NH 03079

NEW HAMPSHIRE KITCHEN
CENTER INC
264 N Broadway
Unit # 201A
Salem, NH 03079

Stratham

THE CABINETWORKS
62 Portsmouth Avenue
Stratham, NH 03885

West Lebanon

JOHNSON'S HOME CENTER
Route 12-A
West Lebanon, NH 03784

NEW JERSEY

Absecon

SCHLOESSER CONSTRUCTION
100 E Seminole Drive
Absecon, NJ 08201

Allendale

EMERALD KITCHENS
10 Elm Street
Allendale, NJ 07401

Bayonne

ABBEY'S KITCHENS & BATHS
INC
685 Broadway
Bayonne, NJ 07002

Belle Mead

MICHAEL J BRUNO
206 Stephen Way
Belle Mead, NJ 08502

NASSAU KITCHEN AND BATH
COMPANY INC
1109 Route 206
Belle Mead, NJ 08502

Belleville

KITCHENS & BATHS BY
MODERN MILLWORK
624 Washington Avenue
Belleville, NJ 07109

Belmar

DU CRAFT INC
1919 Highway 71
Belmar, NJ 07719

Bergenfield

DOVETAIL DESIGNS INC
7 Irving Place
Bergenfield, NJ 07621

Berkeley Height

ALPS CRAFTSMEN &
TECHNOLOGY INC
30 Locust Avenue
Berkeley Height, NJ 07922

Blackwood

BLANCO AMERICA INC
1001 Lower Landing Road
Suite 607
Blackwood, NJ 08012

Bloomfield

BOYETTE KITCHENS &
BATHS
214 Montgomery Street
Bloomfield, NJ 07003

Bridgeport

SUN WAVE U S A COMPANY
LTD
509 Sharptown Road
PO Box 345
Bridgeport, NJ 08014

Bridgeton

MIKE KELLY'S KITCHENS
RD #8 Box 229
Landis Avenue
Bridgeton, NJ 08302

Bridgewater

FOOTHILL CONSTRUCTION
COMPANY
101 Mountainside Lane
Bridgewater, NJ 08807

SOMERVILLE LUMBER
1480 Route 22
Bridgewater, NJ 08807

Butler

RICH'S KITCHENS INC
309 Hamburg Turnpike
Butler, NJ 07405

THE KITCHEN CORNER
Route 23 S & Boonton Avenue
Box 41
Butler, NJ 07405

Cedar Grove

J HARRISON KITCHENS
465 Pompton Avenue
Cedar Grove, NJ 07009

Cherry Hill

APPLE KITCHENS INC
1334 Brace Road
Cherry Hill, NJ 08034

DAVE FILAN PLUMBING &
HEATING INC
1816 Garden Avenue
Cherry Hill, NJ 08003

R BUZZETTA BUILDERS INC
#1 Middle Acre Lane
Cherry Hill, NJ 08003

Chester

KITCHENS UNIQUE BY LOIS
INC
259 Main Street
Box 6899
Chester, NJ 07930

Cliffside Park

AMSTERDAM ASSOCIATES
INC
200 Winston Drive-3103
Cliffside Park, NJ 07010

Cliffwood Beach

FLO DAR INC
Highway 35
Cliffwood Beach, NJ 07735

Clifton

HOME DEPOT #0908
Bloomfield Avenue
Clifton, NJ 07012

R & R REMODELERS INC
423 Hazel Street
Clifton, NJ 07011

THERMCO INC
228 Scoles Avenue
Clifton, NJ 07012

Cranbury

TIMBERLINE KITCHENS
Cranbury Station Road
Cranbury, NJ 08512

Dayton

AFFORDABLE KITCHENS
UNLIMITED
342 George's Road
PO Box 532
Dayton, NJ 08810

HOME DEPOT #5997
Charles Court
Dayton, NJ 08810

Denville

DORWOOD INDUSTRIES INC
30 Estling Lake Road
Denville, NJ 07834

KITCHENS BY SPITALNY
101 Bloomfield Avenue
Denville, NJ 07834

Dover

LAKELAND INDUSTRIES
CABAINET CORNER
408 Route 46
Dover, NJ 07801

Dumont

NICK'S KITCHEN CENTER
71 New Milford Avenue
Dumont, NJ 07628

East Brunswick

KITCHEN DECOR
252 Highway 18
East Brunswick, NJ 08816

East Hanover

HOME DEPOT #0901
Murray Road
East Hanover, NJ 07936

Edison

ANDI CO AEG APPLIANCE
INC RARITAN CENTER
65 Campus Plaza
Edison, NJ 08837

THERMADOR-NORTHWEST
SALES OFFICE
334 Raritan Center Parkway
Edison, NJ 08837

Elizabeth

CRINCOLI WOODWORK
COMPANY INC
160 Spring Street
Elizabeth, NJ 07201

IKEA U.S. INC
1000 Center Drive
Elizabeth, NJ 07201

Elmwood Park

KINZEE INDUSTRIES
1 Paul Kohner Place
Elmwood Park, NJ 07407

Englewood

ALTHERM INC
255 Humphrey Street
Englewood, NJ 07631

HARRINGTON BRASS WORKS
LTD
166 Collidge Avenue
Englewood, NJ 07631

KITCHENAID INC
25 Rockwood Place
Englewood, NJ 07631

PLATON IMPORTS
105 Cedar Lane
Englewood, NJ 07631

Fair Haven

FITZPATRICK BUILDERS INC
188 Fair Haven Road
Fair Haven, NJ 07704

Fairfield

ALLMILMO CORPORATION
70 Clinton Road
Fairfield, NJ 07004

FABRICATORS SUPPLY
COMPANY
425 US Highway 46
Fairfield, NJ 07006

HARDWARE DESIGNS INC
135 New Dutch Lane
Fairfield, NJ 07006

S & A DISTRIBUTORS INC
33 Route 46 W
Fairfield, NJ 07004

Fairlawn

KITCHEN TECHNIQUE INC
14 27 River Road
Fairlawn, NJ 07410

Farmingdale

THE KITCHEN COLLECTION
GERALD SACCA
5105 Highway 33 34
Farmingdale, NJ 07727

Fort Lee

GENERAL ELECTRIC
COMPANY
Two Executive Drive
5th Floor
Fort Lee, NJ 07024

KITCHEN AND BATH
MARKETING GROUP
3 Horizon Road Suite 1033
Fort Lee, NJ 07024

KITCHENETICS
521 Main Street
Fort Lee, NJ 07024

Frenchtown

BATCH & TINSMAN
ASSOCIATES
Rt 29 Box 100
Frenchtown, NJ 08825

Garwood

DUDICK & SON
40 North Avenue
Garwood, NJ 07027

Glen Ridge

ROSEANNE LEANZA SMITH
11 Summit Street
Glen Ridge, NJ 07028

Great Meadows

KARCHER CONSTRUCTION
LTD CORPORATION
PO Box 132
Great Meadows, NJ 07838

Green Brook

BEAUTY CRAFT KITCHENS &
BATHS INC
283 US Highway 22
Green Brook, NJ 08812

Hackensack

GUENTER METSCH
WOODCRAFT INC
200 Atlantic Street
Hackensack, NJ 07601

KITCHEN & BATH DESIGN
NEWS
2 University Plaza
Suite 11
Hackensack, NJ 07601

Hackettstown

HACKETTSTOWN SUPPLY
COMPANY INC
47 Route 46
Hackettstown, NJ 07840

UNION STOVE WORKS INC
Hackettstown Commerce Park
101 Bilby Road PO Box 7141
Hackettstown, NJ 07840

Haddonfield

HADDONFIELD KITCHENS
INC
423 Haddon Avenue
Haddonfield, NJ 08033

HADDONFIELD LUMBER
COMPANY
PO Box 1038
Haddonfield, NJ 08033

Hammonton

UNIVERSAL SUPPLY
COMPANY INC
South Harbor & White Horse Pike
PO Box 266
Hammonton, NJ 08037

Hawthorne

HAWTHORNE KITCHENS INC
Fifth and Utter Avenues
Hawthorne, NJ 07506

HOME SUPPLY & LUMBER
CENTER
160 Vanwinkle Avenue
Hawthorne, NJ 07506

Ho-ho-kus

RICHARD J BELL COMPANY
INC
1 Hollywood Avenue 20B
Ho-ho-kus, NJ 07423

Hopatcong

JAMES P LUZZO JR
114 Tulsa Trail
Hopatcong, NJ 07843

Jobstown

J & L WOODWORKING
COMPANY INC
RR #1 Box 440
Jobstown, NJ 08041

Kearny

AANENSEN'S
142 Midland Avenue
Kearny, NJ 07032

Lake Hiawatha

KITCHENS BATHS INTERIORS
58 N Beverwyck Road
Lake Hiawatha, NJ 07034

Lakewood

HOME DEPOT #0902
Shorrock Road
Lakewood, NJ 08701

Lambertville

MACDONALD KITCHEN &
BATH DESIGNS INC
71 N Main Street
Lambertville, NJ 08530

NIECE LUMBER
Elm Street
Lambertville, NJ 08530

Lebanon

CWI KITCHENS & BATHS INC
Route 22 PO Box 528
Lebanon, NJ 08833

Linden

ECONOMY KITCHENS
431 N Wood Avenue
PO Box 1352
Linden, NJ 07036

MALONEY & CURCIO INC
PO Box 1490
Linden, NJ 07036

Little Silver

LITTLE SILVER KITCHEN &
BATH STUDIO INC
2 Fairview Avenue
Little Silver, NJ 07739

S D DESIGNS INC
116 Oceanport Avenue
Little Silver, NJ 07739

Livingston

RAY RIVERS & ASSOCIATES
INC
34 E Northfield Road
Livingston, NJ 07039

Long Branch

NORDIN CABINETS &
MANUFACTURING
22 Third Avenue
Long Branch, NJ 07740

Manalapan

CABITRON DISTRIBUTORS
INC
Home Fashion Center
520 Route 9 N
Manalapan, NJ 07726

Maplewood

SAWHORSE DESIGNS
119 Baker Street
Maplewood, NJ 07040

Margate

DILLON CUSTOM KITCHENS
1 S Granville Avenue
Margate, NJ 08402

Marmora

A-1 CUSTOM KITCHENS &
BATHS
22 Norwood Road
PO Box 787
Marmora, NJ 08223

Maywood

LOMAR DISTRIBUTON INC
946 Spring Valley Road
Maywood, NJ 07607

Mercerville

DELORENZO AND VERDE
DESIGN T/A THE CABINET
STUDIO
4040 Quakerbridge Road
Mercerville, NJ 08619

Middlesex

MICHAEL GEORGE
KITCHEN'S
679 Bound Brook Road
Middlesex, NJ 08846

Midland Park

KITCHENS BY KUSTOM
KRAFT
22 Paterson Avenue
Midland Park, NJ 07432

PANDORF ASSOCIATES
301 Greenwood Avenue
Midland Park, NJ 07432

Millburn

THE BATH CONNECTION/DIVISION
OF NJ PLUMBING SUPPLY CO
183 Millburn Avenue
Millburn, NJ 07041

Montvale

PASCACK SHOWCASE INC
PO Box 367
33 S Kinderkamack Road
Montvale, NJ 07645

Moorestown

SCOTT INDUSTRIES
PO Box 588
Moorestown, NJ 08057-0588

Morristown

DISTINCTIVE KITCHENS
171 Ridgedale Avenue
Morristown, NJ 07960

Mount Arlington

PATTERN SYSTEMS
INTERNATIONAL INC
200 Valley Road
Suite 302
Mount Arlington, NJ 07856

N Brunswick

ELEGANT BATH SHOPPE
Joyce Kilmer Avenue At 12th
Street
N Brunswick, NJ 08902

N Plainfield

KITCHEN & BATH WORKS
Route 22 & W End Avenue
PO Box 1269
N Plainfield, NJ 07061

New Providence

ROSAN CUSTOM KITCHENS
AND BATH
1294 Springfield Avenue
New Providence, NJ 07974

Newark

COOPER DISTRIBUTING
COMPANY
177 Central Avenue
Newark, NJ 07103

Newfield

KITCHENS N THINGS INC
Route 40
PO Box 346
Newfield, NJ 08344

North Plainfield

KITCHEN IDEAS INC
918 Route 22
North Plainfield, NJ 07060

Northfield

SO JERSEY KIT DIST INC/K &
B DSGN CR
1333 New Road
Plaza 9
Northfield, NJ 08225

Northvale

FOUR SEASONS HOME
REMODELING INC
209 Willow Avenue
Northvale, NJ 07647

Nutley

PARAMOUNT KITCHENS
291 Bloomfield Avenue
Nutley, NJ 07110

Ocean City

REBER MCLEAN KITCHENS
INC
628 West Avenue
Ocean City, NJ 08226

SHOEMAKER LUMBER
COMPANY INC
1200 W Avenue
PO Box 357
Ocean City, NJ 08226

Old Bridge

AFFORDABLE KITCHENS &
BATHS
209 Englishtown Road
Old Bridge, NJ 08857

Paramus

HOME DEPOT #0904
Route 17 N
Paramus, NJ 07652

QUALITY BATH INC
556 Route 17 N
Paramus, NJ 07652

STAR BEKA KUCHEN IDI
NORTH INC
489 Route 17 South
Paramus, NJ 07652

Parlin

HOME DEPOT #0905
Route 9 N Old Bridge
Parlin, NJ 08859

WORLD TRADERS INC
PO Box 308
Parlin, NJ 08859

Parsippany

CERDEL CONSTRUCTION
120 Park Road
Parsippany, NJ 07054

Paterson

CORINTHIAN PRODUCTS INC
421 5th Avenue
Paterson, NJ 07514

Pennsauken

FABRICATORS SUPPLY
COMPANY
1125 Busch Highway
Pennsauken, NJ 08110

FESSENDEN HALL INC
1050 Sherman Avenue
Pennsauken, NJ 08110

RALPH WILSON PLASTICS
COMPANY (WILSONART)
135 Thomas Busch Memorial
Highway
Pennsauken, NJ 08110

Pequannock

THE KITCHEN SHOP INC
35 Newark Pompton Turnpike
Pequannock, NJ 07440

Perth Amboy

WHOLESALE KITCHEN
CABINET DISTRICT INC
533 Krochmally Avenue
Perth Amboy, NJ 08861

Piscataway

AMERICAN STANDARD
PO Box 6820
Piscataway, NJ 08855

FORMICA CORPORATION
One Stranford Road
Piscataway, NJ 08854

STELTON CABINET & SUPPLY
COMPANY
1358 Stelton Road
Piscataway, NJ 08854

Plainsboro

BATH & KITCHEN DESIGNS
PO Box 496
Plainsboro, NJ 08536-0796

Pleasantville

JOTI KITCHENS
413 S Main Street
Pleasantville, NJ 08232

Point Pleasant

IDEAL KITCHENS INC
407 Sea Avenue
Point Pleasant, NJ 08742

Point Pleasant Beach

CAPRICORN KITCHENS &
BATHS
827 Trenton Avenue
Point Pleasant Beach, NJ 08742-
2432

Pompton Lakes

HANS' KITCHENS & BATHS
INC
10 Colfax Avenue
Pompton Lakes, NJ 07442

LORANGER & SONS INC
324 Ringwood Avenue
Pompton Lakes, NJ 07442

Pompton Plains

JEFFREYS & LUTJEN INC
29 Evans Place
Pompton Plains, NJ 07444

Princeton

JEFFERSON BATH &
KITCHEN DIVINSION NC
JEFFERSON PLUMBING
190 Witherspoon Street
Princeton, NJ 08542

Ramsey

BONDI'S WORLD OF
KITCHENS INC
455 Route 17 S
Ramsey, NJ 07446

Raritan

THE CABINET CENTER BY
FLEETWOOD
20 Route 206
Raritan, NJ 08869

Red Bank

ACCENT HARDWARE BY
CREATIVE SPACE
549 Highway 35
Red Bank, NJ 07701

THE KITCHEN GALLERY INC.
24 Mechanic Street
Red Bank, NJ 07701

Ridgewood

ULRICH INC
100 Chestnut Street
Ridgewood, NJ 07450

Riverside

SOLIDSURFACE DESIGNS INC
117 Delaware Avenue
Riverside, NJ 08075

Robbinsville

WILLIAMS BUILDER
2365 Route 33
Robbinsville, NJ 08691

Roselle

PROVEN DESIGN INC
225 E First Avenue
Roselle, NJ 07203

Saddle Brook

CLASSIC KITCHENS & BATHS
479 N Midland Avenue
Saddle Brook, NJ 07662

SALERNO'S KITCHEN
CABINETS INC
599 Midland Avenue
Saddle Brook, NJ 07662

Salem

MANNINGTON RESILIENT
FLOORS
PO Box 30
Salem, NJ 08079

Scotch Plains

THE DESIGN CENTER
1625 E Second Street
Scotch Plains, NJ 07076

Sea Girt

DESIGN LINE KITCHENS
2127 Highway 35
Sea Girt, NJ 08750

Secaucus

THE NEMIROFF CORPORATION
400 Plaza Drive
Secaucus, NJ 07094

Somerdale

THE PURPLE THUMB INC
6 South White Horse Pike
Somerdale, NJ 08083

Somerset

BATHS PLAIN & FANCY J
DOLAN SONS P&H
696 Franklin Boulevard
Somerset, NJ 08873

MIELE APPLIANCES INC
22D Worlds Fair Drive
Somerset, NJ 08873

VILLEROY & BOCH USA INC
1600 Cottontail Lane
PO Box 7490
Somerset, NJ 08875

Somerville

FRESH IMPRESSIONS, INC
882 Route 22 E
Somerville, NJ 08876

South Plainfield

HOME DEPOT #0903
Dept 26 Merchant NE Div
3096 Hamilton Boulevard
South Plainfield, NJ 07080

JOANNE'S KITCHENS
2208 Hamilton Boulevard
PO Box 267
South Plainfield, NJ 07080

South Somerville

ROYAL CABINET COMPANY
INC
14 Park Avenue
South Somerville, NJ 08876

Sparta

SPARTA TRADES KITCHENS
& BATHS
580 Route 15
PO Box 963
Sparta, NJ 07871

Spotswood

ALBECKER'S KITCHENS &
BATHS
272 Main Street
Spotswood, NJ 08884

COMBINED CRAFTMEN INC
168 Manalapan Road
Spotswood, NJ 08884

Springfield

KURT'S CONCEPTS
615 Morris Avenue
Springfield, NJ 07081

Succasunna

HOME DEPOT #0909
Route 10 Roxbury
Succasunna, NJ 07876

Summit

BAZALA KITCHENS INC
37 Maple Street
Summit, NJ 07901

CABRI INC
323 Springfield Avenue
Summit, NJ 07901

THE GALLERY OF KITCHENS
& CARPETS INC
789 Springfield Avenue
Summit, NJ 07901

Sussex

KITCHENS & BATHS BY RAN
COMPANY INC
56 E Main Street
Sussex, NJ 07461

Teaneck

NATIVE WOOD
370 Queen Anne Road
Teaneck, NJ 07666

SUBURBAN CABINET CORP
1465 Palisade Avenue
Teaneck, NJ 07666

Tenafly

ARTISTIC BATH TILE &
HARDWARE INC
136 Piermont Road
Tenafly, NJ 07670

KITCHEN COLLECTION
16 Central Avenue
Tenafly, NJ 07670

Toms River

IZZY'S CUSTOM REMODELING
T/A KITCHENS & MORE
1889 Hooper Avenue
Toms River, NJ 08753

Totowa

REMY'S KITCHEN & BATH
STUDIO
394 Union Boulevard
Totowa, NJ 07512

Trenton

BOB LANG INCORPORATED
1842 S Broad Street
Trenton, NJ 08610

CAMELOT KITCHENS
1589 Reed Road
Trenton, NJ 08628

HAMILTON KITCHENS
4441 Nottingham Way
Hamiliton Square
Trenton, NJ 08690

HAMILTON SUPPLY
COMPANY INC
PO Box 3005
65 Klockner Road
Trenton, NJ 08619

KITCHEN QUEST INCORPORATED
1453 Kuser Road
Trenton, NJ 08619

VERNON'S PENN SUPPLY INC
514 Hamilton Avenue
Trenton, NJ 08609

Union

G R BYRON PLUMBING &
HEATING INC
1171 Jeanette Avenue
Union, NJ 07083

JAEGER LUMBER
2322 Morris Avenue
PO Box 126
Union, NJ 07083

MARVIC CORPORATION
5 Iorio Street
Union, NJ 07083

TOP NOTCH INC
1941 Arbor Lane
Union, NJ 07083

Vineland

B & F KITCHENS
270 N Orchard Road
Vineland, NJ 08360

REMODELING CONCEPTS
319 West Weymouth Road
Vineland, NJ 08360

Wall

DISTINCTIVE RENOVATIONS
INC
1700 Kings Court
Wall, NJ 07719

Warren

KING GEORGE PLUMBING
20 Mountain Boulevard
Warren, NJ 07059

SUPERIOR CUSTOM
KITCHENS
126 Mount Bethel Road
Warren, NJ 07060

Washington

SCHNEIDER'S KITCHENS INC
426 Rt 31 N
Washington, NJ 07882

Wayne

AMERICAN CYANAMID
One Cyanamid Plaza
Wayne, NJ 07470

DOLAN & TRAYNOR
32 Riverview Drive
PO Box 487
Wayne, NJ 07474

West Brunswick

HOME DEPOT #5998
Corporate Road
West Brunswick, NJ 08902

West Caldwell

CARL SCHAEDEL &
COMPANY INC
11 Paton Drive
West Caldwell, NJ 07006

West Orange

ROHL CORPORATION KWC
FAUCETS
454 Prospect Avenue
243
West Orange, NJ 07052-4103

SMALLBONE INC
3 Bradford Avenue
West Orange, NJ 07052-3914

West Paterson

CASTRUCCI CABINET
17 Pompton Avenue
West Paterson, NJ 07424

CENTURY SHOWER DOOR
INC
10 Andrews Drive
West Paterson, NJ 07424

Westcreek

TAYLOR MADE CABINETS
145 Division Street
Westcreek, NJ 08092

Westmont

HADDON TOWNE DESIGN
CENTER
112 Haddon Avenue
Westmont, NJ 08108

Whippany

ARROW CRAFTS INC
71 Route 10
Whippany, NJ 07981

SCHLEIFER CONST INC
20 North Jefferson Road
Whippany, NJ 07981

Windsor

FORM TOPS LAMINATORS
Route 130 Box 389
Windsor, NJ 08561

Wyckoff

A & B KITCHENS & BATHS
INC
279 Franklin Avenue
Wyckoff, NJ 07481

DUSCHQUEEN INC
40 Lawlins Park
Wyckoff, NJ 07481

FARNAN ASSOCIATES
552 Fairmont Road
Wyckoff, NJ 07481

MCCANN'S HOME
IMPROVEMENT
338 Calvin Court
Wyckoff, NJ 07481

THE HAMMER & NAIL
INCORPORATION
232 Madison Avenue
Wyckoff, NJ 07481

NEW MEXICO

Albuquerque

AMERICAN BATH
REMODELING
1540 Juan Tabo NE
Albuquerque, NM 87112

CREATIVE KITCHENS INC
7923 Menaul NE
Albuquerque, NM 87110

DESIGN PROFESSIONALS K &
B CENTER
1309 San Mateo N E
Albuquerque, NM 87110

Belen

AVONITE INC
5100 West Goldleaf Circle
1945 So Highway 304
Belen, NM 87002

Roswell

BUSH WOODWORKS AND
APPLIANCE INC
111 West Country Club Road
Roswell, NM 88201

Santa Fe

CASEWORKS
231 Las Mananitas
Santa Fe, NM 87501

CREATIVE KITCHENS
1209 Cerrillos Road
Santa Fe, NM 87501

KITCHENS FOR LIVING INC
RR #10 Box 91 MLM
Santa Fe, NM 87501

PITTMAN BROTHERS
WOODWORKS
1241 Siler Road
Santa Fe, NM 87501

NEW YORK

Adams

LUNMAN FURNITURE &
APPLIANCE CENTER
70 North Main Street
Adams, NY 13605

Albany

KITCHEN & BATH WORLD
INC
345 New Karner Road
Albany, NY 12205

MARCO'S SHOWCASE
1814 Central Avenue
Albany, NY 12205

MILLWORK SPECIALTIES INC
45 Learned Street
Albany, NY 12207

NATIONAL KITCHENS &
BATHS
476 Central Avenue
Albany, NY 12206

NATIONAL SUPPLY
CORPORATION
476 Central Avenue
Albany, NY 12206

Armonk

IEA INTERNATIONAL INC
5 Hunter Drive
Armonk, NY 10504

Astoria

EURO CONCEPTS LTD
27-50 1st Street #3Floor
Astoria, NY 11102-5020

THE KITCHEN STORE INC
42-16 28th Avenue
Astoria, NY 11103

Auburn

QUIG ENTERPRISES
COMPLETE HOME CENTER
RD 6 Mutton Hill Road
Auburn, NY 13021

Baldwin

BALDWIN SALES CORPORATION
795 Merrick Road
Baldwin, NY 11510

Ballston Spa

CURTIS LUMBER COMPANY
885 Route 67
Ballston Spa, NY 12020-3604

Batavia

GIAMBRONE APPLIANCE
SALES
634 E Main Street
Batavia, NY 14020

Bayshore

ELJAY KITCHEN REMODELING
CORPORATION
1365 Gardiner Drive
Bayshore, NY 11706

HOME DEPOT #1211
Sunrise Highway
Bayshore, NY 11706

Bayside

KITCHEN AND BATHROOM
BY DAVIDSON AND son
214-26 41st Avenue
Bayside, NY 11361

Beacon

UNICO INC
PO Box 850
Beacon, NY 12508

Bedford Hills

DESIGNER KITCHENS BY
PAMELA INC
61 Adams Street
Bedford Hills, NY 10507

WESTCHESTER ARCHITECHT
WOODWORKING Inc
385 Adams Street
Bedford Hills, NY 10507

Bedrord Hills

BEDFORD HILLS SUPPLY INC
332 Adams Street
PO Box 499
Bedrord Hills, NY 10507

Bellmore

WYMAN BUILDING
INDUSTRIES INC
1786 Newbirdge Road
Bellmore, NY 11710

Bellport

SIGNATURE KITCHENS AND
BATHS LTD
143 Main Street
PO Box 82
Bellport, NY 11713

Binghamton

COMPETITION KITCHENS &
BATHS
19 S Washington Street
Binghamton, NY 13905

CREATIVE KITCHENS &
BATHS
331 Main Street
Binghamton, NY 13905

HERB SPACH INC
101 Broad Avenue
Binghamton, NY 13904

MCGOWAN CORPORATION
368 Kattelville Road R D #9
Box 1
Binghamton, NY 13901

Brainardsville

PERRY'S
Route 374
PO Box 8
Brainardsville, NY 12915

Brewster

DILLS BEST BUILDING
CENTER
2 All View Avenue
Brewster, NY 10519

Bridgehampton

BENCHMARK INC
Snake Hollow Road
PO Box 1252
Bridgehampton, NY 11932

Bronx

GRANITES OF ITALY
3451 De Lavall Avenue
Bronx, NY 10475

KITCHEN SOLUTIONS
1086 East Gun Hill Road
Bronx, NY 10469

KOSTER & EVANS
INDUSTRIES INC
2235 Light Street
Bronx, NY 10466

Brooklyn

CARDINAL KITCHENS INC
410 4th Avenue
Brooklyn, NY 11215

COUNTERTOPS INC
2125 Utica Avenue
Brooklyn, NY 11234

FAMCO DISTRIBUTORS INC
166 58th Street
Brooklyn, NY 11220

FOCAL POINT HARDWARD
INC
1950 Coney Island Avenue
Brooklyn, NY 11223

G P A CONTRACTING
CORPORATION
1301 E 57th Street
Brooklyn, NY 11234

GOLD & REISS CORPORATION
312 McDonald Avenue
Brooklyn, NY 11218

LAMINATORS SUPPLY
CORPORATION
6303 Fifth Avenue
Brooklyn, NY 11220

METRO KITCHENS
5407 Foster Avenue
Brooklyn, NY 11234

RAY BARRY & SONS INC
2184 McDonald Avenue
Brooklyn, NY 11223

REGAL KITCHENS & BATHS
INC
966 Mc Donald Avenue
Brooklyn, NY 11230

REGENCY KITCHENS INC
4204-14 Avenue
Brooklyn, NY 11219

SARAH JUNIK
1705 President Street
Brooklyn, NY 11213

TIVOLI TILE & MARBLE
COMPANY INC
883 65th Street
Brooklyn, NY 11220

Buffalo

KEN TON FABRICATORS INC
2505 Main Street
Buffalo, NY 14214

Carle Place

EURO KITCHEN PLUS
222 Glen Cove Road
Carle Place, NY 11514

Carmel

ALPINE KITCHENS INC
220 Brewster Avenue
Route 6
Carmel, NY 10512

Carthage

FARNEY'S INC HOME &
BUILDING CENTER
Deer River Road
PO Box 189
Carthage, NY 13619

Centereach

THERESE MARCEL'S INC
1456 Middle Country Road
Centereach, NY 11720

Central Valley

BHK OF AMERICA
3 Bond Street
PO Box 37
Central Valley, NY 10917

Claverack

THE COOK'S CORNER
Old Lane
Box 200
Claverack, NY 12513

Clifton Park

JOMAR KITCHENS
NORTHEAST WINDOWS
1483 Route 9
Clifton Park, NY 12065

Cohoes

CLOUSER SALES INC
15 Green Mountain Drive
Cohoes, NY 12047

College Point

TRAULSEN & COMPANY INC
114-02 15th Avenue
PO Box 169
College Point, NY 11356

Commack

CONSUMERS WAREHOUSE
CENTER INC
258 Commack Road
Commack, NY 11725

HOME DEPOT 1202
Jericho Turnpike
Commack, NY 11725

MICA ELEGANCE
196 Commack Road
Commack, NY 11725

Congers

RALPH WILSON PLASTICS
COMPANY WILSONART
1 Brenner Drive
Congers, NY 10920

Copiague

CONSUMERS WAREHOUSE
CENTER INC
1250 Sunrise Highway
Copiague, NY 11726

THE BATH FACTORY
1270 Sunrise Highway
Copiague, NY 11726

Corning

ADAMYS INC
PO Box 59
Corning, NY 14830

SULLIVAN KITCHEN & BATH
64 Denison Parkway E
PO Box 378
Corning, NY 14830

THE CORNING BUILDING
COMPANY INC
CBC Plaza Park Avenue
Corning, NY 14830

Cortland

BUILDERS BEST HOME
IMPROVEMENT CENTER
3798 Luker Road
Cortland, NY 13045

ITHACA KITCHEN & BATH
DESIGN CENTER INC
4078 Quail Ridge
Cortland, NY 13045-9113

Deer Park

BROOK INDUSTRIES INC
20 Evergreen
Deer Park, NY 11729

TRIAD COUNTER
CORPORATION
301 Suburban Avenue
Deer Park, NY 11729

E Meadow

KITCHENS UNIQUE BY DELF
482 E Meadow Avenue
E Meadow, NY 11554

East Farmingdale

CAPUANO HOME APPLIANCE
SALES INC
215 A Central Avnue
East Farmingdale, NY 11735

PORCELANOSA VENIS TILE
1970 New Highway
East Farmingdale, NY 11735

East Hampton

RIVERHEAD BUILDING
SUPPLY
15 Railroad Avenue
East Hampton, NY 11937

East Meadow

CONSUMERS WAREHOUSE
CENTER INC
2280 Hempstead Turnpike
East Meadow, NY 11554

HOME DEPOT #1201
Hempstead Turnpike
East Meadow, NY 11554

JARRO BUILDING
INDUSTRIES CORPORATIO
1796 Hempstead Turnpike
East Meadow, NY 11554

East Meadows

ALURE HOME IMPROVEMENTS
1999 Hempstead Turnpike
East Meadows, NY 11554

Elmira

KITCHEN & BATH GALLERY
1055 Walnut Street
Elmira, NY 14905

ROBINSON BUILDING
MATERIALS INC
PO Box 325
Elmira, NY 14902-0325

Elmont

FIORANO CERAMIC TILE
1400 Hempstead Turnpike
Elmont, NY 11003

HOME DEPOT #1208
Hempstead Turnpike
Elmont, NY 11003

Endwell

M & M KITCHEN & BATH
2906 E Main Street
Endwell, NY 13760

Farmingdale

HOME DEPOT #1203
Willow Park Court
Farmingdale, NY 11735

M & N SUPPLY CORPORATION
30 Allen Boulevard
Farmingdale, NY 11735

R PRATO CUSTOM
CARPENTRY & CONSTRUCTION
99 Milbar Boulevard
Farmingdale, NY 11735

REMODELING BY ARTHUR W
LEE LTD
35 Central Drive
Farmingdale, NY 11735

Floral Park

WINDHAM INTERIORS
146 Jericho Turnpike
Floral Park, NY 11001-2006

Flushing

ATLANTIS KITCHEN & HOME
IMPROVEMENT CENTER
40-37 162nd Street
Flushing, NY 11358

HOME IDEAL INC
171 10 39 Avenue
Flushing, NY 11358

Forest Hills

GLENDALE KITCHENS &
BATHS LTD
99-12 Metropolitan Avenue
Forest Hills, NY 11375

Franklin Square

BATHROOMS & KITCHENS BY
ROYAL
958 Hempstead Turnpike
Franklin Square, NY 11010

CONSUMERS WAREHOUSE
CENTER INC
600 Franklin Avenue
Franklin Square, NY 11010

Fredonia

PATTON ELECTRIC
COMPANY
10378 Bennett Road
Fredonia, NY 14063

THE GALLERY
112 W Main Street
Fredonia, NY 14063

Freeport

HOME DEPOT #1206
East Sunrise Highway
Freeport, NY 11520

KITCHEN EXCELLENCE INC
27A West Merrick Road
Freeport, NY 11520

Fresh Meadows

GMJ MAINTENANCE MAGIC
75-11 194th Street
Fresh Meadows, NY 11366

Fulton

JOICE & BURCH
2 West First Street North
Fulton, NY 13069

Garden City

HERBERT P BISULK INC,
KITCHEN OF DISTINCTION
BY MONTE
295 Nassau Boulevard South
Garden City, NY 11530

Garden City Park

GLOBE COVELL
2310 Jericho Turnpike
Garden City Park, NY 11040

Geneva

L A JOHNSON'S KITCHENS &
BATHS
PO Box 129
Route 5 & 20
Geneva, NY 14456

TIMBERLINE ELECTRIC
1902 Route 14 N
Geneva, NY 14456

Glendale

FREDERICK HOME
REMODELING CORPORATION
79-49 Myrtle Avenue.
Glendale, NY 11385

MECHANICS BUILDING
MATERIALS
82-40 73rd Avenue
Glendale, NY 11385

Glens Falls

KITCHEN & BATH
CREATIONS OF BRIAN R
MEURS INC
PO Box 3206
Glens Falls, NY 12801

Goshen

MASTERWORK KITCHES
134 West Main Street
Goshen, NY 10924

Granite Springs

JILCO WINDOW CORPORATION
PO Box 1 Mahopac Avenue
Granite Springs, NY 10527

Great Neck

D & M KITCHENS INC
400 Great Neck Road
Great Neck, NY 11021

KOLSON INC
653 Middle Neck Road
Great Neck, NY 11023

Hauppauge

UNITED CERAMIC TILE
923 Motor Parkway
Hauppauge, NY 11788

Hawthorne

BERGER APPLIANCE INC
PO Box 202
Hawthorne, NY 10532

Henrietta

CAVE'S CABINETRY
CONCEPTS
3081 E Henrietta Road
PO Box 268
Henrietta, NY 14467

Hewlett

DON RODGERS INTERIORS
INC
1159 Broadway
Hewlett, NY 11557

KITCHEN WORKS
1157A Broadway
Hewlett, NY 11557-2321

Hicksville

IKEA U.S. INC.
1100 Broadway Mall
Hicksville, NY 11801

Holbrook

CONSUMERS WAREHOUSE
CENTER INC
717 Broadway Avenue
Holbrook, NY 11741

JOHN ANIUNES CONTRACTING
DISTINCTIVE GRANITE &
MARBLE
331 C Eante Court
Holbrook, NY 11714

Hornell

MAIN PLUMBING HEATING
KITCHENS INC
299 Main Street
Hornell, NY 14843

Huntington

ALAMODE DESIGN
CONCEPTS INC
595 W Jericho Turnpike
Huntington, NY 11743-6362

C.H. JONES Fine Kitchen and
Bath Cabinetry
220 East Main Street
Huntington, NY 11743

CARL R SALMINEN AIA &
ASSOCIATES
29 Young's Hill Road
Huntington, NY 11743

CUSTOM CONCEPTS INC
741-A W Jericho Turnpike
Huntington, NY 11743

EURO CONCEPTS OF
HUNTINGTON LTD
1802 E Jericho Turnpike
Huntington, NY 11743

YANKEE WOODCRAFT INC
160 E Main Street
Huntington, NY 11743

Huntington Station

ARTHUR CHRISTENSEN INC-
CHRISTENSEN'S
545 East Jericho Turnpike
Huntington Station, NY 11746

ARTISTA KITCHEN DESIGNS
206 W Jericho Turnpike
Huntington Station, NY 11746

HUNTINGTON KITCHEN AND
BATH INC
673 E Jericho Turnpike
Huntington Station, NY 11746

Hyde Park

BERTO KITCHEN CABINETS
INC
503 Violet Avenue
Hyde Park, NY 12538

Inwood

EMERSON BUILDERS
131 Doughty Boulevard
Inwood, NY 11696

Island Park

SPECIALTY WOOD AND
MICA CORPORATION
4032 Austin Boulevard
Island Park, NY 11558

Islip

KINGSLEY DISTRIBUTORS
INC
374 Islip Avenue #102
Islip, NY 11751

Islip Terrace

CANDLELIGHT KITCHENS
INC
68 Cedarhusrst Street
Islip Terrace, NY 11752

Ithaca

CAYUGA LUMBER INC
801 W State Street
Ithaca, NY 14850

Jackson Heights

CRS DESIGNS INC
3107 80th Street
Jackson Heights, NY 11370

Jay

WARD LUMBER COMPANY
INC
PO Box 154
Glen Road
Jay, NY 12941

Johnson City

VALLEY CRAFTS INC
753 Harry L Drive
PO Box 676
Johnson City, NY 13790

Kenmore

ORVILLE D WILSON INC
PLUMB & HEATING
845 Englewood Avenue
Kenmore, NY 14223

Lake Placid

HUNTER DESIGNS INC
Cascade Road
PO Box 244
Lake Placid, NY 12946

Lake Success

GOLDMAN ASSOCIATES OF
NEW YORK INC
2323 New Hyde Park Road
Lake Success, NY 11042

Larchmont

LAWRENCE R LOFFREDO
INC
2406 Boston Post Rd
Larchmont, NY 10538-3403

S&C MURPHY CONTRACTORS
INC
19 Revere Road
Larchmont, NY 10538

Latham

GREENS APPLIANCES INC
428 Old Niskayuna Road
Latham, NY 12110

JADE HOUSING CORPORATION
755 Troy Schenectady Road
Latham, NY 12110

SPINDLE CITY DISTRIBUTORS
INC
154 Sicker Road
Latham, NY 12110

Lewiston

HAMILTON PORCELAINS LTD
PO Box 1178
Lewiston, NY 14092

KEN WOODBURN INC
PO Box 643
467 Dutton Drive
Lewiston, NY 14092

Lindenhurst

LAKEVILLE INDUSTRIES INC
100 S Smith Street
Lindenhurst, NY 11757

Liverpool

C & R SUPPLY INC
4483 Buckley Road W
PO Box 2700
Liverpool, NY 13089

MIDSTATE WHOLESALE
CORPORATION
Morgan Place
PO Box 97
Liverpool, NY 13088

Lockport

L J FAERY CUSTOM KITCHEN
& BATH
6620 Lincoln Avenue
Lockport, NY 14094

Long Island City

DI FIORE & SONS CUSTOM
WOODWORKING
42 02 Astoria Boulevard
Long Island City, NY 11103

Mamaronack

REMODELING CONSUL.OF
W'CHESTER INC
545 Fenimore Road
Mamaronack, NY 10543

Mamaroneck

BILOTTA HOME CENTER INC
564 Mamaroneck Avenue
Mamaroneck, NY 10543

FUHRMANN KITCHENS
253 Halstead Avenue
Mamaroneck, NY 10543

WATERCROSS
930 Mamaroneck Avenue
Mamaroneck, NY 10543

Manlius

R E COOPER BUILDING
SPECIALTIES
320 Fayette
PO Box 402
Manlius, NY 13104

Massapequa

KITCHENS BY MR D INC
4163 Merrick Road
Massapequa, NY 11758

PARK PLACE RENOVATIONS
INC
115 Hunter Ridge Road
Massapequa, NY 11758

Massapequa Park

ALADDIN REMODELERS INC
5020 Sunrise Highway
Massapequa Park, NY 11762

Medford

CREATIVE CABINET
CORPORATION OF AMERICA
3731 Horseblock Road
Medford, NY 11763

Merrick

CREATIVE KITCHENS &
BATHS INC
1829 Merrick Avenue
Merrick, NY 11566

Middletown

KITCHENS BY MC CAREY
531 N Street
Middletown, NY 10940

ROWLEY KITCHEN SALES
INC
87 Wisner Avenue
Middletown, NY 10940

Mineola

J R ASSOCIATES
80 2nd Street
Mineola, NY 11501

MERILLON BATH AND
KITCHEN CENTER
550 Jericho Turnpike
Mineola, NY 11501

Mohegan Lake

HOME DESIGNS INC
3766 Briar Hill Street
Mohegan Lake, NY 10547

Montgomery

BRESCIA LUMBER
CORPORATION
DRte 278 & County 99
PO Box 278
Montgomery, NY 12549

Monticello

BOGNER SEITEL LUMBER
COMPANY
76 Saint John Street
PO Box 598
Monticello, NY 12701

Mount Kisco

BEDFORD TILE CORPORATION
510 Lexington Avenue
Mount Kisco, NY 10549

CREATIVE CARPENTRY OF
WESTCHESTER
24 Seth Canyon Drive
Mount Kisco, NY 10549

Mount Morris

MOUNT MORRIS KITCHEN
CENTER
86 Main Street
Mount Morris, NY 14510

Mount Vernon

NU WAY DISTRIBUTING
CORPORATION
210 W Lincoln Avenue
Mount Vernon, NY 10550

WESTCHESTER MARBLE &
GRANITE
31 Warren Place
Mount Vernon, NY 10550

N Bangor

DWYERS HOME IMPROVEMENT
CENTER INC
PO Box 308 Depot Street
N Bangor, NY 12966

Nanuet

NEW ENGLAND REMODELING
CENTER INC
224 S Middle Town Road
Nanuet, NY 10954

Nassau

MILLBROOK CUSTOM
KITCHENS INC
Route 20
Nassau, NY 12123

New Hartford

CHARM KITCHENS BY
SPETTS
Seneca Turnpike
Route 5
New Hartford, NY 13413

NEW HARTFORD PLUMBING
SUPPLY CORP
1103 Commercial Drive
New Hartford, NY 13413

THE WATERWORKS
190 Seneca Turnpike
PO Box 775
New Hartford, NY 13413

New Hyde Park

KITCHEN DESIGNS BY KEN
KELLY INC
2115 Hillside Avenue
New Hyde Park, NY 11040

New Rochelle

RIEMER KITCHENS INC
1327 N Avenue
New Rochelle, NY 10804

New York

ALLIED BRASS MANUFACTURING
COMPANY
149 Wooster Street
New York, NY 10012

BETTER HOMES & GARDENS
SPECIAL INTEREST
PUBLICATION
750 Third Avenue
New York, NY 10017

BUILDING DETAILS
131 Varick Street
New York, NY 10013

CAPITAL KITCHEN CABINET
& DOOR MANUF
14-25 128th Street
College Point
New York, NY 11356

CLEAVES DESIGN
258 Broadway
New York, NY 10007

DECORATING REMODELING
110 Fifth Avenue
New York, NY 10011

ELGOT KITCHENS
937 Lexington Avenue
New York, NY 10021

HASTINGS KITCHEN STUDIO
230 Park Avenue S
New York, NY 10003

JUPITER AFFILIATES LTD
90 Riverside Drive
New York, NY 10024

KITCHEN & BATH BUSINESS
1515 Broadway
New York, NY 10036

KRAFT
306 E 61St Street
New York, NY 10021

LEESAM KITCHEN & BATH
124 7th Avenue
New York, NY 10011

MCGRAW-HILL INC.
1221 Avenue of the Americas
New York, NY 10020

NEMO TILE COMPANY INC
48 E 21 Street
New York, NY 10010

QUINTESSENTIALS
525 Amsterdam Avenue
New York, NY 10024

SAINT CHARLES KITCHENS
OF NEW YORK
150 E 58th Street
New York, NY 10155

T O GRONLUND COMPANY
INC
200 Lexington Avenue
New York, NY 10016

THE KITCHEN & BATH
EXPERTS
473 Amsterdam Avenue
New York, NY 10024

TOWN EAST KITCHEN LTD
DIVISION UNIVERSITY STOVE
COMPANY
225 E 120th Street
New York, NY 10035

North Bayshore

CONTRACTORS KITCHEN
NETWORK
570 Pine Aire Drive
North Bayshore, NY 11706

North Lindenhurst

SELECT BUILDING
910 North Wellwood Avenue
North Lindenhurst, NY 11757

North Syracuse

COUNTRY GENTLEMEN
KITCHEN & BATH CENTER
720 North Main Street
North Syracuse, NY 13212

North Tarrytown

SLEEPY HOLLOW CUSTOM
KITCHENS
42 River Street
North Tarrytown, NY 10591

Northport

BRUCE CABINET
350 A Woodbine Avenue
Northport, NY 11768

SUSAN SERRA ASSOCIATES
INC
15 Starlit Drive
Northport, NY 11768

Norwich

KUNTRISET KITCHENS
Road 2 Box 254
Norwich, NY 13815

Nunda

MODERN HOME CENTER
10 South State Street
PO Box 395
Nunda, NY 14517

Oakdale

NOR'EAST ASSOCIATES
32 Wood Lawn Avenue
Oakdale, NY 11769

Oneonta

DR FRANCES H GAILEY
46 Woodside Avenue
Oneonta, NY 13820

PICKETT BUILDING
MATERIAL
RD 2 Box 2066
Oneonta, NY 13820

Ossining

CREATIVE DESIGNS
34 State Street
Ossining, NY 10562

Oyster Bay

BAY WOODCRAFT INC
85 Pine Hollow Road
Oyster Bay, NY 11771

Patchogue

HOME DEPOT 1205
Sunrise Highway
Patchogue, NY 11772

Peekskill

ULTIMATE DESIGN
CONCEPTS
Crompond Road
Peekskill, NY 10566

Pelham

T J QUATRONI PLUMBING &
HEATING
231 Sixth Avenue
Pelham, NY 10803

Plainview

KITCHEN & BATH
MARKETING
5 Bentley Road
Plainview, NY 11803

LONG ISLAND BATH
WHOLESALERS INC
105 Newtown Road
Plainview, NY 11803

Plattsburgh

E J MONROE
Boynton Avenue
PO Box 847
Plattsburgh, NY 12901

GREGORY SUPPLY
COMPANY INC
PO Box 70
Tom Miller Road
Plattsburgh, NY 12901

Pleasantville

ALPINE CONTRACTING
COMPANY INC
79 Grandview Avenue
Pleasantville, NY 10570

ARNOLD WILE & ASSOCIATES
34 Marble Avenue
Pleasantville, NY 10570

Port Jefferson

CUSTOM CABINETS BY K & I
INC
617-2 Bicycle Path
Port Jefferson, NY 11776

JOHN FRANCIS ASSOCIATES
LTD
524 Jefferson Shopping Plaza
Port Jefferson, NY 11776

Port Jervis

SMITH KITCHEN & BATH
GALLERY
66 Jersey Avenue
Port Jervis, NY 12771

Port Washington

LEE NAJMAN DESIGNS INC
55 Channel Drive
Port Washington, NY 11050

Potsdam

D L THOMAS KITCHENS &
BATHS
Outer Market Street
PO Box 5046
Potsdam, NY 13676

Poughkeepsie

BLAUVELT BROTHERS
FLOOR COVERING &
INTERIORS
360 New Hackensack Road
Poughkeepsie, NY 12603

J F BAHRENBURG INC
35 Manchester Circle
Poughkeepsie, NY 12603

PACE GENERAL CONTRACTING
INC
6 Raymond Avenue
Poughkeepsie, NY 12603

Queens Village

JAC WOODWORKING
235-07 Braddock Avenue
Queens Village, NY 11428

Queensbury

KAIDAS KITCHENS & BATHS
45 Quaker Road
Queensbury, NY 12804

Red Hook

KITCHEN KREATIONS
23 S Broadway
Red Hook, NY 12571

Rego Park

KITCHEN & BATH WORLD
62-43A Woodhaven Boulevard
Rego Park, NY 11374

LINGOLD DESIGN &
CONSTRUCTION CORP
63-76 Woodhaven Boulevard
Rego Park, NY 11374

Rhinebeck

WILLIAMS LUMBER
Route 9 N
PO Box 31
Rhinebeck, NY 12572

Riverhead

CABINETS PLUS
1086 Route 58
Riverhead, NY 11901

RIVERHEAD BUILDING
SUPPLY CORPORATE
CABINET SHOWCASE
1295 Pulaski Street
Riverhead, NY 11901

Rochester

BLOCH INDUSTRIES INC
140 Commerce Drive
Rochester, NY 14623

CHASE PITKIN
3131 Winton Road S
Rochester, NY 14623

E T DONOHUE & SONS INC
1621 Jefferson Road
PO Box 23628
Rochester, NY 14692

MCKENNA'S ROCHESTER
KITCHEN & BATH CENTER
3401 Winton Road
Rochester, NY 14623

SLOAN & COMPANY INC
350 Metro Park
Rochester, NY 14623

Rockville Center

WINDSOR CONTRACTING
CORPORATION
125 Merrick Road
Rockville Center, NY 11570

Rocky Point

DON HICKS WOODCRAFTER
12 Walnut Road
Rocky Point, NY 11778

Rome

GENERAL LUMBER &
HARDWARE
529 Erie Boulevard West
Rome, NY 13440

Ronkonkoma

RICHARD POST INC
701 Koehler Ave #4
Ronkonkoma, NY 11779-7403

TITONE MARBLE WORKS INC
1735 Feuereisen Avenue
Ronkonkoma, NY 11779

Roslyn

BRANDT WOODCRAFT OF
ROSLYN INC
18 Lumber Road
Roslyn, NY 11576

CLASSIC KITCHEN & BATH
CENTER LTD
1062 Northern Boulevard

Roslyn, NY 11576

S Fallsburg

KAPLAN CABINET COMPANY
221 Main Street
PO Box 804
S Fallsburg, NY 12779

Saint James

NORTH COUNTRY KITCHEN
& BATH INC
437 N Country Road
Saint James, NY 11780

Saratoga Spring

ALLERDICE BUILDING
SUPPLY
Division & Wallworth Street
Saratoga Spring, NY 12866

CAPITOL DISTRICT SUPPLY
208 Washington Street
Saratoga Spring, NY 12866

KITCHEN DIMENSIONS
2 Franklin Square
Saratoga Spring, NY 12866

Saugerties

HICKORY MEADOWS
CUSTOM KITCHENS
83 Lauren Tice Road
Saugerties, NY 12477

Sayville

UNITED MARBLE & MICA
LTD
98 Lincoln Avenue
PO Box 366
Sayville, NY 11782

Scarsdale

GARTH CUSTOM KITCHENS
INC
24 Garth Road
Scarsdale, NY 10583

Schenectady

AMERICAN WOODWORK
THE YANKEE BUILDER INC
1702 Chrisler Avenue
Schenectady, NY 12303

BELLVUE BUILDERS SUPPLY
500 Duanesburg Road
Schenectady, NY 12306

MARCO SUPPLY COMPANY
INC
315 Green Street
Schenectady, NY 12305

YOUR KITCHEN & BATH INC
2245 Central Avenue
Schenectady, NY 12304

Scotia

CENTRAL PLUMBING &
HEATTIN SUPPLY COMAPNY
INC
141 Freemans Bridge Road
Scotia, NY 12302

HOMECREST KITCHENS INC
110 Freemans Br Road
Scotia, NY 12302

JAHODA'S CABINET CORNER
443 Saratoga Road
Scotia, NY 12302

Seaford

SCOTTO-BRENNAN
ASSOCIATES LTD
3900 Sunrise Highway
Seaford, NY 11783

Selden

HOME DEPOT #1209
Independance Plaza
Selden, NY 11784

Selkirk

C L HUMMEL CONSTRUCTION
INC
RD #2 Box 196
Selkirk, NY 12158

Sidney

SIDNEY APPLIANCE &
MODERN KITCHENS INC
PO Box 2115
Sidney, NY 13838-2115

Slingerlands

COVENTRY CONSTRUCTION
INC
PO Box 88
1572 New Scotland Road
Slingerlands, NY 12159

Smithtown

GALLO KITCHENS INC
116 W Main Street
Smithtown, NY 11787

Southampton

E T CABINET CORP
106 Mariner Drive
Southampton, NY 11968

SOUTHAMPTON LUMBER
CORP
25 Powell Avenue
Southampton, NY 11968

Specerport

PA FLORAMO'S HOME
IMPROVEMENT SHOWCASE
42 Nichols Street
Specerport, NY 14559

Spring Creek

SEPCO INDUSTRIES
491 Wortman Avenue
Spring Creek, NY 11208

Spring Valley

THE PLUMBING STORE INC
10 E Route 59
Spring Valley, NY 10977

Staten Island

ANDERSON KITCHENS
77 Lincoln Avenue
Staten Island, NY 10306

BUSHNELL'S KITCHENS INC
4707 Arthur Kill Road
Staten Island, NY 10309

COPPOLA ENTERPRISES INC
53 New Dorp Plaza
Staten Island, NY 10306

DESIGN STUDIO
1572 Richmond Road
Staten Island, NY 10304

ISLAND KITCHENS INC
1198 Hylan Boulevard
Staten Island, NY 10305

NEW YORK KITCHEN DESIGN
INC
1076 Bay Street Avenue
Staten Island, NY 10304

Syosset

BATH IMAGES
345 Jericho Turnpike
Syosset, NY 11719

Syracuse

BENJAMEN CRANE
831 W Fayette Street
PO Box 1032
Syracuse, NY 13201

BUSCH PRODUCTS
2083 Park Street
Syracuse, NY 13208

DISTINCTIVE INTERIORS
5891 Firestone Drive
Syracuse, NY 13206

G B STRINGER INC
400 Lodi Street
Syracuse, NY 13203

MKS INDUSTRIES INC
5801 Court Street Road
PO Box 4948
Syracuse, NY 13221

Tarrytown

ZAMBELLETTI'S CUSTOM
KITS & BATHS
92 Central Avenue
Tarrytown, NY 10591

Ticonderoga

NOR'EAST ASSOCIATES
332 The Portage
Ticonderoga, NY 12883

Tonawanda

WEINHEIMERS INC
1888 Niagara Falls Boulevard
Tonawanda, NY 14150

Utica

TRI TEMP REFRIGERATION
EQUIPMENT COMPANY
PO Box 4158
Utica, NY 13504-4158

Valatie

DIECKELMANN HOME
CENTER
Rt 9
Valatie, NY 12184

Valley Stream

BRUCE PLUMBING SUPPLY
650 W Merrick Road
Valley Stream, NY 11580

Victor

DAVID K SMITH ASSOCIATES
6796 Spring Creek Drive
Victor, NY 14564

Vista

RING'S END INC
386 Smith Ridge Road
Route 123
Vista, NY 10590

Voorheesville

CLASSIC RENOVATIONS
45 Maple Avenue
Voorheesville, NY 12186

Wantagh

BLACKMAN HOFFMAN
COMPANY WANTAGH INC
3480 Sunrise Highway
Wantagh, NY 11793

EDGAR SABBETH PLYWOOD
CORPORATION
PO Box 109
Wantagh, NY 11793

GOLD COAST KITCHENS &
BATHS INC
3004 Merrick Road
Wantagh, NY 11793

Wappinger Falls

EMPIRE KITCHEN &
WOODWORKING INC
862 South Road
Wappinger Falls, NY 12590

Warwick

BATHS, KITCHENS & BEYOND
INC
13 Main Street
Warwick, NY 10990

Watertown

MACAR'S
161 Coleman Avenue
Watertown, NY 13601

Waverly

RYNONE KITCHEN & BATH
410 Spaulding Street
Waverly, NY 14892

Webster

KITCHEN & BATH
EXPRESSIONS BY GARY
LARZZARO
1175 Ridge Road
Webster, NY 14580

West Hempstead

ARTISAN CUSTOM
INTERIORS
163 Hempstead Turnpike
West Hempstead, NY 11552

MARCEL'S CUSTOM
KITCHENS & BATHS INC
507 Chestnut Street
West Hempstead, NY 11552

Westbury

LONG ISLAND FABRICATIONS
60 Brooklyn Avenue
Westbury, NY 11590

Westhampton Beach

SHEAHAN PUBLICATIONS INC
Suffolk County Airport
Westhampton Beach, NY 11978

White Plains

MAJESTIC KITCHENS
530 Tarrytown Road
White Plains, NY 10607

Yonkers

QUAKER MAID KITCHENS BY CENTRAL INC
1880 Central Park Avenue
Yonkers, NY 10710

SCHOTT AMERICA GLASS & SCIENTIFIC PR
3 Odell Plaza
Yonkers, NY 10701

Yorktown

BEST PLUMBING SUPPLY INC BUILDING DESIGN CENTER
33331 Crompond Road
Yorktown, NY 10598

Yorktown Heights

YORKTOWN INTERIOR WOODWORKING
1776 Front Street
Yorktown Heights, NY 10598

NORTH CAROLINA

Angier

TIMBERLYNE CABINET COMPANY INC
Rt 4 Box 437 B
Angier, NC 27501

Apex

BEAUTIFUL BATHZ INC
299 North Salem Street
Apex, NC 27502

Asheville

BALLARD APPLIANCE AND CABINET CO INC
1238 Hendersonville Road
Asheville, NC 28803

COOPER HOUSE INC
479 Hendersonville Road
Asheville, NC 28803

NOVA KITCHEN & BATH
1257 Sweeten Creek Road
PO Box 5594
Asheville, NC 28813

Carrboro

FOREST HILL ASSOCIATES
409 E Main Street
Carrboro, NC 27510

Cashiers

HENSON CABINET & WOODWORKING SHOP
Highway 64 E PO Box 163
Cashiers, NC 28717

Charlotte

AMERICAN KITCHENS INC CABINETRY & DESIGN
1123 McAlway Road
Charlotte, NC 28211

BATH STYLE/USCO INC.
2215 Crown Centre Drive
Charlotte, NC 28227

CLASSIC DOORS & KITCHENS
9315 Monroe Road Suite E
Charlotte, NC 28270

CRAFTMASTER KITCHEN AND BATH
PO Box 241491
Charlotte, NC 28224

DEPOT DISTRIBUTORS OF THE SE INC
1132 Pro Am Drive
PO Box 220590
Charlotte, NC 28211

HETTICH AMERICA
PO Box 7664
Charlotte, NC 28241

INTERSTATE KITCHEN & BATH INC
8200 South Boulevard
Charlotte, NC 28273

KITCHENS UNLIMITED INC
1820 S Boulevard
Suite 200
Charlotte, NC 28203

PEERLESS INC
PO Box 668845
Charlotte, NC 28266-8845

THE MARBLE & STONE SHOP INC
PO Box 32773
1001 West Morehead Street
Charlotte, NC 28208

Cherokee

BROBEN ENTERPRISES
PO Box 1108
Cherokee, NC 28719

Cornelius

SOLID SURFACES PRODUCTS
PO Box 1461
Cornelius, NC 28031

Davidson

INTERNATIONAL KITCHEN & BATH INC
18835 B Statesville Road
Davidson, NC 28036

Durham

ACME PLUMB & HEAT COMPANY OF DURHAM INC
PO Box 2288
636 Foster Street
Durham, NC 27702

KITCHENS ET CETERA INC
2514 University Drive
Durham, NC 27707

LE MEYERS BUILDERS
4528 Hillsborough Road
Durham, NC 27705

THE KITCHEN SPECIALIST
3407 University Drive
Durham, NC 27707

Elizabeth City

CARTER'S CABINETS
1219 Little River Drive
Elizabeth City, NC 27909

Fayetteville

CAPE FEAR SUPPLY
645 S Reilly Road
PO Box 40408
Fayetteville, NC 28309

Greensboro

DESIGNER CABINETS
2505 Carroll Street #C
Greensboro, NC 27408

HATCH CABINET DESIGNS
4604 West Market Street
Greensboro, NC 27407

OLD MASTER KIT BURLINGTON DIST CO IN
1401 W Lee Street
Greensboro, NC 27403

Greenville

EAST CAROLINA UNIVERSITY
School Of Human Environmental Science
Greenville, NC 27858

Hickory

PIEDMONT DESIGNS OF HICKORY
2250 Highway 70 South East
Suite 458
Hickory, NC 28602

High Point

MARSH FURNITURE COMPANY
PO Box 870
High Point, NC 27261

OMEGA STUDIOS INC
PO Box 780
High Point, NC 27261

SNOW LUMBER COMPANY INC
PO Box 530
High Point, NC 27261

Jacksonville

KITCHENS BY DESIGN INC
825 Gum Branch Road
Suite 109
Jacksonville, NC 28540

Kernersville

GRASS AMERICA INC
1202 Highway 66 South
Kernersville, NC 27284

Kitty Hawk

COZY HOME CUSTOM CABINETS INC
921 Kitty Hawk Road
Kitty Hawk, NC 27949

Mooresville

CARTER COMPANIES
PO Box 980
Mooresville, NC 28115

New Bern

KITCHEN ART INC
1907 S Glenburnie Road
PO Box 12882
New Bern, NC 28561-2882

P & F CABINETS
Route 1
Box 200C
New Bern, NC 28560

Pinehurst

KITCHEN & BATH SHOWPLACE
PO Box 3880
Pinehurst, NC 28374

Pineville

HOME DEPOT #3601
Centrum Parkway
Pineville, NC 28134

Raleigh

BUILDER PRODUCTS INC
814 Semart Drive
Raleigh, NC 27604

HAMPTON KITCHENS OF RALEIGH
1505 Downtown Boulevard
Raleigh, NC 27603

KITCHEN FACERS KLASSIC KITCHENS
3518 B Wade Avenue
Raleigh, NC 27607

TRIANGLE DESIGN KITCHENS INC
5216 Holly Ridge Drive
Raleigh, NC 27612

Salisbury

GOLD STANDARD KITCHENS & BATHS
228 S Main Street
Salisbury, NC 28144

Shelby

IRON WIND CORPORATION
1414 Chatfield Road
Shelby, NC 28150

Southern Pines

SANDAVIS CUSTOM
KITCHENS
515 F Midland Road
PO Box 1100
Southern Pines, NC 28387

Swansboro

NATIONAL MARBLE
PRODUCTS
PO Box 33
120 Leslie Lane
Swansboro, NC 28485

Wilmington

CREATIVE KITCHEN & BATH
DESIGNS
1717 N 23rd Street
Wilmington, NC 28405

SUPERIOR MILLWORK INC
615 S 17th Street
Wilmington, NC 28401

THE BECKER BUILDERS
SUPPLY COMPANY
PO Box 1697
Wilmington, NC 28405

Winston Salem

AMARR CABINETS
1001 N Liberty
Winston Salem, NC 27101

GREAT KITCHENS AND
BATHS
8001 A North Point Boulevard
Winston Salem, NC 27106

NORTH DAKOTA

Bismarck

CUSTOM WOODWORKING
1535 Park Avenue
Bismarck, ND 58504

Fargo

BACHMAN INC
360 36th Street S
Fargo, ND 58103

BRAATEN CABINETS INC
PO Box 249
Fargo, ND 58107-0249

Minot

GREAT PLAINS SUPPLY
PO Box 1781
Minot, ND 58702

Wahpeton

KITCHENS UNLIMITED
PO Box 903
Wahpeton, ND 58074

PRIME WOOD INC
2217 N 9th Street
Wahpeton, ND 58075

OHIO

Akron

ACCENT SHOWROOM-
DESIGN CENTER
1495 South Main Street
Akron, OH 44301

BUILDER'S KITCHENS
1095 Home Avenue
Akron, OH 44310

LUMBERJACK'S INC
723 E Tallmadge Avenue
Akron, OH 44310

WATERLOO HOME SUPPLY
869 W Waterloo Road
Akron, OH 44314

Alliance

ROBERTSON HEATING
SUPPLY
500 W Main Street
PO Box 2448
Alliance, OH 44601

Barberton

C C SUPPLY
250 S Van Buren Avenue
Barberton, OH 44203

Bay Village

HERON BAY LIMITED INC
660 Dover Center Road
Bay Village, OH 44140

Beachwood

PURDY'S DESIGN STUDIO
2101 Richmond Road
Beachwood, OH 44122

RADIO DISTRIBUTING
COMPANY
23800 Commerce Park Road
Suite G
Beachwood, OH 44122

Bedford Heights

SOMRAK KITCHENS INC
26201 Richmond Road
Bedford Heights, OH 44146

Brecksville

D A BRANCH INC
8921 Brecksville Road
Brecksville, OH 44141

Canfield

KITCHEN & BATH WORLD
INC
Route 224
Canfield, OH 44406

Canton

COUNTER POINT DISTRIBUTOR
1205 5th Street S W
Canton, OH 44702

Chagrin Falls

STONE GATE ASSOCIATES
INC
7181 Chagrin Road
Chagrin Falls, OH 44023

Chardon

RESIDENCE ARTISTS INC
220 Fifth Avenue
Chardon, OH 44024

THE KITCHEN COMPANY
695 South Street
Chardon, OH 44024

Chesterland

FINESSE KITCHEN & BATH
SPECIALISTS
12539 Harold Drive
Chesterland, OH 44026

Cincinnati

BONA DECORATIVE
HARDWARE
3073 Madison Road
Cincinnati, OH 45209

CABINETRY CONCEPTS &
DESIGNS INC
10793 Fallsington Court
Cincinnati, OH 45242

CITY-WIDE KITCHENS &
BATHS
6706 Montgomery Road
Cincinnati, OH 45236

DAYTON SHOWCASE
COMPANY CINCINNATI
10915 Reading Road
Cincinnati, OH 45241

DOMA DESIGNS INC
3573 Bayard Drive
Cincinnati, OH 45208

DRACKETT DESIGNS INC
4905 Burley Hills Drive
Cincinnati, OH 45243

ESQUIRE KITCHEN
SPECIALISTS
2280 Quebec Road
Cincinnati, OH 45214

FORMICA CORPORATION
10155 Reading Road
Cincinnati, OH 45241

FORMICA CORPORATION
10155 Reading Road
Cincinnati, OH 45241

HOME DIMENSIONS INC
4862 Business Center Way
Cincinnati, OH 45246

INTERNATIONAL KITCHEN &
BATH STUDIO
430 Reading Road
Cincinnati, OH 45202

JOHN TISDEL DISTRIBUTING
INC
6995 E Kemper Road
Cincinnati, OH 45249

KEMPER DESIGN CENTER
3200 East Kemper Road
Cincinnati, OH 45241

KITCHEN CONCEPTS INC
6026 Ridge Avenue
Cincinnati, OH 45213

MIAMI CAREY/NUTONE INC
Madison and Redbank Roads
PO Box 275010
Cincinnati, OH 45227

MOELLERING INDUSTRIES
1213 West York Street
Cincinnati, OH 45214

NUTONE INC
Madison & Red Bank Roads
Cincinnati, OH 45227

OHIO VALLEY SUPPLY
COMPANY INC
3512 Spring Grove Avenue
Cincinnati, OH 45223

SIMS LOHMAN CABINET
COMPANY
4333 Mayhew Avenue
Cincinnati, OH 45238

STANLEY DOE KITCHENS &
BATHS INC
5200 Beechmont Avenue
Cincinnati, OH 45230

THE DEVINE COMPANY
6916 Plainfield Road
Cincinnati, OH 45236

VALLEY FLOOR COVERING
BATH KIT SPEC
401 W Wyoming Avenue
Cincinnati, OH 45215

WESTERN HOME CENTER
INC
7600 Colerain Avenue
Cincinnati, OH 45239

Cleveland

ARTISAN CUSTOM-MAID INC.
3321 W 140th Street
Cleveland, OH 44111

BREITS INC
5218 Detroit Avenue
Cleveland, OH 44102

BUILDING WORKS &
COMPANY INCORPORATION
3540 Ridge Road
Cleveland, OH 44109

CENTERIOR ENGERY
PO Box 5000
Room 832
Cleveland, OH 44101

DECORATIVE HARDWARE &
BATH COMPANY
27900 Chagrin Boulevard
Cleveland, OH 44122

EXPOSITIONS INC
Edgewater Branch
PO Box 550
Cleveland, OH 44107-0550

FOREST CITY BABIN
5111 Richmond Road
Cleveland, OH 44146

GENERAL BUILDING
PRODUCT CORPORATION
1281 E 38th Street
Cleveland, OH 44114

MAYFAIR GRANITE
COMPANY INC
4202 Myafield Road
Cleveland, OH 44121

RA MUNSON & ASSOCIATES
INC
21877 Euclid Avenue
Cleveland, OH 44117

SEARS HIPS #4784
6950 W 130th Street
Cleveland, OH 44130

THE BATH SHOWPLACE BY
REX PIPE & SUPPLY
10311 Berea Road
Cleveland, OH 44102

THE EAST OHIO GAS
COMPANY
1201 E 55th Street
Cleveland, OH 44103

WELKER MC KEE SUPPLY
6606 Granger Road
Cleveland, OH 44131

Cleveland Heights

NATIONAL KITCHENS &
BATHS
3962 Mayfield Road
Cleveland Heights, OH 44121

Columbia Station

CHIPPEWA MARBLE
COMPANY INC
27500 Royalton Road
PO Box 965
Columbia Station, OH 44028

Columbus

BIG 8 CO'S INC
2900 Ole Country Lane
Columbus, OH 43219

BUILDER APPLIANCE SUPPLY
INC
39 S Yearling Road
Columbus, OH 43227

CABINET WAREHOUSE INC
2988 East 5th Avenue
Columbus, OH 43219

CARR SUPPLY
280 Fletcher Street
Columbus, OH 43215

CHESTER A SMITH INC
1330 Norton Avenue
Columbus, OH 43212

DAVE FOX CONTRACTING
INC
1151 Bethel Road
Columbus, OH 43220

EASTWAY SUPPLIES
1561 Alum Creek Drive
Columbus, OH 43209

ELLIS KITCHEN & BATH
STUDIO
477 S Front Street
Columbus, OH 43215

EUREKA INC
5156 Sinclair Road
Columbus, OH 43229

HAMILTON PARKER
COMPANY
165 West Vine Street
Columbus, OH 43215

HAYWARD INC
909 W Fifth Avenue
Columbus, OH 43212

HERITAGE MARBLE OF OHIO
INC
7086 Huntley Road
Columbus, OH 43229

JAE COMPANY
955 W Fifth Avenue
Columbus, OH 43212

KITCHEN KRAFT INC
999 Goodale Boulevard
Columbus, OH 43212-3888

LONDON KITCHENS
1065 Dublin Road
Columbus, OH 43215

MASTER WOODWORKS
KITCHEN STUDIO
6323 Busch Boulevard
Columbus, OH 43229

OHIO VALLEY SUPPLY
COMPANY
850 Distribution Drive
Columbus, OH 43228

PALMER-DONAVIN
MANUFACTURING
1200 Steelwood Road
Columbus, OH 43212-1372

PIONEER PLASTICS
CORPORATION
1662 Williams Road
Columbus, OH 43207

R J LANDIS DESIGN &
CONSTURCTION
5027 Avalon Avenue
Columbus, OH 43229

RALPH WILSON PLASTICS
COMPANY (WILSONART)
2500 International Street
Columbus, OH 43228

ROOT REMODELERS
640 N Hague
Columbus, OH 43204

SCIOTO KITCHEN SALES INC
3232 Allegheny Avenue
Columbus, OH 43209

SURFACE STYLE AN EPRO
COMPANY
650 High Street
Columbus, OH 43215

SWAN MANUFACTURING
COMPANY
65 Kingston Avenue
Columbus, OH 43207

THE BATH & BRASS
EMPORIUM
683 E Lincoln Avenue
Columbus, OH 43229

WESTWATER SUPPLY
CORPORATION
PO Box 24127
2945 Silver Drive
Columbus, OH 43224-0127

WORLY PLUMBING SUPPLY
INC
503 S Front Street
Columbus, OH 43215

WRIGHT CONSTRUCTION
COMPANY
3001 Asbury Drive
Columbus, OH 43221

Dayton

A BETTER KITCHEN SUPPLY
3810 Dayton Xenia Road
Dayton, OH 45432

DAYTON SHOWCASE
COMPANY
2601 W Dorothy Lane
Dayton, OH 45439

DESIGN PRO REMODELING,
INC.
214/216 N Springboro Pike
Dayton, OH 45449

SHAWNEE SUPPLY
INCORPORATION
43 Pierce Avenue
Dayton, OH 45449

SUPPLY ONE CORPORATION
210 Wayne Avenue
PO Box 636
Dayton, OH 45401

THE KITCHEN SHOPPE INC
5575 Far Hills Avenue
Dayton, OH 45429

Dublin

CABINETRY BY DESIGN
5813 Springburn Drive
Dublin, OH 43017-8731

East Liverpool

BIRCH SUPPLY COMPANY
INC
16477 Saint Clair Avenue
PO Box 9000
East Liverpool, OH 43920

Elyria

MOEN INCORPORATED
377 Woodland Avenue
Elyria, OH 44036

Fairfield

FLAGG INC
9195 Seward Road
Fairfield, OH 45236

Findlay

CAVINS KITCHEN VILLAGE
215 S Main Street
Findlay, OH 45840

Fort Recovery

HOME IDEA CENTER
111 W Butler
Fort Recovery, OH 45846

Garfield Heights

BUILDERS WORLD INC
4918 NEO Parkway
Garfield Heights, OH 44128

Girard

USA INDUSTRIES INC
115 West Broadway
Girard, OH 44420

Hartville

SCHUMACHER LUMBER
COMPANY
120 Mill Street
Hartville, OH 44632

Huron

FIRELANDS KITCHEN
COMPANY INC
PO Box 66
607 Main Street
Huron, OH 44839

Kettering

A D KISTLER KITCHEN&
BATH SPECIALIST
4638 Wilmington Pike
Kettering, OH 45440

Killbuck

WILSON CABINET COMPANY
INC
Straits Industrial Park
PO Box 305
Killbuck, OH 44637

La Grange

VIRGIL'S KITCHENS INC
100 Public Square
PO Box 625
La Grange, OH 44050

Lakewood

IMPERIAL HOME CENTER
INC
16000 Madison Avenue
Lakewood, OH 44107

Lancaster

DICK PAULUS CUSTOM
BUILDER
1241 Rainbow Drive NW
Lancaster, OH 43130

KARSHNER SALES INC
735 N Slocum
Lancaster, OH 43130

Lima

LIMA BUILDING PRODUCTS
INC
P O Box 1846
227 S Main Street
Lima, OH 45802

Loveland

SPECIALTY CABINETS
COMPANY INC
900 Loveland-Madeira Road
Loveland, OH 45140

Lyndhurst

GEROMES KITCHEN & BATH
5540 Mayfield Road
Lyndhurst, OH 44124

Mantua

76 SUPPLY COMPANY INC
3384 Sr 82
Mantua, OH 44255

Maple Heights

LAMINATED CONCEPTS INC
14300 Industrial Avenue N
Maple Heights, OH 44137

Marion

NU SUPPLY INC
1585 Harding Highway E
Marion, OH 43302

Mayfield Heights

BUILDERS WORLD INC
5885 Mayfield Road
Mayfield Heights, OH 44124

CABINET EN-COUNTERS INC
6265 Mayfield Road
Mayfield Heights, OH 44124

Mentor

FASHION TREND KITCHENS
AND BATHS
7507 Tyler Boulevard
Mentor, OH 44060

MENTOR LUMBER COMPANY
7180 N Center Street
Mentor, OH 44060

MIKE ROSS CONSTRUCTION
INC
9309 Mercantile Drive
Mentor, OH 44060

TRIDELTA INDUSTRIES INC
7350 Corporate Boulevard
Mentor, OH 44060

Middlefield

KRAFTMAID CABINETRY INC
PO Box 1055
Middlefield, OH 44062

Millersburg

ARTWOOD PRODUCTS INC
PO Box 289 CR 407
Millersburg, OH 44654

Mount Vernon

MICHAEL'S WOODWORKS
10015 Bishop Road
Mount Vernon, OH 43050

New Knoxville

HOGE LUMBER COMPANY
PO Box 159
New Knoxville, OH 45871

North Canton

HOME CONCEPTS INC
543 N Main
North Canton, OH 44720

North Olmsted

BUILDERS WORLD INC
24355-57 Lorain Road
North Olmsted, OH 44070

North Ridgeville

BLANCHETTE'S A UNIQUE
KITCHEN & BATH CONCEPT
9425 Avon Beldon Road SR 83
North Ridgeville, OH 44039

Parma Heights

LITT'S PLUMBING KITCHEN
& BATH GALLERY
6510 Pearl Road
Parma Heights, OH 44130

Piqua

HAMPSHIRE COMPANY
PO Box 1195
Piqua, OH 45356

Plain City

THE MILLER CABINET
COMPANY INC
6217 Converse Huff Road
Plain City, OH 43064

Poland

E H DUNCAN THE BATH &
KITCHEN CENTER
108 S Main Street
Poland, OH 44514

Port Clinton

THE CATAWBA COMPANY
5065 Sloan Street
Port Clinton, OH 43452

Reynoldsburg

STOUT SALES INC
6320 E Main Street
Reynoldsburg, OH 43068

Richfield

LINDA WANCATA
5074 Tall Timbers Drive
Richfield, OH 44286

Rocky River

REYMAR SYSTEMS
COMPANY
1150 Linda Street
Rocky River, OH 44116

Rushsylvania

BAYLISS BUILDERS
3500 State Route 274 East
Rushsylvania, OH 43347

Salem

R H HOMEWORKS INC
850 W State Street
Salem, OH 44460

Seville

4-B WOOD SPECIALTIES INC
5125 Greenwich Road
Seville, OH 44273

C C SUPPLY
5129 Greenwich Road
Seville, OH 44273

Steubenville

C B JOHNSON INC
621 Market Street
Steubenville, OH 43952

Streetsboro

SEENO ASSOCIATES
MARKETING INC
8990 State Route 14
Streetsboro, OH 44241

Tiffin

BUCKEYE PANEL PLY INC
2525 W Street Route 18 Box P
Tiffin, OH 44883

Toledo

ADVANCE KITCHEN & BATH
DESIGN
3520 Heatherdowns Boulevard
Suite 1
Toledo, OH 43614

DAVID HAHN FINE
KITCHENS
5345 Heatherdowns Boulevard
Toledo, OH 43614

KITCHEN DESIGN PLUS
5250 Renwyck Drive
Toledo, OH 43615

KITCHENS BY JEROME INC
2138 N Reynolds Road
Toledo, OH 43615

LAGRANGE BUILDERS
SUPPLY INC
702 W Laskey Road
Toledo, OH 43612

LUMA BUILDING PRODUCTS
1607 Coining Drive
Toledo, OH 43612

MAINLINE KITCHEN & BATH
DESIGN CENTER
4730 W Bancroft Street
Toledo, OH 43615

RAM MARKETING
5250 Renwyck Drive #C
Toledo, OH 43615

SUPERIOR KITCHEN
DISTRIBUTORS
6540 W Central Avenue
Toledo, OH 43615

VOLMAR'S KITCHEN & BATH
CENTER
45 W Alexis Road
Toledo, OH 43612

Uniontown

HOSTETLERS CUSTOM
KITCHENS
10233 Cleveland Avenue
Uniontown, OH 44685

Valley View

TREVARROW INC TOP
BRANDS DIVISION
8555 Sweet Valley Drive
Valley View, OH 44125-4211

Van Wert

KITCHENS INC
10098 W Ridge Road
Van Wert, OH 45891

Wadsworth

STEWART CABINET SALES
140 W Walnut Street
PO Box 110
Wadsworth, OH 44281

Warren

MODERN HOME KITCHEN &
BATH CENTER INC
1002 W Market Street
Warren, OH 44481

Warrensville Heights

DANIELS DISTRIBUTION INC
4346 Cranwood Parkway
Warrensville Heights, OH 44128

Waverly

MILL'S PRIDE
423 Hopewell Road
Waverly, OH 45690

Westerville

DESIGNER KITCHENS &
BATHS INC
9020 Columbus Pike
US Route 23 N
Westerville, OH 43081

E & E REMODELERS
3318 Reno Road
Westerville, OH 43081

JOHN MICHOLOK
5611 Longrifle Road
Westerville, OH 43081

Westville

FLEETWOOD CUSTOM
COUNTERTOPS INC
5901 Chandler Court
Westville, OH 43081

Willoughby Hills

FARALLI'S KITCHEN & BATH
DESIGN STUDIO
2804 S O M Center Road
Willoughby Hills, OH 44094

Wooster

HORST CABINET & HOME
CENTER
840 E Milltown Road
Wooster, OH 44691

Worthington

MEBCO
6296 Proprietors Road
Worthington, OH 43085

Youngstown

DON WALTER KITCHEN
DISTRIBUTORS INC
260 Victoria Road
Youngstown, OH 44515

DORRANCE SUPPLY
COMPANY
1140-44 Hubbard Road
Youngstown, OH 44505

Zanesville

ZANESVILLE FABRICATORS
73 Shawnee Avenue
PO Box 1816
Zanesville, OH 43702-1816

OKLAHOMA

Bartlesville

JIM'S CUSTOM KITCHENS
720 NE Washington Boulevard
Bartlesville, OK 74006

Claremore

PIXLEY LUMBER COMPANY
715 West Will Rogers Boulevard
Box 308
Claremore, OK 74018

Lawton

ANDERSON FLETCHER
LIVINGSTON SUPPLY
COMPANY
602 Wallock
Lawton, OK 73501

Oklahoma City

CLASSIC KITCHENS
548 E Memorial Road
Oklahoma City, OK 73114

DESIGNER HARDWARE INC
430 W Wilshire Boulevard
PO Box 14240 73116
Oklahoma City, OK 73113

I T S COMPANY LTD
PO Box 18387
908 NW 71st Street
Oklahoma City, OK 73154

KITCHEN SHOWCASE &
DESIGN CENTER
2761 N Country Club
Oklahoma City, OK 73116

Tulsa

JAY RAMBO COMPANY
8401 E 41st Street
Tulsa, OK 74145

KITCHEN KORNER INC
1001 S Main
Tulsa, OK 74119

OKLAHOMA NATURAL GAS
COMPANY
100 W Fifth Street
Box 871
Tulsa, OK 74102

OREGON

Beaverton

NEIL KELLY DESIGNERS
REMODELERS
8101 S W Numbus Building 11
Beaverton, OR 97005

Bend

KITCHEN CONCEPTS
447 NE Greenwood Avenue
Bend, OR 97701

Boring

PLYMART INC
PO Box 127
Boring, OR 97009

Central Point

THE KITCHEN AND BATH
CENTER
359 S Front
PO Box 3441
Central Point, OR 97502

Corvallis

OREGON STATE UNIV-
APPAREL INT HOUSE
Milam Hall - 224
Corvallis, OR 97331-5101

STEVEN S RICHTER CUSTOM
BUILDER INC
795 SW Hanson Street
Corvallis, OR 97333

Eugene

THE NEW KITCHEN
2817 Oak
Eugene, OR 97405

Hermiston

WINDOWS WALLS &
INTERIORS
256 E Hurlburt Suite 103
Hermiston, OR 97838

Hillsboro

DIAMOND CABINET DIVISION
WHITE CONSOL INDUSTRIAL
600 S W Walnut Street
Hillsboro, OR 97123

Milwaukie

DICK BALLARD REMODELING
11923 SE McLoughlin Boulevard
Milwaukie, OR 97222

Portland

ANN SACHS TILE
500 NW 23rd Avenue
Portland, OR 92710

BASCO
2012 NW Vaughn
Portland, OR 97209

BASSIST COLLEGE
2000 S W 5th
Portland, OR 97201

GEORGE A MORLAN
PLUMBING COMPANY
5529 S E Foster Road
Portland, OR 97206

HALLBERG REMODELING
COMPANY
1710 N E 82nd Avenue
Portland, OR 97220

J GREB & SON INC
5027 N E 42nd Avenue
Portland, OR 97218

NEIL KELLY DESIGNERS
REMODELERS
804 N Alberta
Portland, OR 97217

THE KITCHEN BROKER EAST
3354 S E Powell Boulevard
Portland, OR 97202

THE KITCHEN BROKER WEST
8685 S W Canyon Road
Portland, OR 97225

TILE DISTRIBUTORS
3002 N Wygant
Portland, OR 97217

Salem

CHEMEKETA COMMUNITY
COLLEGE
PO Box 14007
Salem, OR 97309-7070

DIAMOND CAB DIV OF
WHITE CONSOL IND
4897 Indian School Road N E
Salem, OR 97305

SCHULER CORPORATION
560 21st Street SE
PO Box 12245
Salem, OR 97309

Tigard

TOTAL BUILDING PRODUCTS
INC
PO Box 23337
Tigard, OR 97223

PENNSYLVANIA

Adamstown

MARTIN CUSTOM KITCHENS
PO Box 567
Adamstown, PA 19501

Aliquippa

CABINET WAREHOUSE
214 Pleasant Drive
Aliquippa, PA 15001

Allentown

BATHS WITH CLASS INC
3101 Berger Street
Allentown, PA 18103

BELL SUPPLY
1439 Fairmont Street
Allentown, PA 18102

FRANK BIELEN
324 Tamarack Drive
Allentown, PA 18104

KITCHENS BY DESIGN INC
1802 Allen Street
Allentown, PA 18104

KITCHENS BY WIELAND INC
4210 Tilghman Street
Allentown, PA 18104

KNAUSS WOODWORKING
814 N Gilmore Street
Allentown, PA 18103

QUAKER MAID KITCHENS OF
ALLENTOWN
665 Union Boulevard
Allentown, PA 18103

Ambridge

DELUCA CABINET SHOP
998 Merchant Street
Ambridge, PA 15003

Annville

COLONIAL CRAFT KITCHENS
INC
344 W Main Street
Annville, PA 17003

Archbald

THE KITCHEN SHOPPE,
APPLIANCE CENTER LTD
Kennedy Plaza 4 Kelly Avenue
Archbald, PA 18403

Avonmore

DOVERSPIKE CUSTOM
KITCHEN
RD #1
Avonmore, PA 15618

Baden

BERTUS-ARTMAN
ASSOCIATES
224 Bradford Park Road
Baden, PA 15005

Bala Cynwyd

DESIGN MANIFEST INC
5 Maple Avenue
Bala Cynwyd, PA 19004

MOSER CORPORATION
129 Montgomery Avenue
Bala Cynwyd, PA 19004

Bally

LONGACRE ELECTRICAL
SERVICE INC
602 Main Street
PO Box 159
Bally, PA 19503

Beaver Falls

KITCHEN CITY
415 7th Avenue
Beaver Falls, PA 15010

Bensalem

ROBERN INC
1648 Winchester Road
Bensalem, PA 19020

Bentleyville

SAN DELL KITCHENS INC
PO Box 613
Bentleyville, PA 15314

Beth Ayres

A A PERRY & SONS INC
2528 Huntingdon Pike
Beth Ayres, PA 19006

Bethel Park

BROOKSIDE LUMBER AND
SUPPLY COMPANY
500 Logan Road
PO Box 327
Bethel Park, PA 15102

CLARK CONSTRUCTION
COMPANY
3180 Industrial Boulevard
Bethel Park, PA 15102

Bethlehem

OBERHOLTZER KITCHENS
77 W Broad Street #1
Bethlehem, PA 18018

PHILIP J STOFANAK INC
176 Nazareth Pike
Bethlehem, PA 18017

Bloomsburg

BOB JOHNSON COMPANY
1611 New Berwick Highway
Bloomsburg, PA 17815

Bristol

CAMEO KITCHENS
248 Mill Street
Bristol, PA 19007

DOMESTIC DESIGNS
2605 Durham Road
PO Box 702
Bristol, PA 19007

Broomall

MADSEN KITCHENS & BATHS
2901 Springfield Road
Broomall, PA 19008

Bryn Mawr

MAIN LINE CUSTOM
KITCHENS LTD
19 N Merion Avenue
Bryn Mawr, PA 19010

PETERSEN KITCHENS INC
592 Lancaster Avenue
Bryn Mawr, PA 19010

Buckingham

LIVING QUARTERS DESIGNS
INC
Routes 202 & 263
Buckingham Green POB 517
Buckingham, PA 18912

Camp Hill

LEGGETT INC
1989 Hummel Avenue
Camp Hill, PA 17011

Canonsburg

ROBERT JOHNSTON KITCHEN
& BATH
156 Morganza Road
Canonsburg, PA 15317-1719

Carlisle

CARLISLE KITCHEN CENTER
1034 Harrisburg Pike
Carlisle, PA 17013

HOME FASHION CENTER INC
1150 Walnut Bottom Road
Carlisle, PA 17013

Carnegie

DISTRIBUTOR SERVICE INC
1 Dorrington Road
Carnegie, PA 15106

PATETE KITCHENS & BATHS
1105 Washington Avenue
Carnegie, PA 15106

Centre Hall

ASSOCIATED WOODCRAFT
RD 2 Box 9
Centre Hall, PA 16828

Chambersburg

WADEL'S KITCHEN CENTER
1882 Wayne Road
Chambersburg, PA 17201

Chester

CHESTER WOODWORKING
INC
503 E 7th Street
Chester, PA 19013

JOSEPH STONG INC
742 W Front Street
Chester, PA 19013

Christiana

WINDING GLEN WOODCRAFT
INC
PO Box 40
28 South Bridge
Christiana, PA 17509

Clarks Summit

ABINGTON CABINETRY
Route 6 & 11
PO Box 101
Clarks Summit, PA 18411

Collingdale

FRANK'S CUSTOM CRAFT
INC
215-227 Clifton Avenue
Collingdale, PA 19023

Columbia

P N D DISTRIBUTORS INC
207 Chestnut Street
Columbia, PA 17512-1153

Conshohocken

TOWN & COUNTRY
KITCHENS & BATHS INC
123 West Ridge Pike
Po Box 309
Conshohocken, PA 19428

Corry

THE KITCHEN VILLAGE
12275 Route 6
Corry, PA 16407

Danville

C L SNYDER INC
800 Bloom Road
Danville, PA 17821

Darby

JOSEPH J KELSO & SONS INC
1300 Main Street
Darby, PA 19023

Derry

GEORGE BUSH KITCHEN
CENTER INC
1309 West 4th Avenue
Derry, PA 15627

Doylestown

HANKINS & ASSOCIATES
PO Box 113
Doylestown, PA 18901

SUPERIOR WOODCRAFT INC
CUSTOM KITCHEN
243 Harvey Avenue
Doylestown, PA 18901

UNIQUE KITCHENS & BATHS
1715 S Easton Road
Doylestown, PA 18901

Dresher

D L POST INC
1400 Candlebrook Drive
Dresher, PA 19025

Drexel Hill

REBER MC LEAN KITCHENS
4629 State Road
Drexel Hill, PA 19026

REGGIE'S CUSTOM
KITCHENS
3009 Garrett Road
Drexel Hill, PA 19026

REISEN SALES ASSOCIATES
465 Penn Avenue
PO Box 104848
Drexel Hill, PA 19026-1412

Dunmore

TECHNIQUES IN WOOD
419 S Blakely Street
Dunmore, PA 18512-2234

East Earl

CONESTOGA WOOD
SPECIALTIE INC
RD 2
PO Box 158
East Earl, PA 17519

Effort

EFFORT WOODCRAFT INC
Evergreen Hollow Road
PO Box 90
Effort, PA 18330

Eighty Four

84 LUMBER COMPANY
PO Box 8484
Eighty Four, PA 15384

Eighty-Four

ELISH & COMPANY INC
P O Box 4546 Route 519
Eighty-Four, PA 15330

Elizabethtown

MILL CREEK CABINETRY
19 W High Street
Elizabethtown, PA 17022

Ellwood City

DESIGNING INTERIORS
KITCHENS & BATH STUDIO
728 Lawrence Ave PO Box 810
Ellwood City, PA 16117

DOM'S HOME DESIGN
CENTER
739 Portersville Road
Ellwood City, PA 16117

Elysburg

KNOEBEL LUMBER-H H
KNOEBEL SONS INC
RD 1 Route 487
Elysburg, PA 17824

Ephrata

JEMSON CABINETRY INC
27 West Mohler Church Road
Ephrata, PA 17522

WICKES LUMBER COMPANY
82 Garden Spot Road
Ephrata, PA 17522

Erie

KITCHEN CONCEPTS BY
RICK CONSTANTINO
2402 State Street
Erie, PA 16503-1853

KITCHENS BY MEADE INC
2401 West 12th Street
Erie, PA 16505

ROBERTSON'S KITCHEN &
REMODELING SERVICE OF
ERIE
2630 W 12th Street
Box 8112
Erie, PA 16505

Fairless Hills

HERITAGE DISTRIBUTORS
INC CUSTOM KITCHENS &
BATHS
413 Andover Road
Fairless Hills, PA 19030

Feasterville

CENTURY PIONEER
DISTRIBUTORS INC
1707 Bustleton Pike
Feasterville, PA 19047

TED WEILER & SONS INC
90 Bustleton Pike
Feasterville, PA 19047

WEILER'S APPLIANCE &
KITCHEN CENTER
350 Bustleton Pike
Feasterville, PA 19053

Flourtown

OLDE TIME KITCHENS &
BATH RENOVATION
1411 Bethlehem Pike (Rear)
Flourtown, PA 19031

Folsom

CHARLES H GOEBEL AND
SONS INC
100 Sycamore Avenue
Folsom, PA 19033

Frazer

COVENTRY KITCHENS INC
490 Lancaster Avenue
Frazer, PA 19355

Fredonia

BUCHANAN KITCHEN &
BATH BOUTIQUE
109 Second Street
Fredonia, PA 16124

Glen Rock

HALF PRICE BUILDING
SUPPLY
240 Main Street
Glen Rock, PA 17327

Glenolden

JOHN MURPHY'S BATH &
KITCHENS
327 North Chester Pike
Glenolden, PA 19036

Glenside

GAVALA KITCHENS & BATHS
285 Keswick Avenue
Glenside, PA 19038

Goodville

RUTT CUSTOM CABINETRY
1564 Main Street
PO Box 129
Goodville, PA 17528

Greensburg

MANOR HOUSE KITCHENS
INC
589 Rugh Street
Greensburg, PA 15601

PETERSONS CUSTOM
KITCHENS & BATH
BOUTIQUE
503 New Alexandria Road
Route 119N
Greensburg, PA 15601

Grove City

STEIGERWALD'S DESIGN
CENTER
133 S Broad Street
Grove City, PA 16127

Gwynedd Valley

DOUGLAS A VOLK BUILDERS
INC
1407 Crestview Drive
Gwynedd Valley, PA 19437

Hamburg

ERNST KITCHEN CENTER
51 Primrose Street
Hamburg, PA 19526

Hanover

DEL WOOD KITCHENS INC
RD 10 Box 327
Hanover, PA 17331

Harleysville

I T LANDES & SONS
INCORPORATION
247 Main Street
Harleysville, PA 19438

Harrisburg

HARRISBURG ELECTRICAL
SUPPLIES COMPANY
806 S 28th Street
Harrisburg, PA 17111

SCHWALM & FASOLT INC
1649 Bobali Drive
Harrisburg, PA 17104

SEARS HIPS #4294
4600 Jonestown Road
Harrisburg, PA 17109

Hatboro

BONNIE LYNN INTERIORS
531 Warminster Road
Hatboro, PA 19040

Hatfield

ESTATE OF GEORGE S
SNYDER
1700 Hatfield Valley Road
PO Box 130
Hatfield, PA 19440

Havertown

DESIGN CONCEPTS PLUS
CORP
18 E Eagle Road
Havertown, PA 19083

Hermitage

BUD MILLER'S KITCHEN &
BATH DIST INC
3005 E State Street
Hermitage, PA 16148

Hollidaysburg

HOLIDAY KITCHEN & BATH
INC
737 Logan Boulevard
Hollidaysburg, PA 16648

Holmes

MURPHY PLUMBING &
HEATING INC
2357 MacDade Boulevard
Holmes, PA 19043

Honesdale

DESIGNER KITCHENS BY
NARROWSBURG LBR
RD 4 BOX 218
Honesdale, PA 18431

Huntingdon

ENDRES WOOD PLASTICS
INC
11th Susquehanna Avenue
Huntingdon, PA 16652

Jeannette

BACKUS CABINET COMPANY
INC
PO Box 570
Jeannette, PA 15644-0570

Jenkintown

CUSTER KITCHENS
204 Old York Road
Jenkintown, PA 19046

Kennett Square

KITCHENS ETC INC
714 E Baltimore Pike
Kennett Square, PA 19348

MC GRORY INC
PO Box 999
Kennett Square, PA 19348

King Of Prussia

QUEEN KITCHENS AND
BATHS
150 W DeKalb Pike
King Of Prussia, PA 19406

King of Prussia

THE CABINET WORKS
337 E De Kalb Pike
King of Prussia, PA 19406

Kintnersville

KITCHEN COMPLETE
Route 611 & Kintner Road
PO Box 94
Kintnersville, PA 18930

Kreamer

BATTRAM COMPANY
Rt 522 PO Box 582
Kreamer, PA 17833

CHARLES ASSOCIATES INC
Route 522
Kreamer, PA 17833

WOOD-MODE INC
#1 Second Street
Kreamer, PA 17833

Lancaster

ARMSTRONG WORLD
INDUSTRIES INC
PO Box 3001
Lancaster, PA 17604

BRUBAKER INC
1284 Rohrerstown Road
Lancaster, PA 17601

BRUBAKER KITCHENS INC
1121 Manheim Pike
Lancaster, PA 17601

FESSENDEN HALL OF
PENNSYLVANIA INC
3021 Industry Drive
Lancaster, PA 17603

Langhorne

SIEMATIC CORPORATION
886 Town Center Drive
Langhorne, PA 19047

Lansdale

AMERICAN OLEAN TILE
COMPANY
1000 Cannon Avenue
Lansdale, PA 19446

ATEC FABRICATORS
719 W Third Street
Lansdale, PA 19446

M W DONNELLY INC
37 W 2nd Street
Lansdale, PA 19446

Lansdowne

FERNWOOD KITCHENS INC
Baltimore & Union Avenues
Lansdowne, PA 19050

Latrobe

MCBROOM'S HOME CENTER
RD 5 Route 30 E
Latrobe, PA 15627

THREE
125 Hillview Avenue
Latrobe, PA 15650

Leesport

QUAKER MAID DIVISION OF
WCI INC
Route 61
Leesport, PA 19533

Lehigh Valley

MORRIS BLACK & SONS INC
984 Marcon Boulevard
PO Box 20570
Lehigh Valley, PA 18002

ROLAND & ROLAND INC
PO BOX 20344
900 13th Avenue
Lehigh Valley, PA 18002

Lemoyne

ED LANK KITCHENS INC
313 Market Street
Lemoyne, PA 17043

EXCEL INTERIOR CONCEPTS
CONSTRUCTION
570 S 3rd Street
Lemoyne, PA 17043

Levittown

MC HALES KBA
2450 Trenton Road
Levittown, PA 19056

Lionville

GENERAL ECOLOGY INC
151 Sheree Boulevard
Lionville, PA 19353

Lititz

MERLE ZIMMERMAN INC
723 Rothsville Road
Lititz, PA 17543

Littlestown

KITCHENS BY TED RON
1480 White Hall Road
Littlestown, PA 17340

Lock Haven

HW RAYMOND COMPANY
INC
111 Woodward Avenue
PO Box 395
Lock Haven, PA 17745

Lower Burrell

J & J WOOD PRODUCTS INC
102 Craigdell Road
Lower Burrell, PA 15068

Malvern

C I DUNCAN COMPANY
346 East King Street
Malvern, PA 19355

THE CREATIVE NOOK INC
MALVERN DESIGN CENTER
203 E King Street
Malvern, PA 19355

Mars

STIEHLER KITCHEN
CABINETS WINDOWS DOORS
PO Box 817
100 Irvine
Mars, PA 16046

Mc Murray

TOMORROW'S KITCHENS INC
1009 Waterdam Plaza Drive
Mc Murray, PA 15317

McAlisterville

PANNEBAKER CABINET
COMPANY
Box 250
McAlisterville, PA 17049

Mckeesport

LUCAS DISTRIBUTION INC
39 Olympia Shopping Center
Mckeesport, PA 15132-6115

Mechanicsburg

ADVANCED KITCHENS &
BATHS
522 Trindle Road
Mechanicsburg, PA 17055

MOTHER HUBBARD'S
KITCHEN CENTER
5309 E Trindle Road
Mechanicsburg, PA 17055

Media

THE KITCHEN PEOPLE OF
CH MARSHALL IN
PO Box 196
Media, PA 19063

Mifflinburg

C A SHIPTON INC
36 E Chestnut Street
Mifflinburg, PA 17844

Mifflintown

JUNIATA KITCHENS INC
18 N Main Street
PO Box #131
Mifflintown, PA 17059

Milford

JAMES LEIGHTY CONSTRUCTION
402 West Hartford Street
PO Box 222
Milford, PA 18337

Mill Hall

RENNINGER'S CLINTON
COUNTY CABINETRE
RD 1 Box 95E
Mill Hall, PA 17751

Milroy

GEORGE BERUBE
ASSOCIATES
Treaster Valley Run Road
PO Box 476
Milroy, PA 17063

MILROY WOOD PRODUCTS/A
WCI DIVISISON
Route 322
PO Box 367
Milroy, PA 17063

Milton

CLINGER LUMBER COMPANY
PO Box 315
Arch At Locust Street
Milton, PA 17847

Monaca

LUCCI KITCHEN CENTER
INC
1271 N Brodhead Road
Monaca, PA 15061

Mount Pleasant

VALLEY KITCHEN SALES &
SERVICE INC
555 Valley Lane
Mount Pleasant, PA 15666

Munhall

OMNI RENOVATION
114 East James Street
Munhall, PA 15120

Myerstown

BROCKLEHURST ENTERPRISES
334 Yeagley Road
Myerstown, PA 17067

Narvon

CONESTOGA VALLEY
CUSTOM KITCHENS INC
2042 Turkey Hill Road
Narvon, PA 17555

Nazareth

EAST LAWN SUPPLY
COMPANY INC
355 N New Street
Nazareth, PA 18064

New Britain

CANAAN CABINETRY
Route 202 Professional Center
Suite 104 B
New Britain, PA 18901

New Castle

UNIVERSAL RUNDLE CORP
217 North Mill Road
New Castle, PA 16103

New Holland

HERITAGE CUSTOM
KITCHENS
215 Diller Avenue
New Holland, PA 17557

HOMEWERKS
870 E Main Street
New Holland, PA 17557

QUALITY CUSTOM KITCHENS
125 Peters Road
PO Box 189
New Holland, PA 17557-0189

New Kensington

STYLE-RITE KITCHENS
1306 Greensburg Road
New Kensington, PA 15068

Newmanstown

KOUNTRY KRAFT KITCHENS
S Sheridan Street
Box 882 Rd 2
Newmanstown, PA 17073

North Huntingdon

CARUSO CABINET
MANUFACTURING INC
10809 Route 30
North Huntingdon, PA 15642

North Huntington

LAUREL KITCHENS
7740 Route 30
North Huntington, PA 15642

North Wales

FRANKE INC K S D
212 Church Road
North Wales, PA 19454

Oil City

VENANGO PLUMBING
HEATING SUPPLY COMPANY
PO Box 1168
Oil City, PA 16301

Olyphant

RIST CONST KITCHEN &
BATH DESIGN GALLERY
1505 E Lackawana Avenue
Olyphant, PA 18447

Ottsville

BAUMHAUER'S KITCHEN-
BATH DESIGN CTR
Route 611 at 412
PO Box 100
Ottsville, PA 18942

Oxford

MARTIN W SUMNER INC
121 S Third Street
Oxford, PA 19363

Palmyra

BARRY L EHRHART SR
421 E N Chestnut Street
Palmyra, PA 17078

Paradise

PARADISE CUSTOM
KITCHENS
3333 Lincoln Highway E
PO Box 278
Paradise, PA 17562

Parkesburg

LANTZ CUSTOM KITCHENS
Lincoln Highway West
RD 1 Box 337 E
Parkesburg, PA 19365

Peckville

VALLEY CABINET CENTER
505 3rd Street
Peckville, PA 18452

Petaluma

ANDREA CYPRESS
554 Laurel Street
Petaluma, PA 94952

Philadelphia

AMERICAN METAL
MOULDING CORPORATION
PO Box 29277-0977
Philadelphia, PA 19125

COGAN & GORDON INC
2200 N American Street
Philadelphia, PA 19133

EASTERN DISTRIBUTORS
COMPANY INC
34th Street & Indiana Avenue
Philadelphia, PA 19132

JOANNE HUDSON
ASSOCIATES LTD
2400 Market Street
Suite 310
Philadelphia, PA 19103

KULLA KITCHENS
7800 Rockwell Avenue
Philadelphia, PA 19111

MORTON BLOCK ASSOCIATES
DIVISION OF DESIGN
KITCHEN INC
2400 Market Street N S
Suite 205
Philadelphia, PA 19103

PEIRCE-PHELPS COMPANY
INC
2000 N 9th Street
Philadelphia, PA 19131

PENNYPACK SUPPLY
COMPANY INC
8030 Frankford Avenue
Philadelphia, PA 19136

PHILBERN DESIGNS
INCORPORATED
2302 The Rittenhouse
210 West Rittenhouse Square
Philadelphia, PA 19103

PLY GEMS KITCHEN AND
BATH CENTER
6948 Frankford Avenue
Philadelphia, PA 19135

RAIDER ASSOCIATES INC
843 Disston Street
Philadelphia, PA 19111

S S FRETZ JR INC
2001 Woodhaven Road
Philadelphia, PA 19116

Phoenixville

AKER CONTRACTORS INC
15 Benburb Road
Phoenixville, PA 19460

VALLEY FORGE KITCHEN &
BATH
1193 Valley Forge Road
Phoenixville, PA 19460

Pittsburgh

ANGELO ASSOCIATES INC
1125 Forest Way
Pittsburgh, PA 15236

BABCOCK LUMBER
COMPANY
2220 Palmer Street
Pittsburgh, PA 15218

BAXTER REMODELING
1345 Mc Laughlin Run Road
Pittsburgh, PA 15241

BENNETT SUPPLY COMPANY
INC
19th & Main Street
Pittsburgh, PA 15215

BILL GLIVIC KITCHENS
3845 Willow Avenue
Pittsburgh, PA 15234

CRESCENT SUPPLY OF
PENNSYLVANIA INC
6301 Butler Street
PO Box 40110
Pittsburgh, PA 15201

EXCEL KITCHEN CENTER
1800 Fifth Avenue
Pittsburgh, PA 15219

FRANKE'S CABINET SHOP
641 Butler Street
Pittsburgh, PA 15223

HOUSTON STARR COMPANY
300 Brushton Avenue
Pittsburgh, PA 15221

IKEA U.S. INC.
2001 Park Mannor Blvd.
Pittsburgh, PA 15205

JONES & BROWN INC
2515 Preble Avenue
PO Box 99969
Pittsburgh, PA 15233

KITCHEN & BATH CONCEPT
OF PITTSBURGH
7901 Perry Highway N
Pittsburgh, PA 15237

KITCHEN DESIGNS OF
PITTSBURGH
2260 Babcock Boulevard
Pittsburgh, PA 15237

KITCHEN WORKS
1002 Greentree Road
Pittsburgh, PA 15220

MARCUS KITCHENS INC
5954 Baum Boulevard
Pittsburgh, PA 15206

MASTERKRAFT KUSTOM
KITCHEN DIVISON
OF MASTERKRAFT
CONSTRUCTION
100 A Street
100 A Street
Pittsburgh, PA 15235

MORRISON KITCHEN & BATH
INC
5121 Clairton Boulevard
Pittsburgh, PA 15236

NICKLAS SUPPLY INC
1463 Glenn Avenue
Pittsburgh, PA 15116

STEIN'S CUSTOM KITCHENS
& BATHS
3559 Bigelow Boulevard
Pittsburgh, PA 15213

THE KITCHEN COMPANY
9421 Woodcrest Road
Pittsburgh, PA 15237

THE TILE COLLECTION
4031 Bigelow Boulevard
Pittsburgh, PA 15213

TRI STATE REFINISHERS INC
3401 Saw Mill Run Boulevard
Pittsburgh, PA 15227-2717

W T LEGGETT COMPANY
40th & Butler Streets
Pittsburgh, PA 15201

Plymouth Meeting

IKEA US INC
Plymouth Commons
Plymouth Meeting, PA 19462

Pocono Summit

CONTEMPRI KITCHENS
DIVISION CUSTOM DESIGN
& MANUFACTURING
Route 940
PO Box 216
Pocono Summit, PA 18346

Quakertown

MID STATES SUPPLY
461 N W End Boulevard
Quakertown, PA 18951

TRIANGLE BUILDING
CENTERS
472 California Road
Quakertown, PA 18951

Reading

C H BRIGGS HARDWARE
COMPANY
2047 Kutztown Road
Reading, PA 19605

LINCOLN PLUMBING &
HEATING COMPANY
450 Morgantown Road
Reading, PA 19611

Red Lion

KEENER KITCHEN
MANUFACTURING COMPANY
560 W Boundary Avenue
Red Lion, PA 17356

YORKTOWNE INC
100 Redco Avenue
PO Box 231
Red Lion, PA 17356

Reinholds

WIN KIT COMPANY INC
PO Box 90
80 W Main Street
Reinholds, PA 17569

Robesonia

RICH CRAFT DESIGN
CENTER INC
157 W Penn Avenue
Robesonia, PA 19551

Schaefferstown

PLAIN 'N FANCY KITCHENS
PO Box 519
Schaefferstown, PA 17088

Scranton

C B SCOTT COMPANY
400 S Washington Avenue
PO BOX 5909
Scranton, PA 18505

KENN DZIEDZIC
1514 Prospect Avenue
Scranton, PA 18505-4014

Selinsgrove

PENN CRAFT KITCHENS
PO Box 407
Selinsgrove, PA 17870

Sellersville

ELEGANT INTERIORS LTD
1122 Old Route 309
Sellersville, PA 18960

Sewickley

SCHURMANS
One Ohio River Boulevard
Haysville Boro
Sewickley, PA 15143

Shamokin

THE PLUMBING OUTLET INC
Route 61
Shamokin, PA 17872

Sinking Spring

TLC DESIGNS INC
205 Sage Drive
Sinking Spring, PA 19608

Somerset

KITCHEN DESIGNS BY
MARSH
1024 N Center Avenue
Somerset, PA 15501

SDC BUILDING CENTER
S Edgewood Avenue
PO Box 328
Somerset, PA 15501

Southampton

SUBURBAN KITCHEN
COMPANY
650 Street Road
Southampton, PA 18966

Springfield

DONZE KITCHENS &
BATHROOMS INC
512 Baltimore Park
Springfield, PA 19064

EASTERN KITCHENS INC
35 Baltimore Pike
Springfield, PA 19064

Springhouse

BLUE BELL KITCHENS
1104 Bethlehem Pike
Springhouse, PA 19477

State College

HOUSEWRIGHTS INC
2790 W College Avenue
Suite 1000
State College, PA 16801

Stockertown

PEOPLE'S BUILDING SUPPLY
COMPANY
201 East Center Street
Stockertown, PA 18083

Stroudsburg

BENNISON WOOD PRODUCTS
INC
RR 2 Box 2114
Stroudsburg, PA 18360

BEST SUPPLY COMPANY INC
1018 West Main Street
Stroudsburg, PA 18360

Tarrs

C & C BUILDING SUPPLIES
SUPERMARKET
PO Box C
Tarrs, PA 15688

Telford

CHELLEW KITCHENS INC
222 N Hamilton Street
Telford, PA 18969

Trappe

RICK GRAMM KITCHENS &
BATHS
1504 Main Street
Trappe, PA 19426

Turtle Creek

COLE PLUMBING HEATING &
AIR-COND INC
1101 Airbrake Avenue
Turtle Creek, PA 15145

Upper Darby

WALL & WALSH INC
8320 W Chester Pike
Upper Darby, PA 19082

Washington

FAMOUS SUPPLY COMPANY
W Chestnut Street
PO Box 695
Washington, PA 15301

Washington Crossing

KITCHEN CONCEPTS OF
WASHINGTON CROSSING
INCORPORATED
1107 Taylorsville Road
Washington Crossing, PA 18977

Wayne

DONOHUE DESIGNER
KITCHENS
303 W Lancaster Avenue
Wayne, PA 19087

Wellsboro

PATTERSON LUMBER
COMPANY INC
41 45 Charleston Street
Wellsboro, PA 16901

Wellsville

KAMPEL ENTERPRISES INC
8930 Carlisle Road
Wellsville, PA 17365

West Chester

MARBLE CRAFTERS INC
301 E Market Street
West Chester, PA 19382

MCCANNEY & ASSOCIATES
INC
626 Thorncroft Drive
West Chester, PA 19380

MUHLY KBA INC
7 North Five Points Road
West Chester, PA 19380

PACO DISTRIBUTORS
720 East Nields Street
PO Box 375
West Chester, PA 19380

VANGUARD KITCHEN &
BATH DISTRIBUTOR
1105 W Chester Pike
West Chester, PA 19380

West Conshohocken

MAIN LINE DESIGN
539 Ford Steet
West Conshohocken, PA 19428

Wexford

WEXFORD SUPPLY INC
145 Wexford Road
Wexford, PA 15090

Wilkes Barre

WH CONYNGHAM &
COMPANY EASTERN
PENNYSVANYIA SUPPLY
700 Scott Street
Wilkes Barre, PA 18705

Wind Gap

KEEPSAKE KITCHENS INC
112 N Broadway
Wind Gap, PA 18091

Wyoming

BETTERHOUSE INC
1140 Wyoming Avenue
Wyoming, PA 18644

York

BOB HARRY'S KITCHEN
CENTER INC
3602 E Market Street
York, PA 17402

JOHN H MEYERS & SON INC
PO Box 1924
York, PA 17405

SUSQUEHANNA CABINETS
INC
PO Box 3252
York, PA 17402-0252

THE WOLF ORGANIZATION
20 W Market Street
York, PA 17401

THOMAS D KLING INC
2474 N George Street
York, PA 17402

RHODE ISLAND

Barrington

BARRINGTON KITCHENS INC
496 Maple Avenue
Barrington, RI 02806

Central Falls

CREST DISTRIBUTORS
1136 Lonsdale Avenue
Central Falls, RI 02863

Cranston

BUILDERS KITCHEN
CABINET COMPANY
730 Wellington Avenue
Cranston, RI 02910

COLE CABINET COMPANY
INC
530 Wellington Avenue
Cranston, RI 02910

East Greenwich

M AND J KITCHEN SUPPLY
461 Main Street
East Greenwich, RI 02818

Johnston

CREATIVE KITCHENS INC
2656 Hartford Avenue
Johnston, RI 02919

KITCHEN & BATH GALLERY
DIV OF AMERICAN BATH &
SUPPLY INC
1665 Hartford Avenue
Johnston, RI 02919

Pawtucket

DROLET KITCHEN CENTER
122 Benefit Street
Pawtucket, RI 02861

Tiverton

P D HUMPHREY COMPANY
590 Main Road
PO Box 39
Tiverton, RI 02878

Warwick

FERENDO KITCHEN & BATH
SUPPLY COMPANY
110 Jefferson Boulevard
Warwick, RI 02888-3854

HOME DEPOT #4280
Universal Boulevard
Warwick, RI 02893

KB LAMINATE SUPPLY INC
2121 Elmwood Avenue
Warwick, RI 02888

West Warwick

RI KITCHEN & BATH INC
95 Manchester Street
West Warwick, RI 02893

Westerly

VIC MORGAN & SONS INC
42 Canal Street
Westerly, RI 02891

WESTERLY CABINET
COMPANY INC
95 Franklin Street
Westerly, RI 02891

Woonsocket

CABINET GALLERY LTD
520 Social Street
PO Box 336
Woonsocket, RI 02895

HOMESTEAD KITCHEN
CENTER
332 River Street
Woonsocket, RI 02895

SOUTH CAROLINA

Anderson

SMITH CABINET SHOP INC
817 Williamston Road
Anderson, SC 29621

Blythewood

ANDY BATES
114 Holly Grove Road
Blythewood, SC 29016

Charleston

DESIGNS IN WOOD
1533 Folly Road Suite F-4
Charleston, SC 29412

SIGNATURE KITCHEN &
BATHS OF CHARLESTON INC
1926 Savannah Highway
Charleston, SC 29407

Columbia

B & H KITCHENS & INTERIOR
3021 Rosewood Drive
Columbia, SC 29205

HAMPTON KITCHENS
2205 North Main Street
PO Box 7273
Columbia, SC 29201

NORTHEAST KITCHEN AND
BATH
116 N Brickyard Road
Columbia, SC 29223

SOLID SURFACES INC
8019 Sumter Highway
Columbia, SC 29209

Florence

KITCHENS!
1811 Cherokee Road
Florence, SC 29501

MODERN MAID
PO Box 6255
Florence, SC 29502

Greenville

BUILDERWAY INC
PO Drawer 27107
Greenville, SC 29616

HOME DEPOT #1101
Woodruff Road
Greenville, SC 29607

REMODEL AMERICA INC
PO Box 47
Greenville, SC 29602

Hilton Head

CRYSTAL CABINETS OF HHI
PO Box 21993
Hilton Head, SC 29925

Hilton Head Island

PLATATIOIN CAB A
COVENANT ENTERPRISE
COMPANY
8 Bow Circle
PO Box 4737
Hilton Head Island, SC 29938

Marion

CLARK'S DESIGN CENTER
INC
PO Box 659
1302 N Main Street
Marion, SC 29571

Mauldin

DENNIS D SMITH LTD
WOODSMITHS
PO Box 36
319 Neely Ferry Road
Mauldin, SC 29662

SAVAGE CABINET COMPANY
INC
502A North Main Street
Mauldin, SC 29662

Mount Pleasant

KITCHEN CONCEPTS INC
1260 Ben Sawyer Boulevard
Mount Pleasant, SC 29464

KITCHENS BY DESIGN INC
1035 Johnnie Dodds Boulevard
Fairmount Shopping Center
Mount Pleasant, SC 29464

Myrtle Beach

CAROLINA KITCHEN
DESIGNS
PO Box 3544
Myrtle Beach, SC 29578

KREATIVE KITCHENS INC
4923 Highway 17 South ByPass
Myrtle Beach, SC 29577

North Charleston

CAROLINA KITCHENS OF
CHARLESTON
2450 Leeds Avenue
North Charleston, SC 29405

Spartanburg

HOME DEPOT #1102
W O Exell Boulevard
Spartanburg, SC 29301

West Columbia

CREGGER COMPANY INC
629 12th Street Ext
West Columbia, SC 29169

SOUTH DAKOTA

Rapid City

DARLENE'S KITCHEN
GALLERY
3275 Pioneer Drive
Rapid City, SD 57701

Sioux Falls

DEL'S QUALITY BUILT
CABINETS INC
RR2 Box 208
Sioux Falls, SD 57103

HANDY MAN SG SWENSON &
SONS
1103 South Cliff Avenue
PO Box 1201
Sioux Falls, SD 57105

KITCHENS UNLIMITED
525 N Kiwanis Avenue
Sioux Falls, SD 57104

STARMARK INC
700 E 48th Street N
PO Box 84810
Sioux Falls, SD 57118

Yankton

MIDWEST KITCHEN & BATH
200 Walnut
Yankton, SD 57078

TENNESSEE

Antioch

HOME DEPOT #0721
Bell Road
Antioch, TN 37013

Chattanooga

ANA WOODWORKS
10 Meadow Street
Chattanooga, TN 37405

HOME DEPOT #0769
Perimeter Drive
Chattanooga, TN 37421

Clarksville

CITY OF CLARKSVILLE
BUILDING MAINTENANCE
DEPARTMENT
130 N Spring Street
Clarksville, TN 37040

Columbia

R.D. VANN BATHS, KITCHEN
AND PLUMBING
1409 South Main Street
Columbia, TN 38401

Crossville

VILLAGE KITCHENS
PO Box 1396
407 W Avenue S
Crossville, TN 38557

Johnson City

HARRIS-TARKETT INC
2225 Eddie Williams Road
PO Box 300
Johnson City, TN 37605

SUMMERS HARDWARE &
SUPPLY COMPANY
Buffalo & Ashe
PO Box 210
Johnson City, TN 37605

Knoxville

DAVID NEWTON &
ASSOCIATES
PO Box 51706
Knoxville, TN 37950

HOME DEPOT #0730
Kingston Pike
Knoxville, TN 37922

HOME DEPOT #0731
Centerline Drive
Knoxville, TN 37917

JOHN BERETTA TILE CO INC
2706 Sutherland Ave.
Knoxville, TN 37919

MODERN SUPPLY COMPANY
Lovell Road At I 40 W
PO Box 22997
Knoxville, TN 37932

SIGNATURE KITCHENS &
BATHS INC
316 Nancy Lynn Lane
Suite 23B
Knoxville, TN 37919

STANDARD KITCHEN &
HEARTH
8003 Kingston Pike
Knoxville, TN 37919

Madison

HOME DEPOT #0720
Gallatin Pike W
Madison, TN 37115

Memphis

KEVIN WRIGHT INC
5690 Summer Avenue
Memphis, TN 38134

KITCHENS UNLIMITED INC
3550 Summer Avenue
Memphis, TN 38122

Nashville

DEAN'S KITCHEN CENTER
INC
1023-16th Avenue S
Nashville, TN 37212

HENRY KITCHENS & BATH
306 8th Avenue S
Nashville, TN 37203

HERMITAGE KITCHEN &
BATH GALLERY
531 Lafayette Street
Nashville, TN 37203

HOME DEPOT #0722
Highway 70 S
Nashville, TN 37221

KITCHEN & BATH CONCEPTS
INC
3307 Charlotte Avenue
Nashville, TN 37209

LANKFORD HARDWARE &
SUPPLY CO., INC.
800 6th Avenue South
P.O. Box 290457
Nashville, TN 37229

TEXAS

Amarillo

TROOK CABINETS INC
401 N Tyler
Amarillo, TX 79107

Arlington

HOME DEPOT #0541
S Cooper
Arlington, TX 76017

LARRY JONES INC
7900 Valcasi
Arlington, TX 76017

Austin

HOME DEPOT #0520
Research Boulevard
Austin, TX 78759

KITCHENS INC
2712 Bee Caves Road
Suite 122
Austin, TX 78746

THE URBAN KITCHEN INC
1617 W Koenig Lane
Austin, TX 78756

Carrollton

HOME DEPOT #0558
W.Trinity Mill
Carrollton, TX 75006

Conroe

ANNE MOORE LTD MOORE
SUPPLY COMPANY
PO Box 448
Conroe, TX 77305

Corpus Christi

ADVANCE KITCHEN & BATH
4535 S Padre Island Drive
#17
Corpus Christi, TX 78411

CABINET ALTERNATIVES INC
4341 S Alameda
Corpus Christi, TX 78412

Dallas

APEX SUPPLY COMPANY
180 Oak Lawn Avenue
Dallas, TX 75207

BRUCE CABINETS
16803 Dallas Parkway
PO Box 660100
Dallas, TX 75266-0100

CABINETMASTERS INC
5400 E Mockingbird Lane
Suite # 110
Dallas, TX 75206

CONTINENTAL CABINETS
INC
2841 Pierce Street
Dallas, TX 75233

DAL TILE CORPORATION
7834 Hawn Freeway
Dallas, TX 75217

ELJER DESIGN AND
SHOWROOM SERVICES
17120 North Dallas Parkway
Dallas, TX 75248

ELJER INDUSTRIES
17120 Dallas Parkway
Dallas, TX 45248

FORMICA CORPORATIION
1245 Viceroy Drive
Dallas, TX 75247

HERMAN JOHNS &
ASSOCIATES
5301 W Lovers Lane
Dallas, TX 75209

HOME DEPOT #0547
Westmoreland Road
Dallas, TX 75237

HOME DEPOT #0550
Garland Road
Dallas, TX 75218

HOME DEPOT #0557
Forest Lane
Dallas, TX 75243

HOME DEPOT #0559
WNW Highway
Dallas, TX 75220

KITCHEN DISTRIBUTORS OF
AMERICA
6322 Gaston Avenue
Dallas, TX 75214

KITCHENS & BATHS
11055 Plano Road
Dallas, TX 75238

LIVING KITCHENS INC
14448 Midway Road
Dallas, TX 75244

RALPH WILSON PLASTICS
COMPANY Wilsonart
4051 LaReunion
Dallas, TX 75212

Duncanville

QUALITY CABINETS
603 Big Stone Gap Road
Duncanville, TX 75137

El Paso

KITCHENS BY WILLIAMSON
& GELABERT
205 Teramar Way
El Paso, TX 79922

Euless

HOME DEPOT #0537
S Industrial Boulevard
Euless, TX 76040

Fort Worth

BETTIS CONSTRUCTION INC
7341C Vickery Boulevard
Fort Worth, TX 76116-9034

DESIGN'S BY DROSTE
4818 Camp Bowie Boulevard
Fort Worth, TX 76107

FREED APPLIANCE
DISTRIBUTORS
5012 S E Loop 820
Fort Worth, TX 76140

HOME DEPOT 0542
SW Loop 820 Building
Fort Worth, TX 76109

KITCHEN PLANNERS
3300 Airport Freeway
Fort Worth, TX 76111

Grand Prairie

HOME DEPOT #5599
W Sherman
Grand Prairie, TX 75050

Harlingen

PEACOCK'S CUSTOM
KITCHENS
801 E Grimes
PO Box 95
Harlingen, TX 78551

Henderson

SWIRL WAY
PO Box 210
Henderson, TX 75653

Houston

21ST CENTURY MFG INC
10813 Warwana Road #402
Houston, TX 77043

ACCENT CABINETS INC
PO Box 73263
Houston, TX 77273

ALLMILMO DESIGN STUDIO
OF HOUSTON
1705 W Grey
Houston, TX 77019

CABINETS & DESIGNS INC
3637 W Alabama
Suite 380
Houston, TX 77027

CUSTOM ACCESSORIES
4083 Westheimer
Houston, TX 77027

FLECKWAY HOUSEWORKS
612 West Bough Lane
Houston, TX 77024

GAY FLY DESIGNER
KITCHENS AND BATHS
4200 Westheimer Suite 120
Houston, TX 77027

HALLMARK FASHION
KITCHENS INC
3413 E Greenridge Drive
Houston, TX 77057

HOME DEPOT #0569
Market Street
Houston, TX 77015

HOME DEPOT #0570
Bellerive Drive
Houston, TX 77074

HOME DEPOT #0571
Lumpkin Road
Houston, TX 77043

HOME DEPOT #0572
Fm 1960 West
Houston, TX 77070

HOME DEPOT #0573
Gulf Freeway
Houston, TX 77034

HOME DEPOT #0575
Stuebner Airline Road
Houston, TX 77088

HOME DEPOT #5595
Chisholm Trail
Houston, TX 77060

IKEA U.S. INC
7810 Katy Freeway
Houston, TX 77024

KIRK CRAIG COMPANY
2431 Sunset
Houston, TX 77005

KITCHEN & BATH CONCEPTS
2627 Westheimer
Houston, TX 77098

OMNITEK KITCHEN
DISTRIBUTORS
8584 Katy Freeway
Suite 106
Houston, TX 77024

RALPH WILSON PLASTICS
COMPANY Wilsonart
552 Garden Oaks
Houston, TX 77018

ROYAL BATHS MANUFACTURING
COMPANY
PO Box 671666
Houston, TX 77267

SUSAN TAKIFF SCHNEIDER
KITCHENS & BATH
2511 Bellefontaine
Houston, TX 77030

URBAN KITCHEN & BATHS
INC
3601 W Alabama
Houston, TX 77027

VILLAGE PLUMBING SUPPLY
5403 Kirby Drive
Houston, TX 77005

Humble

MEAD ASSOCIATES CUSTOM
KITCHENS & BATHS
203 N Houston Avenue
Humble, TX 77338

Irving

TWENTY FIRST CENTURY
INTERNATIONAL FIRE
EQUIPMENT & SERVICES
CORP
3249 W Story Road
Irving, TX 75038

Keene

BRANDOM MANUFACTURING
COMPANY INC
PO Box 636
Keene, TX 76059

McAllen

DESIGN ALTERNATIVE
706 N McColl
PO Box 326
McAllen, TX 78505

Mesquite

HOME DEPOT #0538
N Towneast
Suite 100
Mesquite, TX 75150

Palestine

TERRY MANUFACTURING
COMPANY
2300 W Reagan Street
Palestine, TX 75801

Plano

HOME DEPOT #0539
N Central Expressway
Plano, TX 75074

Richardson

ASKO INC
903 North Bowser Road # 200
Richardson, TX 75081

HOME DEPOT #0544
South Plano Road #660
Richardson, TX 75081

VENT-A-HOOD COMPANY
1000 N Greenville Avenue
PO Box 830426
Richardson, TX 75080

San Angelo

S & P KITCHEN INTERIORS
3402 Arden Road
San Angelo, TX 76901

San Antonio

BELDON ROOFING &
REMODELING
5039 West Avenue
San Antonio, TX 78213

JOBWARE INC
7344 Caribou
San Antonio, TX 78238

WAGNER & COMPANY
203 W Rhapsody
San Antonio, TX 78216

Sugarland

HOME DEPOT #0574
SW Freeway
Sugarland, TX 77478

Sunset Valley

HOME DEPOT #0521
Brodie Lane
Suite 100
Sunset Valley, TX 78745

Temple

RALPH WILSON PLASTICS
COMPANY WILSONART
600 General Bruce Drive
Temple, TX 76503

RALPH WILSON PLASTICS
COMPANY Wilsonart
500 E Ridge Drive
Temple, TX 76503

W Richland Hil

HOME DEPOT #0549
Grapeview Highway
W Richland Hil, TX 76180

Webster

BAY AREA KITCHENS &
BATHS
17306 Highway 3
Webster, TX 77598

White Settlemen

HOME DEPOT #0548
Cherry Lane
White Settlemen, TX 76108

UTAH

Centerville

ERNST HOME CENTER #234
158 E Pages Lane
Centerville, UT 84014

Draper

COTTONWOOD
12757 S State
Draper, UT 84020

Layton

ERNST HOME CENTER #264
451 West 1500 North
Layton, UT 84041

Logan

ERNST HOME CENTER #233
1224 N Main
Logan, UT 84321

Midvale

ERNST HOME CENTER #232
39 West 7200 South
Midvale, UT 84047

THE KITCHEN CENTER
7515 S State
Midvale, UT 84047

Ogden

WEBER STATE UNIVERSITY
Sales & Service Tech
Ogden, UT 84408-1503

Orem

CATHY MAGLEBY
222 S 760 W
Orem, UT 84058

ERNST HOME CENTER #231
172 East 1300 South
Orem, UT 84058

Salt Lake City

ARENDAL KITCHEN DESIGN
INC
1941 South 1100 East
Salt Lake City, UT 84106

CARLSON KITCHENS
2261 East 3300 South
Salt Lake City, UT 84109

CRAFTSMAN KITCHENS &
BATHS
220 S Main
Salt Lake City, UT 84115

ERNST HOME CENTER #263
1198 Brickyard Road
Salt Lake City, UT 84106

ERNST HOME CENTER #209
2334 East 70th Street
Salt Lake City, UT 84121

EXXEL COMPANY
5975 Stratler Avenue
Salt Lake City, UT 84107

HALLMARK CABINETS INC
4851 Warehouse Road
Salt Lake City, UT 84118

JB TILE COMPANY
PO BOX 65217
Salt Lake City, UT 84165

KARMAN KITCHENS
6000 South Stratler Street
Salt Lake City, UT 84107

MIDWEST FLOOR COVERING
INC
810 W 2500 S
Salt Lake City, UT 84119

THOMAS FRANK INTERIOR
DESIGNERS 7 SPECIFIERS
3369 Highland Drive
Salt Lake City, UT 84106

JEST MAR NEVAMAR
2225 S W Temple
Salt Lake City, UT 84103

Sunset

SUNSET KITCHEN CENTER
INC
1661 N Main Street
Sunset, UT 84015

W Jordon

WASATCH CABINET &
FURNITURE COMPANY INC
3412 West 8600 South
W Jordon, UT 84084

West Valley

ERNST HOME CENTER #228
3749 South 2700 West
West Valley, UT 84119

VERMONT

Barre

ALLEN LUMBER COMPANY
INC
502 N Main Street
Barre, VT 05641

CONCEPTS IN CABINETRY
393 N Main Street
Barre, VT 05641

CORNERSTONE PRODUCTS
OF VERMONT
PO Box 814
Barre, VT 05641

HILLSIDE SAW PLANT INC
Box 134 Gable Place
Barre, VT 05641

INTERIOR CREATIONS
92 S Main Street
Barre, VT 05641

Brattleboro

DJ INC
Putney Road
PO Box 825
Brattleboro, VT 05301

KITCHEN CONCEPTS
RFD 5 Box 228 Putney Road
Black Mountain Square
Brattleboro, VT 05301

Burlington

ACME PAINT & GLASS
COMPANY
1 North Avenue
Burlington, VT 05401

Clarendon

KNIGHT CAB DIVISION NEW
ENGLAND DESK CORP
RR1 Box 231 1 N
Clarendon, VT 05759

Dorset

SUPERIOR KITCHENS &
BATHS
PO Box 899
Meadow Lane
Dorset, VT 05251

Essex Junction

BOUCHARD PIERCE
127 Pearl Street
Essex Junction, VT 05452

WOOD STOCK KITCHENS &
BATHS
163 Pearl Street
Essex Junction, VT 05452

Richford

J J BARKER INC
PO Box 40
Richford, VT 05476

Rutland

MINTZER BROTHERS INC
247 West Street
PO Box 955
Rutland, VT 05701

ROTELLA KITCHEN & BATH
DESIGN CENTER
325 W Street
PO Box 6309
Rutland, VT 05702

Saxtons River

VERMONT CUSTOM WOOD
PRODUCTS INC
Pleasant Valley Road
PO Box 721
Saxtons River, VT 05154

Stowe

COOPER & TURNER INC
17 Towne Farm Lane
Stowe, VT 05672

I M R
PO Box 213
Stowe, VT 05672

VIRGINIA

Alexandria

ALMAR DESIGNER KITCHENS
5930 Tilbury Road
Alexandria, VA 22310

INTERIOR FINISHES OF
VIRGINIA INC
816 N Fairfax Street
Alexandria, VA 22314

Annandale

REGENCY TILE & MARBLE
COMPANY
7106 Columbia Pike
Annandale, VA 22003

Arlington

CUSTOM CRAFTERS INC
6023 Wilson Boulevard
Arlington, VA 22205

VOELL CUSTOM KITCHENS
4788 Lee Highway
Arlington, VA 22207

Blacksburg

HOUSING INTERIOR DESIGN
& RESOURCE MANAGEMENT
VPI & SU
Blacksburg, VA 24061-0424

Bristol

CABINETS INC
111 Goodson Street
Bristol, VA 24201

Charlottesville

CRITZER'S CABINET
CREATIVE
355 W Rio Road
Suite 104 Westpark Plaza
Charlottesville, VA 22901

Chesapeake

THE SAINT CHARLES
COMPANIES One Greenbrier
Point
1401 Greenbrier Parkway
Chesapeake, VA 23320

Christiansburg

IDEAL CABINETS INC
103 N Franklin Street
PO Box 301
Christiansburg, VA 24073

Exmore

THE HERBERT SENN
COMPANY INC
PO Box 547
Exmore, VA 23350

Fairfax

BATH & KITCHEN
CREATIONS
PO Box 370
Fairfax, VA 22039

COURTHOUSE KITCHENS &
BATHS DKB INC
9974 Main Street
Fairfax, VA 22031

RON WHEATON CUSTOM
KITCHENS INC
11244 Waples Mill Road
Suite J-2
Fairfax, VA 22030

Falls Church

CAMEO KITCHENS INC
7297 M Lee Highway
Falls Church, VA 22042

F A MCGONEGAL INC
1061 West Broad Street
Falls Church, VA 22046

Gainesville

KITCHEN DESIGN CENTER
OF HAYES LUMBER
5529 Wellington Road
Gainesville, VA 22065

Great Falls

BETTER BY DESIGN
10114 Sanders Court
Great Falls, VA 22066

COUNTRY KITCHENS &
BATHS INC
774B Walker Road
Great Falls, VA 22066

Hampton

BUILDERS SQUARE 1516
1072 W Mercury Boulevard
Hampton, VA 23663

Harrisonburg

COUNTRYSIDE KITCHENS
40 South Carlton Street
Harrisonburg, VA 22801

HOUSE CALLS
1951 E Evelyn Byrd Avenue
Harrisonburg, VA 22801

Lanexa

RIGHTER CABINET
PO Box 116
Lanexa, VA 23089

Leesburg

J T HIRST & COMPANY INC
41 Catocin Circle S E
Leesburg, VA 22075

Lorton

ABD APPLIANCE DISTRIBUTOR
7371 E Lockport Place
Lorton, VA 22079

CRAFTWOOD CABINET
COMPANY
8815 Telegraph Road
Lorton, VA 22079

Lynchburg

TAYLOR BROTHERS INC
905 Graves Mill Road
PO Box 11198
Lynchburg, VA 24506

Manakin Sabot

LUCK STONE CORP
RICHMOND CENTER
PO Box 174
Manakin Sabot, VA 23103

Manassas

ALLIED PLYWOOD
CORPORATION
7891 Notes Drive
Manassas, VA 22110

Mclean

DIANE H SMALL INC
1969 Massachusetts Avenue
Mclean, VA 22101

KITCHEN GALLERY DESIGN
CENTER INC
6823A Tennyson Drive
Mclean, VA 22101

Middleburg

MIDDLEBURG MILLWORK
INC
106 S Madison Street
PO Box 407
Middleburg, VA 22117

Midlothian

INNOVATIVE KITCHEN &
BATH INC
1127 Alverser Drive
Midlothian, VA 23113

Newington

B & F CERAMICS DESIGN
SHOWROOM INC
8900 Telegraph Road
PO Box 1544
Newington, VA 22122

PMC CONTRACTORS INC
7913 Kincannon Place
PO Box 1415
Newington, VA 22122

Newport News

FERGUSON ENTERPRISES INC
618 Bland Boulevard
Newport News, VA 23602

VIRGINIA MAID KITCHENS
INC
737 Ble Crab Road
Suite 1A
Newport News, VA 23606

WARWICK CUSTOM
KITCHENS MANUFACTURING
COMPANY
497 Denbigh Boulevard
Newport News, VA 23602

Norfolk

CENTRAL WHOLESALE
SUPPLY CORPORATION
1532 Ingleside Road
Norfolk, VA 23509

KITCHENS & BATHS
INTERNATIONAL INC
222 West 21st Street
Norfolk, VA 23517

Petersburg

DAVE'S CABINET SHOP INC
22504 Cox Road
Petersburg, VA 23803

Portsmouth

KITCHEN EMPORIUM
3411 High Street
Portsmouth, VA 23707

Radford

THE CABINET COMPANY
921 First Street
Radford, VA 24141

Reston

KITCHEN CABINET
MANUFACTURERS ASSOC
1899 Preston White Drive
Reston, VA 22091

Richmond

CUSTOM KITCHENS INC
6412 Horsepen Road
Richmond, VA 23226

E A HOLSTEN INC
1400 Overbrook Road
PO Box 26808
Richmond, VA 23261

HI TECH TOPS INC
1728 Arlington Road
Richmond, VA 23230

KITCHEN ART INC
2337 W Broad Street
Richmond, VA 23220

LUCK STONE
PO Box 29682
Richmond, VA 23242

PLYWOOD & PLASTICS INC
1727 Arlington Road
Richmond, VA 23230

RICHMOND CABINETS INC
6305 Hull Street Road
Richmond, VA 23224

THE KITCHEN AND BATH
DESIGN SHOP LTD
2317 West Main Street
Richmond, VA 23220

Roanoke

CARDINAL CABINET
CORPORATION
PO Box 13706
403 Salem Avenue South West
Roanoke, VA 24036

CARTER'S CABINET SHOP OF
ROANOKE INC
2132 Shenandoah Valley
Roanoke, VA 24012

CUSTOM WOOD PRODUCTS
INC
P O Box 4516
Roanoke, VA 24015

PERDUE CABINET SHOP INC
3806 Brambleton Avenue
Southwest
Roanoke, VA 24018

Springfield

COYLE & KLEPPINGER INC
7420 Fullerton Road
Suite 102
Springfield, VA 22153

JOHNSON CONSTRUCTION
DESIGN INC
7705 Hooes Road
Springfield, VA 22152

MID SOUTH BUILDING
SUPPLY
7940 Woodruff Court
Springfield, VA 22151

REICO DISTRIBUTORS
6790 Commercial Drive
Springfield, VA 22153

Sterling

COLLINS & COMPANY INC
22879 Glenn Drive #140
Sterling, VA 20164

H & H CUSTOM CABINETS
22560 Glenn Drive
Suite 115
Sterling, VA 22170

Vienna

KITCHEN DESIGN
CONSULTANTS
129 Park Street North East
Vienna, VA 22180

LINDA SHEARER
406 Course Street NE
Vienna, VA 22180

LYN WEXLER
302 Lewis St., N.W.
Vienna, VA 22180

SUNDANCE KITCHEN DESIGN
INC
394 Park Street SE
Vienna, VA 22180

Virginia Beach

DESIGNER KITCHENS &
BATHS INC
4143 Virginia Beach Boulevard
Virginia Beach, VA 23452

GREENWICH SUPPLY CORP
5789 Arrowhead Drive
PO Box 61737
Virginia Beach, VA 23462

PESTIGE KITCHENS OF
VIRGINIA
2798 Dean Drive
Virginia Beach, VA 23452

Winchester

AMERICAN WOODMARK
CORPORATION
3102 Shawnee Drive
PO Box 1980
Winchester, VA 22601

Woodbridge

DAVE'S DESIGN
13475 Fowke Lane
Woodbridge, VA 22192

IKEA U.S. INC.
Potomac Mills Mall
2700 Potomac Mills Circle
Woodbridge, VA 22192

WASHINGTON

Aberdeen

EENST HOME CENTER #237
1109 E Wishkah
Aberdeen, WA 98520

Algona

RALPH WILSON PLASTICS
COMPANY WILSONART
400 Boundary Boulevard
Algona, WA 98001

Auburn

ERNST HOME CENTER #248
1347 Auburn Way N
Auburn, WA 98002

PACIFIC CREST CABINETS
2709 Auburn Way N
Auburn, WA 98002

WAREHOUSE KITCHEN
SALES DIVISION DEWILS IND
INC
233
Auburn, WA 98002

Bellevue

ERNST HOME CENTER #207
44 Bellevue Way N E
Bellevue, WA 98004

ERNST HOME CENTER #217
Crossroads Shopping Center
Building M
Bellevue, WA 98008

INTERNATIONAL CABINETS
INC
13500 Bel Red Road # 7
Bellevue, WA 98005

LYNN LLOYD CONNER
KITCHEN & BATH
12819 SE 38th Street
Suite 394
Bellevue, WA 98006

RONNELLCO INC
1034 116th Avenue NE
Bellevue, WA 98005

Bellingham

ERNST HOME CENTER #247
3968 Guide-Meridian Avenue
Bellingham, WA 98226

HYDRO SWIRL
2150 Division Street
Bellingham, WA 98226

KITCHEN & BATH CONCEPTS
5980 Meridian
Bellingham, WA 98226

SASH & DOOR
3801 Hannegan Road
Bellingham, WA 98226

Bremerton

BRISTOL KITCHENS
5889 State Highway
303 N E #101
Bremerton, WA 98310

ERNST HOME CENTER #230
3449 Wheaton Way
Bremerton, WA 98310

Centralia

ARISTOCRATIC CABINETS,
INC.
108 South Washington
Centralia, WA 98531

East Wenatchee

ERNST HOME CENTER #238
401 Valley Mall Parkway
East Wenatchee, WA 98801

Everett

ERNST HOME CENTER #210
4920 Evergreen Way
Everett, WA 98203

Federal Way

ERNST HOME CENTER 239
1718 S 320 Street
Federal Way, WA 98003

Friday Harbor

MICHAEL PULLEN
CONSTRUCTION
PO Box 2963
Friday Harbor, WA 98250

Gig Harbor

ERNST HOME CENTER #272
4816 Point Fosdick Drive
Gig Harbor, WA 98335

Hoquiam

MAJOR LINE PRODUCTS
COMPANY
402 Tyler Street
PO Box 478
Hoquiam, WA 98550

Issaquah

ERNST HOME CENTER #278
1025 Gilman Boulevard
Issaquah, WA 98027

LINDA LEE JOHNSON
20412 S E 119th Street
Issaquah, WA 98027

PAC WEST MARKETING
4306 191st Avenue SE
Issaquah, WA 98027

Kennewick

ERNST HOME CENTER #258
3017 W Kennewick Avenue
Kennewick, WA 99336

Kent

CRAWFORD SALES INC
6649 S 216th Street
Kent, WA 98032

ERNST HOME CENTER #229
23662 104th Avenue S E
Kent, WA 98031

GATEWAY APPLIANCE
DISTRIBUTORS
19204 68th Avenue South
Kent, WA 98032-1188

KIMBERLY ACKERMAN
23108 112th Place S E
Kent, WA 98031

NORTHWEST KITCHEN &
BATH QUARTERLY
25713 36th Place South
Kent, WA 98032

TOTAL BUILDING PRODUCTS
8641 S 212 Street
Kent, WA 98031

Kirkland

ERNST HOME & NURSERY
#225
12630A Kingsgate Way N E
Kirkland, WA 98034

KITCHENS FOR DREAM
HOMES
12024 Juanita Drive N E
Kirkland, WA 98034

THURMAN INDUSTRIES INC
PO Box 3359
Kirkland, WA 98083

Lacey

ERNST HOME CENTER #214
25 South Sound Center
Lacey, WA 98503

Longview

ERNST HOME CENTER #216
8 Triangle Shopping Center
Longview, WA 98632

Lynnwood

ERNST HOME CENTER 279
19310 60th Avenue W
Lynnwood, WA 98036

Mercer Island

CLASSIC KITCHENS & BATHS
INC
4800 East Mercer Way
Mercer Island, WA 98040-4736

LLOYD F PUGH &
ASSOCIATES
PO Box 127
Mercer Island, WA 98040

Mill Creek

CONSOLIDATED CABINET
COMPANY
15911 23rd Lane SE
Mill Creek, WA 98012

ERNST HOME CENTER #266
16222 Bothell Everett Highway
Mill Creek, WA 98012

UNITED DEVELOPEMENT
CORPORATION
15714 Country Club Dr., S.E.
Mill Creek, WA 98012

Moses Lake

THE CABINET GALLERY &
DESIGN CENTER
703 West Broadway
Moses Lake, WA 98837

Mount Vernon

ERNST HOME CENTER #226
310 Collage Way
Mount Vernon, WA 98273

Oak Harbor

FINE WOOD CABINETS
645 W Oak Street
Oak Harbor, WA 98277

Olympia

CORNERSTONE KITCHEN &
BATH
3530 Martin Way
Unit 2
Olympia, WA 98506

ERNST HOME CENTER #250
400 Cooper Point Road SW
Olympia, WA 98502

LUMBERMEN'S BUILDING
CENTER
3773 Martin Way E
PO Box 3406
Olympia, WA 98503

Otis Orchards

AFFORDABLE CUSTOM
CABINETS
N 5421 Corrigan
Otis Orchards, WA 99027

Port Angeles

RGS CABINETS
508 S Adler Street
Port Angeles, WA 98362

Port Orchard

ERNST HOME CENTER #265
1700 S E State Highway 160
Building 100
Port Orchard, WA 98366

Puyallup

ERNST HOME CENTER #221
1317 E Main Avenue
Puyallup, WA 98372

ERNST HOME CENTER #277
900 E North Meridian
Suite 35
Puyallup, WA 98371

ERNST HOME CENTER 252
11723 Meridian Street E
Puyallup, WA 98373

Redmond

ERNST HOME CENTER #241
17170 Redmond Way
Redmond, WA 98052

ROZANN CHERRY
17510 N E 33 Street
Redmond, WA 98052

SHOWPLACE KITCHENS &
BATH
PO Box 955
Redmond, WA 98073

Renton

ERNST HOME CENTER #246
4601 North East Sunset
Boulevard
Renton, WA 98056

ERNST HOME CENTERS #201
14068 SE Petrovitsky Road
Renton, WA 98058

Richland

ERNST HOME CENTER #251
1717 George Washington Way
Richland, WA 99352

SE Bellevue

ERNST HOME CENTER #240
4037 Factoria Square Mall
SE Bellevue, WA 98006

Seattle

C A NEWELL COMPANY INC
9877-40th Avenue S
Seattle, WA 98118

CHRISTIANE H D'AIES
220 S W 191st Street
Seattle, WA 98166

CONTEMPORARY
COUNTERTOPS
702 Industry Drive
Seattle, WA 98188

DOMESTIC SUPPLY
COMPANY
6750 S 180th
PO Box 58910
Seattle, WA 98138

ERNST CORPORATE OFFICE
1511 6th Avenue
Seattle, WA 98101

ERNST HOME CENTER #203
4704 25th Avenue N E
Seattle, WA 98105

ERNST HOME CENTER #204
414 Northgate Mall
Seattle, WA 98125

ERNST HOME CENTER #205
1401 N W Leary Way
Seattle, WA 98107

ERNST HOME CENTER #212
2501 SW Trenton
Seattle, WA 98126

ERNST HOME CENTER 215
150 Burien Plaza SW
Seattle, WA 98166

ERNST HOME CENTER 249
15403 Westminister Way N
Seattle, WA 98133

HOLLABAUGH BROTHERS
AND ASSOCIATES
1260 6th Avenue S
Seattle, WA 98134

KITCHEN & BATH DESIGNS
INC
14018 Aurora Ave N
Seattle, WA 98133

KITCHEN & BATHS BY
BLODGETT
4515 44th SW
Seattle, WA 98116

KITCHEN DISTRIBUTING
COMPANY
PO Box 24979
Seattle, WA 98124

MORGAN ELECTRICAL &
PLUMBING SUPPLY
8055 15th NW
Seattle, WA 98117

NORTHWEST CABINETPAK
KITCHENS INC
3809 Stoneway N
Seattle, WA 98103

O'NEILL PLUMBING
COMPANY
6056 California Avenue SW
Seattle, WA 98136

R E WEAVER CONSTRUCTION
1721 First Avenue S
Seattle, WA 98134

RAINER WOODWORKING OF
KING COMPANY INC
1011 NE 65th Street
Seattle, WA 98115

ROBINSON DISTRIBUTING
CORPORATION
1400 Elliott Avenue W
Seattle, WA 98119

ROY RICKETTS INC
3417 1st Avenue S
Seattle, WA 98134

SEATTLE KITCHEN DESIGNS
10002 Holman Road NW
Seattle, WA 98177

THE FIXTURE GALLERY,
BOWLES NW CO.
4302 Stone Way N
Seattle, WA 98103

UNITED TILE
17400 W Valley Highway
PO Box 58204
Seattle, WA 98138

Silverdale

ERNST HOME CENTER #267
PO Box 810
Silverdale, WA 98383

Spokane

DESIGNER KITCHENS &
BATHS
2625 East Trent Avenue
Spokane, WA 99202

ERNST HOME CENTER #218
E 12105 Sprague Avenue
Spokane, WA 99206

ERNST HOME CENTER #227
W 2215 Wellesley
Spokane, WA

ERNST HOME CENTER #254
9960 N Newport Highway
Spokane, WA 99218

ERNST HOME CENTER 219
2910 E 29th Street
Spokane, WA 99203

HUNTWOOD INDUSTRIES
Spokane Industrial Park
Building 26
Spokane, WA 99216

Tacoma

B & D INTERNATIONAL INC
455 E 15th Street
PO Box 1762
Tacoma, WA 98401

CUSTOM DESIGN CABINETRY
INC
701 E 72nd Street
Tacoma, WA 98404

DOUGLAS DESIGN CABINET
& REMODELING COMPANY
4804 Center Street
Tacoma, WA 98409

ERNST HOME CENTER #211
10507 Gravelly Lake Drive SW
Tacoma, WA 94899

ERNST HOME CENTER #224
15615 Pacific Avenue
Tacoma, WA 98444

ERNST HOME CENTER #222
6425 6th Avenue
Tacoma, WA 98406

ERNST HOME CENTER 260
3800 Bridgeport Way W
Tacoma, WA 98466

OLD TIME WOODWORK INC
2105 S
Tacoma, WA 98402

Tukwila

EAGLE HARDWARE &
GARDEN INC
101 Andover Park E Suite 200
Tukwila, WA 98188

WANKE CASCADE
18260 Olympic Avenue S
Tukwila, WA 98188

Union Gap

ERNST HOME CENTER #223
2505 Main Street
Union Gap, WA 98903

Vancouver

DEWILS INDUSTRIES
PO Box 4598
Vancouver, WA 95662

LYNWOOD KITCHENS INC
2300 N E 65th Avenue
PO Box 1539
Vancouver, WA 98668

T SQUARE REMODELING
10600 N E 94th Avenue
Vancouver, WA 98662

TALBOT CONSTRUCTION INC
10602 NW 26th Avenue
Vancouver, WA 98685

Wenatchee

CONCEPTS KITCHEN & BATH
DESIGNS
132 S Mission Street
Wenatchee, WA 98801

Woodinville

BOLIG KITCHEN STUDIO
13110 NE 177th Place
#8-102
Woodinville, WA 98072

CONTAINER HOME SUPPLY
INC
7627 W Bostain Road
Woodinville, WA 98072

ERNST HOME CENTER #275
14501 N E Woodinville & Duvell
Road
Woodinville, WA 98072

WESTERN CABINET &
MILLWORK INC
PO Box 137
Woodinville, WA 98072

WEST VIRGINIA

Barboursville

WOODY'S KITCHENS BATHS
DECORATE STUDIO
5841 Davis Creek Road
Barboursville, WV 25504

Bluefield

KITCHENS PLUS
1130 Bland Street
PO Box 1623
Bluefield, WV 24701

Charleston

SAVE SUPPLY COMPANY INC
PO Box 71
Charleston, WV 25321

Huntington

CREATIVE KITCHENS PLUS
PO Box 2786
Huntington, WV 25727

Martinsburg

J & D KITCHEN DISTRIBUTORS
INC
49 Meadow Lane Plaza
Martinsburg, WV 25401

KITCHENS AND BATHS
UNLIMITED
2035 Shephardstown Road
Martinsburg, WV 25401

Morgantown

GENERAL GLASS COMPANY
INC
275 University Ave.
P.O. Box 618
Morgantown, WV 26505

SHARP KITCHENS
454 Dunkard Avenue
Morgantown, WV 26505

Parkersburg

HARMON'S CABINET SHOP
1933 Ohio Avenue
Parkersburg, WV 26101

WISCONSIN

Appleton

KUSTOM KITCHENS & BATHS
741 W College Avenue
Appleton, WI 54914

PLEUSS MARKETING
W 4511 City Road
Appleton, WI 54915

STOCK LUMBER APPLETON
1924 W College Avenue
Appleton, WI 54914

Baraboo

THE MERCHANDISE CENTER
54066 Highway 12
Baraboo, WI 53913

Beaver Dam

WICKES LUMBER COMPANY
N6543 Highway 151 S
Beaver Dam, WI 53916

Beloit

THE WITTE BARKER
SHOWROOM
419 E Grand Avenue
Beloit, WI 53511

Brookfield

JERRY MAHRT INC
PO Box 792 Suite B&D
2920 N Brookfield Road
Brookfield, WI 53008

RAPHAEL LTD A NORTEK
COMPANY
Po Box 390
Brookfield, WI 53008

S & K PUMP & PLUMBING
INC
20880 W Enterprise Avenue
Brookfield, WI 53045

THE KITCHEN CENTER
4060 N 128th Street
Brookfield, WI 53005

Broukfield

UNDER ROOF BUILDING
12625 W Burleigh
Broukfield, WI 53005

Burlington

COURTYARD CABINETRY
109 Dodge Street
Burlington, WI 53105

Cedarburg

CEDARBURG LUMBER
COMPANY INC
North 144 West 5800 Pioneer
Road
Cedarburg, WI 53012

Combined Locks

US SCHMIDT PLUMBING &
HEATING
425 S Washington Street
Combined Locks, WI 54113

Delavan

KUSTOM KITCHEN DESIGNS
1102 Ann Street
PO BOX 526
Delavan, WI 53115

Eau Claire

CHARLSON'S BUILDING &
DESIGS
97 West Madison Street
Eau Claire, WI 54703

EAU CLAIRE PLUMBING
SUPPLY COMPANY
596 Cameron Avenue
PO Box 166
Eau Claire, WI 54701

Fond Du Lac

AHERN GROSS INC
PO Box 1027
Fond Du Lac, WI 54936-1027

MATRIX INTERIOR SUPPLY
INC
PO Box 1134
243 Morris Court
Fond Du Lac, WI 54936

PERSONAL KITCHENS
PO Box 1738
Fond Du Lac, WI 54936-1738

Franklin

QS REMODELERS INC
11113 W Forest Home Avenue
Franklin, WI 53132

Fremont

CREATIVE DESIGNS
E 7451 Red Oak Road
Fremont, WI 54940

Germantown

DESIGN HOUSE INC
W180 N11691 River Lane
PO Box 1001
Germantown, WI 53022

RIEBAU'S CABINETS LTD
PO Box 458
Germantown, WI 53022

Green Bay

SHOWCASE KITCHEN AND
BATH
2674 Packerland Drive
Green Bay, WI 54313

WILCO CABINET MAKERS
INC
1844 Sal Street
Green Bay, WI 54302

Greendale

CUSTOM DESIGN
ASSOCIATES INC
5101 West Loomis Road
Greendale, WI 53129

GREAT AMERICAN KITCHEN
& BATH CO. INC.
5130 West Loomis Road
Greendale, WI 53129

Gresham

BISLEY FABRICATION INC
700 Industrial Street
Gresham, WI 54128

Hartford

BROAN MANUFACTURING
COMPANY INC
926 W State Street
Hartford, WI 53027

Jackson

EECKES LUMBER CENTER
3650 City Highway P
Jackson, WI 53037

Janesville

MARLING KITCHEN
DISTRIBUTOR
1236 Barberry Drive
Box 999
Janesville, WI 53547

Kenosha

NELSON MILLWORK &
SUPPLIES
6935 14th Avenue
Kenosha, WI 53143

SOUTHPORT DISTRIBUTORS
DIV.OF SOUTHP
2929 75th Street
Kenosha, WI 53140

Kohler

KOHLER COMPANY
444 Highland Drive
Kohler, WI 53044

PAST BASKET
765 F Wood Lake Road
Kohler, WI 53044

La Crosse

LA CROSSE PLUMBING
SUPPLY
106 Cameron Avenue
PO Box 1028
La Crosse, WI 54602

Lacrosse

STOCK LUMBER
1735 Kramer Street
PO Box 2195
Lacrosse, WI 54603

Luck

SAINT CROIX VALLEY
HARDWOODS INC
230 Duncan Street
PO Box 220
Luck, WI 54853

Madison

AUTOMATIC TEMPERATURE
SUPPLIES
1023 E Main Street
Madison, WI 53703

BENJAMIN PLUMBING
COMPANY
6194 Mc Kee Road
Madison, WI 53719

BRUNSELL LUMBER AND
MILLWORK
4611 W Beltline Highway
Madison, WI 53711

CUSTOM COUNTERTOP
FABRICATION INC
56 Corry Drive
Madison, WI 53704

J.R. LUCK & ASSOCIATES INC
1118 Saybrook Road
Madison, WI 53711

KITCHENS OF DISTINCTION
6719 Seybold Road
Madison, WI 53719

MODERN KITCHEN SUPPLY
INC
PO Box 44189
Madison, WI 53744-4189

SUB ZERO FREEZER CO INC
P O Box 44130
Madison, WI 53774-4130

VENETIAN MARBLE OF
WISCONSIN INC
PO Box 7761
Madison, WI 53707

WISCONSIN SUPPLY
CORPORATION
6800 Gisholt Drive
PO Box 8124
Madison, WI 53708

Manitowoc

BRAUN BUILDING CENTER
3303 Menasha Avenue
Manitowoc, WI 54220

LUISIER PLUMBING INC
2510 Marshall Street
Manitowoc, WI 54220

Marshfield

KABINET KONNECTION
1304 N Central
Marshfield, WI 54449

REIGEL PLUMBING &
HEATING INC
1701 S Galvin Avenue
Marshfield, WI 54449

THE CABINET STUDIO
107 North Central Avenue
Marshfield, WI 54449

Medford

CABINETRY BY DESIGN
N3452 Highway 13
Medford, WI 54451

Menasha

DRUCKS PLUMBING &
HEATING COMPANY INC
504 Third Street
PO Box 355
Menasha, WI 54952

WATTERS PLUMBING INC
1303 Midway Road
PO Box 118
Menasha, WI 54952

Menomonee Falls

LIPPERT CORPORATION
W142 N8999 Fountain Boulevard
PO Box 219
Menomonee Falls, WI 53051

LIPPERT MARKETING INC
N 84 W 15787 Menomonee
Avenue
PO Box 496
Menomonee Falls, WI 53051

WOOD SPECIALTIES, INC.
N-94 W-14555 Garwin Mace
Drive
Menomonee Falls, WI 53051

Mequon

THE KITCHEN DESIGN
GROUP LTD
11065 N Port Washington Road
Mequon, WI 53092

Middleton

KITCHEN AND BATH
CONCEPTS
6333 University Avenue
Middleton, WI 53562

Milwaukee

ALPINE PLYWOOD
CORPORATION
12210 W Silver Spring Road
Milwaukee, WI 53225

B & E GENERAL CONTRACTORS
INC
9049 North Lake Drive
Milwaukee, WI 53217

BLAU BATH AND KITCHEN
INC
735 S 108th Street
Milwaukee, WI 53214

BUILT-IN KITCHENS INC
7289 N Teutonia Avenue
Milwaukee, WI 53209

HALLMARK BUILDING
SUPPLIES INC
6060 North 77th Avenue
Milwaukee, WI 53218

MILWAUKEE BUILDING
SUPPLY COMPANY IN
5800 West Douglas Avenue
Milwaukee, WI 53218

MORLEY MURPHY COMPANY
8500 W Bradley Road
Milwaukee, WI 53224

THE KOPFMANN COMPANY
INC
3142 W Mill Road Court
PO Box 9127
Milwaukee, WI 53209

Monroe

GOLDEN OAK WOODWORKS
N3362 Highway 81
Monroe, WI 53566

Mosinee

KITCHENS BY FEATHERSTONE
10606 Tesch Lane
Mosinee, WI 54455

Necedah

JAMES & JEAN SCHMIDT
W5175 Highway 21 E
Necedah, WI 54646

New Berlin

OAKTON DISTRIBUTORS OF
WISCONSIN INC
16600 West Cleveland
PO Box 498
New Berlin, WI 53151

New Richmond

COUNTRYSIDE PLUMBING
AND HEATING INC
753 S Knowles Avenue
New Richmond, WI 54017

Oshkosh

FOX VALLEY KITCHEN
SPECIALISTS
2721 Oregon Street
Oshkosh, WI 54901

KITCHEN GALLERY
1804 Evans Street
Oshkosh, WI 54901

SUPERIOR SURFACES
ANDRESEN'S BUILDERS INC
1423 Monroe
Oshkosh, WI 54901

VAL CORPORATION OF
WISCONSIN VALCO
2056 Dickinson Avenue
Oshkosh, WI 54904

Port Washington

THE STREFF SHOP INC
981 S Spring Street
Port Washington, WI 53074

Racine

CRYSTAL CABINETS &
SUPPLY INC
4639 Douglas Avenue
Racine, WI 53402

IN SINK ERATOR
4700 21st Street
Racine, WI 53406

Rhinelander

FRASIERS SHOWPLACE
INTERIORS INC
130 N Brown Street
Rhinelander, WI 54501

Rib Lake

GREAT NORTHERN
CABINETRY INC
Box 207
Rib Lake, WI 54470

Rice Lake

HOLIDAY KITCHENS DIV
MASTERCRAFT INC
120 West Allen
Rice Lake, WI 54868

Rio

SANDENWOOD PRODUCTS
W4265 Sampson Road
Rio, WI 53960

Saint Nazianz

REINDL PLUMBING &
HEATING INC
403 S Fourth Avenue
Saint Nazianz, WI 54232

Schofield

DE LISLE COMPANY INC
624 Moreland Avenue
Schofield, WI 54476

Sheboygan

CREATIVE KITCHEN
CONCEPTS
1504 Saint Clair Avenue
Sheboygan, WI 53081

DIANE HARBRECHT DESIGNS
1807 Ridge Road
Sheboygan, WI 53083

KBAER DESIGN CENTER-D &
M PLUMBING
1020 Michigan Avenue
Sheboygan, WI 53081

SOHRE'S KITCHENS & BATHS
DIVISION OF
2125 Maryland Avenue
Sheboygan, WI 53081

THE KITCHEN AND THE
BATH BY KYM
1202 North 8th Street
Sheboygan, WI 53081

Sheboygan Falls

RICHARDSON LUMBER
904 Monroe
Box 904
Sheboygan Falls, WI 53085

Stevens Point

CABINETS & MORE INC
2309 Division Street
Stevens Point, WI 54481

CHET'S PLUMBING &
HEATING INCORPORATION
5009 Coye Dr
Stevens Point, WI 54481

DESIGNS BY ELDON
1581 N Skyline Drive
Stevens Point, WI 54481

FALK CABINET SYSTEMS INC
2817 Post Road
Stevens Point, WI 54481

Stratford

STRATFORD BUILDING
SUPPLY INC
PO Box 146
Stratford, WI 54484

Sun Prairie

HENSEN MANUFACTURING
INC
3361 Brooks Drive
Sun Prairie, WI 53590

Twin Lakes

STAN'S LUMBER INC
PO Box 40
Twin Lakes, WI 53181

Waunakee

WINDOWS & DOORS INC
800 S Division Street
PO Box 99
Waunakee, WI 53597

Waupaca

ARROW KITCHEN CABINET
COMPANY
N2331 Highway 22
Waupaca, WI 54981

Wautoma

MID STATE SUPPLY OF
YELLOW THUNDER CORP
PO Box 510
Wautoma, WI 54982

Wauwatosa

KITCHEN DESIGN STUDIO
8932 W North Avenue
Wauwatosa, WI 53226

West Allis

CABINET WHOLESALERS OF
WISCONSIN INC
1013 S 108th
West Allis, WI 53214

DO IT YOURSELF
BATHROOM CENTER
6135 W Greenfield Avenue
West Allis, WI 53214

KNUTSON BROTHERS
BUILDER'S INC
9330 W Lincoln Avenue
West Allis, WI 53227

West Bend

COUNTRY CABINETRY OF
WEST BEND INC
2139 W Washington
West Bend, WI 53095

Wisconsin Rapid

QUALITY KITCHENS
1211 8th Street South
Wisconsin Rapid, WI 54494

WYOMING

Casper

KITCHEN DESIGNS
2381 Belmont
Casper, WY 82604

WYOMING BUILDING SUPPLY
2104 Fairgrounds Road
Casper, WY 82604

Cheyenne

ERNST HOME CENTER #255
3711 E Lincoln Way
Cheyenne, WY 82001

SCHROLL CABINETS INC
821 Bradley Avenue
Cheyenne, WY 82007

Gillette

B & I SUPPLY INC
2724 S Powder Basin Avenue
Gillette, WY 82716

Canada

ALBERTA

Calgary

BATH CLASSICS
2025-41 Avenue NE
Calgary, AB T2E 6P2

DENCA CABINETS
555-60 Avenue SE
Calgary, AB T2H 0R1

HEARTWOOD KITCHEN &
BATH DESIGN
1925 10th Avenue SW
Calgary, AB T3C 0K3

KITCHEN SHOWPLACE LTD
Bay 23 3220-5th Avenue NE
Calgary, AB T2A 5N1

MERIT KITCHENS
Bay 1 6130 4th Street SE
Calgary, AB T2H 2B6

THE KITCHEN CRAFT
CONNECTION
110 495 36th Street N E
Calgary, AB T2A 6K3

Edmonton

ARISTOCRAT KITCHENS
8716 51 Avenue
Edmonton, AB T6E 5E8

BATH CLASSICS
13030 Yellowhead Trail
Edmonton, AB T5L 3C1

MERIT KITCHENS &
RENOVATIONS
12710 Street Albert Trail
Edmonton, AB T5L 4S5

THE KITCHEN CRAFT
CONNECTION
2866 Calgary Trail South
Edmonton, AB T6J 6V7

Fort McMurray

MATT-N-AL WOODWORKING
(1986) LTD
420 MacAlpine Crest
Fort McMurray, AB T9H 4B1

Red Deer

WESTRIDGE CABINETS LTD
#8 7428-49 Avenue
Red Deer, AB T4P 1M2

Sherwood Park

JEAN'S CUSTOM INTERIOR &
DRAPERY
74 993 Fir Street
Sherwood Park, AB T8A 4N5

BRITISH COLUMBIA

Abbotsford

DALE JAMES KITCHENS &
BATHS LTD
#5 1733 Riverside Road
Abbotsford, BC V2S 4J8

NOVA KITCHENS & CUSTOM
CABINETS LTD
31107 Peardonville Road
Abbotsford, BC V2S 5W6

Aldergrove

DURAGLAS PRODUCTS LTD
PO Box 274
Aldergrove, BC V0X 1A0

KITCHEN KORNER
PO Box 370
Aldergrove, BC V0X 1A0

Burnaby

BATH CLASSICS
109 3701 E Hastings
Burnaby, BC V5C 2H6

DUPONT CANADA INC
710 4710 Kingsway
Burnaby, BC V5H 4M2

GPM DISTRIBUTING LTD
8835 Northbrook Court
Burnaby, BC V6M 3W4

MC KILLICAN DISTRIBUTION
LTD
3212 Lake City Way
Burnaby, BC V5A 3A4

PREMIER INSTALLATIONS
LTD
4710 E Hastings Street
Burnaby, BC V5C 2K7

ULTRALINE DISTRIBUTION
INC
8855 Northbrook Court
Burnaby, BC V5J 5G1

Delta

HERTCO KITCHEN
MANUFACTURING LTD
7175 Brown Street RR #5
Delta, BC V4G 1G5

Kamloops

EXCEL INDUSTRIES
670 Kingston Avenue
Kamloops, BC V2B 2C8

Kelowna

CENTURY CABINETS INC
251 Adams Road
Kelowna, BC V1V 1J9

KELOWNA KITCHEN CENTRE
LTD
2791 Highway 97 N
Kelowna, BC V1X 4J8

MERIT KITCHENS LTD
435 Banks Road
Kelowna, BC V1X 6A2

Langley

CHARMAINE LORRISE
7084 197B Street
Langley, BC V3A 4P7

LANGLEY WOODCRAFT LTD
5780-203 Street
Langley, BC V3A 1W3

Nanaimo

KITCHENS UNLIMITED
2520 Bowen Road
Nanaimo, BC V9T 3L3

MERIT KITCHENS
4890 Rutherford Road
Nanaimo, BC V9T 4Z4

New Westminister

WESTERN CAST MARBLE
ASSOCIATION
220 522 7th Street
New Westminister, BC V3M 5T5

New Westminster

EUROPEAN KITCHEN
CABINETS LTD
143 E Columbia Street
New Westminster, BC V3L 3V9

North Vancouver

ALPINE APPLIANCE
INSTALLATIONS LTD
727 Kikeel Place
North Vancouver, BC V7N 2X2

CO-ORDINATED KITCHENS
LTD
225 East First Street
North Vancouver, BC V7L 1B4

KSI (KITCHEN SPACE INC)
15 Chesterfield Place
North Vancouver, BC V7M 3K3

MODERN MATERIALS LTD
125 E First Street
North Vancouver, BC V7L 1B2

Penticton

LEE-LYNN HOLDINGS INC
325 Dawson Avenue
Penticton, BC V2A 3N5

Richmond

MERIT KITCHENS
12331 Bridgeport Road
Richmond, BC V6V 1J4

PANEL PRODUCTS
2600 Viking Way
Richmond, BC V6V 1N2

REG PIKE
10155 Fundy Drive
Richmond, BC V7E 5P9

SUNCREST CABINETS
12580 Vickers Way
Richmond, BC V6V 1H9

THE ROBERTSON FAMILY
KITCHEN IDEA CENTER LTD
106 3860 Jacombs Road
Richmond, BC V6V 1Y6

THUNDERBIRD HOME
CENTERS
2440 Viking Way
Richmond, BC V6V 1N2

WOLF INDUSTRIES LTD
120 4500 Vanguard Road
Richmond, BC V6X 2P4

Sidney

WEDGEWOOD CABINETS
LTD
#1 2051 Malaview Avenue
RR 3
Sidney, BC V8L 2Z1

Surrey

DYNASTY KITCHEN
CABINETS LIMITED
#13 8145 130th Street
Surrey, BC V3W 7X4

MERIT KITCHENS LTD
12185 86th Avenue
Surrey, BC V3W 3H8

TAPLIN MANAGEMENT
COMPANY LTD
5684 Landmark Way
Surrey, BC V3S 7H1

Terrace

TERRACE BUILDERS CENTRE
LTD
3207 Munroe Street
Terrace, BC V8G 3B3

Vancouver

BAY DESIGN COMPANY
8696 Barnard Street
Vancouver, BC V6P 5G5

CACHET KITCHEN
INTERIORS LTD
1080 Mainland Street
Suite 204
Vancouver, BC V6B 2T4

CONTOUR KITCHEN DESIGN
LTD
1128 Mainland Street
Vancouver, BC V6B 5L1

CRONKHITE SUPPLY LTD
126 S E Marine Drive
Vancouver, BC V5X 2S3

DRIMO TILE
#102-333 Terminal Avenue.
Vancouver, BC V6A 2L7

KINGS-WAY KITCHEN
CENTRE LTD
3195 Kingsway
Vancouver, BC V5R 5K2

LONETREE ENTERPRISES
LTD
2990 Artbutus Street
Vancouver, BC V6J 3Y9

MERIT KITCHENS
2401 Burrard Street
Vancouver, BC V6J 3J3

PRESTIGE KITCHENS (1978)
LTD
6158 East Boulevard
Vancouver, BC V6M 3V6

SHOWCASE KITCHENS
1120 Mainland Street
Vancouver, BC V6B 2T9

SUPERIOR COVE-TOPS
3470 Commercial Street
Vancouver, BC V5N 4E9

Vernon

26TH STREET KITCHEN &
BATH LTD
5201 26th Street
Vernon, BC V1T 5G4

LIPILIAN KITCHENS &
MILLWORK
106 2450 14th Avenue
Vernon, BC V1B 2T1

Victoria

ALPHA FINISHERS LTD
568 Alpha Street
Victoria, BC V8Z 1B2

ARTLINE KITCHENS LTD
1838 Oak Bay Avenue
Victoria, BC V8R 1C2

DYNEL PACIFIC MARBLE
BATHROOMS LTD
1035 Alston Street
Victoria, BC V9A 3S6

E ROKO DISTRIBUTING LTD
619 Alpha Street
Victoria, BC V8Z 1B5

KITCHEN CLASSICS
601 Discovery Street
Victoria, BC V8T 5G4

LAZLO ROSSINI DESIGN LTD
CENTRE
141 Skinner
Victoria, BC V9A 6X4

MERIT KITCHENS &
RENOVATIONS
3196 Douglas Street
Victoria, BC V8Z 3K6

PACIFIC CABINETS LTD
3031 Jutland Road
Victoria, BC V8T 2T1

STARTEK BATHING SYSTEMS
LTD
491 A Burnside Road E
Victoria, BC V8T 2X3

West Vancouver

Y FRANKS APPLIANCES LTD
503 15th Street
West Vancouver, BC V7T 2S6

White Rock

KITCHENS ALIVE!
#21-15531-24th Avenue
White Rock, BC V4A 2J4

MANITOBA

Winnipeg

KITCHEN CRAFT OF
CANADA LTD
1180 Springfield Road
Winnipeg, MB R2C 2Z2

THE KITCHEN CRAFT
CONNECTION LTD
1500 Regent Avenue West
Winnipeg, MB R2C 3A8

NEW BRUNSWICK

Moncton

LAWSONS INC
194 Killam Drive
Moncton, NB E1C 3S4

NOVA SCOTIA

Pugwash

SEAGULL PEWTER LTD
Durham Street
PO Box 370
Pugwash, NS B0K 1L0

ONTARIO

Arprior

BOSA'S CUSTOM WOODCRAFTING
Flat Rapids Road
RR #2
Arprior, ON K7S 3G8

Barrie

BRADFORD PLANNED
KITCHENS
35 Cedar Pointe Drive
Barrie, ON L4N 5R7

ECONOMY KITCHENS &
RENOVATIONS INC
110 Anne Street South
Unit 6
Barrie, ON L4N 2E3

Bracebridge

MURRAY'S CUSTOM
KITCHENS LTD
Highway 11 South
PO Box 472
Bracebridge, ON P1L 1T8

Bradford

COUNTRY CABINETS INC
10 Industrial Court
PO Box 459
Bradford, ON L3Z 2B1

Brampton

METEOR PLYWOODS
LIMITED
4 Kenview Boulevard
Brampton, ON L6T 5E4

NEFF KITCHEN MANUFACTURERS
LTD
6 Melanie Drive
Brampton, ON L6T 4K9

UNIQUE KITCHENS INC
25 Rutherford Road S
Brampton, ON L6W 3J3

Brockville

KITCHEN AND BATH
CENTRE R.V. SPRACKLIN &
SONS LTD
Highway 29 N
PO Box 1425
Brockville, ON K6V-5Y6

Burlington

GRAVELLE KITCHEN & BATH
STUDIO
4084 Fairview Street
Burlington, ON L7Y 4Y8

O/B OPAL BATHS & DESIGN
OPAL DESIGN INC
4104 Fairview Street
Unit #3
Burlington, ON L7L 2A4

WILLIS SUPPLY COMPANY
5403 Fairview Street
Burlington, ON L7L 5J7

Cambridge

BECKERMANN KITCHEN
CONCEPTS
240 Holiday Inn Drive
Cambridge, ON N3C 3X4

EUROCLEAN CANADA INC
866 Langs Drive
Cambridge, ON N3H 2N7

SMITTY'S KITCHEN GALLERY
150 Holiday Inn Drive
Cambridge, ON N3C 1Z5

Carleton Place

LATIF CABINETS LTD
110 Industrial Avenue
Box 70
Carleton Place, ON K7C 3P3

Concord

AQUABRASS INC
8899 Jane Street
Concord, ON L4K 2M6

Cornwall

MENARD RENOVATION
CENTER LTD
1100 Marleau Avenue
PO Box 38
Cornwall, ON K6H 5R9

Courtice

BRANDOM KITCHEN
WHOLESALE
1732 Baseline Road W
Courtice, ON L1E 2S8

Don Mills

BATH & KITCHEN
MARKETER
1450 Don Mills Road
Don Mills, ON M3B 2X7

Echo Bay

MAPLE LEAF FOREST
PRODUCTS
Highway 17
Echo Bay, ON P0S 1C0

Gorrie

WATSON HOME HARDWARE
Highway 87
Gorrie, ON N0G 1X0

Guelph

PARAGON KITCHENS
LIMITED
230 Southgate Drive
Guelph, ON N1G 5P5

Hanover

HANOVER KITCHEN & BATH
GALLERY
PO Box 159
655 10th Street
Hanover, ON N4N 3C4

HANOVER KITCHENS
(CANADA) INC
711 - 10th Avenue
Hanover, ON N4N 2P7

Huntsville

GRANITE POINT HOMES INC
Lindgren Road E Highway # 11
PO Box 2767
Huntsville, ON P0A 1K0

Kingston

COUNTRY WIDE KITCHEN &
FLOORING INC
407 Counter
Suite 110
Kingston, ON K7K 6A9

KITCHEN THINK
2780 Princess Street
Kingston, ON K7R 1W9

WINSTON'S KITS/DIV
WINBETT MGT CORP
1469 Princess Street
Unit 3A
Kingston, ON K7M 3E9

Kitchener

ACORN KITCHENS LIMITED
56 Trillium Park Place
Kitchener, ON N2E 1X1

BECKERMANN EXQUISITE
KITCHENS
44 Otonabee Drive
Kitchener, ON N2C 1L6

GREAT CABINETS PLUS INC
1244 Victoria Street N
Kitchener, ON N2B 3C9

HEARTLAND APPLIANCES
INC
5 Hoffman Street
Kitchener, ON N2M 3M5

London

CARDINAL KITCHENS
LIMITED
215 Exeter Road
London, ON N6L 1A4

CONTINENTAL CABINET
COMPANY
547 Clarke Road
London, ON N5V 2E1

DEAN'S KITCHEN CENTRE
LTD
90 Charterhouse Crescent
Unit #7
London, ON N5W 5V5

Midland

KINDRED INDUSTRIES
1000 Kindred Road
Midland, ON L4R 4K9

Mississauga

DOWNSVIEW WOODWORKING
LTD
2635 Rena Road
Mississauga, ON L4T 1G6

INTEGRATED APPLIANCES
LTD BOYD BROWN
APPLIANCE USA
6451 NW Drive
Mississauga, ON L4V 1K2

KITCHENAID CANADA
1901 Minnesota Court
Mississauga, ON L5N 3A7

LEETECH CABINETS INC
5181 Everest Drive
Mississauga, ON L4W 2R2

Nepean

J H ERNEST DALY
3978 Richmond Road
Nepean, ON K2H 8R5

Niagra Falls

NIAGARA ARTCRAFT
WOODWORK COMPANY LTD
4417 Kent Avenue
Niagra Falls, ON L2H 1J1

Oakville

EURO-LINE APPLIANCES LTD
2923 Portland Drive
Oakville, ON L6H 5S4

FAUCCETTE MOEN INC
2816 Bristol Circle
Oakville, ON L6H 5S7

MARKOW & ASSOCIATES
LTD
133 Wilson Street
Oakville, ON L6K 3G9

OAKVILLE KITCHEN CENTRE
599 Third Line
Oakville, ON L6L 4A8

QUALITY KITCHEN & BATH
DIVISION OF 89795 ONTARIO
1480 Speers Road
Units 1 & 2
Oakville, ON L6L 2X6

Oldcastle

KITCHEN KORNER 388456
ONTARIO CANADA
1620 Rossi Drive
Oldcastle, ON N0R 1L0

Orangeville

T.A.L.K. KITCHENS LTD
76 Centennial Road #4
Orangeville, ON L9W 1P9

Orillia

PENISTON INTERIORS (1980)
INC
301 Forest Avenue
PO Box 186
Orillia, ON L3V 6J3

Oshawa

MILLWORK HOME CENTER
1279 Simcoe St. North
Oshawa, ON L1G 4X4

THE KITCHEN PLACE LTD
861 Simcoe Street South
Oshawa, ON L1H 4K8

Ottawa

DESIGN FIRST KITCHEN
INTERIORS
24 Clarence Street
Ottawa, ON K1N 5P3

DOMICILE KITCHENS
202 Dalhousie Street
Ottawa, ON K1N 7C8

MODULAR KITCHENS LTD
16 Pretoria
Ottawa, ON K1S 1W7

THE TOTAL KITCHEN INC
1658 Woodward Drive
Ottawa, ON K2C 3R8

Owen Sound

BATH AND KITCHEN BY
ACTON'S
RR #5
Owen Sound, ON N4K SN7

KEN PHILIP PLUMBING &
HEATING LTD
PO Box 743
Owen Sound, ON N4K 5W9

Peterborough

ART CRAFT CABINETS
655-13 The Queensway
Peterborough, ON K9J 7M1

BALL KITCHEN CENTRE INC
1135 Lansdowne Street W
Peterborough, ON K9J 7M2

EUR OWN STYLE BATH &
KITCHEN
709 Bethune Street
Peterborough, ON K9H 4A5

NHB INDUSTRIES LTD
944 Crawford Drive
Peterborough, ON K9J 3X2

WHITLER INDUSTRIES LTD
789 O'Brien Drive
PO Box 2018
Peterborough, ON K9J 7Y4

Pickering

BINNS DESIGNER KITCHENS
INC
333 Kingston Road
Pickering, ON L1V 1A1

MONARCH KITCHEN
CENTRE DIVISION OF RJF
CUSTOM HOMES
Unit 6
1020 Brock Road
Pickering, ON L1W 3H2

PROBILT KITCHENS LIMITED
1080 Brock Road Unit #8
Pickering, ON L1W 3H3

THE KITCHEN COURT
1755 Pickering Parkway
Unit 13
Pickering, ON L1V 6K5

Renfrew

DESLAURIER CUSTOM
CABINETS INC
405 Hall Avenue Unit 12
Renfrew, ON K7V 2S6

Rexdale

NORTESCO INC
151 Carlingview Drive
Unit 12
Rexdale, ON M9W 5S4

Richmond Hill

PARIS KITCHENS DIVISION
OF SANDERSON-HAROLD
COMPANY
245 West Beaver Creek Road
Richmond Hill, ON L4B 1L1

Saint Catharine

ELMWOOD KITCHEN
LIMITED
445 Eastchester Avenue
Saint Catharine, ON L2M 6S2

Sarnia

SARNIA CABINETS LTD
1321 Plank Road
Sarnia, ON N7W 1A6

Sault Saint Marie

KITCHEN AND HOME
CENTRE
64 Industrial Park Crescent
Sault Saint Marie, ON P6B 5P2

Scarborough

L I K E DISTRIBUTORS LTD
390 Tapscott Road
Scarborough, ON M1B 2H9

Stoneycreek

IMAGES KITCHEN & BATH
DESIGN INC
43 Teal Ave Unit 3
Stoneycreek, ON L8E 3B1

Sudbury

KITCHENS 'N COUNTERS
371 Lorne Street
Sudbury, ON P3C 4R1

Thornhill

CANAC KITCHENS LTD
360 John Street
Thornhill, ON L3T 3M9

RAYWAL LTD
68 Green Lane
Thornhill, ON L3T 6K8

Toronto

CENTURA
53 Apex Road
Toronto, ON M6A 2V6

DUNBAR & ROSS LIMITED
3425 Yonge Street
Toronto, ON M4N 2N1

FERRETTI INTERNATIONAL
4701 Steeles Avenue West
Suite 220
Toronto, ON M9L 1X2

GINGER'S INTERNATIONAL
BATH CENTRE
1275 Castlefield Avenue
Toronto, ON M6B 1G4

HEARTWOOD INC
2760 Yonge Street
Toronto, ON M4N 2J2

INTERNATIONAL DESIGNS
INC
2725 Yonge Street
Toronto, ON M4N 2H8

KINGSWAY KITCHENS
4247 Dundas Street West
Toronto, ON M8X 1Y3

LAURENTIDE DESIGN LTD
945 Eglinton Avenue East
Toronto, ON M4G 4B5

THE KITCHEN COURT
TORONTO
266 Eglington Avenue W
Toronto, ON M4R 1B2

THE ROBINSON GROUP
263 Davenport Road
Toronto, ON M5R 1J9

Victoria

GRIFFIN DESIGN KITCHENS
714 View Street
Victoria, ON V8W 1J8

Waterloo

ELMIRA STOVE WORKS
145 Northfield Drive
Waterloo, ON N2L 5J3

VANITY MART BATH &
KITCHEN CENTER
90 Frobisher Drive
Waterloo, ON N2V 2A1

Weston

MBA MANUFACTURING
175 Toryork Drive
Unit 54
Weston, ON M9L 2Y7

Windsor

NAYLOR'S KITCHEN & BATH
3260 Jefferson Boulevard
Windsor, ON N8Y 2W8

Woodstock

THE KITCHEN EMPORIUM
INC
54 Kent Street
Woodstock, ON N4S 6Y7

QUEBEC

Drummondville

VENMAR VENTILATION INC
1715 Haggerty
Drummondville, PQ J2C 5P7

Lasalle

FABRICATION MODULATEK
INC
295 La Fleur Street
Lasalle, PQ H8R 3H3

Laval

TWENTY TWENTY
1730 Cunard Street
Suite 101
Laval, PQ H7S 2B2

Montreal

ATELIER SINGULIER INC
4621 Salaberry
Montreal, PQ H4J 1H7

LES CUISINES INTERNATIONALES
G M B H
8100 Decarie
Montreal, PQ H4P 2S4

Saint Leonard

M FILIAULT DISTRIBUTOR
LTD
6475 Des Grandes Prairies
Saint Leonard, PQ H1P 1A5

U. S. Territories

PUERTO RICO

San Juan

BATHROOM JEWELS
313 Domenech Avenue
San Juan, PR 00918

RAFAEL J NIDO INC
PO Box 11978
San Juan, PR 00922

APPROVED NKBA
CERTIFIED KITCHEN DESIGNER
AND
CERTIFIED BATH DESIGNER
MEMBERS

ALABAMA

Birmingham

Betsy Hedrick-Smith CKD
705 Morning Sun Drive
Birmingham, AL 35242

Charles R Lambert CKD
3345 Valley Park Drive
Birmingham, AL 35243

Mobile

Tracy M Hooper CKD
BY DESIGN
1 Lancaster Road
PO Box 8567
Mobile, AL 36689

Jeannine S McNeely CKD
5519 Richmond Road
Mobile, AL 36608

Wayne A Williams CKD
PO Box 81486
Mobile, AL 36689

ALASKA

Anchorage

Elizabeth Breon CKD
PO Box 221642
Anchorage, AK 99522

Hot Springs

Marion H Herman CKD
PO Box 1609
Hot Springs, AK 76102

ARIZONA

Catalina

Donald K Paugh Sr CKD
PO Box 8521
Catalina, AZ 85738

Lake Havasu City

Barbara A Gialdini CKD
3501 N. Highway 95, Space 51
Lake Havasu City, AZ 86405

Duane M Leber CKD
CABINETS UNLIMITED INC
703 Enterprise Drive
Lake Havasu City, AZ 86403

Mesa

Rita L Phillips CKD
MASTERCRAFT KITCHEN
PO Box 40910
Mesa, AZ 85274

Phoenix

Dennis L Ayers CKD
6212 N 22nd Drive
Phoenix, AZ 85015

Tucson

Colleen B Langston CKD CBD
ALBRITE BATH & KITCHEN
3640 E. Ft. Lowell
Tucson, AZ 85716

Janice L O'Brien CKD
331 N. El Camino Del Norte
Tucson, AZ 85716

Michael P O'Brien CKD
331 N. El Camino
Tucson, AZ 85716

Michelle A Robinson CKD
8356 N Bayou Dr
Tucson, AZ 85741-1022

ARKANSAS

Jacksonville

Billy C Morden CKD
WRIGHT'S CABINET SHOP
INC
2600 Cory Drive
Jacksonville, AR 72076

Jonesboro

Vilas H Elder Jr CKD
1304 Dupwe
Jonesboro, AR 72401

Little Rock

Kaye M Osburn CKD
5108 West 10th
Little Rock, AR 72204

CALIFORNIA

Alameda

Joy H Wilkins CKD
3000 Central Avenue
Alameda, CA 94501

Berkeley

Carolyn Sell CKD
1529 A Delaware Street
Berkeley, CA 94703

Bermuda Dunes

Mary Grace Satterfield CKD
42630 Maypen
Bermuda Dunes, CA 92201

Carpinteria

Holly G Sommers CKD
5950 Via Real #1
Carpinteria, CA 93013

Chowchilla

Sheron W Bailey CKD
12390 Avenue 18 1/2
Chowchilla, CA 93610

Citrus Heights

Kathy A Maraglio CKD
ORIGINAL DESIGNS
6735 Indian River Drive
Citrus Heights, CA 95621

Clovis

DeAnn Martin-Ray CKD
KITCHENS UNLIMITED
77 Burgan Avenue
Clovis, CA 93612

Concord

Al Drachman CKD
1080 San Miguel
Concord, CA 94518

Corona del Mar

G. Townsend Bradner Jr CKD
KITCHENS DEL MAR
3536 East Coast Highway
Corona del Mar, CA 92625

Costa Mesa

Cynthia Roberts McCue CKD
621 Shasta Lane
Costa Mesa, CA 92626

Daly City

Phillip H Stidham CKD
368 Imperial Way #137
Daly City, CA 94015

Danville

Larry E Cathey CKD
CLASSIC KITCH OF
DANVILLE
301 Hartz Avenue
Suite 217
Danville, CA 94526

El Cajon

Nancy Blandford CKD
475 Murray Drive
El Cajon, CA 92020

El Toro

Jerry E Hagler CKD
24701 Raymond Way, #111
El Toro, CA 92630

Encino

David Lemkin CKD
5211 Yarmouth Avenue #15
Encino, CA 91316

Fillmore

Douglas R Benjamin CKD
Kitchen Design Service
Fillmore, CA 93015

Foster City

Karen L Brown CKD
839 Balboa Lane
Foster City, CA 94404

Fremont

William R Pease CKD
CUSTOM KITCHEN BATH
CENTER
40900 Fremont Boulevard
Fremont, CA 94538

Fresno

Louis A Hall CKD CBD
363 W. Stuart Avenue
Fresno, CA 93704

Fullerton

Carol E Lamkins CKD
3901 Madonna Drive
Fullerton, CA 92635

Glendora

Virginia Griffin CKD
KITCHENS ALPHA OMEGA
1247 E Sierra Madre Avenue
Glendora, CA 91740

Grass Valley

Karen Austin CKD
CREATIVE KITCHENS AND
BATHS
13399 Capitol Drive
Grass Valley, CA 95945

Hacienda Heights

Richard L Pizzuti CKD
2947 Adelita Drive
Hacienda Heights, CA 91745

Edythe I Rabon CKD
2525 Teresina Drive
Hacienda Heights, CA 91745

Hillsborough

Stanley M Macey CKD
2031 Forest View Avenue
Hillsborough, CA 94010

Huntington Beach

Richard B Pulsifer CKD
THE ARTIFACTORY
17142 Gothard Street
Huntington Beach, CA 92647-
5420

Irvine

Shanda K Stephenson CKD
THE JM KITCHEN & BATH
SHOWROOM
15333 Culver Drive
Suite 220
Irvine, CA 92714

La Mesa

Gary D Heidman CKD
KITCHENS PLUS
7943 University Avenue
La Mesa, CA 91941

John De Luca CKD
KITCHENS BY DE LUCA
7872 LaMesa Boulevard
La Mesa, CA 91941

Richard Mikesell CKD
8481 El Paso Street
La Mesa, CA 91942

Laguna Beach

Karen S Costello CKD
SKYLINE KITCHENS & BATHS
31671 South Pacific Coast
Highway
Laguna Beach, CA 92677

Laguna Hills

Edward Rubin CKD
3437-C Bahia Blanca West
Laguna Hills, CA 92653

Gary E White CBD
25251 Calero Avenue
Laguna Hills, CA 92653

Lake Forest

Annabelle Marshall CKD
VALLEY KITCHENS
22541 Aspan Suite A
Lake Forest, CA 92630

Lakewood

George D Alemshah CKD
5209 Knoxville Avenue
Lakewood, CA 90713

Loomis

James M Liston CKD
4965 Del Road
Loomis, CA 95650

Los Angeles

John W Avram CKD
JOHN W AVRAM &
ASSOCIATES
1328 S Santa Fe Avenue
Los Angeles, CA 90021

Garry A Bishop CKD
SHOWCASE KITCHENS
2317 Westwood Boulevard
Los Angeles, CA 90064

William T Boyle CKD
DESIGN STUDIO WEST SAINT
CHARLES
8656 Sunset Boulevard
Los Angeles, CA 90069

Neil R Cooper CKD
COOPER PACIFIC KITCHENS
INC
8687 Melrose Avenue
#G776
Los Angeles, CA 90069-5701

Laurence I Geisser CKD
CLEVELAND WRECKING
COMPANY
3170 E Washington Boulevard
Los Angeles, CA 90023

Michael Goldberg CKD
BRENTWOOD KITCHENS
2378 Westwood Boulevard
Los Angeles, CA 90064

Christine Kosmalski CKD
3549 Hughes Avenue #104
Los Angeles, CA 90034

John A Pace CKD
8700 Burton Way #103
Los Angeles, CA 90048

Donald E Silvers CKD
KITCHENS & OTHER
ENVIRONMENTS BY DES
155 S Orange Drive
Los Angeles, CA 90036

Los Osos

Randolph Ball CKD
INDEPENDENT CONTRACTOR
PO Box 6595
Los Osos, CA 93412

Menlo Park

Iris F Harrell CBD
HARRELL REMODELING INC
108 Gilbert Avenue
Menlo Park, CA 94025

Newcastle

Molly J. Korb CKD CBD
6835 Ravine Court
Newcastle, CA 95658

Newport Beach

James D Maddox CKD
2332 Naples
Newport Beach, CA 92660

Bonnie M Teel CKD
GREENBRIAR KITCHENS
3601 Jamboree Road
Newport Beach, CA 92660

Novato

Edward A Wittig CKD
30 Hickox Road
Novato, CA 94947

Oakland

Carlene Anderson CKD
KITCHEN DESIGN INC
5818 Balboa Drive
Oakland, CA 94611

Fred M Brasch CKD
SUPERIOR HOME REMODELING
CONTRACTORS
4700 Telegraph Avenue
Oakland, CA 94609

Tim W Jollymore CKD
J B TURNER & SONS
3911 Piedmont Avenue
Oakland, CA 94611

Orange

James B Galloway CKD
CAREFREE KITCHENS INC
453 N Anaheim Boulevard
Orange, CA 92668

Orinda

Dagmar T Thiel CKD
KITCHEN AND BATH DESIGN
2 Theater Square
Suite 307
Orinda, CA 94563

Oxnard

Terry Breese CKD
235 Central Avenue
Oxnard, CA 93030

Pacifica

Ernest Weidner CKD
329 3rd Avenue
Pacifica, CA 94044

Palo Alto

Kathleen Claudon CKD
KM DESIGNS
1220 Wilson Street
Palo Alto, CA 94301-7453

Michelle R Seabrook CKD
3747 Ladonna Avenue
Palo Alto, CA 94306

Pasadena

Michael B Baugus CKD
1975 Galbreth Road
Pasadena, CA 91104

Pinole

Gary A Taylor CKD
2810 Wright Avenue
Pinole, CA 94564

Pleasant Hill

Margie Little CKD
INDEPENDENT KITCHEN &
BATH DESIGNER
1432 Stonehedge Drive
Pleasant Hill, CA 94523

Patricia K Stenger CKD
STENGER DESIGN
ASSOCIATES
443 Coleman Court
Pleasant Hill, CA 94523

Rancho Lacosta

Peter M Del Vecchio CKD
INTERPLAN DESIGNS
7720-B El Camino Real #185
Rancho Lacosta, CA 92009

Rancho Palos Verdes

Suzanne J Karbach CKD
5935 Flambeau Road
Rancho Palos Verdes, CA 90274

CKD-Certified Kitchen Designer; CBD-Certified Bath Designer

Redding

Shirley E Anderson CKD
2450 Sacramento Drive
Redding, CA 96001

Redondo Beach

Jacqueline Balint CKD
THE KITCHEN COLLECTION
241 Avendia Del Norte
Redondo Beach, CA 90277

Redwood City

Maureen R Cordoza CKD
1754 Stockbridge Avenue
Redwood City, CA 94061

S San Francisco

Peggy Deras CKD
548 Theresa Drive
S San Francisco, CA 94080

Sacramento

Melissa S Anderson CKD
1941 Iris Avenue
Sacramento, CA 95815

Salinas

Arthur M Brost CKD
9789 Trefoil Place
Salinas, CA 93907

San Clemente

Beth A Marsden CKD
PARK AVENUE WEST
63 Calle De Industrias
#472
San Clemente, CA 92672-3826

San Diego

Dianne L Harsch CKD
EUROPEAN KITCHEN &
BATH
6440 Lusk Boulevard
San Diego, CA 92121

San Leandro

Marilyn S Gray CKD
GRAY & GRAY
16608 Kildare Road
San Leandro, CA 94578

Brian Peck CKD
SOMERSET REMODELING
INC
15255 Hesperian Boulevard
San Leandro, CA 94578

San Pablo

Joseph W Aievoli CKD
142 Westgate Circle
San Pablo, CA 94806

San Rafael

Lyndell Hogan CKD
LAMPERTI ASSOCIATES
1241 Anderson Drive
San Rafael, CA 94901

Santa Ana Heights

Theresa M Matusek CKD
EURO AMERICAN KITCHENS
AND BATHS
20331 Irvine Ave Ste 4
Santa Ana Heights, CA 92707

Santa Barbara

Susan Thielmann CKD
THIELMANN'S KITCHENS
AND BATHS
208 Cottage Grove Avenue
Santa Barbara, CA 93101

Santa Clara

Lila Levinson CKD
ACCENT ON DESIGN
100 Saratoga Avenue
Santa Clara, CA 95051

Santa Maria

Curtis W Crane CKD
1930 South Lincoln #2
Santa Maria, CA 93454

Santa Monica

W E Peterson CKD
BAY CITIES KITCHENS &
APPLIANCES
1302 Santa Monica Boulevard
Santa Monica, CA 90404

Santa Paula

David Johnson CKD
933 Cliff Drive
Santa Paula, CA 93060

Santa Rosa

Nancy Lind Cooper CKD
COOPER KITCHENS INC
1133 Sunnyslope Drive
Santa Rosa, CA 95404

Santee

Michael S De Luca CKD
MICHAEL DE LUCA AND
ASSOCIATES
11355 Canyon Park Drive
Santee, CA 92071

Spring Valley

Timothy L Woods CKD
2135 La Mesa Court
Spring Valley, CA 92078

Sunnyvale

Loren E Wright CKD
614 Conrado Terrace #3
Sunnyvale, CA 94086

Tustin

Todd L Mead CKD
2192 Dogwood Road #A
Tustin, CA 902680

Ayeshah T Morin CKD
DESIGNER KITCHENS INC
17300 E 17th St Ste A
Tustin, CA 92680

Vacaville

Susan S Holbrook CKD
356 Shannon Drive
Vacaville, CA 95688

Vallejo

Mary M Fraser CKD
790 Derr Avenue
Vallejo, CA 94590-7730

Vista

Norman M Allegan CKD
1491 Green Oak Road
Vista, CA 92083

W Sacramento

John B Curtis CKD
CURTIS & COMPANY
1152 Fernwood Street
W Sacramento, CA 95691

Walnut Creek

Sharon R Buffa CKD
2704 Oak Road #76
Walnut Creek, CA 94596

Walnut Criid

Maureen O'Brien-Morsch CKD
1450 Creekside Drive
Walnut Criid, CA 94549

West Hollywood

Paul C Bailly CKD
KITCHEN DESIGN STUDIO
400 North Robertson Boulevard
West Hollywood, CA 90048

Yorba Linda

Patricia J Otto CKD
5081 West Knoll
Yorba Linda, CA 92686

COLORADO

Arvada

Joan M Adducci CKD
8294 Depew Way
Arvada, CO 80003

Aurora

Carryn R. Dyer CKD
PO Box 440093
Aurora, CO 80044-0093

Angela S Lawrence CKD
1917 Hanover Street
Aurora, CO 80010-2323

Robert R Oxley CKD
ROBERT OXLEY TRAINING &
CONSULTING
401 S Kalispell Way
Suite #107
Aurora, CO 80017

Kenneth W Smith CKD CBD
1671 Dunkirk Court
Aurora, CO 80011

Boulder

Kevin A Jean CKD
KITCHEN PLANNERS
1627 28th Street
Boulder, CO 80301

Carbondale

Seth T Fordham CKD
PO Box 1376
Carbondale, CO 81623

Colorado Springs

William B Jordan CKD
1090 Hill Circle
Colorado Springs, CO 80904

Colorado Sprngs

Ed Medran CKD
KITCHEN DESIGN
SPECIALISTS
218 East Monument
Colorado Sprngs, CO 80903

Carl E Varley CKD
4838 Splendid Circle South
Colorado Sprngs, CO 80917

Denver

Ms Cynthia R Buechler CKD
2449 S. Broadway
Denver, CO 80210

Catherine Dulacki CKD
4050 S. Willow Way
Denver, CO 80237

Helen D Francis CKD
540 S Forest Street #Y
Denver, CO 80222

Edward Hanley CKD
EDWARD HANLEY &
COMPANY
1448 Oneida Street
Denver, CO 80220

T J Kesicki CKD
KITCHEN GALLERY LTD
66 S Logan Street
Denver, CO 80209

Cynthia Leonard CKD
THURSTON INC
2920 East 6th Avenue
Denver, CO 80206

Pamela L Ludwig CKD
3060 W. 39th
Denver, CO 80211

Lynne W McMurtry CKD
WM OHS SHOWROOM INC
2900 E 6th Avenue
Denver, CO 80206

Kathryn A Moyse CKD
2205 S. Yosemite Circle
Denver, CO 80231

Bonnie DeGabain Rollin CKD
THE THURSTON KITCHEN
AND BATH
2920 E 6th Avenue
Denver, CO 80206

Klaudia H Spivey CKD
DESIGN TIMES
901 Adams Street
Denver, CO 80206

CKD-Certified Kitchen Designer; CBD-Certified Bath Designer

Englewood

Beverly G Adams CKD
8810 East Mineral Place
Englewood, CO 80112

Kenneth W Savacool CKD
6073 South Krameria
Englewood, CO 80111

Fraser

Lynne Hada Anderson CKD
PO Box 1019
Fraser, CO 80442

Glenwood Sprngs

Robin M Slattery CKD
5050 Road 154
Glenwood Sprngs, CO 81601

Golden

Ed Winger CKD
25318 Foothills Drive, North
Golden, CO 80401-9171

Highlands Ranch

Larry R Lanners CKD
9413 S. Cobblecrest Drive
Highlands Ranch, CO 80126

Lafayette

Diane M Ebeling CKD
1205 Centaur Village Court
Lafayette, CO 80026

Madelin Nelson CKD
613 East Emma Street
Lafayette, CO 80026

Lakewood

Joyce J Combs CKD
701 Harlan Street E4
Lakewood, CO 80214

Julie A Mills CKD
216 Wright Street #106
Lakewood, CO 80228

Norman L Van Nattan CKD
KITCHENS FOR COLORADO
INC
6381 W Alameda Avenue
Lakewood, CO 80226

Littleton

Mikel Altenhofen CKD
7193 S. Cody Way
Littleton, CO 80123-4274

Ronald F Dreyer CKD
451 E. Caley Avenue
Littleton, CO 80121

Esther M Hartman CKD
KITCHEN DISTRIBUTORS INC
1309 W Littleton Boulevard
Littleton, CO 80120

Thomas Hartman CKD
6878 S. Dover Way
Littleton, CO 80123

Ms Diane D Johnson CKD
5504 South Hoyt Street
Littleton, CO 80123

Sharon Reznicek Lamb CKD
4691 W. Lake Circle, North
Littleton, CO 80123-6772

Jo Ann D Roach CKD
7449 S. Clarkson Circle
Littleton, CO 80122

Mary Lynn Rockwell CKD
7826 S. University way
Littleton, CO 80122

Westminster

Charles Martin CKD
7931 Bradburn Blvd.
Westminster, CO 80030

CONNECTICUT

Ansonia

Bruno Pasqualucci CKD
196 North State Street
Ansonia, CT 06401

Bristol

Genard E Dolan CKD
10 Carpenter Avenue
Bristol, CT 06010

Cheshire

Lorey A Cavanaugh CKD
304 Beacon Hill Drive
Cheshire, CT 06410

Chester

George D Crane CKD
PO Box 478
Chester, CT 06412

Clinton

Laurie Eriksson CKD
6 Nod Road
Clinton, CT 06413

Danbury

Terry Scarborough CKD
ETHAN ALLEN INC
Gallery Eathan Allen Drive
Danbury, CT 06811

Easton

Alexander Kasper CKD
38 Palmer Place
Easton, CT 06612

Fairfield

Isidore B Plotkin CKD
93 Old Farm Road
Fairfield, CT 06430

Hamden

Donald W Fioretti CKD
414 Wintergreen Avenue
Hamden, CT 06514

Huntington

Henry Jacoby CKD
DESIGN CONCEPTS INC
314 Aspetuck Village
Huntington, CT 06484

Madison

Richard R Gedney CKD
KITCHENS BY GEDNEY INC
84 Bradley Road
Madison, CT 06443

New Britain

Timothy J Bates CKD
29 North Wellington Street
New Britain, CT 06053

New Canaan

Mark A Rutter CBD
MARK A RUTTER &
COMPANY LTD
PO Box 1530
244 Elm Street
New Canaan, CT 06840

New Milford

Cynthia P Beck CKD
RINGS' END INC
140 Danbury Road
New Milford, CT 06776

Kelly Loyd Stewart CKD
108 Old Ridge Road
New Milford, CT 06776

Old Saybrook

Sue McAlexander CKD
3 Wild Apple Lane
Old Saybrook, CT 06475

Prospect

Thomas D Biron CKD
CASEWORK DESIGNS
10 Roy Mountain Road
Prospect, CT 06712

Putnam

Frederick Kress CKD
9 Milton Street
Putnam, CT 06260

Ridgefield

Tom Bailey CKD
36 Fairview Avenue
Ridgefield, CT 06877

Sherman

Paul Levine CKD
Deer Hill
Sherman, CT 06784

Southington

Gertrude I Greaves CKD
4 Stoughton Road
Southington, CT 06489

Stamford

Joanne M Stage CKD
KITCHENS BY DEANE
1267 E Main Street
Stamford, CT 06902

Wallingford

Ramona Eldridge CKD
84 Brentwood Village
Wallingford, CT 06492

West Hartford

Maurice A Peterson CKD
26 Gloucester Lane
West Hartford, CT 06107

Brita O Peterson CKD
26 Gloucester Lane
West Hartford, CT 06107

Kenneth W Peterson CKD
64 High Farms Road
West Hartford, CT 06110

James D Tate CKD
50 Ridgebrook Drive
West Hartford, CT 06107

Westbrook

Joseph B Ciccarello CKD
COVENANT KITCHENS &
BATHS
1871 Boston Post Road
Westbrook, CT 06498

Winsted

Robert C Aldridge CKD
28 Case Avenue
Winsted, CT 06098

DELAWARE

Seaford

Michael R Griffith CKD
2012 Concord Road
Seaford, DE 19973

Wilmington

Steven J Campbell CKD
BATH/KITCHEN & TILE
CENTER
103 Greenbank Road
Wilmington, DE 19808

Lisa H Greene CKD
1428 Stapler Place
Wilmington, DE 19806

Mark J Pyle CKD
BATH KITCHEN & TILE
CENTER
103 Greenbank Road
Wilmington, DE 19808

Jeanette A Spaeth CKD
3501 Haley Court
Wilmington, DE 19808

CKD-Certified Kitchen Designer; CBD-Certified Bath Designer

DISTRICT OF COLUMBIA

Washington

Nancy R Meyer CKD
4545 Connecticut Avenue, N.W.
Washington, DC 20008

Robert D Schafer CKD
THE KITCHEN GUILD
5027 Connecticut Avenue NW
Washington, DC 20008

FLORIDA

Alachua

Sharon R Diehl CKD
DESIGN CABINETS INC
PO Box 1108
Alachua, FL 32615

Avon Park

Paul Lipkin CKD
1705 N. Homeric Road
Avon Park, FL 33825

Boca Raton

Leonard F Maceli CKD
20795 Boca Ridge Drive North
Boca Raton, FL 33428

Boynton Beach

Robert O Geddes CKD
9796 Pavarotti Terrace #103
Boynton Beach, FL 33437

Brandon

Richard D Arnold CKD
1016 Mandalay Drive
Brandon, FL 33511

Casselberry

Richard P Gerth CKD
PO Box 181424
Casselberry, FL 32707

Charlotte Harbor

Cyril F Schrage CKD
KITCHEN CLASSICS
4265 K Tamiami Trail
Charlotte Harbor, FL 33980

Clearwater

Charlotte Clark CKD
CHARLOTTE CLARK
KITCHENS
PO Box 3039
Clearwater, FL 34630

Deerfield Beach

Paul B Gunter CKD
1509 S.E. 14th Drive
Deerfield Beach, FL 33441

Ellenton

Louis P Scarani CKD
62 Meadowlark Circle
Ellenton, FL 34222

Fort Lauderdale

Charles Poole CKD CBD
DESIGNER KITCHENS &
BATHS INC
2500 Wilton Drive
Fort Lauderdale, FL 33305

Robert L Welky CKD
PO Box 24430
Fort Lauderdale, FL 33307-4430

Fort Myers

Carl E Bergner CKD Jr
1527 Woodford Avenue
Fort Myers, FL 33901

Fort Pierce

Celeste C Bush CKD
DESIGN KITCHENS
412 Farmers Market Road
Fort Pierce, FL 34982

Ft. Lauderdale

Carl R Aden CKD
PO Box 100445
Ft. Lauderdale, FL 33310

Gulf Breeze

John HG Raiser CKD
1371 Players Club Circle
Gulf Breeze, FL 32561

Hialeah

Ivan Parron CKD
7990 W. 25th Avenue
Hialeah, FL 33016

Holiday

George J Baird CKD
1312 Maybury Drive
Holiday, FL 34691-5138

Indian Lake Estates

William T Langohr CKD
TOWNSEND ASSOCIATES
907 Park Avenue
PO Box 7337
Indian Lake Estates, FL 33855

Jacksonville

Paul A Barton CKD CBD
6001-27 Argule Forrest - Bl #235
Jacksonville, FL 32244

Melanie P Hastings CKD
KITCHENS ETC BY REGENCY
8321 Atlantic Boulevard
Jacksonville, FL 32211

William L Oxley Jr CKD
6318 Mercer Circle E
Jacksonville, FL 32217

Lake Placid

Victor L Matousek CKD
904 Golfview Drive
Lake Placid, FL 33852

Lake Wales

John F Werner CKD
96 Tower Lake
Lake Wales, FL 33853

Lakeland

Glenn D Bridges CKD
FLORIDA KITCHEN DESIGNS
608 N Ingraham Avenue
Lakeland, FL 33801

Largo

Clarice E Terepka CKD
THE CABINET CORNER INC
426 W Bay Drive
Largo, FL 34640

Longwood

Sandra L Linn CKD
226 Cambridge Drive
Longwood, FL 32779

Marco Island

Edward M Scardaccione CKD
980 Huron Court PH 1
Marco Island, FL 33937

Margate

Richard B Dettmer CKD
3460 Pinewalk Drive N.
Margate, FL 33063

Miami

Nancy Ware CKD CBD
TRIM LINE KITCHENS &
BATHS
10001 S Dixie Highway
Miami, FL 33156

Miami Shores

G Ann Nunnally CKD
1700 N.E. 105 Street, #106
Miami Shores, FL 33138

Milton

Sharon F Holley CKD
1850 Locust Street
Milton, FL 32570

N Miami Beach

Louis Platsky CKD
920 NE 169th Street
Apartment 614
N Miami Beach, FL 33162

Naples

James C Langan CKD
449 Riviera Blvd.
Naples, FL 33962

New Port Richey

Martin M Frank CKD
MARTIN ASSOCIATES
PO Box 1481
New Port Richey, FL 34656-1481

No. Palm Beach

Frank B Shone CKD
833 Cinnamon Road
No. Palm Beach, FL 33408

Ocala

Thomas W Nelson CKD
516-B Fairway Circle
Ocala, FL 32672

Pensacola

James H Baldwin Jr CKD
4344 Langley Avenue - #G-242
Pensacola, FL 32504

Franklin D Kay CKD
2440 Connell Drive
Pensacola, FL 32503

Rachael L Muller CKD
KAY'S KITCHEN & BATH
DESIGNS
2901 N
Pensacola, FL 32501

Plantation

John M Kennedy CKD
JOHN KENNEDY CKD
MANUFACTURING
REPRENSTATIVE
1550 N W 110th Avenue
Suite 351
Plantation, FL 33322

Port Orange

Hans Schuon CKD
4665 Hidden Lake Drive
Port Orange, FL 32119

Port Richey

Frank Berg CKD
Regency Residence
Port Richey, FL 33568

Port Saint Lucie

Richard V Kucera CKD
1518 S E Pitcher Road
Port Saint Lucie, FL 34952

Saint Petersburg

Sharon Armstrong CKD
KITCHEN & BATH IDEAS
7219 Central Avenue
Saint Petersburg, FL 33710

Sarasota

Bernice Bisulk CKD
7112 Fairway Bend Circle
Sarasota, FL 34243

Herbert P Bisulk CKD
7112 Fairway Bend Circle
Sarasota, FL 34243

Larry E Compton CKD
6585 Tarawa Drive
Sarasota, FL 34241

Robert B Eckert CKD
322 Pearl Avenue
Sarasota, FL 34243

CKD-Certified Kitchen Designer; CBD-Certified Bath Designer

Robert F Gornati CKD
4759 Harvest Bend
Sarasota, FL 34235-6911

St. Petersburg

Betty J Gold CKD
887 65th Avenue, South
St. Petersburg, FL 33705

Stephen E Terepka CKD
THE CABINET CORNER
5562 Central Avenue
St. Petersburg, FL 33707

Stuart

Donald L Davis CKD
4491 SE Cottonwood Terrace
Stuart, FL 34997

Tamarac

Erwin Schwartzberg CKD
7354 Fairfax Drive
Tamarac, FL 33321-4316

Vero Beach

Robert W Stoddard CKD
THE KITCHEN SCENE
89 Royal Palm Boulevard
Vero Beach, FL 32960

West Palm Beach

Thomas G Burns CKD
RYNONE KITCHEN & BATH
CENTRE
7740 Byron Drive
West Palm Beach, FL 33404

Beverly M Wolfe CKD
BMW DESIGNER KITCHENS
INC
1860 Old Okeechobee Road
Suite 510
West Palm Beach, FL 33409

Winter Haven

Ray W Afflerbach CKD
RAY AFFLERBACH CKD
413 Greenfield Road
Winter Haven, FL 33884

Winter Park

Ann Dawson CKD
3733 Goldenrod Road
Winter Park, FL 32792

GEORGIA

Alpharetta

Shirley J McFarlane CKD
5200 Skidaway Drive
Alpharetta, GA 30201

Atlanta

Carlene K Dockery CKD
2882 Ashford Road
Atlanta, GA 30319

Robert F Foltz CKD
BROOKWOOD KITCHENS
2140 Peachtree Road NW
Atlanta, GA 30309

Jacqueline Naylor CKD
JACKIE NAYLOR INTERIORS
4287 Glengary Drive
Atlanta, GA 30342

Herbert H Schmidt CKD
KITCHENSMITH INC
1198 N Highland Avenue NE
Atlanta, GA 30306

Kenneth J Thelen CKD
THELEN KITCHEN & BATH
5566 Chamblee Dunwoody Road
Atlanta, GA 30338

Cailin M Thelen CKD
THELEN KITCHEN AND BATH
STUDIOS
5566 Chamblee Dunwoody Road
Atlanta, GA 30338

Lee Woodall CKD
2122 Abby Lane
Atlanta, GA 30345

Gaithersburg

Robinette Lynch CKD
718 Beacon Hill Terrace
Gaithersburg, GA 20878

Marietta

Patrick J Dunbar CKD
Marietta Kitchen Studio
Marietta, GA 30068

Charlotte Fisher CKD
3582 Clubland Drive
Marietta, GA 30068

Norcross

Jo Alese Ridley CKD
THE CARAPACE CORPORATION
3250 A Peachtree Corners Circle
Norcross, GA 30092

Rosewell

Gertrude E McGinnis CKD
MCGINNIS GROUP
1350 Ridgefield Drive
Rosewell, GA 30075

Roswell

Stanley Kopkin CKD
565 Leather Hinge Trail
Roswell, GA 30075

Saint Simons Island

Patricia B Burgess CKD
KITCHEN & BATH CONCEPTS
OF ST SIMONS INC
105 St Clair Drive
Saint Simons Island, GA 31522

Savannah

Donald B Mc Cullough CKD
KITCHENS BY DON
MCCULLOUGH INC
1311 E 59th Street
Savannah, GA 31404

Smyrna

Joseph V Duket CKD
2528 Oakwood Way
Smyrna, GA 30080

Tucker

Ernie J Giramonti CKD
STANDARD KITCHENS
2725 Mountain Ind Boulevard
Suite A
Tucker, GA 30084

Scott D Purswell CKD
STANDARD KITCHENS OF
GEORGIA
2725 Mountain Industrial
Boulevard
Tucker, GA 30084

Jennifer D Reed CKD
STANDARD KITCHENS OF GA
2725A Mountain Indutrial
Boulevard
Tucker, GA 30084

HAWAII

Honolulu

Judy Dawson CKD
DESIGNER KITCHENS AND
BATHS
3055 Maigret Street
Honolulu, HI 96816

Susan Palmer CKD CBD
KITCHEN CONCEPTS INC
770 Kapiolani Boulevard
Honolulu, HI 96813

Michael L Smith CKD CBD
KITCHEN CONCEPTS PLUS
INC
770 Kapiolani Boulevard
Honolulu, HI 96813

Cheri Villberg CKD CBD
KITCHEN & BATH
DESIGNWORKS
350 Ward Avenue
106 174
Honolulu, HI 96814

Pukalani

Sydney U Zimmerman CKD
2691 Keikilani Street
Pukalani, HI 96768

IDAHO

Boise

Dena Rae Jurries CKD
3511 Mountain View Drive
Boise, ID 83704

Rexburg

Shawna Strobel CKD
SHAWNA INTERIORS
444 Morgan Drive
Rexburg, ID 83440

ILLINOIS

Alsip

Bernice G Greenwald CKD
5024 West 122nd Street
Alsip, IL 60658

Arlington Heights

Edward J Keegan CKD
801 S Beverly Lane
Arlington Heights, IL 60005

Barrington

Helen Lundstrom CKD
260 C Timber Ridge
Barrington, IL 60010

James R Walker CKD
BARRINGTON HOMEWORKS
KITCHEN CENTER
301 E Main Street
Barrington, IL 60010

Batavia

Neal J Conde Jr CKD
210 N. Washington Avenue
Batavia, IL 60510

Belleville

Robert J Davis CKD
13 Eastwood Drive
Belleville, IL 62223

Vince P Schifferdecker CKD
29 Oak Knoll
Belleville, IL 62223

Bensenville

Mary Falkenberg CKD
123 Woodland Avenue
Bensenville, IL 60106

Bloomington

Mary D Sandy CKD
KITCHENS & BATHS BY HOLT
607 Arcadia Drive
Bloomington, IL 61704

Caseyville

Verla M Stratton CKD
629 E. O'Fallon Road
Caseyville, IL 62232

Paul H Stratton CKD
629 O'Fallon Road
Caseyville, IL 62232

Chicago

Susan J Alderson CKD
CITY KITCHENS
2231 N Claybourn
Chicago, IL 60614

Donald C Johnson CKD
KITCHENS & BATHS BY DON
JOHNSON
Merchandise Mart
Suite 1375-53
Chicago, IL 60654

Dale E Johnson CKD
KITCHENS & BATHS BY DON
JOHNSON
Merchandise Mart
Suite 1375
Chicago, IL 60654

Joe Kohn CKD
6549 N. Kedzie
Chicago, IL 60645

Kenneth W Krengel CKD
KRENGEL & ASSOCIATES INC
13101 The Merchandise Mart
Chicago, IL 60654

Joan L Rabinowitz CKD
CITY KITCHENS
2231 N Clybourn
Chicago, IL 60614

Chicago Ridge

Michael J Mikoff CKD
MIKOFF CUSTOM KITCHEN &
BATH
10527 S Ridgeland Avenue
Chicago Ridge, IL 60415

Crystal Lake

Les Svendson CKD
SVENDSON & ASSOCIATES
10 Terra Cotta Avenue
Crystal Lake, IL 60014

Decatur

George E Coutant CKD
899 E. Lake Shore Drive - #3B
Decatur, IL 62521

Dwight

Beverly A Hogan CKD
HOGAN DESIGNS
RR 1 Box 10
Dwight, IL 60420

Edwardsville

Richard V Mueller CKD
EDWARDSVILLE LUMBER
201 W High Street
Edwardsville, IL 62025

Fairview Heights

Richard E Schmitt CKD
8 Briarcliff
Fairview Heights, IL 62208

Fox River Grove

Joyce A Zuelke CKD
9618 E. Witchie Drive
Fox River Grove, IL 60021

Glen Ellyn

Gail Drury CKD
DRURY DESIGNS
244 Exmoor Avenue
Glen Ellyn, IL 60137

Harrisburg

Harold Wilson CKD
101 Southwest Drive
Harrisburg, IL 62946

Humboldt

Mike Spence CKD
AMISH CRAFT
PO Box 38
Humboldt, IL 61931

Jacksonville

Floyd R Taylor CKD
TAYLOR MADE KITCHENS
RR 3 Box 57
Jacksonville, IL 62650

Joliet

Charles W Bidgood CKD
1217 Clement Street
Joliet, IL 60435

Lake Forest

Edwyn L Johnson CKD
290 E. Hilldale Place
Lake Forest, IL 60045

Libertyville

Nancy E Snow CKD
LIBERTY KITCHEN & BATH
INC
627 N Second Street
Libertyville, IL 60048

Lombard

Jacqueline Foersom CKD
362 Eugenia
Lombard, IL 60148

Morton

Ronald L Smallenberger CKD
CREATIVE KITCHENS INC
2001 W Jackson Street
Morton, IL 61550

Morton Grove

Wilma E Wendt CKD
W W DESIGNS INC
9112 Parkside
Morton Grove, IL 60053

Naperville

Judith A Blanks CKD
1032 N Loomis Street
Naperville, IL 60540

Niles

Jules P Kastens CKD
KITCHEN & BATH MART
7755 N Milwaukee Avenue
Niles, IL 60648

Edmund L Zielinski CKD
BETTER KITCHENS INC
7640 Milwaukee Avenue
Niles, IL 60648-3182

Oak Park

Donna Norell CKD
THE KITCHEN STUDIO INC
1107 9 Westgate
Oak Park, IL 60301

Pamela J Polvere CKD
229 S. Cuyler Avenue
Oak Park, IL 60302-3301

Karen Walsh Roberts CKD
THE KITCHEN STUDIO INC
1107 09 Westgate
Oak Park, IL 60301

Laura Trujillo CKD
THE KITCHEN STUDIO INC
1107 9 Westgate
Oak Park, IL 60301

Park Ridge

Howard H Sersen CKD
1608 South Courtland Avenue
Park Ridge, IL 60068

Pawnee

Kathryn E Schultz CKD
89 Michele Drive
Pawnee, IL 62558

Peoria

Jere D Ruwe CKD
JERE'S KITCHENS
1526 E Sunny Lane
Peoria, IL 61615

River Grove

Walter A Reynolds Jr CKD
REYNOLDS ENTERPRISES INC
2936 River Road
River Grove, IL 60171

Rockford

Donald C Johnson CKD
DAHLGREN & JOHNSON INC
1000 Ninth Street
Rockford, IL 61104

Saint Charles

Dennis M Regole CKD
KITCHEN & BATH DESIGN
CONCEPTS
1519 E Main Street
Saint Charles, IL 60174

Skokie

Joe G Tarlos CKD
TARLOS KITCHENS & BATHS
8808 Gross Point Road
Skokie, IL 60077-1809

Springfield

Darlene H Weaver CKD
DISTINCTIVE DESIGNS FOR
KITCHENS & BATHS
226 Highland Avenue
Springfield, IL 62704

St Charles

Robert Best CKD
42 W 596 Steeplechase
St Charles, IL 60175

St. Charles

O.R. Beardsley CKD
1320 South 4th Street
St. Charles, IL 60174

Robert J Rodgers CKD
529 Longmeadow Circle
St. Charles, IL 60174

Louis P Thompson CKD
1303 So. 4th Street
St. Charles, IL 60174

Sullivan

Cathy M Kopel CKD
16 Cotton Tail Lane
Sullivan, IL 61951

Taylorville

Violet J Brown CKD
421 Springfield Road
Taylorville, IL 62568

Wauconda

Star Norini CKD
203 S. Main Street
Wauconda, IL 60084

Wheaton

Claudia Penna CKD
KITCHEN & BATH MART
611 W Roosevelt Road
Wheaton, IL 60187

Wilmette

Maggie F Burke CKD
NORTH SHORE KITCHEN &
BATH CENTER
3207 West Lake Avenue
Wilmette, IL 60091

Michael De Giulio CKD
1121 Central Avenue
Wilmette, IL 60091

Paul R Knobel CKD
KARL G KNOBEL INC
1218 Washington Avenue
Wilmette, IL 60091

K Peter Knobel CKD CBD
KARL G KNOBEL INC
1218 Washington Avenue
Wilmette, IL 60091

Winnetka

John P Descour CKD
818 Elm Street
Winnetka, IL 60093

CKD-Certified Kitchen Designer; CBD-Certified Bath Designer

Yorkville

Richard A Seifrid CKD
204 King Street
Yorkville, IL 60560

INDIANA

Bargersville

Robert E Nichols CKD
PO Box 545
Bargersville, IN 46106

Batesville

Thomas P Walsman CKD
WALSMAN SUPPLY
COMPANY INC
1818 State Road 46 E
PO Box 225
Batesville, IN 47006

Bloomington

Larry G Routen CKD CBD
ROUTEN DESIGN ASSOCIATES
3915 Sugar Lane E
Bloomington, IN 47404

Columbus

Lotus W Alexander CKD
1448 Franklin Street
Columbus, IN 47201

Larry W Alexander CKD
ALEXANDERS' CABINET &
APPLIANCE CENTER
1817 24th Street
Columbus, IN 47201

Evansville

Anna L Skomp CKD
824 Wiltshire Court
Evansville, IN 47715

Clifford E Skomp CKD
824 Wiltshire Court
Evansville, IN 47715

Lynda M Wilhelmus CKD
8909 Petersburg Road
Evansville, IN 47711

Goshin

Carl Kelly Hunsberger CKD
65775 CR #7
Goshin, IN 46526

Greenwood

W.D. Rupel CKD
4011 Tarry Lane
Greenwood, IN 46142

Michael F Teipen CKD CBD
KITCHENS BY TEIPEN
586 S State Road 135
Greenwood, IN 46142-1426

Griffith

Mr Seymour Kaplan CKD
1739 N. Arbogast, Apartment #1-G
Griffith, IN 46319

Indianapolis

Joseph M Boarman CKD
1814 Wyoming Street
Indianapolis, IN 46221

Chester Gray CKD
7444 Lions Head Drive
Indianapolis, IN 46260

James S Jordan CKD
JORDAN SHOWPLACE
KITCHENS
2206 Lafayette Road
Indianapolis, IN 46222

Brenda J Merritt CKD
5949 Ralston Avenue
Indianapolis, IN 46220

Allan C Raup CKD
5249 N. Keystone Avenue
Indianapolis, IN 46220

Lowell

Vernon A Wietbrock CKD
600 West Commercial Avenue
Lowell, IN 46356

Muncie

Carylye P Pippen CKD
PIPPENS HOME CENTER
3400 W Purdue Road
Muncie, IN 47304

Nappanee

Donald P Guckenberger CKD
NAPPANEE WOOD
PRODUCTS
1205 E Lincoln Street
Nappanee, IN 46550

Ronald M Ringenberg CKD
27401 CR 52 R 4
Nappanee, IN 46550

Robert A Waters Sr CKD
507 N. Nappanee Street
Nappanee, IN 46550

Newburgh

Jimmy D Mitchell CKD
EOMPLETE KITCHENS BY
MITCHELL
PO Box 396
4395 Highway #261 N
Newburgh, IN 47629

Shelbyville

Joe L Risley CKD
RISLEY'S KITCHEN
SPECIALISTS
212 E Broadway
Shelbyville, IN 46176

South Bend

David E Carpenter CKD
515 E. Monroe Street
South Bend, IN 46601

Louis M Seago CKD
LOUIE SEAGO AND SONS
REMODELING SERVICE
2506 S Michigan Street
South Bend, IN 46614

Syracuse

William M Beemer CKD
BEEMER ENTERPRISES INC
PO Box 5
Syracuse, IN 46567

Terre Haute

Walter F Frazier CKD
FRAZIER DISTRIBUTING
COMPANY INC
306 Terre Vista Drive
Terre Haute, IN 47803

Vincennes

Douglas G Warren CKD
#52 Warren Estates
Vincennes, IN 47591

Westfield

Carol L Demaree CKD
WICKES LUMBER COMPANY
16708 U S 31 N
Westfield, IN 46074

IOWA

Boone

Kathleen K Cupp CKD
1112 Union
Boone, IA 50036

Burlington

Walter C Fox CKD
2315 Sunnyside Avenue
Burlington, IA 52601

Warren M Hoffman CKD
RFD #1
Burlington, IA 52601

Cedar Rapids

Henry R Ek CKD
2758 Iowa Avenue S.E.
Cedar Rapids, IA 52403

Richard J Felter CKD
AR-JAY BUILDING
PRODUCTS
1515 Blairs Ferry Road N E
PO Box 10017
Cedar Rapids, IA 52410-0017

Joanne L Just CKD
AR JAY BUILDING PRODUCTS
1515 Blairs Ferry Road
PO Box 10017
Cedar Rapids, IA 52410

Richard W Moritz CKD
P H I DISTRIBUTORS
1570 42nd Street NE
Cedar Rapids, IA 52402

Don L Novak CKD
NOVAK CONSTRUCTION
COMPANY
10400 Club Road S W
Cedar Rapids, IA 52404

Ralph H. Palmer CKD
AR JAY BUILDING PRODUCTS
PO Box 10017
1515 Blairs Ferry Road NE
Cedar Rapids, IA 52410

Jodi L Schultz CKD
AR JAY BUILDING PRODUCTS
PO Box 10017
Cedar Rapids, IA 52410-0017

Des Moines

A Arnold Johnson CKD
4114 Leonard Place
Des Moines, IA 50310

Fort Dodge

Phil D Stephenson CKD
ATLAS KITCHEN & BATH
1903 1st Avenue S
Fort Dodge, IA 50501

Iowa City

Ernst Redeker CKD
777 Keswick Drive
Iowa City, IA 52246

Marshalltown

Steven L Fritz CKD
SWANCO ENTERPRISE INC
815 N 3rd Avenue
Box 1030
Marshalltown, IA 50158

Clifford Swanson CKD
1505 Fremont Street
Marshalltown, IA 50158

Mason City

E.G. Jerry Beman Jr CKD
35 N Willowgreen Court
Mason City, IA 50401

Northwood

Sarah L Reep CKD
FIELDSTONE CABINETRY INC
PO Box 109
Highway 105 E
Northwood, IA 50459

Sioux City

Ralph F Hempey CKD
3700-28th Street
Sioux City, IA 51105

Washington

Richard J Widmer CKD
200 E. Polk
Washington, IA 52353

Waterloo

Lucie C Van Metre CKD
2237 Edgemont #10
Waterloo, IA 50702

KANSAS

Independence

Steven W Stark CKD
PRESTIGE INC
201 N Penn
Suite 408
Independence, KS 67301

CKD-Certified Kitchen Designer; CBD-Certified Bath Designer

Leawood

Nancy McLeod CKD
3016 W. 89 Terrace
Leawood, KS 66206

Salina

Robert J Duffield CKD
700 Victoria Heights Terrace
Salina, KS 67401

Richard J Greene CKD
CRESTWOOD INC
353 E Avenue A
Salina, KS 67401

Carl A Long CKD
CRESTWOOD INC
358 E Avenue A
Salina, KS 67401

Wichita

Joe Gordon CKD
GORDON'S HOUSE OF
CABINETRY
1206 E First Street
Wichita, KS 67214

Jan E Parker CKD
15 Douglas Avenue
Wichita, KS 67207

KENTUCKY

Lexington

Mike Butcher CKD
DESIGNER KITCHENS INC
1269 Eastland Drive
Lexington, KY 40505

Robert B Cornett CKD
982 Lakeland Drive
Lexington, KY 40502

Louisville

John U Forst CKD
4906 Raven Road
Louisville, KY 40213

Kurt R Grant CKD
RIVER CITY KITCHEN &
BATH
1805 R Cargo Court
Louisville, KY 40299

Louise A Sachs CKD
504 Ledgeview Court
Louisville, KY 40206

Owensboro

Deborah S Smedley CKD
CABINETS BY DESIGN
3149 Commonwealth Court
Owensboro, KY 42303

Park Hills

Laura M Klein CKD
1030 Park Crest Drive
Park Hills, KY 41011

Prospect

C Jean Mattingly CKD
CJM DESIGNS INC G E
PO Box 708
Prospect, KY 40059

LOUISIANA

Baton Rouge

David W Johnston CKD
ACADIAN HOUSE KITCHENS
& BATHS
9921 Mammoth Avenue
Baton Rouge, LA 70814

Covington

Charles J Wheeler CKD
1216 W. Presidents Drive
Covington, LA 70433

Gretna

Henry P Simon CKD
2145 Gibson Street
Gretna, LA 70056

Lafayette

Marlon D Duhon CKD
TOP'S WOODWORK &
SUPPLY INC
5826 Johnston Street
PO Drawer 31810
Lafayette, LA 70503

New Orleans

Cameron B Gamble CKD
6031 Garfield Street
New Orleans, LA 70118

Belva M Johnson CKD
CAMERON KITCHEN AND
BATH DESIGNS
8019 Palm Street
New Orleans, LA 70125

Gerald C Johnson CKD CBD
CAMERON KITCHEN AND
BATH DESIGNS
8019 Palm Street
New Orleans, LA 70125

Stewart J. Lagarde CKD
CLASSIC CUPBOARDS INC
4747 Earhart Blvd
New Orleans, LA 70125

Shreveport

William J Patten CKD
DESIGNER KITCHENS &
FLOORS INC
6210-B Fairfield Avenue
Shreveport, LA 71106

MAINE

Alfred

Daniel L Roux CKD
ROUX'S KITCHEN & BATH
CENTER
Route 202
PO Box 337
Alfred, ME 04002

Brunswick

Carol E Bartlett CKD
BRUNSWICK COAL &
LUMBER
18 Spring Street
Brunswick, ME 04011

Ellsworth

Gwen M Dewitt CKD
R.R. 5
Ellsworth, ME 04605

Kittery

Pamela P Bold CKD
BOLD CABINETRY
162 State Road
Kittery, ME 03904

Charles E Bold Jr CKD
BOLD CABINETRY
162 State Road
Kittery, ME 03904

Lewiston

Charles Bellegarde Jr CKD
CHARLES BELLEGARDE &
SON INC
23 Columbia Avenue
Lewiston, ME 04240

Peter Clifford CKD
BELLEGARDE CUSTOM
KITCHENS
516 Sabattus Street
Lewiston, ME 04240

Mary E DeCoster CKD
BELLEGARDE CUSTOM
KITCHEN
516 Sabattus Street
Lewiston, ME 04240

Robert O Dion CKD
DION DISTRIBUTORS
PO Box 1668
Lewiston, ME 04241-1668

Norway

Jerald M Foster CKD
PO Box 717
Norway, ME 04268

Rockland

Elaine C Murdoch CKD
MATHEWS BROTHERS
25 31 Rankin Street
Rockland, ME 04841

Sanford

Deborah J Roberge CKD
42 Farview Drive
Sanford, ME 04073

Topsham

Marjorie Otis CKD
Middlesex Road
Topsham, ME 04086

Van Buren

Cynthia M Dufour CKD
GAGNON'S HARDWARE &
FURNITURE INC
184 Main Street
Van Buren, ME 04785

W. Lebanon

Maryterese Russo CKD
PO Box 1063
W. Lebanon, ME 04027

MARYLAND

Accident

Richard L Alexander CKD
PO Box 103
Accident, MD 21520

Annapolis

Max L Coll-Pardo CKD
838 Woodmont Road
Annapolis, MD 21401

Mark T White CKD
KITCHEN ENCOUNTERS
302 Legion Avenue
Annapolis, MD 21401

Joan E Zimmerman CKD
DESIGN SOLUTIONS
300 Legion Avenue
Annapolis, MD 21401

Baltimore

Alan L Caplan CKD
2945 Marnat Road
Baltimore, MD 21209

Jodi Connolly CKD
STUART KITCHENS INC
1858 Reisterstown Road
Baltimore, MD 21208

Robert F Cox CKD
BOB COX TRAINING
SCHOOLS
616 E 33rd Street
Baltimore, MD 21218

Bradley Crockett CKD
6660 Security Blvd.
Baltimore, MD 21207

Stu Dettelbach CKD
S D KITCHENS
1201 Greenwood Road
Baltimore, MD 21208

Robert L Gibbs CKD
COX KITCHENS & BATHS INC
5011 York Road
Baltimore, MD 21212

Ben Kirk CKD
2701 Smith Avenue
Baltimore, MD 21209

Stanley Klein CKD
6800 Westridge Road
Baltimore, MD 21207

D Lester Kuhn CKD
STUART KITCHENS INC
1858 Reisterstown Road
Baltimore, MD 21208

Maxine D Lowy CKD
SD KITCHENS
1201 Greenwood Road
Baltimore, MD 21208

James J Mittelkamp CKD
4546 Ambermill Road
Baltimore, MD 21236

John H Morgan CKD
JOHN H MORGAN &
ASSOCIATES
3800 Timber View Way
Baltimore, MD 21136

Ilene Silberg CKD
SD KITCHENS
1201 Greenwood Road
Baltimore, MD 21208

Michael K Storms CKD
223 E Churchill St.
Baltimore, MD 21230

Alfred V Taylor CKD
6716 Chokeberry Road
Baltimore, MD 21209

Victor P Williams CKD
5004 Edmondson Avenue
Baltimore, MD 21229

Beltsville

Deborah J Miller CKD
BRAY & SCARFF INC
11950 Baltimore Avenue
Beltsville, MD 20705

Rebecca Phillips CKD
BRAY AND SCARFF
11950 Baltimore Avenue
Beltsville, MD 20705

Peggy Reynolds CKD
11803 Macon Street
Beltsville, MD 20705

Debra L Saling CKD
COLONIAL DISTRIBUTORS
5200 Sunnyside Avenue
Beltsville, MD 20705

Kara L Sibley CKD
BRAY & SCARFF
11950 Baltimore Avenue
Beltsville, MD 20705

Mark A Yost CKD
CONTRACT KITCHEN
DISTRIBUTORS INC
12002 Old Baltimore Pike
Beltsville, MD 20705

Bethesda

Peter V Chadik CKD
THE PHOENIX OF BETHESDA
4925 Battery Lane
Apartment 604
Bethesda, MD 20814

Polly W Evans CKD
CASE DESIGN REMODELING
4701 Sangamore Road
N Plaza Suite 40
Bethesda, MD 20816

William C Hurley CKD
SEARS ROEBUCK &
COMPANY
7103 Democracy Boulevard
Bethesda, MD 20817

Bowie

Francine B Blumenfeld CKD
2818 Stoneybrook Drive
Bowie, MD 20715

Chevy Chase

Nancy M Elliott CKD
NANCY ELLIOTT &
ASSOCIATES
37 W Irving Street
Chevy Chase, MD 20815

Jennifer L Gilmer CKD
6919C Strathmore Street
Chevy Chase, MD 20815

Richard M Tunis CKD
RICHARD M TUNIS INC
7032 Wisconsin Avenue
Chevy Chase, MD 20815

Michael Wasserman CKD
RICHARD M TUNIS INC
7032 Wisconsin Avenue
Chevy Chase, MD 20815

Jerry R Weed CKD
RICHARD M TUNIS INC
7032 Wisconsin Avenue
Chevy Chase, MD 20815

Cockeysville

Stuart D Bunyea CKD
1080 Misty Lynn Circle
Cockeysville, MD 21030

Gaithersburg

Gerald E Dionne CKD
SEARS ROEBUCK AND
COMPANY
Lake Forest Mall
701 Russell Avenue
Gaithersburg, MD 20877

Randi J Place CKD
8104 Langport Terrace
Gaithersburg, MD 20877

Carol A Will CKD
9908 Shrewsbury Court
Gaithersburg, MD 20879

Germantown

Steven D Edwards CKD
12830 Kitchen House Way
Germantown, MD 20874

Glenn Dale

Jeffrey R Beynon CKD
11335 Daisey Lane
Glenn Dale, MD 20769

Jarrettsville

Nova Counts CKD
NOVA DESIGNS
3607 N Furnace Road
Jarrettsville, MD 21084

Laurel

Harry C Schuder CKD
12104 Dove Circle
Laurel, MD 20708

Linthicum

William E Murphy Jr CKD
459 Mary Kay Court
Linthicum, MD 21090

Lutherville

John M. Christopher CKD
KITCHEN & BATH CENTER
INC.
1518 York Road
Lutherville, MD 21093

Owings Mills

Robert J Townsend CKD
3505 Gwynnbrook Avenue
Owings Mills, MD 21117

Pasadena

Joseph C Birner CKD
STUART KITCHENS INC
8031 Ritchie Highway
Pasadena, MD 21122

Phoenix

David P Rackl CKD
4004 Sweet Air Road
Phoenix, MD 21131

Potomac

Robert B Cutler CKD
8715 Postoak Road
Potomac, MD 20854

Rockville

Jay Dobbs CKD
CREATIVE KITCHENS INC
1776 E Jefferson Street
Rockville, MD 20852

Severna Park

Carol S Goldring CKD
BAY KITCHENS
688 Ritchie Highway
Severna Park, MD 21146

Donna K Sisson CKD
BAY KITCHENS LTD
688 Ritchie Highway
Severna Park, MD 21146

Robin S Wallace CKD
BAY KITCHENS LTD
688 Ritchie Highway
Severna Park, MD 21146

Shady Side

Walt Fadeley CKD
FADELEY ASSOCIATES INC
PO Box 807
Shady Side, MD 20764

Silver Spring

Linda L Settle CKD
13421 Locksley Lane
Silver Spring, MD 20904

Silver Springs

Nathan Granat CKD
508 Deerfield Avenue
Silver Springs, MD 20910

Timonium

Ken A Freebairn CKD
STUART KITCHENS INC
2221 Greenspring Drive
Timonium, MD 21093

Waldorf

Holmes E Fowler CKD
WALDORF SUPPLY INC
PO Box 578
Waldorf, MD 20604

D Lynne Labanowski CKD
Box 185-3A
Waldorf, MD 20603

Westminster

Gary Wedeking CKD
2409 Raintree Avenue
Westminster, MD 21157

White Plains

Robert Garner CKD
BATH & KITCHEN CONCEPTS
BY WALDORF MARBLE
6309 Theodore Green Boulevard
White Plains, MD 20695

MASSACHUSETTS

Acton

Geleta F Fenton CKD CBD
57 Maple Street
Acton, MA 01720

Agawam

Jerry Herzenberg CKD
KITCHENS BY HERZENBERG
INC
South End Bridge Circle
Agawam, MA 01001

Amherst

Robert F Barnes CKD
265 Pelham Road
Amherst, MA 01002

Andover

Jill A Kehoe CKD
ANDOVER KITCHEN & BATH
CENTER INC
2 Stevens Street
Andover, MA 01810

Bellingham

Gary W Sandford CKD
SCANDIA KITCHENS INC
39 Maple Street
PO Box 85
Bellingham, MA 02019

Boylston

Francis V Garofoli CKD
KITCHENS BY DESIGN
200 Shrewsbury Street
PO Box 670
Boylston, MA 01505

Concord

Rhoda E Miller CKD
53 Monument Street
Concord, MA 01742

Claire Miller CKD
SPECIALTY CRAFTSMEN OF
CONCORD
9 Milldam Lane
Concord, MA 01742

Danvers

Mr Stanley F Brown CKD
56 North Putnam Street
Danvers, MA 01923

Dennisport

Daniel F Stepnik CKD
KITCHEN STUDIO DCM INC
66 Upper County Road
PO Box 1188
Dennisport, MA 02639

Fitchburg

Norman J Thibault CKD
65 Highland Avenue
Fitchburg, MA 01420

Framingham

Kenneth W Doody CKD
KITCHEN CENTER OF
FRAMINGHAM INC
697 Waverly Street
Framingham, MA 01701

Gloucester

Joseph Parisi III CKD
BUILDING CENTER INC
1 Harbor Loop
Gloucester, MA 01930

Great Barrington

Sandra F Beebe CKD
STILLWATER DESIGN
95 West Ave.
Great Barrington, MA 01230

Haverhill

Denyne M Blanchet CKD
89 Broadway
Haverhill, MA 01832

Deborah McQuesten CKD
112 Perkins Court
Haverhill, MA 01832

Hull

Donna Wilfert CKD
11 E Street
Hull, MA 02045

Hyannis

Ronald A Durgin CKD
JOHN HINCKLEY & SON
COMPANY
49 Yarmouth Road
PO Box 2110
Hyannis, MA 02601

Leominster

Robert E Sponenberg CKD
7 Reed Street
Leominster, MA 01453

Lexington

Frank Drake CKD
DRAKE CABINET &
REMODELING INC
401 Lowell Street (Rear)
Lexington, MA 02173

Mashpee

Patricia A Clement CKD
KITCHEN DESIGN CENTER
Summerfield Park
Route 28
Mashpee, MA 02649

Mattapoisett

Wayne Walega CKD
WALEGA ASSOCIATES
92 North Street
PO Box 496
Mattapoisett, MA 02739

Needham

Susan R Brisk CKD
CHARLES RIVER KITCHENS
837 Highland Avenue
Needham, MA 02194

New Bedford

Normand E Robitaille CKD
TAILORED KITCHENS &
BATH
100 Tarkiln Hill Road
PO Box 50004
New Bedford, MA 02745

Newton

Steven M. Levine CKD CBD
621 Watertown Street #24
Newton, MA 02160

No. Attleboro

Dianne P Landry CKD
72 Sutherland Road
No. Attleboro, MA 02760

North Adams

Louis S Gagliardi CKD
56 East Avenue
North Adams, MA 01247

North Andover

Maeve M Cullen CKD
605 Osgood Street
North Andover, MA 01845

Northboro

Melissa A Flahive CKD
128 Northgate Road
Northboro, MA 01532

Norwell

Cameron M Snyder CKD
KITCHEN CONCEPTS INC
159 Washington Street
Norwell, MA 02061

Norwood

George Magyar CKD CBD
19 Malvern Road
Norwood, MA 02062

Onset

William M Joy CKD
PO Box 48
Onset, MA 02558-0048

Osterville

Thomas F Leckstrom CKD
KITCHEN & BATH DESIGNS
UNLIMITED INC
5 Parker Road
Osterville, MA 02655

Plymouth

John F Corcoran CKD
THE CABINET CONNECTION
27 Samoset Street
Plymouth, MA 02360

Eric A Kavanagh CKD
57 West Pond Road
Plymouth, MA 02360

Phillip M Rothschild CKD
THE CABINET CONNECTION
27 Samoset Street
Plymouth, MA 02360

Alan M Sharp CKD
16 Sushala Way
Plymouth, MA 02360

Roslindale

Robert L Norberg CKD
CHARL MARC KITCHEN &
BATH CENTER
4174 Washington Street
Roslindale, MA 02131

S Dennis

Rebecca H Brown CKD
16 Sawyer Circle
S Dennis, MA 02660

Scituate

Trisha Sauve CKD
29 Beaver Dam Road
Scituate, MA 02066

Shrewsbury

Robert A Cuccaro CKD
3 Saxon Lane
Shrewsbury, MA 01545

Kristina L Cullen CKD
12 Phillips Court
Shrewsbury, MA 01545

Peter J Lawton CKD
27 Edgemere Blvd.
Shrewsbury, MA 01545

South Dartmouth

Gilbert W Costa CKD
COSTA'S QUALITY KITCHENS
6 McCabe Street
South Dartmouth, MA 02748

Springfield

Francis E Nataloni CBD
KITCHENS & BATHS BY
CURIO INC
1045 Boston Road
Springfield, MA 01119

Curio Nataloni CKD
KITCHENS & BATHS BY
CURIO INC
1045 Boston Road
Springfield, MA 01119

Stoughton

Richard Kublin CKD
RICHARD KUBLIN KITCHENS
INC
489 Page Street
Stoughton, MA 02072

W Bridgewater

Daniel C Patchett CKD
WOOD-HU INC
343 Manley Street
W Bridgewater, MA 02379

W. Springfield

Susan M Orena CKD
36A Elmwood Avenue
W. Springfield, MA 01089

Wakefield

Dana E Mortensen CKD
10 Meriam Street
Wakefield, MA 01880

Wellesley

Donna S Dami CKD
3 Roberts Road
Wellesley, MA 02181

Payson T Lowell III CKD
17 Durant Road
Wellesley, MA 02181

Westwood

Catherine Pratt CKD
PRATT & SON INC
91 Adler Road
Westwood, MA 02090

Woburn

Leon K Johnson CKD
3 Rehabilitation Way #617
Woburn, MA 01801

Yarmouth Port

James G Robinson CKD
56 Miriah Drive
Yarmouth Port, MA 02675

CKD-Certified Kitchen Designer; CBD-Certified Bath Designer

MICHIGAN

Ann Arbor

Mary Alice Ford CKD
MARY CHRISTENSEN'S
KITCHENS INC
2335 West Stadium Boulevard
Ann Arbor, MI 48103

Birmingham

Thomas A Richards CKD
KITCHENS BY LENORE &
RICHARDS INC
912 S Woodward Avenue
Birmingham, MI 48009

Blissfield

William M Weinlander CKD
212 Pearl Street
Blissfield, MI 49228

Bloomfield Hills

Linda L Roth CKD
7330 Deep Run #1513
Bloomfield Hills, MI 48301

Canton

Michael A Glaser CKD
48315 Ford Road
Canton, MI 48187

Charlevoix

Elizabeth Firebaugh CKD
07999 U.S. Hwy 31 N. #404
Charlevoix, MI 49720

Chesaning

Murray Cox CKD
COX GREGORY AGENCY
16160 Briggs Road
Chesaning, MI 48616

Climax

Daryl A Letts CKD
SHOWCASE KITCHENS &
INTERIORS
12717 P Avenue East
Climax, MI 49034

Coldwater

Donald N Streets CKD
H & S SUPPLY INC
317 N Fiske Road
Coldwater, MI 49036

E Grand Rapids

Marilyn A Nagelkirk CKD
LIFESTYLE KITCHEN & BATH
2216 Wealthy SE
E Grand Rapids, MI 49506

Flint

David B Gavulic CKD
403 W. Philadelphia Blvd
Flint, MI 48504

Flushing

Bernard J Maday CKD
STARLINE DISTRIBUTORS,
INC
65500 W. Pierson Rd.
Flushing, MI 48433

Fraser

Cesar Rastelli CKD
SHOWCASE KITCHEN &
BATH
31435 Utica Road
Fraser, MI 48026

Grand Blanc

Stephen E Allen CKD
5023 Springwell Lane
Grand Blanc, MI 48439

Grand Ledge

Judith A Heinowski CKD
LEDGES TRUE VALUE
522 S Clinton
Grand Ledge, MI 48837

Grand Rapids

Meade E Blake CKD
WILLIAMS DISTRIBUTING
COMPANY
658 Richmond N W
Grand Rapids, MI 49501

Susan L Bloss CKD
LIFESTYLE KITCHEN & BATH
2215 Wealthy S E
Grand Rapids, MI 49506

Jack M Damstra CKD
GALLERY OF KITCHENS INC
5243 Plainfield N E
Grand Rapids, MI 49505

Stephanie Witt CKD
KITCHENS BY STEPHANIE
2880 Thornhills SE
Grand Rapids, MI 49546

Gregory

Richard L Tarantowski CKD
13223 Noah Court
Gregory, MI 48137-9627

Grosse Point Woods

James W Morris CKD
MUTSCHLER KITCHENS INC
20227 Mack Avenue
Grosse Point Woods, MI 48236

Lansing

Dave E Hagerman CKD
THE KITCHEN SHOP
5320 S. Pennsylvania Avenue
Lansing, MI 49306

Mark J Voss CKD
THE KITCHEN SHOP
5320 S Penn Avenue
Lansing, MI 48910

Leslie

Tad E Muscott CKD
2388 Baseline Road
Leslie, MI 49251

Mason

Robert A Ferle CKD
665 N Aurelius Road
Mason, MI 48854

Muskegon

Donald C Nicholson CKD
4764 Maranatha Drive
Muskegon, MI 49441-5289

Okemos

Robert B Vandervoort CKD
2331 Shawnee Trail
Okemos, MI 48864

Petoskey

Robin N Hissong CKD
LIFESTYLES KITCHEN &
BATH
Preston Feather Building Center
900 Spring Street
Petoskey, MI 49770

Petosky

K Stephen Sweet CKD
2449 U.S. Highway 31 North
Petosky, MI 49770

Royal Oak

Rex E Holton CKD
ROYAL OAK KITCHENS INC
4518 N Woodward
Royal Oak, MI 48073

Chris R Holton CKD
ROYAL OAK KITCHENS INC
4518 N Woodward
Royal Oak, MI 48073

Spring Lake

Russell E. Hill CKD
17650 Woodbridge Road
Spring Lake, MI 49456

Swartz Creek

Richard Harris CKD CBD
5405 Don Shenk Drive
Swartz Creek, MI 48473

Sylvan Lake

Scott Grandis CKD
LIVING SPACES
2678 Orchard Lake Road
Sylvan Lake, MI 48320

Kimberly A Saffel CKD
LIVING SPACES
2678 Orchard Lake Road
Sylvan Lake, MI 48320

Traverse City

Barbara B Eager CKD
PO Box 85
Traverse City, MI 49685

W. Bloomfield

Cheryl A Feit CKD
6358 Timberwood S.
W. Bloomfield, MI 48322

West Bloomfield

James R Allcorn CKD
2170 Locklin Lane
West Bloomfield, MI 48324

Wixom

Douglas C Goodhue CKD
E W KITCHEN DISTRIBUTION
29750 Anthony Drive
Wixom, MI 48393

J D House CKD
E W KITCHEN DISTRIBUTORS
29750 Anthony Drive
Wixom, MI 48393

Woodhaven

Jan Logan CKD
GRAHL'S KITCHEN & BATH
DESIGN CENTER
21111 Allen Road
Woodhaven, MI 48183

MINNESOTA

Anoka

Barbara Hirschfeld CKD
357 Mckinley Street, N.W.
Anoka, MN 55303

Apple Valley

Donald T Carman Jr CKD
12785 Ethelton Way
Apple Valley, MN 55124

Duluth

Rebecca G Lindquist CKD
926 East 4th Street
Duluth, MN 55805

Eagan

Susan A Turner CKD
WOODMASTERS INC
990 Lone Oak Road 150
Eagan, MN 55121

Edina

Gary N Conner CKD
NORTH STAR SERVICES
4402 France Avenue S
Edina, MN 55410

Michelle C Rooney CKD
NORTH STAR SERVICES
4402 France Avenue S
Edina, MN 55410

John T Sacarelos CKD
NORTH STAR SERVICES
4402 France Avenue S
Edina, MN 55410

Howard Lake

Glen O Peterson CKD
DURA SUPREME INC
300 Dura Drive
Howard Lake, MN 55349

CKD-Certified Kitchen Designer; CBD-Certified Bath Designer

Lino Lakes

Richard E Petroske CKD
332 Main Street
Lino Lakes, MN 55014

Maplewood

Mark S Peterson CKD
2340 Stillwater Avenue
Maplewood, MN 55119

Minneapolis

Raymond N Pasch CKD
CRYSTAL KITCHEN CENTER
INC
666 N Highway 169
Minneapolis, MN 55427

Steven Ptaszek CKD
STEVEN CABINETS INC
2303 Kennedy Street NE
Minneapolis, MN 55413

Minnetonka

Peter Dukinfield CKD
6085 Rowland Road #206
Minnetonka, MN 55343

New Ulm

Eugene J Altmann CKD
426 South Jefferson
New Ulm, MN 56073

Plymouth

Zee Gee Franzen CKD
1885 Black Oaks Lane
Plymouth, MN 55447

Ramsey

N Timothy Brown CKD
14326 Waco Street N.W.
Ramsey, MN 55303

Saint Paul

James W Krengel CKD CBD
KITCHENS BY KRENGEL INC
1688 Grand Avenue
Saint Paul, MN 55105

Stephen A Lyons CKD
MERLE'S CONSTRUCTION
COMPANY
860 Randolph Avenue
Saint Paul, MN 55102

Michael J Palkowitsch CKD CBD
KITCHENS BY KRENGEL INC
1688 Grand Avenue
Saint Paul, MN 55105

Matthew H Piepkorn CKD
NORTH STAR SERVICES
688 Hague Avenue
Saint Paul, MN 55104

Shoreview

Diana L Berndt CKD
The Kitchenplan Company
Shoreview, MN 55126

Richard J Gorman CKD
838 Sherwood Road
Shoreview, MN 55126

St. Paul

Timothy J Aden CKD CBD
1145 James Avenue
St. Paul, MN 55105

Charles R Geerdes CKD
55 N. Lexington Parkway
St. Paul, MN 55104

Donald G Gustason CKD
355 Marshal Avenue
St. Paul, MN 55102

Karen K Lehmann CKD
LEHMANN & JONES KITCHEN
STUDIO
1672 1/2 Grand Avenue
St. Paul, MN 55105

Willmar

Bruce L Dexter CKD
KITCHEN FAIR
305 W 5th Street
Willmar, MN 56201

MISSISSIPPI

Ackerman

Raymond A Sanders CKD
BELWOOD USA
Highway 15 S
PO Box 901
Ackerman, MS 39735

Jackson

Jerry Burns CKD
5409 Wayneland Drive
Jackson, MS 39211-4044

MISSOURI

Affton

Howard A Baygents CKD
6617 Hurstgreen Lane
Affton, MO 63123

Ballwin

Scott A Schumacher CKD
SCHUMACHER KITCHEN &
BATH STUDIO INC
PO Box 1079
Ballwin, MO 63022

Brentwood

Linda D Gordon CKD
KARR BICK KITCHENS &
BATHS
2715 Mercantile
Brentwood, MO 63144

Crestwood

Joseph L Baldes CKD
9220 Cordoba Lane
Crestwood, MO 63126

Des Peres

Fred L Bueler Jr CKD
2199 Pardoroyal Drive
Des Peres, MO 63131

David W Laurence CKD
THOMPSON'S HOUSE OF
KITCHENS & BATHS
11718 Manchester Road
Des Peres, MO 63131

Doniphan

Leslie E Stewart CKD
Route 1, Box 1190
Doniphan, MO 63935

Ellisville

Susan J Schumacher CKD
808 Surrey Meadows Court
Ellisville, MO 63021

Florissant

Neil E Clark CKD
595 Carrico
Florissant, MO 63034

Four Seasons

Howard Schrock CKD
H & S SALES INC
3 Acacia Court
Four Seasons, MO 65049

Grover

James R Schmidt CKD
2470 Eatherton Road
Grover, MO 63040

Hannibal

Stanley C Keck CKD
1104 Summer Street
Hannibal, MO 63401

Kirkwood

James A Baygents CKD
BAYGENTS COMPANY
117 West Argonne
Kirkwood, MO 63122

Matthew L Chapman CKD
426 Burns
Kirkwood, MO 63122

Charles R Schumacher CKD
10030 Big Bend Blvd.
Kirkwood, MO 63122

Dana E Sheets CKD
BAYGENTS COMPANY
117 W Argonne
Kirkwood, MO 63122

Manchester

Roy E Duenke CKD
ROY E DUENKE CABINET
COMPANY
14436 Manchester Road
Manchester, MO 63011

Pacific

James A Lodderhose CKD
39 Hillside Drive
Pacific, MO 63069

Saint Charles

Jerry E Weaver CKD
KITCHENS BY WEAVER INC
2281 First Capitol Drive
Saint Charles, MO 63301

Saint Louis

Albert Baum CKD
ALBERT BAUM ASSOCIATES
9973 Coddington Way
Saint Louis, MO 63132

J Wallace Morse CKD
PLAIN N FANCY
8133 Maryland
Saint Louis, MO 63105

Thompson C Price CKD CBD
THOMPSON'S HOUSE OF
KITCHENS & BATHS
11718 Manchester Road
Saint Louis, MO 63131

St Louis

Arlene M. Allmeyer CKD
RSI DISTRIBUTING
8110 Eager Road
St Louis, MO 63144

St. Louis

Joyce Bishop CKD
530 West Drive
St. Louis, MO 63130

Douglas C Chapman CKD CBD
863 Twin Pine
St. Louis, MO 63122

Wilbert C Karr CKD
436 Honeysuckle Lane
St. Louis, MO 63119

C J Polley CKD
9332 Warrior Drive
St. Louis, MO 63123-5721

Patricia P. Shelp CKD
1121 Redman Blvd.
St. Louis, MO 63138

Webster Groves

Gerald L Cutter CKD
348 Hazel Avenue
Webster Groves, MO 63119

Pat Duffy CKD
468 Fieldcrest
Webster Groves, MO 63119

MONTANA

Bozeman

Mary K Cichosz CKD CBD
PO Box 1824
Bozeman, MT 59715

Kristie McPhie CKD
MCPHIE CABINETRY
435 E Main Street
Bozeman, MT 59715

CKD-Certified Kitchen Designer; CBD-Certified Bath Designer

Great Falls

Arnie Owen CKD
THE CABINET COMPANY INC
801 9th Street S
Great Falls, MT 59405

NEBRASKA

Kearney

Kenneth E Anderson CKD
TASK LIGHTING CORPORATION
910 E 25th Street
PO Box 1094
Kearney, NE 68848

Todd Halbert CKD
HALBERT & ASSOCIATES
524 W 23rd Street
Kearney, NE 68847

Lincoln

Robert E Crowl CKD
3939 South 58th Street
Lincoln, NE 68506

Gary R Crowl CKD
4315 F Street
Lincoln, NE 68510

Anda R Schmaltz CKD
1121 North Park Blvd.
Lincoln, NE 68521

Mc Cook

Corky D Krizek CKD
Modern Interiors
Mc Cook, NE 69001

Omaha

Bard Goedeker CKD
NEBRASKA CUSTOM
KITCHENS
4601 Dodge Street
Omaha, NE 68132

NEVADA

Las Vegas

Sidney B Wechter CKD
KITCHEN STUDIO INC
610 1/2 E Sahara Avenue
Las Vegas, NV 89104

NEW HAMPSHIRE

Auburn

Joseph R Higgins CKD
21 Deerneck Road
Auburn, NH 03032

Bow

Carole J Neely CKD
1 Hunter Drive
Bow, NH 03304

Concord

Norman D Mabie CKD
6-B Heights Road
Concord, NH 03301

Dover

John Mitrook CKD
411 Dover Point Road
Dover, NH 03820

Epsom

William G Magan CKD
RFD #1, Box 42
Epsom, NH 03234

Belinda J McCubrey CKD
RFD 1, River Road
Epsom, NH 03234

Hooksett

Earl Mabie CKD
60 Sherwood Drive
Hooksett, NH 03106

Lebanon

Robert C Elliott CKD
3 Hough Street
Lebanon, NH 03766

Meredith

Stacy A Morris CKD
MEREDITH BAY CABINETRY
Route 25
Meredith Shopping Center
Meredith, NH 03253

Nashua

Paul L Hackel CKD
139 Daniel Webster Highway
Nashua, NH 03060

Newington

Kathlyn G Box CKD CBD
ADAPTATIONS UNLIMITED
INC
2001 Woodbury Avenue
Newington, NH 03801

Newport

Patricia M Ross CKD
PO Box 115
Newport, NH 03773

North Haverhill

Harold A Lovell CKD
R.R. 1, Box 125A
North Haverhill, NH 03774

Pelham

John C Taylor CKD
TAYLORED CONCETPS LTD
PO Box 6
Pelham, NH 08076

Rye

Walter C Teufel CKD
116 Central Road
Rye, NH 03870

Stratham

Linda Clough CKD
13 Brookside Drive
Stratham, NH 03885

NEW JERSEY

Bayonne

John F Pietruszka CKD
109 Garretson Avenue
Bayonne, NJ 07002

Rudy S Santos CKD
133 West 30th Street
Bayonne, NJ 07002

Bridgeton

Michael R Kelly CKD
MIKE KELLY'S KITCHENS
RR #8 Box 229
Landis Avenue
Bridgeton, NJ 08302

Anne B Miller CKD
MIKE KELLY'S KITCHENS
RR #8 Box 229
Landis Avenue
Bridgeton, NJ 08302

Caldwell

J Richard Taylor CKD
9 Leaycraft Lane
Caldwell, NJ 07006

Cedar Grove

Andrew F Colannino CKD
70 Forest Hills Way
Cedar Grove, NJ 07009

Chatham

Maria Brisco CKD
10 C Heritage Drive
Chatham, NJ 07928

Cherry Hill

Gerald G Hurwitz CKD
121 Uxbridge
Cherry Hill, NJ 08034

Clifton

Ralph F Zielinski CKD
R & R REMODELERS INC
423 Hazel Street
Clifton, NJ 07011

Dumont

Joe D'Aloisio CKD
121 Locust
Dumont, NJ 07628

Fairfield

Lothar C Birkenfeld CKD CBD
ALLMILMO CORPORATION
70 Clinton Road
Fairfield, NJ 07004

Far Hills

Leo H Kelsey CKD
PO Box 931
Far Hills, NJ 07931

Florham Park

Arthur S Franzblau CKD
250 P-1 Ridgedale Avenue
Florham Park, NJ 07932

Franklin Lakes

Michael B. Laido CKD
LAIDO DESIGNS
PO Box 457
Franklin Lakes, NJ 07417

Garwood

M Edward Dudick CKD
DUDICK & SON
40 North Avenue
Garwood, NJ 07027

David N Lugara CKD
DUDICK & SON
40 North Avenue
Garwood, NJ 07027

Glen Rock

Alan S Asarnow CKD
35 Rodney Street
Glen Rock, NJ 07452

Hackettstown

Annette M DePaepe CKD CBD
440 Mansfield Village
Hackettstown, NJ 07840

Nicholas J Geragi Jr CKD CBD
NKBA
687 Willow Grove Street
Hackettstown, NJ 07840

Haddon Heights

Anthony J Terragrossa CKD
CABINET TREE INC
1720 Prospect Ridge Boulevard
Haddon Heights, NJ 08035-1137

Hawthorne

Theodore J Bogusta CKD
19-10th Avenue
Hawthorne, NJ 07506

James Kershaw CKD
JAMES KERSHAW
ASSOCIATES
120 7th Avenue
Hawthorne, NJ 07506

Jacob VanBeuzekom CKD
301 Lafayette Avenue
Hawthorne, NJ 70506

Kinnelon

Hans H Fichtler CKD
16 Birch Road
Kinnelon, NJ 07405

Lake Hiawatha

Ronald G Goldsworth CKD
39 Glenwood Avenue
Lake Hiawatha, NJ 07034

Lakewood

Marc R Eber CKD
MARC R EBER & ASSOCIATES
PO Box 32
Lakewood, NJ 08701

Lynda C Eber CKD
3 Lapsley Lane
Lakewood, NJ 08701

Lambertville

Neil MacDonald CKD
MACDONALD THOMPSON
ASSOCIATES
71 N Main Street
Lambertville, NJ 08530

Linwood

Judith M Schaeffer CKD
408 Lennie Lane
Linwood, NJ 08221-1231

Livingston

Natalie D Raskin CKD
RAY RIVERS & ASSOCIATES
34 E Northfield Road
Livingston, NJ 07039

Margate

Sidney Haifetz CKD
109 South Nassau Avenue
Margate, NJ 08402

Marlton

Conrad A Hidalgo CKD
304 Berkshire Way
Marlton, NJ 08053

Medford

Carol J Cherry CKD
CHERRY'S DESIGNS INC
1 Strafford Court
Medford, NJ 08055

Raymond E Mayer CKD
560 Stokes Road
Medford, NJ 08055

Merchantville

Charles J Curtis CKD
7417 Rudderow Avenue
Merchantville, NJ 08109

Milford

Stephen A Kinon CKD
114 Mountain Circle South
Milford, NJ 07480

Neptune

Barry R Tunbridge CKD
13 Pinewood Drive
Neptune, NJ 07753

Netcong

Ellen Sarra Haspel CKD
CREATIONS IN GLASS
43 Center Street
Netcong, NJ 07857

New Providence

Mary M Banas CKD
40 Dogwood Lane
New Providence, NJ 07974

North Haledon

William F Earnshaw CKD
18 Hillside Drive
North Haledon, NJ 07508

Nutley

John P Castronova CKD
PARAMOUNT KITCHENS
291 Bloomfield Avenue
Nutley, NJ 07110

Oxford

Francis Jones CKD CBD
496 Valley Road
Oxford, NJ 07863

Pequannock

David L Kennedy CKD
BATHS AND KITCHENS BY
KENNEDY
66 Pequannock Avenue
Pequannock, NJ 07440

Perth Amboy

Robert P Kirsten CKD
WHOLESALE KITCHEN
CABINET DISTRIBUTOR INC
533 Krochmally Avneue
Perth Amboy, NJ 08861

Pluckemin

Jeffrey Kennedy CKD
HOME GRAPHICS & DESIGN
PO Box 15
Pluckemin, NJ 07978

Pompton Plains

Theodore E Lutjen CKD
JEFFREYS & LUTJEN INC
29 Evans Place
Pompton Plains, NJ 07444

Princeton

Ethel M Peresett CKD
249 Moore Street
Princeton, NJ 08540

Raritan

Catherine Reed CKD
THE CABINET CENTER BY
FLEETWOOD
20 Route 206
Raritan, NJ 08869

Richard Van Fleet CKD
THE CABINET CENTER BY
FLEETWOOD
20 Route 206
Raritan, NJ 08869

Ridgewood

Sharon L Sherman CKD
ULRICH INC
100 Chestnut Street
Ridgewood, NJ 07450

J David Ulrich CKD
ULRICH INC
100 Chestnut Street
Ridgewood, NJ 07450

River Edge

Herman B Sobel CKD
THE KITCHEN MAN
962 Kinderkamack Road
River Edge, NJ 07661

Roselle

Glenn C Horvath CKD
PROVEN DESIGN INC
225 First Avenue E
Roselle, NJ 07203

Saddle Brook

Peter Salerno CKD
SALERNO'S KITCHEN
CABINET
599 Midland Avneue
Saddle Brook, NJ 07662

Scotch Plains

Paul E Horvath CKD
DESIGNS BY PAUL
1625 E Second Street
Scotch Plains, NJ 07076

Somerdale

Cheryl A Cronce CKD
103 Holyoke Avenue
Somerdale, NJ 08083

Somerville

Christopher Brovich CKD
FRESH IMPRESSIONS INC
882 Route 22 East
Somerville, NJ 08876

Paul Milea CKD
57-1B Taurus Drive
Somerville, NJ 08876

Sparta

Chester Basher CKD
SPARTA TRADES KITCHEN &
BATH
580 Route # 15
PO Box 963
Sparta, NJ 07871

Russell W Platek CKD CBD
744 West Shore Trail
Sparta, NJ 07871

Spotswood

John H Albecker CKD
ALBECKER'S KITCHEN &
BATH
272 Main Street
Spotswood, NJ 08884

Eileen G Jaedicke CKD
ALBECKERS KITCHEN &
BATH
272 Main Street
Spotswood, NJ 08884

Summit

Matt Ezmat CKD
CABRI INC
323 Springfield Avenue
Summit, NJ 07901

Trenton

Charles Eardley CKD
4441 Nottingham Way
Trenton, NJ 08690

Vernon

Gil C Murphy CKD
18 Lauren Lane
Vernon, NJ 07462

Wanamassa

Philip W Fluhr CKD
1117 Jeffrey Avenue
Wanamassa, NJ 07712

West Orange

Leo Lemchen CKD
STRUCTURAL & INTERIOR
DESIGN
200 Mt Pleasant Avenue #G3
West Orange, NJ 07052

West Paterson

Albert Castrucci CKD
CASTRUCCI CABINET
17 Pompton Avenue
West Paterson, NJ 07424

Wyckoff

Herman Brandes CKD CBD
279 Franklin Avenue
Wyckoff, NJ 07481

Randy J Brandes CKD CBD
A & B KITCHENS & BATHS
INC
279 Franklin Avenue
Wyckoff, NJ 07481

Virginia R Loretto CKD
A & B KITCHENS AND BATHS
279 Franklin Avenue
Wyckoff, NJ 07481

Karen L Moyers CKD
HEART OF THE HOME
350 Dartmouth Street
Wyckoff, NJ 07481

CKD-Certified Kitchen Designer; CBD-Certified Bath Designer

NEW MEXICO

Albuquerque

Robert C Carr CKD
DESIGN PROF KITCHEN &
BATH CENTER
1309 San Mateo N E
Albuquerque, NM 87110

Michelle A Carr CKD
DESIGN PROF KITCHEN &
BATH CENTER
1309 San Mateo N E
Albuquerque, NM 87110

Diane Wandmaker CKD
CREATIVE KITCHENS INC
7923 B Menaul NE
Albuquerque, NM 87110

Rio Rancho

Howard L Chapman CKD
532 Eastlake Drive S.E.
Rio Rancho, NM 87124

Santa Fe

Robert M Baker Jr CKD
231 Las Mananitas Street
Santa Fe, NM 87501-1545

Peter G Merrill CKD
CREATIVE KITCHENS
1209 Cerrillos Road
Santa Fe, NM 87501

Elizabeth Munson CKD
RR #10, Box 91 MLM
Santa Fe, NM 87501

Joan Viele CKD
300 E. Houghton
Santa Fe, NM 87501

NEW YORK

Albany

Lawrence H Miller CKD
MARCO'S SHOWCASE
BUILDERS SQUARE PLAZA
1814 Central Avenue
Albany, NY 12205

Clifford M Peterson CKD CBD
122 Hackett Boulevard
Albany, NY 12209

Altamont

Geoffrey Martin CKD
116 Lark Street
Altamont, NY 12009

Amsterdam

John J Miller CKD
R.D. #7
Amsterdam, NY 12010

Auburn

Robert Quigley CKD
QUIG ENTERPRISES
Mutton HIll Road
Route 6
Auburn, NY 13021

Baldwin

Howard Gainsburg CKD
3400 Courtney Place
Baldwin, NY 11510

James P Rupolo CKD
BALDWIN SALES CORPORATION
795 Merrick Road
Baldwin, NY 11510

Boonville

Harold R Myers CKD
HR MYERS LUMBER
COMPANY INC
154 Wood Gate
PO Box 147
Boonville, NY 13309

Boston

Stanley C Gilfoyle CKD
7210 Boston Colden Road
Boston, NY 14025

Brainard

Robert W Baum CKD
Box 84
Brainard, NY 12024

Briarcliff Manor

Joseph S Bracchitta CKD
38 Brookwood Drive
Briarcliff Manor, NY 10510

Canton

John F Hammill CKD
19 Goodrich Street
Canton, NY 13617

Castleton

Robert W Wiltsie CKD
WOOD BROTHERS INC
1954 Pittsfield Road
Castleton, NY 12033

Central Valley

David A Forshay CKD
KITCHENS BY FORSHAY INC
236 Route 32
Central Valley, NY 10917

Cutchogue

Joseph S Dowling CKD
450 Depot Lane
Cutchogue, NY 11935

East Hampton

Robert P Wolfram CKD
RIVERHEAD BUILDING
SUPPLY KITCHEN CABINET
SHOWROOM
15 Railroad Avenue
East Hampton, NY 11937

East Meadow

Lee P Wanaselja CKD
2502 Ramona Street
East Meadow, NY 11554

East Setauket

Richard J Rizzi CKD
6 King Arthur's Court
East Setauket, NY 11733

Elmira

Tammy J Gray CKD
KITCHEN & BATH GALLERY
1055 Walnut Street
Elmira, NY 14905

Fort Salonga

Frank Diliberto CKD
12 Yellow Brick Road
Fort Salonga, NY 11768

Fulton

Jill M Stoughton CKD
JOICE & BURCH INC
2 W First Street N
Fulton, NY 13069

Garden City

Monte G Berkoff CKD
KITS OF DIST BY MONTE/H P
BISULK INC
295 Nassau Boulevard South
Garden City, NY 11530

Glendale

F.P. Frederick CKD
79-49 Myrtle Avenue
Glendale, NY 11385

Great Neck

Don Boico CKD
11 Nassau Road
Great Neck, NY 11021

Christy Mustello CKD
D & M KITCHENS INC
400 Great Neck Road
Great Neck, NY 11021

Hawthorne

Ernest E Berger CKD
BERGER APPLIANCES
Box 202
Hawthorne, NY 10532

Henrietta

Deborah M Ellison CKD
CAVES CABINETRY
CONCEPTS
3081 E Henrietta Road
PO Box 268
Henrietta, NY 14467

Hicksville

Arvids Gulbis CKD
98 East Street
Hicksville, NY 11801

Erna Gulbis CKD
98 East Street
Hicksville, NY 11801-3116

Huntington

Joseph C Ferrara CKD
CUSTOM CONCEPTS INC
741 A W Jericho Turnpike
Huntington, NY 11743

Maria L Ferrara CKD
5 Blue Bird Lane
Huntington, NY 11743

Theodore M Frank CKD
ALAMODE DESIGN
CONCEPTS
595 W Jericho Turnpike
Huntington, NY 11743

Ithaca

David G. Brown CKD
ITHACA KITCHEN & BATH
DESIGN CENTER
401 E State Street
Ithaca, NY 14850

Andrew M Foster CKD
216 Wood Street
Ithaca, NY 14850

Johnson City

Robert F. Carbrey CKD
VALLEY CRAFTS, INC.
753 Harry L Drive
Johnson City, NY 13790

Lake Placid

David W Hunter CKD
HUNTER DESIGNS INC
Cascade Road
PO Box 244
Lake Placid, NY 12946

Malverne

Tino Passaro CKD
176 Rider Avenue
Malverne, NY 11565

Manopac

Greg W Weiss CKD
6 Maple Drive
Manopac, NY 10541

Massapequa Park

Michael Graziano CKD
ALADDIN REMODELERS INC
5000 Sunrise Highway
Massapequa Park, NY 11762

William T Luther CKD
228 Oak Street
Massapequa Park, NY 11762

Middletown

David S McCarey CKD
531 North Street
Middletown, NY 10940

Mineola

Felix M Frank CKD
ALAMODE KITCHEN CENTER
INC
206 E Jericho Turnpike
Mineola, NY 11501

Mohegan Lake

Ralph Fasano Jr CKD
PO Box 425
Mohegan Lake, NY 10547

Montgomery

Jack L Clouser CKD
CLOUSER SALES INC
136 Bracken Road
Montgomery, NY 12549

N Syracuse

Ruth M Lenweaver CKD
COUNTRY GENTLEMEN
KITCHEN & BATH CENTER
720 N Main Street
N Syracuse, NY 13212

New Hartford

Carmen R Spetts CKD
CHARM KITCHENS & BATHS
BY SPETTS
100 Seneca Turnpike
New Hartford, NY 13413

New Paltz

Andre J Venables CKD
KITCHENS BY ANDRE
121 Main Street
New Paltz, NY 12561

New York

Charles F Adams CKD
SAINT CHARLES KITCHENS
OF NEW YORK
150 E 58th Street
New York, NY 10155

Edward C Collier CKD
SAINT CHARLES OF NEW
YORK INC
150 E 58th Street
New York, NY 10155

Theodore B Gronlund CKD
T O GRONLUND COMPANY
INC
200 Lexington Avenue
New York, NY 10016

Florence Perchuk CKD
DESIGNS BY FLORENCE
PERCHUK
127 E 59th Street
Suite 201
New York, NY 10016

Mark L Rosenhaus CKD
321 Avenue C
New York, NY 10009

Michelle F Salinard CKD
60 Gramercy Park North
New York, NY 10010

Norwich

Michael C Stockin CKD
KUNTRISET KITCHENS
RD 2 Box 254
Norwich, NY 13815

Orangeburg

Laurie M Kaplan CKD
Blue Hill Commons - #15L
Orangeburg, NY 10962

Penfield

Jacob J Horvat CKD
CHASE PITKIN HOME
CENTERS
2155 Penfield Road
Penfield, NY 14526

Phoenicia

Edgar W Schlosser CKD
PO Box 159
Phoenicia, NY 12464

Port Chester

Leona S Hess CKD CBD
5 Haines Boulevard
Port Chester, NY 10573

Potsdam

Durward L Thomas CKD
D L THOMAS KITCHENS AND
BATHS
Outer Market Street
PO Box 5046
Potsdam, NY 13676

Poughkeepsie

William H Algier Sr CKD
160 Academy Street #9D
Poughkeepsie, NY 12601

Vincent Cappello CKD
21 Marshall Drive
Poughkeepsie, NY 12601

Dorretta Waite CKD
37 Circular Road
Poughkeepsie, NY 12601

Queensbury

Patricia French CKD
131 Queensbury Avenue
Queensbury, NY 12804

Remsenburg

Thomas J Longo CKD
Box 356
Remsenburg, NY 11960

Mary Jane Longo CKD
BALDWIN SALES CORPORATION
White Birch Lane
Remsenburg, NY 11960

Rhinebeck

George V Krom CKD
WILLIAMS LUMBER & HOME
CENTER
Route 9 N
Rhinebeck, NY 12572

Riverhead

Frank Tommasini CKD
KITCHEN AND BATH INC
1179 Route 58
Riverhead, NY 11901

Rochester

Samuel L Ayres III CKD
122 Saranac Street
Rochester, NY 14621

Sag Harbor

Anthony J De Pinto CKD
KITCHEN FAIR INC
79 Bay View Drive
Sag Harbor, NY 11963

Saugerties

Richard M Downey CKD
HICKORY MEADOWS
CUSTOM KITCHENS
1903 Lauren Tice Road
Saugerties, NY 12477

Scotia

John M Torelli CKD
14 Horstman Drive
Scotia, NY 12302

Seaford

Jo Ann Campo CKD
3935 Darby Lane
Seaford, NY 11783

Searingtown

Lawrence N Newman CKD
105 Serpentine Lane
Searingtown, NY 11507

Sidney

Dominic J Zieno CKD
SIDNEY APPLIANCE &
MODERN KITCHENS
PO Box 2115
Sidney, NY 13838

Stewart Manor

Neal W Deleo CKD
24 Chester Avenue
Stewart Manor, NY 11530

Syracuse

Raymond F Martino Jr CKD
MODERN KITCHENS OF
SYRACUSE
5801 Court Street Road
Syracuse, NY 13221

Paul D Thompson CKD
DISTINCTIVE INTERIORS
5891 Firestone Drive
Syracuse, NY 13206

Troy

Paul R Cloutier CKD
RD #2 Box 239-B
Troy, NY 12182

Vestal

Arthur H Andrews CKD
4508 West Marshall Drive
Vestal, NY 13850

Victor

Sue Smith CKD
DAVID K SMITH ASSOCIATES
6796 Spring Creek Drive
Victor, NY 14564

Wappinger Falls

Frank O Algier CKD
EMPIRE KITCHENS INC
862 South Road
Wappinger Falls, NY 12590

William H Algier Jr CKD
862 South Road
Wappinger Falls, NY 12590

Randall A Thoms CKD
PO Box 221
Wappinger Falls, NY 12590

Warwick

Marisa Panecki CKD
BATHS KITCHENS & BEYOND
13 Main Street
Warwick, NY 10990

Nicholas Papaceno CKD
21 Fairview Avenue
Warwick, NY 10990

Watkins Glen

Karen R Edwards CKD
KAREN EDWARDS DESIGN
PO Box 230
Watkins Glen, NY 14891

White Plains

Frank R Massello CBD
HOME DESIGNS INC
202 Westchester Avenue
White Plains, NY 10601

Yonkers

Daniel J Lowen Jr CKD
QUAKER MAID KITCHENS OF
NEW YORK INC
1880 Central Park Avenue
Yonkers, NY 10710

Yorktown Heights

David A Bourgeois CKD
BOURGEOIS INDUSTRIES INC
3093 Ferncrest Drive
Yorktown Heights, NY 10598

NORTH CAROLINA

Apex

Thomas A Cambron Jr CBD
BEAUTIFUL BATHZ INC
229 North Salem Street
Apex, NC 27502

Asheville

Rex E Ballard CKD
Z-6 Crowfields Drive
Asheville, NC 28803

Robert R Cooper CKD
COOPER HOUSE INC
479 Hendersonville Road
Asheville, NC 28803

CKD-Certified Kitchen Designer; CBD-Certified Bath Designer

Chapel Hill

Janine Jordan CKD
J J INTERIORS
PO Box 5130
Chapel Hill, NC 27514

Charlote

Steven T Maddox CKD
2619 Lytham Drive
Charlote, NC 28210

Charlotte

Elizabeth Brunnemer CKD
809 S. Edgehill Road
Charlotte, NC 28207

Al Herold CKD
700 Ashmeade Road
Charlotte, NC 28211

Wyona Fay Hodges CKD CBD
1911-302 Sharon Oaks Lane
Charlotte, NC 28210

David A Prunczik CKD
INTEXT DIVERSIFIED SALES
INC
11660 Old Surry Lane
Charlotte, NC 28277

Durham

Gary Stephens CKD
4411 E. Emerald Forest Drive
Durham, NC 27713

Fayetteville

Mr Sherman E Holt CKD
Kitchen Kreations
Fayetteville, NC 28304

Greensboro

Robert T Koehler CKD CBD
OLD MASTER KITCHENS
1401 W Lee Street
Greensboro, NC 27403

Joseph P Mitchell Jr CKD
OLD MASTER KITCHENS
1401 W Lee Street
PO Drawer 5486
Greensboro, NC 27403

Jon H White CKD
J & J CUSTOM KITCHENS
3404 A W Wendover Avenue
Greensboro, NC 27407

Greenville

Marjorie Inman CKD PhD.
210 Fairlane
Greenville, NC 27834

Kitty Hawk

Susan M Kirkwood CKD
COZY HOME CUSTOM
CABINETS
921 Kitty Hawk
Kitty Hawk, NC 27949

Raleigh

William J. Camp CKD
TRIANGLE DESIGN
KITCHENS INC
5216 Holly Ridge Drive
Raleigh, NC 27612

Max G Isley Jr CKD
HAMPTON KITCHENS
1505 Capital Boulevard
Raleigh, NC 27603

Southern Pines

Loren J Ryder CKD
565 Fairway Drive
Southern Pines, NC 28387

Waxhaw

Arthur L Wyse CKD
7123 McCaslan Lane
Waxhaw, NC 28173

Wilmington

Mr Theodore L Frank CKD
SUPERIOR MILLWORK INC
615 S Seventeenth Street
Wilmington, NC 28401

Cynthia Sporre CKD
502 Hidden Valley Road
Wilmington, NC 28409

NORTH DAKOTA

Fargo

William Tweten CKD
THE FLOOR TO CEILING
STORE
360 36th Street S
Fargo, ND 58103

OHIO

Akron

Ellyn J Schneier CKD
BUILDER'S KITCHENS
1095 Home Avenue
Akron, OH 44310

Beachwood

Samuel L Besunder CKD
23531 Wendover
Beachwood, OH 44122

Richard M Sheldon CKD
25114 Hazelmere
Beachwood, OH 44122

Bedford Heights

Margaret Vogt Burns CKD
THE CABINET CENTER INC
26901 Richmond Road
Bedford Heights, OH 44146

Chagrin Falls

Alan G Luzius CKD
STONE GATE ASSOCIATES
33 River Street
Chagrin Falls, OH 44022

Chesterland

Darlene J. Hackbart-Somrak
CKD
11844 East Hill Drive
Chesterland, OH 44026

Brenda L Lunka CKD
THE WOODLAND DESIGN
STUDIO INC
8389 Mayfield Road
Chesterland, OH 44026

Lisa M Perfetto CKD
PO Box 283
Chesterland, OH 44026

Cincinnati

Susan E Chenault CKD
CABINETRY CONCEPTS &
DESIGNS INC
10793 Fallingston Court
Cincinnati, OH 45242

R B Davis CKD CBD
SIGNATURE KITCHENS
3004 Harris
Cincinnati, OH 45212

Scott A Kronour CKD
DAYTON SHOWCASE
COMPANY
10915 Reading Road
Cincinnati, OH 45241

Patti A Lawson CKD
DAYTON SHOWCASE
COMPANY
10915 Reading Road
Cincinnati, OH 45241

Cleveland Heights

Arthur C Zigerelli CKD
NATIONAL KITCHENS &
BATHS
3962 Mayfield Road
Cleveland Heights, OH 44121

Columbia Station

Christi S Bechtold CKD
12802 E. River Road
Columbia Station, OH 44028

Columbus

David L Fox CKD
1163 Bethel Road
Columbus, OH 43220

Michael A Noble CKD
LONDON KITCHENS
1065 Dublin Road
Columbus, OH 43215

Dayton

Luellen A Brown CKD
DAYTON SHOWCASE
COMPANY
2601 West Dorothy Lane
Dayton, OH 45439

William Paul Kemna CKD
464 Peachcreek Road
Dayton, OH 45458

Loren D Raines CKD
762 Greenlawn Ave
Dayton, OH 45403-3332

Dublin

Joseph F Fehn CKD
113 Longview Drive
Dublin, OH 43017

East Liverpool

Cynthia K Birch CKD
BIRCH SUPPLY COMPANY
INC
16477 Saint Clair Avenue
PO Box 9000
East Liverpool, OH 43920

Fairfield

Connie M Hampton CKD
HAMPTON CUSTOM
KITCHENS
4838 Dixie Highway
Fairfield, OH 45014

Findlay

Bryan V Cavins CKD
9051 Township Road #95
Findlay, OH 45840

Fort Recovery

Daniel J Schoen CKD
HOME IDEA CENTER INC
111 W Butler Street
Fort Recovery, OH 45846

Hamilton

Arthur R Lingler CKD
100 Fairborn Drive
Hamilton, OH 45013

Highland Height

Peter J Orobello CKD
696 Davidson Drive
Highland Height, OH 44143

Kirkland

Wilbur C Pike CKD
8720 Singlefoot Trail
Kirkland, OH 44094

Mayfield

Alan Abrams CKD
6868 Wildwood Trail
Mayfield, OH 44143

Middlefield

Royce V Hogue CKD
KRAFTMAID CABINETRY INC
PO Box 1055
Middlefield, OH 44162

Middletown

Terry L Hupp CKD
2507 Halifax Court
Middletown, OH 45044

New Knoxville

Evelyn A Flock CKD
HOGE LUMBER COMPANY
PO Box 159
New Knoxville, OH 45871

Oliver H Hoge CKD
HOGE LUMBER COMPANY
307 E Bremen Street
New Knoxville, OH 45871

Plain City

Katherine Miller CKD
THE MILLER CABINET
COMPANY
6217 Converse Huff Road
Plain City, OH 43064

Terrace Park

John F Rugh CKD
159 Wrenwood Lane
Terrace Park, OH 45174

Toledo

Richard A Mc Kimmy CKD
MCKIMMY & ELLIOTT
5250 Renwyck Drive #C
Toledo, OH 43615

Jerome B Waxman CKD
KITCHENS BY JEROME INC
2138 N Reynolds Road
Toledo, OH 43615

Westchester

Richard E Bolte CKD
7763 Oceola Lane
Westchester, OH 45069

Willoughby Hill

John F Hall CKD
STUDIO FARALLI
2804 S O M Center
Willoughby Hill, OH 44094

Youngstown

Ralph M Watson CKD
4414 Euclid Boulevard
Youngstown, OH 44512

OKLAHOMA

Duncan

Billie Latham CKD
LATHAM INCORPORATION
702 Willow
Duncan, OK 73533

Oklahoma City

Karen K Black-Roberts CKD
KITCHEN SHOWCASE &
DESIGN CENTER
2761 North Country Club Drive
Oklahoma City, OK 73116

Donald G Dobbs CKD
10205 Glendover Avenue
Oklahoma City, OK 73162

Zachary Taylor CKD
8225 Northwest 92nd
Oklahoma City, OK 73132

Stephen Wells CKD
CLASSIC KITCHENS INC
584 E Memorial Road
Oklahoma City, OK 73114

Tulsa

Ralph Lackner CKD CBD
JAY RAMBO COMPANY
8401 E 41st
Tulsa, OK 74145

OREGON

Beaverton

Amalia B Parecki CKD
10645 SW 135th Avenue
Beaverton, OR 97005

Corbett

Michelle Heaton Rolens CKD
CBD
2320 NE Corbett Hill Rd.
Corbett, OR 97019

Lake Oswego

Martha Kerr CKD CBD
726 S.W. McVey
Lake Oswego, OR 97034

Oregon City

J Lynette Black CKD
16299 South Eaden Road
Oregon City, OR 97045

Portland

C Faye Cornelison CKD
NEIL KELLY DESIGNERS
REMODELERS
804 North Alberta
Portland, OR 97217

Kathleen F Donohue CKD CBD
4612 SW Pomona
Portland, OR 97219

Victor R Greb CKD
J GREB & SON INC
5027 N E 42nd Avenue
Portland, OR 97218

Neil B Kelly CKD
804 N. Alberta
Portland, OR 97217

Randi Reed CKD
NEIL KELLY DESIGNERS
REMODELERS
804 N Alberta
Portland, OR 97217

Karen Richmond CKD
5828 SW California
Portland, OR 97219-1212

Julia B Spence CKD
NEIL KELLY DESIGNERS
REMODELERS
804 N Alberta Street
Portland, OR 97217

Kenneth P Stanley CKD
NEIL KELLY DESIGNERS
REMODELERS
804 N Alberta
Portland, OR 97217

Tigard

Bob Cone CKD
TOTAL BUILDING PRODUCTS
PO Box 23337
Tigard, OR 97223

Richard C Hallberg CKD
7170 S.W. Lola Lane
Tigard, OR 97223

PENNSYLVANIA

Adamstown

Irvin L Martin CKD
MARTIN CUSTOM KITCHENS
PO Box 567
Adamstown, PA 19501

Aliquidpa

Guy D Lucci Jr CKD
642 North Brodhead Road
Aliquidpa, PA 15001

Aliquippa

Richard Lucci Sr CKD
303 Baker Drive
Aliquippa, PA 15001

Allentown

Susan Y Adams CKD
2000 Linden Street
Allentown, PA 18104

Daniel J Lenner CKD
MORRIS BLACK & SONS
984 Marcon Boulevard LVIP III
Allentown, PA 18103

Robert L Wieland CKD CBD
KITCHENS BY WIELAND INC
4210 Tilghman Street
Allentown, PA 18104

Auburn

Jerald G Heffleger CKD
619 Wynonah Drive
Auburn, PA 17922

Bala Cynwyd

Ted R Moser CKD
MOSER CORPORATION
129 Montgomery Avenue
Bala Cynwyd, PA 19004-2828

Andrew R Stein CBD
Maple Avenue
Bala Cynwyd, PA 19004

Bethayres

Arthur A Perry Jr CKD
A A PERRY & SONS INC
2528 Huntington Pike
Bethayres, PA 19006

Bethel Park

William J Glivic CKD CBD
2875 O'Neill Drive
Bethel Park, PA 15102

Bethlehem

Donna H Lyman CKD
MORRIS BLACK & SON
984 Marcon Boulevard
Bethlehem, PA 18001

Dennis R Oberholtzer CKD
OBERHOLTZER KITCHENS
77 W Board St #1
Bethlehem, PA 18018-5722

Bird In Hand

Sylvia Terry CKD
TERRY'S ENTERPRISES
Railroad Avenue
PO Box 279
Bird In Hand, PA 17505

Bristol

Joseph D'Emidio CKD
212 East Circle
Bristol, PA 19007

Canonsburg

Tracy M Johnston CKD
ROBERT JOHNSTON KITCHEN
& BATH
156 Morganza Road
Canonsburg, PA 15317

Carlisle

Harold B Gibb Jr CKD
CARLISLE KITCHEN CENTER
1034 Harrisburg Pike
Carlisle, PA 17013

James F Goodman CKD
154 West Middlesex Drive
Carlisle, PA 17013

Carnegie

Steven M Erenrich CKD
PATETE KITCHEN & BATH
1105 Washington Avenue
Box 669
Carnegie, PA 15106

Clarks Summit

A Wayne Trivelpiece CKD
ABINGTON CABINETRY
PO Box 101
Clarks Summit, PA 18411

Corry

Raymond A Anderson CKD
THE KITCHEN VILLAGE INC
12275 Route 6
Corry, PA 16407

Drexel Hill

Edmund W McGarvey CKD
2821 Hillcrest Road
Drexel Hill, PA 19026

Duncansville

William Sandrus CKD
846 Broad Avenue Ext.
Duncansville, PA 16635

Jill S Shaw CKD
SHOWCASE KITCHENS INC
921 3rd Avenue
PO Box 713
Duncansville, PA 16635

Dunmore

Fred N Schank CKD
PO Box 617
Dunmore, PA 18512

E. Petersburg

Stephen M Brown CKD
2784 Madison Court
E. Petersburg, PA 17520

Ellwood City

Joseph R DeOtto CKD
PINECREST KITCHEN AND
BATH
728 Lawrence Avenue
PO Box 708
Ellwood City, PA 16117

Erie

Paulette H Hessinger CKD
3244 Willis Street
Erie, PA 16506

Richard V Robertson CKD
5305 Old Sterrettania Road
Erie, PA 16506

James J Robertson CKD
ROBERTSON KITCHENS INC
2630 W 12th Street
PO Box 8112
Erie, PA 16505

Fredonia

Richard L Buchanan CKD
BUCHANAN KITCHEN AND
BATH BOUTIQUE
998 Second Street
Fredonia, PA 16124

Glen Mills

John C Stefanide CKD
155 Gov. Markham Drive
Glen Mills, PA 19342

Glenshaw

Arthur C Winterhalter CKD
3705 Rosebriar Avenue
Glenshaw, PA 15116

Goodville

Barbara R Herr CKD
RUTT CUSTOM CABINETRY
1564 Main Street
PO Box 129
Goodville, PA 17528

Greensburg

Alan Ehrensberger CKD
413 East Pittsburgh Street
Greensburg, PA 15601

Wendell Peterson CKD
1036 Rimrock Road
Greensburg, PA 15601

Harrisburg

Thomas D Kling CKD
1609 N Second Street
Harrisburg, PA 17102

Hermitage

Bud Miller CKD
BUD MILLER'S KITCHEN &
BATH DIST INC
3005 E State Street
Hermitage, PA 16148

Gene Renz CKD
825 Koonce Road
Hermitage, PA 16148

Honesdale

Arlene Hawker CKD
104 Brown Street
Honesdale, PA 18431

Huntingdon

Richard J Endres Sr CKD
760 Bryan Heights
Huntingdon, PA 16652

Johnstown

Patsy J Formica CKD
1256 Franklin Street
Johnstown, PA 15905

Carmen A Formica CKD
RD #5, Box 207A
Johnstown, PA 15905

Kimberton

Carol Crane CKD
Box 126
Kimberton, PA 19442

Lancaster

Michael R Bowers CKD
51 Deer Ford Drive
Lancaster, PA 17601

Elizabeth Dodds CKD
154 Knollwood Drive
Lancaster, PA 17601-5661

Mark F Ehrsam CKD
MARK I KITCHENS & BATHS
134 E Walnut Street
Lancaster, PA 17602

Langhorne

Gary R Ulanowski CKD
SIEMATIC CORPORATION
886 Town Center Drive
Langhorne, PA 19047

Lewisburg

Charles H Lemmerman CKD
82 Fairmount Drive
Lewisburg, PA 17837

Ligonier

L James Frey CKD
1261 Griffith Road
Ligonier, PA 15658

Malvern

Alex R Hall CKD
THE CREATIVE NOOK INC
203 E King Street
Malvern, PA 19355-2517

Marysville

Charles H. Dissinger CKD
1000 Mountaindale Drive
Marysville, PA 17053

Mechanicsburg

Roy McLain CKD CBD
ADVANCED KROWN
KITCHENS & BATHS
5222 E Trindle Road
Mechanicsburg, PA 17055

Les Petrie CKD
MOTHER HUBBARD'S
KITCHEN CENTER
5309 E Trindle Road
Mechanicsburg, PA 17055

John A Petrie CKD
MOTHER HUBBARD'S
KITCHEN CENTER
5309 E Trindle Road
Mechanicsburg, PA 17055

Menhall

M Paul Cook Jr CKD
OMNI RENOVATION
114 East James Street
Menhall, PA 15120

Monroeville

Ida M McConnell CKD
860 MacBeth Drive
Monroeville, PA 15146

Mt. Joy

Sandra L Steiner Houck CKD
313 S. Market Avenue
Mt. Joy, PA 17552

Mt. Pleasant

Frank A Sevcik CKD
R.D. #1 Box 304
Mt. Pleasant, PA 15666

Murrysville

Thomas E Backus CKD
BACKUS CABINET COMPANY
3700 Old William Penn Highway
Murrysville, PA 15668-1800

Narvon

Michael E White CKD
CONESTOGA VALLEY
CUSTOM KITCHENS INC
2042 Turkey Hill Road
Narvon, PA 17555

New Holland

Paul V Weidman CKD
HERITAGE CUSTOM
KITCHENS
215 Diller Avenue
New Holland, PA 17557

New Kensington

Frank R Boyd CKD
1306 Greensburg Road
New Kensington, PA 15068

Newmanstown

Dolores J Hurst CKD
KOUNTRY KRAFT KITCHENS
INC
Box 570
Newmanstown, PA 17073

North Huntingdon

Dennis S Caruso CKD
CARUSO CABINET
MANUFACTURING INC
10809 Route 30
North Huntingdon, PA 15642

Philadelphia

Morton M Block CKD CBD
MORTON BLOCK ASSOCIATES
2400 Market Street
Suite 205
Philadelphia, PA 19103

Marc W Block CKD CBD
MORTON BLOCK ASSOCIATES
2400 Market Street
Suite 205
Philadelphia, PA 19103

Bud Fleet CKD
1009 Grant Avenue
Philadelphia, PA 19115

James S Kaufer CKD
810 Susquehanna Road
Philadelphia, PA 19111

Samuel Kulla CKD
KULLA KITCHENS
7800 Rockwell Avenue
Philadelphia, PA 19111

Linda Pera CKD
PLYGEMS KITCHEN & BATH
CENTER
6948 Frankford Avenue
Philadelphia, PA 19135

Leon A Scarf CKD
2255 Faunce Street
Philadelphia, PA 19152

Pittsburgh

Oscar R Acevedo CKD
MASTERCRAFT KUSTOM
KITCHENS
100 A Street
Pittsburgh, PA 15235

Charles Buchsbaum CKD
MASTERKRAFT KUSTOM
KITCHENS
100 A Street
Pittsburgh, PA 15218

Robert P Butt Jr CKD
KITCHEN WORKS INC
1002 Greentree Road
Pittsburgh, PA 15220

Raymond C Franke Jr CKD
FRANKE'S CABINET SHOP
641 Butler Street
Pittsburgh, PA 15223

August R Lang CKD
EXCEL KITCHEN CENTER
1800 Fifth Avenue
Pittsburgh, PA 15219

Victoria Liscinsky CKD
KITCHEN & BATH CONCEPTS
OF PITTSBURG
7901 Perry Highway
Route 19 North
Pittsburgh, PA 15237

Chester Mandella CKD CBD
800 E. Monroe Circle
Pittsburgh, PA 15229

W Kenneth Niklaus CKD
7005 Ohio River Blvd.
Pittsburgh, PA 15202

Kenneth R Rogg CKD
STRAIGHT LINE CABINET
CORP
101 S Main Street
PO Box 7883
Pittsburgh, PA 15215

Joseph H Safyan CKD
2118 Beechwood Blvd.
Pittsburgh, PA 15217

Abe Sambol CKD
STEIN'S CUSTOM KITCHENS
AND BATHS
3559 Bigelow Boulevard
Pittsburgh, PA 15213

Jerry A Sambol CKD
STEIN'S CUSTOM KITCHENS
AND BATHS
3559 Bigelow Boulevard
Pittsburgh, PA 15213

Simon Z Stein CKD
1317 Shady Avenue
Pittsburgh, PA 15217

William E Takacs Jr CKD
MASTERKRAFT KUSTOM
KITCHENS
100 A Street
Pittsburgh, PA 15235

Thomas D Trzcinski CKD CBD
KITCHEN & BATH CONCEPTS
OF PITTSBURGH
7901 Perry Highway N
Pittsburgh, PA 15237

Regina A Williams CKD
W T LEGGETT COMPANY
INC
40th & Butler Streets
Pittsburgh, PA 15201

Quakertown

Holly March CKD
2455 Old Bethlehem Pike
Quakertown, PA 18951

Robesonia

John A Donohue CKD
RICH CRAFT CUSTOM
KITCHEN
141 W Penn Avenue
PO Box 39
Robesonia, PA 19551

Selinsgrove

David C Broscious CKD
RD 1 Box 316
Selinsgrove, PA 17870

Joseph E. Callender CKD
8 Melody Lane
Selinsgrove, PA 17870

Howard J Campbell CKD
517 North High Street
Selinsgrove, PA 17870

Lawrence J Tempel CKD
2 Bogar Circle
Selinsgrove, PA 17870

Shaefferstown

Joe F Edwards CKD
Box 302
Shaefferstown, PA 17088

Sharon

Barry E Kirby CKD
267 Case Avenue
Sharon, PA 16146

Slippery Rock

Julia A Lorentz CKD
306 Normal Avenue
Slippery Rock, PA 16057

Somerset

Marshall A Trigona CKD
KITCHEN DESIGNS BY
MARSH
1024 N Center Avenue
Somerset, PA 15501

Southampton

Alvin J Moeser CKD
SUBURBAN KITCHEN
COMPANY
650 Street Road
Southampton, PA 18966

Springfield

Sam J Donze CKD
620 Laurel Road
Springfield, PA 19064

Anthony L Donze CKD
254 Lewis Road
Springfield, PA 19064

Ned L Rossi CKD
455 West Woodland Avenue
Springfield, PA 19064

James H Stefanide CKD
812 Crum Creek Road
Springfield, PA 19064

Swarthmore

John C Oliver CKD
808 Girard Avenue
Swarthmore, PA 19081

Tarrs

Jospeh M Barrick Jr CKD
C & C BUILDERS
Off Route 31
Tarrs, PA 15688

Telford

Gretchen L Edwards CKD CBD
276 North Third Street
Telford, PA 18969

Upper Darby

Charles J Walsh Jr CKD
WALL & WALSH INC
8320 W Chester Pike
Upper Darby, PA 19082

W Chester

Conrad E Muhly III CKD CBD
MUHLY KBA INC
7 N Five Point Road
W Chester, PA 19380

Warren

Susan A Reinke CKD
514 Beech Street
Warren, PA 16365

West Chester

Gordon H Davis CKD
1407 Wexford Circle
West Chester, PA 19380

H Richard Hurlbrink CKD
HURLBRINK KITCHENS INC
701 Old Westtown Road
West Chester, PA 19382

Thomas A Ingle CKD
105 Hedgerow Lane
West Chester, PA 19380

West Lawn

Daphne D Frownfelter CKD
2333 Highland Street
West Lawn, PA 19609

White Oak

Ronald R Massung CKD
MASSUNG CABINET
COMPANY
3026 Stewartsville Road
White Oak, PA 15131

Windgap

Larry C Hess CKD
122 No. Broadway
Windgap, PA 18091

Windsor

Donna L Cunningham CKD
RR 2 Box 60
Windsor, PA 17366-9614

Wyoming

Marvin L Weisberger CKD
BETTERHOUSE INC
1140 Wyoming Avenue
Wyoming, PA 18644

York

Jesse Dagenhardt CKD
994 Country Club Road
York, PA 17403

RHODE ISLAND

Barrington

Robert W Chew CKD
BARRINGTON KITCHENS
496 Maple Avenue
Barrington, RI 02806

Carolina

Norman S Fay CKD
PO Box 605
Carolina, RI 02813

Greenville

Richard L Manocchia CKD
14 Kimberly Ann Drive
Greenville, RI 02828

Johnston

Ronald J Finacchiaro CKD
CREATIVE KITCHENS INC
2656 Hartford Avenue
Johnston, RI 02919

Warwick

Frank J Ferendo CKD
FERENDO KITCHENS
110 Jefferson Boulevard
Warwick, RI 02888

Chester H Sandford CKD
16 Beach Avenue
Warwick, RI 02889

Westerly

Gene M Parise CKD
69B Cross Street
Westerly, RI 02891

CKD-Certified Kitchen Designer; CBD-Certified Bath Designer

Wyoming

Elisabeth McHenry CKD
PO Box 67
Wyoming, RI 02898

SOUTH CAROLINA

Beaufort

Raymond C Clausen CKD
77 Dolphin Point Drive
Beaufort, SC 29902

Columbia

James A Clarkson CKD
1011 Laurens Street
Columbia, SC 29201

W Hampton Oliver CKD
HAMPTON KITCHENS
2205 N Main Street
PO Box 7273
Columbia, SC 29201

Hilton Head Island

Norman H Armstrong CKD
37 Old Military Road
Hilton Head Island, SC 29928

Isle Of Palms

Malcolm C Bogan CKD CBD
16 43rd Avenue
Isle Of Palms, SC 29451

Mount Pleasant

Duval B Acker CKD CBD
1035 Johnnie Dodds Blvd.
Mount Pleasant, SC 29464-6154

Myrtle Beach

James E Brunson CKD
CANAC CABINETS
3832 Wesley Street
Myrtle Beach, SC 29577

Rock Hill

William T McPherson CKD
1226 Twin Lakes Road
Rock Hill, SC 29730

Spartanburg

William R Scott CKD
1166 Woodburn Road
Spartanburg, SC 29302

Summerville

Jill Absher Patton CKD
112 Thrush Lane
Summerville, SC 29485

Claudette Pimm CKD
210 Sprucewood Drive
Summerville, SC 29483

Surfside Beach

Lloyd C Rice CKD
14 Sandy Pine Drive
Surfside Beach, SC 29575

SOUTH DAKOTA

Rapid City

Darlene L Davignon CKD
3275 Pioneer Drive
Rapid City, SD 57701

TENNESSEE

Antioch

Dean Potts CKD
108 Stone Bridge Court
Antioch, TN 37103-1283

Chattanooga

Kathy D Massey CKD
FERGUSON ENTERPRISES
4100 Amnicola Highway
Chattanooga, TN 37412

Katharine Powell CKD
INNOVATIVE DESIGNS
1124 Dana Avenue
Chattanooga, TN 37443

Crossville

Lorie K. Smith CKD
VILLAGE KITCHENS BATHS
INTERIORS
W Avenue S
PO Box 1396
Crossville, TN 38557

Germantown

Georgia L Kilpatrick CKD
KITCHENS BY KILPATRICK
2025 Woodgate Drive
Germantown, TN 38138

Knoxville

Jack H. Lady CKD
817 Roderick Road
Knoxville, TN 37923

David H Newton CKD
DAVID NEWTON AND
ASSOCIATES
PO Box 51706
Knoxville, TN 37950

Mitchell L Robinson CKD
MODERN SUPPLY COMPANY
525 Lovell Road
PO Box 22997
Knoxville, TN 37932

Memphis

Wilson M Carruthers CKD
CARRUTHERS KITCHENS INC
2665 Broad Avenue
Memphis, TN 38112

James E Mason CKD
2761 Elmore Park Road
Memphis, TN 38138

Charles A Tracy CKD
231 Lorece Lane
Memphis, TN 38117

Nashville

Gerald Fleischer CKD
221 Page Road
Nashville, TN 37205

James R Henry CKD
HENRY KITCHENS & BATH
306-8th Avenue S
Nashville, TN 37203

Tony Herrera CKD
KITCHEN & BATH CONCEPTS
INC
3307 Charlotte Avenue
Nashville, TN 37209

Caroline A Weismueller CKD
HENRY KITCHENS & BATH
INC
306 8th Avenue S
Nashville, TN 37203

James C Wood CKD
JIM WOOD & ASSOCIATES
1209 Otter Creek Road
Nashville, TN 37215

TEXAS

Amarillo

Ashley M Buck CKD
1300 S Jackson Street
Amarillo, TX 79101-4144

Arlington

Daniel E Domeracki CKD
5617 Louise Way Drive
Arlington, TX 76017

Georgie L Skover CKD
KITCHENS BY DESIGN INC
2905 Greenbrook Drive
Arlington, TX 76016

Austin

R Kent Barnes CKD CBD
KITCHENS INC
2712 Bee Cave Road #122
Austin, TX 78746

Carrollton

Denise M Dick CKD
2101 Kings Road
Carrollton, TX 75007

Corpus Christi

Edward L Bokamper CKD CBD
4918 Calallen Drive
Corpus Christi, TX 78410

Lynna L Simpson CKD
LL SIMPSON SELECT
DESIGNS
1822 Holly Road
110
Corpus Christi, TX 78417

Dallas

Lars S Fredriksen CKD
LIVING KITCHENS INC
14448 Midway Road
Dallas, TX 75244

William R. Gedney CKD
WILLIAM R. GEDNEY & CO.
8422 Swift Avenue
Dallas, TX 75228-5846

Brad Pence CKD
BRAD PENCE COMPANY
4508 Lovers Lane
Dallas, TX 75225

Richard D Walden CKD
SEARS HOME IMPROVEMENT
5334 Ross Avenue
Dallas, TX 75206

Fort Worth

W J Chambless CKD
KITCHEN PLANNERS
3300 Airport Freeway
Fort Worth, TX 76111

Sally Whitson-Salazar CKD
GEARHEART CONSTRUCTION
COMPANY INC
3221 Hulen
Suite E
Fort Worth, TX 76107

Beth M Stribling CKD
KITCHEN PLANNERS
3300 Airport Freeway
Fort Worth, TX 76111

Mark A Wessels CKD
8600 Vanderbilt Court, #108
Fort Worth, TX 76120

Houston

Cherye Burns CKD
EEKITCHEN & BATH
CONCEPTS
2627 Westheimer
Houston, TX 77098

Dorel P Carter CKD
DOREL CARTER KITCHEN
DESIGNS
3655 Wickersham
Houston, TX 77027

Virgil L Church CKD
1803 Althea Drive
Houston, TX 77018

Kirk Craig CKD
KIRK CRAIG COMPANY
2431 Sunset Boulevard
Houston, TX 77005

Robert E Crellen CKD
CABINETS & DESIGNS INC
3637 W Alabama #380
Houston, TX 77027

Aurolyn M Devine CKD
823 South Ripple Creek
Houston, TX 77057

Richard S. Difazzio CKD
12819 Tennis Drive
Houston, TX 77099

W Donald Fleck CKD CBD
FLECKWAY HOUSEWORKS
INC
612 W Bough Lane
Houston, TX 77024

Gay Fly CKD CBD
GAY FLY DESIGNER
KITCHENS & BATHS
4200 Westheimer
Suite 120
Houston, TX 77027

Margaret J Grants CKD
12850 Whittington Drive
Houston, TX 77077

Collin T Hahn CKD
HALLMARK FASHION
KITCHENS INC
3413 E Greenridge Drive
Houston, TX 77057

Peggy McGowen CKD
3126 Robinhood
Houston, TX 77005

Jane S Putman CKD
1953 Ridgemore
Houston, TX 77055

Zena C Wong CKD
URBAN KITCHENS & BATHS
3601 W Alabama 380
Houston, TX 77027

Humble

Jacqueline Mead CKD
MEAD ASSOCIATES
203 N Houston Avenue
Humble, TX 77338

New Braunfels

Linda W Whitworth CKD
KITCHEN DESIGN
318 Clemens Avenue
New Braunfels, TX 78130

San Antonio

Diana H Hawkins CKD
7926 Broadway Street #504
San Antonio, TX 78209

Robert G Thompson CKD
4335 Apple Tree Woods
San Antonio, TX 78249

Spring

Laura H Scott CKD
SCOTT DESIGNS
6503 Inway Drive
Spring, TX 77389

The Woodlands

Catherine Locetta CKD
15 Raintree Crossing
The Woodlands, TX 77381

UTAH

Salt Lake City

Larry A Carlson CKD
CARLSON KITCHENS
2261 East 3300 South
Salt Lake City, UT 84109

Dean Denning CKD
KITCHEN ORIGINALS INC
965 E 3300 S
Salt Lake City, UT 84106

Gary N Sheffield CKD
6205 Rodeo Lane
Salt Lake City, UT 84121

Jeniel E Smith CKD
JENIEL SMITH DESIGNS
4812 Naniloa Drive
Salt Lake City, UT 84117

West Jordan

Howard H Tullis CKD
WABATCH CABINET
COMPANY INC
3412 W 8600 S
West Jordan, UT 84088

VERMONT

Barre

Richard E Fournier CKD
10 Crescent Lane
Barre, VT 05641

Roy D. Kilburn CKD
CONCEPTS IN CABINETRY
393 N Main Street
Barre, VT 05641

Ludlow

Lois A Harken CKD
10 Bridge Street
Ludlow, VT 05149

N Clarendon

George A Ritter CKD
KNIGHT CABINETS
Route 7 B
RR 1 Box 231 1
N Clarendon, VT 05759

North Hero

Paul G Cheeseman CKD
RR #1, Box 2688
North Hero, VT 05474

VIRGINIA

Alexandria

Alvin E Dennis Jr CKD
5930 Tilbury Road
Alexandria, VA 22310

Arlington

Louis E Schucker CKD
VOELL CUSTOM KITCHENS
4788 Lee Highway
Arlington, VA 22207

Chesapeake

Eugene E Bryant CKD
EEB ENTERPRISES
809 Live Oak Drive
Suite #31
Chesapeake, VA 23320

Chesterfield

Rena Lipkind CKD
6032 Baron Drive
Chesterfield, VA 23832

Dunn Loring

Richard H Coyle CKD
8008 Sandburg Court
Dunn Loring, VA 22027

Fairfax

Robert W Clements CBD
C W TILE COMPANY
PO Box 370
Fairfax, VA 22039

Lisa M Foley CKD
3929 Tedrich Boulevard
Fairfax, VA 22031

Falls Church

Nick Bianco CKD
KITCHEN & BATH DESIGNS
BY NICK BIANCO CKD
3304 Brandy Court
Falls Church, VA 22042

James W Bingnear CKD
F A MCGONEGAL
1061 West Broad Street
Falls Church, VA 22046

Judith R Bracht CKD
F A MCGONEGAL INC
1061 West Broad Street
Falls Church, VA 22046

Dee David Fogle CKD CBD
2612 Shelby Lane
Falls Church, VA 22043

Louise E Perini CKD
3008 Cedarwood Lane
Falls Church, VA 22042

Mickey Riemondy CKD
3459 Glavis Road
Falls Church, VA 22044

Inga K Willner CKD
F A MCGONEGAL
1061 W Broad Street
Falls Church, VA 22046

Leesburg

Carolyn K Willingham CKD
PO Box 526
Leesburg, VA 22075

Lynchburg

Albert B Fink Jr CKD
A B FINK INC
118 Madison Street
Lynchburg, VA 24504

McLean

Donna Dougherty CKD
DIANE H SMALL INC
1969 Massachusetts Avenue
McLean, VA 22101

Diane H Small CKD
DIANE H SMALL INC
1969 Massachusetts Avenue
McLean, VA 22101

John C Spitz CKD CBD
DIANE SMALL INC
1969 Massachusetts Avenue
McLean, VA 22101

Mechanicsville

Dayton Leadbetter CKD
2614 Powhickery Drive
Mechanicsville, VA 23111

Newington

Patrick H Padberg CKD CBD
PMC CONTRACTORS INC
7913 Kincannon Place
PO Box 1415
Newington, VA 22122

Newport News

Don R Ligon CKD
VIRGINIA MAID KITCHENS
737 Blue Crab Road
Newport News, VA 23601

Norfolk

Meredith M Crockett CKD
EVENT HORIZON
1220 Manchester Avenue
Norfolk, VA 23508

Ann Hux Johnson CKD
421 Peace Haven Drive
Norfolk, VA 23502

Michael L Lawless CKD
911 Graydon Avenue - Apt. A1
Norfolk, VA 23507

Walter B Neal Jr CKD
CAVALIER KITCHENS INC
5595 Raby Road
Norfolk, VA 23502

Hugh H Parker Jr CKD
8448 Norristown Drive
Norfolk, VA 23518

Petersburg

David J Roane Sr CKD
DAVE'S CABINET SHOP INC
22504 Cox Road
Petersburg, VA 23803

Poquoson

John D Willis CKD
3 Cheryl Circle
Poquoson, VA 23662

CKD-Certified Kitchen Designer; CBD-Certified Bath Designer

Richmond

Robert G Baker CKD
7409 Fairway Avenue
Richmond, VA 23228

Charles H Fleming CKD
CUSTOM KITCHENS INC
6412 Horsepen Road
Richmond, VA 23226

Morris E Gunn Jr CKD
208 Ralston Road
Richmond, VA 23229

Robert E Hammack CKD
7625 Rock Creek Road
Richmond, VA 23229

Richard F Hendrick CKD
CUSTOM KITCHENS INC
6412 Horsepen Road
Richmond, VA 23226

David A Hendrick CKD
CUSTOM KITCHENS INC
6412 Horsepen Road
Richmond, VA 23226

Arthur C Hendrick Jr CKD
1625 Princeton Road
Richmond, VA 23227

W Brian Pilgrim CKD
CUSTOM KITCHENS INC
6412 Horsepen Road
Richmond, VA 23226

Katheryn W Robertson CKD
THE KITCHEN AND BATH
DESIGN SHOP LTD
2317 W Main Street
Richmond, VA 23220

Roanoke

Brownie S Carter CKD
PO Box 12014
Roanoke, VA 24022

Russell D Carter CKD
Carter's Cabinet Shop
Roanoke, VA 24012

Sterling

Lisa M Robey CKD
HARVEY'S KITCHENS &
BATHS
22560 Glenn Drive
Suite 115
Sterling, VA 22170

Vienna

Janis M Magnuson CKD
KITCHENS BY DESIGN INC
394 Park Street S E
Vienna, VA 22180

Virginia Beach

Ray Boggs CKD
4903 Ocean View Avenue
Virginia Beach, VA 23455

Benton Flax CKD
2827 Charlemagne Drive
Virginia Beach, VA 23451

Clark J Janssen CKD
PRESTIGE KITCHENS OF
VIRGINA INC
2798
Virginia Beach, VA 23452

Winchester

Connie Edwards CKD
228 Woodberry Lane
Winchester, VA 22601

WASHINGTON

Bellevue

Lynn Llyod Conner CKD CBD
LYNN LLOYD CONNER
KITCHEN & BATH DESIGN
12819 S E 38th
Suite 394
Bellevue, WA 98006

Jitka M Urban CKD
DESIGN BY JITKA
14590 NE 35th Street
D204
Bellevue, WA 98007

Barbara S Wahler CKD
14630 N.E. 40th Street
Bellevue, WA 98007

Bothell

Martha Kildal CKD
7338 N.E. 140th Place
Bothell, WA 98011

Robert D Mac Donald CKD
21809-35th Avenue, S.E.
Bothell, WA 98021

Bremerton

Stanley E Bajema CKD
C & S DESIGNS
6960 Navajo Trail Northeast
Bremerton, WA 98310

Ronald L Edmondson CKD CBD
BRISTOL KITCHENS
5889 State Highway 303 N E
Suite #101
Bremerton, WA 98310

Everett

Kenneth E Peterson CKD
5104 Fowler
Everett, WA 98203

Issaquah

Leslie J Galvin CKD
4374 242 Place SE
Issaquah, WA 98027

Kirkland

Jerald D Hilzinger CKD
KITCHENS FOR DREAM
HOMES
12024 Juanita Drive N E
Kirkland, WA 98034

Lynnwood

Lynn D Sheffield CKD
SHEFFIELD DESIGNS
4320 196th Street SW B750
Lynnwood, WA 98036

Moxee

Kelly S Petty CKD
PO Box 308
Moxee, WA 98936

Puyallup

Margaret R Stephens CKD
6714 92nd Street, East
Puyallup, WA 98371

Redmond

Bruce R Kelleran CKD
SHOWPLACE KITCHENS &
BATHS
8710 Willows Road
PO Box 955
Redmond, WA 98073

Diana K Valentine CKD
SHOWPLACE KITCHENS &
BATH
8710 Willows Road
PO Box 955
Redmond, WA 98073

Seattle

Charles S Blodgett CBD
KITCHEN & BATHS BY
BLODGETT
4515 44th S W
Seattle, WA 98116

John W Brush CKD
20706 Occidental Avenue South
Seattle, WA 98198

Jeffrey B Case CKD
2466 - 4th Avenue North
Seattle, WA 98109

Jackie A Goedde CKD
3338 Hunter Blvd. South
Seattle, WA 98144

Kimithy H Nagel CKD
KITCHENS & BATHS BY
BLODGETT
4515 44th Avenue SW
Seattle, WA 98116

Snohomish

Delores L Hyden CKD CBD
9106 131st Avenue SE
Snohomish, WA 98298

Tacoma

Mary Ellen Jackl CKD
1646 South Stevens
Tacoma, WA 98405

Jere L Johnson CKD
CUSTOM DESIGN CABINETRY
INC
701 72nd Street E
Tacoma, WA 98404

Robert J Miller CKD
CUSTOM DESIGN CABINETRY
701 East 72nd
Tacoma, WA 98404-1009

Shiela M Off CKD
DOUGLAS DESIGN CABINET
& REMODELING COMPANY
4804 Center Street
Tacoma, WA 98409

Woodinville

Susan M Larsen CKD CBD
BOLIG KITCHEN STUDIO
13110 N E 177th Place
Woodinville, WA 98072

Catherine Larsen CKD CBD
BOLIG KITCHEN STUDIO
13110 NE 177th Place
#B 102
Woodinville, WA 98072

WEST VIRGINIA

Barboursville

Beverly Renee Pauken CKD
WOODY'S KITCHENS
5841 Davis Creek Road
Barboursville, WV 25504

Huntington

Robert E Stepp CKD
300 Holswade Drive
Huntington, WV 25701

Jane Lew

Keith H McCarty CKD
R.D. 1
Jane Lew, WV 26378

Morgantown

John Keith Carr CKD
GENERAL GLASS COMPANY
INC
PO Box 618
Morgantown, WV 26507

Mt. Hope

Lesia B Campbell CKD
Route 2 Box 237A
Mt. Hope, WV 25880

S Charleston

Charles A Arey CKD
WARDEN'S INC
5621 MacCorkle Avenue S W
S Charleston, WV 25309

Vienna

Wayne L Brown CKD
MOORE'S
1502 Grand Central Avenue
Vienna, WV 24021-3708

Williamson

Jennifer A Rowe CKD
310 Slater Street
Williamson, WV 25661

Williamstown

Robert B Ingram CKD
INGRAM & ASSOCIATES
803 W 3rd Street
Williamstown, WV 26187

WISCONSIN

Appleton

John A Klinkert CKD
631 Taft Avenue
Appleton, WI 54915

Dennis L Schwersenka CKD
KUSTOM KITCHENS & BATHS
741 W College Avenue
Appleton, WI 54914

Blue Mounds

Debra Doud CKD
2566 Highway 7
Blue Mounds, WI 53517

Cedarburg

Brent Baker CKD
CEDARBURG LUMBER
COMPANY
North 144 West 5800 Pioneer
Road
Cedarburg, WI 53012

Germantown

Kathie Kroening CKD
W156 N10952 Catskill Lane
Germantown, WI 53022

Leonard E Riebau CKD
N112 W20925 Mequon Road
Germantown, WI 53022

Greendale

Timothy J Benkowski CKD CBD
CUSTOM DESIGN
ASSOCIATES
5101 West Loomis Road
Greendale, WI 53129

Janesville

Marie E Garot CKD
227 Jefferson Avenue
Janesville, WI 53545

Kohler

Peter D Cameron CBD
KOHLER COMPANY
444 Highland Drive
Kohler, WI 53004

James R Dase CKD CBD
KOHLER COMPANY
444 Highland Drive
MSN 002
Kohler, WI 53044

Madison

Mr Steven P Emerson CKD
KITCHENS OF DISTINCTION
6719 Seybold Road
Madison, WI 53719

James R Luck CKD
J R LUCK & ASSOCIATES INC
1118 Saybrook Road
Madison, WI 53711

William R Opalewski CBD
OPALEWSKI BATH &
KITCHEN DESIGN
4333 Portland Parkway
Madison, WI 53714

Lawrence C Thomas CKD
3210 Knollwood Way
Madison, WI 53713

Manitowoc

John J Sleger CKD
1020 S 12th Street
Apartment 309
Manitowoc, WI 54220

Marshfield

David A Burger CKD
1600 North Wood Avenue
Marshfield, WI 54449

Middleton

James E Abrahamson CKD
8689 Airport Road
Middleton, WI 53562

Milwaukee

William M Feradi CKD
BUILT-IN KITCHENS INC
7289 N Teutonia Avenue
Milwaukee, WI 53209

Richard K Rossman CKD
WISCONSIN KITCHEN MART
3601 W Wisconsin Avenue
Milwaukee, WI 53208

Muskego

John R Foat CKD CBD
PO Box 186
Muskego, WI 53150-0186

Oshkosh

John A Lieske CKD
FOX VALLEY KITCHEN
SPECIALISTS LTD
2721 Oregon Street
Oshkosh, WI 54901

Portage

B J Lessner CKD
4544 Allan Road
Portage, WI 53901

Schofield

Thomas E De Lisle CKD
DE LISLE COMPANY INC
624 Moreland Avenue
Schofield, WI 54476

Sheboygan

Arthur B Mather CKD
734 Mayflower Avenue
Sheboygan, WI 53083

Sheboygan Falls

Barbara J Blasing CKD
RICHARDSON LUMBER
COMPANY
904 Monroe Street
PO Box 904
Sheboygan Falls, WI 53085-0904

Ivan Nagode CKD CBD
RICHARDSON LUMBER
904 Monroe
Box 904
Sheboygan Falls, WI 53085

Stevens Point

Ronald J Nowacki CKD
2309 Division Street
Stevens Point, WI 54481

Sun Prairie

Harry Guy Haynes CKD
1811 Oakland Avenue
Sun Prairie, WI 53590

Wautoma

Steven A Weiss CKD
MID STATE SUPPLY
COMPANY
Highway 21 E
PO Box 510
Wautoma, WI 54982

Wauwatosa

Jane A. Altenbach CKD
2729 Mayfair Court
Wauwatosa, WI 53222

Eugene L Delfosse CKD
KITCHEN DESIGN STUDIO
INC
8932 W North Avenue
Wauwatosa, WI 53226

Wisconsin Rapid

Maurice D Petta CKD
530 11th Street S
Wisconsin Rapid, WI 54494

Wisconsin Rapids

Debra DeCaluwe CKD
QUALITY KITCHENS
1211 8th Street S
Wisconsin Rapids, WI 54494

Canada

ALBERTA

Edmonton

Gerald A Dreger CKD
8331 - 120th Street
Edmonton, AB T6G 1X1

Lily D Dreger CKD
8331 120th Street
Edmonton, AB T6E 1X1

BRITISH COLUMBIA

Abbotsford

Allan S Pattison CKD
3457 Mt Blanchard Court
Abbotsford, BC V2S 6T6

N Vancouver

Roger Moras CKD CBD
MERIT KITCHENS LTD
1329 Appin Road
N Vancouver, BC V7J 2T4

Penticton

Gordon H Stark CKD
LEE LYNN HOLDINGS INC
325 Dawson Avenue
Penticton, BC V2A 3N5

Surrey

Peter Mc Bride CKD
MERIT INDUSTRIES LIMITED
12331 Bridgeport Road
Surrey, BC V6V 1J4

Kathi A Gorges CKD
8321 148B Street
Surrey, BC V3S 7S1

Vancouver

Ron A McKee CKD CBD
PRESTIGE KITCHENS LTD
6158 East Boulevard
Vancouver, BC V6M 3V6

Victoria

Debora L Boulding CKD
MERIT KITCHENS LTD
435 Banks Road
Victoria, BC V1X 6A2

Fraser Rose CKD
MERIT KITCHENS LTD
3196 Douglas Street
Victoria, BC V8Z 3K6

MANITOBA

Winnipeg

Joy Myers Piske CKD
MYERS PISKE INTERIOR
DESIGN
Box 22 Group 337
RR 3
Winnipeg, MB R3C 2E7

NEW BRUNSWICK

Frederickton

Eric Di Carlo CKD
131 Colonial Heights
Frederickton, NB E3B 5M2

NOVA SCOTIA

Halifax

Patti A Ford CKD
FULL CIRCLE
6420 Lady Hammond Road
Halifax, NS B3K 2S3

CKD-Certified Kitchen Designer; CBD-Certified Bath Designer

ONTARIO

Michael J Hetherman CKD
759 Cobbler's Court
, ON L1V 3S2

Barrie

Gabrielle Brown CKD
151 Shirley Avenue
Barrie, ON L4N 6E7

William R Brown CKD
151 Shirley Avenue
Barrie, ON L4N 6E9

Glen P Prairie CKD
273 Wellington Street, E.
Barrie, ON L4M 2E4

Burlington

Carol L Watts CKD
206 Lakeview Avenue
Burlington, ON L7N 2Y6

Embro

Reno H Rakutt CKD CBD
THE KITCHEN EMPORIUM
INC
54 Kent Street
Embro, ON N4S 6Y7

Hanover

Linda A Whaling CKD
HANOVER KITCHEN
GALLERY
509 10th Street
Hanover, ON N4N 1R4

Kingston

Denise M Holmes CKD
WINSTON'S KITCHENS &
BATH
1469 Princess Street
Unit 3A
Kingston, ON K7M 3E9

Nancy D Howey CKD
218 Mack Street
Kingston, ON K7L 1P7

Art Warren CKD
PO Box 1832
Kingston, ON K7L 5J7

Marlbank

Robert C Mezzatesta CKD
R.R. #2
Marlbank, ON K0K 2L0

Ottawa

Doris Lacroix CKD CBD
#40 Boteler Street
Ottawa, ON K1N 9C8

Judy A Welsh CKD
DOMICILE KITCHENS
202 Dalhousie Street
Ottawa, ON K1N 7C8

Carolyn J Yost CKD
2199 Deschenes Street
Ottawa, ON K2B 6N2

Owen Sound

Valerie C Meyer CKD
160 7th Street SW
Owen Sound, ON N4K 5S9

Peterborough

Tom C MacKenzie CBD
EUR-OWN-STYLE BATH &
KITCHEN
709 Bethune Street
Peterborough, ON K9H 4A5

Pickering

Anthony S Binns CKD
1948 Parkside Drive
Pickering, ON L1V 1A1

John A Hunter CKD
992 Timmins Gardens
Pickering, ON L1W 2L2

Rory A Mc Lean CKD
BINNS DESIGNER KITCHENS
INC
333 Kingston Road
Pickering, ON L1V 1A1

Saint Thomas

Mary Anne Cormack CKD
CASEY'S CREATIVE
KITCHENS LTD
469-470 Talbot Street
Saint Thomas, ON N5P 1C2

Scarborough

Cetin Ulker CKD
71 Natal Avenue
Scarborough, ON M1N 3V5

Toronto

Jan E Regis CBD
550 Bedford Park
Toronto, ON M5M 1K3

Windsor

Gordon B Wilson CKD CBD
2749 Randolph
Windsor, ON N9E 3E1

CKD-Certified Kitchen Designer; CBD-Certified Bath Designer